RESTATEMENT 2d OF THE LAW: CONTRACTS & UNIDROIT PRINCIPLES OF INTERNATIONAL COMMERCIAL CONTRACTS

THE TEXTS, THE COMMENTS & THE ILLUSTRATIONS

Student Texts
Including Comments and Illustrations

INSTITUTE OF INTERNATIONAL BANKING LAW & PRACTICE, INC.
PUBLICATIONS
P.O. BOX 2235
MONTGOMERY VILLAGE, MD 20886
WWW.IIBLP.ORG

The Institute of International Banking Law & Practice, Inc.
P.O. Box 2235
20405 Ryecroft Ct.
Montgomery Village, MD 20886
Phone: (301) 869-9840
Fax: (301) 926-1265

Website: www.iiblp.org
E-mail: info@iiblp.org

Products and services of the Institute are detailed at the last page.

Summary of Contents

Restatement 2d of the Law: Contracts

UNIDROIT Principles of International Commercial Contracts

Appendix

Publisher's Note

These materials are intended to bring the full richness of the two primary sources of the judicial law of contracts, *The Restatement of the Law 2d of Contracts* and the UNIDROIT *Principals of International Commercial Contracts,* to first year law students.

The Restatement of Contracts, first published in 1932 by the American Law Institute, was revised in 1980. The *Restatement 2d of Contracts* largely reflects the vision of Professors Arthur Corbin and Karl Llewellyn. It includes not only the "Black Letter" provisions contained in the toy versions usually used by first year students, but a wealth of comments, illustrations, and reporters' notes. To make this reproduction of the *Restatement 2d of Contracts* more usable, all of the Reporters' Notes have been omitted. But 95% of the comments and illustrations have been retained. The few omissions are indicated by an ellipsis. The serious scholar will, of course, have recourse to the complete version.

The UNIDROIT *Principals of International Commercial Contracts* was published in 1994. It is the product of an intensive study of contract law in all the major legal systems of the world by an international body of legal professionals. The purpose of the UNIDROIT *Principals* is to provide rules for contracts based on international consensus of leading authorities. It, too, contains black letter rules, supplemented by comments and illustrations. In addition to the black letter rules (available in most toy supplements), the vast majority of comments and illustrations have been reproduced here. Only those relatively few comments and illustrations that were in no way pertinent to the first year study of contracts have been omitted, which are again indicated with an ellipsis.

The benefit of these nearly complete reproductions is that students now have access to the comments and illustrations which explain the often illusive meaning of the black letter law in one manageable volume.

The *Restatement 2d of Contracts* is copyrighted to the American Law Institute. The *Principals of International Commercial Contracts* is copyrighted by UNIDROIT. Both are reproduced here with their respective permissions.

The support of George Mason University School of Law in making this project possible is gratefully acknowledged, as is the able and untiring contribution of my Research Assistant, Phillip R. Blackmon, Jr. Gratitude is also expressed to Professors Donald Wallace, Jr., of Georgetown University Law Center, and Michael Joachim Bonell, Chairman of the Working Group on the UNIDROIT Principles, for their invaluable assistance.

Professor James E. Byrne
Institute of International Banking Law & Practice
and George Mason University School of Law

RESTATEMENT 2D
OF THE LAW:

CONTRACTS

Restatement 2d of Contracts

Table of Contents

Chapter 1

MEANING OF TERMS

Introductory Note A persistent source of difficulty in the law of contracts is the fact that words often have different meanings to the speaker and to the hearer. Most words are commonly used in more than one sense, and the words used in this Restatement are no exception. It is arguable that the difficulty is increased rather than diminished by an attempt to give a word a single definition and to use it only as defined. But where usage varies widely, definition makes it possible to avoid circumlocution in the statement of rules and to hold ambiguity to a minimum.

In the Restatement, an effort has been made to use only words with connotations familiar to the legal profession, and not to use two or more words to express the same legal concept. Where a word frequently used has a variety of distinct meanings, one meaning has been selected and indicated by definition. But it is obviously impossible to capture in a definition an entire complex institution such as "contract" or "promise." The operative facts necessary or sufficient to create legal relations and the legal relations created by those facts will appear with greater fullness in the succeeding chapters.

§ 1. Contract Defined

A contract is a promise or a set of promises for the breach of which the law gives a remedy, or the performance of which the law in some way recognizes as a duty.

Comment:

a. Other meanings. The word "contract" is often used with meanings different from that given here. It is sometimes used as a synonym for "agreement" or "bargain." It may refer to legally ineffective agreements, or to wholly executed transactions such as conveyances; it may refer indifferently to the acts of the parties, to a document which evidences those acts, or to the resulting legal relations. In a statute the word may be given still other meanings by context or explicit definition. As is indicated in the Introductory Note to the Restatement of this Subject, definition in terms of "promise" excludes wholly executed transactions in which no promises are made; such a definition also excludes analogous obligations imposed by law rather than by virtue of a promise.

b. Act and resulting legal relations. As the term is used in the Restatement of this Subject, "contract," like "promise," denotes the act or acts of promising. But, unlike the term "promise," "contract" applies only to those acts which have legal effect as stated in the definition given. Thus the word "contract" is commonly and quite properly also used to refer to the resulting legal obligation, or to the entire resulting complex of legal relations. Compare Uniform Commercial Code § 1-201(11), defining "contract" in terms of "the total legal obligation which results from the parties' agreement."

c. Set of promises. A contract may consist of a single promise by one person to another, or of mutual promises by two persons to one another; or there may be, indeed, any number of persons or any number of promises. One person may make several promises to one person or to several persons, or several persons may join in making promises to one or more persons. To constitute a "set," promises need not be made simultaneously; it is enough that several promises are regarded by the parties as constituting a single contract, or are so related in subject matter and performance that they may be considered and enforced together by a court.

d. Operative acts other than promise. The definition does not attempt to state what acts are essential to create a legal duty to perform a promise. In many situations other acts in addition to the making of a promise are essential, and the formation of the contract is not completed until those acts take place. For example, an act may be done as the consideration for a contract (see § 71), and may be essential to the creation of a legal duty to perform the promise (see § 17). Similarly, delivery is required for the formation of a contract under seal (see § 95). Such acts are not part of the promise, and are not specifically included in the brief definition of contract adopted here.

...

g. "Binding promise." A promise which is a contract is said to be "binding." As the term "contract" is defined, a statement that a promise is binding does not necessarily mean that any particular remedy is available in the event of breach, or indeed that any remedy is available. Because of the limitations inherent in stating or illustrating rules for the legal relations resulting from promises, it frequently becomes necessary to indicate that a legal duty to perform arises from the facts stated, assuming the absence of other facts. In order to avoid the connotation that the duty stated exists under all circumstances, the word "binding" or a statement that the promisor is "bound" is used to indicate that the duty arises if the promisor has full capacity, if there is no illegality or fraud in the transaction, if the duty has not been discharged, and if there are no other similar facts which would defeat the prima facie duty which is stated.

§ 2. Promise; Promisor; Promisee; Beneficiary

(1) A promise is a manifestation of intention to act or refrain from acting in a specified way, so made as to justify a promisee in understanding that a commitment has been made.

(2) The person manifesting the intention is the promisor.

(3) The person to whom the manifestation is addressed is the promisee.

(4) Where performance will benefit a person other than the promisee, that person is a beneficiary.

Comment:

a. Acts and resulting relations. "Promise" as used in the Restatement of this Subject denotes the act of the promisor. If by virtue of other operative facts there is a legal duty to perform, the promise is a contract; but the word "promise" is not limited to acts having legal effect. Like "contract," however, the word "promise" is commonly and quite properly also used to refer to the complex of human relations which results from the promisor's words or acts of assurance, including the justified expectations of the promisee and any moral or legal duty which arises to make good the assurance by performance. The performance may be specified either in terms describing the action of the promisor or in terms of the result which that action or inaction is to bring about.

b. Manifestation of intention. Many contract disputes arise because different people attach different meanings to the same words and conduct. The phrase "manifestation of intention" adopts an external or objective standard for interpreting conduct; it means the external expression of intention as distinguished from undisclosed intention. A promisor manifests an intention if he believes or has reason to believe that the promisee will infer that intention from his words or conduct. Rules governing cases where the promisee could reasonably draw more than one inference as to the promisor's intention are stated in connection with the acceptance of offers (see §§ 19 and 20), and the scope of contractual obligations (see §§ 201, 219).

c. Promise of action by third person; guaranty. Words are often used which in terms promise action or inaction by a third person, or which promise a result obtainable only by such action. Such words are commonly understood as a promise of conduct by the promisor which will be sufficient to bring about the action or inaction or result, or to answer for harm caused by failure. An example is a guaranty that a third person will perform his promise. Such words constitute a promise as here defined only if they justify a promisee in an expectation of some action or inaction on the part of the promisor.

d. Promise of event beyond human control; warranty. Words which in terms promise that an event not within human control will occur may be interpreted to include a promise to answer for harm caused by the failure of the event to occur. An example is a warranty of an existing or past fact, such as a warranty that a horse is sound, or that a ship arrived in a foreign port some days previously. Such promises are often made when the parties are ignorant of the actual facts regarding which they bargain, and may be dealt with as if the warrantor could cause the fact to be as he asserted. It is then immaterial that the actual condition of affairs may be irrevocably fixed before the promise is made.

Words of warranty, like other conduct, must be interpreted in the light of the circumstances and the reasonable expectations of the parties. In an insurance contract, a "warranty" by the insured is usually not a promise at all; it may be merely a representation of fact, or, more commonly, the fact warranted is a condition of the insurer's duty to pay (see § 225(3)). In the sale of goods, on the other hand, a similar warranty normally also includes a promise to answer for damages (see Uniform Commercial Code § 2-715). **Illustrations:**

> 1. A, the builder of a house, or the inventor of the material used in part of its construction, says to B, the owner of the house, "I warrant that this house will never burn down." This includes a promise to pay for harm if the house should burn down.
> 2. A, by a charter-party, undertakes that the "good ship Dove," having sailed from Marseilles a week ago for New York, shall take on a cargo for B on her arrival in New York. The statement of the quality of the ship and the statement of her time of sailing from Marseilles include promises to pay for harm if the statement is untrue.

e. Illusory promises; mere statements of intention. Words of promise which by their terms make performance entirely optional with the "promisor" whatever may happen, or whatever course of conduct in other respects he may pursue, do not constitute a promise. Although such words are often referred to as forming an illusory promise, they do not fall within the present definition of promise. They may not even manifest any intention on the part of the promisor. Even if a present intention is manifested, the reservation of an option to change that intention means that there can be no promisee who is justified in an expectation of performance.

On the other hand, a promise may be made even though no duty of performance can arise unless some event occurs (see §§ 224, 225(1)). Such a conditional promise is no less a promise because there is small likelihood that any duty of performance will arise, as in the case of a promise to insure against fire a thoroughly fireproof building. There may be a promise in such a case even though the duty to perform depends on a state of mind of the promisor other than his own unfettered wish (see §§228), or on an event within the promisor's control. **Illustration:**

> 3. A says to B, "I will employ you for a year at a salary of $ 5,000 if I go into business." This is a promise, even though it is wholly optional with A to go into business or not.

f. Opinions and predictions. A promise must be distinguished from a statement of opinion or a mere prediction of future events. The distinction is not usually difficult in the case of an informal gratuitous opinion, since there is often no manifestation of intention to act or refrain from acting or to bring about a result, no expectation of performance and no consideration. The problem is frequently presented, however, whether words of a seller of goods amount to a warranty. Under Uniform Commercial Code § 2-313(2) a statement purporting to be merely the seller's opinion does not create a warranty, but the buyer's reliance on the seller's skill and judgment may create an implied warranty that the goods are fit for a particular purpose under Uniform Commercial Code § 2-315. In any case where an expert opinion is paid for, there is likely to be an implied promise that the expert will act with reasonable care and skill.

A promise often refers to future events which are predicted or assumed rather than promised. Thus a promise to render personal service at a particular future time commonly rests on an assumption that the promisor will be alive and well at that time; a promise to paint a building may similarly rest on an assumption that the building will be in existence. Such cases are the subject of Chapter 11. The promisor may of course promise to answer for harm caused by the failure of the future event to occur; if he does not, such a failure may discharge any duty of performance. **Illustration:**

> 4. A, on seeing a house of thoroughly fire-proof construction, says to B, the owner, "This house will never burn down." This is not a promise but merely an opinion or prediction. If A had been paid for his opinion as an expert, there might be an implied promise that he would employ reasonable care and skill in forming and giving his opinion.

g. Promisee and beneficiary. The word promisee is used repeatedly in discussion of the law of contracts, and it cannot be avoided here. In common usage the promisee is the person to whom the promise is made; as promise is defined here, the promisee might be the person to whom the manifestation of the promisor's intention is communicated. In many situations, however, a promise is complete and binding before the communication is received (see, for example, §§ 63 and 104(1)). To cover such cases, the promisee is defined here as the addressee. As to agents or purported agents of the addressee, see § 52 Comment *c.*

In the usual situation the promisee also bears other relations to the promisor, and the word promisee is sometimes used to refer to one or more of those relations. Thus, in the simple case of a loan of money, the lender is not only the addressee of the promise but also the person to whom performance is to be rendered, the person who will receive economic benefit, the person who furnished the consideration, and the person to whom the legal duty of the promisor runs. As the word promisee is here defined, none of these relations is essential.

Contractual rights of persons not parties to the contract are the subject of Chapter 14. The promisor and promisee are the "parties" to a promise; a third person who will benefit from performance is a "beneficiary." A beneficiary may or may not have a legal right to performance; like "promisee", the term is neutral with respect to right and duties. A person who is entitled under the terms of a letter of credit to draw or demand payment is commonly called a beneficiary, but such a person is ordinarily a promisee under the present definition. See Uniform Commercial Code § 5-103.

§ 3. Agreement Defined; Bargain Defined

An agreement is a manifestation of mutual assent on the part of two or more persons. A bargain is an agreement to exchange promises or to exchange a promise for a performance or to exchange performances.

Comment:

a. Agreement distinguished from bargain. Agreement has in some respects a wider meaning than contract, bargain or promise. On the other hand, there are contracts which do not require agreement. See, e.g., §§ 82-90, 94, 104. The word "agreement" contains no implication that legal consequences are or are not produced. It applies to transactions executed on one or both sides, and also to those that are wholly executory. The word contains no implication of mental agreement. Such agreement usually but not always exists where the parties manifest assent to a transaction.

b. Manifestation of assent. Manifestation of assent may be made by words or by any other conduct (see §19). Even silence in some circumstances is such a manifestation (see § 69). Compare the definition of "agreement" in Uniform Commercial Code § 1-201(3).

c. Bargain distinguished from agreement. Bargain has a narrower meaning than agreement, since it is applicable only to a particular class of agreements. It includes agreements which are not contracts, such as transactions where one party makes a promise and the other gives something in exchange which is not consideration, or transactions where what would otherwise be a contract is invalidated by illegality. As here defined, it includes completely executed transactions, such as exchanges of goods (barters) or of services, or sales where goods have been transferred and the price paid for them, although such transactions are not within the scope of this Restatement unless a promise is made.

d. Offer. A bargain is ordinarily made by an offer by one party and an acceptance by the other party or parties, the offer specifying the two subjects of exchange to which the offeror is manifesting assent (see §§ 22 and 24).

e. Contract distinguished from bargain. A contract is not necessarily a bargain. Thus, a promise to make a gift, if made under seal, may be a contract (see § 95), but it is not a bargain. Other contracts which are not bargains are the subject of §§ 82-94. Such contracts do not require manifestations of mutual assent in the form of offer and acceptance.

§ 4. How a Promise May Be Made

A promise may be stated in words either oral or written, or may be inferred wholly or partly from conduct.

Comment:

a. Express and implied contracts. Contracts are often spoken of as express or implied. The distinction involves, however, no difference in legal effect, but lies merely in the mode of manifesting assent. Just as assent may be manifested by words or other conduct, sometimes including silence, so intention to make a promise may be manifested in language or by implication from other circumstances, including course of dealing or usage of trade or course of performance. See Uniform Commercial Code § 1-201(3), defining "agreement." **Illustrations:**

    1. A telephones to his grocer, "Send me a ten-pound bag of flour." The grocer sends it. A has thereby promised to pay the grocer's current price therefor.

    2. A, on passing a market, where he has an account, sees a box of apples marked "25 cts. each." A picks up an apple, holds it up so that a clerk of the establishment sees the act. The clerk ods, and A passes on. A has promised to pay twenty-five cents for the apple.

b. Quasi-contracts. Implied contracts are different from quasi-contracts, although in some cases the line between the two is indistinct. See Comment *a* to § 19. Quasi-contracts have often been called implied contracts or contracts implied in law; but, unlike true contracts, quasi-contracts are not based on the apparent intention of the parties to undertake the performances in question, nor are they promises. They are obligations created by law for reasons of justice. Such obligations were ordinarily enforced at common law in the same form of action (assumpsit) that was appropriate to true contracts, and some confusion with reference to the nature of quasi-contracts has been caused thereby. They are dealt with in the Restatement of Restitution. See also §§ 141, 158, 197-99, 272, 370-77. **Illustration:**

    3. A's wife, B, separates from A for justifiable cause, and, in order to secure necessary clothing and supplies, buys them from C and charges their cost to A. A is bound to pay for them, though he has directed C not to furnish his wife with such supplies; but A's duty is quasi-contractual, not contractual. See Restatement of Restitution § 113.

§ 5. Terms of Promise, Agreement, or Contract

(1) A term of a promise or agreement is that portion of the intention or assent manifested which relates to a particular matter.

(2) A term of a contract is that portion of the legal relations resulting from the promise or set of promises which relates to a particular matter, whether or not the parties manifest an intention to create those relations.

Comment:

a. Agreed terms. The terms of a promise or agreement are those expressed in the language of the parties or implied in fact from other conduct. Both language and conduct are to be understood in the light of the circumstances, including course of dealing or usage of trade or course of performance. See Comment *a* to § 4. If a promise is binding, a term of the promise becomes a term of the contract unless it is rendered inoperative by some rule of law.

b. Contract terms supplied by law. Much contract law consists of rules which may be varied by agreement of the parties. Such rules are sometimes stated in terms of presumed intention, and they may be thought of as implied terms of an agreement. They often rest, however, on considerations of public policy rather than on manifestation of the intention of the parties. In the Restatement of this Subject, such rules are stated in terms of the operative facts which make them applicable.

c. Statutory contract terms. Statutes providing for contract terms vary in the extent to which they follow the terminology used here, and in the extent to which they permit variation by agreement. Under Uniform Commercial Code § 1-102(3), for example, the effect of provisions of the Code may be freely varied by agreement, with limited exceptions; at the other extreme are statutes or administrative regulations prescribing standard forms of such documents as insurance policies or bills of lading. Transactions entered into under statutes providing either optional or required terms commonly contain promises within the present definition, but they may also produce obligations which do not rest upon any manifestation of the intention of the obligor.

Such statutory obligations are beyond the scope of the Restatement of this Subject. The statutes are sometimes written in terms of presumed intention, and they are sometimes properly interpreted as imposing the same legal consequences as if one of the parties to a contract had made a promise in the prescribed terms. If so, rules stated here may be applicable. **Illustration:**

1. A contracts to sell B a described automobile. Both parties sign a printed contract form on which the description is typed and which contains the printed words, "Seller hereby excludes all warranties, express or implied." Under Uniform Commercial Code § 2-316 the quoted words do not exclude an implied warranty of merchantability, and under § 2-314 A warrants that the automobile is fit to drive. Under § 2-714 the warranty has the effect of a promise to pay for harm if the warranty is broken.

§ 6. Formal Contracts

The following types of contracts are subject in some respects to special rules that depend on their formal characteristics and differ from those governing contracts in general:

(a) Contracts under seal,

(b) Recognizances,

(c) Negotiable instruments and documents,

(d) Letters of credit.

...

§ 7. Voidable Contracts

A voidable contract is one where one or more parties have the power, by a manifestation of election to do so, to avoid the legal relations created by the contract, or by ratification of the contract to extinguish the power of avoidance.

Comment:

a. "Void contracts." A promise for breach of which the law neither gives a remedy nor otherwise recognizes a duty of performance by the promisor is often called a void contract. Under § 1, however, such a promise is not a contract at all; it is the "promise" or "agreement" that is void of legal effect. If the term "contract" were defined to refer to the acts of the parties without regard to their legal effect, a contract could without inconsistency be referred to as "void."

b. Grounds of avoidance. Typical instances of voidable contracts are those where one party was an infant, or where the contract was induced by fraud, mistake, or duress, or where breach of a warranty or other promise justifies the aggrieved party in putting an end to the contract. Usually the power to avoid is confined to one party to the contract, but where, for instance, both parties are infants, or where both parties enter into a contract under a mutual mistake, the contract may be voidable by either one of the parties. Avoidance is often referred to as "disaffirmance."

c. Consequences of avoidance. The legal relations that exist after avoidance vary with the circumstances. In some cases the party who avoids the contract is entitled to be restored to a position as good as that which he occupied immediately before the formation of the contract; in other cases the parties may be left in the same condition as at the time of the avoidance. In many cases the power of avoidance exists only if the original situation of the parties can be and is restored at least substantially; but this is not necessarily the case. An infant, for instance, in many jurisdictions is allowed to avoid his contract without this qualification, so that when the infant exercises his power the parties frequently are left in a very different situation from that which existed when the contract was made. See § 14; Restatement of Restitution § 62. As to breach of contract, see Chapters 10 and 16 of this Restatement; as to mistake, misrepresentation, duress and undue influence, see Chapters 6 and 7. **Illustration:**

1. A, an infant, sells and delivers his watch to B, an adult, in return for B's promise to pay $ 20. There is a contract whereby B becomes owner of the watch and is under an enforceable duty to pay $ 20 to A. But A has the power to

extinguish his own right to the money and B's duty to pay it and, as against B, to revest in himself the ownership of the watch.

d. Promptness of election. Voidable contracts differ with respect to the requirement that the avoiding party manifest his election promptly. In some cases the power of avoidance may be lost by unreasonable delay in returning benefits received or in manifesting the election to avoid. In other cases, particularly where the contract is entirely executory on both sides, no manifestation of intention is necessary until an action is brought against the party having the power of avoidance. **Illustrations:**

> 2. A, by fraud, induces B to make a promise to pay A money in consideration of goods delivered by A to B. There is a contract, but the fraudulent representations of A give B a power to avoid by tendering back to A within a reasonable time the goods received from him.
> 3. A, an infant, makes an agreement with B, an adult, the infant promising to pay money and the adult promising to deliver a chattel. This is enforceable against B, but not against A. If A has

not previously avoided, he will have the power of ratification upon attaining his majority.

e. Power of ratification. The propriety of calling a transaction a voidable contract rests primarily on the traditional view that the transaction is valid and has its usual legal consequences until the power of avoidance is exercised. Where each party has a power of avoidance, there is no legal duty of performance; but the term voidable contract is appropriate if ratification by one of the parties would terminate his power of avoidance and make the contract enforceable against him. See § 85. Moreover, action may be necessary in order to prevent the contract from producing the ordinary legal consequences of a contract; often such action in order to be effectual must be taken promptly. **Illustration:**

> 4. A, by fraud, induces B to promise to pay for certain advice which A gives. This promise creates no duty in B, but is not wholly void, because it can be validated by B after he learns the facts.

§ 8. Unenforceable Contracts

An unenforceable contract is one for the breach of which neither the remedy of damages nor the remedy of specific performance is available, but which is recognized in some other way as creating a duty of performance, though there has been no ratification.

Comment:

a. Distinction between "voidable" and "unenforceable." Just as a contract may be voidable by one party or by either party, so it may be enforceable by one and not by the other or it may be unenforceable by either. Similarly, one party to an unenforceable contract may have a power to make the contract enforceable by all the usual remedies, and both voidable and unenforceable contracts may have collateral consequences. Voidable contracts might be defined as one type of unenforceable contract. As defined here, however, the term unenforceable contract refers to rules under which the duty of performance does not depend solely on the election of one party. In the transactions here classified as unenforceable, some legal consequences other than the creation of a power of ratification follow without further action by either party. **Illustrations:**

> 1. A, an infant, orally accepts a written offer signed by B, an adult, to sell a tract of land.

A's promise is voidable by him because of his infancy and unenforceable under the Statute of Frauds. Upon attaining his majority, A delivers to B a signed writing stating the terms of the contract and manifesting an election to avoid it. Under § 133, the Statute of Frauds no longer prevents enforcement; but the contract is avoided.

> 2. A is indebted to B, but the statute of limitations has barred a direct remedy. A has the power to make direct remedies available or to make a new contract without consideration by making a new promise or part payment of the debt (see § 82). Even without such further acts, legal consequences may flow from the barred debt. If the creditor has security, he may have a right to apply it towards payment of the debt.

b. Types of unenforceable contracts. Some contracts are unenforceable because they arise out of illegal bargains which are neither wholly void nor voidable. See Comments *b-d* to § 178; §§ 183-84; Comment *b* to § 197. Others are unenforceable because of laws relating primarily to remedies, such as the Statute of Frauds (see Chapter 5) or Statute of Limitations. **Illustrations:**

    3. A agrees to sell specific goods to B, and B agrees to buy them. A has previously contracted to sell the same goods to C, as B knows. The bargain between A and B is unenforceable on grounds of public policy (§ 194), and neither party can enforce it while executory. But if either party performs his promise, he can recover what he has transferred or its value. The return promise, though unenforceable, is given legal effect as showing that the performance was not gratuitous, and is therefore a contract.

    4. A makes an oral purchase of goods from B for an agreed price of $ 500. There is no delivery or part payment, and the bargain is unenforceable under the Statute of Frauds. A insures the goods as owner. The insurer cannot defeat a claim under the policy on the ground that A did not own the goods, although A would have had no direct remedy against B for failure to deliver.

c. Government contracts. Contracts with a government or governmental agency are sometimes unenforceable under remnants of the historic English tradition that the sovereign is immune from suit. Yet the legal consequences of such a contract show that what is promised by the government is due as of right and not as a favor. Thus, a claim against the government arising out of the contract may pass to the executor or trustee in bankruptcy of the claimant. Sometimes such a claim, though not enforceable by action, may be asserted defensively in an action by the government.

. . .

Chapter 2

Formation of Contracts - Parties and Capacity

§ 9. Parties Required

There must be at least two parties to a contract, a promisor and a promisee, but there may be any greater number.

Comment:

a. Promise to oneself. In one sense a person can make a promise to himself, but the law does not provide remedies for breach of such promises. This rule, which is implicit in the definition of "promise" in § 2, has been thought to be a rule of substantive law independent of mere procedural requirements. But it is unlikely to have practical significance unless some other person becomes involved, and in such cases it is an unreliable basis for prediction of legal consequences. Thus a contract may be formed in which the same person is one of several on one side of a bargain, and either alone or with others a party on the other side. See § 11. Again, where one party to a contract becomes both obligor and obligee and there are no other parties to the contract, the contract is not necessarily deprived of all legal consequences. See the provisions on discharge in Chapter 12; compare Uniform Commercial Code §§ 3-208, 3-601.

b. Different capacities. One person may have different capacities, as for instance as trustee, as executor, as partner, and as individual. If he purports to make a promise in one capacity to himself in another capacity, there may be legal consequences. He cannot make a contract by his own undisclosed mental processes; a contract requires a manifestation of intention. Even if his intention is manifested by execution of a formal document or by other conduct, it may not be technically accurate to say that in one capacity he holds a claim against himself in another capacity, but that may be substantially the effect of his acts. Thus if a trust company holds a sum of money in trust, and in accordance with the terms of the trust deposits the money in its banking department, it is under substantially the same duties to the beneficiaries as if it held a claim against a third person in trust. See Restatement, Second, Trusts § 87; compare Restatement, Second, Agency § 24. Such self-dealing by a fiduciary may involve a breach of duty to a beneficiary or principal. See Restatement, Second, Trusts § 170; Restatement, Second, Agency § 387.

c. Multiple parties. Under § 1 a contract may be a "set of promises", and there may be multiple promisors and multiple promisees in one set.

Illustration:

1. A, B, C and D enter into a written contract by which A makes certain promises to B, other promises to C, and other promises to D. In return B, C and D promise a single performance to A, or each promises A a separate performance. In either case there is a contract, and numerous variations may be made from this illustration in regard to the number of parties and the various promises which they may make.

§ 10. Multiple Promisors and Promisees of the Same Performance

(1) Where there are more promisors than one in a contract, some or all of them may promise the same performance, whether or not there are also promises of separate performances.

(2) Where there are more promisees than one in a contract, a promise may be made to some or all of them as a unit, whether or not the same or another performance is separately promised to one or more of them.

Comment:

a. Procedural limitations at common law. Historically it was said that there could be only two sides to an action at law, that of the plaintiff and that of the defendant. There might be more than one person on each side, but it was necessary that all the parties joined as plaintiffs assert a common right and that all the persons joined as defendants be charged with a common duty. In equity, however, there has never been a requirement that the parties to a suit must consist of merely two units, one seeking to enforce a right against the other. On the contrary, any number of parties having diverse and conflicting legal relations could be dealt with under equity procedure; and the same thing is true where under modern statutes or rules of court legal and equitable procedures have been merged in a single form of action. The extent to which remnants of common-law procedure survive in the United States is beyond the scope of the Restatement of this Subject.

b. Multiple promises; suretyship. As a matter of substantive law, an indefinite number of persons may contract with one another, and there may be three or more individuals or groups, each with distinct rights and duties. Promises may be made by individuals or by groups acting together, and they may be made to individuals or to groups acting together.

Rules governing multiple promises of the same performance are stated in Chapter 13. Where promises of the same performance are made by two or more promisors, there is necessarily a relation of suretyship among the promisors. Thus, if there are two promisors, either one is the principal obligor and the other his surety, or each is a principal obligor as to a part and a surety as to the balance. Rules of suretyship are stated in the Restatement of Security; in general they are beyond the scope of the Restatement of this Subject. **Illustration:**

> 1. A promises to convey a tract of land to his three sons, B, C and D. In return B and C promise to build and maintain a home for A; D promises to live with A and to support and care for him; B, C and D promise that A will receive $ 200 a year. As to the home, B is the principal obligor for his share and C for his; B is C's surety for C's share and C is B's surety for B's share. Similarly, as to the $ 200, each is principal as to a third and surety for each of the others. D alone is bound to furnish care and support.

§ 11. When a Person May Be Both Promisor and Promisee

A contract may be formed between two or more persons acting as a unit and one or more but fewer than all of these persons, acting either singly or with other persons.

. . .

Illustrations:

> 1. A becomes a member of an unincorporated society, and by so doing promises to pay dues to the society. He is bound by a contract.
>
> 2. A, a trustee of an estate jointly with B, enters into a written agreement by which he individually promises to buy and A and B as trustees promise to sell a piece of land belonging to the trust. This is a contract; and, thought it is voidable by the beneficiaries if made without ei-

ther their consent or the authority of a court, it is enforceable unless the beneficiaries elect to avoid it.

b. Historically contracts falling within the terms of this Section were said not to be enforceable at common law, but this difficulty could be obviated by resort to a court of equity. The extent to which this procedural distinction survives in the United States is beyond the scope of the Restatement of this Subject.

§ 12. Capacity to Contract

(1) No one can be bound by contract who has not legal capacity to incur at least voidable contractual duties. Capacity to contract may be partial and its existence in respect of a particular transaction may depend upon the nature of the transaction or upon other circumstances.

(2) A natural person who manifests assent to a transaction has full legal capacity to incur contractual duties thereby unless he is

(a) under guardianship, or

(b) an infant, or

(c) mentally ill or defective, or

(d) intoxicated.

Comment:

a. Total and partial incapacity. Capacity, as here used, means the legal power which a normal person would have under the same circumstances. See Restatement, Second, Agency § 20; Restatement, Second, Trusts § 18. Incapacity may be total, as in cases where extreme physical or mental disability prevents manifestation of assent to the transaction, or in cases of mental illness after a guardian has been appointed. Often, however, lack of capacity merely renders contracts voidable. See § 7. Incapacity sometimes relates only to particular types of transactions; on the other hand, persons whose capacity is limited in most circumstances may be bound by particular types of transactions. In cases of partial disability, the law of mistake or of misrepresentation, duress and undue influence may be relevant. See Chapters 6 and 7, particularly §§ 153, 157, 161(d), 163, 164, 167, 169(c) and 177, Comment *b* to § 172 and Comment *c* to § 175.

b. Types of incapacity. Historically, the principal categories of natural persons having no capacity or limited capacity to contract were married women, infants, and insane persons. Those formerly referred to as insane are included in the more modern phrase "mentally ill," and mentally defective persons are treated similarly. Statutes sometimes authorize the appointment of guardians for habitual drunkards, narcotics addicts, spendthrifts, aged persons or convicts as in cases of mental illness. Even without the appointment of a guardian, civil powers of convicts may be suspended in whole or in part during imprisonment; and American Indians are for some purposes treated as wards of the United States government. The contractual powers of convicts and Indians are beyond the scope of the Restatement of this Subject. As to convicts, see Model Penal Code § 306.5.

c. Inability to manifest assent. In order to incur a contractual duty, a party must make a promise, manifesting his intention; in most cases he must manifest assent to a bargain. See §§ 2, 17, 18. The conduct of a party is not effective as a manifestation of his assent unless he intends to engage in the conduct. See § 19. Hence if physical disability prevents a person from acting, or if mental disability is so extreme that he cannot form the necessary intent, there is no contract. Similarly, even if he intends to engage in the conduct, there is no contract if the other party knows or has reason to know that he does not intend the resulting appearance of assent. See § 20. In such cases it is proper to say that incapacity prevents the formation of a contract.

d. Married women. At common law a married woman had no capacity to incur contractual duties, although courts of equity recognized a limited power with respect to property conveyed to her separate use. Modern statutes in most States have given married women full power to contract, and they are therefore omitted from the list in subsection (2) of persons who may not have full capacity. In some States, however, capacity is still denied with respect to particular types of contracts, such as contracts between husband and wife, contracts of suretyship, contracts for the sale of real property, or contracts relating to the management of community property.

e. Artificial persons. The contractual powers of artificial persons such as corporations and governmental agencies are beyond the scope of the Restatement of this Subject. The tendency of modern legislation is to restrict the assertion of the defense of *ultra vires* by business corporations, and in effect to give them full capacity; what was once lack of capacity then resembles lack of authority as used in the law of agency. See Model Business Corporation Act § 6 (1961). Where partnerships or unincorporated associations have no power to contract as such, contracts made in their names bind the members instead. Compare Restatement, Second, Agency § 20; Restatement, Second, Trusts §§ 97, 98. ...

§ 13. Persons Affected by Guardianship

A person has no capacity to incur contractual duties if his property is under guardianship by reason of an adjudication of mental illness or defect.

Comment:

a. Rationale. The reason for appointing a guardian of property is to preserve the property from being squandered or improvidently used. The guardianship proceedings are treated as giving public notice of the ward's incapacity and establish his status with respect to transactions during guardianship even though the other party to a particular transaction may have no knowledge or reason to know of the guardianship: the guardian is not required to give personal notice to all persons who may deal with the ward. The control of the ward's property is vested in the guardian, subject to court supervision; that control and supervision are not to be impaired or avoided by proof that the ward has regained his reason or has had a lucid interval, unless the guardianship is terminated or abandoned.

The rules governing contracts made by a guardian are beyond the scope of the Restatement of this Subject. A contract purporting not to bind the guardian personally but to bind the ward's estate raises problems much like those raised by a similar contract made by a trustee. See Restatement, Second, Trusts §§ 262, 263, 271. But the powers of guardians are usually defined by statute, and are ordinarily much narrower than those of trustees.

b. Non-contractual obligations. Property under guardianship may be reached in some circumstances to redress the torts of the ward or to satisfy his quasi-contractual obligations. See Restatement of Restitution § 139. The guardian is not required, in order to defend the ward against contractual liability arising out of a transaction during guardianship, to restore the other party to his original position, since such a requirement might force the guardian to use other property to replace property dissipated by the ward. Compare Restatement of Restitution § 62. But the other party may be able to reclaim the consideration received by the ward if it can be found. In some cases, as where necessaries have been furnished, the other party, to avoid unjust enrichment, may recover the fair value of the consideration received by the ward. See Comment *f* to § 12.

Illustration:

    1. A, under guardianship by reason of mental illness, buys an old car from B for $ 300, giving a promissory note for that amount. A subsequently abandons the car. A is not liable on the note. B may reclaim the car or, if the car is found to be a necessary, has a claim for having furnished it to A.

  . . .

§ 14. Infants

Unless a statute provides otherwise, a natural person has the capacity to incur only voidable contractual duties until the beginning of the day before the person's eighteenth birthday.

Comment:

a. Who are infants. The common law fixed the age of twenty-one as the age at which both men and women achieve full capacity to contract, and the rule that the critical moment is the beginning of the preceding day was established on the ground that the law disregards fractions of a day. In almost every State these rules have been changed by statute. It appears that 49 States have lowered the age of majority, either generally or for contract capacity, to less than twenty-one; usually, the age is eighteen. See the table in the Reporter's Note to this Comment. The birthday rather than the preceding day is the date of majority in some States; in some both men and women have full capacity upon marriage.

b. Obligations which are not voidable. Infants' contracts were at one time classified as void, voidable or valid, but the modern rule in the absence of statute is that they are voidable by the infant. See § 7. Compare Restatement, Second, Agency § 20. An infant may be bound by obligations imposed by law independently of contract, such as tort and quasi-contractual obligations. See Comment *f* to § 12, Restatement of Restitution § 139. In addition, certain contracts are held binding, ordinarily by statute, such as recognizances for appearance in court or contracts made with judicial approval. Modern statutes also sometimes deny the power of disaffirmance as to such transactions as withdrawal of bank deposits or payment of life insurance premiums.

c. Restoration of consideration. An infant need not take any action to disaffirm his contracts until he comes of age. If sued upon the contract, he may defend on the ground of infancy without returning the consideration received. His disaffirmance revests in the other party the title to any property received by the infant under the contract. If the consideration received by the infant has been dissipated by him, the other party is without remedy unless the infant ratifies the contract after coming of age or is under some non-contractual obligation. But some states, by statute or decision, have restricted the power of disaffirmance, either generally or under particular circumstances, by requiring restoration of the consideration received. Where the infant seeks to enforce the contract, the conditions of the other party's promise must be fulfilled. The problems arising when an infant seeks to disaffirm a conveyance or executed contract are beyond the scope of the Restatement of this Subject, whether the disaffirmance is attempted before or after he comes of age. As to what constitutes ratification, see § 85.

§ 15. Mental Illness or Defect

(1) A person incurs only voidable contractual duties by entering into a transaction if by reason of mental illness or defect

(a) he is unable to understand in a reasonable manner the nature and consequences of the transaction, or

(b) he is unable to act in a reasonable manner in relation to the transaction and the other party has reason to know of his condition.

(2) Where the contract is made on fair terms and the other party is without knowledge of the mental illness or defect, the power of avoidance under Subsection (1) terminates to the extent that the contract has been so performed in whole or in part or the circumstances have so changed that avoidance would be unjust. In such a case a court may grant relief as justice requires.

Comment:

a. Rationale. A contract made by a person who is mentally incompetent requires the reconciliation of two conflicting policies: the protection of justifiable expectations and of the security of transactions, and the protection of persons unable to protect themselves against imposition. Each policy has sometimes prevailed to a greater extent than is stated in this Section. At one extreme, it has been said that a lunatic has no capacity to contract because he has no mind; this view has given way to a better understanding of mental phenomena and to the doctrine that contractual obligation depends on manifestation of assent rather than on mental assent. See §§ 2, 19. At the other extreme, it has been asserted that mental incompetency has no effect on a contract unless other grounds of avoidance are present, such as fraud, undue influence, or gross inadequacy of consideration; it is now widely believed that such a rule gives inadequate protection to the incompetent and his family, particularly where the contract is entirely executory.

b. The standard of competency. It is now recognized that there is a wide variety of types and degrees of mental incompetency. Among them are congenital deficiencies in intelligence, the mental deterioration of old age, the effects of brain damage caused by accident or organic disease, and mental illnesses evidenced by such symptoms as delusions, hallucinations, delirium, confusion and depression. Where no guardian has been appointed, there is full contractual capacity in any case unless the mental illness or defect has affected the particular transaction: a person may be able to understand almost nothing, or only simple or routine transactions, or he may be incompetent only with respect to a particular type of transaction. Even though understanding is complete, he may lack the ability to control his acts in the way that the normal individual can and does control them; in such cases the inability makes the contract voidable only if the other party has reason to know of his condition. Where a person has some understanding of a particular transaction which is affected by mental illness or defect, the controlling consideration is whether the transaction in its result is one which a reasonably competent person might have made.

Illustration:

1. A, a school teacher, is a member of a retirement plan and has elected a lower monthly

benefit in order to provide a benefit to her husband if she dies first. At age 60 she suffers a "nervous breakdown," takes a leave of absence, and is treated for cerebral arteriosclerosis. When the leave expires she applies for retirement, revokes her previous election, and elects a larger annuity with no death benefit. In view of her reduced life expectancy, the change is foolhardy, and there are no other circumstances to explain the change. She fully understands the plan, but by reason of mental illness is unable to make a decision based on the prospect of her dying before her husband. The officers of the plan have reason to know of her condition. Two months after the changed election she dies. The change of election is voidable.

c. Proof of incompetency. Where there has been no previous adjudication of incompetency, the burden of proof is on the party asserting incompetency. Proof of irrational or unintelligent behavior is essential; almost any conduct of the person may be relevant, as may lay and expert opinions and prior and subsequent adjudications of incompetency. Age, bodily infirmity or disease, use of alcohol or drugs, and illiteracy may bolster other evidence of incompetency. Other facts have significance when there is mental illness or defect but some understanding: absence of independent advice, confidential or fiduciary relationship, undue influence, fraud, or secrecy; in such cases the critical fact often is departure from the normal pattern of similar transactions, and particularly inadequacy of consideration.

. . .

Illustration:

> 2. A, an incompetent not under guardianship, contracts to sell land to B, who does not know of the incompetency. A continues to be incompetent. On discovering the incompetency, B may refuse to perform until a guardian is appointed, and if none is appointed within a reasonable time may obtain a decree canceling the contract.

e. Effect of performance. Where the contract has been performed in whole or in part, avoidance is permitted only on equitable terms. In the traditional action at law, the doing of equity by or on behalf of the incompetent was accomplished by a tender before suit, but in equity or under modern merged procedure it is provided for in the decree. Any benefits still retained by the incompetent must be restored or paid for, and restitution must be made for any necessaries furnished under the contract. See Comment *f* to §

12. If the other party knew of the incompetency at the time of contracting, or if he took unfair advantage of the incompetent, consideration not received by the incompetent or dissipated without benefit to him need not be restored. **Illustrations:**

> 3. A, an incompetent not under guardianship, contracts to buy land for a fair price from B, who does not know of the incompetency. Shortly after transfer of title to A and part payment by A, A dies. A's personal representative may recover A's part payment on reconveying the land to B.
>
> 4. The facts being otherwise as stated in Illustration 3, C, with knowledge of A's incompetency, renders legal services to A in the transaction; after learning of A's incompetency, B pays $ 500 to C pursuant to the contract. A's personal representative need not reimburse B for the payment.

f. When avoidance is inequitable. If the contract is made on fair terms and the other party has no reason to know of the incompetency, performance in whole or in part may so change the situation that the parties cannot be restored to their previous positions or may otherwise render avoidance inequitable. The contract then ceases to be voidable. Where the other party, though acting in good faith, had reason to know of the incompetency at the time of contracting or performance, or where the equities can be partially adjusted by the decree, the court may grant or deny relief as the situation requires. Factors to be taken into account in such cases include not only benefits conferred and received on both sides but also the extent to which avoidance will benefit the incompetent and the extent to which others who will benefit from avoidance had opportunities to prevent the situation from arising. **Illustrations:**

> 5. A, an incompetent spouse not under guardianship, mortgages land on fair terms to B, a bank which has no knowledge or reason to know of the incompetency, for a loan of $ 2,000. At A's request the money is paid to the other spouse, C, who absconds with it. The contract is not voidable.
>
> 6. A, a congenital imbecile not under guardianship, has an interest in unimproved land which is contingent on his surviving his father B. A joins B and C, a cousin, in leasing the land on fair terms for 25 years to D, who has no reason to know of the incompetency. Subsequently A assigns his interest in the rent to C in return for C's agreement to support A for life, which C duly

performs. Five years later A joins B and C in an outright sale of the land to D. On B's death avoidance of the sale of A's interest may be equitable if D can be assured of repayment of the price and of retaining improvements made by him after the sale; avoidance of the lease would be inequitable.

7. A, an incompetent not under guardianship, lives on a homestead with his mother B and brother C. A also holds a mortgage on a second tract of land owned by C. To prevent foreclosure of a mortgage on the homestead, A, B and C join in borrowing money from D on a mortgage of both tracts on fair terms. D acts in good faith but has reason to know of A's incompetency. A dies, leaving B his sole heir. The mortgage to D is not voidable for the benefit of B.

§ 16. Intoxicated Persons

A person incurs only voidable contractual duties by entering into a transaction if the other party has reason to know that by reason of intoxication

(a) he is unable to understand in a reasonable manner the nature and consequences of the transaction, or

(b) he is unable to act in a reasonable manner in relation to the transaction.

Comment:

a. Rationale. Compulsive alcoholism may be a form of mental illness; and when a guardian is appointed for the property of a habitual drunkard, his transactions are treated like those of a person under guardianship by reason of mental illness. See §§ 13, 15. If drunkenness is so extreme as to prevent any manifestation of assent, there is no capacity to contract. See §§ 2, 12, 19. It would be possible to treat voluntary intoxication as a temporary mental disorder in all cases, but voluntary intoxication not accompanied by any other disability has been thought less excusable than mental illness. Compare Model Penal Code § 2.08 and Comment. Hence a contract made by an intoxicated person is enforceable by the other party even though entirely executory, unless the other person has reason to know that the intoxicated person lacks capacity. Elements of overreaching or other unfair advantage may be relevant on the issues of competency, of the other party's reason to know, and of the appropriate remedy. Compare Comments *c, e* and *f* to § 15. Use of drugs may raise similar problems.

b. What contracts are voidable. The standard of competency in intoxication cases is the same as that in cases of mental illness. If the intoxication is so extreme as to prevent any manifestation of assent, there is no contract. Otherwise the other party is affected only by intoxication of which he has reason to know. A contract made by a person who is so drunk he does not know what he is doing is voidable if the other party has reason to know of the intoxication.

Where there is some understanding of the transaction despite intoxication, avoidance depends on a showing that the other party induced the drunkenness or that the consideration was inadequate or that the transaction departed from the normal pattern of similar transactions; if the particular transaction in its result is one which a reasonably competent person might have made, it cannot be avoided even though entirely executory. **Illustrations:**

1. A, while in a state of extreme intoxication, signs and mails a written offer on fair terms to B, who has no reason to know of the intoxication. B accepts the offer. A has no right to avoid the contract.

2. A is ill and confined to his bed. B, knowing that the illness is incurable, plies A with intoxicating liquor for a week and then purports to treat him by rubbing him with oil. While intoxicated, A executes by mark a contract to sell land to B for a grossly inadequate consideration. Six days later A dies. A's heirs may avoid the contract.

3. A has been drinking heavily. B, who has also been drinking, meets A, offers to buy A's farm for $ 50,000, a fair price, and offers A a drink which A accepts. In drunken exhilaration A, as a joke, writes out and signs a memorandum of agreement to sell, gets his wife to sign it, and delivers it to B, who understands the transaction as a serious one. A's intoxication is no defense to B's suit for specific performance.

c. Ratification and avoidance. Where a contract is voidable on the ground of intoxication, the rules as to ratification and avoidance are much the same as in cases of misrepresentation.

See Chapter 7. On becoming sober, the intoxicated person must act promptly to disaffirm and must offer to restore consideration received. Such an offer may be excused, however, if the consideration has been dissipated during the period of drunkenness. **Illustration:**

4. A buys a barber shop from B for $ 650. Shortly afterward, A, helplessly drunk and evidently not aware of what he is doing, sells the shop back to B for $ 200. On recovering his senses, A cannot remember the transaction and cannot find out what happened to the $ 200. On prompt disaffirmance, A may recover the shop without repaying the $ 200.

Chapter 3

Formation of Contracts - Mutual Assent

§ 17. Requirement of a Bargain

(1) Except as stated in Subsection (2), the formation of a contract requires a bargain in which there is a manifestation of mutual assent to the exchange and a consideration.

(2) Whether or not there is a bargain a contract may be formed under special rules applicable to formal contracts or under the rules stated in §§ 82-94.

Comment:

a. Formal contracts. The types of contracts listed in § 6 are not necessarily subject to the requirements of manifestation of assent and consideration. Where contracts under seal still have their common-law effect, neither manifestation of assent by the promisee nor consideration is essential. See § 95, 104(1). Under Uniform Commercial Code § 3-408, a negotiable instrument may be binding without consideration in some cases. Under Uniform Commercial Code § 5-105, 5-106, neither manifestation of assent by the customer or the beneficiary nor consideration is necessary to the establishment of a letter of credit.

b. Bargains. Contracts of types enumerated in § 6 can be used in many of the transactions essential to civilized life: e.g., sale or lease of land, goods, or intangible property; the rendering of services for hire; the lending of money. But in modern times less formal contracts are far more important. The typical contract is a bargain, and is binding without regard to form. The governing principle in the typical case is that bargains are enforceable unless some other principle conflicts. This chapter and the next deal with the two essential elements of a bargain: agreement and exchange.

c. "Meeting of the minds." The element of agreement is sometimes referred to as a "meeting of the minds." The parties to most contracts give actual as well as apparent assent, but it is clear that a mental reservation of a party to a bargain does not impair the obligation he purports to undertake. The phrase used here, therefore, is "manifestation of mutual assent," as in the definition of "agreement" in § 3. See also Comment *b* to § 2. Topics 2-5, §§ 18-70, explain this requirement.

d. "Sufficient consideration." The element of exchange is embodied in the concept of consideration. In some cases a promise is not binding for want of consideration, despite the presence of an element of exchange. "Consideration" has sometimes been used to refer to the element of exchange, without regard to whether it is sufficient to make an informal promise legally binding; the consideration which satisfies the legal requirement has then been called "sufficient consideration." As the term "consideration" is used here, however, it refers to an element of exchange which is legally sufficient, and the word "sufficient" would therefore be redundant. The requirement of consideration is the subject of §§ 71-81.

Illustration:

1. A owes B $ 50. In exchange for A's payment of the debt B makes a promise. Under the rule stated in § 73, B's promise is without consideration.

e. Informal contract without bargain. There are numerous atypical cases where informal promises are binding though not made as part of a bargain. In such cases it is often said that there is consideration by virtue of reliance on the promise or by virtue of some circumstance, such as a "past consideration," which does not involve the element of exchange. In this Restatement, however, "consideration" is used only to refer to the element of exchange, and contracts not involving that element are described as promises binding without consideration. There is no requirement of agreement for such contracts. They are the subject of §§ 82-94.

§ 18. Manifestation of Mutual Assent

Manifestation of mutual assent to an exchange requires that each party either make a promise or begin or render a performance.

Comment:

a. Manifestation of assent. Assent to the formation of an informal contract is operative only to the extent that it is manifested. Compare § 3 and Comment *b* to § 2. As to the manifestation of assent by conduct other than words, see §§ 4 and 19. Rules for cases where one party could reasonably draw more than one inference as to the intention of another are stated in the following sections, in connection with the scope of contractual obligations (see §§ 201, 219), and in connection with mistake (see § 151-58).

b. Assent by promise or performance. Where a bargain has been fully performed on one side, there is commonly no need to determine the moment of making of the contract or whether the performing party made a promise before he performed. Those issues ordinarily become important only when a dispute arises at an earlier stage. In the typical case such a dispute involves an exchange of promises before any performance takes place; there is an offer containing a promise and made binding by an acceptance containing a return promise. Section 50. The beginning or tender of performance may operate as such a return promise under § 63. In less common cases, acceptance may be made by a performance under § 54, and the beginning of performance may have an intermediate effect of making the offer irrevocable under § 45.

c. Sham or jest. Where all the parties to what would otherwise be a bargain manifest an intention that the transaction is not to be taken seriously, there is no such manifestation of assent to the exchange as is required by this Section. In some cases the setting makes it clear that there is no contract, as where a business transaction is simulated on a stage during a dramatic performance. In other cases, there may be doubt as to whether there is a joke, or one of the parties may take the joke seriously. If one party is deceived and has no reason to know of the joke the law takes the joker at his word. Even if the deceived party had reason to know of the joke, there may be a claim for fraud or unjust enrichment by virtue of the promise made. Where the parties to a sham transaction intend to deceive third parties, considerations of public policy may sometimes preclude a defense of sham. Cf. Illustration 1 to § 21.

§ 19. Conduct as Manifestation of Assent

(1) The manifestation of assent may be made wholly or partly by written or spoken words or by other acts or by failure to act.

(2) The conduct of a party is not effective as a manifestation of his assent unless he intends to engage in the conduct and knows or has reason to know that the other party may infer from his conduct that he assents.

(3) The conduct of a party may manifest assent even though he does not in fact assent. In such cases a resulting contract may be voidable because of fraud, duress, mistake, or other invalidating cause.

Comment:

a. Conduct other than words. Words are not the only medium of expression. Conduct may often convey as clearly as words a promise or an assent to a proposed promise. See Comment *a* to § 4 and Illustrations. Where no particular requirement of form is made by the law a condition of the validity or enforceability of a contract, there is no distinction in the effect of the promise whether it is expressed in writing, or orally, or in acts, or partly in one of these ways and partly in others. Purely negative conduct is sometimes, though not usually, a sufficient manifestation of assent. See § 69.

Like words, non-verbal conduct often has different meanings to different people. Indeed, the meaning of conduct not used as a conventional symbol is more uncertain and more dependent on its setting than are words. A wide variety of elements of the total situation may be relevant to the interpretation of such conduct. The problem is illustrated in cases of claims against a decedent's estate for services rendered.

In such cases the line between a contractual claim based on agreement and a quasi-contractual claim based on unjust enrichment is often indistinct; on either basis a major question may be whether the services were rendered gratuitously, and the circumstances are often critical. **Illustration:**

> 1. A lives in B's home and renders services to B over a period of years, and after B's death claims the value of the services. By statute A is incompetent to testify to transactions with B, and there is no evidence of a verbal promise. Among the factors relevant to a determination whether the services were gratuitous are the following: a request by B that A render the services, the relation between A and B, the value of the services to B, the alternatives foregone and hardship suffered by A, the financial circumstances of the parties, the relation between B and his legatees or distributees, and their connection with A's services.

b. "Reason to know." A person has reason to know a fact, present or future, if he has information from which a person of ordinary intelligence would infer that the fact in question does or will exist. A person of superior intelligence has reason to know a fact if he has information from which a person of his intelligence would draw the inference. There is also reason to know if the inference would be that there is such a substantial chance of the existence of the fact that, if exercising reasonable care with reference to the matter in question, the person would predicate his action upon the assumption of its possible existence.

Reason to know is to be distinguished from knowledge and from "should know." Knowledge means conscious belief in the truth of a fact; reason to know need not be conscious. "Should know" imports a duty to others to ascertain facts; the words " reason to know" are used both where the actor has a duty to another and where he would not be acting adequately in the protection of his own interests were he not acting with reference to the facts which he has reason to know. See Restatement, Second, Agency § 9; Restatement, Second, Torts § 12; Uniform Commercial Code § 1-201(25).

c. Responsibility for unintended appearance of assent. A "manifestation" of assent is not a mere appearance; the party must in some way be responsible for the appearance. There must be conduct and a conscious will to engage in that conduct. Thus, when a party is used as a mere mechanical instrument, his apparent assent does not affect his contractual relations. See the rules on duress in §§ 174-77. This is true even though the other party reasonably believes that the assent is genuine.

Similarly, even though the intentional conduct of a party creates an appearance of assent on his part, he is not responsible for that appearance unless he knows or has reason to know that his conduct may cause the other party to understand that he assents. In effect there must be either intentional or negligent creation of an appearance of assent. Compare § 20 and the rules on mistake, misrepresentation, duress and undue influence in Chapters 6 and 7. The other party must also manifest assent, but no further change of position on his part is necessary to the formation of a bargain. Change of position may of course be relevant to the existence of a power of avoidance, but the law must take account of the fact that in a society largely founded on credit bargains will be relied on in subtle ways, difficult or incapable of proof. **Illustrations:**

> 2. A offers to sell B his library at a stated price, forgetting that his favorite Shakespeare, which he did not intend to sell, is in the library. B accepts the offer. There is a contract including the Shakespeare, unless B knows or has reason to know of A's temporary forgetfulness. Whether the contract is voidable for mistake depends on the rules stated in Chapter 6.

> 3. A writes an offer to B, which he encloses in an envelope, addresses and stamps. Shortly afterwards, he decides not to send the offer, but by mistake he deposits it in the mail. It is delivered to B, who accepts the offer. There is a contract unless B knows or has reason to know of A's error. Whether the contract is voidable for mistake is governed by the rules stated in Chapter 6.

d. Voidable manifestations distinguished. Actual mental assent is not essential to the formation of an informal contract enforceable as a bargain. This is made clear by the definitions of "bargain" and "agreement" in terms of "manifestation" of mutual assent. See §§ 3, 17, 18; compare Comment *b* to § 2. But the fact that apparent assent is not genuine may have legal significance in rendering the contract voidable or unenforceable for mistake, misrepresentation, duress, or undue influence. See Chapters 6 and 7. In such cases it is often necessary to inquire whether the power of avoidance has been exercised with sufficient promptness, or whether the other party has so changed his position that avoidance would be inequitable. Where there is no manifestation of mutual assent, on the other hand, the contractual relations of the parties are not affected, and such inquiries are unnecessary.

§ 20. Effect of Misunderstanding

(1) There is no manifestation of mutual assent to an exchange if the parties attach materially different meanings to their manifestations and

(a) neither party knows or has reason to know the meaning attached by the other; or

(b) each party knows or each party has reason to know the meaning attached by the other.

(2) The manifestations of the parties are operative in accordance with the meaning attached to them by one of the parties if

(a) that party does not know of any different meaning attached by the other, and the other knows the meaning attached by the first party; or

(b) that party has no reason to know of any different meaning attached by the other, and the other has reason to know the meaning attached by the first party.

Comment:

a. Scope. Subsection (1) states the implications of the rule of § 19(2) as to the meaning of "manifestation of mutual assent" in cases of mistake in the expression of assent. The subject-matter of this Section is more fully treated in Chapter 9 on the scope of contractual obligations. Rules are stated here only for two-party transactions; multi-party transactions are more complex, but are governed by the same principles. As to the meaning of "reason to know," see Comment *b* to § 19.

b. The need for interpretation. The meaning given to words or other conduct depends to a varying extent on the context and on the prior experience of the parties. Almost never are all the connotations of a bargain exactly identical for both parties; it is enough that there is a core of common meaning sufficient to determine their performances with reasonable certainty or to give a reasonably certain basis for an appropriate legal remedy. See § 33. But material differences of meaning are a standard cause of contract disputes, and the decision of such disputes necessarily requires interpretation of the language and other conduct of the parties in the light of the circumstances.

c. Interpretation and agreement. There is a problem of interpretation in determining whether a contract has been made as well as in determining what obligations a contract imposes. Where one party makes a precise and detailed offer and the other accepts it, or where both parties sign the same written agreement, there may be an "integrated" agreement (see § 209) and the problem is then one of interpreting the offer or written agreement. In other cases agreement may be found in a jumble of letters, telegrams, acts and spoken words. In either type of case, the parties may have different understandings, intentions and meanings. Even though the parties manifest mutual assent to the same words of agreement, there may be no contract because of a material difference of understanding as to the terms of the exchange. Where there is no integration, the parties may also differ as to whether there was an offer of any kind, or whether there was an acceptance. Rules of interpretation governing various situations are stated in Chapter 9 on the scope of contractual obligations; those rules are applicable in the determination of what each party "knows or has reason to know."

d. Error in expression. The basic principle governing material misunderstanding is stated in Subsection (1): no contract is formed if neither party is at fault or if both parties are equally at fault. Subsection (2) deals with cases where both parties are not equally at fault. If one party knows the other's meaning and manifests assent intending to insist on a different meaning, he may be guilty of misrepresentation. Whether or not there is such misrepresentation as would give the other party a power of avoidance, there is a contract under Subsection (2) (a), and the mere negligence of the other party is immaterial. See § 166 as to reformation of a written contract in such a case. Under Subsection (2) (b) a party may be bound by a merely negligent manifestation of assent, if the other party is not negligent. The question whether such a contract is voidable for mistake is dealt with in §§ 151-58. **Illustrations:**

1. A offers to sell B goods shipped from Bombay ex steamer "Peerless". B accepts. There are two steamers of the name "Peerless", sailing from Bombay at materially different times. If both parties intend the same Peerless, there is a contract, and it is immaterial whether they know or have reason to know that two ships are named Peerless.

2. The facts being otherwise as stated in Illustration 1, A means Peerless No. 1 and B means Peerless No. 2. If neither A nor B knows or has reason to know that they mean different ships, or if they both know or if they both have reason to know, there is no contract.

3. The facts being otherwise as stated in Illustration 1, A knows that B means Peerless No. 2 and B does not know that there are two ships named Peerless. There is a contract for the sale of the goods from Peerless No. 2, and it is immaterial whether B has reason to know that A means Peerless No. 1. If A makes the contract with the undisclosed intention of not performing it, it is voidable by B for misrepresentation (see §§ 159-64). Conversely, if B knows that A

means Peerless No. 1 and A does not know that there are two ships named Peerless, there is a contract for the sale of the goods from Peerless No. 1, and it is immaterial whether A has reason to know that B means Peerless No. 2, but the contract may be voidable by A for misrepresentation.

4. The facts being otherwise as stated in Illustration 1, neither party knows that there are two ships Peerless. A has reason to know that B means Peerless No. 2 and B has no reason to know that A means Peerless No. 1. There is a contract for the sale of goods from Peerless No. 2. In the converse case, where B has reason to know and A does not, there is a contract for sale from Peerless No. 1. In either case the question whether the contract is voidable for mistake is governed by the rules stated in §§ 151-58.

5. A says to B, "I offer to sell you my horse for $ 100." B, knowing that A intends to offer to sell his cow for that price, not his horse, and that the word "horse" is a slip of the tongue, replies, "I accept." The price is a fair one for either the horse or the cow. There is a contract for the sale of the cow and not of the horse. If B makes the contract with the undisclosed intention of not performing it, it is voidable by A for misrepresentation. See §§ 159-64.

§ 21. Intention to Be Legally Bound

Neither real nor apparent intention that a promise be legally binding is essential to the formation of a contract, but a manifestation of intention that a promise shall not affect legal relations may prevent the formation of a contract.

Comment:

a. Intent to be legally bound. Most persons are now aware of the existence of courts and rules of law and of the fact that some promises are binding. The parties to a transaction often have a reasonably accurate understanding of the applicable law, and an intention to affect legal relations. Such facts may be important in interpreting their manifestations of intention and in determining legal consequences, but they are not essential to the formation of a contract. The parties are often quite mistaken about particular rules of law, but such mistakes do not necessarily deprive their acts of legal effect. **Illustrations:**

1. A draws a check for $ 300 payable to B and delivers it to B in return for an old silver watch worth about $ 15. Both A and B understand the transaction as a frolic and a banter, but each believes that he would be legally bound if the other dishonestly so asserted. There is no contract.

2. A orally promises to sell B a book in return for B's promise to pay $ 5. A and B both think such promises are not binding unless in writing. Nevertheless there is a contract, unless one of them intends not to be legally bound and the other knows or has reason to know of that intention.

b. Agreement not to be legally bound. Parties to what would otherwise be a bargain and a contract sometimes agree that their legal relations are not to be affected. In the absence of any invalidating cause, such a term is respected by the law like any other term, but such an agreement may present difficult questions of interpretation: it may mean that no bargain has been reached, or that a particular manifestation of intention is not a promise; it may reserve a power to revoke or terminate a promise under certain circumstances but not others. In a written document prepared by one party it may raise a question of misrepresentation or mistake or overreaching; to avoid such questions it may be read against the party who prepared it.

The parties to such an agreement may intend to deny legal effect to their subsequent acts. But where a bargain has been fully or partly performed on one side, a failure to perform on the other side may result in unjust enrichment, and the term may then be unenforceable as a provision for a penalty or forfeiture. See §§ 185, 229, 356. In other cases the term may be unenforceable as against public policy because it unreasonably limits recourse to the courts or as unconscionably limiting the remedies for breach of contract. See §§ 178-79, 208; Uniform Commercial Code §§ 2-302, 2-719 and Comment 1. **Illustrations:**

    3. A, an employer, issues to B, an employee, a "certificate of benefit", promising stated sums increasing yearly, payable to a named beneficiary if B dies while still in A's employ. The certificate provides that it "constitutes no contract" and "confers no legal right." The quoted language may be read as reserving a power of revocation only until B dies.

    4. A and B, two business corporations, have a contract by which B is the exclusive distributor in a certain territory of goods made by A. By a detailed written agreement they agree to continue the distributorship for three years. The writing provides that it is not to be a legal agreement or subject to legal jurisdiction in the law courts. The written agreement may be read and given effect to terminate the prior contract and to prevent any legal duty arising from the making of the agreement or from the acceptance of orders under it; but it does not excuse B from paying for goods delivered under it.

. . .

§ 22. Mode of Assent: Offer and Acceptance

(1) The manifestation of mutual assent to an exchange ordinarily takes the form of an offer or proposal by one party followed by an acceptance by the other party or parties.

(2) A manifestation of mutual assent may be made even though neither offer nor acceptance can be identified and even though the moment of formation cannot be determined.

Comment:

    a. The usual practice. Subsection (1) states the usual practice in the making of bargains. One party ordinarily first announces what he will do and what he requires in exchange, and the other then agrees. Where there are more than two parties, the second party to agree may be regarded as accepting the offer made by the first party and as making a similar offer to subsequent parties, and so on. It is theoretically possible for a third person to state a suggested contract to the parties and for them to say simultaneously that they assent. Or two parties may sign separate duplicates of the same agreement, each manifesting assent whether the other signs before or after him. Compare Illustration 5 to § 23.

    b. Assent by course of conduct. Problems of offer and acceptance are important primarily in cases where advance commitment serves to shift a risk from one party to the other, as in sales of goods which are subject to rapid price fluctuations, in sales of land, and in insurance contracts. Controversies as to whether and when the commitment is made are less likely to be important even in such cases once performance is well under way. Offer and acceptance become still less important after there have been repeated occasions for performance by one party where the other knows the nature of the performance and has an opportunity for objection to it. See Uniform Commercial Code § 2-208 (1); compare Comment *a* to § 19. In such cases it is unnecessary to determine the moment of making of the contract, or which party made the offer and which the acceptance. Thus, Uniform Commercial Code §§ 2-204 and 2-207(3), relating to contracts for the sale of goods, provide that conduct by both parties which recognizes the existence of a contract is sufficient to establish it although the writings of the parties do not otherwise establish a contract. The principle has also been applied in non-sales contexts. **Illustration:**

    1. A, a general contractor preparing a bid on a government construction contract, receives a bid by a proposed subcontractor, B, in a given amount. A names B as a subcontractor in A's bid, but after A receives the government con-

tract, A unsuccessfully asks B to reduce its bid, and also unsuccessfully seeks permission from the Government to replace B as a subcontractor. Pursuant to A's instructions, B proceedswith the work, but refuses to accept a work order from A which recites that A is still seeking permission to replace B. No new work order is issued. A does issue "change orders" using B's bid as the base "contract amount." B completes the job, but A refuses to pay the full amount, contending that B is entitled only to restitutionary damages because there never was a contract. There is an enforceable contract based upon A's assent to B's bid, as manifested by A's conduct, and B is entitled to the amount it bid, as modified by the change orders.

§ 23. Necessity That Manifestations Have Reference to Each Other

It is essential to a bargain that each party manifest assent with reference to the manifestation of the other.

Comment:

a. Mutuality of assent. Two manifestations of willingness to make a bargain, though having the same terms, do not constitute a bargain unless each is made with reference to the other. Ordinarily one party, by making an offer, assents in advance; the other, upon learning of the offer, assents by accepting it and thereby forms the contract. The offer may be communicated directly or through an agent; but information received by one party that another is willing to enter into a bargain is not necessarily an offer. The test is whether the offer is so made as to justify the accepting party in a belief that the offer is made to him. **Illustration:**

> 1. A advertises in a large New York newspaper that he will pay a specified reward to anyone who will give him certain information within one year. B sees a copy of this advertisement in a Tokyo newspaper, correctly translated into Japanese, and sends A the information within the year. There is a contract.

b. Unintended appearance of mutual assent. Either the offeror or the offeree may be bound by an unintended appearance of assent created by his intentional conduct. See §§ 19. The mutual reference required by this Section is ordinarily intended by both parties to a contract, but if one party believes that there is such reference and the other knows that his conduct creates that appearance, the requirement is satisfied. Similarly, if one party believes that there is such reference and has no reason to know that the other has a different understanding, the requirement is satisfied if the other has reason to know that his conduct creates the unintended appearance. Section 20. Thus where an offer is contained in a writing either the offeror or the offeree may, without reading the writing, manifest assent to it and bind himself without knowing its terms. Again, where goods are sent by a seller as an offer to a buyer, the buyer, without examining them or knowing precisely what they are or that a bargain is proposed, can bind himself by accepting the goods. So in many cases usages of business or of local exchanges are annexed as terms to an offer, and an offeror or offeree who should be aware of those terms may be bound in accordance with them if he manifests assent. See §§ 219-23; Uniform Commercial Code §§ 1-205, 2-104.

c. Unknown offers of rewards. Obligations arising from unintended manifestations of assent by an offeree are imposed in order to protect the offeror in justifiable reliance on the offeree's promise. If the offer clearly contemplates no commitment by the offeree, so that no binding return promise can be made and justifiable reliance by the offeror is impossible, this reason disappears. Thus if a general offer of reward to anyone who does a certain act or achieves a certain result is treated as contemplating a bargain, the only expectations to be fulfilled are those of the offeree, and he may have none unless he knows of the offer.

Such an offer is commonly interpreted as intended to induce action by people who know of the reward. A person who acts without such knowledge is then not within the terms of the offer, even though he intends to accept any offer which may be outstanding and thus does not act gratuitously. Standing offers of rewards made by governmental bodies, however, may be regarded as intended to create a climate in which people do certain acts in the hope of earning unknown rewards. Theoretically, an act so done might create a bargain, but recovery of the reward can be justified just as well by treating the offer as a promise binding without mutual assent or consideration or as creating a non-contractual obligation. **Illustrations:**

> 2. A advertises that he will give a specified reward for certain information, or writes B a similar proposal. B gives the information in ignorance of the advertisement, or without having received the letter. There is no contract enforceable as a bargain.

> 3. A city ordinance provides that a standing reward of $ 1000 will be paid for information leading to the arrest and conviction of anyone guilty of arson within the city limits. A furnishes such information. A is entitled to the reward whether or not he knew of the reward or was motivated by hope of reward.

. . .

e. Acceptance of unknown terms. An offeree, knowing that an offer has been made to him, need not know all its terms. Knowing that an offer has been made, he can accept without investigation of the exact terms, either intentionally or by words or conduct creating an unintended appearance of intention to accept. The governing principles are the same as those for unrecognized offers, explained in Comment *b*. **Illustration:**

> 7. A sends to B an offer to sell a specified lot for $ 5,000, also stating terms as to time of payment, mortgage security, taxes and insurance. B is so anxious to buy the lot that, without reading any of these additional terms, he sends to A an unconditional acceptance. There is a contract on the terms stated in A's offer.

§ 24. Offer Defined

An offer is the manifestation of willingness to enter into a bargain, so made as to justify another person in understanding that his assent to that bargain is invited and will conclude it.

Comment:

a. Offer as promise. An offer may propose an executed sale or barter rather than a contract, or it may propose the exchange of a promise for a performance or an exchange of promises, or it may propose two or more such transactions in combination or in the alternative. In the normal case of an offer of an exchange of promises, or in the case of an offer of a promise for an act, the offer itself is a promise, revocable until accepted. There may also be an offer of a performance, to be exchanged either for a return promise (§ 55) or for a return performance; in such cases the offer is not necessarily a promise, but there are often warranties or other incidental promises. **Illustration:**

> 1. A says to B, "That book you are holding is yours if you promise to pay me $ 5 for it." This is an offer empowering B, by making the requested promise, to make himself owner of the book and thus complete A's performance. In that

event there is also an implied warranty of title made by A. See Uniform Commercial Code §§ 2-312, 2-401.

b. Proposal of contingent gift. A proposal of a gift is not an offer within the present definition; there must be an element of exchange. Whether or not a proposal is a promise, it is not an offer unless it specifies a promise or performance by the offeree as the price or consideration to be given by him. It is not enough that there is a promise performable on a certain contingency. **Illustration:**

> 2. A promises B $ 100 if B goes to college. If the circumstances give B reason to know that A is not undertaking to pay B to go to college but is promising a gratuity, there is no offer.

c. Offer as contract. A promise made by the offeror as part of his offer may itself be a contract. Such a contract is commonly called an "option". See § 25.

§ 25. Option Contracts

An option contract is a promise which meets the requirements for the formation of a contract and limits the promisor's power to revoke an offer.

Comment:

a. "Option." A promise which constitutes an option contract may be contained in the offer itself, or it may be made separately in a collateral

offer to keep the main offer open. Such promises are commonly called "options." But the word "option" is also often used for any continuing offer, even though revocable, and indeed is sometimes used to refer to any power to make a choice. To avoid ambiguity the phrase "option contract" is used in this Restatement.

Illustrations:

> 1. A promises B under seal or in return for $ 100 paid or promised by B that A will sell B 100 shares of stock in a specified corporation for $ 5,000 at any time within thirty days that B selects. There is an option contract under which B has an option.

> 2. A offers to sell B Blackacre for $ 5,000 at any time within thirty days. Subsequently A promises under seal or in return for $ 100 paid or promised by B that the offer will not be revoked. There is an option contract under which B has an option.

b. The need for irrevocable offers. To provide the offeree with a dependable basis for decision whether or not to accept, the rule in many legal systems is that an offer is irrevocable unless it provides otherwise. The common-law rule, on the other hand, resting on the requirement of consideration, permits the revocation of offers even though stated to be firm. See Comment *a* to § 42. The offeree's need for a dependable basis for decision is met in part by the common-law rule that mailed acceptance prevents revocation. See § 63. Where more is needed, the option contract is available.

c. Types of option contracts. The traditional common-law devices for making an offer irrevocable are the giving of consideration and the affixing of a seal. The requirement of consideration may be met in any of the ways permitted by the rules stated in §§ 71-81: payment of money or some other performance by the offeree is effective, as is a promise of such performance; one option may furnish consideration for another, and a single consideration may support both a present contract and a future option. Compare Illustration 3 to § 47; see § 45 as to the beginning or tender of performance.

The option under seal is the traditional mode of making an offer irrevocable without consideration. Cf. § 95. In some cases a negotiable instrument or a letter of credit may operate as an offer binding without consideration. See Uniform Commercial Code §§ 3-408, 5-105, 5-106. Offers may also be irrevocable by statute or by virtue of reliance by the offeree or other circumstances bringing into play one of the rules stated in §§ 82-94. See, especially, § 87.

d. Effect of option contract. The principal legal consequence of an option contract is that stated in this Section: it limits the promisor's power to revoke an offer. The termination of the offeree's power of acceptance is subject to the requirements for discharge of a contractual duty. See § 37. A revocation by the offeror is not of itself effective, and the offer is properly referred to as an irrevocable offer.

§ 26. Preliminary Negotiations

A manifestation of willingness to enter into a bargain is not an offer if the person to whom it is addressed knows or has reason to know that the person making it does not intend to conclude a bargain until he has made a further manifestation of assent.

Comment:

a. Interpretation of proposals for exchange. The rule stated in this Section is a special application of the definition in § 24 and of the principles governing the interpretation of manifestations of assent. See § 20 and Chapter 9. Conduct which resembles an offer may not be so intended either because there is an intent not to affect legal relations (see § 18), or because the actor does not intend to engage in the conduct (see § 19), or because the proposal is not addressed to the recipient or is not received by the addressee (see § 23), or because the proposal contemplates a gift rather than a bargain (see Comment *b* to § 24). This Section deals rather with the case where the actor intends to make a bargain in the future, but only if he makes some further manifestation of assent. If the addressee of a proposal has reason to know that no offer is intended, there is no offer even though he understands it to be an offer. "Reason to know" depends not only on the words or other conduct, but also on the circumstances, including previous communications of the parties and the usages of their community or line of business.

b. Advertising. Business enterprises commonly secure general publicity for the goods or services they supply or purchase. Advertisements of goods by display, sign, handbill, newspaper, radio or television are not ordinarily intended or understood as offers to sell. The same is true of catalogues, price lists and circulars, even though the terms of suggested bargains may be stated in some detail. It is of course possible to make an offer by an advertisement directed to the general public (see § 29), but there must ordinarily be some language of commitment or some invitation to take action without further communication. **Illustrations:**

> 1. A, a clothing merchant, advertises over-coats of a certain kind for sale at $ 50. This is not an offer, but an invitation to the public to come and purchase. The addition of the words "Out they go Saturday; First Come First Served" might make the advertisement an offer.
>
> 2. A advertises that he will pay $ 5 for every copy of a certain book that may be sent to him. This is an offer, and A is bound to pay $ 5 for every copy sent while the offer is unrevoked.

c. Quotation of price. A "quotation" of price is usually a statement of price per unit of quantity; it may omit the quantity to be sold, time and place of delivery, terms of payment, and other terms. It is sometimes associated with a price list or circular, but the word "quote" is commonly understood as inviting an offer rather than as making one, even when directed to a particular customer. But just as the word "offer" does not necessarily mean that an offer is intended, so the word "quote" may be used in an offer. In determining whether an offer is made relevant factors include the terms of any previous inquiry, the completeness of the terms of the suggested bargain, and the number of persons to whom a communication is addressed. **Illustration:**

> 3. A writes to B, "I can quote you flour at $ 5 a barrel in carload lots." This is not an offer, in view of the word "quote" and incompleteness of the terms. The same words, in response to an inquiry specifying detailed terms, would probably be an offer; and if A added "for immediate acceptance" the intent to make an offer would be unmistakable.

d. Invitation of bids or other offers. Even though terms are specified in detail, it is common for one party to request the other to make an offer. The words "Make me an offer" would normally indicate that no offer is being made, and other conduct such as the announcement of an auction may have similar effect. See § 28. A request for bids on a construction project is similar, even though the practice may be to accept the lowest bid conforming to specifications and other requirements. And forms used or statements made by a traveling salesman may make it clear that the customer is making an offer to be accepted at the salesman's home office. See § 69. **Illustration:**

> 4. A writes B, "I am eager to sell my house. I would consider $ 20,000 for it." B promptly answers, "I will buy your house for $ 20,000 cash." There is no contract. A's letter is a request or suggestion that an offer be made to him. B has made an offer.

e. Written contract documents. A standard method of making an offer is to submit to the offeree a written agreement signed by the offeror and to invite the offeree to sign on a line provided for that purpose. See § 27. But the signature even in such a case is not conclusive if the other party has reason to know that no offer is intended. More common is the use of promissory expressions or words of assent in unsigned documents or letters where the document is intended not as an offer but only as a step in the preliminary negotiation of terms, or as a specimen for use in other transactions, or as something to be shown to a third person to influence his action. Reason to know that such is the intention may exist even though the document on its face seems to be clear and unambiguous.

f. Preliminary manifestations as terms of later offer. Even though a communication is not an offer, it may contain promises or representations which are incorporated in a subsequent offer and hence become part of the contract made when the offer is accepted. Indeed, the preliminary communication may thus form part of a written contract, or of a memorandum satisfying the Statute of Frauds, or of an integrated contract. See Comment *c* to § 20, §§ 132, 202.

§ 27. Existence of Contract Where Written Memorial Is Contemplated

Manifestations of assent that are in themselves sufficient to conclude a contract will not be prevented from so operating by the fact that the parties also manifest an intention to prepare and adopt a written memorial thereof; but the circumstances may show that the agreements are preliminary negotiations.

Comment:

a. Parties who plan to make a final written instrument as the expression of their contract necessarily discuss the proposed terms of the contract before they enter into it and often, before the final writing is made, agree upon all the terms which they plan to incorporate therein. This they may do orally or by exchange of several writings. It is possible thus to make a contract the terms of which include an obligation to execute subsequently a final writing which shall contain certain provisions. If parties have definitely agreed that they will do so, and that the final writing shall contain these provisions and no others, they have then concluded the contract.

b. On the other hand, if either party knows or has reason to know that the other party regards the agreement as incomplete and intends that no obligation shall exist until other terms are assented to or until the whole has been reduced to another written form, the preliminary negotiations and agreements do not constitute a contract.

c. Among the circumstances which may be helpful in determining whether a contract has been concluded are the following: the extent to which express agreement has been reached on all the terms to be included, whether the contract is of a type usually put in writing, whether it needs a formal writing for its full expression, whether it has few or many details, whether the amount involved is large or small, whether it is a common or unusual contract, whether a standard form of contract is widely used in similar transactions, and whether either party takes any action in preparation for performance during the negotiations. Such circumstances may be shown by oral testimony or by correspondence or other preliminary or partially complete writings.

d. Even though a binding contract is made before a contemplated written memorial is prepared and adopted, the subsequent written document may make a binding modification of the terms previously agreed to.

§ 28. Auctions

(1) At an auction, unless a contrary intention is manifested,

(a) the auctioneer invites offers from successive bidders which he may accept or reject;

(b) when goods are put up without reserve, the auctioneer makes an offer to sell at any price bid by the highest bidder, and after the auctioneer calls for bids the goods cannot be withdrawn unless no bid is made within a reasonable time;

(c) whether or not the auction is without reserve, a bidder may withdraw his bid until the auctioneer's announcement of completion of the sale, but a bidder's retraction does not revive any previous bid.

(2) Unless a contrary intention is manifested, bids at an auction embody terms made known by advertisement, posting or other publication of which bidders are or should be aware, as modified by any announcement made by the auctioneer when the goods are put up.

Comment:

a. Manifestation of contrary intention. The rules stated in this Section reflect the usual understanding at an auction sale. Established auctions often have their own customary rules, made known by publication or by announcement at the commencement of the auction. Such rules prevail even though they are contrary to the rules stated here. Compare the phrase, "unless otherwise agreed," explained in the Introductory Note to this Restatement; see Uniform Commercial Code §§ 1-102, 1-205, 2-328. But where an auction is held pursuant to statute or court order, there may be requirements or terms which cannot be varied by private agreement.

b. Auction with reserve. An auction as ordinarily conducted furnishes an illustration of the principle stated in § 26. The auctioneer, by beginning to auction property, does not impliedly say: "I offer to sell this property to which ever of you makes the highest bid," but rather requests that the bidders make offers to him, as indeed he frequently states in his remarks to those before him. Hence, it is understood that he may reject all bids and withdraw the goods from sale until he announces completion of the sale. Similarly, under § 42, a bidder may withdraw his bid at any time before the announcement of completion. See Uniform Commercial Code § 2-328(3).

. . .

c. Advertisement for bids. Governmental agencies or private persons often advertise for bids from construction contractors prepared to undertake the building of a building or other structure, or from persons prepared to supply goods or services. It may be customary or required by law that the contract be awarded to the lowest responsible bidder whose bid conforms to published specifications. A bidder in such a case may seek bids from subcontractors for part of the work. The rule in such cases is much like that governing auctions -- unless a contrary intention is manifested, the advertisement is not an offer but a request for offers; bidders on both prime contract and subcontract make offers when they submit bids; and all bids may be rejected. As to irrevocable bids, see § 25.

. . .

d. Auction without reserve. Where an auction is advertised as "without reserve" and the goods are put up without any contrary announcement, or where the auctioneer opens the sale by announcing that the sale will be "without reserve," the normal understanding is that the goods are not to be withdrawn. There is an offer, and it is made irrevocable by Uniform Commercial Code § 2-328(3), unless no bid is made within a reasonable time. See § 25. Nevertheless, unless a contrary intention is manifested, bids can be withdrawn until the auctioneer announces completion of the sale, as in other auctions; and a bid is discharged when a higher bid is made, even though the higher bid is later withdrawn. Uniform Commercial Code § 2-328(3).

. . .

§ 29. To Whom an Offer Is Addressed

(1) The manifested intention of the offeror determines the person or persons in whom is created a power of acceptance.

(2) An offer may create a power of acceptance in a specified person or in one or more of a specified group or class of persons, acting separately or together, or in anyone or everyone who makes a specified promise or renders a specified performance.

Comment:

a. Terms of offer control. The rule stated in Subsection (1) is an elaboration of the definition of offer in § 24, and it is to be read in the light of the rules stated in §§ 23 and 26. The offeror is the master of his offer; just as the making of any offer at all can be avoided by appropriate language or other conduct, so the power of acceptance can be narrowly limited. The offeror is bound only in accordance with his manifested assent; he is not bound just because he receives a consideration as good as or better than the one he bargained for. But if he knows or has reason to know that he is creating an appearance of assent, he may be bound by that appearance. These considerations apply to the identity of the offeree or offerees as well as to the mode of manifesting acceptance (see § 30) and the substance of the exchange (see §§ 31, 32, 58).

b. General offers. An offer may create separate powers of acceptance in an unlimited number of persons, and the exercise of the power by one person may or may not extinguish the power of another. Where one acceptor only is to be selected, various methods of selection are possible: for example, "first come, first served" (see Illustration 1 to § 26), the highest bidder (see Illustration 3 to § 28), or the winner of a contest. Who can accept, and how, is determined by interpretation of the offer. **Illustrations:**

1. A publishes an offer of reward to whoever will give him certain information. There is no indication that A intends to pay more than

once. Any person learning of the offer has power to accept (see Comments *a* and *c* to § 23), but the giving of the information by one terminates the power of every other person.

2. A, a bank, issues a traveler's letter of credit promising to repay anyone who makes advances to a named beneficiary, up to a certain amount, the amounts advanced to be noted on the letter of credit. This creates a power of acceptance in anyone to whom the letter is presented, but only if the notation is made and only so long as the noted amounts do not exceed the maximum. See Uniform Commercial Code § 5-108.

3. A, the proprietor of a medical preparation, offers $ 100 to anyone who contracts a certain disease after using the preparation as directed. B, C and D use it as directed. Each has made a contract independent of the others, and is entitled to the $ 100 if he later contracts the disease.

§ 30. Form of Acceptance Invited

(1) An offer may invite or require acceptance to be made by an affirmative answer in words, or by performing or refraining from performing a specified act, or may empower the offeree to make a selection of terms in his acceptance.

(2) Unless otherwise indicated by the language or the circumstances, an offer invites acceptance in any manner and by any medium reasonable in the circumstances.

Comment:

a. Required form. The offeror is the master of his offer. See Comment *a* to § 29. The form of acceptance is less likely to affect the substance of the bargain than the identity of the offeree, and is often quite immaterial. But the offeror is entitled to insist on a particular mode of manifestation of assent. The terms of the offer may limit acceptance to a particular mode; whether it does so is a matter of interpretation.

Illustration:

1. A sends a letter to B stating the terms of a proposed contract. At the end he writes, "You can accept this offer only by signing on the dotted line below my own signature." a replies by telegram, "I accept your offer." There is no contract.

b. Invited form. Insistence on a particular form of acceptance is unusual. Offers often make no express reference to the form of acceptance; sometimes ambiguous language is used. Language referring to a particular mode of acceptance is often intended and understood as suggestion rather than limitation; the suggested mode is then authorized, but other modes are not precluded. In other cases language which in terms refers to the mode of acceptance is intended and understood as referring to some more important aspect of the transaction, such as the time limit for acceptance. See §§ 60, 63.

c. Term supplied in acceptance. An offer may contain a choice of terms, and may invite or require an acceptance making a selection among the terms stated. Or the offer may indicate a term such as quantity to be filled in by the offeree. An acceptance to be effective must comply with the terms of the offer, and those terms or the circumstances may make it plain that the acceptance must specify terms. Section 60. In such cases the offer does not fail for indefiniteness, but no contract is made by an attempted acceptance which does not supply the term as indicated. See § 33. The offer assents in advance to the term chosen or filled in by the offeree. **Illustration:**

2. A offers to deliver to B at any time during the next 30 days any amount of coal, up to 100 tons, for which B will promise to pay $ 15 a ton. In order to accept this offer B must specify the amount of coal he desires and must promise to pay $ 15 a ton for it. An order for 50 tons by B concludes a definite agreement.

d. Form not specified. Interpretation of the offer is necessary in order to determine whether there is any limitation on the mode of acceptance. The meaning given the offer by the offeree controls if it is a meaning of which the offeror knew or had reason to know. See §§ 19, 20. Since limitation is not customary, the offeror has reason to know that the offeree may understand that the offer can be accepted in any reasonable manner, and a contrary intention is not operative unless manifested. See Uniform Commercial Code § 2-206(1). **Illustrations:**

3. A orally offers to sell and deliver to B 100 tons of coal at $ 20 a ton payable 30 days after delivery. B replies, "I accept your offer." B has manifested assent in a sufficient form, even though A neither suggested nor required that form.

4. A makes a bid at an auction sale. By the usual custom at auctions, the auctioneer may accept by letting the hammer fall, by saying "Sold", or by any words manifesting acceptance.

e. Reasonable manner. As to acceptance by promise or nonpromissory performance, see § 32. Cases where the contract leaves terms to be chosen in the course of performance are the subject of § 34. What manner and medium are reasonable is governed by the rules stated in §§ 60 and 65. Sometimes, though not ordinarily, even silent inaction may be effective as a mode of acceptance. See § 69.

§ 31. Offer Proposing a Single Contract or a Number of Contracts

An offer may propose the formation of a single contract by a single acceptance or the formation of a number of contracts by successive acceptances from time to time.

. . .

§ 32. Invitation of Promise or Performance

In case of doubt an offer is interpreted as inviting the offeree to accept either by promising to perform what the offer requests or by rendering the performance, as the offeree chooses.

Comment:

a. Promise or performance. In the ordinary commercial bargain a party expects to be bound only if the other party either renders the return performance or binds himself to do so either by express words or by part performance or other conduct. Unless the language or the circumstances indicate that one party is to have an option, therefore, the usual offer invites an acceptance which either amounts to performance or constitutes a promise. The act of acceptance may be merely symbolic of assent and promise, or it may also be part or all of the performance bargained for. See §§ 2, 4, 18, 19. In either case notification of the offeror may be necessary. See §§ 54, 56.

The rule of this Section is a particular application of the rule stated in § 30(2). The offeror is often indifferent as to whether acceptance takes the form of words of promise or acts of performance, and his words literally referring to one are often intended and understood to refer to either. Where performance takes time, however, the beginning of performance may constitute a promise to complete it. See § 62.

Illustrations:

1. A writes B, "If you will mow my lawn next week, I will pay you $ 10." B can accept A's offer either by promptly promising to mow the lawn or by mowing it as requested.

2. A says to B: "If you finish that table you are making and deliver it to my house today, I will give you $ 100 for it." B replies, "I'll do it." There is a contract. B could also accept by delivering the table as requested.

b. Offer limited to acceptance by performance only. Language or circumstances sometimes make it clear that the offeree is not to bind himself in advance of performance. His promise may be worthless to the offeror, or the circumstances may make it unreasonable for the offeror to expect a firm commitment from the offeree. In such cases, the offer does not invite a promissory acceptance, and a promise is ineffective as an acceptance. Examples are found in offers of reward or of prizes in a contest, made to a large number of people but to be accepted by only one. See § 29. Non-commercial arrangements among relatives and friends (see Comment *a* to § 19, Comment *c* to § 21) and offers which leave important terms to be fixed by the offeree in the course of performance (see §§ 33, 34) provide other examples.

It is a separate question whether the offeree undertakes any responsibility to complete performance once begun, or whether he takes any responsibility for the quality of the performance when completed. **Illustrations:**

3. A publishes the following offer: "I will pay $ 50 for the return of my diamond bracelet lost yesterday on State Street." B sees this advertisement and at once sends a letter to A, saying "I accept your offer and will search for this

bracelet." There is no acceptance.

4. A writes to B, his nephew aged 16, that if B will refrain from drinking, using tobacco, swearing, and playing cards or billiards for money until he becomes 21 years of age, A will pay B $ 5,000. B makes a written reply promising so to refrain. There is probably no contract. But if B begins to refrain, A may be bound by an option contract under §§ 45; and if B refrains until he becomes 21, A is bound to pay him $ 5,000.

c. Shipment of goods. An order or other offer to buy goods for prompt or current shipment normally invites acceptance either by a prompt promise to ship or by prompt or current shipment. Uniform Commercial Code § 2-206(1)(b). If nonconforming goods are shipped, the shipment may be an acceptance and at the same time a breach. But there is no acceptance if the offeror has reason to know that none is intended, as where the offeree promptly notifies him that nonconforming goods are being shipped and are offered only as an accommodation to him.

Illustrations:

5. A mails a written order to B, offering to buy specified machinery on specified terms. The order provides, "Ship at once." B immediately mails a letter to A, saying "I accept your offer and will ship at once." This is a sufficient acceptance to form a contract. See Uniform Commercial Code § 2-206(1).

6. In Illustration 5, instead of mailing a letter of acceptance, B immediately ships the machinery as requested. This is a sufficient acceptance to form a contract. If the machinery is defective, the shipment is both an acceptance forming a contract and a breach of that contract, unless B promptly notifies A that the shipment is offered only as an accommodation to A. See Uniform Commercial Code § 2-206(1).

§ 33. Certainty

(1) Even though a manifestation of intention is intended to be understood as an offer, it cannot be accepted so as to form a contract unless the terms of the contract are reasonably certain.

(2) The terms of a contract are reasonably certain if they provide a basis for determining the existence of a breach and for giving an appropriate remedy.

(3) The fact that one or more terms of a proposed bargain are left open or uncertain may show that a manifestation of intention is not intended to be understood as an offer or as an acceptance.

Comment:

a. Certainty of terms. It is sometimes said that the agreement must be capable of being given an exact meaning and that all the performances to be rendered must be certain. Such statements may be appropriate in determining whether a manifestation of intention is intended to be understood as an offer. But the actions of the parties may show conclusively that they have intended to conclude a binding agreement, even though one or more terms are missing or are left to be agreed upon. In such cases courts endeavor, if possible, to attach a sufficiently definite meaning to the bargain.

An offer which appears to be indefinite may be given precision by usage of trade or by course of dealing between the parties. Terms may be supplied by factual implication, and in recurring situations the law often supplies a term in the absence of agreement to the contrary. See § 5, defining "term." Where the parties have intended to conclude a bargain, uncertainty as to incidental or collateral matters is seldom fatal to the existence of the contract. If the essential terms are so uncertain that there is no basis for deciding whether the agreement has been kept or broken, there is no contract. But even in such cases partial performance or other action in reliance on the agreement may reinforce it under § 34.

b. Certainty in basis for remedy. The rule stated in Subsection (2) reflects the fundamental policy that contracts should be made by the parties, not by the courts, and hence that remedies for breach of contract must have a basis in the agreement of the parties. Where the parties have intended to make a contract and there is a reasonably certain basis for granting a remedy, the same policy supports the granting of the remedy. The test is not certainty as to what the parties were to do nor as to the exact amount of damages due to the plaintiff; uncertainty may preclude one remedy without affecting another. See Uniform Commercial Code § 2-204(3) and Comment.

Thus the degree of certainty required may be affected by the dispute which arises and by the remedy sought. Courts decide the disputes before them, not other hypothetical disputes which might have arisen. It is less likely that a reasonably certain term will be supplied by construction as to a matter which has been the subject of controversy between the parties than as to one which is raised only as an afterthought. In some cases greater definiteness may be required for specific performance than for an award of damages; in others the impossibility of accurate assessment of damages may furnish a reason for specific relief. Partial relief may sometimes be granted when uncertainty prevents full-scale enforcement through normal remedies. See §§ 357-62. **Illustrations:**

1. A agrees to sell and B to buy goods for $ 2,000, $ 1,000 in cash and the "balance on installment terms over a period of two years," with a provision for liquidated damages. If it is found that both parties manifested an intent to conclude a binding agreement, the indefiniteness of the quoted language does not prevent the award of the liquidated damages.

2. A agrees to sell and B to buy a specific tract of land for $ 10,000, $ 4,000 in cash and $ 6,000 on mortgage. A agrees to obtain the mortgage loan for B or, if unable to do so, to lend B the amount, but the terms of loan are not stated, although both parties manifest an intent to conclude a binding agreement. The contract is too indefinite to support a decree of specific performance against B, but B may obtain such a decree if he offers to pay the full price in cash.

c. Preliminary negotiations. The rule stated in Subsection (3) is a particular application of the rule stated in § 26 on preliminary negotiations. Incompleteness of terms is one of the principal reasons why advertisements and price quotations are ordinarily not interpreted as offers. Similarly, if the parties to negotiations for sale manifest an intention not to be bound until the price is fixed or agreed, the law gives effect to that intention. Uniform Commercial Code § 2-305(4). The more terms the parties leave open, the less likely it is that they have intended to conclude a binding agreement. See Uniform Commercial Code § 2-204 and Comment.

d. Uncertain time of performance. Valid contracts are often made which do not specify the time for performance. Where the contract calls for a single performance such as the rendering of a service or the delivery of goods, the time for performance is a "reasonable time." Compare § 41 on the time for accepting an offer; see Uniform Commercial Code §§ 1-204, 2-309(1). Payment is due when the service is completed or the goods received. Uniform Commercial Code § 2-310. When the contract calls for successive performances but is indefinite in duration, it is commonly terminable by either party, with or without a requirement of reasonable notice. Uniform Commercial Code § 2-309(2), (3).
Illustrations:

3. A and B promise that certain performances shall be mutually rendered by them "immediately" or "at once," or "promptly," or "as soon as possible," or "in about one month." All these promises are sufficiently definite to form contracts.

4. A promises B to sell certain goods to him, and B promises to pay a specified price therefor. No time of performance is fixed. The time for delivery and payment is a reasonable time. Uniform Commercial Code §§ 2-309(1), 2-310(a). What is a reasonable time depends on the nature, purpose and circumstances of the action to be taken. Uniform Commercial Code §§ 1-204(2).

5. A offers to employ B for a stated compensation as long as B is able to do specified work, or as long as a specified business is carried on, and B accepts the terms offered. The length of the engagement is sufficiently definite for the formation of a contract.

6. A promises B to serve B as chauffeur, and B promises to pay him $ 100 a month. Nothing further is stated as to the duration of the employment. There is at once a contract for one month's service. At the end of the first month, in the absence of revocation, there is a contract for a second month. But circumstances may show that such an agreement merely specifies the rate of compensation for an employment at will.

e. Indefinite price. Where the parties manifest an intention not to be bound unless the amount of money to be paid by one of them is fixed or agreed and it is not fixed or agreed there is no contract. Uniform Commercial Code §§ 2-305(4). Where they intend to conclude a contract for the sale of goods, however, and the price is not settled, the price is a reasonable price at the time of delivery if (a) nothing is said as to price, or (b) the price is left to be agreed by the parties and they fail to agree, or (c) the price is to be fixed in terms of some agreed market or other standard as set or recorded by a third person or agency and it is not so set or recorded. Uniform Commercial Code § 2-305(1). Or one party may be given power to fix the price within limits set by agreement or custom or good faith. Similar principles apply to contracts for the rendition of service. But substantial damages cannot be recovered unless they can be estimated with reasonable certainty (§ 352), and if the contract is entirely executory and specific performance is not an appropriate remedy, relief may be limited to the recovery of benefits conferred and specific expense incurred in reliance on the contract.

Illustrations:

7. A promises to sell and B to buy goods "at cost plus a nice profit." The quoted words strongly indicate that the parties have not yet concluded a bargain.

8. A promises to do a specified piece of work and B promises to pay a price to be thereafter mutually agreed. The provision for future agreement as to price strongly indicates that the parties do not intend to be bound. If they manifest an intent to be bound, the price is a reasonable price at the time for doing the work.

f. Other indefinite terms. Promises may be indefinite in other aspects than time and price. The more important the uncertainty, the stronger the indication is that the parties do not intend to be bound; minor items are more likely to be left to the option of one of the parties or to what is customary or reasonable. Even when the parties intend to enter into a contract, uncertainty may be so great as to frustrate their intention. Thus a promise by A to give B employment, even though consideration is paid for it, does not provide a basis for any remedy if neither the character of the employment nor the compensation therefor is stated. In such cases the consideration paid, or its value, can be recovered. Restatement of Restitution §§ 15, 40, 47, 53. **Illustrations:**

9. A promises B to execute a conveyance in fee or a lease for a year of specified land and B promises to make specified payments therefor. Although the terms of leases and conveyances vary, the promises are interpreted as providing for documents in the form in common local use, and are sufficiently definite to form contracts.

10. A promises to sell and B to buy all goods of a certain character which B shall need in his business during the ensuing year. The quantity to be sold is sufficiently definite to provide a basis for remedy, since the promises are interpreted to refer to B's actual good-faith requirements. Uniform Commercial Code § 2-306.

11. A promises B to construct a building according to stated plans and specifications, and B promises A to pay $ 30,000 therefor. It is also provided that the character of the window fastenings shall be subject to further agreement of the parties. Unless a contrary intention is manifested, the indefiniteness of the agreement with reference to this matter will not prevent the formation of a contract.

12. A and B have a settlement of accounts, and A promises to pay B a stated balance, "errors and omissions excepted." A's promise is reasonably certain in the absence of a showing of error or omission, but it may be corrected on such a showing.

§ 34. Certainty and Choice of Terms; Effect of Performance or Reliance

(1) The terms of a contract may be reasonably certain even though it empowers one or both parties to make a selection of terms in the course of performance.

(2) Part performance under an agreement may remove uncertainty and establish that a contract enforceable as a bargain has been formed.

(3) Action in reliance on an agreement may make a contractual remedy appropriate even though uncertainty is not removed.

Comment:

a. Choice in the course of performance. A bargain may be concluded which leaves a choice of terms to be made by one party or the other. If the agreement is otherwise sufficiently definite to be a contract, it is not made invalid by the fact that it leaves particulars of performance to be specified by one of the parties. Uniform Commercial Code § 2-311(1). The more important the choice is, the more it is likely that the parties do not intend to be bound until the choice is made. But even on such matters as subject matter and price, one party is often given a wide choice. If the parties intend to make a contract and there is a reasonably certain basis for granting an appropriate remedy, such alternative terms do not invalidate the contract. See § 33. Often a basis for remedy can be found in the rule of Comment *b* to § 362, permitting a remedy in accordance with the alternative chosen or in accordance with the alternative that will result in the smallest recovery. In other cases the failure of one party to choose may shift the right to choose to the other party or to an arbitrator or to the court. **Illustrations:**

1. A promises B to give him any one of a number of specified things which A shall choose, and B promises A to pay a specified price. The agreement is sufficiently definite to be a contract. A method is provided for determining what A is to give; though what he gives is subject to his choice, he must give some one of the things specified.

2. A agrees to sell and B to buy 50,000 pounds of white worsted yarn on a basis which enables the parties to compute 48 prices for 48 styles and sizes. The agreement is sufficiently definite to be a contract. Unless otherwise agreed specifications relating to assortment of the goods are at the buyer's option, but if B does not make a seasonable specification, A may proceed to perform in any reasonable manner. Uniform Commercial Code § 2-311.

b. Unlimited choice; good faith and fair dealing. If one party to an agreement is given an unlimited choice, that party may not be a promisor (see Comment *e* to § 2), and the contract may fail for want of consideration. See § 79. The other party's promise may be unconscionable and may be wholly or partly illegal. Compare §§ 178, 208; see Uniform Commercial Code § 2-302. These difficulties are commonly avoided, however, by the fact that the choice granted is limited. Just as the power of selection may be given not only by explicit agreement but also by course of dealing or usage of trade or course of performance under the particular agreement or by other implication from circumstances, so limits on the power may be either express or implied. Often the choice made must be reasonable in the circumstances. See § 228; Uniform Commercial Code §§ 2-306, 2-311(1). And in any event discretionary power granted by a commercial contract must be exercised in good faith and in accordance with fair dealing. Uniform Commercial Code § 1-203, 2-103(1)(b). A price to be fixed by a seller or buyer of goods, for example, means a price for him to fix in good faith. Uniform Commercial Code § 2-305(2). **Illustration:**

3. A promises B to do specified work or to transfer certain goods or land and B promises A to make specified payments if the work or property is satisfactory to B in specified respects. These promises are sufficiently definite to form contracts, since B's duty depends not on his mere whim but on his exercise of an honest judgment, or in some cases of a reasonable judgment. See § 228.

c. Subsequent conduct removing uncertainty. Indefiniteness may prevent enforcement of a contract in two different ways: it may mean that a manifestation of intention is not intended to be understood as an offer; or, even though the parties intended to enter into a contract, there may be no sufficient basis for giving an appropriate remedy. See § 33. Subsequent conduct of one or both parties may remove either obstacle or both. Preliminary manifestations may propose terms which are incorporated in a subsequent offer and become part of a contract. See Comment *f* to § 26. The contract may then be thought of as concluded only at the time of the acceptance of the subsequent offer. Or part performance may give meaning to indefinite terms of an agreement, or may have the effect of eliminating indefinite alternatives by waiver or modification. Uniform Commercial Code § 2-208. In such cases a bargain may be concluded, but it may be impossible to identify offer or acceptance or to determine the moment of formation. See § 22(2). The obstacle of indefiniteness may nevertheless be removed.

d. Reliance and appropriate remedies. The need for a particular remedy may sometimes become apparent as a result of part performance or other action in reliance on an indefinite agreement, even though the original uncertainty remains. The appropriate remedy may be non-contractual. Thus benefits conferred on the other party under an agreement void for indefiniteness may ordinarily be recovered. Restatement of Restitution §§ 15, 40, 47, 53. In some such cases the measure of benefit may appropriately be the value of the plaintiff's performance rather than the economic benefit to the defendant. See Restatement of Restitution § 155 and Caveat; compare § 370 of this Restatement. Where one party has suffered loss because of his reliance on such an agreement, the other party may be subject to liability in tort. See Restatement, Second, Torts § 323, and Caveat; Restatement, Second, Agency § 378.

In many cases, however, reliance makes appropriate a contractual remedy. Thus the agreement may be treated as divisible and recovery for benefits conferred may then be permitted at the promised rate. An express or implied promise may be found to reimburse expenses incurred pursuant to the indefinite agreement. In some cases partial or full enforcement through an award of damages for breach of contract or a decree of specific performance may become appropriate. See § 90. As to detrimental reliance not consisting of the performance of the agreement, compare Comment *a* to § 129. **Illustrations:**

    4. A says to B: "I will employ you for some time at $ 10 a day." An acceptance by B either orally or in writing will not create a con-tract. But if B serves one or more days with A's assent A is bound to pay $ 10 for each day's service.

    5. A agrees to sell and B to buy a specific house and lot for $ 10,000, mortgage terms to be agreed. At B's request, reinforced by a threat not to perform, A makes certain alterations in the house, which add nothing to its value. B then repudiates the agreement without reference to mortgage terms. A may recover the cost of the alterations. See § 349.

    6. A leases land to B for three years, giving B an option to buy the land for $ 10,000 "on terms to be agreed on." B occupies the land for three years, making extensive improvements, and seeks to exercise the option, offering to pay "either in cash or upon such terms as A may impose." B may obtain a decree of specific performance. See Illustration 2 to § 362.

§ 35. The Offeree's Power of Acceptance

(1) An offer gives to the offeree a continuing power to complete the manifestation of mutual assent by acceptance of the offer.

(2) A contract cannot be created by acceptance of an offer after the power of acceptance has been terminated in one of the ways listed in § 36.

Comment:

    a. "Duration of an offer." It is common to speak of the duration "of an offer." But "offer" is defined in § 24 as a manifestation of assent, and the reference here is not to the time occupied by the offeror's conduct but to the duration of its legal operation. Hence this topic speaks of the duration and termination of the offeree's power rather than the duration and termination of the offer.

    b. Continuing power. Under Subsection (1) the offeree's power arises when the offeror's manifestation of assent is complete. Since the acceptance must have reference to the offer it is ordinarily necessary that the offeree have knowledge of the offer. See § 23. Once the power arises it continues until terminated. Methods of termination are listed in § 36 and explained in the following sections. There is no requirement that the offer be accompanied by the mental assent of the offeror, or that mental assent which exists at the time of the offer continue until the time of acceptance. See § 19.

    c. Creation of contract. Exercise of the power of acceptance concludes an agreement and a bargain, and thus satisfies one of the requirements for formation of an informal contract enforceable as a bargain. See §§ 17, 18. But a contract is not created unless the other requirements are met. Thus there may be no consideration; or impossibility or illegality may prevent any duty of performance from arising.

§ 36. Methods of Termination of the Power of Acceptance

(1) An offeree's power of acceptance may be terminated by

(a) rejection or counter-offer by the offeree, or

(b) lapse of time, or

(c) revocation by the offeror, or

(d) death or incapacity of the offeror or offeree.

(2) In addition, an offeree's power of acceptance is terminated by the non-occurrence of any condition of acceptance under the terms of the offer.

Comment:

a. Scope. This Section merely lists the methods of termination which are possible. The circumstances under which each method operates are stated in §§ 36-49.

b. Conditions of acceptance. Subsection (2) provides for any condition of acceptance arising under the terms of the offer itself. Compare the definition of "condition" in § 224. A condition of acceptance, like a condition, may be express or implied in fact or constructive. See Comment *c* to § 226. Thus by common understanding a reward offer can ordinarily be accepted only once; the first acceptance terminates the power of acceptance of other offerees. See Illustration 1 to § 29. Compare the effect on a bid at an auction when a higher bid is made. See § 28(1)(c).

c. Impossibility and illegality. The power of acceptance may be terminated by the death or destruction of a person or thing essential for performance or by supervening legal prohibition. The extent to which such events have the effect of a failure of a condition of acceptance depends on the terms of the offer and on the circumstances. Such events may also prevent a duty of performance from arising from an acceptance if they occur before the offer is made, or may discharge a duty of performance if they occur after acceptance. The effects of such events are therefore stated in Chapters 6-12, which deal with Mistake (Chapter 6), Misrepresentation, Duress and Undue Influence (Chapter 7), Unenforceability on Grounds of Public Policy (Chapter 8), The Scope of Contractual Obligations (including conditions and similar events) (Chapter 9), Performance and Non-performance (Chapter 10), Impracticability of Performance and Frustration of Purpose (Chapter 11) and Discharge by Assent or Alteration (Chapter 12).

§ 37. Termination of Power of Acceptance Under Option Contract

Notwithstanding §§ 38-49, the power of acceptance under an option contract is not terminated by rejection or counter-offer, by revocation, or by death or incapacity of the offeror, unless the requirements are met for the discharge of a contractual duty.

Comment:

a. Option contracts. An option contract is a promise which meets the requisites of a contract and limits the promisor's power to revoke an offer. See § 25. The power given the offeree by such an option differs from a power to specify particulars of performance after a contract is made, since the offeree under an option contract can choose not to undertake any contractual duties at all. But both types of choice may be given to the same offeree at the same time. See § 34(1).

b. Requirements for discharge. An option contract binds the offeror and gives rise to a duty of performance conditional on the offeree's acceptance exercising the option. The rules governing discharge of contractual duties therefore apply. See Chapter 12; compare Comment *c* to § 42; § 256 on the nullification of a repudiation. **Illustrations:**

1. A leases land to B, giving B an option to purchase the land for $ 10,000 in cash during the term of the lease. Misinterpreting the lease, B attempts to exercise the option by tendering a mortgage for $ 10,000. A refuses to accept the mortgage. B retains power to exercise the option by a tender conforming to the terms of the lease.

2. A gives B the same option as that stated in Illustration 1. A receives an offer from C to purchase the land and so informs B. B states that he will not exercise the option and A conveys the land to C. B's power to exercise the option is terminated. See §§ 89; 273-85.

§ 38. Rejection

(1) An offeree's power of acceptance is terminated by his rejection of the offer, unless the offeror has manifested a contrary intention.

(2) A manifestation of intention not to accept an offer is a rejection unless the offeree manifests an intention to take it under further advisement.

Comment:

a. The probability of reliance. The legal consequences of a rejection rest on its probable effect on the offeror. An offeror commonly takes steps to prepare for performance in the event that the offer is accepted. If the offeree states in effect that he declines to accept the offer, it is highly probable that the offeror will change his plans in reliance on the statement. The reliance is likely to take such negative forms as failure to prepare or failure to send a notice of revocation, and hence is likely to be difficult or impossible to prove. To protect the offeror in such reliance, the power of acceptance is terminated without proof of reliance. This rule also protects the offeree in accordance with his manifested intention that his subsequent conduct is not to be understood as an acceptance. **Illustrations:**

1. A makes an offer to B and adds: "This offer will remain open for a week." B rejects the offer the following day, but later in the week purports to accept it. There is no contract unless the offer was itself a contract. B's purported acceptance is itself a new offer.

2. A makes an offer to sell water rights to B, and states, "You may accept this offer by applying to the appropriate authority for a permit to use the water." B rejects the offer, obtains water rights elsewhere, and later applies for the permit contemplated by the offer. There is no contract. Even if A's offer was a binding option, B has not exercised it.

b. Contrary statement of offeror or offeree. The rule of this Section is designed to give effect to the intentions of the parties, and a manifestation of intention on the part of either that the offeree's power of acceptance is to continue is effective. Thus if the offeree states that he rejects the offer for the present but will reconsider it at a future time, there is no basis for a change of position by the offeror in reliance on a rejection, and under Subsection (2) there is no rejection. Similarly a statement in the offer that it will continue in effect despite a rejection is effective, and a similar statement after a rejection makes a new offer.

Where the manifestation of intention of either party is misunderstood by the other, the principles underlying § 20 apply. If the offeror is justified in inferring from the words or conduct of the offeree, interpreted in the light of the offeror's prior words or conduct, that the offeree intends not to accept the offer and not to take it under further advisement, the power of acceptance is terminated. Compare § 39.

§ 39. Counter-Offers

(1) A counter-offer is an offer made by an offeree to his offeror relating to the same matter as the original offer and proposing a substituted bargain differing from that proposed by the original offer.

(2) An offeree's power of acceptance is terminated by his making of a counter-offer, unless the offeror has manifested a contrary intention or unless the counter-offer manifests a contrary intention of the offeree.

Comment:

a. Counter-offer as rejection. It is often said that a counter-offer is a rejection, and it does have the same effect in terminating the offeree's power of acceptance. But in other respects a counter-offer differs from a rejection. A counter-offer must be capable of being accepted; it carries negotiations on rather than breaking them off. The termination of the power of acceptance by a counter-offer merely carries out the usual understanding of bargainers that one proposal is dropped when another is taken under consideration; if alternative proposals are to be under consideration at the same time, warning is expected. **Illustration:**

1. A offers B to sell him a parcel of land for $ 5,000, stating that the offer will remain open for thirty days. B replies, "I will pay $ 4,800 for the parcel," and on A's declining that, B writes, within the thirty day period, "I accept your of-

fer to sell for $ 5,000." There is no contract unless A's offer was itself a contract (see § 37), or unless A's reply to the counter-offer manifested an intention to renew his original offer.

b. Qualified acceptance, inquiry or separate offer. A common type of counter-offer is the qualified or conditional acceptance, which purports to accept the original offer but makes acceptance expressly conditional on assent to additional or different terms. See § 59. Such a counter-offer must be distinguished from an unqualified acceptance which is accompanied by a proposal for modification of the agreement or for a separate agreement. A mere inquiry regarding the possibility of different terms, a request for a better offer, or a comment upon the terms of the offer, is ordinarily not a counter-offer. Such responses to an offer may be too tentative or indefinite to be offers of any kind; or they may deal with new matters rather than a substitution for the original offer; or their language may manifest an intention to keep the original offer under consideration. **Illustration:**

2. A makes the same offer to B as that stated in Illustration 1, and B replies, "Won't you take less?" A answers, "No." An acceptance thereafter by B within the thirty-day period is effective. B's inquiry was not a counter-offer, and A's original offer stands.

c. Contrary statement of offeror or offeree. An offeror may state in his offer that it shall continue for a stated time in any event and that in the meanwhile he will be glad to receive counter-offers. Likewise an offeree may state that he is holding the offer under advisement, but that if the offeror desires to close a bargain at once the offeree makes a specific counter-offer. Such an answer will not extend the time that the original offer remains open, but will not cut that time short. Compare § 38. **Illustration:**

3. A makes the same offer to B as that stated in Illustration 1. B replies, "I am keeping your offer under advisement, but if you wish to close the matter at once I will give you $ 4,800." A does not reply, and within the thirty-day period B accepts the original offer. B's acceptance is effective.

§ 40. Time When Rejection or Counter-Offer Terminates the Power of Acceptance

> Rejection or counter-offer by mail or telegram does not terminate the power of acceptance until received by the offeror, but limits the power so that a letter or telegram of acceptance started after the sending of an otherwise effective rejection or counter-offer is only a counter-offer unless the acceptance is received by the offeror before he receives the rejection or counter-offer.

Comment:

a. Receipt essential. A rejection terminates the offeree's power of acceptance because of the probability of reliance by the offeror, and there is no possibility of reliance until the rejection is received. See § 38. Hence the power continues until receipt. The same rule is applied by analogy to a counter-offer, although the reason is somewhat different: a counter-offer cannot be taken under consideration as a substitute proposal until it is received. See § 39. As to when a rejection is received, see § 68; compare Restatement, Second, Agency §§ 268-83, Uniform Commercial Code § 1-201(25) to (27).

b. Subsequent acceptance. Since a rejection or counter-offer is not effective until received, it may until that time be superseded by an acceptance. But the probability remains that the offeror will rely on the rejection or counter-offer

if it is received before the acceptance. To protect the offeror in such reliance, the offeree who has dispatched a rejection is deprived of the benefit of the rule that an acceptance may take effect on dispatch (§ 63). The rule of this Section only applies, however, to a rejection or counter-offer which is otherwise effective. A rejection or counter-offer may be denied effect to terminate the power of acceptance if the original offer is itself a contract or if the offeror or offeree manifests an intention that the power continue. See §§ 37-39. Similarly, a purported rejection or counter-offer dispatched after an effective acceptance is in effect a revocation of acceptance, governed by § 63 rather than by this Section. **Illustration:**

1. A makes B an offer by mail. B immediately after receiving the offer mails a letter of

rejection. Within the time permitted by the offer B accepts. This acceptance creates a contract only if received before the rejection, or if the power of acceptance continues under §§ 37-39.

§ 41. Lapse of Time

(1) An offeree's power of acceptance is terminated at the time specified in the offer, or, if no time is specified, at the end of a reasonable time.

(2) What is a reasonable time is a question of fact, depending on all the circumstances existing when the offer and attempted acceptance are made.

(3) Unless otherwise indicated by the language or the circumstances, and subject to the rule stated in § 49, an offer sent by mail is seasonably accepted if an acceptance is mailed at any time before midnight on the day on which the offer is received.

Comment:

a. Specified time. Just as the offer may prescribe the identity of the offeree (§ 29) or the form of acceptance (§ 30), so it may prescribe a time limit for acceptance. Such a limitation must be complied with. See § 60. In cases of misunderstanding, the principles underlying § 20 are applicable. See Chapter 9.

b. Reasonable time. In the absence of a contrary indication, just as acceptance may be made in any manner and by any medium which is reasonable in the circumstances (§ 30), so it may be made at any time which is reasonable in the circumstances. The circumstances to be considered have a wide range: they include the nature of the proposed contract, the purposes of the parties, the course of dealing between them, and any relevant usages of trade. In general, the question is what time would be thought satisfactory to the offeror by a reasonable man in the position of the offeree; but circumstances not known to the offeree may be relevant to show that the time actually taken by the offeree was satisfactory to the offeror. See Illustration 6 to § 23.

c. Time for acceptance by act; rewards. Where the offeree is invited to accept by performing or refraining from performing an act, a reasonable time for so doing is ordinarily a reasonable time for accepting. But the purposes of the offeror, if the offeree knows or has reason to know of them, must also be taken into account. Thus an offer of reward for the capture of the person guilty of a specific crime cannot ordinarily be accepted after the statute of limitations has barred prosecution. **Illustrations:**

1. A publishes an offer of reward for information leading to the arrest and conviction of the person guilty of a specified murder. B, intending to obtain the reward, gives the requested information a year after the publication of the offer.

The acceptance is timely.

2. After a series of incendiary attempts, a city publishes each day for a week an offer of reward for information leading to the arrest and conviction of any person who shall set fire to any building within the city. The responsible city officials serve for one year terms. A fire set three years after the last publication is not within the terms of the offer.

3. A bank posts in its office an offer of reward for information leading to the arrest and conviction of any person who robs any bank which is a member of an association of banks in the same county. After several years the poster is removed. A robbery three years after the removal may be found to be within the terms of the offer.

d. Direct negotiations. Where the parties bargain face to face or over the telephone, the time for acceptance does not ordinarily extend beyond the end of the conversation unless a contrary intention is indicated. A contrary intention may be indicated either by express words or by the circumstances. For example, the delivery of a written offer to the offeree, or an expectation that some action will be taken before acceptance, may indicate that a delayed acceptance is invited. **Illustration:**

4. While A and B are engaged in conversation, A makes B an offer to which B then makes no reply, out on meeting A again a few hours later B states that he accepts the offer. There is no contract unless the offer or the circumstances indicate that the offer is intended to continue beyond the immediate conversation.

e. Offers made by mail or telegram. Where the parties are at a distance from each other, the normal understanding is that the time for acceptance is extended at least by the normal time for transmission of the offer and for the sending of the offeree's reply. Compare § 49. Subsection (3) reflects the normal understanding that mail is promptly answered if a reply is mailed at any time on the day of receipt. Compare Uniform Commercial Code §§ 4-301, 4-302, fixing the time for settlement by a bank for demand items. But in the absence of a significant speculative element in the situation, a considerably longer time may be reasonable. The fact that an offer is made by telegram or mailgram may or may not indicate that the time for reply is shorter than it would be if the mail were used. Compare § 65. **Illustration:**

> 5. A makes B an offer by mail to sell goods. B receives the offer at the close of business hours and accepts it by letter promptly the next morning. The acceptance is timely.

. . .

§ 42. Revocation by Communication From Offeror Received by Offeree

An offeree's power of acceptance is terminated when the offeree receives from the offeror a manifestation of an intention not to enter into the proposed contract.

Comment:

a. Revocability of offers. Most offers are revocable. Revocability may rest on the express or implied terms of the offer, as in the case of bids at an auction. See § 28. But the ordinary offer is revocable even though it expressly states the contrary, because of the doctrine that an informal agreement is binding as a bargain only if supported by consideration. Inroads have been made on that doctrine by statute and by rules giving effect to nominal consideration and to action in reliance on a promise. Where such rules are applicable, or where the offer is itself a formal contract or an agreement binding as a bargain, the case is governed by § 37 rather than by this Section. See § 25. **Illustration:**

> 1. A makes a written offer to B to sell him a piece of land. The offer states that it will remain open for thirty days and is not subject to countermand. The next day A orally informs B that the offer is terminated. B's power of acceptance is terminated unless the offer is a contract under § 25.

b. Necessity that communication be received. An offeror may reserve the power to revoke the offer without notice, and such a reservation will be given effect whether contained in the offer or in a later communication received by the offeree before a contract is created. But such a reservation is unusual; it deprives the offeree of a dependable basis for decision whether to accept and greatly impairs the usefulness of the offer. In the absence of such a reservation, the offeree is justified in relying on the offeror's manifested intention regardless of any undisclosed change in the offeror's state of mind. As to when a revocation is received by the offeree, see § 68; compare Restatement, Second, Agency §§ 268-83, Uniform Commercial Code § 1-201(25) to (27).

c. Purported revocation after acceptance. Once the offeree has exercised his power to create a contract by accepting the offer, a purported revocation is ineffective as such. Where an acceptance by mail is effective on dispatch, for example, it is not deprived of effect by a revocation subsequently received by the offeree. See § 63. But the revocation may have effect, depending on its terms, as a failure of condition discharging the offeree's duty of performance, as a breach by anticipatory repudiation, or as an offer to modify or rescind the contract. **Illustrations:**

> 2. A sends B an offer by mail to buy a piece of land for $ 5000. The next day A sends B a letter stating that unless B has already accepted A revokes the offer and makes a new offer to buy the same land for $ 4800. B receives A's second letter after he has duly mailed a letter of acceptance, but promptly sells the land to C without further communication with A. The sale is a breach of contract by B.
>
> 3. A sends B an offer by mail to buy a piece of land. The next day A sends B a letter stating that A has changed his mind and will not buy the land even if B has already accepted the offer. B receives A's second letter after he has duly mailed a letter of acceptance, but promptly sells the land to C. B's duty of performance is discharged. See Comment *a* to § 283.

d. What constitutes revocation. The word "revoke" is not essential to a revocation. Any clear manifestation of unwillingness to enter into the proposed bargain is sufficient. Thus a statement that property offered for sale has been otherwise disposed of is a revocation. But equivocal language may not be sufficient.

Illustrations:

4. A makes an offer to buy goods from B, and later requests B not to deliver the goods until A is in a better condition to handle them. The request does not revoke the offer.

5. A makes an offer to B, and later says to B, "Well, I don't know if we are ready. We have not decided, we might not want to go through with it." The offer is revoked.

§ 43. Indirect Communication of Revocation

An offeree's power of acceptance is terminated when the offeror takes definite action inconsistent with an intention to enter into the proposed contract and the offeree acquires reliable information to that effect.

Comment:

a. Direct and indirect communication. This Section extends the principle giving effect to a revocation communicated directly by the offeror to the offeree, and is subject to the same qualifications. See § 42. Thus a revocation is ineffective, whether communication is direct or indirect, if the offer is itself a contract, or after the power of acceptance has been duly exercised. On the other hand, no communication at all is necessary for revocation if the offer so provides. Where a revocation is communicated through a person or persons having power to act for the offeror or offeree, the case is governed by § 42, supplemented by the law of agency.

. . .

d. Definite action; reliable information. This Section does not apply to cases where the offeror takes no action or takes equivocal action. Thus mere negotiations with a third person, or even a definite offer to a second offeree, may be consistent with an intention on the part of the offeror to honor an acceptance by the original offeree. Even a binding contract with a third person may be expressly subject to any rights arising under the outstanding offer. Moreover, a mere rumor does not terminate the power of acceptance, if the offeree disbelieves it and is reasonable in doing so, even though the rumor is later verified. The basic standard to which the offeree is held is that of a reasonable person acting in good faith. **Illustration:**

3. A offers to sell B a hundred shares of stock at a fixed price, and states that the offer will not be revoked for a week. Within the week C offers A a higher price for the same stock, and B learns of the higher offer. B's power of acceptance is not terminated, since he is entitled to assume that A will honor his commitment regardless of its legal effect.

§ 44. Effect of Deposit on Revocability of Offer

An offeror's power of revocation is not limited by the deposit of money or other property to be forfeited in the event of revocation, but the deposit may be forfeited to the extent that it is not a penalty.

Comment:

a. Deposits. Money or other property is often transferred by an offeror to the account of the offeree, and such property may ordinarily be recovered if the offer is not accepted. See Restatement of Restitution § 56. If it is agreed that the property may be forfeited in the event of revocation of the offer, the agreement is subject to the rules governing liquidated damages and penalties. See § 356; Uniform Commercial Code § 2-718. The agreement may be valid as a provision for liquidated damages, or as a provision of security for the payment of actual damages. In either case, the offer is treated as irrevocable for the purpose of determining rights in the deposit, but the offeror's power of revocation is not otherwise impaired. In cases of bids on government contracts, statutes often authorize forfeiture without regard to the distinction between liquidated damages and penalty.

...

§ 45. Option Contract Created by Part Performance or Tender

(1) Where an offer invites an offeree to accept by rendering a performance and does not invite a promissory acceptance, an option contract is created when the offeree tenders or begins the invited performance or tenders a beginning of it.

(2) The offeror's duty of performance under any option contract so created is conditional on completion or tender of the invited performance in accordance with the terms of the offer.

Comment:

a. Offer limited to acceptance by performance only. This Section is limited to cases where the offer does not invite a promissory acceptance. Such an offer has often been referred to as an "offer for a unilateral contract." Typical illustrations are found in offers of rewards or prizes and in non-commercial arrangements among relatives and friends. See Comment *b* to § 32. As to analogous cases arising under offers which give the offeree power to accept either by performing or by promising to perform, as he chooses, see §§ 32, 62.

b. Manifestation of contrary intention. The rule of this Section is designed to protect the offeree in justifiable reliance on the offeror's promise, and the rule yields to a manifestation of intention which makes reliance unjustified. A reservation of power to revoke after performance has begun means that as yet there is no promise and no offer. See §§ 2, 24. In particular, if the performance is one which requires the cooperation of both parties, such as the payment of money or the manual delivery of goods, a person who reserves the right to refuse to receive the performance has not made an offer. See § 26.

Illustrations:

1. B owes A $ 5000 payable in installments over a five-year period. A proposes that B discharge the debt by paying $ 4,500 cash within one month, but reserves the right to refuse any such payment. A has not made an offer. A tender by B in accordance with the proposal is an offer by B.

2. A, an insurance company, issues a bulletin to its agents, entitled "Extra Earnings Agreement," providing for annual bonus payments to the agents varying according to "monthly premiums in force" and "lapse ratio," but reserving the right to change or discontinue the bonus, individually or collectively, with or without notice, at any time before payment. There is no offer or promise.

c. Tender of performance. A proposal to receive a payment of money or a delivery of goods is an offer only if acceptance can be completed without further cooperation by the offeror. If there is an offer, it follows that acceptance must be complete at the latest when performance is tendered. A tender of performance, so bargained for and given in exchange for the offer, ordinarily furnishes consideration and creates a contract. See §§ 17, 71, 72.

This is so whether or not the tender carries with it any incidental promises. See §§ 54, 62. If no commitment is made by the offeree, the contract is an option contract. See § 25.

Illustration:

3. A promises B to sell him a specified chattel for $ 5, stating that B is not to be bound until he pays the money. B tenders $ 5 within a reasonable time, but A refuses to accept the tender. There is a breach of contract.

d. Beginning to perform. If the invited performance takes time, the invitation to perform necessarily includes an invitation to begin performance. In most such cases the beginning of performance carries with it an express or implied promise to complete performance. See § 62. In the less common case where the offer does not contemplate or invite a promise by the offeree, the beginning of performance nevertheless completes the manifestation of mutual assent and furnishes consideration for an option contract. See § 25. If the beginning of performance requires the cooperation of the offeror, tender of part performance has the same effect. Part performance or tender may also create an option contract in a situation where the offeree is invited to take up the option by making a promise, if the offer invites a preliminary performance before the time for the offeree's final commitment. **Illustrations:**

4. A offers a reward for the return of lost property. In response to the offer, B searches for the property and finds it. A then notifies B that the offer is revoked. B makes a tender of the property to A conditional on payment of the

reward, and A refuses. There is a breach of contract by A.

5. A, a magazine, offers prizes in a subscription contest. At a time when B has submitted the largest number of subscriptions, A cancels the contest. A has broken its contract with B.

6. A writes to her daughter B, living in another state, an offer to leave A's farm to B if B gives up her home and cares for A during A's life, B remaining free to terminate the arrangement at any time. B gives up her home, moves to A's farm, and begins caring for A. A is bound by an option contract.

7. A offers to sell a piece of land to B, and promises that if B incurs expense in employing experts to appraise the property the offer will be irrevocable for 30 days. B hires experts and pays for their transportation to the land. A is bound by an option contract.

8. In January A, an employer, publishes a notice to his employees, promising a stated Christmas bonus to any employee who is continuously in A's employ from January to Christmas. B, an employee hired by the week, reads the notice and continues at work beyond the expiration of the current week. A is bound by an option contract, and if B is continuously in A's employ until Christmas a notice of revocation of the bonus is ineffective.

e. Completion of performance. Where part performance or tender by the offeree creates an option contract, the offeree is not bound to complete performance. The offeror alone is bound, but his duty of performance is conditional on completion of the offeree's performance. If the offeree abandons performance, the offeror's duty to perform never arises. See § 224, defining "condition," and Illustration 4 to that Section. But the condition may be excused, for example, if the offeror prevents performance, waives it, or repudiates. See Comment *b* to § 225 and §§ 239, 278.

f. Preparations for performance. What is begun or tendered must be part of the actual performance invited in order to preclude revocation under this Section. Beginning preparations, though they may be essential to carrying out the contract or to accepting the offer, is not enough. Preparations to perform may, however, constitute justifiable reliance sufficient to make the offeror's promise binding under § 87(2).

In many cases what is invited depends on what is a reasonable mode of acceptance. See § 30. The distinction between preparing for performance and beginning performance in such cases may turn on many factors: the extent to which the offeree's conduct is clearly referable to the offer, the definite and substantial character of that conduct, and the extent to which it is of actual or prospective benefit to the offeror rather than the offeree, as well as the terms of the communications between the parties, their prior course of dealing, and any relevant usages of trade. **Illustration:**

9. A makes a written promise to pay $ 5000 to B, a hospital, "to aid B in its humanitarian work." Relying upon this and other like promises, B proceeds in its humanitarian work, expending large sums of money and incurring large liabilities. Performance by B has begun, and A's offer is irrevocable.

§ 46. Revocation of General Offer

Where an offer is made by advertisement in a newspaper or other general notification to the public or to a number of persons whose identity is unknown to the offeror, the offeree's power of acceptance is terminated when a notice of termination is given publicity by advertisement or other general notification equal to that given to the offer and no better means of notification is reasonably available.

Comment:

a. Revocability. This Section is an extension of the principle giving effect to a communicated revocation, and is subject to the same limitations. See § 42; compare § 43. Theoretically, a general offer may be made irrevocable under §§ 25 and 37 in the same ways as any other offer, but irrevocable offers to a number of unidentified persons are rare except where such documents as letters of credit are issued. See Illustration 2 to § 29. An irrevocable offer, or a revocable offer which has been duly accepted, cannot of course be revoked under this Section. On the other hand, this Section does not exclude revocation under § 42 or § 43 or under a power to revoke expressly reserved in the offer; a published notice of revocation which does not comply with this Section is nonetheless effective as to an offeree who actually learns of it.

b. *Available means of notice.* The rule of this Section reconciles the principle that an offer is ordinarily revocable with the fact that general publication is not a reliable means of informing offerees of the revocation of an offer. Revocation by a notification not actually received is given effect only where such revocation is provided for in the offer or where the alternative is that the offer is as a practical matter irrevocable. Where a feasible and customary substitute is available which is better calculated to produce actual receipt of notice, newspaper publication is not enough. Even where publication is the only or the best available means of giving notice, it may not be effective immediately. There must be publicity equivalent to that given the offer, including in appropriate cases a reasonable time for equivalent indirect circulation. Compare Illustration 1 to § 23. **Illustrations:**

1. A, a newspaper, publishes an offer of prizes to the persons who procure the largest number of subscriptions as evidenced by cash or checks received by a specified time. B completes and mails an entry blank giving his name and address, which is received by A. Thereafter, during the contest, A publishes a notice that personal checks will not be counted; B does not see the notice. Unless the original offer provided otherwise, B is not bound by the later notice, since A could have given B personal notice. ...

§ 47. Revocation of Divisible Offer

An offer contemplating a series of independent contracts by separate acceptances may be effectively revoked so as to terminate the power to create future contracts, though one or more of the proposed contracts have already been formed by the offeree's acceptance.

   ...

§ 48. Death or Incapacity of Offeror or Offeree

An offeree's power of acceptance is terminated when the offeree or offeror dies or is deprived of legal capacity to enter into the proposed contract.

Comment:

a. *Death of offeror.* The offeror's death terminates the power of the offeree without notice to him. This rule seems to be a relic of the obsolete view that a contract requires a "meeting of minds," and it is out of harmony with the modern doctrine that a manifestation of assent is effective without regard to actual mental assent. See § 19. Some inroads have been made on the rule by statutes and decisions with respect to bank deposits and collections, and by legislation with respect to powers of attorney given by servicemen. See Uniform Commercial Code § 4-405; Restatement, Second, Agency § 120 and Comment a. In the absence of legislation, the rule remains in effect. See also Restatement of Security § 87.

b. *Incapacity of offeror.* The common types of incapacity and their effects are indicated in the Comment to § 12. The offeror's permanent lack of capacity to enter into a contract terminates the offeree's power of acceptance in the same manner as the offeror's death. Compare Restatement, Second, Agency §§ 122, 133; Restatement of Security § 84. But persons under a disability often have power to enter into voidable contracts. See § 7 and Comment; §§ 12-16.

c. *Death or incapacity of offeree.* Only the offeree can accept an offer which is not also a contract. See § 52. When the offeree dies or lacks capacity, therefore, acceptance is impossible. Compare Comment b to § 36. By the terms of the offer, however, the personal representative or distributee of the offeree may be made an additional offeree.

d. *Option contracts.* The rule stated in this Section does not affect option contracts. See § 37. But the death or incapacity of one of the parties may discharge any contractual duty by reason of failure of consideration, frustration, impossibility or failure of condition. See § 36 and Comment.

§ 49. Effect of Delay in Communication of Offer

If communication of an offer to the offeree is delayed, the period within which a contract can be created by acceptance is not thereby extended if the offeree knows or has reason to know of the delay, though it is due to the fault of the offeror; but if the delay is due to the fault of the offeror or to the means of transmission adopted by him, and the offeree neither knows nor has reason to know that there has been delay, a contract can be created by acceptance within the period which would have been permissible if the offer had been dispatched at the time that its arrival seems to indicate.

Illustration:

1. A sends B a misdirected offer which is delayed in delivery, as is apparent from the date of the letter or the postmark on the envelope, so that the offeree does not receive the offer until some time later than he would have received it had the direction been correct. The offeree cannot accept the offer unless he can do so within the time which would have been permissible had the offer arrived seasonably.

§ 50. Acceptance of Offer Defined; Acceptance by Performance; Acceptance by Promise

(1) Acceptance of an offer is a manifestation of assent to the terms thereof made by the offeree in a manner invited or required by the offer.

(2) Acceptance by performance requires that at least part of what the offer requests be performed or tendered and includes acceptance by a performance which operates as a return promise.

(3) Acceptance by a promise requires that the offeree complete every act essential to the making of the promise.

Comment:

a. Mode of acceptance. The acceptance must manifest assent to the same bargain proposed by the offer, and must also comply with the terms of the offer as to the identity of the offeree and the mode of manifesting acceptance. Offers commonly invite acceptance in any reasonable manner, but a particular mode of acceptance may be required. See § 30. In case of doubt, the offeree may choose to accept either by promising or by rendering the requested performance. See § 32.

b. Acceptance by performance. Where the offer requires acceptance by performance and does not invite a return promise, as in the ordinary case of an offer of a reward, a contract can be created only by the offeree's performance. See Comment *b* to § 32. In such cases the act requested and performed as consideration for the offeror's promise ordinarily also constitutes acceptance; under § 45 the beginning of performance or the tender of part performance of what is requested may both indicate assent and furnish consideration for an option contract. In some other cases the offeree may choose to create a contract either by making a promise or by rendering or tendering performance; in most such cases the beginning of performance or a tender of part performance operates as a promise to render complete performance. See § 32, 62. Mere preparation to perform, however, is not acceptance, although in some cases preparation may make the offeror's promise binding under § 87(2). **Illustrations:**

1. A, who is about to leave on a month's vacation, tells B that A will pay B $ 50 if B will paint A's porch while A is away. B says he may not have time, and A says B may decide after A leaves. If B begins the painting, there is an acceptance by performance which operates as a promise to complete the job. See §§ 32, 62.

2. In Illustration 1, B also expresses doubt whether he will be able to finish the job, and it is agreed that B may quit at any time but will be paid only if he finishes the job during A's vacation. If B begins the painting, there is an acceptance by performance creating an option contract. See § 45.

c. Acceptance by promise. The typical contract consists of mutual promises and is formed by an acceptance constituting a return promise by the offeree. A promissory acceptance may be explicitly required by the offer, or may be the only type of acceptance which is reasonable under the circumstances, or the offeree may choose to accept by promise an offer which invites acceptance either by promise or by performance. See §§ 30, 32. The promise may be made in words or other symbols of assent, or it may be implied from conduct, other than acts of performance, provided only that it is in a form invited or required by the offer. An act of performance may also operate as a return promise, but the acceptance in such a case is treated as an acceptance by performance rather than an acceptance by promise; thus the requirement of notification is governed by § 54 rather than by § 56. As appears from § 63, acceptance by promise may be effective when a written promise is started on its way, but the offeree must complete the acts necessary on his part to constitute a promise by him. Similarly, in cases where communication to the offeror is unnecessary under § 69, the acts constituting the promise must be complete.

Illustrations:

3. A sends to B plans for a summer cottage to be built on A's land in a remote wilderness area, and writes, "If you will undertake to build a cottage in accordance with the enclosed plans, I will pay you $ 5,000." B cannot accept by beginning or completing performance, since A's letter calls for acceptance by promise. See § 58.

4. A mails a written order to B, offering to buy on specified terms a machine of a type which B regularly sells from stock. The order provides, "Ship at once." B immediately mails a letter of acceptance. This is an acceptance by promise, even though under § 32 B might have accepted by performance.

5. A gives an order to B Company's traveling salesman which provides, "This proposal becomes a contract without further notification when approval by an executive officer of B Company is noted hereon at its home office." The notation of approval is an acceptance by promise. See §§ 56, 69 as to the requirement of notification.

§ 51. Effect of Part Performance Without Knowledge of Offer

Unless the offeror manifests a contrary intention, an offeree who learns of an offer after he has rendered part of the performance requested by the offer may accept by completing the requested performance.

Comment:

a. Performance without knowledge. Where an offer invites a return promise, the offeree may manifest assent and thereby make a return promise even though he does not have actual knowledge of the offer. See § 23 Comment *c*; § 69. But when an offer contemplates no commitment, as in cases of offers of reward, it is ordinarily essential to the acceptance of the offer that the offeree know of the proposal made. In general, performance completed before the offer comes to the offeree's knowledge does not have reference to the offer, and the terms of the offer are not satisfied by such action. See §§ 23, 71.

b. Completion of performance with knowledge. Where part performance has been rendered by a person ignorant of the existence of an offer, the offer can no longer serve the purpose of inducing that performance. But it can induce the completion of performance. It is commonly intended by the offeror to have that effect and so understood by the offeree. The

inference that the offeror so intends is strengthened when the part performance is valueless to him unless completed, or when the offeror knows of the offeree's continuing performance and fails to revoke. In the absence of contrary indications, the law gives effect to the common understanding. But there may be no consideration if the offeree is under a legal duty to the offeror to complete the performance. See § 73. **Illustrations:**

1. A offers a reward for the apprehension and delivery into police custody of a criminal. Before learning of the reward, B arrests the criminal. After learning of the reward, B delivers the criminal into police custody. B is entitled to the reward.

2. A posts a notice on his bulletin board offering a specified bonus to any employee who remains in A's employment for four months. B, one of the employees, continues to work for one month before learning of the offer. Thereafter, B completes the four-month period of employment. B is entitled to the bonus.

§ 52. Who May Accept an Offer

An offer can be accepted only by a person whom it invites to furnish the consideration.

Comment:

a. Rationale. This Section states a negative fairly implied in § 29. The offeror is the master of his offer, and the power of acceptance rests on his manifested intention. The rule that the power of acceptance is personal to the offeree is applied strictly, even in cases where the offeree after acceptance could assign his rights and delegate performance to the assignee under §§ 317(2) and 318(1). As to death of the offeree, compare § 37 with § 48. **Illustrations:**

     1. A makes an offer to B, who dies after receiving it. His executor, though acting within the permitted time, cannot accept.

     2. A offers to guarantee payment for goods delivered to B by C. D cannot accept by delivering goods to B.

     . . .

c. Agency. The rules stated in the Restatement of this Subject are supplemented by the law of agency, and in the absence of contrary statement it is assumed that any necessary act may be performed on behalf of a contracting party by his agent. Thus an offer may be accepted by an agent of the offeree. See Restatement, Second, Agency § 292. Even an acceptance by a purported agent, acting without agency power, may in appropriate cases be ratified by the offeree. See Restatement, Second, Agency §§ 82-104. Ratification must occur, however, before the offeror manifests withdrawal from the transaction and before the termination of the offeree's power of acceptance. See Restatement, Second, Agency § 88.

Under the law of agency, an offeree who purports to act on his own behalf may in fact be acting for an undisclosed principal, and the undisclosed principal may be bound by the contract and may have rights under it. See Restatement, Second, Agency §§ 186 Comment *a*, 302-10, 372.

§ 53. Acceptance by Performance; Manifestation of Intention Not to Accept

     (1) An offer can be accepted by the rendering of a performance only if the offer invites such an acceptance.

     (2) Except as stated in § 69, the rendering of a performance does not constitute an acceptance if within a reasonable time the offeree exercises reasonable diligence to notify the offeror of non-acceptance.

     (3) Where an offer of a promise invites acceptance by performance and does not invite a promissory acceptance, the rendering of the invited performance does not constitute an acceptance if before the offeror performs his promise the offeree manifests an intention not to accept.

Comment:

a. Invitation of acceptance by performance. Subsection (1) makes explicit with respect to acceptance by performance the offeror's power to control the mode of acceptance. See §§ 30(1), 50(1). In the absence of contrary indication, the question is whether acceptance by performance is reasonable under the circumstances. See § 30(2). Where either acceptance by performance or acceptance by promise is reasonable, the offeree may choose between them. Where no return commitment is invited and the invited performance takes time, the beginning of performance creates an option contract. See § 45. In other cases the beginning of performance may carry with it a promise to complete performance. See § 62.

b. Rejection by the performing offeree. Subsection (2) states the power of the offeree to reject an offer even though he engages in conduct invited by the offer. Compare §§ 38-40. Ordinarily the making of an offer does not limit the offeree's freedom of action or inaction; he may act or forbear without reference to the offer. But if he has reason to know that the offeror may reasonably infer from his conduct that he assents, he runs the risk of being bound by his manifestation of assent. See §§ 19, 20. He may guard against that risk by manifesting an intention not to accept. Although a rejection does not terminate the power of acceptance until received by the offeror (§ 40), reasonable diligence to notify the offeror is sufficient to protect the offeree against an unintended acceptance, except as stated in § 69. Thus Uniform Commercial Code § 2-206(1)(b) provides that a shipment of nonconforming goods in response to an offer to buy is not an acceptance if the seller seasonably notifies the buyer that the shipment is offered only as an accommodation to the buyer. See Illustrations 5 and 6 to § 32. The exceptional cases covered by § 69 involve taking the benefit of offered goods or services, or prior conduct of the offeree justifying the offeror in inferring assent.

c. Rejection or disclaimer where return promise is not contemplated. Where no promise by the offeree is contemplated, there is no problem of justifiable reliance by the offeror. See Comment *d* to § 23. The offeree's conduct ordinarily constitutes an acceptance in such cases only if he knows of the offer. His rendering of the invited performance with knowledge of the offer is a sufficient manifestation of assent, and inquiry into his motives is unnecessary. But the meaning of non-verbal conduct is even more dependent on its setting than the meaning of words. See Comment *a* to § 19. The words or conduct of the offeree may show that he acts gratuitously, or otherwise without reference to the offer. There is then no bargain. See § 23. Moreover, as in other cases where it is assumed that a promisee accepts a promise beneficial to him, disclaimer renders the promise inoperative from the beginning.

Compare §§ 104, 306. The effect of disclaimer in violation of duty to third persons and the effect of disclaimer on the rights of third persons are beyond the scope of this Restatement. See, e.g., Restatement, Second, Trusts §§ 35, 102.

Illustrations:

1. A offers a reward for information leading to the conviction of a criminal. B, a friend of the criminal, knows of the reward and gives the information voluntarily. B is entitled to the reward even though he acts because he thinks he is about to die and wants both to ease his conscience and to revenge himself for a beating received from the criminal.

2. The facts being otherwise as stated in Illustration 1, B is interrogated by the police and threatened with arrest as an accomplice of the criminal. During the interrogation, without any mention of the reward, B is tricked into giving the information to clear himself. B is not entitled to the reward.

3. The facts being otherwise as stated in Illustration 1, B states after giving the information that he does not claim the reward. B is not entitled to the reward.

4. A, an elderly widow apparently in dire poverty, promises B, a distant relative of her deceased husband, that she will pay for board and lodging in B's home. B furnishes board and lodging to A for a year without requesting or receiving any payment, and on A's death states that nothing is due to B. It is a question of fact on all the circumstances whether B has manifested an intention not to seek payment even if A is found to have left a substantial bank account.

§ 54. Acceptance by Performance; Necessity of Notification to Offeror

(1) Where an offer invites an offeree to accept by rendering a performance, no notification is necessary to make such an acceptance effective unless the offer requests such a notification.

(2) If an offeree who accepts by rendering a performance has reason to know that the offeror has no adequate means of learning of the performance with reasonable promptness and certainty, the contractual duty of the offeror is discharged unless

(a) the offeree exercises reasonable diligence to notify the offeror of acceptance, or

(b) the offeror learns of the performance within a reasonable time, or

(c) the offer indicates that notification of acceptance is not required.

Comment:

a. Rationale. In the usual commercial bargain the offeror expects and receives prompt notification of acceptance, and such notification is ordinarily essential to an acceptance by promise. See § 56. But where an offer invites the offeree to accept by rendering a performance, the offeree needs a dependable basis for his decision whether to accept. Compare § 63 and Comment *a*. When the offeree performs or begins to perform in response to such an offer, there is need for protection of his justifiable reliance. Compare § 45. Those needs are met by giving the performance the effect of temporarily barring revocation of the offer; but ordinarily notification of the offeror must follow in due course. See Uniform Commercial Code § 2-206 Comment 3.

b. Performance operating as return promise. This Section applies only to offers which invite acceptance by performance. Where the offeree is empowered to choose between acceptance by performance and acceptance by promise (see § 32), this Section applies only if he chooses to accept by performance. See § 50(2). In such a case the acceptance often carries with it a return commitment (see § 62), and it is rare that the offer dispenses with notification of such a commitment. Compare §§ 56, 69. Unless the performance will come to the offeror's attention in normal course, it is not likely to be a reasonable mode of acceptance. See § 30. In the exceptional case where acceptance is invited by a performance which will not come promptly to the offeror's attention, Subsection (2) usually requires notification of acceptance. Uniform Commercial Code § 2-206(2) provides that if no notification is sent within a reasonable time in such a case, the offeror may treat the offer as having lapsed before acceptance. Compare § 41. **Illustration:**

> 1. A mails a written order to B for goods to be manufactured specially for A, and requests B to begin at once since manufacture will take several weeks. Under § 62 acceptance is complete when B begins, but A's contractual duty is discharged and he may treat the offer as having lapsed before acceptance unless within a reasonable time

B sends notification of acceptance or unless the offer or a prior course of dealing indicates that notification is not required.

c. Where no return promise is contemplated. Performance may be invited as an alternative mode of acceptance or as the exclusive mode of acceptance. See §§ 30, 32. Where no return commitment is involved, the only notification of acceptance called for is often that necessarily involved in performance by the offeree, or that which accompanies the offeree's request for performance by the offeror. Performance itself both manifests assent and furnishes consideration. Notification is requisite only where the offeror has no convenient means of ascertaining whether the requisite performance has taken place. Even then, it is not the notification which creates the contract, but lack of notification which ends the duty. Compare § 224. Moreover, the offeror may effectively waive notification either before or after the time when it would otherwise be due. See § 84. **Illustrations:**

> 2. A, the proprietor of a medical preparation, offers $ 100 to anyone who contracts a certain disease after using the preparation as directed. B uses it as directed. B has accepted the offer, and is entitled to the $ 100 if she later contracts the disease. No notification to A is required until after B has contracted the disease.
>
> 3. A, a newspaper, requests B to discontinue distribution of a rival newspaper, and offers to pay B $ 10 per week as long as B abstains from such distribution. B discontinues the distribution. B has accepted the offer, and no notification to A is required.

. . .

§ 55. Acceptance of Non-Promissory Offers

Acceptance by promise may create a contract in which the offeror's performance is completed when the offeree's promise is made.

Comment:

a. "Reverse unilateral contracts." It is possible to offer a performance without making any promise. Like other offers, a non-promissory offer may require acceptance by performance or acceptance by promise or a combination of the two, or it may leave the mode of acceptance to the offeree's choice. An exchange of performances is not within the definition of "contract" in § 1 and is beyond the scope of the Restatement of this Subject. But where a non-promissory offer is accepted by promise, there is

a contract if the requirements other than manifestation of mutual assent are met. Since the contract formed by a performance in response to an offer of a promise such as an offer of reward is often called a "unilateral contract," the type of contract referred to in this Section is sometimes referred to as a "reverse unilateral contract." Contracts so referred to often involve incidental promises by the performing offeror, and in that event the word "unilateral" is not entirely appropriate.

. . .

Illustrations:

1. A applies to B, an insurance company, for a policy of life insurance, and pays the first premium on an understanding that the insurance must be approved at B's home office. B's notification that the approval has been given is an acceptance of A's offer and forms a contract of insurance.

. . .

3. A, the owner of a horse in B's possession, offers to sell the horse to B for $ 100 payable in thirty days. On B's promise to pay in accordance with the offer, ownership of the horse is transferred to him and there is a contract. Uniform Commercial Code § 2-401(3).

. . .

§ 56. Acceptance by Promise; Necessity of Notification to Offeror

Except as stated in § 69 or where the offer manifests a contrary intention, it is essential to an acceptance by promise either that the offeree exercise reasonable diligence to notify the offeror of acceptance or that the offeror receive the acceptance seasonably.

Comment:

a. Necessity of notification. Where the offeree has performed in whole or in part, notification to the offeror is not essential to acceptance, although failure to notify may discharge the offeror's duty of performance. See § 54. Similarly, where the offeror has rendered a performance and the offeree has taken the benefit of that performance, the offeree may be bound without notification to the offeror. See § 69. In such cases the enforcement of the promise rests in part on a change of position in justifiable reliance on a promise, often reinforced by a corresponding benefit received by the promisor. Section 69 also provides for some cases of offers which manifest an intention to dispense with notification. In other cases of the exchange of promises which are entirely executory on both sides, the offeror is entitled to notification of acceptance unless the offer manifests a contrary intention.

Illustrations:

1. A gives an order to B Company's traveling salesman for a $ 2000 machine "to purify water of the character shown by sample to be submitted," shipment to be made in one month. The order provides: "This proposal becomes a contract when approved by an executive officer of B Company at its home office." Notation of such approval on the order is an acceptance by promise without any notification, but A's duty to perform is conditional on reasonable notification to send the sample.

2. A makes written application for life insurance through an agent for B Insurance Company, pays the first premium, and is given a receipt stating that the insurance "shall take effect as of the date of approval of the application" at B's home office. Approval at the home office in accordance with B's usual practice is an acceptance of A's offer even though no steps are taken to notify A.

b. Failure of communication. It is sometimes said that the acceptance must be communicated to the offeror, and when the parties deal face to face communication is ordinarily required. The rule is more accurately stated as one requiring reasonable diligence on the part of the offeree, however, since in cases of misunderstanding acceptance turns on what each party knew or had reason to know. See § 20. In cases of communication by mail or telegram, moreover, an acceptance may be effective on dispatch even though it fails to reach the addressee. See § 63. Failure of diligence becomes immaterial if the offeror receives the acceptance seasonably. See § 67. As to when a written acceptance is received, see § 68. Compare Restatement, Second, Agency §§ 268-83, Uniform Commercial Code § 1-201(25)-(27). Of course reasonable diligence, or even receipt, is not enough if the terms of the offer require more. See § 58.

§ 57. Effect of Equivocal Acceptance

Where notification is essential to acceptance by promise, the offeror is not bound by an acceptance in equivocal terms unless he reasonably understands it as an acceptance.

Comment:

a. Requirement of notification. Notification of acceptance by promise is required in most circumstances. See § 56. Where notification is dispensed with by the terms of the offer, the offeror cannot complain of the resulting uncertainty of his position. See § 69. In cases of acceptance by performance, the reliance of the offeree or the unjust enrichment of the offeror may justify a legal remedy for breach in spite of uncertainty in the offeror's position. Compare §§ 34, 54. Hence this Section is limited to cases of acceptance by promise in which notification is required.

b. Equivocation. This Section is a particular application of the general principles stated in § 20. Where notification is essential to acceptance by promise, the offeror is entitled to know in clear terms whether the offeree accepts his proposal. It is not enough that the words of a reply justify a probable inference of assent. But the circumstances may make it proper to protect an offeror who acts on such an inference. Or subsequent conduct of one or both parties may bind one to an agreement in accordance with the understanding of the other. Compare § 70.

Illustrations:

1. A gives an order for goods to B's traveling salesman, subject to approval by B at his home office. B sends a letter to A stating that the order has been received and will receive B's attention. A promptly sends a letter of revocation to B, which B receives before doing anything further. There is no contract.

2. The facts being otherwise as stated in Illustration 1, A does not revoke, but after two months, when it is too late for A to procure substitute goods, B writes a letter to A stating that "it is necessary to cancel this order." B has broken a contract with A.

. . .

§ 58. Necessity of Acceptance Complying with Terms of Offer

An acceptance must comply with the requirements of the offer as to the promise to be made or the performance to be rendered.

Comment:

a. Scope. This rule applies to the substance of the bargain the basic principle that the offeror is the master of his offer. See Comment *a* to § 29. That principle rests on the concept of private autonomy underlying contract law. It is mitigated by the interpretation of offers, in accordance with common understanding, as inviting acceptance in any reasonable manner unless there is contrary indication. See §§ 20, 30(2), 32. Usage of trade or course of dealing may permit inconsequential variations; or a variation clearly to the offeror's advantage, such as a reduction in the price of ordered goods, may be within the scope of the offer. But even in such cases the offeror is entitled, if he makes his meaning clear, to insist on a prescribed type of acceptance. **Illustrations:**

1. A offers to sell a book to B for $ 5 and states that no other acceptance will be honored but the mailing of B's personal check for exactly $ 5. B personally tenders $ 5 in legal tender, or mails a personal check for $ 10. There is no contract.

2. A offers to pay B $ 100 for plowing Flodden field, and states that acceptance is to be made only by posting a letter before beginning work and before the next Monday noon. Before Monday noon B completes the requested plowing and mails to A a letter stating that the work is complete. There is no contract.

§ 59. Purported Acceptance Which Adds Qualifications

A reply to an offer which purports to accept it but is conditional on the offeror's assent to terms additional to or different from those offered is not an acceptance but is a counter-offer.

Comment:

a. Qualified acceptance. A qualified or conditional acceptance proposes an exchange different from that proposed by the original offeror. Such a proposal is a counter-offer and ordinarily terminates the power of acceptance of the original offeree. See § 39. The effect of the qualification or condition is to deprive the purported acceptance of effect. But a definite and seasonable expression of acceptance is operative despite the statement of additional or different terms if the acceptance is not made to depend on assent to the additional or different terms. See § 61; Uniform Commercial Code § 2-207(1). The additional or different terms are then to be construed as proposals for modification of the contract. See Uniform Commercial Code § 2-207(2). Such proposals may sometimes be accepted by the silence of the original offeror. See § 69. **Illustration:**

1. A makes an offer to B, and B in terms accepts but adds, "This acceptance is not effective unless prompt acknowledgement is made of receipt of this letter." There is no contract, but a counter-offer.

b. Statement of conditions implied in offer. To accept, the offeree must assent unconditionally to the offer as made, but the fact that the offeree makes a conditional promise is not sufficient to show that his acceptance is conditional. The offer itself may either expressly or by implication propose that the offeree make a conditional promise as his part of the exchange. By assenting to such a proposal the offeree makes a conditional promise, but his acceptance is unconditional. The offeror's promise may also be conditional on the same or a different fact or event. **Illustrations:**

2. A makes a written offer to sell B a patent in exchange for B's promise to pay $ 10,000 if B's adviser X approves the purchase. B signs the writing in a space labelled "Accepted:" and returns the writing to A. B has made a conditional promise and an unconditional acceptance. There is a contract, but B's duty to pay the price is conditional on X's approval.

3. A makes a written offer to B to sell him Blackacre. By usage the offer is understood as promising a marketable title. B replies, "I accept your offer if you can convey me a marketable title." There is a contract.

§ 60. Acceptance of Offer Which States Place, Time or Manner of Acceptance

If an offer prescribes the place, time or manner of acceptance its terms in this respect must be complied with in order to create a contract. If an offer merely suggests a permitted place, time or manner of acceptance, another method of acceptance is not precluded.

Comment:

a. Interpretation of offer. If the offeror prescribes the only way in which his offer may be accepted, an acceptance in any other way is a counter-offer. But frequently in regard to the details of methods of acceptance, the offeror's language, if fairly interpreted, amounts merely to a statement of a satisfactory method of acceptance, without positive requirement that this method shall be followed. **Illustrations:**

1. A mails an offer to B in which A says, "I must receive your acceptance by return mail." An acceptance sent within a reasonable time by any other means, which reaches A as soon as a letter sent by return mail would normally arrive,

creates a contract on arrival. As to what is a reasonable time, see Illustration 8 to § 41.

2. A makes an offer to B and adds, "Send your office boy around with an answer to this by twelve o'clock." The offeree comes himself before twelve o'clock and accepts. There is a contract.

3. A offers to sell his land to B on certain terms, also saying: "You must accept this, if at all, in person at my office at ten o'clock tomorrow." B's power is strictly limited to one method of acceptance.

4. A offers to sell his land to B on certain terms, also saying: "You may accept by leaving word at my house." This indicates one operative

mode of acceptance; but B's power is not limited to that mode alone. A personal statement to A would serve just as well.

    5. A makes an offer to B and adds, "my address is 53 State Street." This is a business address. B sends an acceptance to A's home which A receives promptly. Unless the circumstances indicate that A has made a positive requirement of the place where the acceptance must be sent, there is a contract.

§ 61. Acceptance Which Requests Change of Terms

An acceptance which requests a change or addition to the terms of the offer is not thereby invalidated unless the acceptance is made to depend on an assent to the changed or added terms.

Comment:

    a. Interpretation of acceptance. An acceptance must be unequivocal. But the mere inclusion of words requesting a modification of the proposed terms does not prevent a purported acceptance from closing the contract unless, if fairly interpreted, the offeree's assent depends on the offeror's further acquiescence in the modification. See Uniform Commercial Code § 2-207(1). **Illustrations:**

    1. A offers to sell B 100 tons of steel at a certain price. B replies, "I accept your offer. I hope that if you can arrange to deliver the steel in weekly installments of 25 tons you will do so." There is a contract, but A is not bound to deliver in installments.

    2. A offers to sell specified hardware to B on stated terms. B replies: "I accept your offer; ship in accordance with your statement. Please send me also one No. 5 hand saw at your list price." The request for the saw is a separate offer, not a counter-offer.

§ 62. Effect of Performance by Offeree Where Offer Invites Either Performance or Promise

(1) Where an offer invites an offeree to choose between acceptance by promise and acceptance by performance, the tender or beginning of the invited performance or a tender of a beginning of it is an acceptance by performance.

(2) Such an acceptance operates as a promise to render complete performance.

Comment:

    a. The offeree's power to choose. The offeror normally invites a promise by the offeree for the purpose of obtaining performance of the promise. Full performance fulfills that purpose more directly than the promise invited, and hence constitutes a reasonable mode of acceptance. The offeror can insist on any mode of acceptance, but ordinarily he invites acceptance in any reasonable manner; in case of doubt, an offer is interpreted as inviting the offeree to choose between acceptance by promise and acceptance by performance. See §§ 30, 32, 58.

    b. Part performance or tender. Where acceptance by performance is invited and no promise is invited, the beginning of performance or the tender of part performance creates an option contract and renders the offer irrevocable. See §§ 37, 45. Under Subsection (1) of this Section the offer is similarly rendered irrevocable where it invites the offeree to choose between acceptance by promise and acceptance by performance. In both types of cases, if the invited performance takes time, the invitation to perform necessarily includes an invitation to begin performance; if performance requires cooperation by the offeror, there is an offer only if acceptance can be completed by tender of performance. But unless an option contract is contemplated, the offeree is expected to be bound as well as the offeror, and Subsection (2) of this Section states the implication of promise which results from that expectation. See Illustration 5 to § 32. In such standard cases as the shipment of goods in response to an order, the acceptance will come to the offeror's attention in normal course; in other cases, the rule of § 54(2) ordinarily requires prompt notification.

    c. Manifestation of contrary intention. The rule of Subsection (1), like the rule of § 45, is designed to protect the offeree in justifiable reliance on the offeror's promise; both rules yield to a manifestation of intention which makes such reliance unjustified. Moreover, in most cases of both types the offeree may prevent the formation of a contract by seasonably notifying the offeror of non-acceptance. Section 53(2). Similarly, the rule of Subsection (2) is designed to preclude the offeree from speculating at the offeror's expense where no option contract is contemplated by the offer (compare § 63), and to protect the offeror in justifiable reliance on the offeree's implied promise; this rule also yields to a manifestation of contrary intention under § 53(2).

d. Preparations for performance. As under § 45, what is begun or tendered must be part of the actual performance invited, rather than preparation for performance, in order to make the rule of this Section applicable. See Comment *f* to § 45. But preparations to perform may bring the case within § 87(2) on justifiable reliance.

Illustrations:

1. A, a merchant, mails B, a carpenter in the same city, an offer to employ B to fit up A's office in accordance with A's specifications and B's estimate previously submitted, the work to be completed in two weeks. The offer says, "You may begin at once," and B immediately buys lumber and begins to work on it in his own shop. The next day, before B as sent a notice of acceptance or begun work at A's office or rendered the lumber unfit for other jobs, A revokes the offer. The revocation is timely, since B has not begun to perform.

2. A, a regular customer of B, orders fragile goods from B which B carries in stock and ships in his own trucks. Following his usual practice, B selects the goods ordered, tags them as A's, crates them and loads them on a truck at substantial expense. Performance has begun, and A's offer is irrevocable. See Uniform Commercial Code § 2-206 and Comment 2.

§ 63. Time When Acceptance Takes Effect

Unless the offer provides otherwise,

(a) an acceptance made in a manner and by a medium invited by an offer is operative and completes the manifestation of mutual assent as soon as put out of the offeree's possession, without regard to whether it ever reaches the offeror; but

(b) an acceptance under an option contract is not operative until received by the offeror.

Comment:

a. Rationale. It is often said that an offeror who makes an offer by mail makes the post office his agent to receive the acceptance, or that the mailing of a letter of acceptance puts it irrevocably out of the offeree's control. Under United States postal regulations, however, the sender of a letter has long had the power to stop delivery and reclaim the letter. A better explanation of the rule that the acceptance takes effect on dispatch is that the offeree needs a dependable basis for his decision whether to accept. In many legal systems such a basis is provided by a general rule that an offer is irrevocable unless it provides otherwise. The common law provides such a basis through the rule that a revocation of an offer is ineffective if received after an acceptance has been properly dispatched. See Comment *c* to § 42. Acceptance by telegram is governed in this respect by the same considerations as acceptance by mail. **Illustration:**

1. A makes B an offer, inviting acceptance by telegram, and B duly telegraphs an accep-

tance. A purports to revoke the offer in person or by telephone or telegraph, but the attempted revocation is received by B after the telegram of acceptance is dispatched. There is no effective revocation.

b. Loss or delay in transit. In the interest of simplicity and clarity, the rule has been extended to cases where an acceptance is lost or delayed in the course of transmission. The convenience of the rule is less clear in such cases than in cases of attempted revocation of the offer, however, and the language of the offer is often properly interpreted as making the offeror's duty of performance conditional upon receipt of the acceptance. Indeed, where the receipt of notice is essential to enable the offeror to perform, such a condition is normally implied. See Comment *c* to § 226. **Illustrations:**

2. A offers to buy cotton from B, the operator of a cotton gin, B to accept by specifying the number of bales in a telegram sent before 8 p.m. thesame day. B duly sends a telegram of

acceptance and ships the cotton, but the telegram is not delivered. There is a contract, and A is bound to take and pay for the cotton.

3. A mails to B an offer to lease land, stating, "Telegraph me Yes or No. If I do not hear from you by noon on Friday, I shall conclude No." B duly telegraphs "Yes," but the telegram is not delivered until after noon on Friday. Any contract formed by the telegraphic acceptance is discharged. 4. A offers to buy cattle for B, on an understanding that if B telegraphs "Yes" A will notify B of the amount of money needed and B will supply it. B's "Yes" telegram is duly dispatched but does not arrive within a reasonable time. Any contract formed by the dispatch of the telegram is discharged.

c. Revocation of acceptance. The fact that the offeree has power to reclaim his acceptance from the post office or telegraph company does not prevent the acceptance from taking effect on dispatch. Nor, in the absence of additional circumstances, does the actual recapture of the acceptance deprive it of legal effect, though as a practical matter the offeror cannot assert his rights unless he learns of them. An attempt to revoke the acceptance by an overtaking communication is similarly ineffective, even though the revocation is received before the acceptance is received. After mailing an acceptance of a revocable offer, the offeree is not permitted to speculate at the offeror's expense during the time required for the letter to arrive.

A purported revocation of acceptance may, however, affect the rights of the parties. It may amount to an offer to rescind the contract or to a repudiation of it, or it may bar the offeree by estoppel from enforcing it. In some cases it may be justified as an exercise of a right of stoppage in transit or a demand for assurance of performance. Compare Uniform Commercial Code §§ 2-609, 2-702, 2-705. Or the contract may be voidable for mistake or misrepresentation, §§ 151-54, 164. See particularly the provisions of § 153 on unilateral mistake. **Illustrations:**

5. A mails to B a note payable by C with instructions to collect the amount of the note and remit by mailing B's own check. At C's request B mails his own check as instructed. Subsequently, at C's request, B recovers his letter and check from the post office. The recovery does not discharge the contract formed by the mailing of B's check. But if B is a bank, its remittance may be provisional under Uniform Commercial Code § 4-211.

6. The facts being otherwise as stated in Illustration 5, B recovers his letter and check from the post office because he has learned that C is insolvent and cannot reimburse B. B is entitled to rescind the contract for mistake. See §§ 153-54; compare Uniform Commercial Code § 4-212.

7. A mails an offer to B to appoint B A's exclusive distributor in a specified area. B duly mails an acceptance. Thereafter B mails a letter which is received by A before the acceptance is received and which rejects the offer and makes a counter-offer. On receiving the rejection and before receiving the acceptance, A executes a contract appointing C as exclusive distributor instead of B. B is estopped to enforce the contract. Compare § 40.

8. The Government mails to A an offer to pay the amount quoted by him for the manufacture of two sets of ship propellers, and A mails an acceptance. A then discovers that by mistake he has quoted the price for a single set, and so informs the Government by a telegram which arrives before the acceptance. A's mailing the acceptance created a contract. The question whether the contract is voidable for mistake is governed by the rules stated in §§ 153-54.

d. Other types of cases. The question when and where an acceptance takes effect may arise in determining the application of tax and regulatory laws, choice of governing law, venue of litigation, and other issues. Such cases often turn on policies beyond the scope of the Restatement of this Subject. To the extent that the issue is referred to the rule governing private contract disputes, the rules stated in this Section are applicable. Where the issue is what obligation is imposed by a contract, whether those rules apply is ordinarily a matter of interpretation. **Illustrations:**

9. A mails to B an offer to buy goods, and B mails an acceptance. The application of a new tax statute depends on when title to the goods passes to A, and under Uniform Commercial Code § 2-401(3) (b) title passes at the time of contracting. The time of contracting is the time when B's acceptance is mailed.

10. A offers to insure B's house against fire, the insurance to take effect upon actual payment of the premium, and invites B to reply by mailing his check for a specified amount. B duly mails the check. While B's letter is in transit, the house burns. The loss is within the period of insurance coverage.

e. The offeree's possession. The rule of Subsection (1) gives effect to an acceptance when "put out of the offeree's possession." Its principal application is to the use of mail and telegraph, but it would apply equally to any other similar public service instrumentality, even though the instrumentality may for some purposes be the offeree's agent. See Restatement, Second, Agency § 1. It may also apply to a private messenger service which is independent of the offeree and can be relied on to keep accurate records. But, except where the Government or a telegraph company can make use of its own postal or telegraph facilities, communication by means of the offeree's employee is excluded; the employee's possession is treated as that of the employer. **Illustration:**

> 11. A makes B an offer by mail, or messenger, and B promptly sends an acceptance by his own employee. There is no contract until the acceptance is received by the offeror. As to receipt, see § 68.

f. Option contracts. An option contract provides a dependable basis for decision whether to exercise the option, and removes the primary reason for the rule of Subsection (1). Moreover, there is no objection to speculation at the expense of a party who has irrevocably assumed that risk. Option contracts are commonly subject to a definite time limit, and the usual understanding is that the notification that the option has been exercised must be received by the offeror before that time. Whether or not there is such a time limit, in the absence of a contrary provision in the option contract, the offeree takes the risk of loss or delay in the transmission of the acceptance and remains free to revoke the acceptance until it arrives. Similarly, if there is such a mistake on the part of the offeror as justifies the rescission of his unilateral obligation, the right to rescind is not lost merely because a letter of acceptance is posted. See §§ 151-54. **Illustrations:**

> 12. A, for consideration, gives B an option to buy property, written notice to be given on or before a specified date. Notice dispatched before but not received until after that date is not effective to exercise the option.

> 13. A submits a bid to supply goods to the Government, which becomes irrevocable when bids are opened. Within a reasonable time the Government mails a notice of award of the contract to A. Until A receives the notice, there is no contract binding on the Government.

§ 64. Acceptance by Telephone or Teletype

Acceptance given by telephone or other medium of substantially instantaneous two-way communication is governed by the principles applicable to acceptances where the parties are in the presence of each other.

Comment:

a. Rationale. Where the parties are in each other's presence, the offeree can accept without being in doubt as to whether the offeror has attempted to revoke his offer or whether the offeror has received the acceptance. His need of a dependable basis for decision whether to accept is therefore met without the rules stated in § 63. The situation prevents the question from arising whether a revocation of the offer or acceptance can be effective during the period required for communication of the acceptance, and all that remains is the risk of misunderstanding. Where the parties are not in each other's presence, but are able to communicate with each other without any substantial lapse of time, the situation is similar and the governing principles are the same.

b. Failure of communication. Where the parties are in each other's presence, ambiguities and misunderstandings, if perceived by either party, can be cleared up on the spot. The governing rules where a misunderstanding is not corrected are stated in § 20. The risk of failure of telephone, teletype or other similar communication is similar in that ordinarily one or both parties will know or have reason to know of the failure, and the same principles apply. If one party has reason to know of a failure of communication and hence that the other party's understanding may be different from his own, he runs the risk of being held to a manifestation of assent unless he takes immediate steps to clear up any misunderstanding. But if both parties are equally innocent or equally at fault, there is no contract. **Illustrations:**

. . .

2. A makes an offer to B by teletype. B transmits an acceptance, and A knows that a reply has been transmitted; but a mechanical fail-ure at A's end, unknown to B, prevents A from learning the contents of the reply. There is a con-tract.

. . .

§ 65. Reasonableness of Medium of Acceptance

Unless circumstances known to the offeree indicate otherwise, a medium of acceptance is reasonable if it is the one used by the offeror or one customary in similar transactions at the time and place the offer is received.

Comment:

a. Significance of use of reasonable medium. Under § 30 an offer invites acceptance by any reasonable medium unless there is contrary indication; under § 63 an acceptance so invited is ordinarily effective upon dispatch. If an unreasonable medium of acceptance is used, on the other hand, the governing rule is that stated in § 67. Thus if an offer is made by mail, an acceptance by mail is ordinarily effective on dispatch. Exception is made by this section if circumstances known to the offeree indicate otherwise, by § 63 if the offer otherwise provides, and by § 30 if the offer or circumstances forbid acceptance by mail regardless of reasonableness.

b. Circumstances relevant to reasonableness. This Section specifies certain circumstances which ordinarily indicate that a particular medium of acceptance is reasonable, but it does not exhaust the circumstances which may be relevant. Among the relevant circumstances not specified in this Section may be the speed and reliability of the medium, a prior course of dealing between the parties, and a usage of trade. See Chapter 9. The concept of reasonableness is flexible, and its applicability may be enlarged as newmedia develop or existing media become more speedy or reliable or come into more general use. See Comment 1 to Uniform Commercial Code § 2-206.

c. Mail. Acceptance by mail is ordinarily reasonable where the parties are negotiating at a distance, unless there is some special reason for speed such as rapid price fluctuation. Compare § 41. The same is true when the parties are located in the same city, if the offer is in writing, even though it is left with the offeree in person or delivered to his messenger. Even though an offer is transmitted by telephone or telegraph, acceptance by mail may well be reasonable.

Illustration:

1. By telegram A in Oklahoma orders two car-loads of potatoes from B in Wisconsin. B wires back an acceptance "if you will give us time to fill." Immediately on receiving B's reply A mails a confirming letter stating "we wish if possible you would ship at once" and giving shipping instructions. A has accepted B's counter-offer by a reasonable medium of acceptance.

d. Telegraph. Acceptance by telegram or mailgram is affected by the same considerations as acceptance by mail. In addition, there is a risk of mistake in transmission which may be provided for by agreement or may be reduced by a practice of confirmation by mail or by use of repeated messages. Notwithstanding that risk, telegraphic communication is now sufficiently reliable that telegraphic acceptance of an offer made by mail is ordinarily reasonable. But a contrary provision in the offer or a course of dealing or usage of trade requiring confirmation by mail is effective. See Comment *c* to § 221.

§ 66. Acceptance Must Be Properly Dispatched

An acceptance sent by mail or otherwise from a distance is not operative when dispatched, unless it is properly addressed and such other precautions taken as are ordinarily observed to insure safe transmission of similar messages.

Comment:

a. Rationale. Under § 50, acceptance by promise is not effective until the offeree has completed every act essential to the making of the promise. Reasonable diligence to notify is essential under § 56, except as stated in § 69. It follows that, notwithstanding § 63, acceptance by mail or telegram is not effective on dispatch unless the acceptor exercises reasonable diligence to notify the offeror. Compare the rules as to acceptance by performance stated in § 54. This Section specifies what constitutes reasonable diligence: it would be most unusual for an offer to invite acceptance by the sending, for example, of a misdirected letter or telegram.

. . .

§ 67. Effect of Receipt of Acceptance Improperly Dispatched

Where an acceptance is seasonably dispatched but the offeree uses means of transmission not invited by the offer or fails to exercise reasonable diligence to insure safe transmission, it is treated as operative upon dispatch if received within the time in which a properly dispatched acceptance would normally have arrived.

Comment:

a. Improper medium of transmission. Ordinarily an offer invites acceptance by any reasonable medium, and acceptance by such a medium is operative on dispatch. See §§ 30, 63, 65. An acceptance which is not operative on dispatch may be operative on its receipt by the offeror. The rule stated in this Section goes further: once the acceptance reaches the offeror, the means of transmission becomes immaterial. Compare Uniform Commercial Code § 1-201(38). Since the offeror's interest in receiving notification is satisfied, the offeree is not permitted to disavow his own act, and the usual rules are applied to bind both parties at the same instant. Just as if the acceptance had been properly dispatched, a revocation of the offer which crosses the acceptance in the mail, or an overtaking letter revoking the acceptance, is ineffective. Of course the offer may provide for a contrary rule. And the rule is limited to acceptance seasonably dispatched: the offeree is not empowered to use for speculation the time allowed for communication. See Comment *f* to § 41. **Illustration:**

    1. A makes an offer to B by telegram on Monday, requesting a reply by telegram to be sent no later than Thursday noon. B mails an acceptance on Monday which A receives on Thursday morning. Even if the mail is an unreasonable medium of acceptance under the circumstances, a revocation of the offer by A by telephone on Tuesday, or a revocation of the acceptance by B by telephone, is ineffective.

b. Misdirection and the like. The same rule applies to cases where the offeree uses the wrong address or fails to provide for postage or other cost of transmission. In such cases the offeree takes the risk of loss or delay in transmission. See §§ 63, 66. But it is not uncommon for communications to arrive promptly despite misdirection or the omission of ordinary precautions to insure safe transmission. In such cases the improper dispatch becomes immaterial.

§ 68. What Constitutes Receipt of Revocation, Rejection, or Acceptance

A written revocation, rejection, or acceptance is received when the writing comes into the possession of the person addressed, or of some person authorized by him to receive it for him, or when it is deposited in some place which he has authorized as the place for this or similar communications to be deposited for him.

. . .

Illustrations:

1. A sends B by mail an offer dated from A's house and states as a condition of the offer that an acceptance must be received within three days. B mails an acceptance which reaches A's house and is delivered to a servant or is deposited in a mail box at the door within three days; but A has been called away from home and does not personally receive the letter for a week. There is a contract.

. . .

§ 69. Acceptance by Silence or Exercise of Dominion

(1) Where an offeree fails to reply to an offer, his silence and inaction operate as an acceptance in the following cases only:

(a) Where an offeree takes the benefit of offered services with reasonable opportunity to reject them and reason to know that they were offered with the expectation of compensation.

(b) Where the offeror has stated or given the offeree reason to understand that assent may be manifested by silence or inaction, and the offeree in remaining silent and inactive intends to accept the offer.

(c) Where because of previous dealings or otherwise, it is reasonable that the offeree should notify the offeror if he does not intend to accept.

(2) An offeree who does any act inconsistent with the offeror's ownership of offered property is bound in accordance with the offered terms unless they are manifestly unreasonable. But if the act is wrongful as against the offeror it is an acceptance only if ratified by him.

Comment:

a. Acceptance by silence is exceptional. Ordinarily an offeror does not have power to cause the silence of the offeree to operate as acceptance. See Comment *b* to § 53. The usual requirement of notification is stated in § 54 on acceptance by performance and § 56 on acceptance by promise. The mere receipt of an unsolicited offer does not impair the offeree's freedom of action or inaction or impose on him any duty to speak. The exceptional cases where silence is acceptance fall into two main classes: those where the offeree silently takes offered benefits, and those where one party relies on the other party's manifestation of intention that silence may operate as acceptance. Even in those cases the contract may be unenforceable under the Statute of Frauds. See Chapter 5.

b. Acceptance of offered services. Services rendered cannot be recovered in specie, and there is in general no right to restitution of the value of services rendered officiously or gratuitously. Even where services are rendered by mistake, the right to restitution is limited. See Restatement of Restitution §§ 40-42, 56. But when the recipient knows or has reason to know that the services are being rendered with an expectation of compensation, and by a word could prevent the mistake, his privilege of inaction gives way; under Subsection (1) (a) he is held to an acceptance if he fails to speak. The resulting duty is not merely a duty to pay fair value, but a duty to pay or perform according to the terms of the offer.

. . .

c. Intent to accept. The mere fact that an offeror states that silence will constitute acceptance does not deprive the offeree of his privilege to remain silent without accepting. But the offeree is entitled to rely on such a statement if he chooses. The case for acceptance is strongest when the reliance is definite and substantial or when the intent to accept is objectively manifested though not communicated to the offeror. Compare §§ 54, 87(2). Even though the intent to accept is manifested only by silent inaction, however, the offeror who has invited such an acceptance cannot complain of the resulting uncertainty in his position. **Illustrations:**

> 2. A offers by mail to sell to B a horse already in B's possession for $ 250, saying: "I am so sure that you will accept that you need not trouble to write me. Your silence alone will operate as acceptance." B makes no reply, but he does not intend to accept. There is no contract.

> 3. The facts being otherwise as stated in Illustration 2, B replies by return mail, saying: "I accept your offer." There is a contract.

> . . .

d. Prior conduct of the offeree. Explicit statement by the offeree, usage of trade, or a course of dealing between the parties may give the offeror reason to understand that silence will constitute acceptance. In such a situation the offer may tacitly incorporate that understanding, and if the offeree intends to accept the case then falls within Subsection (1) (b). Under Subsection (1) (c) the offeree's silence is acceptance, regardless of his actual intent, unless both parties understand that no acceptance is intended. See § 20.

In a number of recurring situations, statutes have codified the application of theses rules. See Uniform Commercial Code § 2-207(2) on additional terms proposed in an acceptance or written confirmation of a contract between merchants for the sale of goods, §§ 2-327(1) on retention of goods sold on approval, § 4-302 on retention by a bank of commercial paper received for payment or acceptance. In many states by statute or decision an insurance company is under a duty to act without unreasonable delay on insurance applications solicited by its agents; circumstances may be such as to give the applicant reason to understand that he is insured if that duty is not performed, particularly where a premium payment has been made. Compare § 56. **Illustrations:**

> 5. A, through salesmen, has frequently solicited orders for goods from B, the orders to be subject to A's personal approval. In every case A has shipped the goods ordered within a week and without other notification to B than billing the goods to him on shipment. A's salesman solicits and receives another order from B. A receives the order and remains silent. B relies on the order and forbears to buy elsewhere for a week. A is bound to fill the order.

> . . .

e. Exercise of dominion. An offeree in possession of offered property commonly has a duty or privilege to hold it for the offeror, or, if storage, is inconvenient or hazardous, to return it, sell it for the offeror's account, or otherwise dispose of it. Compare Uniform Commercial Code §§§§ 2-602 through 2-604, 7-206. But the offeree's privilege to remain silent without accepting does not extend to acts of ownership not assented to by the offeror. Hence exercise of dominion, even though not intended as acceptance under Subsection (1) (b) and not given meaning by prior conduct under Subsection (1) (c), is a sufficient manifestation of assent under Subsection (2). Compare Uniform Commercial Code § 2-606.

Where the exercise of dominion does not comply with the terms of the offer, the offeror is not bound to treat it as an acceptance but may instead pursue his remedies for tortious interference with his property. But the offeree is not ordinarily permitted to avoid contract obligation by asserting that he is a tortfeasor rather than a promisor; atthe option of the offeror he may be held to an acceptance despite his manifestation of a contrary intention. Such an obligation may fairly be characterized as quasi-contractual rather than contractual, but its terms are fixed by the offer rather than by the fair value of the property. Compare Restatement of Restitution § 56.

An exception is made where the offered terms are manifestly unreasonable. In such cases the offeror has reason to know that no acceptance is intended, and the offered terms do not serve as an administratively convenient substitute for fair value. Particularly where the offeror seeks to take unconscionable advantage of a mistake made in good faith, no social purpose is served by an award plainly in excess of reasonable value even though the exercise of dominion is tortious. **Illustrations:**

> 7. A sends B a one-volume edition of Shakespeare with a letter, saying, "If you wish to buy this book send me $ 6.50 within one week after receipt hereof, otherwise notify me and I will forward postage for return." B examines the book and without replying makes a gift of it to his wife. B owes A $ 6.50. 8. The facts being otherwise as stated in Illustration 7, B examines the book and without replying carefully lays it on a shelf to await A's messenger. There is no contract.

> . . .

§ 70. Effect of Receipt by Offeror of a Late or Otherwise Defective Acceptance

A late or otherwise defective acceptance may be effective as an offer to the original offeror, but his silence operates as an acceptance in such a case only as stated in § 69.

Comment:

a. Counter-offers. A purported acceptance conditional on a change of terms commonly has the effect of a counter-offer. In such cases the original offeror has not ordinarily given the original offeree reason to understand that silence will operate as an acceptance of a counter-offer. Moreover, although an acceptance would not call for a reply, a purported acceptance is not ordinarily a sufficient manifestation of assent to silence as acceptance of the counter-offer. Nor can the original offeror "waive" his right to reject, or at his election regard the counter-offer as an acceptance. But the original offeror may have a duty to speak, for example, if the purported acceptance embodies a plausible but erroneous reading of the original offer. Compare § 20.

Illustration:

1. A offers by mail to sell B 100 acres of land "for $ 15 per acre cash and give you till July 18 to accept." On July 1 A receives from B a purported acceptance not accompanied by the cash. A waits until after July 18 and then notifies B that his acceptance was ineffective because the price was not paid by July 18. There is a contract. Any ambiguity in the quoted language is resolved against A in view of his failure to object to B's interpretation.

b. Late acceptance. Where an offer is subject to a definite time limit, the offeree commonly is in as good a position as the offeror to ascertain whether he has made a timely acceptance. A late acceptance may be an offer which can be accepted by the original offeror, but there is no more reason to treat silence as acceptance than in any other case. But if the original offer lapses only on the expiration of an indefinite reasonable time, the failure of the original offeror to object to an acceptance and his subsequent preparations for performance may be evidence that the acceptance was made within a reasonable time.

Illustration:

2. A invites B to make an offer to buy hay in A's barn. On Friday B inspects the hay and mails A an offer which is received the following day. The following Thursday A mails B an acceptance which is received the following day, and B then employs a third party to haul the hay. There is a contract.

Chapter 4

Formation of Contracts - Consideration

Topic 1. The Requirement of Consideration

§ 71. Requirement of Exchange; Types of Exchange

(1) To constitute consideration, a performance or a return promise must be bargained for.

(2) A performance or return promise is bargained for if it is sought by the promisor in exchange for his promise and is given by the promisee in exchange for that promise.

(3) The performance may consist of

(a) an act other than a promise, or

(b) a forbearance, or

(c) the creation, modification, or destruction of a legal relation.

(4) The performance or return promise may be given to the promisor or to some other person. It may be given by the promisee or by some other person.

Comment:

a. Other meanings of "consideration." The word "consideration" has often been used with meanings different from that given here. It is often used merely to express the legal conclusion that a promise is enforceable. Historically, its primary meaning may have been that the conditions were met under which an action of assumpsit would lie. It was also used as the equivalent of the *quid pro quo* required in an action of debt. A seal, it has been said, "imports a consideration," although the law was clear that no element of bargain was necessary to enforcement of a promise under seal. On the other hand, consideration has sometimes been used to refer to almost any reason asserted for enforcing a promise, even though the reason was insufficient. In this sense we find references to promises "in consideration of love and affection," to "illegal consideration," to "past consideration," and to consideration furnished by reliance on a gratuitous promise.

Consideration has also been used to refer to the element of exchange without regard to legal consequences. Consistent with that usage has been the use of the phrase "sufficient consideration" to express the legal conclusion that one requirement for an enforceable bargain is met. Here § 17 states the element of exchange required for a contract enforceable as a bargain as "a consideration." Thus "consideration" refers to an element of exchange which is sufficient to satisfy the legal requirement; the word "sufficient" would be redundant and is not used.

b. "Bargained for." In the typical bargain, the consideration and the promise bear a reciprocal relation of motive or inducement: the consideration induces the making of the promise and the promise induces the furnishing of the consideration. Here, as in the matter of mutual assent, the law is concerned with the external manifestation rather than the undisclosed mental state: it is enough that one party manifests an intention to induce the other's response and to be induced by it and that the other responds in accordance with the inducement. See § 81; compare §§ 19, 20. But it is not enough that the promise induces the conduct of the promisee or that the conduct of the promisee induces the making of the promise; both elements must be present, or there is no bargain. Moreover, a mere pretense of bargain does not suffice, as where there is a false recital of consideration or where the purported consideration is merely nominal. In such cases there is no consideration and the promise is enforced, if at all, as a promise binding without consideration under §§ 82-94. See Comments *b* and *c* to § 87. **Illustrations:**

1. A offers to buy a book owned by B and to pay B $ 10 in exchange therefor. B accepts the offer and delivers the book to A. The transfer and delivery of the book constitute a performance and are consideration for A's promise. See Uniform Commercial Code § 2-106, 2-301. This is so even though A at the time he makes the offer secretly intends to pay B $ 10 whether or not he gets the book, or even though B at the time he accepts secretly intends not to collect the $ 10.

2. A receives a gift from B of a book worth $ 10. Subsequently A promises to pay B the value of the book. There is no consideration for A's promise. This is so even though B at the time he makes the gift secretly hopes that A will pay him for it. As to the enforcement of such promises, see § 86.

3. A promises to make a gift of $ 10 to B. In reliance on the promise B buys a book from C and promises to pay C $ 10 for it. There is no consideration for A's promise. As to the enforcement of such promises, see § 90.

4. A desires to make a binding promise to give $ 1000 to his son B. Being advised that a gratuitous promise is not binding, A writes out and signs a false recital that B has sold him a car for $ 1000 and a promise to pay that amount. There is no consideration for A's promise.

5. A desires to make a binding promise to give $ 1000 to his son B. Being advised that a gratuitous promise is not binding, A offers to buy from B for $ 1000 a book worth less than $ 1. B accepts the offer knowing that the purchase of the book is a mere pretense. There is no consideration for A's promise to pay $ 1000.

c. Mixture of bargain and gift. In most commercial bargains there is a rough equivalence between the value promised and the value received as consideration. But the social functions of bargains include the provision of opportunity for free individual action and exercise of judgment and the fixing of values by private action, either generally or for purposes of the particular transaction. Those functions would be impaired by judicial review of the values so fixed. Ordinarily, therefore, courts do not inquire into the adequacy of consideration, particularly where one or both of the values exchanged are difficult to measure. See § 79. Even where both parties know that a transaction is in part a bargain and in part a gift, the element of bargain may nevertheless furnish consideration for the entire transaction.

On the other hand, a gift is not ordinarily treated as a bargain, and a promise to make a gift is not made a bargain by the promise of the prospective donee to accept the gift, or by his acceptance of part of it. This may be true even though the terms of gift impose a burden on the donee as well as the donor. See Illustration 2 to § 24. In such cases the distinction between bargain and gift may be a fine one, depending on the motives manifested by the parties. In some cases there may be no bargain so long as the agreement is entirely executory, but performance may furnish consideration or the agreement may become fully or partly enforceable by virtue of the reliance of one party or the unjust enrichment of the other. Compare § 90. **Illustrations:**

6. A offers to buy a book owned by B and to pay B $ 10 in exchange therefor. B's transfer and delivery of the book are consideration for A's promise even though both parties know that such books regularly sell for $ 5 and that part of A's motive in making the offer is to make a gift to B. See §§ 79, 81.

7. A owns land worth $ 10,000 which is subject to a mortgage to secure a debt of $ 5,000. A promises to make a gift of the land to his son B and to pay off the mortgage, and later gives B a deed subject to the mortgage. B's acceptance of the deed is not consideration for A's promise to pay the mortgage debt.

8. A and B agree that A will advance $ 1000 to B as a gratuitous loan. B's promise to accept the loan is not consideration for A's promise to make it. But the loan when made is consideration for B's promise to repay.

d. Types of consideration. Consideration may consist of a performance or of a return promise. Consideration by way of performance may be a specified act of forbearance, or any one of several specified acts or forbearances of which the offeree is given the choice, or such conduct as will produce a specified result. Or either the offeror or the offeree may request as consideration the creation, modification or destruction of a purely intangible legal relation. Not infrequently the consideration bargained for is an act with the added requirement that a certain legal result shall be produced. Consideration by way of return promise requires a promise as defined in § 2. Consideration may consist partly of promise and partly of other acts or forbearances, and the consideration invited may be a performance or a return promise in the alternative. Though a promise is itself an act, it is treated separately from other acts. See § 75. **Illustrations:**

9. A promises B, his nephew aged 16, that A will pay B $ 1000 when B becomes 21 if B does not smoke before then. B's forbearance to smoke is a performance and if bargained for is consideration for A's promise.

10. A says to B, the owner of a garage, "I will pay you $ 100 if you will make my car run properly." The production of this result is consideration for A's promise.

11. A has B's horse in his possession. B

writes to A, "If you will promise me $ 100 for the horse, he is yours." A promptly replies making the requested promise. The property in the horse at once passes to A. The change in ownership is consideration for A's promise.

12. A promises to pay B $ 1,000 if B will make an offer to C to sell C certain land for $ 25,000 and will leave the offer open for 24 hours. B makes the requested offer and forbears to revoke it for 24 hours, but C does not accept. The creation of a power of acceptance in C is consideration for A's promise.

13. A mails a written order to B, offering to buy specified machinery on specified terms. The order provides "Ship at once." B's prompt shipment or promise to ship is consideration for A's promise to pay the price. See § 32; Uniform Commercial Code § 2-206(1) (b).

e. Consideration moving from or to a third person. It matters not from whom the consideration moves or to whom it goes. If it is bargained for and given in exchange for the promise, the promise is not gratuitous.
Illustrations:

14. A promises B to guarantee payment of a bill of goods if B sells the goods to C. Selling the goods to C is consideration for A's promise.

15. A makes a promissory note payable to B in return for a payment by B to C. The payment is consideration for the note.

16. A, at C's request and in exchange for $ 1 paid by C, promises B to give him a book. The payment is consideration for A's promise.

17. A promises B to pay B $ 1, in exchange for C's promise to A to give A a book. The promises are consideration for one another.

18. A promises to pay $ 1,000 to B, a bank, in exchange for the delivery of a car by C to A's son D. The delivery of the car is consideration for A's promise.

§ 72. Exchange of Promise for Performance

Except as stated in §§ 73 and 74, any performance which is bargained for is consideration.

Comment:

a. Enforcement of bargains. Section 17(1) embodies the principle that bargains are enforceable unless some other principle conflicts. Chapter 3 on Formation of Contracts-Mutual Assent deals with one essential element of a bargain, agreement; this Topic on the Requirement of Consideration deals with the other essential element, exchange. See § 3. The requirement laid down in § 17(1) is that there be a "consideration." Under § 71 "consideration" requires an element of exchange. This Section states the general rule that exchange of performance for promise is an enforceable bargain; Sections 73 and 74 deny enforcement to certain bargains despite the presence of an element of exchange. Sections 75-78 state corresponding rules for the exchange of promise for promise.

b. Substantive bases for enforcement; the half-completed exchange. Bargains are widely believed to be beneficial to the community in the provision of opportunities for freedom of individual action and exercise of judgment and as a means by which productive energy and product are apportioned in the economy. The enforcement of bargains rests in part on the common belief that enforcement enhances that utility. Where one party has performed, there are additional grounds for enforcement. Where, for example, one party has received goods from the other and has broken his promise to pay for them, enforcement of the promise not only encourages the making of socially useful bargains; it also reimburses the seller for a loss incurred in reliance on the promise and prevents the unjust enrichment of the buyer at the seller's expense. Each of these three grounds of enforcement, bargain, reliance and unjust enrichment, has independent force, but the bargain element alone satisfies the requirement of consideration except in the cases covered by §§ 73, 74, 76 and 77. Cases of promises binding by virtue of reliance or unjust enrichment are dealt with in §§ 82-94.

c. Formality. Consideration furnishes a substantive rather than a formal basis for the enforcement of a promise. Many bargains, particularly when fully performed on one side, involve acts in the course of performance which satisfy some or all of the functions of form and thus may be thought of as natural formalities. Four principal functions have been identified which legal formalities in general may serve: the *evidentiary* function, to provide evidence of the existence and terms of the contract; the *cautionary* function, to guard the promisor against ill-considered action; the *deterrent* function, to discourage transactions of doubtful utility; and the *channeling* or signalizing function, to distinguish a particular type of transaction from other types and from tentative or exploratory expressions of intention in the way that coinage distinguishes money from other metal. But formality is not essential to consideration; nor does formality supply consideration where the element of exchange is absent. Rules under which formality makes binding a promise not supported by consideration are stated in §§ 82-94 and in §§ 95-109 on contracts under seal.

d. Unconscionable and illegal bargains. The rule stated in this Section does not require that consideration have an economic value equivalent to that of the promise. See § 79. Nor does the Section require that the consideration or the promise be lawful. The problems raised by unconscionable and illegal bargains are dealt with in § 208 on unconscionability, Chapter 6 on mistake, Chapter 7 on misrepresentation, duress and undue influence, and Chapter 8 on unenforceability on grounds of public policy. In addition, particular types of bargains which are likely to be unconscionable are the subject of §§ 73 and 74.

§ 73. Performance of Legal Duty

Performance of a legal duty owed to a promisor which is neither doubtful nor the subject of honest dispute is not consideration; but a similar performance is consideration if it differs from what was required by the duty in a way which reflects more than a pretense of bargain.

Comment:

a. Rationale. A claim that the performance of a legal duty furnished consideration for a promise often raises a suspicion that the transaction was gratuitous or mistaken or unconscionable. If the performance was not in fact bargained for and given in exchange for the promise, the case is not within this Section: in such cases there is no consideration under the rule stated in § 71(1). Mistake, misrepresentation, duress, undue influence, or public policy may invalidate the transaction even though there is consideration. See Chapters 6-8. But the rule of this Section renders unnecessary any inquiry into the existence of such an invalidating cause, and denies enforcement to some promises which would otherwise be valid. Because of the likelihood that the promise was obtained by an express or implied threat to withhold performance of a legal duty, the promise does not have the presumptive social utility normally found in a bargain. Enforcement must therefore rest on some substantive or formal basis other than the mere fact of bargain. See Comments *b* and *c* to § 72. As to such bases, see Topics 2 and 3, and particularly § 89.

b. Public duties; torts and crimes. A legal duty may be owed to the promisor as a member of the public, as when the promisee is a public official. In such cases there is often no direct

sanction available to a member of the public to compel performance of the duty, and the danger of express or implied threats to withhold performance affects public as well as private interests. A bargain by a public official to obtain private advantage for performing his duty is therefore unenforceable as against public policy. See Chapter 8. And under this Section performance of the duty is not consideration for a promise.

Similar reasoning may apply to duties of public utilities, duties of fiduciaries, and in some cases to duties of citizens generally. Thus a bargain to pay a witness for testimony may be unenforceable as against public policy. See §§ 178-80. A bargain induced by an improper threat may be voidable for duress. See §§ 175-76. If the only thing bargained for is forbearance to commit a crime or tort, the bargain may be unenforceable as against public policy. See § 178. The performance of legal duty is not consideration for a promise in any such case if the duty is owed to the promisor. If the legal duty is not owed to the promisor, there is consideration but the violation of public policy or other invalidating cause may remain.

In applying this Section it is first necessary to define the legal duty. The requirement of consideration is satisfied if the duty is doubtful or is the subject of honest dispute, or if the consideration includes a performance in addition to or materially different from the performance of the duty. Whether such facts eliminate duress or violation of public policy or other invalidating cause depends on the circumstances. Ordinarily a mere formality such as the affixing of a seal, though sufficient to render consideration unnecessary, does not cure such defects. In some situations, however, where there is no other invalidating cause but lack of consideration, the bargain may be enforceable by virtue of reliance or unjust enrichment or formality. See §§ 82-109. **Illustrations:**

> 1. A offers a reward to whoever produces evidence leading to the arrest and conviction of the murderer of B. C produces such evidence in the performance of his duty as a police officer. C's performance is not consideration for A's promise.
>
> 2. In Illustration 1, C's duties as a police officer are limited to crimes committed in a particular State, and while on vacation he gathers evidence as to a crime committed elsewhere. C's performance is consideration for the promise.
>
> 3. In a State where contracts between husband and wife are enforced and spouses are under a duty not to leave without just cause, A's wife, B, leaves him without just cause. A promises to pay B $ 1,000 if she will return. Induced thereby, B returns. Her return is not consideration. Compare §§ 175-77, 190.

c. Contractual duty to the promisor. Legal remedies for breach of contract ordinarily involve delay and expense and rarely put the promisee in fully as good a position as voluntary performance. It is therefore often to a promisee's advantage to offer a bonus to a recalcitrant promisor to induce performance without legal proceedings, and an unscrupulous promisor may threaten breach in order to obtain such a bonus. In extreme cases, a bargain for additional compensation under such circumstances may be voidable for duress. See §§ 175-76. And the lack of social utility in such bargains provides what modern justification there is for the rule that performance of a contractual duty is not consideration for a new promise.

But the rule has not been limited to cases where there was a possibility of unfair pressure, and it has been much criticized as resting on scholastic logic. Slight variations of circumstance are commonly held to take a case out of the rule,

particularly where the parties have made an equitable adjustment in the course of performance of a continuing contract, or where an impecunious debtor has paid part of his debt in satisfaction of the whole. See §§ 89, 273-77. And in some states the rule has simply been repudiated. **Illustrations:**

> 4. A, an architect, agrees with B to superintend a construction project for a fixed fee. During the course of the project, without excuse, A takes away his plans and refuses to continue, and B promises him an extra fee if A will resume work. A's resumption of work is not consideration for B's promise of an extra fee.
>
> 5. A files a claim for total disability under an accident insurance policy written by B. Without investigation, discussion or dispute, B pays A the lesser amount which would be payable for partial disability, and A signs a receipt for "full payment" of the claim. The payment is not consideration for A's promise to accept it in full satisfaction of his claim for total disability.
>
> 6. A, being insolvent and contemplating bankruptcy, offers B $ 30 in full settlement of a debt of $ 100. B dissuades A from going into bankruptcy, accepts the offer, receives the money, and closes the account. A's forbearance to seek a discharge in bankruptcy is consideration for B's promise not to seek further payment.
>
> . . .

d. Contractual duty to third person. The rule that performance of legal duty is not consideration for a promise has often been applied in cases involving a contractual duty owed to a person other than the promisor. In such cases, however, there is less likelihood of economic coercion or other unfair pressure than there is if the duty is owed to the promisee. In some cases consideration can be found in the fact that the promisee gives up his right to propose to the third person the rescission or modification of the contractual duty. But the tendency of the law has been simply to hold that performance of contractual duty can be consideration if the duty is not owed to the promisor. Relief may still be given to the promisor in appropriate cases under the rules governing duress and other invalidating causes. **Illustrations:**

> 9. A and B are engaged to be married. In an antenuptial agreement C, A's father, promises B that C will pay an annuity to A, and A and B marry in reliance on the promise. The marriage is consideration for C's promise.

10. A and her husband B are employed as domestic servants of C. B having become ill, C employs A to care for B in the home of A and B. A's care for B is consideration for C's promise to pay wages to A.

11. A contracts with B to install heating units in houses being built by B for C. B becomes insolvent and discontinues work, and C promises to pay A if A completes the installation in accordance with the contract between A and B. A's performance is consideration for C's promise.

. . .

e. Voidable and unenforceable duties. The duty referred to in the Section is confined to a duty for which any remedy ordinarily allowed by the law for that kind of duty is still available. One who may at will avoid a legal relation or refrain from any performance without legal consequences, or against whom all remedies appropriate to the enforcement of his duty have become barred, is not under a duty within the meaning of the Section. **Illustrations:**

13. A, an infant, promises B to pay B $ 50 for a set of books which A does not need. B delivers the books. A becomes of age and threatens to rescind the bargain, as the law permits him to do. B promises A that if A will pay the $ 50 as originally agreed, B will give A another book. A, induced thereby, pays the $ 50. The payment is consideration.

14. A sells goods to B, who becomes indebted therefor in the sum of $ 100. The Statute of Limitations bars any remedy of A to recover the debt. A promises B that if B will pay the debt, A will give B a specified book. B pays the debt. The payment is consideration.

. . .

§ 74. Settlement of Claims

(1) Forbearance to assert or the surrender of a claim or defense which proves to be invalid is not consideration unless

(a) the claim or defense is in fact doubtful because of uncertainty as to the facts or the law, or

(b) the forbearing or surrendering party believes that the claim or defense may be fairly determined to be valid.

(2) The execution of a written instrument surrendering a claim or defense by one who is under no duty to execute it is consideration if the execution of the written instrument is bargained for even though he is not asserting the claim or defense and believes that no valid claim or defense exists.

Comment:

a. Relation to legal-duty rule. Subsection (1) elaborates a limitation on the scope of the legal-duty rule stated in § 73. That limitation is based on the traditional policy of favoring compromises of disputed claims in order to reduce the volume of litigation. Surrender of an invalid defense commonly means that a legal duty is performed, but in cases of invalid claims Subsection (1) may go beyond the legal-duty rule, since in many situations any legal duty not to litigate unfounded claims is likely to be unenforceable. In any event, the subject of compromise agreements is of sufficient importance to deserve separate treatment. Subsection (2) is clearly beyond the scope of the legal-duty rule, and merely states for greater clarity an application of § 72.

b. Requirement of good faith. The policy favoring compromise of disputed claims is clearest, perhaps, where a claim is surrendered at a time when it is uncertain whether it is valid or not. Even though the invalidity later becomes clear, the bargain is to be judged as it appeared to the parties at the time; if the claim was then doubtful, no inquiry is necessary as to their good faith. Even though the invalidity should have been clear at the time, the settlement of an honest dispute is upheld. But a mere assertion or denial of liability does not make a claim doubtful, and the fact that invalidity is obvious may indicate that it was known. In such cases Subsection (1) (b) requires a showing of good faith. **Illustrations:**

1. A, a shipowner, has a legal duty to provide maintenance and cure for B, a seaman. B honestly but unreasonably claims that adequate care is not available in a free public hospital and that he is entitled to treatment by a private physician. B's forbearance to press this claim is consideration for A's promise to be responsible for

the consequences of any improper treatment in the public hospital.

    2. A, knowing that he has no legal basis for complaint, frequently complains to B, his father, that B has made more gifts to B's other children than to A. B promises that if A will cease complaining, B will forgive a debt owed by A to B. A's forbearance to assert his claim of discrimination is not consideration for B's promise.

    3. A, knowing that B is a married man, cohabits with him for several years. During that time B promises to marry A as soon as he is divorced. After the cohabitation ceases, A surrenders all her claims on account of the promise to marry in consideration of B's promise to pay her $ 1000 a month during her life. Under applicable state law A has no valid claim. If it is found that A knew there was no valid claim, there is no consideration for B's promise of payment. Compare § 189-90.

c. Unliquidated obligations. An undisputed obligation may be unliquidated, that is uncertain or disputed in amount. The settlement of such a claim is governed by the same principles as settlement of a claim the existence of which is doubtful or disputed. The payment of any definite sum of money on account of a single claim which is entirely unliquidated is consideration for a return promise. An admission by the obligor that a minimum amount is due does not liquidate the claim even partially unless he is contractually bound to the admission. But payment of less than is admittedly due may in some circumstances tend to show that a partial defense or offset was not asserted in good faith.

    Payment of an obligation which is liquidated and undisputed is not consideration for a promise to surrender an unliquidated claim which is wholly distinct. See § 73. Whether in a particular case there is a single unliquidated claim or a combination of separate claims, some liquidated and some not, depends on the circumstances and the agreements of the parties. If there are no circumstances of unfair pressure or economic coercion and a disputed item is closely related to an undisputed item, the two are treated as making up a single unliquidated claim; and payment of the amount admittedly due can be consideration for a promise to surrender the entire claim. **Illustrations:**

    4. A, a real estate broker, is entitled to a commission for selling B's land, amounting to five per cent or $ 1,500. B claims in good faith that he owes only one per cent or $ 300, and offers to pay that amount in full settlement of the claim for commission. A accepts the offer. The payment is consideration for B's promise to surrender his entire claim.

    5. A owes B at least $ 4,280 on a logging contract. Additional items in the account are unliquidated, and some of them are the subject of honest dispute. A disputes B's right to all above $ 4,280 on grounds he knows to be untrue, and offers $ 4,000 in full settlement. A's payment of $ 4,000 is not consideration for B's promise to surrender his entire claim.   ...

    d. Forbearance without surrender. Forbearance to assert a valid claim or a doubtful or honestly-asserted claim may be consideration for a promise, just as surrender of the claim would be. Where the forbearance is temporary and it is contemplated that the claim will be asserted later, there is sometimes a question whether the forbearance is bargained for and given in exchange for the promise. If an offer specifies a return promise to forbear as the requested consideration, forbearance without promise is not an acceptance. Compare § 53. But a promise to forbear may be implied. Compare §§ 32, 62. Whether a promise is consideration depends on the rules stated in §§ 75-78. Forbearance which is not bargained for may in some cases be reliance sufficient to bring § 90 into play. **Illustrations:**

    8. A owes B $ 120. Without requesting B to forbear suit, C promises B in April that if A does not pay by October 1 C will pay $ 100. B's forbearance to sue until October is not consideration for C's promise.   9. A owes B a debt secured by mortgage, and B begins foreclosure proceedings. C requests B to forbear and promises to pay the debt. B's forbearance for a reasonable time is consideration for C's promise.

. . .

§ 75. Exchange of Promise for Promise

    Except as stated in §§ 76 and 77, a promise which is bargained for is consideration if, but only if, the promised performance would be consideration.

Comment:

a. The executory exchange. In modern times the enforcement of bargains is not limited to those partly completed, but is extended to the wholly executory exchange in which promise is exchanged for promise. In such a case the element of unjust enrichment is not present; the element of reliance, if present at all, is less tangible and direct than in the case of the half-completed exchange. The promise is enforced by virtue of the fact of bargain, without more. Since the principle that bargains are binding is widely understood and is reinforced in many situations by custom and convention, the fact of bargain also tends to satisfy the cautionary and channeling functions of form. Compare Comments *b* and *c* to § 72. Evidentiary safeguards, however, are largely left to the Statute of Frauds rather than to the requirement of consideration. See Chapter 5.

b. Promise and performance. The principle of this Section is that, in determining whether there is consideration, one's word is as good as one's deed but no better. More detailed rules are stated in §§ 76-78 for cases in which the application of this principle has produced problems. Certain cases which have sometimes been thought to be exceptions to the principle are commented upon below.

c. Performance of legal duty and settlement of claims. A promise to perform a legal duty is not consideration for a return promise unless performance would be. Similarly, a promise to surrender a claim or defense or to forbear from asserting it is consideration only if performance would be. Thus a promise of such performance may raise the same questions as the performance would: Is the duty owed to the maker of the return promise? Is the claim or defense known to be invalid? See §§ 73, 74. **Illustrations:**

1. A promises to pay a debt to B, or to perform an existing contractual duty to B, or to perform his duty as a public official. The legal duty is neither doubtful nor the subject of honest dispute, but A would not have fulfilled the duty but for B's return promise. A's promise is not consideration for B's return promise. Compare § 73.

2. A promises B to surrender or to forbear suit upon a claim either against B or against C. A knows the claim is invalid. A's promise is not consideration for a return promise by B. Compare § 74.

d. "Void" promises. The value of a promise does not necessarily depend upon the availability of a legal remedy for breach, and bargains are often made in consideration of promises which are voidable or unenforceable. Such a promise may be consideration for a return promise. See § 78. But it is sometimes suggested that a promise is not consideration if it is not binding, or if it is "void." The examples used commonly involve total lack of capacity to contract (see §§ 12, 13), indefinite promises (see §§ 33-34), promises lacking consideration, or promises unenforceable as against public policy (see Chapter 8). Such cases are not exceptions to the rule stated in this Section. In some of them there is no promise within the definition in § 2, in others the return promise would not be binding whether the consideration consisted of a promise or of performance, in some the invalidity of the return promise rests on other policies than those embodied in the requirement of consideration.

Illustrations:

3. While A's property is under guardianship by reason of an adjudication of mental illness, A makes an agreement with B in which B makes a promise. B's promise is not a contract, whether the consideration consists of a promise by A or performance by A. Compare § 13; Restatement of Restitution § 139.

4. A promises to forbear suit against B in exchange for B's promise to pay a liquidated and undisputed debt to A. A's promise is not binding because B's promise is not consideration under § 73, but A's promise is nevertheless consideration for B's. Moreover, B's promise would be enforceable without consideration under § 82. On either basis, B's promise is conditional on A's forbearance and can be enforced only if the condition is met.

5. A, a married man, and B, an unmarried woman, make mutual promises to marry. B neither knows nor has reason to know that A is married. B's promise is consideration and B may recover damages from A for breach of his promise though B would have a defense to a similar action by A. See § 180.

6. A promises B $ 100 in return for B's promise to cut timber on land upon which A is a trespasser. B neither knows nor has reason to know that A is not privileged to cut the timber. B's promise is consideration and B may recover damages from A for breach of his promise though B would have a defense to a similar action by A. See Illustration 2 to § 180.

§ 76. Conditional Promise

(1) A conditional promise is not consideration if the promisor knows at the time of making the promise that the condition cannot occur.

(2) A promise conditional on a performance by the promisor is a promise of alternative performances within § 77 unless occurrence of the condition is also promised.

Comment:

a. *"Conditional promise."* Conditions and similar events are the subject of Topic 5 of Chapter 9. A promise is "conditional" for the purposes of this Section if an event must occur before a duty of immediateperformance of the promise arises, and the "condition" is the event which must occur. See § 224. A condition may be provided for by a term of a promise, either in words or by virtue of other conduct or the circumstances, or it may be supplied by law. See § 5.

b. *Impossible conditions.* Words of conditional promise do not constitute a promise within the definition in § 2 if both promisor and promisee know that the condition cannot occur. If the promisor has such knowledge but the promisee does not, there may be a promise, but the promisee receives only the false appearance of a commitment by the promisor; in such cases the promise is not consideration for a return promise. But if the promisor honestly believes he is making a commitment, the promise may be consideration even though the facts are such that no duty of immediate performance can ever arise. Thus in dealing with promises conditional on past events the law takes the standpoint of the promisor and treats as uncertain that which is uncertain to him. For this purpose, an event is uncertain to a promisor who does not know even though he has reason to know. **Illustrations:**

1. A promises B to pay him $ 5,000 if B's ship now at sea has already been lost, knowing that the ship has not been lost. A's promise is illusory and is not consideration for a return promise.

2. The facts being otherwise as stated in Illustration 1, A makes the promise not knowing whether the ship has been lost or not. A's promise is consideration even though A has reason to know that the ship has not been lost.

3. A sells to B a tract of land said to contain 500 acres. Later A and B agree to have the land surveyed; A promises to pay B $ 16 for each acre of deficiency; B promises to pay A $ 16 for each acre of excess. A's promise is consideration for B's promise, and B's promise is consideration for A's.

c. *Aleatory promises.* A party may make an aleatory promise, under which his duty to perform is conditional on the occurrence of a fortuitous event. See §§ 225, 226, 239. Such a promise may be consideration for a return promise. **Illustrations:**

4. A promises to sell and B to buy goods if A's employees do not strike before the time for delivery. The promises are consideration for each other.

5. A promises to convey to B immediately a patent owned by A; B promises to pay A $ 10,000 when pending litigation is terminated, if the patent is not held invalid. B's promise is consideration for A's promise.

6. A promises B to pay him $ 5000 if his house burns within a year. This is consideration for a return promise.

d. *Conditions within the promisor's control.* Words of promise do not constitute a promise if they make performance entirely optional with the purported promisor. See Comment *e* to § 2. Such words, often referred to as forming an illusory promise, do not constitute consideration for a return promise. See § 77. But a promise may be conditional on an event within the control of the promisor. Such a promise may be consideration if he has also promised that the condition will occur. Similarly, even though he does not promise occurrence of the condition, there may be consideration if forbearance from causing the condition to occur would itself have been consideration if it alone had been bargained for. In such a case, there is in effect a promise in the alternative, and the rules stated in § 77 apply. **Illustrations:**

7. A promises B to pay him $ 5000 if A enters a competing business within three years. This is consideration for a return promise, since forbearance to compete would be consideration. See § 77.

8. A promises B that, "subject to purchase" of a certain ship, he will charter it to B, and B promises to accept the charter. A's promise is consideration for B's. A's forbearance to buy the ship could have been consideration for a different promise, such as a promise to pay money. See § 77.

§ 77. Illusory and Alternative Promises

A promise or apparent promise is not consideration if by its terms the promisor or purported promisor reserves a choice of alternative performances unless

(a) each of the alternative performances would have been consideration if it alone had been bargained for; or

(b) one of the alternative performances would have been consideration and there is or appears to the parties to be a substantial possibility that before the promisor exercises his choice events may eliminate the alternatives which would not have been consideration.

Comment:

a. Illusory promises. Words of promise which by their terms make performance entirely optional with the "promisor" do not constitute a promise. See Comment *e* to § 2; compare § 76. In such cases there might theoretically be a bargain to pay for the utterance of the words, but in practice it is performance which is bargained for. Where the apparent assurance of performance is illusory, it is not consideration for a return promise. A different rule applies, however, where performance is optional, not by the terms of the agreement, but by virtue of a rule of law. See § 5 (defining "term"), § 78. **Illustrations:**

> 1. A offers to deliver to B at $ 2 a bushel as many bushels of wheat, not exceeding 5,000, as B may choose to order within the next 30 days. B accepts, agreeing to buy at that price as much as he shall order from A within that time. B's acceptance involves no promise by him, and is not consideration. Compare §§ 31, 34.

> 2. A promises B to act as B's agent for three years from a future date on certain terms; B agrees that A may so act, but reserves the power to terminate the agreement at any time. B's agreement is not consideration, since it involves no promise by him.

b. Alternative promises. A promise in the alternative may be made because each of the alternative performances is the object of desire to the promisee. Or the promisee may desire one performance only, but the promisor may reserve an alternative which he may deem advantageous. In either type of case the promise is consideration if it cannot be kept without some action or forbearance which would be consideration if it alone were bargained for. But if the promisor has an unfettered choice of alternatives, and one alternative would not have been consideration if separately bargained for, the promise in the alternative is not consideration. **Illustrations:**

> 3. A offers to deliver to B at $ 2 a bushel as many bushels of wheat, not exceeding 5,000, as B may choose to order within the next 30 days, if B will promise to order at least 1,000 bushels

within that time. B accepts. B's promise is consideration since it reserves only a limited option and cannot be performed without doing something which would be consideration if it alone were bargained for.

> 4. A agrees to sell and B to buy between 400 and 600 tons of fertilizer in installments as ordered by B, A reserving the right to terminate the agreement at any time without notice. B's promise is without consideration.

> 5. A promises B to act as B's agent for three years on certain terms, starting immediately; B agrees that A may so act, but reserves the power to terminate the agreement on 30 days notice. B's agreement is consideration, since he promises to continue the agency for at least 30 days.

> 6. A owes B an undisputed debt of $ 5,000 payable in five years. A makes a subsequent promise that he will either pay $ 4,000 at the end of the first year or pay the debt at maturity; in return B promises to accept the $ 4,000, if paid at the end of the first year, in full satisfaction of the debt. A's subsequent promise is not consideration for B's return promise, since the alternative of performing his legal duty is not consideration. See §§ 73, 75.

c. Alternatives not dependent on promisor's free choice. A promise may give the promisee a right to choose one of several stated performances. Or the selection among alternative performances may be left to events not within the control of either party. In such cases the promise, if bargained for, is consideration if any one of the alternatives would have been, unless the promisor knows that all such alternatives are subject to conditions which cannot exist or occur. See § 76(1). Similarly, the promise may be consideration even though a conditional power of choice is left to the promisor. For example, the promisor may reserve an option to terminate only after he has rendered performance which would be consideration, or only in a contingency which may never occur, or only on a condition of forbearance by him which would have been consideration. Compare Comment *d* to § 76.

Illustration:

7. A orders goods from B for shipment within three months, reserving the right to cancel the order before shipment. B has the goods in stock and accepts the order. A's promise to pay for the goods is consideration for B's promise to ship, since B can prevent cancellation by shipping immediately.

d. Implied limitations on promisor's choice. A limitation on the promisor's freedom of choice need not be stated in words. It may be an implicit term of the promise, or it may be supplied by law. Thus a power to terminate a contract for the sale of goods may be subject to a statutory requirement of reasonable notification, and an agreement dispensing with notification may be unconscionable and invalid. See Uniform Commercial Code § 2-309(3). Again, an alternative promise may cease to be alternative when performance of one alternative becomes impossible or unenforceable on grounds of public policy. See §§ 270, 184. If such a contingency is within the contemplation of the parties so that it is part of what is bargained for, the promise is consideration. **Illustrations:**

8. A promises to sell his output or buy his requirements of a specified type of goods from B on specified terms. A's promise is consideration for a return promise by B. A must operate his plant or conduct his business in good faith and according to commercial standards of fair dealing in the trade so that his output or requirements will approximate a reasonably foreseeable figure. See Comment 2 to Uniform Commercial Code § 2-306.

9. A promises to pay B half of any profits he derives from the sale of goods manufactured by B; in return B promises that A shall have the exclusive right to market such goods. The promises are consideration for each other, since the agreement for exclusive dealing imposes an obligation on A to use best efforts to promote sale of the goods and on B to use best efforts to supply them. See Uniform Commercial Code § 2-306(2).

10. A owes B a matured liquidated debt bearing interest. In an agreement to extend the debt for a year at a lower rate of interest, B reserves the right to accelerate payment "at will," but under Uniform Commercial Code § 1-208, B may accelerate payment only if he in good faith believes that the prospect of payment is impaired. B's surrender of the unconditional right to demand immediate payment is consideration. Compare Illustration 8 to § 73.

11. A is under a contractual duty to deliver to B a described automobile. Because it is doubtful whether such a car will be available at the agreed time, A promises that if he cannot obtain it he will deliver a described substitute; B agrees to accept the substitute if delivered. A's promise is consideration.

§ 78. Voidable and Unenforceable Promises

The fact that a rule of law renders a promise voidable or unenforceable does not prevent it from being consideration.

Comment:

a. Rationale. The value of a promise depends on its terms and on the probability that it will be performed. The value is not necessarily affected adversely by the fact that no legal remedy will be available in the event of breach; the probability of performance may be greater for a voidable or unenforceable promise, or even for a promise which is not binding or is against public policy, than for the judgment or decree of a court. In general the law of contracts leaves to the parties the valuation of a promise in the formation of a bargain. See § 79. The fact that no legal remedy is available for breach of a promise does not prevent it from being a part of a bargain or remove the bargain from the scope of the general principle that bargains are enforceable. See §§ 17, 71. As to "void" promises, see Comment *d* to § 75.

b. Voidable promises. A contract may be voidable by one party by reason of his incapacity or mistake, or by reason of the fraud, breach or other fault of the other party. See § 7. In many such cases a reservation of a similar power by the terms of the agreement would mean that he had made no promise or that his promise was not consideration for a return promise. See § 77. But where the power of avoidance is given by the law to protect one party from actual or possible imposition, he often regards himself as bound in conscience if not in law. He may in some circumstance lose the power by ratification without consideration. See § 85. Until the power is exercised, it does not prevent enforcement of a return promise. **Illustration:**

> 1. A makes a promise in exchange for a return promise by B. The fact that the contract is voidable by A because of his own infancy or because of B's fraud does not prevent A's promise from being consideration for B's promise.

c. Unenforceable promises. A promise may be unenforceable by reason of lack of consideration or public policy, or because of a statute relating to remedies, such as the Statute of Frauds, or because of the traditional immunity of the sovereign from suit. See § 8. In such cases a return promise may or may not be unenforceable on the same or other grounds. But the fact that a promise is unenforceable does not mean that the return promise lacks consideration. See Illustrations 4-6 to § 75. **Illustrations:**

> 2. A makes a promise in exchange for a return promise by B. The fact that A's promise is unenforceable under the local Statute of Frauds does not prevent it from being consideration for B's promise.
>
> 3. A makes a promise in exchange for a promise by B, a foreign government not subject to suit. The fact that B's promise is unenforceable does not prevent it from being consideration for A's promise.

§ 79. Adequacy of Consideration; Mutuality of Obligation

If the requirement of consideration is met, there is no additional requirement of

(a) a gain, advantage, or benefit to the promisor or a loss, disadvantage, or detriment to the promisee; or

(b) equivalence in the values exchanged; or

(c) "mutuality of obligation."

Comment:

a. Rationale. In such typical bargains as the ordinary sale of goods each party gives up something of economic value, and the values exchanged are often roughly or exactly equivalent by standards independent of the particular bargain. Quite often promise is exchanged for promise, and the promised performances are sometimes divisible into matching parts. See § 31. Hence it has sometimes been said that consideration must consist of a "benefit to the promisor" or a "detriment to the promisee"; it has frequently been claimed that there was no consideration because the economic value given in exchange was much less than that of the promise or the promised performance; "mutuality of obligation" has been said to be essential to a contract. But experience has shown that these are not essential elements of a bargain or of an enforceable contract, and they are negated as requirements by the rules stated in §§ 71-78. This Section makes that negation explicit.

b. Benefit and detriment. Historically, the common law action of debt was said to require a *quid pro quo,* and that requirement may have led to statements that consideration must be a benefit to the promisor. But contracts were enforced in the common-law action of assumpsit without any such requirement; in actions of assumpsit the emphasis was rather on the harm to the promisee, and detrimental reliance on a promise may still be the basis of contractual relief. See § 90. But reliance is not essential to the formation of a bargain, and remedies for breach have long been given in cases of exchange of promise for promise where neither party has begun to perform. Today when it is said that consideration must involve a detriment to the promisee, the supposed requirement is often qualified by a statement that a "legal detriment" is sufficient even though there is no economic detriment or other actual loss. It is more realistic to say simply that there is no requirement of detriment. **Illustrations:**

> 1. A contracts to sell property to B. As a favor to B, who is C's friend, and in consideration of A's performance of the contract, C guarantees that B will pay the agreed price. A's performance is consideration for C's promise. See § 73.
>
> 2. A has executed a document in the form of a guaranty which imposes no obligation on A and has no value. B's surrender of the document to A, if bargained for, is consideration for a promise by A to pay $ 10,000. Compare § 74.

c. Exchange of unequal values. To the extent that the apportionment of productive energy and product in the economy are left to private action, the parties to transactions are free to fix their own valuations. The resolution of disputes often requires a determination of value in the more general sense of market value, and such values are commonly fixed as an approximation based on a multitude of private valuations. But in many situations there is no reliable external standard of value, or the general standard is inappropriate to the precise circumstances of the parties. Valuation is left to private action in part because the parties are thought to be better able than others to evaluate the circumstances of particular transactions. In any event, they are not ordinarily bound to follow the valuations of others.

Ordinarily, therefore, courts do not inquire into the adequacy of consideration. This is particularly so when one or both of the values exchanged are uncertain or difficult to measure. But it is also applied even when it is clear that the transaction is a mixture of bargain and gift. See Comment *c* to § 71. Gross inadequacy of consideration may be relevant to issues of capacity, fraud and the like, but the requirement of consideration is not a safeguard against imprudent and improvident contracts except in cases where it appears that there is no bargain in fact. **Illustrations:**

> 3. A borrows $ 300 from B to enable A to begin litigation to recover a gold mine through litigation, and promises to repay $ 10,000 when he recovers the mine. The loan is consideration for the promise.
>
> 4. A is pregnant with the illegitimate child of B, a wealthy man. A promises to give the child A's surname and B's given name, and B promises to provide for the support and education of the child and to set up a trust of securities to provide the child with a minimum net income of $ 100 per week until he reaches the age of 21. The naming of the child is consideration for B's promise.

d. Pretended exchange. Disparity in value, with or without other circumstances, sometimes indicates that the purported consideration was not in fact bargained for but was a mere formality or pretense. Such a sham or "nominal" consideration does not satisfy the requirement of § 71. Promises are enforced in such cases, if at all, either as promises binding without consideration under §§ 82-94 or as promises binding by virtue of their formal characteristics under § 6. See, for example, §§ 95-109 on contracts under seal. **Illustrations:**

> 5. In consideration of one cent received, A promises to pay $ 600 in three yearly install-

ments of $ 200 each. The one cent is merely nominal and is not consideration for A's promise.

> 6. A dies leaving no assets and owing $ 4000 to the B bank. C, A's widow, promises to pay the debt, and B promises to make no claim against A's estate. Without some further showing, B's promise is a mere formality and is not consideration for C's promise.

e. Effects of gross inadequacy. Although the requirement of consideration may be met despite a great difference in the values exchanged, gross inadequacy of consideration may be relevant in the application of other rules. Inadequacy "such as shocks the conscience" is often said to be a "badge of fraud," justifying a denial of specific performance. See § 364(1)(c). Inadequacy may also help to justify rescission or cancellation on the ground of lack of capacity (see §§ 15, 16), mistake, misrepresentation, duress or undue influence (see Chapters 6 and 7). Unequal bargains are also limited by the statutory law of usury, by regulation of the rates of public utilities and some other enterprises, and by special rules developed for the sale of an expectation of inheritance, for contractual penalties and forfeitures (see §§ 229, 356), and for agreements between secured lender and borrower (see Restatement of Security § 55, Uniform Commercial Code § 9-501).

f. Mutuality. The word "mutuality," though often used in connection with the law of Contracts, has no definite meaning. "Mutual assent" as one element of a bargain is the subject of Topic 2 of this Chapter. "Mutuality of remedy" is dealt with in Comment *c* to § 363. Clause (c) of this Section negates any supposed requirement of "mutuality of obligation." Such a requirement has sometimes been asserted in the form, "Both parties must be bound or neither is bound." That statement is obviously erroneous as applied to an exchange of promise for performance; it is equally inapplicable to contracts governed by §§ 82-94 and to contracts enforceable by virtue of their formal characteristics under § 6. Even in the ordinary case of the exchange of promise for promise, § 78 makes it clear that voidable and unenforceable promises may be consideration. The only requirement of "mutuality of obligation" even in cases of mutual promises is that stated in §§ 76-77.

§ 80. Multiple Exchanges

(1) There is consideration for a set of promises if what is bargained for and given in exchange would have been consideration for each promise in the set if exchanged for that promise alone.

(2) The fact that part of what is bargained for would not have been consideration if that part alone had been bargained for does not prevent the whole from being consideration.

Comment:

a. One consideration for a number of promises. Since consideration is not required to be adequate in value (see § 79), two or more promises may be binding even though made for the price of one. A single performance or return promise may thus furnish consideration for any number of promises. But if the performance or return promise would not be consideration for a single promise, it is not consideration for that promise as part of a set of promises, or for the other promises in the set. **Illustrations:**

1. A pays B or promises B to pay him $ 5, not then owed by A, in consideration of which B promises A to give him a book and also promises to surrender a letter. Both of B's promises are supported by consideration.

2. A pays B or promises B to pay him $ 50 not then owed by A, in exchange for the following promises: a promise by C to dig a well for D, a promise by E to discharge F from a debt of $ 100 owing by F to E. All the promises are supported by consideration.

b. Several performances or return promises as consideration. In cases within Subsection (2) the promisor has received all he bargained for. The fact that part of it would not have been consideration standing alone does not make enforcement of the bargain unjust to the promisor or contrary to the public interest. The effect of public policy on part of the consideration, however, may invalidate the entire bargain under some circumstances. See §§ 178, 183-85.

Illustration:

3. A owes B $ 5. B promises to give A a book if A will pay the $ 5 and $ 1 in addition. A pays the $ 6. B's promise is binding, although A's payment of the $ 5 which he owed would not of itself have been consideration.

c. Compositions with creditors. Composition agreements between a debtor and his creditors illustrate Subsection (2). The consideration for which each assenting creditor bargains may be any or all of the following: (1) part payment of the sum due him, (2) the promise of each other creditor to forego a portion of his claim, (3) forbearance or promise of forbearance by the debtor to pay the assenting creditors more than equal proportions, (4) the action of the debtor in securing the assent of the other creditors, (5) the part payments made to the other creditors. The first is not consideration, but each of the others may be consideration. The last two are seldom bargained for in fact, but (2) and (3) are practically always bargained for by implication if not in so many words. Still other considerations may be agreed upon in any case.

Illustration:

4. A makes a composition with B, C and D, three of his creditors, whereby each of them promises to accept forty cents on the dollar as full satisfaction, A promising to treat all assenting creditors equally. A's promise and the promises of the other two creditors are consideration for the promise of each creditor, even though there are other non-assenting creditors.

§ 81. Consideration as Motive or Inducing Cause

(1) The fact that what is bargained for does not of itself induce the making of a promise does not prevent it from being consideration for the promise.

(2) The fact that a promise does not of itself induce a performance or return promise does not prevent the performance or return promise from being consideration for the promise.

Comment:

a. "Bargained for." Consideration requires that a performance or return promise be "bargained for" in exchange for a promise; this means that the promisor must manifest an intention to induce the performance or return promise and to be induced by it, and that the promisee must manifest an intention to induce the making of the promise and to be induced by it. See § 71 and Comment *b*. In most commercial bargains the consideration is the object of the promisor's desire and that desire is a material motive or cause inducing the making of the promise, and the reciprocal desire of the promisee for the making of the promise similarly induces the furnishing of the consideration.

    b. Immateriality of motive or cause. This Section makes explicit a limitation on the requirement that consideration be bargained for. Even in the typical commercial bargain, the promisor may have more than one motive, and the person furnishing the consideration need not inquire into the promisor's motives. Unless both parties know that the purported consideration is mere pretense, it is immaterial that the promisor's desire for the consideration is incidental to other objectives and even that the other party knows this to be so. Compare § 79 and Illustrations. Subsection (2) states a similar rule with respect to the motives of the promisee.

Topic 2. Contracts Without Consideration

Introductory Note *Bases for enforcement.* The rules of this Topic are exceptions to the general requirement of a bargain stated in § 17. The elements in a transaction which justify enforcement of a promise which is not part of a bargain are also often present in bargains. The principal substantive bases for enforcement are reliance and unjust enrichment. Also relevant is the extent to which the evidentiary, cautionary, deterrent and channeling functions of formalities are satisfied. See Comment *c* to § 72. Additional justification for the enforcement of some promises is found in the fact that they are preliminary steps toward bargain or are otherwise ancillary to the making or performance of a bargain. *Omitted cases.* In the absence of bargain, the factors bearing on the enforcement of promises appear in widely varying combinations, and no general principle has emerged which distinguishes the binding promise from the non-binding. Sections 82-94 state rules for certain cases which have arisen often enough so that rules have crystallized, and §§ 86 and 90 state general principles with respect to the effect of unjust enrichment and reliance, respectively. In some States, by statute or decision, additional categories of promises are binding without consideration.

    Promises conditional on mutual assent and consideration. Sections 82-94 state the circumstances under which certain types of promises are binding. Where the stated circumstances do not include mutual assent or consideration, those elements are not required by law. But a promise may be in terms conditional on acceptance or performance or return promise by the promisee, and such a condition is effective. See § 91. Where such a condition is met, there may be a transaction enforceable as a bargain; if so, limitations stated in §§ 82-94, relating to enforcement in the absence of bargain, may be inappropriate and inapplicable

§ 82. Promise to Pay Indebtedness; Effect on the Statute of Limitations

    (1) A promise to pay all or part of an antecedent contractual or quasi-contractual indebtedness owed by the promisor is binding if the indebtedness is still enforceable or would be except for the effect of a statute of limitations. (2) The following facts operate as such a promise unless other facts indicate a different intention: (a) A voluntary acknowledgment to the obligee, admitting the present existence of the antecedent indebtedness; or

    (b) A voluntary transfer of money, a negotiable instrument, or other thing by the obligor to the obligee, made as interest on or part payment of or collateral security for the antecedent indebtedness; or

    (c) A statement to the obligee that the statute of limitations will not be pleaded as a defense.

Comment:

    a. Requirement of a writing. Statutes enacted in most States provide that a promise included in the Section is not binding unless it is in writing and signed by or on behalf of the promisor, except where the promise is inferred from part payment or from the giving of a negotiable instrument or collateral security as stated in Subsection (2) (b). See § 110. In a few States, no writing is required in any case. In a few other States, the rule is more stringent than that generally prevailing and even part payment or giving of security imposes no promissory duty on a debtor unless there is also a signed writing. Most of the statutes requiring a writing are inapplicable to promises supported by consideration or made enforceable by reliance. See § 90.

b. *Historical note: types of indebtedness.* The rule of Subsection (1) was established in the action of general or indebitatus assumpsit, based on a fictitious promise to pay an antecedent debt. Such an action could be brought on a simple contract debt, and the subsequent promise could be set up by way of replication to a plea of the statute of limitations. The rule was the same whether the new promise was made before or after the statute of limitations had run on the original debt; it was enough that the new promise was made within the statutory period before the bringing of the action. General assumpsit was extended to unliquidated contractual obligations and later to quasi-contractual obligations; it was not available for claims to damages for breach of a promissory bargain not performed on either side or for tort claims not involving unjust enrichment. The word "indebtedness" is intended to carry forward the distinction: a promise to pay damages for a tort or breach of contract may be made binding by consideration or reliance, but it is not within the rule stated in Subsection (1).

General assumpsit was extended to foreign judgments, but it did not lie for debts founded on domestic judgments or on contracts under seal. Some American courts have therefore denied effect to new promises to pay judgment debts or obligations under seal. In England there was no statute of limitations for such obligations until the nineteenth century, and the nineteenth-century statutes expressly gave effect to acknowledgments and part payments. Modern American statutes have changed the setting in which the question of the effect of a new promise arises. Statutes in many States have abrogated some or all of the common-law effects of the seal, and have thus weakened the basis for distinguishing contracts under seal from other contracts. Statutes also commonly make explicit provision for the extension or revival of judgments; such statutes may affect the question

whether a new promise to pay a judgment can be the basis of an action. **Illustrations:**

1. A owes B $ 100 and the claim is not yet barred by the statute of limitations. A promises B in a signed writing to pay the debt. The promise is binding, and the statute of limitations will not bar the claim for the statutory period after the making of the new promise.

2. A owes B three debts of $ 500 each. All of the debts are barred by the statute of limitations. A writes to B, "I promise to pay you one of those $ 500 debts which I owe; the other two I shall not pay." A's promise of $ 500 is binding.

3. A owes B a debt for some work which B has done but the amount due is in dispute. A writes to B, "I will pay you whatever I owe." The promise is binding during the statutory period of limitation from the time when it was made, and subjects A to a duty to pay whatever amount B can prove was due him.

...

d. *Acknowledgment.* An unqualified admission that a debt is owing operates as a promise to pay it for the purposes of the rule stated in Subsection (1). It does not so operate for all purposes. See § 83; Uniform Commercial Code § 3-102(1) (c). The implication of a promise from an acknowledgment may be a survival of the view that the statute of limitations raises a presumption of payment, and in some States an acknowledgment is still said to be effective without any promise to pay. But circumstances indicating an intention not to pay deprive the acknowledgment of effect in most States. **Illustrations:**

10. A owes B a debt, and lists the debt in a sworn schedule required to be filed in his voluntary bankruptcy proceeding. A's admission that he owes the debt does not impose a new obligation on him, whether the statute of limitations has or has not completely run on the original obligation when the admission is made. See Comment *a* to § 83.

11. A owes B $ 500, and writes B, "I admit that I owe you $ 500, but I am unable to pay it." A's letter imposes no duty upon him.

e. *Part payment and giving of collateral.* Part payment of a debt amounts to an admission that it is owing and thus has the same effect as an acknowledgment, except that most of the statutes requiring a writing expressly preserve the effect previously given to a part payment. See § 110. Payment on account of interest is treated as part payment for this purpose, and the giving of a negotiable instrument or of collateral security has the same effect. There must be a voluntary transfer by the debtor; the creditor's exercise of a power given by law or of a power irrevocably given at a previous time does not operate as a promise by the debtor. See Restatement, Second, Agency §§ 14H, 138-39. Nor does a voluntary transfer so operate if the circumstances indicate that the debtor has no such intention. If the debtor makes a part payment in performance of a promise to pay in installments or on condition, he is bound only in accordance with the promise. **Illustrations:**

> 12. A owes B $ 500 and without comment sends B a check for $ 300. Absent other facts establishing that the check is referrable to the larger debt, it does not operate as a new promise.
>
> 13. A owes B $ 5,000, secured by a pledge of corporate bonds. On A's default B sells the bonds under a power given by law or by the pledge agreement and applies the proceeds to the debt, leaving a balance of $ 2000. The part payment does not operate as a new promise by A.
>
> 14. A owes B $ 500 and sends B a post-dated check for $ 200, stating that it is sent as part payment of the debt. The delivery of the check operates as a new promise to pay the debt, and payment of the check by the drawee bank on the subsequent date shown on the check oper-

ates as a second new promise. The bank's authority to pay was revocable, and A could have stopped payment.

> 15. A owes B a debt of $ 1000, barred by the statute of limitations. A orally promises to pay the debt in monthly installments of $ 10, and subsequently pays $ 5 on account of the first installment. The part payment, though excepted from a statute requiring a writing, binds A only to pay in monthly installments.

. . .

g. New promise by agent, co-debtor or fiduciary. Despite early English decisions that a joint debtor was bound by a part payment made by his co-debtor, the modern rule by statute or decision is that a new promise binds a debtor only if made by him or by a person having power to bind him under the law of agency. An assignee for creditors or like fiduciary does not ordinarily have power to bind the debtor by a new promise. In the absence of consideration or reliance a fiduciary does not bind himself personally unless he was bound by the original obligation. Whether a fiduciary has power to bind the estate he administers by a new promise depends on the terms of the statute or instrument under which he acts. In many States statutes deny such a power to the executor or administrator of a decedent.

§ 83. Promise to Pay Indebtedness Discharged in Bankruptcy

An express promise to pay all or part of an indebtedness of the promisor, discharged or dischargeable in bankruptcy proceedings begun before the promise is made, is binding.

Comment:

a. Rationale. The early history of the rule of this Section is the same as that of the rule of § 82, relating to the statute of limitations, and the two rules are similar in many respects. But only a few States have enacted statutes requiring the promises described in this Section to be in writing. In modern times discharge in bankruptcy has been thought to reflect a somewhat stronger public policy than the statute of limitations, and a promise implied from acknowledgment or part payment does not revive a debt discharged in

bankruptcy. Although in the absence of a statute an oral promise is effective, the courts have insisted on the formality of express promise, denying effect to expressions of expectation or of good intention. **Illustrations:**

> 1. A owes B $ 100 and is about to go into bankruptcy. Immediately before filing his petition he promises B to pay the debt in spite of any discharge that he may get in bankruptcy. The promise is not binding but would have been binding if it had been made after the petition in bankruptcy was filed.

. . .

§ 84. Promise to Perform a Duty in Spite of Non-Occurrence Of a Condition

(1) Except as stated in Subsection

(2), a promise to perform all or part of a conditional duty under an antecedent contract in spite of the non-occurrence of the condition is binding, whether the promise is made before or after the time for the condition to occur, unless

(a) occurrence of the condition was a material part of the agreed exchange for the performance of the duty and the promisee was under no duty that it occur; or

(b) uncertainty of the occurrence of the condition was an element of the risk assumed by the promisor.

(2) If such a promise is made before the time for the occurrence of the condition has expired and the condition is within the control of the promisee or a beneficiary, the promisor can make his duty again subject to the condition by notifying the promisee or beneficiary of his intention to do so if

(a) the notification is received while there is still a reasonable time to cause the condition to occur under the antecedent terms or an extension given by the promisor; and

(b) reinstatement of the requirement of the condition is not unjust because of a material change of position by the promisee or beneficiary; and

(c) the promise is not binding apart from the rule stated in Subsection (1).

Comment:

a. Rationale. Like the rules stated in §§ 82 and 83, the rule of Subsection (1) can be thought of in terms of waiver of a defense not addressed to the merits, and rests in large part on the policies against forfeiture and unjust enrichment. Where the waiver is made before the time for the occurrence of the condition, it may induce non-occurrence of the condition, and enforcement may also rest on reliance or on excuse by prevention or hindrance. See §§ 89, 90, and Comment *d* to § 205. But a waiver made after the original duty has been discharged, though it is sometimes said to "reinstate" the duty, in fact creates a new duty unqualified by the condition.

Conditions are the subject of more detailed treatment in §§ 224-29. In many situations an agreement or a rule of law, in the interest of simplicity and certainty, provides for absolute discharge of the promisor although a discharge to the extent of loss caused by a non-occurrence of condition might seem more equitable. See, e.g., Uniform Commercial Code §§ 3-502. The likelihood of waiver and the pressure to find waiver or other excuse increase in proportion to the extent and unfairness of the forfeiture involved; in extreme cases the non-occurrence of the condition may be excused without other reason. See § 229.

b. "Waiver" and "estoppel"; mistake. "Waiver" is often inexactly defined as "the voluntary relinquishment of a known right." When the waiver is reinforced by reliance, enforcement is often said to rest on "estoppel." Compare §§ 89, 90. Since the more common definition of estoppel is limited to reliance on a misrepresentation of an existing fact, reliance on a waiver or promise as to the future is sometimes said to create a "promissory estoppel." The common definition of waiver may lead to the incorrect inference that the promisor must know his legal rights and must intend the legal effect of the promise. But under § 93 it is sufficient if he has reason to know the essential facts. And if the waiver is supported by reliance or by consideration, the effect of mistake on the part of the promisor depends on the rules stated in Chapter 6.

c. Conditions material to the exchange or risk. A promise is often conditional on the receipt of some performance regarded as the equivalent of the performance promised, as in the case of an option contract to sell a horse if the promisee pays $ 500 for him. A promise may also be conditional on a fortuitous event, and the risk or burden assumed by the promisor may depend on the probability that the condition will occur, as in a promise to insure a house against fire. In both types of cases, where a promise to disregard the non-occurrence of the condition materially affects the value received by the promisor or the burden or risk assumed by him, the promise is not binding under Subsection (1). Such a promise may be binding by virtue of reliance or for some other reason. See §§ 89, 90. See also § 246. But a waiver of the price of a horse or of the fire required by an insurance policy is not within this Section.

Illustration:

> 1. In an insurance policy the insurer promises to pay $ 1000 if the insured is killed on a railroad. The insurer's subsequent promise to pay $ 1000 even though the insured is not killed on a railroad is not binding under this Section, whether the promise is made before or after the death of the insured.

d. Conditions which may be waived. The rule of Subsection (1) applies primarily to conditions which may be thought of as procedural or technical, or to instances in which the non-occurrence of condition is comparatively minor. Examples are conditions which merely relate to the time or manner of the return performance or provide for the giving of notice or the supplying of proofs. Insurance policies ordinarily contain conditions of notice and proof of loss and of time for suit; and guarantors, indorsers and other sureties may be discharged by an agreement varying the duty of the principal debtor, by failure of diligence in presentment or prosecution, or by failure to give a required notice. In such cases, even though a promise to disregard the non-occurrence of the condition subjects the promisor to a new duty, the new duty is not regarded as significantly different from the old and the promise is binding without consideration, reliance, or formality. See, e.g., Uniform Commercial Code § 3-606, Comment 2.

Illustrations:

> 2. A is surety for B on a debt due C. C makes a contract with B, the principal debtor, extending the time for payment. Thereafter A, with knowledge of that fact, promises C to pay the debt. The promise is binding, and A has no power to retract it.

> 3. A employs B to build a house, promising to pay therefor $ 10,000 on the production of a certificate from A's architect, C, stating that the work has been satisfactorily completed. B builds the house but the work is defective in certain trivial particulars. C refuses to give B a certificate. A says to B, "My architect rightfully refuses to give you a certificate but the defects are not serious; I will pay you the full price which I promised." A is bound to do so, and has no power to restore the requirement of the condition.

> . . .

e. Form. Adjustments in an on-going transaction commonly take place in a setting which fulfills some of the functions of legal formalities, and the probability of reliance is high. Compare § 89. Even when the requirement of a technical condition is waived after the non-occurrence of that condition, the effect is often to achieve a result which seems fair without regard to waiver. The Statute of Frauds may make unenforceable an oral promise which has not been relied on. See § 150; compare Uniform Commercial Code § 2-209, Comment 4. Otherwise, formal requirements are at a minimum. It is immaterial how the promisor manifests his intention to fulfill the prior duty without the performance of the condition. Words of promise or waiver, though often used, are unnecessary; in many situations nonverbal conduct is enough. A mere acknowledgment of the antecedent duty does not suffice unless there is a manifestation of intention to disregard the condition, and a conditional or partial waiver is effective only according to its terms. **Illustration:**

> 5. A, an insurance company, issues to B a policy of automobile liability insurance, under which it is a condition of A's duty to pay that B notify A "as soon as practicable" after an accident. An accident occurs, but B does not notify A as soon as practicable. Without any statement concerning the non-occurrence of the condition, A begins to defend B in an action brought against B as a result of the accident. A's beginning to defend B operates as a promise to pay in spite of the non-occurrence of the condition.

f. Reinstatement after waiver. If the requirement of a condition has been eliminated from a contract by an agreement supported by consideration it cannot be reinstated by unilateral action of the promisor. Nor can it be reinstated if a new unconditional duty has been created by a promise made after the original duty was discharged by non-occurrence of the condition, or if reinstatement would be unjust in view of a change of position by the other party. Compare Uniform Commercial Code § 2-209(5); Restatement of Restitution § 142. But where the requirement of a condition is waived in advance, the promisor may reinstate the requirement by giving notice to the other party before the latter has materially changed his position. Whether delay alone makes reinstatement unjust depends upon the circumstances: in some cases a reasonable extension of time sufficiently protects the other party; in others the extension may be required to be both definite and reasonable; in some no extension can put him in as good a position to perform as before the waiver.

Illustrations:

6. In Illustration 4, A can restore the requirement of the condition by notifying B of his intention to do so if there still remains a reasonable time for the occurrence of the condition before the expiration of the thirty-day period, unless such action would be unjust in view of a material change of position by B in reliance on A's waiver. If a reasonable time does not remain, A cannot restore the requirement of the condition by extending the time.

7. A, an insurance company, insures B's house against loss by fire. The insurance policy provides that unless suit is brought on the policy within twelve months after a loss, no recovery can be had. An insured loss occurs and A tells B that it is unnecessary to bring suit within that time. Unless B has so changed his position that it would be unjust to restore the time limitation, A can do so by giving B notice. Thereafter B has a reasonable time to bring suit. In the absence of special circumstances, the reasonable time will expire twelve months after the notice is received.

. . .

§ 85. Promise to Perform a Voidable Duty

Except as stated in § 93, a promise to perform all or part of an antecedent contract of the promisor, previously voidable by him, but not avoided prior to the making of the promise, is binding.

Comment:

a. Types of voidable contracts. The rule of this Section may be thought of as implicit in the definition of "voidable contract" in § 7. Such a contract is distinguished from the "unenforceable contract" defined in § 8 by the existence of a power of ratification. The power of avoidance may rest on lack of capacity under the rules stated in §§ 12-16, on mistake, misrepresentation, duress or undue influence under Chapters 6 and 7. In such cases exercise of the power of avoidance discharges the contractual duty and terminates the power of ratification; conversely, exercise of the power of ratification terminates the power of avoidance. See §§ 378-85.

b. Ratification and new promise. This Section relates only to action which constitutes a promise under the definition in § 2. Such a promise may be binding under this Section or because of its formal character or because it is supported by consideration or reliance. Even though it is "binding" under this Section, the new promise may itself be voidable for the same reason as the original promise, or it may be voidable or unenforceable for some other reason. See § 1, Comment *g.* In particular, a few states require the new promise of a former infant to be in writing and signed. A power of avoidance may also be lost in various other ways: by delay in giving notice, by failure to restore performance received, by exercise of dominion over things received, or by change of circumstances. See, e.g., as to avoidance for misrepresentation, § 164.

Illustrations:

1. A is induced by B's fraud to promise $ 100 in return for a worthless chattel. After discovering the fraud A promises B to pay as agreed. The promise is binding.

2. A, an infant, promises B to pay him $ 100 in consideration of a bicycle which B transfers to him. The bicycle is worth $ 60. On coming of age A promises to pay B the sum he originally agreed to pay. He is bound to do so. If instead of such a promise he promises to pay a smaller sum, as $ 40, he is also bound, but only to that extent.

§ 86. Promise for Benefit Received

(1) A promise made in recognition of a benefit previously received by the promisor from the promisee is binding to the extent necessary to prevent injustice.

(2) A promise is not binding under Subsection (1)

(a) if the promisee conferred the benefit as a gift or for other reasons the promisor has not been unjustly enriched; or

(b) to the extent that its value is disproportionate to the benefit.

Comment:

a. "Past consideration"; "moral obligation." Enforcement of promises to pay for benefit received has sometimes been said to rest on "past consideration" or on the "moral obligation" of the promisor, and there are statutes in such terms in a few states. Those terms are not used here: "past consideration" is inconsistent with the meaning of consideration stated in § 71, and there seems to be no consensus as to what constitutes a "moral obligation." The mere fact of promise has been thought to create a moral obligation, but it is clear that not all promises are enforced. Nor are moral obligations based solely on gratitude or sentiment sufficient of themselves to support a subsequent promise. **Illustrations:**

    1. A gives emergency care to B's adult son while the son is sick and without funds far from home. B subsequently promises to reimburse A for his expenses. The promise is not binding under this Section.

    2. A lends money to B, who later dies. B's widow promises to pay the debt. The promise is not binding under this Section.

    3. A has immoral relations with B, a woman not his wife, to her injury. A's subsequent promise to reimburse B for her loss is not binding under this Section.

b. Rationale. Although in general a person who has been unjustly enriched at the expense of another is required to make restitution, restitution is denied in many cases in order to protect persons who have had benefits thrust upon them. See Restatement of Restitution §§ 1, 2, 112. In other cases restitution is denied by virtue of rules designed to guard against false claims, stale claims, claims already litigated, and the like. In many such cases a subsequent promise to make restitution removes the reason for the denial of relief, and the policy against unjust enrichment then prevails. Compare Restatement, Second, Agency § 462 on ratification of the acts of a person who officiously purports to act as an agent. Enforcement of the subsequent promise sometimes makes it unnecessary to decide a difficult question as to the limits on quasi-contractual relief.

Many of the cases governed by the rules stated in §§ 82-85 are within the broader principle stated in this Section. But the broader principle is not so firmly established as those rules, and it may not be applied if there is doubt whether the objections to restitution are fully met by the subsequent promise. Facts such as the definite and substantial character of the benefit received, formality in the making of the promise, part performance of the promise, reliance on the promise or the probability of such reliance may be relevant to show that no imposition results from enforcement.

c. Promise to correct a mistake. One who makes a mistake in the conferring of a benefit is commonly entitled to restitution regardless of any promise. But restitution is often denied to avoid prejudice to the recipient of the benefit. Thus restitution of the value of services or of improvements to land or chattels may require a payment which the recipient cannot afford. See Restatement of Restitution §§ 41, 42. Where a subsequent promise shows that the usual protection is not needed in the particular case, restitution is granted to the extent promised. **Illustrations:**

    4. A is employed by B to repair a vacant house. By mistake A repairs the house next door, which belongs to C. A subsequent promise by C to pay A the value of the repairs is binding.

    5. A pays B a debt and gets a signed receipt. Later B obtains a default judgment against A for the amount of the debt, and A pays again. B's subsequent promise to refund the second payment if A has a receipt is binding.

d. Emergency services and necessaries. The law of restitution in the absence of promise severely limits recovery for necessaries furnished to a person under disability and for emergency services. See Restatement of Restitution §§ 113-17, 139. A subsequent promise in such a case may remove doubt as to the reality of the benefit and as to its value, and may negate any danger of imposition or false claim. A positive showing that payment was expected is not then required; an intention to make a gift must be shown to defeat restitution. **Illustrations:**

    6. A finds B's escaped bull and feeds and cares for it. B's subsequent promise to pay reasonable compensation to A is binding.

    7. A saves B's life in an emergency and is totally and permanently disabled in so doing. One month later B promises to pay A $ 15 every two weeks for the rest of A's life, and B makes the payments for 8 years until he dies. The promise is binding.

e. Benefit conferred as a gift. In the absence of mistake or the like, there is no element of unjust enrichment in the receipt of a gift, and the rule of this Section has no application to a promise to pay for a past gift. Similarly, when a debt is discharged by a binding agreement, the transaction is closed even though full payment is not made. But marginal cases arise in which both parties understand that what is in form a gift is intended to be reimbursed indirectly, or in which a subsequent promise to pay is expressly contemplated. See Illustration 3 to § 83. Enforcement of the subsequent promise is proper in some such cases. **Illustrations:**

> 8. A submits to B at B's request a plan for advertising products manufactured by B, expecting payment only if the plan is adopted. Because of a change in B's selling arrangements, B rejects the plan without giving it fair consideration. B's subsequent promise to reimburse A's expenses in preparing the plan is binding.

> 9. A contributes capital to B, an insurance company, on the understanding that B is not liable to reimburse A but that A will be reimbursed through salary and commissions. Later A withdraws from the company and B promises to pay him ten percent of premiums received until he is reimbursed. The promise is binding.

f. Benefit conferred pursuant to contract. By virtue of the policy of enforcing bargains, the enrichment of one party as a result of an unequal exchange is not regarded as unjust, and this Section has no application to a promise to pay or perform more or to accept less than is called for by a pre-existing bargain between the same parties. Compare §§ 79, 89. Similarly, if a third person receives a benefit as a result of the performance of a bargain, this Section does not make binding the subsequent promise of the third person to pay extra compensation to the performing party. But a promise to pay in substitution for the return performance called for by the bargain may be binding under this Section. **Illustration:**

> 10. A digs a well on B's land in performance of a bargain with B's tenant C. C is unable to pay as agreed, and B promises to pay A the reasonable value of the well. The promise is binding.

g. Obligation unenforceable under the Statute of Frauds. A promise to pay a debt unenforceable under the Statute of Frauds is very similar to the promises governed by §§ 82-85. But the problem seldom arises. Part performance often renders the Statute inapplicable; if it does

not, the contract can be made enforceable by a subsequent memorandum. See § 136. In any event, the Statute does not ordinarily foreclose the remedy of restitution. See § 375. Where the question does arise, the new promise is binding if the policy of the Statute is satisfied. **Illustration:**

> 11. By statute an agreement authorizing a real estate broker to sell land for compensation is void unless the agreement or a memorandum thereof is in writing. A, a real estate broker, procures a purchaser for B's land without any written agreement. In the written sale agreement, signed by B, B promises to pay A $ 200, the usual commission, "for services rendered." The promise is binding.

> . . .

i. Partial enforcement. The rules stated in §§ 82-85 refer to promises to perform all or part of an antecedent duty, and do not make enforceable a promise to do more. Similarly, where a benefit received is a liquidated sum of money, a promise is not enforceable under this Section beyond the amount of the benefit. Where the value of the benefit is uncertain, a promise to pay the value is binding and a promise to pay a liquidated sum may serve to fix the amount due if in all the circumstances it is not disproportionate to the benefit. See Illustration 7. A promise which is excessive may sometimes be enforced to the extent of the value of the benefit, and the remedy may be thought of as quasi-contractual rather than contractual. In other cases a promise of disproportionate value may tend to show unfair pressure or other conduct by the promisee such that justice does not require any enforcement of the promise. Compare Comment *c* to § 72. **Illustrations:**

> 12. A, a married woman of sixty, has rendered household services without compensation over a period of years for B, a man of eighty living alone and having no close relatives. B has a net worth of three million dollars and has often assured A that she will be well paid for her services, whose reasonable value is not in excess of $ 6,000. B executes and delivers to A a written promise to pay A $ 25,000 "to be taken from my estate." The promise is binding.

> 13. The facts being otherwise as stated in Illustration 12, B's promise is made orally and is to leave A his entire estate. A cannot recover more than the reasonable value of her services.

§ 87. Option Contract

(1) An offer is binding as an option contract if it

(a) is in writing and signed by the offeror, recites a purported consideration for the making of the offer, and proposes an exchange on fair terms within a reasonable time; or

(b) is made irrevocable by statute.

(2) An offer which the offeror should reasonably expect to induce action or forbearance of a substantial character on the part of the offeree before acceptance and which does induce such action or forbearance is binding as an option contract to the extent necessary to avoid injustice.

Comment:

a. Consideration and form. The traditional common-law devices for making a firm offer or option contract are the giving of consideration and the affixing of a seal. See §§ 25, 95. But the firm offer serves a useful purpose even though no preliminary bargain is made: it is often a necessary step in the making of the main bargain proposed, and it partakes of the natural formalities inherent in business transactions. The erosion of the formality of the seal has made it less and less satisfactory as a universal formality. As literacy has spread, the personal signature has become the natural formality and the seal has become more and more anachronistic. The rules stated in this section reflect the judicial and legislative response to this situation.

b. Nominal consideration. Offers made in consideration of one dollar paid or promised are often irrevocable under Subsection (1)(a). The irrevocability of an offer may be worth much or little to the offeree, and the courts do not ordinarily inquire into the adequacy of the consideration bargained for. See § 79. Hence a comparatively small payment may furnish consideration for the irrevocability of an offer proposing a transaction involving much larger sums. But gross disproportion between the payment and the value of the option commonly indicates that the payment was not in fact bargained for but was a mere formality or pretense. In such a case there is no consideration as that term is defined in § 71.

Nevertheless, such a nominal consideration is regularly held sufficient to support a short-time option proposing an exchange on fair terms. The fact that the option is an appropriate preliminary step in the conclusion of a socially useful transaction provides a sufficient substantive basis for enforcement, and a signed writing taking a form appropriate to a bargain satisfies the desiderata of form. In the absence of statute, however, the bargaining form is essential: a payment of one dollar by each party to the other is so obviously not a bargaining transaction that it does not provide even the form of an exchange. **Illustrations:**

1. In consideration of twenty-five cents paid by B, A executes and delivers to B a written option agreement giving B the right to buy a piece of land for $ 100,000 if B gives notice of intention to buy within 120 days. The price and terms of sale are fair. A has made an irrevocable offer.

2. In consideration of one dollar paid by B, A, a widow who owns land worth $ 25,000 as a farm, gives B a ten-year option to take phosphate rock from the land on paying a royalty of twenty-five cents per ton. As B knows but A does not, the prevailing royalty in such transactions ranges from $ 1.00 to $ 1.10 per ton. The offer is not made irrevocable by the one-dollar payment.

c. False recital of nominal consideration. A recital in a written agreement that a stated consideration has been given is evidence of that fact as against a party to the agreement, but such a recital may ordinarily be contradicted by evidence that no such consideration was given or expected. See §§ 218. In cases within Subsection (1)(a), however, the giving and recital of nominal consideration performs a formal function only. The signed writing has vital significance as a formality, while the ceremonial manual delivery of a dollar or a peppercorn is an inconsequential formality. In view of the dangers of permitting a solemn written agreement to be invalidated by oral testimony which is easily fabricated, therefore, the option agreement is not invalidated by proof that the recited consideration was not in fact given. A fictitious rationalization has sometimes been used for this rule: acceptance of delivery of the written instrument conclusively imports a promise to make good the recital, it is said, and that promise furnishes consideration. Compare § 218. But the sound basis for the rule is that stated above.

Illustration:

> 3. A executes and delivers to B a written agreement "in consideration of one dollar in hand paid" giving B an option to buy described land belonging to A for $ 15,000, the option to expire at noon six days later. The fact that the dollar is not in fact paid does not prevent the offer from being irrevocable.

d. Statutory firm offers. In many states the seal is no longer an effective substitute for consideration, see Introductory Note to Topic 3 of this Chapter. In addition, Uniform Commercial Code § 2-203 withdraws contracts and offers for the sale of goods from the law of sealed instruments. Statutes have sometimes given effect to a signed writing as a substitute formality, either generally or in cases of offers made in a signed writing and stated to be irrevocable. More common, however, are statutes dealing with particular types of offers. Thus when goods are put up at auction without reserve, an offer is made which is irrevocable under Uniform Commercial Code § 2-328(3). See § 28. Again, when statutes authorize or require that government work be awarded to contractors on the basis of competitive bidding, it may be fairly implied that the public officials in charge may protect the integrity of the competition by refusing to allow a bid to be withdrawn after the bids are opened. A similar implication may be drawn when an offer is required to be submitted to a court for approval. A more general provision for irrevocable offers is found in Uniform Commercial Code § 2-205, giving effect for a reasonable time not exceeding three months to a firm offer to buy or sell goods, made by a merchant in a signed writing.

e. Reliance. Subsection (2) states the application of § 90 to reliance on an unaccepted offer, with qualifications which would not be appropriate in some other types of cases covered by § 90. It is important chiefly in cases of reliance that is not part performance. If the beginning of performance is a reasonable mode of acceptance, it makes the offer fully enforceable under § 45 or § 62; if not, the offeror commonly has no reason to expect part performance before acceptance. But circumstances may be such that the offeree must undergo substantial expense, or undertake substantial commitments, or forego alternatives, in order to put himself in a position to accept by either promise or performance. The offer may be made expressly irrevocable in contemplation of reliance by the offeree. If reliance follows in such cases, justice may require a remedy. Compare Restatement, Second, Torts § 325; Restatement, Second, Agency § 378. But the reliance must be substantial as well as foreseeable.

Full-scale enforcement of the offered contract is not necessarily appropriate in such cases. Restitution of benefits conferred may be enough, or partial or full reimbursement of losses may be proper. Various factors may influence the remedy: the formality of the offer, its commercial or social context, the extent to which the offeree's reliance was understood to be at his own risk, the relative competence and the bargaining position of the parties, the degree of fault on the part of the offeror, the ease and certainty of proof of particular items of damage and the likelihood that unprovable damages have been suffered.

Illustrations:

> 4. A leases a farm to B and later gives B an "option" to buy the farm for $ 15,500 within five years. With A's approval, B makes permanent improvements in the farm buildings, builds roads, drains and dams, and contours plow land, using his own labor and expending several thousand dollars. Toward the end of the five years, A purports to revoke the option, demanding a higher price. B then gives written notice of acceptance in accordance with the terms of the offer. Specific performance by A may be decreed.
>
> 5. A offers to B a "blanket arrangement" to buy "poultry grown by you" at stated prices. As contemplated, B buys 7,000 baby chicks and begins raising them for sale to A as "broilers." Thereafter A purports to revoke the offer. B has the rights of an aggrieved seller under a contract for the sale of 7,000 "broilers."
>
> 6. A submits a written offer for paving work to be used by B as a partial basis for B's bid as general contractor on a large building. As A knows, B is required to name his subcontractors in his general bid. B uses A's offer and B's bid is accepted. A's offer is irrevocable until B has had a reasonable opportunity to notify A of the award and B's acceptance of A's offer.

§ 88. Guaranty

A promise to be surety for the performance of a contractual obligation, made to the obligee, is binding if

(a) the promise is in writing and signed by the promisor and recites a purported consideration; or

(b) the promise is made binding by statute; or

(c) the promisor should reasonably expect the promise to induce action or forbearance of a substantial character on the part of the promisee or a third person, and the promise does induce such action or forbearance.

Comment:

a. Rationale. Like option contracts, guaranties are ancillary to bargains, and have some of the same presumptive utility. See §§ 72 and 87 and Comments. A guaranty is commonly supported by the consideration which supports the obligation guaranteed. See § 80. Or it may be binding because it is under seal. But there has been much confusion where a guaranty not under seal is given after the principal obligor has received the consideration for his promise. The elements of a bargain with the guarantor can sometimes be found in such cases, either because the original bargain was not completed until the guaranty was furnished or by virtue of forbearance to pursue the principal debtor. The rules stated in this Section often render the search for such elements unnecessary. Where applicable, the formal requirements of the Statute of Frauds must of course be met. See §§ 112-23.

b. Nominal consideration and recital thereof. A contract of suretyship is aleatory, like familiar forms of insurance, and if the surety is called upon to pay he commonly has recourse against the principal obligor by way of reimbursement or subrogation. See Restatement of Security § 104, 141. The amount paid for a guaranty is often only a small fraction of the amount of the principal obligation; indeed, consideration may be furnished by the mere extension of credit to the principal obligor. Hence it would often be difficult to say whether a consideration of one dollar is adequate in amount, and courts do not ordinarily inquire into that question. See § 79. Like § 87 on option contracts, this Section goes further and precludes inquiry into the question whether the consideration recited in a written contract of guaranty was mere formality or pretense, or whether it was in fact given. **Illustration:**

    1. A executes a written guaranty to B of a debt then due from C. The guaranty is stated to be "in consideration of one dollar paid to me by B, the receipt of which is hereby acknowledged." The guaranty is binding whether the dollar is in fact paid or not.

c. Statutes. A guaranty may be binding by virtue of a seal or a statutory substitute for the seal. Although Uniform Commercial Code § 2-203 withdraws contracts for the sale of goods from the law of sealed instruments, § 2-701 provides that remedies for breach of collateral or ancillary obligations or promises are not impaired. Again, Uniform Commercial Code § 3-113 makes the provisions of the Code relating to commercial paper applicable despite the presence of a seal, but § 3-408 makes consideration unnecessary for an instrument or obligation thereon given in payment of or as security for an antecedent obligation of any kind.

d. Reliance. Paragraph (c) states the application of § 90 to reliance on a guaranty, with modifications appropriate to the particular type of case. Reliance commonly takes the form of an extension of new credit to the principal obligor or of forbearance to pursue him, and often can be found to have been bargained for. Where a written guaranty is executed in a commercial context, such reliance is extremely probable, though mixed motives on the part of the obligee may make specific proof difficult. Whether the guarantor is entitled to notice of the obligee's intention to act in such cases depends on the terms of the guaranty and on the circumstances. See § 54. Even in a non-commercial context, if the reliance is foreseeable and substantial, no further inquiry is necessary as to whether justice requires enforcement.

If the conditions of enforcement are met, the appropriate remedy is enforcement of the guaranty according to its terms. Difficult problems of measurement of the extent of the reliance are thereby avoided, and the guarantor is left to his recourse against the principal obligor.

The effect of repudiation of a guaranty on action taken by the obligee thereafter depends on the divisibility of the guaranty and rules relating to avoidable consequences and assurance of counter-performance. See §§ 31, 255, 350, 363.

Illustrations:

2. A owes $ 10,000 to B, a stockbroker. To prevent sale of A's stock held by B as collateral, C executes a written guaranty to B of A's account. A's father D subsequently executes a written guaranty to C against losses in the account. There are no further transactions in the account, but in reliance on D's guaranty C for two years refrains from liquidating the account, while the stock fluctuates in value. The guaranty is binding.

. . .

4. A draws checks on the B bank, forging the signature of A's father-in-law C as drawer. After the checks are paid and the forgeries discovered C promises B to make good the amount, since C wants no prosecution of A and no publicity about the matter. In reliance on C's promise B forbears for a month to seek evidence of the forgery or to seek recourse against A and solvent indorsers. C's promise is binding. Under Uniform Commercial Code § 3-404(2) the promise is binding without regard to reliance.

. . .

§ 89. Modification of Executory Contract

A promise modifying a duty under a contract not fully performed on either side is binding
(a) if the modification is fair and equitable in view of circumstances not anticipated by the parties when the contract was made; or
(b) to the extent provided by statute; or
(c) to the extent that justice requires enforcement in view of material change of position in reliance on the promise.

Comment:

a. Rationale. This Section relates primarily to adjustments in on-going transactions. Like offers and guaranties, such adjustments are ancillary to exchanges and have some of the same presumptive utility. See §§ 72, 87, 88. Indeed, paragraph (a) deals with bargains which are without consideration only because of the rule that performance of a legal duty to the promisor is not consideration. See § 73. This Section is also related to § 84 on waiver of conditions: it may apply to cases in which § 84 is inapplicable because a condition is material to the exchange or risk. As in cases governed by § 84, relation to a bargain tends to satisfy the cautionary and channeling functions of legal formalities. See Comment *c* to § 72. The Statute of Frauds may prevent enforcement in the absence of reliance. See §§ 149-50. Otherwise formal requirements are at a minimum.

b. Performance of legal duty. The rule of § 73 finds its modern justification in cases of promises made by mistake or induced by unfair pressure. Its application to cases where those elements are absent has been much criticized and is avoided if paragraph (a) of this Section is applicable. The limitation to a modification which is "fair and equitable" goes beyond absence of coercion and requires an objectively demonstrable reason for seeking a modification. Compare Uniform Commercial Code § 2-209 Comment. The reason for modification must rest in circumstances not "anticipated" as part of the context in which the contract was made, but a frustrating event may be unanticipated for this purpose if it was not adequately covered, even though it was foreseen as a remote possibility. When such a reason is present, the relative financial strength of the parties, the formality with which the modification is made, the extent to which it is performed or relied on and other circumstances may be relevant to show or negate imposition or unfair surprise.

The same result called for by paragraph (a) is sometimes reached on the ground that the original contract was "rescinded" by mutual agreement and that new promises were then made which furnished consideration for each other. That theory is rejected here because it is fictitious when the "rescission" and new agreement are simultaneous, and because if logically carried out it might uphold unfair and inequitable modifications. **Illustrations:**

1. By a written contract A agrees to excavate a cellar for B for a stated price. Solid rock is unexpectedly encountered and A so notifies B. A and B then orally agree that A will remove the rock at a unit price which is reasonable but nine times that used in computing the original price, and A completes the job. B is bound to pay the increased amount.

2. A contracts with B to supply for $ 300 a laundry chute for a building B has contracted to build for the Government for $ 150,000. Later A discovers that he made an error as to the type of material to be used and should have bid $ 1,200. A offers to supply the chute for $ 1000, eliminating overhead and profit. After ascertaining that other suppliers would charge more, B agrees. The new agreement is binding.

3. A is employed by B as a designer of coats at $ 90 a week for a year beginning November 1 under a written contract executed September 1. A is offered $ 115 a week by another employer and so informs B. A and B then agree that A will be paid $ 100 a week and in October execute a new written contract to that effect, simultaneously tearing up the prior contract. The new contract is binding.

4. A contracts to manufacture and sell to B 2,000 steel roofs for corn cribs at $ 60. Before A begins manufacture a threat of a nationwide steel strike raises the cost of steel about $ 10 per roof, and A and B agree orally to increase the price to $ 70 per roof. A thereafter manufactures and delivers 1700 of the roofs, and B pays for 1,500 of them at the increased price without protest, increasing the selling price of the corn cribs by $ 10. The new agreement is binding.

. . .

c. Statutes. Uniform Commercial Code § 2-209 dispenses with the requirement of consideration for an agreement modifying a contract for the sale of goods. Under that section the original contract can provide against oral modification, and the requirements of the Statute of Frauds must be met if the contract as modified is within its provisions; but an ineffective modification can operate as a waiver. The Comment indicates that extortion of a modification without legitimate commercial reason is ineffective as a violation of the duty of good faith imposed by the Code. A similar limitation may be applicable under statutes which give effect to a signed writing as a substitute for the seal, or under statutes which give effect to acceptance by the promisee of the modified performance. In some States statutes or constitutional provisions flatly forbid the payment of extra compensation to Government contractors.

d. Reliance. Paragraph (c) states the application of § 90 to modification of an executory contract in language adapted from Uniform Commercial Code § 2-209. Even though the promise is not binding when made, it may become binding in whole or in part by reason of action or forbearance by the promisee or third persons in reliance on it. In some cases the result can be viewed as based either on estoppel to contradict a representation of fact or on reliance on a promise. Ordinarily reliance by the promisee is reasonably foreseeable and makes the modification binding with respect to performance by the promisee under it and any return performance owed by the promisor. But as under § 84 the original terms can be reinstated for the future by reasonable notification received by the promisee unless reinstatement would be unjust in view of a change of position on his part. Compare Uniform Commercial Code § 2-209(5).

Illustrations:

6. A defaults in payment of a premium on a life insurance policy issued by B, an insurance company. Pursuant to the terms of the policy, B notifies A of the lapse of the policy and undertakes to continue the insurance until a specified future date, but by mistake specifies a date two months later than the insured would be entitled to under the policy. On inquiry by A two years later, B repeats the mistake, offering A an option to take a cash payment. A fails to do so, and dies one month before the specified date. B is bound to pay the insurance.

7. A is the lessee of an apartment house under a 99-year lease from B at a rent of $ 10,000 per year. Because of war conditions many of the apartments become vacant, and in order to enable A to stay in business B agrees to reduce the rent to $ 5,000. The reduced rent is paid for five years. The war being over, the apartments are then fully rented, and B notifies A that the full rent called for by the lease must be paid. A is bound to pay the full rent only from a reasonable time after the receipt of the notification.

. . .

§ 90. Promise Reasonably Inducing Action or Forbearance

(1) A promise which the promisor should reasonably expect to induce action or forbearance on the part of the promisee or a third person and which does induce such action or forbearance is binding if injustice can be avoided only by enforcement of the promise. The remedy granted for breach may be limited as justice requires.

(2) A charitable subscription or a marriage settlement is binding under Subsection (1) without proof that the promise induced action or forbearance.

Comment:

a. Relation to other rules. Obligations and remedies based on reliance are not peculiar to the law of contracts. This Section is often referred to in terms of "promissory estoppel," a phrase suggesting an extension of the doctrine of estoppel. Estoppel prevents a person from showing the truth contrary to a representation of fact made by him after another has relied on the representation. See Restatement, Second, Agency § 8B; Restatement, Second, Torts §§ 872, 894. Reliance is also a significant feature of numerous rules in the law of negligence, deceit and restitution. See, e.g., Restatement, Second, Agency §§ 354, 378; Restatement, Second, Torts §§ 323, 537; Restatement of Restitution § 55. In some cases those rules and this Section overlap; in others they provide analogies useful in determining the extent to which enforcement is necessary to avoid injustice.

It is fairly arguable that the enforcement of informal contracts in the action of assumpsit rested historically on justifiable reliance on a promise. Certainly reliance is one of the main bases for enforcement of the half-completed exchange, and the probability of reliance lends support to the enforcement of the executory exchange. See Comments to §§ 72, 75. This Section thus states a basic principle which often renders inquiry unnecessary as to the precise scope of the policy of enforcing bargains. Sections 87-89 state particular applications of the same principle to promises ancillary to bargains, and it also applies in a wide variety of non-commercial situations. See, e.g., § 94. **Illustration:**

1. A, knowing that B is going to college, promises B that A will give him $ 5,000 on completion of his course. B goes to college, and borrows and spends more than $ 5,000 for college expenses. When he has nearly completed his course, A notifies him of an intention to revoke the promise. A's promise is binding and B is entitled to payment on completion of the course without regard to whether his performance was "bargained for" under § 71.

b. Character of reliance protected. The principle of this Section is flexible. The promisor is affected only by reliance which he does or should foresee, and enforcement must be necessary to avoid injustice. Satisfaction of the latter requirement may depend on the reasonableness of the promisee's reliance, on its definite and substantial character in relation to the remedy sought, on the formality with which the promise is made, on the extent to which the evidentiary, cautionary, deterrent and channeling functions of form are met by the commercial setting or otherwise, and on the extent to which such other policies as the enforcement of bargains and the prevention of unjust enrichment are relevant. Compare Comment to § 72. The force of particular factors varies in different types of cases: thus reliance need not be of substantial character in charitable subscription cases, but must in cases of firm offers and guaranties. Compare Subsection (2) with §§ 87, 88. **Illustrations:**

2. A promises B not to foreclose, for a specified time, a mortgage which A holds on B's land. B thereafter makes improvements on the land. A's promise is binding and may be enforced by denial of foreclosure before the time has elapsed.

3. A sues B in a municipal court for damages for personal injuries caused by B's negligence. After the one year statute of limitations has run, B requests A to discontinue the action and start again in the superior court where the action can be consolidated with other actions against B arising out of the same accident. A does so. B's implied promise that no harm to A will result bars B from asserting the statute of limitations as a defense.

4. A has been employed by B for 40 years. B promises to pay A a pension of $ 200 per month when A retires. A retires and forbears to work elsewhere for several years while B pays the pension. B's promise is binding.

c. Reliance by third persons. If a promise is made to one party for the benefit of another, it is often foreseeable that the beneficiary will rely on the promise. Enforcement of the promise in such cases rests on the same basis and depends on the same factors as in cases of reliance by the promisee. Justifiable reliance by third persons who are not beneficiaries is less likely, but may sometimes reinforce the claim of the promisee or beneficiary. **Illustrations:**

5. A holds a mortgage on B's land. To enable B to obtain a loan, A promises B in writing to release part of the land from the mortgage upon payment of a stated sum. As A contemplated, C lends money to B on a second mortgage, relying on A's promise. The promise is binding and may be enforced by C.

6. A executes and delivers a promissory note to B, a bank, to give B a false appearance of assets, deceive the banking authorities, and enable the bank to continue to operate. After several years B fails and is taken over by C, a representative of B's creditors. A's note is enforceable by C.

7. A and B, husband and wife, are tenants by the entirety of a tract of land. They make an oral promise to B's niece C to give her the tract. B, C and C's husband expend money in building a house on the tract and C and her husband take possession and live there for several years until B dies. The expenditures by B and by C's husband are treated like those by C in determining whether justice requires enforcement of the promise against A.

d. Partial enforcement. A promise binding under this section is a contract, and full-scale enforcement by normal remedies is often appropriate. But the same factors which bear on whether any relief should be granted also bear on the character and extent of the remedy. In particular, relief may sometimes be limited to restitution or to damages or specific relief measured by the extent of the promisee's reliance rather than by the terms of the promise. See §§ 84, 89; compare Restatement, Second, Torts § 549 on damages for fraud. Unless there is unjust enrichment of the promisor, damages should not put the promisee in a better position than performance of the promise would have put him. See §§ 344, 349. In the case of a promise to make a gift it would rarely be proper to award consequential damages which would place a greater burden on the promisor than performance would have imposed. **Illustrations:**

8. A applies to B, a distributor of radios manufactured by C, for a "dealer franchise" to sell C's products. Such franchises are revocable at will. B erroneously informs A that C has ac-

cepted the application and will soon award the franchise, that A can proceed to employ salesmen and solicit orders, and that A will receive an initial delivery of at least 30 radios. A expends $ 1,150 in preparing to do business, but does not receive the franchise or any radios. B is liable to A for the $ 1,150 but not for the lost profit on 30 radios. Compare Restatement, Second, Agency § 329.

9. The facts being otherwise as stated in Illustration 8, B gives A the erroneous information deliberately and with C's approval and requires A to buy the assets of a deceased former dealer and thus discharge C's "moral obligation" to the widow. C is liable to A not only for A's expenses but also for the lost profit on 30 radios.

10. A, who owns and operates a bakery, desires to go into the grocery business. He approaches B, a franchisor of supermarkets. B states to A that for $ 18,000 B will establish A in a store. B also advises A to move to another town and buy a small grocery to gain experience. A does so. Later B advises A to sell the grocery, which A does, taking a capital loss and foregoing expected profits from the summer tourist trade. B also advises A to sell his bakery to raise capital for the supermarket franchise, saying "Everything is ready to go. Get your money together and we are set." A sells the bakery taking a capital loss on this sale as well. Still later, B tells A that considerably more than an $ 18,000 investment will be needed, and the negotiations between the parties collapse. At the point of collapse many details of the proposed agreement between the parties are unresolved. The assurances from B to A are promises on which B reasonably should have expected A to rely, and A is entitled to his actual losses on the sales of the bakery and grocery and for his moving and temporary living expenses. Since the proposed agreement was never made, however, A is not entitled to lost profits from the sale of the grocery or to his expectation interest in the proposed franchise from B.

11. A is about to buy a house on a hill. Before buying he obtains a promise from B, who owns adjoining land, that B will not build on a particular portion of his lot, where a building would obstruct the view from the house. A then buys the house in reliance on the promise. B's promise is binding, but will be specifically enforced only so long as A and his successors do not permanently terminate the use of the view.

12. A promises to make a gift of a tract of land to B, his son-in-law. B takes possession and lives on the land for 17 years, making valuable improvements. A then dispossesses B, and

specific performance is denied because the proof of the terms of the promise is not sufficiently clear and definite. B is entitled to a lien on the land for the value of the improvements, not exceeding their cost.

e. Gratuitous promises to procure insurance. This Section is to be applied with caution to promises to procure insurance. The appropriate remedy for breach of such a promise makes the promisor an insurer, and thus may result in a liability which is very large in relation to the value of the promised service. Often the promise is properly to be construed merely as a promise to use reasonable efforts to procure the insurance, and reliance by the promisee may be unjustified or may be justified only for a short time. Or it may be doubtful whether he did in fact rely. Such difficulties may be removed if the proof of the promise and the reliance are clear, or if the promise is made with some formality, or if part performance or a commercial setting or a potential benefit to the promisor provide a substitute for formality. **Illustrations:**

13. A, a bank, lends money to B on the security of a mortgage on B's new home. The mortgage requires B to insure the property. At the closing of the transaction A promises to arrange for the required insurance, and in reliance on the promise B fails to insure. Six months later the property, still uninsured, is destroyed by fire. The promise is binding.

14. A sells an airplane to B, retaining title to secure payment of the price. After the closing A promises to keep the airplane covered by insurance until B can obtain insurance. B could obtain insurance in three days but makes no effort to do so, and the airplane is destroyed after six days. A is not subject to liability by virtue of the promise.

f. Charitable subscriptions, marriage settlements, and other gifts. One of the functions of the doctrine of consideration is to deny enforcement to a promise to make a gift. Such a promise is ordinarily enforced by virtue of the promisee's reliance only if his conduct is foreseeable and reasonable and involves a definite and substantial change of position which would not have occurred if the promise had not been made. In some cases, however, other policies reinforce the promisee's claim. Thus the promisor might be unjustly enriched if he could reclaim the subject of the promised gift after the promisee has improved it.

Subsection (2) identifies two other classes of cases in which the promisee's claim is similarly reinforced. American courts have traditionally favored charitable subscriptions and marriage settlements, and have found consideration in many cases where the element of exchange was doubtful or nonexistent. Where recovery is rested on reliance in such cases, a probability of reliance is enough, and no effort is made to sort out mixed motives or to consider whether partial enforcement would be appropriate. **Illustrations:**

15. A promises B $ 5000, knowing that B desires thatsum for the purchase of a parcel of land. Induced thereby, B secures without any payment an option to buy the parcel. A then tells B that he withdraws his promise. A's promise is not binding.

16. A orally promises to give her son B a tract of land to live on. As A intended, B gives up a homestead elsewhere, takes possession of the land, lives there for a year and makes substantial improvements. A's promise is binding.

17. A orally promises to pay B, a university, $ 100,000 in five annual installments for the purposes of its fund-raising campaign then in progress. The promise is confirmed in writing by A's agent, and two annual installments are paid before A dies. The continuance of the fund-raising campaign by B is sufficient reliance to make the promise binding on A and his estate.

18. A and B are engaged to be married. In anticipation of the marriage A and his father C enter into a formal written agreement by which C promises to leave certain property to A by will. A's subsequent marriage to B is sufficient reliance to make the promise binding on C and his estate.

§ 91. Effect of Promises Enumerated in 82-90 When Conditional

If a promise within the terms of § 82-90 is in terms conditional or performable at a future time the promisor is bound thereby, but performance becomes due only upon the occurrence of the condition or upon the arrival of the specified time.

Illustration:

1. A owes B a debt of $ 60, but B's claim is barred by the statute of limitations. A promises in a signed writing to pay B in satisfaction of the claim $ 5 monthly for a year. The promise is binding but B's only right is to the payment of $ 5 at the end of each month.

§ 92. To Whom Promises Enumerated in 82-85 Must Be Made

The new promise referred to in §§ 82-85 is not binding unless it is made to a person who is then an obligee of the antecedent duty.

Comment:

a. Rationale. The promises referred to in §§ 82-85 are binding without mutual assent or consideration. In the absence of consideration or reliance, there is need to distinguish between promises and expressions of expectation or good intention. Even a writing in the form of a promise is not effective if it is not delivered to anyone or is delivered only to the agent of the writer. An informal statement to a third person is likewise ineffective, even though words of promise are used, until there is communication to the promisee or to someone acting on his behalf. But a written promise is made when it is mailed to the promisee. Compare § 63. And delivery to a third person may have the same effect if no power of revocation is reserved and the promisor manifests an intention that the contents of the writing be communicated to the promisee. Compare §§ 101-03. **Illustrations:**

1. A holds bonds issued by B, a city, which are overdue as to principal and interest. B's city treasurer writes a letter to B's fiscal agents in another city, acknowledging B's indebtedness on the bonds held by A and instructing the fiscal agents to redeem the bonds to the extent of the fund in their hands. The letter is not binding as a new promise by B to A.

. . .

b. Obligees: promisee, beneficiary and surety. The new promise must be made to a person to whom the antecedent duty runs at the time of the new promise. Where the duty was created by a contract for the benefit of a third person, both the original promisee and the beneficiary may be obligees. See §§ 305-06. If there are several obligees of the same duty, a new promise to one may be binding for the benefit of all. A surety of the promisor is an obligee to the extent of any right to exoneration which would exist in the absence of the defenses referred to in §§ 82-85. See Restatement of Security §§ 108, 112. **Illustration:**

3. A owes B $ 500 on a negotiable note. C, an indorser of the note, was duly charged at maturity. B's rights against A and C are barred by the statute of limitations. A promises C to pay B the amount of the note. The promise is binding for the benefit of B.

c. Obligees: assignor, assignee and distributee. When an obligation is assigned or transferred by operation of law the assignee or transferee becomes an obligee and a new promise to him is binding. In some cases the assignor may also be an obligee, as where he retains a beneficial interest after making an assignment as collateral security. In other cases the assignor may act as agent of the assignee. In cases of transfers to a trustee or other representative there may be ambiguity as to who is an obligee, and a new promise to one beneficially interested in the obligation may be binding. Thus after the death of an obligee a new promise to a distributee of his estate may be binding. **Illustrations:**

4. A, induced by B's fraud, contracts to pay B $ 100. B assigns to C who knows of the fraud. A with knowledge of the fraud now promises C to pay C $ 100 as promised originally to B. The promise to C is binding.

5. A owes B $ 500 on a negotiable promissory note. B's right against A is barred by the statute of limitations. A promises B to pay the note. Subsequently B indorses the note to C. C may recover from A.

. . .

§ 93. Promises Enumerated in 82-85 Made in Ignorance of Facts

A promise within the terms of §§ 82-85 is not binding unless the promisor knew or had reason to know the essential facts of the previous transaction to which the promise relates, but his knowledge of the legal effect of the facts is immaterial.

Illustrations:

1. A secures from B a promise to pay $ 100 by fraudulently representing that a watch given as consideration for the promise is made of gold. B, knowing the facts but not knowing that A's fraud justifies him in avoiding the transaction, promises to pay the $ 100. The promise is binding.

2. A, an indorser of a note, did not receive due notification of its dishonor by the maker. Subsequently, in ignorance of the fact that the lack of notification had discharged him, A promises B, the holder of the note, to pay it. The promise is binding.

Topic 3. Contracts Under Seal; Writing as a Statutory Substitute for the Seal

§ 94. Stipulations

A promise or agreement with reference to a pending judicial proceeding, made by a party to the proceeding or his attorney, is binding without consideration. By statute or rule of court such an agreement is generally binding only

(a) if it is in writing and signed by the party or attorney, or

(b) if it is made or admitted in the presence of the court, or

(c) to the extent that justice requires enforcement in view of material change of position in reliance on the promise or agreement.

Comment:

a. Consideration. Such agreements as are within the rules stated in the Section are called stipulations. Stipulations with respect to matters of form and procedure serve the convenience of the parties to litigation and often serve to simplify and expedite the proceeding. In some cases they are supported by the policy of favoring compromise in order to reduce the volume of litigation. Hence they are favored by the courts and enforced without regard to consideration.

b. Formality. Statutes or rules of court in most jurisdictions require stipulations to be in writing. In some States other formalities, such as filing in court, are also required. Such requirements relieve the courts of the duty to decide unseemly disputes between attorneys whose memories differ as to the terms of the agreement, disputes which would often be highly technical, time-consuming, and collateral to the matter in litigation. But a lawyer must comply with local customs of courtesy and practice unless he gives timely notice of his intent not to comply. American Bar Association, Code of Professional Responsibility, Disciplinary Rule 7-106(c)(5). Thus, it appears that it is dishonorable for an attorney to avoid performance of an agreement fairly made because it is not reduced to writing. Cf. American Bar Association, Former Canons of Professional Ethics 25. Admitted stipulations and stipulations made in open court are enforced without regard to form. And where a stipulation has been acted on, the court will not let a party take unfair advantage of the action he has induced. See § 90. **Illustration:**

1. A owes a debt to B secured by a mortgage. In foreclosure proceedings A signs and files in court a stipulation waiving service of all papers, relying on B's oral promise to bid the amount of the debt and costs at a sale of the mortgaged premises. At the sale B bids less and a judgment is entered against A for the deficiency. Notwithstanding a rule of court requiring a writing, the court may order a resale on A's application.

95. Requirements for Sealed Contract or Written Contract or Instrument

(1) In the absence of statute a promise is binding without consideration if

(a) it is in writing and sealed; and

(b) the document containing the promise is delivered; and (c) the promisor and promisee are named in the document or so described as to be capable of identification when it is delivered.

(2) When a statute provides in effect that a written contract or instrument is binding without consideration or that lack of consideration is an affirmative defense to an action on a written contract or instrument, in order to be subject to the statute a promise must either

(a) be expressed in a document signed or otherwise assented to by the promisor and delivered; or

(b) be expressed in a writing or writings to which both promisor and promisee manifest assent.

. . .

§ 96. What Constitutes a Seal

(1) A seal is a manifestation in tangible and conventional form of an intention that a document be sealed.

(2) A seal may take the form of a piece of wax, a wafer or other substance affixed to the document or of an impression made on the document.

(3) By statute or decision in most States in which the seal retains significance a seal may take the form of a written or printed seal, word, scrawl or other sign.

. . .

§ 97. When a Promise Is Sealed

A written promise is sealed if the promisor affixes or impresses a seal on the document or adopts a seal already thereon.

. . .

98. Adoption of a Seal by Delivery

Unless extrinsic circumstances manifest a contrary intention, the delivery of a written promise by the promisor amounts to the adoption of any seal then on the document which has apparent reference to his signature or to the signature of another party to the document.

. . .

§ 99. Adoption of the Same Seal by Several Parties

Any number of parties to the same instrument may adopt one seal.

. . .

§ 100. Recital of Sealing or Delivery

A recital of the sealing or of the delivery of a written promise is not essential to its validity as a contract under seal and is not conclusive of the fact of sealing or delivery unless a statute makes a recital of sealing the equivalent of a seal.

. . .

§ 101. Delivery

A written promise, sealed or unsealed, may be delivered by the promisor in escrow, conditionally to the promisee, or unconditionally.

. . .

§ 102. Unconditional Delivery

A written promise is delivered unconditionally when the promisor puts it out of his possession and manifests an intention that it is to take effect at once according to its terms.

Comment:

a. Transfer of possession without delivery. "Delivery" is often used in the sense of voluntary transfer of possession. See Uniform Commercial Code § 1-201(14). But as it is used in this Section more is required. There is no delivery if the promisor manifests an intention to reserve a power of revocation. Thus manual tradition to the promisor's own servant or agent is not delivery; nor is a transfer of possession for the purpose of inspection or discussion, for use as a sample or model, or merely for safekeeping. But mailing to the promisee is sufficient if the promisor manifests an intention that the promise take immediate effect. Compare § 63. **Illustrations:**

1. A hands to B a sealed promise by A in which C is named as promisee, and requests B to give the document to C unless B receives contrary instructions from A. There is no delivery and no contract under seal until the document is delivered to C.

. . .

§ 103. Delivery in Escrow; Conditional Delivery to the Promisee

(1) A written promise is delivered in escrow by the promisor when he puts it into the possession of a person other than the promisee without reserving a power of revocation and manifests an intention that the document is to take effect according to its terms upon the occurrence of a stated condition but not otherwise.

(2) A written promise is delivered conditionally to the promisee when the promisor puts it into the possession of the promisee without reserving a power of revocation and manifests an intention that the document is to take effect according to its terms upon the occurrence of a stated condition but not otherwise.

(3) Delivery of a written promise in escrow or its conditional delivery to the promisee has the same effect as unconditional delivery would have if the requirement of the condition were expressed in the writing.

(4) In the absence of a statute modifying the significance of a seal, delivery of a sealed promise in escrow or its conditional delivery to the promisee is irrevocable for the time specified by the promisor for the occurrence of the condition, or, if no time is specified, for a reasonable time.

Comment:

a. Escrow. Like "scroll" and "scrawl," the word "escrow" is derived from the Norman-French word for a writing or a written instrument. It has come in practice to refer to a security device: one or both parties to a transaction deposit property or an instrument with a third party until some condition has occurred. The property or instrument may be referred to as "the escrow"; the delivery is said to be "in escrow."

. . .

§ 104. Acceptance or Disclaimer by the Promisee

(1) Neither acceptance by the promisee nor knowledge by him of the existence of a promise is essential to the formation of a contract by the delivery of a written promise which is binding without consideration.

(2) A promisee who has not manifested assent to a written promise may, within a reasonable time after learning of its existence and terms, render it inoperative by disclaimer. (3) Acceptance or disclaimer is irrevocable.

. . .

§ 105. Acceptance Where Return Promise Is Contemplated

Where a conveyance or a document containing a promise also purports to contain a return promise by the grantee or promisee, acceptance by the grantee or promisee is essential to create any contractual obligation other than an option contract binding on the grantor or promisor.

. . .

§ 106. What Amounts to Acceptance of Instrument

Acceptance of a conveyance or of a document containing a promise is a manifestation of assent to the terms thereof made, either before or after delivery, in accordance with any requirements imposed by the grantor or promisor. If the acceptance occurs before delivery and is not binding as an option contract, it is revocable until the moment of delivery.

. . .

§ 107. Creation of Unsealed Contract by Acceptance by Promisee

Where a grantee or promisee accepts a sealed document which purports to contain a return promise by him, he makes the return promise. But if he does not sign or seal the document his promise is not under seal, and whether it is binding depends on the rules governing unsealed contracts.

. . .

§ 108. Requirement of Naming or Describing Promisor and Promisee

A promise under seal is not binding without consideration unless both the promisor and the promisee are named in the document or so described as to be capable of identification when it is delivered.

Comment:

a. Historical Note. In the common-law courts of medieval England the sealed instrument was treated as almost complete in itself, and evidence of extrinsic circumstances was not permitted even to show that the instrument was voidable for fraud. A different view was taken in equity, and in modern times extrinsic evidence may be relevant to show conditional delivery or for a variety of other purposes. The rule of this Section is a remnant of the former strictness, and it may not be followed where the law of seals has been changed by statute or decision. Compare Restatement, Second, Agency §§ 151, 191, 296, under which a principal is not a party to a sealed instrument unless he appears in the instrument as a party. Where the seal is not essential to the validity of the contract, it may be treated as superfluous, and a party not named in the writing may then have rights or duties under the rules governing unsealed contracts.

. . .

§ 109. Enforcement of a Sealed Contract by Promisee Who Does Not Sign or Seal It

The promisee of a promise under seal is not precluded from enforcing it as a sealed contract because he has not signed or sealed the document, unless his doing so was a condition of the delivery, whether or not the document contains a promise by him.

. . .

Chapter 5

The Statute of Frauds

§ 110. Classes of Contracts Covered

(1) The following classes of contracts are subject to a statute, commonly called the Statute of Frauds, forbidding enforcement unless there is a written memorandum or an applicable exception:

(a) a contract of an executor or administrator to answer for a duty of his decedent (the executor administrator provision);

(b) a contract to answer for the duty of another (the suretyship provision);

(c) a contract made upon consideration of marriage (the marriage provision);

(d) a contract for the sale of an interest in land (the land contract provision);

(e) a contract that is not to be performed within one year from the making thereof (the one-year provision).

(2) The following classes of contracts, which were traditionally subject to the Statute of Frauds, are now governed by Statute of Frauds provisions of the Uniform Commercial Code:

(a) a contract for the sale of goods for the price of $ 500 or more (Uniform Commercial Code § 2-201);

(b) a contract for the sale of securities (Uniform Commercial Code § 8-319);

(c) a contract for the sale of personal property not otherwise covered, to the extent of enforcement by way of action or defense beyond $ 5,000 in amount or value of remedy (Uniform Commercial Code § 1-206).

(3) In addition the Uniform Commercial Code requires a writing signed by the debtor for an agreement which creates or provides for a security interest in personal property or fixtures not in the possession of the secured party.

(4) Statutes in most states provide that no acknowledgment or promise is sufficient evidence of a new or continuing contract to take a case out of the operation of a statute of limitations unless made in some writing signed by the party to be charged, but that the statute does not alter the effect of any payment of principal or interest.

(5) In many states other classes of contracts are subject to a requirement of a writing.

Comment:

a. Classes of contracts. The five classes of contracts listed in Subsection (1) were included in different language in § 4 of the English Statute of Frauds, enacted in 1677. The English Statute was repealed in 1954 except for the suretyship and land contract provisions. Subsections (2) and (3) refer to four separate Statute of Frauds sections found in the Uniform Commercial Code, which displace § 4 of the Uniform Sales Act and § 17 of the English statute. The Code sections are not elaborated in this Restatement. Subsection (4) is a statement of a provision of Lord Tenterden's Act, 1828, which has been widely copied in the United States. As to the extent of enactment of these and other similar statutes, see the Statutory Note preceding this Section. The formal contracts referred to in § 6 of this Restatement are not affected by the Statute of Frauds, but in some cases are subject to separate statutes containing formal requirements.

b. Overlap of classes. The clauses of the English statute apply separately; one contract may be within more than one clause of the statute, and facts which except it from one class may not except it from another. Thus contracts in consideration of marriage or for the sale of land or goods may also be contracts not to be performed within a year, and the statutory requirements in one clause may be satisfied and those of another clause unsatisfied. **Illustration:**

1. A and B orally agree to marry three years later. The contract is unenforceable because not to be performed within a year, even though it is excepted from the provision for contracts in consideration of marriage.

c. Variations in the statutes. The English Statute of Frauds and many American statutes take the form, "No action shall be brought whereby to charge . . . unless . . . . " In some states non-complying contracts are said to be "void" or "invalid" or "not binding," but in spite of such differences there is much similarity in the interpretation given. Lord Tenterden's Act and statutes modeled on it, however, are generally construed to require the acknowledgment or promise itself to be in writing; under such statutes a subsequent memorandum does not render enforceable a prior oral promise. See § 136.

d. Consequences of non-compliance. The consequences of non-compliance are the subject of Topic 7, §§ 138-47. In general a contract subject to the Statute of Frauds is unenforceable if the requirements of the statute are not satisfied. See § 8. The Statute does not in general bar the remedy of restitution; indeed, recovery of benefits conferred pursuant to an unenforceable contract is a standard remedy. See § 375; Restatement of Restitution § 108. Where there has been part performance or other action in reliance on an unenforceable contract, the effect is in some situations to make the contract fully enforceable, in others to make particular remedies available. See, e.g., § 129. Even though no such rule is applicable, the circumstances may be such that justice requires enforcement of the promise. To the extent that justice so requires, the promise is then enforced by virtue of the doctrine of estoppel or by virtue of reliance on a promise notwithstanding the Statute. See § 139.

§ 111. Contract of Executor or Administrator

A contract of an executor or administrator to answer personally for a duty of his decedent is within the Statute of Frauds if a similar contract to answer for the duty of a living person would be within the Statute as a contract to answer for the duty of another.

Comment:

a. Analogy to suretyship. The first clause of § 4 of the English Statute of Frauds is treated as a special application of the suretyship provision of the second clause. Where the principal obligor dies before the promise in question is made, the case may not fall precisely within the usual definition of suretyship. See Restatement of Security § 82. But the situation is similar, and similar rules are applied. If there was no obligation before the death of the decedent, the promise is not within this clause. Where the executor or administrator makes a contract on behalf of the estate, the creditor's right against the estate ordinarily depends on the right of the executor or administrator to exoneration. Compare Restatement, Second, Trusts §§ 266-71A.

Illustrations:

1. S, executor of D, promises C, a creditor of D at the time of D's death, in consideration of C's promise to forego part of the debt, to guarantee payment of the balance by the estate. S's promise is within the executor provision.

. . .

b. Exceptions. The executor provision is subject to the same exceptions as the suretyship provision. See Topic 2, §§ 112-23; Restatement of Security §§ 89-100. Thus the rule relating to novations stated in § 115 and the "main purpose" rule stated in § 116 are similarly applied to promises of executors or administrators.

Illustrations:

3. S, executor of D, promises C, a creditor of D at the time of D's death, in consideration of C's promise never to prove his claim against D's estate, to pay the debt. S's promise is not within the executor provision. See § 115.

. . .

§ 112. Requirement of Suretyship

A contract is not within the Statute of Frauds as a contract to answer for the duty of another unless the promisee is an obligee of the other's duty, the promisor is a surety for the other, and the promisee knows or has reason to know of the suretyship relation.

Comment:

a. The statutory purpose. In general the primary purpose of the Statute of Frauds is assumed to be evidentiary. See Statutory Note preceding § 110. In the case of suretyship contracts, however, the Statute also serves the cautionary function of guarding the promisor against ill-considered action. The suretyship provision is not limited to important or complex contracts, but is limited to suretyship and to promises made to an obligee of the principal obligation. Such promises serve a useful purpose, and the requirement of consideration is commonly met by the same promise or performance which is consideration for the principal obligation. See Comment to § 72; compare § 88. But the motivation of the surety is often essentially gratuitous, his obligation depends on a contingency which may seem remote at the time of contracting, and natural formalities which often attend an extension of credit are likely not to provide reliable evidence of the existence and terms of the surety's undertaking. Hence the requirement of a writing. Reliance of the kinds usual in suretyship situations -- extension of credit or forbearance to pursue the principal obligor -- does not render the requirement inapplicable.

b. *"Debt, default or miscarriages."* The word "duty" is used here as a substitute for the words "debt, default or miscarriages" used in the English statute to describe the principal obligation. Those words and corresponding words in American statutes include all kinds of duties recognized by law, whether or not contractual and whether already incurred or to be incurred in the future. The person owing the duty is called the principal debtor or obligor. The duty may be conditional, voidable or unenforceable; but if there is no duty at all, the Statute does not apply. **Illustrations:**

1. D commits a tort against C. S promises C orally for consideration to pay C the damages which C has suffered from the tort if D fails to do so. S's promise is within the Statute of Frauds, since D is under a direct duty to C, and S's promise is to perform D's duty if D fails to do so.

2. S promises C orally to guarantee the performance of any duty that D may incur to C within the ensuing year. Relying on this promise, C enters into contracts with D, by which D undertakes within the year to sell materials for a house and to act as supervising architect during its construction. D, without excuse, fails to perform his contract. S's promise is within the Statute of Frauds.

3. D, an infant, obtains goods on credit from C, who is induced to part with them by S's oral guaranty that D will pay the price as agreed. The

goods are not necessaries but D is subject to a duty, though it is voidable. S's promise is within the Statute of Frauds.

. . .

c. *Promisor must be surety.* The suretyship provision applies only if there is a principal obligation "of another" than the promisor. The promisor must promise as a surety for the principal obligor. Whether the promisor and the other are surety and principal depends on their contract or relation to each other. The essential elements of the relation are that they are bound for the same performance and that as between them the other rather than the promisor should perform. See Restatement of Security § 82. A promise to be surety for part of the principal obligation is within the Statute, but a promise of a distinct performance is not, even though its purpose is to render more certain the performance of the principal obligation. **Illustrations:**

5. S obtains goods from C on this oral promise: "Charge them to D, and, if he does not pay for them, I will." S has no authority to charge the goods to D, and D makes no promise to pay for them. S's promise is not within the suretyship provision of the Statute of Frauds, since D is under no duty, and hence is not a principal obligor.

6. In consideration of the delivery of goods by C to D at S's request, S orally promises to pay the price of them. S's promise is not within the Statute of Frauds, since D is under no duty.

. . .

d. *Promisee must be obligee; "reason to know."* The suretyship provision does not apply to a promise unless the promisee is the person to whom the principal obligation is owed, or who is entitled to damages for the default or miscarriage. Moreover, the obligee-promisee must know or have reason to know of the suretyship relation, either from the terms of his contract with the principal or with the surety or from extrinsic facts. As to what constitutes "reason to know," see Comment *b* to § 19. **Illustrations:**

9. S, for consideration, orally promises E to pay a debt of E's son D to C, if D fails to pay it at maturity. S's promise is not within the Statute of Frauds because it was made to E, not to the creditor C.

. . .

§ 113. Promises of the Same Performance for the Same Consideration

Where promises of the same performance are made by two persons for a consideration which inures to the benefit of only one of them, the promise of the other is within the Statute of Frauds as a contract to answer for the duty of another, whether or not the promise is in terms conditional on default by the one to whose benefit the consideration inures, unless

(a) the other is not a surety for the one to whose benefit the consideration inures; or

(b) the promises are in terms joint and do not create several duties or joint and several duties; or

(c) the promisee neither knows nor has reason to know that the consideration does not inure to the benefit of both promisors.

Comment:

a. Rationale. This Section provides for the application of the rule of § 112 to a common situation, and makes an exception for cases of joint duties. Unless a contrary intention is manifested, the fact that promises of the same performance are made by two persons for a consideration which inures to the benefit of only one of them sufficiently shows that the other is a surety. A promisee who has reason to know that the consideration inures to the benefit of only one has sufficient reason to know of the suretyship relation to satisfy the requirement of § 112.

b. Joint obligations. Historically, joint promisors were treated for many purposes as a unit. Hence as against one joint promisor the obligation of his co-promisor was not treated as that "of another" within the Statute of Frauds, even though a suretyship relation in fact existed between them. In modern times the historic rules governing joint obligations have been greatly modified by statute or decision in most states. See Chapter 13. But where the distinction between joint duties and joint and several duties retains significance, the suretyship provision of the Statute of Frauds does not apply to suretyship between joint promisors.

Illustrations:

1. D and S jointly and orally promise C to pay C for goods which C knows are to be delivered for the exclusive benefit of D. If S is under no several duty, his promise is not within the Statute of Frauds.

2. The facts being otherwise as stated in Illustration 1, the promise is joint and several. S's promise is within the Statute of Frauds.

3. The facts being otherwise as stated in Illustration 2, C has no reason to know that the goods are not for the benefit of both parties. S's promise is not within the Statute of Frauds.

§ 114. Independent Duty of Promisor

A contract to perform or otherwise to satisfy all or part of a duty of a third person to the promisee is not within the Statute of Frauds as a contract to answer for the duty of another if, by the terms of the promise when it is made, performance thereof can involve no more than

(a) the application of funds or property held by the promisor for the purpose, or

(b) performance of any other duty owing, irrespective of his promise, by the promisor to the promisee, or

(c) performance of a duty which is either owing, irrespective of his promise, by the promisor to the third person, or which the promisee reasonably believes to be so owing.

Comment:

a. Rationale. Where the promisor, if he keeps his promise, will be doing no more than he is bound to do by reason of a duty other than that imposed by the promise, the promise is not within the Statute. Even though the promisor is a surety, he promises to answer for his own obligation as well as that of another and is not within the reason of the Statute. The terms of the promise will commonly refer to the independent duty, but need not do so. The independent duty may exist when the promise is made or may arise subsequently.

b. Application of funds. Subsection (a) deals

primarily with cases where the promisor is a trustee and the promisee a beneficiary of the trust, although the trust relationship is not essential. In such cases the promise usually shows by its terms the independent duty and the limitation of the promise. To the extent that the promise goes beyond the duty, the case is not within Subsection (a).

Illustrations:

    1. D owes C $ 100 and pays that sum to S in trust to pay it to C. Then or thereafter S orally promises C to pay D's debt. Whether or not C knows of the trust, C acquires an enforceable right against S.

. . .

c. Other independent duties. Where the promisor merely promises to perform an independent duty owed to the promisee or to the principal obligor, the promise is not within the Statute. In such cases the terms of the promise often do not disclose the independent duty. Where the promisee in good faith believes, when the promise is made, that such a duty is owed by the promisor to his co-obligor, the same rule is applied even though the duty does not in fact exist. **Illustrations:**

    3. S is a member of a partnership. After he retires but before the debts of the partnership are paid, S orally promises C, a partnership creditor, to pay the amount due him. The promise is not within the Statute of Frauds.

    4. S, at D's request, orally promises C to guarantee the payment by D to C of the price of any goods sold by C to D, to the extent of the indebtedness S may owe D at the time when C notifies S that D has made default. C thereupon sells goods to D. S's promise is not within the Statute of Frauds.

. . .

§ 115. Novation

A contract that is itself accepted in satisfaction of a previously existing duty of a third person to the promisee is not within the Statute of Frauds as a contract to answer for the duty of another.

Comment:

a. This Section relates to novations. It makes no difference whether the new promisor promises the same performance as that formerly due from the first obligor or a different performance. The promise is not one to answer for another's duty since that other ceases to be under a duty when the new promise becomes binding, and the promisor is not a surety. The case must be distinguished where performance of the new promise -- not the promise itself -- is to be taken in satisfaction of the old duty.

§ 116. Main Purpose; Advantage to Surety

A contract that all or part of a duty of a third person to the promisee shall be satisfied is not within the Statute of Frauds as a promise to answer for the duty of another if the consideration for the promise is in fact or apparently desired by the promisor mainly for his own economic advantage, rather than in order to benefit the third person. If, however, the consideration is merely a premium for insurance, the contract is within the Statute.

Comment:

a. Rationale. This Section states what is often called the "main purpose" or "leading object" rule. Where the surety-promisor's main purpose is his own pecuniary or business advantage, the gratuitous or sentimental element often present in suretyship is eliminated, the likelihood of disproportion in the values exchanged between promisor and promisee is reduced, and the commercial context commonly provides evidentiary safeguards. Thus there is less need for cautionary or evidentiary formality than in other cases of suretyship. The situation is comparable to a sale or purchase of a third person's obligation, which is also outside the purposes of the suretyship provision of the Statute of Frauds. See §§ 121, 122. Historically, the rule could be reconciled with the words of the Statute on the ground that a promisor who received a bargained-for benefit could be sued in debt or *indebitatus assumpsit*; hence he promised to pay his own debt rather than the debt "of another", and the promise was not "special" in the sense that special assumpsit was the only appropriate remedy. In modern times, however, the rule is applied in terms of its reason rather than to accord with abandoned procedural categories.

b. *Factors affecting application of the rule.* The fact that there is consideration for the surety's promise is insufficient to bring the rule into play. Slight and indirect possible advantage to the promisor is similarly insufficient. The expected advantage must be such as to justify the conclusion that his main purpose in making the promise is to advance his own interests. Facts such as the following tend to indicate such a main purpose when there is an expected pecuniary or business advantage: prior default, inability or repudiation of the principal obligor; forbearance of the creditor to enforce a lien on property in which the promisor has an interest or which he intends to use; equivalence between the value of the benefit and the amount promised; lack of participation by the principal obligor in the making of the surety's promise; a larger transaction to which the suretyship is incidental. The benefit may be supplied to the promisor by the promisee, by the principal obligor, or by some

other person; if it is substantial and meets the main purpose test it may come indirectly through benefit to the principal obligor. **Illustrations:**

1. D owes C $ 1,000. C is about to levy an attachment on D's factory. S, who is a friend of D's desiring to prevent his friend's financial ruin, orally promises C that if C will forbear to take legal proceedings against D for three months S will pay D's debt if D fails to do so. S has no purpose to benefit himself and C has no reason to suppose so. S's promise is not enforceable.

2. D owes C $ 1,000. C is about to levy an attachment on D's factory. S, who is also a creditor of D's, fearing that the attachment will ruin D's business and thereby destroy his own chance of collecting his claim, orally promises C that if C will forbear to take legal proceedings against D for three months, S will pay D's debt if D fails to do so. S's promise is enforceable.

3. D contracts with S to build a house for S. C contracts with D to furnish materials for the purpose. D, in violation of his contract with C, fails to pay C for some of the materials furnished. C justifiably refuses to furnish further materials. S orally promises C, that if C will continue to furnish D with materials that C had previously agreed to furnish, S will pay the price not only for the materials already furnished but also for the remaining materials if D fails to do so. S's promise is enforceable.

. . .

§ 117. Promise to Sign a Written Contract of Suretyship

A promise to sign a written contract as a surety for the performance of a duty owed to the promisee or to sign a negotiable instrument for the accommodation of a person other than the promisee is within the Statute of Frauds.

Comment:

a. *Scope.* The promises covered by the Section are not in terms promises to answer for a duty of another. They are promises to execute written instruments by which the promisor will on signing undertake to answer for such a duty. In substance, however, such promises, if binding, subject the promisor to an action if the performance due from the obligor is not rendered. The Section is applicable whether the promise

relates to an existing duty or to one expected to arise in the future. **Illustrations:**

1. In consideration of a loan by C to D, S orally promises C to execute a written instrument guaranteeing the debt. S's promise is within the Statute.

2. D owes C $ 1,000. In consideration of C's forbearance to sue D, S orally promises C that S will sign as acceptor for the accommodation of D a draft for $ 1,000 to be drawn by D. S's promise is within the Statute.

§ 118. Promise to Indemnify a Surety

A promise to indemnify against liability or loss made to induce the promisee to become a surety is not within the Statute of Frauds as a contract to answer for the duty of another.

Comment:

a. Non-surety indemnitor. Where an indemnitor is not a surety, his promise to indemnify is not within the Statute of Frauds. See § 112. For example, a promise to indemnify a surety may be made by the principal obligor or by a person who has assumed the obligation as principal obligor. Or the person assumed to be principal obligor may not be subject to the assumed duty. **Illustrations:**

     1. I promises to indemnify S if he will guarantee I's obligation to C. I's promise is not within the Statute of Frauds. S's promise is.

     2. I promises to indemnify S if he will sign an accommodation note to C for I's benefit. I's promise is not within the Statute of Frauds.

. . .

b. Indemnitor as surety. The principal obligor has a duty to exonerate or reimburse a surety. See Restatement of Security §§ 104, 112. A promise to indemnify the surety has sometimes been treated as a promise to answer for the default of the principal obligor in the event of his failure to exonerate or reimburse the surety. Such treatment is appropriate when it accords with the understanding of the parties. But commonly the parties treat the promise to indemnify as a promise to a prospective debtor rather than as a promise to a prospective creditor. So viewed, the promise is not within the Statute. See §§ 112, 123. Many such cases are also within the main purpose rule. See § 116. In any event they do not ordinarily present the need for cautionary and evidentiary formalities which the Statute is designed to meet.

Illustrations:

     5. To induce C, a commercial surety company, to file a bond in an action against D company, S gives C a written guaranty against loss. After judgment against D company, I, a stockholder, orally promises S to indemnify him against loss. Unless I's promise is within the main purpose rule, it is within the Statute of Frauds.

. . .

§ 119. Assumption of Duty by Another

A contract not within the Statute of Frauds as a contract to answer for the duty of another when made is not brought within it by a subsequent promise of another person to assume performance of the duty as principal obligor.

Comment:

a. Scope. An obligor originally bound as a principal debtor may become a surety by agreement with another who subsequently assumes the duty, but this will not make the original promise subject to the Statute of Frauds. The rule stated in this Section applies, for example, where a partner retires from a partnership and the remaining partners agree to assume all of the partnership obligations. If the obligation on which the retiring partner was originally bound was oral, it does not become unenforceable merely because, as between the retiring partner and the others, the retiring partner becomes a surety.

§ 120. Obligations on Negotiable Instruments

(1) An obligation on a negotiable instrument or a guaranty written on the instrument is not within the Statute of Frauds.

(2) A promise to pay a negotiable instrument, made by a party to it who has been or may be discharged by the holder's failure or delay in making presentment or giving notice of dishonor or in making protest, is not within the Statute of Frauds.

. . .

§ 121. Contract of Assignor or Factor

(1) A contract by the assignor of a right that the obligor of the assigned right will perform his duty is not within the Statute of Frauds as a contract to answer for the duty of another.
(2) A contract by an agent with his principal that a purchaser of the principal's goods through the agent will pay their price to the principal is not within the Statute of Frauds as a contract to answer for the duty of another.

Comment:

a. Rationale. The promisors referred to in this Section become sureties for the debts of others, but the promises are commonly made in contexts which provide evidence and eliminate the need of cautionary formality. The assignor's promise is ordinarily made for a consideration wholly for his own benefit. See § 116. The selling agent who guarantees customers' accounts is commonly called a *"del credere* factor"; an important inducement for the promise is his desire to advance his own interest. In addition, the guaranty is likely to be part of a course of business rather than an isolated transaction.

Illustrations:

1. S holds a note made by D payable to bearer, and sells and delivers it to C, orally guaranteeing that D will pay the note. S's promise is not within the Statute.

...

§ 122. Contract to Buy a Right From the Obligee

A contract to purchase a right which the promisee has or may acquire against a third person is not within the Statute of Frauds as a contract to answer for the duty of another.

Comment:

a. Contract to buy. Ordinarily a promise to buy a right and a promise to pay the debt of another are quite different transactions. A promise to buy is not within the suretyship provision of the Statute of Frauds, but it may be within other provisions, particularly Uniform Commercial Code §§ 1-206, 8-319, 9-203. See § 110; Statutory Note preceding § 110. **Illustration:**

1. D owes C $ 1,000 on open account. S, who specializes in the purchase of slow accounts, orally promises to buy C's right against D for $ 800 if assignment is made within three months. At the end of three months, C tenders S an assignment of the account. S's promise is not within the suretyship provision of the Statute of Frauds.

b. Suretyship in form of purchase. Where a promise to buy a debt is conditional on the debtor's default and the amount to be paid is the same as if the debt had been guaranteed, the consequences of a contract to purchase and a contract of a surety are the same. The distinction between a contract to buy and a contract of a surety does not lie in the formal difference in the words used but in the reality of the transaction. For the purposes of the Statute of Frauds, the test is whether in all the circumstances the promisor is acquiring a right or protecting a creditor against a default. Compare § 116.

Illustration:

2. D corporation owes C $ 1,000 which is due. S orally promises C that if C will grant D an extension of 60 days, S will purchase the debt at that time if it is not then paid. The circumstances indicate that S is really guaranteeing the account, and the promise is unenforceable.

§ 123. Contract to Discharge the Promisee's Duty

A contract to discharge a duty owed by the promisee to a third person is not within the Statute of Frauds as a contract to answer for the duty of another.

Comment:

a. Rationale. In most jurisdictions the promise described in this Section gives the creditor as beneficiary a direct right against the promisor without destroying his right against the original debtor. The promise is not within the Statute of Frauds, however, because the Statute is designed to require written evidence only in the case where the promise is made to the creditor.

See § 112. In contrast to the language of the Statute, the contract here considered is one to answer for the default of the promisee, not for the default "of another," that is of a third person. **Illustration:**

1. D owes C $ 100. S orally promises D that S will discharge the debt, or promises to lend D money with which to pay it. In either case, S's promise is not within the Statute of Frauds.

§ 124. Contract Made Upon Consideration of Marriage

A promise for which all or part of the consideration is either marriage or a promise to marry is within the Statute of Frauds, except in the case of an agreement which consists only of mutual promises of two persons to marry each other.

Comment:

a. Engagement to marry. Mutual promises to marry were within the words of the English statute, but were not within the statutory purpose and were soon excluded by judicial interpretation. A number of American statutes explicitly except such promises from the marriage provision. They may, however, fall within the one-year provision. Statutes in many states bar actions for breach of a promise to marry.

b. Marriage settlements. A promise to transfer property to a husband or wife or to a third person or a promise regulating the property interests of husband and wife is within the Statute of Frauds if the consideration includes marriage or a promise to marry, whether or not mutual promises to marry are part of the agreement. Such a promise may be made by one of the parties to the contemplated marriage or by a third person. **Illustrations:**

1. In consideration of A's promise to marry B, B orally promises to marry A and to settle Blackacre upon A. B's promise is within the Statute of Frauds.

2. B offers to marry A. To induce A to accept the offer, B orally promises to settle property upon A. A accepts the offer. Both promises to marry and B's promise to make a settlement are within the Statute of Frauds.

. . .

c. Promise in contemplation of marriage. A promise is not within the Statute merely because it is conditional on marriage, or because marriage is contemplated by the promisor or the promisee or both. The marriage or promise to marry must be bargained for and given in exchange for the promise. See § 71. **Illustrations:**

5. A and B mutually promise that each will settle $ 5,000 on A's daughter when she marries B's son. The promises are not within the Statute of Frauds, since the marriage is a condition rather than consideration.

. . .

d. Part performance; subsequent memorandum. An oral contract between prospective spouses made upon consideration of marriage does not become enforceable merely because the marriage has taken place in reliance on it, nor by virtue of subsequent action incident to the marriage relation, since a contrary rule would deprive the marriage provision of the Statute of any significant effect. But the agreement may be enforced if there has been such additional part performance or action in reliance that justice requires enforcement. See § 139. A promise of a marriage settlement made by a third person involves less danger of interference in the marriage relation and may be enforced as in other cases of reliance. See, e.g., § 129. Particularly in the latter type of case the marriage provision of the Statute performs a cautionary as well as an evidentiary function, and a subsequent writing is not sufficient compliance with the Statute unless made as a memorandum of the agreement. See § 133. A new agreement not in consideration of the marriage may fail for want of consideration or as a fraud on creditors even though an antenuptial agreement would have been binding and enforceable but for the Statute.

§ 125. Contract to Transfer, Buy, or Pay for an Interest in Land

(1) A promise to transfer to any person any interest in land is within the Statute of Frauds.

(2) A promise to buy any interest in land is within the Statute of Frauds, irrespective of the person to whom the transfer is to be made.

(3) When a transfer of an interest in land has been made, a promise to pay the price, if originally within the Statute of Frauds, ceases to be within it unless the promised price is itself in whole or in part an interest in land.

(4) Statutes in most states except from the land contract and one-year provisions of the Statute of Frauds short-term leases and contracts to lease, usually for a term not longer than one year.

Comment:

a. Conveyance of land. The English Statute of Frauds in §§ 1 and 3 required a writing for the creation, transfer or surrender of an interest in land. The words "contract or sale" in § 4, therefore, have been read as "contract for sale" and not applied to present conveyances. American statutes modeled on § 4 commonly use such phrases as "any agreement for the sale of real estate or any interest in or concerning it," and are similarly read to exclude present conveyances. The formal requisites of a conveyance of land are beyond the scope of this Restatement. See § 1; Restatement of Property §§ 467, 522. What is an interest in land is the subject of § 127.

b. Short-term leases. A lease is both a conveyance and a contract. As conveyances, leases "not exceeding the term of three years from the making thereof" were excepted by § 2 from § 1 of the English statute, providing that interests in land created without a writing had the effect of estates at will. Leases thus exempted as conveyances were also held not within either the land contract provision or the one-year provision of § 4. In most states statutes reduce to one year the term of a valid oral lease and eliminate the words "from the making thereof." The usual result is to validate an oral lease or contract to lease for a one-year term even though made before the term begins. In some states the statute modeled on § 4 of the English statute applies expressly to "an agreement for the leasing for a longer period than one year" of real property and thus applies neither to a lease nor to a contract to make a lease for a year or less, even though made before the term begins. An agreement related to a lease, however, if it is not itself a lease or contract to lease, is not within the exception.

. . .

c. Contract to sell. The land contract provision applies to any executory promise to transfer an interest in land, whether the consideration is money, chattels, services, other land, or something else, and whether the land is to be transferred to the promisee or to someone else. "Transfer" for this purpose includes the creation or extinguishing of an interest with the effect of giving another an interest he did not previously have, and "promise to transfer" includes an option contract. But the provision does not apply to a promise to refrain from making a transfer, or to a promise to divide profits if land is sold. In some cases, despite a failure to satisfy the Statute, a resulting or constructive trust is imposed on one who has acquired land or other property under the contract. See Restatement, Second, Trusts §§ 404-60; Restatement of Restitution §§ 180-83. **Illustrations:**

> 2. A promises B to transfer Blackacre to B or to C for a price to be paid by B. A's promise is within the Statute of Frauds, whether or not B is committed to buy.

. . .

§ 126. Contract to Procure Transfer or to Act as Agent

(1) A contract to procure the transfer of an interest in land by a person other than the promisor is within the Statute of Frauds.

(2) A contract to act as agent for another in endeavoring to procure the transfer of any interest in land by someone other than the promisor is not within the Statute of Frauds as a contract for the sale of an interest in land.

Comment:

a. Contract to procure transfer. A promise that a third person will convey land to the promisee is within the Statute, even though the promisee is to pay the price. The Statute also applies if the third person is to convey the land to the promisor for the benefit of the promisee or his nominee, or is to convey directly to the promisee's nominee. But if the conveyance is made, the contract may cease to be within the Statute under the rule stated in § 125, or a resulting or constructive trust may arise.

. . .

b. Agency contracts. A contract to employ a real estate broker and to pay him a commission is not within the Statute of Frauds as a contract for the sale of an interest in land unless the commission is to take the form of an interest in land. In such a case the broker's promise to act as agent is not within the Statute, unless he promises to make or procure a transfer. A promise to use best efforts to procure a transfer is not such a promise. In many states, however, statutes explicitly require a writing for a contract to pay a commission to a real estate broker or business opportunity broker. See Statutory Note preceding § 110. **Illustrations:**

     4. A orally promises B to pay him $ 500 if he succeeds in inducing C to agree to transfer Blackacre to A for $ 5,000. A's promise is not within the Statute of Frauds as a contract for the sale of an interest in land. In many states, however, a separate statute makes such a promise unenforceable in the absence of a writing.

. . .

§ 127. Interest in Land

An interest in land within the meaning of the Statute is any right, privilege, power or immunity, or combination thereof, which is an interest in land under the law of property and is not "goods" within the Uniform Commercial Code.

Comment:

a. Property interests. In applying the land contract provision of the Statute of Frauds, the test of what is an interest in land is in general that furnished by the law of property. See Restatement of Property §§ 1-9. Leaseholds are included unless within an exception for short-term leases. Both present and future interests, legal and equitable, are interests in land for this purpose, including the interests of mortgagor and mortgagee or of vendor and purchaser under a specifically enforceable contract.

. . .

§ 128. Boundary and Partition Agreements

(1) A contract between owners of adjoining tracts of land fixing a dividing boundary is within the Statute of Frauds but if the location of the boundary was honestly disputed the contract becomes enforceable notwithstanding the Statute when the agreed boundary has been marked or has been recognized in the subsequent use of the tracts.

(2) A contract by joint tenants or tenants in common to partition land into separate tracts for each tenant is within the Statute of Frauds but becomes enforceable notwithstanding the Statute as to each tract when possession of it is taken in severalty in accordance with the agreement.

. . .

§ 129. Action in Reliance; Specific Performance

A contract for the transfer of an interest in land may be specifically enforced notwithstanding failure to comply with the Statute of Frauds if it is established that the party seeking enforcement, in reasonable reliance on the contract and on the continuing assent of the party against whom enforcement is sought, has so changed his position that injustice can be avoided only by specific enforcement.

Comment:

a. Historical note and modern justifications. This Section restates what is widely known as the "part performance doctrine." Part performance is not an accurate designation of such acts as taking possession and making improvements when the contract does not provide for such acts, but such acts regularly bring the doctrine into play. The doctrine is contrary to the words of the Statute of Frauds, but it was established by English courts of equity soon after the enactment of the Statute. Payment of purchase-money, without more, was once thought sufficient to justify specific enforcement, but a contrary view now prevails, since in such cases restitution is an adequate remedy. English decisions treated a transfer of possession of the land as sufficient, if unequivocally referable to the oral agreement, apparently on the ground that the promise to transfer had been executed by a common-law conveyance. Such decisions are not generally followed in the United States. Enforcement has instead been justified on the ground that repudiation after "part performance" amounts to a "virtual fraud." A more accurate statement is that courts with equitable powers are vested by tradition with what in substance is a dispensing power based on the promisee's reliance, a discretion to be exercised with caution in the light of all the circumstances. Compare § 90.

b. Rationale. Two distinct elements enter into the application of the rule of this Section: first, the extent to which the evidentiary function of the statutory formalities is fulfilled by the conduct of the parties; second, the reliance of the promisee, providing a compelling substantive basis for relief in addition to the expectations created by the promise. The evidentiary element can be satisfied by painstaking examination of the evidence and realistic appraisal of the probabilities on the part of the trier of fact; this is commonly summarized in a standard that calls upon the trier of the facts to be satisfied by "clear and convincing evidence." The substantive element requires consideration of the adequacy of the remedy of restitution. **Illustrations:**

1. A and B agree by an unsigned writing that A will sell Blackacre to B for $ 5,000. B pays the price to A as agreed, and A accepts the payment but refuses to transfer the land as agreed. B is not entitled to specific performance, but can recover the amount of the payment.

2. A orally leases A's farm to B for five years, agreeing that B will repair the premises at prevailing wages to be credited on the rent. B takes possession of the farm and does $ 1,000 worth of repair work, using material furnished by A. A then seeks to evict B. B is entitled to $ 1,000 less the fair rental of the farm for the period of his occupancy, but is not entitled to specific performance or damages.

. . .

c. Monetary relief. Unlike the rule of § 125(3), under which a contract ceases to be subject to the Statute of Frauds when the land is conveyed, the present rule is limited to equitable relief, and does not make available an ordinary action for damages for breach of contract. The remedy of restitution is not ordinarily affected by the Statute of Frauds. See § 375. Where a contract is specifically enforceable under the rule of this Section, damages or other relief may be awarded if specific performance is prevented by the intervention of an innocent purchase for value, by condemnation of the land, or by other circumstances. Or monetary relief may be granted on the basis of fraud, estoppel, or other doctrines. See § 139. Even in jurisdictions where the rule of this Section is repudiated, an equitable lien may be imposed on the land as security for restitution of the value of benefits conferred.

d. Transfer of possession and reasonable reliance. Where specific enforcement is rested on a transfer of possession plus either part payment of the price or the making of improvements, it is commonly said that the action taken by the purchaser must be unequivocally referable to the oral agreement. But this requirement is not insisted on if the making of the promise is admitted or is clearly proved. The promisee must act in reasonable reliance on the promise, before the promisor has repudiated it, and the action must be such that the remedy of restitution is inadequate. If these requirements are met, neither taking of possession nor payment of money nor the making of improvements is essential. Thus, the rendering of peculiar services not readily compensable in money may justify specific performance, particularly if the promisee has also taken other action in reliance on the promise. **Illustrations:**

5. A owns an unsightly vacant lot adjoining B's home in a residential suburb. A's agent and B orally agree that A will sell the lot to B for $

1,500. B, a lawyer aware of the doctrine of part performance, expends $ 1,000 in grading and planting on the lot, but makes no payments and does not communicate with A for two years. A observes the grading and planting, but later denies concluding a contract or knowing that B claimed under a contract. B is not entitled to specific performance, since his actions are not unequivocally referable to a contract for sale and recovery of the value of the improvements is an adequate remedy.

. . .

e. Action by landowner. Specific performance may be granted to a seller or lessor of land under the rule of this Section. But it must be justified by his own part performance or other action in reliance on the contract rather than by the avoidance of injustice to the buyer or lessee.

Illustrations:

11. A and B orally agree that A will sell a house and lot to B for $ 10,000. A signs a memorandum of the contract but B does not; B pays $ 1,000 on account of the price. A prepares a conveyance and delivers it in escrow to await payment, delivers possession of the land to B, and sells him the furniture in the house. B lives in the house for six months and plants a substantial garden, but refuses to pay the balance of the price because of defects in A's title, and finally repudiates the contract shortly after the defects are cured. Whether or not B would have been entitled to specific performance, A is not.

12. A orally leases a storeroom to B for six years at a rental of $ 400 per month. In accordance with the agreement A builds a balcony at a cost of $ 1500 which does not add to the value of the premises. B takes possession and pays rent for three years, and then repudiates the lease at a time when tenants have become scarce. A is entitled to specific performance.

f. Other clauses of the Statute. Ordinarily the various clauses of the Statute of Frauds apply separately. See Comment *b* to § 110. Thus a contract for the sale of land may also be a contract in consideration of marriage, a contract not to be performed within a year, and a contract for the sale of goods. When the contract is specifically enforceable under the rule of this Section, however, the other clauses of the Statute do not prevent enforcement.

§ 130. Contract Not to Be Performed Within a Year

(1) Where any promise in a contract cannot be fully performed within a year from the time the contract is made, all promises in the contract are within the Statute of Frauds until one party to the contract completes his performance.

(2) When one party to a contract has completed his performance, the one-year provision of the Statute does not prevent enforcement of the promises of other parties.

Comment:

a. Possibility of performance within one year. The English Statute of Frauds applied to an action "upon any agreement that is not to be performed within the space of one year from the making thereof." The design was said to be not to trust to the memory of witnesses for a longer time than one year, but the statutory language was not appropriate to carry out that purpose. The result has been a tendency to construction narrowing the application of the statute. Under the prevailing interpretation, the enforceability of a contract under the one-year provision does not turn on the actual course of subsequent events, nor on the expectations of the parties as to the probabilities. Contracts of uncertain duration are simply excluded; the provision covers only those contracts whose performance cannot possibly be completed within a year.

Illustrations:

1. A, an insurance company, orally promises to insure B's house against fire for five years, B promising to pay the premium therefor within the week. The contract is not within the Statute of Frauds, since if the house burns and the insurer pays within a year the contract will be fully performed.

2. A orally promises to work for B, and B promises to employ A during A's life at a stated salary. The promises are not within the one-year provision of the Statute, since A's life may terminate within a year.

3. A and B, a railway, agree that A will provide grading and ties and B will construct a switch and maintain it as long as A needs it for shipping purposes. A plans to use it for shipping lumber from adjoining land which contains enough lumber to run a mill for 30 years, and uses the switch for 15 years. The contract is not within the one-year provision of the Statute.

4. A orally promises B to sell him five crops

of potatoes to be grown on a specified farm in Minnesota, and B promises to pay a stated price on delivery. The contract is within the Statute of Frauds. It is impossible in Minnesota for five crops of potatoes to mature in one year.

b. Discharge within a year. Any contract may be discharged by a subsequent agreement of the parties, and performance of many contracts may be excused by supervening events or by the exercise of a power to cancel granted by the contract. The possibility that such a discharge or excuse may occur within a year is not a possibility that the contract will be "performed" within a year. This is so even though the excuse is articulated in the agreement. This distinction between performance and excuse for nonperformance is sometimes tenuous; it depends on the terms and the circumstances, particularly on whether the essential purposes of the parties will be attained. Discharge by death of the promisor may be the equivalent of performance in the case of a promise to forbear, such as a contract not to compete. **Illustrations:**

5. A orally promises to work for B, and B promises to employ A for five years at a stated salary. The promises are within the Statute of Frauds. Though the duties of both parties will be discharged if A dies within a year, the duties cannot be "performed" within a year. This conclusion is not affected by a term in the oral agreement that the employment shall terminate on A's death.

6. The facts being otherwise as stated in Illustration 5, the agreement provides that either party may terminate the contract by giving 30 days notice at any time. The agreement is one of uncertain duration and is not within the one-year provision of the Statute.

7. The facts being otherwise as stated in Illustration 5, the agreement provides that A may quit at any time. The agreement is within the Statute.

8. A, the maternal grandmother of a newborn illegitimate child, agrees with B, the father, that A will care for the child and B will make support payments until the child becomes 21 years old. The agreement is not within the one-year provision of the Statute. If the child dies within a year, the primary object of furnishing necessaries to the child will be fully "performed".

9. A sells his grocery business to B, who pays part of the price and promises to pay the balance in a month, A agreeing orally not to engage in the grocery business in the same town for five years. The contract is not within the one-

year provision of the Statute, since A's death within one year will give B the equivalent of full performance.

c. The one-year period. The period of a year begins when agreement is complete, ordinarily when the offer is accepted. Compare §§ 63, 64. But a subsequent restatement of the terms starts the period again if the manifestation of mutual assent is such that it would be sufficient in the absence of prior agreement. The one-year period ends at midnight of the anniversary of the day on which the contract is made, on the theory that fractions of a day are disregarded in the way most favorable to the enforceability of the contract. If complete performance is possible before that time, the contract is not within the one-year provision, regardless of what hour of the day the contract is entered into. **Illustrations:**

10. Without consideration A promises B that, so long as B buys through A B's requirements for gasoline and A accepts B's orders, A will pay B an amount equal to the discount other distributors would allow B. For several years A accepts orders from B. A's promise is not within the one-year provision, since a separate contract is made each time A accepts an order.

11. On December 1, 1966, A and B contract orally for A's employment by B at a stated salary for a year beginning the following day. The contract is not within the one-year provision, since the promised performance will be fully rendered before midnight of December 1, 1967.

12. On December 1, 1966, A and B enter into an oral contract for the employment of A at a stated salary for the calendar year 1967. On the first working day in 1967, A presents himself for work, says "I understand these are the terms on which I am to be employed," and restates the terms. B replies, "That is right." Though the original contract was within the Statute of Frauds, the subsequent restatement makes a new contract performable within a year.

d. Full performance on one side. If either party promises a performance that cannot be completed within a year, the Statute applies to all promises in the contract, including those which can or even must be performed within a year. But unlike other provisions of the Statute, the one-year provision does not apply to a contract which is performed on one side at the time it is made, such as a loan of money, nor to any contract which has been fully performed on one side, whether the performance is completed within a year or not. This rule, by permitting an action for the agreed price, avoids the problem of valuation which would otherwise arise in an action for the value of benefits conferred; but the rule goes further and makes available the usual contract remedies. **Illustrations:**

13. A sells and delivers goods to B in return for B's promise to pay $ 1,000 in six months, $ 1,000 in a year and $ 1,000 in eighteen months. B's promises are not within the one-year provision of the Statute.

14. A promises to pay B $ 5,000 in two years in return for B's promise to render a stated performance for five years. A pays the $ 5,000 as agreed. B then refuses further performance. The contract is withdrawn from the operation of the Statute.

e. Part performance. Part performance not amounting to full performance on one side does not in general take a contract out of the one-year provision. Restitution is available in such cases, and doctrines of estoppel and fraud may be applicable. See §§ 139, 375. Where the contract provides the price or rate to be paid for the part performance, the performing party will normally recover according to the contract; in other cases,

the contract terms are evidence of reasonable value. **Illustrations:**

15. A and B contract orally for A's employment by B at a stated salary for the ensuing two years. A works under the contract for 15 months when B discharges him without cause. The contract is not withdrawn from the operation of the Statute, and A may not recover damages for wrongful discharge. But A may recover any unpaid salary.

16. A and B agree on the sale of the output of A's creamery to B for five years at stated prices. After four years B refuses further deliveries. The contract is not withdrawn from the operation of the Statute, but A may recover the contract price of goods delivered and accepted.

f. Other clauses of the Statute. Ordinarily the one-year provision of the Statute applies independently of the other provisions. See Comment *b* to § 110. But statutes in most states have the effect of excepting leases of land for one year even though they begin at a future date. See § 125. And the one-year provision does not prevent specific enforcement of a land contract under the rule stated in § 129.

§ 131. General Requisites of a Memorandum

Unless additional requirements are prescribed by the particular statute, a contract within the Statute of Frauds is enforceable if it is evidenced by any writing, signed by or on behalf of the party to be charged, which

(a) reasonably identifies the subject matter of the contract,

(b) is sufficient to indicate that a contract with respect thereto has been made between the parties or offered by the signer to the other party, and

(c) states with reasonable certainty the essential terms of the unperformed promises in the contract.

Comment:

a. The statutory language. This Section restates the law developed by judicial interpretation of the requirement of § 4 of the English Statute of Frauds that "the agreement . . . or some memorandum or note thereof" be in writing and signed. Despite slight variations in wording in § 17 of the English Statute and in American statutes, they have generally been read to establish the same requisites. Where the statute requires that "the contract" be in writing, however, a mere memorandum is not sufficient; and statutory provisions sometimes explicitly require a statement of the consideration or explicitly negate such a requirement, either with respect to contracts of suretyship or in all cases.

b. The Uniform Commercial Code. Paragraphs (a) and (b) follow the phrasing of Uniform Commercial Code §§ 1-206 and 2-201. Compare §§ 8-319, 9-203. Section 1-206 requires in addition an indication that the contract has been made "at a defined or stated price." Section 2-201 omits this requirement and also any reference to identification of subject matter, and adds "A writing is not insufficient because it omits or incorrectly states a term agreed upon but the contract is not enforceable under this paragraph beyond the quantity of goods shown in such writing." Section 8-319 refers to "a stated quantity of described securities at a defined or stated price." Section 9-203 requires "a security agreement which contains a description of the collateral" and in certain cases "a description of the land concerned." The description is sufficient "if it reasonably identifies what is described." See § 9-110.

c. *Rationale*. The primary purpose of the Statute is evidentiary, to require reliable evidence of the existence and terms of the contract and to prevent enforcement through fraud or perjury of contracts never in fact made. The contents of the writing must be such as to make successful fraud unlikely, but the possibility need not be excluded that some other subject matter or person than those intended will also fall within the words of the writing. Where only an evidentiary purpose is served, the requirement of a memorandum is read in the light of the dispute which arises and the admissions of the party to be charged; there is no need for evidence on points not in dispute.

The suretyship and marriage provisions of the Statute perform a cautionary as well as an evidentiary function. See §§ 112, 124. The land contract provision performs a channeling function. See Statutory Note preceding § 110. Even where these provisions are involved, however, there is no evidence of a statutory purpose to facilitate repudiation of firm oral agreements fairly made, to protect a promisor from temptation to perjure himself by false denial of the promise, or to reward a candid contract-breaker by denying enforcement.

d. *Types of documents*. The statutory memorandum may be a written contract, but under the traditional statutory language any writing, formal or informal, may be sufficient, including a will, a notation on a check, a receipt, a pleading, or an informal letter. Neither delivery nor

reduction to tangible form. See Uniform Commercial Code § 1-201. **Illustrations:**

1. A makes an oral contract with B to devise Blackacre to B, and executes a will containing the devise and a recital of the contract. The will is revoked by a later will. The revoked will is a sufficient memorandum to charge A's estate.

2. A publishes in a newspaper an offer to buy certain goods, stating the terms of his proposal, and his name is printed under the advertisement. B accepts the offer. The advertisement is a sufficient memorandum to charge A. See § 136.

3. A writes and signs in pencil a receipt for $ 1,000 which recites that the money is received from B as part payment of the price of $ 5,000 for a parcel of land. The receipt is a sufficient memorandum to charge A on the agreement recited.

e. *Subject matter*. A memorandum, like a contract, must be read in its context and need not be comprehensible to persons not familiar with the particular type of transaction. Without reference to executory oral promises, the memorandum in context must indicate with reasonable certainty the nature of the transaction and must provide a basis for identifying the land, goods or other subject matter. **Illustrations:**

4. A Company executes a written contract with B by which B purchases certain accounts owned by A Company. As part of the same transaction, C, the president of A Company, signs a contract of guaranty printed at the foot of the same paper: "In order to induce B to enter into an agreement dated with (hereinafter referred to as the client), the undersigned agrees to be liable for due performance of all the client's agreements with B." The blanks are not filled in. The quoted words are sufficient to identify the obligation guaranteed.

5. A and B make an oral contract for the sale of goods and sign the following memorandum:

```
"Sept. 19th B,                                    12 mos.
300 bales S. F. drills                              7 1/4
100 cases blue do                                   8 3/4
     Credit to commence when ship sails;
     not after December 1 -- delivered free
     of charge for truckage.

                                        (Signed) A
                                                 B"
```

communication is essential. See § 133. Writing for this purpose includes any intentional

If persons acquainted with the usages of the business would understand its meaning, the memorandum is sufficient.

6. A and B enter into an oral contract by which A promises to sell and B to buy such of A's iron in his millyard as he may decide to sell. A memorandum describes the subject matter of the contract as "all A's iron which he may decide to sell." The description is sufficient.

7. A and B enter into a contract by which A promises to sell and B to buy a certain lot of hops belonging to A. A telegram from B refers to the subject matter as "number 13." This refers to a sample submitted by A to B by mail with a numbered tag attached and referring by trade usage to a specific lot. The description is sufficient.

8. A and B enter into an oral contract for the sale and purchase of Blackacre. An otherwise sufficient memorandum, signed by A and B, describes the subject matter as "the land on the corner of X and Y Streets," omitting any statement as to the city or state. A owns only one of the four lots at the intersection. The description is sufficient.

9. A and B enter into a written contract for the employment of B as A's sales manager for a term of two years. At the end of the two years, A and B orally agree to extend the employment for three more years at an increased salary. A year later A signs the following memorandum: "It is understood that the arrangements made for employment of B in our business on January 1, 1977, for a period of three years from that date at a salary of $ 30,000 per year, continues in force until January 1, 1980." The memorandum sufficiently identifies the nature of B's employment.

f. Contract between the parties. A memorandum must be sufficient to indicate that a contract has been made between the parties with respect to an identified subject matter or that the signer has offered such a contract to the other party. The parties must be reasonably identified; the identification may consist of a name or initials, even though there may be others with the same name or initials, or of any other reasonably accurate mode of description. Identification of the agent of a party in the memorandum sufficiently refers to the party, whether or not the agent is himself a party. See Restatement, Second, Agency § 153. Where there is no dispute as to the parties, a party may be sufficiently identified by possession of a memorandum signed by the other party. A signed written offer to the public may be sufficient even though the offeree is not identified. **Illustrations:**

10. A and B are negotiating for the sale of A's restaurant to B. B gives A a check for $ 500 bearing the notation "Tentative deposit on tentative purchase of 1415 City Line Ave., Phila. Restaurant, Fixtures, Equipment, Good Will." Later A and B orally agree on terms of sale. The quoted memorandum is not sufficient to indicate that a contract for sale has been made.

11. C and D make an oral contract for the sale of Blackacre and sign the following memorandum: "C agrees to sell and D agrees to buy Blackacre for $ 10,000." C is agent for A, D is agent for B, and each is acting on behalf of his principal. The memorandum is sufficient to charge A and B.

12. An otherwise sufficient memorandum of an oral contract for the sale of Blackacre states that "the owner of Blackacre" promises to sell it. The memorandum is signed by B, and B is the agent of A, the owner of Blackacre, acting on A's behalf. The memorandum is sufficient to charge A.

13. A, president and principal stockholder of A Company, gives B his personal check for $ 10,000 and a written offer to buy Blackacre from B on stated terms. The offer, signed by A, states that "the offer to purchase is from a company owned by A." B accepts the offer by a signed writing. Neither the offer nor the acceptance identifies the purchaser except by the quoted language. The identification is sufficient.

14. A and B make an oral agreement for the sale of a parcel of land by A to B. B pays A $ 50 and A signs and delivers to B a receipt which identifies the parcel and accurately states the terms of payment but does not name or describe B or his agent. In B's suit for specific performance, A defends on the ground of B's inequitable conduct in the negotiations. B is sufficiently identified by his possession of the memorandum.

g. Terms; accuracy. The degree of particularity with which the terms of the contract must be set out cannot be reduced to a formula. The writing must be the agreement or a memorandum "thereof"; a memorandum of a different agreement will not suffice. The "essential" terms of unperformed promises must be stated; "details or particulars" need not. What is essential depends on the agreement and its context and also on the subsequent conduct of the parties, including the dispute which arises and the remedy sought. Omission or erroneous statement of an agreed term makes no difference if the same term is supplied by implication or by rule of law. Erroneous statement of a term can sometimes be corrected by reformation. See § 155. Otherwise omission or misstatement of an essential term means that the memorandum is insufficient. Uniform Commercial Code § 2-201, however, states a different rule for sale of goods. **Illustrations:**

> 15. A and B enter into an oral contract for the sale of Blackacre by A to B. A memorandum is made and signed which states sufficiently the parties, subject matter and terms of the oral bargain except that, though the parties in fact orally agreed that the price should be payable on delivery of a deed, the memorandum contains no statement as to when the price is payable. The memorandum is sufficient.

> 16. A and B enter into an oral contract for the sale of Blackacre by A to B, and both sign a memorandum providing for a "purchase money mortgage in the amount of $ 18,000 payable for 15 years at 5%." B claims a right to pay $ 142.35 per month; A claims a payment of $ 100 a month plus monthly interest at 5%. No usage is shown. The memorandum is not sufficient to support an action by B for specific performance on his terms.

h. Statement of consideration. In Wain v. Warlters, 5 East 10 (K.B. 1804), a promise in writing to pay the debt of another was held unenforceable because the writing failed to state the consideration, which had been fully executed. Where that view is followed, the words "for value received" or an implication of consideration may validate the memorandum. But the decision has not been generally followed in the United States, and the English law was changed by statute in 1856. Uniform Commercial Code § 3-408 eliminates the requirement of consideration for a negotiable

instrument or obligation thereon given in payment of or as security for an antecedent obligation, and § 3-416 exempts from the Statute of Frauds any guaranty written on a negotiable instrument. Aside from explicit statutory provisions, the prevailing view is that error or omission in the recital of past events does not affect the sufficiency of a memorandum.

Where, on the other hand, the consideration for a promise consists of a return promise not yet performed, performance of the return promise is commonly a condition of the promisor's duty, and an adequate memorandum will ordinarily reveal the consideration. A memorandum of a contract for the sale of land for an agreed price is not sufficient unless it discloses the price. Compare Uniform Commercial Code §§ 1-206 and 3-319, referring to "a defined or stated price" for intangible personal property or for investment securities. But § 2-201 dispenses with statement of the price of goods sold. **Illustrations:**

> 17. A lends $ 1,000 to B, and as part of the transaction C orally agrees to guarantee repayment. To evidence the guaranty, C signs a written promise to pay A $ 1,000. The written promise is a sufficient memorandum without any statement of consideration.

> 18. A agrees not to sue B Company on a debt for goods sold and delivered, in consideration of C's guaranty of payment for past and future deliveries to B up to $ 3,000. C signs the following guaranty: "I, C, do hereby guarantee to A the payment of any sums due or that may become due up to the sum of $ 3,000 on such goods as B may have bought or shall buy from A. [Signed] C." A makes no further deliveries. The memorandum is not sufficient to charge C, since it omits any mention of A's return promise.

§ 132. Several Writings

The memorandum may consist of several writings if one of the writings is signed and the writings in the circumstances clearly indicate that they relate to the same transaction.

Comment:

a. Rationale. The requirements of the Statute of Frauds, designed primarily to serve an evidentiary purpose, are less rigorous than those of the Statute of Wills, which is designed to serve cautionary and channeling purposes as well. See Comment *c* to § 72; Statutory Note preceding § 110. A will may refer to facts which have independent significance, and in some States a will may incorporate by reference an unattested

existing document. See Restatement Second, Trusts § 54. A memorandum of a contract need only give assurance that the contract enforced was in fact made and provide evidence of its terms. It may consist of several separate documents, even though not all of them are signed and even though no one of them is itself a sufficient memorandum. At least one must be signed by the party to be charged, and the documents and circumstances must be such that the documents can be read together as "some memorandum or note" of the agreement. Explicit incorporation by reference is unnecessary, but if the connection depends on evidence outside the writings, the evidence of connection must be clear and convincing.

b. Several signed writings. Where two or more documents are signed by the party to be charged, they may be read together even though neither contains any reference to the other. The question whether they constitute a sufficient memorandum is substantially the same as if they had been incorporated in a single document.

Illustration:

1. A signs and sends to B a letter stating that he is interested in leasing aparcel of land from B. After six months of negotiations A and B orally agree on an eight-year lease of the parcel with an option to purchase, and both sign a memorandum which is sufficient except that it does not identify the land. The two documents together constitute a sufficient memorandum to charge A.

c. Reference to unsigned writing: physical connection. Where the signature of the party to be charged is made or adopted with reference to an unsigned writing, the signed and unsigned writings together may constitute a memorandum. It is sufficient that the signed writing refers to the unsigned writing explicitly or by implication, or that the party to be charged physically attaches one document to the other or encloses them in the same envelope. Even if there is no internal reference or physical connection, the documents may be read together if in the circumstances they clearly relate to the same transaction and the party to be charged has acquiesced in the contents of the unsigned writing. **Illustrations:**

2. A and B make an oral contract within the Statute. A writes and signs a letter to B which is a sufficient memorandum except that it does not identify B. The deficiency may be supplied by the name and address on the envelope in which the letter arrives.

3. A and B make an oral contract within the Statute. A memorandum of the contract is made on two sheets of paper which are not connected physically, and A signs one of the sheets. The two sheets may be read together as a memorandum to charge A if an incomplete sentence on one is completed on the other, if the contract partially disclosed by one is clearly the same

contract partially disclosed by the other, or if the fact that one is a continuation of the other is otherwise shown by clear and convincing evidence.

4. A and B enter into an oral contract within the Statute. A memorandum of the contract is made on two sheets of paper. The contents of the sheets do not show that they belong together, but A signs one and then fastens the sheets together with a clip. Even though the clip is later removed, the fastening is a sufficient adoption of A's signature with reference to both sheets to charge A, but only if the evidence of the fastening is clear and convincing.

5. A agrees orally to employ B for two years. An unsigned memorandum of the contract, stating its terms, is prepared at A's direction. Later B begins work and payroll cards are made and initialed by A which state some of the terms but not the duration of the employment. If it is clear that the unsigned memorandum and the payroll cards refer to the same agreement, they may be read together as a sufficient memorandum to charge A.

d. Reference to future writings. Ordinarily a signature does not authenticate a document not in existence at the time the signature is made. But when several documents are executed by different parties in a single transaction, the signature of one may have reference to a subsequent signature of another. In some such cases the earlier signature may be adopted with reference to a document prepared later, whether signed by anyone or not. In other cases the reference is to an event of independent significance, or to the exercise of a power granted by the signer. Thus a signed offer authenticates the acceptance invited by it. **Illustrations:**

6. A and B enter into a contract within the Statute and sign a memorandum, otherwise sufficient, stating that the price to be paid shall be the same as the price agreed upon by C and D in a similar contract expected to be made on the following day. The memorandum is sufficient if it accurately states the entire agreement between A and B. The contract made between C and D is an event of independent significance, and may be referred to for the price whether or not there is a memorandum signed by C or D.

7. A and B enter into an oral contract for the purchase and sale of a tract of land and sign a memorandum, otherwise sufficient, stating that the contract is "contingent upon A's ability to arrange $ 7,000 purchase money mortgage." A subsequently applies in writing to a financial

institution for such a mortgage loan on specific terms as to duration, interest rate and payment.

The mortgage loan application may be read with the memorandum to satisfy the Statute against either party.

§ 133. Memorandum Not Made as Such

Except in the case of a writing evidencing a contract upon consideration of marriage, the Statute may be satisfied by a signed writing not made as a memorandum of a contract.

Comment:

a. Rationale. The rule of this Section reflects the general assumption that the primary purpose of the Statute is evidentiary, that it was not intended to facilitate repudiation of oral contracts. The marriage provision, however, performs a cautionary function as well, and a subsequent writing does not satisfy the Statute unless made as a memorandum of the agreement. See § 124 Comment *d.* More than a merely evidentiary writing is also required to satisfy a statutory provision that "the contract" be in writing.

b. Communication; delivery. There is no requirement that a memorandum be communicated or delivered to the other party to the contract, or even that it be known to him or to anyone but the signer. A memorandum may consist of an entry in a diary or in the minutes of a meeting, of a communication to or from an agent of the party, of a public record, or of an informal letter to a third person. Where a written offer serves as a memorandum to charge the offeror, however, communication of the offer is essential; written instructions to an agent to make an offer do not suffice. And where the statute requires only the vendor's signature the memorandum is not effective to charge the vendee until he manifests assent to it. **Illustrations:**

1. A and B enter into an oral contract for the sale of Blackacre. A writes and signs a letter to his friend C containing an accurate statement of the contract. The letter is a sufficient memorandum to charge A even though it is never mailed.

2. A writes to B the following letter: "Dear B: I will employ you as superintendent of my mill for a term of three years from date, at a salary of $ 28,000 a year. Let me know if you wish to accept this offer. [Signed] A."

B accepts the offer orally. The letter is a sufficient memorandum to charge A.

3. A writes and signs a letter to his agent C authorizing C to make the offer stated in Illustration 2. C orally makes the offer, and B orally accepts it. A's letter is not a sufficient memorandum to charge him.

c. Repudiating memorandum. A signed writing which is otherwise a sufficient memorandum of a contract is not rendered insufficient by the fact that it also repudiates or cancels the contract, or asserts that it is not binding because not in writing. But a writing denying the making of the contract is not a memorandum of it. **Illustration:**

4. A and B enter into an oral contract by which A promises to sell and B promises to buy Blackacre for $ 5,000. A writes and signs a letter to B in which he states accurately the terms of the bargain, but adds "our agreement was oral. It, therefore, is not binding upon me, and I shall not carry it out." The letter is a sufficient memorandum to charge A.

d. Pleadings and testimony. A written pleading, stipulation or deposition may serve as a memorandum if otherwise sufficient as to contents and signature. An oral statement before the court is treated in some states as the equivalent of a signed writing. See Uniform Commercial Code §§ 2-201(3)(b), 8-319(d). Where the writing or oral statement is made under legal compulsion, it is nonetheless effective unless there is a contrary procedural policy in the state. But a motion to dismiss a complaint or a failure to deny an allegation, though given the procedural effect of an admission, is not the equivalent of a signed writing for the purposes of the Statute of Frauds.

§ 134. Signature

The signature to a memorandum may be any symbol made or adopted with an intention, actual or apparent, to authenticate the writing as that of the signer.

Comment:

a. Types of symbol. The traditional form of signature is of course the name of the signer, handwritten in ink. But initials, thumbprint or an arbitrary code sign may also be used; and the signature may be written in pencil, typed, printed, made with a rubber stamp, or impressed into the paper. Signed copies may be made with carbon paper or by photographic process. *b. Place of signature; "subscribed."* Under a statute in the traditional English form, the signature need not appear on any particular part of the writing. Although it is usual to sign at the end of a document, a printed letterhead or billhead may be adopted as a signature. See Uniform Commercial Code § 1-201(39) Comment. Even where the statute uses the word "subscribe," there is an ambiguity: the word "subscribe" is sometimes read as a synonym for "sign," sometimes as requiring signing at the end or foot. Wherever the signature appears, it must be made or adopted with the requisite intention, but in the absence of contrary evidence the intention may be inferred from the conventional form of the writing. **Illustrations:**

    1. A and B make an oral contract within the Statute. A sends to B a written acceptance, stating the terms, on a form bearing A's name as a printed heading. At the foot of the form is the word "Accepted" followed by a blank space for signature, which is not filled in. In the absence of other evidence of intention, the form is not signed by A.

    2. A and B make an oral contract within the Statute. A writes a memorandum stating the terms which begins, "I, A, make the following contract with B." A then delivers the memorandum to B. This is A's signature if the trier of fact infers A's intent to authenticate the writing.

    3. A and B make an oral contract within the Statute. A clerk makes a written statement of the contract, and A writes at the top thereof -- "O.K." followed by A's initials. This is a signature by A.

c. Time of signing; blanks and alterations. Commonly a document is signed after it is completed, but blanks may be left to be filled in later. If the signer fills a blank or adds a postscript or if another does so with his authority, the prior signature is effectively adopted with reference to the added portion. Alterations are often separately initialed, but re-adoption of the prior signature is equally effective for the purposes of the Statute of Frauds. Compare Uniform Commercial Code §§ 3-115, 3-407. **Illustration:**

    4. A has a number of forms of letters printed ending with the words, "Yours very truly, A." With A's authority a clerk fills in one of the forms with the terms of an offer to B and sends it to B. B accepts orally. A's printed name is his signature.

§ 135. Who Must Sign

Where a memorandum of a contract within the Statute is signed by fewer than all parties to the contract and the Statute is not otherwise satisfied, the contract is enforceable against the signers but not against the others.

Comment:

    a. The "party to be charged." Section 4 of the English Statute of Frauds required signature of the agreement, or some memorandum or note thereof, "by the party to be charged therewith, or some other person thereunto by him lawfully authorized." Section 17 referred to signature "by the parties to be charged by such contract or their agents thereunto lawfully authorized." Both forms of words are generally read to refer to the party to be charged in the legal proceeding, not the party or parties to be bound by the contract. In a few states, however, either by statute or by decision, the memorandum of a land contract is required to be signed only by the lessor or vendor. See Comment *b* to § 133.

    b. Agency. A memorandum may be signed by an agent of a party with the same effect as if the party had signed personally. Unless the Statute so provides, written authorization is unnecessary, but the power to sign cannot be orally conferred on the other party to the transaction. The same third person may be the agent of both parties to sign a memorandum, and an auctioneer has irrevocable power to sign for both buyer and seller for a reasonable time on the day of sale. See Restatement, Second, Agency §§ 24, 30.

§ 136. Time of Memorandum

A memorandum sufficient to satisfy the Statute may be made or signed at any time before or after the formation of the contract.

Comment:

a. Pre-contract memorandum. A written offer signed by the offeror may constitute a sufficient memorandum to bind him. See Illustration 2 to § 131; Illustrations 2 and 3 to § 133. In other cases a memorandum or signature made before the formation of the contract may be adopted thereafter. See §§ 132, 134.

b. Subsequent memorandum. There is no requirement that the memorandum be made contemporaneously with the contract. It may be made even after breach or repudiation. The language "No action shall be brought" has sometimes been read to require a memorandum made before the action is begun, but such a procedural defect is curable under modern statutes or rules of court. See Comment *d* to § 133.

§ 137. Loss or Destruction of a Memorandum

The loss or destruction of a memorandum does not deprive it of effect under the Statute.

Comment:

a. Not a rule of evidence. Although the Statute of Frauds was designed to serve an evidentiary purpose, it is not a rule of evidence. In cases of loss or destruction, the contents of a memorandum may be shown by an unsigned copy or by oral evidence. See Uniform Rules of Evidence Rule 70; cf. Fed. R. Ev. 1001-04; compare Uniform Commercial Code § 3-804 (negotiable instrument).

§ 138. Unenforceability

Where a contract within the Statute of Frauds is not enforceable against the party to be charged by an action against him, it is not enforceable by a set-off or counterclaim in an action brought by him, or as a defense to a claim by him.

Comment:

a. Contracts within the Statute. Section 110 lists the classes of contracts which are subject to the Statute of Frauds, and Topics 1-5, §§ 111-30 elaborate the descriptions of some of those classes and the circumstances in which certain contracts originally within the Statute may cease to be within it.

b. Unenforceability. Despite variations in wording, the American statutes based on the English Statute of Frauds are read to make contracts unenforceable by action or defense unless the Statute is satisfied by a signed memorandum. See § 8, defining "unenforceable contract." Satisfaction by a memorandum is the subject of Topic 6, §§ 131-37. Under the rule stated in § 135, the Statute may be satisfied as against one party and not as against another; in that event the Statute does not prevent enforcement by action, set-off, counterclaim or defense against the former party.

c. Exceptions. In many situations a contract within the Statute becomes enforceable even though the Statute is not satisfied by a memorandum. Of particular importance are cases where denial of enforcement would be unjust because of part or full performance or other reliance by the aggrieved party. Some such cases are dealt with by rules withdrawing the case from the class of contracts within the Statute (see, e.g., §§ 125, 130), others by a rule making particular remedies available (see, e.g., §§ 129, 375). Exceptions relating to particular classes of contracts are stated in appropriate sections in the Topics relating to those classes.

§ 139. Enforcement by Virtue of Action in Reliance

(1) A promise which the promisor should reasonably expect to induce action or forbearance on the part of the promisee or a third person and which does induce the action or forbearance is enforceable notwithstanding the Statute of Frauds if injustice can be avoided only by enforcement of the promise. The remedy granted for breach is to be limited as justice requires.

(2) In determining whether injustice can be avoided only by enforcement of the promise, the following circumstances are significant:

(a) the availability and adequacy of other remedies, particularly cancellation and restitution;

(b) the definite and substantial character of the action or forbearance in relation to the remedy sought;

(c) the extent to which the action or forbearance corroborates evidence of the making and terms of the promise, or the making and terms are otherwise established by clear and convincing evidence;

(d) the reasonableness of the action or forbearance;

(e) the extent to which the action or forbearance was foreseeable by the promisor.

Comment:

a. Relation to other rules. This Section is complementary to § 90, which dispenses with the requirement of consideration if the same conditions are met, but it also applies to promises supported by consideration. Like § 90, this Section overlaps in some cases with rules based on estoppel or fraud; it states a basic principle which sometimes renders inquiry unnecessary as to the precise scope of other policies. Sections 128 and 129 state particular applications of the same principle to land contracts; §§ 125(3) and 130(2) also rest on it in part. See also Uniform Commercial Code §§ 2-201(3), 8-319(b). Where a promise is made without intention to perform, remedies under this Section may be alternative to remedies for fraud. See Comment *b* to § 313; Restatement, Second, Torts § 530.

b. Avoidance of injustice. Like § 90 this Section states a flexible principle, but the requirement of consideration is more easily displaced than the requirement of a writing. The reliance must be foreseeable by the promisor, and enforcement must be necessary to avoid injustice. Subsection (2) lists some of the relevant factors in applying the latter requirement. Each factor relates either to the extent to which reliance furnishes a compelling substantive basis for relief in addition to the expectations created by the promise or to the extent to which the circumstances satisfy the evidentiary purpose of the Statute and fulfill any cautionary, deterrent and channeling functions it may serve.

Illustrations:

1. A is lessee of a building for five years at $ 75 per month and has sublet it for three years at $ 100 per month. A seeks to induce B to purchase the building, and to that end orally promises to assign to B the lease and sublease and to execute a written assignment as soon as B obtains a deed. B purchases the building in reliance on the promise. B is entitled to the rentals from the sublease.

2. A is a pilot with an established airline having rights to continued employment, and could take up to six months leave without prejudice to those rights. He takes such leave to become general manager of B, a small airline which hopes to expand if a certificate to operate over an important route is granted. When his six months leave is about to expire, A demands definite employment because of that fact, and B orally agrees to employ A for two years and on the granting of the certificate to give A an increase in salary and a written contract. In reliance on this agreement A lets his right to return to his prior employer expire. The certificate is soon granted, but A is discharged in breach of the agreement. The Statute of Frauds does not prevent recovery of damages by A.

c. Particular factors. The force of the factors listed varies in different types of cases, and additional factors may affect particular types of contracts. Thus reliance of the kinds usual in suretyship transactions is not sufficient to justify enforcement of an oral guaranty, where the evidentiary and cautionary functions performed by the statutory formalities are not fulfilled. See Comment *a* to § 112. In the case of a contract between prospective spouses made upon consideration of marriage, the policy of the Statute is reinforced by a policy against legal interference in the marriage relation, and reliance incident to the marriage relation does not make the contract enforceable. See Comment *d* to § 124. Where restitution is an unavailable remedy because to grant it would nullify the statutory purpose, a remedy based on reliance will ordinarily also be denied. See Comment *a* to § 375. **Illustration:**

    3. A orally promises to pay B a commission for services in negotiating the sale of a business opportunity, and B finds a purchaser to whom A sells the business opportunity. A statute extends the Statute of Frauds to such promises, and is interpreted to preclude recovery of the reasonable value of such services. The promise is not made enforceable by B's reliance on it.
    . . .

§ 140. Defense of Failure to Perform

The Statute of Frauds does not invalidate defenses based on the plaintiff's failure to perform a condition of his claim or defenses based on his present or prospective breach of the contract he seeks to enforce.

Comment:

    a. Affirmative relief; independent claims. Since the Statute of Frauds requires signature "by the party to be charged," the question whether a contract is enforceable against the plaintiff in an action is distinct from the question whether it is enforceable against the defendant. See § 135. If a contract is unenforceable against the plaintiff, the defendant cannot use it as a basis for affirmative relief by way of counterclaim. Nor can he assert it defensively against an independent claim of the plaintiff. **Illustration:**

    1. A owes B $ 1,000. In consideration of B's oral agreement to discharge the debt, A promises to transfer Blackacre to B. A tenders B a deed of Blackacre. B refuses the tender and sues for $ 1,000. Whether or not A has signed a memorandum sufficient to charge him, B can recover.

    b. Conditions; present or prospective breach. A contractual right may be limited by the agreed terms or by virtue of considerations of fairness or public policy. Thus a failure of the promisee to perform a return promise commonly discharges the promisor's duty in whole or in part or gives him an offsetting claim. Where a plaintiff seeks to enforce a contract, the defendant may assert defensively any defense or claim arising from the terms of that contract, whether or not the Statute makes the contract unenforceable against the plaintiff, and whether or not the defendant has or asserts a defense under the Statute. **Illustration:**

    2. A promises to sell Blackacre to B, and B promises to pay $ 5,000 for it. B signs a memorandum sufficient to charge him, but A does not and the contract is not enforceable against A. A sues B for damages for breach of the contract. B may defend on the ground that A repudiated the contract before tendering a deed, or may recoup damages resulting from a defect in A's title.

§ 141. Action for Value of Performance Under Unenforceable Contract

(1) In an action for the value of performance under a contract, except as stated in Subsection (2), the Statute of Frauds does not invalidate any defense which would be available if the contract were enforceable against both parties.

(2) Where a party to a contract which is unenforceable against him refuses either to perform the contract or to sign a sufficient memorandum, the other party is justified in suspending any performance for which he has not already received the agreed return, and such a suspension is not a defense in an action for the value of performance rendered before the suspension.

Comment:

    a. Restitution as a contract remedy. Subsection (1) applies to the remedy of restitution the same rule stated in § 140 for actions for damages or specific performance. Restitution is a standard remedy for breach of contract, and is dealt with in §§ 370-77. In some situations a plaintiff who has broken a contract is nevertheless entitled to restitution of the value of his part performance, less the harm caused by his breach. See § 374. An action for restitution in either type of case is not regarded as an action "upon" the contract within the meaning or purpose of the Statute of Frauds, and the remedy is not in general affected by the Statute. See § 375. Whether or not the contract is enforceable against the plaintiff, his action is subject to the same limitations and defenses as if the contract were fully enforceable against both parties.

Illustration:

> 1. A contracts to transfer land to B for $ 10,000, and B pays $ 1,000. B does not sign a memorandum, and sues to recover the $ 1000 payment on the ground that the contract is un-enforceable under the Statute of Frauds. A is willing and able to perform. B cannot recover. See § 375.

b. Refusal to sign a memorandum. The Statute of Frauds does not affect the defense of actual or prospective failure of consideration. See § 140. Where a contract is unenforceable against one party, whether or not it is enforceable against the other, the latter has reasonable grounds for insecurity and may demand performance or adequate assurance of performance, including the signing of a sufficient memorandum. Compare Uniform Commercial Code § 2-609; § 251. If his demand for such assurance is refused without excuse, he may suspend his own performance and maintain an action for the reasonable value of any part performance he has rendered. In such an action, his suspension of performance is neither a complete nor a partial defense. Compare §§ 251, 253, 255; Restatement, Second, Agency § 468(3); Restatement of Restitution § 108(d).

Illustration:

> 2. A and B enter into an oral contract for the performance of services by A extending over a period of two years, B promising to pay $ 5,000 on completion of the services. After six months work A demands that B sign a written memorandum of the contract. B refuses, and A quits work and sues for the value of the work done. A can recover without deduction for damages caused by A's quitting.

§ 142. Tort Liability for Acts Under Unenforceable Contract

Where because of the existence of a contract conduct would not be tortious, unenforceability of the contract under the Statute of Frauds does not make the conduct tortious if it occurs without notice of repudiation of the contract.

Comment:

a. Scope. An unenforceable contract may include authority or consent to do acts which would otherwise constitute a tort. The authority or consent is effective notwithstanding the Statute of Frauds to bar tort remedies for acts done pursuant to the contract, but the authority or consent may be revoked without liability. Acts subsequent to revocation are not protected.

Illustration:

> 1. A enters into an oral contract with B by which A promises to transfer Blackacre to B and B promises to pay $ 5,000, B to have an immediate license to go upon land. B does so. A sues for trespass; B tenders $ 5,000 and demands a transfer. A need not accept the money or make a transfer, but B has a good defense to A's action for trespass.

§ 143. Unenforceable Contract as Evidence

The Statute of Frauds does not make an unenforceable contract inadmissible in evidence for any purpose other than its enforcement in violation of the Statute.

Comment:

a. Procedure. The Statute of Frauds makes non-complying contracts unenforceable by action or defense, subject to certain exceptions. See § 138. The procedure for asserting the bar of the Statute is beyond the scope of this Restatement. Rule 8(c) of the Federal Rules of Civil Procedure requires it to be pleaded as an affirmative defense. If the defense is properly pleaded, or if it is not required to be pleaded, evidence offered for the purpose of enforcing an unenforceablecontract may be excluded as immaterial. But the Statute, despite occasional statements to the contrary, does not lay down a rule of evidence, and an unenforceable contract may be proved for any legitimate purpose.

Illustrations:

> 1. A renders services to B under an oral contract within the Statute by which B promises to pay for the services. On B's refusal to pay, A sues for the value of the services. The oral con-

tract is admissible as evidence that the services were not rendered officiously or as a gift, and as evidence of the value of the services.

2. A sues B on a debt and garnishes C, who had borrowed money from B. In defense C offers to prove an oral contract with B whereby B agreed to discharge C in return for C's oral promise to transfer Blackacre to D at a future day. Since the oral contract, though unenforceable, would establish a good defense to the garnishment under § 144, it is admissible in evidence against A.

. . .

§ 144. Effect of Unenforceable Contract as to Third Parties

Only a party to a contract or a transferee or successor of a party to the contract can assert that the contract is unenforceable under the Statute of Frauds.

Comment:

a. Successor to contract duty. Where a contract is unenforceable under the Statute, the Statute provides a defense to a party who is sued for specific performance of the contract or for damages for its breach. A person who assumes the contractual duty and agrees to perform it may assert the defense only if the terms of the contract of assumption permit. See § 309. The personal representative, trustee in bankruptcy or like successor to the duty has the benefit of the defense. See, e.g., Bankruptcy Reform Act of 1978, 11 U.S.C. § 541(e)(1978).

b. Assignee or successor to claim. Where an unenforceable contract is asserted as a defense to an independent claim by a party to the contract, the Statute enables the party to reply that the defense is invalid. See § 140. The same reply is available to an assignee of the claim or to a successor such as a personal representative or trustee in bankruptcy.

c. Transferee of property. Where a party who has made an unenforceable contract to sell property transfers the property to a third person, the third person has the benefit of the Statute as a defense to any claim based on the contract. See §§ 146. A successor such as a personal representative or trustee in bankruptcy of the seller also has the benefit of the defense. Bankruptcy Reform Act of 1978, 11 U.S.C. § 544(a)(3)(1978).

d. Other third parties. Only parties to a contract and their transferees and successors can take advantage of the Statute of Frauds. As against others the unenforceable contract creates the same rights, powers, privileges and immunities as if it were enforceable. See Uniform Commercial Code § 2-201 Comment. For this purpose, where one party has sold or contracted to sell property to the other and has not repudiated the sale or contract, the seller's attaching or levying creditor is a successor only to the interest the seller has apart from the Statute. See § 143 Illustration 2. **Illustrations:**

1. A and B make a contract which is unenforceable by virtue of the Statute. C prevents B from performing, and C's conduct would be tortious if the contract were enforceable. The Statute does not impair C's tort liability to A or B.

2. A contracts to sell a ship to B. The Statute is not satisfied. B insures the ship with C, an insurance company. The ship is lost. The Statute provides no defense to C.

3. A contracts to sell specific goods to B, title to pass at once. A retains possession and the contract is unenforceable, but the sale is not fraudulent under any rule of law. C, A's creditor, attaches the goods as A's before any repudiation of the contract. The attachment is invalid as against B.

4. A promises orally to sell Blackacre to B and B pays A the price. Later A incurs debts which render him insolvent. A then signs a sufficient memorandum, or conveys the land to B. A's creditor cannot set aside the contract or the transfer as in fraud of creditors.

§ 145. Effect of Full Performance

Where the promises in a contract have been fully performed by all parties, the Statute of Frauds does not affect the legal relations of the parties.

Comment:

a. Rationale. The Statute of Frauds renders certain contracts unenforceable by action or defense; it does not forbid the making or performance of such contracts, or authorize their rescission after full performance on both sides. After such full performance, neither party can maintain an action for restitution merely because the contract was unenforceable under the Statute. See § 141. The Statute has no further function to perform, and the legal relations of the parties are the same as if the contract had been enforceable. Compare § 147. **Illustrations:**

    1. A owes B a debt of $ 20,000. A's land, worth $ 10,000, is about to be sold on foreclosure under a mortgage held by C. B contracts to bid in the land and to deduct from A's debt to B $ 10,000 less the amount B pays. B bids in the land for $ 6,000. A's debt is reduced by $ 4,000.

    2. At D's request S orally guarantees to C that D will pay a debt D owes to C. On D's failure to pay at maturity, S pays the debt. C's claim against D is discharged, and S has the same rights against D as if S's promise to C had been enforceable.

§ 146. Rights of Competing Transferees of Property

(1) Where a contract to transfer property or a transfer was unenforceable against the transferor under the Statute of Frauds but subsequently becomes enforceable, the contract or transfer has whatever priority it would have had aside from the Statute of Frauds over an intervening contract by the transferor to transfer the same property to a third person.

(2) If the third person obtains title to the property by an enforceable transaction before the prior contract becomes enforceable, the prior contract is unenforceable against him and does not affect his title.

Comment:

    a. Competing contracts. Where an owner of property makes two agreements to sell the same property to two different buyers, both agreements may be enforceable against him, or the second agreement may be unenforceable as a bargain interfering with a contract with a third person. See § 194. Where each agreement standing alone would be specifically enforceable, the first in time ordinarily has priority, but the second may achieve priority by consent of the first transferee, by estoppel, by a recording act, or by the doctrine of bona fide purchase. See, e.g., § 342.

    b. Priority of unenforceable contract. Where the first contract is unenforceable by virtue of the Statute of Frauds, it does not render the second agreement illegal or prevent the second agreement from being an enforceable contract, unless enforcement of the second would be a tortious interference with the first. See §§ 179, 180, 194. The second transferee, as a successor of the transferor, has the benefit of the transferor's statutory defense. See § 144. But the unenforceable contract is not void or voidable; if the Statute is satisfied by a memorandum or the contract becomes enforceable by virtue of action taken in reliance on it, it has the same priority as if it had been enforceable from the beginning. Compare Restatement, Second, Trusts §§ 41, 42. **Illustration:**

    1. A orally contracts to sell Blackacre to B. Later A contracts in a signed writing to sell Blackacre to C. Thereafter A signs a memorandum of his contract with B. B can enforce the contract specifically against A and C, whether or not C entered into his contract with knowledge of B's, and whether or not B knew of C's contract when the memorandum was signed. C may recover damages from A.

    c. Rights of a transferee. Where the second transferee obtains title to the property, he becomes a successor of the transferor, and has the benefit of the transferor's statutory defense. See § 144. He need not be a bona fide purchaser; whether or not he gives value and whether or not he knows of the prior unenforceable contract, he is given the benefit of the defense so as to preserve the value of the defense to the transferor. Compare Restatement, Second, Trusts §§ 41, 42. For this purpose an attaching or levying creditor is not treated as a transferee unless the property has been sold on execution before the prior contract becomes enforceable. An interest arising by virtue of the transferor's marriage is not protected by the rule. **Illustrations:**

    2. A orally contracts to sell Blackacre to B. He transfers Blackacre to C by deed as a gift, C having knowledge of the contract with B. A subsequently signs a memorandum of the contract with B. B may recover damages from A, but cannot enforce the contract specifically against C.

    . . .

§ 147. Contract Containing Multiple Promises

(1) Where performance of the promises in a contract which subject it to the Statute of Frauds is exclusively beneficial to one party, that party by agreeing to forego the performance may render the remainder of the contract enforceable, but this rule does not apply to a contract to transfer property on the promisor's death.

(2) Where the promises in a contract which subject it to the Statute have become enforceable or where the duty to perform them has been discharged by performance or otherwise, the Statute does not prevent enforcement of the remaining promises.

(3) Except as stated in this Section, where some of the unperformed promises in a contract are unenforceable against a party under the Statute of Frauds, all the promises in the contract are unenforceable against him.

Comment:

a. Waiver of unenforceable part by party seeking enforcement. Where the part of the contract which renders it subject to the Statute is exclusively beneficial to the party seeking enforcement, he may agree to forego that part and enforce the rest. This rule has particular application to cases where the party seeking enforcement has paid the entire consideration. But the rule is not applied to a promise to make a will covering both real and personal property for a single consideration, even though the entire consideration has been given, presumably because of the policy of the Statute of Wills and because of the availability of the remedy of restitution. **Illustrations:**

1. In consideration of A's oral promise to marry B and to settle $ 5,000 upon her, B promises to marry A. If A refuses to marry B after B expresses assent to forego the settlement, the Statute of Frauds does not preclude an action by B against A for breach of promise to marry.

2. For a single premium A orally insures a shipment of B's goods against fire and also orally agrees to answer for certain defaults of the carrier. The goods are damaged by fire. The Statute of Frauds does not prevent enforcement of the fire insurance.

. . .

b. Performance or discharge of the part within the Statute. Where a contract includes promises within the Statute and also promises not within it, the objection to enforcement disappears when the part within the Statute becomes enforceable or is performed or where performance is excused. The part remaining unperformed, if not of itself within the Statute, can be enforced as if it were a separate contract. On the effect of part performance, compare §§ 125(3), 129, 130, 139; Uniform Commercial Code §§ 2-201(3), 8-319(b). **Illustrations:**

4. A and B orally agree that A will work for B for six months and that B will transfer to A an automobile valued at $ 2,400 and pay A $ 600 a month salary. Later the Statute is satisfied with respect to the sale of the automobile by receipt and acceptance. The balance of the contract becomes enforceable.

5. A employs B as plant manager under an oral agreement that B will be paid $ 600 a month and given an option to buy the plant, including real and personal property, on stated terms, but that A may substitute for the option an additional payment of $ 900 per month from the time B starts work. The amounts involved are not disproportionate. B works for several months and gives notice of his exercise of the option, but A refuses to sell. The Statute of Frauds does not prevent B's recovery of the additional payment.

c. Unenforceability of multiple promises. Where an undischarged part of a contract is unenforceable by virtue of the Statute of Frauds, the whole contract is unenforceable, unless the party to be charged has signed a memorandum. As to the situation where a memorandum is signed by fewer than all parties to the contract, see § 135. Whether an agreement creates a single contract or more than one for the present purpose depends primarily on the terms of the agreement, the interdependence of its parts, and the possibility of apportioning the consideration on one side among several promises on the other without doing violence to the expectations of the parties. **Illustrations:**

6. A and B orally agree that A will work for B for six months and that B will transfer to A an automobile worth $ 2,400 and pay A $ 600 a month salary. The Statute is not satisfied with respect to the sale of the automobile. In the absence of a waiver by A, the entire contract is unenforceable.

7. A written agreement between A and B provides that A's manufacturing facilities will be shipped to B and set up and operated by B, that within one year A will buy from B for $ 70,000 certain goods to be manufactured by B, and that for two years A and B will engage in a joint selling enterprise with respect to other goods on terms to be mutually agreed upon. A and B later agree orally on the terms for the joint enterprise. After B begins manufacture, A repudiates the agreement. The Statute of Frauds does not prevent B's recovery of damages for refusal to complete the $ 70,000 purchases.

§ 148. Rescission by Oral Agreement

Notwithstanding the Statute of Frauds, all unperformed duties under an enforceable contract may be discharged by an oral agreement of rescission. The Statute may, however, apply to a contract to rescind a transfer of property.

Comment:

a. Rescission of an executory contract. This Section may be regarded as a particular application of the rules stated in §§ 145 and 149. In determining whether the Statute applies to a contract modifying a prior contract, the second contract is treated as creating a single new contract containing the terms as modified. So treated, it is not within the Statute if there is no remaining unperformed promise. **Illustration:**

1. A and B enter into a written contract of employment for a term exceeding a year. Later they orally agree to rescind the contract. The oral agreement is effective and the written contract is rescinded.

b. Sale of goods. A contract for the sale of goods may be unenforceable under Uniform Commercial Code § 2-201 or because the contract is also a contract to answer for the debt of another or a land contract or a contract not to be performed within a year. Each provision of the Statute of Frauds must be considered separately, and this Section is applicable no matter which provision is under consideration. Uniform Commercial Code § 2-209(2), however, gives effect to a signed agreement which excludes modification "or rescission" except by a signed writing. That provision, applicable to "transactions in goods" (§ 2-102), by its terms negates the rule stated in this Section.

Where title to goods passes to the buyer under a contract for sale, or where the buyer acquires a special property in the goods (Uniform Commercial Code § 2-401), the rule stated in the first sentence of this Section applies if the contract is unenforceable. If the contract is enforceable by virtue of a sufficient memorandum, a contract to rescind the transfer of property may be within the Statute. Compare Uniform Commercial Code § 2-326(4) on contracts for "sale or return." If the seller retains possession, the contract to rescind may be enforceable on the ground that the goods "have been received and accepted" by the seller. See Uniform Commercial Code § 2-201(3)(c). But if the original contract for sale is enforceable because the buyer has "received and accepted" the goods, a contract to rescind is treated as a contract for resale by the buyer to the seller in applying the Statute of Frauds. **Illustration:**

2. A contracts to sell and B to buy a refrigerator for the price of $ 500, and the refrigerator is delivered and paid for. One week later A and B orally agree that if B is not satisfied after a week's further trial the transaction will be rescinded. There is no redelivery or repayment. The contract of rescission is unenforceable.

c. Land contracts; right to specific performance. Where land has been transferred by an effective deed, an agreement to rescind the transaction is a contract for the transfer of an interest in land within the Statute of Frauds. The same rule has sometimes been applied to executory land contracts which were enforceable by virtue of a memorandum or of action in reliance, on the ground that a specifically enforceable contract creates an equitable property interest in the purchaser. But the reasoning is circular: if the rule of the first sentence of this Section is applied, an oral contract to rescind is a defense to an action for specific enforcement of the executory contract, and there is no equitable property interest. The prevailing rule is that an executory land contract may be rescinded orally like other contracts within the Statute, even though enforceable. Compare Restatement of Property § 557, Comment *e*. In any event the contract to rescind becomes enforceable when there has been a material change of position in reliance on it. See

§ 150. The same reasoning applies to specifically enforceable contracts to transfer property other than land. **Illustration:**

§ 149. Oral Modification

(1) For the purpose of determining whether the Statute of Frauds applies to a contract modifying but not rescinding a prior contract, the second contract is treated as containing the originally agreed terms as modified. The Statute may, however, apply independently of the original terms to a contract to modify a transfer of property.

(2) Where the second contract is unenforceable by virtue of the Statute of Frauds and there has been no material change of position in reliance on it, the prior contract is not modified.

Comment:

a. Modification. Where one contract modifies another, the terms of the new contract are found partly in the original contract and partly in the modifying contract. In applying the Statute of Frauds, the new contract is viewed as a whole. See Uniform Commercial Code § 2-209(3) (sale of goods). But where a transfer of property has been made, the modifying contract must be viewed separately in applying the Statute insofar as there is a new transfer of property. See § 148; compare Restatement of Property § 557, Comment *e*; Restatement, Second, Property (Landlord and Tenant) § 2.4 (modification of a lease).

Illustrations:

1. A and B make a written contract that A will employ B for two years at $ 500 a month. At the time B begins work, they agree orally to substitute a contract for six months at $ 600 a month. The second contract is not within the Statute, is enforceable, and at once discharges the prior contract.

2. A and B make a written contract that A will repair and sell to B two specific appliances for $ 3,000. Later they agree orally to eliminate one appliance and to reduce the price. Whether the second contract is within the Statute depends on whether the reduced price is $ 500 or more. See Uniform Commercial Code § 2-201.

3. A and B make mutual promises to marry within one month. Later they orally agree that the marriage will be postponed for two years. The oral agreement is not enforceable.

3. A and B contract in writing that A will sell and B will buy Blackacre for $ 140,000. Later A and B orally rescind the written contract. The written contract is not enforceable.

b. Effect of unenforceable modification. Subsection (2) is an application of the rule stated in § 147: where part of a contract is unenforceable by virtue of the Statute, the whole contract is ordinarily unenforceable. An agreement to rescind a prior contract and to substitute a new contract is normally indivisible; if the substitution is unenforceable, the rescission is also unenforceable. There is no difference for this purpose between modification of a term and substitution of an entire new contract. But it is possible for the parties to include in a single agreement two separate contracts, one to rescind a prior contract and the other to make a new contract; in such a case they may intend the rescission to be effective even though the new contract is unenforceable. See § 148.

Illustrations:

4. In Illustration 3 the original promises to marry are not within the Statute. They remain enforceable unless there is a material change of position. See § 150.

5. A promises to sell and B to buy a specific automobile for $ 3,000, delivery to be made in 30 days and payment in 60 days. Both parties sign a sufficient memorandum. The next day they orally agree on delivery in 45 days and payment in 90 days. Before any change of position B repudiates the oral agreement. The oral agreement is not enforceable; the original contract remains enforceable.

. . .

§ 150. Reliance on Oral Modification

Where the parties to an enforceable contract subsequently agree that all or part of a duty need not be performed or of a condition need not occur, the Statute of Frauds does not prevent enforcement of the subsequent agreement if reinstatement of the original terms would be unjust in view of a material change of position in reliance on the subsequent agreement.

Comment:

a. Relation to other rules. This Section states a particular application of the broader principle stated in § 139. Just as § 139 is complementary to § 90, so this Section is complementary to §§ 84 and 89, which like § 90 dispense with the requirement of consideration in similar circumstances. But this Section like § 139 also applies to promises supported by consideration. Enforcement of a promise or agreement under the present rule is often said to rest on "waiver" or "estoppel," or on excuse by prevention or hindrance. See § 84, 153; Uniform Commercial Code § 2-209(5).

b. Waiver. Where a contract is modified by subsequent agreement and the contract as modified is within a provision of the Statute of Frauds, the modified contract is unenforceable unless the Statute is satisfied. In such a case, if the original contract was enforceable it is not rescinded or modified but remains enforceable. See § 149. But the unenforceable modification may operate as a waiver. See Uniform Commercial Code § 2-209(4). To the extent that the waiver is acted on before it is revoked, it excuses the other party from performance of his own duty and of conditions of the duty of the waiving party. Cf. §§ 246, 247, 278-80. **Illustration:**

1. A and B contract in writing that A will sell specific goods to B for $ 1,000, delivery to be made in 30 days and payment in 60 days. Ten days later B orally requests that delivery be delayed until 45 days, and A so delays in reliance on the request. The delay is not a breach of A's duty and does not excuse B from performing.

c. Reinstatement after waiver. Where an unenforceable modification of an enforceable contract operates as a waiver affecting an executory portion of the contract, the waiving party may retract the waiver by reasonable notification received by the other party. The original terms are then reinstated unless reinstatement would be unjust in view of a material change of position in reliance on the waiver. See Uniform Commercial Code § 2-209(5).

Illustration:

2. The facts being otherwise as stated in Illustration 1, B retracts his request for delay early enough to enable A without difficulty to deliver in accordance with the original terms. A is no longer justified in relying on B's request for delay, either to excuse performance of A's duty or to deny B an excuse for nonperformance.

d. Requirement of reliance. The change of position which prevents retraction of the waiver and reinstatement of the original terms may consist of action or forbearance, and may result from reliance either by the other party to the modifying agreement or by a beneficiary. But it must be a change of position in reliance on the modifying agreement, and it must be such that reinstatement of the original terms would be unjust. See § 84 on the effect of an extension of time by the party retracting a waiver. If the duty or condition would not have been performed in any event, or if there is a waiver of performance after a failure of performance, the failure is not in reliance on the modifying agreement.

Illustrations:

3. The facts being otherwise as stated in Illustration 1, A is unable to deliver for reasons independent of B's request for delay. The request does not excuse A's delay.

4. A and B contract in writing that A will sell and B will buy a parcel of land on stated terms. B's promise to buy is conditional on delivery by A within three days of a certificate showing his title. A does not furnish the certificate, and after three days B orally tells A that he need not furnish the certificate. Though B's implied promise to buy without the certificate is binding without consideration (see § 84), in the absence of reliance the promise is unenforceable by virtue of the Statute of Frauds.

e. Interpretation, modification and waiver. A waiver under this Section may be found in a course of performance. Where there are repeated occasions for performance by one party and the other has knowledge of the nature of the performance and opportunity to object, a course of performance accepted or not objected to may be relevant to show the meaning of the contract, or a modification of it, or a waiver. Where a claim or defense based on interpretation fails, and a claim or defense based on modification is unenforceable by virtue of the Statute of Frauds, a claim or defense based on waiver may nevertheless succeed. But the waiver, unlike the other bases, is subject to the possibility of reinstatement of rights waived. In case of doubt, the policy of the Statute combines with the need for flexibility in an on-going relationship to establish a preference for the claim or defense based on waiver. See Uniform Commercial Code § 2-208 and Comment.

Chapter 6

MISTAKE

Introductory Note The law of contracts supports the finality of transactions lest justifiable expectations be disappointed. This Chapter deals with exceptional situations in which the law departs from this policy favoring finality and allows either avoidance or reformation on the ground of mistake. As § 151 makes clear, the word "mistake" is here used to refer to a belief that is not in accord with existing facts, rather than to an act that is the result of such an erroneous belief.

The type of mistake dealt with in this Chapter is one that relates to existing facts that the parties regard as a basis for making an agreement. An important sub-category of such mistake is mistake as to expression, in which the mistake relates to the contents or effect of a writing that expresses an agreement. In general, the appropriate relief for mistake takes the form of avoidance of the contract. Where, however, because of a mistake of both parties as to expression the writing fails to express an agreement that they have reached previously, the appropriate relief ordinarily takes the form of reformation of the writing to make it conform to their intention. To the extent that reformation is available, as it usually will be, to correct the effects of such a mistake, it is the exclusive remedy and avoidance is unnecessary and unavailable. See § 152. A mistake of only one party as to expression, however, may be a basis for avoidance under the rule stated in § 153. See Illustrations 5 and 6 to § 153.

The basic rule for mistake of both parties is stated in §§ 152. It allows avoidance by the adversely affected party if the mistake was one as to a basic assumption on which the contract was made, if it had a material effect on the agreed exchange of performances, and if he does not bear the risk of the mistake. The situations to which this rule is applicable are often similar to those governed by § 266 on existing impracticability or frustration, since those latter situations also involve mistake. However, the justification underlying the two sections is significantly different. Underlying § 266 is the notion of unexpected extreme hardship, either through impracticability of performance or frustration of purpose, and the legal consequence is that no duty to render performance arises. Underlying § 152 is the notion of an unexpected material imbalance in the exchange, and the legal consequence is merely that the contract is voidable by the party adversely affected. The consequences of impracticability of performance or frustration of purpose are so extreme that it is relatively unusual for a party to agree to perform in spite of mistake that results in such unexpected hardship as would justify his non-performance on one of these grounds. Therefore, § 266 provides for an exception only in the relatively narrow case where "the language or the circumstances indicate the contrary." See Comment *c* to § 261. The consequences of a mistake that materially affects the exchange of performances may be, on the contrary, much less extreme. It is, therefore, much more common for a party to undertake to perform in spite of mistake that would justify his avoidance on this ground. (Indeed, in the absence of provision to the contrary and aside from the exceptional cases of supervening impracticability (§ 261) and frustration (§ 265), a party generally bears the entire risk of subsequent changes that affect the agreed exchange.) Therefore, § 152 provides for an exception, much broader than that in § 266, in all cases where the adversely affected party "bears the risk of mistake." The scope of this exception is spelled out in more detail in a separate section, §§ 154, since the notion of allocation of risk plays a much more significant role in connection with the law of mistake than it does in connection with the law of impracticability and frustration.

The basic rule for mistake of only one party is stated in § 153. In situations where the rule stated in § 153 allows the mistaken party to avoid the contract, avoidance will more clearly disappoint the expectations of the other party, who was not mistaken, than will avoidance under the rule stated in § 152, where he too was mistaken. Therefore, the rule stated in § 153 is more restrictive than that stated in § 152 and generally allows the mistaken party to avoid only in extreme cases where it would be unconscionable to require him to perform, or where the other party had reason to know of the mistake or his fault caused it.

The rules stated in §§ 152 and 153 tell only whether a contract is voidable (§ 7) on the ground of mistake. A party wishing to exercise a power of avoidance will usually simply notify the other party of his rescission, offering to return what he has received or the equivalent. He may then either sue for the return of his own performance or the equivalent or set up his rescission as a defense to a suit on the contract. Sometimes he will instead institute direct proceedings for rescission of the contract. In any case there may be limitations on his power of avoidance. The rules governing this power are stated elsewhere (§§ 380-85), together with those for contracts voidable on the ground of incapacity (§§ 12-16) or misrepresentation, duress or undue influence (Chapter 7).

The basic rule for mistake of both parties as to expression is stated in § 155. It allows reformation where the parties are mistaken in thinking that a writing correctly expresses an agreement that they have previously reached. Avoidance is not an appropriate remedy where the mistake can be corrected by reformation. Under the rule stated in § 214(d), the parol evidence rule does not prevent reformation in such a case, and, under the rule stated in § 156, the Statute of Frauds does not prevent reformation. However, since reformation is a discretionary equitable remedy, the rule stated in § 155 tells only when a court "may" grant such relief, leaving open the possibility that it might deny it on equitable grounds. See Comment *d* to § 155.

If there is a mistake of only one party as to expression, avoidance may be an appropriate remedy under the rule stated in § 153. See Illustrations 5 and 6 to § 153. If, however, his mistake is in believing that a writing correctly expresses a prior agreement and the other party knows that it does not correctly express that agreement, the problem is one of the effect of the latter's failure to disclose this fact. This is dealt with in §§ 160-61, together with other instances in which nondisclosure may be tantamount to misrepresentation.

The rules governing all of the situations dealt with in this Chapter have traditionally been marked by flexibility and have conferred considerable discretion on the court. In part, this has been due to the protean character of the situations involved and the circumstance that they are almost inevitably unforeseen by the parties. In part it has been due to the fact that the law of mistake was shaped largely by courts of equity which had broad discretionary powers. This characteristic of flexibility marks the rules stated in this Chapter, as is evidenced by such necessarily imprecise language as "materially" (§ 152), "unconscionable" (§ 153), and "bears the risk" (§§ 152, 153, 154). In addition, § 158 makes it clear that if these rules will not suffice to do substantial justice, it is within the discretion of the court to grant relief on such terms as justice requires. Compare § 272, which makes this clear in cases of impracticability and frustration.

A number of problems closely related to those dealt with in this Chapter are found elsewhere in the Restatement of this Subject. Some of these, in contrast to those dealt with here, involve the question whether a contract was formed at all. Thus, the effect of misunderstanding, where the parties attach such different meanings to their language or other manifestations that there is no manifestation of mutual assent, is governed by the rule stated in § 20. But cf. Illustration 6 to § 153. Similarly, the effect of a mistake of the offeree as to the fact of a delay in the transmission of an offer is dealt with in § 49, and the effect of a mistake of the offeree as to the terms of the offer, caused by defective transmission, would be determined by analogous principles. As to the effect of a mistake of a party who makes a contract unaware of the death or insanity of the other, see §§ 15 and 48. Other problems, involving a mistake of one party caused by the fraud or misrepresentation of the other, are dealt with in § 161.

Only those aspects of mistake that affect contract law are dealt with in the Restatement of this Subject. Important questions may arise as to money paid or other performance rendered by mistake, for example, under a mistaken belief that such performance is due under an actual or supposed contract. These questions, however, are not dealt with here unless they are inextricably bound up with the enforceability of contract duties, as may be the case for restitution in connection with avoidance of a contract. Similarly, the Restatement of this Subject does not generally cover present transfers, as by assignment or deed. Such matters are, for the most part, left to the Restatement of Restitution. (As to the effect of mistake on equitable remedies, see § 364(a).)

Furthermore, for the sake of simplicity, the rules stated in this Chapter have been formulated in terms of the typical contract based on an exchange of consideration by two parties. It does not, therefore, deal exhaustively with situations involving several parties (§ 9) including intended beneficiaries (§ 302), promises enforceable because of reliance (§ 90), promises enforceable because under seal (§ 95), and other less typical situations. See Comment *c* to § 158

§ 151. Mistake Defined

A mistake is a belief that is not in accord with the facts.

Comment:

a. Belief as to facts. In this Restatement the word "mistake" is used to refer to an erroneous belief. A party's erroneous belief is therefore said to be a "mistake" of that party. The belief need not be an articulated one, and a party may have a belief as to a fact when he merely makes an assumption with respect to it, without being aware of alternatives. The word "mistake" is not used here, as it is sometimes used in common speech, to refer to an improvident act, including the making of a contract, that is the result of such an erroneous belief. This usage is avoided here for the sake of clarity and consistency. Furthermore, the erroneous belief must relate to the facts as they exist at the time of the making of the contract. A party's prediction or judgment as to events to occur in the future, even if erroneous, is not a "mistake" as that word is defined here. An erroneous belief as to the contents or effect of a writing that expresses the agreement is, however, a mistake. Mistake alone, in the sense in which the word is used here, has no legal consequences. The legal consequences of mistake in connection with the creation of contractual liability are determined by the rules stated in the rest of this Chapter. **Illustrations:**

1. A contracts with B to raise and float B's boat which has run aground on a reef. At the time of making the contract, A believes that the sea will remain calm until the work is completed. Several days later, during a sudden storm, the boat slips into deep water and fills with mud, making it more difficult for A to raise it. Although A may have shown poor judgment in making the contract, there was no mistake of either A or B, and the rules stated in this Chapter do not apply. Whether A is discharged by

supervening impracticability is governed by the rules stated in Chapter 11. See Illustration 5 to § 261. If, however, the boat had already slipped into deep water at the time the contract was made, although they both believed that it was still on the reef, there would have been a mistake of both A and B. Its legal consequences, if any, would be governed by the rule stated in § 152.

2. A contracts to sell and B to buy stock amounting to a controlling interest in C Corporation. At the time of making the contract, both A and B believe that C Corporation will have earnings of $ 1,000,000 during the following fiscal year. Because of a subsequent economic recession, C Corporation earns less than $ 500,000 during that year. Although B may have shown poor judgment in making the contract, there was no mistake of either A or B, and the rules stated in this Chapter do not apply. See Uniform Commercial Code § 8-306(2).

b. Facts include law. The rules stated in this Chapter do not draw the distinction that is sometimes made between "fact" and "law." They treat the law in existence at the time of the making of the contract as part of the total state of facts at that time. A party's erroneous belief with respect to the law, as found in statute, regulation, judicial decision, or elsewhere, or with respect to the legal consequences of his acts, may, therefore, come within these rules. **Illustration:**

3. A contracts to sell a tract of land to B. Both parties understand that B plans to erect an office building on the land and believe that he can lawfully do so. Unknown to them, two days earlier a municipal ordinance was enacted requiring a permit for lawful erection of such a building. There is a mistake of both A and B. Its legal consequences, if any, are governed by the rule stated in § 152. See Illustration 7 to § 152.

§ 152. When Mistake of Both Parties Makes a Contract Voidable

(1) Where a mistake of both parties at the time a contract was made as to a basic assumption on which the contract was made has a material effect on the agreed exchange of performances, the contract is voidable by the adversely affected party unless he bears the risk of the mistake under the rule stated in § 154.

(2) In determining whether the mistake has a material effect on the agreed exchange of performances, account is taken of any relief by way of reformation, restitution, or otherwise.

Comment:

a. Rationale. Before making a contract, a party ordinarily evaluates the proposed exchange of performances on the basis of a variety of assumptions with respect to existing facts. Many of these assumptions are shared by the other party, in the sense that the other party is aware that they are made. The mere fact that both parties are mistaken with respect to such an assumption does not, of itself, afford a reason for avoidance of the contract by the adversely affected party. Relief is only appropriate in situations where a mistake of both parties has such a material effect on the agreed exchange of performances as to upset the very basis for the contract.

This Section applies to such situations. Under it, the contract is voidable by the adversely affected party if three conditions are met. First, the mistake must relate to a "basic assumption on which the contract was made." Second, the party seeking avoidance must show that the mistake has a material effect on the agreed exchange of performances. Third, the mistake must not be one as to which the party seeking relief bears the risk. The parol evidence rule does not preclude the use of prior or contemporaneous agreements or negotiations to establish that the parties were mistaken. See § 214(d). However, since mistakes are the exception rather than the rule, the trier of the facts should examine the evidence with particular care when a party attempts to avoid liability by proving mistake. See Comment *c* to § 155. The rule stated in this Section is subject to that in § 157 on fault of the party seeking relief. It is also subject to the rules on exercise of the power of avoidance stated in §§ 378-85.

b. Basic assumption. A mistake of both parties does not make the contract voidable unless it is one as to a basic assumption on which both parties made the contract. The term "basic assumption" has the same meaning here as it does in Chapter 11 in connection with impracticability (§§ 261, 266(1)) and frustration (§§ 265, 266(2)). See Uniform Commercial Code § 2-615(a). For example, market conditions and the financial situation of the parties are ordinarily not such assumptions, and, generally, just as shifts in market conditions or financial ability do not effect discharge under the rules governing impracticability, mistakes as to market conditions or financial ability do not justify avoidance under the rules governing mistake. See Comment *b* to § 261. The parties may have had such a "basic assumption," even though they were not conscious of alternatives. See Introductory Note to Chapter 11. Where, for example, a party purchases an annuity on the life of another person, it can be said that it was a basic assumption that the other person was alive at the time, even though the parties never consciously addressed themselves to the possibility that he was dead. See Illustration 6.

Illustrations:

    1. A contracts to sell and B to buy a tract of land, the value of which has depended mainly on the timber on it. Both A and B believe that the timber is still there, but in fact it has been destroyed by fire. The contract is voidable by B.

    2. A contracts to sell and B to buy a tract of land, on the basis of the report of a surveyor whom A has employed to determine the acreage. The price is, however, a lump sum not calculated from the acreage. Because of an error in computation by the surveyor, the tract contains ten per cent more acreage than he reports. The contract is voidable by A. Compare Illustrations 8 and 11 to this Section and Illustration 2 to § 158.

    3. A contracts to sell and B to buy a tract of land. B agrees to pay A $ 100,000 in cash and to assume a mortgage that C holds on the tract. Both A and B believe that the amount of the mortgage is $ 50,000, but in fact it is only $ 10,000. The contract is voidable by A, unless the court supplies a term under which B is entitled to enforce the contract if he agrees to pay an appropriate additional sum, and B does so. See Illustration 2 to § 158.

    . . .

c. Material effect on agreed exchange. A party cannot avoid a contract merely because both parties were mistaken as to a basic assumption on which it was made. He must, in addition, show that the mistake has a material effect on the agreed exchange of performances. It is not enough for him to prove that he would not have made the contract had it not been for the mistake. He must show that the resulting imbalance in the agreed exchange is so severe that he can not fairly be required to carry it out. Ordinarily he will be able to do this by showing that the exchange is not only less desirable to him but is also more advantageous to the other party. Sometimes this is so because the adversely affected party will give, and the other party will receive, something more than they supposed. Sometimes it is so because the other party will give, and the adversely affected party will receive, something less than they supposed. In such cases the materiality of the effect on the agreed exchange will be determined by the overall impact on both parties. In exceptional cases the adversely affected party may be able to show that the effect on the agreed exchange has been material simply on the ground that the exchange has become less desirable for him, even though there has been no effect on the other party. Cases of hardship that result in no advantage to the other party are, however, ordinarily appropriately left to the rules on impracticability and frustration. See Illustration 9 and § 266. The standard of materiality here, as elsewhere in this Restatement (e.g., § 237), is a flexible one to be applied in the light of all the circumstances. **Illustrations:**

7. The facts being as stated in Illustration 3 to § 151, in determining whether the effect on the agreed exchange is material, and the contract therefore voidable by B, the court will consider not only the decrease in its desirability to B but also any advantage to A through his receiving a higher price than the land would have brought on the market had the facts been known. See Illustration 3 to § 151.

8. A contracts to sell and B to buy a tract of land, which they believe contains 100 acres, at a price of $ 1,000 an acre. In fact the tract contains 110 acres. The contract is not voidable by either A or B, unless additional facts show that the effect on the agreed exchange of performances is material.

9. A contracts to sell and B to buy a dredge which B tells A he intends to use for a special and unusual purpose, but B does not rely on A's skill and judgment. A and B believe that the dredge is fit for B's purpose, but in fact it is not, although it is merchantable. The contract is not voidable by B because the effect on the agreed exchange of performances is not material. If B's purpose is substantially frustrated, he may have relief under § 266(2). See also Uniform Commercial Code §§ 2-314, 2-315.

d. Significance of other relief. Under the rule stated in Subsection (2), before determining the effect on the agreed exchange, the court will first take account of any relief that may be available to him or granted to the other party under the rules stated in §§ 155 (see Illustration 10) and 158 (see Illustration 11). A party may choose to seek relief by means of reformation even though it makes his own performance more onerous when, absent reformation, the contract would be voidable by the other party. See Introductory Note and Comment *e* to § 155. **Illustrations:**

10. A and B agree that A will sell and B will buy a tract of land for $ 100,000, payable by $ 50,000 in cash and the assumption of an existing mortgage of $ 50,000. In reducing the agreement to writing, B's lawyer erroneously omits the provision for assumption of the mortgage, and neither A nor B notices the omission. Under the rule stated in § 155, at the request of either party, the court will decree that the writing be reformed to add the provision for assumption of the mortgage. The contract is, therefore, not voidable by A because, when account is taken of the availability to him of reformation, the effect on the agreed exchange of performances is not material. See Illustration 1 to § 155.

11. A contracts to sell and B to buy a tract of land, described in the contract as containing 100 acres, at a price of $ 100,000, calculated from the acreage at $ 1,000 an acre. In fact the tract contains only 90 acres. If B is entitled to a reduction in price of $ 10,000, under the rule stated in § 158(2), the contract is not voidable by B because when account is taken of the availability to him of a reduction in price, the effect on the agreed exchange of performances is not material. See Illustration 1 to § 158. As to the possibility of an argument based on frustration, see § 266(2).

e. Allocation of risk. A party may be considered to have undertaken to perform in spite of a mistake that has a material effect on the agreed exchange of performances. He then bears the risk of the mistake. Because of the significance of the allocation of risk in the law of mistake, the scope of this exception is spelled out in detail in § 154. (It is assumed in the illustrations to the present Section that the adversely affected party does not bear the risk of the mistake under the rule stated in § 154. See, e.g., Illustration 14.)

f. Releases. Releases of claims have afforded particularly fertile ground for the invocation of the rule stated in this Section. It is, of course, a traditional policy of the law to favor compromises as a means of settling claims without resort to litigation. See Comment *a* to § 74. Nevertheless, a claimant who has executed such a release may later wish to attack it. The situation may arise with respect to any claim, but a particularly common example involves claims for personal injury, where the claimant may have executed the release without full knowledge of the extent or, perhaps, even of the nature of his injuries. Such a claimant has a variety of possible grounds for attacking the release on discovering that his injuries are more serious than he had initially supposed. He may seek to have the release interpreted against the draftsman so as to be inapplicable to the newly discovered injuries (§ 206). He may seek to have the release reformed on the ground that it does not correctly express the prior agreement of the parties (§ 155). He may seek to avoid the release on the ground that it was unfairly obtained through misrepresentation, duress or undue influence (Chapter 7). He may seek to have the release, or at least that part purporting to cover the newly discovered injuries, held unenforceable as unconscionable (§ 208). Or he may seek to avoid the release on the ground that both he and the other party were mistaken as to the nature or extent of his injuries. Assuming that the release is properly interpreted to cover unknown injuries and that it was not unfairly obtained or unconscionable, his case will turn on the application of the rule stated in this Section to his claim of mistake. In dealing with such attacks on releases, a court should be particularly sensitive to obscure or misleading language and especially alert to the possibility of unfairness or unconscionability. However, the same rules relating to mistake apply to such releases as apply to other contracts, and if the results sometimes seem at variance with those rules, the variance can usually be attributed to the presence of one of the alternative grounds listed above.

A claimant's attempt at avoidance based on mistake of both parties, therefore, will frequently turn on a determination, in the light of all the circumstances, of the basic assumptions of the parties at the time of the release. These circumstances may include the fair amount that would be required to compensate the claimant for his known injuries, the probability that the other party would be held liable on that claim, the amount received by the claimant in settlement of his claim, and the relationship between the known injuries and the newly discovered injuries. If, for example, the amount received by the claimant is reasonable in comparison with the fair amount required to compensate him for his known injuries and the probability of the other party being held liable on that claim, this suggests that the parties assumed that his injuries were only those known. Furthermore, even if the parties do not assume that his injuries are only those known, they may assume that any unknown injuries are of the same general nature as the known ones, while differing in extent. Although the parties may fix the assumptions on which the contract is based by an express provision, fairly bargained for, the common recital that the release covers all injuries, known or unknown and of whatever nature or extent, may be disregarded as unconscionable if, in view of the circumstances of the parties, their legal representation, and the setting of the negotiations, it flies in the face of what would otherwise be regarded as a basic assumption of the parties. What has been said here with respect to releases of claims for personal injury is generally true for releases executed in other contexts. **Illustrations:**

> 12. A has a claim against B for B's admitted negligence, which appears to have caused damage to A's automobile in an amount fairly valued at $ 600. In consideration of B's payment of $ 600, A executes a release of "all claims for injury to person or property" that he may have against B. Both A and B believe that A has suffered damage to property only, but A later discovers that he has also suffered personal injuries in the extent of $ 20,000. The release is voidable by A.
>
> . . .

g. Relation to breach of warranty. The rule stated in this Section has a close relationship to the rules governing warranties sale by a seller of goods or of other kinds of property. A buyer usually finds it more advantageous to rely on the law of warranty than on the law of mistake. Because of the broad scope of a seller's warranties, a buyer is more often entitled to relief based on a claim of breach of warranty than on a claim based on mistake. Furthermore, because relief for breach of warranty is generally based on the value that the property would have had if it had been as warranted (see Uniform Commercial Code § 2-714(2)), it is ordinarily more extensive than that afforded if he merely seeks to avoid the contract on the ground of mistake. Nevertheless, the warranties are not necessarily exclusive and, even absent a warranty, a buyer may be able to avoid on the ground of mistake if he brings himself within the rule stated in this Section. The effect, on a buyer's claim of mistake, of language purporting to disclaim the seller's responsibility for the goods is governed by the rules on interpretation stated in Chapter 9. **Illustration:**

> 14. A, a violinist, contracts to sell and B, another violinist, to buy a violin. Both A and B believe that the violin is a Stradivarius, but in fact it is a clever imitation. A makes no express warranty and, because he is not a merchant with respect to violins, makes no implied warranty of merchantibility under Uniform Commercial Code § 2-314. The contract is voidable by B.

h. Mistakes as to different assumptions. The rule stated in this Section applies only where both parties are mistaken as to the same basic assumption. Their mistakes need not be, and often they will not be, identical. If, however, the parties are mistaken as to different assumptions, the rule stated in § 153, rather than that stated in this Section, applies.

§ 153. When Mistake of One Party Makes a Contract Voidable

Where a mistake of one party at the time a contract was made as to a basic assumption on which he made the contract has a material effect on the agreed exchange of performances that is adverse to him, the contract is voidable by him if he does not bear the risk of the mistake under the rule stated in § 154, and (a) the effect of the mistake is such that enforcement of the contract would be unconscionable, or (b) the other party had reason to know of the mistake or his fault caused the mistake.

Comment:

a. Rationale. Courts have traditionally been reluctant to allow a party to avoid a contract on the ground of mistake, even as to a basic assumption, if the mistake was not shared by the other party. Nevertheless, relief has been granted where the other party actually knew (see §§ 160, 161) or had reason to know of the mistake at the time the contract was made or where his fault caused the mistake. There has, in addition, been a growing willingness to allow avoidance where the consequences of the mistake are so grave that enforcement of the contract would be unconscionable. This Section states a rule that permits avoidance on this latter basis, as well as on the more traditional grounds. The rules stated in this Section also apply to option contracts, under which a party's offer is irrevocable either under a statute, such as one applying to bids for public works, or on other grounds. The parol evidence rule does not preclude the use of prior or contemporaneous agreements or negotiations to establish that a party was mistaken. See § 214(d). Nevertheless, because mistakes are the exception rather than the rule, the trier of the facts should examine the evidence with particular care when a party attempts to avoid liability by proving mistake. See Comment *c* to § 155. The rule stated in this Section is subject to that stated in § 157 on fault of the party seeking relief. It is also subject to the rules on exercise of the power of avoidance stated in §§ 380-85.

b. Similarity to rule where both are mistaken. In order for a party to have the power to avoid a contract for a mistake that he alone made, he must at least meet the same requirements that he would have had to meet had both parties been mistaken (§ 152). The mistake must be one as to a basic assumption on which the contract was made; it must have a material effect on the agreed exchange of performances; and the mistaken party must not bear the risk of the mistake. The most common sorts of such mistakes occur in bids on construction contracts and result from clerical errors in the computation of the price or in the omission of component items. See Illustration 1. The rule stated in this Section is not, however, limited to such cases. It also applies, for example, to a misreading of specifications (see Illustration 4) or such misunderstanding as does not prevent a manifestation of mutual assent (see Illustrations 5 and 6). Where only one party is mistaken, however, he must meet either the additional requirement stated in Subparagraph (a) or one of the additional requirements stated in Subparagraph (b).

c. Additional requirement of unconscionability. Under Subparagraph (a), the mistaken party must in addition show that enforcement of the contract would be unconscionable. The reason for this additional requirement is that, if only one party was mistaken, avoidance of the contract will more clearly disappoint the expectations of the other party than if he too was mistaken. See Introductory Note. Although § 208, Unconscionable Contract or Term, is not itself applicable to such cases since the unconscionability does not appear at the time the contract is made, the standards of unconscionability in such cases are similar to those under § 208 (see Comment *c* to § 208). The mistaken party bears the substantial burden of establishing unconscionability and must ordinarily show not only the position he would have been in had the facts been as he believed them to be but also the position in which he finds himself as a result of his mistake. For example, in the typical case of a mistake as to the price in a bid, the builder must show the profit or loss that will result if he is required to perform, as well as the profit that he would have made had there been no mistake. **Illustrations:**

    1. In response to B's invitation for bids on the construction of a building according to stated specifications, A submits an offer to do the work for $ 150,000. A believes that this is the total of a column of figures, but he has made an error by inadvertently omitting a $ 50,000 item, and in fact the total is $ 200,000. B, having no reason to know of A's mistake, accepts A's bid. If A performs for $ 150,000, he will sustain a loss of $ 20,000 instead of making an expected profit of $ 30,000. If the court determines that enforcement of the contract would be unconscionable, it is voidable by A.

    2. The facts being otherwise as stated in Illustration 1, the item that A inadvertently omits is a $ 35,000 item which would have made the total $ 185,000, so that if he does the work for $ 150,000 he will sustain a loss of $ 5,000 rather than make a profit of $ 30,000. The court may reach a result contrary to that in Illustration 1, on the ground that enforcement of the contract would not be unconscionable, and hold that it is not voidable by A.

    3. The facts being otherwise as stated in Illustration 1, B has not accepted A's bid before notification of the mistake, but by statute A's bid is an irrevocable option contract because B is a state agency. In addition, A has posted a $ 10,000 bidder's bond with S as surety. If the court determines that enforcement of the option contract would be unconscionable, it is voidable by A and, on avoidance by A, S is not liable on the bond.

    4. The facts being otherwise as stated in Illustration 1, the $ 50,000 error in A's bid is the result of A's mistake in interpreting B's specifications. If the court determines that enforcement of the contract would be unconscionable, it is voidable by A.

    5. A writes B offering to sell for $ 100,000 a tract of land that A owns known as "201 Lincoln Street." B, who mistakenly believes that this description includes an additional tract of land worth $ 30,000, accepts A's offer. If the court determines that enforcement of the contract would be unconscionable, it is voidable by B.

    6. A offers to sell B goods shipped from Bombay ex steamer "Peerless." B accepts. There are two steamers of the name "Peerless" sailing from Bombay at materially different times. B means Peerless No. 2, and A has reason to know this. A means Peerless No. 1, but B has no reason to know this. Under the rule stated in § 20 there is a contract for the sale of goods from Peerless No. 2, but, under the rule stated in this Section, if the court determines that its enforcement would be unconscionable, it is voidable by A. See Illustration 4 to § 20.

d. Effect of reliance on unconscionability. Reliance by the other party may make enforcement of a contract proper although enforcement would otherwise be unconscionable. If the mistake is discovered and the other party notified before he has relied on the contract, avoidance by the mistaken party deprives the other party only of his expectation, the "benefit of the bargain," (see § 344). If, however, the other party has relied on the contract in some substantial way, avoidance may leave that reliance uncompensated. In such a case, enforcement of the contract would not be unconscionable, even if it otherwise would be.

If, however, the court can adequately protect the other party by compensating him for his reliance under the rules stated in § 158, avoidance is not then precluded on this ground. **Illustrations:**

7. In response to an invitation from B, a general contractor, for bids from subcontractors, A submits an offer to B to do paving work for $ 10,000, to be used by B as a partial basis for B's bid on a large building. As A knows, B is required to name his subcontractors in his general bid. Because of the short time in which A has to prepare his bid, A inadvertently totals his bid as $ 10,000 rather than $ 15,000. B uses A's bid in arriving at his offer of $ 100,000, making A's offer irrevocable as an option contract (§ 87). B's offer is accepted, but A discovers his mistake before B accepts his bid. The option contract is not voidable by A because of B's reliance by using A's offer in making up his own offer. See Illustration 6 to § 87.

8. The facts being otherwise as stated in Illustration 1, on A's refusal to perform for $ 150,000, B is no longer able to accept the next lowest bid and has to re-advertise for bids at a cost of $ 1,000 before getting a bid that he accepts. If the court determines that enforcement of the contract would be unconscionable, the contract is voidable by A in spite of B's reliance, because B can be adequately protected by holding A liable for the $ 1,000 cost of re-advertising (see §§ 158(1) and Comment *b* to that Section).

e. Had reason to know of or caused the mistake. If the other party had reason to know of the mistake, the mistaken party can avoid the contract regardless of whether its enforcement would be unconscionable. (The terminology "reason to know" is used instead of "should know" on the ground explained in Comment *b* to § 19. The situation in which the other party actually knows of the mistake is covered in § 161. See Comment *d* to § 161.) Similar results follow where the other party's fault caused the mistake. (If the mistake was the fault of both parties, it was not caused by the other party within the meaning of this Section and the court may exercise its discretion under the rule stated in § 158(2). See Comment *c* to § 158.) In attempting to unscramble a partially or completely executed transaction, the court may allow the mistaken party recovery under the rules stated in § 158(1). **Illustrations:**

9. The facts being otherwise as stated in Illustration 1, A does not prove what his profit or loss will be if he performs, but B had esti-

mated the expected cost as $ 180,000 before advertising for bids and the ten other bids were all in the range between $ 180,000 and $ 200,000. If it is determined, because of the discrepancy between A's bid on the one hand and B's estimate and the ten other bids on the other, that B had reason to know of A's mistake, the contract is voidable by A.

10. The facts being otherwise as stated in Illustration 7, if it is determined that B had reason to know of A's mistake, the contract is voidable by A.

f. Allocation of risk. Here, as under § 152, a party may undertake to perform in spite of a mistake that would otherwise allow him to avoid the contract. It is, of course, unusual for a party to bear the risk of a mistake that the other party had reason to know of or that was caused by his fault within Subparagraph (b). Because of the significance of allocation of risk in the law of mistake, the scope of this exception is spelled out in detail in § 154. (It is assumed in the illustrations to the present Section that the adversely affected party does not bear the risk under the rule stated in § 154.)

g. Mistake as to identity. Mistakes as to the identity of a party have sometimes been treated as distinct from other mistakes, but the modern trend is to apply the rules applicable to other mistakes. Cf. Uniform Commercial Code § 2-403(1)(a). Such a mistake is therefore subject generally to the rules stated in this Chapter and, since it is by its nature a mistake of only one of the parties, particularly to the rule stated in this Section. The identity of the other party, as distinguished, for example, from his financial standing (see Comment *b* to § 152), is usually a basic assumption on which a contract is made. If the other party knows that he is not the intended offeree, he cannot accept an offer. That case is governed by § 52. If, however, he accepts without knowing that he is not the intended offeree, a contract may result. See Comment *b* to § 52. Whether that contract is voidable by the offeror on the ground of mistake is governed by the rule stated in this Section. The contract is voidable by the mistaken party, under the rule stated in Subparagraph (b), if the other party has caused a mistake as to his identity or if he had reason to know of the mistake, as long as it has a material effect on the agreed exchange of performances. Otherwise it is not voidable unless enforcement of the contract would be unconscionable, under the rule stated in Subparagraph (a). In some transactions the identity of the other party is of sufficient importance that he will be able to show unconscionability, but often he will not.

The situation in which a party deals with an agent acting secretly for an undisclosed principal is governed by the Restatement, Second, of Agency and not by the Restatement of this Subject. The basic principles there applied are not, however, inconsistent with the rule stated in this Section. The party who deals with such an agent gets that which he expects, the liability of the agent on the contract. See Restatement, Second, Agency § 322. Indeed, he gets more, for on disclosure of the agent's principal he can also hold the principal. See Restatement, Second, Agency § 186. Although it is also true that he may himself be liable to the principal, as well as to the agent, on the contract, this additional burden has not been regarded by the law of agency as sufficiently important to make enforcement of the contract against him

unconscionable, since it does not change the terms of the contract. **Illustrations:**

11. In answer to an inquiry from "J. B. Smith Company," A offers to sell goods for cash on delivery. A mistakenly believes that the offeree is John B. Smith, who has an established business of good repute, but in fact it is a business run by his son, whose business is new and near insolvency. The son accepts, not knowing of A's mistake. If the court concludes that, because payment is to be cash on delivery, enforcement of the contract would not be unconscionable, the contract is not voidable by A.

12. The facts being otherwise as stated in Illustration 11, A's offer is to sell goods on 90 days credit. If the court determines that, because payment is to be on 90 days credit, enforcement of the contract would be unconscionable, the contract is voidable by A. See §§ 251, 252; Uniform Commercial Code §§ 2-609, 2-702(1).

13. The facts being otherwise as stated in Illustration 11, A's offer contains references to "your long established business" from which the son had reason to know of A's mistake. The contract is voidable by A.

§ 154. When a Party Bears the Risk of a Mistake

A party bears the risk of a mistake when (a) the risk is allocated to him by agreement of the parties, or (b) he is aware, at the time the contract is made, that he has only limited knowledge with respect to the facts to which the mistake relates but treats his limited knowledge as sufficient, or (c) the risk is allocated to him by the court on the ground that it is reasonable in the circumstances to do so.

Comment:

a. Rationale. Absent provision to the contrary, a contracting party takes the risk of most supervening changes in circumstances, even though they upset basic assumptions and unexpectedly affect the agreed exchange of performances, unless there is such extreme hardship as will justify relief on the ground of impracticability of performance or frustration of purpose. A party also bears the risk of many mistakes as to existing circumstances even though they upset basic assumptions and unexpectedly affect the agreed exchange of performances. For example, it is commonly understood that the seller of farm land generally cannot avoid the contract of sale upon later discovery by both parties that the land contains valuable mineral deposits, even though the price was negotiated on the basic assumption that the land was suitable only for farming and the effect

on the agreed exchange of performances is material. In such a case a court will ordinarily allocate the risk of the mistake to the seller, so that he is under a duty to perform regardless of the mistake. The rule stated in this Section determines whether a party bears the risk of a mistake for the purposes of both §§ 152 and 153. Stating these rules in terms of the allocation of risk avoids such artificial and specious distinctions as are sometimes drawn between "intrinsic" and "extrinsic" mistakes or between mistakes that go to the "identity" or "existence" of thesubject matter and those that go merely to its "attributes," "quality" or "value." Even though a mistaken party does not bear the risk of a mistake, he may be barred from avoidance if the mistake was the result of his failure to act in good faith and in accordance with reasonable standards of fair dealing. See § 157.

b. Allocation by agreement. The most obvious case of allocation of the risk of a mistake is one in which the parties themselves provide for it by their agreement. Just as a party may agree to perform in spite of impracticability or frustration that would otherwise justify his non-performance, he may also agree, by appropriate language or other manifestations, to perform in spite of mistake that would otherwise justify his avoidance. An insurer, for example, may expressly undertake the risk of loss of property covered as of a date already past. Whether the agreement places the risk on the mistaken party is a question to be answered under the rules generally applicable to the scope of contractual obligations, including those on interpretation, usage and unconscionability. See Chapter 9. **Illustration:**

> 1. A contracts to sell and B to buy a tract of land. A and B both believe that A has good title, but neither has made a title search. The contract provides that A will convey only such title as he has, and A makes no representation with respect to title. In fact, A's title is defective. The contract is not voidable by B, because the risk of the mistake is allocated to B by agreement of the parties.

c. Conscious ignorance. Even though the mistaken party did not agree to bear the risk, he may have been aware when he made the contract that his knowledge with respect to the facts to which the mistake relates was limited. If he was not only so aware that his knowledge was limited but undertook to perform in the face of that awareness, he bears the risk of the mistake. It is sometimes said in such a situation that, in a sense, there was not mistake but "conscious ignorance." **Illustration:**

> 2. The facts being otherwise as stated in Illustration 2 to § 152, A proposes to B during the negotiations the inclusion of a provision under which the adversely affected party can cancel the contract in the event of a material error in the surveyor's report, but B refuses to agree to such a provision. The contract is not voidable by A, because A bears the risk of the mistake.

d. Risk allocated by the court. In some instances it is reasonably clear that a party should bear the risk of a mistake for reasons other than those stated in Subparagraphs (a) and (b). In such instances, under the rule stated in Subparagraph (c), the court will allocate the risk to that party on the ground that it is reasonable to do so. A court will generally do this, for example, where the seller of farm land seeks to avoid the contract of sale on the ground that valuable mineral rights have newly been found. See Comment *a*. In dealing with such issues, the court will consider the purposes of the parties and will have recourse to its own general knowledge of human behavior in bargain transactions, as it will in the analogous situation in which it is asked to supply a term under the rule stated in § 204. The rule stated in Subsection (c) is subject to contrary agreement and to usage (§ 221). **Illustrations:**

> 3. The facts being otherwise as stated in Illustration 6 to § 152, C is not dead but is afflicted with an incurable fatal disease and cannot live more than a year. The contract is not voidable by A, because the court will allocate to A the risk of the mistake.

> 4. A, an owner of land, and B, a builder, make a contract under which B is to take from A's land, at a stated rate per cubic yard, all the gravel and earth necessary for the construction of a bridge, an amount estimated to be 114,000 cubic yards. A and B believe that all of the gravel and earth is above water level and can be removed by ordinary means, but in fact about one quarter of it is below water level, so that removal will require special equipment at an additional cost of about twenty percent. The contract is not voidable by B, because the court will allocate to B the risk of the mistake. Compare Illustration 5 to § 266.

> 5. A contracts with B to build a house on B's land. A and B believe that subsoil conditions are normal, but in fact some of the land must be drained at an expense that will leave A no profit under the contract. The contract is not voidable by A, because the court will allocate to A the risk of the mistake. Compare Illustration 8 to § 266.

> 6. The facts being otherwise as stated in Illustration 1 to § 153, the $ 50,000 error in A's bid is the result of A's mistaken estimate as to the amount of labor required to do the work. A cannot avoid the contract, because the court will allocate to A the risk of the mistake.

§ 155. When Mistake of Both Parties as to Written Expression Justifies Reformation

Where a writing that evidences or embodies an agreement in whole or in part fails to express the agreement because of a mistake of both parties as to the contents or effect of the writing, the court may at the request of a party reform the writing to express the agreement, except to the extent that rights of third parties such as good faith purchasers for value will be unfairly affected.

Comment:

a. Scope. The province of reformation is to make a writing express the agreement that the parties intended it should. Under the rule stated in this Section, reformation is available when the parties, having reached an agreement and having then attempted to reduce it to writing, fail to express it correctly in the writing. Their mistake is one as to expression -- one that relates to the contents or effect of the writing that is intended to express their agreement -- and the appropriate remedy is reformation of that writing properly to reflect their agreement. For the rule stated in this Section to be invoked, therefore, there must have been some agreement between the parties prior to the writing. The prior agreement need not, however, be complete and certain enough to be a contract. Compare § 1 with § 3; see § 33. If the parties reach agreement as to only part of a prospective bargain, and if they are later mistaken in their attempt to put in writing this agreement together with such other terms as will make a contract, reformation is still an appropriate remedy. The agreement must, of course, be certain enough to permit a court to frame relief in terms of reformation. The writing that is reformed may purport to embody their entire agreement (i.e., a completely integrated agreement under § 210(1)), or only part of their agreement (i.e., a partially integrated agreement under § 210(2)), since the parol evidence rule does not preclude such a showing of mistake. See § 214(d). It may be a writing evidencing a contract within the Statute of Frauds, since the Statute does not bar reformation. See § 156. (If neither the parol evidence rule nor the Statute of Frauds applies, the writing itself will not ordinarily have sufficient legal significance for its reformation to be necessary.) The error in expressing the agreement may consist in the omission or erroneous reduction to writing of a term agreed upon or the inclusion of a term not agreed upon. If the parties are mistaken with respect to the legal effect of the language that they have used, the writing

may be reformed to reflect the intended effect. Reformation is available even though the effect of the error is to make it appear from the writing that there is no enforceable agreement. See Illustration 2 and Comment *a* and Illustration 3 to § 156. Reformation is not precluded by the mere fact that the party who seeks it failed to exercise reasonable care in reading the writing, but the right to reformation is subject to the rule on fault stated in § 157. With the merger of law and equity under modern codes of procedure, it is generally unnecessary to seek reformation as a condition to enforcing the true contract, and a party may be granted both reformation and enforcement in a single suit. **Illustrations:**

    1. A and B agree that A will sell and B will buy a tract of land for $ 100,000 and that B will assume an existing mortgage of $ 50,000. In reducing the agreement to writing, B's lawyer erroneously omits the provision for assumption, and neither A nor B notices the omission. At the request of either A or B, the court will reform the writing to add the provision for assumption. 2. A and B agree that A will sell and B will buy all the coal that B shall require in his business during a five year period. In reducing the agreement to writing, B mistakenly provides that he will buy all the coal that he shall desire to buy during that period, and A fails to notice the error. At the request of either A or B, the court will reform the writing to provide that B will buy all the coal that he shall require rather than all that he shall desire to buy.

. . .

b. Relation to other rules. The rule stated in this Section applies only where both parties are mistaken with respect to the reduction to writing. (In the case of a promise under seal to make a gift, since the intention of only one party is involved, his mistake alone will entitle him to reformation, at least if there has been no reliance by the donee that cannot be compensated for. See Comment *d*.) A mistake as to expression is a mistake as to a basic assumption, but the contract is not voidable unless reformation is unavailable to protect the interests of the parties. See §§ 152. One party may, therefore, seek reformation in order to prevent avoidance by the other. See Comment *e* to this Section and Illustration 10 to §§ 152. If, however, the parties make a written agreement that they would not otherwise have made because of a mistake other than one as to expression, the court will not reform a writing to reflect the agreement that it thinks they would have made. The remedy in that case is avoidance. See Illustrations 4 and 5. The discretionary relief authorized under the rule stated in § 158 may involve some reshaping of the contract duties by the court but is different from reformation.

Several other related cases must also be distinguished. If one party sends to the other an offer which, because of a mistake, does not reflect the offeror's intention, the rule stated in this Section does not apply both because only one party is mistaken and because there was no prior agreement. The mistaken party's remedy, if any, in that case is not reformation but avoidance under the rule stated in § 153. See Illustration 6 to § 153. Similarly, when the parties to a bargain, sufficiently certain to be a contract, are silent with respect to a term that is essential to a determination of their rights and duties, the court will not decree reformation but will supply a term under the rule stated in § 204. See Illustration 6. Furthermore, even where there is a prior agreement that is not properly expressed in the writing, if only one party is mistaken and the other actually knows this, the mistaken party's right to reformation is governed by the rule on fraudulent misrepresentation stated in § 166.

In some instances where it might appear that both parties are mistaken with respect to the reduction to writing of a prior agreement, interpretation of the writing will show that the mistake is only apparent and not real. Where, for example, the parties use language in the writing in an unusual way, interpretation of the writing in accord with the meaning attached by the parties will protect their expectations, and reformation is unnecessary. See Illustration 7. In a borderline case a court may avoid the necessity of reforming the writing by viewing the issue as one of interpretation. Finally, in the case of a standardized agreement, the special rule stated in § 211(3) may operate to exclude a term that is not only unknown to a party but beyond the range of reasonable expectations. See Comment *f* to § 211. **Illustrations:**

4. A and B make a written contract for the sale by A to B for $ 15,000 of a claim by A against C. Both parties mistakenly believe that the claim is an unliquidated one for about $ 20,000, but in fact it does not exceed $ 10,000. A court will not, at the request of B, reform the writing, because the mistake of the parties was not one as to its contents or effect. B's right to avoidance is governed by the rule stated in § 152. See Illustration 4 to § 152.

5. A contracts to sell and B to buy a tract of land, described in the contract as containing 100 acres, at a price of $ 100,000. Both parties believe that the area is 100 acres but in fact it is only 90 acres. The court will not, at the request of B, reform the writing, because the mistake of the parties was not one as to its contents or effect. B's right to avoidance is governed by the rules stated in §§ 152 and 158. See Illustration 11 to § 152 and Illustration 1 to § 158.

6. A and B agree that A shall have the exclusive right to market goods manufactured by B and that A shall pay B half of any profits he derives from their sale. The agreement is then reduced to writing. Each party understands that A is to use best efforts to promote sale of the goods and that B will use best efforts to supply them, but nothing is said on this subject. Under the rule stated in § 204 a court will supply a term imposing on both A and B an obligation to use best efforts, and it will not reform the writing. See Illustration 9 to § 77 and Uniform Commercial Code § 2-306(2).

. . .

c. Proof required. Because experience teaches that mistakes are the exception and not the rule, the trier of the facts should examine the evidence with particular care when it relates to a party's assertion of mistake as the basis for his claim or defense. Care is all the more necessary when the asserted mistake relates to a writing, because the law of contracts, as is indicated by the parol evidence rule and the Statute of Frauds, attaches great weight to the written expression of an agreement. This is commonly summarized in a standard that requires the trier of the facts to be satisfied by "clear and convincing evidence" before reformation is granted. Each case must, however, turn on its particular facts, and the evidentiary weight to be attached to a writing will depend, in part, on its inherent credibility in the light of those facts. Once the court is convinced that the writing fails to express the agreement of the parties, the writing loses its usual evidentiary effect with respect to other matters, such as the ascertainment of the parties' actual agreement. Because this Restatement is concerned with rules of substantive law and not with rules of procedure, including proof, this question of the proof required for reformation is not dealt with in this Section.

d. Equitable discretion. This Section states the circumstances in which a court "may" grant reformation. Since the remedy of reformation is equitable in nature, a court has the discretion to withhold it, even if it would otherwise be appropriate, on grounds that have traditionally justified courts of equity in withholding relief. No attempt is made here to define the limits of this traditional equitable discretion. One such limit, however, has been that equity will not ordinarily aid a volunteer, and it is for this reason that the promisee of a promise under seal to make a gift is generally barred from obtaining reformation. See Comment *b*.

e. Who is entitled to reformation. Reformation may be granted at the request of any party to the contract, including an intended beneficiary, or of a party's successor in interest. In contrast to the rules for avoidance stated in §§ 152 and 153, the party seeking relief need not show that the mistake has resulted in an inequality that adversely affects him. A party may, for example, seek and be granted reformation even though it makes his own performance more onerous when, absent reformation, the agreement would be unenforceable for lack of consideration (see Illustration 2) or where the agreement would be voidable by the other party (see Illustration 10 to § 152). A court will, however, deny reformation where the effect of the mistake is trivial.

f. Protection of innocent third parties. The claim of a mistaken party to reformation, being equitable in its origin, is subject to the rights of good faith purchasers for value and other third parties who have similarly relied on the finality of a consensual transaction in which they have acquired an interest in property. Cf. Restatement of Restitution § 13. Such other third parties include those who have given value and come within the definition of "purchaser" in Uniform Commercial Code § 1-201(33), (32), notably mortgagees, pledgees and other holders of a security interest. Judgment creditors and trustees in bankruptcy are not included. **Illustrations:**

8. A gives B a note for $ 50,000, loaned to him by B, and also gives B a written contract by which A promises to execute a mortgage on land that he owns as security for the note. Because of a mistake of both parties as to the contents of the writing, it fails to express their agreement that the mortgage is to be subject to another mortgage for $ 30,000 for which A is then bargaining. B negotiates the note and assigns the contract to C, a good faith purchaser for value. The court will not, at the request of A, reform the writing because to do so would adversely affect C, a good faith purchaser.

. . .

§ 156 Mistake as to Contract Within the Statute of Frauds

    If reformation of a writing is otherwise appropriate, it is not precluded by the fact that the contract is within the Statute of Frauds.

Comment:

a. Rationale and scope. The premise underlying the rule stated in this Section is that a writing evidencing an agreement may be reformed under the rule stated in § 155 before it is subjected to the requirements of the Statute of Frauds. If the parties have prepared an integrated agreement which, because of a mistake of both of them, incorrectly states an essential term that would have to be contained in a writing in order to satisfy the Statute, the court will reform the writing before determining whether it satisfies the Statute. The Statute of Frauds does not bar reformation in such a case. See Illustration 1. The court will similarly reform a writing that is a mere memorandum and not an integrated agreement before determining whether it satisfies the Statute. See Illustration 2. Reformation is also available where the parties have by mistake omitted an essential term, as distinguished from stating it incorrectly. No meaningful distinction can be drawn in this respect between errors of omission and those of commission. See Illustration 3. If reformation is to be an appropriate remedy in the case of omission, however, the failure of the writing to contain the omitted term must, under the rule stated in §§ 155, be the result of mistake of both parties as to its contents; they must have believed that the writing contained the term. Reformation will not be granted where the parties simply failed to include a required term in the writing and one party, having discovered the failure, later seeks to reform it so that it will satisfy the Statute. The Statute is neither a basis for denying nor one for granting reformation. See Illustration 4. The rule stated in this Section applies to reformation under the rules stated in § 166 as well as under the rules stated in this Chapter. **Illustrations:**

1. A agrees to sell and B to buy a tract of land for $ 100,000. In preparing a writing that the parties intend to be a completely integrated agreement, A's secretary erroneously types "$ 10,000" instead of "$ 100,000," and both A and B sign without noticing the error. Although the agreement is within the Statute of Frauds (§ 125), at the request of either A or B, the court will reform the writing to read "$ 100,000."

2. The facts being otherwise as stated in Illustration 1, the parties do not intend the writing to be an integrated agreement but a mere memorandum evidencing the agreement. Although the agreement is within the Statute of Frauds (§ 125), at the request of either A or B, the court will reform the writing to read "$ 100,000" before determining whether the statute is satisfied.

. . .

§ 157 Effect of Fault of Party Seeking Relief

A mistaken party's fault in failing to know or discover the facts before making the contract does not bar him from avoidance or reformation under the rules stated in this Chapter, unless his fault amounts to a failure to act in good faith and in accordance with reasonable standards of fair dealing.

Comments:

a. Rationale. The mere fact that a mistaken party could have avoided the mistake by the exercise of reasonable care does not preclude either avoidance (§§ 152, 153) or reformation (§ 155). Indeed, since a party can often avoid a mistake by the exercise of such care, the availability of relief would be severely circumscribed if he were to be barred by his negligence. Nevertheless, in extreme cases the mistaken party's fault is a proper ground for denying him relief for a mistake that he otherwise could have avoided. Although the critical degree of fault is sometimes described as "gross" negligence, that term is not well defined and is avoided in this Section as it is in the Restatement, Second, of Torts. Instead, the rule is stated in terms of good faith and fair dealing. The general duty of good faith and fair dealing, imposed under the rule stated in § 205, extends only to the performance and enforcement of a contract and does not apply to the negotiation stage prior to the formation of the contract. See Comment *c* to § 205. Therefore, a failure to act in good faith and in accordance with reasonable standards of fair dealing during pre-contractual negotiations does not amount to a breach. Nevertheless, under the rule stated in this Section, the failure bars a mistaken party from relief based on a mistake that otherwise would not have been made. During the negotiation stage each party is held to a degree of responsibility appropriate to the justifiable expectations of the other. The terms "good faith" and "fair dealing" are used, in this context, in much the same sense as in § 205 and Uniform Commercial Code § 1-203. **Illustrations:**

1. The facts being otherwise as stated in Illustration 1 to § 153, A's mistake is caused by his failure to exercise reasonable care in totalling and verifying his figures. A's negligence does not amount to a failure to act in good faith and in accordance with reasonable standards of fair dealing, and he is not precluded from avoiding the contract.

2. The facts being otherwise as stated in Illustration 1 to § 153, B, on finding that A's bid is the lowest, asks A to check his figures to make certain that there has been no mistake. A states that he has done so although he has not and although such a check would have revealed his mistake. B then accepts A's bid. A's conduct amounts to a failure to act in good faith and in accordance with reasonable standards of fair dealing, and he cannot avoid the contract.

b. Failure to read writing. Generally, one who assents to a writing is presumed to know its contents and cannot escape being bound by its terms merely by contending that he did not read them; his assent is deemed to cover unknown as well as known terms. See Comment *b* to § 23; Comment *b* to § 211. But see the special rule of § 211(3) for the case of standardized agreements. The exceptional rule stated in the present Section with regard to reformation has no application to the common case in which the term in question was not the subject of prior negotiations. It only affects cases that come within the scope of § 155, under which there must have been an agreement that preceded the writing. In such a case, a party's negligence in failing to read the writing does not preclude reformation if the writing does not correctly express the prior agreement. See Illustration 3. Where there was no prior agreement, however, this Section does not apply because reformation is not available under § 155. See Illustration 4. **Illustrations:**

> 3. The facts being otherwise as stated in Illustration 1 to § 155, neither A nor B reads the writing before signing it, although the omission would be obvious to either if he read it. Neither A's nor B's conduct amounts to a failure to act in good faith and in accordance with reasonable standards of fair dealing, and neither A nor B is precluded from obtaining a decree reforming the writing.

. . .

§ 158. Relief Including Restitution

(1) In any case governed by the rules stated in this Chapter, either party may have a claim for relief including restitution under the rules stated in §§ 240 and 376.

(2) In any case governed by the rules stated in this Chapter, if those rules together with the rules stated in Chapter 16 will not avoid injustice, the court may grant relief on such terms as justice requires including protection of the parties' reliance interests.

Comment:

a. Scope. A court may use several techniques to adjust the rights of the parties after discovery of a mistake. Subsection (1) speaks to claims for relief such as that provided by the rule on part performances as agreed equivalents stated in § 240 and those on restitution and other relief stated in Chapter 16. Subsection (2) speaks to supplying a term to avoid injustice. See the analogous rule stated in § 272.

b. Relief including restitution. Avoidance of a contract ideally involves a reversal of any steps that the parties may have taken by way of performance, so that each party returns such benefit as he may have received. This is not, however, possible in all cases. Occasionally a party who has performed may be entitled to recover on the contract for the part that he has performed under the rule on part performances as agreed equivalents (§ 240). Even where this is not so, it may be appropriate to permit avoidance coupled with a money claim for restitution to the extent that one party's performance has benefited the other. Such claims are governed by the rules stated in §§ 370-77. A party may also have a claim that goes beyond mere restitution and includes elements of reliance by the claimant. See, e.g., Illustration 8 to § 153.

c. Supplying a term to avoid injustice. Under the rule stated in § 204, when the parties have not agreed with respect to a term that is essential to a determination of their rights and duties, the court will supply a term that is reasonable in the circumstances. Ordinarily the rules stated in this Chapter, coupled with those stated in Chapter 16, will be adequate to allow the court to arrive at a just result. See Subsection (1). If, however, these rules will not suffice to avoid injustice, the court may supply a term just as it may in cases of impracticability of performance and frustration of purpose. See § 272(2) and Comment *c* to that section. Here, as there, a particularly significant application occurs when the just solution is to "sever" the agreement and require that some unexecuted part of it be performed on both sides, rather than to relieve both parties of all their duties. The situation differs from that envisioned in § 240, under which the court merely allows recovery at the contract rate for performance that has already been rendered. The question under this Section is whether the court can salvage a part of the agreement that is still executory on both sides. See Illustration 1.

Sometimes the party who is not adversely affected by a mistake can, by assenting to a modification of the contract, eliminate the effect of the mistake on the agreed exchange. He should generally be allowed to do so and thereby to preclude avoidance by the party who would otherwise be adversely affected. A court may, under Subsection (2), grant the party who has not been adversely affected what is, in effect, an option to enforce the contract on new terms. See Illustration 2.

The Court may also exercise its discretion under Subsection (2) where both parties have been responsible for the mistake. It may do so, for example, where a mistake of one party resulted both from his failure to act in good faith and in accordance with reasonable standards of fair dealing (§ 157) and from the fault of the other party (§ 153(b)). See Comment *f* to § 153. Furthermore, for the sake of simplicity, the rules stated in this Chapter have been formulated in terms of the typical contract based on an exchange of consideration by two parties, and it does not, therefore, deal exhaustively with problems of mistake involving several parties (§ 9) including intended beneficiaries (§ 302), promises enforceable because of reliance (§ 90), promises enforceable because under seal (§ 95), and other less typical situations. In such cases, the court will apply rules analogous to those stated in this Chapter. See Comments *b, d,* and *e* to § 155. The situations dealt with in Subsection (2) are to be distinguished from those envisioned by § 155, where a writing is reformed to carry out the intentions of the parties. **Illustrations:**

1. A contracts to sell and B to buy a tract of land, described in the contract as containing 100 acres, at a price of $ 100,000, calculated from the acreage at $ 1,000 an acre. In fact the tract contains only 90 acres. Under the rule stated in § 152, the contract would be voidable by B. If, however, the court decides that this rule will not avoid injustice, it is within the discretion of the court to grant relief on such terms as justice requires. The contract is not then voidable by B. See Illustration 11 to § 152.

2. The facts being otherwise as stated in Illustration 1, the tract in fact contains 110 acres. Under the rule stated in § 152, the contract would be voidable by A. If, however, the court decides that this rule will not avoid injustice, it is within the discretion of the court to grant relief on such terms as justice requires. Compare Illustration 2 to § 152.

3. A sends B two different offers of a contract, one with an option for renewal by A and one without such an option. B signs the one with an option, believing that it is the other one. Under the rule stated in § 153, if the court found that enforcement of the contract would be unconscionable, the contract would be voidable by B. If, however, the court decides that this rule will not avoid injustice, it may supply a term, if reasonable, under which B is entitled to avoid the contract only if he accepts the other offer.

Chapter 7

Misrepresentation, Duress and undue Influence

Introductory Note Contract law has traditionally relied in large part on the premise that the parties should be able to make legally enforceable agreements on their own terms, freely arrived at by the process of bargaining. This premise presupposes that the integrity of the bargaining process has not been impaired by misrepresentation, duress or undue influence.

Topic 1 of this Chapter deals with situations in which a party has been induced to make a contract by a misrepresentation, that is, an assertion, either fraudulent or non-fraudulent, that is not in accord with existing facts. Topic 2 deals with situations in which a party has been influenced to make a contract by improper pressure. This pressure may take the form of duress by physical compulsion or by threat, or may take the form of undue influence.

Only those aspects of these subjects that deal with contract law are treated in the Restatement of this Subject. Important questions may arise, for example, as to the payment of money or other performance induced by misrepresentation, duress or undue influence. These questions are not dealt with here unless they are inextricably bound up with the enforceability of contract duties, as in the case of restitution in connection with avoidance of a contract on one of these grounds. Similarly, the Restatement of this Subject does not generally cover present transfers, as by assignment or deed. Such matters are, for the most part, left to the Restatement of Restitution. Furthermore, for the sake of simplicity, the rules stated in this Chapter have been formulated in terms of the typical contract involving only two parties and supported by consideration and do not deal exhaustively with less typical situations such as those involving several parties (§ 9) or promises enforceable because of reliance (§ 90) or because under seal (§ 95). As to the possibility that misconduct short of that required by the rules stated in this Chapter may nevertheless be sufficient to preclude equitable relief, see § 364. As to the effect of unconscionability, see § 208.

At most, the rules stated in this Chapter make the contract voidable, rather than giving the aggrieved party the right to a claim for damages. Compare Restatement, Second, Torts chs. 22, 23.

Topic 1. Misrepresentation

Introductory Note A misrepresentation is an assertion that is not in accord with the facts (§ 159). Concealment (§ 160) and in some cases non-disclosure (§ 161) of a fact are equivalent to such an assertion. A misrepresentation may have three distinct effects under the rules stated in this Chapter. First, in rare cases, it may prevent the formation of any contract at all (§ 163). Second, it may make a contract voidable (§ 164). Third, it may be the grounds for a decree reforming the contract (§ 166). In the case of non-disclosure by a fiduciary, making a contract with his beneficiary, these rules are supplemented by the rule stated in § 173.

A misrepresentation may also be the basis for an affirmative claim for liability for misrepresentation under the law of torts. Such liability for misrepresentation is dealt with in the Restatement, Second, Torts. See Restatement, Second, Torts chs. 22, 23. The rules stated there conform generally to those stated here. However, because tort law imposes liability in damages for misrepresentation, while contract law does not, the requirements imposed by contract law are in some instances less stringent. Notably, under tort law a misrepresentation does not give rise to liability for fraudulent misrepresentation unless it is both fraudulent and material, while under contract law a misrepresentation may make a contract voidable if it is either fraudulent or material. See Comment *a* to § 164, and compare § 164 with Restatement, Second, Torts § 538

The most common of the three possible effects of a misrepresentation under the rules stated in this Chapter is that of making the resulting contract voidable. In order for this effect to follow, four things must be shown. First, there must have been a misrepresentation (§§ 159, 160, 161). Second, the misrepresentation must have been either fraudulent or material (§ 162). Third, the misrepresentation must have induced the recipient to make the contract (§ 167). Fourth, the recipient's reliance on the misrepresentation must have been justified. Specific aspects of the last requirement are treated in connection with assertions of opinion (§§ 168, 169), assertions as to matters of law (§ 170), assertions of intention (§ 171), and fault (§ 172).

Assertions of opinion pose particularly difficult problems. If such an assertion is solely one of opinion and carries with it no assertion of fact beyond one as to the maker's state of mind, the recipient's reliance on it is usually unjustified, since a party is generally expected to form his own opinions as to the proposed bargain. Exceptional situations, where reliance on such an assertion is justified, are enumerated in § 169. However, the recipient may properly interpret a statement of a person's opinion as to facts not known to the recipient as more than a statement of opinion only. He may interpret it as, in addition, an assertion that that person knows of facts sufficient to justify him in forming the opinion, or at least that he knows of no facts incompatible with it (§ 168(2)). To this extent, the recipient may be justified in relying on that assertion, even if reliance on the assertion as one of opinion only would not be justified under the rule stated in § 169.

Because a misrepresentation induces the recipient to make a contract while under a mistake, the rules on mistake stated in Chapter 6 also apply to many cases of misrepresentation. However, a mistaken party who can show the elements required for avoidance on the ground of misrepresentation will ordinarily prefer to base his claim on this ground rather than attempting to establish the additional elements required by the law of mistake.

Special rules of law, applicable to particular types of contracts, also supplement or qualify the rules stated in this Topic. Examples include the provisions of the Uniform Commercial Code relating to warranties in contracts for the sale of goods and those of statutes requiring disclosure in consumer transactions or regulating transactions in securities (see Federal Securities Code, Parts XVI, XVII). These special rules are not dealt with in this Restatement

§ 159. Misrepresentation Defined

A misrepresentation is an assertion that is not in accord with the facts.

Comment:

a. Nature of the assertion. A misrepresentation, being a false assertion of fact, commonly takes the form of spoken or written words. Whether a statement is false depends on the meaning of the words in all the circumstances, including what may fairly be inferred from them. An assertion may also be inferred from conduct other than words. Concealment or even non-disclosure may have the effect of a misrepresentation under the rules stated in §§ 160 and 161. Whether a misrepresentation is fraudulent is determined by the rule stated in § 162(1). However, an assertion need not be fraudulent to be a misrepresentation. Thus a statement intended to be truthful may be a misrepresentation because of ignorance or carelessness, as when the word "not" is inadvertently omitted or when inaccurate language is used. But a misrepresentation that is not fraudulent has no consequences under this Chapter unless it is material. Whether an assertion

is material is determined by the rule stated in § 162(2). The consequences of a misrepresentation are dealt with in §§ 163, 164 and 166.

Illustrations:

1. A, seeking to induce B to make a contract to buy a used car, turns the odometer back from 60,000 to 18,000 miles. B makes the contract. A's conduct in setting the odometer is a misrepresentation. Whether the contract is voidable by B is determined by the rule stated in § 164.

2. A, seeking to induce B to make a contract to lease a particular generator, writes B a letter with the intention of describing its output correctly as "1200 kilowatts." Because of an error of A's typist, unnoticed by A, the letter states that the output of the generator is "2100 kilowatts." B makes the contract. A's statement is a misrepresentation. Whether the contract is voidable by B is determined by the rule stated in § 164.

b. Half-truths. A statement may be true with respect to the facts stated, but may fail to include qualifying matter necessary to prevent the implication of an assertion that is false with respect to other facts. For example, a true statement that an event has recently occurred may carry the false implication that the situation has not changed since its occurrence. Such a half-truth may be as misleading as an assertion that is wholly false. **Illustrations:**

    3. A, seeking to induce B to make a contract to buy land, tells B that his title to the land has been upheld in a court decision. A knows that the decision has been appealed but does not tell this to B. B makes the contract. A's statement omits matter necessary to prevent the implied assertion that A's title is clearly established, and this assertion is a misrepresentation. Whether the contract is voidable by B is determined by the rule stated in § 164.

    4. A, seeking to induce B to make a contract to buy an apartment house, tells B that the apartments are all rented to tenants at $ 200 a month. A knows that the rent of $ 200 has not been approved by the local rent control authorities and that without this approval it is illegal but does not tell this to B. B makes the contract. A's statement omits matter needed to prevent the implied assertion that the rent is legal, and this assertion is a misrepresentation (see § 170). Whether the contract is voidable by B is determined by the rules stated in § 164.

    c. Meaning of "fact." An assertion must relate to something that is a fact at the time the assertion is made in order to be a misrepresentation. Such facts include past events as well as present circumstances but do not include future events. An assertion limited to future events (see § 2), may be a basis of liability for breach of contract, but not of relief for misrepresentation. However, a promise or a prediction of future events may by implication

involve an assertion that facts exist from which the promised or predicted consequences will follow, which may be a misrepresentation as to those facts. Thus, from a statement that a particular machine will attain a specified level of performance when it is used, it may be inferred that its present design and condition make it capable of such a level. Such an inference may be drawn even if the statement is not legally binding as a promise. **Illustrations:**

    5. A, seeking to induce B to make a contract to buy land, promises B to build an expensive house on an adjoining tract. A knows that he neither owns nor has such an interest in the tract that he can perform the promise, although he hopes to perform it. B makes the contract. A's promise implies an assertion that he owns the tract or has such an interest in the adjoining tract that he can perform his promise, and this assertion is a misrepresentation. Whether the contract is voidable by B is determined by the rule stated in § 164.

    6. A, seeking to induce B to buy a furnace, tells B that it will give a stated amount of heat while consuming only a stated amount of fuel. A knows that the furnace is not capable of such efficiency. B makes the contract. A's statement implies an assertion that the furnace has an existing capability of such efficiency, and this assertion is a misrepresentation. Whether the contract is voidable by B is determined by the rule stated in § 164.

    d. State of mind as a fact. A person's state of mind is a fact, and an assertion as to one's opinion or intention, including an intention to perform a promise, is a misrepresentation if the state of mind is other than as asserted. The extent to which the recipient is justified in relying on an assertion of opinion or intention is dealt with in §§ 168, 169 and 171.

§ 160. When Action Is Equivalent to an Assertion (Concealment)

Action intended or known to be likely to prevent another from learning a fact is equivalent to an assertion that the fact does not exist.

Comments:

    a. Scope. Concealment is an affirmative act intended or known to be likely to keep another from learning of a fact of which he would otherwise have learned. Such affirmative action is always equivalent to a misrepresentation and has any effect that a misrepresentation would have under the rules stated in §§ 163, 164 and 166. The rule stated in the following section

applies to non-disclosure, where one person simply fails to inform another of a fact relating to the transaction. Non-disclosure is equivalent to a misrepresentation only in the circumstances enumerated in that section.

    b. Common situations. The rule stated in this Section is commonly applied in two situations, although it is not limited to them. In the first, a party actively hides something from the other, as when the seller of a building paints over a defect. See Illustration 1. In such a case his conduct has the same effect as an assertion that the defect does not exist, and it is therefore a misrepresentation. Similarly, if the offeror reads a written offer to the offeree and omits a portion of it, his conduct has the same effect as an assertion that the omitted portion is not contained in the writing and is therefore a misrepresentation. In the second situation, a party prevents the other from making an investigation that would have disclosed a defect. An analogous situation arises where a party frustrates an investigation made by the other, for example by sending him in search of information where it cannot be found. Even a false denial of knowledge by a party who has possession of the facts may amount to a misrepresentation as to the facts that he knows, just as if he had actually misstated them, if its effect on the other is to lead him to believe that the facts do not exist or cannot be discovered.

Action may be considered as likely to prevent another from learning of a fact even though it does not make it impossible to learn of it.

Illustrations:

    1. A, seeking to induce B to make a contract to buy his house, paints the basement floor in order to prevent B from discovering that the foundation is cracked. B is prevented from discovering the defect and makes the contract. The concealment is equivalent to an assertion that the foundation is not cracked, and this assertion is a misrepresentation. Whether the contract is voidable by B is determined by the rule stated in § 164.

    2. A, seeking to induce B to make a contract to buy his house, convinces C, who, as A knows, is about to tell B that the foundation is cracked, to say nothing to B about the foundation. B is prevented from discovering the defect and makes the contract. A's conduct is equivalent to an assertion that the foundation is not cracked, and this assertion is a misrepresentation. Whether the contract is voidable by B is determined by the rule stated in § 164.

§ 161. When Non-Disclosure Is Equivalent to an Assertion

A person's non-disclosure of a fact known to him is equivalent to an assertion that the fact does not exist in the following cases only:

(a) where he knows that disclosure of the fact is necessary to prevent some previous assertion from being a misrepresentation or from being fraudulent or material.

(b) where he knows that disclosure of the fact would correct a mistake of the other party as to a basic assumption on which that party is making the contract and if non-disclosure of the fact amounts to a failure to act in good faith and in accordance with reasonable standards of fair dealing.

(c) where he knows that disclosure of the fact would correct a mistake of the other party as to the contents or effect of a writing, evidencing or embodying an agreement in whole or in part.

(d) where the other person is entitled to know the fact because of a relation of trust and confidence between them.

Comment:

    a. Concealment distinguished. Like concealment, non-disclosure of a fact may be equivalent to a misrepresentation. Concealment necessarily involves an element of non-disclosure, but it is the act of preventing another from learning of a fact that is significant and this act is always equivalent to a misrepresentation (§ 160). Non-disclosure without concealment is equivalent to a misrepresentation only in special situations. A party making a contract is not expected to tell all that he knows to the other party, even if he knows that the other party lacks knowledge on some aspects of the transaction. His nondisclosure, as such, has no legal effect except in the situations enumerated in this Section. He may not, of course, tell half-truths and his assertion of only some of the facts without the inclusion of such additional matters as he knows or believes to be necessary to prevent it from being misleading is itself a misrepresentation. See Comment *a* to § 159. In contrast to the rule applicable to liability in tort for misrepresentation, it is not enough, where disclosure is expected, merely to make reasonable efforts to disclose the relevant facts. Actual disclosure is required. Compare Restatement, Second, Torts § 551, Comment *d*.

b. Fraudulent or material. In order to make the contract voidable under the rule stated in § 164(1), the non-disclosure must be either fraudulent or material. The notion of disclosure necessarily implies that the fact in question is known to the person expected to disclose it. But the failure to disclose the fact may be unintentional, as when one forgets to disclose a known fact, and it is then equivalent to an innocent misrepresentation. Furthermore, one is expected to disclose only such facts as he knows or has reason to know will influence the other in determining his course of action. See § 162(2). Therefore, he need not disclose facts that the ordinary person would regard as unimportant unless he knows of some peculiarity of the other person that is likely to lead him to attach importance to them. There is, however, no such requirement of materiality if it can be shown that the non-disclosure was actually fraudulent. If a fact is intentionally withheld for the purpose of inducing action, this is equivalent to a fraudulent misrepresentation.

c. Failure to correct. One who has made an assertion that is neither a fraudulent nor a material misrepresentation may subsequently acquire knowledge that bears significantly on his earlier assertion. He is expected to speak up and correct the earlier assertion in three cases. First, if his assertion was not a misrepresentation because it was true, he may later learn that it is no longer true. See Illustration 1. Second, his assertion may have been a misrepresentation but may not have been fraudulent. If this was because he believed that it was true, he may later learn that it was not true. See Illustration 2. If this was because he did not intend that it be relied upon, he may later learn that the other is about to rely on it. See Illustration 3. Third, if his assertion was a misrepresentation but was not material because he had no reason to know of the other's special characteristics that made reliance likely, he may later learn of such characteristics. If a person fails to correct his earlier assertion in these situations, the result is the same as it would have been had he had his newly acquired knowledge at the time he made the assertion. The rule stated in Clause (a), like that stated in Clause (d), extends to non-disclosure by persons who are not parties to the transaction. **Illustrations:**

1. A makes to B, a credit rating company, a true statement of his financial condition, intending that its substance be published to B's subscribers. B summarizes the information and transmits the summary to C, a subscriber. Shortly thereafter, A's financial condition becomes seriously impaired, but he does not disclose this to B. C makes a contract to lend money to A. A's non-disclosure is equivalent to an assertion that his financial condition is not seriously impaired, and this assertion is a misrepresentation. Whether the contract is voidable by B is determined by the rule stated in § 164.

2. A, seeking to induce B to make a contract to buy a thoroughbred mare, tells B that the mare is in foal to a well-known stallion. Unknown to A, the mare has miscarried. A learns of the miscarriage but does not disclose it to B. B makes the contract. A's non-disclosure is equivalent to an assertion that the mare has not miscarried, and this assertion is a misrepresentation. Whether the contract is voidable by B is determined by the rule stated in § 164.

. . .

d. Known mistake as to a basic assumption. In many situations, if one party knows that the other is mistaken as to a basic assumption, he is expected to disclose the fact that would correct the mistake. A seller of real or personal property is, for example, ordinarily expected to disclose a known latent defect of quality or title that is of such a character as would probably prevent the buyer from buying at the contract price. An owner is ordinarily expected to disclose a known error in a bid that he has received from a contractor. See Comment *e* to § 153. The mistake must be as to a basic assumption, as is also required by the rules on mistake stated in § 152 (see Illustrations 4, 5 and 6) and § 153 (see Illustrations 8 and 9). The rule stated in Clause (b), is, however, broader than these rules for mistake because it does not require a showing of a material effect on the agreed exchange and is not affected by the fact that the party seeking relief bears the risk of the mistake (§ 154). Nevertheless, a party need not correct all mistakes of the other and is expected only to act in good faith and in accordance with reasonable standards of fair dealing, as reflected in prevailing business ethics. A party may, therefore, reasonably expect the other to take normal steps to inform himself and to draw his own conclusions. If the other is indolent, inexperienced or ignorant, or if his judgment is bad or he lacks access to adequate information, his adversary is not generally expected to compensate for these deficiencies. A buyer of property, for example, is not ordinarily expected to disclose circumstances that make the property more valuable than the seller supposes. Compare Illustrations 10 and 11. In contrast to the rules stated in Clauses (a) and (d), that stated in Clause (b) is limited to non-disclosure by a party to the transaction. Actual knowledge is required for the application of the rule stated in Clause (b). The case of a party who does not know but has reason to know of a mistake is governed by the rule stated in § 153(b). As to knowledge in the case of an organization, see the analogous rule in Uniform Commercial Code § 1-201(27). **Illustrations:**

4. A, seeking to induce B to make a contract to buy land, knows that B does not know that the land has been filled with debris and covered but does not disclose this to B. B makes the contract. A's non-disclosure is equivalent to an assertion that the land has not been filled with debris and covered, and this assertion is a misrepresentation. Whether the contract is voidable by B is determined by the rule stated in § 164.

5. A, seeking to induce B to make a contract to buy A's house, knows that B does not know that the house is riddled with termites but does not disclose this to B. B makes the contract. A's non-disclosure is equivalent to an assertion that the house is not riddled with termites, and this assertion is a misrepresentation. Whether the contract is voidable by B is determined by the rule stated in § 164.

. . .

7. A, seeking to induce B to make a contract to sell land, knows that B does not know that the land has appreciably increased in value because of a proposed shopping center but does not disclose this to B. B makes the contract. Since B's mistake is not one as to a basic assumption (see Comment b to § 152 and Comment b to § 261), A's non-disclosure is not equivalent to an assertion that the value of the land has not appreciably increased, and this assertion is not a misrepresentation. The contract is not voidable by B. See Illustration 13.

8. In response to B's invitation for bids on the construction of a building according to stated specifications, A submits an offer to do the work for $ 150,000. A believes that this is the total of a column of figures, but he has made an error by inadvertently omitting a $ 5,000 item, and in fact the total is $ 155,000. B knows this but accepts

A's bid without disclosing it. B's non-disclosure is equivalent to an assertion that no error has been made in the total, and this assertion is a misrepresentation. Whether the contract is voidable by A is determined by the rule stated in § 164. See Illustrations 1 and 2 to § 153. See also Comment a to § 167.

. . .

10. A, seeking to induce B to make a contract to sell A land, learns from government surveys that the land contains valuable mineral deposits and knows that B does not know this, but does not disclose this to B. B makes the contract. A's non-disclosure does not amount to a failure to act in good faith and in accordance with reasonable standards of fair dealing and is therefore not equivalent to an assertion that the land does not contain valuable mineral deposits. The contract is not voidable by B.

11. The facts being otherwise as stated in Illustration 10, A learns of the valuable mineral deposits from trespassing on B's land and not from government surveys. A's non-disclosure is equivalent to an assertion that the land does not contain valuable mineral deposits, and this assertion is a misrepresentation. Whether the contract is voidable by B is determined by the rule stated in § 164.

e. Known mistake as to a writing. One party cannot hold the other to a writing if he knew that the other was mistaken as to its contents or as to its legal effect. He is expected to correct such mistakes of the other party and his failure to do so is equivalent to a misrepresentation, which may be grounds either for avoidance under § 164 or for reformation under § 166. (Compare the rule on reformation for mistake of both parties as to their written expression stated in § 155. See Comment a to § 155.) The failure of a party to use care in reading the writing so as to discover the mistake may not preclude such relief (§ 172). In the case of standardized agreements, these rules supplement that of § 211(3), which applies, regardless of actual knowledge, if there is reason to believe that the other party would not manifest assent if he knew that the writing contained a particular term. Like the rule stated in Clause (b), that stated in Clause (c) requires actual knowledge and is limited to non-disclosure by a party to the transaction. See Comment d. **Illustration:**

12. A, seeking to induce B to make a contract to sell a tract of land to A for $ 100,000, makes a written offer to B. A knows that B mistakenly thinks that the offer contains a provi-

sion under which A assumes an existing mortgage, and he knows that it does not contain such a provision but does not disclose this to B. B signs the writing, which is an integrated agreement. A's non-disclosure is equivalent to an assertion that the writing contains such a provision, and this assertion is a misrepresentation. Whether the contract is voidable by B is determined by the rule stated in § 164. Whether, at the request of B, the court will decree that the writing be reformed to add the provision for assumption is determined by the rule stated in § 166. See Illustration 4 to § 166.

f. Relation of trust and confidence. The rule stated in Clause (d) supplements that stated in § 173 with respect to contracts between parties in a fiduciary relation. Where the latter rule applies, as in the case of a trustee, an agent, a guardian, or an executor or administrator, its more stringent requirements govern. Even where a party is not, strictly speaking, a fiduciary, he may stand in such a relation of trust and confidence to the other as to give the other the right to expect disclosure. Such a relationship normally exists between members of the same family and may

arise, in other situations as, for example, between physician and patient. In addition, some types of contracts, such as those of suretyship or guaranty, marine insurance and joint adventure, are recognized as creating in themselves confidential relations and hence as requiring the utmost good faith and full and fair disclosure. As to contracts of suretyship, see Restatement of Security § 124.

The rule stated in Clause (d) is not limited to cases in which the non-disclosure is by a party to the transaction. In contrast, the rule stated in § 173 applies only to non-disclosure by a fiduciary who is a party. Therefore the rule stated in Clause (d) covers the residual case of a fiduciary who is not a party. As to the duty of a trustee to disclose to his beneficiary matters important for him to know in dealing with others, see Restatement, Second, Trusts § 173, Comment *d.* As to the duty of an agent to disclose to his principal matters important for him to know in dealing with others, see Restatement, Second, Agency § 381.

. . .

§ 162. When a Misrepresentation Is Fraudulent or Material

(1) A misrepresentation is fraudulent if the maker intends his assertion to induce a party to manifest his assent and the maker

(a) knows or believes that the assertion is not in accord with the facts, or

(b) does not have the confidence that he states or implies in the truth of the assertion, or

(c) knows that he does not have the basis that he states or implies for the assertion.

(2) A misrepresentation is material if it would be likely to induce a reasonable person to manifest his assent, or if the maker knows that it would be likely to induce the recipient to do so.

Comment:

a. Meaning of "fraudulent." The word "fraudulent" is used in various senses in the law. In order that a misrepresentation be fraudulent within the meaning of this Section, it must not only be consciously false but must also be intended to mislead another. Compare Restatement, Second, Torts § 526. Consequences are intended if a person either acts with the desire to cause them or acts believing that they are substantially certain to result. See Restatement, Second, Torts § 8A. Thus one who believes that another is substantially certain to be misled as a result of a misrepresentation intends to mislead even though he may not desire to do so. See Comment *c* to Restatement, Second, Torts § 531.

If the maker knows that his statement is misleading because it is subject to two interpretations, it is fraudulent if he makes it with the intention that it be understood in the false sense. See Restatement, Second, Torts § 527. If the recipient continues to rely on a misrepresentation made in an earlier transaction, the misrepresentation is fraudulent if the maker knows that the recipient is still relying. See Restatement, Second, Torts § 535. Furthermore, the maker need not have a particular person in mind as the recipient at the time the misrepresentation is made. He may merely have reason to expect that it will reach any of a class of persons, of which the recipient is a member, as in the case of the merchant who furnishes information to a credit agency. See Illustration 1. In order that a fraudulent representation have legal effect within this Chapter, it need not be material. Compare §§ 163, 164, 166 with Restatement, Second, Torts § 538. It is, however, essential that it actually induce assent. See §§ 163, 164, 166. **Illustration:**

> 1. A makes to B, a credit rating company, a statement of his financial condition that he knows is untrue, intending that its substance be published to B's subscribers. B summarizes the information and transmits the summary to C, a subscriber. C is thereby induced to make a contract to lend money to A. A's statement is a fraudulent misrepresentation and the contract is voidable by C under the rule stated in § 164.

b. "Scienter." The word "scienter" is often used by courts to refer to the requirement that the maker know of the untrue character of his assertion. Subsection (1) states three ways in which this requirement can be met. First, it is clearly met if the maker knows the fact to be otherwise than as stated. However, knowledge of falsity is not essential, and it is sufficient under the rule stated in Clause (a) if he believes the assertion to be false. It will not suffice merely to show that the misrepresentation is one that a person of ordinary care and intelligence would have recognized as false, although this is evidence from which his belief in its falsity may be inferred. Second, the requirement is met under the rule stated in Clause (b), if the maker, lacking confidence in the truth of his assertion that he states or implies, nevertheless chooses to make it as one of his own knowledge rather than one merely of his opinion. This is so when he is conscious that he has only a belief in its truth and recognizes that there is some chance that it may not be true. This conclusion is often expressed by saying that the misrepresentation has been made without belief in its truth or that it has been made recklessly, without regard to whether it is true or false. Third, the requirement is met under the rule stated in Clause (c), if the maker has said or implied that the assertion is made on some particular basis, such as his personal knowledge or his personal investigation, when it is not so made. This is so even though the maker is honestly convinced of its truth from hearsay or other source that he believes is reliable. **Illustration:**

> 2. A, seeking to induce B to make a contract to buy his house, tells B that the plumbing is of pipe of a specified quality. A does not know the quality of the pipe, and it is not of the specified quality. B is induced by A's statement to make the contract. The statement is a fraudulent misrepresentation, both because A does not have the confidence that he implies in its truth, and because he knows that he does not have the basis for it that he implies. The contract is voidable by B under the rule stated in § 164.

c. Meaning of "material." Although a fraudulent misrepresentation need not be material in order to entitle the recipient to relief under the rule stated in § 164, a non-fraudulent misrepresentation will not entitle him to relief unless it is material. The materiality of a misrepresentation is determined from the viewpoint of the maker, while the justification of reliance is determined from the viewpoint of the recipient. (Contrast also the concept of a "material" failure to perform. See § 241.) The requirement of materiality may be met in either of two ways. First, a misrepresentation is material if it would be likely to induce a reasonable person to manifest his assent. Second, it is material if the maker knows that for some special reason it is likely to induce the particular recipient to manifest his assent. There may be personal considerations that the recipient regards as important even though they would not be expected to affect others in his situation, and if the maker is aware of this the misrepresentation may be material even though it would not be expected to induce a reasonable person to make the proposed contract. One who preys upon another's known idiosyncrasies cannot complain if the contract is held voidable when he succeeds in what he is endeavoring to accomplish. Cf. Restatement, Second, Torts § 538. Although a nonfraudulent misrepresentation that is not material does not make the contract voidable under the rules stated in this Chapter, the recipient may have a claim to relief under other rules, such as those relating to breach of warranty. See Introductory Note to this Topic. **Illustrations:**

> 3. A, while negotiating with B for the sale of A's race horse, tells him that the horse has run a mile in a specified time. A is honestly mistaken, and, unknown to him, the horse has never

come close to that time. B is induced by A's assertion to make a contract to buy the horse. A's statement, although not fraudulent, is a ma-terial misrepresentation, and the contract is voidable by B under the rule stated in § 164.

. . .

§ 163. When a Misrepresentation Prevents Formation of a Contract

If a misrepresentation as to the character or essential terms of a proposed contract induces conduct that appears to be a manifestation of assent by one who neither knows nor has reasonable opportunity to know of the character or essential terms of the proposed contract, his conduct is not effective as a manifestation of assent.

Comment:

a. Rationale. Under the general principle stated in § 19(2), a party's conduct is not effective as a manifestation of his assent unless he knows or has reason to know that the other party may infer from it that he assents. This Section involves an application of that principle where a misrepresentation goes to what is sometimes called the "factum" or the "execution" rather than merely the "inducement." If, because of a misrepresentation as to the character or essential terms of a proposed contract, a party does not know or have reasonable opportunity to know of its character or essential terms, then he neither knows nor has reason to know that the other party may infer from his conduct that he assents to that contract. In such a case there is no effective manifestation of assent and no contract at all. Compare § 174. This result only follows, however, if the misrepresentation relates to the very nature of the proposed contract itself and not merely to one of its nonessential terms. The party may believe that he is not assenting to any contract or that he is assenting to a contract entirely different from the proposed contract. The mere fact that a party is deceived as to the identity of the other party, as when a buyer of goods obtains credit by impersonating a person of means, does not bring the case within the present Section, unless it affects the very nature of the contract. See Uniform Commercial Code § 2-403(1)(a). It is immaterial under the rule stated in this Section whether the misrepresentation is made by a party to the transaction or by a third person. See Comment *e* to § 164. **Illustration:**

    1. A, seeking to induce B to make a contract to sell him goods on credit, tells B that he is C, a well-known millionaire. B is induced by the statement to make the proposed contract with A. B's apparent manifestation of assent is effective.

However, the contract is voidable by B under the rule stated in § 164(1). Contrast Illustrations 2 and 4.

b. Effect of fault. If the recipient had a reasonable opportunity to know the character or essential terms of the proposed contract, the rule stated in this Section does not apply, and his conduct is effective as a manifestation of assent. Compare § 172. The case then comes within § 164 on avoidance or § 166 on reformation. In deciding whether the recipient has had such an opportunity, less care will ordinarily be expected of him if he did not intend to assume a legal obligation at all than if he intended to assume a legal obligation, although one of a different nature. **Illustrations:**

    2. A and B reach an understanding that they will execute a written contract containing terms on which they have agreed. It is properly prepared and is read by B, but A substitutes a writing containing essential terms that are different from those agreed upon and thereby induces B to sign it in the belief that it is the one he has read. B's apparent manifestation of assent is not effective.

    3. A and B reach an understanding that they will execute a written contract containing terms on which they have agreed. A prepares a writing containing essential terms that are different from those agreed upon and induces B to sign it by telling him that it contains the terms agreed upon and that it is not necessary for him to read it. B's apparent manifestation of assent is effective if B had a reasonable opportunity to read the writing. However, the contract is voidable by B under the rule stated in § 164. See Illustration 3 to § 164. In the alternative, at the request of B, the court will decree that the writing be reformed to conform to their understanding under the rule stated in § 166. See Illustration 1 to § 166.

. . .

c. "Void" rather than voidable. It is sometimes loosely said that, where the rule stated in this Section applies, there is a "void contract" as distinguished from a voidable one. See Comment *a* to § 7. This distinction has important consequences. For example, the recipient of a misrepresentation may be held to have ratified the contract if it is voidable but not if it is "void." Furthermore, a good faith purchaser may acquire good title to property if he takes it from one who obtained voidable title by misrepresentation but not if he takes it from one who obtained "void title" by misrepresentation.

§ 164. When a Misrepresentation Makes a Contract Voidable

(1) If a party's manifestation of assent is induced by either a fraudulent or a material misrepresentation by the other party upon which the recipient is justified in relying, the contract is voidable by the recipient.

(2) If a party's manifestation of assent is induced by either a fraudulent or a material misrepresentation by one who is not a party to the transaction upon which the recipient is justified in relying, the contract is voidable by the recipient, unless the other party to the transaction in good faith and without reason to know of the misrepresentation either gives value or relies materially on the transaction.

Comment:

a. Requirements. A misrepresentation may make a contract voidable under the rule stated in this Section, even though it does not prevent the formation of a contract under the rule stated in the previous section. Three requirements must be met in addition to the requirement that there must have been a misrepresentation. First, the misrepresentation must have been either fraudulent or material. See Comment *b.* Second, the misrepresentation must have induced the recipient to make the contract. See Comment *c.* Third, the recipient must have been justified in relying on the misrepresentation. See Comment *d.* Even if the contract is voidable, exercise of the power of avoidance is subject to the limitations stated in Chapter 16 on remedies.

b. Fraudulent and non-fraudulent misrepresentation. A representation need not be fraudulent in order to make a contract voidable under the rule stated in this Section. However, a non-fraudulent misrepresentation does not make the contract voidable unless it is material, while materiality is not essential in the case of a fraudulent misrepresentation. One who makes a non-fraudulent misrepresentation of a seemingly unimportant fact has no reason to suppose that his assertion will induce assent. But a fraudulent misrepresentation is directed to attaining that very end, and the maker cannot insist on his bargain if it is attained, however unexpectedly, as long as the additional requirements of inducement and justifiable reliance are met. See

Illustration 1. Compare Restatement, Second, Torts § 538, which limits liability for fraudulent misrepresentation to cases in which the matter misrepresented is material. **Illustrations:**

1. A, seeking to induce B to make a contract to buy a tract of land at a price of $ 1,000 an acre, tells B that the tract contains 100 acres. A knows that it contains only 90 acres. B is induced by the statement to make the contract. Because the statement is a fraudulent misrepresentation (§ 162(1)), the contract is voidable by B, regardless of whether the misrepresentation is material.

2. The facts being otherwise as stated in Illustration 1, A is mistaken and does not know that the tract contains only 90 acres. Because the statement is not a fraudulent misrepresentation, the contract is voidable by B only if the misrepresentation is material (§ 162(2)).

3. A and B agree that A will buy a tract of land from B for $ 100,000 and will assume an existing mortgage of $ 50,000. In reducing the agreement to writing, A intentionally omits the provision for assumption but tells B that the writing correctly expresses their agreement. B does not notice the omission and is induced by A's statement to sign the writing. The misrepresentation is both fraudulent and material, and the contract is voidable by B. Compare Illustration 1 to § 166 and see Illustration 10 to § 161.

c. Inducement. No legal effect flows from either a non-fraudulent or a fraudulent misrepresentation unless it induces action by the recipient, that is, unless he manifests his assent to the contract in reliance on it. Whether a misrepresentation is an inducement is a question of fact governed by the rule stated in § 167. In general, the recipient of a misrepresentation need not show that he has actually been harmed by relying on it in order to avoid the contract. But see § 165.

d. Justification. A misrepresentation, even if relied upon, has no legal effect unless the recipient's reliance on it is justified. The most significant and troublesome applications of this principle occur in connection with assertions of opinion (§§ 168, 169), assertions as to matters of law (§ 170), assertions of intention (§ 171), and fault (§ 172). In other situations the requirement of justification is usually met unless, for example, the fact to which the misrepresentation relates is of only peripheral importance to the transaction or is one as to which the maker's assertion would not be expected to be taken seriously.

e. Misrepresentation by a third party. The rule stated in Subsection (2) makes a contract voidable for a misrepresentation by a third party, subject to the general principle of law that if an innocent person has in good faith and without notice given value or changed his position in reliance on the contract, it is not voidable on that ground. This is the same principle that protects an innocent person who purchases goods or commercial paper in good faith, without notice and for value from one who has obtained them from the original owner by a misrepresentation. See Uniform Commercial Code §§ 2-403(1), 3-305.

In the cases that fall within Subsection (2), however, the innocent person deals directly with the recipient of the misrepresentation, which is made by one not a party to their contract. The contract is not voidable by the recipient if the innocent person gives value or relies materially on the transaction before learning or acquiring reason to know of the misrepresentation. The term "value" has the same meaning here as it does under Uniform Commercial Code § 1-201(44), and therefore the consideration given by the innocent party is value for this purpose. The rule does not protect a person who is responsible under the law of agency for the maker's misrepresentation. See Restatement, Second, Agency § 259. Assignees and intended beneficiaries, who derive their rights from a contract that is voidable for misrepresentation, take subject to the right of avoidance under § 309, 336. The rule stated in Subsection (2) does not preclude avoidance for mistake under the rules stated in Chapter 6. **Illustrations:**

> 4. A, who is not C's agent, induces B by a fraudulent misrepresentation to make a contract with C to sell land to C. C promises to pay the agreed price, not knowing or having reason to know of the fraudulent misrepresentation. Since C's promise to pay is value, the contract is not voidable by B. The contract would be voidable by B if C learned or acquired reason to know of the fraudulent misrepresentation before promising to pay the price.

> . . .

§ 165. Cure by Change of Circumstances

If a contract is voidable because of a misrepresentation and, before notice of an intention to avoid the contract, the facts come into accord with the assertion, the contract is no longer voidable unless the recipient has been harmed by relying on the misrepresentation.

Comment:

a. Rationale. In general, the recipient of a misrepresentation need not show that he has actually been harmed by relying on it in order to avoid the contract. If, however, the effect of misrepresentation has been cured because the facts have been brought or have otherwise come into accord with the assertion before he has notified the maker of his intention to avoid the contract, there is ordinarily little likelihood of harm. The rule stated in this Section precludes

avoidance in such a case, unless the recipient shows that he has actually been harmed. It applies to fraudulent as well as to non-fraudulent misrepresentations. **Illustrations:**

> 1. A, seeking to induce B to make a contract to buy land, tells B that the land is unencumbered. A knows that the land is subject to a lien. B is induced by A's statement to make the proposed contract. A then removes the lien. If B has not been harmed by the misrepresentation, the contract is no longer voidable by B.

§ 166. When a Misrepresentation as to a Writing Justifies Reformation

If a party's manifestation of assent is induced by the other party's fraudulent misrepresentation as to the contents or effect of a writing evidencing or embodying in whole or in part an agreement, the court at the request of the recipient may reform the writing to express the terms of the agreement as asserted, (a) if the recipient was justified in relying on the misrepresentation, and (b) except to the extent that rights of third parties such as good faith purchasers for value will be unfairly affected.

Comment:

a. Scope. Reformation is more broadly available for fraudulent misrepresentation than for mistake. Compare § 155. Reformation for mistake is limited to the situation in which the parties, having already reached an agreement, later fail to express it correctly in a writing. That limitation, stated in § 155, applies to all cases where both parties are mistaken, including those where one of the mistaken parties has made a non-fraudulent misrepresentation as to the contents or effect of a writing. Where, however, only one party is mistaken and the other has fraudulently misrepresented the writing's contents or effect, reformation may be granted even though there was no prior agreement. Compare Comment *a* to § 155. The writing must be one that evidences or embodies, at least in part, the agreement of the parties. Otherwise it will not ordinarily have sufficient legal significance for its reformation to be necessary, and the dispute can be resolved simply in accordance with the general rules applicable to offer and acceptance. The rule stated in this Section also applies to the case where only one party is mistaken and the other, although aware of the mistake, says nothing to correct it. In that case his non-disclosure is equivalent to an assertion that the writing is as the other understands it to be (§ 161(c)). (Where only one party is mistaken and the other is not aware of the mistake, the rule stated in § 153, on mistake of only one party, applies.) The misrepresentation must, of course, be certain enough to permit a court to know how the writing should be reformed. Reformation is not precluded by the mere fact that the party who seeks it failed to exercise reasonable care in reading the writing, but his reliance on the misrepresentation must be justified and the right to reformation is therefore subject to the rule on fault stated in § 172. This Section, like § 155, only states the circumstances in which a court "may" grant reformation, and, since the remedy is equitable, a court has the discretion to withhold it, even if it would otherwise be appropriate, on grounds traditionally considered by courts of equity in exercising their discretion. See Comment *d* to § 155. **Illustrations:**

1. A and B agree that A will buy a tract of land from B for $ 100,000 and will assume an existing mortgage of $ 50,000. In reducing the agreement to writing, A intentionally omits the provision for assumption and tells B that the writing correctly expresses their agreement. B does not notice the omission and is induced by A's fraudulent misrepresentation to sign the writing, which is an integrated agreement. At the request of B, the court will reform the writing to add the provision for assumption. Compare Illustration 3 to § 164. See Illustration 1 to § 155.

2. A, seeking to induce B to make a contract to sell a tract of land to A for $ 100,000, makes a written offer to B and tells B that it includes a provision under which A assumes an existing mortgage. A knows that the writing does not contain such a provision. B does not notice the omission and is induced by A's fraudulent misrepresentation to sign the writing, which is an integrated agreement. At the request of B, the court will reform the writing to add the provision for assumption.

. . .

b. Relation to other rules. The rule stated in this Section applies only to misrepresentations as to the contents or effect of a writing. If the misrepresentation relates to some other fact, the contract may be voidable under § 164, but reformation is not appropriate. See also § 163. The availability of reformation based on a fraudulent misrepresentation does not, however, preclude the alternative of avoidance, and the recipient has a choice of remedies. See Illustration 12 to § 161 and compare Illustration 3 to § 164 with Illustration 1 to the present Section. This is in contrast to the rule for mutual mistake. See Introductory Note to Chapter 6 and Comment *d* to § 152. In some instances, however, the problem may be merely one of interpretation of the writing, so that neither reformation nor avoidance is appropriate. See § 20. **Illustration:**

> 5. A, seeking to induce B to make a contract to buy a tract of land at a price of $ 100,000, makes a written offer to B and tells B that the tract contains 100 acres. A knows that it contains only 90 acres. B is induced by A's fraudulent misrepresentation to sign the writing. The court will not, at the request of B, reform the writing because the mistake of the parties was not one as to the contents or effect of the writing. B's right to avoidance is governed by the rule stated in § 164(1). See Illustration 1 to § 164 and Illustration 5 to § 155.

c. Parol evidence rule and Statute of Frauds. The parol evidence rule does not preclude proof of a fraudulent misrepresentation to justify reformation. See § 214(d). Furthermore, if reformation of a writing is otherwise appropriate, it is not precluded by the fact that the contract is within the Statute of Frauds. See § 156.

d. Protection of innocent third parties. The right to reformation under the rule stated in this Section is subject to the rights of good faith purchasers for value and other third parties who have similarly relied on the finality of a consensual transaction in which they have acquired an interest in property. Such other third parties include those who have given value and come within the definition of "purchaser" in Uniform Commercial Code § 1-201(33), (32), notably mortgagees, pledgees and other holders of a security interest. Judgment creditors and trustees in bankruptcy are not included. This is thesame exception as that under § 155 where third parties have intervened. See Comment *f* to § 155 and Illustrations 8 and 9 to that Section.

§ 167. When a Misrepresentation Is an Inducing Cause

A misrepresentation induces a party's manifestation of assent if it substantially contributes to his decision to manifest his assent.

Comment:

a. Scope. The rule stated in this Section determines whether a misrepresentation in fact induced a party's actual or apparent manifestation of assent, as required under §§ 163, 164 and 166. A misrepresentation is not a cause of a party's making a contract unless he relied on the misrepresentation in manifesting his assent. His reliance will usually consist of his acceptance, an affirmative act, but may also consist of his refraining from revoking an outstanding offer. See Illustrations 8 and 9 to § 161. It is not necessary that this reliance have been the sole or even the predominant factor in influencing his conduct. It is not even necessary that he would not have acted as he did had he not relied on the assertion. It is enough that the manifestation substantially contributed to his decision to make the contract. It is, therefore, immaterial that he may also have been influenced by other considerations. As to the effect of the recipient's fault, see § 172. The misrepresentation need not be made directly to the recipient but may be made to a third person for the purpose of having him transmit it, or its substance, to the recipient in order to induce action. See Illustration 1 to § 162. **Illustrations:**

> 1. A, seeking to induce B to make a contract to buy land, makes a fraudulent misrepresenta-tion. Although he believes A's assertion, B wishes to confirm it and therefore inspects the land and inquires of third persons. B then makes the contract. The misrepresentation substantially contributes to his decision to make the contract, although he is also induced to do so by his investigation and inquiries. B's manifestation of assent is induced by the misrepresentation, and the contract is voidable by B.

> . . .

b. Criteria. Circumstantial evidence is often important in determining whether a misrepresentation has been an inducing cause. The materiality of the misrepresentation is a particularly significant factor in this determination. It is assumed, in the absence of facts showing the contrary, that the recipient attached importance to the truth of a misrepresentation if it was material, but not if it was immaterial. The extent of a party's investigation also bears on the question of causation. If he relies solely on his investigation and not on the misrepresentation, he is not entitled to relief. One who makes an investigation will often be taken to rely on it alone as to all facts disclosed to him in the course of it. On the other hand, if the fact is not one that the investigation disclosed or would have been likely to disclose, the recipient may still be relying on the misrepresentation as well as on the investigation. Particularly when the investigation produces results that tend to confirm the misrepresentation but are still somewhat inconclusive, it may be found that the recipient relied on both and that he attached importance to the truth of the misrepresentation in making the contract. A party who, having made a misrepresentation, intentionally frustrates the other's investigation of its truth, will be precluded from claiming that the other relied on the investigation to the exclusion of the

misrepresentation. See Restatement, Second, Torts § 547(2). **Illustrations:**

> 3. A, seeking to induce B to make a contract to buy his race horse, tells him that the horse has run a mile in a specified time. A is honestly mistaken, and, unknown to him, the horse has never come close to that time. B makes the contract. Because A's misrepresentation is material, it will be assumed, in the absence of facts showing the contrary, that B attached importance to its truth in deciding to make the contract. The contract is therefore voidable by B. See Illustration 3 to § 162.

. . .

§ 168. Reliance on Assertions of Opinion

(1) An assertion is one of opinion if it expresses only a belief, without certainty, as to the existence of a fact or expresses only a judgment as to quality, value, authenticity, or similar matters. (2) If it is reasonable to do so, the recipient of an assertion of a person's opinion as to facts not disclosed and not otherwise known to the recipient may properly interpret it as an assertion (a) that the facts known to that person are not incompatible with his opinion, or (b) that he knows facts sufficient to justify him in forming it.

Comment:

a. Knowledge and opinion. A statement of opinion is also a statement of fact because it states that a person has a particular state of mind concerning the matter to which his opinion relates. But it also implies that he does not have such definite information, that he is not certain enough of what he says, to make an assertion of his own knowledge as to that matter. It implies atmost that he knows of no facts incompatible with the belief or that he knows of facts that justify him in holding it. The difference is that between "This is true," and "I think this is true, but I am not sure." The important distinction is between assertions of knowledge and those of opinion, rather than assertions of fact and those of opinion. The person whose opinion is asserted is usually the maker of the assertion himself, but the opinion may also be that of a third person. See Comment *b* to § 169.

b. Criteria. The fact that points of view may be expected to differ on the subject of a statement suggests that the statement is one of opinion. Statements of judgment as to quality, value, authenticity, or similar matters are common examples. For instance, the statement that an automobile is a "good" car relates to a matter on which views may be expected to differ. The maker of such a statement will normally be understood

as expressing only his own judgment and not as making assertions concerning such matters as horsepower or riding qualities. But see Comment *d* and Illustration 3. The form of the statement is important but not controlling. A statement that is in form an assertion of the maker's knowledge may be made in circumstances that suggest that it expresses only a belief, that he is not free from doubt. This may be so, for example, when the recipient knows that the maker has no information concerning the fact asserted and therefore can be stating only his belief. The problem is one of interpretation of the language used.

c. Statements of quantity, quality, value and price. A seller's statement of the quantity of land or goods is virtually never a statement of opinion, even though he does not suggest that it is based on a survey, weighing or other measurement. The words "more or less" do not change such a statement into one of opinion, and the recipient is justified in believing that the quantity is substantially as stated although the measurement expressed may not be exact. In contrast, a seller's general statement of quality is usually one of opinion. There are, however, instances in which the gradations of quality are so marked that goods are usually sold as of a specified grade and an assertion of grade is not one of opinion. A statement of value is, like one of quality, ordinarily a statement of opinion. However, a statement of the price at which something has been offered for sale or sold is not one of opinion. **Illustrations:**

    1. A, seeking to induce B to make a contract to buy goods, tells B that he paid $ 10,000 for them. A knows that he paid only $ 8,000 for the goods. The statement is not one of opinion.

    2. The facts being otherwise as stated in Illustration 1, A tells B only that the goods are worth $ 10,000. The statement is one of opinion.

    d. Implication of a statement of opinion. In some circumstances the recipient may reasonably understand a statement of opinion to be more than an assertion as to the maker's state of mind. Under the rule stated in Subsection (2), if the statement of opinion relates to facts not known to the recipient, he may be justified in inferring that there are facts that justify the opinion, or at least that there are no facts that are incompatible with it. In such a case, the statement of opinion becomes, in effect, an assertion as to those facts and may be relied on as such. The rule is, however, applied in the light of the realities of the market place. The propensity of sellers and buyers to exaggerate the advantages to the other party of the bargains they promise is well recognized, and to some extent their assertions of opinion must be discounted. Nevertheless, while some allowance must be made for seller's puffing and buyer's depreciation, the other party is entitled to assume that a statement of opinion is not so far removed from the truth as to be incompatible with the facts known to the maker. Where circumstances justify it, a statement of

opinion may also be reasonably understood as carrying with it an assertion that the maker knows facts sufficient to justify him in forming it. However, the rule stated in Subsection (2) applies only when the facts to which the opinion relates are not disclosed and not otherwise known to the recipient. An assertion of opinion that does not fall within Subsection (2) is one of opinion only. As to the circumstances in which reliance on such an assertion is justified, see § 169. **Illustrations:**

    3. A, seeking to induce B to make a contract to buy real property, tells B that the sewage system is "good." A knows that the sewage system is unworkable. B interprets A's statement of opinion as an assertion that the facts known to A are not incompatible with his opinion and is induced by this assertion to make the contract. B's interpretation is reasonable, the assertion is a fraudulent misrepresentation, and the contract is voidable by B.

    4. The facts being otherwise as stated in Illustration 3, A knows that the sewage system is not very good but is workable. There is no misrepresentation because the facts known to A are not incompatible with his opinion, and the contract is not voidable by B.

    5. A, seeking to induce B to make a contract to become A's partner in A's business, tells B that the business is "a money-maker." A knows that the business has been unprofitable since its inception. B interprets A's statement of opinion as an assertion that the facts known to A are not incompatible with his opinion and is induced by this assertion to make the contract. B's interpretation is reasonable, the assertion is a fraudulent misrepresentation, and the contract is voidable by B.

. . .

§ 169. When Reliance on an Assertion of Opinion Is Not Justified

To the extent that an assertion is one of opinion only, the recipient is not justified in relying on it unless the recipient (a) stands in such a relation of trust and confidence to the person whose opinion is asserted that the recipient is reasonable in relying on it, or (b) reasonably believes that, as compared with himself, the person whose opinion is asserted has special skill, judgment or objectivity with respect to the subject matter, or (c) is for some other special reason particularly susceptible to a misrepresentation of the type involved.

Comment:

    a. Scope: The rule stated in this Section applies only to the extent that an assertion amounts to nothing more than an assertion of

opinion, whether that of the maker or a third person. As is stated in § 168(2), an assertion of opinion as to facts not known to the recipient may, in proper circumstances, reasonably be interpreted to include an assertion as to those facts themselves. If that assertion is false, it may be the basis of avoidance regardless of the rule stated in this Section. The rule stated here determines whether reliance is justified whenever the assertion of opinion does not carry with it an assertion as to facts under the rule stated in § 168(2).

b. Rationale. If the subject matter of the transaction is one on which the two parties have roughly equal skill and judgment, each must generally form his own opinions and neither is justified in relying on the other's. The law assumes that the ordinary person is reasonably competent to form his own opinions as to the advisability of entering into those transactions that form part of the ordinary routine of life. The mere fact that one of the parties is less astute than the other does not justify him in relying on the other's opinion. This is true even though one party knows that the other is somewhat more conversant with the value and quality of the subject matter, since expressions of opinion by the other party are generally to be discounted. It may be assumed, for example, that a seller will express a favorable opinion concerning what he has to sell. When he praises it in general terms, commonly known as "puffing" or "sales talk," without specific content or reference to facts, buyers are expected to understand that they are not entitled to rely. See Uniform Commercial Code § 2-313(2). A similar assumption applies to deprecating statements by buyers. See Comment *d* to § 168.

c. Confidential relationship. In some situations a relationship of trust and confidence between the parties justifies the reliance of one on the other's opinion. Where there is a true fiduciary relation, the more stringent requirements of § 173 apply. But even where a party is not, strictly speaking, a fiduciary, he may stand in a relation of trust and confidence to the recipient. Such a relation often arises, for example, between members of the same family. See Comment *f* to § 161. It may also arise where one party has taken steps to induce the other to believe that he can safely rely on the first party's judgment, as where he has gained the other's confidence by stressing their common membership in a religious denomination, fraternal order or social group, or the fact that they were born in the same locality. In addition, some types of contracts, such as marine insurance and joint adventure, are recognized as creating in themselves a confidential relation and hence as requiring the utmost good faith and full and fair disclosure. As to contracts of suretyship, see Restatement of Security § 124(1). As to undue influence, see § 177. **Illustration:**

1. A, professing friendship, offers to advise B, an elderly widow inexperienced in business, concerning her investments. He does so for five years, giving her good advice and acquiring her trust and confidence. At the end of this time he advises her to buy his worthless shares of stock, telling her that in his opinion it is a "good investment." B is induced by A's statement to make the contract. B's reliance on A's statement is justified, and the contract is voidable by B.

d. Special skill, judgment or objectivity. Ordinarily the recipient is not justified in relying on the other party's assertion of opinion because the recipient has as good a basis for forming his own opinion and the other party's opinion must be discounted because of his self-interest. Clause (b) applies to situations where this is not the case because the recipient reasonably believes that the other party has special skill or judgment, relative to that of the recipient, with respect to the subject matter. In modern commercial life, situations often occur in which special training or experience are necessary to the formation of a sound judgment. Often, in such a case, the recipient will be able to base a claim to relief on one of the assertions as to facts that arise under the rule stated in § 168(2). This will not be so, however, if the facts are known to both parties. In that event, the recipient's reliance may be justified under the rule stated in Clause (b). Compare Uniform Commercial Code § 2-315.

Clause (b) also applies to instances in which the recipient reasonably believes that the person whose opinion is asserted has special objectivity with respect to the subject matter that would give his opinion particular weight. This includes situations in which one who is not a party to the transaction and has no other adversary interest misrepresents his opinion. See § 164(2). It also includes situations in which the maker has an adversary interest but conceals this from the recipient. In such cases, the recipient's reasonable although erroneous belief that the maker is disinterested may be sufficient to justify his reliance. Finally, it applies to situations where a party to the transaction misrepresents that an apparently disinterested person holds a particular opinion. Thus an assertion that a third person has paid or offered a particular price for something, in addition to being a misrepresentation as to the conduct of that person, implies that that person holds an appropriate opinion of its value, and a prospective purchaser may be justified in taking this into account in determining whether to buy. Whether a person's apparent disinterest gives him the special objectivity required to justify reliance on this implied assertion of opinion depends on the circumstances of the particular case, including any special skill or judgment that may accompany his disinterest. **Illustrations:**

2. A, the proprietor of a dance studio, seeking to induce B, a 60-year-old widow with no background in dancing, to make a contract for dance lessons, tells B that she has "dance potential" and would develop into a "beautiful dancer." A knows that B has little aptitude as a dancer. B is induced by A's statement of opinion to make the proposed contract. B's reliance on A's statement of opinion is justified, and the contract is voidable by B.

3. A, seeking to induce B to make a contract to buy land, tells B that C, a local businessman, shortly before his death offered him $ 50,000 for the land. A knows that C offered only $ 40,000 for the land. B infers from A's statement that in C's opinion the land was worth $ 50,000 and, believing that C had special objectivity, is induced by the statement to make the contract. B's reliance is justified, and the contract is voidable by B.

e. Particularly susceptible recipient. If the recipient is for some special reason, other than those covered by Clause (b), particularly vulnerable to misrepresentation of the kind practiced on him, his reliance on it is justified under Clause (c). Examples of such reasons include lack of intelligence, illiteracy, and unusual credulity or gullibility. One whose misrepresentation of opinion induces reliance because of such a characteristic will not be heard to say that the reliance he sought to induce was not justified because his statement was one of opinion and therefore should have been mistrusted. **Illustration:**

4. A, seeking to induce B, who is particularly inexperienced and gullible, to make a contract to buy property, tells B that its value is $ 35,000. A knows that it is practically worthless. B is induced by A's statement to make the contract. If B's reliance is justified because his inexperience and gullibility make him particularly susceptible to such a misrepresentation, the contract is voidable by B.

§ 170. Reliance on Assertions as to Matters of Law

If an assertion is one as to a matter of law, the same rules that apply in the case of other assertions determine whether the recipient is justified in relying on it.

Comment:

a. Law as fact. A statement as to a matter of law is subject to the same rules as are other assertions. Such a statement may or may not be one of opinion. Thus, an assertion that a particular statute has been enacted or repealed or that a particular decision has been rendered by a court is generally not a statement of opinion. The rules that determine the consequences of a misrepresentation of such a matter of law are the same as those that determine the consequences of a similar misrepresentation of any other fact. **Illustration:**

1. A, seeking to sell goods to B, tells B that the government authorities have not fixed a maximum price for such goods. A knows that the authorities have fixed a maximum price for the goods. The assertion is a fraudulent misrepresentation, and the contract is voidable by B.

b. Law as opinion. Many statements of law involve assertions as to what a court would determine to be the legal consequences of a dispute if it were litigated, and such a statement is one of opinion. Such a statement may, as may any other statement of opinion, carry with it the assertion that the facts known to the maker are not incompatible with his opinion, or that he does know facts that justify him in forming it. See § 168(2). However, a statement that is limited to the maker's opinion as to the legal consequences of a state of facts and does not amount to an assertion as to the facts themselves is an assertion of opinion only. This is particularly true if all of the facts are known to both parties or are assumed by both of them to exist. Such a statement may be relied on, but to no greater extent than any other statement of opinion only (§ 169). Thus, as between the two parties to a contract, the recipient is ordinarily expected to draw his own conclusions or to seek his own independent legal advice. On the other hand, if the maker of the representation purports to have special expertise in the law which the recipient does not have, reliance on the opinion may be justified (§ 167(b)). If a lawyer states his opinion of law to a layman, the layman is entitled to assume his professional honesty and may justifiably rely on his opinion even though the two have an adverse relation in negotiating a contract. Even if the maker is not a lawyer, he may purport to have special knowledge that will enable him to form a reliable opinion, as where a real estate broker or an insurance agent gives his opinion on a routine problem within his competence to a layman. **Illustration:**

> 2. A, seeking to induce B to make a contract to buy land from him tells B, "I have good title to this land." Unknown to A, the person from whom he purchased the land had no title to it. B interprets A's statement as an assertion that he

knows of conveyances sufficient to vest good title in him and is induced to make the contract. Although A's statement is in the form of a legal conclusion, B's interpretation is reasonable, the assertion is a material misrepresentation, and the contract is voidable by B. See § 168(2).

c. Foreign law. The rule stated in this Section applies to statements of foreign as well as domestic law. Some courts have refused to recognize that statements of the law of a state or country where the recipient neither resides nor habitually does business are mere statements of opinion, even though they purport to cover only the legal consequences of facts known to both parties. This refusal may often be explained on the ground that, although the statement is of opinion only, the recipient's reliance is more likely to be justified because he is less able to draw his own conclusions as to foreign law. Nevertheless, he is not justified in relying on a statement of opinion as to foreign law absent one of the circumstances enumerated in § 169. If the maker resides or habitually does business in the foreign jurisdiction, he may be expected to have special expertise as to its law. See § 169(b).

§ 171. When Reliance on an Assertion of Intention Is Not Justified

(1) to the extent that an assertion is one of intention only, the recipient is not justified in relying on it if in the circumstances a misrepresentation of intention is consistent with reasonable standards of dealing.

(2) If it is reasonable to do so, the promisee may properly interpret a promise as an assertion that the promisor intends to perform the promise.

Comment:

a. Assertions of intention. A statement as to the intention of either the maker or a third person is an assertion of a fact, his state of mind, just as a statement of his opinion is such an assertion. It is therefore a misrepresentation if that state of mind is not as asserted. However, the truth of a statement as to a person's intention depends on his intention at the time that the statement is made and is not affected if he subsequently, for any reason, changes his mind. In order for reliance on an assertion of intention to be justified, the recipient's expectation that the maker's intention will be carried out must be reasonable. If he knows facts that will make it impossible for the maker to carry out his intention, then his reliance cannot be justified. See Illustration 1. As with statements of opinion (§ 169), not all statements of intention are to be taken seriously. In some situations,

courts have accorded the maker considerable latitude in misrepresenting his intention, for the reason that such statements are generally regarded as unreliable. A court will take account of all the circumstances, including any usage and the relationship of the parties. A prospective buyer of land may, for example, misrepresent his intended use of the land in order to conceal from the seller some special advantage that the buyer will derive from its purchase, which if known to the seller, would cause him to demand a higher price. The contract is not voidable on this ground if the court concludes that, in all the circumstances, the buyer's misrepresentation is not contrary to reasonable standards of dealing. See Illustration 2. The result will ordinarily be different, however, if the prospective buyer misrepresents his intended use so as to conceal from the seller some harm to the seller's other interests that will be caused if the buyer carries out his actual intention. See Illustration 3.

Illustrations:

1. A, the owner of a real estate development, seeking to induce B to make a contract to buy a lot in it, tells B that he intends to construct a golf course in the development. A has no such intention. B is induced by A's statement to make the contract. The contract is voidable by B. If, however, B knows that the terrain is not suitable for a golf course, that there is not enough land for it, and that it could only be constructed by purchase of a large quantity of additional land quite beyond A's means, B's reliance is not justified, and the contract is not voidable by B.

. . .

b. A promise as a statement of intention. It is ordinarily reasonable for the promisee to infer from the making of a promise that the promisor intends to perform it. If, therefore, the promise is made with the intention of not performing it, this implied assertion is false and is a misrepresentation. The promise itself need not be made in words but may be inferred from conduct or even supplied by law. Nor does it need to be a legally enforceable promise. The promisor's intention not to perform his promise cannot be established merely by proof of its non-performance. Nevertheless, the probable inability of a party, at the time the contract is made, to perform it, for instance the insolvency of one who buys land, is evidence bearing on the question of intent not to perform. If the promisor knows or should know that he cannot at least substantially perform his promise, this is strong although not conclusive evidence of an intent not to carry it out. (The effect of a buyer's misrepresentation of solvency or of intent to pay in the case of a contract for the sale of goods is the subject of the special rule of Uniform Commercial Code § 2-702(2).) If a party is entitled to avoid the contract on this ground, he may do so immediately and need not await the time for performance. The application of the rule stated in Subsection (2) does not turn on whether the promisor is the offeror or the offeree. When the parties exchange promises as consideration for each other, each promise is properly regarded as the inducement for the other. Therefore, if the offeree has no intention of performing his promise when he accepts, the contract is voidable by the offeror on the ground that his promise was made in reliance on that of the offeree. See Comment *a* to § 167. As with other assertions, the recipient's reliance must be justified. It is not justified if the promisor has disclosed his intention not to perform or if performance is known not to be within his control.

. . .

§ 172. When Fault Makes Reliance Unjustified

A recipient's fault in not knowing or discovering the facts before making the contract does not make his reliance unjustified unless it amounts to a failure to act in good faith and in accordance with reasonable standards of fair dealing.

Comment:

a. Rationale. The recipient's reliance on the misrepresentation must be justified in order to entitle him to avoidance (§ 164) or reformation (§ 166). He is not entitled to relief if his reliance was unreasonable in the light of his particular circumstances. See Comment *b* to § 164. But the mere fact that he could, by the exercise of reasonable care, have avoided the mistake caused by the misrepresentation does not bar him from relief. The rule is similar to that applicable to mistake in general (§ 157), and its justification is particularly strong since here the recipient's mistake is the result of a misrepresentation. However, the recipient's fault will prevent the application of the rule stated in § 163, under which a misrepresentation as to the very nature of a proposed contract makes his apparent manifestation of assent ineffective. That rule applies only if he has neither knowledge nor reasonable opportunity to obtain knowledge of the character or essential terms of the proposed contract. But even in such a case, lack of reasonable care will not preclude the recipient from avoiding or from obtaining reformation. See Illustration 1. The recipient's fault makes his reliance unjustified only in extreme cases where he has failed to act in good faith and in accordance with reasonable standards of fair dealing. **Illustration:**

1. A and B reach an understanding that they will execute a written contract containing terms on which they have agreed. A prepares a writing

containing essential terms different from those agreed upon and induces B to sign it by telling him that it contains the agreed terms and that it is not necessary for him to read it. Although B's apparent manifestation of assent is effective if he had a reasonable opportunity to read the writing (see Illustration 3 to § 163), his reliance is justified since his fault does not amount to a failure to act in good faith and in accordance with reasonable standards of fair dealing. The contract is voidable by B. In the alternative he may have the writing reformed.

b. Good faith and fair dealing. In determining whether the recipient of a misrepresentation has conformed to the standard of good faith and fair dealing, account is taken of his peculiar qualities and characteristics, including his credulity and gullibility, and the circumstances of the particular case, including the fraudulent or innocent nature of the misrepresentation. However, in contrast to the rules that govern a damage action in deceit, the rule stated in this Section applies to innocent as well as to fraudulent misrepresentations. Compare Restatement, Second, Torts § 545A with § 552A. If the recipient knows that the assertion is false or should have discovered its falsity by making a cursory examination, his reliance is clearly not justified and he is not entitled to relief. See Restatement, Second, Torts § 541. He is expected to use his senses and not rely blindly on the maker's assertion. On the other hand, he is not barred by the mere failure to investigate the truth of a misrepresentation, even where it might be reasonable to do so. See Restatement, Second,

Torts § 540. The fact that the recipient took advantage of an opportunity to investigate may be relevant under the rules relating to assertions of opinion (see Comment *b* to § 168) or as indicating that he did not rely on the misrepresentation (see Comment *b* to § 167). For the purposes of the rule stated in this Section, however, the recipient is generally entitled to rely on the maker's assertions as to his knowledge without undertaking an investigation as to their truthfulness. **Illustrations:**

2. A, seeking to induce B to make a contract to buy land, tells B that the land is free from encumbrances. Unknown to either A or B, C holds a recorded and unsatisfied mortgage on the land. B could easily learn this by walking across the street to the register of deeds in the courthouse but does not do so. B is induced by A's statement to make the contract. B's reliance is justified since his fault does not amount to a failure to act in good faith and in accordance with reasonable standards of fair dealing, and the contract is voidable by B.

3. A, seeking to induce B to make a contract to buy furniture for B's house, hands B a printed order form and tells B that the total price for the furniture is $ 550 and that this is stated in the form. A knows that in the form additional furniture is described and that the total price stated is $ 1,050. B is induced by A's statement to sign the form without reading it, and A accepts B's offer. B's reliance is justified since his fault does not amount to a failure to act in good faith and in accordance with reasonable standards of fair dealing. The contract is voidable by B. In the alternative he may have the writing reformed.

§ 173. When Abuse of a Fiduciary Relation Makes a Contract Voidable

If a fiduciary makes a contract with his beneficiary relating to matters within the scope of the fiduciary relation, the contract is voidable by the beneficiary, unless (a) it is on fair terms, and (b) all parties beneficially interested manifest assent with full understanding of their legal rights and of all relevant facts that the fiduciary knows or should know.

Comment:

a. Equal footing. The rule stated in this Section applies to any fiduciary, including a trustee, an agent, a guardian, or an executor or administrator. See Restatement, Second, Trusts § 170(2). It is more severe than the rule relating to non-disclosure in the case of one who stands in a relation of trust and confidence but who is not a fiduciary. See § 161(b); cf. § 169(a). When a fiduciary makes a contract with the person beneficially interested, it is not enough that he

make a complete disclosure of the facts known to him. The person beneficially interested must be put on an equal footing, with full understanding of his legal rights and of all relevant facts that the fiduciary knows or should know. If that person is not of competent age and understanding, this may be difficult if not impossible to achieve. If it is impossible, the fiduciary is precluded from making a contract with him within the scope of the fiduciary relation.

b. Fairness. In addition to assuring itself that the parties were placed on an equal footing, a court will inquire into the fairness of the resulting agreement. What is required is not merely the absence of unconscionability, as is the case for contracts in general. The contract is voidable unless it is shown to be on fair terms in the light of the circumstances at the time of its making.

Illustration:

    1. A, the executor of a will under which a tract of land has been devised to B, makes a contract with B to buy the tract from him. Before making the contract, A tells B all relevant facts about the transaction. The contract is voidable by B unless the court concludes that it is on fair terms.

c. Relation to other rules. The rule stated in this Section applies only where the fiduciary is a party to the contract. As to the effect of misrepresentation or non-disclosure by a fiduciary who is not a party to the contract, see §§ 161(a), 169(a), which apply to any relation of trust and confidence, including a fiduciary relation. The rule stated in this Section, like those stated in §§ 164, 175 and 177, only makes the contract voidable, and the power of avoidance is subject to the rights of good faith purchasers and to the rules stated in Chapter 16 on remedies.

Topic 2. Duress and Undue Influence

Introductory Note This Topic deals with improper pressure in the bargaining process, in the form of either duress or undue influence. Duress takes two forms. In one, a person physically compels conduct that appears to be a manifestation of assent by a party who has no intention of engaging in that conduct. The result of this type of duress is that the conduct is not effective to create a contract (§ 174). In the other, a person makes an improper threat that induces a party who has no reasonable alternative to manifesting his assent. The result of this type of duress is that the contract that is created is voidable by the victim (§ 175). This latter type of duress is in practice the more common and more important. Either type may be exercised by one who is not a party to the contract as well as by one who is, but if the duress is of the latter type, avoidance is precluded if the other party to the transaction has in good faith and without reason to know of the duress either given value or relied materially (§ 175(2)).

Over the course of centuries, courts have greatly expanded the classes of threats that will be characterized as improper. The rule stated in § 176 which determines whether a threat is improper, therefore includes types of pressure commonly known as "economic duress" or "business compulsion."

Undue influence involves unfair persuasion, a milder form of pressure than duress. Such persuasion nevertheless makes the contract voidable if it is exercised on a party who is under the domination of the person exercising it or is, by virtue of his relation with that person, justified in assuming that this person will not act in a manner inconsistent with his welfare. This rule is subject to an exception similar to that applicable to duress where the undue influence is exercised by one who is not a party (§ 177 (2)).

Since duress and undue influence, unlike deceit, are not generally of themselves actionable torts, the victim of duress or undue influence is usually limited to avoidance and does not have an affirmative action for damages. But see Comment *f* to Restatement, Torts § 871.

§ 174. When Duress by Physical Compulsion Prevents Formation of a Contract

If conduct that appears to be a manifestation of assent by a party who does not intend to engage in that conduct is physically compelled by duress, the conduct is not effective as a manifestation of assent.

Comment:

a. Rationale. Under the general principle stated in § 21(2), a party's conduct is not effective as a manifestation of his assent if he does not intend to engage in it. This Section involves an application of that principle to those relatively rare situations in which actual physical force has been used to compel a party to appear to assent to a contract. Compare § 163. The essence of this type of duress is that a party is compelled by physical force to do an act that he has no intention of doing. He is, it is sometimes said, "a mere mechanical instrument." The result is that there is no contract at all, or a "void contract" as distinguished from a voidable one. See Comment *a* to § 7. Cases, such as those involving hypnosis, in which conduct is compelled without physical force, are left to be governed by the general rule stated in § 19(2). **Illustration:**

> 1. A presents to B, who is physically weaker than A, a written contract prepared for B's signature and demands that B sign it. B refuses. A grasps B's hand and compels B by physical force

to write his name. B's signature is not effective as a manifestation of his assent, and there is no contract.

b. "Void" rather than voidable. The distinction between "void contract" and a voidable contract has important consequences. For example, a victim of duress may be held to have ratified the contract if it is voidable, but not if it is "void." Furthermore, a good faith purchaser may acquire good title to property if he takes it from one who obtained voidable title by duress but not if he takes it from one who obtained "void title" by duress. It is immaterial under the rule stated in this Section whether the duress is exercised by a party to the transaction or by a third person. See Comment *d* to § 175.

§ 175. When Duress by Threat Makes a Contract Voidable

(1) If a party's manifestation of assent is induced by an improper threat by the other party that leaves the victim no reasonable alternative, the contract is voidable by the victim.

(2) If a party's manifestation of assent is induced by one who is not a party to the transaction, the contract is voidable by the victim unless the other party to the transaction in good faith and without reason to know of the duress either gives value or relies materially on the transaction.

Comment:

a. Improper threat. The essence of the type of duress dealt with in this Section is inducement by an improper threat. The threat may be expressed in words or it may be inferred from words or other conduct. Past events often import a threat. Thus, if one person strikes or imprisons another, the conduct may amount to duress because of the threat of further blows or continued imprisonment that is implied. Courts originally restricted duress to threats involving loss of life, mayhem or imprisonment, but these restrictions have been greatly relaxed and, in order to constitute duress, the threat need only be improper within the rule stated in § 176.

b. No reasonable alternative. A threat, even if improper, does not amount to duress if the victim has a reasonable alternative to succumbing and fails to take advantage of it. It is sometimes said that the threat must arouse such fear as precludes a party from exercising free will and judgment or that it must be such as would induce assent on the part of a brave man or a man of ordinary firmness. The rule stated in this Section omits any such requirement because of its vagueness and impracticability. It is enough if the threat

actually induces assent (see Comment *c*) on the part of one who has no reasonable alternative. The alternative may take the form of a legal remedy. For example, the threat of commencing an ordinary civil action to enforce a claim to money may be improper. See § 176(1)(c). However, it does not usually amount to duress because the victim can assert his rights in the threatened action, and this is ordinarily a reasonable alternative to succumbing to the threat, making the proposed contract, and then asserting his rights in a later civil action. See Illustration 1; cf. Restatement of Restitution § 71. This alternative may not, however, be reasonable if the threat involves, for instance, the seizure of property, the use of oppressive tactics, or the possibility of emotional consequences. See Illustration 2. The standard is a practical one under which account must be taken of the exigencies in which the victim finds himself, and the mere availability of a legal remedy is not controlling if it will not afford effective relief to one in the victim's circumstances. See Illustrations 3 and 4. The alternative to succumbing to the threat need not, however, involve a legal remedy at all. In the case of a threatened denial of needed goods or services, the availability on the market of similar goods or services may afford a reasonable means of avoiding the threat. Compare Illustrations 5 and 6. Since alternative sources of funds are ordinarily available, a refusal to pay money is not duress, absent a showing of peculiar necessity. See Illustration 7. Where the threat is one of minor vexation only, toleration of the inconvenience involved may be a reasonable alternative. Whether the victim has a reasonable alternative is a mixed question of law and fact, to be answered in clear cases by the court. **Illustrations:**

1. A makes an improper threat to commence civil proceedings against B unless B agrees to discharge a claim that B has against A. In order to avoid defending the threatened suit, B is induced to make the contract. Defense of the threatened suit is a reasonable alternative, the threat does not amount to duress, and the contract is not voidable by B.

2. A makes an improper threat to commence a civil action and to file a lis pendens against a tract of land owned by B, unless B agrees to discharge a claim that B has against A. Because B is about to make a contract with C for the sale of the land and C refuses to make the contract if the levy is made, B agrees to discharge the claim. B has no reasonable alternative, A's threat is duress, and the contract is voidable by B.

3. A, with whom B has left a machine for repairs, makes an improper threat to refuse to deliver the machine to B, although B has paid for the repairs, unless B agrees to make a contract to have additional repair work done. B can replevy the machine, but because he is in urgent need of it and delay would cause him heavy financial loss, he is induced by A's threat to make the contract. B has no reasonable alternative, A's threat amounts to duress, and the contract is voidable by B.

4. A, who has promised B to vacate leased premises in return for $ 10,000 in order to permit B to demolish the building and construct another, refuses to do so unless B agrees to purchase his worthless furniture for $ 5,000. B can resort to regular eviction proceedings, but because this will materially delay his construction schedule and cause him heavy financial loss, he is induced by A's threat to make the contract. B has no reasonable alternative, A's threat amounts to duress, and the contract is voidable by B.

. . .

c. Subjective test of inducement. In order to constitute duress, the improper threat must induce the making of the contract. The rule for causation in cases of misrepresentation stated in § 167 is also applied to analogous cases of duress. No special rule for causation in cases of duress is stated here because of the infrequency with which the problem arises. A party's manifestation of assent is induced by duress if the duress substantially contributes to his decision to manifest his assent. Compare § 167. The test is subjective and the question is, did the threat actually induce assent on the part of the person claiming to be the victim of duress. Threats that would suffice to induce assent by one person may not suffice to induce assent by another. All attendant circumstances must be considered, including such matters as the age, background and relationship of the parties. Persons of a weak or cowardly nature are the very ones that need protection; the courageous can usually protect themselves. Timid and inexperienced persons are particularly subject to threats, and it does not lie in the mouths of the unscrupulous to excuse their imposition on such persons on the ground of their victims' infirmities. However, here as under §§ 167 circumstantial evidence may be useful in determining whether a threat did in fact induce assent. For example, although it is not essential that a reasonable person would have believed that the maker of the threat had the ability to execute it, this may be relevant in determining whether the threat actually induced assent. Similarly, such factors as the availability of disinterested advice and the length of time that elapses between the making of the threat and the assent may also be relevant in determining whether the threat actually induced the assent. **Illustrations:**

8. A, seeking to induce B to make a contract to sell land to A, threatens to poison B unless B makes the contract. The threat would not be taken seriously by a reasonable person, but B is easily frightened and attaches importance to the threat in deciding to make the contract. The contract is voidable by B.

9. A seeks to induce B, A's wife, who has a history of severe emotional disturbances, to sign a separation agreement on unfavorable terms. B has no lawyer, while A does. A tells B that if she does not sign the agreement he will charge her with desertion, she will never see her children again and she will get back none of her personal property, which is in A's possession. B signs the separation agreement. The agreement is voidable by B.

d. Voidable. Duress by threat results in a contract voidable by the victim. It differs in this important respect from duress by physical compulsion, which results in there being no contract at all. See Comment *b* to § 174. The power of avoidance for duress is subject to limitations that are similar to those applicable to avoidance on other grounds, such as mistake and misrepresentation. These limitations are stated in §§ 378-84. The person making the threat may, of course, pursue any civil claim that he has against the victim independently of the contract induced by the threat. Furthermore, to the extent that such a claim is valid, the maker of the threat may be entitled to retain what he has actually received through performance of such a contract. These matters are not dealt with in this Section.

e. Duress by a third person. If a party's assent has been induced by the duress of a third person, rather than that of the other party to the contract, the contract is nevertheless voidable by the victim. There is, however, an important exception if the other party has, in good faith and without reason to know of the duress, given value or changed his position materially in reliance on the transaction. "Value" includes a performance or a return promise that is consideration under the definition stated in § 71, so that the other party is protected if he has made the contract in good faith before learning of the duress. See Uniform Commercial Code § 1-201(44). The rule stated in this Section does not, however, protect a party to whom the duress is attributable under the law of agency. The rule is similar to that for misrepresentation (§ 163) and is analogous to the rule that protects against the original owner the good faith purchaser of property from another who obtained it by duress.

Illustrations:

10. A, who is not C's agent, induces B by duress to contract with C to sell land to C. C, in good faith, promises B to pay the agreed price. The contract is not voidable by B.

11. The facts being otherwise as stated in Illustration 10, C learns of the duress before he promises to pay the agreed price. The contract is voidable by B.

§ 176. When a Threat Is Improper

(1) A threat is improper if

(a) what is threatened is a crime or a tort, or the threat itself would be a crime or a tort if it resulted in obtaining property,

(b) what is threatened is a criminal prosecution,

(c) what is threatened is the use of civil process and the threat is made in bad faith, or

(d) the threat is a breach of the duty of good faith and fair dealing under a contract with the recipient.

(2) A threat is improper if the resulting exchange is not on fair terms, and

(a) the threatened act would harm the recipient and would not significantly benefit the party making the threat,

(b) the effectiveness of the threat in inducing the manifestation of assent is significantly increased by prior unfair dealing by the party making the threat, or

(c) what is threatened is otherwise a use of power for illegitimate ends.

Comment:

a. Rationale. An ordinary offer to make a contract commonly involves an implied threat by one party, the offeror, not to make the contract unless his terms are accepted by the other party, the offeree. Such threats are an accepted part of the bargaining process. A threat does not amount to duress unless it is so improper as to amount to an abuse of that process. Courts first recognized as improper threats of physical violence and later included wrongful seizure or detention of goods. Modern decisions have recognized as improper a much broader range of threats, notably those to cause economic harm. The rules stated in this Section recognize as improper both the older categories and their modern extensions under developing notions of "economic duress" or "business compulsion." The fairness of the resulting exchange is often a critical factor in cases involving threats. The categories within Subsection (1) involve threats that are either so shocking that the court will not inquire into the fairness of the resulting exchange (see Clauses

(a) and (b)) or that in themselves necessarily involve some element of unfairness (see Clauses (c) and (d)). Those within Subsection (2) involve threats in which the impropriety consists of the threat in combination with resulting unfairness. Such a threat is not improper if it can be shown that the exchange is one on fair terms. Of course a threat may be improper for more than one reason. Any threat that comes within Subsection (1) as well as Subsection (2) is improper without an inquiry, under the rule stated in Subsection (2), into the fairness of the resulting exchange.

b. Crime or tort. A threat is improper if the threatened act is a crime or a tort, as in the traditional examples of threats of physical violence and of wrongful seizure or retention of goods. See Comment *a.* Where physical violence is threatened, it need not be to the recipient of the threat, nor even to a person related to him, if the threat in fact induces the recipient to manifest his assent. See Illustration 2. The threatened act need not involve harm to person or goods but may, for example, involve a tortious interference with another's contractual rights. Where the crime or tort is a minor one, however, the claim of duress may fail, even though the threat is improper, on the ground that the victim had a reasonable alternative (see Comment *b* to § 175) or that the threat was not an inducing cause (see Comment *c* to § 175). The threatened act need not be a crime or tort if the threat itself would have been one had it resulted in the obtaining of property.

Therefore, in jurisdictions where a broad modern extortion statute has been enacted, many of the threats that come within Subsection (2) are elements of the crime of extortion and therefore also fall within Clause (1)(a). See Model Penal Code § 223.4. The fairness of the exchange is immaterial in such cases. **Illustrations:**

> 1. A is a good faith purchaser for value of a valuable painting stolen from B. When B demands the return of the painting, A threatens to poison B unless he releases all rights to the painting for $ 1,000. B, having no reasonable alternative, is induced by A's threat to sign the release, and A pays him $ 1,000. The threatened act is both a crime and a tort, and the release is voidable by B.
> 2. A threatens B that he will kill C, an employee of B, unless B makes a contract to sell A a tract of land that B owns. B, having no reasonable alternative, is induced by A's threat to make the contract. The threatened act is both a crime and a tort, and the contract is voidable by B.

. . .

c. Threat of prosecution. Under the rule stated in Clause (1)(b), a threat of criminal prosecution is improper as a means of inducing the recipient to make a contract. An explanation in good faith of the criminal consequences of another's conduct may not involve a threat. But if a threat is made, the fact that the one who makes it honestly believes that the recipient is guilty is not material. The threat involves a misuse, for personal gain, of power given for other legitimate ends. See Comment *f.* The threat may be to instigate prosecution against the recipient or some third person, who is commonly although not necessarily a relative of the recipient. The guilt or innocence of the person whose prosecution is threatened is immaterial in determining whether the threat is improper, although it may be easier to show that the threat actually induced assent in the case of guilt. A bargain to suppress prosecution may be unenforceable on grounds of public policy. See the Introductory Note to Chapter 8 on agreements against public policy.

. . .

d. Threat of civil process. The policy in favor of free access to the judicial system militates against the characterization as improper of threats to commence civil process, even if the claim on which the process is based eventually proves to be without foundation. Nevertheless, if the threat is shown to have been made in bad faith, it is improper. Bad faith may be shown by proving that the person making the threat did not believe there was a reasonable basis for the threatened process, that he knew the threat would involve a misuse of the process or that he realized the demand he made was exorbitant. See Comment *f.* However, a threat to commence civil process, even if improper, may not amount to duress since defense of the threatened action is often a reasonable alternative. See Comment *b* to § 175. **Illustrations:**

> 6. A threatens to commence a civil action and file a lis pendens against a tract of land owned by B, unless B makes a contract to discharge a disputed claim that B has against A. A knows that the threatened action is without foundation. B, having no reasonable alternative, is induced by A's threat to make the contract. Since A does not believe that there is a reasonable basis for the threatened process, his threat is made in bad faith.

A's threat is improper, and the contract is void-able by B. If, however, A believes that there is a reasonable basis for the threatened process and if the proposed contract is not exorbitant, the threat is not improper, and the contract is not voidable by B.

. . .

e. Breach of contract. A threat by a party to a contract not to perform his contractual duty is not, of itself, improper. Indeed, a modification induced by such a threat may be binding, even in the absence of consideration, if it is fair and equitable in view of unanticipated circumstances. See § 89. The mere fact that the modification induced by the threat fails to meet this test does not mean that the threat is necessarily improper. However, the threat is improper if it amounts to a breach of the duty of good faith and fair dealing imposed by the contract. See §§ 205. As under the Uniform Commercial Code, the "extortion of a 'modification' without legitimate commercial reason is ineffective as a violation of the duty of good faith. . . . The test of 'good faith' between merchants or as against merchants includes 'observance of reasonable commercial standards of fair dealing in the trade' (Section 2-103), and may in some situations require an objectively demonstrable reason for seeking a modification. But such matters as a market shift which makes performance come to involve a loss may provide such a reason even though there is no such unforeseen difficulty as would make out a legal excuse from performance under Sections 2-615 and 2-616." Comment 2 to Uniform Commercial Code § 2-209. However, a threat of non-performance made for some purpose unrelated to the contract, such as to induce the recipient to make an entirely separate contract, is ordinarily improper. See Illustration 9. Furthermore, a threat may be a breach of the duty of good faith and fair dealing under the contract even though the threatened act is not itself a breach of the contract. See Illustrations 10 and 11. This is particularly likely to be the case if the threat is effective because of power not derived from the contract itself. See Comment *f.* **Illustrations:**

    8. A contracts to excavate a cellar for B at a stated price. A unexpectedly encounters solid rock and threatens not to finish the excavation unless B modifies the contract to state a new price that is reasonable but is nine times the origi-nal price. B, having no reasonable alternative, is induced by A's threat to make the modification by a signed writing that is enforceable by statute without consideration. A's threat is not a breach of his duty of good faith and fair dealing, and the modification is not voidable by B. See Illustra-tion 1 to § 89.

    9. A contracts to excavate a cellar for B at a stated price. A begins the excavation and then threatens not to finish it unless B makes a sepa-rate contract to excavate the cellar of another building. B, having no reasonable alternative, is induced by A's threat to make the contract. A's threat is a breach of his duty of good faith and fair dealing, and the proposed contract is void-able by B. See Illustration 5 to § 175.

    10. A contracts to sell part of a tract of land to B. B, solely to induce A to discharge him from his contract duty on favorable terms, threatens to resell the land to a purchaser whose industrial use will have an undesirable effect on A's re-maining land, unless A releases B in return for a stated sum. A, having no reasonable alternative, signs the release. B's threat is a breach of his duty of good faith and fair dealing, and the modi-fication is voidable by A.

  . . .

f. Other improper threats. The proper limits of bargaining are difficult to define with precision. Hard bargaining between experienced adversaries of relatively equal power ought not to be discouraged. Parties are generally held to the resulting agreement, even though one has taken advantage of the other's adversity, as long as the contract has been dictated by general economic forces. See Illustration 14. Where, however, a party has been induced to make a contract by some power exercised by the other for illegitimate ends, the transaction is suspect. For example, absent statute, a threat of refusal to deal with another party is ordinarily not duress, but if other factors are present an agreement that results from such a threat may be called into question. Subsection (2) deals with threats that are improper if the resulting exchange is not on fair terms. Clause (a) is concerned with cases in which a party threatens to do an act that would not significantly benefit him but would harm the other party. If, on the recipient's refusal to contract, the maker of the threat were to do the threatened act, it would therefore be done maliciously and unconscionably, out of pure vindictiveness. A typical example is a threat to make public embarrassing information concerning the recipient unless he makes a proposed contract. See Illustration 12 and Model Penal

Code § 223.4(g). Clause (b) is concerned with cases in which the party making the threat has by unfair dealing achieved an advantage over the recipient that makes his threat unusually effective. Typical examples involve manipulative conduct during the bargaining stage that leaves one person at the mercy of the other. See Illustration 13. Clause (c) is concerned with other cases in which the threatened act involves the use of power for illegitimate ends. Many of the situations encompassed by clauses (1)(b), (1)(c), (2)(a) and (2)(b) involve extreme applications of this general rule, but it is more broadly applicable to analogous cases. See Illustrations 15 and 16. If, in any of these cases, the threat comes within Subsection (1), as where the threatened act or the threat itself is criminal or tortious (Clause (1)(a)), it is improper without an inquiry into the fairness of the resulting exchange under Subsection 2. See Comment *a*. **Illustrations:**

12. A makes a threat to B, his former employee, that he will try to prevent B's employment elsewhere unless B agrees to release a claim that he has against A. B, having no reasonable alternative, is thereby induced to make the contract. If the court concludes that the attempt to prevent B's employment elsewhere would harm B and would not significantly benefit A, A's threat is improper and the contract is voidable by B.

13. A, who has sold goods to B on several previous occasions, intentionally misleads B into thinking that he will supply the goods at the usual price and thereby causes B to delay in attempting to buy them elsewhere until it is too late to do so. A then threatens not to sell the goods to B unless he agrees to pay a price greatly in excess of that charged previously. B, being in urgent need of the goods, makes the contract. If the court concludes that the effectiveness of A's threat in inducing B to make the contract was significantly increased by A's prior unfair dealing, A's threat is improper and the contract is voidable by B.

14. The facts being otherwise as stated in Illustration 13, A merely discovers that B is in great need of the goods and that they are in short supply but does not mislead B into thinking that he will supply them. A's threat is not improper, and the contract is not voidable by B.

. . .

§ 177. When Undue Influence Makes a Contract Voidable

(1) Undue influence is unfair persuasion of a party who is under the domination of the person exercising the persuasion or who by virtue of the relation between them is justified in assuming that that person will not act in a manner inconsistent with his welfare.

(2) If a party's manifestation of assent is induced by undue influence by the other party, the contract is voidable by the victim.

(3) If a party's manifestation of assent is induced by one who is not a party to the transaction, the contract is voidable by the victim unless the other party to the transaction in good faith and without reason to know of the undue influence either gives value or relies materially on the transaction.

Comment:

a. Required domination or relation. The rule stated in this Section protects a person only if he is under the domination of another or is justified, by virtue of his relation with another in assuming that the other will not act inconsistently with his welfare. Relations that often fall within the rule include those of parent and child, husband and wife, clergyman and parishioner, and physician and patient. In each case it is a question of fact whether the relation is such as to give undue weight to the other's attempts at persuasion. The required relation may be found in situations other than those enumerated. However, the mere fact that a party is weak, infirm or aged does not of itself suffice, although it may be a factor in determining whether the required relation existed.

b. Unfair persuasion. Where the required domination or relation is present, the contract is voidable if it was induced by any unfair persuasion on the part of the stronger party. The law of undue influence therefore affords protection in situations where the rules on duress and misrepresentation give no relief. The degree of persuasion that is unfair depends on a variety of circumstances. The ultimate question is whether the result was produced by means that seriously impaired the free and competent exercise of judgment. Such factors as the unfairness of the resulting bargain, the unavailability of independent advice, and the susceptibility of the person persuaded are circumstances to be taken into account in determining whether there was unfair persuasion, but they are not in themselves controlling. Compare § 173. **Illustrations:**

    1. A, who is not experienced in business, has for years been accustomed to rely in business matters on the advice of his friend, B, who is experienced in business. B constantly urges A to make a contract to sell to C, B's confederate, a tract of land at a price that is well below its fair value. A is thereby induced to make the contract. Even though B's conduct does not amount to misrepresentation, it amounts to undue influence because A is justified in assuming that B will not act in a manner inconsistent with his welfare, and the contract is voidable.

    2. A, an elderly and illiterate man, lives with and depends for his support on B, his nephew. B tells A that he will no longer support him unless A makes a contract to sell B a tract of land. A is thereby induced to make the proposed contract. Even though B's conduct does not amount to duress, it amounts to undue influence because A is under the domination of B, and the contract is voidable by A.

    c. Undue influence by a third person. If a party's assent has been induced by the undue influence of a third person rather than that of the other party to the contract, the contract is nevertheless voidable by the victim, unless the other party has in good faith either given value or changed his position materially in reliance on the transaction. The rule is similar to that for misrepresentation (see Comment *c* to § 164) and duress (see Comment *b* to § 175). Compare Illustration 1.

Chapter 8

Unenforceability on Grounds of Public Policy Introductory Note

Introductory Note: In general, parties may contract as they wish, and courts will enforce their agreements without passing on their substance. Sometimes, however, a court will decide that the interest in freedom of contract is outweighed by some overriding interest of society and will refuse to enforce a promise or other term on grounds of public policy. Such a decision is based on a reluctance to aid the promisee rather than on solicitude for the promisor as such. Two reasons lie behind this reluctance. First, a refusal to enforce the promise may be an appropriate sanction to discourage undesirable conduct, either by the parties themselves or by others. Second, enforcement of the promise may be an inappropriate use of the judicial process in carrying out an unsavory transaction. The decision in a particular case will often turn on a delicate balancing of these considerations against those that favor supporting transactions freely entered into by the parties. This Chapter states the rules by which courts are guided in making such decisions.

These are not, to be sure, the only rules relating to contracts that are based on public policy. The principle of freedom of contract is itself rooted in the notion that it is in the public interest to recognize that individuals have broad powers to order their own affairs by making legally enforceable promises. Similarly, the rules relating to consideration manifest a policy in favor of limiting that enforcement to those promises that are arrived at by bargain. Other rules, such as those that treat of misrepresentation, duress and undue influence, serve to insure that bargaining has taken place in a suitable climate. The policies behind all of these rules are, however, related to the very process by which the promise itself is made. In contrast, the policies with which this Chapter is concerned touch upon matters of substance related to the public welfare rather than aspects of the bargaining process between the parties. Because of the myriad of such policies, this Chapter does not purport to deal in detail with all of the many kinds of promises that may be unenforceable on grounds of public policy. Nor does it catalog promises that are enforceable in spite of arguments to the contrary based on public policy.

Some policies are purely the product of judicial development. No attempt is made here to present a complete catalog of these, although rules are included in three major areas that have often been before the courts, relating to restraint of trade (Topic 2), impairment of family relations (Topic 3), and interference with other protected interests (Topic 4). Other judicially developed policies are dealt with in the Restatements of other subjects. See Restatement, Second, Conflict of Laws §§ 32, 80 (choice of forum clauses), 187 (choice of law clauses); Restatement of Property, Division IV, Part II (restraints on alienation); Restatement, Second, Property (Landlord and Tenant) § 9.1 (property leased for illegal purposes). See also § 317(2)(b) of this Restatement (assignments).

Other policies are implemented by courts for the reason that they have been manifested by legislation. Such legislation may vary widely from one jurisdiction to another, and no attempt is made here to deal with questions of its interpretation. The law of the particular jurisdiction must determine whether there has been a violation of a statute of that jurisdiction that, for example, prohibits the conduct of some activity without a license. Once it is decided that the statute has been violated, the rules stated in this Chapter give guidance as to the effect of that violation on any contractual rights claimed by the parties.

For this reason, no detailed rules are included in this Chapter on fields in which legislation has become preeminent. Labor agreements are not touched upon, nor are agreements in restraint of trade except to the limited extent that legislation is not dominant. See Introductory Note to Topic 2. Older laws prohibiting usury have been supplemented by new ones that focus on consumer transactions, just as older laws prohibiting gambling have been subjected to more modern exceptions. Bargains tending to obstruct the administration of justice or in violation of a public duty have also come under extensive legislative control. Thus penal laws condemn bribery and corrupt influence, perjury and other falsification in official matters, and obstructing governmental operation (see Model Penal

Code Arts. 240-42), and legislation has replaced the common law of maintenance and champerty in many states. A particularly important change has been effected by statutes relating to arbitration, which have now been enacted in so many jurisdictions that it seems likely that even in the remaining states, there has been a change in the former judicial attitude of hostility toward agreements to arbitrate future disputes (see Restatement, Second, Conflict of Laws, Introductory Note to Topic 5, Chapter 8). Such agreements are now widely used and serve the public interest by saving court time. The rules stated in this Chapter do not preclude their enforcement, even in the absence of legislation. Because each of these subjects has a heavy legislative ingredient, none is specifically dealt with in this Chapter. They are however, subject to the general rules relating to unenforceability (Topic 1) and restitution (Topic 5), to the extent that the governing legislation does not dictate otherwise.

All of the rules stated in this Chapter are subject to contrary provision by legislation. The possibility of such modification cannot be overlooked, even in areas where legislation is not extensive

Topic 1. Unenforceability in General

Introductory Note: This Topic states rules that determine when a promise or other term is unenforceable on grounds of public policy. In stating these rules, it avoids the common characterization of such promises or terms as "illegal." This Restatement is concerned with whether a promise is enforceable and not with whether some other sanction has been attached to the act of making or performing it in such a way as to make that act "illegal." The rules stated here are therefore formulated in terms of "unenforceability" rather than "illegality."

They are also broadly formulated to apply to all promises and other terms (§§ 2(1), 5), including those where there is no agreement or bargain (§ 3). See Topic 2 of Chapter 4. Even where both parties make promises, the analysis usually begins with the question of the enforceability of one promise or term of it. Sometimes the unenforceability of that promise or term will result in the unenforceability of other promises and the denial of any relief to either party.

The law, however, is not necessarily so severe. In some situations, one party's promise may be enforceable even though the other party's is not. See, for example,§ 180. In other situations, part of an agreement may be enforceable even though the rest is unenforceable on grounds of public policy. See §§ 183, 184, 185. Finally, a court may allow restitution under one of the exceptions to the general rule that denies restitution in such cases (Topic 5). In reading the rule stated in § 178, it is important to realize not only that it is itself a flexible one, but that it is subject to these mitigating doctrines.

The rules of substantive law stated in this Topic do not turn on niceties of pleading or of proof. Although it is sometimes said that a party's ability to enforce a promise depends on whether he can state his case in his pleadings without disclosing a contravention of public policy, such arbitrary criteria are not satisfactory ones for resolving matters of significant public interest. Even if neither party's pleading or proof reveals the contravention, the court may ordinarily inquire into it and decide the case on the basis of it if it finds it just to do so, subject to any relevant rules of pleading or proof by which it is bound. Those rules are beyond the scope of this Restatement.

Some related problems are dealt with in other parts of this Restatement. Even though enforcement of a promise is not precluded on grounds of public policy, a governmental regulation or order may give rise to a defense based on supervening or even existing impracticability or frustration. See Chapter 11, Illustration 1 to § 261, Illustrations 2 and 6 to § 264, Illustration 4 to § 265, Illustration 2 to § 266. A court may decide that, although enforcement of a promise is not precluded on grounds of public policy, the promisee is not entitled to equitable relief such as specific performance. See § 365. Or it may avoid the problem of unenforceability by so interpreting the promise that no contravention of public policy is involved. See §§ 203(a), 207. That a promise that is unenforceable on grounds of public policy may nevertheless be consideration for a return promise, see § 78 and Comment *d* to § 75

§ 178. When a Term Is Unenforceable on Grounds of Public Policy

(1) A promise or other term of an agreement is unenforceable on grounds of public policy if legislation provides that it is unenforceable or the interest in its enforcement is clearly outweighed in the circumstances by a public policy against the enforcement of such terms.

(2) In weighing the interest in the enforcement of a term, account is taken of

(a) the parties' justified expectations,

(b) any forfeiture that would result if enforcement were denied, and

(c) any special public interest in the enforcement of the particular term.

(3) In weighing a public policy against enforcement of a term, account is taken of

(a) the strength of that policy as manifested by legislation or judicial decisions,

(b) the likelihood that a refusal to enforce the term will further that policy,

(c) the seriousness of any misconduct involved and the extent to which it was deliberate, and

(d) the directness of the connection between that misconduct and the term.

Comment:

a. Legislation providing for unenforceability. Occasionally, on grounds of public policy, legislation provides that specified kinds of promises or other terms are unenforceable. Whether such legislation is valid and applicable to the particular term in dispute is beyond the scope of this Restatement. Assuming that it is, the court is bound to carry out the legislative mandate with respect to the enforceability of the term. But with respect to such other matters as the enforceability of the rest of the agreement (§§ 183, 184) and the possibility of restitution (Topic 5), a court will be guided by the same rules that apply to other terms unenforceable on grounds of public policy (see Illustration 1), absent contrary provision in the legislation itself (see Illustration 3). The term "legislation" is used here in the broadest sense to include any fixed text enacted by a body with authority to promulgate rules, including not only statutes, but constitutions and local ordinances, as well as administrative regulations issued pursuant to them. It also encompasses foreign laws to the extent that they are applicable under conflict of laws rules. See Restatement, Second, Conflict of Laws §§ 202, 203. **Illustrations:**

1. A promises to pay B $ 1,000 if the Buckets win their basketball game with the Hoops, and B promises to pay A $ 2,000 if the Hoops win. A state statute makes wagering a crime and provides that a promise such as A's or B's is "void." A's and B's promises are unenforceable on grounds of public policy. Any claims of A or B to restitution for money paid under the agreement are governed by the rules stated in Topic 5. See § 199(b) and Illustrations 4 and 5 to that section.

2. A and B make an agreement by which A agrees to sell and B to buy, at a fixed price per bushel, one thousand bushels of wheat from A at any time that A shall choose during the following month. The state statute that makes wagering a crime does not apply to such an agreement and it does not offend any judicially declared public policy. Enforcement of A's and B's promises is not precluded on grounds of public policy.

. . .

b. Balancing of interests. Only infrequently does legislation, on grounds of public policy, provide that a term is unenforceable. When a court reaches that conclusion, it usually does so on the basis of a public policy derived either from its own perception of the need to protect some aspect of the public welfare or from legislation that is relevant to that policy although it says nothing explicitly about unenforceability. See § 179. In some cases the contravention of public policy is so grave, as when an agreement involves a serious crime or tort, that unenforceability is plain. In other cases the contravention is so trivial as that it plainly does not preclude enforcement. In doubtful cases, however, a decision as to enforceability is reached only after a careful balancing, in the light of all the circumstances, of the interest in the enforcement of the particular promise against the policy against the enforcement of such terms. The most common factors in the balancing process are set out in Subsections (2) and (3). Enforcement will be denied only if the factors that argue against enforcement clearly outweigh the law's traditional interest in protecting the expectations of the parties, its abhorrence of any unjust enrichment, and any public interest in the enforcement of the particular term.

c. Strength of policy. The strength of the public policy involved is a critical factor in the balancing process. Even when the policy is one manifested by legislation, it may be too insubstantial to outweigh the interest in the enforcement of the term in question. See Illustrations 4 and 5. A court should be particularly alert to this possibility in the case of minor administrative regulations or local ordinances that may not be indicative of the general welfare. A disparity between a relatively modest criminal sanction provided by the legislature and a much larger forfeiture that will result if enforcement of the promise is refused may suggest that the policy is not substantial enough to justify the refusal. See Illustration 4. **Illustrations:**

    4. A and B make an agreement for the sale of goods for $ 10,000, in which A promises to deliver the goods in his own truck at a designated time and place. A municipal parking ordinance makes unloading of a truck at that time and place an offense punishable by a fine of up to $ 50. A delivers the goods to B as provided. Because the public policy manifested by the ordinance is not sufficiently substantial to outweigh the interest in the enforcement of B's promise, enforcement of his promise is not precluded on grounds of public policy.

    5. A promises to employ B and B promises to work for A, all work to be done on weekdays. The agreement is made on Sunday in violation of a statute that makes the doing of business on Sunday a misdemeanor. If the court decides that the public policy manifested by the statute is not sufficiently substantial to outweigh the interests in enforcement of A's and B's promises, it will hold that enforcement of their promises is not precluded on grounds of public policy.

d. Connection with term. The extent to which a refusal to enforce a promise or other term on grounds of public policy will further that policy depends not only on the strength of the policy but also on the relation of the term to that policy and to any misconduct involved. In most cases there is a promise that involves conduct offensive to the policy. The promise may be one to engage in such conduct

    . . .

Or it may be one that tends to induce the other party to engage in such conduct. This tendency may result from the fact that the promise is made in return for the promisee's engaging in the conduct...or in return for the promisee's return promise to engage in the conduct.

    . . .

Or it may result from the fact that the duty to perform the promise is conditional on the promisee's engaging in the conduct (see Illustration 9). In such cases, it is the tendency itself that makes the promise unenforceable, even though the promise does not actually induce the conduct. There are other situations in which the conduct is not itself against public policy, but it is against public policy to promise to engage in such conduct or to attempt to induce it. It is sometimes objectionable to make a commitment to engage in conduct that is not in itself objectionable. This is the case, for example, for a promise to vote in a particular way. See Illustration 10. It is sometimes objectionable to attempt to induce conduct that is not in itself objectionable. This is the case, for example, for a promise made in consideration of the promisee's voting in a particular way. See Illustration 11. This list does not exhaust all of the possible relations between the conduct and the promise that may justify a decision that the promise is unenforceable. But as the relation between the conduct and the promise becomes tenuous, it becomes difficult to justify unenforceability unless serious misconduct is involved. A party will not be barred from enforcing a promise because of misconduct that is so remote or collateral that refusal to enforce the promise will not deter such conduct and enforcement will not amount to an inappropriate use of the judicial process. See Illustrations 15 and 16. However, a new promise to perform an earlier promise that was unenforceable on grounds of public policy is also unenforceable on those grounds unless the circumstances that made the first promise unenforceable no longer exist. The rules stated in §§ 183 and 184 involve special applications of these general principles concerning the relation between the conduct and the promise.

    . . .

e. Other factors. A court will be reluctant to frustrate a party's legitimate expectations unless there is a corresponding benefit to be gained in deterring misconduct or avoiding an inappropriate use of the judicial process. See Illustration 17. The promisee's ignorance or inadvertence, even if it does not bring him within the rule stated in § 180, is one factor in determining the weight to be attached to his expectations. See Illustration 4 to § 181. To the extent, however, that he engaged in misconduct that was serious or deliberate, his claim to protection of his expectations fails. The interest in favor of enforcement becomes much stronger after the promisee has relied substantially on those expectations as by preparation or performance. The court will then take into account any enrichment of the promisor and any forfeiture by the promisee if he should lose his right to the agreed exchange after he has relied substantially on those expectations. See Comment *b* to § 227. The possibility of restitution may be significant in this connection. See Topic 5. In addition to the interest of the promisee, the court will also weigh any interest that the public or third parties may have in the enforcement of the term in question. Such an interest may be particularly evident where the policy involved is designed to protect third parties. See Illustrations 18 and 19.

Illustrations:

17. A agrees to reimburse B for any legal expenses incurred if B will go on C's land in order to test a right of way that is disputed by A and C. B goes on C's land. Enforcement of A's promise is not precluded on grounds of public policy, even if it is later determined that B has committed a trespass. Compare § 192.

18. A, a trustee under a will, makes an agreement with B in violation of A's fiduciary duty. If enforcement of A's and B's promises is desirable for the protection of the beneficiaries, it is not precluded on grounds of public policy. Compare § 193.

19. A, B, and C, directors of a bank, make notes payable to the bank in order to deceive the bank examiner. They agree that the notes shall be returned and cancelled after they have served their purpose. Enforcement of the promises of A, B and C embodied in the notes is not precluded on grounds of public policy.

f. Effect on rest of agreement. The rules stated in this Section determine only whether a particular promise or other term is unenforceable. The question of the effect of such a determination on the rest of the agreement is sometimes a complex one. If there is only one promise in the transaction and it is unenforceable, then the question will not arise. (As to the divisibility of such a promise, however, see §§ 184, 185). This is the case for offers that have been accepted by a performance rather than by a promise (§ 53), for promises enforceable because of reliance by the promisee (§ 90), and for promises under seal (§ 95). Furthermore, even when there is another promise, it too is often unenforceable under the rules stated in this Section. This is the case, for example, where one party's promise is unenforceable because the promised conduct offends public policy and the other party's return promise is unenforceable because it tends to induce that conduct. See Illustration 8. There are, however, situations in which only one party's promise is unenforceable while the other party's return promise is enforceable, as is the case where the promisee of the return promise belongs to the class sought to be protected by the policy in question. See Illustrations 3, 4 and 5 to § 179 and Illustration 5 to § 181. (That an unenforceable promise may be consideration for a return promise, see § 78.) Finally, there are circumstances in which the unenforceability of one part of an agreement does not entail the unenforceability of the rest of the agreement, and these are dealt with in §§ 183 and 184. As to the effect of public policy on conditions, see § 185.

§ 179. Bases of Public Policies Against Enforcement

A public policy against the enforcement of promises or other terms may be derived by the court from

(a) legislation relevant to such a policy, or

(b) the need to protect some aspect of the public welfare, as is the case for the judicial policies against, for example,

(i) restraint of trade (§§ 186-188),

(ii) impairment of family relations (§§ 189-191), and

(iii) interference with other protected interests (§§ 192-196, 356).

Comment:

a. Development of the judicial role. Historically, the public policies against enforcement of terms were developed by judges themselves on the basis of their own perception of the need to protect some aspect of the public welfare. Some of these policies are now rooted in precedents accumulated over centuries. Important examples are the policies against restraint of trade, impairment of domestic relations, and interference with duties owed to individuals. These are singled out for mention in Paragraph (b) because they are dealt with in detail in Topics 2-4 of this Chapter. Society has, however, many other interests that are worthy of protection, and as society changes so do these interests. Courts remain alert to other and sometimes novel situations in which enforcement of a term may contravene those interests. See Illustration 1. At the same time, courts should not implement obsolete policies that have lost their vigor over the course of years. The rule of this Section is therefore an open-ended one that does not purport to exhaust the categories of recognized public policies. **Illustration:**

> 1. A and B make a written agreement that contains a term providing that "no prior negotiations shall be used to interpret this agreement." Prior negotiations would otherwise be admissible to establish the meaning of the writing (§ 214(c)). If the court decides that the term would unreasonably deprive it of relevant evidence that would enable it to resolve an ambiguity in the agreement and thereby hamper it in the fair administration of justice, it will hold that the term is unenforceable on grounds of public policy.

b. Modern role of legislation. The declaration of public policy has now become largely the province of legislators rather than judges. This is in part because legislators are supported by facilities for factual investigations and can be more responsive to the general public. When proscribing conduct, however, legislators seldom address themselves explicitly to the problems of contract law that may arise in connection with such conduct. See § 178(a). Usually they do not even have these problems in mind and say nothing as to the enforceability of terms. In such situations it is pointless to search for the "intention of the legislature," and the court's task is to determine on its own whether it should, by refusing to enforce the promise, add a sanction to those already provided by the legislature. This is a question of "law," in the conventional sense, rather than one of "fact." The legislation is significant, not as controlling the disposition of the case, but as enlightening the court concerning some specific policy to which it is relevant. A court will examine the particular statute in the light of the whole

legislative scheme in the jurisdiction to see, for example, if similar statutes in the same area contain explicit provisions making comparable promises unenforceable. It will look to the purpose and history of the statute. The fact that the statute explicitly prohibits the making of a promise or the engaging in the promised conduct may be persuasive in showing a policy against enforcement of a promise but it is not necessarily conclusive. On the other hand, the fact that the statute provides a civil sanction, whether in addition to a criminal penalty or not, may suggest that no other civil sanction such as unenforceability is intended, but this is not necessarily conclusive either. See Illustration 2. Furthermore, even though a field is the subject of legislation, a court may decide that the legislature has not entirely occupied the field and may refuse to enforce a term on grounds of a judicially developed public policy even though there is no contravention of the legislation. The term "legislation" is used here in the same broad sense as in the preceding section. See Comment *a* to § 178. Although no attempt is made in this Restatement to state rules to deal with any of the myriad of specific pieces of legislation that may be involved in such controversies, § 181 deals with the important cases involving licensing requirements. **Illustration:**

> 2. A induces B to make an agreement to buy goods on credit from A by bribing B's purchasing agent. A delivers the goods to B. A state statute makes such bribery a crime and gives B a civil action to recover the amount of the bribe against A. Although the statute already provides for a civil sanction, a court may decide that B's promise to pay the price is unenforceable on grounds of public policy. Cf. Illustration 12 to § 178.

c. When refusal to enforce may frustrate policy. In some instances, refusal to enforce a term may frustrate rather than further public policy. This is likely to be the case where legislation was enacted to protect a class of persons to which the promisee belongs in transactions of the kind involved. In such instances, there is no policy against the enforcement of the promise by one who belongs to that class. **Illustrations:**

> 3. A, a corporation, makes an agreement to do work for B, a city. C, an official of B, is also a principal shareholder of A, and a statute prohibits the making of such agreements and sub-

jects those who make them to penalties. A's performance of the agreement is defective. Since the statute was enacted to protect a class of persons to which B belongs against a class to which A belongs, enforcement of A's promise is not precluded on grounds of public policy and B can recover damages from A for breach of contract.

4. A, an insurance company, issues a policy of fire insurance to B on his house. The policy differs from that required by a state statute prescribing a standard fire policy. B's house is destroyed by fire. Since the statute was enacted to protect a class of persons to which B belongs against a class to which A belongs, enforcement of A's promise is not precluded on grounds of public policy and B can recover the insurance proceeds from A.

. . .

d. Change of circumstances. Whether a promise is unenforceable on grounds of public policy is determined as of the time that the promise is made and is not ordinarily affected by a subsequent change of circumstances, whether of fact or law. If, however, both parties were excusably ignorant of facts or of legislation of a minor character that made it unenforceable, a change as to these may make the promise enforceable. Compare § 180.

§ 180. Effect of Excusable Ignorance

If a promisee is excusably ignorant of facts or of legislation of a minor character, of which the promisor is not excusably ignorant and in the absence of which the promise would be enforceable, the promisee has a claim for damages for its breach but cannot recover damages for anything that he has done after he learns of the facts or legislation.

Comment:

a. Excusable ignorance. At the time a promise is made, the promisee may be excusably ignorant of facts that contravene the public policy in question. Furthermore, although for the purposes of this Chapter, parties are generally charged with knowledge of policies affecting enforceability, this Section states a limited exception for a party who is excusably ignorant of legislation of a minor character from which the policy is derived. Such ignorance is more likely to be excusable where the legislation is of a local, specialized or technical nature and where the other party may be assumed to have knowledge as to such matters. In determining whether ignorance of fact or law is excusable, any misrepresentations made by the other party are relevant. However, good faith is expected on the part of the party who claims ignorance and he cannot blind his eyes because he does not wish to see. Furthermore, the matter of which he is ignorant must not be one as to which he is expected to have knowledge because of his expertise or his relation to the transaction.

b. Promisor must not be excusably ignorant. The promisee's excusable ignorance is not by itself enough to give him the right to enforce the promise under this Section. The promisor must not be excusably ignorant as to the matter in question. (That an unenforceable promise can be consideration for a return promise, see § 78.) If the promisor has specialized knowledge of the field involved, he is likely to be charged with knowledge as to legislation of even a minor character. It is not necessary that the promisor make any misrepresentation, although a misrepresentation by him may be significant as bearing on whether the promisee's ignorance is excusable. See Comment *a.* Furthermore, on learning the truth, the promisee is expected promptly to withdraw from the transaction and render no further performance. **Illustrations:**

1. A and B make an agreement under which B promises to deliver to A goods. B already has a contract to deliver the goods to C, but A neither knows nor has reason to know this. On learning of B's contract with C, A refuses to take the goods or pay the price. Enforcement of B's promise to deliver the goods to A is not precluded on grounds of public policy and A has a claim against B for damages. But see § 194.

2. A and B make an agreement under which A promises to pay B $ 10,000 in return for B's promise to cut down trees on a specified tract of land. A knows that the land belongs to C rather than to A, but B neither knows nor has reason to know this. C prohibits entry on the land. Enforcement of A's promise to pay B $ 10,000 is not precluded on grounds of public policy and B has a claim against A for damages. As to the rights of A and B if A neither knows nor has reason to know that C is the owner, see § 198(b).

. . .

§ 181. Effect of Failure to Comply with Licensing or Similar Requirement

If a party is prohibited from doing an act because of his failure to comply with a licensing, registration or similar requirement, a promise in consideration of his doing that act or of his promise to do it is unenforceable on grounds of public policy if (a) the requirement has a regulatory purpose, and (b) the interest in the enforcement of the promise is clearly outweighed by the public policy behind the requirement.

Comment:

a. Scope. One of the most frequent applications of the general rule stated in § 178 occurs where a party seeks to enforce an agreement although he has failed to obtain a license, to register or to comply with a similar requirement. This Section states a specific version of that general rule as it applies to such cases. Whether there has been a violation of legislation that imposes the requirement is a matter of interpretation of the legislation itself and is beyond the scope of this Restatement.

b. Regulatory purpose. In deciding whether a party can enforce an agreement in spite of his failure to comply with such a requirement, courts distinguish between requirements that have a regulatory purpose and those that do not. The policy behind a requirement that has a regulatory purpose may be regarded as sufficiently substantial to preclude enforcement, while the policy behind one that is merely designed to raise revenue will not be. In determining whether a measure has a regulatory purpose, a court will consider the entire legislative scheme, including any relevant declaration of purpose. Common indications of regulation include provisions for examination or apprenticeship to ensure minimum standards on entrance and provisions for the posting of a bond or procedures for license revocation to ensure that standards are maintained. **Illustration:**

> 1. A, an unlicensed broker, agrees to arrange a transaction for B, for which B promises to pay A $ 1,000. A city ordinance requires persons arranging such transactions to be licensed as a result of paying a fee, with no inquiry into competence or responsibility. A arranges the transaction. Since the licensing requirement is designed merely to raise revenue and does not have a regulatory purpose, enforcement of B's promise is not precluded on grounds of public policy.

c. Balancing where purpose is regulatory. If the court decides that the requirement has a regulatory purpose, it must then weigh the interests favoring enforcement of the promise against the public policy behind the requirement.

The factors listed in § 178 are taken into account in this process. If the party who has failed to comply with the requirement has done nothing by way of preparation or performance, the interest in enforcement of the promise is easily outweighed. But if, as is usually the case, he has completely performed and is seeking the promised compensation for that performance, forfeiture to himself and enrichment to the other party may result from a refusal to enforce the other party's promise. In determining the extent to which forfeiture and enrichment will result, a court will consider the possibilities that part of the agreement may be enforceable (see § 183 and Illustration 1 to that section) and that restitution may be available (see § 197 and Illustration 4 to that section). In evaluating the gravity of the public policy involved, the court will look to the interest that the regulation is designed to protect and will give greater weight, for example, to a measure intended to protect the public health or safety than one intended to have only an economic effect. Compare Illustrations 2 and 3. It will consider the magnitude of the penalty provided by the legislature as some indication of the weight that it attached to that interest. It will also take account of the extent to which the misconduct was deliberate or inadvertent. See Illustration 4. **Illustrations:**

> 2. A, an unlicensed plumber, agrees to repair plumbing in B's home, for which B promises to pay A $ 1,000. A state statute, enacted to prevent the public from being victimized by incompetent plumbers and to protect the public health, requires persons doing plumbing to be licensed on the basis of an examination, the posting of a bond, and the payment of a fee, and makes violation a crime. A does the agreed work. A court may decide that the public policy against enforcement of B's promise outweighs the interest in its enforcement, and that B's promise is unenforceable on grounds of public policy. Compare Illustration 1 to § 183.
>
> . . .

d. Enforcement by the other party. The rule stated in this Section deals only with the right of the non-complying party to enforce the other party's promise. The enforceability of the non-complying party's promise is governed by the general rule stated in § 178. Regulatory legislation may be designed to protect a class of persons to which the other party belongs against a class to which the non-complying party belongs. See Comment *c* to § 179. In that case the policy behind the legislation will usually best be served by holding the non-complying party liable in damages for any defective performance. See Illustration 5.

. . .

§ 182. Effect of Performance

If Intended Use Is Improper If the promisee has substantially performed, enforcement of a promise is not precluded on grounds of public policy because of some improper use that the promisor intends to make of what he obtains unless the promisee

(a) acted for the purpose of furthering the improper use, or

(b) knew of the use and the use involves grave social harm.

Comment:

a. Scope. A significant application of the general rule stated in § 178 occurs where one party intends to use goods, money, or something else that he acquires in the transaction in a manner contrary to public policy. Whether that party's promise to render his own performance is unenforceable on grounds of public policy depends on the balancing process required under that rule. Even if his promise would be unenforceable if the agreement were wholly executory, however, his receipt of performance may justify enforcement. This Section states a rule that determines when this is so by resolving the problem of balancing in such a case. Situations that do not come within it because the promisee has not substantially performed are governed by the general rule stated in §§ 178.

b. Action for purpose of furthering use. If the improper use involves grave social harm, as where it threatens human life, the promisee's mere knowledge of the use is sufficient to bar him from recovering for his performance. If the improper use does not involve grave social harm, the promisee is not barred from recovery unless he not only knew of the use but acted for the purpose of furthering it. Whether the promisee acted for such a purpose is a question of fact. It may be evidenced by his doing of specific acts to facilitate the improper use. It may also be evidenced by a course of dealing with persons engaged in improper conduct. In close cases, a court will consider whether denial of recovery will deter the improper conduct or, on the contrary, encourage persons engaging in such conduct to enter into transactions knowing that their promises are unenforceable. **Illustrations:**

1. A sells and delivers to B a shotgun on credit. The sale of firearms is legal, but B plans to use the gun in hunting without a license required by law and A knows this. Enforcement of B's promise to pay the price is not precluded on grounds of public policy. If B planned to use the gun to commit a robbery and A knew this, B's promise to pay the price would be unenforceable on those grounds.

2. A, who has lost $ 1,000 by playing faro, promises B, who regularly makes loans to gamblers, that he will repay B with interest in thirty days if B will make him three loans: $ 1,000 to cover his losses, $ 4,000 to recoup them by continuing to play faro, and $ 2,000 to support his family while he does so. B lends A a total of $ 7,000, and A loses it all playing faro. A state statute makes playing faro for money a crime. Enforcement of A's promise to repay the $ 1,000 to cover his losses and the $ 2,000 to support his family is not precluded on grounds of public policy. Since A lent him the $ 4,000 for the purpose of furthering B's gambling, B's promise to repay the $ 4,000 is unenforceable on those grounds.

. . .

§ 183. When Agreement Is Enforceable as to Agreed Equivalents

If the parties' performances can be apportioned into corresponding pairs of part performances so that the parts of each pair are properly regarded as agreed equivalents and one pair is not offensive to public policy, that portion of the agreement is enforceable by a party who did not engage in serious misconduct.

Comment:

a. Concept of "divisibility" or "severability." This Section deals with the situation in which a party is allowed to enforce one part of an agreement even though another part of the same agreement is unenforceable on grounds of public policy, for the reason that the first part does not materially advance the improper purpose. It illustrates a general technique by which a court can mitigate the harshness of a rule that bars a party from enforcing an agreement by apportioning the performances into corresponding pairs of part performances and then enforcing the agreement as to only one part. Another common illustration of this technique occurs when a party is allowed to insist on his right to a return performance under one part of an agreement even though he has committed a material breach under another part of the same agreement. See § 240. In situations where this mitigating technique is applied, the agreement is sometimes said to be "divisible" or "severable." This terminology is avoided here as wrongly suggesting that an agreement itself can be characterized as "divisible" or "severable" for all purposes and in any circumstances. A court may conclude that an agreement that is "divisible" or "severable" for one purpose or in some circumstances is not "divisible" or "severable" for another purpose or in other circumstances. The concept is a flexible one, to be applied on a case by case basis.

b. Requirements. The rule stated in this Section applies when four requirements are met. The first is that it must be possible to apportion the parties' performances into corresponding pairs of part performances. This process of apportionment is essentially one of calculation and the rule cannot be applied unless calculation is feasible. But it is enough in a contract for the sale of goods, for example, if the price of separate items is separately stated in the agreement itself or in a price list on which the agreement was based, or can be reliably ascertained from stated prices for components or from a total price for similar items. See Comment *d* to § 240. The second

requirement is that the corresponding pairs of part performances must be properly regarded as agreed equivalents. This means that the parts of the pair must be of roughly equivalent value to the injured party in terms of his expectation with respect to the total agreed exchange. Fairness requires that a party, having received only a fraction of the performance that he expected under an agreement, not be asked to pay an identical fraction of the price that he originally promised on the expectation of full performance, unless it appears that the performance that he actually received is worth to him roughly the same fraction of what full performance would have been worth to him. Because the rule is based on considerations of fairness, it is necessarily somewhat imprecise and flexible. Its application may be especially attractive where it will avoid forfeiture by a party who has already relied on the agreement, as by preparation or performance. In this connection, the availability of restitution as an alternative means of avoiding forfeiture is relevant. See Topic 5. Decisions holding that part performances are not properly regarded as agreed equivalents for some other purpose, for example in the case of material breach (§ 240) are not determinative under this Section. See Comment *a*; Comment *e* to § 240. The third requirement is that one of the pairs of performances must not be offensive to public policy. If the entire agreement is part of an integrated scheme to contravene public policy, none of it will be enforced. The fourth requirement is that the party seeking enforcement must not have engaged in serious misconduct. This will depend on the gravity of the public policy involved and the extent of the party's involvement in its contravention. A court will not use the mitigating technique of this Section in favor of a party whose misconduct is so serious that a refusal to enforce the entire agreement is a proper sanction to discourage such conduct. In such a case enforcement of any part of the agreement would amount to a misuse of official authority. **Illustrations:**

1. A, an unlicensed plumber, agrees to install plumbing in B's home for which B agrees to pay $ 1,000 for labor and $ 500 for materials. A city ordinance, designed to prevent the public from being victimized by incompetent plumbers and to protect the public health, requires persons doing plumbing to be licensed on the basis of an examination, the posting of a bond, and the payment of a fee, and makes violation a misdemeanor. A does the agreed work. Even if the court decides that B's promise to pay $ 1,000 for labor is unenforceable on grounds of public policy, it may decide that B's promise to pay $ 500 for materials is not. If the price for materials is not separately stated, the court may reach the same decision if it can reliably ascertain it from A's price lists or from market prices.

. . .

c. When apportionment not possible. Even if the parties' performances cannot be apportioned into corresponding pairs of part performances under the rule stated in this Section, the unenforceability of a single promise or other term on grounds of public policy does not necessarily mean that the entire agreement is unenforceable. If the unenforceable term is relatively unimportant in relation to the entire agreement, the rest of the agreement may be salvaged under the rule stated in the following section.

§ 184. When Rest of Agreement Is Enforceable

(1) If less than all of an agreement is unenforceable under the rule stated in § 178, a court may nevertheless enforce the rest of the agreement in favor of a party who did not engage in serious misconduct if the performance as to which the agreement is unenforceable is not an essential part of the agreed exchange.

(2) A court may treat only part of a term as unenforceable under the rule stated in Subsection (1) if the party who seeks to enforce the term obtained it in good faith and in accordance with reasonable standards of fair dealing.

Comment:

a. Refusal to enforce a promise. Under the rule stated in the preceding Section, an agreement may be unenforceable as to corresponding equivalents on each side but enforceable as to the rest. If it is not possible to apportion the parties' performances in this way so that corresponding concessions are made on both sides, a refusal to enforce only part of the agreement will necessarily result in some inequality. If the performance as to which the agreement is unenforceable is an essential part of the agreed exchange, the inequality will be so great as to make the entire agreement unenforceable. Under Subsection (1), however, if that performance is not an essential part of the agreed exchange, a court may enforce all but the part that contravenes public policy. For example, a promise not to compete that is unreasonably in restraint of trade will often not invalidate the entire agreement of which it is a part. Whether the performance is an essential part of the agreed exchange depends on its relative importance in the light of the entire agreement between the parties. A party who has engaged in such serious misconduct that the entire agreement is unenforceable cannot take advantage of the rule stated in Subsection (1). See Comment *d* to § 178. **Illustration:**

1. A employs B as head bookkeeper of his retail clothing store under an employment agreement in which B promises not to work in the retail clothing business in the same town for three years after the termination of his employment. B works for A for five years but does not deal directly with customers and acquires no confidential information in his work. Although B's promise is unreasonably in restraint of trade and is unenforceable on grounds of public policy, enforcement of the rest of the employment agreement is not precluded on those grounds. See Illustration 8 to § 188.

b. Refusal to enforce part of a term. Sometimes a term is unenforceable on grounds of public policy because it is too broad, even though a narrower term would be enforceable. In such a situation, under Subsection (2), the court may refuse to enforce only part of the term, while enforcing the other part of the term as well as the rest of the agreement. The court's power in such a case is not a power of reformation, however, and it will not, in the course of determining what part of the term to enforce, add to the scope of the term in any way. A court will not exercise this discretion in favor of a party unless it appears that he made the agreement in good faith and in accordance with reasonable standards of fair dealing. Compare §§ 157, 205. For example, a court will not aid a party who has taken advantage of his dominant bargaining power to extract from the other party a promise that is clearly so broad as to offend public policy by redrafting the agreement so as to make a part of the promise enforceable. The fact that the term is contained in a standard form supplied by the dominant party argues against aiding him in this request. Whether a particular dispute involves a single term, so that it comes under Subsection (2), or separate terms, so that it comes under Subsection (1), will be determined from the substance of the agreement as well as from its language.

Illustrations:

2. A, who is engaged in business as a baker and confectioner, sells the business to B, and as part of the bargain promises not to engage in the business of "baker, confectioner, or other business" within the same town for three years. The provision is fairly bargained for. A's promise is so broad as to be unreasonably in restraint of trade because A's business is only that of baker and confectioner. Although part of A's promise is unenforceable on grounds of public policy (§ 188), it is enforceable with respect to the business of baker or confectioner.

3. A sells his grocery business to B and as part of the agreement promises not to engage in that business "within the city where the business is situated or within a radius of fifty miles." The provision is fairly bargained for. A's promise involves an unreasonable restraint of trade because the business extends within the city and over a radius of only twenty-five miles. Although part of A's promise is unenforceable on grounds of public policy (§ 188), it is enforceable with respect to the city and twenty-five miles.

. . .

§ 185. Excuse of a Condition on Grounds of Public Policy

To the extent that a term requiring the occurrence of a condition is unenforceable under the rule stated in § 178, a court may excuse the non-occurrence of the condition unless its occurrence was an essential part of the agreed exchange.

Comment:

a. Relationship to other rules. This Section is concerned with the situation in which a promisor seeks to induce the promisee to do an act by conditioning his own promise on the promisee's doing that act. If it is contrary to public policy to do the act or to encourage the doing of it, the court will first go through the same process of balancing competing interests as it does under the rule stated in § 178. If it concludes that the public interest is paramount, it may react in one of two ways. First, it may hold that the promise itself is unenforceable on grounds of public policy under the rule stated in § 178. See Comment *d* to § 178 and Illustration 9 to that Section. Whether the rest of the agreement is also unenforceable is then determined by the rules stated in §§ 183 and 184. Second, it may disregard the term requiring the occurrence of the condition by excusing the non-occurrence of the condition under the rule stated in this Section. See Illustration 1. The promise itself is not then unenforceable on grounds of public policy and the rest of the agreement is not affected.

b. Essential part of the agreed exchange. Whether a court will take the first or the second course will depend on whether occurrence of the condition was an essential part of the agreed exchange. If it was an essential part, the court will hold that the promise itself, and perhaps the entire agreement, is unenforceable on grounds of public policy under the rule stated in § 178. If it was not an essential part, the court will simply disregard the term by excusing the non-occurrence of the condition on grounds of public policy under the rule stated in this Section. In determining whether occurrence of a condition is an essential part of the agreed exchange, a court will look at the entire agreement in the light of all the circumstances and will be guided by basically the same factors that govern that determination under the rules stated in §§ 84 and 229. The fundamental question is, how central was the condition to the agreement reached by the parties? It is not enough that the actual non-occurrence happened to involve a departure that was not an essential part of the agreed exchange, if the occurrence of the condition was an essential part of that exchange. A court need not entirely excuse the non-occurrence of the condition, but may merely excuse it to the extent required by public policy. In doing so it will be guided by principles analogous to those applicable under § 184. See Illustration 2. **Illustrations:**

    1. A employs B as advertising manager of his retail clothing store. As part of the employment agreement, A promises to pay B a pension on B's retirement on condition that B not work in the retail clothing business in the same town. B works for A for fifteen years, but does not deal with customers and acquires no confidential trade information in his work. The restraint is unreasonable under the rule stated in § 188, but the condition is not an essential part of the agreed exchange and its non-occurrence will be excused. A's promise to pay the pension is enforceable even though B works as an advertising manager in the retail clothing business in the same town. Compare Illustration 8 to § 188.

    2. A employs B as a research chemist in his nationwide pharmaceutical business. As part of the employment agreement, A promises to pay B a pension on B's retirement on condition that B not work in any branch of the chemical industry at any place in the country for three years after retirement. B works for fifteen years and acquires valuable confidential information that would be useful to A's competitors and would harm A's business. B can find employment as a research chemist outside of the pharmaceutical industry. The restraint is unreasonably broad under the rule stated in § 188, but the condition is not an essential part of the agreed exchange and its non-occurrence will be excused. If the court concludes that the confidential information acquired by B is such as unreasonably to harm A's business, that B can find employment as a research chemist outside the pharmaceutical industry, and that B obtained the term in good faith and in accordance with fair dealing (see § 184), the court will hold that A's promise to pay the pension is conditional on B's not working in the pharmaceutical industry at any place in the country within three years of his retirement. Compare Illustration 7 to § 188.

Topic 2. Restraint of Trade

Introductory Note The common law's policy against restraint of trade is one of its oldest and best established. Nevertheless, the statement in this Chapter of the rules that implement that policy is severely circumscribed in two respects.

    First, those rules are included only to the extent that they concern the law of contracts. Although activities such as organizing a corporation or refusing to deal with another may be in restraint of trade, they are outside the scope of this Restatement if no promise is involved. However, a promise to organize a corporation or to refuse to deal comes within its purview.

    Second, the Restatement does not deal with those aspects of the subject that are largely legislative. See Introductory Note to this Chapter. Promises in restraint of trade are governed by extensive federal and state statutes, under which the promise may not only be unenforceable, as at common law, but may give rise to both civil and criminal responsibility. The substance of that legislation is beyond the scope of this Restatement. With respect to most aspects of the restraint of trade, federal legislation has so completely occupied the field as to make the common law rules of little or no consequence except as they may give meaning to some of the more general terms of that legislation. Examples are the creation of monopoly, the substantial lessening of competition by, for example, tying purchases of one product to another, or the imposition of non-ancillary restraints controlling prices or limiting production. Specific aspects of the subject may also be governed by state statutes.

    The first section in this Topic, § 186, treats in general terms of promises in restraint of trade and is intended to complement federal and state legislation in those instances in which recourse to a common law rule may be useful. The other two sections, §§ 187 and 188, are concerned with the one type of promise in restraint of trade that has traditionally been left to be dealt with under judicially developed rules -- the promise to refrain from competition. This Topic, like the rest of this Chapter, does not attempt to catalog promises that are enforceable in spite of arguments to the contrary based on public policy

§ 186. Promise in Restraint of Trade

(1) A promise is unenforceable on grounds of public policy if it is unreasonably in restraint of trade.

(2) A promise is in restraint of trade if its performance would limit competition in any business or restrict the promisor in the exercise of a gainful occupation.

Comment:

a. Rule of reason. Every promise that relates to business dealings or to a professional or other gainful occupation operates as a restraint in the sense that it restricts the promisor's future activity. Such a promise is not, however, unenforceable unless the restraint that it imposes is unreasonably detrimental to the smooth operation of a freely competitive private economy. A rule of reason of this kind necessarily has somewhat vague outlines. Whether a restraint is reasonable is determined in the light of the circumstances of the transaction, including not only the particular facts but general social and economic conditions as well. The promise is viewed in terms of the effects that it could have had and not merely what actually occurred. Account is taken of such factors as the protection that it affords for the promisee's legitimate interests, the hardship that it imposes on the promisor, and the likely injury to the public. See § 188 and Comments *b* and *c* to that Section. A restraint that is reasonable in some circumstances may be unreasonable in others.

. . .

§ 187. Non-Ancillary Restraints on Competition

A promise to refrain from competition that imposes a restraint that is not ancillary to an otherwise valid transaction or relationship is unreasonably in restraint of trade.

Comment:

a. Importance of rules. The common law on restraint of trade has played a particularly important role with respect to promises to refrain from competition. Parties who have challenged such promises have ordinarily been content to assert their unenforceability under the common law and have not sought relief under federal or state legislation. There is, therefore, an especially well-developed and significant body of judicial decisions applying the general rule of reason stated in the preceding section to such promises. Because of the importance of these decisions, the rules that they embody are given special attention in this Section and the one that follows. (No implication is intended with respect to the application of federal or state legislation to such promises.)

. . .

§ 188. Ancillary Restraints on Competition

(1) A promise to refrain from competition that imposes a restraint that is ancillary to an otherwise valid transaction or relationship is unreasonably in restraint of trade if

(a) the restraint is greater than is needed to protect the promisee's legitimate interest, or

(b) the promisee's need is outweighed by the hardship to the promisor and the likely injury to the public.

(2) Promises imposing restraints that are ancillary to a valid transaction or relationship include the following:

(a) a promise by the seller of a business not to compete with the buyer in such a way as to injure the value of the business sold;

(b) a promise by an employee or other agent not to compete with his employer or other principal;

(c) a promise by a partner not to compete with the partnership.

Comment:

a. Rule of reason. The rules stated in this Section apply to promises not to compete that, because they impose ancillary restraints, are not necessarily invalid. Subsection (1) restates in more detail the general rule of reason of § 186 as it applies to such promises. Under this formulation the restraint may be unreasonable in either of two situations. The first occurs when the restraint is greater than necessary to protect the legitimate interests of the promisee. The second occurs when, even though the restraint is not greater than necessary to protect those interests, the promisee's need for protection is outweighed by the hardship to the promisor and the likely injury to the public. In the second situation the court may be faced with a particularly difficult task of balancing competing interests. No mathematical formula can be offered for this process.

b. *Need of the promisee.* If a restraint is not ancillary to some transaction or relationship that gives rise to an interest worthy of protection, the promise is necessarily unreasonable under the rule stated in the preceding Section. In some instances, however, a promise to refrain from competition is a natural and reasonable means of protecting a legitimate interest of the promisee arising out of the transaction to which the restraint is ancillary. In those instances the same reasons argue for its enforceability as in the case of any other promise. For example, competitors who are combining their efforts in a partnership may promise as part of the transaction not to compete with the partnership. Assuming that the combination is not monopolistic, such promises, reasonable in scope, will be upheld in view of the interest of each party as promisee. See Subsection (2)(c) and Comment *h*. (It is assumed in the Illustrations to this Section that the arrangements are not objectionable on grounds other than those that come within its scope.) The extent to which the restraint is needed to protect the promisee's interests will vary with the nature of the transaction. Where a sale of good will is involved, for example, the buyer's interest in what he has acquired cannot be effectively realized unless the seller engages not to act so as unreasonably to diminish the value of what he has sold. The same is true of any other property interest of which exclusive use is part of the value. See Subsection (2)(a) and Comment *f*. In the case of a post-employment restraint, however, the promisee's interest is less clear. Such a restraint, in contrast to one accompanying a sale of good will, is not necessary in order for the employer to get the full value of what he has acquired. Instead, it must usually be justified on the ground that the employer has a legitimate interest in restraining the employee from appropriating valuable trade information and customer relationships to which he has had access in the

course of his employment. Arguably the employer does not get the full value of the employment contract if he cannot confidently give the employee access to confidential information needed for most efficient performance of his job. But it is often difficult to distinguish between such information and normal skills of the trade, and preventing use of one may well prevent or inhibit use of the other. See Subsection (2)(b) and Comment *g*. Because of this difference in the interest of the promisee, courts have generally been more willing to uphold promises to refrain from competition made in connection with sales of good will than those made in connection with contracts of employment.

c. *Harm to the promisor and injury to the public.* Even if the restraint is no greater than is needed to protect the promisee's interest, the promisee's need may be outweighed by the harm to the promisor and the likely injury to the public. In the case of a sale of a business, the harm caused to the seller may be excessive if the restraint necessitates his complete withdrawal from business; the likely injury to the public may be too great if it has the effect of removing a former competitor from competition. See Comment *f*. In the case of a post-employment restraint, the harm caused to the employee may be excessive if the restraint inhibits his personal freedom by preventing him from earning his livelihood if he quits; the likely injury to the public may be too great if it is seriously harmed by the impairment of his economic mobility or by the unavailability of the skills developed in his employment. See Comment *g*. Not every restraint causes injury to the public, however, and even a post-employment restraint may increase efficiency by encouraging the employer to entrust confidential information to the employee.

d. *Extent of the restraint.* The extent of the restraint is a critical factor in determining its reasonableness. The extent may be limited in three ways: by type of activity, by geographical area, and by time. If the promise proscribes types of activity more extensive than necessary to protect those engaged in by the promisee, it goes beyond what is necessary to protect his legitimate interests and is unreasonable. If it covers a geographical area more extensive than necessary to protect his interests, it is also unreasonable. And if the restraint is to last longer than is required in light of those interests, taking account of such factors as the permanent or transitory nature of technology and information, it is unreasonable. Since, in any of these cases, the restraint is too broad to be justified by the promisee's need, a court may hold it to be unreasonable without the necessity of weighing the countervailing interests of the promisor and the public. What limits as to activity, geographical area, and time are appropriate in a particular case depends on all the circumstances. As to the possibility of divisibility, see § 183.

e. Examples of ancillary restraints. The rule stated in Subsection (1) has its most significant applications with respect to the three types of promises set out in Subsection (2). In each of these situations the promisee may have need for protection sufficient to sustain a promise to refrain from competition as long as it is reasonable in extent. They involve promises by the seller of a business, by an employee or agent, and by a partner. The list is not an exclusive one and there may be other situations in which a valid transaction or relationship gives the promisee a legitimate interest sufficient to sustain a promise not to compete.

. . .

Topic 3. Impairment of Family Relations

Introductory Note The power of individuals by legally enforceable private agreement to alter the incidents of marriage or to shape legal relationships within the family has traditionally been regarded as very limited. Moreover, courts exercise broad and continuing discretionary powers in cases of separation and divorce with respect to obligations of support and custody of children. Disposition of property, on the other hand, is subject to far greater control by the parties.

This area of law is currently one in flux, and the reassessment and change is particularly noticeable in connection with the law relating to divorce and to the rights of women. The rules stated in this Topic are intended to meet current needs and are therefore illustrative rather than exhaustive in their content and are flexible rather than rigid in their statement. They deal with three areas of particular importance: the freedom of unmarried persons to marry (§ 189), the integrity of the relationship between married persons (§ 190), and the protection of custodial rights over children (§ 191). In many states this Topic is the subject of important statutory provisions that vary the rules stated here. As to similar restraints in the law of property, see Restatement of Property, Chapter 32, Provisions in Restraint of Marriage.

§ 189. Promise in Restraint of Marriage

A promise is unenforceable on grounds of public policy if it is unreasonably in restraint of marriage.

Comment:

a. Rule of reason. Marriage is regarded by the common law as of concern to the state as well as to the individual, and the freedom of individuals to marry should not be impaired except for good reason. A promise in restraint of marriage is not necessarily unenforceable, but is subject to a rule of reason, analogous to that applicable to promises in restraint of trade. See § 186. Here, as there, the duration of the restraint and its extent, in terms of the narrowing of the likely area of choice, are important. In order for the restraint to be reasonable, it must serve some purpose other than that of merely discouraging marriage. The most common acceptable purpose is that of providing support until marriage. Courts are, therefore, relatively tolerant of restraints on marriages that condition a promise of support on the promisee's not marrying and thereby acquiring another provider. Particularly is this so when the restraint is imposed by one spouse on remarriage by the other spouse, since both the close family relationship and the limitation of the restraint to a subsequent marriage argue in favor of enforceability. **Illustrations:**

     1. A pays B, his twenty-one-year-old child, $ 100,000 in return for B's promise not to marry for ten years. B's promise is unreasonably in restraint of marriage and is unenforceable on grounds of public policy.

. . .

§ 190. Promise Detrimental to Marital Relationship

(1) A promise by a person contemplating marriage or by a married person, other than as part of an enforceable separation agreement, is unenforceable on grounds of public policy if it would change some essential incident of the marital relationship in a way detrimental to the public interest in the marriage relationship. A separation agreement is unenforceable on grounds of public policy unless it is made after separation or in contemplation of an immediate separation and is fair in the circumstances.

(2) A promise that tends unreasonably to encourage divorce or separation is unenforceable on grounds of public policy.

Comment:

a. Change in essential incident of marital relationship. Although marriage is sometimes loosely referred to as a "contract," the marital relationship has not been regarded by the common law as contractual in the usual sense. Many terms of the relationship are seen as largely fixed by the state and beyond the power of the parties to modify. Two reasons support this view. One is that there is a public interest in the relationship, and particularly in such matters as support and child custody, that makes it inappropriate to subject it to modification by the parties. Another is that the courts lack workable standards and are not an appropriate forum for the types of contract disputes that would arise if such promises were enforceable. The rule stated in Subsection (1) reflects this view by making a promise unenforceable if it changes an essential incident of marriage in a way detrimental to the public interest in the relationship. This rule, however, does not prevent persons contemplating marriage or married persons from making contracts between themselves for the disposition of property, since this is not ordinarily regarded as an essential incident of the marital relationship. Nor does it prevent their making contracts for services that are not an essential incident of the marital relationship within the rule stated here. But it does, for example, preclude them from changing in a way detrimental to the public interest in the relationship the duty imposed by law on one spouse to support the other. Whether a change in the duty of support is detrimental in this way will depend on the circumstances of each case. The presence of an unenforceable promise in an otherwise enforceable antenuptial or separation agreement does not, of course, necessarily entail the unenforceability of the entire agreement. See §§ 183, 184. The principles underlying this Section also apply to an agreement under which a third person as trustee is to hold sums in trust for the other spouse on separation. The rules stated in this Section apply only to the relations between the parties and do not govern the enforceability of promises relating to the duty of support owed to children. Even though enforcement of a promise is not precluded under the rule stated in Subsection (1), it may be precluded under the rule stated in Subsection (2). **Illustration:**

1. A and B, who are about to marry, make an antenuptial agreement in which A promises to leave their home at any time on notice by B and to make no further claims against B, and B promises thereupon to pay A $ 100,000. The promises of A and B alter an essential incident of the marital relationship in a way detrimental to the public interest in that relationship and are unenforceable on grounds of public policy.

b. Separation agreements. The policy that limits the parties in modifying the marital relationship does not apply if that relationship has ended. The rule stated in Subsection (1) thus does not apply to a promise that is part of an enforceable separation agreement. A separation agreement, to be enforceable, must be made after the parties have separated or when they contemplate immediate separation, so that the marriage has, in effect, already disintegrated. It must also be fair in the circumstances, a matter as to which the court may exercise its continuing discretionary powers. Separation agreements commonly deal with such matters as support and are generally enforceable because the parties could usually accomplish the same result through a judicial separation. They are still subject to the rule stated in Subsection (2) if they tend unreasonably to encourage divorce. **Illustration:**

2. A and B, who are married but have decided to separate, make a separation agreement that is fair in the circumstances, in which A promises to pay B a stated sum each month in return for B's promise to relinquish all other claims to

support. Although the promises of A and B change an essential incident of the marital relationship, their enforcement is not for that reason precluded on grounds of public policy because they are part of a separation agreement. But see Subsection (2) and Comment *c*.

c. Tending to encourage divorce or separation. When persons contemplating marriage or married persons seek to determine by agreement their rights in the event of a divorce or separation, the rule stated in Subsection (2) comes into play, along with that stated in Subsection (1). See Illustration 2. Because of the public interest in the marriage relationship (see Comment *a*), a promise that undermines that relationship by tending unreasonably to encourage divorce or separation is unenforceable. Although the parties are free, if they choose, to terminate their relationship under the law providing for divorce or separation, a commitment that tends unreasonably in this direction will not be enforced. Whether a promise tends unreasonably to encourage divorce or

separation in a particular case is a question of fact that depends on all the circumstances, including the state of disintegration of the marriage at the time the promise is made. A promise that merely disposes of property rights in the event of divorce or separation does not of itself tend unreasonably to encourage either.

Illustrations:

3. A, who is married to B, promises to pay B $ 50,000 in return for B's promise to obtain a divorce. The promises of A and B tend unreasonably to encourage divorce and are unenforceable on grounds of public policy. The result does not depend on whether or not there are grounds for divorce or on whether or not B has performed.

4. A, who was married to B but has obtained a divorce that can possibly be set aside for fraud, promises to pay B $ 50,000 in return for B's promise not to attempt to have the divorce set aside. The promises of both A and B tend unreasonably to encourage divorce and are unenforceable on grounds of public policy. The result does not depend on whether or not B has performed.

. . .

§ 191. Promise Affecting Custody

A promise affecting the right of custody of a minor child is unenforceable on grounds of public policy unless the disposition as to custody is consistent with the best interest of the child.

Comment:

a. Rationale. The custody of minor children is, like marriage, an important subject of public concern. A promise by one entitled to the custody of a minor child to transfer the custody to another or not to reclaim custody already transferred to another is unenforceable unless it is consistent with the child's best interest. Such promises are typically found in separation agreements between parents, and the fact that the person to

whom custody is transferred is a parent is an important, although not controlling, factor in showing that the transfer is in the interest of the child. Even where enforcement of a promise disposing of custody is not precluded on grounds of public policy, the disposition is still subject to the plenary supervision of the court. Similar rules apply to visitation rights.

. . .

Topic 4. Interference with Other Protected Interests

Introductory Note: Just as parties are generally free by agreement to impose new duties on each other, they are generally free by agreement to modify existing duties that they owe each other as a matter of law. One party can ordinarily, for example, contract out of his duty to exercise reasonable care with respect to the other party and thereby exonerate himself of liability to him for negligence (§ 195(2)). There are, however, important limitations imposed on grounds of public policy on the parties' power to interfere with such duties. He cannot, for example, exonerate himself of tort liability for harm caused intentionally or recklessly (§ 195(1)). Other significant limitations relate to a party's duty to refrain from conduct that is tortious (§ 192), including violation of a fiduciary duty (§ 193) or interference with a contract (§ 194). These and related rules are collected in this Topic. They are not intended to be exhaustive. In many instances legislation, such as the Uniform Commercial Code and consumer protection statutes, prohibits derogation from the rights it creates. See also § 356 on liquidated damages and penalties

§ 192. Promise Involving Commission of a Tort

A promise to commit a tort or to induce the commission of a tort is unenforceable on grounds of public policy.

Comment:

a. Scope. A promise to commit a tort is plainly unenforceable on grounds of public policy. See Illustration 6 and 8 to § 178. So is a promise made in return for the commission of a tort or a promise to commit a tort. See Illustrations 7, 8 and 9 to § 178. The same is true if the act is a tortious interference with a third person's interest in property. The rule does not, however, apply to an agreement made in good faith merely to test another's claim to property. See Illustration 17 to § 178. It is also subject to the rule on excusable ignorance stated in § 180. See Illustration 2 to § 180. This Section does not purport to be exhaustive and there are other types of conduct, involving neither the commission of a tort nor the interference with property, that so jeopardize an individual's life or freedom as to render promises involving them unenforceable on grounds of public policy. See Restatement, Second, Torts § 892-92D. **Illustrations:**

1. A and B make an agreement under which A promises to bring an action against a corporation, and have its assets seized, although there is no reasonable ground to believe that there is a cause of action, for the sole purpose of lowering the price of its stock so that B can buy it at an advantageous price. A's promise is to commit a tort and is unenforceable on grounds of public policy.

2. A makes an agreement with B under which A promises that he will excavate a city street without permission from the city. A's promise is to interfere tortiously with an interest in property of the city and is unenforceable on grounds of public policy. *b. Promise to indemnify.* A promise to indemnify another against the consequences of his committing a tort is unobjectionable if the tortious act is only an undesired possibility and the promise does not tend to induce its commission. See Illustrations 3 and 4. In some circumstances, however, the promise may tend to induce the commission of the act. Where this is so, it is unenforceable for the same reason as is a promise to commit a tort or a promise in return for the commission of a tort. See Illustration 5. **Illustrations:**

3. A, an insurance company, in consideration of a premium paid by B, promises to indemnify B against liability for injury to the persons or property of others whether caused by B's negligence or not. Enforcement of A's promise is not precluded on grounds of public policy.

. . .

§ 193. Promise Inducing Violation of Fiduciary Duty

A promise by a fiduciary to violate his fiduciary duty or a promise that tends to induce such a violation is unenforceable on grounds of public policy.

. . .

§ 194. Promise Interfering with Contract with Another

A promise that tortiously interferes with performance of a contract with a third person or a tortiously induced promise to commit a breach of contract is unenforceable on grounds of public policy.

Comment:

a. Scope. Interfering with performance of a contract may be a tort. See Restatement, Second, Torts § 766. A promise that tortiously interferes with performance of a contract with a third person is therefore unenforceable on grounds of public policy. The same is true of a promise to commit a breach of contract that has been tortiously induced. The rule stated in this Section applies even though the contract interfered with is unenforceable because of the Statute of Frauds.

Illustrations:

1. A and B make an agreement under which A promises to employ B to work full time and B promises to begin to work immediately. As A knows, B is under an existing contract of full time employment with C. A's promise tends tortiously to interfere with B's contract with C, and B's is a tortiously induced promise to commit a breach of that contract. Both promises are unenforceable on grounds of public policy. Compare Illustration 1 to § 180. 2. A induces B, a member of a stock exchange, to make an agreement under which B promises to charge A reduced commissions that A knows are in violation of the rules of the exchange by which B agreed to be bound when he became a member. B's promise is a tortiously induced promise to commit a breach of his contract with the exchange and is unenforceable on grounds of public policy. Compare Illustration 1 to § 180.

§ 195. Term Exempting From Liability for Harm Caused Intentionally, Recklessly or Negligently

(1) A term exempting a party from tort liability for harm caused intentionally or recklessly is unenforceable on grounds of public policy.

(2) A term exempting a party from tort liability for harm caused negligently is unenforceable on grounds of public policy if

(a) the term exempts an employer from liability to an employee for injury in the course of his employment;

(b) the term exempts one charged with a duty of public service from liability to one to whom that duty is owed for compensation for breach of that duty, or

(c) the other party is similarly a member of a class protected against the class to which the first party belongs.

(3) A term exempting a seller of a product from his special tort liability for physical harm to a user or consumer is unenforceable on grounds of public policy unless the term is fairly bargained for and is consistent with the policy underlying that liability.

Comment:

a. Rationale. The law of torts imposes standards of conduct for the protection of others against unreasonable risk of harm. One cannot exempt himself from such liability for harm that is caused either intentionally or recklessly. See Restatement, Second, Torts § 500. (As to the possibility that one party's consent may give the other a defense under the law of torts, see Restatement, Second, Torts §§ 892-92D.) However, a party to a contract can ordinarily exempt himself from liability for harm caused by his failure to observe the standard of reasonable care imposed by the law of negligence. See Restatement, Second, Torts § 282. This rule is subject to an exception if the other party is a member of a protected class. Two examples of this exception are widely recognized. First, an employer is not permitted to exempt himself from liability to his employee for negligently caused injury (paragraph (a)). Second, one who is charged with a duty of public service, such as a common carrier or a public utility, and who undertakes to perform it for compensation, is not permitted to exempt himself from liability to the one to be served for negligent breach of that duty (paragraph (b)). The rigor of this rule may, however, be mitigated by a fairly bargained for agreement to limit liability to a reasonable agreed value in return for a lower rate. In most jurisdictions legislation has altered the rule in specific situations, usually by restricting the power to limit liability. The two examples given under Subsection (2) are not intended as an exhaustive list of situations in which such terms are unenforceable. If, for example, a statute imposes a standard of conduct, a court may decide on the basis of an analysis of the statute, that a term exempting a party from liability for failure to conform to that standard is unenforceable. See § 179(a). **Illustrations:**

1. A, a common carrier, issues a pass to B, one of its employees. A term of the pass exempts A from liability to B for any injury caused by A's negligence. The term is unenforceable on grounds of public policy. Enforcement of a similar term in a pass given gratuitously to one who is not an employee would not be precluded on those grounds.

2. A term in an agreement between A, a railroad, and B, an adjacent land owner, exempts A from liability to B for fires negligently caused by sparks from its engines. Because the term does not exempt A from liability for breach of its duty of public service, its enforcement is not precluded on grounds of public policy. The term would be unenforceable on those grounds if it exempted A from liability for harm caused either willfully, intentionally or recklessly.

b. Relation to other rules. Language inserted by a party in an agreement for the purpose of exempting him from liability for negligent conduct is scrutinized with particular care and a court may require specific and conspicuous reference to negligence under the general principle that language is interpreted against the draftsman. See § 206. Furthermore, a party's attempt to exempt himself from liability for negligent conduct may fail as unconscionable. See § 208. The rule stated in this Section does not apply to an agreement by a third person to indemnify a party against liability in tort. The effect of a term purporting to exempt a party from the consequences of a misrepresentation is governed by the rule stated in § 196.

c. Strict product liability. One who sells a product in a defective condition unreasonably dangerous to the user or consumer or to his property is subjected to liability for resulting physical harm under the rule stated in Restatement, Second, Torts § 402A. In general, a term exempting the seller from this liability is unenforceable on grounds of public policy. See Comment *m* to Restatement, Second, Torts § 402A. Subsection (3) states an exception for the rare situation in which the term is consistent with the policy underlying the liability. This might be the case, for example, for a term in a fairly negotiated contract between two merchants for the sale of an experimental product. Such a term would not, however, affect the rights of one who was not a party to the contract.

§ 196. Term Exempting From Consequences of Misrepresentation

A term unreasonably exempting a party from the legal consequences of a misrepresentation is unenforceable on grounds of public policy.

Comment:

. . .

Topic 5. Restitution

Introductory Note: Of the cases that raise the question of the unenforceability of promises on grounds of public policy, the hardest are those in which the promisee has performed and not been paid, but is involved in the wrong with the promisor. In deciding whether to enforce the promise, the court faces a dilemma. On the one hand, if it allows the promisee to enforce the promise, it lends its aid to the promisee in spite of *his* involvement in the wrong. On the other hand, if it refuses to allow the promisee to enforce the promise, it leaves the benefit that he has conferred by performance in the hands of the promisor in spite of *his* involvement in the wrong. The dilemma is aggravated by the general principle that a court will not aid one wrongdoer by granting him restitution of a benefit conferred upon the other party, even if the other is also a wrongdoer. See § 197. But courts have made important exceptions to this general principle out of a desire to avoid unjust enrichment, when consistent with other goals. These exceptions are set out in the following three sections and relate to claims for restitution by one who would otherwise suffer forfeiture that is disproportionate to the contravention of public policy involved (§ 197), by one who is not equally in the wrong with the other party or is excusably ignorant (§ 198), and by one who has withdrawn or where the situation is contrary to the public interest (§ 199). If a claim for restitution is allowed under one of these sections, it is subject to the general rules on restitution stated in §§ 370-77. If it is within the power of the court to fashion a form of relief in which the benefit conferred on one wrongdoer is transferred, not to the other wrongdoer, but to an appropriate and innocent third party, the rules stated in this Topic do not prevent it from doing so. As to the effect of public policy on claims in restitution arising out of transactions in which no promise within this Chapter is involved, see Restatement of Restitution § 140.

§ 197. Restitution Generally Unavailable

Except as stated in §§ 198 and 199, a party has no claim in restitution for performance that he has rendered under or in return for a promise that is unenforceable on grounds of public policy unless denial of restitution would cause disproportionate forfeiture.

Comment:

a. Rationale. In general, if a court will not, on grounds of public policy, aid a promisee by enforcing the promise, it will not aid him by granting him restitution for performance that he has rendered in return for the unenforceable promise. Neither will it aid the promisor by allowing a claim in restitution for performance that he has rendered under the unenforceable promise. It will simply leave both parties as it finds them, even though this may result in one of them retaining a benefit that he has received as a result of the transaction. **Illustrations:**

1. A, the owner of a newspaper, promises B that he will publish a statement about C known to A and B to be false and defamatory, if B pays him $ 10,000. B pays A $ 10,000. Since A's promise is unenforceable on grounds of public policy (§ 192), B has no claim in restitution against A. See Illustration 6 to § 178.

2. A induces B to make an agreement to buy goods on credit from A by bribing B's purchasing agent. A's bribe tends to induce the agent to violate his fiduciary duty. A delivers the goods to B. Since B's promise to pay the price is unenforceable on grounds of public policy, A has no claim in restitution against B. See § 193 and Illustration 14 to § 178.

. . .

§ 198. Restitution in Favor of Party Who Is Excusably Ignorant or Is Not Equally in the Wrong

A party has a claim in restitution for performance that he has rendered under or in return for a promise that is unenforceable on grounds of public policy if
(a) he was excusably ignorant of the facts or of legislation of a minor character, in the absence of which the promise would be enforceable, or
(b) he was not equally in the wrong with the promisor.

Comment:

a. Ignorance of facts or legislation. A party's excusable ignorance of facts or of legislation of a minor character may enable him to enforce a promise that would otherwise be unenforceable on grounds of public policy. See § 180. In the alternative, he may have a claim in restitution under the rule stated in paragraph (a). In some cases, however, he will not be able to enforce the promise because the other party is also excusably ignorant of the facts or legislation. See Comment *b* to § 180. In such cases, he is nevertheless entitled to restitution under the rule stated in paragraph (b). Whether ignorance is excusable is governed by the same considerations that apply under the rule stated in § 180. Restitution under this Subsection is subject to the rules of §§ 370-77. **Illustration:**

1. A, an insurance company, issues a policy of fire insurance to B on a building. A state statute makes A's promise unenforceable as a wager because B has no insurable interest in the building. B pays A the premium but neither A nor B knows nor has reason to know that B has no legally insurable interest in the building. Although A's promise is unenforceable on grounds of public policy, B was excusably ignorant of the facts that make it unenforceable, and B has a claim in restitution against A for the amount of the premium paid.

. . .

§ 199. Restitution Where Party Withdraws or Situation Is Contrary to Public Interest

A party has a claim in restitution for performance that he has rendered under or in return for a promise that is unenforceable on grounds of public policy if he did not engage in serious misconduct and

(a) he withdraws from the transaction before the improper purpose has been achieved, or

(b) allowance of the claim would put an end to a continuing situation that is contrary to the public interest.

. . .

Chapter 9

The Scope of Contractual Obligations

Introductory Note: The typical contract is a bargain -- an agreement in which a promise is exchanged for a consideration; in atypical cases a promise is binding because of its formal characteristics, because of reliance by the promisee, or for some other reason. See § 17. The terms of the agreement or promise to a large extent define the obligation created. Certain types of contracts or terms, however, are forbidden or otherwise regulated, and rules of law must fill the gap when the parties have not provided for the situation which arises. Where the parties have adopted a writing as the final expression of all or part of their agreement, interpretation focuses on the writing, and its terms may supersede other manifestations of intention. Whether or not there is a writing, the parties' intention is read in its context, and usages common to the parties are often an important part of the context.

General rules relating to these matters are stated in this chapter. Bargains unenforceable on grounds of public policy, however, are the subject of a separate chapter. See Chapter 8. The scope of a contractual obligation may be determined or affected by the meaning of the promise or agreement (Topic 1), by considerations of fairness and the public interest (Topic 2), by the adoption of a writing (Topic 3), and by usage (Topic 4). Some special rules relating to conditions and their effect on the scope of contractual obligations are stated at the end of this Chapter (Topic 5).

This Chapter analyzes the process of interpreting and applying agreements, stating separately rules with respect to various aspects of the process. Such a separate statement may convey an erroneous impression of the psychological reality of the judicial process in which many elements are typically combined in a single ruling. Nevertheless, where evidence of an oral term is excluded in an action based on a written agreement with simply the imprecise explanation that "the writing speaks for itself," the ruling, when analyzed, may sum up the following determinations: the contract was integrated (§ 209); the integration was complete (§ 210); the oral term is inconsistent with the written agreement, is within its scope, does not bear on its interpretation, and would not naturally be omitted from the writing (§§ 213-16).

§ 200. Interpretation of Promise or Agreement

> **Interpretation of a promise or agreement or a term thereof is the ascertainment of its meaning.**

Comment:

a. Formation of contract. Questions of interpretation arise in determining whether there is a contract as well as in determining rights and duties under a contract. Chapter 3 states rules applicable in determining whether the parties have manifested the mutual assent necessary to a contract enforceable as a bargain. The rules stated in the present Topic overlap with those rules, but also apply where the making of a contract is not disputed.

b. Manifestation of intention. As is made clear in Chapter 3, particularly §§ 17-20, the intention of a party that is relevant to formation of a contract is the intention manifested by him rather than any different undisclosed intention. The definitions of "promise," "agreement," and

"term" in §§ 2, 3 and 5 also refer to "manifestation of intention." It follows that the meaning of the words or other conduct of a party is not necessarily the meaning he expects or understands. He is not bound by a meaning unless he has reason to know of it, but the expectation and understanding of the other party must also be taken into account. See § 201.

c. Interpretation and legal operation. Interpretation is not a determination of the legal effect of words or other conduct. Properly interpreted, an agreement may not be enforceable as a contract, or a term such as a promise to pay a penalty may be denied legal effect, or it may have a legal effect different from that agreed upon, as in a case of employment at less than a statutory minimum wage.

§ 201. Whose Meaning Prevails

(1) Where the parties have attached the same meaning to a promise or agreement or a term thereof, it is interpreted in accordance with that meaning.

(2) Where the parties have attached different meanings to a promise or agreement or a term thereof, it is interpreted in accordance with the meaning attached by one of them if at the time the agreement was made

(a) that party did not know of any different meaning attached by the other, and the other knew the meaning attached by the first party; or

(b) that party had no reason to know of any different meaning attached by the other, and the other had reason to know the meaning attached by the first party.

(3) Except as stated in this Section, neither party is bound by the meaning attached by the other, even though the result may be a failure of mutual assent.

Comment:

a. The meaning of words. Words are used as conventional symbols of mental states, with standardized meanings based on habitual or customary practice. Unless a different intention is shown, language is interpreted in accordance with its generally prevailing meaning. See § 202(3). Usages of varying degrees of generality are recorded in dictionaries, but there are substantial differences between English and American usages and between usages in different parts of the United States. Differences of usage also exist in various localities and in different social, economic, religious and ethnic groups. All these usages change over time, and persons engaged in transactions with each other often develop temporary usages peculiar to themselves. Moreover, most words are commonly used in more than one sense.

b. The problem of context. Uncertainties in the meaning of words are ordinarily greatly reduced by the context in which they are used. The same is true of other conventional symbols, and the meaning of conduct not used as a conventional symbol is even more dependent on its setting. But the context of words and other conduct is seldom exactly the same for two different people, since connotations depend on the entire past experience and the attitudes and expectations of the person whose understanding is in question. In general, the context relevant to interpretation of a bargain is the context common to both parties. More precisely, the question of meaning in cases of misunderstanding depends on an inquiry into what each party knew or had reason to know, as stated in Subsections (2) and (3). See § 20 and Illustrations. Ordinarily a party has reason to know of meanings in general usage.

c. Mutual understanding. Subsection (1) makes it clear that the primary search is for a common meaning of the parties, not a meaning imposed on them by the law. To the extent that a mutual understanding is displaced by government regulation, the resulting obligation does not rest on "interpretation" in the sense used here. The objective of interpretation in the general law of contracts is to carry out the understanding of the parties rather than to impose obligations on them contrary to their understanding: "the courts do not make a contract for the parties." Ordinarily, therefore, the mutual understanding of the parties prevails even where the contractual term has been defined differently by statute or administrative regulation. But parties who used a standardized term in an unusual sense obviously run the risk that their agreement will be misinterpreted in litigation.

Illustrations:

1. A and B agree that A will sell goods to B "f.o.b." the place of destination. Prior correspondence shows that the price has been adjusted on the assumption that B's insurance policies will cover the goods during shipment. Notwithstanding the normal meaning of the "f.o.b." term declared in Uniform Commercial Code § 2-319, it may be found that the parties have "otherwise agreed" under that section and that B bears the risk in transit.

2. A signs a negotiable promissory note payable to B's order, and C signs his name on the back without more. Under Uniform Commercial Code § 3-402, C's signature is an indorsement, and evidence of a contrary understanding is not admissible except for the purpose of reformation of the instrument. This conclusion does not rest on interpretation of the writing.

3. A agrees to sell beer to B at a specified price per barrel. At the time of the agreement both parties and others in their trade use as standard barrels wooden barrels which originally hold 31 gallons and hold less as they continue in use.

A statute defines a barrel as 31 1/2 gallons. The statute does not prevent interpretation of the agreement as referring to the barrels in use.

d. Misunderstanding. Subsection (2) follows the terminology of § 20, referring to the understanding of each party as the meaning "attached" by him to a term of a promise or agreement. Where the rules stated in Subsections (1) and (2) do not apply, neither party is bound by the understanding of the other. The result may be an entire failure of agreement or a failure to agree as to a term. There may be a binding contract despite failure to agree as to a term, if the term is not essential or if it can be supplied. See § 204. In some cases a party can waive the misunderstanding and enforce the contract in accordance with the understanding of the other party. **Illustrations:**

    4. A agrees to sell and B to buy a quantity of eviscerated "chicken." A tenders "stewing chicken" or "fowl"; B rejects on the ground that the contract calls for "broilers" or "fryers." Each party makes a claim for damages against the other. It is found that each acted in good faith and that neither had reason to know of the difference in meaning. Both claims fail.

    5. A orders goods from B, using A's standard form. B acknowledges the order, using his own standard form. Each form provides that no terms are agreed to except those on the form and that the other party agrees to the form. One form contains an arbitration clause; the other does not. The goods are delivered and paid for. Later a dispute arises as to their quality. There is no agreement to arbitrate the dispute.

§ 202. Rules in Aid of Interpretation

(1) Words and other conduct are interpreted in the light of all the circumstances, and if the principal purpose of the parties is ascertainable it is given great weight.

(2) A writing is interpreted as a whole, and all writings that are part of the same transaction are interpreted together.

(3) Unless a different intention is manifested,

(a) where language has a generally prevailing meaning, it is interpreted in accordance with that meaning;

(b) technical terms and words of art are given their technical meaning when used in a transaction within their technical field.

(4) Where an agreement involves repeated occasions for performance by either party with knowledge of the nature of the performance and opportunity for objection to it by the other, any course of performance accepted or acquiesced in without objection is given great weight in the interpretation of the agreement.

(5) Wherever reasonable, the manifestations of intention of the parties to a promise or agreement are interpreted as consistent with each other and with any relevant course of performance, course of dealing, or usage of trade.

Comment:

a. Scope of special rules. The rules in this Section are applicable to all manifestations of intention and all transactions. The rules are general in character, and serve merely as guides in the process of interpretation. They do not depend upon any determination that there is an ambiguity, but are used in determining what meanings are reasonably possible as well as in choosing among possible meanings.

b. Circumstances. The meaning of words and other symbols commonly depends on their context; the meaning of other conduct is even more dependent on the circumstances. In interpreting the words and conduct of the parties to a contract, a court seeks to put itself in the position they occupied at the time the contract was made. When the parties have adopted a writing as a final expression of their agreement, interpretation is directed to the meaning of that writing in the light of the circumstances. See §§ 209, 212. The circumstances for this purpose include the entire situation, as it appeared to the parties, and in appropriate cases may include facts known to one party of which the other had reason to know. See § 201. **Illustrations:**

    1. A contracts with B to do concrete work on a bridge, to be paid for according to "the number of square yards of concrete surface included in the bridge deck." An estimate included in the proposal for bids and an estimate submitted by

A to B after award are shown to have been based on the top surface only, not including the side and bottom surfaces. On a finding that this was the mutual understanding, the contract is to be so interpreted.

2. In a written agreement between A and B it is stated that B owns half of the stock of C Company, that "A has rendered valuable services to C Company for which B desires to compensate A in the sum of $ 25,000 payable in the manner hereinafter set forth," and that B will pay A "one-half of all money received from C Company, such as dividends, or profits until A has been paid the said amount of $ 25,000." It is shown that the written agreement was executed after the services were rendered, that there was no prior explicit understanding that A would be compensated, and that before signing the written agreement A and B orally agreed that the $ 25,000 was to be a "bonus out of B's profit," "double or nothing," "a gamble." The written agreement is to be interpreted in accordance with the oral agreement.

c. *Principal purpose.* The purposes of the parties to a contract are not always identical; particularly in business transactions, the parties often have divergent or even conflicting interests. But up to a point they commonly join in a common purpose of attaining a specific factual or legal result which each regards as necessary to the attainment of his ultimate purposes. Moreover, one party may know or have reason to know the purpose of the other and thus that his meaning is one consistent with that purpose. Determination that the parties have a principal purpose in common requires interpretation, but if such a purpose is disclosed further interpretation is guided by it. Even language which is otherwise explicit may be read with a modification needed to make it consistent with such a purpose. **Illustrations:**

3. A promises B as follows: "In consideration of your supplying my nephew C with china and earthenware during the coming year, I guarantee the payment of any bills you may draw on him on account thereof to the amount of $ 200." C is engaged in the business of selling such goods. B sells C $ 2,000 of china during the year and draws bills for their price in varying amounts. C pays $ 1,000 and then defaults. A's promise is to be interpreted as a continuing undertaking, not limited to the first $ 200 of purchases.

4. A agrees with his divorced wife B and C, trustee, to pay to C $ 1,200 each year for the benefit of D, the 10-year-old son of A and B, until D enters college, and to pay $ 2,200 each

year for the period of D's higher education but not more than four years. At age 19 D completes high school and is inducted into the army. Upon a finding that the main purpose of the agreement is to provide for D's maintenance and education, the agreement is to be interpreted as not requiring payments during D's military service.

d. *Interpretation of the whole.* Meaning is inevitably dependent on context. A word changes meaning when it becomes part of a sentence, the sentence when it becomes part of a paragraph. A longer writing similarly affects the paragraph, other related writings affect the particular writing, and the circumstances affect the whole. Where the whole can be read to give significance to each part, that reading is preferred; if such a reading would be unreasonable, a choice must be made. See § 203. To fit the immediate verbal context or the more remote total context particular words or punctuation may be disregarded or supplied; clerical or grammatical errors may be corrected; singular may be treated as plural or plural as singular. **Illustrations:**

5. A written agreement between A and B for the exchange of real estate provides that A and B will each pay a $ 200 commission to C, a broker, "upon the signing of this agreement by both parties hereto." The last sentence of the agreement states, "The commission being due and payable upon the transfer of the properties." It is shown that A refused to sign the agreement until the last sentence was added. The agreement is to be interpreted to make the commission due only when both the signing and the transfer take place.

6. A agrees to appoint B exclusive distributor in a specified area for a new product to be manufactured by A, and B agrees to use his best efforts to promote sale of the product. The written agreement includes an initial retail price list and a provision that A will sell to B at the lowest price and highest discount it gives to any distributor. Whether the parties intend to be bound before any other distributor is appointed or any price fixed is a question of the meaning of the entire agreement in its context. If they do, the agreement has the effect of an agreement to sell at a reasonable price at the time for delivery. See Uniform Commercial Code § 2-305.

7. A contracts in writing to build a house for B according to specifications, and C, a surety company, guarantees A's performance. After completion and acceptance the house and its contents are damaged by hot water because of defective work by the plumbing and heating subcontractor. In determining the responsibility of

A and C, the contract, specifications and surety bond are to be read together.

e. General usage. In the United States the English language is used far more often in a sense which would be generally understood throughout the country than in a sense peculiar to some locality or group. In the absence of some contrary indication, therefore, English words are read as having the meaning given them by general usage, if there is one. This rule is a rule of interpretation in the absence of contrary evidence, not a rule excluding contrary evidence. It may also yield to internal indications such as inconsistency, absurdity, or departure from normal grammar, punctuation, or word order. **Illustrations:**

8. A issues to B a fire insurance policy covering lumber stored in "sheds." In the absence of contrary indication, lumber in the basement of a two-story warehouse is not covered.

9. A leases restaurant premises to B. The lease provides that A will pay for electricity and that B will "pay for gas or fuel used in the preparation of food." In the absence of contrary indication, "fuel" should be read not to include electricity.

f. Technical terms. Parties to an agreement often use the vocabulary of a particular place, vocation or trade, in which new words are coined and common words are assigned new meanings. But technical terms are often misused, and it may be shown that a technical word or phrase was used in a non-technical sense. Moreover, the same word may have a variety of technical and other meanings. "Mules" may mean animals, shoes or machines; a "ram" may mean an animal or a hydraulic ram; "zebra" may refer to a mammal, a butterfly, a lizard, a fish, a type of plant, tree or wood, or merely to the letter "Z". **Illustrations:**

10. The facts being otherwise as stated in Illustration 9, there is a local usage in the restaurant trade that "fuel" includes electricity used in cooking. In the absence of contrary indication, "fuel" may be read in accordance with the usage. But a provision in the lease that if B installs a new electric range he will also install a special meter and pay for electricity used by the range would show that the parties did not adopt the local usage.

11. A contract for the sale of horsemeat scraps calls for "minimum 50% protein." As both parties know, by a usage of the business in which they are engaged, 49.5 per cent is treated as the equivalent of 50 per cent. The contract is to be interpreted in accordance with the usage.

g. Course of performance. The parties to an agreement know best what they meant, and their action under it is often the strongest evidence of their meaning. But such "practical construction" is not conclusive of meaning. Conduct must be weighed in the light of the terms of the agreement and their possible meanings. Where it is unreasonable to interpret the contract in accordance with the course of performance, the conduct of the parties may be evidence of an agreed modification or of a waiver by one party. See Uniform Commercial Code § 2-208. Or there may be simply a mistake which should be corrected. The rule of Subsection (4) does not apply to action on a single occasion or to action of one party only; in such cases the conduct of a party may be evidence against him that he had knowledge or reason to know of the other party's meaning, but self-serving conduct is not entitled to weight. **Illustrations:**

12. A discloses to B a secret formula for an antiseptic liquid and B agrees to pay monthly royalties based on amounts sold. Fifty years later the formula has been published in medical journals. After continuing to pay for 25 years more, B contends that the duty to pay royalties ended when the formula ceased to be secret. B's conduct strongly negates the contention.

13. Several railroads agree in writing to share working expenses and taxes of X, another railroad, on a "wheelage basis." For several years they pay shares in proportion to their stock ownership in the other railroad. Then all but one agree that they have been mistaken and that future payments will be made on a basis of use of X's physical properties. Stock ownership is so plainly unrelated to any possible meaning of "wheelage" that the course of performance does not support an interpretation of "wheelage basis" as requiring payments in proportion to stock ownership.

h. Preference for consistency. Subsection (5) states a rule fairly implied in Subsections (1) and (2); words and conduct are interpreted in the light of the circumstances, and writings are interpreted as a whole. A meaning consistent with all the circumstances is preferred to a meaning which requires that part of the context be disregarded. But the parties may have agreed to displace normal meanings, may have modified a prior understanding, or may have agreed to confusing or self-contradictory terms. They may even have entirely failed to agree, though each thought there was an agreement. See §§ 20, 201.

§ 203. Standards of Preference in Interpretation

In the interpretation of a promise or agreement or a term thereof, the following standards of preference are generally applicable:

(a) an interpretation which gives a reasonable, lawful, and effective meaning to all the terms is preferred to an interpretation which leaves a part unreasonable, unlawful, or of no effect;

(b) express terms are given greater weight than course of performance, course of dealing, and usage of trade, course of performance is given greater weight than course of dealing or usage of trade, and course of dealing is given greater weight than usage of trade;

(c) specific terms and exact terms are given greater weight than general language;

(d) separately negotiated or added terms are given greater weight than standardized terms or other terms not separately negotiated.

Comment:

a. Scope. The rules of this Section are applicable to all manifestations of intention and all transactions. They apply only in choosing among reasonable interpretations. They do not override evidence of the meaning of the parties, but aid in determining meaning or prescribe legal effect when meaning is in doubt.

b. Superfluous terms. Since an agreement is interpreted as a whole, it is assumed in the first instance that no part of it is superfluous. The parties may of course agree to supersede prior manifestations of intention; indeed, this is the normal effect of an integrated agreement. See § 213. But, particularly in cases of integrated agreements, terms are rarely agreed to without reason. Where an integrated agreement has been negotiated with care and in detail and has been expertly drafted for the particular transaction, an interpretation is very strongly negated if it would render some provisions superfluous. On the other hand, a standard form may include provisions appropriate only to some of the transactions in which the form is to be used; or the form may be used for an inappropriate transaction. Even agreements tailored to particular transactions sometimes include overlapping or redundant or meaningless provisions.

The preference for an interpretation which gives meaning to every part of an agreement does not mean that every part is assumed to have legal consequences. Parties commonly direct their attention to performance rather than breach, and it is enough that each provision has meaning to them as a guide to performance. Stipulations against particular legal consequences are not uncommon. Thus it is not unusual to define the intended performance with precision and then to provide for tolerances within which variation is permitted. See Uniform Commercial Code § 2-508(2).

c. Unreasonable and unlawful terms. In the absence of contrary indication, it is assumed that each term of an agreement has a reasonable rather than an unreasonable meaning, and that the agreement is intended to be lawful rather than unconscionable, fraudulent or otherwise illegal. But parties are free to make agreements which seem unreasonable to others, and circumstances may show that even an agreement innocent on its face has an illegal purpose. The search is for the manifested intention of the parties. If a term or a contract is unconscionable or otherwise against public policy, it should be dealt with directly rather than by spurious interpretation. See § 208 and Uniform Commercial Code § 2-302 and Comment. **Illustration:**

1. A licenses B to manufacture pipes under A's patents, and B agrees to pay "a royalty of 50 cents per 1,000 feet for an output of 5,000,000 or less feet per year, and for an output of over 5,000,000 feet per year at the rate of 30 cents per thousand feet." The 50 cent rate is payable on the first 5,000,000 feet, the 30 cent rate only on the excess. The more literal reading is unreasonable, since it would involve a smaller payment for 6,000,000 feet than for 4,000,000 feet.

d. Priority of express terms. Just as parties to agreements often depart from general usage as to the meaning of words or other conduct, so they may depart from a usage of trade. Similarly, they may change a pattern established by their own prior course of dealing. Their meaning in such cases is ordinarily to be ascertained as a fact; no penalty is attached by the law of contracts to their failure to conform to the usages of others or to their own prior usage. Course of performance may establish meaning, or it may show mistake or oversight or modification or waiver. See § 202. The priorities stated in Subsection (b) are those stated in Uniform Commercial Code §§ 1-205 and 2-208, rephrased to fit the different context of the Restatement.

e. General and specific terms. People commonly use general language without a clear consciousness of its full scope and without awareness that an exception should be made. Attention and understanding are likely to be in better focus when language is specific or exact, and in case of conflict the specific or exact term is more likely to express the meaning of the parties with respect to the situation than the general language. If the specific or exact can be read as an exception or qualification of the general, both are given some effect, in accordance with the rule stated in Subsection (a). Compare Uniform Commercial Code § 2-317. But the rule yields to manifestation of a contrary intention.

f. Superseded standard terms. The rule stated in Subsection (d) has frequent application in cases of standardized documents. Printed forms are often misused, and there may be a question whether the parties manifested assent to a printed term on a writing. A printed provision that is clearly part of an integrated contract is normally to be interpreted as consistent with other terms, but in cases of inconsistency a handwritten or typewritten term inserted in connection with the particular transaction ordinarily prevails.

Similarly, a typewritten term may be superseded by drawing a line through it, modified by interlineation, or controlled by an inconsistent handwritten insertion in another part of the agreement. It is sometimes said generally that handwritten terms control typewritten and printed terms, and typewritten control printed. See Uniform Commercial Code § 3-118(b); compare § 2-316(1) (disclaimer of express warranty), §§ 3-110(3) (instrument payable both to order and to bearer). But the rule yields to manifestation of a contrary intention. **Illustrations:**

2. A, an agent of C, authorized to make contracts for C, writes a letter to B beginning "We offer," and stating a proposal in detailed and clear language, signed "C by A, Agent." At the bottom of the office stationery which A uses for the offer there is printed "All contracts and orders taken are subject to the approval of the executive office." A portion of the letter is typed over a portion of this printing. A jury's finding that the printed words were not part of the letter and that it is therefore an offer will not be set aside.

3. A charter party contains the printed provision "vessel to have turn in loading." There is written below this, "vessel to be loaded promptly." The printed and written provisions are given the consistent meaning that the vessel shall take its turn in loading, though this involves considerable delay, but when its turn arrives, the vessel shall be loaded promptly.

. . .

§ 204. Supplying an Omitted Essential Term

When the parties to a bargain sufficiently defined to be a contract have not agreed with respect to a term which is essential to a determination of their rights and duties, a term which is reasonable in the circumstances is supplied by the court.

Comment:

a. Scope; relation to other rules. This Section states a principle governing the legal effect of a binding agreement. The supplying of an omitted term is not technically interpretation, but the two are closely related; courts often speak of an "implied" term. In many common situations the principle has been elaborated in more detailed rules, applicable unless otherwise agreed. See the rules on the effect of failure of performance stated in §§ 231-49 and the rules on impossibility and frustration stated in Chapter 11, and compare §§ 158 and 272, regarding the supplying of terms in cases of mistake and impracticability or frustration. A similar principle is often applicable

in determining whether the terms of an agreement are sufficiently certain to constitute a contract. See §§ 33, 34. In both situations the supplying of an omitted term may resemble or overlap interpretation (see § 200) or the effect given to usage (see §§ 219-23).

b. How omission occurs. The parties to an agreement may entirely fail to foresee the situation which later arises and gives rise to a dispute; they then have no expectations with respect to that situation, and a search for their meaning with respect to it is fruitless. Or they may have expectations but fail to manifest them, either because the expectation rests on an assumption which is unconscious or only partly conscious, or because the situation seems to be unimportant or unlikely, or because discussion of it might be unpleasant or might produce delay or impasse.

c. Interpretation and omission. Interpretation may be necessary to determine that the parties have not agreed with respect to a particular term, but the supplying of an omitted term is not within the definition of interpretation in §§ 200. Where there is tacit agreement or a common tacit assumption or where a term can be supplied by logical deduction from agreed terms and the circumstances, interpretation may be enough. But interpretation may result in the conclusion that there was in fact no agreement on a particular point, and that conclusion should be accepted even though the omitted term could be supplied by giving agreed language a meaning different from the meaning or meanings given it by the parties.

d. Supplying a term. The process of supplying an omitted term has sometimes been disguised as a literal or a purposive reading of contract language directed to a situation other than the situation that arises. Sometimes it is said that the search is for the term the parties would have agreed to if the question had been brought to their attention. Both the meaning of the words used and the probability that a particular term would have been used if the question had been raised may be factors in determining what term is reasonable in the circumstances. But where there is in fact no agreement, the court should supply a term which comports with community standards of fairness and policy rather than analyze a hypothetical model of the bargaining process.

Thus where a contract calls for a single performance such as the rendering of a service or the delivery of goods, the parties are most unlikely to agree explicitly that performance will be rendered within a "reasonable time;" but if no time is specified, a term calling for performance within a reasonable time is supplied. See Uniform Commercial Code §§ 1-204, 2-309(1). Similarly, where there is a contract for the sale of goods but nothing is said as to price the price is a reasonable price at the time for delivery. See Uniform Commercial Code § 2-305.

e. Effect of the parol evidence rule. The fact that an essential term is omitted may indicate that the agreement is not integrated or that there is partial rather than complete integration. In such cases the omitted term may be supplied by prior negotiations or a prior agreement. See § 216. But omission of a term does not show conclusively that integration was not complete and a completely integrated agreement, if binding, discharges prior agreements within its scope. See § 213. Where there is complete integration and interpretation of the writing discloses a failure to agree on an essential term, evidence of prior negotiations or agreements is not admissible to supply the omitted term, but such evidence may be admissible, if relevant, on the question of what is reasonable in the circumstances. **Illustration:**

> 1. A and his wife convey their ranch to A's sister and her husband, reserving an option to repurchase. The parties agree orally that the property will be kept in the family, but the deed says nothing as to assignment of the option. If the deed is found to be a partial integration, the oral agreement is effective to show that the option is not assignable. If the deed is found to be a complete integration, the oral agreement is discharged and the option is assignable.

§ 205. Duty of Good Faith and Fair Dealing

Every contract imposes upon each party a duty of good faith and fair dealing in its performance and its enforcement.

Comment:

a. Meanings of "good faith." Good faith is defined in Uniform Commercial Code §§ 1-201(19) as "honesty in fact in the conduct or transaction concerned." "In the case of a merchant" Uniform Commercial Code § 2-103(1)(b) provides that good faith means "honesty in fact and the observance of reasonable commercial standards of fair dealing in the trade." The phrase "good

faith" is used in a variety of contexts, and its meaning varies somewhat with the context. Good faith performance or enforcement of a contract emphasizes faithfulness to an agreed common purpose and consistency with the justified expectations of the other party; it excludes a variety of types of conduct characterized as involving "bad faith" because they violate community standards of decency, fairness or reasonableness. The appropriate remedy for a breach of the duty of good faith also varies with the circumstances.

b. *Good faith purchase*. In many situations a good faith purchaser of property for value can acquire better rights in the property than his transferor had. See, e.g., § 342. In this context "good faith" focuses on the honesty of the purchaser, as distinguished from his care or negligence. Particularly in the law of negotiable instruments inquiry may be limited to "good faith" under what has been called "the rule of the pure heart and the empty head." When diligence or inquiry is a condition of the purchaser's right, it is said that good faith is not enough. This focus on honesty is appropriate to cases of good faith purchase; it is less so in cases of good faith performance.

c. *Good faith in negotiation*. This Section, like Uniform Commercial Code § 1-203, does not deal with good faith in the formation of a contract. Bad faith in negotiation, although not within the scope of this Section, may be subject to sanctions. Particular forms of bad faith in bargaining are the subjects of rules as to capacity to contract, mutual assent and consideration and of rules as to invalidating causes such as fraud and duress. See, for example, §§ 90 and 208. Moreover, remedies for bad faith in the absence of agreement are found in the law of torts or restitution. For examples of a statutory duty to bargain in good faith, see, e.g., National Labor Relations Act § 8(d) and the federal Truth in Lending Act. In cases of negotiation for modification of an existing contractual relationship, the rule stated in this Section may overlap with more specific rules requiring negotiation in good faith. See §§ 73, 89; Uniform Commercial Code § 2-209 and Comment.

d. *Good faith performance*. Subterfuges and evasions violate the obligation of good faith in performance even though the actor believes his conduct to be justified. But the obligation goes further: bad faith may be overt or may consist of inaction, and fair dealing may require more than honesty. A complete catalogue of types of bad faith is impossible, but the following types are among those which have been recognized in judicial decisions: evasion of the spirit of the bargain, lack of diligence and slacking off, willful rendering of imperfect performance, abuse of a power to specify terms, and interference with or failure to cooperate in the other party's performance. **Illustrations:**

1. A, an oil dealer, borrows $ 100,000 from B, a supplier, and agrees to buy all his requirements of certain oil products from B on stated terms until the debt is repaid. Before the debt is repaid, A makes a new arrangement with C, a competitor of B. Under the new arrangement A's business is conducted by a corporation formed and owned by A and C and managed by A, and the corporation buys all its oil products from C. The new arrangement may be found to be a subterfuge or evasion and a breach of contract by A.

2. A, owner of a shopping center, leases part of it to B, giving B the exclusive right to conduct a supermarket, the rent to be a percentage of B's gross receipts. During the term of the lease A acquires adjoining land, expands the shopping center, and leases part of the adjoining land to C for a competing supermarket. Unless such action was contemplated or is otherwise justified, there is a breach of contract by A.

3. A Insurance Company insures B against legal liability for certain bodily injuries to third persons, with a limit of liability of $ 10,000 for an accident to any one person. The policy provides that A will defend any suit covered by it but may settle. C sues B on a claim covered by the policy and offers to settle for $ 9,500. A refuses to settle on the ground that the amount is excessive, and judgment is rendered against B for $ 20,000 after a trial defended by A. A then refuses to appeal, and offers to pay $ 10,000 only if B satisfies the judgment, impairing B's opportunity to negotiate for settlement. B prosecutes an appeal, reasonably expending $ 7,500, and obtains dismissal of the claim. A has failed to deal fairly and in good faith with B and is liable for B's appeal expense.

4. A and B contract that A will perform certain demolition work for B and pay B a specified sum for materials salvaged, the contract not to "become effective until" certain insurance policies "are in full force and effect." A makes a good faith effort to obtain the insurance, but financial difficulty arising from injury to an employee of A on another job prevents A from obtaining them. A's duty to perform is discharged.

5. B submits and A accepts a bid to supply approximately 4000 tons of trap rock for an airport at a unit price. The parties execute a standard form of "Invitation, Bid, and Acceptance (Short Form Contract)" supplied by A, including typed terms "to be delivered to project as required," "delivery to start immediately," "cancellation by A may be effected at any time." Good faith requires that A order and accept the

rock within a reasonable time unless A has given B notice of intent to cancel.

6. A contracts to perform services for B for such compensation "as you, in your sole judgment, may decide is reasonable." After A has performed the services, B refuses to make any determination of the value of the services. A is entitled to their value as determined by a court.

7. A suffers a loss of property covered by an insurance policy issued by B, and submits to B notice and proof of loss. The notice and proof fail to comply with requirements of the policy as to form and detail. B does not point out the defects, but remains silent and evasive, telling A broadly to perfect his claim. The defects do not bar recovery on the policy.

e. Good faith in enforcement. The obligation of good faith and fair dealing extends to the assertion, settlement and litigation of contract claims and defenses. See, e.g., §§ 73, 89. The obligation is violated by dishonest conduct such as conjuring up a pretended dispute, asserting an interpretation contrary to one's own understanding, or falsification of facts. It also extends to dealing which is candid but unfair, such as taking advantage of the necessitous circumstances of the other party to extort a

modification of a contract for the sale of goods without legitimate commercial reason. See Uniform Commercial Code § 2-209, Comment 2. Other types of violation have been recognized in judicial decisions: harassing demands for assurances of performance, rejection of performance for unstated reasons, willful failure to mitigate damages, and abuse of a power to determine compliance or to terminate the contract. For a statutory duty of good faith in termination, see the federal Automobile Dealer's Day in Court Act, 15 U.S.C. §§ 1221-25 (1976).

Illustrations:

8. A contracts to sell and ship goods to B on credit. The contract provides that, if B's credit or financial responsibility becomes impaired or unsatisfactory to A, A may demand cash or security before making shipment and may cancel if the demand is not met. A may properly demand cash or security only if he honestly believes, with reason, that the prospect of payment is impaired.

9. A contracts to sell and ship goods to B. On arrival B rejects the goods on the erroneous ground that delivery was late. B is thereafter precluded from asserting other unstated grounds then known to him which A could have cured if stated seasonably.

§ 206. Interpretation Against the Draftsman

In choosing among the reasonable meanings of a promise or agreement or a term thereof, that meaning is generally preferred which operates against the party who supplies the words or from whom a writing otherwise proceeds.

Comment:

a. Rationale. Where one party chooses the terms of a contract, he is likely to provide more carefully for the protection of his own interests than for those of the other party. He is also more likely than the other party to have reason to know of uncertainties of meaning. Indeed, he may leave meaning deliberately obscure, intending to decide at a later date what meaning to assert. In cases of doubt, therefore, so long as other factors are not decisive, there is substantial reason for preferring the meaning of the other party. The rule is often invoked in cases of standardized contracts and in cases where the drafting party has the stronger bargaining position, but it is not limited to such cases. It is in strictness a rule of legal effect, sometimes called construction, as well as interpretation: its operation depends on the positions of the parties as they appear in

litigation, and sometimes the result is hard to distinguish from a denial of effect to an unconscionable clause.

b. Compulsory contract or term. The rule that language is interpreted against the party who chose it has no direct application to cases where the language is prescribed by law, as is sometimes true with respect to insurance policies, bills of lading and other standardized documents. In some cases, however, the statute or regulation adopts language which was previously used without compulsion and was interpreted against the drafting party, and there is normally no intention to change the established meaning. Moreover, insurers are more likely than insures to participate in drafting prescribed forms and to review them carefully before putting them into use.

§ 207. Interpretation Favoring the Public

In choosing among the reasonable meanings of a promise or agreement or a term thereof, a meaning that serves the public interest is generally preferred.

Comment:

a. Scope. The rule preferring an interpretation which favors an interest of the public applies only to agreements which affect a public interest. It is a rule of legal effect as well as interpretation, and rests more on considerations of public policy than on the probable intention of the parties. It has often been relied on to justify narrow construction of a grant of a public franchise or an agreement for a tax exemption. In general, it does not prefer the interest of a governmental agency as a party to a contract; government contracts are likely to be construed against the government as the drafting party. **Illustration:**

1. A is employed by B as an inventor. In an agreement settling their disputes on termination of the employment, A promises to assign to B all A's rights in a pending patent application and all improvements on the invention covered. Thereafter A makes an invention and applies for a patent, and B claims it as an improvement. The public interest in encouraging invention supports an interpretation of the agreement excluding future improvements unless future improvements were specifically included.

§ 208. Unconscionable Contract or Term

If a contract or term thereof is unconscionable at the time the contract is made a court may refuse to enforce the contract, or may enforce the remainder of the contract without the unconscionable term, or may so limit the application of any unconscionable term as to avoid any unconscionable result.

Comment:

a. Scope. Like the obligation of good faith and fair dealing (§ 205), the policy against unconscionable contracts or terms applies to a wide variety of types of conduct. The determination that a contract or term is or is not unconscionable is made in the light of its setting, purpose and effect. Relevant factors include weaknesses in the contracting process like those involved in more specific rules as to contractual capacity, fraud, and other invalidating causes; the policy also overlaps with rules which render particular bargains or terms unenforceable on grounds of public policy. Policing against unconscionable contracts or terms has sometimes been accomplished "by adverse construction of language, by manipulation of the rules of offer and acceptance or by determinations that the clause is contrary to public policy or to the dominant purpose of the contract." Uniform Commercial Code § 2-302 Comment 1. Particularly in the case of standardized agreements, the rule of this Section permits the court to pass directly on the unconscionability of the contract or clause rather than to avoid unconscionable results by interpretation. Compare § 211.

b. Historic standards. Traditionally, a bargain was said to be unconscionable in an action at law if it was "such as no man in his senses and not under delusion would make on the one hand, and as no honest and fair man would accept on the other;" damages were then limited to those to which the aggrieved party was "equitably" entitled. Hume v. United States, 132 U.S. 406 (1889), quoting Earl of Chesterfield v. Janssen, 2 Ves. Sen. 125, 155, 28 Eng. Rep. 82, 100 (Ch. 1750). Even though a contract was fully enforceable in an action for damages, equitable remedies such as specific performance were refused where "the sum total of its provisions drives too hard a bargain for a court of conscience to assist." Campbell Soup Co. v. Wentz, 172 F.2d 80, 84 (3d Cir. 1948). Modern procedural reforms have blurred the distinction between remedies at law and in equity. For contracts for the sale of goods, Uniform Commercial Code § 2-302 states the rule of this Section without distinction between law and equity. Comment 1 to that section adds, "The principle is one of the prevention of oppression and unfair surprise (Cf. Campbell Soup Co. v. Wentz, . . .) and not of disturbance of allocation of risks because of superior bargaining power."

c. Overall imbalance. Inadequacy of consideration does not of itself invalidate a bargain, but gross disparity in the values exchanged may be an important factor in a determination that a contract is unconscionable and may be sufficient ground, without more, for denying specific performance. See §§ 79, 364. Such a disparity may also corroborate indications of defects in the bargaining process, or may affect the remedy to be granted when there is a violation of a more specific rule. Theoretically it is possible for a contract to be oppressive taken as a whole, even though there is no weakness in the bargaining process and no single term which is in itself unconscionable. Ordinarily, however, an unconscionable contract involves other factors as well as overall imbalance. **Illustrations:**

> 1. A, an individual, contracts in June to sell at a fixed price per ton to B, a large soup manufacturer, the carrots to be grown on A's farm. The contract, written on B's standard printed form, is obviously drawn to protect B's interests and not A's; it contains numerous provisions to protect B against various contingencies and none giving analogous protection to A. Each of the clauses can be read restrictively so that it is not unconscionable, but several can be read literally to give unrestricted discretion to B. In January, when the market price has risen above the contract price, A repudiates the contract, and B seeks specific performance. In the absence of justification by evidence of commercial setting, purpose, or effect, the court may determine that the contract as a whole was unconscionable when made, and may then deny specific performance.

> 2. A, a homeowner, executes a standard printed form used by B, a merchant, agreeing to pay $ 1,700 for specified home improvements. A also executes a credit application asking for payment in 60 monthly installments but specifying no rate. Four days later A is informed that the credit application has been approved and is given a payment schedule calling for finance and insurance charges amounting to $ 800 in addition to the $ 1,700. Before B does any of the work, A repudiates the agreement, and B sues A for $ 800 damages, claiming that a commission of $ 800 was paid to B's salesman in reliance on the agreement. The court may determine that the agreement was unconscionable when made, and may then dismiss the claim.

d. Weakness in the bargaining process. A bargain is not unconscionable merely because the parties to it are unequal in bargaining position, nor even because the inequality results in an allocation of risks to the weaker party. But gross inequality of bargaining power, together with terms unreasonably favorable to the stronger party, may confirm indications that the transaction involved elements of deception or compulsion, or may show that the weaker party had no meaningful choice, no real alternative, or did not in fact assent or appear to assent to the unfair terms. Factors which may contribute to a finding of unconscionability in the bargaining process include the following: belief by the stronger party that there is no reasonable probability that the weaker party will fully perform the contract; knowledge of the stronger party that the weaker party will be unable to receive substantial benefits from the contract; knowledge of the stronger party that the weaker party is unable reasonably to protect his interests by reason of physical or mental infirmities, ignorance, illiteracy or inability to understand the language of the agreement, or similar factors. See Uniform Consumer Credit Code § 6.111. **Illustration:**

> 3. A, literate only in Spanish, is visited in his home by a salesman of refrigerator-freezers for B. They negotiate in Spanish; A tells the salesman he cannot afford to buy the appliance because his job will end in one week, and the salesman tells A that A will be paid numerous $ 25 commissions on sales to his friends. A signs a complex installment contract printed in English. The contract provides for a cash price of $ 900 plus a finance charge of $ 250. A defaults after paying $ 32, and B sues for the balance plus late charges and a 20% attorney's fee authorized by the contract. The appliance cost B $ 350. The court may determine that the contract was unconscionable when made, and may then limit B's recovery to a reasonable sum.

e. Unconscionable terms. Particular terms may be unconscionable whether or not the contract as a whole is unconscionable. Some types of terms are not enforced, regardless of context; examples are provisions for unreasonably large liquidated damages, or limitations on a debtor's right to redeem collateral. See Uniform Commercial Code §§ 2-718, 9-501(3). Other terms may be unconscionable in some contexts but not in others. Overall imbalance and weaknesses in the bargaining process are then important. **Illustrations:**

> 4. A, a packer, sells and ships 300 cases of canned catsup to B, a wholesale grocer. The contract provides, "All claims other than swells must be made within ten days from receipt of goods." Six months later a government inspector, upon microscopic examination of samples, finds excessive mold in the cans and obtains a court or-

der for destruction of the 270 remaining cases in B's warehouse. In the absence of justifying evidence, the court may determine that the quoted clause is unconscionable as applied to latent defects and does not bar a claim for damages for breach of warranty by B against A.

5. A, a retail furniture store, sells furniture on installment credit to B, retaining a security interest. As A knows, B is a woman of limited education, separated from her husband, maintaining herself and seven children by means of $ 218 per month public assistance. After 13 purchases over a period of five years for a total of $ 1,200, B owes A $ 164. B then buys a stereo set for $ 514. Each contract contains a paragraph of some 800 words in extremely fine print, in the middle of which are the words "all payments . . . shall be credited pro rata on all outstanding . . . accounts." The effect of this language is to keep a balance due on each item until all are paid for. On B's default, A sues for possession of all the items sold. It may be determined that either the quoted clause or the contract as a whole was unconscionable when made.

6. A, a corporation with its principal office in State X, contracts with B, a resident of State X, to make improvements on B's home in State X. The contract is made on A's standard printed form, which contains a clause by which the parties submit to the jurisdiction of a court in State Y, 200 miles away. No reason for the clause appears except to make litigation inconvenient and expensive for B. The clause is unconscionable.

f. Law and fact. A determination that a contract or term is unconscionable is made by the court in the light of all the material facts. Under Uniform Commercial Code § 2-302, the determination is made "as a matter of law," but the parties are to be afforded an opportunity to present evidence as to commercial setting, purpose and effect to aid the court in its determination. Incidental findings of fact are made by the court rather than by a jury, but are accorded the usual weight given to such findings of fact in appellate review. An appellate court will also consider whether proper standards were applied. **Illustration:**

7. A, a finance company, lends money to B, a manufacturing company, on the security of an assignment by B of its accounts receivable. The agreement provides for loans of 75% of the value of assigned accounts acceptable to A, and forbids B to dispose of or hypothecate any assets without A's written consent. The agreed interest rate of 18% would be usurious but for a statute precluding a corporation from raising the defense of usury. Substantial advances are made, and the balance owed is $ 14,000 when B becomes bankrupt, three months after the first advance. A determination that the agreement is unconscionable on its face, without regard to context, is error. The agreement is unconscionable only if it is not a reasonable commercial device in the light of all the circumstances when it was made.

g. Remedies. Perhaps the simplest application of the policy against unconscionable agreements is the denial of specific performance where the contract as a whole was unconscionable when made. If such a contract is entirely executory, denial of money damages may also be appropriate. But the policy is not penal: unless the parties can be restored to their pre-contract positions, the offending party will ordinarily be awarded at least the reasonable value of performance rendered by him. Where a term rather than the entire contract is unconscionable, the appropriate remedy is ordinarily to deny effect to the unconscionable term. In such cases as that of an exculpatory term, the effect may be to enlarge the liability of the offending party.

Topic 3. Effect of Adoption of a Writing

Introductory Note The parties to an agreement often reduce all or part of it to writing. Their purpose in so doing is commonly to provide reliable evidence of its making and its terms and to avoid trusting to uncertain memory. Such a purpose is so common that it is often not discussed; it may not even be conscious. In the interest of certainty and security of transactions, the law gives special effect to a writing adopted as a final expression of an agreement. Such a writing is here referred to as an "integrated agreement" (§ 209).

The principal effects of a binding integrated agreement are to focus interpretation on the meaning of the terms embodied in the writing (§ 212), to discharge prior inconsistent agreements, and, in a case of complete integration, to discharge prior agreements within its scope regardless of consistency

(§ 213). Evidence of prior agreements and negotiations is admissible for a variety of purposes, but the admissibility of evidence to contradict an integrated agreement or to add to a completely integrated agreement is restricted, and a limit is thus placed on the power of the trier of fact to exercise a dispensing power in the guise of a finding of fact. The effect of usage on an integrated agreement is treated in Topic 4, §§ 219-23.

§ 209. Integrated Agreements

(1) An integrated agreement is a writing or writings constituting a final expression of one or more terms of an agreement.

(2) Whether there is an integrated agreement is to be determined by the court as a question preliminary to determination of a question of interpretation or to application of the parol evidence rule.

(3) Where the parties reduce an agreement to a writing which in view of its completeness and specificity reasonably appears to be a complete agreement, it is taken to be an integrated agreement unless it is established by other evidence that the writing did not constitute a final expression.

Comment:

a. Significance of integration. Where the parties to an agreement have reduced a term of the agreement to specific words or other symbols, interpretation of that term relates to the meaning of the words and symbols used. See § 212. An integrated agreement supersedes contrary prior statements, and a completely integrated agreement supersedes even consistent additional terms. See §§ 213-16. But both integrated and unintegrated agreements are to be read in the light of the circumstances and may be explained or supplemented by operative usages of trade, by the course of dealing between the parties, and by the course of performance of the agreement.

b. Form of integrated agreement. No particular form is required for an integrated agreement. Written contracts, signed by both parties, may include an explicit declaration that there are no other agreements between the parties, but such a declaration may not be conclusive. The intention of the parties may also be manifested without explicit statement and without signature. A letter, telegram or other informal document written by one party may be orally assented to by the other as a final expression of some or all of the terms of their agreement. Indeed, the parties to an oral agreement may choose their words with such explicit precision and completeness that the same legal consequences follow as where there is a completely integrated agreement. **Illustrations:**

1. A and B enter into an oral contract, and prepare and sign a writing to incorporate its terms. Though the writing contains substantially all the orally agreed terms, they are not fully satisfied with it, and they agree to have it re-drafted. There is no integrated agreement.

2. A orally agrees to employ B on certain terms. B immediately writes and A receives a letter beginning, "Confirming our oral arrangement this morning," and fully stating the contract as he understands it. A makes no reply but with knowledge of B's understanding accepts services from B under the contract. The letter is a completely integrated agreement. Even though the letter is not in all respects accurate, it operates as an offer of substituted terms, and A's acquiescence manifests assent to those terms.

c. Proof of integration. Whether a writing has been adopted as an integrated agreement is a question of fact to be determined in accordance with all relevant evidence. The issue is distinct from the issues whether an agreement was made and whether the document is genuine, and also from the issue whether it was intended as a complete and exclusive statement of the agreement. See § 210; compare Uniform Commercial Code § 2-202. Ordinarily the issue whether there is an integrated agreement is determined by the trial judge in the first instance as a question preliminary to an interpretative ruling or to the application of the parol evidence rule. See §§ 212, 213. After the preliminary determination, such questions as whether the agreement was in fact made may remain to be decided by the trier of fact. Subsection (3) states the rule that a written agreement complete on its face is taken to be an integrated agreement in the absence of contrary evidence. **Illustration:**

> 3. A sells and delivers a hotel to B. Later A takes possession of the hotel furniture, and B sues to recover it. B claims the furniture under an oral agreement; A proves an apparently complete written agreement for the sale of the real property, and objects to consideration of the oral agreement. In the absence of contrary evidence, the writing is taken to be an integration; whether it is a complete integration is decided on the basis of all relevant evidence. If the oral agreement contradicts the writing, or if the writing is a complete integration, evidence of the oral agreement is excluded; otherwise the trier of fact is to decide whether the oral agreement was made.

§ 210. Completely and Partially Integrated Agreements

(1) A completely integrated agreement is an integrated agreement adopted by the parties as a complete and exclusive statement of the terms of the agreement.

(2) A partially integrated agreement is an integrated agreement other than a completely integrated agreement.

(3) Whether an agreement is completely or partially integrated is to be determined by the court as a question preliminary to determination of a question of interpretation or to application of the parol evidence rule.

Comment:

a. Complete integration. The definition in Subsection (1) is to be read with the definition of integrated agreement in § 209, to reject the assumption sometimes made that because a writing has been worked out which is final on some matters, it is to be taken as including all the matters agreed upon. Even though there is an integrated agreement, consistent additional terms not reduced to writing may be shown, unless the court finds that the writing was assented to by both parties as a complete and exclusive statement of all the terms. Upon such a finding, however, evidence of the alleged making of consistent additional terms must be kept from the trier of fact. See § 216; Uniform Commercial Code § 2-202 Comment 3.

b. Proof of complete integration. That a writing was or was not adopted as a completely integrated agreement may be proved by any relevant evidence. A document in the form of a written contract, signed by both parties and apparently complete on its face, may be decisive of the issue in the absence of credible contrary evidence. But a writing cannot of itself prove its own completeness, and wide latitude must be allowed for inquiry into circumstances bearing on the intention of the parties. **Illustration:**

> 1. A, a college, owns premises which have no toilet or plumbing facilities or heating equipment. In negotiating a lease to B for use of the premises as a radio station, A orally agrees to permit the use of facilities in an adjacent building and to provide heat. The parties subsequently execute a written lease agreement which makes no mention of facilities or heat. The question whether the written lease was adopted as a completely integrated agreement is to be decided on the basis of all relevant evidence of the prior and contemporaneous conduct and language of the parties.

c. Partial integration. It is often clear from the face of a writing that it is incomplete and cannot be more than a partially integrated agreement. Incompleteness may also be shown by other writings, which may or may not become part of a completely or partially integrated agreement. Or it may be shown by any relevant evidence, oral or written, that an apparently complete writing never became fully effective, or that it was modified after initial adoption. **Illustration:**

> 2. A writes to B a letter offer containing four provisions. B replies by letter that three of the provisions are satisfactory, but makes a counter proposal as to the fourth. After further discussion of the fourth provision, the parties come to oral agreement on a revision of it, but make no further statements as to the other three terms. A's letter is a partially integrated agreement with respect to the first three provisions.

§ 211. Standardized Agreements

(1) Except as stated in Subsection (3), where a party to an agreement signs or otherwise manifests assent to a writing and has reason to believe that like writings are regularly used to embody terms of agreements of the same type, he adopts the writing as an integrated agreement with respect to the terms included in the writing.

(2) Such a writing is interpreted wherever reasonable as treating alike all those similarly situated, without regard to their knowledge or understanding of the standard terms of the writing.

(3) Where the other party has reason to believe that the party manifesting such assent would not do so if he knew that the writing contained a particular term, the term is not part of the agreement.

Comment:

a. Utility of standardization. Standardization of agreements serves many of the same functions as standardization of goods and services; both are essential to a system of mass production and distribution. Scarce and costly time and skill can be devoted to a class of transactions rather than to details of individual transactions. Legal rules which would apply in the absence of agreement can be shaped to fit the particular type of transaction, and extra copies of the form can be used for purposes such as record-keeping, coordination and supervision. Forms can be tailored to office routines, the training of personnel, and the requirements of mechanical equipment. Sales personnel and customers are freed from attention to numberless variations and can focus on meaningful choice among a limited number of significant features: transaction-type, style, quantity, price, or the like. Operations are simplified and costs reduced, to the advantage of all concerned.

b. Assent to unknown terms. A party who makes regular use of a standardized form of agreement does not ordinarily expect his customers to understand or even to read the standard terms. One of the purposes of standardization is to eliminate bargaining over details of individual transactions, and that purpose would not be served if a substantial number of customers retained counsel and reviewed the standard terms. Employees regularly using a form often have only a limited understanding of its terms and limited authority to vary them. Customers do not in fact ordinarily understand or even read the standard terms. They trust to the good faith of the party using the form and to the tacit representation that like terms are being accepted regularly by others similarly situated. But they understand that they are assenting to the terms not read or not understood, subject to such limitations as the law may impose.

c. Review of unfair terms. Standardized agreements are commonly prepared by one party. The customer assents to a few terms, typically inserted in blanks on the printed form, and gives blanket assent to the type of transaction embodied in the standard form. He is commonly not represented in the drafting, and the draftsman may be tempted to overdraw in the interest of his employer. The obvious danger of overreaching has resulted in government regulation of insurance policies, bills of lading, retail installment sales, small loans, and other particular types of contracts. Regulation sometimes includes administrative review of standard terms, or even prescription of terms. Apart from such regulation, standard terms imposed by one party are enforced. But standard terms may be superseded by separately negotiated or added terms (§ 203), they are construed against the draftsman (§ 206), and they are subject to the overriding obligation of good faith (§ 205) and to the power of the court to refuse to enforce an unconscionable contract or term (§ 208). Moreover, various contracts and terms are against public policy and unenforceable. See Chapter 8.

d. Non-contractual documents. The same document may serve both contractual and other purposes, and a party may assent to it for other purposes without understanding that it embodies contract terms. He may nevertheless be bound if he has reason to know that it is used to embody contract terms. Insurance policies, steamship tickets, bills of lading, and warehouse receipts are commonly so obviously contractual in form as to give the customer reason to know their character. But baggage checks or automobile parking lot tickets may appear to be mere identification tokens, and a party without knowledge or reason to know that the token purports to be a contract is then not bound by terms printed on the token. Documents such as invoices, instructions for use, and the like, delivered after a contract is made, may raise similar problems. **Illustrations:**

1. A delivers a fur coat to B for storage and receives a warehouse receipt which purports on its face to set forth the terms of the storage contract. By accepting the receipt, whether or not A reads it or understands it, A assents to its terms.

2. A pays ten cents and checks a parcel in a parcel room in a bus terminal, and receives a parcel check three inches long and two and one-half inches wide. The check bears an identifying number and the word "contract," both conspicuous, and contractual terms in fine print, but A does not read it or know of the terms until later. The terms are not part of the checking agreement.

3. A sells plant bulbs to B. Later A delivers the bulbs with an invoice containing contractual language. B writes on a copy of the invoice "picked up October 27th" and signs his name. The invoice terms are not part of the contract.

e. Equality of treatment. One who assents to standard contract terms normally assumes that others are doing likewise and that all who do so are on an equal footing. In the case of a public utility, that assumption is fortified by statutory and common law limitations on discrimination among customers; a term prescribed by statute or regulation in the case of an insurance policy also carries an assurance of equal treatment. Apart from government regulation, courts in construing and applying a standardized contract seek to effectuate the reasonable expectations of the average member of the public who accepts it. The result may be to give the advantage of a restrictive reading to some sophisticated customers who contracted with knowledge of an ambiguity or dispute. **Illustration:**

4. A, an insurance company, issues an insurance policy to B covering injuries "by accidental means." A clause in the policy excludes "disability or other loss resulting from or contributed to by any disease or ailment." B believes himself to be in good health, but has a latent Parkinson's disease. Later an accidental blow activates the disease into a disabling condi-

tion. B is covered by the policy without regard to his knowledge or understanding of the quoted language at the time of contracting.

f. Terms excluded. Subsection (3) applies to standardized agreements the general principles stated in §§ 20 and 201. Although customers typically adhere to standardized agreements and are bound by them without even appearing to know the standard terms in detail, they are not bound to unknown terms which are beyond the range of reasonable expectation. A debtor who delivers a check to his creditor with the amount blank does not authorize the insertion of an infinite figure. Similarly, a party who adheres to the other party's standard terms does not assent to a term if the other party has reason to believe that the adhering party would not have accepted the agreement if he had known that the agreement contained the particular term. Such a belief or assumption may be shown by the prior negotiations or inferred from the circumstances. Reason to believe may be inferred from the fact that the term is bizarre or oppressive, from the fact that it eviscerates the non-standard terms explicitly agreed to, or from the fact that it eliminates the dominant purpose of the transaction. The inference is reinforced if the adhering party never had an opportunity to read the term, or if it is illegible or otherwise hidden from view. This rule is closely related to the policy against unconscionable terms and the rule of interpretation against the draftsman. See §§ 206 and 208. **Illustrations:**

5. A applies to B, an insurance company, for burglary insurance. B issues to A a written binder by which B "agrees to insure property as herein described for amounts subscribed" until a policy is issued. The policy in ordinary use by B includes a provision for cancellation by B on written notice and requires suit within one year after loss. Those terms are part of the contract.

6. A ships goods via B, a carrier. B carries an insurance policy with C, an insurance company, and with C's authority issues to A a certificate that A's shipment is insured under the policy. The policy contains a clause excluding coverage of trips on the Great Lakes unless approved by D, an individual, but this clause is not referred to in the certificate or known to A. It is not part of the contract between A and C.

. . .

§ 212. Interpretation of Integrated Agreement

(1) The interpretation of an integrated agreement is directed to the meaning of the terms of the writing or writings in the light of the circumstances, in accordance with the rules stated in this Chapter.

(2) A question of interpretation of an integrated agreement is to be determined by the trier of fact if it depends on the credibility of extrinsic evidence or on a choice among reasonable inferences to be drawn from extrinsic evidence. Otherwise a question of interpretation of an integrated agreement is to be determined as a question of law.

Comment:

a. "Objective" and "subjective" meaning. Interpretation of contracts deals with the meaning given to language and other conduct by the parties rather than with meanings established by law. But the relevant intention of a party is that manifested by him rather than any different undisclosed intention. In cases of misunderstanding, there may be a contract in accordance with the meaning of one party if the other knows or has reason to know of the misunderstanding and the first party does not. See §§ 200, 201. The meaning of one party may prevail as to one term and the meaning of the other as to another term; thus the contract as a whole may not be entirely in accordance with the understanding of either. When a party is thus held to a meaning of which he had reason to know, it is sometimes said that the "objective" meaning of his language or other conduct prevails over his "subjective" meaning. Even so, the operative meaning is found in the transaction and its context rather than in the law or in the usages of people other than the parties. **Illustrations:**

1. In an integrated agreement A promises to sell and B to buy described real estate. A intends to sell Blackacre; B intends to buy Whiteacre. The writing reasonably describes Greenacre, and neither party has any more reason that the other to know of the misdescription. There is no contract.

2. In an integrated agreement A agrees to sell and B to buy certain patent rights. A intends to sell only the rights under the British patent on a certain invention; B intends also to buy rights under American and French patents. If A has reason to know that B intends to buy the American rights, B has reason to know that A does not intend to sell the French rights, and the language used can be read to cover the British and American but not the French rights, that may be determined to be the proper interpretation.

b. Plain meaning and extrinsic evidence. It is sometimes said that extrinsic evidence cannot change the plain meaning of a writing, but meaning can almost never be plain except in a context. Accordingly, the rule stated in Subsection (1) is not limited to cases where it is determined that the language used is ambiguous. Any determination of meaning or ambiguity should only be made in the light of the relevant evidence of the situation and relations of the parties, the subject matter of the transaction, preliminary negotiations and statements made therein, usages of trade, and the course of dealing between the parties. See §§ 202, 219-23. But after the transaction has been shown in all its length and breadth, the words of an integrated agreement remain the most important evidence of intention. Standards of preference among reasonable meanings are stated in §§ 203, 206, 207. **Illustrations:**

3. A agrees orally with B, a stockbroker, that in transactions between them "abracadabra" shall mean X Company. A sends a signed written order to B to buy 100 shares "abracadabra," and B buys 100 shares of X Company. The parties are bound in accordance with the oral agreement.

4. A and B are engaged in buying and selling shares of stock from each other, and agree orally to conceal the nature of their dealings by using the word "sell" to mean "buy" and using the word "buy" to mean "sell." A sends a written offer to B to "sell" certain shares, and B accepts. The parties are bound in accordance with the oral agreement.

c. Statements of intention. The rule of Subsection (1) permits reference to the negotiations of the parties, including statements of intention and even positive promises, so long as they are used to show the meaning of the writing. A contrary rule in the interpretation of wills is sometimes stated broadly enough to apply to the interpretation of contracts, but that rule is subject to exceptions and rests in part on the more rigorous formal requirements to which wills are subject. Statements of a contracting party subsequent to the adoption of an integration are admissible against him to show his understanding of the meaning asserted by the other party. **Illustrations:**

> 5. In an integrated agreement A promises B to insert B's "business card" in A's "advertising chart" for a price to be paid when the chart is "published." The quoted terms are to be read in the light of the circumstances known to the parties, including their oral statements as to their meaning.

> 6. In an integrated agreement A contracts to sell "my horse," and B contracts to buy it. A owns two horses. It may be shown by oral evidence, including statements of the parties, that both A and B meant the same horse.

d. "Question of law." Analytically, what meaning is attached to a word or other symbol by one or more people is a question of fact. But general usage as to the meaning of words in the English language is commonly a proper subject for judicial notice without the aid of evidence extrinsic to the writing. Historically, moreover, partly perhaps because of the fact that jurors were often illiterate, questions of interpretation of written documents have been treated as questions of law in the sense that they are decided by the trial judge rather than by the jury. Likewise, since an appellate court is commonly in as good a position to decide such questions as the trial judge, they have been treated as questions of law for purposes of appellate review. Such treatment has the effect of limiting the power of the trier of fact to exercise a dispensing power in the guise of a finding of fact, and thus contributes to the stability and predictability of contractual relations. In cases of standardized contracts such as insurance policies, it also provides a method of assuring that like cases will be decided alike.

e. Evaluation of extrinsic evidence. Even though an agreement is not integrated, or even though the meaning of an integrated agreement depends on extrinsic evidence, a question of interpretation is not left to the trier of fact where the evidence is so clear that no reasonable person would determine the issue in any way but one. But if the issue depends on evidence outside the writing, and the possible inferences are conflicting, the choice is for the trier of fact.

§ 213. Effect of Integrated Agreement on Prior Agreements (Parol Evidence Rule)

(1) A binding integrated agreement discharges prior agreements to the extent that it is inconsistent with them.

(2) A binding completely integrated agreement discharges prior agreements to the extent that they are within its scope.

(3) An integrated agreement that is not binding or that is voidable and avoided does not discharge a prior agreement. But an integrated agreement, even though not binding, may be effective to render inoperative a term which would have been part of the agreement if it had not been integrated.

Comment:

a. Parol evidence rule. This Section states what is commonly known as the parol evidence rule. It is not a rule of evidence but a rule of substantive law. Nor is it a rule of interpretation; it defines the subject matter of interpretation. It renders inoperative prior written agreements as well as prior oral agreements. Where writings relating to the same subject matter are assented to as parts of one transaction, both form part of the integrated agreement. Where an agreement is partly oral and partly written, the writing is at most a partially integrated agreement. See § 209.

b. Inconsistent terms. Whether a binding agreement is completely integrated or partially integrated, it supersedes inconsistent terms of prior agreements. To apply this rule, the court must make preliminary determinations that there is an integrated agreement and that it is inconsistent with the term in question. See § 209. Those determinations are made in accordance with all relevant evidence, and require interpretation both of the integrated agreement and of the prior agreement. The existence of the prior agreement may be a circumstance which sheds light on the meaning of the integrated agreement, but the integrated agreement must be given a meaning to which its language is reasonably susceptible when read in the light of all the circumstances. See §§ 212, 214. **Illustrations:**

1. D Corporation regularly borrows money from C Bank. S, the principal stockholder in D, offers to guarantee payment if C will increase the amounts lent. There is a bank custom to make such loans only on adequate collateral supplied by the borrower, and C promises S to follow the custom. S then executes a written agreement with C guaranteeing payment of future loans to D "with or without security." If the written agreement is a binding integrated agreement, C's prior promise is discharged.

2. A orally agrees to sell a city lot to B. The city is installing a sidewalk in front of the lot, and A orally agrees to pay the cost to be assessed by the city in an amount not exceeding $ 45. B then retains a lawyer to draw up a written agreement, and A and B execute it, A without reading it. The agreement provides that A will pay all costs of the installation of the sidewalk, but does not mention any dollar limit. If the written agreement is a binding integrated agreement, any agreement for a $ 45 limit is discharged.

c. Scope of a completely integrated agreement. Where the parties have adopted a writing as a complete and exclusive statement of the terms of the agreement, even consistent additional terms are superseded. See § 216. But there may still be a separate agreement between the same parties which is not affected. To apply the rule of Subsection (2) the court in addition to determining that there is an integrated agreement and that it is completely integrated, must determine that the asserted prior agreement is within the scope of the integrated agreement. Those determinations are made in accordance with all relevant evidence, and require interpretation both of the integrated agreement and of the prior agreement. **Illustrations:**

3. In May A and B exchange properties and agree orally that A will make certain repairs on the property to be conveyed by A to B, the repairs to be finished by October 1. A and B then draw up and sign a memorandum of the repair agreement, specifying all the terms except that the memorandum is silent as to time of performance. If the memorandum is a binding completely integrated agreement, the agreement to finish by October 1 is discharged, and the repairs are to be finished within a reasonable time.

The oral agreement as to October 1 may be relevant evidence as to what is a reasonable time.

4. A and B make an oral agreement for the sale of land and a hotel thereon, together with the hotel furniture. They employ a lawyer to prepare a written contract. He does so, and they sign it. It contains no mention of personal property. The agreement as to furniture is discharged if there is a binding completely integrated agreement covering the entire transaction, but not if only the part of the agreement relating to real property is integrated.

d. Effect of non-binding integration. An integrated agreement does not supersede prior agreements if it is not binding, for example, by reason of lack of consideration, or if it is voidable and avoided. The circumstances may, however, show an agreement to discharge a prior agreement without regard to whether the integrated agreement is binding, and such an agreement may be effective. Moreover, an integrated agreement may be effective to render inoperative an oral term which would have been part of the agreement if it had not been integrated. The integrated agreement may then be without consideration, even though the inoperative oral term would have furnished consideration. **Illustrations:**

5. A and B enter into a contract that B will build a house on A's land for a price. Later they enter into an oral contract by which B promises to add a porch and A promises to pay an extra $ 2,000. Still later they enter into an integrated agreement in which B promises to build according to the original plans and A promises to pay the extra $ 2,000. The integrated agreement is not binding for lack of consideration, and the oral intermediate agreement is not discharged.

6. A and B enter into a contract that B will build a house on A's land for a price. Later B offers to add a porch if A will sign a new contract. They then enter into an integrated agreement in which B promises to build according to the original plans and A promises to pay an extra $ 2,000. If the integrated agreement is inconsistent with the porch offer, or if it is a completely integrated agreement and the matter of the porch is within its scope, the integrated agreement is effective to discharge the porch offer but is not binding for lack of consideration.

§ 214. Evidence of Prior or Contemporaneous Agreements and Negotiations

Agreements and negotiations prior to or contemporaneous with the adoption of a writing are admissible in evidence to establish

(a) that the writing is or is not an integrated agreement;

(b) that the integrated agreement, if any, is completely or partially integrated;

(c) the meaning of the writing, whether or not integrated;

(d) illegality, fraud, duress, mistake, lack of consideration, or other invalidating cause;

(e) ground for granting or denying rescission, reformation, specific performance, or other remedy.

Comment:

a. Integrated agreement and completely integrated agreement. Whether a writing has been adopted as an integrated agreement and, if so, whether the agreement is completely or partially integrated are questions determined by the court preliminary to determination of a question of interpretation or to application of the parol evidence rule. See § 209-13. Writings do not prove themselves; ordinarily, if there is dispute, there must be testimony that there was a signature or other manifestation of assent. The preliminary determination is made in accordance with all relevant evidence, including the circumstances in which the writing was made or adopted. It may require preliminary interpretation of the writing; the court must then consider the evidence which is relevant to the question of interpretation.

b. Interpretation. Words, written or oral, cannot apply themselves to the subject matter. The expressions and general tenor of speech used in negotiations are admissible to show the conditions existing when the writing was made, the application of the words, and the meaning or meanings of the parties. Even though words seem on their face to have only a single possible meaning, other meanings often appear when the circumstances are disclosed. In cases of misunderstanding, there must be inquiry into the meaning attached to the words by each party and into what each knew or had reason to know. See § 201. **Illustrations:**

1. A and B in an integrated contract agree that A shall serve as captain of B's ship, and shall have a certain rate of pay instead of "privilege and primage." Previous negotiations showing that the meaning to the parties of the quoted words when used was the privilege of transporting goods in the captain's cabin establish that as the meaning in the contract.   2 .

In an integrated contract with A, B promises to buy "your wool." Previous negotiations of the parties related to both wool from A's sheep and wool that A had contracted to buy from other persons. The negotiations are admissible to establish both classes as the meaning of the words "your wool" in the contract.

. . .

4. A and B make an integrated contract by which A promises to sell and B to buy goods "ex Peerless." Evidence is admissible to show that there are two ships of that name, which one each party meant, and, in case of misunderstanding, whether either had knowledge or reason to know of the other's meaning.

c. Invalidating cause. What appears to be a complete and binding integrated agreement may be a forgery, a joke, a sham, or an agreement without consideration, or it may be voidable for fraud, duress, mistake, or the like, or it may be illegal. Such invalidating causes need not and commonly do not appear on the face of the writing. They are not affected even by a "merger" clause. See Comment *e* to § 216. **Illustrations:**

5. A and B make an integrated agreement by which A promises to complete an unfinished building according to certain plans and specifications, and B promises to pay A $ 2,000 for so doing. It may be shown that, by a contract made previously with B, A had promised to erect and complete the building for $ 10,000; that he had not fully completed it though paid the whole price. This evidence is admissible to show that there is no consideration for B's new promise, since A is promising no more than he is bound by his original contract to perform.

6. A and B make an integrated agreement by which A promises to sell and B promises to buy a large quantity of rifles. It may be shown that A and B had previously agreed that the rifles when bought by B should be used in fomenting a rebellion in violation of law.

d. Remedies. A contract which is fully enforceable in an action for damages may be subject to equitable remedies such as rescission or reformation by reason of fraud, mistake or the like. Specific performance may be denied by reason of oppression or unfairness, or other remedies may be withheld or limited where the contract or a term is unconscionable. See § 208. Evidence of the circumstances in which the contract was made may be relevant to such remedial issues, even though it also shows an agreement or proposal superseded by a later integrated contract. **Illustration:**

7. A and B make an integrated agreement by which A promises to sell and B promises to buy a tract of land described in the agreement. Owing to a mutual mistake the description is not an accurate one of the tract in regard to which both A and B were bargaining. Prior oral agreements may be shown to establish the right to reformation of the integration so that it shall accurately describe the tract intended.

§ 215. Contradiction of Integrated Terms

Except as stated in the preceding Section, where there is a binding agreement, either completely or partially integrated, evidence of prior or contemporaneous agreements or negotiations is not admissible in evidence to contradict a term of the writing.

Comment:

a. Relation to other rules. Like § 216, this Section states an evidentiary consequence of § 213. A binding integrated agreement discharges inconsistent prior agreements, and evidence of a prior agreement is therefore irrelevant to the rights of the parties when offered to contradict a term of the writing. The same evidence may be properly considered on the preliminary issues whether there is an integrated agreement and whether it is completely or partially integrated. See §§ 209, 210. If there is a finding that there is an integrated agreement or a completely integrated agreement, the evidence may nevertheless be relevant to a question of interpretation, to a question of invalidating cause, or to a question of remedy. See § 214. But the earlier agreement, no matter how clear, cannot override a later agreement which supersedes or amends it.

b. Interpretation and contradiction. An earlier agreement may help the interpretation of a later one, but it may not contradict a binding later integrated agreement. Whether there is contradiction depends, as is stated in § 213, on whether the two are consistent or inconsistent. This is a question which often cannot be determined from the face of the writing; the writing must first be applied to its subject matter and placed in context. The question is then decided by the court as part of a question of interpretation. Where reasonable people could differ as to the credibility of the evidence offered and the evidence if believed could lead a reasonable person to interpret the writing as claimed by the proponent of the evidence, the question of credibility and the choice among reasonable inferences should be treated as questions of fact. But the asserted meaning must be one to which the language of the writing, read in context, is reasonably susceptible. If no other meaning is reasonable, the court should rule as a matter of law that the meaning is established. See § 212(2).

§ 216. Consistent Additional Terms

(1) Evidence of a consistent additional term is admissible to supplement an integrated agreement unless the court finds that the agreement was completely integrated.

(2) An agreement is not completely integrated if the writing omits a consistent additional agreed term which is

(a) agreed to for separate consideration, or

(b) such a term as in the circumstances might naturally be omitted from the writing.

Comment:

a. Relation to other rules. Like § 215, this Section states an evidentiary consequence of § 213. It also limits the concept of a completely integrated agreement set forth in § 210. Compare Uniform Commercial Code § 2-202(b). Where the limitation is not applicable, the court must decide whether the agreement is completely integrated on the basis of all relevant evidence, including the evidence of consistent additional terms.

b. Consistency. Terms of prior agreements are superseded to the extent that they are inconsistent with an integrated agreement, and evidence of them is not admissible to contradict a term of the integration. See §§ 213, 215. The determination whether an alleged additional term is consistent or inconsistent with the integrated agreement requires interpretation of the writing in the light of all the circumstances, including the evidence of the additional term. For this purpose, the meaning of the writing includes not only the terms explicitly stated but also those fairly implied as part of the bargain of the parties in fact. It does not include a term supplied by a rule of law designed to fill gaps where the parties have not agreed otherwise, unless it can be inferred that the parties contracted with reference to the rule of law. There is no clear line between implications of fact and rules of law filling gaps; although fairly clear examples of each can be given, other cases will involve almost imperceptible shadings. See § 204. **Illustrations:**

> 1. A check states no date of payment, but it is orally agreed that the check will be paid only after six months. The oral agreement contradicts the check. Under Uniform Commercial Code § 3-108 the check is payable on demand, and most competent adults in the United States have reason to know the rule.
>
> 2. A owes B two debts, and sends a check for an amount less than the amount of either. In the absence of any contrary manifestation of intention by either party, the rule of law would be that the check is applied to the debt which first matured. An agreement that the other debt is to be paid is not inconsistent with the check.

c. Separate consideration. Where there is a binding completely integrated agreement, even consistent additional terms are superseded if they are within the scope of the agreement. See § 213. A separate contract, not covered by the integrated agreement, is not superseded. The rule of Subsection (2)(a) goes further; it limits the scope of the integrated agreement by excluding a consistent additional term made for separate consideration even though the additional term and its consideration are part of the same contract. This rule may be regarded as a particular application of the rule of Subsection (2)(b). **Illustration:**

> 3. A and B in an integrated writing promise to sell and buy a specific automobile. As part of the transaction they orally agree that B may keep the automobile in A's garage for one year, paying $ 15 a month. The oral agreement is not within the scope of the integration and is not superseded.

d. Terms omitted naturally. If it is claimed that a consistent additional term was omitted from an integrated agreement and the omission seems natural in the circumstances, it is not necessary to consider further the questions whether the agreement is completely integrated and whether the omitted term is within its scope, although factual questions may remain. This situation is especially likely to arise when the writing is in a standardized form which does not lend itself to the insertion of additional terms. Thus agreements collateral to a negotiable instrument if written on the instrument might destroy its negotiability or otherwise make it less acceptable to third parties; the instrument may not have space for the additional term. Leases and conveyances are also often in a standard form which leads naturally to the omission of terms which are not standard. These examples are not exclusive. Moreover, there is no rule or policy penalizing a party merely because his mode of agreement does not seem natural to others. Even though the omission does not seem natural, evidence of the consistent additional terms is admissible unless the court finds that the writing was intended as a complete and exclusive statement of the terms of the agreement. See § 210. **Illustrations:**

> 4. A owes B $ 1,000. They agree orally that A will sell B Blackacre for $ 3,000 and that the $ 1,000 will be credited against the price, and then sign a written agreement, complete on its face, which does not mention the $ 1,000 debt or the credit. The written agreement is not completely integrated, and the oral agreement for a credit is admissible in evidence to supplement the written agreement.
>
> 5. A and B sign a written agreement, complete on its face, that A will sell B Blackacre for $ 3,000, conveyance and payment to be made within 60 days. It is claimed that B was about to render services for A and that the written agreement was signed on the oral understanding that B would be permitted to pay the price by rendering the services at $ 50 an hour. The oral understanding is admissible in evidence unless it is found that the written agreement was completely integrated.
>
> . . .

e. Written term excluding oral terms ("merger" clause). Written agreements often contain clauses stating that there are no representations, promises or agreements between the parties except those found in the writing. Such a clause may negate the apparent authority of an agent to vary orally the written terms, and if agreed to is likely to conclude the issue whether the agreement is completely integrated. Consistent additional terms may then be excluded even though their omission would have been natural in the absence of such a clause. But such a clause does not control the question whether the writing was assented to as an integrated agreement, the scope of the writing if completely integrated, or the interpretation of the written terms.

§ 217. Integrated Agreement Subject to Oral Requirement of a Condition Where the parties to a written agreement agree orally that performance of the agreement is subject to the occurrence of a stated condition, the agreement is not integrated with respect to the oral condition.
Comment:

a. Relation to other rules. This Section states a rule for unsealed writings which is similar in operation to the rules governing delivery of a sealed promise in escrow or its conditional delivery to the promisee. See § 103. If an unrestricted power of revocation is reserved by either party, there is no contract until he acts further. But if performance of the written agreement is subject to an oral requirement of a condition not within the control of either party, there may be a binding contract creating immediate conditional rights. In such a case the precise legal consequences may turn on inquiry into what the parties in fact agreed to. The writing, if so intended, may be a partially integrated agreement and may automatically become a completely integrated agreement on the occurrence of the oral requirement of a condition. See §§ 209, 210. **Illustrations:**

   1. A and B agree that A will sell a patent to B for $ 10,000 if C, an engineer advising B, approves. A and B sign a written agreement covering all of the agreement except C's approval, and agree orally that it will take effect only if C approves. There is an immediate contract, but B's duty is conditional on C's approval.
   . . .

b. Requirement of a condition inconsistent with a written term. The rule of this Section may be regarded as a particular application of the rule of § 216(2)(b), giving effect to consistent additional terms omitted naturally from a writing. So regarded, it has sometimes been limited to requirements of conditions consistent with the written terms. But an oral requirement of a condition is never completely consistent with a signed written agreement which is complete on its face; in such cases evidence of the oral requirement bears directly on the issues whether the writing was adopted as an integrated agreement and if so whether the agreement was completely integrated or partially integrated. Inconsistency is merely one factor in the preliminary determination of those issues. If the parties orally agreed that performance of the written agreement was subject to a condition, either the writing is not an integrated agreement or the agreement is only partially integrated until the condition occurs. Even a "merger" clause in the writing, explicitly negating oral terms, does not control the question whether there is an integrated agreement or the scope of the writing. See Comment *e* to § 216. **Illustrations:**

   3. A and B sign a written agreement for the sale of goods, and orally agree that the writing shall not take effect unless railroad cars are available within ten days. The oral agreement is effective.
   4. Evidence of the facts stated in Illustration 3 is offered, and the writing contains a provision that "delivery shall be made within 30 days." Evidence of the oral agreement is excluded only if the court makes a preliminary determination that performance of the written agreement could not in the circumstances reasonably be found to have been subject to the oral agreement.
   . . .

§ 218. Untrue Recitals; Evidence of Consideration

(1) A recital of a fact in an integrated agreement may be shown to be untrue.

(2) Evidence is admissible to prove whether or not there is consideration for a promise, even though the parties have reduced their agreement to a writing which appears to be a completely integrated agreement.

Comment:

a. Fact and transaction. The parol evidence rule (§ 213) relates to the effect of an integrated agreement on prior agreements. An integrated agreement may have the effect of discharging a prior promise, conveyance or discharge; it does not establish fictitious events.

b. Effect of recital. A recital of fact in an integrated agreement is evidence of the fact, and its weight depends on the circumstances. Contrary facts may be proved. The result may be that the integrated agreement is not binding, or that it has a different effect from the effect if the recital had been true. In the absence of estoppel, the true facts have the same operation as if stated in the writing.

c. Estoppel. In some circumstances a recital may embody a representation of fact by one party to the other, and the party making such a representation may be barred by estoppel from showing the truth contrary to the representation after another has relied on the representation. See Comment *a* to § 90.

d. Omission of consideration. Where a written agreement requires consideration and none is stated in the writing, a finding that the writing is a completely integrated agreement would mean that it is not binding for want of consideration. Since only a binding integrated agreement brings the parol evidence rule into operation, evidence is admissible to show that there was consideration and what it was.

Illustration:

1. A gives B a written promise to pay $ 100. The writing states no consideration. B promises orally to build a fence in consideration of the promise of $ 100. Both promises are operative.

e. Incorrect recital of consideration. Where a writing shows a promise in consideration of a return promise and it is determined that the writing is a binding integrated agreement, inconsistent prior agreements are discharged. See § 213. But an integrated agreement which is not binding does not ordinarily discharge prior agreements, and the parol evidence rule does not apply to recitals of facts. Where consideration is required, the requirement is not satisfied by a false recital of consideration, although in some circumstances a recital of consideration may make a promise binding without consideration. See §§ 71, 87, 88. An incorrect statement of a consideration does not prevent proof either that there was no consideration or that there was a consideration different from that stated. In some such cases the recital may imply a promise not explicitly stated. **Illustrations:**

2. A, an insurance company, issues a fire insurance policy to B. The policy provides that A is not bound until the premium is paid, and falsely recites payment. On accepting the policy, B impliedly promises to pay the premium and A is bound by the policy.

. . .

§ 219. Usage Usage is habitual or customary practice.

Comment:

a. Scope of usage. Although rules of law are often founded on usage, usage is not in itself a legal rule but merely habit or practice in fact. A particular usage may be more or less widespread. It may prevail throughout an area, and the area may be small or large -- a city, a state or a larger region. A usage may prevail among all people in the area, or only in a special trade or other group. Usages change over time, and persons in close association often develop temporary usages peculiar to themselves.

b. Usage of words. A word usage exists when few or many people use a word or phrase to convey a standard meaning or several standard meanings and develop a common understanding of the meaning or meanings. Dictionaries record word usages which have achieved some generality, with varying degrees of completeness and accuracy. See § 201.

§ 220. Usage Relevant to Interpretation

(1) An agreement is interpreted in accordance with a relevant usage if each party knew or had reason to know of the usage and neither party knew or had reason to know that the meaning attached by the other was inconsistent with the usage.

(2) When the meaning attached by one party accorded with a relevant usage and the other knew or had reason to know of the usage, the other is treated as having known or had reason to know the meaning attached by the first party.

Comment:

a. Relation to other rules. Usage may "give particular meaning to" an agreement, or may "supplement or qualify" it. See Uniform Commercial Code § 1-205. This Section deals with usage as an element in interpretation and states rules consistent with the general rules on agreement and interpretation stated in §§ 20 and 201. Usage supplementing or qualifying an agreement is the subject of the following section, and §§ 222 and 223 apply the general rules of this Section and § 221 to the particular cases of usage of trade and course of dealing. Where there are conflicting usages of words and no different intention is shown, § 202 provides guides for the process of interpretation; where there is conflict between usage of trade and express terms, course of performance or course of dealing, § 203 states standards of preference.

b. Interpretation of language. An agreement may have a legal effect not intended by either party, but interpretation is limited to meanings intended by at least one party. Neither party is bound by a meaning unless he knows or has reason to know of it. See §§ 200, 201. Usage is subject to the same rule: a party is not bound by a usage unless he knows or has reason to know of it. Hence a party who asserts a meaning based on usage must show either that the other party knew of the usage or that the other party had reason to know of it. Analytically, the meaning of language is a question of fact, but in the absence of extrinsic evidence the meaning of language in an integrated writing is to be determined as a question of law. See § 212. Where a usage of words is sufficiently well known, a court will take judicial cognizance of it without proof; otherwise the burden of establishing a usage is on the party asserting it. See § 202. Ordinarily there is no requirement that a usage relevant to the interpretation of language be pleaded, but a party against whom evidence of usage is offered may be entitled to a continuance or to notice sufficient to prevent unfair surprise.

See Uniform Commercial Code § 1-205(6).

Illustrations:

1. A contracts to sell and B to buy ten bushels of oats. By very general usage 32 pounds constitutes a bushel of oats. In the absence of contrary evidence, ten bushels in the contract means 320 pounds.

2. A contracts with B to "sponsor" a bowling team and to pay B "the usual sponsoring fees." In an action against A for repudiating the contract in a dispute over the fees, B cannot recover without proving a usage as to "usual sponsoring fees."

3. A employs B as exclusive broker to sell business premises subject to a one-year lease back to A. B submits an agreement for sale to C subject to a one-year lease, with a provision for termination of the lease on six months notice. A rejects the agreement. In an action for the agreed commission B claims that by local usage all business leases contain such a provision. B has the burden of establishing the usage and A's knowledge or reason to know of it.

c. Agreed but unstated terms. An agreement or term thereof need not be stated in words if the parties manifest assent to it by other conduct, and such assent is often manifested by conduct in accordance with usage. Where there is an integrated agreement, an agreed but unstated term may be annexed by usage on the same principle which controls consistent additional terms generally. See § 216. But it is so common to contract with reference to usage, leaving the usage unstated, that no inquiry is necessary as to whether it is natural in the particular circumstances to omit the term from the writing. See Uniform Commercial Code § 2-202(a). Where it is claimed that the usage contradicts the express terms, the issue is resolved as a question of interpretation. See § 203(b). Whether a usage is reasonable may bear on the issue whether the parties contracted with reference to it, but if they did they are not in general forbidden to make agreements which seem unreasonable to others.

Illustrations:

4. A and B contract for a year's employment of B by A. As both parties know, there is a usage that such a contract may be terminated by a month's notice. Unless a contrary intention is manifested, the usage is part of the contract.

5. A sends goods to B by C, a private carrier, receiving a bill of lading from C. B rejects the shipment. The usage of such carriers, known to A and C, is to notify the shipper of such a rejection. Unless a contrary intention is manifested, the requirement of notification is added to the terms of the bill of lading.

6. A contracts to sell and B to buy 100 barrels of flour at$ 8 a barrel. By a usage of the trade known to A and B payment under such contracts is due ten days after delivery unless otherwise agreed. The usage is part of the contract.

7. A contracts to sell and B to buy 100 barrels of mackerel. By a usage of trade known to A and B, sellers of mackerel, unless they agree otherwise, warrant that the fish are not below a certain size. The usage is part of the contract. See Uniform Commercial Code §§ 2-314(3), 2-316(3)(c).

d. Ambiguity and contradiction. Language and conduct are in general given meaning by usage rather than by the law, and ambiguity and contradiction likewise depend upon usage. Hence usage relevant to interpretation is treated as part of the context of an agreement in determining whether there is ambiguity or contradiction as well as in resolving ambiguity or contradiction. There is no requirement that an ambiguity be shown before usage can be shown, and no prohibition against showing that language or conduct have a different meaning in the light of usage from the meaning they might have apart from the usage. The normal effect of a usage on a written contract is to vary its meaning from the meaning it would otherwise have. **Illustrations:**

8. A leases a rabbit warren to B. The written lease contains a covenant that at the end of the term A will buy and B will sell the rabbits at "60 ££ per thousand." The parties contract with reference to a local usage that 1,000 rabbits means 100 dozen. The usage is part of the contract.

9. In an integrated contract, A promises to sell and B to buy a certain quantity of "white arsenic" for a stated price. The parties contract with reference to a usage of trade that "white arsenic" includes arsenic colored with lamp black. The usage is part of the contract.

10. A, a bank in New York City, issues to B a letter of credit promising a payment on presentation of documents including a "full set of bills of lading." By a general banking usage in New York City, banks accept less than a full set in such cases if there is a guaranty by a responsible New York bank in lieu of the missing part. Unless otherwise agreed, the usage is part of the contract. Uniform Commercial Code § 5-109.

§ 221. Usage Supplementing an Agreement

An agreement is supplemented or qualified by a reasonable usage with respect to agreements of the same type if each party knows or has reason to know of the usage and neither party knows or has reason to know that the other party has an intention inconsistent with the usage.

Comment:

a. Agreed terms and omitted terms. Where the parties have in fact agreed to incorporate a usage into their agreement, the case is within § 220. This Section extends the same principle to cases where the parties did not advert to the problem with which the usage deals, or where one or each separately foresaw the problem but failed to manifest any intention with respect to it. In such cases, in the absence of usage, the court would supply a reasonable term. See § 204. But if there is a reasonable usage which supplies an omitted term and the parties know or have reason to know of the usage, it is a surer guide than the court's own judgment of what is reasonable. Thus a usage may make it unnecessary to inquire into or prove what the actual intentions of the parties were with respect to an unstated term. Compare Uniform Commercial Code §§ 1-205(3), 2-202(a). **Illustrations:**

1. A, a canner, and B, a wholesale grocer, contract for the sale by A to B of canned fruit products, using a standard form of contract approved by canning and wholesale grocer trade associations. By uniform usage among canners, where the standard form is used title to unshipped goods passes on billing dates specified on the form. In the absence of contrary indication, the usage is part of the contract.

2. A, an ordained rabbi, is employed by B, an orthodox Jewish congregation, to officiate as cantor at specified religious services. At the time

the contract is made, it is the practice of such congregations to seat men and women separately at services, and a contrary practice would violate A's religious beliefs. At a time when it is too late for A to obtain substitute employment, B adopts a contrary practice. A refuses to officiate. The practice is part of the contract, and A is entitled to the agreed compensation.

b. Reason to know and reasonableness. The more general and well-established a usage is, the stronger is the inference that a party knew or had reason to know of it. Similarly, the fact that a usage is reasonable may tend to show that the parties contracted with reference to it or that a particular party knew or had reason to know of it. Where the parties in fact agree to a usage, there is no general requirement that their usage seem reasonable to others; but where there is no agreement only a reasonable usage supplies an omitted term. What is reasonable for this purpose depends on the circumstances; it may be reasonable to hold a nonmerchant to mercantile standards if he is represented by a mercantile agent. See Uniform Commercial Code § 2-104, defining "merchant." Ordinarily an agent is authorized to comply with relevant usages of business if the principal has notice that usages of such a nature may exist. See Restatement, Second, of Agency § 36. **Illustrations:**

3. A, in Washington, sends an order to B, a broker in Baltimore, to be executed on the New York Stock Exchange. Unless both A and B give the order a different and identical interpretation or B has reason to know that A has a different intention, the order is interpreted in accordance with the reasonable usages of the New York Stock Exchange.

4. A, a publisher, contracts with B to publish a two-volume work. The contract provides for binding "10,000 copies at .538," which by usage of the publishing business refers to the number of volumes rather than the number of sets. The usage is part of the contract even though the work is B's first and he does not know of the usage.

c. Effect of usage on law. It is often said that usage cannot change a rule of law, but a distinction must be drawn. If the rule of law is one which overrides contrary agreement, it also overrides usage; but if the law merely supplies a term in the absence of contrary agreement, usage can have the same effect as contrary agreement. See Uniform Commercial Code § 1-201(3). **Illustrations:**

5. A and B, both members of a Mercantile Exchange, enter into an oral contract within the Statute of Frauds. By usage of the Exchange oral agreements between members of the Exchange are enforceable. The usage does not make the contract enforceable if it is otherwise unenforceable.

6. A makes B a promise without consideration. By usage such promises are binding without consideration. The usage does not make the promise legally binding.

7. A makes an offer to B by telephone, and B accepts by telephone. By usage known to both parties such an agreement is not binding unless promptly confirmed in writing by the acceptor. Unless a contrary intention is indicated, the usage is part of the agreement, and there is no contract unless B gives prompt written confirmation.

d. Intention inconsistent with usage. The parties to an agreement are not bound to follow the usages of others or their own prior usages. If either party has reason to know that the other has an intention inconsistent with a particular usage, the usage is not applicable. Such an intention need not be manifested in any particular way; whether the parties contracted with reference to a usage is determined on the basis of all the circumstances, and a usage may be excluded by the same type of proof which would include it. **Illustrations:**

8. A, a resident of Philadelphia, makes a contract with B, a resident of New York, by which A promises to build a brick wall in Philadelphia. There is a local usage in Philadelphia as to measuring brick which differs from that elsewhere. B is not aware of the Philadelphia usage, as A has reason to know. The usage is not part of the contract.

9. A, a bank, issues a letter of credit promising to honor drafts accompanied by bills of lading covering "Coromandel groundnuts." Dealers in groundnuts understand "Coromandel groundnuts" to mean "machine-shelled groundnut kernels." A is not bound to honor drafts accompanied by bills of lading covering "machine-shelled groundnut kernels." See Uniform Commercial Code § 5-109(1)(c).

§ 222. Usage of Trade

(1) A usage of trade is a usage having such regularity of observance in a place, vocation, or trade as to justify an expectation that it will be observed with respect to a particular agreement. It may include a system of rules regularly observed even though particular rules are changed from time to time.

(2) The existence and scope of a usage of trade are to be determined as questions of fact. If a usage is embodied in a written trade code or similar writing the interpretation of the writing is to be determined by the court as a question of law.

(3) Unless otherwise agreed, a usage of trade in the vocation or trade in which the parties are engaged or a usage of trade of which they know or have reason to know gives meaning to or supplements or qualifies their agreement.

Comment:

a. Relation to other rules. This Section follows Uniform Commercial Code § 1-205 and states a particular application of the rules stated in §§ 220 and 221. As to conflicting usages of words, see § 202; as to conflict between usage of trade and express terms, course of performance or course of dealing, see § 203.

b. Regularity of observance. A usage of trade need not be "ancient or immemorial," "universal," or the like. Unless agreed to in fact, it must be reasonable, but commercial acceptance by regular observance makes out a prima facie case that a usage of trade is reasonable. There is no requirement that an agreement be ambiguous before evidence of a usage of trade can be shown, nor is it required that the usage of trade be consistent with the meaning the agreement would have apart from the usage. When the usage consists of a system of rules, the parties need not be aware of a particular rule if they know or have reason to know the system and the particular rule is within the scheme of the system. A change within the system may have effect promptly, even though there has been no time for regular observance of the change. **Illustrations:**

1. A contracts to sell B 10,000 shingles. By usage of the lumber trade, in which both are engaged, two packs of a certain size constitute 1,000, though not containing that exact number. Unless otherwise agreed, 1,000 in the contract means two packs.

2. A contracts to sell B 1,000 feet of San Domingo mahogany. By usage of dealers in mahogany, known to A and B, good figured mahogany of a certain density is known as San Domingo mahogany, though it does not come from San Domingo. Unless otherwise agreed, the usage is part of the contract.

3. A promises to act as B's agent in a certain business, and B promises to pay a certain commission for each "order." By a local usage in that business, "order" means only an order on which the purchaser has paid a certain price. Unless otherwise agreed, the usage is part of the contract.

4. A and B enter into a contract for the sawing of logs during the "winter season." Usage in the logging business may show that "winter season" means the period between the closing of a sawmill in the autumn and the arrival of logs in the spring.

5. A and B enter into a contract of charter party in which A promises to discharge the vessel "in 14 days." Usage in the shipping business may show this means 14 working days.

6. A and B enter into a contract for the purchase and sale of "No. 1 heavy book paper guaranteed free from ground wood." Usage in the paper trade may show that this means paper not containing over 3% ground wood.

c. Local usages of trade. Where usages vary from place to place, there may be a problem in deciding which usage is applicable. Even though local residents regularly contract with reference to a local usage of trade, others are not bound by the usage unless they know or have reason to know of it. If that condition is satisfied and no contrary intention is shown, a usage of trade in a particular place is ordinarily used to interpret the agreement as to that part of the performance which is to occur there. See Uniform Commercial Code § 1-205(5). **Illustrations:**

7. A contracts to employ B for 20 days. In the kind of work to which the employment relates, in the place where both reside and the work is to be performed, a day's work is eight hours. Unless otherwise agreed, B's employment is for 20 eight-hour days.

8. A leases to B a portion of a building for "confectionery store purposes." By local usage at the time and place where the lease is made and the building is located, "confectionery store purposes" include the giving of light lunches. Un-

less otherwise agreed, the usage is part of the contract.

9. A promises B to keep certain premises "fully insured." At the time and place where the contract is made and to be performed and where the parties reside, insurance companies will not insure such premises for more than three-fourths of their value, and such premises insured for three-fourths of their value are called "fully insured." Unless otherwise agreed, the local usage is part of the contract.

10. A of Chicago negotiates and concludes in South Carolina an integrated contract to sell and deliver to B in South Carolina "ground sheep manure." These words mean a finer grinding in South Carolina than they do in Chicago, and A has reason to know of the South Carolina usage. Unless otherwise agreed, the contract is taken to refer to the South Carolina usage.

§ 223. Course of Dealing

(1) A course of dealing is a sequence of previous conduct between the parties to an agreement which is fairly to be regarded as establishing a common basis of understanding for interpreting their expressions and other conduct.

(2) Unless otherwise agreed, a course of dealing between the parties gives meaning to or supplements or qualifies their agreement.

Comment:

a. Relation to other rules. This Section follows Uniform Commercial Code § 1-205 and states a particular application of the rules stated in §§ 220 and 221. As to conflict between course of dealing and express terms, course of performance or usage of trade, see § 203.

b. Common basis of understanding. Course of dealing may become part of an agreement either by explicit provision or by tacit recognition, or it may guide the court in supplying an omitted term. Like usage of trade, it may determine the meaning of language or it may annex an agreed but unstated term. There is no requirement that an agreement be ambiguous before evidence of a course of dealing can be shown, nor is it required that the course of dealing be consistent with the meaning the agreement would have apart from the course of dealing. **Illustrations:**

1. A, a sugar company, enters into a written agreement with B, a grower of sugar beets, by which B agrees to raise and deliver and A to purchase specified quantities of beets during the coming season. No price is fixed. The agreement is on a standard form used for B and many other growers in prior years. A's practice is to pay all growers uniformly on a formula based on A's "net return" according to A's established accounting system. Unless otherwise agreed, the established pattern of pricing is part of the agreement.

2. A, a manufacturer, sends a price quotation on goods to B, a dealer, together with printed "conditions of sale." B then sends orders to A; and A fills them. B takes advantage of discount terms of the quotation not referred to in B's orders. Unless otherwise agreed, the "conditions of sale" are part of each contract.

Topic 5. Conditions and Similar Events

Introductory Note: The preceding sections of this Chapter have been primarily concerned with duties. This Topic is concerned with conditions. An obligor will often qualify his duty by providing that performance will not become due unless a stated event, which is not certain to occur, does occur. Such an event is called a condition. An obligor may make an event a condition of his duty in order to shift to the obligee the risk of its non-occurrence. In this case the event may be within the control of the obligee (e.g., his furnishing security), or of the obligor (e.g., his satisfaction with the obligee's performance), or of neither (e.g., the accidental destruction of the subject matter). An obligor may also make an event a condition of his duty in order to induce the obligee to cause the event to occur. In this case the event is presumably within the control of the obligee (e.g., his performance within a specified time). And even when the party has not qualified his duty in this way, a court may supply a term (§ 204) making an event a condition.

When a court determines whether the agreement makes an event a condition, or whether, if the agreement does not, the court itself should supply a term making an event a condition, it follows the general rules already stated in this Chapter. The same rules are used to ascertain the meaning of the agreement (Topic 1), and the same considerations of fairness and the public interest apply (Topic 2); the adoption of a writing has the same consequences (Topic 3; but see § 217), and usage has the same effect (Topic 4).

Conditions have, however, traditionally been the subject of a distinctive terminology, and there are some special rules in aid of interpretation with regard to conditions. This Topic deals with this terminology and these rules. The terminology includes the word "condition" itself (§ 224 and Comment *a*), the terms "express," "implied in fact" and "constructive" conditions (Comment *c* to § 226), the phrase "excuse of the non-occurrence of a condition" (Comment *b* to § 225), and the terms "condition precedent" and "condition subsequent," which are not used in this Restatement (Comment *e* to §224; Comment *a* to § 230). The rules speak to the effect of the non-occurrence of a condition (§ 225), to whether an event is a condition and, if so, the nature of that event (§§ 226-28), and to the excuse of the non-occurrence of a condition to avoid forfeiture (§ 229). Where performances are to be exchanged under an exchange of promises, a failure of performance by one party may have the same effect as the non-occurrence of a condition, but this matter is covered in Chapter 10 and not in this Topic.

CONDITIONS

§ 224. Condition Defined

A condition is an event, not certain to occur, which must occur, unless its non-occurrence is excused, before performance under a contract becomes due.

Comment:

a. "Condition" limited to event. "Condition" is used in this Restatement to denote an event which qualifies a duty under a contract. See the Introductory Note to this Topic. It is recognized that "condition" is used with a wide variety of other meanings in legal discourse. Sometimes it is used to denote an event that limits or qualifies a transfer of property. In the law of trusts, for example, it is used to denote an event such as the death of the settlor that qualifies his disposition of property in trust. See Restatement, Second, Trusts § 360. See also the rules on "conditional" delivery (§ 103) and "conditional" assignment (§§ 103, 331). Sometimes it is used to refer to a term (§ 5) in an agreement that makes an event a condition, or more broadly to refer to any term in an agreement (e.g., "standard conditions of sale"). For the sake of precision, "condition" is not used here in these other senses.

Illustration:

1. A contracts to sell and B to buy goods pursuant to a writing which provides, under the heading "Conditions of Sale," that "the obligations of the parties are conditional on B obtaining from X Bank by June 30 a letter of credit" on stated terms. The quoted language is a term of the agreement (§ 5), not a condition. The event referred to by the term, obtaining the letter of credit by June 30, is a condition.

b. Uncertainty of event. Whether the reason for making an event a condition is to shift to the obligee the risk of its non-occurrence, or whether it is to induce the obligee to cause the event to occur (see Introductory Note to this Topic), there is inherent in the concept of condition some degree of uncertainty as to the occurrence of the event. Therefore, the mere passage of time, as to which there is no uncertainty, is not a condition and a duty is unconditional if nothing but the passage of time is necessary to give rise to a duty of performance. Moreover, an event is not a condition, even though its occurrence is uncertain, if it is referred to merely to measure the passage of time after which an obligor is to perform. See Comment *b* to § 227. Performance under a contract becomes due when all necessary events, including any conditions and the passage of any required time, have occurred so that a failure of performance will be a breach. See §§ 231-43.

The event need not, in order to be a condition, be one that is to occur after the making of the contract, although that is commonly the case. It may relate to the present or even to the past, as is the case where a marine policy insures against a loss that may already have occurred. Furthermore, a duty may be conditioned upon the failure of something to happen rather than upon its happening, and in that case its failure to happen is the event that is the condition. **Illustrations:**

    2. A tells B, "If you will paint my house, I will pay you $ 1,000 on condition that 30 days have passed after you have finished." B paints A's house. Although A is not under a duty to pay B $ 1,000 until 30 days have passed, the passage of that time is not a condition of A's duty to pay B $ 1,000.

    3. A contracts to sell and B to buy goods to be shipped "C.I.F.," payment to be "on arrival of goods." Risk of loss of the goods passes from A to B when A, having otherwise complied with the C.I.F. term of the contract, puts the goods in the possession of the carrier (Uniform Commercial Code § 2-320(2)). If the goods are lost in transit, B is under a duty to pay the price when the goods should have arrived (Uniform Commercial Code §§ 2-709(1)(a), 2-321(3)). The arrival of the goods is not a condition of B's duty to pay for the goods.

  c. Necessity of a contract. In order for an event to be a condition, it must qualify a duty under an existing contract. Events which are part of the process of formation of a contract, such as offer and acceptance, are therefore excluded under the definition in this section. It is not customary to call such events conditions. But cf. § 36(2) ("condition of acceptance"). For the most part, they are required by law and may not be dispensed with by the parties, while conditions are the result of, or at least subject to, agreement. Where, however, an offer has become an option contract, e.g., by the payment of a dollar (§ 87), the acceptance is a condition under the definition in this section. **Illustration:**

    4. A tells B, "I promise to pay you $ 1,000 if you paint my house." B begins to paint A's house. Since B's beginning of the invited performance gives rise to an option contract, B's completion of performance is a condition of A's duty under that contract to pay B $ 1,000. See § 45.

  d. Relationship of conditions. A duty may be subject to any number of conditions, which may be related to each other in various ways. They may be cumulative so that performance will not become due unless all of them occur. They may be alternative so that performance may become due if any one of them occurs. Or some may be cumulative and some alternative. Furthermore, a condition may qualify the duties of both parties. Cf. § 217. **Illustrations:**

    5. A, as the result of financial reverses, sells B a valuable painting for $ 1,000,000, but reserves a right to repurchase it by tendering the same price on or before August 18 if he again finds himself in such a financial condition that he can keep it for his personal enjoyment. A's tender of $ 1,000,000 by August 18 and his being in such financial condition that he can keep the painting for his personal enjoyment are cumulative conditions and redelivery of the painting does not become due unless both of them occur.

    6. A purchases land from Mrs. B, who is unable to get Mr. B to join her in signing the deed because they are engaged in divorce proceedings. A takes possession under a deed signed by Mrs. B, pays Mrs. B $ 10,000 and promises to pay an additional $ 5,000 "if, within one year, (1) Mr. and Mrs. B execute a quitclaim deed to A, or (2) Mrs. B furnishes A with a certificate of the death of Mr. B with Mrs. B surviving him, or (3) Mrs. B as a single person executes a quitclaim deed to A after having been awarded the land following the entry of a final decree of divorce from Mr. B." The three enumerated events are alternative conditions and A's payment of $ 5,000 to Mrs. B becomes due if any of them occurs.

    7. A and B contract to merge their corporate holdings into a single new company. It is agreed that the project is not to be operative unless the parties raise $ 600,000 additional capital. The raising of the additional capital is a condition of the duties of both A and B. If it is not raised, neither A's nor B's performance becomes due.

  e. Occurrence of event as discharge. Parties sometimes provide that the occurrence of an event, such as the failure of one of them to commence an action within a prescribed time, will extinguish a duty after performance has become due, along with any claim for breach. Such an event has often been called a "condition subsequent," while an event of the kind defined in this section has been called a "condition precedent." This terminology is not followed here. Since a "condition subsequent," so-called, is subject to the rules on discharge in § 230, and not to the following rules on conditions, it is not called a "condition" in this Restatement. Occasionally, although the language of an agreement says that if an event does not occur a duty is "extinguished," "discharged," or "terminated," it can be seen from the circumstances that the event must ordinarily occur before performance of the duty can be expected. When a court concludes that, for this reason, performance is not to become due unless the event occurs, the event is, in spite of the language, a condition of the duty. See § 227(3). See also Comment *a* to § 230. **Illustrations:**

8. A insures B's property against theft. The policy provides that B's failure to notify A within 30 days after loss shall "terminate" A's duty to pay and that suit must be brought within one year after loss. Since it can be seen from the circumstances that notice must ordinarily be given before payment by A can be expected, B's notification of A within 30 days after loss is a condition of A's duty. B's bringing suit against A within a year after loss is not a condition of A's duty. B's failure to bring suit within that time will discharge A's duty after payment has become due, along with any claim for breach.

9. A and B make a contract under which A promises to pay B $ 10,000 in annual installments of $ 1,000 each, beginning the following January 1, with a provision that "no installments whether or not overdue and unpaid shall be payable in case of A's death within the 10 years." A's being alive is a condition of his duty to pay any installment. A's death within ten years will discharge his duty to pay any installment after payment has become due, along with any claim for breach.

f. Sealed contracts. The rules governing conditions stated in the Restatement of this Subject are applicable to sealed as well as unsealed contracts. The same rules have traditionally been applied to both types of contract with technical exceptions that are no longer of significance.

§ 225. Effects of the Non-Occurrence of a Condition

(1) Performance of a duty subject to a condition cannot become due unless the condition occurs or its non-occurrence is excused.

(2) Unless it has been excused, the non-occurrence of a condition discharges the duty when the condition can no longer occur.

(3) Non-occurrence of a condition is not a breach by a party unless he is under a duty that the condition occur.

Comment:

a. Two effects. The unexcused non-occurrence of a condition has two possible effects on the duty subject to that condition. The first effect always follows and the second often does. The first, stated in Subsection (1), is that of preventing performance of the duty from becoming due. This follows from the definition of "condition" in § 224. Performance of the duty may still become due, however, if the condition occurs later within the time for its occurrence. The non-occurrence of the condition within that time has the additional effect, stated in Subsection (2), of discharging the duty. The time within which the condition can occur in order for the performance of the duty to become due may be fixed by a term of the agreement or, in the absence of such a term, by one supplied by the court (§ 204). Where discharge would produce harsh results, this second effect may be avoided by rules of interpretation (§§ 226, 228) or of excuse of conditions (Comment *b* and § 229).

Illustrations:

1. A contracts to sell and B to buy A's business. The contract provides that B is to pay in installments over a five-year period following the conveyance, and that A is to convey on condition that B pledge specified collateral to secure his payment. Conveyance by A does not become due until B pledges the collateral. If the agreement does not provide for the time within which the collateral is to be pledged, A's duty is discharged if it is not pledged within a reasonable time.

2. B gives A $ 10,000 to use in perfecting an invention, and A promises to repay it only out of royalties received during his lifetime from the sale of the patent rights. In spite of diligent efforts, A is unable to perfect his invention and obtain a patent, and no royalties are received. A dies after six years. B has no claim against A's estate. Receipt of royalties is a condition of A's duty to repay the money and A's duty is dis-

charged by the non-occurrence of that condition during his lifetime.

b. Excuse. The non-occurrence of a condition of a duty is said to be "excused" when the condition need no longer occur in order for performance of the duty to become due. The non-occurrence of a condition may be excused on a variety of grounds. It may be excused by a subsequent promise, even without consideration, to perform the duty in spite of the non-occurrence of the condition. See the treatment of "waiver" in § 84, and the treatment of discharge in §§ 273-85. It may be excused by acceptance of performance in spite of the non-occurrence of the condition, or by rejection following its non-occurrence accompanied by an inadequate statement of reasons. See §§ 246-48. It may be excused by a repudiation of the conditional duty or by a manifestation of an inability to perform it. See § 255; § 250-51. It may be excused by prevention or hindrance of its occurrence through a breach of the duty of good faith and fair dealing (§ 205). See § 239. And it may be excused by impracticability. See § 271. These and other grounds for excuse are dealt with in other chapters of this Restatement. This Chapter deals only with one general ground, excuse to avoid forfeiture. See § 229.

c. Effect of excuse. When the non-occurrence of a condition of a duty is excused, the damages for breach of the duty will depend on whether or not the occurrence of the condition was also part of the performances to be exchanged under the exchange of promises. If it was not part of the agreed exchange, the obligor is liable for the same damages for which he would have been liable had the duty originally been unconditional. If it was part of the agreed exchange, however, the saving to the obligee resulting from the non-occurrence of the condition must be subtracted in determining the obligor's liability for damages. Rules for determining damages are set out in § 347; see generally §§ 346-56. If the obligee is under a duty that the condition occur, the ground for the excuse of the non-occurrence of the condition may not be a ground for discharge of that duty. He may therefore be liable for breach of the duty in spite of the excuse of the non-occurrence of the condition. Not only may a party excuse entirely the non-occurrence of a condition of his duty, but he may merely excuse its non-

occurrence during the period of time in which it would otherwise have to occur. If he does this, the non-occurrence of the condition during that period will not discharge the duty under Subsection (2), although its non-occurrence will ultimately have that effect. See Illustration 8 to § 84. **Illustrations:**

3. A contracts with B to build a house for $ 50,000, payable on condition that A present a certificate from C, B's architect, showing that the work has been properly completed. A properly completes the work, but C refuses to give the certificate because of collusion with B, and the non-occurrence of the condition is therefore excused. See § 239. Since the presentation of the architect's certificate is not part of the performances to be exchanged under the exchange of promises, A has a claim against B for $ 50,000.

4. Under an option contract, A promises to sell B a painting "on condition that B pay $ 100,000" by a stated date. Before that date, the non-occurrence of the condition is excused by A's repudiation of the contract. See § 255. Since the payment of the $ 100,000 is B's part of the performances to be exchanged under the exchange of promises, B saved that amount when the non-occurrence of the condition was excused, and it should be subtracted in determining damages. B has a claim against A for the value of the painting to B less $ 100,000.

5. A leases property to B for a stated monthly rental. The lease provides that A is under a duty to remove described property from the premises, and that its removal is a condition of B's duty to pay the rent. After A has removed most of the property from the premises, B says that he will pay the rent even though not all of it has been removed. The non-occurrence of the condition is excused and B is under a duty to pay the rent even though A does not remove the rest of the property. See § 84. But A's duty to remove the rest of the property is not discharged and his failure to remove the rest is a breach.

d. Imposition of duty distinguished. When one party chooses to use the institution of contract to induce the other party to cause an event to occur, he may do so by making the event a condition of his own duty (Introductory Note to this Topic). Or he may do so by having the other party undertake a duty that the event occur. Or he may do both. But, as Subsection (3) makes clear, a term making an event a condition of an obligor's duty does not of itself impose a duty on the obligee and the non-occurrence of the event is not of itself a breach by the obligee. Unless the obligee is under such a duty, the non-occurrence of the event gives rise to no claim against him. The same term may, however, be interpreted not only to make an event a condition of the obligor's duty, but also to impose a duty on the obligee that it occur. And even where no term of the agreement imposes a duty that a condition occur, the court may supply such a term. See § 204. **Illustrations:**

6. A, a shipowner, promises to carry B's cargo on his ship to Portsmouth. B promises to pay A the stipulated freight on condition that A's ship sail directly there on its next sailing. A's ship carries B's cargo to Portsmouth, but puts into port on the way. Since carrying B's cargo directly to Portsmouth is a condition of B's duty, no duty to pay arises, and, since the condition can no longer occur, B's duty is discharged. Since A is under no duty to carry B's cargo directly to Portsmouth, however, his failure to do so is not a breach.

7. The facts being otherwise as stated in Illustration 6, A promises to carry B's cargo on his ship directly to Portsmouth on its next sail-ing. Since carrying B's cargo directly to Portsmouth is a condition of B's duty, no duty to pay arises and, since the condition can no longer occur, B's duty is discharged. Since A is under a duty to carry B's cargo directly to Portsmouth, his failure to do so is also a breach.

8. A contracts to sell and B to buy a house for $ 50,000, with the provision, "This contract is conditional on approval by X Bank of B's pending mortgage application." Approval by X Bank is a condition of B's duty. B is under no duty that the X Bank approve his application, but a court will supply a term imposing on him a duty to make reasonable efforts to obtain approval. See §§ 204, 205.

e. Ignorance immaterial. The rules stated in this Section apply without regard to whether a party knows or does not know of the non-occurrence of a condition of his duty. **Illustration:**

9. The facts being otherwise as stated in Illustration 6, B refuses to pay the freight without knowing that A's ship has put into port on the way. B's refusal is not a breach since his duty is discharged.

§ 226. How an Event May Be Made a Condition

An event may be made a condition either by the agreement of the parties or by a term supplied by the court.

Comment:

a. By agreement of the parties. No particular form of language is necessary to make an event a condition, although such words as "on condition that," "provided that" and "if" are often used for this purpose. An intention to make a duty conditional may be manifested by the general nature of an agreement, as well as by specific language. Whether the parties have, by their agreement, made an event a condition is determined by the process of interpretation. That process is subject to the general rules that are contained in previous topics of this Chapter. For example, as in other instances of interpretation, the purpose of the parties is given great weight (§ 202(1)), and, in choosing between reasonable meanings, that meaning is generally preferred which operates against the draftsman (§ 206). There are also some special standards of preference that are of particular applicability to conditions, and these are set out in § 227.

Illustrations:

1. A partnership agreement among physicians provides that A may withdraw from the partnership on three months' written notice to the partnership's executive committee, "but in the event that the committee requests him to revoke his notice of withdrawal prior to its effective date, and he refuses to comply, he shall not upon his withdrawal engage in the practice of medicine within a twenty-five mile radius." A gives notice of his withdrawal. A request by the committee that A revoke his notice is a condition of A's duty not to practice medicine within a twenty-five mile radius.

2. A, a tenant of B, promises to pay $ 1,000 for "such repairs as an architect appointed by B shall approve." The appointment by B of an architect and the architect's approval of repairs are conditions of A's duty to pay for repairs.

3. A sells an automobile to B, for which B promises to pay $ 5,000 "on demand." A sues B for the $ 5,000 without first making a demand. A can recover. The quoted language is to be inter-

preted in the light of the purpose of the parties (§ 202(1)), and the purpose of such language, in connection with a promise that is one to pay money and is otherwise unconditional, is to fix the time after which interest at the legal rate is payable. A's suit should therefore not be dismissed merely because he did not demand payment, and a demand by A is not a condition of B's duty. The same interpretation follows by analogy from the rule of Uniform Commercial Code § 3-122(1)(b), under which a claim on a demand instrument arises on its date or date of issue.

4. A contracts to sell and B to buy a house for $ 50,000. The contract contains the provision, "This contract is conditional on approval by X Bank of B's pending mortgage application." Approval by X Bank is a condition of B's duty but not of A's duty. The quoted language is to be interpreted in the light of the purpose of the parties (§ 202(1)), and their purpose in including such a provision is to protect B and not A in the event that the application is not approved. If X Bank does not approve B's application, performance by B will not become due even if A makes a conditional offer to deliver a deed, but performance by A will become due if, in spite of X Bank's failure to approve B's application, B makes a conditional offer to pay the $ 50,000. Cf. Illustration 8 to § 225.

b. Nature of event. Just as the process of interpretation determines whether the parties have by their agreement made an event a condition, it also determines the nature of that event. Here too the process is subject to the general rules of interpretation stated earlier in the present Chapter, and here too there are some special standards of preference. These standards are set out in §§ 227(1) and 228. **Illustrations:**

5. A, an insurance company, insures B, a storekeeper, against safe burglary, "provided entry be made by actual force and violence, of which there are visible marks upon the exterior of all of the doors of the safe if entry is made through such doors." A burglar robs B's safe by picking the lock of the outer door, leaving no visible marks, and punching out the lock of the inner door. If the requirement of visible marks on both doors is merely evidentiary, the condition occurs when there is as here, adequate evidence of force and violence to prevent fraudulent claims, even though there are no visible marks on the outer door. Since A was the draftsman of the policy, the meaning favorable to B is preferred (§ 206).

6. A contracts to sell and B to buy a house for $ 50,000. The contract recites that financing is to take the form of "$ 30,000 mortgage from X Bank" on stated terms and provides that B's duty is "conditional upon B's ability to arrange above described financing." B is unable to get the mortgage from X Bank but A offers to take a $ 30,000 purchase money mortgage on the stated terms and makes a conditional offer to deliver a deed. B refuses to perform. Although circumstances may show a contrary intention, the quoted language will ordinarily be interpreted so that the condition occurs only if B is able to get the mortgage from X Bank, and not if B is able to get a similar mortgage from A. Under this interpretation, B's refusal is not a breach.

c. By a term supplied by court. When the parties have omitted a term that is essential to a determination of their rights and duties, the court may supply a term which is reasonable in the circumstances (§ 204). Where that term makes an event a condition, it is often described as a "constructive" (or "implied in law") condition. This serves to distinguish it from events which are made conditions by the agreement of the parties, either by their words or by other conduct, and which are described as "express" and as "implied in fact" (inferred from fact) conditions. See Comments *a* and *b* to § 4. It is useful to distinguish "constructive" conditions, even though the distinction is necessarily somewhat arbitrary. For one thing, it is helpful in analysis and description to have terminology that reflects the two distinctive processes, sometimes called "interpretation" and "construction," that give rise to conditions. See Uniform Commercial Code §§ 2-313 to 2-315, in which an analogous distinction is made between express and implied warranties. For another, to the extent that the parties have, by a term of their agreement, clearly made an event a condition, they can be confident that a court will ordinarily feel constrained strictly to apply that term, while the same court may regard itself as having considerable latitude in tailoring a similar term that it has itself supplied.

One example of such a term supplied by the court is the requirement of § 45(2) that the offeree, under an option contract, complete or tender the invited performance as a condition of the offeror's duty. A more common example occurs where an obligor's duty cannot be performed without some act by the obligee, and the court supplies a term making that act a condition of the obligor's duty. In most such situations, the obligee's own obligation of good faith and fair dealing (§ 205) imposes on him a duty to do the act, so that a material failure to perform that duty would, in any case, have the same effect as the non-occurrence of a condition under the rules relating to performances to be exchanged under an exchange of promises (§ 239). The examples given in the following illustrations involve situations where no duty to do the act is imposed.

Illustrations:

7. A promises to make necessary interior repairs on a building that he has leased to B, but reserves no privilege of entering the building. B's giving reasonable notice to A of any necessary interior repairs of which A would otherwise be unaware is a condition of A's duty to make those repairs, although B is under no duty to give notice.

8. A, a general contractor, contracts with B, a town, to construct a sewer system, agreeing in addition to defend any action against the town arising out of the work and to pay any damages recovered in such an action. B's giving reasonable notice to A of the commencement of any action of which A would otherwise be unaware is a condition of A's duties to defend and pay damages, although B is under no duty to give notice.

§ 227. Standards of Preference with Regard to Conditions

(1) In resolving doubts as to whether an event is made a condition of an obligor's duty, and as to the nature of such an event, an interpretation is preferred that will reduce the obligee's risk of forfeiture, unless the event is within the obligee's control or the circumstances indicate that he has assumed the risk.

(2) Unless the contract is of a type under which only one party generally undertakes duties, when it is doubtful whether

(a) a duty is imposed on an obligee that an event occur, or

(b) the event is made a condition of the obligor's duty, or

(c) the event is made a condition of the obligor's duty and a duty is imposed on the obligee that the event occur, the first interpretation is preferred if the event is within the obligee's control.

(3) In case of doubt, an interpretation under which an event is a condition of an obligor's duty is preferred over an interpretation under which the non-occurrence of the event is a ground for discharge of that duty after it has become a duty to perform.

Comment:

a. Scope. The present Section states three standards of preference used in the process of interpretation with regard to conditions. They supplement the standards of preference in § 203, as well as the other rules set out in Topics 1 through 4 of this Chapter.

b. Condition or not. The non-occurrence of a condition of an obligor's duty may cause the obligee to lose his right to the agreed exchange after he has relied substantially on the expectation of that exchange, as by preparation or performance. The word "forfeiture" is used in this Restatement to refer to the denial of compensation that results in such a case. The policy favoring freedom of contract requires that, within broad limits (see § 229), the agreement of the parties should be honored even though forfeiture results. When, however, it is doubtful whether or not the agreement makes an event a condition of an obligor's duty, an interpretation is preferred that will reduce the risk of forfeiture. For example, under a provision that a duty is to be performed "when" an event occurs, it may be doubtful whether it is to be performed only if that event occurs, in which case the event is a condition, or at such time as it would ordinarily occur, in which case the event is referred to merely to measure the passage of time. In the latter case, if the event does not occur some alternative means will be found to measure the passage of time, and the non-occurrence of the event will not prevent the obligor's duty from becoming one of performance. If the event is a condition, however, the obligee takes the risk that its non-occurrence will discharge the obligor's duty. See § 225(2). When the nature of the condition is such that the uncertainty as to the event will be resolved before either party has relied on its anticipated occurrence, both parties can be entirely relieved of their duties, and the obligee risks only the loss of his expectations. When, however, the nature of the condition is such that the uncertainty is not likely to be resolved until after the obligee has relied by preparing to perform or by performing at least in part, he risks forfeiture. If the event is within his control, he will often assume this risk. If it is not within his control, it is sufficiently unusual for him to assume the risk that, in case of doubt, an interpretation is preferred under which the event is not a condition. The rule is, of course, subject to a showing of a contrary intention, and even without clear language, circumstances may show that he assumed the risk of its non-occurrence.

Although the rule is consistent with a policy of avoiding forfeiture and unjust enrichment, it is not directed at the avoidance of actual forfeiture and unjust enrichment. Since the intentions of the parties must be taken as of the time the contract was made, the test is whether a particular interpretation would have avoided the risk of forfeiture viewed as of that time, not whether it will avoid actual forfeiture in the resolution of a dispute that has arisen later. Excuse of the non-occurrence of a condition because of actual forfeiture is dealt with in § 229, and rules for the avoidance of unjust enrichment as such are dealt with in the Restatement of Restitution and in Chapter 16 of this Restatement, particularly §§ 370-77. **Illustrations:**

    1. A, a general contractor, contracts with B, a sub-contractor, for the plumbing work on a construction project. B is to receive $ 100,000, "no part of which shall be due until five days after Owner shall have paid Contractor therefor." B does the plumbing work, but the owner becomes insolvent and fails to pay A. A is under a duty to pay B after a reasonable time.

    2. A, a mining company, hires B, an engineer, to help reopen one of its mines for "$ 10,000to be payable as soon as the mine is in successful operation." $ 10,000 is a reasonable compensation for B's service. B performs the required services, but the attempt to reopen the mine is unsuccessful and A abandons it. A is under a duty to pay B $ 10,000 after the passage of a reasonable time.

    3. A, a mining company, contracts with B, the owner of an untested experimental patented process, to help reopen one of its mines for $ 5,000 paid in advance and an additional "$ 15,000

to be payable as soon as the mine is in successful operation." $ 10,000 is a reasonable compensation for B's services. B performs the required services, but because the process proves to be unsuccessful, A abandons the attempt to reopen the mine. A is under no duty to pay B any additional amount. In all the circumstances the risk of failure of the process was, to that extent, assumed by B.

    4. A contracts to sell and B to buy land for $ 100,000. At the same time, A contracts to pay C, a real estate broker, as his commission, $ 5,000 "on the closing of title." B refuses to consummate the sale. Absent a showing of a contrary intention, a court may conclude that C assumed this risk, and that A's duty is conditional on the sale being consummated. A is then under no duty to pay C.

    c. Nature of event. In determining the nature of the event that is made a condition by the agreement, as in determining whether the agreement makes an event a condition in the first place (see Comment *b*), it will not ordinarily be supposed that a party has assumed the risk of forfeiture. Where the language is doubtful, an interpretation is generally preferred that will avoid this risk. This standard of preference finds an important application in the case of promises to pay for work done if some independent third party, such as an architect, surveyor or engineer, is satisfied with it, where the risk of forfeiture in the case of a judgment that is dishonest or based on a gross mistake as to the facts is substantial. The standard does not, however, help a party if the condition is within his control or if the circumstances otherwise indicate that he assumed that risk. **Illustrations:**

    5. A contracts with B to repair B's building for $ 20,000, payment to be made "on the satisfaction of C, B's architect, and the issuance of his certificate." A makes the repairs, but C refuses to issue his certificate, and explains why he is not satisfied. Other experts in the field consider A's performance to be satisfactory and disagree with C's explanation. A has no claim against B. The quoted language is sufficiently clear that Subsection (1) does not apply. If C is honestly not satisfied, B is under no duty to pay A, and it makes no difference if his dissatisfaction was not reasonable.

    6. The facts being otherwise as stated in Illustration 5, C refuses to issue his certificate although he admits that he is satisfied. A has a claim against B for $ 20,000. The quoted language will be interpreted so that the requirement

of the certificate is merely evidentiary and the condition occurs when there is, as here, adequate evidence that C is honestly satisfied.

7. The facts being otherwise as stated in Illustration 5, C does not make a proper inspection of the work and gives no reasons for his dissatisfaction. A has a claim against B for $ 20,000. In using the quoted language, A and B assumed that C would exercise an honest judgment and by failing to make a proper inspection, C did not exercise such a judgment. Since the parties have omitted an essential term to cover this situation, the court will supply a term (see § 204) requiring A to pay B if C ought reasonably to have been satisfied.

8. The facts being otherwise as stated in Illustration 5, C makes a gross mistake with reference to the facts on which his refusal to give a certificate is based. A has a claim against B for $ 20,000. In using the quoted language, A and B assumed that C would exercise his judgment without a gross mistake as to the facts. Since the parties have omitted an essential term to cover this situation, the court will supply a term (see § 204) requiring A to pay B if C ought reasonably to have been satisfied.

d. Condition or duty. When an obligor wants the obligee to do an act, the obligor may make his own duty conditional on the obligee doing it and may also have the obligee promise to do it. Or he may merely make his own duty conditional on the obligee doing it. Or he may merely have the obligee promise to do it. (See Introductory Note to this Topic and Comment *d* to § 225). It may not be clear, however, which he has done. The rule in Subsection (2) states a preference for an interpretation that merely imposes a duty on the obligee to do the act and does not make the doing of the act a condition of the obligor's duty. The preferred interpretation avoids the harsh results that might otherwise result from the non-occurrence of a condition and still gives adequate protection to the obligor under the rules of Chapter 10 relating to performances to be exchanged under an exchange of promises. Under those rules, particularly §§237-41, the obligee's failure to perform his duty has, if it is material, the effect of the non-occurrence of a condition of the obligor's duty. Unless the agreement makes it clear that the event is required as a condition, it is fairer to apply these more flexible rules. The obligor will, in any case, have a remedy for breach. In many instances the rule in Subsection (1) will also apply and will reinforce

the preference stated in Subsection (2).

This standard of preference applies only where the event is within the obligee's control. Where it is within the obligor's control (e.g., his honest satisfaction with the obligee's performance), within a third party's control (e.g., an architect's satisfaction with performance), or within no one's control (e.g., the accidental destruction of the subject matter), the preferential rule does not apply since it is not usual for the obligee to undertake a duty that such an event will occur. Although the obligee can, by appropriate language, undertake a duty that an event that is not within his control will occur, such an undertaking must be derived from the agreement of the parties under the general rules of interpretation stated earlier in the present Chapter without resort to this standard of preference.

Furthermore, this standard of preference does not apply when the contract is of a type under which only the obligor generally undertakes duties. It therefore does not apply to the typical insurance contract under which only the insurer generally undertakes duties, and a term requiring an act to be done by the insured is not subject to this standard of preference. In view of the general understanding that only the insurer undertakes duties, the term will be interpreted as making that event a condition of the insurer's duty rather than as imposing a duty on the insured. **Illustrations:**

9. On August 1, A contracts to sell and B to buy goods, "selection to be made by buyer before September 1." B merely has a duty to make his selection by September 1, and his making it by that date is not a condition of A's duty. A failure by B to make a selection by September 1 is a breach, and if material it operates as the non-occurrence of a condition of A's duty. See §§237, 241.

10. A, B, and C make a contract under which A agrees to buy the inventory of B's grocery business, C agrees to finance A's down payment, and B agrees to subordinate A's obligation to him to pay the balance to A's obligation to C to repay the amount of the down payment. The contract provides that "C shall maintain the books of account for A, and shall inventory A's stock of merchandise every two months, rendering statements to B." C merely has a duty to do these acts and doing them is not a condition of B's duty. A failure by C to do them is a breach,

and if material it operates as the non-occurrence of a condition of B's duty. See §§237, 241.

11. A insures B's house against fire for $ 50,000 under a policy providing, "other insurance is prohibited." Because the insured has undertaken no other duties under the contract, Subsection (2) does not apply. Because a policy of fire insurance is a type of contract under which only the insurer generally undertakes duties, the absence of other insurance is merely a condition of A's duty, and B is not under a duty not to procure other insurance.

e. Condition or discharge. Circumstances may show that the parties intended to make an event a condition of an obligor's duty even though their language appears to make the non-occurrence of the event a ground for discharge of his duty after performance has become due. See Comment *e* to § 224. An example is the traditional form of bond, which states that the obligor is under a duty to perform, but that the duty will be discharged if something happens. The language, in spite of its form, is interpreted so that the failure of that thing to happen is a condition of the obligor's duty. Unless that condition occurs, no performance is due. Although this form of expression persists in legal documents, only rarely do the parties intend that one of them shall be under a duty to perform which is to cease on the occurrence of something that is still uncertain. The clearest language is therefore necessary to justify such an interpretation, and if the language is doubtful a contrary interpretation is preferred. **Illustrations:**

12. In return for a fee paid by X, A signs and delivers to B a bond which reads: "I acknowledge myself to be indebted to B in the sum of $ 50,000. The condition of this obligation is such that if X shall faithfully perform his duties as executor of the will of Y, this obligation shall be void, but otherwise of full effect." X's failure faithfully to perform his duties is a condition of A's duty under the bond.

13. A promises to pay B $ 10,000 for a quantity of oil, and promises to pay B an additional $ 5,000 "but if a greater quantity of oil arrives in vessels during the first quarter of the year than arrived during the same quarter last year, then this obligation to be void." A's payment of the additional $ 5,000 is not due until the end of the first quarter, and the failure of a greater quantity of oil to arrive by that time is a condition of A's duty to pay the additional $ 5,000.

§ 228. Satisfaction of the Obligor as a Condition

When it is a condition of an obligor's duty that he be satisfied with respect to the obligee's performance or with respect to something else, and it is practicable to determine whether a reasonable person in the position of the obligor would be satisfied, an interpretation is preferred under which the condition occurs if such a reasonable person in the position of the obligor would be satisfied.

Comment:

a. Conditions of satisfaction. This Section sets out a special standard of preference for a type of condition that has long been of particular interest and importance -- the satisfaction of the obligor himself, rather than a third party. Usually it is the obligee's performance as to which the obligor is to be satisfied, but it may also be something else, such as the propitiousness of circumstances for his enterprise. The agreement will often use language such as "satisfaction" or "complete satisfaction," without making it clear that the test is merely one of honest satisfaction rather than of reasonable satisfaction. Under any interpretation, the exercise of judgment must be in accordance with the duty of good faith and fair dealing (§205), and for this reason, the agreement is not illusory (§77). If the agreement leaves no doubt that it is only honest satisfaction that is meant and no more, it will be so interpreted, and the condition does not occur if the obligor is honestly, even though unreasonably, dissatisfied. Even so, the dissatisfaction must be with the circumstance and not with the bargain and the mere statement of the obligor that he is not satisfied is not conclusive on the question of his honest satisfaction. **Illustrations:**

1. A grants to B an exclusive license in a designated territory to bottle and sell a soft drink on specified terms for a five-year period. The contract describes in detail B's duty diligently to represent A in the territory and provides that A may terminate the license at any time if in A's "sole, exclusive and final judgment made in good faith" B does not perform that duty. After a year,

A terminates, honestly telling B that in A's judgment B has not performed his duty under the contract. B has no claim against A since the agreement clearly provides a test of honest satisfaction.

2. A contracts to sell and B to buy 500 barrels of cherries in syrup "quality to be satisfactory in buyer's honest judgment," delivery to be in installments. After deliveries of and payments for a total of 100 barrels, B states that he is not satisfied and refuses to take more. Since the agreement clearly provides a test of honest satisfaction, B's termination is effective if his judgment is in fact made honestly in accordance with his duty of good faith and fair dealing (§205). However, A may show that B's rejection was for other reasons by proving, for example, that B expressed satisfaction at the time of the first deliveries, that B's demand had dropped sharply, and that A's cherries are selected and put up with great care and are of the highest quality.

b. Preference for objective standard. When, however, the agreement does not make it clear that it requires merely honest satisfaction, it will not usually be supposed that the obligee has assumed the risk of the obligor's unreasonable, even if honest, dissatisfaction. In such a case, to the extent that it is practicable to apply an objective test of reasonable satisfaction, such a test will be applied. The situation differs from that where the satisfaction of a third party such as an architect, surveyor or engineer is concerned. See Comment *c* to §227. These professionals, even though employed by the obligor, are assumed to be capable of independent judgment, free from the selfish interests of the obligor. But if the obligor would subject the obligee's right to compensation to his own idiosyncrasies, he must use clear language. When, as is often the case, the preferred interpretation will reduce the obligee's risk of forfeiture, so that §227(1) also applies, there is an additional argument in its favor. This argument is particularly strong where the obligor will be left with a benefit which he cannot return. If, however, the circumstance with respect to which a party is to be satisfied is such that the application of an objective test is impracticable, the rule of this Section is not applicable. A court will then, for practical reasons, apply a subjective test of honest satisfaction, even if the agreement admits of doubt on the point and even if the result will be to increase the obligee's risk of forfeiture.

Illustrations:

3. A contracts with B to install a heating system in B's factory, for a price of $ 20,000 to be paid "on condition of satisfactory completion." A installs the heating system, but B states that he is not satisfied with it and refuses to pay the $ 20,000. B gives no reason except that he does not approve of the heating system, and according to experts in the field the system as installed is entirely satisfactory. A has a claim against B for $ 20,000 since it is practicable to apply an objective test to the installation of the heating system. This interpretation is also preferred because it reduces A's risk of forfeiture.

4. A contracts with B to paint a portrait of B's daughter, for which B promises to pay $ 5,000 "if entirely satisfied." A paints the portrait, but B honestly states that he is not satisfied with it and refuses to pay the $ 5,000. B gives no reason except that the portrait does not please him, and according to experts in the field the portrait is an admirable work of art. A has no claim against B since it is not practicable to apply an objective test to the painting.

. . .

§ 229. Excuse of a Condition to Avoid Forfeiture

To the extent that the non-occurrence of a condition would cause disproportionate forfeiture, a court may excuse the non-occurrence of that condition unless its occurrence was a material part of the agreed exchange.

Comment:

a. Relation to other rules. As is pointed out in Comment *b* to § 227, the non-occurrence of a condition of the obligor's duty may result in forfeiture by the obligee. Forfeiture may sometimes be avoided by application of the general rules of interpretation stated in the present Chapter, such as the rule on interpretation against the draftsman (§ 206). It may sometimes be avoided by application of the special rules on interpretation stated in the present Topic with regard to conditions (§§ 227(1), 228). But if the term that requires the occurrence of the event as a condition is expressed in unmistakable language, the possibility of forfeiture will not affect the interpretation of that language. See Comment *b* to § 227. Nevertheless, forfeiture may sometimes still be avoided by application of the rules on excuse of conditions. See Comment *b* to § 225. Under the present Section a court may, in appropriate circumstances, excuse the non-occurrence of a condition solely on the basis of the forfeiture that would otherwise result. Although both this Section and § 208, on unconscionable contract or term, limit freedom of contract, they are designed to reach different types of situations. While § 208 speaks of unconscionability "at the time the contract is made," this Section is concerned with forfeiture that would actually result if the condition were not excused. It is intended to deal with a term that does not appear to be unconscionable at the time the contract is made but that would, because of ensuing events, cause forfeiture.

b. Disproportionate forfeiture. The rule stated in the present Section is, of necessity, a flexible one, and its application is within the sound discretion of the court. Here, as in § 227(1), "forfeiture" is used to refer to the denial of compensation that results when the obligee loses his right to the agreed exchange after he has relied substantially, as by preparation or performance on the expectation of that exchange. See Comment *b* to § 227. The extent of the forfeiture in any particular case will depend on the extent of that denial of compensation. In determining whether the forfeiture is "disproportionate," a court must weigh the extent of the forfeiture by the obligee against the importance to the obligor of the risk from which he sought to be protected and the degree to which that protection will be lost if the non-occurrence of the condition is excused to the extent required to prevent forfeiture. The character of the agreement may, as in the case of insurance agreements, affect the rigor with which the requirement is applied. **Illustrations:**

1. A contracts to build a house for B, using pipe of Reading manufacture. In return, B agrees to pay $ 75,000 in progress payments, each payment to be made "on condition that no pipe other than that of Reading manufacture has been used." Without A's knowledge, a subcontractor mistakenly uses pipe of Cohoes manufacture which is identical in quality and is distinguishable only by the name of the manufacturer which is stamped on it. The mistake is not discovered until the house is completed, when replacement of the pipe will require destruction of substantial parts of the house. B refuses to pay the unpaid balance of $ 10,000. A court may conclude

that the use of Reading rather than Cohoes pipe is so relatively unimportant to B that the forfeiture that would result from denying A the entire balance would be disproportionate, and may allow recovery by A subject to any claim for damages for A's breach of his duty to use Reading pipe.

2. A, an ocean carrier, carries B's goods under a contract providing that it is a condition of A's liability for damage to cargo that "written notice of claim for loss or damage must be given within 10 days after removal of goods." B's cargo is damaged during carriage and A knows of this. On removal of the goods, B notes in writing on the delivery record that the cargo is damaged, and five days later informs A over the telephone of a claim for that damage and invites A to participate in an inspection within the ten day period. A inspects the goods within the period, but B does not give written notice of its claim until 25 days after removal of the goods. Since the purpose of requiring the condition of written notice is to alert the carrier and enable it to make a prompt investigation, and since this purpose had been served by the written notice of damage and the oral notice of claim, the court may excuse the non-occurrence of the condition to the extent required to allow recovery by B.

c. Limitation on scope. The rule of this Section applies only where occurrence of the condition was not a material part of the agreed exchange. These are situations where, under § 84, the non-occurrence of the condition could have been excused by a promise to perform the duty in spite of its non-occurrence. It is not enough that the actual non-occurrence happened to involve a departure that was not a material part of the agreed exchange, if the occurrence of the condition was a material part of that exchange. A court may, of course, ignore trifling departures.

A court need not excuse entirely the non-occurrence of the condition, but may merely excuse its non-occurrence during the period of time in which it would otherwise have to occur (see Comment *c* to § 225), if it concludes that the time of its occurrence is not a material part of the agreed exchange. This conclusion is sometimes summed up by the phrase that "time is not of the essence." **Illustrations:**

3. A contracts to make repairs on B's house, in return for which B agrees to pay $ 10,000 "on condition that the repairs are completed by October 1." The repairs are not completed until October 2. A court may decide that there are two cumulative conditions, repair of the house

and completion of the repairs by October 1, and that the non-occurrence of the second condition is excused to the extent of one day.

4. On July 1, A makes an option contract with B, under which B has the right to buy land for $ 200,000, on condition that he exercise it no later than June 30 five years later. B makes an initial payment of $ 10,000 and agrees to make additional $ 10,000 payments on or before June 30 of each of the four succeeding years, unless he has already exercised the option, his right being "conditional on his paying the $ 10,000 on or before the prescribed date." These payments are not to be applied to the purchase price. After paying for two years and building on adjacent land, substantially increasing the value of the land subject to the option, B mails a $ 10,000 check for the third year on June 30. A receives it on July 1 and returns it to B, stating that the option contract is cancelled. A court may decide that there are two cumulative conditions, payment of $ 10,000 and payment on or before June 30, and that the non-occurrence of the second condition is excused to the extent of one day.

. . .

§ 230. Event That Terminates a Duty

(1) Except as stated in Subsection (2), if under the terms of the contract the occurrence of an event is to terminate an obligor's duty of immediate performance or one to pay damages for breach, that duty is discharged if the event occurs.

(2) The obligor's duty is not discharged if occurrence of the event

(a) is the result of a breach by the obligor of his duty of good faith and fair dealing, or

(b) could not have been prevented because of impracticability and continuance of the duty does not subject the obligor to a materially increased burden.

(3) The obligor's duty is not discharged if, before the event occurs, the obligor promises to perform the duty even if the event occurs and does not revoke his promise before the obligee materially changes his position in reliance on it.

Comment:

a. Scope. Parties sometimes provide that an obligor's matured duty will be extinguished on the occurrence of a specified event, which is sometimes referred to as a "condition subsequent." See Comment *e* to § 224. They may, for example, provide that an obligor's duty to reimburse the obligee for some loss or to compensate him for a breach will be extinguished if the obligee does not take some action, such as bringing suit, within a stated period of time. Under such a provision, the duty is generally discharged if the event occurs. The same result follows if its occurrence becomes inevitable. Subsection (2) states exceptions to this general rule for cases in which the occurrence of the event is due to the obligor's breach of his duty of good faith and fair dealing (§ 205) or could not have been prevented by the obligee because of impracticability (§ 261). See Subsection (2). The rule stated in this Section applies only to matured duties and to duties to make compensation. If performance under the contract is not to become due until occurrence of an event, that event is a condition of the duty and is governed by the rules stated in §§ 224-29. The difference is one of substance and not merely of the form in which the provision is stated. **Illustrations:**

1. A, an insurance company, insures the property of B under a policy providing that no recovery can be had if suit is not brought on the policy within two years after a loss. A loss occurs and B lets two years pass before bringing suit. A's duty to pay B for the loss is discharged and B cannot maintain the action on the policy.

. . .

b. Promise to perform in spite of occurrence. Under the rule stated in Subsection (3), a promise by the obligor to perform the duty regardless of the occurrence of the event is binding if the obligee has materially changed his position in reliance on it. The promise need not be in words and may be inferred from other conduct. The rule, like that stated in § 84, is sometimes thought of in terms of "waiver" or "estoppel." See Comments *a* and *b* to § 84. It supplements the general rules on modification of contracts by agreement of the parties. **Illustration:**

3. The facts being otherwise as stated in Illustration 1, after the loss occurs, A tells B that it is not necessary to bring suit within two years, and B relies on the statement in refraining from suing for two years. A's duty to pay B for the loss is not discharged and B can maintain an action on the policy even after two years have passed.

Chapter 10

Performance and Non-Performance

Introductory Note Because contracting parties ordinarily expect that they will perform their obligations, they are usually more explicit in defining those obligations than in stating the consequences of their non-performance. During the course of performance, problems may arise that require a clear definition of the obligations of the parties under the contract and that may make it appropriate for them to adjust those obligations in the light of a situation not contemplated when the contract was made. When such problems arise, the parties should be encouraged to communicate with each other and seek to resolve them without outside intervention. Should their efforts fail, a court may be asked to define their obligations. See § 204. This Chapter states rules for this purpose.

In general, these rules are based on fundamental principles of fairness and justice. The provisions of Article 2 of the Uniform Commercial Code that relate to performance and non-performance show the application of these principles to contracts for the sale of goods. They serve therefore both as illustrations of the principles on which the rules stated in this Chapter are based and as sources, by analogy, of those principles. Compare, e.g., § 233 with Uniform Commercial Code § 2-307, and § 251 with Uniform Commercial Code § 2-609.

The most important and complex of the rules stated in this Chapter apply to the most significant type of contract, that in which the parties have exchanged promises in the expectation that there will be a subsequent exchange of performances. Rules for identifying contracts of this type are stated in §§ 231 and 232. The principal objective of the rules applicable to such contracts is to secure the parties' expectation that a subsequent exchange of performances will actually take place.

When a party fails to receive the performance that he expects, the wisest course is ordinarily for the parties to attempt to resolve their differences by negotiations, including clarification of expectations, cure of past defaults, and assurance as to future performance. If these efforts fail, the injured party may pursue his claim in court. It is, of course, always possible to leave a party who is aggrieved by his failure to receive the expected exchange to pursue a claim for damages against the other party. But contracting parties ordinarily bargain for performance rather than for a lawsuit. It is therefore generally fairer to give the injured party, to the extent that it is possible, the right to suspend his own performance and ultimately to refuse it and, if the other party's non-performance is not justified, to claim damages for total breach of contract. This the injured party is permitted to do under §§ 237 and 238, which make performance, or at least an offer of performance, by the other party a condition of the aggrieved party's remaining duty under the contract.

When the rules stated in these sections apply, their effect is to deny to the other party any right to compensation under the contract itself (as distinguished from any possible claim to restitution) for what he has done. To minimize the risk of forfeiture, they are tempered by provision that only a material failure by the other party operates as the non-occurrence of a condition which justifies the injured party in suspending his own performance and ultimately in treating his duties as discharged. Considerations for determining whether a failure is material and the time after which a material failure discharges the injured party's remaining duties and may also give him a claim for damages for total breach are stated in §§ 241 and 242. The risk of forfeiture is also reduced by the rule stated in § 240, which allows recovery for performance of only a part of what is due subject to any claim for breach as to the remainder, where part performances are agreed equivalents.

In applying these rules it is essential to know the order in which the parties' performances are to be given, so that it can be determined at any particular time whether there has been a material failure by either party with respect to any performance that is due at an earlier time. Where the language or the circumstances indicate the time for performance, that is of course controlling. Otherwise, the rules stated in §§ 233 and 234 govern. To the extent possible, simultaneous performance by both parties is desirable, since this gives each party the opportunity to withhold his own performance until he is sure that the other party's performance will be forthcoming and requires neither party to finance the transaction before he receives the other's performance.

Other sections in Topic 2 of this Chapter state rules that are applicable to contracts generally and are not limited to performances that are to be exchanged under an exchange of promises. They deal with the effects on contract duties of performance and non-performance (§ 235), with claims for total and partial breach (§§ 236, 243), and with the excuse of the non-occurrence of conditions in the course of performance (§§ 245-49). Topic 3 deals with prospective non-performance. See Introductory Note to Topic 3.

The rules stated in this Chapter are not intended to apply to performance as a means of acceptance of an offer, including an option contract (§§ 45, 62), although in some instances the same underlying considerations may apply

§ 231. Criterion for Determining When Performances Are to Be Exchanged Under an Exchange of Promises

Performances are to be exchanged under an exchange of promises if each promise is at least part of the consideration for the other and the performance of each promise is to be exchanged at least in part for the performance of the other.

Comment:

a. Expectation of an exchange of performances. Agreements involving an exchange of promises play a vital role in an economically advanced society. Ordinarily when parties make such an agreement, they not only regard the promises themselves as the subject of an exchange (§ 71(2)), but they also intend that the performances of those promises shall subsequently be exchanged for each other. Even without a showing of such an actual intention, a court will often, out of a sense of fairness, assume that it was their expectation that there would be a subsequent exchange of the performance of each party for that of the other. Cf. § 204. This Chapter consists, in substantial part, of rules designed to secure that expectation of a subsequent exchange of performances.

b. Performances need not be simultaneous. It is often expected that performances will be exchanged under an exchange of promises even though those performances are not to take place at the same time. Under a contract for the sale of goods, for example, the parties expect an exchange of the delivery of the goods by the seller and the payment of the price by the buyer, regardless of whether the price is payable before, at the same time as, or after delivery of the goods. As long as this is their expectation, the delivery of the goods and the payment of the price are to be exchanged under the exchange of promises, and it is immaterial when the price is payable.

Illustrations:

1. A, a shipowner, promises to carry B's cargo on his ship. B promises to pay A the stipulated freight. They exchange these promises in the expectation that there will be a subsequent exchange of those performances. A fails to carry B's cargo, and B thereupon refuses to pay the freight. A's carrying the cargo and B's paying the freight are to be exchanged under the exchange of promises. Therefore, under the rule stated in § 237, A has no claim against B.

2. In return for A's promise to deliver a machine, B promises to pay A $ 10,000 within 30 days. They exchange these promises in the expectation that there will be a subsequent exchange of those performances. A fails to deliver the machine, and B thereupon refuses to pay any part of the $ 10,000. A's delivery of the machine and B's payment of the $ 10,000 are to be exchanged under the exchange of promises. Therefore, under the rule stated in § 237, A has no claim against B.

c. Consideration need not be exclusively promises. The parties may expect that their performances will be exchanged under their exchange of promises even though that exchange does not consist exclusively of promises. The consideration given by one or both parties may consist in part of some performance. **Illustration:**

3. In return for A's promise to deliver a machine priced at $ 10,000, B pays A $ 5,000 as a down payment and promises to pay A the $ 5,000 balance within 30 days after delivery of the

machine. They exchange these promises in the expectation that delivery of the machine will be exchanged, at least in part, for the $ 5,000 balance and that the $ 5,000 balance will be exchanged for the machine. A fails to deliver the machine, and B thereupon refuses to pay the $ 5,000 balance. A's delivery of the machine and B's payment of the $ 5,000 balance within 30 days are to be exchanged under the exchange of promises. Therefore, under the rule stated in § 237, A has no claim against B. B is entitled to restitution of the $ 5,000 he paid (see §§ 370-77) in addition to his claim against A for damages for breach (§ 243).

d. Separate contracts. The rules that protect parties whose performances are to be exchanged under an exchange of promises apply only when the promises are exchanged as part of a single contract. When each party gives more than one promise, or gives some performance in addition to a promise, it may not be clear whether there is a single exchange of promises resulting in a single contract or separate exchanges resulting in separate contracts. If every promise by one party is at least part of the consideration for every promise by the other party, there is a single exchange in which all of the promises on each side are exchanged for all of those on the other side. This is so, for example, where a buyer and a seller make a single bargain for the sale of several related kinds of goods. But if one or more promises by each party are no part of the consideration for one or more promises by the other party, there are instead separate exchanges. In that case all of the promises on each side cannot be regarded as exchanged for all of those on the other side. This is so, for example, where a buyer and a seller make several bargains at the same time for the sale of several unrelated kinds of goods. In deciding whether there is a single contract rather than separate contracts, the court must look to the actual bargain of the parties, in accordance with § 71(2), to decide whether each promise on one side was sought and given as at least part of the exchange for each promise on the other side. The form of the agreement is not controlling, and the actual bargain of the parties is not to be determined merely by reference to such criteria as whether separate performances are made the subject of a single promise or of separate promises, whether separate promises are contained in a single writing or in separate writings, or whether the understanding of the parties is entirely written or oral or is partly written and partly oral. **Illustrations:**

    4. A promises to sell and B to buy a food freezer priced at $ 1,200 to be paid for in monthly installments over an eighteen-month period. A also promises to sell B frozen food at greatly reduced prices, and B promises to buy an initial quantity, deliverable at the same time as the freezer, for $ 200, with additional quantities to be available in the future at B's option. Although two separate writings are executed, one entitled "Freezer Contract" and, the other, entitled "Food Contract," the promises are made as part of the same bargain, and payment for the freezer, for example, is to be exchanged at least in part for the delivery of the food. A tenders the freezer but fails to supply the food although B tenders the $ 200. B thereupon refuses to take the freezer or to pay anything. The performances promised in the two writings, A's delivery of the freezer and the food and B's payment for the freezer and the food, are to be exchanged under a single exchange of promises. Therefore, under the rule stated in § 238, A has no claim against B.

    · · ·

§ 232. When It Is Presumed That Performances Are to Be Exchanged Under an Exchange of Promises

Where the consideration given by each party to a contract consists in whole or in part of promises, all the performances to be rendered by each party taken collectively are treated as performances to be exchanged under an exchange of promises, unless a contrary intention is clearly manifested.

Comment:

    a. Reason for presumption. The rules applicable to performances to be exchanged under an exchange of promises are designed to give the parties maximum protection, consistent with freedom of contract, against disappointment of their expectation of a subsequent exchange of those performances. When the parties have exchanged promises, there is ordinarily every reason to suppose that they contracted on the basis of such an expectation since the exchange of promises would otherwise have little purpose. Even absent a showing of their actual intentions, fairness dictates that such an expectation be assumed. This Section therefore states a presumption in favor of the conclusion that, in such a case, the performances are to be exchanged under the exchange of promises. For one of the parties to show that the expectation was otherwise, the contrary intention must be clearly manifested. The presumption applies regardless of whether the promises are written or oral or both, and even where a negotiable instrument is involved. See Uniform Commercial Code § 3-408. It also applies even though the consideration given by a party consists partly of some performance and only partly of a promise (see Comment *c* to § 231), although it is possible that in such a case the promise may be so minor and incidental that its non-performance would not be a material failure of performance. See Comment *b* to § 241. **Illustrations:**

    1. A, a wholesaler, promises to sell and B, a retailer, promises to buy goods together with related advertising material, payment to be made within 30 days of delivery. A also promises not to sell similar advertising material to any other retailer in B's city. A sells similar advertising material to another retailer in B's city, and B thereupon refuses to take or pay for the goods. A's selling B goods together with advertising material and not selling others similar advertising material, taken collectively, and B's payment are to be exchanged under the exchange of promises. Therefore, under the rule stated in § 237, if A's failure of performance is material, A has no claim against B.

    2. A promises to sell to B a lot in a subdivision for $ 8,000. B promises to pay in four annual installments of $ 2,000 each, beginning one year after execution of the contract. A promises to begin to make improvements and pave the streets within 60 days and to complete work within a reasonable time and promises to deliver a deed at the time of the final payment. A fails to pave the streets, and B thereupon refuses to pay any installments. A's making improvements, paving streets, and delivering a deed, taken collectively, and B's paying installments are to be exchanged under the exchange of promises. Therefore, under the rule stated in § 237, if A's failure of performance is material, A has no claim against B.

. . .

§ 233. Performance at One Time or in Installments

(1) Where performances are to be exchanged under an exchange of promises, and the whole of one party's performance can be rendered at one time, it is due at one time, unless the language or the circumstances indicate the contrary.

(2) Where only a part of one party's performance is due at one time under Subsection (1), if the other party's performance can be so apportioned that there is a comparable part that can also be rendered at that time, it is due at that time, unless the language or the circumstances indicate the contrary.

Comment:

    a. Performance at one time. Subsection (1) states the established rule that a party who can give his whole performance at one time is expected to do so. He is not entitled to perform a part at a time, nor is the other party entitled to demand that he do so. Uniform Commercial Code § 2-307 so provides for contracts for the sale of goods. The rule expresses the usual understanding of parties in such cases. A party who asserts a different understanding may establish a contrary intention by an express agreement such as one for delivery in installments, or by usage of trade (§ 221; Uniform Commercial Code § 1-205) or by course of dealing (§ 223; Uniform Commercial Code § 1-205). Or he may establish it by showing special circumstances, as where under a contract for brick to be used to build a building it is understood that the buyer's storage space is so limited that it would be impossible for him to receive the entire amount at once. See Comment 3 to Uniform Commercial Code § 2-307. The rule does not apply where performance requires a period of time. The requirement that performance be possible at one time may, however, be met even though the performance, as in the case of delivery of a large quantity of bulky goods, cannot be instantaneous. **Illustrations:**

1. A contracts to sell and B to buy ten identical carloads of coal for $ 100,000. Delivery by A of all ten carloads is due in a single lot.

2. The facts being otherwise as stated in Illustration 1, it is known by both A and B that only one carload of coal will be available at a time. A may deliver one carload at a time.

b. Right to other party's performance. If the language or circumstances indicate that, contrary to the general rule stated in Subsection (1), only a part of one party's performance is due at one time, a question then arises as to when the other party's performance is due. Under the rule stated in Subsection (2), if the other party's performance can be so apportioned that there is a comparable part that can also be given at that time, part performance by both parties is due at that time. See § 234(1). In the typical case the other party's performance will consist of the price and the question is whether the price can be apportioned. See Comment *d* to § 240. This is the way in which the rule is stated for the sale of goods in Uniform Commercial Code § 2-307. **Illustration:**

3. The facts being as stated in Illustration 2, payment of $ 10,000 by B is due at the same time that A delivers each carload of coal.

§ 234. Order of Performances

(1) Where all or part of the performances to be exchanged under an exchange of promises can be rendered simultaneously, they are to that extent due simultaneously, unless the language or the circumstances indicate the contrary.

(2) Except to the extent stated in Subsection (1), where the performance of only one party under such an exchange requires a period of time, his performance is due at an earlier time than that of the other party, unless the language or the circumstances indicate the contrary.

Comment:

a. Advantages of simultaneous performance. A requirement that the parties perform simultaneously where their performances are to be exchanged under an exchange of promises is fair for two reasons. First, it offers both parties maximum security against disappointment of their expectations of a subsequent exchange of performances by allowing each party to defer his own performance until he has been assured that the other will perform. This advantage is implemented by the rule stated in § 238, which deals with offers to perform. Second, it avoids placing on either party the burden of financing the other before the latter has performed. Subsection (1) therefore imposes a requirement of simultaneous performance whenever this is feasible under the contract, in the absence of language or circumstances indicating a contrary intention. A notable example of such a requirement is that laid down for contracts for the sale of goods by Uniform Commercial Code §§ 2-507 and 2-511. The requirement is subject to the agreement of the parties, as by an express provision extending credit to the buyer, or one requiring him to pay against documents or to furnish a letter of credit. Even absent an express provision, a contrary intention may be shown by circumstances including usage of trade and course of dealing (§§ 221, 223; Uniform Commercial Code § 1-205).

b. When simultaneous performance possible under agreement. In the absence of language or circumstances showing a contrary intention, the requirement of simultaneous performance stated in Subsection (1) applies whenever such performance is possible, consistent with the terms of the contract. A major instance where simultaneous performance is not possible occurs when one party's performance is continuous over some substantial period of time, a situation that is dealt with in Subsection (2). However, as is the case for the requirement of the preceding section that the whole performance be possible at one time, the requirement of simultaneous performance is not to be applied so literally as to exclude instances in which the objectives of the requirement can be fulfilled although performance cannot be instantaneous. See Comment *a* to § 233. A less important instance where simultaneous performance is not possible occurs when distance and lack of adequate communications make it impossible to assure the parties that performance is taking place at the same time, so that although the performance of each party can be instantaneous, the two performances cannot be simultaneous within the meaning of Subsection (1). Cases in which simultaneous performance is possible under the terms of the contract can be grouped into five categories: (1) where the same time is fixed for the performance of each party; (2) where a time is fixed for the performance of one of the parties and no time is fixed for the other; (3) where no time is fixed for the performance of either party; (4) where the same period is fixed within which each party is to perform; (5) where different periods are fixed within which each party is to perform. The requirement of simultaneous performance applies to the first four categories. The requirement does not apply to the fifth category, even if simultaneous performance is possible, because in fixing different periods for performance the parties must have contemplated the possibility of performance at different times under their agreement. Therefore in cases in the fifth category the circumstances show an intention contrary to the rule stated in Subsection (1). **Illustrations:**

> 1. A promises to sell land to B, delivery of the deed to be on July 1. B promises to pay A $ 50,000, payment to be made on July 1. Delivery of the deed and payment of the price are due simultaneously.
> 2. A promises to sell land to B, the deed to be delivered on July 1. B promises to pay A $ 50,000, no provision being made for the time of payment. Delivery of the deed and payment of the price are due simultaneously.
> 3. A promises to sell land to B and B promises to pay A $ 50,000, no provision being made for the time either of delivery of the deed or of payment. Delivery of the deed and payment of the price are due simultaneously.
> 4. A promises to sell land to B, delivery of the deed to be on or before July 1. B promises to pay A $ 50,000, payment to be on or before July 1. Delivery of the deed and payment of the price are due simultaneously.
> 5. A promises to sell land to B, delivery of the deed to be on or before July 1. B promises to pay A $ 50,000, payment to be on or before August 1. Delivery of the deed and payment of the prices are not due simultaneously.

c. When simultaneous performance possible in part. The requirement of simultaneous performance stated in Subsection (1) also applies where only part rather than all of the performance of one party can be performed simultaneously with either part or all of the performance of the other party. It therefore applies to the situations discussed in Comment *b* to § 233 and exemplified by Illustration 3 to that section. But it is broader than this and also applies, for example, to instances where some part performance of one party can be rendered simultaneously with the entire performance of the other party. See Comment *f* and Illustration 12. **Illustrations:**

> 6. A promises to sell land to B, delivery of the deed to be four years from the following July 1. B promises to pay A $ 50,000 in installments of $ 10,000 on each July 1 for five years. Delivery of the deed and payment of the last installment are due simultaneously.
> 7. A promises to sell land to B, delivery of the deed to be one year from July 1. B promises to pay A $ 50,000 in installments of $ 10,000 on each July 1 for five years. Delivery of the deed and payment of the second installment are due simultaneously.

d. When simultaneous performance later becomes possible. Although different times or periods were originally fixed for the performance of each party, performance by the party who is to perform first may sometimes be delayed until the time for performance by the other party has arrived. If the latter party is entitled to and does assert that his remaining duties of performance are discharged because of the delay, under the rule stated in § 237, no question of the order of performance remains. Unless the delay is justified, he will also have a claim for damages for total breach based on all of his remaining rights to performance. (§§ 236(1), 243(1)). If, however, he is not entitled to assert that his remaining duties of performance are discharged, or if he does not assert this even though he is entitled to do so, a question of the order of performances remains. Unless the delay is justified he will, of course, have a claim for damages for partial breach because of the delay. Whether or not the delay is justified, he can at least insist on simultaneous performance. (As to judicial supervision of the requirement of simultaneous performance where the injured party has brought an action before the time when his own performance is due and that time then arrives before he has obtained and enforced a judgment, see Comment *c* and Illustration 5 to § 238.) There may be circumstances, however, in which it is appropriate for him to require the other party to perform first, as where the parties to a sale of goods contemplate that the buyer will need the time specified between delivery and payment to resell the goods in order to pay the price. In such a case the right of the party in delay to receive payment may be subject to postponement. **Illustration:**

. . .

e. Where performance requires a period of time. Where the performance of one party requires a period of time and the performance of the other party does not, their performance can not be simultaneous. Since one of the parties must perform first, he must forego the security that a requirement of simultaneous performance affords against disappointment of his expectation of an exchange of performances, and he must bear the burden of financing the other party before the latter has performed. See Comment *a*. Of course the parties can by express provision mitigate the harshness of a rule that requires that one completely perform before the other perform at all. They often do this, for example, in construction contracts by stating a formula under which payment is to be made at stated intervals as work progresses. But it is not feasible for courts to devise such formulas for the wide variety of such cases that come before them in which the parties have made no provision. Centuries ago, the principle became settled that where work is to be done by one party and payment is to be made by the other, the performance of the work must precede payment, in the absence of a showing of a contrary intention. It is sometimes supposed, that this principle grew out of employment contracts, and reflects a conviction that employers as a class are more likely to be responsible than are workmen paid in advance. Whether or not the explanation is correct, most parties today contract with reference to the principle, and unless they have evidenced a contrary intention it is at least as fair as the opposite rule would be.

f. Applicability of rule. The rule stated in Subsection (2) usually finds its application to contracts involving services, such as construction and employment contracts. The common practice of making express provision for progress payments has diminished its importance with regard to the former, and the widespread enactment of state wage statutes giving the employee a right to the frequent periodic payment of wages has lessened its significance with regard to the latter. Nevertheless, it is a helpful rule for residual cases not otherwise provided for. It applies not only to contracts under which the performance of one party is more or less continuous, but also to contracts where performance consists of a series of acts with an interval of time between them. See Comment *c*. Under a contract of the latter type, simultaneity may be possible in part and, to the extent that it is possible, the rule stated in Subsection (2) is subject to that stated in Subsection (1). See Illustrations 6 and 12. **Illustrations:**

9. A contracts to do the concrete work on a building being constructed by B for $ 10 a cubic yard. In the absence of language or circumstances indicating the contrary, payment by B is not due until A has finished the concrete work.

. . .

§ 235. Effect of Performance as Discharge and of Non-Performance As Breach

(1) Full performance of a duty under a contract discharges the duty.

(2) When performance of a duty under a contract is due any non-performance is a breach.

Comment:

a. Discharge by performance. Under the rule stated in Subsection (1), a duty is discharged when it is fully performed. Nothing less than full performance, however, has this effect and any defect in performance, even an insubstantial one, prevents discharge on this ground. The defect need not be wilful or even negligent. Although a court may ignore trifling departures, performance that is merely substantial does not result in discharge under Subsection (1). See Comment *d* to § 237. A duty may, of course, be discharged on some other ground. See Chapter 12. For example, a duty that has not been fully performed may be discharged on the ground of impracticability of performance. See Chapter 11. **Illustration:**

1. A contracts to build a house for B for $ 50,000 according to specifications furnished by B. A builds the house according to the specifications. A's duty to build the house is discharged.

b. Effect of non-performance. Non-performance is not a breach unless performance is due. Performance may not be due because a required period of time has not passed, or because a condition has not occurred (§ 225), or because the duty has already been discharged (Chapter 12) as, for example, by impracticability of performance (Chapter 11). In such a case non-performance is justified. When performance is due, however, anything short of full performance is a breach, even if the party who does not fully perform was not at fault and even if the defect in his performance was not substantial. Non-performance of a duty when performance is due is a breach whether the duty is imposed by a promise stated in the agreement or by a term supplied by the court (§ 204), as in the case of the duty of good faith and fair dealing (§ 205). Non-performance includes defective performance as well as an absence of performance.

Illustrations:

2. The facts being otherwise as stated in Illustration 1, A builds the house according to the specifications except for an inadvertent variation in kitchen fixtures which can easily be remedied for $ 100. A's non-performance is a breach.

3. A contracts with B to manufacture and deliver 100,000 plastic containers for a price of $ 100,000. The colors of the containers are to be selected by B from among those specified in the contract. B delays in making his selection for an unreasonable time, holding up their manufacture and causing A loss. B's delay is a breach. His duty of good faith and fair dealing (§ 205) includes a duty to make his selection within a reasonable time.

. . .

c. Statute of Frauds. Non-performance can be a breach of a contract even though, at the time of the non-performance, the contract is unenforceable because of the Statute of Frauds (§§ 8, 138). Non-performance when performance is due still gives rise to a claim for damages for which a court will grant relief if the Statute is subsequently satisfied as, for example, by the later signing of a memorandum or by an admission in court. See Comments *c* and *d* to § 133 and Comment *b* to § 136. If the Statute is subsequently satisfied, the claim is one for damages for a breach that occurred previously, at the time of the actual non-performance, and not for one that occurred at the time of the later satisfaction of the Statute. **Illustration:**

5. A and B make an oral contract, unenforceable under the Statute of Frauds (§ 125), by which A promises to sell and B to buy land for $ 50,000. Although B tenders the money, A fails to tender a deed and later writes a letter to B which satisfies the Statute of Frauds. A's non-performance is a breach and gives rise to a claim for damages, even though the claim is unenforceable until A writes the letter. See Illustration 4 to § 133.

§ 236. Claims for Damages for Total and for Partial Breach

(1) A claim for damages for total breach is one for damages based on all of the injured party's remaining rights to performance.

(2) A claim for damages for partial breach is one for damages based on only part of the injured party's remaining rights to performance.

Comment:

a. Breach. A breach may be one by non-performance (§ 235(2)), or by repudiation (§ 253), or by both (§ 243). Every breach gives rise to a claim for damages, and may give rise to other remedies. Even if the injured party sustains no pecuniary loss or is unable to show such loss with sufficient certainty, he has at least a claim for nominal damages. See § 346(2). If a court chooses to ignore a trifling departure (Comment *a* to § 235), there is no breach and no claim arises.

b. Total and partial breach distinguished. Although every breach gives rise to a claim for damages, not every claim for damages is one for damages based on all of the injured party's remaining rights to performance under the contract. Such a claim is said to be one for damages for total breach. (The injured party's remaining duties under the contract are not necessarily discharged, however. Even if performances are to be exchanged under an exchange of promises, a duty of the injured party to give a performance that is not part of that exchange of performances is not discharged (§ 237). And a duty of the injured party to give a performance that is the agreed equivalent of performance that has been given by the other party is not discharged (§ 240).) If the injured party elects to or is required to await the balance of the other party's performance under the contract, his claim is said instead to be one for damages for partial breach. For example, an injured party who claims damages in addition to specific performance claims damages for partial breach. Rules for determining whether a particular breach gives rise to a claim for damages for partial breach, for total breach, or for either partial or total breach at the election of the injured party are stated in §§ 243 and 253. **Illustrations:**

     1. A contracts with B to build a building on B's land, work to commence on May 1 and to be completed by October 1. On May 10, A has not yet commenced work. If the court concludes that A's breach, although material (§ 241), has not continued for such a length of time that B is discharged (§ 242), B has a claim against A for damages caused by the delay, but this is not a claim for damages based on all of B's remaining rights to performance. B's claim is one for damages for partial breach. See § 243.

     2. The facts being otherwise as stated in Illustration 1, B cancels the contract. If the court concludes that A's breach is not only material but has continued for such a length of time that B is discharged (§ 242), B has a claim against A for damages based on all of his remaining rights to performance. B's claim is one for damages for total breach. See § 243.

§ 237. Effect on Other Party's Duties of a Failure to Render Performance

Except as stated in § 240, it is a condition of each party's remaining duties to render performances to be exchanged under an exchange of promises that there be no uncured material failure by the other party to render any such performance due at an earlier time.

Comment:

     a. Effect of non-occurrence of condition. Under the rule stated in this Section, a material failure of performance, including defective performance as well as an absence of performance, operates as the non-occurrence of a condition. Under § 225, the non-occurrence of a condition has two possible effects on the duty subject to that condition. See Comment *a* to § 225. The first is that of preventing performance of the duty from becoming due, at least temporarily (§ 225(1)). The second is that of discharging the duty when the condition can no longer occur (§ 225(2)). A material failure of performance has, under this Section, these effects on the other party's remaining duties of performance with respect to the exchange. It prevents performance of those duties from becoming due, at least temporarily, and it discharges those duties if it has not been cured during the time in which performance can occur. The occurrence of conditions of the type dealt with in this Section is required out of a sense of fairness rather than as a result of the agreement of the parties. Such conditions are therefore sometimes referred to as "constructive conditions of exchange." Cf. § 204. What is sometimes referred to as "failure of consideration" by courts and statutes (e.g., Uniform Commercial Code § 3-408) is referred to in this Restatement as "failure of performance" to avoid confusion with the absence of consideration. Circumstances significant in determining whether a failure is material are set out in § 241. Circumstances significant in determining the period of time after which remaining duties are discharged, if a material failure has not been cured, are set out in § 242. The rules stated in this Section and the one following apply without regard to whether or not the failure of performance is a breach. They apply, for example, even though the failure is justified on the ground of impracticability of performance (Chapter 11). Illustrations of the operation of these rules in situations in which the failure is justified are given in other chapters under the sections that deal with the particular justification, such as impracticability. See, e.g., § 267, 268. The illustrations in this Chapter concern, for the most part, their operation in situations where the failure is a breach. But see, e.g., Illustration 3. The rules of this Section and the one following apply even when the promise of the party in default is unenforceable under the Statute of Frauds, while the promise of the other party is enforceable. See § 140. They are, of course, subject to variation by agreement of the parties. **Illustrations:**

     1. A contracts to build a house for B for $50,000, progress payments to be made monthly in an amount equal to 85% of the price of the

work performed during the preceding month, the balance to be paid on the architect's certificate of satisfactory completion of the house. Without justification B fails to make a $ 5,000 progress payment. A thereupon stops work on the house and a week goes by. A's failure to continue the work is not a breach and B has no claim against A. B's failure to make the progress payment is an uncured material failure of performance which operates as the non-occurrence of a condition of A's remaining duties of performance under the exchange. If B offers to make the delayed payment and in all the circumstances it is not too late to cure the material breach, A's duties to continue the work are not discharged. A has a claim against B for damages for partial breach because of the delay.

2. The facts being otherwise as stated in Illustration 1, B fails to make the progress payment or to give any explanation or assurances for one month. If, in all the circumstances, it is now too late for B to cure his material failure of performance by making the delayed payment, A's duties to continue the work are discharged. Because B's failure to make the progress payment was a breach, A also has a claim against B for total breach of contract (§ 243).

3. A, a theater manager, contracts with B, an actress, for performance by her for a period of six months in a play that A is about to present. B dies during the first week of the performance. A's remaining duties with respect to the exchange of performances are discharged by B's uncured material failure of performance. Because B's failure is justified on the ground of impossibility (§ 262), A has no claim against B's estate.

. . .

d. Substantial performance. In an important category of disputes over failure of performance, one party asserts the right to payment on the ground that he has completed his performance, while the other party refuses to pay on the ground that there is an uncured material failure of performance. (Compare Comment *b*.) A typical example is that of the building contractor who claims from the owner payment of the unpaid balance under a construction contract. In such cases it is common to state the issue, not in terms of whether there has been an uncured material failure by the contractor, but in terms of whether there has been substantial performance by him. This manner of stating the issue does not change its substance, however, and the rule stated in this Section also applies to such cases. If there has been substantial although not full performance, the building contractor has a claim for the unpaid balance and the owner has a claim only for damages. If there has not been substantial performance, the building contractor has no claim for the unpaid balance, although he may have a claim in restitution (§ 374). The considerations in determining whether performance is substantial are those listed in § 241 for determining whether a failure is material. See Comment *b* to § 241. If, however, the parties have made an event a condition of their agreement, there is no mitigating standard of materiality or substantiality applicable to the non-occurrence of that event. If, therefore, the agreement makes full performance a condition, substantial performance is not sufficient and if relief is to be had under the contract, it must be through excuse of the non-occurrence of the condition to avoid forfeiture. See § 229 and Illustration 1 to that section. **Illustration:**

11. A contracts to build a house for B, for which B promises to pay $ 50,000 in monthly progress payments equal to 85% of the value of the work with the balance to be paid on completion. When A completes construction, B refuses to pay the $ 7,500 balance claiming that there are defects that amount to an uncured material breach. If the breach is material, A's performance is not substantial and he has no claim under the contract against B, although he may have a claim in restitution (§ 374). If the breach is not material, A's performance is said to be substantial, he has a claim under the contract against B for $ 7,500, and B has a claim against A for damages because of the defects.

. . .

§ 238. Effect on Other Party's Duties of a Failure to Offer Performance

Where all or part of the performances to be exchanged under an exchange of promises are due simultaneously, it is a condition of each party's duties to render such performance that the other party either render or, with manifested present ability to do so, offer performance of his part of the simultaneous exchange.

Comment:

a. Effect of offer to perform. Where the performances are to be exchanged simultaneously under an exchange of promises, each party is entitled to refuse to proceed with that simultaneous exchange until he is reasonably assured that the other party will perform at the same time. If a party actually performs, his performance both discharges his own duty (§ 235(1)) and amounts to the occurrence of a condition of the other party's duty (§ 237). But it is not necessary that he actually perform in order to produce this latter effect. It is enough that he make an appropriate offer to perform, since it is a condition of each party's duties of performance with respect to the exchange that there be no uncured material failure by the other party at least to offer performance. Circumstances significant in determining whether a failure is material are set out in § 241. Such an offer of performance by a party amounts to the occurrence of a condition of the other party's duty to render performance, although it does not amount to performance by the former. Until a party has at least made such an offer, however, the other party is under no duty to perform, and if both parties fail to make such an offer, neither party's failure is a breach. (If one of the parties is already in breach, as where he has repudiated or has failed to go to the place appointed for the simultaneous exchange, the other party's duty to render performance may already have been discharged under §§ 253(2) or 237, giving him a claim for damages for total breach under §§ 253(1) or 243(1).) When it is too late for either to make such an offer, both parties are discharged by the non-occurrence of a condition. A failure to offer performance can be cured, if an appropriate offer is made in time (§ 242). Cf. Comment *b* to § 237. The fact that a party is ignorant of a defect in the other party's offer is immaterial. See Comment *c* to § 237.

Illustrations:

    1. A contracts to sell and B to buy a machine for $ 10,000, delivery of the machine and payment of the price to be made at a stated place on July 1. On July 1 both parties are present at that place, but A neither delivers nor offers to deliver the machine and B neither pays nor offers to pay the price. A has no claim against B, and B has no claim against A. See Uniform Commercial Code §§ 2-507(1) and 2-511(1). If, however, B had committed a material breach by fail-

ing to go to the stated place, A would have had a claim against B for damages for total breach. See §§ 237, 243.

    2. The facts being otherwise as stated in Illustration 1, on July 2, B, with manifested present ability to do so, offers to pay the price if A simultaneously delivers the machine, but A refuses to deliver the machine. If the delay of one day does not exceed the time after which A is discharged (§ 242), A's refusal is a breach. If it exceeds that time, B has no claim against A.

b. What amounts to an offer to perform. An offer of performance meets the requirement stated in this Section even though it is conditional on simultaneous performance by the other party. The offer must be accompanied with manifested present ability to make it good, but the offeror need not go so far as actually to hold out that which he is to deliver. (On the meaning of the term "manifested," see Comment *b* to § 2.) Thus the Uniform Commercial Code § 2-503(1) requires only "that the seller put and hold conforming goods at the buyer's disposition and give the buyer any notice reasonably necessary to enable him to take delivery." In this respect the requirement of this Section is less exacting than that of tender under, for example, § 45 or § 62. Any conduct, including tender, that goes beyond an offer of performance will, of course, also satisfy the requirement. The requirement of an offer of performance is to be applied in the light of what is reasonably to be expected by the parties in view of the practical difficulties of absolute simultaneity (see Comment *b* to § 234) and is subject to the agreement of the parties, as supplemented or qualified by usage (§§ 221, 222) and course of dealing (§ 223). **Illustration:**

    3. A contracts to sell and B to buy land for $ 50,000. The land is to be conveyed free of liens and encumbrances, but B knows that it is subject to a $ 30,000 mortgage held by C which A expects to satisfy out of the $ 50,000 purchase price. A, in the presence of B and C, makes a conditional offer of a deed of the property subject to the mortgage, and both A and C present documents that are legally sufficient to satisfy the mortgage debt to be delivered immediately on payment of the price by B. B thereupon refuses to pay the price. In view of the circumstances at the time the contract was made, A's offer is sufficient, and A has a claim against B for damages for total breach of contract.

    . . .

§ 239. Effect on Other Party's Duties of a Failure Justified by Non-Occurrence Of a Condition

(1) A party's failure to render or to offer performance may, except as stated in Subsection (2), affect the other party's duties under the rules stated in §§ 237 and 238 even though failure is justified by the non-occurrence of a condition.

(2) The rule stated in Subsection (1) does not apply if the other party assumed the risk that he would have to perform in spite of such a failure.

Comment:

a. General rule. The rules stated in §§ 237 and 238 apply to any uncured material failure, whether or not it is a breach. They therefore apply even when a party's failure is justified on the ground that performance has not become due because of the non-occurrence of a condition of his duty (§ 224). Subsection (1) makes it clear that this is so, as a general rule. The general rule is based on the premise that the other party did not assume the risk that he would have to perform even if the expected exchange was not forthcoming because of the non-occurrence of the condition. His expectation is that even if the condition does not occur, he will not be called upon to perform unless that exchange is forthcoming. He is therefore entitled to refuse to perform if there is a failure of the return performance, even if that failure is not a breach because of the non-occurrence of the condition. In that case, he has, of course, no claim for damages, although he may have one in restitution. See §§ 370-77. **Illustration:**

> 1. A contracts to sell and B to buy a house for $ 50,000. The contract contains the provision, "This contract is conditional on approval by X Bank of B's pending mortgage application." Approval by X Bank is a condition of B's duty, and therefore if X Bank does not approve B's application, performance by B will not become due, even if A makes an offer of a deed. But it is not a condition of A's duty and therefore performance by A will become due if, although X Bank does not approve B's application, B makes an offer to pay $ 50,000. See Illustration 4 to § 226. Under the rule stated in this Section, performance by A will not become due if B does not pay or offer to pay $ 50,000 because A did not assume the risk that he would nonetheless have to perform.

b. Assumption of risk. Subsection (2) states an exception to the general rule to cover the case in which a party assumes the risk that he will have to perform even if the agreed exchange is not forthcoming because of the non-occurrence of a condition. Since a condition is by definition not certain to occur (§ 224), every obligee of a conditional duty assumes a risk. It is the premise of the general rule that he assumes only the risk that if the condition does not occur, the expected exchange will not be carried out on either side. See Illustration 1. But sometimes he assumes the greater risk that, if the condition does not occur, he will have to carry out his side of the exchange even though it is not carried out on the other side. If he has assumed this greater risk, then conduct on the other side which would otherwise operate as a failure to perform under § 237 or to offer to perform under § 238 does not so operate. The nature of the risk taken by a party who enters into such an exchange of promises is sometimes indicated by describing the promise that he receives as "aleatory." See Comment *c* to § 232.

Illustrations:

> 2. A, a general contractor, contracts with B, a subcontractor, for the plumbing work on a construction project. B is to receive $ 100,000, payable monthly as the work progresses "on condition that Owner shall have paid Contractor therefor." B works for three months and makes monthly requests for payment of a total of $ 60,000 from A. When A does not pay B because the owner has not paid A for the plumbing work, B stops work and a month later notifies A that he cancels the contract. If the court determines, in the light of the quoted language and other circumstances, that B assumed the risk that he would have to perform even if A did not pay him on the ground that the owner did not pay A, A's justifiable non-payment on that ground does not operate as a failure to perform under § 237 and therefore B's cancellation is a breach. Compare Illustration 1 to § 227 and Illustration 2 to § 237.

> 3. The facts being otherwise as stated in Illustration 2, A unjustifiably refuses to pay B, although the owner has paid A for the plumbing work. Although B assumed the risk that he would have to perform even if A did not pay on the ground that the owner did not pay A, A's non-payment is not justified on that ground and therefore operates as a failure to perform under § 237. If a court concludes that the failure is material

and that B's cancellation came when it was too late for A to cure it, B's cancellation is not a breach. Compare Illustration 1 to § 227 and Illustration 2 to § 237.

§ 240. Part Performances as Agreed Equivalents

If the performances to be exchanged under an exchange of promises can be apportioned into corresponding pairs of part performances so that the parts of each pair are properly regarded as agreed equivalents, a party's performance of his part of such a pair has the same effect on the other's duties to render performance of the agreed equivalent as it would have if only that pair of performances had been promised.

Comment:

a. Mitigating effect of the rule. Under the rule stated in § 237, a party's failure to perform may cause him to lose his right to the agreed exchange after he has relied substantially on the expectation of that exchange, as by either preparation or performance. The risk of forfeiture is similar to that which arises on the non-occurrence of a condition stated in the agreement. See Comment *a* to § 227. But because the failure must be material in order to have this effect under § 237, courts can temper the application of those sections in appropriate cases to avoid forfeiture in a way that is not possible where the agreement itself states the condition. Compare §§ 241 and 242 with § 229. In addition, forfeiture may sometimes be reduced or avoided by allowing a party whose failure has been material to have restitution in accordance with the policy favoring avoidance of unjust enrichment. See §§ 370-77. This Section embodies another mitigating doctrine which reduces the risk of forfeiture in that important class of cases in which it is proper to regard corresponding parts of the performances of each party as agreed equivalents. Its effect is to give a party who has performed one of these parts the right to its agreed equivalent just as if the parties had made a separate contract with regard to that pair of corresponding parts. A failure as to some other part does not affect this right. See Comment *d* to § 231. Of course, if the failure amounts to a breach, the injured party has a claim for damages. Substantial performance of such a part has the same effect with regard to such a pair of agreed equivalents as substantial performance of the whole has under § 237 with respect to the entire contract. See Comment *d* to § 237.

b. Separate contracts distinguished. When it is proper to regard parts of pairs of corresponding performances under a contract as agreed equivalents, the contract is sometimes loosely said to be "divisible" or "severable." But under the rule stated in this Section, the pairs of corresponding parts are not treated as if they were separate contracts. If there are two separate contracts, one party's performance under the first and the other party's performance under the second are not to be exchanged under a single exchange of promises, and even a total failure of performance by one party as to the first has no necessary effect on the other party's duty to perform the second. Comment *d* to § 231. (On the situation if the failure gives reasonable grounds to believe that the other party will commit a breach of the second, see §§ 251 and 252.) This is not so, however, if there is a single contract under which the parties are to exchange performances, even though it is proper to regard pairs of corresponding parts of those performances as agreed equivalents. If there is an uncured material failure by either party, he can claim compensation for any parts that he has already performed, but he cannot enforce the contract with respect to any other pair of corresponding parts, including the part or parts that he has failed to perform. See Illustration 3. With respect to those parts the rule of § 237 still applies, for the parties are bound by a single contract and not by a series of separate contracts for each pair of corresponding parts. Although the pairs of performances may be regarded as agreed equivalents, the parties exchanged promises for an exchange of their whole performances. **Illustrations:**

1. A contracts to sell and B to buy a quantity of dressed hogs and a quantity of live hogs at stated prices for each quantity. A is to deliver the dressed hogs first and the live hogs 15 days later, and B is to pay for each delivery within 30 days after it is made. A delivers the dressed hogs, but unjustifiably refuses to deliver the live ones. If a court finds that delivery of the dressed hogs and payment of the price stated for them are agreed equivalents, A can recover the stated price

for the dressed hogs under the contract. B then has a claim against A for damages for his failure to deliver the live hogs.

. . .

c. Order of performance distinguished. The terms "divisible" and "severable" are sometimes used, not only in determining whether the rule stated in this Section is applicable, but also in determining whether a party's performance is due at one time or in installments (§ 233). Many of the contracts covered by the rule stated in this Section happen also to be contracts in which performance of each party is to be given in installments, corresponding to the times of the other party's performance. Indeed, the fact that the order of performance involves such pairs of corresponding parts may suggest that it is proper to regard those pairs as agreed equivalents. But it does not necessarily follow that it is proper, and in many contracts under which performance is to be in pairs of corresponding parts, it is not proper to regard the parts of those pairs as agreed equivalents. See Illustrations 7 and 9. Conversely, in many contracts under which performance of one or both parties is to be at one time, it is proper to regard those performances as composed of pairs of agreed equivalents. See Illustrations 2, 8 and 10. Two distinct determinations are involved and it is undesirable to obscure this by employing the same terminology for both.

d. Apportionment. The rule stated in this Section cannot be applied unless the parties' performances can be apportioned into corresponding pairs of part performances. The process of apportionment is essentially one of calculation and the rule can only be applied where calculation is feasible. It is enough, however, if the price of separate items is separately stated in the agreement itself or in a price list on which the agreement was based, or can be reliably ascertained from stated prices for components or from a total price for similar items.

Illustrations:

    4. A contracts with B to work for one year as a real estate salesman and to devote his full time to this work. A is to receive half of the real estate commission on all sales that he effects. A devotes full time to this work for ten months, but unjustifiably devotes only part time for the last two months. A court may apportion the unpaid commissions earned by A into those earned during the first ten months and those earned under the last two months according to the formula stated in the contract and, if it finds that working full time for ten months and the commissions on the sales over those months are agreed equivalents, A can recover the unpaid commissions for those months under the contract. B then has a claim against A for damages for his failure to devote full time during the last two months.

    . . .

§ 241. Circumstances Significant in Determining Whether a Failure Is Material

In determining whether a failure to render or to offer performance is material, the following circumstances are significant: (a) the extent to which the injured party will be deprived of the benefit which he reasonably expected; (b) the extent to which the injured party can be adequately compensated for the part of that benefit of which he will be deprived; (c) the extent to which the party failing to perform or to offer to perform will suffer forfeiture; (d) the likelihood that the party failing to perform or to offer to perform will cure his failure, taking account of all the circumstances including any reasonable assurances; (e) the extent to which the behavior of the party failing to perform or to offer to perform comports with standards of good faith and fair dealing.

Comment:

a. Nature of significant circumstances. The application of the rules stated in § 237 and 238 turns on a standard of materiality that is necessarily imprecise and flexible. (Contrast the situation where the parties have, by their agreement, made an event a condition. See § 226 and Comments *a* and *c* thereto and § 229.) The standard of materiality applies to contracts of all types and without regard to whether the whole performance of either party is to be rendered at one time or part performances are to be rendered at different times. See Uniform Commercial Code § 2-612. It also applies to pairs of agreed equivalents under § 240. See Illustration 2. It is to be applied in the light of the facts of each case in such a way as to further the purpose of securing for each party his expectation of an exchange of performances. This Section therefore states circumstances, not rules, which are to be considered in determining whether a particular failure is material. A determination that a failure is not material means only that it does not have the effect of the non-occurrence of a condition under §§ 237 and 238. Even if not material, the failure may be a breach and give rise to a claim for damages for partial breach (§§ 236, 243).

Illustrations:

> 1. A, a subcontractor, contracts to do excavation and earth moving on a housing subdivision project for B, the owner and general contractor, and to do all work "in a workmanlike manner." B is to make monthly progress payments for the work performed during the preceding month less a retainer of ten percent. A negligently damages a building with his bulldozer causing serious damage and denies any liability for B's loss. When B refuses to make further progress payments until A repairs the damage or admits liability, A notifies B that he cancels the contract. If the court determines that A's breach is material, A has no claim against B. B has a claim against A for damages for breach of contract.

> 2. The facts being otherwise as stated in Illustration 6 to § 240, A completes the part concerned with the excavation and grading of lots and streets but fails in a minor respect to comply with the specifications. If a court determines that the failure is not material, A has a claim against B for $ 75,000 under the contract for the excavation and grading. B has a claim for damages against A for his failure fully to perform as to excavation and grading and also for his unjustified refusal to make street improvements.

b. Loss of benefit to injured party. Since the purpose of the rules stated in §§ 237 and 238 is to secure the parties' expectation of an exchange of performances, an important circumstance in determining whether a failure is material is the extent to which the injured party will be deprived of the benefit which he reasonably expected from the exchange (Subsection (a)). If the consideration given by either party consists partly of some performance and only partly of a promise (see Comment *a* to § 232), regard must be had to the entire exchange, including that performance, in applying this criterion. Although the relationship between the monetary loss to the injured party as a result of the failure and the contract price may be significant, no simple rule based on the ratio of the one to the other can be laid down, and here, as elsewhere under this Section, all

relevant circumstances must be considered. In construction contracts, for example, defects affecting structural soundness are ordinarily regarded as particularly significant. In the sale of goods a particularly exacting standard has evolved. There it has long been established that, in the absence of a showing of a contrary intention, a buyer is entitled to expect strict performance of the contract, and Uniform Commercial Code § 2-601 carries forward this expectation by allowing the buyer to reject "if the goods or the tender of delivery fail in any respect to conform to the contract." The Code, however, compensates to some extent for the severity of this standard by extending the seller's right to cure beyond the point when the time for performance has expired in some instances (§ 2-508(2)), by allowing revocation of acceptance only if a nonconformity "substantially impairs" the value of the goods to the buyer (§ 2-608(1)), and by allowing the injured party to treat a nonconformity or default as to one installment under an installment contract as a breach of the whole only if it "substantially impairs" the value of the whole (§ 2-612(3)).

c. Adequacy of compensation for loss. The second circumstance, the extent to which the injured party can be adequately compensated for his loss of benefit (Subsection (b)), is a corollary of the first. Difficulty that he may have in proving with sufficient certainty the amount of that loss will affect the adequacy of compensation. If the failure is a breach, the injured party always has a claim for damages, and the question becomes one of the adequacy of that claim to compensate him for the lost benefit. Where the failure is not a breach, the question becomes one of the adequacy of any claim, such as one in restitution, to which the injured party may be entitled. This is a particularly important circumstance when the party in breach seeks specific performance. Such relief may be granted if damages can adequately compensate the injured party for the defect in performance. See Comment *c* to § 242.

d. Forfeiture by party who fails. Because a material failure acts as the non-occurrence of a condition, the same risk of forfeiture obtains as in the case of conditions generally if the party who fails to perform or tender has relied substantially on the expectation of the exchange, as through preparation or performance. Therefore a third circumstance is the extent to which the party failing to perform or to make an offer to perform will suffer forfeiture if the failure is treated as material. For this reason a failure is less likely to be regarded as material if it occurs late, after substantial preparation or performance, and more likely to be regarded as material if it occurs early, before such reliance. For the same reason the failure is more likely to be regarded as material if such preparation or performance as has taken place can be returned to and salvaged by the party failing to perform or tender, and less likely to be regarded as material if it cannot. These factors argue against a finding of material failure and in favor of one of substantial performance where a builder has completed performance under a construction contract and, because the building is on the owner's land, can salvage nothing if he is denied recovery of the balance of the price. Even in such a case, however, the potential forfeiture may be mitigated if the builder has a claim in restitution (§§ 370-77, especially § 374) or if he has already received progress payments under a provision of the contract. The same factors argue for a finding of material failure where a seller tenders goods and can salvage them by resale to others if they are rejected and he is denied recovery of the price. This helps to explain the severity of the rule as applied to the sale of goods. See Comment *b*. Even in such a case, however, the potential forfeiture may be aggravated if the seller has manufactured the goods specially for the buyer or has spent substantial sums in shipment. **Illustrations:**

> 3. A contracts to sell and B to buy 300 crates of Australian onions, shipment to be from Australia in March. A has 300 crates ready for shipment in March, but government requisitions prevent him from loading more than 240 crates on the only ship available in March. B refuses to accept or pay for the onions when they are tendered. Under the circumstances stated in Subsections (a) and (c), A's failure is material and A has no claim against B. If A's failure is unjustified, B has a claim against A for damages for partial breach because of the delay even if A cures his failure, and has a claim against A for damages for total breach if A does not cure his failure (§ 243).
>
> . . .

e. Uncertainty. A material failure by one party gives the other party the right to withhold further performance as a means of securing his expectation of an exchange of performances. To the extent that that expectation is already reasonably secure, in spite of the failure, there is less reason to conclude that the failure is material. The likelihood that the failure will be cured is therefore a significant circumstance in determining whether it is material (Subsection (d)). The fact that the injured party already has some security for the other party's performance argues against a determination that the failure is material. So do reasonable assurances of performance given by the other party after his failure. So does a shift in the market that makes performance of the contract more favorable to the other party. On the other hand, defaults by the other party under other contracts or as to other installments under the same contract argue for a determination of materiality. So does such financial weakness of the other party as suggests an inability to cure. This circumstance differs from the notion of reasonable grounds for insecurity (§ 251), in that the former can become relevant only after there has been an actual failure to perform or to tender. On discharge by repudiation, see § 253(2). **Illustration:**

> 5. A contracts to sell and B to buy land for $ 25,000. B is to make a $ 5,000 down payment and pay the balance in four annual installments of $ 5,000 each. A is to proceed immediately to have abstracts of title prepared showing a marketable title and to deliver them prior to the time for payment of the first annual installment. Without explanation, A fails to have abstracts prepared for delivery prior to the time for payment of the first annual installment. B refuses to pay that installment. Under the circumstances stated in Subsections (a)-(d), the failure of performance is material and A has no claim against B. B has a claim against A for damages for partial breach based on the delay if A cures his failure and a claim for damages for total breach if he does not (§ 243).

f. Absence of good faith or fair dealing. A party's adherence to standards of good faith and fair dealing (§ 205) will not prevent his failure to perform a duty from amounting to a breach (§ 236(2)). Nor will his adherence to such standards necessarily prevent his failure from having the effect of the non-occurrence of a condition (§ 237; cf. § 238). The extent to which the behavior of the party failing to perform or to offer to perform comports with standards of good faith and fair dealing is, however, a significant circumstance in determining whether the failure is material (Subsection (e)). In giving weight to this factor courts have often used such less precise terms as "wilful." Adherence to the standards stated in Subsection (e) is not conclusive, since other circumstances may cause a failure to be material in spite of such adherence. Nor is non-adherence conclusive, and other circumstances may cause a failure not to be material in spite of such non-adherence.

Illustrations:

6. A contracts to build a house for B, using pipe of Reading manufacture. In return, B agrees to pay $ 75,000, with provision for progress payments. Without B's knowledge, a subcontractor mistakenly uses pipe of Cohoes manufacture which is identical in quality and is distinguishable only by the name of the manufacturer which is stamped on it. The substitution is not discovered until the house is completed, when replacement of the pipe will require destruction of substantial parts of the house. B refuses to pay the unpaid balance of $ 10,000. Under the circumstances stated in Subsections (a), (c), and (e), the failure of performance is not material and A has a claim against B for the unpaid balance of $ 10,000, subject to a claim by B against A for damages for A's breach of his duty to use Reading pipe. See Illustration 1 to § 229.

. . .

§ 242. Circumstances Significant in Determining When Remaining Duties Are Discharged

In determining the time after which a party's uncured material failure to render or to offer performance discharges the other party's remaining duties to render performance under the rules stated in §§ 237 and 238, the following circumstances are significant:

(a) those stated in § 241;

(b) the extent to which it reasonably appears to the injured party that delay may prevent or hinder him in making reasonable substitute arrangements;

(c) the extent to which the agreement provides for performance without delay, but a material failure to perform or to offer to perform on a stated day does not of itself discharge the other party's remaining duties unless the circumstances, including the language of the agreement, indicate that performance or an offer to perform by that day is important.

Comment:

a. Cure. Under §§ 237 and 238, a party's uncured material failure to perform or to offer to perform not only has the effect of suspending the other party's duties (§ 225(1)) but, when it is too late for the performance or the offer to perform to occur, the failure also has the effect of discharging those duties (§ 225(2)). Ordinarily there is some period of time between suspension and discharge, and during this period a party may cure his failure. Even then, since any breach gives rise to a claim, a party who has cured a material breach has still committed a breach, by his delay, for which he is liable in damages. Furthermore, in some instances timely performance is so essential that any delay immediately results in discharge and there is no period of time during which the injured party's duties are merely suspended and the other party can cure his failure.

b. Significant circumstances. This Section states circumstances which are to be considered in determining whether there is still time to cure a particular failure, or whether the period of time for discharge has expired. They are similar to the circumstances stated in the preceding section. The importance of delay to the injured party will depend on the extent to which it will deprive him of the benefit which he reasonably expected (§ 241(a)) and on the extent to which he can be adequately compensated (§ 241(b)). The extent of the forfeiture by the party failing to perform or to offer to perform (§ 241(c)) is also significant in determining the importance of delay. The likelihood that the injured party's withholding of performance will induce the other party to cure his failure is particularly important (§ 241(d)), because the very reason for suspending rather than immediately discharging the injured party's duties is that this will induce cure. The reasonableness of the injured party's conduct in communicating his grievances and in seeking satisfaction is a factor to be considered in this connection. Where performance is to extend over a period of time, as where delivery of goods is to be in installments, so that a continuing relationship between the parties is contemplated, the injured party may be expected to give more opportunity for cure than in the case of an isolated exchange. On discharge by repudiation, see § 253(2). Finally, the nature of the behavior of the party failing to perform or to offer to perform may be considered here as under the preceding section (§ 241(e)). **Illustration:**

    1. The facts being otherwise as stated in Illustration 1 to § 237, B tenders the progress payment after a two-day delay along with damages for the delay. A refuses to accept the payment and resume work and notifies B that he

cancels the contract. B's tender cured his breach before A's remaining duties to render performance were discharged, and B has a claim against A for total breach of contract, subject to a claim by A against B for damages for partial breach because of the delay.

. . .

e. Excuse and reinstatement. Just as a party may under § 84 promise to perform in spite of the complete non-occurrence of a condition, he may under that section promise to perform in spite of a delay in its occurrence. If he places no limit on the delay, his power to impose a time limit by later notification of the other party is subject to the rules on reinstatement stated in § 84(2).

§ 243. Effect of a Breach by Non-Performance As Giving Rise to a Claim for Damages for Total Breach

(1) With respect to performances to be exchanged under an exchange of promises, a breach by non-performance gives rise to a claim for damages for total breach only if it discharges the injured party's remaining duties to render such performance, other than a duty to render an agreed equivalent under § 240.

(2) Except as stated in Subsection (3), a breach by non-performance accompanied or followed by a repudiation gives rise to a claim for damages for total breach.

(3) Where at the time of the breach the only remaining duties of performance are those of the party in breach and are for the payment of money in installments not related to one another, his breach by non-performance as to less than the whole, whether or not accompanied or followed by a repudiation, does not give rise to a claim for damages for total breach. (4) In any case other than those stated in the preceding subsections, a breach by non-performance gives rise to a claim for total breach only if it so substantially impairs the value of the contract to the injured party at the time of the breach that it is just in the circumstances to allow him to recover damages based on all his remaining rights to performance.

Comment:

a. Promises exchanged in an expectation of an exchange of performances. Under § 236, a claim for damages for total breach is one for damages based on all of the injured party's remaining rights to performance while a claim for damages for partial breach is one that is based on only part of those rights. No precise general rule can be stated for determining in all cases when a breach gives rise to a claim for damages for total breach and when it gives rise to a claim merely for damages for partial breach. Subsection (1), however, states a rule for the most significant type of case -- the case in which performances are to be exchanged under an exchange of promises, and the breach occurs before the injured party has fully performed his duties with respect to the expected exchange. The breach, if

it is material (§ 241), will operate as the non-occurrence of a condition of those remaining duties (§ 237). This will at least justify the injured party in suspending his performance (§ 225(1)), and will, if the breach is not cured in time (§ 242), discharge his remaining duties of performance (§ 225(2)). Under the rule stated in Subsection (1), the injured party has a claim for damages for total breach if, but only if, those remaining duties are discharged. See Comment *b* to § 236 and Illustration 2 to § 237. (The injured party also has a claim for damages for total breach as the result of a material breach in, for example, Illustrations 4, 5, and 6 to § 237 and Illustrations 2 and 6 to § 240). There is, of course, an exception where the injured party has already, at the time of the breach, come under a duty to render performance of an agreed equivalent under the rule stated in § 240. Such a duty is not discharged, even if there is a material breach, and its survival does not prevent the injured party from claiming damages for total breach under Subsection (1). In contrast to the situation where there is a repudiation (see Comment *b*), the injured party has a choice in the situation contemplated in Subsection (1). If, in spite of the breach, he wishes to await performance by the party in breach and to have merely a claim for damages for partial breach rather than for total breach, he can excuse the non-occurrence of the condition of his remaining duties (§ 237) by promising to perform them in spite of its non-occurrence (§ 84). His remaining duties are then not discharged, and the rule stated in Subsection (1) does not apply. The injured party need not do this expressly (see Comment *e* to § 84), but may do so by his actions in the course of performance. See §§246, 247. **Illustrations:**

    1. A promises to sell to B a lot in a subdivision for $ 8,000. B promises to pay in four installments of $ 2,000 each, beginning one year after execution of the contract. A promises to begin to make improvements and pave the streets within 60 days and to complete work within a reasonable time and promises to deliver a deed at the time of the final payment. A commits a material breach by unjustifiably failing to pave the streets, and B thereupon refuses to pay any installments. After a reasonable time for A to cure his material breach has passed (§ 242), B's duty to pay the price is discharged, and he has a claim against A for damages for total breach.

    2. The facts being otherwise as stated in Illustration 1, B pays the first installment although he knows of A's material breach. B's payment operates as a promise to pay the remaining installments in spite of the non-occurrence of a condition of his duty to do so. See § 237; Illustration 5 to § 84. B's duty to pay the price is not discharged, and he has a claim against A merely for damages for partial breach because of the delay.

b. Effect of repudiation. Under the rule stated in Subsection (2), if a repudiation (§ 250) accompanies or follows a breach by non-performance, the injured party generally has a claim for damages for total breach. A repudiation does not, however, have this effect in those circumstances in which, under the rule stated in Subsection (3), nothing less than a breach as to the whole gives rise to such a claim (see Comment *c* and Illustrations 4 and 5). A

repudiation together with a breach by non-performance, therefore, has this effect in all cases in which a repudiation alone would give rise to a claim for total breach (§ 253) and in some additional cases (see Illustrations 3 and 8). An injured party who has a claim for damages for total breach as a result of a repudiation, and who asserts a claim merely for damages for partial breach, runs the risk that if he prevails he will be barred under the doctrine of merger from further recovery, even in the event of a subsequent breach, because he has "split a cause of action." See Restatement, Second, Judgments §§24-26. His position differs from that of the injured party under the rule stated in Subsection (1), who can, by promising to perform in spite of a breach (§ 84), prevent the breach from discharging his remaining duties of performance, avoid its giving rise to a claim for damages for total breach at all, and thereby treat it as giving rise to a claim merely for damages for partial breach (see Comment *a*). Where a repudiation accompanies or follows a breach that would, if the injured party so chose, give rise to a claim for damages for total breach under Subsection (1), both Subsections (1) and (2) apply. In that case, the injured party cannot avoid the consequence described above of having a claim for damages for total breach under the rule stated in Subsection (2). Even under the rule stated in Subsection (2), however, the injured party can assert a claim for damages for a partial breach without prejudice to a claim for damages arising out of a subsequent breach if he and the repudiator agree that the latter's performance under the contract is to be continued. Furthermore, he is not barred from claiming specific relief under the contract merely because he has a claim for damages for total breach (see Comment *a* to § 359). If the repudiator nullifies his repudiation (§ 256(1)), the injured party still has a claim for damages for the breach by nonperformance but it may then be a claim merely for damages for partial breach (see Comment *a* to § 256). **Illustration:**

    3. A contracts to sell and B to buy for $ 8,000 a subdivision lot on which B plans to build a house for himself. Delivery of the deed and payment of the price are to be made within 30 days, and A promises to make improvements and pave the streets within one year. A delivers the deed and B pays the price within 30 days. A paves the streets and makes most but not all of

the improvements within one year, but then re-pudiates by unjustifiably telling B that he re-fuses to make the rest of the improvements. B has a claim against A for damages for total breach, even though absent a repudiation B's claim might be merely one for damages for partial breach. See Illustration 8. If A and B then agree that A will make the rest of the improvements, B has a claim against A merely for damages for partial breach because of the delay.

c. Duties on one side. The rule stated in Subsection (3) applies only where all the remaining duties at the time of the breach are those of the party in breach. It therefore applies where the parties have exchanged promise for performance (§ 72), and where the parties have exchanged promise for promise (§ 74) and the injured party has fully performed. It is well established that if those duties of the party in breach at the time of the breach are simply to pay money in installments, not related to one another in some way, as by the requirement of the occurrence of a condition with respect to more than one of them, then a breach as to any number less than the whole of such installments gives rise to a claim merely for damages for partial breach. Whether there is a relationship between installments or other acts depends on the extent to which, in the circumstances, a breach as to less than the whole of such installments or acts can substantially affect the injured party's expectation under the contract.

. . .

e. General criterion. The rules stated in Subsections (1), (2) and (3) cover most of the significant cases. Subsection (4) states a general rule for residual cases. Under that rule the criterion is whether the breach so substantially impairs the value of the contract to the injured party at the time of the breach that it is just to allow him to recover damages based on all his remaining rights to performance. This determination is to be made in the light of all the circumstances, taking account of the difficulty of calculating damages for total breach and of any uncertainties that could be avoided if the injured party were given a claim merely for damages for partial breach. The criterion is essentially that of Uniform Commercial Code § 2-610 and, here as there, "The most useful test of substantial value is to determine whether material inconvenience or injustice will result if the aggrieved party is forced to wait . . ." (Comment 3). Although the considerations listed in §§241 and 242 are intended for use in determining whether the injured party is discharged, not in determining whether he has a claim for damages for total breach, some of them are relevant to this latter determination. Among these are the extent to which the injured party will be deprived of the benefit that he reasonably expected (§ 241(a)), the likelihood that the party in breach will cure his breach (§ 241(d)), the extent to which the behavior of the party in breach comports with standards of good faith and fair dealing (§ 241(e)), and the extent to which further delay will prevent or hinder the injured party in making reasonable substitute arrangements (§ 242(b)). **Illustrations:**

6. For a fee of $ 25,000, paid in advance, A contracts with B, an impresario, to sing in five concerts offered to the public as a series. A unjustifiably fails to sing in the first two concerts. A's breach so substantially impairs the value of the contract to B that B has a claim against A for damages for total breach.

7. The facts being otherwise as stated in Illustration 3, A does not repudiate but, in spite of repeated requests from B, does not make improvements or pave streets for two years. A's breach so substantially impairs the value of the contract to B that B has a claim against A for damages for total breach.

8. The facts being otherwise as stated in Illustration 3, A does not repudiate and gives B reasonable assurances that the remaining improvements will be completed with a delay of no more than one month. B has a claim against A merely for damages for partial breach because of the delay.

§ 244. Effect of Subsequent Events on Duty to Pay Damages

A party's duty to pay damages for total breach by non-performance is discharged if it appears after the breach that there would have been a total failure by the injured party to perform his return promise.

Comment:

a. Rationale. If the parties are to exchange performances under an exchange of promises, each party's duties to render performance are generally regarded as conditional on the other party's performance, or at least on his readiness to perform (§§ 237, 238, 251, 253). This principle applies even though one party is already in breach by non-performance. His duty to pay damages is discharged if it subsequently appears that there would have been a total failure of performance by the injured party. A failure is total in this context if it would have been sufficient to have discharged any remaining duties of the party in breach to render his performance. See § 242. The result follows even if it appears that the failure would have been justified and not a breach. Cf. § 254 (1). **Illustration:**

> 1. A contracts to sell and B to buy a particular machine. B is to pay the price on June 15 and A is to deliver the machine on July 1, at which time risk of loss is to pass to B. B does not pay on June 15, and on June 20 the machine is accidentally destroyed. B's duty to pay damages to A for his non-payment is discharged.

§ 245. Effect of a Breach by Non-Performance As Excusing the Non-Occurrence Of a Condition

Where a party's breach by non-performance contributes materially to the non-occurrence of a condition of one of his duties, the non-occurrence is excused.

Comment:

a. Excuse of non-occurrence of condition. Where a duty of one party is subject to the occurrence of a condition, the additional duty of good faith and fair dealing imposed on him under § 205 may require some cooperation on his part, either by refraining from conduct that will prevent or hinder the occurrence of that condition or by taking affirmative steps to cause its occurrence. Under § 235(2), non-performance of that duty when performance is due is a breach. See Illustration 3 to § 235. Under this Section it has the further effect of excusing the non-occurrence of the condition itself, so that performance of the duty that was originally subject to its occurrence can become due in spite of its non-occurrence. See Comments *b* and *c* to § 225. The rule stated in this Section only applies, however, where the lack of cooperation constitutes a breach, either of a duty imposed by the terms of the agreement itself or of a duty imposed by a term supplied by the court. There is no breach if the risk of such a lack of cooperation was assumed by the other party or if the lack of cooperation is justifiable.

Illustrations:

> 1. A contracts with B to repair B's building for $ 20,000, payment to be made "on the satisfaction of C, B's architect, and the issuance of his certificate." A fully performs his duty to make the repairs, but B induces C to refuse to issue his certificate. A has a claim against B for $ 20,000. B's breach of his duty of good faith and fair dealing contributed materially to the non-occurrence of the condition, the issuance of the certificate, excusing it. Cf. Illustrations 5, 6, 7, and 8 to § 227.

> 2. A contracts to sell and B to buy land for $ 100,000. At the same time A contracts to pay C, a real estate broker, as his commission, $ 5,000 "on the closing of title." A unjustifiably refuses to consummate the sale. C has a claim against A for $ 5,000, less any expenses that C saved because the sale was not consummated. A's breach of his duty of good faith and fair dealing contributed materially to the non-occurrence of the condition, the closing of title, excusing it. See Illustration 4 to § 227.

> . . .

b. Contribute materially. Although it is implicit in the rule that the condition has not occurred, it is not necessary to show that it would have occurred but for the lack of cooperation. It is only required that the breach have contributed materially to the non-occurrence. Nevertheless, if it can be shown that the condition would not have occurred regardless of the lack of cooperation, the failure of performance did not contribute materially to its non-occurrence and the rule does not apply. The burden of showing this is properly thrown on the party in breach.

Illustrations:

> . . .

> 6. A, the owner of a manufacturing plant, contracts to transfer the plant to B. B is to pay A $ 500,000 plus a bonus of $ 100,000 if the profits from the plant exceed a stated amount during the first year of its operation. Six months after the transfer B sells the plant to C, who

dismantles it. B refuses to pay the bonus. Whether A has a claim against B depends on whether B's failure to operate the plant for a year is a breach of his duty of good faith and fair dealing which contributed materially to the non-occurrence of the condition, the profits exceeding the stated amount during the first year, excusing it. The fact that A cannot show that the profits would otherwise have exceeded the stated amount does not prevent him from recovering. If, however, B shows that they would not have exceeded that amount, A cannot recover. Compare the rule on certainty in § 352.

. . .

c. Exceptions. Under §§ 237 and 238, it may be required as a condition of one party's duty that the other party perform or offer to perform his duty. A breach by the first party of his duty of good faith and fair dealing will, if material and not cured in time, discharge that duty of the other party (§237), eliminating the requirement that the other party perform or offer to perform it. The discharge of the duty has the additional effect of excusing the non-occurrence of the condition. But non-occurrence of the condition is excused only if the duty is discharged. The rule stated in this Section is, therefore, not applicable to such situations. See Illustrations 4, 5, and 7 to § 237.

§ 246. Effect of Acceptance as Excusing the Non-Occurrence Of a Condition

(1) Except as stated in Subsection (2), an obligor's acceptance or his retention for an unreasonable time of the obligee's performance, with knowledge of or reason to know of the non-occurrence of a condition of the obligor's duty, operates as a promise to perform in spite of that non-occurrence, under the rules stated in § 84.

(2) If at the time of its acceptance or retention the obligee's performance involves such attachment to the obligor's property that removal would cause material loss, the obligor's acceptance or retention of that performance operates as a promise to perform in spite of the non-occurrence of the condition, under the rules stated in § 84, only if the obligor with knowledge of or reason to know of the defects manifests assent to the performance.

Comment:

a. Acceptance or retention as a promise. Section 84 states the circumstances in which a promise to perform a duty in spite of the non-occurrence of a condition is binding. Non-verbal conduct, such as continued performance with knowledge of the non-occurrence, may amount to a promise under that section. See Comment *e* and Illustration 4 to § 84. Because acceptance and retention of the other party's performance in spite of the non-occurrence of a condition are both particularly important kinds of such conduct, this Section sets out in detail the circumstances in which acceptance or retention amounts to a promise under the rules stated in § 84. In this context, acceptance of performance means merely voluntary receipt of it, with no implication that it is received in full satisfaction. The acceptance or retention must, of course, be with knowledge of or reason to know of the non-occurrence of the condition.

b. Effect of promise. The rule stated in this Section applies to all conditions other than those excepted by § 84. A particularly important situation in which it finds application occurs

where performances are being exchanged under an exchange of promises, and the party who has accepted or retained the other's performance asserts that because of defects in that performance there has been a non-occurrence of a condition of his remaining duties to perform (§ 237). If the rule stated in this Section applies, however, the non-occurrence of the condition is excused, and even if the defects amount to a material failure they do not have the asserted effect. Under the Uniform Commercial Code §§ 2-607, 2-608, and 2-709, for example, the buyer must pay the price for goods accepted and retained in spite of a defective tender if the acceptance was with knowledge of or reason to know of the defect. But it does not follow from one party's mere voluntary receipt of performance that the other party's defective performance has discharged his own duty under § 235(1). Therefore, subject to the rules on discharge in Chapter 12, he is liable for damages for partial breach because of his defective performance. Under Uniform Commercial Code §§ 2-607(2) and 2-714, for example, the buyer's acceptance and retention of the goods does not preclude him from recovering damages for any non-conformity of tender. Not only may a party excuse entirely the non-occurrence of a condition of his duty, but he may excuse a delay in its occurrence. See Comment *c* to § 225. He may then claim damages for partial breach because of the delay. See Illustration 1.

. . .

§ 247. Effect of Acceptance of Part Performance as Excusing the Subsequent Non-Occurrence Of a Condition

An obligor's acceptance of part of the obligee's performance, with knowledge or reason to know of the non-occurrence of a condition of the obligor's duty, operates as a promise to perform in spite of a subsequent non-occurrence of the condition under the rules stated in § 84 to the extent that it justifies the obligee in believing that subsequent performances will be accepted in spite of that non-occurrence.

Comment:

a. Acceptance or retention of part. An obligor's acceptance or retention of part performance in spite of the non-occurrence of a condition of his duty may have two effects. First, it may operate as a promise to perform that duty in spite of that non-occurrence under the rule stated in the preceding section. Second, it may operate as a promise to perform in spite of a subsequent non-occurrence of the condition under the rule stated in this Section. It only has this second effect, however, to the extent that it justifies the obligee in believing that subsequent performance will be accepted in spite of that non-occurrence. Where, for example, there have been successive acceptances of defective installments, the obligee may be justified in believing that subsequent installments will be accepted in spite of similar defects. Not only may a party excuse entirely the non-occurrence of a condition of his duty, but he may excuse its non-occurrence during the period of time in which it would otherwise have to occur. See Comment *c* to § 225 and Illustration 1. **Illustrations:**

    1. A contracts to sell and B to buy land for $ 10,000, the price to be payable in a down payment and 36 monthly installments and the deed to be delivered on payment of the last installment. The agreement provides that payment of installments on the dates due is a condition of A's duty to deliver a deed. B does not pay any of the first twelve installments on the dates due, but A accepts them without comment. B tenders the thirteenth installment after the date due, but not later than was generally the case for the previous payments. The non-occurrence of the condition during the period of time in which it would otherwise have to occur, failure to pay the thirteenth installment on the date due, is excused and A's duty is not discharged. A has, however, a claim against B for damages for partial breach because of the delay.

    2. A contracts to build a house for B for $ 50,000, payable in part in monthly progress payments with the balance due on completion, all payments to be made on condition that A present a certificate from B's architect showing that the work has been properly completed. B makes the last six out of seven progress payments without presentation of an architect's certificate and without asking for one, and A materially changes his position in reliance on this. Although A fully performs, B refuses to pay the $ 10,000 balance because of A's failure to present an architect's certificate. The non-occurrence of the condition, presentation of the architect's certificate, is excused and A has a claim against B for $ 10,000.

b. Reinstatement. Since, under this Section, acceptance or retention amounts to a promise under the rules stated in § 84, the obligor can again make his duty subject to the condition by notifying the obligee of his intention to do so. His right to reinstate the requirement of the condition is, however, subject to the restrictions stated in § 84(2), and he cannot reinstate it if, for example, to do so will be unjust because of a material change of position by the obligee. **Illustrations:**

    3. The facts being otherwise as stated in Illustration 1, A notifies B at the time that the twelfth installment is due that he intends to require prompt payment of the thirteenth and subsequent installments. The non-occurrence of the condition during the period of time in which it would otherwise have to occur, failure to pay the thirteenth installment on the date due, is not excused by A's previous acceptance without comment of delayed installments.

. . .

§ 248. Effect of Insufficient Reason for Rejection as Excusing the Non-Occurrence Of a Condition

Where a party rejecting a defective performance or offer of performance gives an insufficient reason for rejection, the non-occurrence of a condition of his duty is excused only if he knew or had reason to know of that non-occurrence and then only to the extent that the giving of an insufficient reason substantially contributes to a failure by the other party to cure.

Comment:

a. Failure to give a reason for rejection. Ordinarily a party whose performance or offer of performance has been rejected must determine at his peril the reason for that rejection. Whether or not he is under a duty to give that performance, he is not entitled to a statement of reasons from the other party and the other party is not prejudiced if he refuses to give such a statement. The following section states a limited exception to this for the case in which the payment of legal tender is required. (And cf. Uniform Commercial Code § 2-605, under which a buyer who fails to particularize his reasons for rejection is precluded, in some circumstances, from relying on an unstated defect.)

b. Giving insufficient reason for rejection. Just as the injured party is not, as a general rule, precluded from relying on a reason for rejection because he stated no reasons (Comment *a*), he is not precluded by the mere fact that he stated an insufficient reason, even though he knew or had reason to know of a sufficient one. The giving of an insufficient reason may, however, so mislead the other party as to induce his failure to cure the defective performance or offer of performance within the time allowed by the agreement. If it does so, the non-occurrence of the condition is excused, although the injured party still has a claim for damages. This is a specific application of the general rule that requires good faith and fair dealing in the enforcement of contracts. See § 205 and Illustration 10 to that section. As to the requirement that the giving of the insufficient reason contribute materially to the failure to cure, see Comment *b* to § 245. Where there is a question of fact as to whether performance was defective or not, the failure to state a reason or the stating of an insufficient reason may be considered in resolving that question, but this Section does not deal with such problems of proof. **Illustrations:**

1. The facts being otherwise as stated in Illustration 6 to § 246, on moving into the house B gives Isa list of seventeen defects to be cured, but omits three others of which he knew or had reason to know. Absent a showing that A could have cured the three defects in time if B had specified them then, B can rely on all of the defects to show that A's breach is material and that A has no claim to $ 10,000 under the contract.

2. A, a subcontractor, makes a contract with B, a contractor, to install a roof on a school that B is building. After A has begun work, B notifies him that the contract is cancelled because of A's failure to provide enough skilled workmen as required by the contract. A sues B. B attempts to show that, although A may have provided enough skilled workmen, A so failed to follow specifications as to constitute a material breach. B is not precluded from showing this, even if he knew it at the time of the cancellation, unless A could have cured the defects in time if B had specified them then.

§ 249. When Payment Other Than by Legal Tender Is Sufficient

Where the payment or offer of payment of money is made a condition of an obligor's duty, payment or offer of payment in any manner current in the ordinary course of business satisfies the requirement unless the obligee demands payment in legal tender and gives any extension of time reasonably necessary to procure it.

Comment:

a. Rationale. Ordinarily a party whose performance or offer of performance has been rejected is not entitled to a reason for its rejection (Comment *a* to § 248). However, money claims are so generally paid by means other than legal tender that, absent a specific demand, the debtor is not likely to suppose that an insistence on legal tender is the reason behind a refusal to accept payment or offer to pay by check or in some other manner current in the ordinary course of business. Moreover, if the debtor is informed that this is the reason for rejection, he can ordinarily obtain legal tender and cure his defective performance or offer of performance, at least if he is given a reasonable extension of time. This Section, therefore, states an exceptional rule applicable to such cases. What manner of payment is current in the ordinary course of business depends on the nature of the transaction involved. Whether payment or an offer of payment must be in money is beyond the scope of this Section, and is to be determined by the rules of Chapter 9 on interpretation, including those on usage (§§ 221, 222) and course of dealing (§ 223). Cf. Comment *b* to § 238. If the contract explicitly requires payment in legal tender, this requirement will be given effect as a demand for legal tender given in advance of the time for performance, and renders any further demand or extension of time unnecessary.

Illustrations:

1. A contracts to sell and B to buy land for $ 10,000, payment of the price and delivery of the deed to be "not later than July 30." On the morning of July 30, B offers to give A his certified check for $ 10,000. A, giving no reason, rejects B's check and refuses to offer to deliver a deed. B's offer to give his certified check satisfies the requirement of § 238 that B offer to pay A $ 10,000.

2. The facts being otherwise as stated in Illustration 1, A demands legal tender when he rejects B's certified check, but his demand comes after banking hours and he refuses to give B the necessary time to procure it. B's offer to give his certified check satisfies the requirement of § 238 that B offer to pay A $ 10,000.

Introductory Note A contracting party expects that the other party will not only perform his duties under the contract when the time for performance comes, but will do nothing substantially to impair this expectation before that time comes. The rules stated in this Topic are designed primarily to afford protection against such impairment.

The first two sections state rules for determining whether there is a repudiation. Section 250 tells when a statement or other voluntary act is a repudiation. Section 251 tells when one party may treat the other party's failure to give assurance as a repudiation. It protects an obligee when, although there has been no repudiation by the obligor, reasonable grounds have nevertheless arisen to believe that the obligor will commit a serious breach. The obligee may demand assurance of due performance, may in a proper case suspend his own performance while he awaits such assurance, and may treat the failure of the obligor to give such assurance as a repudiation. Section 252 states a special rule that gives the obligee broader protection when it is the obligor's insolvency that gives rise to his belief that the obligor will commit a breach.

Sections 253 and 255 deal with the three possible effects of a repudiation. First, a repudiation may, before any breach by non-performance, give rise to a claim for damages for total breach (§ 253(1)). (As to when a repudiation coupled with a breach by non-performance gives rise to such a claim, see § 243(2).) Second, a repudiation may discharge the other party's remaining duties of performance (§ 253(2)). Third, a repudiation may excuse the non-occurrence of a condition of the repudiator's duty (§ 255).

The effect of subsequent events on the repudiator's duty to pay damages is dealt with in § 254, while §§ 256 and 257 deal with the possible effects of subsequent events on the repudiation, itself. Section 256 tells when subsequent events nullify a statement or other event that would otherwise amount to a repudiation under § 250 or the basis for a repudiation under § 251. Section 257 states that efforts by the injured party to obtain performance in spite of a repudiation do not change its effect.

§ 250. When a Statement or an Act Is a Repudiation

A repudiation is

(a) a statement by the obligor to the obligee indicating that the obligor will commit a breach that would of itself give the obligee a claim for damages for total breach under § 243, or

(b) a voluntary affirmative act which renders the obligor unable or apparently unable to perform without such a breach.

Comment:

a. Consequences of repudiation. A statement by a party to the other that he will not or cannot perform without a breach, or a voluntary affirmative act that renders him unable or apparently unable to perform without a breach may impair the value of the contract to the other party. It may have several consequences under this Restatement. If it accompanies a breach by non-performance that would otherwise give rise to only a claim for damages for partial breach, it may give rise to a claim for damages for total breach instead (§ 243). Even if it occurs before any breach by non-performance, it may give rise to a claim for damages for total breach (§ 253(1)), discharge the other party's duties (§ 253(2)), or excuse the non-occurrence of a condition (§ 255).

b. Nature of statement. In order to constitute a repudiation, a party's language must be sufficiently positive to be reasonably interpreted to mean that the party will not or cannot perform. Mere expression of doubt as to his willingness or ability to perform is not enough to constitute a repudiation, although such an expression may give an obligee reasonable grounds to believe that the obligor will commit a serious breach and may ultimately result in a repudiation under the rule stated in § 251. However, language that under a fair reading "amounts to a statement of intention not to perform except on conditions which go beyond the contract" constitutes a repudiation. Comment 2 to Uniform Commercial Code § 2-610. Language that is accompanied by a breach by non-performance may amount to a repudiation even though, standing alone, it would not be sufficiently positive. See § 243(2). The statement must be made to an obligee under the contract, including a third party beneficiary or an assignee.

Illustrations:

1. On April 1, A contracts to sell and B to buy land, delivery of the deed and payment of the price to be on July 30. On May 1, A tells B that he will not perform. A's statement is a repudiation.

2. A contracts to build a house for B for $ 50,000, progress payments to be made monthly in an amount equal to 85% of the price of the work performed during the preceding month, the balance to be paid on the architect's certificate of satisfactory completion of the house. Without justification B fails to make a $ 5,000 progress payment and tells A that because of financial difficulties he will be unable to pay him anything for at least another month. If, after a month, it would be too late for B to cure his material failure of performance by making the delayed payment, B's statement is a repudiation. See Illustration 2 to § 237.

3. The facts being otherwise as stated in Illustration 1, A does not tell B that he will not perform but says, "I am not sure that I can perform, and I do not intend to do so unless I am legally bound to." A's statement is not a repudiation.

4. The facts being otherwise as in Illustration 1, A tells C, a third person having no right under the contract, and not B, that he will not perform. C informs B of this conversation, although not requested by A to do so. A's statement is not a repudiation. But see Comments *b* and *c* to § 251.

c. Nature of act. In order to constitute a repudiation, a party's act must be both voluntary and affirmative, and must make it actually or apparently impossible for him to perform. An act that falls short of these requirements may, however, give reasonable grounds to believe that the obligor will commit a serious breach for the purposes of the rule stated in § 251. The effect of bankruptcy is governed in large part by federal law. In liquidation cases, for example, Bankruptcy Reform Act § 365(a), (d) and (e) gives the trustee the power to assume or reject an executory contract within a statutory period, and the obligee must give him the time to exercise this power. A contract not assumed during this period is deemed to be rejected. Under Bankruptcy Reform Act § 365(g)(1), notwithstanding state law, the trustee's rejection of a contract "constitutes a breach of such contract . . . immediately before the date of the filing of the petition . . . ." The rules stated in this Restatement apply to the extent that they are consistent with federal bankruptcy law. **Illustrations:**

5. The facts being otherwise as stated in Illustration 1, A says nothing to B on May 1,

but on that date he contracts to sell the land to C. A's making of the contract with C is a repudiation.

6. The facts being otherwise as stated in Illustration 1, A says nothing to B on May 1, but on that date he mortgages the land to C as security for a $ 40,000 loan which is not payable until one year later. A's mortgaging the land is a repudiation. Compare Illustration 4 to § 251.

7. A contracts to employ B, and B to work for A, the employment to last a year beginning in ten days. Three days after making the contract B embarks on a ship for a voyage around the world. B's embarking for the voyage is a repudiation.

d. Gravity of threatened breach. In order for a statement or an act to be a repudiation, the threatened breach must be of sufficient gravity that, if the breach actually occurred, it would of itself give the obligee a claim for damages for total breach under § 243(1). Generally, a party acts at his peril if, insisting on what he mistakenly believes to be his rights, he refuses to perform his duty. His statement is a repudiation if the threatened breach would, without more, have given the injured party a claim for damages for total breach. Modern procedural devices, such as the declaratory judgment, may be used to mitigate the harsh results that might otherwise result from this rule. Furthermore, if the

threatened breach would not itself have given the injured party a claim for damages for total breach, the statement or voluntary act that threatens it is not a repudiation. But where a party wrongfully states that he will not perform at all unless the other party consents to a modification of his contract rights, the statement is a repudiation even though the concession that he seeks is a minor one, because the breach that he threatens in order to exact it is a complete refusal of performance. **Illustrations:**

8. On April 1, A contracts to sell and B to buy land for $ 50,000, delivery of the deed and payment of the price to be on August 1. On May 1, the parties make an enforceable modification under which delivery of the deed and payment of the price are to be on July 30 instead of August 1. On June 1, A tells B that he will not deliver a deed until August 1. A's statement is not a repudiation unless the one-day delay would, in the absence of a repudiation, have given B a claim for damages for total breach. See Illustration 4 to § 242.

9. The facts being otherwise as stated in Illustration 8, A tells B that he will not deliver a deed at all unless B agrees to accept it on August 1. A's statement is a repudiation. The result is the same even though A acts in the erroneous belief that the modification has no legal effect.

§ 251. When a Failure to Give Assurance May Be Treated as a Repudiation

(1) Where reasonable grounds arise to believe that the obligor will commit a breach by non-performance that would of itself give the obligee a claim for damages for total breach under § 243, the obligee may demand adequate assurance of due performance and may, if reasonable, suspend any performance for which he has not already received the agreed exchange until he receives such assurance.

(2) The obligee may treat as a repudiation the obligor's failure to provide within a reasonable time such assurance of due performance as is adequate in the circumstances of the particular case.

Comment:

a. Rationale. Ordinarily an obligee has no right to demand reassurance by the obligor that the latter will perform when his performance is due. However, a contract "imposes an obligation on each party that the other's expectation of receiving due performance will not be impaired." Uniform Commercial Code § 2-609(1). When, therefore, an obligee reasonably believes that the obligor will commit a breach by non-performance that would of itself give him a claim for damages for total breach (§ 243), he may, under the rule stated in this Section, be entitled to demand

assurance of performance. The rule is a generalization, applicable without regard to the subject matter of the contract, from that of Uniform Commercial Code § 2-609. The latter applies only to contracts for the sale of goods and gives a party a right to adequate assurance of performance where "reasonable grounds for insecurity arise with respect to the performance" of the other party. Both rules rest on the principle that the parties to a contract look to actual performance "and that a continuing sense of reliance and security that the promised performance will be forthcoming when due, is an important feature of the bargain." Comment 1 to Uniform Commercial Code § 2-609. This principle is closely related to the duty of good faith and fair dealing in the performance of the contract (§ 205). See also Comment *b* to § 141. The rule stated in this Section may be modified by agreement of the parties, and where they have done so their rights depend on the application of the rules on interpretation stated in Chapter 9, The Scope of Contractual Obligations.

b. Relation to other rules. An obligee who believes, for whatever reason, that the obligor will not or cannot perform without a breach, is always free to act on that belief. If he is not himself under a duty to perform before the obligor, he may simply await the obligor's performance and, if his belief is confirmed, he will have a claim for damages for breach by non-performance. If he can prove that his belief would have been confirmed, he is at least shielded from liability even if he has failed to give a performance that is due before that of the obligor or has, by making alternative arrangements, done an act that amounts to a repudiation. For example, under § 254, the obligee's duty to pay damages for total breach by repudiation is discharged if the obligor himself would not or could not have performed when his performance was due. If, however, the obligee's belief is incorrect, his own failure to perform or his making of alternate arrangements may subject him to a claim for damages for total breach. This Section affords him an opportunity, in appropriate cases, to demand assurance of due performance and thereby avoid the uncertainties that would otherwise inhere in acting on his belief. If it is then reasonable for the obligee to suspend his own performance while he awaits assurance by the obligor, he may do so under Subsection (1). Under the special rule stated in § 252, the obligee may always suspend his own performance where his belief that the obligor will commit a breach is based on the obligor's insolvency. If the obligee does not, within a reasonable time, obtain adequate assurance of due performance, he may under Subsection (2) treat the obligor's failure to provide such an assurance as a repudiation. His right to do so is, however, subject to the rule stated in § 256 under which the manifestation of doubt or the apparent inability, on which the obligee bases his belief

that the obligor will commit a breach, may be nullified. In contrast to the situation where the obligor has actually repudiated under § 250, the obligee may choose not to treat the failure to provide assurances as a repudiation and may continue to perform without affecting his right to recover damages for subsequent loss that he could have avoided by so treating it. See Comment *a* to § 257 and § 350. If he chooses to treat the obligor's failure as a repudiation, it may have any of the three effects that any other repudiation may have: it may give him a claim for damages for total breach (§ 253(1)), it may discharge his own remaining duties of performance (§ 253(2)), and it may excuse the non-occurrence of a condition of the other party's duty (§ 255). The effect on the obligee's remaining duties of performance of prospective non-performance by the obligor that would not be a breach because it would be justified on the ground of impracticability of performance is dealt with in § 268. **Illustrations:**

    1. A contracts to let B use his concert hall on the evening of May 7 for a performance by B's string quartet, in return for B's promise to perform and to pay A a percentage of the receipts. The contract provides that B is not discharged even if he is unable to transport his quartet to A's hall. On May 6, because of an unexpected airline strike, A reasonably believes that B's quartet will be unable to come the 3,000 miles necessary to perform in his hall as scheduled. Without demanding adequate assurance of due performance under the rule stated in this Section, A then contracts with C to let C hold a meeting in the hall on the evening of May 7. A's contract with C is a repudiation of his contract with B (§ 250), which gives rise to a claim by B against A for damages for total breach (§ 253). If, however, B is in fact unable to bring his quartet to A's hall on May 7, B's claim against A is discharged (§ 254).

    2. The facts being otherwise as stated in Illustration 1, B succeeds in chartering a plane and flies the 3,000 miles with his quartet in his private plane. He arrives in time to perform, but is unable to do so because C is using the hall. B has a claim against A for damages for total breach (§ 243).

c. Reasonable grounds for belief. Whether "reasonable grounds" have arisen for an obligee's belief that there will be a breach must be determined in the light of all the circumstances of the particular case. The grounds for his belief must have arisen after the time when the contract was made and cannot be based on facts known to him at that time. Nor, since the grounds must be reasonable, can they be based on events that occurred after that time but as to which he took the risk when he made the contract. But minor breaches may give reasonable grounds for a belief that there will be more serious breaches, and the mere failure of the obligee to press a claim for damages for those minor breaches will not preclude him from basing a demand for assurances on them. Compare § 241(d), Comment *e* to that section, and Comment *b* to § 242. Even circumstances that do not relate to the particular contract, such as defaults under other contracts, may give reasonable grounds for such a belief. See Comment *a* to § 252. Conduct by a party that indicates his doubt as to his willingness or ability to perform but that is not sufficiently positive to amount to a repudiation (see Comment *b* to § 250), may give reasonable grounds for such a belief. And events that indicate a party's apparent inability, but do not amount to a repudiation because they are not voluntary acts, may also give reasonable grounds for such a belief. One important application of the rule stated in this Section occurs when a party who has contracted to buy specific property, land or goods, discovers that the seller has neither present ownership of the property nor a right to become or at least a reasonable expectation of becoming the owner in time to perform. Another important application of the rule occurs when an obligor who is allowed a period of time within which to perform makes an offer of defective performance. It may still be possible for him, if the offer is refused, to make an offer of conforming performance within the period allowed. Nevertheless, the offer of defective performance may give the obligee reasonable grounds to believe that the obligor will commit a breach under this Section. A third important application of the rule occurs when a party becomes insolvent. The effect of insolvency will vary according to the nature of the obligor's duty. If, for example, it is merely to perform personal services, the fact of insolvency alone may not give reasonable grounds to believe that the obligor will commit a breach, but if it is to pay for goods on credit it will. See Uniform Commercial Code § 2-702(1). A special rule on insolvency is stated in § 252. In any case, in order for this Section to apply, the breach that the obligee believes the obligor will commit must be a breach by non-performance that would so substantially impair the value of the contract to the obligee that it would of itself, unaccompanied by a repudiation, give him a claim for damages for total breach under § 243. **Illustrations:**

　　3. On May 1, A contracts to sell and B to buy a parcel of land for $ 50,000, delivery of the deed and payment of the price to be on July 30. Unknown to both A and B, C has a dower interest in the land. On May 15, B discovers this and demands that A give him adequate assurance of due performance. A fails to do so, and B commences an action against A on July 1. B had reasonable grounds to believe that A would commit a breach by non-performance that would of itself have given B a claim for damages for total breach. If the court concludes that a reasonable time for A to give assurances had passed on July 1, B properly treated A's failure to give assurances as a repudiation. B then has a claim for damages against A for total breach.

　　4. The facts being otherwise as stated in Illustration 3, C's interest in the land is that of mortgagee under a mortgage that A can discharge at any time by payment of the mortgage debt. B had no reasonable grounds to believe that A would commit a breach, B could not treat A's failure to give assurances as a repudiation, and B has no claim for damages against A. Compare Illustration 6 to § 250.

. . .

d. Nature of demand. A party who demands assurances must do so in accordance with his duty of good faith and fair dealing in the enforcement of the contract (§ 205). Whether a particular demand for assurance conforms to that duty will depend on the circumstances. The demand need not be in writing. Although a written demand is usually preferable to an oral one, if time is of particular importance the additional time required for a written demand might necessitate an oral one. Compare Uniform Commercial Code § 2-609(1), which controls in the case of a sale of goods and which requires a demand "in writing." Harrassment by means of frequent unjustified demands may amount to a violation of the duty of good faith and fair dealing.

. . .

e. Nature and time of assurance. Whether an assurance of due performance is "adequate" depends on what it is reasonable to require in a particular case taking account of the circumstances of that case. The relationship between the parties, any prior dealings that they have had, the reputation of the party whose performance has been called into question, the nature of the grounds for insecurity, and the time within which the assurance must be furnished are all relevant factors. (If the obligor's insolvency constitutes the grounds for the obligee's insecurity, the special rule stated in § 252 empowers him to suspend performance until he receives assurance in the form of actual performance, an offer of performance, or reasonable security.) What is a "reasonable time" within which to give assurance under Subsection (2) will also depend on the particular circumstances. Like the demand, the assurance is subject to the general requirement of good faith and fair dealing in the enforcement of the contract (§ 205; see Comment *d*).

. . .

§ 252. Effect of Insolvency

(1) Where the obligor's insolvency gives the obligee reasonable grounds to believe that the obligor will commit a breach under the rule stated in § 251, the obligee may suspend any performance for which he has not already received the agreed exchange until he receives assurance in the form of performance itself, an offer of performance, or adequate security.

(2) A person is insolvent who either has ceased to pay his debts in the ordinary course of business or cannot pay his debts as they become due or is insolvent within the meaning of the federal bankruptcy law.

Comment:

a. Insolvency. An obligor's insolvency is not a repudiation (Comment *c* to § 250) and may not even give the obligee reasonable grounds to believe that the obligor will commit a breach (Comment *c* to § 251). It does, however, have this latter effect when the obligee is to pay for goods on credit, and Uniform Commercial Code § 2-702(1) states a specific statutory rule for that situation. This Section states a rule that applies more broadly to similar situations in which insolvency gives reasonable grounds to believe that the obligor will commit a breach. It supplements the rule stated in § 251 by giving the obligee the unqualified power to suspend his own performance until he receives from the obligor performance, an offer of performance (see Comment *b* to § 238), or reasonable security, which may, in an appropriate case, be by a guarantee of performance. He need not show, as he must under § 251(1), that it is "reasonable" to suspend, and he need not perform unless he receives the assurance required by this Section. Mere evidence of an ability to perform in spite of insolvency or a favorable report from a credit rating agency will not suffice. However, the rule stated in this Section only empowers the obligee to suspend his own performance. If he would treat the failure to give assurance as a repudiation, he must proceed under § 251. Furthermore, in order for the obligee to have the benefit of this Section, the obligor must actually be insolvent. The obligee who merely has doubts as to the obligor's solvency should also proceed under § 251. See Comment *b* to § 251. A party is insolvent for the purpose of this Section only if one of the three tests of insolvency stated in Subsection (2) is satisfied. This statement follows the definition of insolvency under Uniform Commercial Code § 1-201(23). Mere doubts about the solvency of the other party or uncertainty as to his ability to perform may amount, under the rule stated in § 251, to reasonable grounds to believe that he will commit a serious breach, but they do not amount to insolvency. The rule stated in this Section may be modified by agreement of the parties. **Illustrations:**

    1. On April 1, A, a subcontractor, contracts with B, a contractor, to furnish labor and materials for the floors of an apartment building that B is building. A is to begin work on May 1 and be paid 85% of the price in monthly payments as the work progresses and the balance on his completion of the work. On April 10, A discovers that B is insolvent and demands that B pay for the work in advance or give reasonable security. When B refuses to do so, A refuses to begin work on May 1. B has no claim against A.

. . .

§ 253. Effect of a Repudiation as a Breach and on Other Party's Duties

(1) Where an obligor repudiates a duty before he has committed a breach by non-performance and before he has received all of the agreed exchange for it, his repudiation alone gives rise to a claim for damages for total breach.

(2) Where performances are to be exchanged under an exchange of promises, one party's repudiation of a duty to render performance discharges the other party's remaining duties to render performance.

Comment:

a. Breach. An obligee under a contract is ordinarily entitled to the protection of his expectation that the obligor will perform. For this reason, a repudiation by the obligor under § 250 or § 251 generally gives rise to a claim for damages for total breach even though it is not accompanied or preceded by a breach by non-performance. Such a repudiation is sometimes elliptically called an "anticipatory breach," meaning a breach by anticipatory repudiation, because it occurs before there is any breach by non-performance. If there is a breach by non-performance, in addition to the repudiation under § 250 or § 251 the breach is not one by repudiation alone and the rules stated in § 243 rather than those stated in Subsection (1) apply. If, under § 251, it was a breach by non-performance that gave the obligee grounds to believe that the obligor would commit a more serious breach, the obligor's failure to give assurances cannot give rise to a breach by repudiation alone. The measure of damages in the case of a claim under this Section is governed by the rules stated in Topic 2 of Chapter 16. **Illustrations:**

> 1. On April 1, A and B make a contract under which B is to work for A for three months beginning on June 1. On May 1, A repudiates by telling B he will not employ him. On May 15, B commences an action against A. B's duty to work for A is discharged and he has a claim against A for damages for total breach.
>
> . . .

b. Discharge. Under Subsection (1) a breach by repudiation alone can only give rise to a claim for total breach, although a breach by non-performance, even if coupled with a repudiation, can generally give rise to either a claim for partial breach or to one for total breach (§§ 236, 237). Of course, in appropriate circumstances, the injured party can, after a breach by repudiation alone, pursue alternative relief by seeking, for example, a decree of specific performance or an injunction. See Topic 3 of Chapter 16. Nevertheless, the rule stated in Subsection (1) is one of those rules that

are peculiar to breach by repudiation alone and differ from those applicable to a breach by non-performance. (Another such rule is that a breach by repudiation alone can be totally nullified by the party in breach (§ 257), while a breach by non-performance, whether coupled with a repudiation or not, cannot be.) Subsection (2) states a corollary of this rule that a breach by repudiation always gives rise to a claim for damages for total breach: where performances are to be exchanged under an exchange of promises, one party's repudiation discharges any remaining duties of performance of the other party with respect to the expected exchange.

c. Scope. If an obligor repudiates under § 250 or § 251 before he has received all of the agreed exchange for his promise, the repudiation alone gives rise to a claim for damages for total breach under Subsection (1). The most important example of such a case occurs when performances are to be exchanged under an exchange of promises and one party repudiates a duty with respect to the expected exchange before the other party has fully performed that exchange. See Illustrations 1 and 2. (A repudiation of a duty whose performance is not part of the expected exchange, and for which there is therefore no agreed exchange, does not come within the rule stated in Subsection (1). See, e.g., Illustration 3 to § 232.) Another example occurs when one party repudiates a duty under an option contract before the other party has exercised the option by giving the agreed exchange. See Illustration 3. However, it is one of the established limits on the doctrine of "anticipatory breach" that an obligor's repudiation alone, whether under § 250 or § 251, gives rise to no claim for damages at all if he has already received all of the agreed exchange for it. The rule stated in Subsection (1) does not, therefore, allow a claim for damages for total breach in such a case. **Illustrations:**

> 3. On February 1, A and B make an option contract under which, in consideration for B's

payment of $ 100, A promises to convey to B a parcel of land on May 1 for $ 50,000, if B tenders that sum by that date. On March 1, A repudiates by selling the parcel to C. On April 1, B commences an action against A. Since A has not received the $ 50,000, the agreed exchange for his duty to sell the parcel to B, B has a claim against A for damages for total breach.

4. On February 1, A and B make a contract under which, as consideration for B's immediate payment of $ 50,000, A promises to convey to B a parcel of land on May 1. On March 1, A repudiates by selling the parcel to C. On April 1, B commences an action against A. Since A has received the $ 50,000, the agreed exchange for his duty to sell the parcel to B, B has no claim against A for damages for breach of contract until performance is due on May 1.

. . .

§ 254. Effect of Subsequent Events on Duty to Pay Damages

(1) A party's duty to pay damages for total breach by repudiation is discharged if it appears after the breach that there would have been a total failure by the injured party to perform his return promise.

(2) A party's duty to pay damages for total breach by repudiation is discharged if it appears after the breach that the duty that he repudiated would have been discharged by impracticability or frustration before any breach by non-performance.

Comment:

a. Non-performance by injured party after repudiation. If the parties are to exchange performances under an exchange of promises, each party's duties to render performance are generally regarded as conditional on the other party's performance, or at least on his readiness to perform (§§ 237, 238, 251, 253). This principle applies even though one party is already in breach by repudiation. His duty to pay damages is discharged if it subsequently appears that there would have been a total failure of performance by the injured party. A failure is total in this context if it would have been sufficient to have discharged any remaining duties of the party in breach to render his performance. See § 242. The result follows even if it appears that the failure would have been justified and not a breach. Cf. § 244. **Illustration:**

1. On April 1, A and B make a personal service contract under which A promises to employ B for six months beginning July 1 and B promises to work for A during that period. On May 1, A repudiates the contract. On June 1, B falls ill and is unable to perform during the entire

period. A's duty to pay B damages for total breach by repudiation is discharged.

b. Impracticability or frustration after repudiation. Under the rule stated in § 253(1), a party's breach by anticipatory repudiation immediately gives rise to a claim for damages for total breach. If it subsequently appears that the duty that he repudiated would have been discharged by supervening impracticability (§ 261) or frustration (§ 265) before any breach by non-performance, his duty to pay damages is discharged. Impracticability or frustration that would have occurred after breach by non-performance may affect the measure of damages but does not discharge the duty to pay damages; cf. §§ 344, 347, 352. **Illustration:**

2. On April 1, A and B make a personal service contract under which A promises to employ B for 6 months beginning July 1 and B promises to work for A during that period. On May 1, B repudiates the contract. On June 1, B falls ill and is unable to perform during the entire period. B's duty to pay damages to A for his anticipatory repudiation is discharged.

§ 255. Effect of a Repudiation as Excusing the Non-Occurrence Of a Condition

Where a party's repudiation contributes materially to the non-occurrence of a condition of one of his duties, the non-occurrence is excused.

Comment:

a. Rationale. This Section accords the same effect to a repudiation that § 245 accords to a breach by non-performance. No one should be required to do a useless act, and if, because of a party's repudiation, it appears that the occurrence of a condition of a duty would not be followed by performance of the duty, the non-occurrence of the condition is generally excused. In judging whether occurrence of the condition would be followed by performance of the duty the obligee may take the obligor at his word. Nevertheless, the repudiation must contribute materially to the non-occurrence of the condition, and if the condition would not have occurred in any event, its non-occurrence is not excused. In such a case both parties are discharged.

Illustrations:

     1. A, an insurance company, issues a policy insuring B against theft, and providing that no payment will be made unless written notice is given within 60 days after loss. A loss occurs, and B immediately notifies A by telephone. A repudiates by informing B without adequate reason that it will not pay the loss. Because of this, B does not give written notice to A. B has a claim against A for the amount of the loss.

     2. On February 1, A contracts to sell and B to buy a house for $ 50,000, B's duty being "conditional on approval by X Bank of B's pending mortgage application." On March 1, B repudiates by telling A that he will not buy the house. On March 10, the X Bank, which is unaware of B's repudiation, disapproves B's application on financial grounds. A has no claim against B. The non-occurrence of the condition, approval by X Bank, is not excused because B's repudiation did not contribute materially to its non-occurrence.

b. Exceptions. Under §§ 237 and 238, it may be required as a condition of one party's duty that the other party perform or offer to perform his duty. A repudiation by the first party will, in those circumstances, discharge that duty of the other party (§ 253(2)), eliminating the requirement that the other party perform or offer to perform it. The discharge has the additional effect of excusing the non-occurrence of the condition. But non-occurrence of the condition is excused only if the duty is discharged. See Comment *c* to § 245 and Illustrations 1 and 2 to § 253.

Illustration:

     3. A, a contractor, makes a contract with B, a subcontractor, under which B is to be paid $ 300,000 for furnishing heating and air conditioning units for a housing project to be built by A, "on condition that Contractor is furnished with a performance bond within two weeks." No provision is made for progress payments. A week after the making of the contract, A repudiates by telling B that he will not perform the contract. Because of the repudiation, B does not furnish a performance bond. B has a claim against A for damages for total breach. The non-occurrence of one condition, B's furnishing of a performance bond, is excused under this Section because A's repudiation contributed materially to its non-occurrence. The non-occurrence of another condition, B's furnishing heating and air conditioning units, is excused because B's duty to furnish the units was discharged when A repudiated (§ 253(2)), and its performance was therefore no longer a condition under § 237.

§ 256. Nullification of Repudiation or Basis for Repudiation

(1) The effect of a statement as constituting a repudiation under § 250 or the basis for a repudiation under § 251 is nullified by a retraction of the statement if notification of the retraction comes to the attention of the injured party before he materially changes his position in reliance on the repudiation or indicates to the other party that he considers the repudiation to be final.

(2) The effect of events other than a statement as constituting a repudiation under § 250 or the basis for a repudiation under § 251 is nullified if, to the knowledge of the injured party, those events have ceased to exist before he materially changes his position in reliance on the repudiation or indicates to the other party that he considers the repudiation to be final.

Comment:

     a. Effect of nullification. A repudiation may have three consequences: it may give rise to a claim for damages for total breach (§ 253(1)), discharge duties (§ 253(2)), and excuse the non-occurrence of a condition (§ 255). A party's manifestation of doubt or apparent inability may entitle the other party to demand adequate assurance of due performance and to treat a failure to give such assurance as a repudiation under the rule stated in § 251. If, however, the effect of the statement or other events constituting the repudiation under § 250 or the basis for the repudiation under § 251 is nullified as provided in this Section, none of these consequences follows. Such a nullification does not, of course, alter the consequences of any breach by non-performance that may have taken place. If, for example, a repudiation accompanies a breach by non-performance, nullification of the repudiation leaves the injured party a claim for damages for the breach, although the claim may no longer be one for damages for total breach (see Comment *b* to § 243). If the repudiation is wholly anticipatory, nullification leaves the injured party with no claim at all. Compare the effect of events subsequent to a total breach by repudiation (§ 254). **Illustrations:**

1. On February 1, A contracts to supply B with natural gas for one year beginning on May 1, payment to be made each month. On June 1, A repudiates and fails to supply gas under the contract. On June 2, before B has taken any action in response to the repudiation, A resumes the supply of gas and notifies B that he retracts his repudiation. B has no claim against A based on the repudiation. B has a claim against A for damages for A's breach by non-performance for one day. Whether B's claim is one for damages for partial breach or for total breach is determined by the rule stated in § 243(1).

2. On February 1, A contracts to supply B with natural gas for one year beginning on May 1, payment to be made each month. On March 1,

A repudiates. On April 1, before B has taken any action in response to the repudiation, A notifies B that he retracts his repudiation. B's duties under the contract are not discharged, and B has no claim against A. *b. Manner of retraction.* It is not necessary for the repudiator to use words in order to retract his statement. Conduct, such as an offer of performance, may be adequate to convey the idea of retraction to the injured party.

c. Time for nullification. Once the injured party has materially changed his position in reliance on the repudiation, nullification would clearly be unjust. In the interest of certainty, however, it is undesirable to make the injured party's rights turn exclusively on such a vague criterion, and he may therefore prevent subsequent nullification by indicating to the other party that he considers the repudiation final. It is, for example, enough under Uniform Commercial Code § 2-612 that "the aggrieved party has since the repudiation cancelled or materially changed his position or otherwise indicated that he considers the repudiation final." Cancellation of the contract or the commencement of an action claiming damages for total breach would be sufficient. (See Comment 1 to Uniform Commercial Code § 2-611.) **Illustrations:**

3. The facts being otherwise as stated in Illustration 2, on March 15, B makes a contract with C for the supply of gas to replace that which he was to receive from A. B's duties under the contract are discharged and B has a claim against A for damages for total breach (§ 253).

. . .

§ 257. Effect of Urging Performance in Spite of Repudiation

The injured party does not change the effect of a repudiation by urging the repudiator to perform in spite of his repudiation or to retract his repudiation.

Comment:

a. Effects of rule. Although the effects of a repudiation may be nullified as stated in § 256, a repudiation operates until nullified not only as a breach (§ 253(1)), but as a ground for discharge (§ 253(2)) and for excuse of the non-occurrence of a condition (§ 255). Under the rule stated in this Section, these effects continue although the injured party has urged that the repudiator perform or that he retract his repudiation. This rule is in accord with that of Uniform Commercial Code § 2-610(b), which allows the injured party to "resort to any remedy for breach . . . even though he has notified the repudiating party that

he would await the latter's performance and has urged retraction." Any possibility that the injured party might unfairly mislead the repudiator is avoided by the duty of good faith and fair dealing (§ 205). An injured party who continues to perform in spite of a repudiation may, however, be precluded under § 350 from claiming damages for loss that he could have avoided. **Illustration:**

1. A contracts to sell and B to buy a parcel of land for $ 50,000, delivery of the deed and payment of the price to be on July 1. On June 1, A repudiates the contract. B writes A urging him to perform, but A does not reply. B thereupon

buys another parcel of land in its place and makes no conditional offer of the $ 50,000 on July 1. A, however, having changed his mind makes a con-ditional offer of a deed on July 1. B has a claim against A for damages for total breach. A has no claim against B.

Introductory Note: If an obligor who owes two or more duties to the same obligee renders a performance that is not sufficient to discharge all of them, it may be important to determine which are discharged. This Topic states rules for the application of performances in that situation. In many states these rules have been modified by statutes governing the application of payments in consumer credit transactions. See, e.g., Uniform Consumer Credit Code § 3.303 (1974 ed.), which provides for the application of payments on debts secured by cross-collateral.

The obligor generally has the power to direct application of his performance and often does so explicitly if his intention is not evident from the nature of the performance itself. This rule is stated in § 258. Sections 259 and 260 state rules that apply where the obligor has not exercised this power. If the obligor's duties are to render immediate performances of identical character, the obligee generally has the power to apply it as he chooses. If he does not, the performance is applied according to rules of law. In practice the questions dealt with in §§ 259 and 260 arise almost exclusively in connection with duties to pay money. This is because, even after breach, a duty to pay money continues unchanged, except for the added duty to pay interest, and may still be discharged by payment. However, once a duty to render a performance of another kind has been transformed into a duty to pay damages for total breach, the duty to pay damages cannot be discharged simply by rendering the performance originally called for. Because performances other than payment rarely present questions of the kind dealt with in §§ 259 and 260, those sections refer only to payment. The principles extend, however, to the occasional instances of other performances of an identical character.

The rules stated in this Topic do not apply to cases in which the obligee accepts a performance different from that owed by the obligor. Rules for those cases are stated in Topic 2 of Chapter 12, Discharge By Assent or Alteration. Nor do the rules stated in this Topic extend to performances that are not rendered voluntarily, such as payments made by the receiver of an insolvent obligor or by the insurer of an obligor under an insurance policy. The rights that an obligor may have to restitution of a payment on grounds such as mistake, misrepresentation or duress at the time of payment are stated in the Restatement of Restitution.

§ 258. Obligor's Direction of Application

(1) Except as stated in Subsection (2), as between two or more contractual duties owed by an obligor to the same obligee, a performance is applied according to a direction made by the obligor to the obligee at or before the time of performance.

(2) If the obligor is under a duty to a third person to devote a performance to the discharge of a particular duty that the obligor owes to the obligee and the obligee knows or has reason to know this, the obligor's performance is applied to that duty.

Comment:

a. Obligor's power. As a general rule, an obligor has the power to direct the obligee's application of a payment or other performance. The direction is effective immediately on the obligee's acceptance of the performance, the performance is considered to be applied as directed, and the obligor's duty is discharged accordingly. A contrary statement or other inconsistent action by an obligee who has accepted the performance does not affect this result. The obligor cannot, however, effectively direct an application in breach of a contract with the obligee as to how performances should be applied if the contract is specifically enforceable, as may be the case if application as directed will deprive the obligee of security. See § 363.

The obligor can effectively direct that a performance be applied to a duty that is not matured, to one that is unsecured, and even to one that is unenforceable on grounds of public policy. As to state statutes governing consumer credit transactions, see the Introductory Note to this Topic. **Illustrations:**

1. A makes two contracts to sell identical cargoes of sugar to B, delivery under the first to be not later than July 1 and under the second not later than August 1. In June A delivers a conforming cargo of sugar, directing that it be applied to the second contract. A's duty under that contract is discharged.

2. A owes B two debts of $ 1,000 each, one secured and the other unsecured. A sends B $ 1,000 with a letter stating that the payment is to discharge the secured debt. B keeps the money but replies, "I shall apply your payment to the unsecured debt." The secured debt is discharged.

3. A owes B $ 1,000 for goods sold. He has also promised to pay B $ 1,000 that he lost to B at gambling, but his promise is unenforceable on grounds of public policy. A pays B $ 1,000, stating that it is in payment of his gambling losses. A's duty to pay B $ 1,000 for goods sold is not discharged.

. . .

c. Interests of third persons. Sometimes an obligor owes a duty to a third person to devote a performance to the discharge of a particular duty that the obligor owes to the obligee. If the obligee knows or has reason to know that this is so, an inconsistent direction by the obligor is ineffective and the performance is applied to that duty to the obligee. The obligor's duty to the third person may be a fiduciary one, as where the obligor is a trustee who has received money in trust to pay a debt. Or it may be a contractual duty, as where a debtor has a duty to devote to the debt the very money received from the third party. But the duty to the third party must relate to the disposition of the third party's performance and not be merely one to pay the debt. Compare Illustrations 7 and 8; cf. § 260(2)(a). **Illustrations:**

7. A contracts with B to build a building, to be completed free of liens. C obtains a mechanic's lien on the building to secure payment for labor and materials that he has furnished under a subcontract with A. A owes C on other accounts as well as under this subcontract. A, on receiving progress payments from B, uses the money to pay C, and directs C, who knows its source, to apply it to the other accounts. If A is under no duty to B to use the progress payments in a particular way, A's direction is effective regardless of C's knowledge. A's duty to pay the other accounts is discharged to the extent of the payments to C. Compare Illustration 1 to § 260.

. . .

§ 259. Creditor's Application

(1) Except as stated in Subsections (2) and (3), if the debtor has not directed application of a payment as between two or more matured debts, the payment is applied according to a manifestation of intention made within a reasonable time by the creditor to the debtor.

(2) A creditor cannot apply such a payment to a debt if

(a) the debtor could not have directed its application to that debt, or

(b) a forfeiture would result from a failure to apply it to another debt and the creditor knows or has reason to know this, or

(c) the debt is disputed or is unenforceable on grounds of public policy.

(3) If a creditor is owed one such debt in his own right and another in a fiduciary capacity, he cannot, unless empowered to do so by the beneficiary, effectively apply to the debt in his own right a greater proportion of a payment than that borne by the unsecured portion of that debt to the unsecured portions of both claims.

Comment:

a. Creditor's power of application. If the debtor has not directed the application of his payment by the time payment is made, the creditor has a power to apply it himself. Subject to some limitations (see Comments *c* and *d*), he can apply it to any matured debt or distribute it among several matured debts and can do so to his own advantage, without regard to the effect on the debtor. He can, for example, apply it to an unsecured debt, to one that is barred by a statute of limitations, or to one that is unenforceable because of the Statute of Frauds. He cannot, however, apply it to a debt that is not matured at the time of payment. The creditor's power may be limited by a direction given by the debtor at or before the time of payment that it not be applied to a particular debt or debts. As to the extension of these principles to performances other than payments and as to state statutes governing consumer credit transactions, see the Introductory Note to this Topic.

. . .

§ 260. Application of Payments Where Neither Party Exercises His Power

(1) If neither the debtor nor the creditor has exercised his power with respect to the application of a payment as between two or more matured debts, the payment is applied to debts to which the creditor could have applied it with just regard to the interests of third persons, the debtor and the creditor.

(2) In applying payments under the rule stated in Subsection (1), a payment is applied to the earliest matured debt and ratably among debts of the same maturity, except that preference is given

(a) to a debt that the debtor is under a duty to a third person to pay immediately, and

(b) if he is not under such a duty,

(i) to overdue interest rather than principal, and (ii) to an unsecured or precarious debt rather than one that is secured or certain of payment.

Comment:

a. General rule. If neither the debtor nor the creditor exercises his power with respect to the application of a payment it is applied with just regard to the interests of third persons, the debtor and the creditor. This general principle supplements the specific rules stated in Subsection (2) and gives guidance in their application. However, a payment will not be applied to a duty to which the creditor himself could not have applied it because of the limitations stated in § 259. As to the extension of these principles to performances other than payments and as to state statutes governing consumer credit transactions other than payments, see the Introductory Note to this Topic.

. . .

Chapter 11

Impractibility of Performance and Furstration of Purpose

Introductory Note Contract liability is strict liability. It is an accepted maxim that *pacta sunt servanda*, contracts are to be kept. The obligor is therefore liable in damages for breach of contract even if he is without fault and even if circumstances have made the contract more burdensome or less desirable than he had anticipated. (As to the effect of hardship on equitable remedies, see § 364(b).) The obligor who does not wish to undertake so extensive an obligation may contract for a lesser one by using one of a variety of common clauses: he may agree only to use his "best efforts"; he may restrict his obligation to his output or requirements; he may reserve a right to cancel the contract; he may use a flexible pricing arrangement such as a "cost plus" term; he may insert a *force majeure* clause; or he may limit his damages for breach. The extent of his obligation then depends on the application of the rules on interpretation stated in Chapter 9, The Scope of Contractual Obligations.

Even where the obligor has not limited his obligation by agreement, a court may grant him relief. An extraordinary circumstance may make performance so vitally different from what was reasonably to be expected as to alter the essential nature of that performance. In such a case the court must determine whether justice requires a departure from the general rule that the obligor bear the risk that the contract may become more burdensome or less desirable. This Chapter is concerned with the principles that guide that determination. The question is generally considered to be one of law rather than fact, for the court rather than the jury. Cf. Comment *d* to § 212. In recent years courts have shown increasing liberality in discharging obligors on the basis of such extraordinary circumstances.

Three distinct grounds for discharge of the obligor's duty must be distinguished. First, the obligor may claim that some circumstance has made his own performance impracticable. The general rule governing impracticability of performance is stated in § 261, and three common specific instances of impracticability are dealt with in §§ 262, 263 and 264. Second, the obligor may claim that some circumstance has so destroyed the value to him of the other party's performance as to frustrate his own purpose in making the contract. The rule governing frustration of purpose is stated in § 265. Third, the obligor may claim that he will not receive the agreed exchange for his own performance because some circumstance has discharged the obligee's duty to render that agreed exchange, on the ground of either impracticability or frustration. The general rules on the effect of failure of performance on the other party's duties are stated in Chapter 10 and particularly in §§ 237 and 238. A special rule for cases in which non-performance is justified by impracticability or frustration is stated in § 267.

Usually the impracticability or frustration that is relied upon as a justification for non-performance occurred after the contract was made. The rule stated in § 261 applies to such instances of supervening impracticability or frustration. The impracticability or frustration may, however, already have existed, unknown to the obligor, at the time of contracting. The rule stated in § 266 applies to such instances of existing impracticability and frustration, and provides for results that are substantially the same as those that would be reached under the rule stated in § 261 in analogous cases of supervening impracticability or frustration. The rules stated in §§ 262, 263 and 264 for specific instances of impracticability apply under § 266 as well as under § 261. See Chapter 6 for the extent to which rules relating to mistake may also be available to an obligor who seeks to avoid liability on the basis of existing impracticability or frustration.

The rationale behind the doctrines of impracticability and frustration is sometimes said to be that there is an "implied term" of the contract that such extraordinary circumstances will not occur. This Restatement rejects this analysis in favor of that of Uniform Commercial Code § 2-615, under which the central inquiry is whether the non-occurrence of the circumstance was a "basic assumption on which the contract was made." See Comment *f* to § 2. In order for the parties to have had such a "basic assumption" it is not necessary for them to have been conscious of alternatives. Where, for example, an artist contracts to paint a painting, it can be said that the death of the artist is an event the non-occurrence of which was a basic assumption on which the contract was made, even though the parties never consciously addressed themselves to that possibility.

Determining whether the non-occurrence of a particular event was or was not a basic assumption involves a judgment as to which party assumed the risk of its occurrence. In contracting for the manufacture and delivery of goods at a price fixed in the contract, for example, the seller assumes the risk of increased costs within the normal range. If, however, a disaster results in an abrupt tenfold increase in cost to the seller, a court might determine that the seller did not assume this risk by concluding that the non-occurrence of the disaster was a "basic assumption" on which the contract was made. In making such determinations, a court will look at all circumstances, including the terms of the contract. The fact that the event was unforeseeable is significant as suggesting that its non-occurrence was a basic assumption. However, the fact that it was foreseeable, or even foreseen, does not, of itself, argue for a contrary conclusion, since the parties may not have thought it sufficiently important a risk to have made it a subject of their bargaining. Another significant factor may be the relative bargaining positions of the parties and the relative ease with which either party could have included a clause. Another may be the effectiveness of the market in spreading such risks as, for example, where the obligor is a middleman who has an opportunity to adjust his prices to cover them.

Under the rationale of this Restatement, the obligor is relieved of his duty because the contract, having been made on a different "basic assumption," is regarded as not covering the case that has arisen. It is an omitted case, falling within a "gap" in the contract. Ordinarily, the just way to deal with the omitted case is to hold that the obligor's duty is discharged, in the case of changed circumstances, or has never arisen, in the case of existing circumstances, and to shift the risk to the obligee. In some cases a party who has already partly performed is entitled to recovery for what he has done under the rule on part performances as agreed equivalents (§ 240). Even where this is not so, relief may be available in the form of a claim for restitution or expenses incurred in reliance on the contract (§ 377). These possibilities are dealt with in § 272(1). Since the case is properly regarded as an omitted one, however, if none of these techniques will suffice to do substantial justice, it is within the discretion of the court to supply an omitted essential term under the rule stated in § 204. This is made clear in § 272(2). Other matters dealt with in this Chapter include: the effect on the other party's duties of a prospective non-performance that is justified by impracticability or frustration (§ 268), temporary impracticability and frustration (§ 269), partial impracticability (§ 270), and excuse of a condition by impracticability (§ 271).

§ 261. Discharge by Supervening Impracticability

Where, after a contract is made, a party's performance is made impracticable without his fault by the occurrence of an event the non-occurrence of which was a basic assumption on which the contract was made, his duty to render that performance is discharged, unless the language or the circumstances indicate the contrary.

Comment:

a. Scope. Even though a party, in assuming a duty, has not qualified the language of his undertaking, a court may relieve him of that duty if performance has unexpectedly become impracticable as a result of a supervening event (see Introductory Note to this Chapter). This Section states the general principle under which a party's duty may be so discharged. The following three sections deal with the three categories of cases where this general principle has traditionally been applied: supervening death or incapacity of a person necessary for performance (§ 262), supervening destruction of a specific thing necessary for performance (§ 263), and supervening prohibition or prevention by law (§ 264). But, like Uniform Commercial Code § 2-615(a), this Section states a principle broadly applicable to all types of impracticability and it "deliberately refrains from any effort at an exhaustive expression of contingencies" (Comment 2 to Uniform Commercial Code § 2-615). The principle, like others in this Chapter, yields to a contrary agreement by which a party may assume a greater as well as a lesser obligation. By such an agreement, for example, a party may undertake to achieve a result irrespective of supervening events that may render its achievement impossible, and if he does so his non-performance is a breach even if it is caused by such an event. See Comment *c*. The rule stated in this Section applies only to discharge a duty to render a performance and does not affect a claim for breach that has already arisen. The effect of events subsequent to a breach on the amount of damages recoverable is governed by the rules on remedies stated in Chapter 16. See Comment *e* to § 347. Their effect on a claim for breach by anticipatory repudiation is governed by the rules on discharge stated in Chapter 12. Cases of existing, as opposed to supervening, impracticability are governed by § 266 rather than this Section.

b. Basic assumption. In order for a supervening event to discharge a duty under this Section, the non-occurrence of that event must have been a "basic assumption" on which both parties made the contract (see Introductory Note to this Chapter). This is the criterion used by Uniform Commercial Code § 2-615(a). Its application is simple enough in the cases of the death of a person or destruction of a specific thing necessary for performance. The continued existence of the person or thing (the non-occurrence of the death of destruction) is ordinarily a basic assumption on which the contract was made, so that death or destruction effects a discharge. Its application is also simple enough in the cases of market shifts or the financial inability of one of the parties. The continuation of existing market conditions and of the financial situation of the parties are ordinarily not such assumptions, so that mere market shifts or financial inability do not usually effect discharge under the rule stated in this Section. In borderline cases this criterion is sufficiently flexible to take account of factors that bear on a just allocation of risk. The fact that the event was foreseeable, or even foreseen, does not necessarily compel a conclusion that its non-occurrence was not a basic assumption. See Comment *c* to this Section and Comment *a* to § 265. **Illustrations:**

    1. On June 1, A agrees to sell and B to buy goods to be delivered in October at a designated port. The port is subsequently closed by quarantine regulations during the entire month of October, no commercially reasonable substitute performance is available (see Uniform Commercial Code § 2-614(1)), and A fails to deliver the goods. A's duty to deliver the goods is discharged, and A is not liable to B for breach of contract.

    2. A contracts to produce a movie for B. As B knows, A's only source of funds is a $ 100,000 deposit in C bank. C bank fails, and A does not produce the movie. A's duty to produce the movie is not discharged, and A is liable to B for breach of contract.

    3. A and B make a contract under which B is to work for A for two years at a salary of $ 50,000 a year. At the end of one year, A discontinues his business because governmental regulations have made it unprofitable and fires B. A's duty to employ B is not discharged, and A is liable to B for breach of contract.

    4. A contracts to sell and B to buy a specific machine owned by A to be delivered on July 30. On July 29, as a result of a creditor's suit against A, a receiver is appointed and takes charge of all of A's assets, and A does not deliver the goods on July 30. A's duty to deliver the goods is not discharged, and A is liable to B for breach of contract.

c. Contrary indication. A party may, by appropriate language, agree to perform in spite of impracticability that would otherwise justify his non-performance under the rule stated in this Section. He can then be held liable for damages although he cannot perform. Even absent an express agreement, a court may decide, after considering all the circumstances, that a party impliedly assumed such a greater obligation. In this respect the rule stated in this Section parallels that of Uniform Commercial Code § 2-615, which applies "Except so far as a seller may have assumed a greater obligation . . . ." Circumstances relevant in deciding whether a party has assumed a greater obligation include his ability to have inserted a provision in the contract expressly shifting the risk of impracticability to the other party. This will depend on the extent to which the agreement was standardized (cf. § 211), the degree to which the other party supplied the terms (cf. § 206), and, in the case of a particular trade or other group, the frequency with which language so allocating the risk is used in that trade or group (cf. § 219). The fact that a supplier has not taken advantage of his opportunity expressly to shift the risk of a shortage in his supply by means of contract language may be regarded as more significant where he is middleman, with a variety of sources of supply and an opportunity to spread the risk among many customers on many transactions by slight adjustment of his prices, than where he is a producer with a limited source of supply, few outlets, and no comparable opportunity. A commercial practice under which a party might be expected to insure or otherwise secure himself against a risk also militates against shifting it to the other party. If the supervening event was not reasonably foreseeable when the contract was made, the party claiming discharge can hardly be expected to have provided against its occurrence. However, if it was reasonably foreseeable, or even foreseen, the opposite conclusion does not necessarily follow. Factors such as the practical difficulty of reaching agreement on the myriad of conceivable terms of a complex agreement may excuse a failure to deal with improbable contingencies. See Comment *b* to this Section and Comment *a* to § 265.

Illustration:

> 5. A, who has had many years of experience in the field of salvage, contracts to raise and float B's boat, which has run aground. The contract, prepared by A, contains no clause limiting A's duty in the case of unfavorable weather, unforeseen circumstances, or otherwise. The boat then slips into deep water and fills with mud, making it impracticable for A to raise it. If the court concludes, on the basis of such circumstances as A's experience and the absence of any limitation in the contract that A prepared, that A assumed an absolute duty, it will decide that A's duty to raise and float the boat is not discharged and that A is liable to B for breach of contract.

d. Impracticability. Events that come within the rule stated in this Section are generally due either to "acts of God" or to acts of third parties. If the event that prevents the obligor's performance is caused by the obligee, it will ordinarily amount to a breach by the latter and the situation will be governed by the rules stated in Chapter 10, without regard to this Section. See Illustrations 4-7 to § 237. If the event is due to the fault of the obligor himself, this Section does not apply. As used here "fault" may include not only "willful" wrongs, but such other types of conduct as that amounting to breach of contract or to negligence. See Comment 1 to Uniform Commercial Code § 2-613. Although the rule stated in this Section is sometimes phrased in terms of "impossibility," it has long been recognized that

it may operate to discharge a party's duty even though the event has not made performance absolutely impossible. This Section, therefore, uses "impracticable," the term employed by Uniform Commercial Code § 2-615(a), to describe the required extent of the impediment to performance. Performance may be impracticable because extreme and unreasonable difficulty, expense, injury, or loss to one of the parties will be involved. A severe shortage of raw materials or of supplies due to war, embargo, local crop failure, unforeseen shutdown of major sources of supply, or the like, which either causes a marked increase in cost or prevents performance altogether may bring the case within the rule stated in this Section. Performance may also be impracticable because it will involve a risk of injury to person or to property, of one of the parties or of others, that is disproportionate to the ends to be attained by performance. However, "impracticability" means more than "impracticality." A mere change in the degree of difficulty or expense due to such causes as increased wages, prices of raw materials, or costs of construction, unless well beyond the normal range, does not amount to impracticability since it is this sort of risk that a fixed-price contract is intended to cover. Furthermore, a party is expected to use reasonable efforts to surmount obstacles to performance (see § 205), and a performance is impracticable only if it is so in spite of such efforts. **Illustrations:**

> 6. A contracts to repair B's grain elevator. While A is engaged in making repairs, a fire destroys the elevator without A's fault, and A does not finish the repairs. A's duty to repair the elevator is discharged, and A is not liable to B for breach of contract. See Illustration 3 to § 263.

> 7. A contracts with B to carry B's goods on his ship to a designated foreign port. A civil war then unexpectedly breaks out in that country and the rebels announce that they will try to sink all vessels bound for that port. A refuses to perform. Although A did not contract to sail on the vessel, the risk of injury to others is sufficient to make A's performance impracticable. A's duty to carry the goods to the designated port is discharged, and A is not liable to B for breach of contract. Compare Illustration 5 to § 262.

> 8. The facts being otherwise as stated in Illustration 7, the rebels announce merely that they will confiscate all vessels found in the designated port. The goods can be bought and sold

on markets throughout the world. A refuses to perform. Although there is no risk of injury to persons, the court may conclude that the risk of injury to property is disproportionate to the ends to be attained. A's duty to carry the goods to the designated port is then discharged, and A is not liable to B for breach of contract. If, however, B is a health organization and the goods are scarce medical supplies vital to the health of the population of the designated port, the court may conclude that the risk is not disproportionate to the ends to be attained and may reach a contrary decision.

9. Several months after the nationalization of the Suez Canal, during the international crisis resulting from its seizure, A contracts to carry a cargo of B's wheat on A's ship from Galveston, Texas to Bandar Shapur, Iran for a flat rate. The contract does not specify the route, but the voyage would normally be through the Straits of Gibraltar and the Suez Canal, a distance of 10,000 miles. A month later, and several days after the ship has left Galveston, the Suez Canal is closed by an outbreak of hostilities, so that the only route to Bandar Shapur is the longer 13,000 mile voyage around the Cape of Good Hope. A refuses to complete the voyage unless B pays additional compensation. A's duty to carry B's cargo is not discharged, and A is liable to B for breach of contract.

10. The facts being otherwise as in Illustration 9, the Suez Canal is closed while A's ship is in the Canal, preventing the completion of the voyage. A's duty to carry B's cargo is discharged, and A is not liable to B for breach of contract.

11. A contracts to construct and lease to B a gasoline service station. A valid zoning ordinance is subsequently enacted forbidding the construction of such a station but permitting variances in appropriate cases. A, in breach of his duty of good faith and fair dealing (§ 205), makes no effort to obtain a variance, although variances have been granted in similar cases, and fails to construct the station. A's performance has not been made impracticable. A's duty to construct is not discharged, and A is liable to B for breach of contract.

e. "Subjective" and "objective" impracticability. It is sometimes said that the rule stated in this Section applies only when the performance itself is made impracticable, without regard to the particular party who is to perform. The difference has been described as that between "the thing cannot be done" and "I cannot do it," and the former has been characterized as "objective" and the latter as "subjective." This Section recognizes that if the performance remains practicable and it is merely beyond the party's capacity to render it, he is ordinarily not discharged, but it does not use the terms "objective" and "subjective" to express this. Instead, the rationale is that a party generally assumes the risk of his own inability to perform his duty. Even if a party contracts to render a performance that depends on some act by a third party, he is not ordinarily discharged because of a failure by that party because this is also a risk that is commonly understood to be on the obligor. See Comment c. But see Comment a to § 262.

Illustrations:

12. A, a milkman, and B, a dairy farmer, make a contract under which B is to sell and A to buy all of A's requirements of milk, but not less than 200 quarts a day, for one year. B may deliver milk from any source but expects to deliver milk from his own herd. B's herd is destroyed because of hoof and mouth disease and he fails to deliver any milk. B's duty to deliver milk is not discharged, and B is liable to A for breach of contract. See Illustration 1 to § 263; compare Illustration 7 to § 263.

13. A contracts to sell and B to buy on credit 1,500,000 gallons of molasses "of the usual run from the C sugar refinery." C delivers molasses to others but fails to deliver any to A, and A fails to deliver any to B. A's duty to deliver molasses is not discharged, and A is liable to B for breach of contract. If A has a contract with C, C may be liable to A for breach of contract.

14. A, a general contractor, is bidding on a construction contract with B which gives B the right to disapprove the choice of subcontractors. A makes a contract with C, a subcontractor, under which, if B awards A the contract, A will obtain B's approval of C and C will do the excavation for A. A is awarded the contract by B, but B disapproves A's choice of C, and A has the excavation work done by another subcontractor. A's duty to have C do the excavation is not discharged, and A is liable to C for breach of contract.

f. Alternative performances. A contract may permit a party to choose to perform in one of several different ways, any of which will discharge his duty. Where the duty is to render such an alternative performance, the fact that one or more of the alternatives has become impracticable will not discharge the party's duty to perform if at least one of them remains practicable. The form of the promise is not controlling, however, and not every promise that is expressed in alternative form gives rise to a duty to render an alternative performance. For example, a surety's undertaking that either the principal will perform or the surety will compensate the creditor does not ordinarily impose such a duty. See Restatement of Security § 117. Nor does a promise either to render a performance or pay liquidated damages impose such a duty. Furthermore, a duty that is originally one to render alternative performances ceases to be such a duty if all but one means of performance have been foreclosed, as by the lapse of time or the occurrence of a condition including election by the obligor, or on the grounds of public policy (Chapter 8) or unconscionability (§ 208).

Illustrations:

15. On June 1, A contracts to sell and B to buy whichever of three specified machines A chooses to deliver on October 1. Two of the machines are destroyed by fire on July 1, and A fails to deliver the third on October 1. A's duty to deliver a machine is not discharged, and A is liable to B for breach of contract. If all three machines had been destroyed, A's duty to deliver a machine would have been discharged, and A would not have been liable to B for breach of contract. See Uniform Commercial Code § 2-613.

16. A contracts to repair B's building. The contract contains a valid provision requiring A to pay liquidated damages if he fails to make any of the repairs. S is surety for A's performance. Before A is able to begin, B's building is destroyed by fire. Neither A's nor S's duty is one to render an alternative performance. A's duty to repair the building is discharged, and A is not liable to B for liquidated damages or otherwise for breach of contract. S's duty as surety for A is also discharged, and S is not liable to B for breach of contract.

§ 262. Death or Incapacity of Person Necessary for Performance

If the existence of a particular person is necessary for the performance of a duty, his death or such incapacity as makes performance impracticable is an event the non-occurrence of which was a basic assumption on which the contract was made.

Comment:

a. Rationale. This Section states a common specific instance for the application of the rule stated in § 261. If, as both parties understand, the existence of a particular person is necessary for the performance of a duty, it is a "basic assumption on which the contract was made" that he will neither die nor be deprived of the necessary capacity before the time for performance. Therefore, the death of that person or his loss of capacity discharges the obligor's duty to render the performance, subject to the qualifications stated in § 261. Usually, the person in question will be the obligor, but he may also be the obligee or a third person. Where the obligor is personally to perform the duty, his death or incapacity results in "objective," not merely in "subjective," impracticability (Comment *e* to § 261), since it is no longer practicable for anyone to perform the duty. The result is, of course, different if the language or the circumstances indicate the contrary (Comment *c* to § 261), but it is sufficiently rare for a party to undertake a duty to render personal service in spite of his death or incapacity that an intention to do so must be clearly manifested. Although the obligor's fault will prevent his disability from discharging that duty, it is often so difficult to foresee the effect of conduct on health that fault in bringing about disability must be clear in order to prevent the disability from resulting in discharge. The rule applies not only to the disability of a natural person but also, by analogy, to the dissolution of a legal person such as a corporation. However, it is seldom applicable to such cases in practice because the dissolution ordinarily must not be due to its financial inability (see Comment *b* to § 261) and, since it must not be due to its own fault, it must not be within its control. If the disability exists at the time the contract is made, the rule stated in § 266(1) rather than that stated in § 261 controls, and this Section applies for the purpose of that rule as well. **Illustrations:**

1. A contracts to employ B as his confidential secretary for a year. B dies before the end of the year. B's duty to work for A is discharged, and B's estate is not liable to A for breach of contract.

2. The facts being otherwise as stated in Illustration 1, A rather than B dies before the end of the year, and B takes other employment. B's duty to work for A is discharged, and B is

not liable to A's estate for breach of contract.

3. A, a corporation, contracts to employ B as its secretary for five years. Within that time the state legislature enacts a law requiring the dissolution of corporations engaged in A's business. On dissolution, A's duty to employ B is discharged, and A is not liable to B for breach of contract. See also § 264. B may have a claim against A under the rule stated in § 272(1).

4. The facts being otherwise as in Illustration 3, A's dissolution is voluntary or the result of insolvency. A's duty to employ B is not discharged, and A is liable to B for breach of contract. See Comment b and Illustration 3 to § 261. Cf. Illustration 5 to § 319.

5. A contracts with B to produce a play starring C, a famous actor, in B's theater on December 16. Early in December, while the play is being performed elsewhere, C experiences a worsening throat condition and, although it does not prevent his performing, he is advised by his doctor to cancel his further performances and have a minor operation. On December 12, A notifies B that the December 16 performance of the play is cancelled for this reason. A's duty to produce the play is discharged, and A is not liable to B for breach of contract. Compare Illustration 7 to § 261.

b. *Where particular person is necessary.* The parties may effectively provide that a particular person is or is not necessary for performance. The agreement may, for example, require the obligor's personal service. Where, as is often the case, the agreement is silent on the subject, all the circumstances will be considered to determine whether the duty, as understood by the parties, sufficiently involves elements of personal service or discretion to require performance by a particular person. In this connection, resort may be had to the rules laid down in Chapter 9, The Scope of Contractual Obligations, including those on usage and course of dealing (§§ 219-23). The question whether a duty requires performance by a particular person is essentially the same question that arises where a party seeks to delegate performance of his duty to another and is to be determined by the same criteria. See § 318 and Comment b to that Section. If an obligor can discharge his duty by the performance of another, his own disability will not discharge him.

Illustrations:

6. A contracts with B to cut a tract of standing timber. A dies, and his estate refuses to complete performance. In the absence of special circumstances showing that A's personal service or supervision is necessary to performance of his duty, A's duty to cut the timber is not discharged, and A's estate is liable to B for breach of contract.

7. A and B make a contract under which A is to devote full time to prospecting for coal on B's land, and, if he is successful, B personally is to finance and manage a corporation for the exploitation of the coal. B is to pay A a salary and convey to him a one-quarter interest in any resulting corporation. A locates coal and is paid his salary, but B dies before he is able to finance and manage a corporation to exploit it, and no such corporation is formed. Whether performance of B's duty to finance and manage a corporation became impracticable on B's death depends on whether that duty, as understood by the parties, could only be performed by B himself. If the court concludes that it could, B's duty to convey an interest in any resulting corporation is discharged, and B's estate is not liable to A for breach of contract. A may have a claim against B under the rule stated in § 272(1).

8. A and B, a firm of architects, contract with C to design a building for C. It is understood by the parties that both A and B shall render services under the contract. A dies and B fails to complete performance. Both A's and B's duties to design the building are discharged, and neither A's estate nor B is liable to C for breach of contract.

9. A and B, a firm of contractors doing an extensive business in many localities, contract with C to fill a tract of low land. A dies and B fails to complete performance. Neither A's nor B's duty to fill the land is discharged, and both A's estate and B are liable to C for breach of contract.

§ 263. Destruction, Deterioration or Failure to Come Into Existence of Thing Necessary for Performance

If the existence of a specific thing is necessary for the performance of a duty, its failure to come into existence, destruction, or such deterioration as makes performance impracticable is an event the non-occurrence of which was a basic assumption on which the contract was made.

Comment:

a. Rationale. This Section, like the preceding one, states a common specific instance for the application of the rule stated in § 261. If, as both parties understand, the existence of a specific thing is necessary for the performance of a duty it is "a basic assumption on which the contract was made" that that thing will come into existence if it does not already exist and will remain in existence until the time for performance. Therefore, if its failure to come into existence or its destruction or deterioration makes performance impracticable, the obligor's duty to render that performance is discharged, subject to the qualifications stated in § 261. Each party bears some of the risk that the transaction will not be carried out for such a reason. The rule does not apply, however, where an obligor merely happens to have at his disposal only one means of performance, which is destroyed, since the parties do not then make the contract on the basis of such an assumption. See Comment *b* to § 261. Nor does it apply if the language or the circumstances indicate the contrary. See Comment *c* to § 261. If the parties contract on an erroneous assumption that a specific thing necessary for performance is then in existence, the rule stated in § 266(1) rather than that stated in § 261 controls, and this Section applies for the purpose of that rule as well. **Illustrations:**

1. A contracts to sell and B to buy cloth. A expects to manufacture the cloth in his factory, but before he begins manufacture the factory is destroyed by fire without his fault. Although cloth meeting the contract description is available on the market, A refuses to buy and deliver it to B. A's duty to deliver the cloth is not discharged, and A is liable to B for breach of contract. See Illustration 12 to § 261; compare Illustration 7 to this Section.

2. The facts being otherwise as stated in Illustration 1, A contracts to sell cloth to be manufactured in the factory that is later destroyed. A's duty to deliver the cloth is discharged, and A is not liable to B for breach of contract. Cf. Illustration 13 to § 261.

3. A contracts with B to shingle the roof of B's house. When A has done part of the work, much of the house including the roof is destroyed by fire without his fault, so that he is unable to complete the work. A's duty to shingle the roof is discharged, and A is not liable to B for breach of contract. Compare Illustration 6 to § 261.

4. A contracts with B to build a house for B. When A has done part of the work, much of the structure is destroyed by fire without his fault. A refuses to finish building the house. A's duty to build the house is not discharged, and A is liable to B for breach of contract.

. . .

b. When specific thing is necessary. The rule stated in this Section applies not only when the terms of the contract make the specific thing necessary, but also when, although the contract is silent, the parties understand that it is necessary. In proving such an understanding, prior negotiations may be used to show the meaning of a writing, even though it takes the form of a completely integrated agreement. See § 214(c). **Illustrations:**

6. A contracts with B to drive logs to B's mill during the following spring. Although the contract does not specify a particular stream, the parties know that there is only one stream down which the logs can be driven. An extraordinary drought dries that stream up during the time for performance. A's duty to drive the logs is discharged, and A is not liable to B for breach of contract.

7. A, a farmer, contracts with B in the spring to sell a large quantity of beans to B during the following season. Although the contract does not state where the beans are to be grown, A owns but one tract of land, on which he has in the past raised beans, and both parties understand that the beans will be raised on this tract. A properly plants and cultivates beans on the tract in sufficient quantity to perform the contract, but an extraordinary flood destroys the crop. A delivers no beans to B. A's duty to deliver beans is discharged, and A is not liable to B for breach of contract. Compare Illustration 1 to this Section; Illustration 12 to § 261.

8. The facts being otherwise as stated in Illustration 7, A and B have no common understanding as to where the beans will be grown. A's duty to deliver beans is not discharged, and A is liable to B for breach of contract. Cf. Comment *f* to § 261.

§ 264. Prevention by Governmental Regulation or Order

If the performance of a duty is made impracticable by having to comply with a domestic or foreign governmental regulation or order, that regulation or order is an event the non-occurrence of which was a basic assumption on which the contract was made.

Comment:

a. Rationale. This Section, like the two that precede it, states a specific instance for the application of the rule stated in § 261. It is "a basic assumption on which the contract was made" that the law will not directly intervene to make performance impracticable when it is due. Therefore, if supervening governmental action prohibits a performance or imposes requirements that make it impracticable, the duty to render that performance is discharged, subject to the qualifications stated in § 261. The fact that it is still possible for a party to perform if he is willing to break the law and risk the consequences does not bar him from claiming discharge. The rule stated in this Section does not apply if the language or the circumstances indicate the contrary. With the trend toward greater governmental regulation, however, parties are increasingly aware of such risks, and a party may undertake a duty that is not discharged by such supervening governmental actions, as where governmental approval is required for his performance and he assumes the risk that approval will be denied (Illustration 3). Such an agreement is usually interpreted as one to pay damages if performance is prevented rather than one to render a performance in violation of law. See §§ 180, 198. If the prohibition or prevention already exists at the time of the making of the contract, the rule stated in § 266(1) rather than that stated in § 261 controls, and this Section applies for the purpose of that rule as well. See Comment *a* to § 266. See also Chapter 8 on agreements unenforceable on grounds of public policy. The effect of a governmental regulation or order on a claim for breach is governed by the rules on discharge stated in Chapter 12.

Illustrations:

1. A sells land to B, who, as part of the contract, promises that the land shall not be built upon. The land is taken by eminent domain under statutory authority and a building is built on it. B's duty not to build on the land is discharged, and B is not liable to A for breach of contract.

2. A, a railroad, promises to give B annual passes for life, in consideration for a conveyance of land by B to A. After thirteen years, a statute is enacted forbidding railroads to grant such passes, and A refuses to give further passes to B. A's duty to give passes is discharged, and A is not liable to B for breach of contract. B may have a claim against A under the rule stated in § 272(1).

3. A, a manufacturer of sewage treatment equipment, contracts to design and install a central sewage treatment plant, for which B, a developer of a residential subdivision, contracts to pay. The parties understand that A must obtain the approval of the state Department of Health before installation. A is unable to install the plant because the Department of Health disapproves the plans. If the court concludes, on the basis of A's experience and the absence of any limitation in the contract, that A assumed the risk that approval would be denied, it will decide that A's duty to install the plant is not discharged and that A is liable to B for breach of contract. Cf. Illustration 3 to § 266.

4. A contracts with B to sell him a specific machine on a stated day, time being of the essence. C, by false allegations of ownership of the machine, induces a court to enjoin A from delivering the machine. In spite of diligent efforts, A is unable to have the injunction dissolved in time to fulfill his contract with B. A's duty to deliver the machine is discharged, and A is not liable to B for breach of contract. The result would be different if due to A's fault C had just grounds for obtaining the injunction, or if A, in breach of his duty of good faith and fair dealing (§ 205), failed to use diligent efforts which could have secured its dissolution. See Comment *d* to § 261 and Illustration 11 to that section.

5. A and B make a contract under which A is to employ B for a year. B is unable to complete his performance because he is arrested and imprisoned for a burglary that he has committed. Because his inability was due to his own fault, B's duty to work for a year is not discharged, and B is liable to A for breach of contract. See Comment *d* to § 261.

b. Nature of regulation or order. Under the rule stated in this Section, the regulation or order may be domestic or foreign. It may emanate from any level of government and may be, for example, a municipal ordinance or an order of an administrative agency. Any governmental action is included and technical distinctions between "law," "regulation," "order" and the like are disregarded. It is not necessary that the regulation or order be valid, but a party who seeks to justify his non-performance under this Section must have observed the duty of good faith and fair dealing imposed by § 205 in attempting, where appropriate, to avoid its application. The requirement is like that of Uniform Commercial Code § 2-615, under which compliance in good faith is sufficient regardless of the validity of the regulation or order. See Comment 10 to Uniform Commercial Code § 2-615. The regulation or order must directly affect a party's performance in such a way that it is impracticable for him both to comply with the regulation or order and to perform. Governmental action that has the indirect effect of making performance more burdensome by, for example, contributing to a scarcity of supply, is governed by the general rule stated in § 261 and not by the specific rule stated in this Section. **Illustration:**

> 6. A, a citizen of a foreign country, contracts with B to sell him the output of A's mill for one year. War breaks out, and A's government orders him to sell the output of his mill to it instead. A complies with the order in good faith and fails to deliver to B. A's duty to deliver his output to B is discharged, and A is not liable for breach of contract. The result does not depend on the legal validity of the order.

§ 265. Discharge by Supervening Frustration

Where, after a contract is made, a party's principal purpose is substantially frustrated without his fault by the occurrence of an event the non-occurrence of which was a basic assumption on which the contract was made, his remaining duties to render performance are discharged, unless the language or the circumstances indicate the contrary.

Comment:

a. Rationale. This Section deals with the problem that arises when a change in circumstances makes one party's performance virtually worthless to the other, frustrating his purpose in making the contract. It is distinct from the problem of impracticability dealt with in the four preceding sections because there is no impediment to performance by either party. Although there has been no true failure of performance in the sense required for the application of the rule stated in § 237, the impact on the party adversely affected will be similar. The rule stated in this Section sets out the requirements for the discharge of that party's duty. First, the purpose that is frustrated must have been a principal purpose of that party in making the contract. It is not enough that he had in mind some specific object without which he would not have made the contract. The object must be so completely the basis of the contract that, as both parties understand, without it the transaction would make little sense. Second, the frustration must be substantial. It is not enough that the transaction has become less profitable for the affected party or even that he will sustain a loss. The frustration must be so severe that it is not fairly to be regarded as within the risks that he assumed under the contract. Third, the non-occurrence of the frustrating event must have been a basic assumption on which the contract was made. This involves essentially the same sorts of determinations that are involved under the general rule on impracticability. See Comments *b* and *c* to § 261. The foreseeability of the event is here, as it is there, a factor in that determination, but the mere fact that the event was foreseeable does not compel the conclusion that its non-occurrence was not such a basic assumption. **Illustrations:**

> 1. A and B make a contract under which B is to pay A $ 1,000 and is to have the use of A's window on January 10 to view a parade that has been scheduled for that day. Because of the illness of an important official, the parade is cancelled. B refuses to use the window or pay the $ 1,000. B's duty to pay $ 1,000 is discharged, and B is not liable to A for breach of contract.

> 2. A contracts with B to print an advertisement in a souvenir program of an international yacht race, which has been scheduled by a yacht club, for a price of $ 10,000. The yacht club cancels the race because of the outbreak of war. A has already printed the programs, but B refuses to pay the $ 10,000. B's duty to pay $ 10,000 is discharged, and B is not liable to A for breach of contract. A may have a claim under the rule stated in §§ 272(1).

> 3. A, who owns a hotel, and B, who owns a country club, make a contract under which A is to pay $ 1,000 a month and B is to make the club's membership privileges available to the guests in A's hotel free of charge to them. A's

building is destroyed by fire without his fault, and A is unable to remain in the hotel business. A refuses to make further monthly payments. A's duty to make monthly payments is discharged, and A is not liable to B for breach of contract.

4. A leases neon sign installations to B for three years to advertise and illuminate B's place of business. After one year, a government regulation prohibits the lighting of such signs. B refuses to make further payments of rent. B's duty to pay rent is discharged, and B is not liable to A for breach of contract. See Illustration 7.

5. A contracts to sell and B to buy a machine, to be delivered to B in the United States. B, as A knows, intends to export the machine to a particular country for resale. Before delivery to B, a government regulation prohibits export of the machine to that country. B refuses to take or pay for the machine. If B can reasonably make other disposition of the machine, even though at some loss, his principal purpose of putting the machine to commercial use is not substantially frustrated. B's duty to take and pay for the machine is not discharged, and B is liable to A for breach of contract.

6. A leases a gasoline station to B. A change in traffic regulations so reduces B's business that he is unable to operate the station except at a substantial loss. B refuses to make further payments of rent. If B can still operate the station,

even though at such a loss, his principal purpose of operating a gasoline station is not substantially frustrated. B's duty to pay rent is not discharged, and B is liable to A for breach of contract. The result would be the same if substantial loss were caused instead by a government regulation rationing gasoline or a termination of the franchise under which B obtained gasoline.

b. Limitations on scope. The rule stated in this Section is subject to limitations similar to those stated in § 261 with respect to impracticability. It applies only when the frustration is without the fault of the party who seeks to take advantage of the rule, and it does not apply if the language or circumstances indicate the contrary. Frustration by circumstances existing at the time of the making of the contract rather than by supervening circumstances is governed by the similar rule stated in § 266(2). **Illustration:**

7. The facts being otherwise as in Illustration 4, the government regulation provides for a procedure under which B can apply for an exemption, but B, in breach of his duty of good faith and fair dealing (§ 205), fails to make such an application. Unless it is found that such an application would have been unsuccessful, B's duty to pay rent is not discharged, and B is liable to A for breach of contract. Cf. Illustration 11 to § 261; Illustration 3 to § 264.

§ 266. Existing Impracticability or Frustration

(1) Where, at the time a contract is made, a party's performance under it is impracticable without his fault because of a fact of which he has no reason to know and the non-existence of which is a basic assumption on which the contract is made, no duty to render that performance arises, unless the language or circumstances indicate the contrary.

(2) Where, at the time a contract is made, a party's principal purpose is substantially frustrated without his fault by a fact of which he has no reason to know and the non-existence of which is a basic assumption on which the contract is made, no duty of that party to render performance arises, unless the language or circumstances indicate the contrary.

Comment:

a. Relation to other rules. A party's performance may be as easily affected by impracticability existing at the time the contract was made, because of some fact of which he was ignorant, as by supervening impracticability. Indeed, it is sometimes difficult to characterize a situation as involving either existing or changed circumstances, as, for example, where a judicial decision is handed down after the time that the contract was made giving an unanticipated interpretation to a statute enacted before that

time. Cf. Illustration 3. The rules stated in this Section for cases of existing impracticability and frustration therefore parallel those for supervening impracticability and frustration (§§ 261, 265). The rules stated in §§ 262-64 for determining when the non-occurrence of an event is a basic assumption on which a contract is made for the purpose of § 261 apply by analogy in determining when the non-existence of a fact is such a basic assumption for the purpose of this Section. There are two respects in which the rules stated in this Section differ from those applicable to supervening impracticability and frustration. First, under the rules stated in this Section, the affected party must have had no reason to know at the time the contract was made of the facts on which he later relies. Second, the effect of these rules is to prevent a duty from arising in the first place rather than to discharge a duty that has already arisen. Where a party has partly performed before discovery of the impracticability or frustration, he may claim relief including restitution under the rules stated in §§ 240 and 370-77. See Illustration 5 and § 272(1). In many of the cases that come under this Section, relief based on the rules relating to mistake stated in Chapter 6 will also be appropriate. See Introductory Note to Chapter 6. In that event, the party entitled to relief may, of course, choose the ground on which he will rely. In other cases that come under the rules stated in this Section, the rules on agreements unenforceable on grounds of public policy stated in Chapter 8 will also apply. To the extent that the latter bar relief for reasons based on public policy, they are controlling. **Illustrations:**

    1. A contracts to sell a specified machine to B for $ 10,000. At the time the contract is made, the machine has been destroyed by fire without A's fault but A has no reason to know this. Under the rule stated in Subsection (1) no duty arose under which A is to deliver the machine, and A is not liable to B for breach of contract. Cf. Illustration 7 to this Section and Illustration 5 to § 263.

    2. A and B make a contract under which A is to sell B a house. B, an experienced real estate dealer, insists on the inclusion of a provision under which A is to procure a permit for its conversion into a two family dwelling. Two days earlier, a local zoning ordinance was enacted prohibiting such a conversion, but A has no reason to know this. A is unable to procure the permit. Under the rule stated in Subsection (1), no duty arose under which A is to procure the permit, and A is not liable to B for breach of contract. See § 264.

    3. A, in public bidding, is awarded a contract to build a hospital for the State. A makes a subcontract with B for the installation of glass. Before B begins performance, a court declares the contract between A and the State to be invalid because of departures, of which A had no reason to know, from administrative procedure required for public bidding. A notifies B that he

will be unable to perform his contract with B. Under the rule stated in Subsection (1), no duty arose under which A is to perform his contract with B, and A is not liable to B for breach of contract. See § 264. Cf. Illustration 3 to § 264. B may have a claim against A under the rule stated in § 272(1).

    4. A, an engineering firm, contracts with B to lay water mains under a river. After diligent effort, A is unable to do the work, although other, more experienced firms could do it. Performance is not impracticable. A is under a duty to lay the mains, and A is liable to B for breach of contract. See Comment *e* to § 261.

    5. A, an owner of land, and B, a builder, make a contract under which B is to take from A's land, at a stated rate per cubic yard, all the gravel and earth necessary for the construction of a bridge, an amount estimated to be 114,000 cubic yards. Much of the gravel and earth is below water level and cannot be removed by ordinary means, so that removal would require the use of special equipment at ten times the usual cost per cubic yard, but B has no reason to know this. After removing 50,000 yards, B discovers that this is the case for the remaining gravel and earth, and refuses to take or pay for it. Under the rule stated in Subsection (1), no duty arose under which B is to take or pay for the gravel, and B is not liable to A for breach of contract. A may have a claim against B under the rule stated in § 272(1).

    6. A contracts to sell land to B for B's use as a health resort and milk farm. Two days earlier, a local zoning ordinance was enacted forbidding its use for this purpose, but B has no reason to know this. On discovery of the ordinance, B refuses to take or pay for the land. Under the rule stated in Subsection (2), no duty arose under which B is to take or pay for the land, and B is not liable to A for breach of contract.

    b. Contrary indication. As under the rules stated in §§ 261 and 265, the language or circumstances may indicate that a party has assumed a greater obligation than that imposed on him under this Section. It is somewhat more usual for a party to undertake such an obligation with respect to existing facts than it is with respect to supervening events. A common and important instance occurs when a seller warrants specific goods against defects (Illustration 7). Whether a party has assumed such an obligation is a particularly troublesome question where the parties make a contract calling for technological development under a mistaken assumption that such development either is feasible under the existing state of the art or will become feasible as a result of a technological breakthrough (Illustrations 9 and 10). In such a case the court will determine whether the obligor took the risk that development might not be practicable by looking at such factors as the history of the negotiations, the relative expertise and bargaining power of the parties, their respective roles with regard to plans and specifications, the nature of the performances and the state of technology in the industry. If the obligee has undertaken an obligation as to the accuracy and sufficiency of the plans and specifications, then the consequences of their inaccuracy or insufficiency are governed by the rules stated in Chapter 10, Performance and Non-Performance.

Illustrations:

7. A contracts to sell a specified machine to B for $ 10,000, warranting its merchantability. At the time the contract is made, the machine is not merchantable because of an uncurable defect not due to the fault of A, but A has no reason to know this. Because of A's warranty, he is under a duty to deliver a merchantable machine in spite of the impracticability of doing so, and A is liable to B for breach of contract.

8. A contracts with B to build a house on B's land according to plans furnished by A. Because of subsoil conditions, of which A has no reason to know, this cannot be done unless the land is drained at great expense. After the house is partly completed, it collapses because of these conditions, and A refuses to continue the work. The court may determine from all the circumstances, including the fact that A furnished the plans, that A is under a duty to build the house in spite of the impracticability of doing so, and that A is liable to B for breach of contract. Compare Illustration 4 to § 263.

9. A contracts with B to develop, manufacture, and deliver a light weight electronic device according to A's own specifications by means of what both A and B understand will be a revolutionary technological breakthrough. No breakthrough occurs, and A is unable to deliver the device because it is not possible for any manufacturer, under the state of the art, to keep the weight within the contract specifications. The court may determine from all the circumstances, including the facts that A furnished the specifications and that the parties understand that A will achieve a breakthrough, that A is under a duty to deliver the device in spite of the impracticability of doing so, and that A is liable to B for breach of contract.

10. A contracts with B to manufacture and deliver a light weight electronic device according to specifications furnished by B's engineers. It is not possible for any manufacturer to keep the weight within the contract specifications, but A has no reason to know this. A does not deliver the device. The court may determine from all the circumstances, including the fact that B furnished the specifications, that A is under no duty to deliver the device because of the impracticability of doing so and that A is not liable to B for breach of contract.

§ 267. Effect on Other Party's Duties of a Failure Justified by Impracticability or Frustration

(1) A party's failure to render or to offer performance may, except as stated in Subsection (2), affect the other party's duties under the rules stated in §§ 237 and 238 even though the failure is justified under the rules stated in this Chapter.

(2) The rule stated in Subsection (1) does not apply if the other party assumed the risk that he would have to perform despite such a failure.

Comment:

a. General rule. The rules stated in §§ 237 and 238 apply to any uncured material failure, whether or not it is a breach. They therefore apply even when a party's non-performance is justified because performance has not become due, his duty having been discharged or not having arisen on the ground of impracticability or frustration (§§ 261, 265, 266). Subsection (1) makes it clear that this is so, as a general rule. Its function in this Chapter is similar to that of § 239(1) in Chapter 10, Performance and Non-Performance. See Comment *a* to § 239. **Illustrations:**

1. A contracts with B to paint a continuous mural around a room in B's house for $ 10,000. A dies after he has finished three of the four walls, and B refuses to pay A's estate anything. Although A's duty as to the fourth wall has been discharged, with the result that his performance never became due, his failure to render it nevertheless may affect B's duty under the rule stated in § 237. Since his failure was material and can-

309

not be cured, A's estate has no claim under the contract for the three painted walls. The estate may have a claim under the rule stated in § 272(1).

2. A, a school teacher, contracts with B to teach in B's school for a year. A is to work from September through May, with June, July and August as vacation, during which A's duties are insignificant. B is to pay A monthly from September through August. A dies at the beginning of June, and B refuses to pay A's salary for June, July or August. A's estate has a claim against B under the contract for the salary for those three months. Although A's duty as to the last three months has been discharged with the result that his performance as to those months never became due, his failure to render performance nevertheless may affect B's duty under the rule stated in § 237. But since his failure was not material, A's estate has a claim against B for the salary for those three months.

b. Assumption of risk. The rule stated in Subsection (2) is similar to that of § 239(2). Sometimes a party will undertake a greater obligation than that imposed by Subsection (1) and will assume the risk that he will have to carry out his side of the exchange even though it is not carried out on the other side. If he has assumed this greater risk, then conduct on the other side which would otherwise affect his duty under the rules stated in § 237 or § 238 does not affect his duty. See Comment *b* to § 239.

Illustrations:

3. A contracts with B to furnish bus service to students attending B's school during the school year, from September through May, for a stated sum payable monthly. In March the school is closed until further notice because of an epidemic. Although the school remains closed during April and May, A is required under the contract to remain ready to resume performance. B refuses to pay A for April and May. Since in the circumstances, including the requirement that A remain ready to resume performance, B assumed the risk that he would have to perform in spite of such non-performance by A, the rule stated in Subsection (1) does not apply and A's failure to render performance does not affect B's duty under the rule stated in § 237. A has a claim against B under the contract for the monthly sums for April and May.

4. A, who is not a merchant, contracts to sell a specified machine to B for $ 10,000 on 30 days credit. Before A tenders the machine to B, a fire destroys it without A's fault. Under Uniform Commercial Code § 2-509(3), risk of loss does not pass to the buyer until tender if the seller is not a merchant. Since the risk of loss did not pass to B until tender, the rule stated in Subsection (1) applies and A's failure of performance may affect B's duty under the rule stated in § 237. Since his failure was material and cannot be cured, A has no claim against B under the contract. Compare Illustration 5 to § 263.

5. The facts being otherwise as stated in Illustration 4, the machine is destroyed after A tenders it to B, but before B receives it. Since the risk of loss passed to B on tender, the rule stated in Subsection (1) does not apply, and A's failure to render performance does not affect B's duty under the rule stated in § 237. A has a claim against B under the contract, even though B does not receive the machine.

. . .

§ 268. Effect on Other Party's Duties of a Prospective Failure Justified by Impracticability or Frustration

(1) A party's prospective failure of performance may, except as stated in Subsection (2), discharge the other party's duties or allow him to suspend performance under the rules stated in §§ 251(1) and 253(2) even though the failure would be justified under the rules stated in this Chapter.

(2) The rule stated in Subsection (1) does not apply if the other party assumed the risk that he would have to perform in spite of such a failure.

Comment:

a. Relation to other rules. This Restatement adopts the principle "that a continuing sense of reliance and security that the promised performance will be forthcoming when due, is an important feature of the bargain." Comment 1 to Uniform Commercial Code § 2-609; see Comment *a* to § 251. If there is reason to expect that a party will not perform as promised, the other party has the protection afforded by the rules stated in §§ 250 and 253 if the first party has repudiated, and by the rule stated in § 251 if reasonable grounds for insecurity have arisen with respect to the first party's future performance. However, those sections apply only if such prospective non-performance would amount to a breach. This Section applies when the prospective non-performance would not be a breach because of the rules on impracticability of performance or frustration of purpose stated in this Chapter. Subsection (2) makes it clear that if the other party has assumed the risk that he will have to perform although he receives no return performance, his duties are not discharged.

b. Statement or voluntary act. If a party properly states that he will not perform because of impracticability of his performance or frustration of his purpose, the other party cannot treat that statement as a repudiation under the rule stated in § 250(a) because the threatened non-performance would not be a breach. It therefore gives him no claim for breach of contract. Nevertheless, under the rule stated in this Section it discharges his remaining duties to render the agreed exchange. The same rule applies to a voluntary affirmative act that would otherwise be a repudiation under the rule stated in § 250(b). The rules on nullification of a repudiation (§ 256) and urging performance (§ 257) also apply to situations that come under this Section.

Illustration:

    1. A, an impresario, contracts with B, a singer, for an engagement for three months beginning on January 1. On the preceding November 30, B contracts pneumonia, and states to A that he will be unable to sing before February 1. A employs another singer to fill B's place. On January 1, B, having recovered, offers to perform but A refuses. Since B's statement would have been a repudiation under the rule stated in § 250 but for the operation of the rules on imprac-

ticability of performance stated in §§ 261 and 262, A's duty to employ B is discharged, and A is not liable to B for breach of contract. Cf. Illustration 2 to § 242.

c. Failure to give assurances. If reasonable grounds arise to believe that a party will not perform because of impracticability of his performance or frustration of his purpose, the other party cannot demand assurances and treat a failure to give them as a repudiation under the rule stated in § 251, because the prospective non-performance would not be a breach. It therefore gives him no claim for breach of contract. Nevertheless, under the rule stated in this Section, he may in a proper case suspend his own performance and treat a failure to give assurance as discharging any remaining duties that he has to render the agreed exchange.

Illustrations:

    2. A, an impresario, contracts with B, a singer, for an engagement for three months beginning on January 1. On the preceding November 30, B contracts pneumonia, and A is advised by competent medical authority that B will not be able to sing before February 1. A reasonably demands assurances of due performance by B. B ignores the demand, and A employs another singer to fill B's place. On January 1, B, having recovered, offers to perform, but A refuses. Since B's failure to furnish assurance of due performance would have been a repudiation under the rule stated in § 251 but for the operation of the rules on impracticability of performance stated in §§ 261 and 262, A's duty to employ B is discharged, and A is not liable to B for breach of contract.

   . . .

§ 269. Temporary Impracticability or Frustration

Impracticability of performance or frustration of purpose that is only temporary suspends the obligor's duty to perform while the impracticability or frustration exists but does not discharge his duty or prevent it from arising unless his performance after the cessation of the impracticability or frustration would be materially more burdensome than had there been no impracticability or frustration.

Comment:

a. Rationale. Impracticability of performance or frustration of purpose may be only temporary. While it lasts, the affected party's duty is at least suspended. When the circumstances giving rise to the impracticability or frustration cease to exist, he must then perform. He is usually expected to perform in full and is entitled to an appropriate

extension of time for performance. When the delay has made full performance impracticable, the rules stated in § 270 for partial impracticability and in § 272(2) on supplying a term apply. In some cases, however, delay will make his performance materially more burdensome for him than had there been no impracticability or frustration, and when it appears that this will be so, his duty is discharged and not merely suspended. In applying the standard of materiality, a court will consider whether the delay has seriously upset the allocation of risks under the agreement of the parties. The rule stated in this Section is, of course, subject to contrary agreement. It applies only to the duty of the party adversely affected by the impracticability or frustration; the effect on the duty of the other party, as to a performance to be exchanged under an exchange of promises, is governed by the rules stated in §§ 267, 268, 237 and 238. Compare Illustration 2 to § 242. **Illustrations:**

    1. A contracts with B to build an electric power plant, completion to be within two years, for $ 10,000,000. Before the commencement of performance, a shortage of materials due to a sudden outbreak of war makes it temporarily impracticable for A to perform. A's duty is suspended until it is no longer impracticable for him to obtain materials, and he is then under a duty

to perform with an appropriate extension of time, unless B's duty to pay is discharged by the delay under the rules stated in §§ 237 and 267. However, if circumstances including increased prices then make it materially more burdensome for A to perform, A's duty to build the plant is discharged regardless of whether B's duty would otherwise be discharged by the delay.

    2. On July 5, A charters his vessel to B for a voyage from New York to Liverpool, contracting that the vessel shall be ready for loading July 10. On July 8, the government requisitions the vessel for the stated period of a week, returning the vessel to A in New York on July 15. A's duty to have the vessel ready is suspended until July 15 and he is then under a duty to perform with an appropriate extension of time, unless B's duty to pay is then discharged by the delay under the rules stated in §§ 237 and 267. However, if circumstances including his other contracts then make it materially more burdensome for A to perform, A's duty is discharged regardless of whether B's duty would otherwise be discharged by the delay.

§ 270. Partial Impracticability

Where only part of an obligor's performance is impracticable, his duty to render the remaining part is unaffected if (a) it is still practicable for him to render performance that is substantial, taking account of any reasonable substitute performance that he is under a duty to render; or (b) the obligee, within a reasonable time, agrees to render any remaining performance in full and to allow the obligor to retain any performance that has already been rendered.

Comment:

    a. Relation to other rules. An obligor's performance may be impracticable only in part. (If impracticability as to part makes his performance of the rest so much more burdensome that it is also impracticable, then the entire performance is impracticable and the rules stated in §§ 261 and 266 apply.) If he has done all that is practicable, he may have a claim for relief including restitution under the rules stated in §§ 240 and 370-77. See § 272(1) and Comment *a.* If, however, further performance is practicable, it may be possible to salvage at least some of the unexecuted part of the agreement. This Section states rules for two situations in which it is relatively easy to do this because the obligee has already performed in full, or is willing to do so, or can be required to do so. In more complex situations where the obligee's duty to perform must be adjusted to avoid injustice, a court may nevertheless salvage some of the agreement by

supplying a term under the rule stated in § 272(2). Analogous problems involving frustration of purpose are also dealt with in § 272(2).

    b. Substantial performance practicable. If the part of the obligor's performance that is impracticable is so minor that it is still practicable for him to render substantial performance, his duty to do so is unaffected. Whether his performance would be substantial depends on the impact on the reasonable expectations of the obligee, who either has performed in full or remains liable to perform in full (§ 237). Two means of reducing this impact are significant. First, if the obligor can render a reasonable substitute performance in place of the impracticable part, he must do so under his duty of good faith in performance (§ 205), and that substitute performance will be considered in determining whether his performance would be substantial. Second, if the obligee has a claim in restitution against the obligor under the rules stated in § 272(1), on the ground that the obligor will otherwise receive a performance from the obligee for which he has not rendered the agreed exchange in full, the adequacy of this claim as compensation for the obligee must also be considered in determining whether the obligor's performance would be substantial. In the common case where performances are to be exchanged under an exchange of promises, performance would be substantial if the failure of performance would not be material. See Comment *d* to § 237. Both parties then remain bound to complete the exchange, subject to discharge of the duty to perform the impracticable part and a compensating claim for restitution. **Illustrations:**

1. A contracts to build a supermarket for B for $ 250,000. Included in the plans are numerous lighted signs, including one next to an adjacent highway. Before A begins performance, a local ordinance prohibits the installation of this sign. Since A's failure to install it would not be material, his performance would be substantial, and A's duty to build the rest of the supermarket is unaffected. B is still under a duty to pay $ 250,000, subject to a claim under the rule stated in § 272(1) based on A's failure to build the sign for which he has been paid.

2. A contracts with B to deliver all of B's requirements of milk during the following year at B's loading platform at 200 Lincoln Street. Before A begins performance, the loading platform is accidentally destroyed by fire, but B has an equally suitable platform across the street at 201 Lincoln Street. Neither A's nor B's duties are affected, except that A is to deliver and B is to accept milk at 201 Lincoln Street.

3. A contracts to sell and B to buy a quantity of wheat "f.o.b. Kosmos Steamer at Seattle." Before delivery, an outbreak of war makes Kosmos line ships unavailable at Seattle, but delivery on that line's loading dock remains possible and is a commercially reasonable substitute. Neither A's nor B's duties are affected, ex-

cept that A is to deliver and B is to accept wheat at the Kosmos line's loading dock. B may have a claim under the rules stated in § 272(1) based on A's failure to load the wheat for which he has been paid.

c. Agreement. Even if it is not practicable to render substantial performance, the obligee may salvage the agreement under the rule stated in Subsection (b). If he assures the obligor that the latter will receive in full the performance that he originally expected from the obligee, the obligor must render the rest of his performance. The obligee can make a legally binding commitment of this kind by agreeing (cf. § 3) to render to the obligor any remaining performance and to allow the obligor to retain any performance that has already been rendered. See §§ 18, 19, 89. When performances are to be exchanged under an exchange of promises, and the obligor's non-performance will be a material failure, such agreement will prevent the discharge of the obligee's duties (§§ 237, 238) and the consequent discharge of the obligor's duties, and the agreement will be salvaged. It will also bar any claim for restitution with respect to the obligor's non-performance. See Comment *b*. Under an exchange of any type, such agreement will bar a claim by the obligee for restitution with respect to any performance that he has already rendered. **Illustration:**

4. A contracts with B to service seven different areas at B's airport for a lump sum. Before performance is to begin, a government regulation forbids the servicing of one of the areas, discharging A's duty as to that area under the rules stated in §§ 261 and 264. Under § 267(1), A's non-performance would operate as a failure of performance for the purpose of the rule stated in § 237, and B's remaining duties would be discharged. If, however, B within a reasonable time agrees to pay A the lump sum in full, B's remaining duties are not discharged and A's duty to service the other six areas is unaffected.

§ 271. Impracticability as Excuse for Non-Occurrence Of a Condition

Impracticability excuses the non-occurrence of a condition if the occurrence of the condition is not a material part of the agreed exchange and forfeiture would otherwise result.

Comment:

a. Relation to other rules. This is one of several sections in this Restatement that serve to avoid the forfeiture that might otherwise result from the non-occurrence of a condition. Under

the rule stated in § 227(1), when it is doubtful whether or not an agreement makes an event a condition of an obligor's duty, an interpretation that it does not do so is generally preferred if this will reduce the obligee's risk of forfeiture (see Comment *b* to § 227). Under the rule stated in § 229, even if the parties do make an event a condition in spite of the risk of forfeiture, the non-occurrence of the condition may still be excused if actual forfeiture would otherwise result, but only if the forfeiture would be extreme. Under the rule stated in this Section, if the non-occurrence of the condition is the result of impracticability, it is excused if forfeiture, even if not extreme, would otherwise result. The impracticability must, of course, be such as would suffice to discharge a duty or prevent it from arising. See §§ 261, 262, 263, 264, 266(1). Here, as in §§ 227 and 229, "forfeiture" is used to refer to the denial of compensation that results when the obligee loses his right to the agreed exchange, after he has relied substantially on the expectation of that exchange, as by preparation or performance. See Comment *b* to § 227 and Comment *b* to § 229. **Illustrations:**

1. A contracts with B to repair B's building for $ 20,000, payment to be made "on the satisfaction of C, B's architect, and the issuance of his certificate." A properly makes the repairs, but C dies before he is able to give a certificate. Since presentation of the architect's certificate is not a material part of the agreed exchange and forfeiture would otherwise result, the occurrence of the condition is excused, and A has a claim against B for $ 20,000. Cf. Illustration 3 to § 225.

2. A, an insurance company, issues to B a policy of accidental injury insurance which provides that notice within 14 days of an accident is a condition of A's duty. B is injured as a result of an accident covered by the policy but is so mentally deranged that he is unable to give notice for 20 days. B gives notice as soon as he is able. Since the giving of notice within 14 days is not a material part of the agreed exchange, and forfeiture would otherwise result, the non-occurrence of the condition is excused and B has a claim against A under the policy.

b. Limitation on scope. The rule of this Section, like that of § 229, applies only where occurrence of the condition was not a material part of the agreed exchange. See § 84 and Comment *c* to § 229. If the occurrence of the condition is impracticable only in part, its non-occurrence is, of course, excused only to that extent. **Illustration:**

3. A, an insurance company, issues to B a policy of whole life insurance making it a condition of A's duty that premiums be paid annually. B is imprisoned in a foreign country for five years, and is unable to pay the premiums during that time. On his release, he tenders the overdue premiums, but A refuses to accept them. Since the annual payment of premiums is a material part of the agreed exchange, its non-occurrence is not excused because of impracticability even though forfeiture will result. B has no claim against A.

§ 272. Relief Including Restitution

(1) In any case governed by the rules stated in this Chapter, either party may have a claim for relief including restitution under the rules stated in §§ 240 and 377.

(2) In any case governed by the rules stated in this Chapter, if those rules together with the rules stated in Chapter 16 will not avoid injustice, the court may grant relief on such terms as justice requires including protection of the parties' reliance interests.

Comment:

a. Mitigating doctrines. Because the rules stated in this Chapter might otherwise appear to have the harsh effect of denying either party any recovery following the discharge of one party's duty based on impracticability or frustration, this Section makes it clear that several mitigating doctrines may be used to allow at least some recovery in a proper case. Subsection (1) speaks to claims for relief such as that provided by the rule on part performances as agreed equivalents stated in § 240 and those on restitution and other relief stated in § 377. Subsection (2) speaks to supplying a term to avoid injustice.

b. Relief including restitution. A party whose duty has never arisen or has been discharged because of impracticability of performance or frustration of purpose may already have rendered some of his own performance or received some of the other party's performance or both. In some cases the party who has performed is entitled to recovery for what he has done under the rule on part performances as agreed equivalents (§ 240). See Illustration 8 to § 240. Even where this is not so, it will generally be appropriate to allow him a claim for restitution to the extent that his performance has benefited the other. Such claims, whether for restitution in kind or for the equivalent in money, are governed by the rules stated in Chapter 16. In a proper case recovery may go beyond mere restitution and include elements of reliance by the claimant even though they have not benefited the other party. See § 377. Special mention has been made of the possibility of such claims in those illustrations in the present Chapter in which the facts make it likely that one party's performance has benefited the other (Illustrations 3 and 7 to § 262, Illustration 2 to § 264, Illustration 2 to § 265, Illustration 1 to § 267). In appropriate circumstances such claims might be allowed in other illustrations as well. The rule stated in Subsection (1) is, of course, subject to the agreement of the parties and does not apply if a contrary intention is manifested.

    c. Supplying a term to avoid injustice. Under the rule stated in § 204, when the parties have not agreed with respect to a term that is essential to a determination of their rights and duties, the court will supply a term that is reasonable in the circumstances. Since it is the rationale of this Chapter that, in a case of impracticability or frustration, the contract does not cover the case that has arisen, the court's function can be viewed generally as that set out in § 204 of supplying a term to deal with that omitted case. See Introductory Note to this Chapter. Ordinarily the rules stated in this Chapter, coupled with those stated in Chapter 16, will be adequate to allow the court to arrive at a just result (Subsection (1)). In some instances, however, these rules will not suffice to avoid injustice. A particularly significant example occurs where the just solution is to "sever" the agreement and require that some unexecuted part of it be performed on both sides, rather than to relieve both parties of all of their duties. This situation differs from that envisioned in § 240, under which the court merely allows recovery at the contract rate for performance that has already been rendered. The question under this Section is whether the court can salvage a part of the agreement that is still executory on both sides. See Illustrations 1, 2, 3 and 4. The rule stated in Subsection (2) makes it clear that it can do so by supplying a term which is reasonable in the circumstances when the rules stated in this Chapter together with those stated in Chapter 16 will not avoid injustice. The rule operates in other situations as well and may, for

example, be invoked to require an obligor to prorate among several obligees that part of his performance that remains practicable. See Illustration 5. **Illustrations:**

    1. A contracts with B to work for him for one year for $ 60,000. Illness prevents A from working for the first eleven months, and he refuses to work for the twelfth month although B manifests his assent to paying him $ 5,000. Under the rule stated in § 270, only a manifestation of assent to payment of $ 60,000, B's remaining performance in full, would prevent the discharge of A's duty to work for the twelfth month. If, however, the court decides that this rule will not avoid injustice, it may supply a term, if reasonable, under which A is to work for the twelfth month in return for B's payment of $ 5,000. A would then be liable to B for breach of contract.

    2. A contracts with B to service seven different areas at B's airport at prices that are stated separately for each area. Before performance is to begin, a government regulation forbids the servicing of one of the areas. A does not service that area, but offers to service the other six areas in return for the stated prices. B refuses to allow A to do so. Under § 267(1), A's non-performance would operate as a failure of performance for the purpose of the rule stated in § 237, and B's remaining duties would be discharged. If, however, the court decides that this rule will not avoid injustice, it may supply a term, if reasonable, under which B is to accept A's servicing of the other areas and pay the stated prices. B would then be liable to A for breach of contract.

    3. A contracts to sell and B to buy A's accounting business for a specified sum. A agrees to remain active in the business for two years during which B agrees to pay A an additional specified sum. After transferring the business to B and receiving a down payment, A dies. B offers to transfer the business to A's estate, refuses to pay the balance due, and demands the return of his down payment. Under the rule stated in § 267(1), not remaining active in the business would operate as a failure of performance for the purpose of the rule stated in § 237, and B's remaining duties would be discharged. If, however, the court decides that this rule will not avoid injustice, it may supply a term, if reasonable, under which B is to keep and pay for the business, but both parties' duties with respect to the two-year period are discharged. B would then be liable to A's estate for breach of contract.

    . . .

    6. A, the owner of an opera company that is heavily in debt, transfers half of its stock to B, who promises to manage the company. B is to

have the right to sell the stock only if through his management the debt is paid off. After seven years, during which B is able to pay off only 15 per cent of the debt, the opera house is accidentally destroyed by fire. The insurance proceeds are used to pay off the debt, leaving a balance in the treasury, and the opera house is not rebuilt, preventing the occurrence of the condition of B's right to sell his stock. A seeks an accounting for the stock transferred to B. Under the rule stated in § 271, the non-occurrence of the condition is not excused because its occurrence is a material part of the agreed exchange. If, however, the court decides that this rule will not avoid injustice, it may supply a term, under which B is entitled to a reasonable compensation for his services, giving due regard to the terms of the contract.

Chapter 12

Discharge by Assent or Alteration

Introductory Note This Chapter is concerned mainly with the discharge of duties by assent of the obligee. The word "duty," when used in this Chapter without qualifying words, refers not only to contract duties but to other duties as well, and it includes a duty to pay damages for breach of contract or for a tort. It refers to duties that are undisputed as well as those that are disputed, to duties that are liquidated as well as unliquidated, and to duties that are matured as well as unmatured.

Discharge of a duty extinguishes the obligor's duty and terminates the obligee's correlative right and any claim based on that right. Discharge of a duty to pay damages for breach of contract terminates the correlative right including any right to specific performance or other equitable relief. However, discharge of a duty of performance does not of itself extinguish a duty to pay damages for breach or a duty to make restitution.

Courts have generally required consideration or a substitute for consideration to support a discharge by the obligee's assent, even if the discharge is immediate and involves no promise to discharge. Topic 1 deals with this general requirement and the exceptions to it. Topic 2 states rules for substituted performance, substituted contract, accord and account stated. In all but the last of these the obligee receives a substituted performance or promise in satisfaction of the duty, and this furnishes the consideration for the discharge. Topic 3 states rules for rescission, release and covenant not to sue. Here the consideration for the discharge is something other than a substitute performance or promise. Topic 4 deals with discharge of a duty by the obligee's alteration of a writing.

Other methods of discharge. Other Chapters of this Restatement deal with other methods of discharge of contract duties. These include: discharge by performance in full (§§ 235, 258-60), discharge on grounds of impracticability or frustration (§§ 261, 265), discharge by non-occurrence of a condition or the occurrence of a similar event (§§ 224, 230), discharge by assignment of the correlative right (§ 317), discharge by the union of a right and duty in the same party (Comment *a* to § 9), and discharge by exercise of a power of avoidance (§ 7) on grounds of lack of capacity (§§ 14-16), mistake (§§ 152, 153), misrepresentation (§ 164), a fiduciary relation (§ 173), duress (§ 175) or undue influence (§ 177). Contract provisions giving a power of termination to one or both parties may pose questions of consideration (§ 77) or interpretation (Chapter 9) that are dealt with in connection with those topics.

Other methods of discharge are beyond the scope of this Restatement. A duty may, for example, be discharged by the running of a statute of limitations or by the operation of the bankruptcy laws and the duty of a surety may be discharged under the laws of suretyship. See Restatement of Security ch. 5. (But see Chapter 13 of this Restatement as to discharge of joint and several promisors.) A duty may be discharged by merger or bar resulting from a judgment or an arbitral award. As to judgments, see Restatement, Second, Judgments §§ 18, 19.

§ 273. Requirement of Consideration or a Substitute

> Except as stated in §§ 274-77, an obligee's manifestation of assent to a discharge is not effective unless
> (a) it is made for consideration,
> (b) it is made in circumstances in which a promise would be enforceable without consideration, or
> (c) it has induced such action or forbearance as would make a promise enforceable.

Comment:

a. Rationale. This Section states the traditional requirement of consideration or one of its substitutes in order that the obligee's assent to even a present discharge be effective. The requirement is analogous to that of consideration or some substitute in order that even a present transfer of a right by assignment be irrevocable (§ 332). Subject to some exceptions, a gratuitous discharge is not effective, just as a gratuitous promise is not enforceable and a gratuitous assignment is not irrevocable. The use of words suggesting present transfer, such as those of gift or of assignment, does not affect the result. See Illustration 1. **Illustration:**

> 1. A, whom B owes $ 1,000 for goods delivered, gives B a signed writing that states, "I hereby irrevocably give, transfer, assign and release my right to the $ 1,000 that you owe me." B's debt is not discharged. Compare § 284 with § 332(1)(a).

b. Consideration and its substitutes. For centuries the seal was used to make a discharge of a duty effective, and in a few states the legislation that has generally deprived the seal of its effect makes an exception for executed transactions such as releases. See Reporter's Note to Introductory Note, Topic 3, Chapter 4. In a few other states legislation makes a signed writing a substitute for a seal in this respect. Today, however, the requirement stated in this Section is usually satisfied by consideration. The rules on consideration that apply generally to the enforceability of promises apply here. These include those set out in Topic 2 of Chapter 4 for situations where a promise is enforceable without consideration. A transaction need not follow one of the traditional forms set out in Topics 4 and 5 in order to be effective. Furthermore, a discharge that is originally ineffective may become effective if it has induced such action or forbearance as would make a promise enforceable (§ 90). See Illustration 2. The rule stated in this Section does not preclude the discharge of a duty by means of a gift of tangible property. See Illustration 3.

Illustrations:

> 2. A pays B $ 1,000 in return for B's promise to paint a landscape for A. Before B is to begin, A says, "I don't want the painting, but you can keep the $ 1,000." B relies on A's statement by making conflicting commitments to do other work. B's duty to A is discharged. Compare § 275.

> 3. A contracts to sell to B a particular machine that B has in his possession as bailee in return for B's promise to pay $ 1,000. Before B pays the $ 1,000, A says, "You can keep the machine as a gift." Since A has made an effective gift of the machine to B, B's duty to pay for it is discharged. Compare § 276.

§ 274. Cancellation, Destruction or Surrender of a Writing

An obligee's cancellation, destruction or surrender to the obligor of a writing of a type customarily accepted as a symbol or as evidence of his right discharges without consideration the obligor's duty if it is done with the manifested intention to discharge it.

. . .

§ 275. Assent to Discharge Duty of Return Performance

If a party, before he has fully performed his duty under a contract, manifests to the other party his assent to discharge the other party's duty to render part or all of the agreed exchange, the duty is to that extent discharged without consideration.

§ 276. Assent to Discharge Duty to Transfer Property

A duty of an obligor in possession of identified personal property to transfer an interest in that property is discharged without consideration if the obligee manifests to the obligor his assent to the discharge of that duty.

. . .

§ 277. Renunciation

(1) A written renunciation signed and delivered by the obligee discharges without consideration a duty arising out of a breach of contract.

(2) A renunciation by the obligee on his acceptance from the obligor of some performance under a contract discharges without consideration a duty to pay damages for a breach that gives rise only to a claim for damages for partial breach of contract.

Comment:

a. Scope. Under the rules stated in this Section, a party injured by a breach of contract can renounce his claim for damages for that breach and thereby discharge without consideration the other party's duty. He can do so in whole or in part. The concept of renunciation presupposes that the injured party is aware of his claim at the time he renounces it. Furthermore, because these rules apply only to duties arising under a contract, the obligor is held to a duty of good faith and fair dealing with respect to the obligee (§ 205). Discharge by renunciation of a negotiable instrument is beyond the scope of this Restatement. See Uniform Commercial Code § 3-605.

b. Written renunciation. Under the rule stated in Subsection (1), the obligee can renounce a claim arising out of a breach of contract, including a claim for damages for either partial or total breach (§ 236), and may do so even though the obligor renders no further performance under the contract. Although no consideration is required, the obligee must deliver a signed writing to the obligor. **Illustrations:**

1. A and B make a contract under which A promises to employ B and B promises to work for A for six months beginning on June 1. After B has begun work, A wrongfully discharges B. B writes A, "I am glad to leave you and I give up any right to sue you." A's duty to pay B damages for total breach is discharged. A's duty to pay B wages earned during the time B has worked is not discharged.

. . .

c. Oral renunciation. Under the rule stated in Subsection (2), the obligee can renounce his right to damages for a breach that is sufficient to give rise to a claim for damages for partial breach but not serious enough to give rise to a claim for damages for total breach (§ 236). However, he can do so only on his acceptance from the obligor of some performance under the contract. A renunciation may occur before performance as long as it continues to the time of performance. No consideration is required and the renunciation may be oral. Mere silent acceptance, however, is not a renunciation. A claim for the unpaid balance of a debt is not one for damages for partial breach under the rule stated in this Section, but a claim for damages caused by delay in payment of a debt is such a claim. See Illustration 3 to § 278. See § 246 for the effect of acceptance of performance on the obligee's right to claim damages for total breach. **Illustrations:**

. . .

5. A and B make a contract under which A promises to employ B and B promises to work for A for six months. After B has begun work, he commits a breach of the contract giving A a claim for damages for partial breach. A says, "Never mind, I excuse that failure in view of your generally excellent performance," and B continues to work for A. A's claim for damages for partial breach is discharged. The result would be different if A's renunciation occurred after B had finished working for A.

d. Other situations distinguished. If the injured party's renunciation is supported by consideration or by reliance, it can be sustained without resort to the rule stated in this Section. If, for example, each of the parties believes that he has a claim against the other for damages for total breach, the renunciation by one of his disputed claim for damages will furnish the consideration for the renunciation by the other of his disputed claim. If a party having a claim for damages for partial breach renounces his claim and the other party relies on the renunciation so that it would be unjust not to enforce the renunciation, the reliance will make the renunciation enforceable.

. . .

Introductory Note A duty may be discharged by the obligee's acceptance of either a performance or a contract in substitution for performance of that duty. This may happen in several ways. First, the obligee may accept a substituted performance in present satisfaction of the duty. The rules for discharge by substituted performance are stated in § 278. Second, the obligee may accept a promise of a substituted performance in present satisfaction of the duty. The rules for discharge by substituted contracts are stated in § 279. A substituted contract in which the obligor or obligee is replaced by a third person is known as a novation and is dealt with in § 280. Third, the obligee may bind himself by a contract known as an accord to accept a substituted performance in future satisfaction of the duty. The rules for discharge by accord and satisfaction are stated in § 281. The concept of account stated, which results in an admission but not a discharge, is dealt with in § 282.

Although much of this terminology is peculiar to the field of discharge, the substantive rules are essentially the same as those generally applicable to the formation of contracts. Under the rules stated in §§ 279-81, which speak of a "contract," all of the requirements for enforceability of promises are imported, so that a party may raise such defenses as mistake, misrepresentation, duress and lack of consideration or one of its substitutes. See Comment *b* to § 279, Comment *c* to § 280 and Comment *d* to § 281.

§ 278. Substituted Performance

(1) If an obligee accepts in satisfaction of the obligor's duty a performance offered by the obligor that differs from what is due, the duty is discharged.

(2) If an obligee accepts in satisfaction of the obligor's duty a performance offered by a third person, the duty is discharged, but an obligor who has not previously assented to the performance for his benefit may in a reasonable time after learning of it render the discharge inoperative from the beginning by disclaimer.

Comment:

a. Substituted performance by the obligor. If the obligor offers a performance that differs from what is due in full or partial satisfaction of his duty, the obligee need not accept it. If he chooses to accept it, however, the obligor is discharged in accordance with the terms of the offer. The obligee generally cannot avoid the consequences of such an exercise of dominion by a declaration that he does not assent to the condition attached by the debtor. Uniform Commercial Code § 1-207, providing for acceptance of performance under reservation of rights, need not be read as changing this well-established rule. See Comment *d* to § 281.

Illustration:

    1. A owes B $ 1,000. A offers B a machine in full satisfaction of his debt, and B accepts it. A's debt is discharged. The result is the same if, before accepting the machine, B writes A that he does not accept it in full satisfaction of the debt.

b. Substituted performance by third person. The obligee need not accept a performance that is offered in full or partial satisfaction of the obligor's duty by a third person who does not do so on behalf of the obligor. If he chooses to accept it, however, the obligor is discharged in accordance with the terms of the third person's offer. The performance may be the same as or different from that originally due from the obligor. The transaction is regarded as one for the benefit of the obligor, who, like any intended beneficiary, has the power to disclaim the benefit of the third person's performance and deprive it of its effect as a discharge. See § 306. **Illustration:**

    2. A owes B $ 1,000. C offers B a machine in full satisfaction of A's debt, and B accepts it. A's debt is discharged.

    . . .

§ 279. Substituted Contract

(1) A substituted contract is a contract that is itself accepted by the obligee in satisfaction of the obligor's existing duty.

(2) The substituted contract discharges the original duty and breach of the substituted contract by the obligor does not give the obligee a right to enforce the original duty.

Comment:

a. Nature and effect of a substituted contract. A substituted contract is one that is itself accepted by the obligee in satisfaction of the original duty and thereby discharges it. A common type of substituted contract is one that contains a term that is inconsistent with a term of an earlier contract between the parties. If the parties intend the new contract to replace all of the provisions of the earlier contract, the contract is a substituted contract. If a substituted contract brings in a new party it is called a "novation" (§ 280). **Illustrations:**

1. A is under a duty to deliver a tractor to B on July 1. On June 1, A offers to deliver a bulldozer to B on July 1 if B will accept his promise in satisfaction of A's duty to deliver the tractor, and B accepts. The contract is a substituted contract. A's duty to deliver the tractor is discharged. If A does not deliver the bulldozer, B can enforce the duty to deliver it but not the original duty to deliver the tractor.

2. A and B make a contract under which A promises to build on a designated spot a building, for which B promises to pay $ 100,000. Later, before this contract is performed, A and B make a new contract under which A is to build on the same spot a different building, for which B is to pay $ 200,000. The new contract is a substituted contract and the duties of A and B under the original contract are discharged.

b. Validity of substituted contract. Under the rule stated in § 273, although the discharge that results from a substituted contract is an immediate change in the legal relations between the obligor and the obligee and involves no promise by the obligee, it is not effective unless it is supported by consideration or some substitute for consideration. See Comment *c* to §

278. Furthermore, to the extent that the substituted contract is vulnerable on such grounds as mistake, misrepresentation, duress or unconscionability, recourse may be had on the original duty. Thus, if the substituted contract is voidable, it discharges the original duty until avoidance, but on avoidance of the substituted contract the original duty is again enforceable. If the substituted contract is unenforceable because of the Statute of Frauds, it does not bar enforcement of the original duty. Cf. § 149. **Illustrations:**

3. A owes B a liquidated and undisputed matured debt of $ 1,000. A offers to pay B $ 500 in 30 days if B will accept his promise in full satisfaction of the debt, and B accepts. A's debt is not discharged. See Illustration 3 to § 278.

. . .

c. Accord distinguished. Because the original duty is discharged regardless of whether the substituted contract is performed, a substituted contract differs from an accord, under which the original duty is discharged only if the accord is performed. See § 281. Whether a contract is a substituted contract or an accord is a question of interpretation, subject to the general rules stated in Chapter 9. In resolving doubts in this regard, a court is less likely to conclude that an obligee was willing to accept a mere promise in satisfaction of an original duty that was clear than in satisfaction of one that was doubtful. It will therefore be less likely to find a substituted contract and more likely to find an accord if the original duty was one to pay money, if it was undisputed, if it was liquidated and if it was matured. Compare Illustration 1 with Illustration 1 to § 281.

§ 280. Novation

A novation is a substituted contract that includes as a party one who was neither the obligor nor the obligee of the original duty.

Comment:

a. Definition of novation. The word "novation" is used in this Restatement to refer to a type of substituted contract that has the effect of adding a party, either as obligor or obligee, who was not a party to the original duty. See Comment *a* to § 279. A novation may involve more than three parties. The performance to be rendered under the new duty may be the same as or different from that to be rendered under the original duty. It is also possible to have an accord that adds a new party, but that is less often the case and such an accord is not termed a novation. See Illustration 1.

b. *Effect of novation.* A novation discharges the original duty, just as any other substituted contract does, so that breach of the new duty gives no right of action on the old duty. Most novations simply substitute a new obligor for an old obligor or, less commonly, a new obligee for an old obligee. Sometimes these are termed simple novations, to distinguish them from more complex transactions that are termed compound novations.

c. *Consideration.* A novation is subject to the same requirements as any other contract, including that of consideration. However, since consideration need not be given to the promisor and need not be given by the promisee (§ 71 (4)), consideration to support the discharge of the original duty can usually be found in the promise to undertake a new duty. It is not necessary for this purpose that all of the parties to the novation manifest their assent simultaneously nor that they all be in the same place, but their manifestations of assent must have reference to one another (§ 23). Although all parties usually assent to a novation, a novation is possible without the assent of the obligor of the original duty or of the obligee of the new duty if that party is an intended beneficiary and does not disclaim (§ 306). See Illustrations 2 and 5. Assent of the obligee of the original duty and of the obligor of the new duty is always necessary.

d. *Substitution of obligor.* A simple novation involving a substitution of obligors results when an obligee promises the obligor that he will discharge the obligor's duty in consideration for a third person's promise to pay the obligee. See Illustration 1. As to the analogous situation of an obligee who takes in payment from the obligor a negotiable instrument on which a third person is liable, see Uniform Commercial Code § 3-802. A substitution of obligors may also result when an obligee promises a third person that he will discharge the obligor's duty in consideration for the third person's promise to render either the performance that was due from the obligor or

some other performance. Even a promise to render part performance is consideration in that situation. See Comment *c* to § 278. If the obligor is an intended beneficiary (§ 302), there is a novation. The assent of the obligor is not required. However, his rights are governed by the rules stated in Chapter 14, Contract Beneficiaries, and if he has not assented he can by disclaimer render the transaction inoperative from the beginning (§ 306). See Illustration 2. Such a novation also results when a third person promises an obligor to assume, immediately and in substitution for the obligor's duty, a duty to the obligee to render the performance that was due from the obligor or some other performance, and the obligee agrees with the obligor or with the third person to that substitution. The third person then comes under a new duty to the obligee, who is an intended beneficiary of his promise to assume (§ 302), and this is consideration for the obligee's agreement to discharge the original obligor. The obligee, having already assented to the discharge of the duty in this way, has no power to disclaim it. See Illustration 3. However, a mere promise by a third party to assume the obligor's duty, not offered in substitution for that duty, does not result in a novation, and the new duty that the third party may owe to the obligee as an intended beneficiary is in addition to and not in substitution for the obligor's original duty. For a novation to take place, the obligee must assent to the discharge of the obligor's duty in consideration for the promise of the third party to undertake that duty. As to the effect of an obligee's acceptance of performance from an assignee after a repudiation by the obligor, see § 329(2). **Illustrations:**

1. A owes B $ 1,000. B promises A that he will discharge the debt immediately if C will promise B to pay B $ 1,000. C so promises. There is a novation under which B's and C's promises are consideration for each other and A is discharged.

2. A owes B $ 1,000. B promises C that he will discharge the debt immediately if C will promise him to pay him $ 1,000. Intending to benefit A, C so promises. There is a novation under which B's and C's promises are consideration for each other, and A's duty to pay B is discharged. A is an intended beneficiary of B's promise (§ 302) and can by disclaimer render the transaction, including the discharge, inoperative from the beginning (§ 306). The result is the same if B's promise is made in return for C's promise to

pay $ 500. See Illustration 4 to § 278.

3. A owes B a duty to service B's machine for a year. A sells part of his business to C, who promises A that he will assume A's duty to B if B promises to accept it immediately and in substitution for A's duty. B so promises A. There is a novation under which B's and C's promises are consideration for each other, and A's duty to service B's machine is discharged. B is an intended beneficiary of C's promise (§ 302), but cannot disclaim because he has assented. The result is the same if B's promise is made to C.

e. Substitution of obligee. A simple novation involving a substitution of obligees results when an obligee promises his obligor to discharge the obligor's duty in consideration for the obligor's promise to a third person to render either the performance that was due from the obligor or some other performance. See Illustration 4. A substitution of obligees may also result when the obligor's promise is one made directly to the obligee but is one to render the performance to a third person as beneficiary. If the third person is an intended beneficiary (§ 302), there is a novation. Illustration 5. The assent of the third person is not required. However, his rights are subject to the rules stated in Chapter 14, Contract Beneficiaries, and if he has not assented he can by disclaimer render the transaction, including the discharge, inoperative from the beginning. Obligees may also be substituted by assignment of a right, which differs from novation in that assignment requires neither the knowledge nor the assent of the obligor and cannot change the performance to be rendered by him. For other differences, see Chapter 15, Assignment and Delegation. **Illustrations:**

4. A owes B $ 1,000. B promises A that he will discharge the debt immediately if A will promise C to perform stated services to C. A so promises C. There is a novation under which A's and B's promises are consideration for each other and A's duty to pay B is discharged. If B's promise were to discharge A when A performed the services, there would be an accord rather than a novation.

5. A owes B $ 1,000. Intending to benefit C, B promises A that he will discharge the debt immediately if A will promise him to perform stated services to C. A so promises B. There is a novation under which A's and B's promises are consideration for each other and A's duty to pay B is discharged. C is an intended beneficiary of A's promise (§ 302) and can by disclaimer render the transaction, including the discharge, inoperative from the beginning.

f. Compound novations. The novations already described involve a simple substitution of one obligor or obligee for another. More complex transactions, sometimes called compound novations, are possible. If, for example, there are two duties and the obligee of the first is the obligor of the second, the three parties may agree that one party shall drop out altogether. See Illustration 6. Furthermore, if each of two parties has a right against the other, they may agree with a third party that the third party shall immediately acquire a right against and be subject to a duty to one of them in substitution for the original right of and duty due the other. The new right and duty may be for performances that are the same as or different from the original ones. See Illustration 7. **Illustrations:**

6. A owes B $ 1,000 and B owes C $ 1,000. A promises B and C that he will assume B's debt to C if B promises to discharge A's debt to B and if C promises to discharge B's debt to C and accept A as his debtor. B and C so promise. There is a novation under which A's promise and B's and C's promises are consideration for each other, and A's debt to B and B's debt to C are discharged.

7. A and B make a contract under which A promises to deliver a tractor to B and B promises to pay A $ 1,000. A promises to deliver a bulldozer to C and to discharge B's duty if B promises to discharge A's duty and C promises to pay A $ 2,000. B and C so promise. There is a novation and A's duty to deliver a tractor to B and B's duty to pay $ 1,000 are discharged.

§ 281. Accord and Satisfaction

(1) An accord is a contract under which an obligee promises to accept a stated performance in satisfaction of the obligor's existing duty. Performance of the accord discharges the original duty.

(2) Until performance of the accord, the original duty is suspended unless there is such a breach of the accord by the obligor as discharges the new duty of the obligee to accept the performance in satisfaction. If there is such a breach, the obligee may enforce either the original duty or any duty under the accord.

(3) Breach of the accord by the obligee does not discharge the original duty, but the obligor may maintain a suit for specific performance of the accord, in addition to any claim for damages for partial breach.

Comment:

a. Nature of an accord. An accord is a contract under which an obligee promises to accept a substituted performance in future satisfaction of the obligor's duty. Because an accord is a contract, it differs from a mere revocable offer by the obligee to accept a substituted performance in satisfaction of the duty (§ 278). The typical accord involves an exchange of promises (Illustration 1), although an accord may also take the form of an option contract (Illustration 2). It is the essence of an accord that the original duty is not satisfied until the accord is performed, a result that is sometimes suggested by use of the term "executory accord." See Comment *e.*

b. Suspensory effect. The accord entitles the obligor to a chance to render the substituted performance in satisfaction of the original duty. Under the rule stated in Subsection (2), the obligee's right to enforce that duty is suspended subject to the terms of the accord until the obligor has had that chance. If the obligor is under a duty to perform the accord, his performance discharges both his original duty and his duty under the accord (§ 235). If, however, there is such a breach of the accord by the obligor as discharges the obligee's duty under the accord to accept the stated performance in satisfaction, he is no longer bound by the accord. He may then choose between enforcement of the original duty and any duty under the accord. Whether a breach by the obligor discharges the obligee's duty under the accord is governed by the rules stated in Chapter 10, Performance and Non-Performance. **Illustrations:**

1. A owes B $ 10,000. They make a contract under which A promises to deliver to B a specific machine within 30 days and B promises to accept it in satisfaction of the debt. The con-tract is an accord. A's debt is suspended and is discharged if A delivers the machine within 30 days.

2. A owes B $ 10,000. In consideration of $ 10 paid by A, not as part of the debt, B prom-ises to accept in satisfaction of the debt a spe-cific machine from A within 30 days. The con-tract is an accord. A's debt is suspended for 30 days and is discharged if A delivers the machine within 30 days, although A is under no duty to deliver the machine.

3. A, B and C, who are creditors of D, enter into a voluntary composition with D under which D promises to pay and A, B and C promise to accept 50% of their debts in full satisfaction. The composition is an accord. D's debts are sus-pended and are discharged if D pays the 50%.

. . .

c. Effect of obligee's breach. If a breach of the accord by the obligee prevents the obligor from performing the accord, the original duty is not discharged, but the obligor has a claim for damages for total breach of the accord. However, the obligor's damages cannot be measured simply by his original duty, but must take account of what he has saved by not performing. To avoid imposing on the innocent obligor the burden of proving these damages, specific performance of the accord will be granted unless for some reason that remedy is inappropriate. In addition, the obligor may have a claim for damages for partial breach. **Illustration:**

5. The facts being otherwise as stated in Illustration 1, A tenders the machine within 30 days, but B refuses to receive it. If B then sues on the original $ 10,000 debt, A can obtain a decree of specific performance providing for the concurrent delivery of the machine and the dis-charge of the debt.

d. Validity of accord. The enforceability of an accord is governed by the rules applicable to the enforceability of contracts in general. The obligee's promise to accept the substituted performance in satisfaction of the original duty may be supported by consideration because that performance differs significantly from that required by the original duty (§ 73) or because the original duty is in fact doubtful or is believed by the obligor to be so (§ 74). It may also be supported by the obligor's reliance even in the absence of consideration (§ 90). A recurring situation involves the creditor who indorses and cashes a check sent by the debtor and marked "payment in full." The debtor then argues that the creditor, by exercising dominion over the check, has made an accord under which he has promised to accept payment of the check in satisfaction of the debt. Assuming that the transaction is not subject to objections such as those based on the absence of consideration (§§ 73, 74), on lack of good faith and fair dealing (§ 205) and on unconscionability (§ 208), such a notation by the debtor, if prominent enough to meet the requirements of § 19(2), may form the basis of an enforceable accord pursuant to the general rule stated in § 69(2). The creditor cannot generally avoid the consequences of his exercise of dominion by a declaration that he does not assent to the condition attached by the debtor. Uniform Commercial Code § 1-207, providing for acceptance of performance under reservation of rights, need not be read as changing this well-established rule. See Comment *a* to § 278. **Illustration:**

6. A contracts with B to have repairs made on A's house, no price being fixed. B sends A a bill for $ 1,000. A honestly disputes this amount and sends a letter explaining that he thinks the amount excessive and is enclosing a check for $ 800 as payment in full. B, after reading the letter, indorses the check and deposits it in his bank for collection. B is bound by an accord under which he promises to accept payment of the check as satisfaction of A's debt for repairs. The result is the same if, before indorsing the check, B adds the words "Accepted under protest as part payment." The result would be different, however, if B's claim were liquidated, undisputed and matured. See § 74.

e. Substituted contract distinguished. Because the obligor's original duty is not satisfied until the accord is performed, an accord differs from a substituted contract, under which a promise of substituted performance is accepted in satisfaction of the original duty. See § 279. Whether a contract is an accord or a substituted contract is a question of interpretation, subject to the general rules stated in Chapter 9. In resolving doubts in this regard, a court is less likely to conclude that an obligee was willing to accept a mere promise in satisfaction of an original duty that was clear than in satisfaction of one that was doubtful. It is therefore less likely to find a substituted contract and more likely to find an accord if the original duty was one to pay money, if it was undisputed, if it was liquidated and if it was matured. Compare Illustration 1 with Illustration 1 to § 279.

§ 282. Account Stated

(1) An account stated is a manifestation of assent by debtor and creditor to a stated sum as an accurate computation of an amount due the creditor. A party's retention without objection for an unreasonably long time of a statement of account rendered by the other party is a manifestation of assent.

(2) The account stated does not itself discharge any duty but is an admission by each party of the facts asserted and a promise by the debtor to pay according to its terms.

Comment:

a. Computation not compromise or liquidation. If a debtor and a creditor make an agreement in the nature of a compromise or liquidation of a disputed or unliquidated debt, the agreement may be either a substituted contract or an accord resulting in discharge under the rules stated in §§ 279 and 280. If, however, they make an agreement in the nature of a computation rather than of compromise of the

debt, the agreement is called an "account stated." An account stated must be founded on previous transactions that have given rise to the relation of debtor and creditor and is usually based on a number of items. If each party is indebted to the other an account stated may be founded on the difference between their indebtedness.

b. Manifestation of assent. Usually it is the creditor who submits the statement, but it may be the debtor who does so. In either case, the recipient's assent may be inferred from his conduct. Under the rule stated in Subsection (1), his retention of the statement for an unreasonably long time is a manifestation of his assent. How long a time is unreasonable is a question of fact to be answered in the light of all the circumstances. The parties, subject to rules such as that on unconscionability (§ 208), may fix by agreement a time after which the recipient will be considered to have assented to a statement of account. However, the party sending the statement cannot impose such a time limit on the recipient merely by a clause on the statement. For federal legislation on credit billing, see 15 U.S.C. § 1666 (1975).

c. Effect of account stated. An account stated does not itself result in discharge, but operates as an admission of its contents for evidentiary purposes. It also operates as a promise to pay. It may therefore become binding as the result of reliance under the rule stated in § 90. It may also be effective as a promise to pay an antecedent indebtedness under the rule stated in § 82, although statutes in many states require that it be in writing and signed if it is to have this effect. See Comment *a* to § 82. If it is in writing it may also satisfy the Statute of Frauds. In the absence of a requirement of a writing, however, an account stated may be oral. The effect of an account stated as a promise is subject to the rules on mistake (Chapter 6). **Illustrations:**

1. A regularly sells goods to B. From time to time B returns some of the goods for credit and makes payments for the rest. At the end of each month, A sends B itemized statements of B's outstanding balance. One of the statements incorrectly gives an outstanding balance of $ 5,500 because of A's oversight in failing to debit B with a $ 1,000 delivery and to credit B with a $ 500 payment both made during the preceding month. Before either mistake is discovered, B writes A that the statement is "correct." There is an account stated, but it does not prevent A from proving the $ 1,000 delivery or B from proving the $ 500 payment. B owes A $ 6,000.

2. A regularly sells goods to B. From time to time B returns some of the goods for credit and makes payments for the rest. At the end of each month, A sends B itemized statements of B's outstanding balance. One of the statements incorrectly gives an outstanding balance of $ 5,500 because of A's failure to credit B with a $ 1,000 payment that was stolen by one of A's employees. B writes A that the statement is "correct" without verifying it, and the resulting delay in discovering the mistake prevents A from obtaining restitution from the employee. B is precluded from showing the mistake. B owes A $ 5,500.

. . .

Introductory Note This Topic deals with three important types of agreements by which duties are discharged. They differ from those in Topic 2 in that they do not involve the obligee's acceptance of either a performance or a contract in substitution for the performance of the duty. They are, however, contractual in nature and must be supported by consideration or one of its substitutes. Agreements of rescission are dealt with in § 283, releases in § 284 and contracts not to sue in § 285.

§ 283. Agreement of Rescission

(1) An agreement of rescission is an agreement under which each party agrees to discharge all of the other party's remaining duties of performance under an existing contract.

(2) An agreement of rescission discharges all remaining duties of performance of both parties. It is a question of interpretation whether the parties also agree to make restitution with respect to performance that has been rendered.

Comment:

a. Nature of agreement of rescission. Sometimes the parties to a contract that is at least partly executory on each side make an agreement under which each party agrees to discharge all of the other party's duties of performance. Such an agreement is called an "agreement of rescission" in this Restatement. Consideration is provided by each party's discharge of the duties of the other. This is so even though one or both parties have partly performed their duties or one or both have a claim for damages for partial breach. The surrender of a doubtful claim may be enough under the rule stated in § 74. The agreement need not be expressed in words. Other conduct may show an intent by both parties to abandon their contract. If one party, even wrongfully, expresses a wish or an intention to cease performance and the other party fails to object, circumstances may justify the inference that there has been an agreement of rescission. Sometimes mere inaction on both sides, such as the failure to take any steps looking toward performance or enforcement, may indicate an intent to abandon the contract. Mere failure to object to a repudiation, however, is not a manifestation of assent to an agreement of rescission. See § 257. The term "agreement of rescission" is used in this Restatement to avoid confusion with the word "rescission," which courts sometimes use to refer to the exercise by one party of a power of avoidance (§ 7). An agreement of "partial rescission" that would discharge less than all the parties' remaining duties of performance is treated as a modification. See Comment *b*. An agreement of rescission differs from a "termination," which "occurs when either party pursuant to a power created by agreement or law puts an end to the contract otherwise than for its breach" and from a "cancellation," which "occurs when either party puts an end to the contract for breach by the other." Uniform Commercial Code § 2-106.

Illustrations:

    1. A and B make a contract under which A promises to paint B's house and B promises to pay A $ 1,000. A finds, after beginning the work, that he will lose more money by finishing than by giving up at once and makes B an offer to rescind the contract. B accepts. There is an agreement of rescission and the duties of both A and B are discharged.

. . .

    b. The Statute of Frauds and oral agreement of rescission. Under the rule stated in § 148, the Statute of Frauds does not affect the enforceability of an oral agreement of rescission unless rescission of a transfer of property is involved. An attempt to make an agreement of "partial rescission" that would discharge less than all of their remaining duties under the existing contract is considered a modification, subject to the rule stated in § 149, and not an agreement of rescission. Even a provision of the earlier contract to the effect that it can be rescinded only in writing does not impair the effectiveness of an oral agreement of rescission. In the absence of statute, such a self-imposed limitation does not limit the power of the parties subsequently to contract. A different rule is laid down in Uniform Commercial Code § 2-209(2) for contracts for the sale of goods.

    c. Whether promise of restitution is included. If the original contract has been partly performed on one or both sides at the time of the agreement of rescission, a question arises as to whether a party is entitled to restitution for such performance as he has rendered. There is no rule of law establishing a presumption to answer this question. It is a question of interpretation of the agreement of rescission that is to be determined on the facts of each case. **Illustration:**

    3. A and B make a contract under which A promises to sell B land for $ 100,000, payable in five installments of $ 20,000 each. B pays the first installment and takes possession under the contract. A and B then make an agreement of rescission. Whether A has a duty to return the $ 20,000 payment, either in full or less the fair rental value of the land for the time that B was in possession, is a question of interpretation of the agreement of rescission.

§ 284. Release

    (1) A release is a writing providing that a duty owed to the maker of the release is discharged immediately or on the occurrence of a condition.

    (2) The release takes effect on delivery as stated in §§ 101-03 and, subject to the occurrence of any condition, discharges the duty.

Comment:

    a. Nature of release. Although no particular form is required for an agreement to discharge a duty, the term "release" has traditionally been reserved for a formal written statement by an obligee that the obligor's duty is discharged. That usage is preserved in this Section. No special words are required and the writing may state, for example, that it releases the obligor, that it releases the obligor's duties or that it releases the obligee's rights. It must, however, take effect immediately or on the occurrence of a condition. A promise to discharge in the future an existing duty merely creates a new duty that can itself be discharged by the parties. Such a promise is not a release. The duty that is released need not be matured. A purported release of a duty that does not yet exist, however, is not a release but a promise to discharge a duty in the future. See Illustration 3. A purported release of a duty that is revived on the occurrence of a condition is not a release but a contract not to sue.

b. Effectiveness of release. A release was traditionally made under seal and this may still be done in jurisdictions where the seal has not been deprived of its effect in this respect. A release may also be supported by consideration or the obligor's reliance. Furthermore, statutes in some states give an unsealed release the same effect that a sealed release had at common law. As a formal instrument, a release is subject to the same requirements of delivery as is a contract under seal. Delivery may be to the obligor conditionally or unconditionally or in escrow. See §§ 101-03. A release is usually authenticated by the obligee's signature. **Illustrations:**

. . .

3. A, who is engaged in business transactions with B, receives from B a writing supported by consideration stating that B releases A from all debts that A owes or may in the future owe to B. One month later B sells goods to A, for which A promises to pay $ 10,000. With respect to debts not yet in existence, the writing is not a release but a contract to discharge A. The subsequent inconsistent contract operates as a modification of this earlier contract and A is under a duty to pay B $ 10,000.

c. Interpretation. The rules of interpretation that apply to contracts generally apply also to writings that purport to be releases. The principal purpose of the obligee is given great weight if it can be ascertained (§ 202(1)).If a literal interpretation of a writing that purports to be a release would frustrate that purpose, the writing may be interpreted as a contract not to sue. This is particularly likely in the case of a purported release of one joint debtor that states that all rights against another joint debtor are reserved. If the effect of a literal interpretation of the writing as a release would be to release the other joint debtor (§ 294) and frustrate the obligee's purpose as indicated by his attempted reservation of rights, the writing will be interpreted as a contract not to sue. See also Restatement of Security § 122. **Illustration:**

4. A and B are bound jointly to pay C $ 1,000. C delivers to A a writing supported by consideration stating that C releases A from the debt but that C reserves his rights against B. If a release of A would discharge B under the rules stated in § 294, the writing will be interpreted as a contract not to sue and not as a release.

§ 285. Contract Not to Sue

(1) A contract not to sue is a contract under which the obligee of a duty promises never to sue the obligor or a third person to enforce the duty or not to do so for a limited time.

(2) Except as stated in Subsection (3), a contract never to sue discharges the duty and a contract not to sue for a limited time bars an action to enforce the duty during that time.

(3) A contract not to sue one co-obligor bars levy of execution on the property of the promisee during the agreed time but does not bar an action or the recovery of judgment against any co-obligor.

Comment:

a. Nature of contract not to sue. Sometimes an obligee does not manifest an intention to discharge the obligor but merely makes a contract by which he promises not to sue him. See § 295. Such a contract is often called "a covenant not to sue," a term that is not used in this Restatement in order to avoid any suggestion that it must be under seal. Although a contract never to sue an obligor does not in terms discharge the obligor's duty immediately, it is given this effect in order to avoid circuity of action. A contract not to sue for a limited time bars an action to enforce the duty during that time. As to a contract not to sue one co-obligor, see Comment *b.* **Illustration:**

1. A owes B $ 1,000 payable immediately. B assigns his right to C, receiving in return C's

promise not to sue A for one year. C cannot maintain an action against A before the end of the year.

b. Co-obligors. If an obligee makes a contract not to sue one co-obligor and then joins that co-obligor in an action merely for the purpose of obtaining judgment against the other co-obligors, this is not regarded as a breach of the contract not to sue the one co-obligor if none of his assets are seized in satisfaction of the judgment. See Comment *b* to § 295. Therefore, the effect of the contract is merely to bar levy of execution on his property during the agreed time.

Introductory Note: The rules on alteration that developed in order to discourage tampering with writings embodying formal contracts were extended to cover the alteration of writings that are completely or partially integrated agreements under the parol evidence rule (§§ 209, 210) and of memoranda that are necessary under the Statute of Frauds (§ 131). The effect of an alteration has been limited, however, so that it results in discharge only if the alteration is both fraudulent and material. In view of the forfeiture that results upon discharge of an obligor if the obligee has already performed, the effect of an alteration may undergo further limitations in the future. See Uniform Commercial Code §§ 7-208, 7-306, under which even a fraudulent and material alteration of a document of title does not discharge the issuer's duty to deliver the goods according to the original terms of the document. The rules stated here, however, reflect the present state of the law. The effect of an alteration is dealt with in § 286 and the effect of assent to or forgiveness of an alteration is dealt with in § 287.

§ 286. Alteration of Writing

(1) If one to whom a duty is owed under a contract alters a writing that is an integrated agreement or that satisfies the Statute of Frauds with respect to that contract, the duty is discharged if the alteration is fraudulent and material.

(2) An alteration is material if it would, if effective, vary any party's legal relations with the maker of the alteration or adversely affect that party's legal relations with a third person. The unauthorized insertion in a blank space in a writing is an alteration.

Comment:

a. Effect of alteration. The rule on alteration stated in this Section applies to writings that are completely or partially integrated agreements under the parol evidence rule (§§ 209, 210) and to memoranda that are necessary to satisfy the Statute of Frauds (§ 131). If a party to whom a duty is owed under a contract represented by such a writing fraudulently and materially alters the writing, that duty is discharged. An alteration that is not both fraudulent and material does not have this effect and the duty remains enforceable according to its original terms. Once a duty has been discharged by alteration, an attempt by the maker of the alteration to revive the duty by restoring the writing is ineffective unless the party whose duty is discharged forgives the alteration (§ 287(2)). An alteration by one who is not a party to the contract does not result in a discharge, however, even if it is fraudulent and material. An alteration by a party never discharges his own duty and therefore never terminates any right of the other party, unless the other manifests his assent under the rule stated in § 287(1). This Restatement does not apply to the alteration of commercial paper or documents of title, which are the subjects of Uniform Commercial Code §§ 3-407, 7-208, 7-306.

b. What is a material alteration. An alteration may be by addition, deletion or substitution. An unauthorized insertion in a space that has been left blank in a writing is an alteration, but to come within the rule stated in Subsection (1) the writing must, in spite of the blank space, be an integrated agreement or satisfy the Statute of Frauds. An alteration is not material, however, unless it purports to change the legal relationships under the contract. If two or more persons are under duties to perform separate acts, an alteration that affects the duty of only one of them does not discharge the duty of another. An alteration may be material even though it purports to be to the disadvantage of the person making it, although such an alteration will rarely be fraudulent as required by the rule stated in Subsection (1). A mere change in the spelling of a party's name or the addition of the date of the writing is not material if it does not purport to have legal effect. **Illustrations:**

    1. A and B make an integrated agreement for the sale of goods to be delivered by A for which B is to pay the price of $ 1,100 on July 1. A fraudulently erases "July 1" and substitutes "June 1." The alteration is both fraudulent and material, and B's duty is discharged.

. . .

    3. The facts being otherwise as stated in Illustration 1, the agreement, although partially integrated, contains a blank for the amount of interest if the price is not paid when due, and A, instead of altering the date, fraudulently and without authority from B inserts "8%" although they had agreed on 6%. The insertion without authority is an alteration that is both fraudulent and material, and B's duty is discharged.

. . .

§ 287. Assent to or Forgiveness of Alteration

(1) If a party, knowing of an alteration that discharges his duty, manifests assent to the altered terms, his manifestation is equivalent to an acceptance of an offer to substitute those terms.

(2) If a party, knowing of an alteration that discharges his duty, asserts a right under the original contract or otherwise manifests a willingness to remain subject to the original contract or to forgive the alteration, the original contract is revived.

Comment:

   a. Assent to alteration. An alteration may be regarded as manifesting a desire on the part of its maker to have a contract in the altered form, and assent by the other party will be treated as if it were acceptance of an offer to substitute the altered terms. The same requirements must be met as in the case of any substituted contract, including those imposed by the doctrine of consideration and by the Statute of Frauds. If two or more persons are under duties to perform the same act and only one of them assents to an alteration, the fact that the others are discharged does not affect the liability of the one who assents, and his assent has the same effect as to him as it would have had if no duties of the others had been discharged.

. . .

   b. Forgiveness of alteration. The innocent party loses none of his rights as the result of an alteration made without his consent and can always assert them under the original contract. If he does assert them, however, he is regarded as having forgiven the alteration and the original contract is revived. Any other manifestation of a willingness to remain subject to the duties under the original contract or to forgive the alteration has the same effect. Forgiveness need not be supported by consideration. If two or more persons are under duties to perform the same act, the effect of forgiveness by one of them is the same as the effect of assent as discussed in Comment *a.*

. . .

Chapter 13

Joint and Several Promisors and Promisees

Introductory Note This Chapter deals with the rights and duties created by multiple promises of the same performance, and with the traditional distinctions between "joint," "several," and "joint and several" rights and duties so created. Multiple promises of the same performance are fully recognized by the substantive law. See §§ 10. They are very common and are of great practical importance. But their remedial and procedural consequences are affected by remnants of outworn conceptions only partially corrected by statutory reforms or by judicial decisions made with or without statutory aid.

Promises of the same performance. Whether or not multiple promises have reference to the same performance is entirely a question of interpretation. For example, A and B may each promise to pay C $ 500, making a total of $ 1,000; or A and B together may promise to pay C a total of $ 1,000, each to be fully responsible for the entire payment. Likewise, A may promise C that he will pay C $ 500 and promise D that he will pay D $ 500; or he may promise C and D together that he will pay them $ 1,000. Interpretation determines from whom and to whom the promises run and in what amounts. The rights and duties between the promisors A and B and between the promisees C and D in such cases present distinct questions dealt with only incidentally in this Chapter.

"Joint and several." There is a basic ambiguity in the use of the words "joint" and "several." In one usage, promissory duties are said to be "joint" if two or more promisors promise the same performance, "several" if they promise separate performances, even though similar. In the same way, promises are sometimes said to create "joint" rights if the same performance is promised to more than one promisee, "several" rights if each promisee is promised a different performance. In the second usage, both "joint" and "several" refer to rights and duties created by promises of the same performance. The second usage is more common in judicial and statutory language, and is the usage followed here.

Joinder of parties. Before the procedural reforms of the nineteenth century, common-law pleading was designed to present a single issue between two parties or groups of parties. Parties could be joined in an action only if they had the same interest, and all parties having a "joint" interest had to be joined. From early times the rule requiring joinder of all living joint promisors could be avoided by making the promise "joint and several" in form; and the impact of this and some related rules was mitigated by judicial decision as stated in this Chapter. But the law governing "joint" contractual duties remained unsatisfactory in almost every respect, and even the law of "joint and several" duties was defective.

Statutory Note: Modern procedural reforms have made provision for permissive joinder of parties without regard to the question whether their interests are "joint," and compulsory joinder based solely on "joint" interest has become an anachronism. The common-law rules relating to joint promisees, as supplemented by rules developed in courts of equity, seem not to have caused undue difficulty; but statutes affect the common-law rules on joint promisors in almost every state.

The principal common-law rules which have been found unsatisfactory are (1) compulsory joinder of joint promisors (see § 290), (2) the requirement of judgment for or against all joint promisors (see § 291), (3) the discharge of joint promisors by a judgment against co-promisors (see § 292), (4) the rule of survivorship, barring actions against estates of deceased joint promisors while co-promisors survive (see § 296), and (5) the rule that discharge of some joint promisors by release, rescission or accord and satisfaction discharges all (see § 294).

The first four of these rules could be and were changed in many states by statutes converting "joint" obligations into "joint and several" obligations. But the fifth was applied in many States to the several liability of joint and several promisors, contrary to § 294; in those states it could only be changed by overruling precedents or by an additional statutory provision. Largely for this reason the Model Joint Obligations Act deals specifically with discharge by judgment and with survivorship and release. The Model Act does not deal with joinder or with the requirement of a joint judgment; its sponsors thought those difficulties had largely been met without statute, but it has been supplemented on those points in the six states which have enacted it.

This Chapter states a number of the prestatutory rules which have been widely repudiated by statute. Such statement reflects the present state of the authorities; it does not reflect disapproval of judicial decisions which have adopted more modern rules without statutory compulsion.

Complete reform. All five of the common-law rules referred to above seem to have been substantially abolished in the jurisdictions listed below. Hawaii, Maine, Nevada, New York, Utah and Wisconsin have enacted the Model Joint Obligations Act, supplemented by separate statutes authorizing judgments against less than all joint promisors. Connecticut, Michigan, Mississippi, New Jersey, Ohio, South Carolina, Texas and Virginia seem to have effected substantially similar reforms by separate statutes. In Colorado, the District of Columbia, Kansas, Minnesota, Missouri and Montana, statutes making "joint" obligations "joint and several" are supplemented by statutes on releases. California, North Dakota and South Dakota are similar, but contracts of co-obligors are merely presumed "joint and several" if all promisors receive a benefit from the consideration or the promise is in the singular.

. . .

Reform except for releases. In the following states, all of the common-law rules referred to above seem to have been substantially abolished except the rule relating to releases. In Alabama, Arizona, Arkansas, Illinois, New Mexico and Tennessee statutes make "joint" obligations "joint and several." In Louisiana the terminology is different, but the same result seems to follow. In Delaware obligations of several persons are "joint and several, unless otherwise expressed"; in Oklahoma there is a presumption of "joint and several" obligation if all promisors receive a benefit from the consideration or the promise is in the singular. Indiana, Iowa, Kentucky, Nebraska, Washington, West Virginia and Wyoming seem to have effected substantially similar reforms by separate statutes.

. . .

Other partial reforms. In the following states important consequences still flow from common-law rules on joint promisors. The consequences retained in some of these states include compulsory joinder, discharge by judgment against co-obligors, survivorship and the common-law rule on releases. Alaska, Florida, Georgia, Idaho, Maryland, Massachusetts, New Hampshire, North Carolina, Oregon*, Rhode Island, Vermont.

Particular types of contracts. When two or more promisors promise the same performance, some or all of them are inevitably sureties for all or part of the resulting obligation, and a number of the statutes referred to above include provisions applicable to guarantors or other sureties. The rules of suretyship are stated in the Restatement of Security and are beyond the scope of this Chapter. See §§ 293-95. The rules stated in this Chapter are also subject to statutes relating to partnership obligations and to negotiable instruments. Section 15 of the Uniform Partnership Act provides that partners are liable jointly and severally for tort or breach of trust, but jointly on partnership contracts. On the other hand, Section 3-118(e) of the Uniform Commercial Code provides that "unless the instrument otherwise specifies" two or more persons who sign commercial paper as maker, acceptor or drawer or indorser and as part of the same transaction are jointly and severally liable.

§ 288. Promises of the Same Performance

(1) Where two or more parties to a contract make a promise or promises to the same promisee, the manifested intention of the parties determines whether they promise that the same performance or separate performances shall be given.

(2) Unless a contrary intention is manifested, a promise by two or more promisors is a promise that the same performance shall be given.

Comment:

a. "Same performance." Where there are more promisors than one in a contract, some or all of them may promise the same performance. See § 10. Thus A and B may both promise that $ 100 lent by C will be repaid, or that certain goods will be delivered to C, or that certain services will be rendered to C. On the other hand, each promisor may promise a separate performance, which may be similar to that promised by another. Thus where C lends $ 100 to A and B, A may promise to repay $ 50 and B may promise to repay $ 50. As used in §§ 288-96, "same performance" refers to the first of these two types of situations but not to the second.

. . .

d. "Several" promises. The word "several" is used in two different senses with reference to promises and duties. First, if one party promises one performance, and another promises a different performance, each may be bound independently of the other and the promisee may be entitled to both performances. The promises and the duties of the promisors may then be described as "several," but this Chapter does not hereafter deal with promises which are "several" in this sense. Second, in traditional usage promises of the same performance by different promisors are said to create "several" duties if "words of severance" are used, even though performance by any one of the promisors is to discharge the duties of all. The legal consequences of such promises of the same performance are the subject of §§ 289-96. Promises of the same performance may be treated as "joint," "several," or "joint and several."

§ 289. Joint, Several, and Joint and Several Promisors of the Same Performance

(1) Where two or more parties to a contract promise the same performance to the same promisee, each is bound for the whole performance thereof, whether his duty is joint, several, or joint and several.

(2) Where two or more parties to a contract promise the same performance to the same promisee, they incur only a joint duty unless an intention is manifested to create several duties or joint and several duties.

(3) By statute in most states some or all promises which would otherwise create only joint duties create joint and several duties.

Comment:

a. Liability of each for the whole performance. In the civil-law system of Louisiana, derived from the Roman and French law, promises of the same performance create "joint" liability on the part of each promisor unless an intention is manifested to create a "solidary" obligation. "Joint" liability means liability only for an aliquot share of the total obligation; a "solidary" obligation is substantially the same as a "joint and several" obligation at common law. Common-law terminology and results are quite different: promises of the same performance may create joint duties, several duties, or joint and several duties; and each promisor is liable for the whole performance promised. A contrary agreement may be effective either to show that separate performances are promised or to limit the liability which would otherwise be created. **Illustrations:**

    1. A and B owe $ 100 to C jointly, and C obtains a judgment against A and B for $ 100. Execution may be levied wholly on the property of either A or B, or partially on the property of each.

    2. A and B severally promise to pay C the same $ 100. C may obtain separate judgments against each for $ 100, and may levy execution under either judgment until $ 100 is collected.

. . .

b. The presumption of joint obligation. The question whether promisors of the same performance undertake "several" duties in addition to or instead of a "joint" duty has traditionally been treated as a question of the application of deductions from legal concepts rather than as a question of manifested intention. Where a "joint" duty differs from "joint and several" duties, the joint duty is invariably less advantageous to the promisee, while the advantage to the promisor does not normally serve any legitimate interest. Joint duties, as distinguished from joint and several duties, are likely to reflect ignorance or inadvertence on the part of the promisee. But in the absence of statute both common-law courts and courts of equity long held promises of the same performance to be joint only unless the promises took a linguistic form appropriate to several duties. The modern tendency is to treat the question as one of interpretation and therefore to give weight to manifestations of contrary intention in whatever form. Subsection (2) reflects this tendency.

c. Severance. The fact that one promisor is under a duty to another to perform the promise or that one promisor has received all or the greater portion of the consideration does not prevent their duty from being joint rather than several or joint and several. But the fact that the promises are made in separate documents or are separately stated in the same document sufficiently shows an intention to undertake several duties. The standard modern form to create duties which are both joint and several is "We jointly and severally promise," but any equivalent words will do as well. In particular, a promise in the first person singular, signed by several persons, creates joint and several duties. **Illustrations:**

4. A, B and C sign a contract stating that "A as principal, and B and C as sureties, promise" a certain performance. A, B and C are jointly bound. In the absence of statute, the statement of the suretyship relation does not manifest an intention to create several duties or joint and several duties.

5. A and B sign a contract in these terms: "We, and each of us, promise D that C hall be paid the sum of $ 100" on a certain date. This creates joint and several duties on the part of the signers.

. . .

§ 290. Compulsory Joinder of Joint Promisors

(1) By statute in most states where the distinction between joint duties and joint and several duties retains significance, an action can be maintained against one or more promisors who incur only a joint duty, even though other promisors subject to the same duty are not served with process.

(2) In the absence of statute, an action can be maintained against promisors who incur only a joint duty without joinder of those beyond the jurisdiction of the court, the representatives of deceased promisors, or those against whom the duty is not enforceable at the time of suit.

. . .

§ 291. Judgment in an Action Against Co-Promisors

In an action against promisors of the same performance, whether their duties are joint, several, or joint and several, judgment can properly be entered for or against one even though no judgment or a different judgment is entered with respect to another, except that judgment for one and against another is improper where there has been a determination on the merits and the liability of one cannot exist without the liability of the other.

. . .

§ 292. Effect of Judgment for or Against Co-Promisors

(1) A judgment against one or more promisors does not discharge other promisors of the same performance unless joinder of the other promisors is required by the rule stated in § 290. By statute in most states judgment against one promisor does not discharge co-promisors even where such joinder is required.

(2) The effect of judgment for one or more promisors of the same performance is determined by the rules of res judicata relating to suretyship or vicarious liability.

Comment:

a. Merger of joint duties by judgment. During the nineteenth century the rule was established, contrary to earlier authority, that judgment against one joint promisor merged the entire claim and barred a subsequent action against a co-promisor. The co-promisor remained liable for contribution if the defendant in the action satisfied the judgment. Yet the discharge was rigorously enforced both at law and in equity: no exception was made when the plaintiff had judgment against the only promisors known to him, they proved insolvent, and suit was brought against a subsequently discovered partner. The same logic applied to the joint duty of joint and several promisors: either a joint judgment or a several judgment against one barred a subsequent joint action, but not a several action against a promisor not joined in the first action.

b. Mitigation of the merger doctrine. Procedural reforms have permitted joinder of defendants whose duty is not joint. Thus in cases of joint and several promisors claims based on the several promises of those not joined in a prior action can be joined, and the merger of the joint duty is academic. As to joint promises, the doctrine did not apply when the omitted promisor was dead (see § 296), and exceptions were made for promisors out of the jurisdiction, for foreign judgments, for cases of estoppel, for judgments on promises given as conditional payment or collateral security. Today statutes in most states have given some or all joint promises the effect of joint and several promises, or have directly provided that judgment against one or more joint promisors does not bar an action against the others, or have permitted judgments binding the joint property of those not served, who may later be summoned to show cause why they should not be bound. See the Introductory Note to this Chapter.

c. Judgment based on personal defense. Also in the nineteenth century, it was established that a judgment for one joint promisor did not discharge the joint duty of all if it was based on a defense peculiar to him. Originally applied to cases of lack of jurisdiction, contractual incapacity, discharge in bankruptcy, and statute of limitations, this rule now applies to any defense not applicable to the co-promisors. Compare § 291.

. . .

§ 293. Effect of Performance or Satisfaction on Co-Promisors

Full or partial performance or other satisfaction of the contractual duty of a promisor discharges the duty to the obligee of each other promisor of the same performance to the extent of the amount or value applied to the discharge of the duty of the promisor who renders it.

Comment:

a. Rationale. This Section makes explicit what is meant by "promises of the same performance": performance by any one of the promisors discharges the duty of the others. See § 288. Satisfaction by the acceptance of a substituted performance (§ 278) has the same effect, since the promisee or beneficiary has a right only to the single performance or to an agreed equivalent. For this purpose it does not matter whether the promisors are bound jointly, severally, or jointly and severally. One of the promisors is not permitted by a subsequent agreement with a promisee or beneficiary to confer on him a right against the other promisors to receive more than was originally promised. A release (§ 284) or contract not to sue (§ 285) is not of itself satisfaction within the meaning of this Section, but is dealt with in §§ 294 and 295.

Illustrations:

1. A borrows $ 100 from D for the common benefit of A, B and C in equal shares, and A, B and C promise that D will be repaid. A pays $ 25 to D pursuant to an express agreement that it shall apply only to A's duty and shall not limit D's rights against B or C. D's rights against B and C, as well as his right against A, are reduced by $ 25.

2. The facts being otherwise as stated in Illustration 1, A delivers to D a set of books worth $ 25, and D accepts the books in full satisfaction of A's duty. A, B and C are discharged.

. . .

b. "Obligee." The word "obligee" is used in this Section and in succeeding sections of this Chapter to include both a promisee and a beneficiary who under the rules of §§ 302-15 has the right to enforce a promise.

§ 294. Effect of Discharge on Co-Promisors

(1) Except as stated in § 295, where the obligee of promises of the same performance discharges one promisor by release, rescission or accord and satisfaction,

(a) co-promisors who are bound only by a joint duty are discharged unless the discharged promisor is a surety for the co-promisor;

(b) co-promisors who are bound by joint and several duties or by several duties are not discharged except to the extent required by the law of suretyship.

(2) By statute in many states a discharge of one promisor does not discharge other promisors of the same performance except to the extent required by the law of suretyship.

(3) Any consideration received by the obligee for discharge of one promisor discharges the duty of each other promisor of the same performance to the extent of the amount or value received. An agreement to the contrary is not effective unless it is made with a surety and expressly preserves the duty of his principal.

Comment:

a. The common-law rule. The English rule that release of one joint obligor releases all was applied to joint and several obligations as well as joint obligations, and to tort as well as contract obligations. See Restatement, Second, Torts § 885. Historically the rule rested on the unitary character of the obligee's right and possibly on the principle that a deed is construed against the grantor. It has been suggested that a contrary rule might permit the obligee to obtain more than just compensation, and that the legitimate expectations of the released obligor might be frustrated by claims of co-obligors for contribution. None of these considerations justifies the rule, however, and it has often been denounced as anomalous and unjust. It has long been possible to avoid it by use of the form of a contract not to sue. See § 295(1). Modern decisions have converted it from a rule defeating intention to a rule of presumptive intention: where an intention contrary to the rule of Subsection (1)(a) is manifested, the purported release or other discharge has the effect of a contract not to sue. See § 295(2).

b. Discharge of a surety. Where the released promisor is surety for a co-promisor, the co-promisor is adequately protected against double recovery by the rule of Subsection (3), since the surety loses his right to reimbursement to the extent that he agrees that consideration given by him is not credited to the principal. There is no danger of indirect attack on the surety, since the principal has no right to contribution from the surety. Thus the only basis for discharge of the co-promisor is the unitary character of the obligation. The obsolescence of that concept has therefore led to the exception stated in Subsection (1)(a).

c. Joint and several promises. Where the English view is followed, joint and several promisors have the benefit of the rule stated in Subsection (1)(a) for joint promisors. Statutes converting joint obligations into joint and several obligations do not, in this view, affect the rule on releases. See Introductory Note to this Chapter. But the English view is out of harmony with the rule stated in § 292(1) as to the effect of a judgment against one joint and several obligor, and is not supported either by logic or by convenience. Subsection (1)(b) therefore rejects the English view and follows the contrary authorities and the analogy of the rule governing judgments.

. . .

§ 295. Effect of Contract Not to Sue; Reservation of Rights

(1) Where the obligee of promises of the same performance contracts not to sue one promisor, the other promisors are not discharged except to the extent required by the law of suretyship.

(2) Words which purport to release or discharge a promisor and also to reserve rights against other promisors of the same performance have the effect of a contract not to sue rather than a release or discharge.

(3) Any consideration received by the obligee for a contract not to sue one promisor

discharges the duty of each other promisor of the same performance to the extent of the amount or value received. An agreement to the contrary is not effective unless it is made with a surety and expressly preserves the duty of his principal.

Comment:

a. The distinction between discharge and contract not to sue. Discharge by release, rescission or accord and satisfaction has long been regarded as an executed transaction rather than an executory promise. It has also long been held that release of one joint promisor discharges his co-promisors, and the rule has been extended to other types of discharges. See § 294. In its origin the rule was regarded as a logical consequence of the nature of the right created by a joint promise; it did not depend on the intention of the parties to the release, and regularly operated to defeat their manifest intention. But the rule could be avoided by use of the form of a contract not to sue, also known as a covenant not to sue. Such a contract was treated as an executory promise; although a single promisor could plead the contract as a defense to prevent circuity of action, it did not discharge the right and hence did not discharge co-promisors.

. . .

c. Reservation of rights. Until the nineteenth century, words in a release of one joint promisor which purported to reserve rights against co-promisors were regarded as repugnant to the nature of the release and void. But in modern times, in order to give effect to the manifested intention, courts have interpreted releases containing such words as contracts not to sue. This rule has been extended to other types of discharge, and has greatly reduced the significance of the rule that release of one releases all. So far as the rules governing joint promisors are concerned, no reservation of rights is necessary in an instrument taking the form of a contract not to sue. But for the purposes of the law of suretyship, which developed independently, a contract not to sue is treated like a release: an unqualified contract not to sue the principal debtor is treated as impairing the surety's right to assert the creditor's right by way of subrogation and hence as discharging the surety. See Comment *d* to § 294. This result can be avoided by a reservation of rights, which is regarded as preserving not only the surety's right to reimbursement from the principal but also his right to subrogation. Thus the reservation subjects the one not to be sued to the risk that the protection the contract affords may be illusory. See Restatement of Security § 122; Uniform Commercial Code § 3-606.

. . .

§ 296. Survivorship of Joint Duties

On the death of one of two or more promisors of the same performance in a contract, the estate of the deceased promisor is bound by the contract, whether the duty was joint, several, or joint and several.

Comment:

. . .

b. The modern rule. The survivorship rule has been abolished in most states by statute or decision. Statutes making joint duties joint and several have this effect, and specific statutes on the point have been widely enacted. See Introductory Note to this Chapter. General statutes on the survival of actions have sometimes been given the same effect, and a number of judicial decisions have simply negated the rule. The question whether the representatives of deceased promisors may be joined in an action against survivors may be resolved by specific statute or left to general procedural statutes or rules.

§ 297. Obligees of the Same Promised Performance

(1) Where a party to a contract makes a promise to two or more promisees or for the benefit of two or more beneficiaries, the manifested intention of the parties determines whether he promises the same performance to all, a separate performance to each, or some combination.

(2) Except to the extent that a different intention is manifested or that the interests of the obligees in the performance or in the remedies for breach are distinct, the rights of obligees of the same performance are joint.

Comment:

a. "Several" rights. The word "several" is used in two different senses with reference to rights created by a promise. First, the promisor may promise a distinct performance to each obligee, creating entirely separate rights. Second, even though the same performance is promised to a number of obligees, they may in the event of breach have separate claims for relief. In the first sense, the same right cannot be both "several" and "joint;" which it is is entirely a question of interpretation. In the second sense, rights may be either "joint" or "several" or some combination, but the parties cannot control entirely the remedies and procedures available.

. . .

§ 298. Compulsory Joinder of Joint Obligees

(1) In an action based on a joint right created by a promise, the promisor by making appropriate objection can prevent recovery of judgment against him unless there are joined either as plaintiffs or as defendants all the surviving joint obligees.

(2) Except in actions on negotiable instruments and except as stated in § 300, any joint obligee unless limited by agreement may sue in the name of all the joint obligees for the enforcement of the promise by a money judgment.

. . .

§ 299. Discharge by or Tender to One Joint Obligee

Except where the promise is made in a negotiable instrument and except as stated in § 300, any joint obligee, unless limited by agreement, has power to discharge the promisor by receipt of the promised performance or by release or otherwise, and tender to one joint obligee is equivalent to a tender to all.

. . .

§ 300. Effect of Violation of Duty to a Co-Obligee

(1) If an obligee attempts or threatens to discharge the promisor in violation of his duty to a co-obligee of the same performance, the co-obligee may obtain an injunction forbidding the discharge.

(2) A discharge of the promisor by an obligee in violation of his duty to a co-obligee of the same performance is voidable to the extent necessary to protect the co-obligee's interest in the performance, except to the extent that the promisor has given value or otherwise changed his position in good faith and without knowledge or reason to know of the violation.

Comment:

a. Duties among co-obligees. The interests of co-obligees among themselves depend upon the agreement or other relation among them. Commonly each has a beneficial interest, but one or more may be a nominal party or a mere agent. An obligee who has power to affect the rights of co-obligees has at least a duty to act in good faith; often he is subject to more rigorous fiduciary duties. For example, he may be an agent for a co-obligee, or they may be partners or co-trustees.

. . .

§ 301. Survivorship of Joint Rights

On the death of a joint obligee, unless a contrary intention was manifested, the surviving obligees are solely entitled as against the promisor to receive performance, to discharge the promisor, or to sue for the enforcement of the promise by a money judgment. On the death of the last surviving obligee, only his estate is so entitled.

. . .

Chapter 14

Contract Beneficiaries

Introductory Note Historically, the rights of contract beneficiaries have been the subject of doctrinal difficulties in both England and the United States. In both countries, decisions in the latter part of the nineteenth century overruled or limited earlier precedents recognizing such rights. In England, but not in the United States (see § 71), the rule was established that consideration must move from the plaintiff. That rule has sometimes been avoided by an artificial holding that the promisee held a contract right in trust for the beneficiary, but it seems to retain some force.

In the United States the principal difficulty was that the beneficiary was not a party to the contract, since the promise was not addressed to him. Some decisions recognized a right only in a "sole" beneficiary or "donee" beneficiary, such as the person to whom the proceeds of a life insurance policy are made payable. Others recognized the beneficiary's right only if the promisor was to satisfy a duty of the promisee to the beneficiary, who was then called a "creditor" beneficiary, or if there was some other relationship between promisee and beneficiary.

These difficulties have now been largely resolved in the United States by recognition of the power of promisor and promisee to create rights in a beneficiary by manifesting an intention to do so. Since the terms "donee" beneficiary and "creditor" beneficiary carry overtones of obsolete doctrinal difficulties, they are avoided in the statement of rules in this Chapter. Instead, the terms "intended" beneficiary and "incidental" beneficiary are used to distinguish beneficiaries who have rights from those who do not.

Difficulties of interpretation of course remain. Where the manifested intention is unclear, rules of law may fill the gap. And in some situations overriding social policies may limit the parties' freedom of contract. Thus Uniform Commercial Code § 2-318 provides for "third party beneficiaries of warranties express or implied," and includes a provision that "A seller may not exclude or limit the effect of this section." Restatement, Second, Torts § 402A deals with the same problem in non-contractual terms. Again, the rights of employees under a collective bargaining agreement are sometimes treated as rights of contract beneficiaries, sometimes as rights based on agency principles, sometimes as rights analogous to the rights of trust beneficiaries. Or the collective bargaining agreement may be treated as establishing a usage incorporated in individual employment contracts, or as analogous to legislation. In any case they are substantially affected by the national labor policy. Such policies are of course beyond the scope of this Restatement.

§ 302. Intended and Incidental Beneficiaries

(1) Unless otherwise agreed between promisor and promisee, a beneficiary of a promise is an intended beneficiary if recognition of a right to performance in the beneficiary is appropriate to effectuate the intention of the parties and either

(a) the performance of the promise will satisfy an obligation of the promisee to pay money to the beneficiary; or

(b) the circumstances indicate that the promisee intends to give the beneficiary the benefit of the promised performance.

(2) An incidental beneficiary is a beneficiary who is not an intended beneficiary.

Comment:

a. Promisee and beneficiary. This Section distinguishes an "intended" beneficiary, who acquires a right by virtue of a promise, from an "incidental" beneficiary, who does not. See §§ 304, 315. Section 2 defines "promisee" as the person to whom a promise is addressed, and "beneficiary" as a person other than the promisee who will be benefitted by performance of the promise. Both terms are neutral with respect to rights and duties: either or both or neither may have a legal right to performance. Either promisee or beneficiary may but need not be connected with the transaction in other ways: neither promisee nor beneficiary is necessarily the person to whom performance is to be rendered, the person who will receive economic benefit, or the person who furnished the consideration.

b. Promise to pay the promisee's debt. The type of beneficiary covered by Subsection (1)(a) is often referred to as a "creditor beneficiary." In such cases the promisee is surety for the promisor, the promise is an asset of the promisee, and a direct action by beneficiary against promisor is normally appropriate to carry out the intention of promisor and promisee, even though no intention is manifested to give the beneficiary the benefit of the promised performance. Promise of a performance other than the payment of money may be governed by the same principle if the promisee's obligation is regarded as easily convertible into money, as in cases of obligations to deliver commodities or securities which are actively traded in organized markets. Less liquid obligations are left to Subsection (1)(b).

A suretyship relation may exist even though the duty of the promisee is voidable or is unenforceable by reason of the statute of limitations, the Statute of Frauds, or a discharge in bankruptcy, and Subsection (1)(a) covers such cases. The term "creditor beneficiary" has also sometimes been used with reference to promises to satisfy a supposed or asserted duty of the promisee, but there is no suretyship if the promisee has never been under any duty to the beneficiary. Hence such cases are not covered by Subsection (1)(a). The beneficiary of a promise to discharge a lien on the promisee's property, or of a promise to satisfy a duty of a third person, is similarly excluded from Subsection (1)(a). Such beneficiaries may, however, be "intended beneficiaries" under Subsection (1)(b).

Illustrations:

    1. A owes C a debt of $ 100. The debt is barred by the statute of limitations or by a discharge in bankruptcy, or is unenforceable because of the Statute of Frauds. B promises A to pay the barred or unenforceable debt. C is an intended beneficiary under Subsection (1)(a).

    2. B promises A to furnish support for A's minor child C, whom A is bound by law to support. C is an intended beneficiary under Subsection (1)(a).

    3. B promises A to pay whatever debts A may incur in a certain undertaking. A incurs in the undertaking debts to C, D and E. If the promise is interpreted as a promise that B will pay C, D and E, they are intended beneficiaries under Subsection (1)(a); if the money is to be paid to A in order that he may be provided with money to pay C, D and E, they are at most incidental beneficiaries.

c. Gift promise. Where the promised performance is not paid for by the recipient, discharges no right that he has against anyone, and is apparently designed to benefit him, the promise is often referred to as a "gift promise." The beneficiary of such a promise is often referred to as a "donee beneficiary"; he is an intended beneficiary under Subsection (1)(b). The contract need not provide that performance is to be rendered directly to the beneficiary: a gift may be made to the beneficiary, for example, by payment of his debt. Nor is any contact or communication with the beneficiary essential.

Illustrations:

    4. A, an insurance company, promises B in a policy of insurance to pay $ 10,000 on B's death to C, B's wife. C is an intended beneficiary under Subsection (1)(b).

    5. C is a troublesome person who is annoying A. A dislikes him but, believing the best way to obtain freedom from annoyance is to make a present, secures from B a promise to give C a box of cigars. C is an intended beneficiary under Subsection (1)(b).

    6. A's son C is indebted to D. With the purpose of assisting C, A secures from B a promise to pay the debt to D. Both C and D are intended beneficiaries under Subsection (1)(b).

    7. A owes C $ 100 for money lent. B promises A to pay C $ 200, both as a discharge of the debt and as an indication of A's gratitude to C for making the loan. C is an intended beneficiary under Subsection (1)(a) as to the amount of the debt and under Subsection (1)(b) as to the excess.

    8. A conveys land to B in consideration of B's promise to pay $ 15,000 as follows: $ 5,000 to C, A's wife, on whom A wishes to make a settlement, $ 5,000 to D to whom A is indebted in that amount, and $ 5,000 to E, a life insurance company, to purchase an annuity payable to A during his life. C is an intended beneficiary under Subsection (1)(b); D is an intended beneficiary under Subsection (1)(a); E is an incidental beneficiary.

9. A owes C $ 100. Not knowing of any such debt, B promises A to pay $ 100 to C. C is an intended beneficiary under Subsection (1)(a) if A manifests an intention that the payment is to satisfy the debt, an intended beneficiary under Subsection (1)(b) if A manifests an intention to make a gift of $ 100, leaving outstanding the original debt.

d. Other intended beneficiaries. Either a promise to pay the promisee's debt to a beneficiary or a gift promise involves a manifestation of intention by the promisee and promisor sufficient, in a contractual setting, to make reliance by the beneficiary both reasonable and probable. Other cases may be quite similar in this respect. Examples are a promise to perform a supposed or asserted duty of the promisee, a promise to discharge a lien on the promisee's property, or a promise to satisfy the duty of a third person. In such cases, if the beneficiary would be reasonable in relying on the promise as manifesting an intention to confer a right on him, he is an intended beneficiary. Where there is doubt whether such reliance would be reasonable, considerations of procedural convenience and other factors not strictly dependent on the manifested intention of the parties may affect the question whether under Subsection (1) recognition of a right in the beneficiary is appropriate. In some cases an overriding policy, which may be embodied in a statute, requires recognition of such a right without regard to the intention of the parties.

Illustrations:

10. A, the operator of a chicken processing and fertilizer plant, contracts with B, a municipality, to use B's sewage system. With the purpose of preventing harm to landowners downstream from its system, B obtains from A a promise to remove specified types of waste from its deposits into the system. C, a downstream landowner, is an intended beneficiary under Subsection (1)(b).

11. A, a corporation, contracts with B, an insurance company, that B shall pay to any future buyer of a car from A the loss he may suffer by the burning or theft of the car within one year after sale. Later A sells a car to C, telling C about the insurance. C is an intended beneficiary.

12. B contracts to build a house for A. Pursuant to the contract, B and his surety S execute a payment bond to A by which they promise A that all of B's debts for labor and materials on the house will be paid. B later employs C as a carpenter and buys lumber from D. C and D are intended beneficiaries of S's promise to A, whether or not they have power to create liens on the house.

13. C asserts that A owes him $ 100. A does not owe this money, or think that he owes it, but rather than engage in litigation and in order to obtain peace of mind A secures a promise from B to pay C $ 100. C is an intended beneficiary.

14. A, a labor union, enters into a collective bargaining agreement with B, an employer, in which B promises not to discriminate against any employee because of his membership in A. All B's employees who are members of A are intended beneficiaries of the promise.

15. A buys food from B, a grocer, for household use, relying on B's express warranty. C, A's minor child, is injured in person by breach of the warranty. Under Uniform Commercial Code § 2-318, without regard to the intention of A or B, the warranty extends to C.

e. Incidental beneficiaries. Performance of a contract will often benefit a third person. But unless the third person is an intended beneficiary as here defined, no duty to him is created. See § 315. **Illustrations:**

16. B contracts with A to erect an expensive building on A's land. C's adjoining land would be enhanced in value by the performance of the contract. C is an incidental beneficiary.

17. B contracts with A to buy a new car manufactured by C. C is an incidental beneficiary, even though the promise can only be performed if money is paid to C.

18. A, a labor union, promises B, a trade association, not to strike against any member of B during a certain period. One of the members of B charters a ship from C on terms under which such a strike would cause financial loss to C. C is an incidental beneficiary of A's promise.

19. A contracts to erect a building for C. B then contracts with A to supply lumber needed for the building. C is an incidental beneficiary of B's promise, and B is an incidental beneficiary of C's promise to pay A for the building.

f. Trust and agency. Where money or property is transferred from one person to another with an intention to benefit a third person, the manifested intention of the parties determines whether the transferee is an agent for the transferor or the third person or a trustee for the third person or whether the third person is the beneficiary of a promise made by the transferee. See Restatement, Second, Agency §§ 14B, 14L;

Restatement, Second, Trusts §§ 8, 14. Similarly, an agreement between two parties may constitute one the agent of the other to confer a benefit on a third person, or the promise of one may be made to the other as trustee for a third person, or a third person may be the beneficiary of a promise of either or both; the manifested intention of the parties determines which of these possible relations is created for the particular purpose involved. There is a fiduciary relation between agent and principal or between trustee and beneficiary, but not between promisor or promisee and beneficiary of a contract. Agency requires the consent of the principal and the agent; a trust or a contract for the benefit of a third person does not require the consent of the beneficiary. Either the promisee or the beneficiary of a promise may be made a trustee of rights arising by virtue of the promise; although the beneficiary of such a trust is a beneficiary of the promise under this Section, his rights must be enforced in accordance with the law of Trusts. See Restatement, Second, Trusts §§ 26, 177, 199.

Illustration:

20. A, an insurance company, promises B in a policy of insurance to pay $ 10,000 on B's death to C as trustee for B's wife D. C is an intended beneficiary and may enforce his rights as trustee; D's rights as beneficiary of the trust and the contract are enforceable only in the manner in which rights of other trust beneficiaries are enforced.

§ 303. Conditional Promises; Promises Under Seal

The statements in this Chapter are applicable to both conditional and unconditional promises and to sealed and unsealed promises.

Comment:

a. Conditional promises. A conditional promise may be made for the benefit of the beneficiary of a promise to pay a debt, or the beneficiary of a gift promise, or one who is otherwise an intended beneficiary. It is enough that the debt will be satisfied or the gift made or the right conferred if the condition occurs so that the promised performance becomes due.

Illustrations:

1. A owes C $ 100. B promises A to pay the debt if Dancer wins the Derby. C is an intended beneficiary of the conditional promise.

2. C asserts and A denies that A owes C $ 100. B promises to pay the debt if it is legally recoverable. C is an intended beneficiary of B's conditional promise.

3. A obtains from B, an insurance company, a policy on A's life, payable to A's wife, C. The policy is conditional on the payment of annual premiums. C is an intended beneficiary, but her right is conditional.

4. A's son C has formed the X Automobile Company. For the stated purpose of benefiting C, A obtains B's promise to buy twenty automobiles from the company. The company is an intended beneficiary, though B's duty to pay the price is conditional on delivery of the automobiles. Compare Illustration 17 to § 302.

. . .

§ 304. Creation of Duty to Beneficiary

A promise in a contract creates a duty in the promisor to any intended beneficiary to perform the promise, and the intended beneficiary may enforce the duty.

Comment:

a. Intended and incidental beneficiaries. "Beneficiary" is defined in § 2, "intended beneficiary" and "incidental beneficiary" in § 302. The terms are defined in relation to a "promise," a term which is neutral with respect to legal consequences; this Section states that a duty to an intended beneficiary is created if the promise is otherwise binding. The related proposition that an incidental beneficiary acquires no right is stated in § 315.

b. Creation and termination of duty. This Section reflects the basic principle that the parties to a contract have the power, if they so intend, to create a right in a third person. The requirements for formation of a contract must of course be met, and the right of the beneficiary, like that of the promisee, may be conditional, voidable, or unenforceable. See § 309. Whether the right of the beneficiary can be varied without his consent by action taken by the promisee or by agreement between promisee and promisor is a separate question which depends on the terms of the contract. See § 311.

c. Promise to pay the promisee's debt. Where the performance of the promise will satisfy an obligation of the promisee to pay money to the beneficiary, the promisee is surety for the promisor. The contract is an asset of the promisee, and on grounds of simplicity and convenience of remedy the beneficiary is allowed a direct action against the promisor without joining the promisee, instead of a procedure like garnishment or a suit to realize on an asset of the debtor not available to seizure by ordinary legal process. The direct remedy also protects the beneficiary in reliance on the promise; his reliance is likely to take the form of inaction and to be difficult or impossible to prove. Promises to render performances other than the payment of money may be similar but require a manifestation of intention to give the benefit of the performance to the beneficiary. **Illustrations:**

    1. A owes C $ 100. For consideration B promises A to pay the debt. B breaks his contract. C may sue B and obtain judgment for the amount of the debt.

    2. A transfers Blackacre to B subject to a mortgage in favor of C, which B assumes and agrees to pay. After default C may sue B and get judgment for the amount of the mortgage debt, or, after foreclosure by sale, for the amount of any deficiency in the sum realized by the sale.

    3. A owes C $ 100. For consideration B promises A to pay $ 100 to C in satisfaction of the debt. Later the statute of limitations bars an action by C against A. That fact is not of itself a defense in an action by C against B.

    4. A promises C to have a fence built between their lands, and C pays A the price. B contracts with A to assume A's obligation to C, and A promises to pay B on completion of the work. On B's failure to build the fence, C may recover damages from B. But a contract by B to build the fence for A would ordinarily not be a contract to assume A's obligation to C.

d. Gift promise. Where the promisee manifests an intention to make a gift of the promised performance to a beneficiary, recognition of a duty to the beneficiary means that the beneficiary has available for his own benefit the usual remedies for breach of contract. An action by the beneficiary is commonly a convenient way to enforce the right of the promisee as well as to redress any injury to the

beneficiary. This is so even though the promisee has reserved a power to vary the beneficiary's right, so long as that power has not been exercised. **Illustration:**

    5. A gives money to B, his son, who promises in consideration thereof to pay A's daughter C, $ 5000 on A's death. A dies and B fails to pay C. C may sue on the promise and obtain judgment for $ 5000.

e. Other intended beneficiaries. The considerations which lead to the recognition of the right of a beneficiary of a promise to pay the promisee's debt or of a gift promise operate in varying degrees in other cases. Where the promisee clearly manifests an intention to confer on the beneficiary a legal right to enforce the contract, recognition of the beneficiary's right rests on the same grounds as recognition of the promisee's right. In cases of doubt, the question whether such an intention is to be attributed to the promisee may be influenced by the likelihood that recognition of the right will further the legitimate expectations of the promisee, make available a simple and convenient procedure for enforcement, or protect the beneficiary in his reasonable reliance on the promise. **Illustrations:**

    6. A owes C $ 1000. For consideration B promises A to pay C $ 1000 for an assignment of C's right. On tender of such an assignment C can recover from B on his promise.

    7. A's son C is indebted to D. With the purpose of assisting C, A secures from B for consideration a promise to pay the debt to D. D may enforce B's promise for D's own benefit.

    8. A owns property subject to a mortgage in favor of C. C asserts and A denies that A is personally liable for the mortgage debt. To resolve the dispute, A transfers the property to B on B's promise to pay the mortgage debt. C may enforce B's promise for C's own benefit whether or not A is personally liable.

    9. A, a common carrier, is required as a condition of its license to maintain liability insurance covering claims for bodily injury arising out of A's operations, and files a policy written by B. C claims to have been injured under circumstances covered by the policy. C may maintain a direct action against B.

    10. A transfers property to B. A promises to use money received from B to discharge all A's obligations "including C's fees" up to $ 20,000; B promises to discharge all obligations in excess of $ 20,000 which A "is found to be responsible to pay including C's fees." C cannot maintain an action against B on the promise before A's liability has been established.

§ 305. Overlapping Duties to Beneficiary and Promisee

(1) A promise in a contract creates a duty in the promisor to the promisee to perform the promise even though he also has a similar duty to an intended beneficiary.

(2) Whole or partial satisfaction of the promisor's duty to the beneficiary satisfies to that extent the promisor's duty to the promisee.

Comment:

a. The promisee's right. The promisee of a promise for the benefit of a beneficiary has the same right to performance as any other promisee, whether the promise is binding because part of a bargain, because of his reliance, or because of its formal characteristics. If the promisee has no economic interest in the performance, as in many cases involving gift promises, the ordinary remedy of damages for breach of contract is an inadequate remedy, since only nominal damages can be recovered. In such cases specific performance is commonly appropriate. See § 307. In the ordinary case of a promise to pay the promisee's debt, on the other hand, the promisee may suffer substantial damages as a result of breach by the promisor. So long as there is no conflict with rights of the beneficiary or the promisor, he is entitled to recover such damages. See § 310. **Illustrations:**

1. In consideration of A's promise to transfer to his brother C A's interest in his mother's estate, A's father B promises A to pay a like amount to C. A makes the promised transfer, but B dies without performing his promise. A may maintain a suit for specific performance against B's personal representative.

2. A owes C an unliquidated sum. In consideration of $ 100 paid to B by A, B promises A to pay C whatever is due. B breaks his promise, and A pays C a reasonable sum in discharge of C's claim. A can at his election recover from B either $ 100 or the amount paid C.

3. A promises C to have a fence built between their lands, and C pays A the price of the fence. A informs B of the contract between A and C and of the danger that C's cattle will harm A's property if the fence is not properly built, and B contracts with A to carry out A's contract with C to build the fence. Because of B's breach of contract C's cattle damage A's property. A may recover the damage from B.

b. Conflicting claims and double liability. In the ordinary case of a promise to pay a debt owed by the promisee to a beneficiary, a single payment by the promisor will discharge both his duty to the promisee and his duty to the beneficiary. But a breach by the promisor can damage both promisee and beneficiary in the full amount of the debt. The promisor and his other creditors are entitled to protection against such doubling of liability so long as the injuries to both promisee and beneficiary can be redressed by a single payment. Moreover, when the promisor is insolvent, the promisee as surety is not permitted to compete with the beneficiary for the assets of the principal debtor. Hence the general creditors of the promisee, so far as they are asserting his rights, cannot reach his claim against the promisor until the beneficiary's claim is satisfied. **Illustrations:**

4. A owes C $ 100. For consideration B promises A to pay the debt to C. On B's breach A may obtain a judgment for $ 100 against B. But the court may protect B against double payment by permitting joinder of C, by an order that money collected by A is to be applied to reduce A's debt to C, by giving B credit on the judgment for payments to C which reduce A's obligation, or by enjoining enforcement of the judgment to the extent of such payment.

. . .

c. Variation of beneficiary's right. Subsection (2) states that satisfaction of the duty to the beneficiary satisfies the duty to the promisee. The converse is not always true: satisfaction of the duty to the promisee may not satisfy the duty to the beneficiary. Whether and to what extent the promisor's duty to the beneficiary is subject to variation or discharge by the promisee or by agreement between promisor and promisee is governed by the rules stated in § 311. One consequence of a right not subject to such variation or discharge is that the promisor's duty to the beneficiary cannot be satisfied without the beneficiary's consent except by rendering the promised performance. **Illustration:**

6. A deposits money in B, a bank, to the joint credit of A and his wife C, payable to either A or C or the survivor. A and C make withdrawals. On A's death B owes the balance to C, and is not entitled to credit for a payment to A's personal representative.

§ 306. Disclaimer by a Beneficiary

A beneficiary who has not previously assented to the promise for his benefit may in a reasonable time after learning of its existence and terms render any duty to himself inoperative from the beginning by disclaimer.

Comment:

a. Acceptance unnecessary. No assent by a beneficiary to the contract and no knowledge on his part is necessary to give him a right of action on it. Compare §§ 53, 104; Restatement, Second, Trusts § 36. Of course, the promise may be conditional on knowledge or assent, or the performance promised may be such that it can only be rendered with the cooperation of the beneficiary.

b. Disclaimer. Like an offeree, a beneficiary is entitled to reject a promised benefit, whether or not there is a related burden. Compare § 38. No particular formality is required for disclaimer, and its effect on the promisor's duty to the beneficiary is the same as if no promise had been made. But once the beneficiary has manifested assent, disclaimer is operative only if the requirements are met for discharge of a contractual duty. Compare § 37.

. . .

§ 307. Remedy of Specific Performance

Where specific performance is otherwise an appropriate remedy, either the promisee or the beneficiary may maintain a suit for specific enforcement of a duty owed to an intended beneficiary.

Comment:

a. Suit by beneficiary. Whether specific performance is an appropriate remedy is determined by the rules stated in §§ 357-69. Where a contract creates a duty to a beneficiary under the rule stated in § 304, the beneficiary is a proper party plaintiff either in an action for damages or in a suit for specific performance. He is the real party in interest within the meaning of any statute requiring suit to be brought by such a party. There is no general requirement that the promisee be made a party, but the promisee is ordinarily a proper party and the circumstances may be such that a final decree should await joinder of the promisee. As to grant of an injunction instead of specific performance, see § 357(2).

b. Suit by promisee. Even though a contract creates a duty to a beneficiary, the promisee has a right to performance. See § 305. The promisee cannot recover damages suffered by the beneficiary, but the promisee is a proper party to sue for specific performance if that remedy is otherwise appropriate under the rules stated in §§ 357-69. Where a statute requires suit to be prosecuted in the name of the real party in interest, the promisee is commonly permitted to sue either as the "trustee of an express trust" or by an express provision for "a party with whom or in whose name a contract has been made for

the benefit of another." See Federal Rules of Civil Procedure Rule 17. There is no general requirement that the beneficiary be joined in such a suit; whether he should or must be made a party depends on the circumstances.

c. Promise to pay the promisee's debt. Where the promised performance will satisfy an obligation of the promisee to pay money to the beneficiary, the promisee may suffer substantial damages as a result of breach. He is entitled to recover such damages so long as there is no conflict with rights of the beneficiary or the promisor. But the promisee as surety for the promisor is not permitted to compete with the beneficiary for the assets of the promisor, and the promisor is ordinarily entitled to protection against enforced double liability. See §§ 305, 310. These difficulties can be avoided by specific performance of the surety's right to exoneration. See Restatement of Security § 112. **Illustration:**

    1. A, a stockholder of X, a corporation, guarantees payment of a debt owed by X to C. A sells his stock to B, who agrees to assume and pay A's obligation on the guaranty. B fails to pay, and C sues A on the guaranty. A may obtain a decree directing B to pay the debt to C.

d. Gift promise. Where the promisee intends to make a gift of the promised performance to the beneficiary, the beneficiary ordinarily has an economic interest in the performance but the promisee does not. Thus the promisee may suffer no damages as the result of breach by the promisor. In such cases the promisee's remedy in damages is not an adequate remedy within the rules stated in §§ 359 and 360, and specific performance may be appropriate. See Illustration 1 to § 305. The court may of course so fashion its decree as to protect the interests of the promisee and beneficiary without unnecessary injury to the promisor or innocent third persons. See § 358. **Illustration:**

　　2. As part of a separation agreement B promises his wife A not to change the provision in B's will for C, their son. A dies and B changes his will to C's detriment, adding also a provision that C will forfeit any bequest if he questions the change before any tribunal. A's personal representative may sue for specific performance of B's promise.

§ 308. Identification of Beneficiaries

It is not essential to the creation of a right in an intended beneficiary that he be identified when a contract containing the promise is made.

Comment:

　　a. The fact that a beneficiary cannot be identified when the contract is made may have a bearing on the question whether the promisee intended to make a gift to him or otherwise to confer on him a right to the promised performance, and thus may determine whether he is an intended beneficiary or an incidental beneficiary. See § 302. It may also bear on the question whether the right created is revocable or not. See § 311. But there is no requirement of identification prior to the time for enforcement of the right. Notwithstanding the rule stated in § 108 as to promisees, the rule of this Section applies to beneficiaries of sealed as well as unsealed promises. See § 303. **Illustrations:**

　　1. A takes out a policy issued by B, an insurance company, the principal sum being payable to A at the age of 60, or if he dies before that age to his wife C, if she survives him; otherwise to such children as he may have surviving at the time of his death. C dies when A is 50. A dies at the age of 55. D, A's only child then surviving, is entitled to the policy and its proceeds to the exclusion of the estates of A and C.

　　2. B promises A to pay anyone to whom A may become indebted for the purchase of an automobile. A buys an automobile from C. B is under a duty to C.

§ 309. Defenses Against the Beneficiary

(1) A promise creates no duty to a beneficiary unless a contract is formed between the promisor and the promisee; and if a contract is voidable or unenforceable at the time of its formation the right of any beneficiary is subject to the infirmity.

(2) If a contract ceases to be binding in whole or in part because of impracticability, public policy, nonoccurrence of a condition, or present or prospective failure of performance, the right of any beneficiary is to that extent discharged or modified.

(3) Except as stated in Subsections (1) and (2) and in § 311 or as provided by the contract, the right of any beneficiary against the promisor is not subject to the promisor's claims or defenses against the promisee or to the promisee's claims or defenses against the beneficiary.

(4) A beneficiary's right against the promisor is subject to any claim or defense arising from his own conduct or agreement.

Comment:

　　a. Necessity of contract. Subsection (1) makes explicit a negative fairly implied in § 304: the right of an intended beneficiary is created by contract, and in the absence of contract there is no such right. Moreover, where there is a contract, the beneficiary's right is subject to any limitations imposed by the law. Thus absence of mutual assent or consideration, lack of capacity, fraud, mistake and the like may be asserted by the promisor against the beneficiary. **Illustrations:**

1. B promises A to pay C $ 100. B's promise, owing to lack of consideration or illegality, gives A no right. Whether at the time of B's promise C had a right against A to be paid $ 100 or not, C acquires no right against B.

2. B orally contracts with A to convey Blackacre to C. The promise is unenforceable because not in writing. Whether or not at the time of B's promise C had a right against A to have Blackacre conveyed to him, C cannot maintain an action on B's promise.

3. The facts being otherwise as stated in Illustration 2, B subsequently delivers to A a written memorandum of the contract. C can now maintain an action on B's promise.

b. Conditions; failure of performance. Where there is a contract, the right of a beneficiary is subject to any limitations imposed by the terms of the contract. Such a limitation may be imposed by the agreed terms, or it may be imposed in the absence of contrary agreement by virtue of considerations of fairness and public policy. Thus a failure of the promisee to perform a return promise ordinarily discharges the promisor's duty to a beneficiary to the same extent that it discharges his duty to the promisee. But not every condition of the promisee's right is necessarily a condition of the right of the beneficiary. The agreement may effectively provide that the right of the beneficiary is not to be affected by the act or neglect of the promisee. Aside from such an agreed term, where the beneficiary's right is not subject to variation by agreement between promisor and promisee under the rules stated in § 311 there may be an implicit limitation on the extent to which such variation can be effected by the act or neglect of the promisee. **Illustrations:**

4. B, a life insurance company, issues a policy to A insuring A's life, the insurance money being payable to C. The policy reserves to A a power to change the beneficiary. C's right is subject to termination by A's changing the beneficiary before the maturity of the policy.

5. B promises A to pay C $ 100 in consideration of A's promise to B to perform stated services for him. A substantially breaks his promise to perform these services. Whether or not at the time of B's promise C had a right against A to be paid $ 100 he has no right against B.

6. A insures goods against fire with B, an insurance company. Later A mortgages the goods to C to secure a loan, and the insurance policy is amended to provide that loss is payable to A and C "as their interest may appear, subject to all the terms and conditions of the policy." A deliberately sets fire to the goods. Neither A nor C may recover from B for the resulting damage.

. . .

8. B and his surety S contract with A, a city, to grade streets and to pay all laborers and materialmen on the job. The contract provides that any laborer working under the contract shall be entitled to sue and recover from S. A extends B's time for performance without S's consent. In a suit by C, a laborer, against S, the extension of time is not a defense.

c. Other claims and defenses. The position of a beneficiary is comparable to that of an assignee after knowledge of the assignment by the obligor. See § 336. His right, like that of an assignee, is subject to limitations inherent in the contract, and to supervening defenses arising by virtue of its terms. Partial defenses by way of recoupment for breach by the promisee may be asserted against the beneficiary, unless precluded by the terms of the agreement or considerations of fairness or public policy. Compare Uniform Commercial Code § 2-717. But the beneficiary's right is direct, not merely derivative, and claims and defenses of the promisor against the promisee arising out of separate transactions do not affect the right of the beneficiary except in accordance with the terms of the contract. Similarly, the beneficiary's right against the promisor is not subject to claims and defenses of the promisee against the beneficiary unless the contract so provides. The conduct of the beneficiary, however, like that of any obligee, may give rise to claims and defenses which may be asserted against him by the obligor, and his right may be affected by the terms of an agreement made by him. **Illustrations:**

9. In exchange for a conveyance of one parcel of land by B to A, A conveys another parcel of land to B subject to a mortgage in favor of C, which B assumes and agrees to pay, and A also agrees to pay money to B at a later date. In an action by C on B's promise, B can offset any part of the sum payable by A which is due and unpaid.

10. A collective bargaining agreement between A, a labor union, and many coal operators including B provides that each operator will pay 40 cents to C, trustee of a welfare fund for coal miners, for each ton of coal mined. In violation of the agreement A calls a strike of B's employees. B is not entitled to deduct the resulting damage from the payments due to C.

. . .

§ 310. Remedies of the Beneficiary of a Promise to Pay the Promisee's Debt; Reimbursement of Promisee

(1) Where an intended beneficiary has an enforceable claim against the promisee, he can obtain a judgment or judgments against either the promisee or the promisor or both based on their respective duties to him. Satisfaction in whole or in part of either of these duties, or of a judgment thereon, satisfies to that extent the other duty or judgment, subject to the promisee's right of subrogation.

(2) To the extent that the claim of an intended beneficiary is satisfied from assets of the promisee, the promisee has a right of reimbursement from the promisor, which may be enforced directly and also, if the beneficiary's claim is fully satisfied, by subrogation to the claim of the beneficiary against the promisor, and to any judgment thereon and to any security therefor.

Comment:

a. Promisee as surety. The claim of a beneficiary against the promisee is not discharged by the promisor's agreement to assume the promisee's obligation. Unless the beneficiary consents to a novation, the promisee remains liable as surety for the promisor. In accordance with the usual rule of suretyship, the creditor may enforce his claim against both surety and principal obligor and need not first have recourse against the principal. See Restatement of Security § 130. The question whether joinder of surety and principal in a single action is permitted or required, and the form of the judgment in case of joinder are beyond the scope of this Restatement. **Illustrations:**

1. A owes C $ 100. For consideration B promises A to pay the debt. B breaks his contract. C can sue A and can also sue B and get judgment against each of them for $ 100, and can enforce either judgment until he has collected $ 100. Entire or partial satisfaction of a judgment against either A or B precludes to that extent enforcement of a judgment against the other, subject to A's right of subrogation.

2. A transfers Blackacre to B subject to a mortgage in favor of C, which B assumes and contracts to pay. C can sue A and he can also sue B and get judgment against each for the amount of the mortgage or, if the mortgaged property has been sold on foreclosure, for the amount of any deficiency in the sum realized by the sale.

3. B contracts with A to pay A's debt to C. D contracts with B to pay the debt. E contracts with D to pay it. C can bring actions against A, B, D and E and obtain judgment against each of them.

b. Suretyship defenses. Once a creditor knows that his debtor has become a surety, he is required to take account of the suretyship in his subsequent dealings. See § 314; Restatement of Security § 114; compare Uniform Commercial Code §§ 3-415, 3-604, 3-606. Thus a release of the promisor, or a binding extension of his time to perform, may discharge the surety-promisee. See Restatement of Security §§ 122, 129. Where the surety is threatened with unusual hardship and prior enforcement of the creditor's right against the promisor will not prejudice the creditor, the creditor may be required to utilize available assets of the promisor before having recourse to the surety. See Restatement of Security § 131.

c. Reimbursement of the promisee. Like any surety, the promisee who pays a debt to a beneficiary is entitled to reimbursement from the principal obligor, the promisor. The promisee is not permitted to compete with the beneficiary for the assets of the promisor, but once the beneficiary's claim is satisfied the promisee is entitled as subrogee to assert the beneficiary's claim against the promisor. See Restatement of Restitution § 162; Restatement of Security § 141. In addition, the promisee has a right to exoneration. See § 307. **Illustration:**

4. A owes C $ 1000. For consideration B promises A to pay the debt. B gives C a bond as security, but fails to pay the debt. C sues A and B and obtains a judgment against each of them, and obtains full payment by a levy of execution on A's property. A is subrogated to C's judgment against B and to the security of the bond.

§ 311. Variation of a Duty to a Beneficiary

(1) Discharge or modification of a duty to an intended beneficiary by conduct of the promisee or by a subsequent agreement between promisor and promisee is ineffective if a term of the promise creating the duty so provides.

(2) In the absence of such a term, the promisor and promisee retain power to discharge or modify the duty by subsequent agreement.

(3) Such a power terminates when the beneficiary, before he receives notification of the discharge or modification, materially changes his position in justifiable reliance on the promise or brings suit on it or manifests assent to it at the request of the promisor or promisee.

(4) If the promisee receives consideration for an attempted discharge or modification of the promisor's duty which is ineffective against the beneficiary, the beneficiary can assert a right to the consideration so received. The promisor's duty is discharged to the extent of the amount received by the beneficiary.

Comment:

a. The power to create an irrevocable duty. The parties to a contract cannot by agreement preclude themselves from varying their duties to each other by subsequent agreement. Nor can they force a right on an unwilling beneficiary, or prevent the beneficiary from joining with them in an agreement varying the duty to him. Compare Restatement, Second, Trusts § 338. But they can by agreement create a duty to a beneficiary which cannot be varied without the beneficiary's consent. Compare § 104; Restatement, Second, Trusts §§ 330, 331.

b. Express and implied terms. Agreements precluding variation of a duty to a beneficiary before the beneficiary knows of the promise are unusual and would often be unwise. See Comment *f.* But the power of the parties to make such an agreement is not restricted by special formal requirements. The agreement need not be explicit: omission of a standard clause reserving a power of modification may manifest an intention to preclude modification; reservation of a limited power may negate a broader power; usage of trade or course of dealing may supply a term precluding modification. See § 5, defining "term."

c. Life insurance. Partly on the basis of statutes, the rule was established in a number of states in the latter part of the nineteenth century that the ordinary life insurance policy in the form then in use belonged to the beneficiary the moment it was issued, and that the insured had no power to transfer the right to any other person unless the power was reserved. That rule was not applied to fraternal benefit insurance, partly again because of statutes and partly because of charter and by-law provisions. Standard policy forms were revised to avoid the rule by reserving to the insured the power to change the beneficiary. Modern policies also provide for powers to surrender for cash, to borrow against the policy, and to assign the policy. Deletion of such a standard provision may manifest an intention that the power is not to exist.

Illustrations:

1. A insures his life for $ 10,000 with the B Insurance Company, designating C as beneficiary but reserving power to change the beneficiary. The policy provides for surrender of the policy by the insured for a stated cash value. Subsequently A by appropriate indorsement on the policy irrevocably designates C as beneficiary. A's power to surrender for cash is terminated.

2. A insures his life for $ 10,000 with the B Insurance Company, designating C as beneficiary but reserving power to change the beneficiary. The policy provides for assignment by the insured, and A assigns it to D as security for a loan. On A's death C's right is limited to the excess over the amount due to D.

d. Infant beneficiaries. Where the beneficiary has full contractual capacity, a duty to him can be made irrevocable by his assent under Subsection (3). Or he may be made a promisee. See § 71(4) as to consideration in such cases. Failure to procure such assent or to make him a promisee may be an indication that the right is to be revocable. But where the beneficiary lacks capacity, as in the case of an infant, such an inference is less clearly justified. It is therefore sometimes said that in such a case the infant's assent is "presumed." The true test rests not on fictitious assent but on the manifested intention of the original parties; other circumstances, such as the fact that the consideration for the promise is executory, may rebut the inference that the beneficiary's right is irrevocable. **Illustrations:**

3. A is employed by the B corporation, and designates his infant son C as beneficiary of a death benefit under a plan set up by B. No provision is made for a power to change the beneficiary. A later notifies B that the designation of C is revoked and that the benefit is to be paid to D, to whom A is newly married. C's right is not affected.

4. A and his wife and his infant son C move onto the farm of A's uncle B under an agreement between A and B that they will care for B and the farm until B dies and that B will pay A good wages and will convey a specified portion of the farm to C when C becomes 21 years old. B is unable to pay wages and conveys a different portion of the farm to A in satisfaction of his obligations under the original agreement. C's right is discharged.

...

g. *Reliance.* In the absence of some contrary indication, an intended beneficiary is justified in relying on the promise. It is immaterial whether he learns of the promise from the promisor, the promisee or a third party, and whether the promise is one to satisfy the promisee's duty or is a gift promise or is neither. If there is a material change of position in justifiable reliance on the promise, the change of position precludes discharge or modification of the contract without the beneficiary's consent. In the case of a promise to pay a debt of the promisee or another person, it is not necessary that the beneficiary enter into a novation with the promisor, though a novation would *a fortiori* be effective. See § 280. As to what constitutes receipt of a notification sufficient to preclude reliance, see § 68; compare Uniform Commercial Code § 1-201(26) and (27).

h. *Assent.* Even though there is no novation and no change of position by the beneficiary, the power of promisor and promisee to vary the promisor's duty to an intended beneficiary is terminated when the beneficiary manifests assent to the promise in a manner invited by the promisor or promisee. This rule rests in part on an analogy to the law of offer and acceptance and in part on the probability that the beneficiary will rely in ways difficult or impossible to prove. In the case of a promise to discharge a duty of the promisee or a third person, the latter basis is supported by the analogy of the rule that a creditor gives "value" for rights acquired as security for a pre-

existing claim. See Uniform Commercial Code § 1-201(44). As to terms of the promise inviting or requiring the beneficiary to manifest assent in a particular way, the law of offer and acceptance provides appropriate analogies. See §§ 60, 63-67. Indeed, the promise may in some cases be an offer to the beneficiary by the promisor or promisee or both. The bringing of suit against the promisor is a sufficient manifestation of assent to preclude discharge or modification. **Illustrations:**

9. The facts being otherwise as stated in Illustration 6, 7 or 8, C brings suit against B before receiving notification of the rescission or release. Judgment should be given for C.

10. B contracts with A to pay C $ 200 which A owes C, and A notifies C of the contract by mail. C mails a letter to A assenting to the contract before receiving notification of a rescission by A and B. The rescission is ineffective against C. Compare §§ 42, 63.

11. A and B, two affiliated corporations, contract that upon surrender of outstanding bonds issued by A new bonds will be issued, bond for bond, paying less interest but guaranteed by B. Forty years later, shortly before the old bonds mature, only a small number of the old bonds have been surrendered, and A and B release each other from the contract with respect to any new bonds not yet issued. The releases are effective against any holder of old bonds who receives notification of the releases before he surrenders his bonds.

i. *Fraud on creditors.* The rules of Subsections (1) and (2) refer to a subsequent agreement which is otherwise valid, and are subject to the law relating to any invalidating cause. In particular, a promise for the benefit of a creditor of the promisee is an asset of the promisee. A release of the promisor may be a fraud on the beneficiary or on other creditors of the promisee if the promisee is insolvent and the release is made without fair consideration, or if the release is made with actual intent to hinder, delay or defraud creditors. See Uniform Fraudulent Conveyance Act §§ 4, 7. In that event, even though the beneficiary has not assented or relied, the release is not effective except to the extent that the promisor has innocently given consideration for it. See Uniform Fraudulent Conveyance Act § 9(2). Similar considerations may be applicable in a case of a promise to satisfy the duty of another person than the promisee.

Illustration:

12. B contracts with A to pay C $ 200 which A owes C. Before C learns of this contract, A, in consideration of B's proposing him for admission to a social club, releases B from his contract. A has no assets other than this contract worth $ 200. The release does not impair C's right against B.

j. The beneficiary's right to proceeds. Where a promise creates rights in a beneficiary, the promisee may retain power to discharge or modify the promisor's duty. Whether the exercise of such a power is rightful or wrongful may depend on facts other than the promise. If it is wrongful, the promisee is under a duty of restitution to the beneficiary for any amount received by him therefor. See Restatement of Restitution §§ 131, 165. Subsection (4) applies a similar principle to cases where the beneficiary's right against the promisor is not discharged or modified. In the latter type of case, the promisor may also have a right of restitution. Compare Restatement of Restitution §§ 124, 126. Which right prevails in the event of conflict and the extent to which assertion of the right against the promisee bars a claim against the promisor depends on what is equitable in the circumstances.

§ 312. Mistake as to Duty to Beneficiary

The effect of an erroneous belief of the promisor or promisee as to the existence or extent of a duty owed to an intended beneficiary is determined by the rules making contracts voidable for mistake.

Comment:

a. Supposed creditor as beneficiary. When performance of the promise will satisfy an obligation of the promisee to pay money to a beneficiary, the beneficiary is normally treated as an intended beneficiary. In cases of a duty other than to pay money, in cases of a duty of someone other than the promisee, or in cases of a supposed or asserted duty of the promisee, whether the beneficiary is an intended beneficiary depends on the intention manifested by the promisee. See §§ 302, 304 and Comments. If the beneficiary would be reasonable in relying on the promise as manifesting an intention to confer a right on him, he is an intended beneficiary. Compare § 20.

b. Existence of mistake. Nonexistence of the supposed duty does not establish a mistake where the terms of the promise provide for the case. Thus if the promisor promises to perform whatever duty is owed and none is owed, the beneficiary has no right against the promisor. Likewise, a promise to render a performance whether or not there is a pre-existing duty is effective according to its terms. *Prima facie* an unqualified promise to render the performance has the same effect, but mistake as to the existence of the duty may make the contract voidable. See §§ 309, 151-58. **Illustrations:**

1. A, a stockholder in X, a corporation, guarantees the payment of a debt owed by X to C and agrees to pay interest and an attorney's fee. Subsequently A sells his stock to B, who agrees to assume and pay the debt owed by X. B is liable for interest and an attorney's fee only to the extent of X's liability.

2. The facts being otherwise as stated in Illustration 1, B agrees to assume and pay the debt owed by X and to pay interest and an attorney's fee. B's liability for interest and an attorney's fee is not affected by the nonliability of X or A or both.

. . .

§ 313. Government Contracts

(1) The rules stated in this Chapter apply to contracts with a government or governmental agency except to the extent that application would contravene the policy of the law authorizing the contract or prescribing remedies for its breach.

(2) In particular, a promisor who contracts with a government or governmental agency to do an act for or render a service to the public is not subject to contractual liability to a member of the public for consequential damages resulting from performance or failure to perform unless

(a) the terms of the promise provide for such liability; or

(b) the promisee is subject to liability to the member of the public for the damages and a

direct action against the promisor is consistent with the terms of the contract and with the policy of the law authorizing the contract and prescribing remedies for its breach.

Comment:

a. Rationale. Beneficiaries of government contracts have often been denied rights because of the doctrinal difficulties referred to in the Introductory Note to this Chapter. Subsection (1) reflects the disappearance of those difficulties, but leaves room for the weighing of considerations peculiar to particular situations. Subsection (2) applies to a particular class of contracts the classification of beneficiaries in § 302. Government contracts often benefit the public, but individual members of the public are treated as incidental beneficiaries unless a different intention is manifested. In case of doubt, a promise to do an act for or render a service to the public does not have the effect of a promise to pay consequential damages to individual members of the public unless the conditions of Subsection (2)(b) are met. Among factors which may make inappropriate a direct action against the promisor are arrangements for governmental control over the litigation and settlement of claims, the likelihood of impairment of service or of excessive financial burden, and the availability of alternatives such as insurance.

. . .

§ 314. Suretyship Defenses

An intended beneficiary who has an enforceable claim against the promisee is affected by the incidents of the suretyship of the promisee from the time he has knowledge of it.

Comment:

a. Effect of knowledge. This Section states a principle of suretyship. See Restatement of Security § 114; compare Uniform Commercial Code § 3-415. Under the definitions in § 302 a contract to satisfy a duty of the promisee to an intended beneficiary makes the promisee a surety for the promisor. Even though he has not consented to the suretyship relation, the beneficiary must recognize it and take it into account when he learns of it.

b. Impairment of recourse or collateral. Where the beneficiary knows that the promisee is surety for the promisor, release of the promisor discharges the surety unless the surety consents or the beneficiary reserves his rights against the surety. Compare § 293-94; see Restatement of Security § 122. Similar rules apply to agreements between beneficiary and promisor modifying their contract, including agreements to extend the time of payment, and to surrender or other impairment of collateral security. See Restatement of Security § 128, 129, 132; Uniform Commercial Code § 3-606. These rules of suretyship are beyond the scope of this Restatement.

Illustration:

1. A owes C a debt of $ 10,000, secured by a mortgage on A's land. A sells Blackacre to B, who assumes and agrees to pay the mortgage debt. C, knowing of this assumption, releases a portion of the mortgaged premises from the lien of the mortgage. The remaining portion of Blackacre is then worth $ 12,000, but at the date of maturity of the mortgage is worth $ 8,000. The released land is then worth $ 2,000. B makes default in paying the debt. C can recover from A only $ 8,000. Since C's own act has diminished by $ 2,000 the value of the security applicable to the debt, his right against A is subject to diminution by that amount. If the released land is then worth $ 1,000, C can recover $ 9,000 from A.

§ 315. Effect of a Promise of Incidental Benefit

An incidental beneficiary acquires by virtue of the promise no right against the promisor or the promisee.

Comment:

a. An incidental beneficiary is a person who will be benefited by performance of a promise but who is neither a promisee nor an intended beneficiary. See §§ 2, 302. Illustrations 3, 8, 16-19 to § 302 also illustrate the rule stated in this Section.

Chapter 15

Assignment and Delegation

Introductory Note The subject matter of this Chapter is part of the larger subject of the transfer of intangible property. The historic rule in the common-rule courts of England was that a "chose in action" could not be assigned. The scope of that rule was progressively narrowed by the reception into the common law of doctrines developed in the law merchant and in the courts of equity and by statute. Little remains of it today, but modern rules, both decisional and statutory, must often be read in the light of the development.

The law merchant. The law merchant is a tradition with an international and maritime flavor. It was followed in special merchant tribunals in England; during the seventeenth century it became part of the common law of England. Under its influence mercantile instruments such as the bill of exchange were held transferable by delivery, or by indorsement and delivery, and similar rules have been extended in modern times, by decision and by statute, to documents of title and to investment securities. See Uniform Commercial Code Articles 3, 7, 8. The rules governing such instruments are beyond the scope of this Restatement. See § 6.

Law and equity. Also during the seventeenth century, it was established that an assignment could take effect in the common-law courts as a power of attorney enabling the assignee to sue in the assignor's name, and that courts of equity would protect the assignee in cases of death or bankruptcy of the assignor or revocation by him. During the eighteenth century the common-law courts began to give effect to the equitable rights of the assignee. In the United States statutes generally require actions to be brought in the name of the real party in interest, and the assignee of a contract right can sue in his own name without regard to the distinction between actions at law and suits in equity. That distinction is therefore not employed in the statement of rules in this Chapter, although references to the "equitable" character of an assignee's rights can be found in the modern literature on the subject.

Statutory Note: The extent to which remnants of common-law procedure survive in the United States is beyond the scope of the Restatement of this Subject. Statutes or rules of court in most States require an action to be prosecuted in the name of the real party in interest, as does Rule 17(a) of the Federal Rules of Civil Procedure. In addition most states have statutes providing for set-offs and other defenses against an assignee, and a number of States have statutes relating to other aspects of the assignment of contractual rights. Article 9 of the Uniform Commercial Code deals comprehensively with transactions intended to create security interests in personal property, including defined types of rights under contracts, and with sales of "accounts and chattel paper." The Code also provides a Statute of Frauds for the sale of personal property not otherwise covered and codifies part of the law governing assignments of contracts for the sale of goods. §§ 1-206, 2-210. Most states also have additional statutes regulating assignment of particular types of claims, such as claims for wages or claims against the Government.

Real-party-in-interest and related provisions. In most states an action by the assignee of a contractual right is required or permitted to be prosecuted in his own name. In many of these this is accomplished by a mandatory general real-party-in-interest statute or rule similar to Rule 17(a) of the Federal Rules of Civil Procedure. In Florida and New Jersey there are general real-party-in-interest provisions which are permissive. Connecticut, Hawaii, Illinois, Vermont and Virginia have statutes permitting the assignee of a non-negotiable chose in action to sue in his own name.

Additional statutes in some of these states, largely redundant, permit the assignment in writing or indorsement of particular types of contracts, such as bonds, promissory notes or non-negotiable written instruments for the payment of money, and provide that the rights of the assignor vest in the assignee and that the assignee may sue in his own name. Compare, as to negotiable instruments, Uniform Commercial Code §§ 3-201, 3-301.

In all the states listed below except Michigan and Delaware there are also statutes providing that an assignment is without prejudice to any set-off or defense existing before notice of the assignment. Some of these statutes refer to counterclaims as well; some refer only to defined classes of contracts such as non-negotiable written instruments for the payment of money.

. . .

Most of the remaining jurisdictions have less comprehensive statutes, limited either to assignments in writing (e.g., Alabama, District of Columbia, Georgia, Mississippi, Rhode Island), or to the assignment of written instruments, contracts for the payment of money, or the like (e.g., Alabama, Mississippi, Tennessee). In Tennessee the assignee who sues in the assignor's name is treated as the real plaintiff of record. Each of these states has a related provision on defenses.

. . .

A number of additional statutory provisions are included in the above tables. Four states provide for recovery from the assignor where the assignee is unable to recover from the obligor (Idaho, Maryland, Missouri, Tennessee). Two states permit such recovery subject to defenses the assignor had against any intermediate assignee (Virginia, West Virginia). In Vermont a defendant may set off a claim against the plaintiff acquired by assignment only if notice of the assignment was given to the plaintiff before suit. In New York an assignment in writing and signed by the assignor is not revocable because of the absence of consideration. In New Jersey the assignment of a sealed instrument by an unsealed writing is as valid as if under seal.

The Uniform Commercial Code. Article 9 of the Uniform Commercial Code establishes a comprehensive scheme for the regulation of security interests in personal property and fixtures, "including goods, documents, instruments, general intangibles, chattel paper or accounts." Because of difficulty in distinguishing between security transactions and outright sales, the scheme also applies "to any sale of accounts or chattel paper," and the interest of the buyer is treated as a "security interest." §§ 1-201(37), 9-102. Documents, instruments and chattel paper are beyond the scope of this Restatement, but accounts and general intangibles include many of the rights which are the subject of this Chapter.

Most contractual rights are covered by Article 9 of the Uniform Commercial Code unless excluded by § 9-104. Where the right is not evidenced by an instrument or chattel paper, "'account' means any right to payment for goods sold or leased or for services rendered . . . whether or not it has been earned by performance," and "general intangibles" is a residual category including contractual rights to performance other than payment. Section 9-106.

Section 9-104 provides that Article 9 "does not apply" to listed types of transactions. Among the excluded types are transfer of a claim for wages, salary, or other compensation of an employee, of an interest or claim in or under any policy of insurance (other than proceeds), of an interest in or lien on real estate, including a lease or rents thereunder, or of any deposit account maintained with a bank, savings and loan association, credit union or like organization. Also excluded is "a sale of accounts or chattel paper as part of a sale of the business out of which they arose, or an assignment of accounts or chattel paper which is for the purpose of collection only, or a transfer of a right to payment under a contract to an assignee who is also to do the performance under the contract or a transfer of a single account to an assignee in whole or partial satisfaction of a preexisting indebtedness." Section 9-104(f).

As to transactions covered, § 9-201 provides generally that except as otherwise provided "a security agreement is effective according to its terms." Section 9-203 provides a Statute of Frauds. See Chapter 5 of this Restatement. Section 9-203 also states rules as to when a security interest "attaches" as between the parties, and § 9-204 provides for a security interest in after-acquired collateral and for security for future advances. Section 9-301 subordinates "unperfected" security interests to the rights of certain third persons; Section 9-302 provides generally for perfection by filing, but exempts "an assignment of accounts which does not alone or in conjunction with other assignments to the same assignee transfer a significant part of the outstanding accounts of the assignor." Section 9-303 provides that if filing occurs before the security interest attaches, it is perfected at the time when it attaches. Subsequent sections provide for priorities, for the mechanics of filing a financing statement in a public office, and for the enforcement of the secured party's rights. Of particular relevance to the subject matter of this Chapter is § 9-318 on the obligor's defenses against the assignee.

The provisions referred to above are far more than a restatement of the common law on assignment of contractual rights although in some respects they adhere to common-law rules. In view of their widespread enactment, statements in this Chapter are applicable primarily to sales of general intangibles which are contractual, to the residue of assignments excluded from Article 9 by § 9-104, and to questions not resolved by Article 9. Outside Article 9, § 1-206 provides a Statute of Frauds for kinds of personal property not otherwise covered, and § 2-210 covers the assignment of rights and delegation of duties under contracts for the sale of goods. Appropriate reference to the Code rules is made in the Comments to this Chapter, but no attempt is made to incorporate the provisions of the Code into the rules stated or to take account of variations in the Code as enacted in various states.

Wage assignments. Virtually every state has statutory restrictions on the assignment of wages. The most common type of provision applies only to assignments as security for loans under a stated amount, or to assignments for a consideration less than a stated amount. Other states, in addition to such statutes, have statutes relating to wage assignments generally, often without clear indication whether both statutes can apply to the same transaction. Still other states have statutory restrictions not limited to small loans.

Five states and the District of Columbia generally prohibit the assignment of future wages. In California and Connecticut separate prohibitions apply to lenders licensed under the small-loan laws.

. . .

Five states have no small-loan provisions on wage assignments, but regulate wage assignments without regard to amount involved. The regulation in Indiana is limited to "wage brokers." Mississippi requires written consent of the employer for assignments for the purchase of goods. The other three states provide for written consent of the employer in all cases, and New Hampshire adds a provision for recording.

. . .

Examples of states having both general regulation of wage assignments and wage-assignment provisions of the small-loan type are given below. The general statutes lay down a variety of formal requirements for assignment such as writing, signature, acknowledgment and witnessing. There are also requirements of consent of or notice to the employer, consent of the assignor's spouse, and recording. Assignments are limited to a percentage of the wages, or to the excess over a dollar amount, or to a period of time such as thirty days or two years.

. . .

Retail installment sales. Uniform Commercial Code §§ 9-201 and 9-203 subordinate the provisions of Article 9 to statutes regulating retail installment sales, and many states have enacted one or more such statutes which contain provisions affecting assignment by the seller of his rights under a regulated contract. In some states only motor vehicle sales are covered; in others there are separate statutes for motor vehicles and for other goods.

Common provisions validate assignments to a financing agency on such terms as may be agreed upon by the seller and the financing agency. Many of these further provide that, as against creditors of or purchasers from the seller, no requirement of filing, notice to the buyer, or limitation of the seller's dominion over payments or over repossessed goods shall be necessary to the validity of a written assignment. By another common provision, unless the buyer has notice of the assignment, payment to the last known holder of the contract is binding on all subsequent assignees. A few states have further limitations on who may be an assignee and how much the seller may receive from the assignee.

Section 9-206(1) of the Uniform Commercial Code relates to "an agreement by a buyer or lessee that he will not assert against an assignee any claim or defense which he may have against the seller or lessor." Such an agreement is made enforceable by an assignee without notice, "[s]ubject to any

statute or decision which establishes a different rule for buyers or lessees of consumer goods."
Retail installment sales acts sometimes protect innocent assignees against particular hazards. In
many states, for example, the buyer's written acknowledgment of delivery of a completed copy of the
contract is conclusive or presumptive evidence in an action by or against an assignee that a
requirement of such delivery has been met.

In 1975, the Federal Trade Commission promulgated a very important Trade Regulation Rule
barring such agreements in transactions involving consumers. See 16 C.F.R. § 433.1-.3 (1975); Comment
f to § 336.

In addition, in several states a statute establishes a "different rule" of the type referred to in
Uniform Commercial Code § 9-206. Some of the statutes forbid the execution of negotiable instruments
cutting off the buyer's defenses. Some forbid contractual waivers, and in some the buyer's defenses
can be cut off unless within ten or fifteen days of receiving written notice of the assignment he or she
gives notice of facts giving rise to a claim or defense.

. . .

Government contracts. Federal statutes forbid the assignment of claims against the United
States before the issuance of a warrant for payment, and the assignment of any public contract or
order. Both statutes contain an exception, called the Assignment of Claims Act of 1940, permitting a
single assignment to a financial institution where the contract does not forbid assignment and
written notice is filed with appropriate Government officers and with any surety on a bond in
connection with the contract. An assignment pursuant to the exception protects the assignee against
liability to repay the United States, and in certain cases against setoff of a liability of the assignor to
the United States.

Several jurisdictions also have limitations on the assignment of public contracts, or of particular
types of public contracts.

. . .

§ 316. Scope of This Chapter

**(1) In this Chapter, references to assignment of a right or delegation of a duty or condition,
to the obligee or obligor of an assigned right or delegated duty, or to an assignor or
assignee, are limited to rights, duties, and conditions arising under a contract or for
breach of a contract.**

**(2) The statements in this Chapter are qualified in some respects by statutory and other
rules governing negotiable instruments and documents, relating to interests in land, and
affecting other classes of contracts.**

Comment:

a. Contractual right; chose in action.
Statements in this Chapter are limited to
contractual rights and duties. Such rights include
debts, rights to non-monetary performance and
rights to damages and other contractual remedies,
whether or not a right to payment has been
earned. On the other hand, "chose in action" is a
much broader term. In its primary sense it includes
debts of all kinds, tort claims, and rights to
recover ownership or possession of real or
personal property; it has been extended to
instruments and documents embodying
intangible property rights, to such intangible
property as patents and copyrights, and even to
equitable rights in tangible property. The rules

stated here may have some application to non-
contractual choses in action, but the transfer of
non-contractual rights is beyond the scope of
the Restatement of this Subject.

*b. Negotiable instruments and documents;
conveyances of land.* The rules governing
negotiable instruments and documents and the
benefits and burdens attached to successive
owners of real property by virtue of a contract in
a prior conveyance or lease are to some extent
different from the law governing contracts in
general. The law governing negotiable
instruments and documents derives from the law
merchant and is now largely statutory. See
Comment to § 6. The law relating to covenants in

conveyances and leases of land grew up as part of the law of real property and is left to the Restatement, Second, of Property.

c. Assignment and delegation. In this Chapter rights are said to be "assigned"; duties are said to be "delegated." The phrase "assignment of the contract," which may refer to either or both, is avoided because "contract" is defined in § 1 in terms of the act or acts of promising. See § 328. "Assignment" is the transfer of a right by the owner (the obligee or assignor) to another person (the assignee). See § 317. A person subject to a duty (the obligor) does not ordinarily have such a power to substitute another in his place without the consent of the obligee; this is what is meant when it is said that duties cannot be assigned. "Delegation" of performance may be effective to empower a substitute to perform on behalf of the obligor, but the obligor remains subject to the duty until it has been discharged by performance or otherwise. Compare the usage of terms in Uniform Commercial Code § 2-210. Delegation of performance of a condition is similar in effect to delegation of performance of duty.

d. Involuntary transfer. In accordance with common usage, assignment and delegation in this Chapter include only transfers made or powers created by virtue of a manifestation of intention of the assignor or obligor. The manifestation may be made to the assignee or the person delegated or to another person on his behalf, but transfers made and powers created by operation of law are excluded. Such transfers and powers, including transfers to and powers of an executor, administrator, trustee in bankruptcy or receiver by virtue of his office, are in general beyond the scope of this Restatement. As to the equitable remedies of constructive trust, equitable lien, and subrogation, which sometimes operate much like an assignment, see Restatement of Restitution §§ 160-62; Restatement of Security § 141.

§ 317. Assignment of a Right

(1) An assignment of a right is a manifestation of the assignor's intention to transfer it by virtue of which the assignor's right to performance by the obligor is extinguished in whole or in part and the assignee acquires a right to such performance.

(2) A contractual right can be assigned unless

(a) the substitution of a right of the assignee for the right of the assignor would materially change the duty of the obligor, or materially increase the burden or risk imposed on him by his contract, or materially impair his chance of obtaining return performance, or materially reduce its value to him, or

(b) the assignment is forbidden by statute or is otherwise inoperative on grounds of public policy, or

(c) assignment is validly precluded by contract.

Comment:

a. "Assignment." The word "assignment" is sometimes used to refer to the act of the owner of a right (the obligee or assignor) purporting to transfer it, sometimes to the resulting change in legal relations, sometimes to a document evidencing the act or change. In this Chapter "assign" and "assignment" refer to an act which has the effect stated in Subsection (1). To avoid ambiguity, such an assignment is said to be "effective"; a similar act which does not have the stated effect is referred to as an "attempted" or "purported" assignment. In either case the actor is referred to as the "assignor" and the transferee or intended or purported transferee is referred to as the "assignee." **Illustrations:**

1. A has a right to $ 100 against B. A assigns his right to C. A's right is thereby extinguished, and C acquires a right against B to receive $ 100.

2. A purports to assign to C a right to receive $ 100 from B. A has no such right. The assignment is ineffective, and C can recover damages from A under the rules stated in § 333.

b. Assignment to obligor. A purported assignment by a creditor to his debtor of the indebtedness owed by the debtor is not covered by this Chapter. Such an "assignment" may or may not be effective to extinguish the assignor's right and thus to discharge the debtor; it cannot create in the debtor a right to performance by himself. Compare § 9.

c. Historical note. As is indicated in the Introductory Note to this Chapter, the historic common-law rule that a chose in action could not be assigned has largely disappeared. It remains applicable to some non-contractual rights, particularly claims for damages for personal injury, and to certain claims against the Government. This Section is limited by § 316 to contractual rights, and the historic rule now has very limited application to such rights. Except as stated in this Section, they may be effectively assigned. Notwithstanding the historical background, recourse need no longer be had to the law merchant, to doctrines peculiar to courts of equity, or to the concept of a power of attorney irrevocable because coupled with an interest. The restrictions in paragraphs (2)(a) and (c) rest on the basic principle that rights based on agreement are limited by the agreement.

d. Material variation. What is a material variation, an increase in burden or risk, or an impairment of the obligor's expectation of counter-performance under paragraph (2)(a) depends on the nature of the contract and on the circumstances. Both assignment of rights and delegation of performance are normal and permissible incidents of many types of contracts. See, for example, as to contracts for the sale of goods, Uniform Commercial Code § 2-210 Comment. When the obligor's duty is to pay money, a change in the person to whom the payment is to be made is not ordinarily material. Compare § 322; Uniform Commercial Code § 9-318. But if the duty is to depend on the personal discretion of one person, substitution of the personal discretion of another is likely to be a material change. The clause on material impairment of the chance of obtaining return performance operates primarily in cases where the assignment is accompanied by an improper delegation under § 318 or § 319: if the obligor is to perform in exchange for the promise of one person to render a return performance at a future time, substitution of the return promise of another impairs the obligor's expectation of counter-performance. But in cases of doubt, adequate assurance of due performance may prevent such an impairment. Compare § 251; Uniform Commercial Code § 2-609. **Illustrations:**

3. B contracts to support A for the remainder of A's life. A cannot by assignment confer on C a right to have B support C.

4. B contracts to support A for the remainder of A's life. B commits a material breach of the contract, and A assigns his right of action to C. The assignment is effective.

5. B contracts to sell to A for three years 250 tons of ice a week, and A contracts to pay on delivery a stated price per ton. A assigns his right under the contract to C. The assignment is effective. C's right to delivery is conditional on payment, but payment by C satisfies the condition.

6. B sells his business to A and makes a valid contract not to compete. A sells the business to C and assigns to C the right to have B refrain from competition. The assignment is effective with respect to competition with the business derived from B. The good will of the business, with contractual protection against its impairment, is treated as an assignable asset.

e. Public policy and statutory limitations. The rules for promises and other terms of an agreement stated in Chapter 8 apply by analogy in determining whether an assignment is inoperative on grounds of public policy under paragraph (2)(b) of this Section. Additional statutory restrictions are common. Uniform Commercial Code § 5-116 prevents assignment of the right to draw under a letter of credit unless the credit is expressly designated as transferable or assignable, and renders ineffective an assignment of the beneficiary's right to proceeds until the letter of credit or advice of credit is delivered to the assignee. As is stated in the Statutory Note preceding § 316, wage-assignment statutes often contain a variety of limitations, and there are statutes forbidding or limiting the assignment of rights under government contracts. **Illustrations:**

7. For value A, a public official, assigns to C salary or fees already earned and also his unearned salary for the ensuing month. The assignment of the earned salary or fees is effective, in the absence of a contrary statute, but the assignment of unearned salary is against public policy.

8. A contracts with B, a physician, for medical services, and later claims that B's negligence in performing the services caused personal injury to A in violation of B's contractual duty to use due care. A assigns the claim to C. The assignment is ineffective.

9. A, a retired officer of the United States Army, borrows money from C and as security for the loan assigns to C whatever is due or shall become due to A as retired pay. The assignment is ineffective except as permitted by statute un-

der regulations prescribed by the Secretary of the Army.

f. Contractual prohibition. The effect of a term in a contract forbidding the assignment of rights arising under the contract is the subject of § 322. Such a term may resolve doubts as to whether an assignment violates paragraph (2)(a) of this Section. Where it seems to forbid an assignment clearly outside the scope of paragraph (2)(a), it may be read restrictively to permit the assignment, or to give the obligor a claim against the assignor rather than a defense against the assignee, or the term may be invalid by statute or decision. See Uniform Commercial Code §§ 2-210, 9-318. Even if the term gives the obligor a defense against the assignee, the assignment is usually partially effective as an assignment conditional on the assent of the obligor.

§ 318. Delegation of Performance of Duty

(1) An obligor can properly delegate the performance of his duty to another unless the delegation is contrary to public policy or the terms of his promise.

(2) Unless otherwise agreed, a promise requires performance by a particular person only to the extent that the obligee has a substantial interest in having that person perform or control the acts promised.

(3) Unless the obligee agrees otherwise, neither delegation of performance nor a contract to assume the duty made with the obligor by the person delegated discharges any duty or liability of the delegating obligor.

Comment:

a. Duty and condition. A contractual performance may discharge the duty of a performing obligor, or it may satisfy a condition of the right of a performing obligee to a return performance. Where the same person is both obligor and obligee, the same performance may both discharge his duty and satisfy a condition of his right. The propriety of delegation is in general governed by the same standard whether the issue is performance of a duty or performance of a condition. In the interest of simplicity of statement, however, the rules are stated in two separate sections. This Section deals with delegation of performance of a duty; delegation of performance of a condition is the subject of § 319. **Illustrations:**

     1. A owes B $ 100, and asks C to pay B. Payment or tender to B by C has the effect of payment or tender by A.

     2. A contracts to deliver to B coal of specified kind and quality. A delegates the performance of this duty to C, who tenders to B coal of the specified kind and quality. The tender has the effect of a tender by A.

     3. A contracts to build a building for B in accordance with specifications, and delegates the plumbing work to C. Performance by C has the effect of performance by A.

b. The duty of the person delegated. The rules stated in this Section apply without regard to whether the person delegated has a legal duty to render the performance in question or whether he acquires a legal right to render it or to receive a return performance. The person delegated may be an agent, gratuitous or otherwise, of the delegating obligor. For such cases this Section is a particular application of Restatement, Second, Agency § 17. Or the person delegated may be an assignee of a related right, entitled to enforce it for his own benefit. See Restatement, Second, Agency §§ 14G, 14H. In either case he may or may not promise the obligor to render the performance. If he does so promise, the obligee may in some cases be an intended beneficiary of the promise, with the consequences stated in Chapter 14. **Illustration:**

     4. In Illustrations 1, 2 and 3, the stated consequences are not affected by the fact that C is an agent of A or an assignee of A's right to return performance or that C has or has not assumed A's duty.

c. Non-delegable duties. Delegation of performance is a normal and permissible incident of many types of contract. See Uniform Commercial Code § 2-210, Comment. The principal exceptions relate to contracts for personal services and to contracts for the exercise of personal skill or discretion. Compare § 317. Even where delegation is normal, a particular contract may call for personal performance. Or the contract may permit delegation where personal performance is normally required. In the absence of contrary agreement, Subsection (2) precludes delegation only where a substantial reason is shown why delegated performance is not as satisfactory as personal performance.

Illustrations:

    5. A, a teacher employed in a public or private school, attempts to delegate the performance of his duties to B, a competent person. An offer by B to perform A's duties need not be accepted, and actual performance by B without the assent of the employer will create no right in either A or B to the salary stated in A's contract.

    6. A contracts with B, a corporation, to sing three songs over the radio as part of an advertisement of B's product. A's performance is not delegable unless B assents.

    7. A contracts with B that A will personally cut the grass on B's meadow. A cannot effectively delegate performance of the duty to C, however competent C may be.

    8. A, a corporation, contracts with B to build a building. A delegates the entire performance to X and Y, the sole stockholders of A. Performance by X and Y in accordance with specifications discharges A's duty, since the supervision is not materially changed.

d. Delegation and novation. An obligor is discharged by the substitution of a new obligor only if the contract so provides or if the obligee makes a binding manifestation of assent, forming a novation. See §§ 280, 328 and 329. Otherwise, the obligee retains his original right against the obligor, even though the obligor manifests an intention to substitute another obligor in his place and the other purports to assume the duty. The obligee may, however, have rights against the other as an intended beneficiary of the promise to assume the duty. See Chapter 14.

Illustrations:

    9. A borrows $ 50,000 from B and contracts to repay it. The contract provides that, if a corporation C is organized and assumes the debt under described conditions, A will be under no further obligation. C is organized and in good faith assumes the debt as provided. A is discharged.

    10. A contracts with B to cut the grass on B's meadow. A delegates performance to C, who contracts with A to assume A's duty and perform the work. C begins performance with B's assent, but later breaks the contract. C is liable to B, but A is not discharged.

§ 319. Delegation of Performance of Condition

(1) Where a performance by a person is made a condition of a duty, performance by a person delegated by him satisfies that requirement unless the delegation is contrary to public policy or the terms of the agreement.

(2) Unless otherwise agreed, an agreement requires performance of a condition by a particular person only to the extent that the obligor has a substantial interest in having that person perform or control the acts required.

Comment:

    a. Type of conditions; related duties. A promissory duty may be subject to a condition either by virtue of a term of the promise or agreement or by virtue of a term of the contract supplied by a rule of law. See § 5; Comment *c* to § 226. This Section applies only to a particular type of condition, a performance by the obligee or some other person. When a promise is subject to such a condition, there may or may not be a return promise by the obligee or another that the performance will be rendered. If there is such a return promise, a breach of it often does not have the effect of the non-occurrence of a condition unless the failure of performance is material. See § 245. This Section deals with delegation as it affects performance of a condition; delegation

affecting performance of a duty is the subject of § 318. **Illustration:**

    1. A contracts with B, a city, to clean the streets of B weekly for five years in return for monthly payments. A delegates performance to C, and C substantially performs until B cancels the contract. C's performance satisfies the condition of B's duty to pay, whether C is A's agent or an assignee from A.

    b. Non-delegable performance. The propriety of delegation of performance that is made a condition is in general governed by the same standard as the propriety of delegation of performance of a duty. Indeed, the same delegation may involve both. See, e.g., Illustration 5 to § 318. Delegation is generally permissible unless otherwise agreed, but performance of personal services and the exercise of personal skill and discretion are not ordinarily delegable. Where the condition consists of the making of a promise, delegation substituting a different promisor is ordinarily not effective. **Illustrations:**

2. Under an option contract A has a right to a conveyance of Blackacre on terms including execution of a promissory note secured by a mortgage on Blackacre. A assigns the contract to C, and C tenders a note executed by C but not by A. B is not bound to convey.

3. A, a corporation, contracts with B to convey Blackacre to B upon completion of installment payments B contracts to make. The deed is to include a covenant against incumbrances which gives rights only to the immediate grantee. A assigns the contract and conveys the land to C. B's duty is conditional on adequate assurance that he will receive a deed directly from A.

4. The facts being otherwise as stated in Illustration 3, B defaults and A becomes insolvent because land values are greatly reduced. The assignment and conveyance to C are made as a result of insolvency proceedings in which A is dissolved. In the absence of a showing that an incumbrance exists, C may obtain a decree of specific performance against B conditional on deposit by C of a deed containing a covenant against incumbrances by C only.

5. A, a corporation of State X, has a contract to act as B's exclusive sales agent for two years in a region including State X. A liquidates and assigns the contract and delegates the duties under it to C, a corporation of State Y, a state outside the region. B can properly treat the contract as terminated.

§ 320. Assignment of Conditional Rights

The fact that a right is created by an option contract or is conditional on the performance of a return promise or is otherwise conditional does not prevent its assignment before the condition occurs.

Comment:

a. Offers and option contracts. An offer can be accepted only by a person whom it invites to furnish the consideration, or by his agent. See §§ 29, 52. The power to accept can be exercised by a transferee only if the transferee is such a person. But an option contract, limiting the power to revoke an offer, is treated as creating a right which is assignable like other contractual rights. See § 25. Of course the assignment may be ineffective if it materially varies the obligor's duty, or if it is contrary to the terms of the option contract. See § 317. **Illustrations:**

1. In return for $ 100 paid by A, B promises to convey Blackacre for $ 10,000 on receipt of that amount within thirty days. A assigns the option to C. On C's tender of $ 10,000 within thirty days, B is under a duty to convey Blackacre to C.

2. In return for $ 100 paid by A, B promises to convey Blackacre to A, if A gives notice of acceptance within thirty days, for $ 10,000 of which $ 2,000 is to be paid on conveyance and the balance in four annual installments represented by notes. A assigns the option to C. The assignment is effective, but C's right is conditional on tender of notes signed by A.

b. Conditional right and conditional assignment. Not every conditional right is capable of effective assignment. The fact that

the right is conditional does not prevent effective assignment, but assignment is subject to the same restrictions as in cases of unconditional rights. See § 317. Either the assignment or the right assigned, or both, may be subject to a condition. See § 331. Thus there may be a conditional assignment of a conditional right. **Illustrations:**

3. A holds an insurance policy in which the insurer promises to pay him $ 1000 at the end of twenty years if A makes specified payments of premiums. A can assign his conditional right.

4. A has a contract with B under which certain payments are to be made to A by B under a fixed schedule and other payments are to be made if B's earnings exceed stated amounts. As security for a loan to A by C, A assigns to C A's rights to payments by B, A to retain any payments falling due before default by A under the loan agreement. The assignment is effective according to its terms.

c. Return performance. The parties to an exchange of promises ordinarily contemplate an exchange of performances, and the right of each is often conditional on his own performance. See §§ 231-39. Or the right may be conditional on a performance by another, or on some other event. Such a condition does not prevent assignment by a promisee or beneficiary of his conditional right. Whether or not the return performance is delegable, and whether or not the assignor is under a duty to render it, the assignee's right is subject to the same conditions as was the assignor's. **Illustrations:**

    5. a, A builder, and B, an owner of land, enter into a building contract. A assigns to C payments due or to become due him under the contract. The assignment is effective.

    6. In Illustration 5, B sells the land to D and assigns to D his right to performance by A. The assignment is effective.

    . . .

    d. Delegation and assumption. The question whether a return performance is delegable arises only if the assignor attempts to delegate it. Often an assignor delegates performance to the assignee, and the assignee assumes the assignor's duty to perform, promising the assignor that the delegated performance will be rendered. See §§ 318-19. If the performance is delegable, such an assignment does not of itself materially vary a condition of the right assigned. The assignor remains subject to the same duty as before, and the obligor of the assigned right acquires a new right as an intended beneficiary of the assignee's promise. In effect the assignor becomes a surety for the assignee. **Illustrations:**

    8. A contracts with B, a city, to clean the streets of B weekly for five years in return for monthly payments. A assigns his rights under the contract to C, and C promises A to perform A's duties under it. The assignment is effective. A is still bound to B, but as surety for C.

    9. A, a builder, and B, an owner of land, enter into a building contract. A enters into a contract with C that C will take A's place in the building contract and that A will be freed from his obligation under it. B does not manifest assent or accept any performance from C. A is still bound to B.

    10. A and B contract that B will sell and deliver goods to A in monthly installments for six months and A will pay for them on delivery. A assigns his rights under the contract to C, who assumes the duty of payment. C refuses to accept any goods from B. Both A and C are subject to liability to B, A as surety for C.

    11. After the assignment in Illustration 10, C and B, without consulting A, agree to and do postpone deliveries for three months. A's duty is discharged.

    e. Prospective failure of performance. An assignment is not effective if its effect is to impair materially the obligor's chance of obtaining return performance. See § 317. Thus an assignment accompanied by the assignor's repudiation of his duty to render a return performance may justify the obligor in suspending his own performance, in so changing his position that his duty is discharged, or even in bringing an immediate action for breach. See §§ 329 and 235-38. An attempt to delegate to an assignee a non-delegable performance may have a similar effect. Under Uniform Commercial Code § 2-210, the obligor may treat any assignment of rights under a contract for the sale of goods as creating reasonable grounds for insecurity if the assignor delegates performance. Under § 2-609 of the Code, the obligor may then demand adequate assurance of due performance, and failure of the assignor or assignee to furnish such assurance within a reasonable time has the effect of a repudiation. See also § 251. **Illustrations:**

    12. A and C, partners, contract with B to act as the exclusive distributor of B's product in a specified territory. The contract is to last for one year, and they are to have an option to renew it from year to year. After six months A sells his interest in the contract to C and withdraws from the business. C gives notice of intention to renew, and B refuses to renew. B is not subject to liability to C for the refusal.

    13. A, a corporation, leases railway cars to B by a contract providing that A will keep the cars in repair. A becomes insolvent, and as a result of insolvency proceedings A's rights under the lease contract and A's repair facilities and staff are transferred to C, a solvent corporation, which assumes the duty of repair and assures B of its readiness and willingness to carry out the terms of the lease. A remains in existence under court supervision. B remains obligated by the lease.

§ 321. Assignment of Future Rights

    (1) Except as otherwise provided by statute, an assignment of a right to payment expected to arise out of an existing employment or other continuing business relationship is effective in the same way as an assignment of an existing right.

    (2) Except as otherwise provided by statute and as stated in Subsection (1), a purported

assignment of a right expected to arise under a contract not in existence operates only as a promise to assign the right when it arises and as a power to enforce it.

Comment:

a. Rights under existing contracts. This Section does not apply to rights in existence at the time of assignment. Such rights are assignable under the rules stated in §§ 317 and 320 even though they are conditional or have not matured. For this purpose rights arising under a contract are treated as existing from the moment of its formation, even though the chance is slight that there will ever be a duty of immediate performance. **Illustration:**

    1. A contracts to build a house for B for a stated price. The contract provides that if A performs any work on the house beyond what the specifications require, he shall have compensation therefor, to be determined by the architect. Before any such work has been agreed upon, A, for value, assigns his right to compensation for extra work to C. Subsequently A becomes bankrupt, and still later extra work under the contract is agreed upon and performed. Immediately on completion of the work A assigns the right to compensation to D. The assignment to C is effective and is not defeated by A's bankruptcy or the assignment to D.

 b. Rationale. The conceptual difficulty posed by transfer of a right which does not exist can be met by giving effect to the attempted transfer when the right later arises. Uniform Commercial Code § 9-204, for example, provides that with certain exceptions a security agreement may provide that all obligations covered by the security agreement are to be secured by after-acquired collateral; in an appropriate case, the security interest is said by § 9-203 to "attach" when it becomes enforceable against the debtor with respect to the collateral. The effect given in such cases is limited, not because of any logical necessity, but by virtue of a public policy which seeks to protect the assignor and third parties against transfers which may be improvident or fraudulent. Similar limitations are placed on attempted transfers of future rights in property other than contractual rights. See Restatement of Property § 316; Restatement of Security § 10; Restatement, Second, Trusts § 86; Uniform Commercial Code §§ 2-401, 2-501, 9-203(4), 9-204(2).

c. Continuing relationships. Subsection (1) gives effect to an assignment of a right to compensation for services expected to be rendered in the course of an existing employment, even though there is no contract to continue the employment, and states a similar rule for rights expected to arise out of other continuing business relationships. Even where there is no continuing relationship, a purported assignment of a right expected to arise out of a subsequent transaction may sometimes become a part of the subsequent transaction and take effect as such a part. **Illustrations:**

    2. B employs A from week to week in his factory at a salary of $ 50 a week. A, in the first week of January, assigns to C any salary which he may earn during the last week in that month in his employment by B. The assignment is effective, and if A works for B during that week B will come under a duty to C to pay him $ 50.

    3. B employs A at a stated rate of pay from day to day. A assigns to C whatever A may become entitled to from work done for B during the ensuing month. During the ensuing month A not only earns his regular pay but acquires a right to extra compensation in the course of his employment. The assignment is effective both as to the right to regular pay and the right to extra compensation.

    . . .

d. Other future rights. In the absence of statute, a purported assignment of a future right not within the rule stated in Subsection (1) has only the effect stated in Subsection (2). That effect is that the assignee has enforceable rights against the assignor only to the extent that contractual remedies are available, as in the case of a promise to make a future assignment. See § 330. As against third parties, the purported assignment operates as a grant to the assignee of the assignor's power to enforce the right. But unless specific enforcement against the assignor is appropriate, the grant of power is revocable and can be defeated by the assignor's creditors until it is exercised. **Illustrations:**

    7. A is employed as a teacher for the school year by X, a municipality. A, in the expectation of employment by B, another municipality, for the following school year, assigns to C the salary for the first month of service which A may render for B. A is subsequently employed by B as expected, and A's salary for the first month becomes due. C makes demand upon B for payment of the salary. B refuses and pays A. In the

absence of statute, B has violated no right of C.

8. The facts being otherwise as stated in Illustration 7, D, a creditor of A, garnishes A's salary after it becomes due. C intervenes, claiming the funds as assignee. In the absence of statute, D's claim is prior to C's.

e. Statutory provisions. The limitations imposed by this Section on the assignment of future rights are not the only possible mode of safeguarding the interests of the assignor and third parties. Particularly when a method is provided for giving public notice of the transaction, statutes commonly relax the limitations stated here. For transactions subject to Article 9 of the Uniform Commercial Code, the Code provides a notice-filing system, and § 9-204 gives effect to a security agreement (not involving consumer goods) providing that a security interest shall attach to after-acquired collateral. Such collateral may include contractual rights. Somewhat similar variations from the rules of this Section have been made in other statutes relating to the assignment of accounts receivable. Again, wage-assignment statutes sometimes limit amount and duration, but within the limits set may permit assignment of wages to be earned under future engagements. See Introductory Note to Chapter 15.

§ 322. Contractual Prohibition of Assignment

(1) Unless the circumstances indicate the contrary, a contract term prohibiting assignment of "the contract" bars only the delegation to an assignee of the performance by the assignor of a duty or condition.

(2) A contract term prohibiting assignment of rights under the contract, unless a different intention is manifested,

(a) does not forbid assignment of a right to damages for breach of the whole contract or a right arising out of the assignor's due performance of his entire obligation;

(b) gives the obligor a right to damages for breach of the terms forbidding assignment but does not render the assignment ineffective;

(c) is for the benefit of the obligor, and does not prevent the assignee from acquiring rights against the assignor or the obligor from discharging his duty as if there were no such prohibition.

Comment:

a. Rationale. In the absence of statute or other contrary public policy, the parties to a contract have power to limit the rights created by their agreement. The policy against restraints on the alienation of property has limited application to contractual rights. Compare Restatement of Property §§ 404-17. A term in a contract prohibiting assignment of the rights created may resolve doubts as to whether assignment would materially change the obligor's duty or whether he has a substantial interest in personal performance by the obligee (see §§ 317-19); or it may serve to protect the obligor against conflicting claims and the hazard of double liability (see §§ 338-43). But as assignment has become a common practice, the policy which limits the validity of restraints on alienation has been applied to the construction of contractual terms open to two or more possible constructions. Compare Restatement of Property §§ 418-23.

b. Ineffective terms. In some circumstances where contractual prohibitions of assignment are regularly limited by construction, explicit contractual provision would not change the result. Where a right to the payment of money is fully earned by performance, for example, a provision that an attempt to assign forfeits the right may be invalid as a contractual penalty. See § 356. If there is no forfeiture, and the obligee joins in demanding payment to the assignee, a contractual prohibition which serves no legitimate interest of the obligor is disregarded. Uniform Commercial Code §§ 2-210 and 9-318 render contractual prohibitions ineffective in additional circumstances, and in some situations a prohibition is invalid as a restraint on alienation aside from statute. See Uniform Commercial Code § 9-311. **Illustrations:**

1. A holds a policy of industrial insurance issued to him by the B Insurance Company. After lapse for failure to pay premiums, B refuses to pay the "cash surrender value" provided for in the policy. A and others similarly situated assign their claims to C for collection. The as-

signment is effective without regard to any contractual prohibition of assignment.

2. A and B contract for the sale of land by B to A. A fully performs the contract, becomes entitled to specific performance on B's refusal to convey the land, and then assigns his rights to C. C is entitled to specific performance against B without regard to any contractual prohibition of assignment. See Restatement of Property § 416.

c. Construction. The rules stated in this Section do not exhaust the factors to be taken into account in construing and applying a prohibition against assignment. "Not transferable" has a clear meaning in a theatre ticket; in a certificate of deposit the same words may refer to negotiability rather than assignability. Where there is a promise not to assign but no provision that an assignment is ineffective, the question whether breach of the promise discharges the obligor's duty depends on all the circumstances. See §§ 237, 241.

d. Consent of the obligor. Ordinarily a contractual prohibition of assignment is for the benefit of the obligor. In such cases third parties cannot assert the invalidity of a prohibited assignment if the obligor makes no objection.

Where, however, the prohibition is not solely for the benefit of the obligor, waiver by the obligor may not validate the assignment. The validity of restraints on alienation in such cases is governed by considerations similar to those governing the validity of spendthrift trusts. See Restatement, Second, Trusts §§ 153-57. **Illustrations:**

3. B contracts to transfer land to A on payment of $ 5000. The contract provides that A shall not assign his right. A assigns his right to C. B, on receiving $ 5000 from C, conveys the land to him. B's duty under his contract with A is discharged.

4. A Manufacturing Company contracts with B Insurance Company for group insurance on the lives of A's employees. The policy and certificates issued under it to individual employees limit the class of permitted beneficiaries, permit the employee to change the beneficiary, forbid irrevocable designation of a beneficiary, and provide that the certificate is not assignable. A certificate is issued to C, a widower, who designates his son D as beneficiary and delivers the certificate to D as a gift. Later C remarries and designates his second wife E as beneficiary. On C's death B interpleads D and E, paying the insurance money into court. E is entitled to the fund.

§ 323. Obligor's Assent to Assignment or Delegation

(1) A term of a contract manifesting an obligor's assent to the future assignment of a right or an obligee's assent to the future delegation of the performance of a duty or condition is effective despite any subsequent objection.

(2) A manifestation of such assent after the formation of a contract is similarly effective if made for consideration or in circumstances in which a promise would be binding without consideration, or if a material change of position takes place in reliance on the manifestation.

Comment:

a. Effect of assent. The assent of the obligor is not ordinarily necessary to make an assignment effective. But his assent may operate to preclude objection based on a change in his duty, burden or risk or in his chance of obtaining return performance. See § 317. It may permit a separate action by a partial assignee. See § 326. It may be an offer of a new contract by novation, or the acceptance of an offer of novation, and may thus terminate the assignor's power to revoke a gratuitous assignment (see § 332), or may discharge or modify a duty of the assignor or a condition of the right assigned (see §§ 318-19). Which of these effects is produced depends on the circumstances and the scope of the assent manifested.

b. Promises to or by "assigns." Contracts often refer to the "assigns" of one or both parties. A purported promise by a promisor "and his assigns" does not mean that the promisor can terminate his duty by making an assignment, nor does it of itself show an assumption of duties by any assignee. It tends to indicate that the promised performance is not personal, just as a promise to a promisee "and his assigns" tends to indicate that the promisor is willing to render performance to an assignee. Whether there is a manifestation of assent to assignment or delegation, however, depends on the interpretation of the contract as a whole. Notwithstanding references to "assigns," other terms and the circumstances may show that the assent is limited or even that there is no assent. **Illustration:**

>   1. A and C, partners, contract with B to act as exclusive distributor of B's product in a specified territory. The terms of the contract show that B reposes personal trust and confidence in both A and C. A term, "This agreement shall bind and benefit the respective successors and assigns of the parties hereto," may be read as inapplicable to an assignment by A or C which delegates performance unless B makes a further manifestation of assent.

c. Assent subsequent to contract. Assent to assignment or delegation may be manifested after the formation of a contract, and may have effects similar to those of a term in the contract. Indeed, such assent may be a practical construction of the contract, relevant to determine its meaning. See Uniform Commercial Code § 2-208. In addition, subsequent assent may waive a prohibition contained in the contract. Unless consideration is given or unless the circumstances are such as to make a new promise binding without consideration, however, such a manifestation of assent can be withdrawn before it has been acted on. See §§ 84, 89, 90. Assent to assignment and delegation, even though irrevocable, does not of itself establish a novation discharging duties of the assignor. **Illustrations:**

>   2. A and B enter into a contract binding A personally to do some delicate cabinet work. A assigns his rights and delegates performance of his duties to C. On being informed of this, B agrees with C in consideration of C's promise to do the work that B will accept C's work, if properly done, instead of the performance promised by A. Later without cause B refuses to allow C to proceed with the work, though C is ready to do so, and makes demand on A that A perform. A refuses. C can recover damages from B and B cannot recover from A.
>
>   3. A contracts to employ B in A's business for one year at a specified salary. A contemplates selling the business, and the contract provides that the contract may be transferred with the business, but B is not informed of the identity of the purchaser. A month later A sells the business to C and assigns his rights and delegates his duties under the contract to C, who agrees to assume A's duties. After the sale B works for C and is paid by C for two weeks. C then discharges B because B refuses to accept a reduction in salary. There is a breach of contract by A as well as C.

§ 324. Mode of Assignment in General

It is essential to an assignment of a right that the obligee manifest an intention to transfer the right to another person without further action or manifestation of intention by the obligee. The manifestation may be made to the other or to a third person on his behalf and, except as provided by statute or by contract, may be made either orally or by a writing.

Comment:

a. Requisites of assignment. Assignment requires an assignable right. See § 317. Aside from statute, the assignor of such a right may make an assignment by manifestation of intention without any particular formality. A manifestation of intention or a promise to make a transfer in the future is not an assignment, however. See § 330. Where the manifestation is made to a third person on behalf of the assignee, the assignment may not take effect unless there is an acceptance by the assignee; or it may take effect subject to disclaimer by the assignee. See § 327. Lack of formality may mean that the assignment is revocable (see § 332), or that it is subject to defenses or claims of the obligor which accrue subsequently (see §§ 336, 338), or that it can be defeated by creditors of the assignor or by subsequent assignees of the same right (see §§ 341, 342).

b. Statutory formalities: the Statute of Frauds. The Statute of Frauds is the subject of Chapter 5 of this Restatement. Section 4 of the Uniform Sales Act included a Statute of Frauds for "a contract to sell or a sale of any . . . choses in action of the value of five hundred dollars or upwards." The Uniform Commercial Code substitutes a general provision that "a contract for the sale of personal property is not enforceable by way of action or defense beyond five thousand dollars in amount or value of remedy" in the absence of a writing, with exceptions for the sale of goods or investment securities and for "security agreements," which are covered by more specific sections. Uniform

Commercial Code § 1-206. Such provisions prevent enforcement against an assignor unless there is a memorandum in writing or some substitute formality, but under the rule stated in § 144 of this Restatement they cannot ordinarily be asserted by third persons, including the obligor of an assigned right. Notwithstanding non-compliance with the Statute, therefore, the assignment is effective against the obligor. Moreover, the obligor discharges his duty by performing in accordance with the assignment, and the assignee can keep the benefit of the performance.

　　c. Security agreements; wage assignments. Uniform Commercial Code § 9-203 provides that with stated exceptions "a security interest is not enforceable against the debtor or third parties" unless the collateral is in the possession of the secured party or the debtor has signed a security agreement. This provision applies not only where the "debtor" assigns contractual rights as security for an obligation, but also where the "debtor" is a "seller of accounts or chattel paper." §§ 1-201(37), 9-102(1)(b), 9-105(1)(d); see the Statutory Note at the beginning of this Chapter and the Reporter's Note to § 317. Transactions subject to this provision are not enforceable against anyone unless the statutory formalities are met. Statutes regulating assignments of wages may go further and deny all effect to a non-complying assignment.

§ 325. Order as Assignment

　　(1) A written order drawn upon an obligor and signed and delivered to another person by the obligee is an assignment if it is conditional on the existence of a duty of the drawee to the drawer to comply with the order and the drawer manifests an intention that a person other than the drawer is to retain the performance.

　　(2) An order which directs the drawee to render a performance without reference to any duty of the drawee is not of itself an assignment, even though the drawee is under a duty to the drawer to comply with the order and even though the order indicates a particular account to be debited or any other fund or source from which reimbursement is expected.

Comment:

　　a. Order on particular fund. The principal application of Subsection (1) is to rights to the payment of money, but it also applies to other rights. The creditor typically delivers to the assignee a written instrument addressed to the debtor, directing the debtor to pay all or part of the debt to the assignee. The instrument may be delivered instead to some other person on the assignee's behalf. See § 327. It may or may not indicate the ultimate disposition of the proceeds. Facts aside from the instrument may show that the recipient is to act as the creditor's agent rather than as assignee. An order communicated only to the debtor is not an assignment unless there is some additional manifestation of intention to assign. **Illustrations:**

　　1. A delivers to C the following writing addressed to B, "Pay C for his own use $ 100 out of the amount you owe me." The writing is an assignment.

　　2. A gives C, acting as A's agent, an order to collect from B whatever B owes A. The order is not an assignment.

　　3. A writes to B, "Please pay to C the balance due me." This is insufficient to establish an assignment or to give B notice of an assignment. But the letter would be an effective assignment if delivered to C to pay or secure a debt owed by A to C.

　　b. Drafts and delivery orders. A check or other draft is an unconditional order for the payment of money meeting formal requisites of certainty in amount and time of payment. If payable to order or bearer, it is negotiable; whether or not negotiable, it is not of itself an assignment of a right against the drawee, and the drawee is not liable on the instrument until he accepts it. Additional facts may show that an assignment is intended, and the instrument may then be the means by which the assignment is effected. See Uniform Commercial Code §§ 3-104, 3-409, 3-805. Similar principles apply to unaccepted orders for the delivery of goods, whether or not conditional, if in negotiable form. See Uniform Commercial Code §§ 7-502, 7-503, 7-504. They also apply to any order which is treated as chargeable against the general credit of the drawer and independent of any particular fund or obligation. As to what terms render an order conditional for this purpose, see Uniform Commercial Code § 3-105. **Illustrations:**

4. A draws and delivers to C for value either a negotiable or a non-negotiable check upon his bank, B, payable to C, for the full amount of A's balance, or for part of it. B dishonors the check in violation of its duty to A. C has no right against B.

5. In Illustration 4, B accepts the check by signing a certification on its face and redelivering it to C. There is a novation substituting C for A as B's creditor to the amount of the check.

. . .

§ 326. Partial Assignment

(1) Except as stated in Subsection (2), an assignment of a part of a right, whether the part is specified as a fraction, as an amount, or otherwise, is operative as to that part to the same extent and in the same manner as if the part had been a separate right.

(2) If the obligor has not contracted to perform separately the assigned part of a right, no legal proceeding can be maintained by the assignor or assignee against the obligor over his objection, unless all the persons entitled to the promised performance are joined in the proceeding, or unless joinder is not feasible and it is equitable to proceed without joinder.

Comment:

a. Other types of divided interests. The partial assignment covered by this Section is to be distinguished from other transactions creating divided interests in a contractual right: (1) A conditional assignment leaves the assignor with an interest if the condition is not met. (2) A total assignment may empower the assignee to enforce the entire right wholly or partially for the benefit of the assignor or others. Examples are assignment to secure an obligation and assignment to a trustee. (3) The obligee may promise to enforce the right wholly or partially for the benefit of others, or to pay to others all or part of any proceeds collected. Such a promise may amount to a declaration of trust or may create an equitable interest in the promisee by virtue of a right to specific performance of the promise.

b. Partial assignment. The distinguishing feature of a partial assignment is a manifestation of intention to make an immediate transfer of part but not all of the assignor's right, and to confer on the assignee a direct right against the obligor to the performance of that part. Historically, the right of a partial assignee could be enforced only by a suit in a court of equity, and it was therefore sometimes described as an "equitable" right. But the right of a total assignee also had historically an "equitable" character. Under the rule stated in Subsection (1), a partial assignment and a total assignment are equally effective, subject to the protection of the obligor under the rule stated in Subsection (2). **Illustrations:**

1. B owes A $ 100. A assigns $ 25 to C. With knowledge of the assignment, B pays the entire debt to A. B's duty to C is not discharged. See § 338.

2. B owes A $ 100. A assigns $ 25 to C, and later assigns the entire debt to D, who pays value without notice of the assignment to C. C has the same priority as to the $ 25 assigned to him as if the entire debt had been assigned to him. See § 342.

. . .

§ 327. Acceptance or Disclaimer by the Assignee

(1) A manifestation of assent by an assignee to the assignment is essential to make it effective unless

(a) a third person gives consideration for the assignment, or

(b) the assignment is irrevocable by virtue of the delivery of a writing to a third person.

(2) An assignee who has not manifested assent to an assignment may, within a reasonable time after learning of its existence and terms, render it inoperative from the beginning by disclaimer.

Comment:

a. Necessity of acceptance. Sale of a contractual right, like sale of goods, requires a bargain in which there is a manifestation of mutual assent to the exchange. Ordinarily the person who furnishes the consideration is the transferee of the right sold, but where consideration is given by one person for an assignment to another, it is not necessary that the assignee know of the bargain or assent to it. Compare §§ 17, 71(2). Where there is no bargain, an irrevocable gift can be made without the assent of the donee by the delivery of a written assignment or a symbolic or evidentiary writing to a third person. Compare §§ 104, 306; Restatement, Second, Trusts §§ 35, 36. The circumstances in which such a delivery makes the assignment irrevocable are stated in § 332. **Illustrations:**

1. A has a contractual right against D. For consideration received from B, A assigns the right to B's son C. C has no knowledge of the assignment. The assignment is effective immediately, subject to C's power of disclaimer.

2. A delivers his savings bank book to B, saying "I deliver this book to you as a gift to C." C has no knowledge of the gift. An attempted revocation by A before C learns of the gift is ineffective.

b. Disclaimer. As in other cases of rights created without the assent of the obligee, an assignee is entitled to reject the right, whether or not there is a related burden. Compare §§ 38, 104, 306. No particular formality is required for disclaimer, and its usual effect is the same as if no assignment had been made. But it cannot make tortious acts lawful when done, and in some cases it may give rise to a right of restitution. See Comment *a* to § 306. The effect of intervening claims of third persons is beyond the scope of this Restatement. **Illustration:**

3. A, the payee of a negotiable or non-negotiable note or certificate of deposit, delivers it to B without indorsement as a gift to C, who has no knowledge of the delivery. Upon learning of the gift C refuses it. A is the owner of the note or certificate.

§ 328. Interpretation of Words of Assignment; Effect of Acceptance of Assignment

(1) Unless the language or the circumstances indicate the contrary, as in an assignment for security, an assignment of "the contract" or of "all my rights under the contract" or an assignment in similar general terms is an assignment of the assignor's rights and a delegation of his unperformed duties under the contract.

(2) Unless the language or the circumstances indicate the contrary, the acceptance by an assignee of such an assignment operates as a promise to the assignor to perform the assignor's unperformed duties, and the obligor of the assigned rights is an intended beneficiary of the promise.

CAVEAT: Caveat: The Institute expresses no opinion as to whether the rule stated in Subsection (2) applies to an assignment by a purchaser of his rights under a contract for the sale of land.

Comment:

a. "Assignment" of duty. A duty cannot be "assigned" in the sense in which "assignment" is used in this Chapter. The parties to an assignment, however, may not distinguish between assignment of rights and delegation of duties. A purported "assignment" of duties may simply manifest an intention that the assignee shall be substituted for the assignor. Such an intention is not completely effective unless the obligor of the assigned right joins in a novation, but the rules of this Section give as full effect as can be given without the obligor's assent. As to contracts for the sale of goods, see Uniform Commercial Code § 2-210. **Illustration:**

1. A, an oil company, has a contract to sell and deliver oil to B. A delivers to C, another oil company, a writing assigning to C "the contract" or "all A's rights and duties under the contract." C is under a duty to B to deliver the oil called for by the contract, and A is surety for C.

b. Contrary agreement; assignment for security. This Section states rules of presumptive interpretation which yield to a manifestation of a different intention. In particular delegation and assumption of the assignor's duties is not ordinarily implied where the contract calls for personal performance by the assignor. Again, an assignment as security does not ordinarily delegate performance to the secured party, and the secured party does not assume the assignor's duties. See Uniform Commercial Code §§ 2-210, 9-317. Under §§ 9-102 and 9-104 of the Code a sale of "accounts or chattel paper" is treated as a secured transaction unless it is part of the sale of a business or unless the assignee is to perform the contract. The quoted terms are limited by definitions in §§ 9-105 and 9-106 to "monetary obligations" or "rights to payment." See Reporter's Note to § 317. **Illustrations:**

2. In Illustration 1, A assigns "the contract" or "all A's rights under the contract" to C, a financial institution. Delivery of the oil is not delegated to C, and C is under no duty to deliver oil.

3. A sells and delivers an automobile to B, the price to be paid in installments, and assigns to C for value "all A's rights under the contract." After B has made all the payments, the automobile is discovered to have been stolen and is retaken by the owner. C is not liable to B for breach of warranty of title; A is.

. . .

§ 329. Repudiation by Assignor and Novation with Assignee

(1) The legal effect of a repudiation by an assignor of his duty to the obligor of the assigned right is not limited by the fact that the assignee is a competent person and has promised to perform the duty.

(2) If the obligor, with knowledge of such a repudiation, accepts any performance from the assignee without reserving his rights against the assignor, a novation arises by which the duty of the assignor is discharged and a similar duty of the assignee is substituted.

Comment:

a. Repudiation and its effects. In some cases a repudiation by one party to a contract discharges the duty of the other party; in some cases it requires the other to treat as total a breach which might otherwise be partial, or it may itself be a total breach. See § 253; Uniform Commercial Code § 2-610. For these purposes repudiation includes a positive statement by an assignor that he will not or cannot substantially perform his duties, or any voluntary affirmative action which renders substantial performance apparently impossible. In some circumstances a statement that he doubts whether he will substantially perform, or that he takes no responsibility for performance, or even a failure to give adequate assurance of performance may have a similar effect. See §§ 250-51.

b. Scope of obligor's assent. The assignment of a contractual right and delegation to the assignee of the assignor's duty is often a matter of course. The obligor of the assigned right may then have a right to withhold performance until he receives adequate assurance of performance by the assignee. Section 251. Failure to demand such assurance and acceptance of performance by the assignee manifest the obligor's assent to the assignment and delegation (see § 323), but not to the discharge of the assignor's duty. However, when the obligor knows that the delegating assignor has repudiated his duty he has reason to know that the performance of the assignee is offered by way of novation, and his silent acceptance of the performance operates as acceptance of the offer of novation. Compare § 69. **Illustrations:**

1. A is under a contract with B to build a house for $ 10,000. A assigns his rights under the contract to C, who agrees to assume A's duty to build the house. B is informed of the assignment and assumption, and makes no objection as C partly performs. A remains bound to B as surety for C's performance.

2. In Illustration 1, A withdraws from the construction business and informs B that he takes no further responsibility for C's performance. B makes no objection and C proceeds with the work. A is discharged.

c. Reservation of rights. The obligor of an assigned right cannot be forced to assent to a repudiation by the assignor or to an offer of a substituted contract with the assignee. To avoid the implication that his silence gives assent, he must manifest either to the assignor or to the assignee his intention to retain unimpaired his rights against the assignor, but no particular form is required. See Uniform Commercial Code §§ 1-207, 3-606; § 281. If the terms of the assignment so provide, the delegation or assumption of duty may be defeated in such a case, and the repudiation may be retracted before it has been acted on. See Uniform Commercial Code § 2-611. Where the assignee continues performance, the reservation of rights by the obligor means that the assignor, if compelled to pay for the assignee's default, will have a right over against the assignee. **Illustration:**

3. In Illustration 2, on being informed of A's repudiation, B notifies A or C that further performance is "without prejudice." A is not discharged.

§ 330. Contracts to Assign in the Future, or to Transfer Proceeds to Be Received

(1) A contract to make a future assignment of a right, or to transfer proceeds to be received in the future by the promisor, is not an assignment.

(2) Except as provided by statute, the effect of such a contract on the rights and duties of the obligor and third persons is determined by the rules relating to specific performance of contracts.

Comment:

a. Contract to assign. As to a right in existence, it is a question of interpretation whether the obligee manifests an intention to make a present transfer or only an intention to bind himself to make a future transfer. A present assignment may be coupled with a promise to provide future evidence of the transfer, but there is no assignment if the transfer is not to take place until the obligee acts further. Whether or not there is a present assignment, the assignee may be empowered to enforce the right. Such a power is ordinarily fairly implied when there is a purported present assignment of a future right, and once the right arises in such a case the situation is substantially similar to that created by a revocable assignment. See § 321. **Illustration:**

1. A holds a promissory note made by B and secured by a mortgage on Blackacre. A enters into a written agreement with C which recites that A has sold the note and mortgage to C for a price payable in installments and that A is to hold the note and mortgage as security for the price and to indorse the note and execute an assignment of the mortgage when the price is paid. There is a present assignment to C, subject to the security interest retained by A.

b. Contract to transfer proceeds. A promise by an obligee that he will collect money due him and pay over all or part of it to the promisee is not an assignment. The same rule applies to a promise to transfer proceeds other than money. Thus if a purchaser under a contract for the sale of land contracts to resell the land, there is a subcontract rather than an assignment of the original contract. But if the prospective transferee is authorized to receive performance on behalf of the obligee-transferor and to retain it, there may be an assignment of the contractual right. The test is whether an intention is manifested to transfer present ownership of the right. **Illustrations:**

2. A sells property to B and authorizes B to pay the price to X, a bank, on A's behalf. Later A borrows money from C and agrees to repay C out of the money received from B. A then instructs X to hold for the account of A and C all sums received from B, stating "C does not claim this money as owner, but you are to hold it until you have been advised in writing by both parties." There is no assignment to C.

3. A, the holder of a note payable by B, delivers it to C, A's attorney, for collection, agreeing that C is co-owner of the claim to the extent of half of what he collects. C is a partial assignee of the right against B.

c. Contracts specifically enforceable. In some circumstances a contract to assign or a contract to transfer proceeds may create a right in the promisee very similar to that of an assignee. Even though there is no present assignment, the promisee may have a right to specific performance of the promise. If it can be enforced against third parties, such a right resembles that of an assignee, and it is sometimes referred to as an "equitable assignment" or "equitable lien." In general the remedy of specific performance is available if the promisee's remedy in damages would be inadequate. See §§ 359, 360. In particular, specific performance is decreed if the promise is one to transfer an interest in specific land or to transfer a specified right as security for an obligation. **Illustrations:**

4. A, a real estate broker, is employed by B to find a purchaser for B's land. In consideration of C's help in finding a purchaser, A promises to pay C one-half of the commission earned. The land is sold and the commission earned. C has no right against B.

5. B, the owner of a parcel of land, contracts to sell the parcel to A. A contracts to assign the contract to C or to convey the parcel to C. Even though C is not an assignee, C can sue A and B to compel A to assert for C's benefit A's right to specific performance by B.

. . .

d. After-acquired rights. In general a contract to give security is specifically enforceable as between the parties even as to rights arising after the contract is made. By statute or decision, however, an exception has been made for contracts to assign wages under future employments. See § 321. And in some states, on the analogy of rules applied to mortgages of after-acquired tangible property, an "equitable assignment" of rights not in existence is subordinate to the claims of creditors of the assignor whose rights attach after the rights have arisen and before the assignor has made a present assignment. In the absence of statutory provision for public notice, the rights of the promisee are inferior to those of a subsequent good faith purchaser for value without notice of the prior contract. **Illustrations:**

7. A "assigns" to C as security for a loan "all the book debts due and owing or which may during the continuance of this security become due and owing" to A. B subsequently becomes indebted to A on a contract made after the "assignment," and thereafter a creditor of A garnishes the debt. In the absence of a statute, C is entitled to the debt to the exclusion of the creditor.

8. The facts being otherwise as stated in Illustration 7, A assigns the debt to D after it arises. D takes the assignment in good faith as a purchaser for value, without notice of the "assignment" to C. In the absence of statute, D is entitled to the debt to the exclusion of C.

e. The Uniform Commercial Code. The provisions of Article 9 of the Uniform Commercial Code apply to "accounts" and "general intangibles," but not to insurance, bank accounts or wages. See Introductory Note to this Chapter. Under § 9-204(1) a security agreement "may provide that any or all obligations covered by the security agreement are to be secured by after-acquired collateral." When a security interest "attaches" is governed by § 9-203, "unless explicit agreement postpones the time of attaching." § 9-203(2). The security interest is subordinate to the rights of creditors of the debtor and purchasers from him if it is unperfected. See § 9-301. But if the filing provisions of the Code have been complied with beforehand, the security interest is perfected when it attaches. See § 9-303.

§ 331. Partially Effective Assignments

An assignment may be conditional, revocable, or voidable by the assignor, or unenforceable by virtue of a Statute of Frauds.

Comment:

a. Assignor's power to destroy assignee's right. In this Restatement "assignment" is used to refer to an act which extinguishes in whole or in part the assignor's right and creates a similar right in the assignee. See §§ 317, 324. On proof of an unconditional assignment, the assignee can recover on an assigned right; the assignor cannot. The assignor may be entitled to revoke the assignment because it is gratuitous or by virtue of a reserved power, or the assignment may be voidable for fraud or other invalidating cause. Even if destruction of the assignee's right is a violation of the assignor's duty, he retains by virtue of his former ownership certain powers which may have that effect. See §§ 338, 342.

b. Conditional assignment; conditional and future rights. A conditional assignment does not wholly extinguish the assignor's right until the condition occurs. A conditional right may be effectively assigned either conditionally or unconditionally; a conditional assignment of a conditional right means that the rights of the assignee and assignor are both subject to one condition and that the right of the assignee is subject to an additional condition. See § 323. Strictly there cannot be an effective assignment of a right not yet in existence, but after the right arises the assignment may for some purposes be treated as if it had been effective when made. See §§ 321, 330. **Illustration:**

1. A has a right to $ 400 against B and assigns the right to C in payment for an automobile on condition that the car run 1,000 miles without needing repairs. The assignment is conditional and is effective according to its terms. If the car does not run 1,000 miles without needing repairs, the right to the $ 400 belongs to A, not to C.

§ 332. Revocability of Gratuitous Assignments

(1) Unless a contrary intention is manifested, a gratuitous assignment is irrevocable if

(a) the assignment is in a writing either signed or under seal that is delivered by the assignor; or

(b) the assignment is accompanied by delivery of a writing of a type customarily accepted as a symbol or as evidence of the right assigned.

(2) Except as stated in this Section, a gratuitous assignment is revocable and the right of the assignee is terminated by the assignor's death or incapacity, by a subsequent assignment by the assignor, or by notification from the assignor received by the assignee or by the obligor.

(3) A gratuitous assignment ceases to be revocable to the extent that before the assignee's right is terminated he obtains

(a) payment or satisfaction of the obligation, or

(b) judgment against the obligor, or

(c) a new contract of the obligor by novation.

(4) A gratuitous assignment is irrevocable to the extent necessary to avoid injustice where the assignor should reasonably expect the assignment to induce action or forbearance by the assignee or a subassignee and the assignment does induce such action or forbearance.

(5) An assignment is gratuitous unless it is given or taken

(a) in exchange for a performance or return promise that would be consideration for a promise; or

(b) as security for or in total or partial satisfaction of a pre-existing debt or other obligation.

Comment:

a. Historical note. Before the assignment of a contractual right was recognized as effective by common-law courts, an assignment was treated as a power of attorney. Exercise of the power to create a new legal right in the assignee was recognized as effective by the common-law courts in the seventeenth century. But in the event of revocation by the assignor before the power was exercised, the assignee's right was enforceable only by a court of equity. See the Introductory Note to this Chapter. A power of attorney requires no consideration, but the maxim that equity will not aid a volunteer precluded relief to a gratuitous assignee in the event of revocation before the power was exercised. In modern times an assignment is recognized as an effective conveyance without regard to the distinction between law and equity. But a gratuitous conveyance remains revocable unless the formal requisites of a valid gift are met. The owner of a contractual right, like the owner of a chattel, can effectively and irrevocably declare himself trustee of it without consideration or formality, but an attempted informal gift which is ineffective does not create a trust. See Restatement, Second, Trusts §§ 28, 31. In certain cases, however, where the donor has died believing he has made an effective gratuitous conveyance to a natural object of his bounty, a constructive trust for the intended donee may arise. See Restatement of Restitution § 164

. *b. Formal requisites of gift; written assignment.* Historically, a gift of a chattel could be made either by delivery of the chattel or by delivery of a deed of gift under seal. This rule has been extended by analogy to gifts of intangible personal property, including contractual rights. As the seal has come to seem archaic, the delivery of a signed written assignment has by statute or decision been given the same effect. The assignment may be delivered either conditionally or unconditionally, and either to the donee or to a third person on his behalf. Compare §§ 101-103. The writing must of course fully manifest an intention to make a present transfer rather than to promise or authorize a future transfer. Compare §§ 325, 330. As to investment securities, Uniform Commercial Code § 8-309 requires delivery of a certificated security, and an attempted transfer without delivery amounts only to a promise to transfer.

Illustrations:

1. B owes A four million dollars. A signs, seals and delivers to C a deed of gift of the debt to the extent of one million dollars. There is an effective and irrevocable assignment.

2. B owes A $ 70,000 represented by a promissory note payable to the order of A in installments. A signs and delivers to C, his sister, a written instrument not under seal reciting that in consideration of love and affection for C A gives and assigns to C fifty per cent of the note, reserving all installments due or paid during A's life. The note is retained in A's possession. The gift is effective and irrevocable.

. . .

c. Delivery of a symbolic writing. In the regular course of business certain writings are treated as adequately evidencing that a person in possession of the writing is entitled to receive performance and to dispose of the right and its proceeds. See Uniform Commercial Code § 1-201(15), defining "document of title," § 3-104, defining certain types of negotiable instrument, § 8-102, defining "security," § 9-105(1)(b), defining "chattel paper." In some circumstances the right to performance is conditional on exhibition or surrender of such a writing. See Uniform Commercial Code § 3-505 (negotiable instrument), § 5-116 (letter of credit), § 7-403(3) (negotiable document of title), § 8-401 (certificated security). A gift of a right embodied in such a writing may be made by delivery in accordance with rules governing gifts of chattels by delivery. **Illustration:**

4. A gratuitously delivers to B a savings bank book, a nonnegotiable promissory note, a life insurance policy and a registered bond with the expressed intent of making B the owner of the rights of which these documents are evidence. The delivery operates as an effective and irrevocable assignment of both the rights and the documents.

d. Delivery of an evidentiary writing. Even though a right is not conditional on exhibition or surrender of a document, it may be so integrated in a writing that contradictory terms of prior agreements and contemporaneous oral agreements are superseded. See §§ 213, 216; Uniform Commercial Code § 2-202. The "best evidence" or original document rule, permitting secondary evidence to prove the contents of a writing only when an explanation is given for nonproduction of the original, has been largely eviscerated by modern evidence practice. See, e.g., Fed. R. Evidence 1001-04. Even though the traditional rule does not apply, an evidentiary writing may be of such importance in the enforcement of the right that its delivery is an appropriate formality to validate a gift of the right. Accordingly, the rule validating a gift by delivery of an essential instrument has been extended to some evidentiary writings. The test is whether the writing is of a type customarily accepted as evidence of the right. **Illustrations:**

5. A makes a written contract with B to convey land to B for $ 25,000. Later A gratuitously delivers to C the written contract, signed by B, with the expressed intent of making C the owner of the right to the purchase money. The gift is effective and irrevocable.

6. A deposits a draft with B bank for collection and is given a receipt signed by B which describes the draft and recites that it is "received from A for collection." A writes on the receipt, "Pay this to C," signs his name, and delivers the receipt to C with the expressed intent of making a gift to C of the proceeds of the draft. The gift is effective and irrevocable.

7. A has a checking account in B bank and delivers the bank pass book to C with the expressed intent of making a gift to C of the balance in the account. The gift is revocable in view of the customary practice of making withdrawals without notation in the pass book, even though A has in fact made no such withdrawals.

8. A deposits various sums of money with B, and keeps a list of the amounts on a sheet of paper. A delivers the list, bearing a total and a date but no signature or other writing, to C with the expressed intent of making a gift to C of the amount due. The gift is revocable.

e. What constitutes delivery. Where a gift of a contractual right by delivery of a symbolic or evidentiary writing is in issue, the concept of delivery is the same as that employed with respect to gifts of tangible personal property. Delivery may be made either conditionally or unconditionally, and either to the donee or to a third person on his behalf. Compare §§ 101-03. A writing in the possession of a third person may be delivered by means of a symbolic or evidentiary writing or by means of a token or symbol such as a key to a safe deposit box. Or the third person may agree to hold on behalf of the donee. A gift of a writing already in the possession of the donee for another purpose may be made by mere oral manifestation of intention. Redelivery to the donor for safekeeping does not defeat the delivery. Where a different rule is applied to gifts of chattels, it is applied equally to gifts of contractual rights by delivery: thus if it is held that a gift *causa mortis* by mere spoken words is ineffective in the case of a chattel in the donee's possession, the same rule is applied to a gift of a contractual writing.

f. Effect of acts subsequent to assignment. A gratuitous assignment, even though revocable, may authorize the assignee to take action which will complete the gift. If, pursuant to the authority given, the assignee obtains performance or other satisfaction from the obligor or a judgment against the obligor or a new contract by novation, the assignor's power of revocation terminates and the assignee may keep for his own benefit what he has acquired. Whatever he obtains after revocation can be recovered from him by the assignor. Revocation is also precluded to the extent that it would be unjust in view of a material change of position in reliance on the assignment. Compare § 90. **Illustration:**

> 9. A draws a check on his account in B bank payable to the order of C and delivers it to C with the expressed intent of making a gift to C of part of the account. C negotiates the check to D for value, or obtains payment from B. Meanwhile A dies. C can retain what he received before the death, but A's personal representative can recover what C received thereafter.

. . .

h. Gratuitous assignment. Whether an assignment is gratuitous for the purposes of the rules stated in this Section is not necessarily the same question as whether the assignment is for value so as to constitute the assignee a bona fide purchaser for value within such rules as that stated in § 342. See Comment *c* to § 338. For example, where an assignment is made in exchange for a return promise which would be consideration under the rule stated in § 75, the assignment is not gratuitous, whether or not the promise is value under the rules stated in Restatement, Second, Trusts § 302. A new loan or other obligation is consideration for this purpose if bargained for and given in exchange for the assignment. Moreover, an assignment as security for or in total or partial satisfaction of a pre-existing obligation is not gratuitous, whether or not there is consideration under § 73 or value under Restatement, Second, Trusts § 304 and Restatement of Restitution § 173. Such an assignment is not gratuitous even if the preexisting obligation is unenforceable, to the extent that in the circumstances a promise to pay the obligation would be binding under §§ 82-85.

§ 333. Warranties of an Assignor

(1) Unless a contrary intention is manifested, one who assigns or purports to assign a right by assignment under seal or for value warrants to the assignee

(a) that he will do nothing to defeat or impair the value of the assignment and has no knowledge of any fact which would do so;

(b) that the right, as assigned, actually exists and is subject to no limitations or defenses good against the assignor other than those stated or apparent at the time of the assignment;

(c) that any writing evidencing the right which is delivered to the assignee or exhibited to him to induce him to accept the assignment is genuine and what it purports to be.

(2) An assignment does not of itself operate as a warranty that the obligor is solvent or that he will perform his obligation.

(3) An assignor is bound by affirmations and promises to the assignee with reference to the right assigned in the same way and to the same extent that one who transfers goods is bound in like circumstances.

(4) An assignment of a right to a sub-assignee does not operate as an assignment of the assignee's rights under his assignor's warranties unless an intention is manifested to assign the rights under the warranties.

Comment:

a. Implied warranties. The warranties of an assignor of a contractual right arise by operation by law and are similar to those of one who transfers a negotiable instrument without indorsement or who transfers a document of title or investment security. See Uniform Commercial Code §§ 3-417, 7-507, 8-306. Unlike an indorser of commercial paper or a collecting bank or its customer, an assignor is not liable for defaults of the obligor and does not warrant his solvency. Compare Uniform Commercial Code §§ 3-414, 4-207 with § 7-505 (document of title), § 8-308(9) (certificated investment security). An assignor does warrant his lack of knowledge of facts and his future abstention from conduct which would impair the value of the assigned right.

Illustrations:

1. A has a right against B and assigns it for value to C. Thereafter A gives B a release. C can recover damages from A for any harm this causes C. The amount of harm may be greater if B is released for value before he receives notification of the assignment than if B remains liable to C.

2. A has a right against B, performance of which B has repudiated without excuse. A assigns his right to C for value without disclosing B's repudiation. C can recover from A damages for any harm the repudiation causes C.

3. A reasonably and in good faith believes he has a right against B, and assigns it to C for value as an actual right. In fact the right does not exist. C can recover damages from A.

b. Express warranties and disclaimers. The rules stated in this Section can be varied by express or implied agreement. Express warranties are created in the same ways as express warranties in the transfer of goods, and implied warranties may be excluded or modified in the same ways. See Uniform Commercial Code §§ 2-312, 2-313, 2-316, 2-317. The words "without recourse" may be ambiguous in this context: ordinarily they are used to disclaim the liability of an indorser but do not eliminate implied warranties. See Uniform Commercial Code §§ 3-414, 3-417(3). **Illustration:**

4. A believes that there is only a slight possibility that he may have a right against B. A assigns to C for value "Any claim or right" which he may have against B without disclosing how seriously he doubts the validity of the claim. A is under no duty to C if the claim is invalid.

c. Warranty to a sub-assignee. A sub-assignee may be an intended beneficiary of an assignor's warranty to an intermediate assignee, or the intermediate assignee may assign to the sub-assignee a claim for breach of warranty. But unless such an intention is manifested, the warranties of an assignor run only to his assignee, and are not transferred by a sub-assignment. Compare Uniform Commercial Code §§ 2-318, 2-607(5), 3-803.

d. Remedies. When a warranty of an assignor is broken, the assignee is entitled to the usual remedies for breach of contract. He can recover damages not only for harm caused but also for the amount by which he would have been benefited if the assigned right had been as warranted. But if the assigned right would have been worthless aside from the breach of warranty, there are no damages. The assignor is also subject to liability, at the assignee's election, for the value of anything received by him from the assignee on account of the assignment, or for any amount wrongfully collected from the obligor. In an appropriate case such equitable remedies as injunction and constructive trust are also available.

§ 334. Variation of Obligor's Duty by Assignment

(1) If the obligor's duty is conditional on the personal cooperation of the original obligee or another person, an assignee's right is subject to the same condition.

(2) If the obligor's duty is conditional on cooperation which the obligee could properly delegate to an agent, the condition may occur if there is similar cooperation by an assignee.

Comment:

a. Scope. This Section relates to the consequences of assignment of a right, stating corollaries of the statement in § 317 that a right cannot be assigned if the effect would be to change materially the duty of the obligor. Delegation of the performance of a duty or requirement of a condition is the subject of §§ 318 and 319. Those Sections apply the same principles applied by this Section to determine when the obligor's duty is conditional on the obligee's personal cooperation and when the

obligee could properly delegate cooperation to an agent. See also Restatement, Second, Agency § 17.

b. Terms of assignment. Whether there is a material change in the obligor's duty depends not only on the terms of the contract creating the duty and on the circumstances, but also on the terms of the assignment. Commonly an assignment manifests an intention that the obligor render performance to the assignee rather than to the assignor. Such a change is immaterial in the usual case of a duty to pay money, but material where personal cooperation is made a condition of the duty. Even in the latter case, however, it is at least theoretically possible to assign the right without departing from the requirement. **Illustrations:**

    1. B contracts to sell A specified goods for a stated price. A effectively assigns his right to C. On tender of the agreed price, C has a right to take delivery of the goods at the agreed time and place.

    2. B contracts to sell and deliver 100 gallons of fuel oil to A at A's house. C lives next door to A and has equal facility for receiving delivery of oil. A assigns his right under the contract to C and directs B to deliver the oil at C's house. B is under a duty to do so. The change in the required performance is too slight to give B a valid objection.

    3. B contracts with A to furnish A's family with all the oil it shall need for the ensuing year at a fixed price. A assigns his rights under the contract to C. C can acquire no right against B that C's family shall be supplied with oil, but may acquire a right that A's family shall be supplied, if such is the intention of the parties.

    4. B contracts with A to serve A as a valet. A, for value, assigns his rights under the contract to C. C acquires no right to have B act as valet to C. If the assignment manifests an intent to give C a right to have B act as valet to A, C acquires such a right.

c. Conditions of cooperation. This Section refers to conditions of cooperation, and does not apply to performances which do not involve the cooperation of anyone, such as going to Rome, forbearing from suit, or refraining from competition. Performances involving the cooperation of third persons, such as paying money to, selling to, buying from, or working for a third person, may bring into play the same

principles as conditions of cooperation by the obligee. Contracts to pay money to the obligee or to sell to or buy from him seldom require his personal cooperation, but may do so. Typically, Subsection (1) applies to contracts to serve under the personal direction of the obligee or to give personal direction to his work. **Illustrations:**

    5. B, a silver mining company, contracts with A, a smelting company, to deliver B's ore to A for smelting. A contracts to smelt the ore and to deliver the metal thereby obtained to B, receiving an agreed price for the work. A's right to receive the ore is assigned for value by him to C. A remains financially responsible but ceases to operate a smelter. The assignment is ineffective. The contract to deliver valuable ore to the assignor involves a degree of personal confidence which precludes the substitution of an assignee to receive the ore. C, therefore, has no right to have the ore delivered to himself, and as A has ceased to carry on the smelting business, C has no right to require B to deliver the ore to A.

    6. B contracts to sell to A, an ice cream manufacturer, the amount of ice A may need in his business for the ensuing three years, to the extent of not more than 250 tons a week, at a stated price a ton. A makes a corresponding promise to B to buy such an amount of ice. A sells his ice cream plant to C and assigns to C all A's rights under the contract with B. Whether the assignment is effective depends on the terms of the contract between A and B and on the likelihood that C's requirements will be different from A's. If the contract is read as a contract to furnish such ice as the plant requires, B is bound to furnish C ice up to the agreed maximum even though C requires more or less ice than B would have required.

    7. B contracts to build a wall on A's land at a place to be selected by A personally. A sells the land and assigns his rights under the contract to C and joins C in selecting the place. B is bound to build the wall.

§ 335. Assignment by a Joint Obligee

    A joint obligee may effectively assign his right, but the assignee can enforce it only in the same manner and to the same extent as the assignor could have enforced it.

Comment:

    a. The extent to which the rights of obligees of the same performance are joint depends on the intention manifested and on the extent to which their interests in the performance or in the remedies for breach are distinct. See § 297(2). In an action based on a joint right, the obligor can require joinder of all surviving joint obligees, but

any joint obligee may sue in the name of all. See § 298. This power to enforce the joint right, the related power to discharge the obligor, and any right to receive and retain the proceeds as against the co-obligees are assignable, subject to limitations imposed by the relationship of the obligees. See §§ 299-301.

§ 336. Defenses Against an Assignee

(1) By an assignment the assignee acquires a right against the obligor only to the extent that the obligor is under a duty to the assignor; and if the right of the assignor would be voidable by the obligor or unenforceable against him if no assignment had been made, the right of the assignee is subject to the infirmity.

(2) The right of an assignee is subject to any defense or claim of the obligor which accrues before the obligor receives notification of the assignment, but not to defenses or claims which accrue thereafter except as stated in this Section or as provided by statute.

(3) Where the right of an assignor is subject to discharge or modification in whole or in part by impracticability, public policy, non-occurrence of a condition, or present or prospective failure of performance by an obligee, the right of the assignee is to that extent subject to discharge or modification even after the obligor receives notification of the assignment.

(4) An assignee's right against the obligor is subject to any defense or claim arising from his conduct or to which he was subject as a party or a prior assignee because he had notice.

Comment:

a. Negotiable instruments and documents. The rules stated in this Section do not apply to the negotiation or transfer of a negotiable instrument or document. See § 316. The Uniform Commercial Code provides for the rights of a holder in due course of a negotiable instrument, a holder to whom a negotiable document has been duly negotiated and a purchaser for value who has taken an investment security without notice of a particular defense. Such a holder or purchaser takes free of many defenses of the obligor. See §§ 3-305, 7-502, 8-202. Compare Comment *f.* Where those provisions do not apply, transfer of a negotiable instrument or document vests in the transferee the rights which the transferor had or had authority to convey. See §§ 3-201, 3-306, 7-504, 8-301.

b. Accrued defenses. Unlike the negotiation of a negotiable instrument, the assignment of a non-negotiable contractual right ordinarily transfers what the assignor has but only what he has. The assignee's right depends on the validity and enforceability of the contract creating the right, and is subject to limitations imposed by the terms of that contract and to defenses which would have been available against the obligee had there been no assignment. Until the obligor receives notification of an assignment, he is entitled to treat the obligee as owner of the right, and the assignee's right is subject to defenses and claims arising from dealings between assignor and obligor in relation to the contract before notification. See § 338. **Illustrations:**

1. A holds B's unsealed written promise, unenforceable because given without consideration. A assigns this to C, who pays value on the faith of the writing, with reasonable belief that A had given B consideration and that the promise is legally binding. C has no right against B.

2. A has a right against B voidable because created when B was an infant. A assigns his right to C, who is ignorant of the facts making the right voidable. C's right against B is voidable.

3. A lends money to B and assigns his right to C. C's right is barred by the Statute of Limitations when A's right would have been.

. . .

c. Accrued claims. Statutes or rules of court commonly permit an obligor when sued to assert by way of set-off or counterclaim in the same action such claims as he has against the plaintiff, whether related to the plaintiff's claim or not. See, e.g., Rule 13 of the Federal Rules of Civil Procedure. In appropriate circumstances the obligor may use defensively against an assignee an offsetting claim against the assignor, although the assignee is not subject to affirmative liability on such a claim unless he contracts to assume such liability. See § 328; Uniform Commercial Code §§ 2-210, 9-317. Courts of equity exercised jurisdiction in set-off at an early date, but set-off in actions at law stems from an English statute enacted in 1729 and applicable to "mutual debts"; counterclaim statutes first appeared in the nineteenth century. Set-off against an assignee has sometimes been limited to cases where both offsetting claims were fully matured at the time of assignment. The modern rule, however, unless a statute provides otherwise, turns on the time the obligor receives notification of assignment and applies even though the assigned right has not then matured. See Uniform Commercial Code § 9-318. **Illustration:**

5. A lends money to B, who regularly sells goods to A on credit and expects to repay the loan by making such sales. A assigns his right to C. Thereafter B sells goods to A as expected, and the price becomes due before B receives notification of the assignment. Unless a statute provides otherwise, B can set off his claim for the price in an action by C as assignee.

d. Defenses and claims accruing after notification. After receiving notification of an assignment, an obligor must treat the assignee as owner of the right and cannot assert against him a defense or claim arising out of a subsequent transaction except as stated in § 338. Moreover, the obligor cannot under the usual statute or rule of court set off an unrelated claim which matures after notification is received. Section 553of the Bankruptcy Reform Act of 1978, 11 U.S.C. § 553 (1978), provides for the set-off of unmatured claims. The extent to which a similar rule is applicable to assignment for the benefit of creditors or to other insolvency proceedings is often affected by statute and is beyond the scope of this Restatement. Notification, however, does not enlarge the obligor's duty, and the possibility remains that the assigned right will become subject to a defense or to a claim by way of recoupment. The assignee's right is subject to such a defense or claim if it arises from the terms of the contract between the assignor and the obligor. See Uniform Commercial Code § 9-318. **Illustrations:**

6. A contracts to market goods for B in return for payment to be made by B. A then assigns his right to payment to C, and B receives notification of the assignment. Subsequently A becomes insolvent and wholly fails to perform the contract. B has a defense against C.

7. A contracts to build a structure for B, and becomes entitled to progress payments. A assigns the money due to C, and B receives notification of the assignment. Thereafter, in breach of his contract, A abandons the work. In an action by C against B, B is entitled to recoup damages caused by A's breach.

e. Claims against a prior assignee. The rules stated in this Section apply to a sub-assignee. Just as an assignee is subject to defenses and claims accruing before the obligor receives notification, so a sub-assignee is subject to defenses and claims accruing between assignee and obligor before the obligor receives notification of a sub-assignment. Defenses and claims arising from the terms of the contract creating the right are available to the obligor regardless of when they accrue. **Illustration:**

8. B owes A $ 100. A assigns the right to C, and C assigns it to D. C owes B $ 50. Unless a statute provides otherwise, B can set off against D the debt owed by C only if it becomes due before B receives notification of the assignment by C.

f. Agreement not to assert defenses. The obligor may undertake a greater obligation to an assignee than to the assignor by direct contract with the assignee, and may confer on the assignor an agency power to bind him to such an agreement. Section 9-206 of the Uniform Commercial Code gives effect to an agreement by a buyer or lessee that he will not assert against an assignee any claim or defense which he may have against the seller or lessor, making it enforceable by a good faith assignee for value without notice of a claim or defense, except as to defenses of a type which may be asserted against a holder in due course of a negotiable instrument. The Assignment of Claims Act of 1940, 31 U.S.C. § 203 (1979), contains a more limited authorization for a no-setoff agreement by the United States. The Code provision is subject to any statute or decision which establishes a different rule for buyers or lessees of consumer goods, and a number of retail installment sales acts limit the power of a buyer to make such an agreement. In addition, the Federal Trade Commission has issued a Trade Regulation Rule barring such agreements with respect to consumers. See 16 C.F.R. §§ 433.1-.3 (1975). In the absence of statute, administrative rule or court decision, such an agreement can take effect to give the assignee greater rights than the assignor as to matters governed by the terms of the contract; but if the agreement not to assert defenses or claims is itself voidable or unenforceable, the assignee takes subject to the defect. **Illustrations:**

9. B, doing business under the name A, executes a purported contract with A reciting the delivery of goods by A to B and B's promise to pay A for them. B then executes on behalf of A an assignment to C of A's rights under the contract and delivers it to C for consideration. Whether or not C knows the facts, B's purported promise is binding in favor of C.

10. A sells and delivers goods to B, and B agrees that in the event of an assignment to C, B will pay the price to C without asserting any defense or claim based on breach of warranty by

A. A assigns his rights under the contract to C, who takes in good faith and without notice of any defense or claim. In the absence of statute or administrative rule, B is barred from asserting against C a defense or claim based on breach of warranty by A.

. . .

g. *Estoppel.* Even though an obligor's agreement not to assert a defense or claim is not binding or is voidable or unenforceable, he may be estopped to assert the claim or defense against an assignee. Where he makes a representation of fact with the intention of inducing an assignee or prospective assignee to act in reliance on the representation, and an assignee does so act, the doctrine of estoppel bars the obligor from contradicting the representation in litigation against the assignee if contradiction would be inequitable. Compare § 90. Application of the doctrine depends on all the circumstances. The representation may be express or it may be implied from conduct, in unusual cases even from failure to act. In some circumstances estoppel may rest on the obligor's reason to know that the assignee may rely, even though there is no intention to induce reliance. **Illustrations:**

> 12. A contracts to do construction work for B, a subcontractor, and becomes entitled to progress payments. A assigns the progress payments to C, who advances money to A in reliance on B's assertion to C that the work has been done and that the payments will be made

when received from the general contractor. In an action by C for the payments, B is estopped to offset B's claim against A for A's defaults subsequent to the assignment.

> 13. A contracts to sell furniture to B for a price payable in installments. A assigns his rights under the contract to C, who buys the rights and pays for them in reliance on B's written statement addressed to C that the furniture has been received and accepted by B. In an action by C for the balance due on the price, B is estopped to assert that no furniture had been received. But there is no such estoppel if at the time of the assignment C has reason to know that A has made a practice of obtaining false statements of receipt and acceptance.

. . .

h. *Conduct of the assignee.* The conduct of the assignee or his agents may, like that of any obligee, give rise to defenses and claims which may be asserted against him by the obligor. An obligee who is subject to such a defense or claim cannot improve his position by assigning the right to an assignee who is not subject to the defense or claim and then taking a reassignment. Compare Uniform Commercial Code § 3-201. **Illustration:**

> 15. A is fraudulently induced by B, the agent of C, to sell goods to C. C assigns his rights to D, who pays value in good faith and without notice. D assigns to E, who knows of the fraud. A cannot avoid the contract as against E, who succeeded to D's rights. But if E assigns to C, A's power of avoidance will revive.

§ 337. Elimination of Defenses by Subsequent Events

Where the right of an assignor is limited or voidable or unenforceable or subject to discharge or modification, subsequent events which would eliminate the limitation or defense have the same effect on the right of the assignee.

Comment:

a. *Rationale.* The rule of this Section is the converse of the rules stated in § 336. An assignment ordinarily transfers only what the assignor has, but limitations and defenses are not enlarged by the transfer. If a condition of the obligor's duty is met or excused, for example, the condition ceases to limit the assignee's right just as it would have ceased to limit the right of the assignor in the absence of assignment. **Illustrations:**

> 1. A has a right against B, voidable for A's fraud. A assigns the right to C. Thereafter B learns of the fraud but does not within a reason-

able time notify either A or C of his intention to avoid the transaction. Whether or not B knows of the assignment, C's right ceases to be voidable.

> 2. A has a right against B, unenforceable because of noncompliance with the Statute of Frauds. A assigns the right to C. Thereafter B makes a memorandum sufficient to satisfy the Statute. Whether or not B knows of the assignment, C's right is enforceable.

b. *New promises.* The rule of this Section does not apply to new transactions between the obligor and the assignor after the obligor has received notification of the assignment. See §

338. Moreover, the effect of a new promise by the obligor of a kind referred to in §§ 82-85 is governed by those Sections. A new promise of such a kind, made to the assignor, is binding only if the assignor is then an obligee of the antecedent duty or is acting as agent for the assignee. See § 92. **Illustration:**

3. A is the payee of B's negotiable note for $ 200. A indorses and delivers the note to C. After maturity, without knowledge of C's rights, B pays A $ 50 on account of the note. The part payment is not effective to extend the period of the statute of limitations in favor of C. If the part payment were made before assignment, the period would be so extended.

§ 338. Discharge of an Obligor After Assignment

(1) Except as stated in this Section, notwithstanding an assignment, the assignor retains his power to discharge or modify the duty of the obligor to the extent that the obligor performs or otherwise gives value until but not after the obligor receives notification that the right has been assigned and that performance is to be rendered to the assignee.

(2) So far as an assigned right is conditional on the performance of a return promise, and notwithstanding notification of the assignment, any modification of or substitution for the contract made by the assignor and obligor in good faith and in accordance with reasonable commercial standards is effective against the assignee. The assignee acquires corresponding rights under the modified or substituted contract.

(3) Notwithstanding a defect in the right of an assignee, he has the same power his assignor had to discharge or modify the duty of the obligor to the extent that the obligor gives value or otherwise changes his position in good faith and without knowledge or reason to know of the defect.

(4) Where there is a writing of a type customarily accepted as a symbol or as evidence of the right assigned, a discharge or modification is not effective

(a) against the owner or an assignor having a power of avoidance, unless given by him or by a person in possession of the writing with his consent and any necessary indorsement or assignment;

(b) against a subsequent assignee who takes possession of the writing and gives value in good faith and without knowledge or reason to know of the discharge or modification.

Comment:

a. Discharge by true obligee. Rules governing the discharge of a contractual right by one who is actually the owner of the right are stated in Chapter 12. Such a discharge is effective against the obligee who gives it, whether he is the original promisee, a beneficiary, or an assignee, and against any person who has no greater rights. Under § 336 a subsequent assignee is ordinarily such a person; but the law governing negotiable instruments and documents in some circumstances gives to a bona fide holder a greater right than his transferor had. See Uniform Commercial Code §§ 3-305, 7-502, 8-202. Estoppel and related doctrines have a similar effect. See Subsection (4)(b); § 336 Comments *f, g;* Uniform Commercial Code § 9-206. **Illustration:**

1. B owes A $ 100. A assigns the right to C. C gives B a gratuitous release under seal and subsequently assigns the right to D for value. D acquires no right against B.

b. Discharge by apparent obligee. This Section covers discharge by one who reasonably seems to the obligor to own the right, though in fact he does not. The obligor is ordinarily protected in such a case of a discharge wrongfully given, but only if he renders performance or otherwise gives value or changes his position in good faith and without knowledge or reason to know that the appearance is false. **Illustrations:**

2. B owes A $ 100. A assigns the right to C. C assigns it to D, and D assigns it to E. Before receiving notification of the assignment to E, B pays D. B is discharged.

3. B owes A $ 100. A assigns the right for value to C and subsequently by way of oral gift to D. Before receiving notification of the assignment to C, B pays D. B is discharged.

c. Value; antecedent debt. The rules as to what constitutes value in this Chapter are the same as the rules stated in §§ 298-309 of the Restatement, Second, of Trusts, except as stated in § 173 of the Restatement of Restitution and except as modified by statute. See also Restatement of Security § 10 Comment *e*. The exception, which conforms to the provisions of Uniform Commercial Code §§ 1-201(44) and 3-303 and earlier uniform acts, is that a transfer of property other than land in satisfaction of or as security for a preexisting debt or other obligation is a transfer for value. Compare § 332.

d. Promise as value. Restatement, Second, Trusts § 302 and Restatement of Restitution § 173 state that a transfer of property in consideration of a promise to make payment in the future is not a transfer for value unless the transferee would be liable upon his promise even if he were compelled to surrender the property, or unless he has so changed his position that it would be inequitable to compel him to surrender the property. Uniform Commercial Code § 3-303 embodies a similar rule for some transactions in negotiable instruments. But for other transactions Uniform Commercial Code § 1-201(44) provides that value is given for rights acquired "in return for a binding commitment to extend credit or for the extension of immediately available credit whether or not drawn upon and whether or not a chargeback is provided for in the event of difficulties in collection"; or "generally, in return for any consideration sufficient to support a simple contract." Compare §§ 4-208 and 4-209 on bank collections. Under those provisions an executory promise is value for the purposes of bona fide purchase of goods, negotiable documents, or investment securities from a person with voidable title. Uniform Commercial Code §§ 2-403(1), 7-501(4), 7-502, 8-301, 8-302. The extent to which by analogy this statutory rule may be applicable to purchases of contractual rights not subject to the statutory provisions is beyond the scope of this Restatement.

e. Receipt of notification. Subsection (1), like § 336, follows Uniform Commercial Code § 9-318 in stating that the assignor's power to discharge terminates when the obligor "receives notification." This phrase is used with the meaning prescribed by Uniform Commercial Code § 1-201(26): a person receives a notification when it comes to his attention or is duly delivered at a place held out by him as the place for receipt of such communications. No particular formality is required, but under § 9-318 the notification must

reasonably identify the rights assigned, and if the assignee fails upon request to furnish reasonable proof an account debtor may pay the assignor. For the greater protection given to banks of deposit, see§ 339 Comment *c*. Receipt of notification does not include all facts which would give "reason to know." See Restatement, Second, Agency §§ 9, 268. **Illustration:**

    4. A assigns to C a debt owed by B. Pursuant to Uniform Commercial Code §§ 9-401 and 9-402, C files a financing statement describing the collateral as "debt owed by B." Without knowledge of the filing and without any other reason to know of the assignment, B pays A. B is discharged.

f. Modification of executory contract. Subsection (2) follows Uniform Commercial Code § 9-318 in stating that so far as a contract is executory the assignor and obligor retain power to make good faith modifications without the assignee's consent even after notification. The assignee is protected by automatic corresponding rights in the modified or substituted contract. As in the case of a discharge by the assignor before notification, exercise of the power may be a breach of the contract of assignment. See § 333. Contrary agreement between obligor and assignee is effective. **Illustrations:**

    5. A contracts to do construction work for B, and assigns to C the payments to become due. C notifies B of the assignment. A becomes financially unable to perform, and B makes advance payments to A which are necessary to enable A to perform. B is liable to C only for the balance due after deducting the amount of the advances.

    6. A Company contracts to supply electricity to B for twenty years. Later A assigns to C for value certain fixed monthly payments to be made by B under the contract. After ten years B ceases to require electricity and A and B agree in good faith to terminate all performance under the contract. B is not liable to C for payments which would have accrued thereafter.

g. Revocable or voidable assignment. Where an assignment is revocable because gratuitous or is voidable because of infancy, insanity, fraud, duress, mistake, or public policy, the assignee nevertheless has power to discharge or modify the duty of an obligor who pays value in good faith and without notice. In the case of a revocable gratuitous assignment, the obligor may assume until he has reason to know otherwise that the assignor desires him to complete the gift by performance or novation. See § 332. But if the obligor has reason to know that a revocable assignment has been revoked or that the assignment is voidable by the assignor, he cannot safely perform. If the facts or law are in dispute in such a case, or if the assignor has not yet exercised a power to avoid, the obligor is entitled to protection by interpleader or like remedy. See § 339. Where an assignor's right is voidable by or held in trust for a third person, an assignee may or may not take subject to the defect. See § 343. If he is subject to it, the same principles apply as in a case of voidable assignment. **Illustrations:**

> 7. B owes A $ 100. A makes a revocable gratuitous assignment to C, and subsequently makes a similar assignment to D. B with knowledge of the facts pays C. B is not discharged. The assignment to D gives B reason to know that A intends to revoke the assignment to C.

> 8. B owes A $ 100. A is induced by C's fraud to assign the right to C. B in good faith and without notice of the fraud enters into a novation with C in satisfaction of the debt. B's duty under the original contract is discharged. But if C holds a substituted right under the novation in constructive trust for A, performance by B with reason to know the facts does not discharge his duty to A.

> 9. A, as trustee for X, has a right against B. A, in violation of his trust, assigns his right to C gratuitously. B pays C with reason to know of A's breach of trust. B's duty to X is not discharged.

> . . .

§ 339. Protection of Obligor in Cases of Adverse Claims

Where a claim adverse to that of an assignee subjects the obligor to a substantial risk beyond that imposed on him by his contract, the obligor will be granted such relief as is equitable in the circumstances.

Comment:

a. Rationale. Like the rules stated in §§ 317 and 334, the rule of this Section rests on the basic principle that rights based on agreement are limited by the agreement. An obligor who has contracted to render a performance should not be required to render it twice because of uncertainties of law and fact relating to the person entitled to receive it, or because a person having a power of avoidance has not yet elected whether to exercise it. In most situations the obligor is protected against double liability by the rules permitting him to disregard an assignment until he receives notification of it and to honor it thereafter. See §§ 336, 338. But additional safeguards may be needed when the obligor has received such notification and also has reason to know of an adverse claim.

b. Proof of assignment. Even in the absence of an adverse claim, the obligor may request that the assignee furnish reasonable proof that the assignment has been made. Uniform Commercial Code § 9-318(3) permits an account debtor to pay the assignor in such a case unless the proof is seasonably furnished. Compare § 5-116 (letters of credit). Where the obligation is embodied in a commercial instrument or document, the obligor may without dishonor require its production. See Uniform Commercial Code §§ 3-505 (commercial paper), 5-116 (letters of credit), 7-403(3) (negotiable document of title). If it is lost, security may be required indemnifying the obligor against loss by reason of further claims. See Uniform Commercial Code §§ 3-804 (commercial paper), 7-601 (documents of title), 8-405 (investment securities). **Illustration:**

> 1. A assigns to C a debt owed A by B, and C notifies B of the assignment. B requests C to furnish reasonable proof of the assignment, but C fails to do so. After a reasonable time B pays A. B's duty to C is discharged.

> . . .

§ 340. Effect of Assignment on Priority and Security

(1) An assignee is entitled to priority of payment from the obligor's insolvent estate to the extent that the assignor would have been so entitled in the absence of assignment.

(2) Where an assignor holds collateral as security for the assigned right and does not effectively transfer the collateral to the assignee, the assignor is a constructive trustee of the collateral for the assignee in accordance with the rules stated for pledges in §§ 29-34 of the Restatement of Security.

. . .

§ 341. Creditors of an Assignor

(1) Except as provided by statute, the right of an assignee is superior to a judicial lien subsequently obtained against the property of the assignor, unless the assignment is ineffective or revocable or is voidable by the assignor or by the person obtaining the lien or is in fraud of creditors.

(2) Notwithstanding the superiority of the right of an assignee, an obligor who does not receive notification of the assignment until after he has lost his opportunity to assert the assignment as a defense in the proceeding in which the judicial lien was obtained is discharged from his duty to the assignee to the extent of his satisfaction of the lien.

Comment:

a. Priority of assignee. An effective assignment extinguishes the assignor's right without any notification of the obligor. Any proceeds of the assigned right received by the assignor thereafter are held in constructive trust for the assignee. See Restatement of Restitution § 165. A creditor of the assignor who claims the assigned right by garnishment, levy of execution or like process is not a bona fide purchaser, even though he has no notice of the assignment. Unless protected by statute or by estoppel or like doctrine, he is subject to the assignee's right. Compare § 342; see Restatement of Restitution § 173. "Judicial lien," as used in this Section, has the same meaning as it does in the Bankruptcy Reform Act of 1978.

b. Defective assignment. An assignor's trustee in bankruptcy can in general reach all of the assignor's legal or equitable interest in any of his property, including powers that he might have exercised for his own benefit and property transferred by him in fraud of creditors. See Bankruptcy Reform Act of 1978, 11 U.S.C. §§ 541(a), (b), 548 (1978). In addition, a person against whom a transfer is voidable can reach the property transferred. In such cases, therefore, the assignee's right is not superior to that of the lien obtained by garnishment or like process. A revocable gratuitous assignment, for example, does not limit the power of the assignor's creditors to levy on the assigned claim. See § 332.

c. Protection of obligor. An obligor garnished by a creditor of the assignor cannot safely pay even in response to a judgment if he has received notification of the assignment, but he is entitled to protection against double liability by interpleader or like remedy. See § 339. If the garnished obligor has not received notification, the assignee's right against him is discharged to the same extent as the assignor's right would have been in the absence of assignment. See §§ 336, 338.

Such a discharge of the obligor does not necessarily terminate the assignee's rights against the assignor and the garnishing creditor. The assignee is entitled to restitution from the assignor to the extent that the assignor has been unjustly enriched by the discharge of his debt. See Restatement of Restitution § 118. The garnishing creditor takes free of the assignee's right to the extent that he becomes a bona fide purchaser or that the assignee is barred by estoppel, laches, *res judicata*, or other defense. See Restatement of Restitution §§ 131, 173, 179.

Illustration:

1. A has a right against B and assigns it to C for value. X, a creditor of A, serves garnishment process on B in an action against A, and obtains judgment against B before B receives notification of the assignment. A month later, before any payment or satisfaction or issue of execution and within the time specified in local procedural rules, B and C move to reopen the judg-

ment. The motion should be granted, and C is entitled to judgment against B to the exclusion of X.

d. Filing statutes. Creditors are commonly among the beneficiaries of statutes requiring public filing of notices of certain types of transactions. The Uniform Commercial Code makes a general requirement of filing to "perfect" a nonpossessory "security interest" in personal property, including "any sale of accounts or chattel paper." See §§ 9-102, 9-302. An unperfected security interest is subordinate to the rights of "a person who becomes a lien creditor before the security interest is perfected." See § 9-301. Transfers of wage claims, rights under insurance policies or deposit accounts, and various other transactions are excluded from coverage. See § 9-104. With respect to certain international open accounts receivable, § 9-103(3)(c) provides alternatives of the application of the filing law of the American jurisdiction in which the debtor has its executive offices or perfection "by notification to the account debtor." Wage assignment statutes also often provide for public filing or for notification of the obligor or both. See Statutory Note preceding § 316.

§ 342. Successive Assignees From the Same Assignor

Except as otherwise provided by statute, the right of an assignee is superior to that of a subsequent assignee of the same right from the same assignor, unless

(a) the first assignment is ineffective or revocable or is voidable by the assignor or by the subsequent assignee; or

(b) the subsequent assignee in good faith and without knowledge or reason to know of the prior assignment gives value and obtains

(i) payment or satisfaction of the obligation,

(ii) judgment against the obligor,

(iii) a new contract with the obligor by novation, or

(iv) possession of a writing of a type customarily accepted as a symbol or as evidence of the right assigned.

Comment:

a. Scope. No attempt is made in this Section to state the effect of statutory changes, which often make priority depend on filing in a public office. In the absence of statute, the rules stated in this Section are applicable to both total and partial assignments and to assignments as security for an obligation as well as to outright sales of contractual rights. If the first assignment is partial, or if the assignor retains a beneficial interest, the subsequent assignee is entitled to any balance after the first assignee has been satisfied.

b. Dearle v. Hall. In England and in a number of states, aside from statute, a different rule has been followed, giving priority to the assignee who first gives notice to the obligor, regardless of the order in which the assignments were made. That rule stems from the leading case of Dearle v. Hall, 3 Russ. 1, 48 (1828), involving successive assignments of the interest of a beneficiary of a trust. The English rule has consequences similar to that of a system of public filing, except that the obligor acts as the filing office; it is somewhat more convenient where a single obligor is involved such as a trustee or the owner or prime contractor on a construction project than in cases of multiple obligors, as where a business concern assigns its accounts receivable. The English rule was not adopted in Restatement, Second, Trusts § 163.

c. Filing statutes. In modern times the rules of this Section have been greatly affected by statute. From 1938 to 1950 Section 60 of the Bankruptcy Act made the validity of an assignment in the assignor's bankruptcy turn on perfection of the assignment as against a hypothetical subsequent assignee. As a result numerous state statutes were enacted, directed particularly at assignments of accounts receivable. In 1950 amendments to the Bankruptcy Act reduced the significance of the problem of successive assignments. The current formulation is found in Bankruptcy Reform Act of 1978, 11 U.S.C. § 547(e)(1)(B) (1978):

a transfer of a fixture or property other than real property is perfected when a creditor on a simple contract cannot acquire a judicial lien that is superior to the interest of the transferee.

The subject is now largely governed by the Uniform Commercial Code, except in cases of wage claims, some rights under insurance polices, deposit accounts, and certain other excluded types of transactions. See § 9-104.

Under the Code, filing or the taking of possession is generally required to "perfect" a "security interest," which includes the interest of a buyer of accounts or chattel paper. Sections 1-201(37), 9-302. An unperfected security interest is subordinate to the rights of a person who is not a secured party to the extent that he gives value for accounts or general intangibles without knowledge of the security interest and before it is perfected. Section 9-301. As between secured parties, priority is determined by the order of filing or perfection, or if neither security interest is filed or perfected, by the order of attachment. Sections 9-312(5) and (6).

d. Defective assignment. If the prior assignment is revocable or voidable by the assignor a subsequent assignment is an effective manifestation of an intent to revoke or avoid. The subsequent assignment therefore has priority. A subsequent assignment may be similarly used to effectuate a power of avoidance of the subsequent assignee. **Illustrations:**

> 1. A has a right to the payment of $ 100 by B, and orally assigns it to C by way of gift. Subsequently A assigns the right to D, who gives value but knows of the assignment to C. Unless B has paid C without notice of D's assignment, B must pay D.
>
> 2. B owes A $ 100. A is an infant in a state where an infant may avoid his contract without restoring any consideration received. A assigns his right to C for value. Subsequently, on becoming of age, A assigns his right to D, who gives value but knows of the assignment to C. Unless B has paid C without notice of D's assignment, B must pay D.

e. Payment, judgment or novation. Where the subsequent assignee as a bona fide purchaser for value obtains performance by the obligor, judgment against him, or a new contract with him by novation, he is entitled to retain what he has received and to enforce the judgment or novation against the obligor, free of any obligation to account to the prior assignee. Historically, this rule was justified on the ground that the right of an assignee was equitable and

was not enforceable against a bona fide purchaser of the legal right. In modern times the doctrine of bona fide purchase has been extended in the interest of the security of transactions. But where the interest of the first assignee has been perfected pursuant to statute, whether by filing or otherwise, subsequent bona fide purchasers are not protected unless the statute so provides or there is an estoppel. See Uniform Commercial Code §§ 1-103, 9-306, 9-309, 9-312.
Illustration:

> 3. B owes $ 100 to A. A assigns the right to C for value. Later A assigns it for value to D, who takes it in good faith. D notifies B of the assignment to him before C notifies B of his assignment. C's right is superior to D's. But if D, still without knowledge or reason to know of the assignment to C, receives $ 50 from B, D can retain what he receives.

f. Symbolic writings. Certain writings are treated in the ordinary course of business as symbols of contractual rights. See Comment *c* to § 332; Comment *h* to § 338. To the extent that such writings are negotiable by common law or by statute, they are beyond the scope of this Section. The rights of bona fide purchasers of some such writings, both negotiable and non-negotiable, are governed by the Uniform Commercial Code. See, *e.g.,* § 9-308 (chattel paper). Aside from statute, a person who takes possession of such a writing as a bona fide purchaser is protected in his reasonable expectations arising from the apparent ownership of his assignor. This rule may be regarded as an application of a broader doctrine of estoppel. See Restatement, Second, Agency §§ 8B, 176.
Illustrations:

> 4. A, the holder of a savings bank book which records a deposit of $ 100 in the B savings bank, assigns the deposit to C for value without delivering the book. A then delivers the book to D, who pays value therefore in ignorance of the assignment to C. D is entitled to the deposit.
>
> 5. A holds a life insurance policy issued by the B insurance company. By written assignment A assigns the policy to C as security for a debt, but does not deliver the policy. Later A assigns the policy to D as security for a loan of $ 3,000, and delivers the policy to D. Still later D lends an additional $ 1,000 to A on A's note, relying in good faith on a notation added to the note without A's authority that the note is secured by the policy. C is entitled to redeem the policy from D on payment of $ 3,000.

g. Relation to discharge of obligor. Priority between successive assignees is independent of the protection of the obligor under § 338. An assignee who acts in good faith may take priority under this Section by receiving payment from an obligor who acts in bad faith and hence is not discharged. Conversely, an assignee who receives a payment with knowledge of a prior assignment must account to the prior assignor even though the obligor acts in good faith and is discharged to the extent of the payment.

h. Value. As to what constitutes value, see Comments *c* and *d* to § 338.

§ 343. Latent Equities

If an assignor's right against the obligor is held in trust or constructive trust for or subject to a right of avoidance or equitable lien of another than the obligor, an assignee does not so hold it if he gives value and becomes an assignee in good faith and without notice of the right of the other.

Comment:

a. Scope. The rule stated in this Section is an application to contractual rights of the rules stated in Restatement, Second, Trusts §§ 284-85 and Restatement of Restitution § 172 as applying to property generally. See also Restatement, Second, Agency § 307A. The rule does not apply to defenses or claims of the obligor, but protects the bona fide purchaser against all other equitable claims adverse to the right of the assignor. The bona fide purchaser may be a purchaser for value of the entire right or only of a fractional or otherwise limited interest, such as a security interest. But the rule does not apply to cases of successive assignments by the same assignor, and does not protect a promisee or beneficiary of a contract to assign or a declaration of trust until he becomes an assignee. See Restatement, Second, Trusts § 286; Restatement of Restitution § 175. **Illustrations:**

    1. A, as trustee for X, has a right against B. In violation of his trust A assigns the right gratuitously to C. C assigns to D, a purchaser for value in good faith and without notice of the breach of trust. D holds the right free of the trust.

    2. A has a right against B and is induced to assign it to C by C's fraud. C assigns it to D, a purchaser for value in good faith and without notice of the fraud. Even after discovering the fraud D can enforce the right against B and retain the proceeds free of A's claim.

b. Equities of the obligor. The rule of this Section is not applied where the protection of the bona fide purchaser would impair the rights of the obligor. Thus where the assignor of a debt holds collateral in constructive trust for the assignee under the rule stated in § 340, a subsequent bona fide purchaser of the collateral from the assignor takes subject to the debtor's right to redeem the collateral by paying the debt to the assignee; the rule of this Section is not applicable unless the collateral is negotiable or the debtor is bound by agreement or estoppel. See Restatement of Security §§ 29, 31. Again, where a surety for the assignor is subrogated to the rights of the obligor, the assignee does not have priority by virtue of the rule stated in this Section. Priorities in such cases arising in connection with public construction contracts are affected by statute and are beyond the scope of this Restatement. Compare Restatement of Restitution § 162; Restatement of Security §§ 141, 165-68.

c. Negotiable instruments and documents. The rule of this Section is negated with respect to negotiable instruments and documents of title which are transferred but not duly negotiated by Uniform Commercial Code §§ 3-306, 7-504, 8-301. Compare § 9-308 (chattel paper).

. . .

Chapter 16

Remedies

Introductory Note This Chapter deals with remedies that are of special importance in disputes arising out of contracts, including restitution as well as damages and equitable relief. Topic 1 sets out the interests protected by these remedies and enumerates the remedies themselves. The next two topics deal with the enforcement of contracts, by the award of damages under the rules stated in Topic 2 and by specific performance or injunction under the rules in Topic 3. Topic 4 is concerned with restitution when an agreement is, for some reason, not to be enforced under the rules stated in Topic 2 and 3. Finally, Topic 5 deals with those circumstances in which a party is precluded from pursuing a remedy by conduct inconsistent with it.

This Chapter is not exhaustive. It does not treat in detail those forms of relief, such as declaration of the rights of the parties or enforcement of an arbitration award, that are largely statutory and are not limited to contracts cases. See Comments *d* and *e* to § 345. It does not deal with some specialized remedies, such as reformation of a writing or replevin of property. Nor does it deal with the extent to which a party to a contract is empowered to protect himself or to obtain satisfaction by methods not involving recourse to a court, such as deducting damages that he claims from the price that he owes, retaking goods, or foreclosing on security. See Uniform Commercial Code §§ 2-717, 9-503, 9-504. Also omitted are the rights of third parties such as those of a good faith purchaser against one who has a power to avoid a contract through which the purchaser derives his title. See Uniform Commercial Code §§ 2-403, 3-305.

The important role that the institution of contract plays in the economy has drawn the attention of economists to the law of contract remedies. In classic economic theory the mechanism of exchange resulting from bargain is essential to the voluntary reallocation of goods, labor and other resources in a socially desirable manner. However, a party may err in calculating the net benefit to be expected from the performance of a bargain, or circumstances may so change as to disappoint his expectations. A contract that he once thought would be profitable may therefore become unprofitable for him. If the contract is still profitable for the other party, however, a question arises as to whether the reluctant party should be compelled to perform. The answer provided by at least some economic analysis tends to confirm the traditional response of common-law judges in dealing with this question.

The traditional goal of the law of contract remedies has not been compulsion of the promisor to perform his promise but compensation of the promisee for the loss resulting from breach. "Willful" breaches have not been distinguished from other breaches, punitive damages have not been awarded for breach of contract, and specific performance has not been granted where compensation in damages is an adequate substitute for the injured party. In general, therefore, a party may find it advantageous to refuse to perform a contract if he will still have a net gain after he has fully compensated the injured party for the resulting loss.

This traditional response is not without its shortcomings. Its focus on the pecuniary aspects of breach fails to take account of notions of the sanctity of contract and the resulting moral obligation to honor one's promises. The analysis of breach of contract in purely economic terms assumes an ability to measure value with a certainty that is not often possible in the judicial process. The analysis also ignores the "transaction costs" inherent in the bargaining process and in the resolution of disputes, a defect that is especially significant where the amount in controversy is small. However, the main thrust of the preceding economic analysis lends some support to traditional contract doctrine in this area.

§ 344. Purposes of Remedies

Judicial remedies under the rules stated in this Restatement serve to protect one or more of the following interests of a promisee:

(a) his "expectation interest," which is his interest in having the benefit of his bargain by being put in as good a position as he would have been in had the contract been performed,

(b) his "reliance interest," which is his interest in being reimbursed for loss caused by reliance on the contract by being put in as good a position as he would have been in had the contract not been made, or

(c) his "restitution interest," which is his interest in having restored to him any benefit that he has conferred on the other party.

Comment:

a. Three interests. The law of contract remedies implements the policy in favor of allowing individuals to order their own affairs by making legally enforceable promises. Ordinarily, when a court concludes that there has been a breach of contract, it enforces the broken promise by protecting the expectation that the injured party had when he made the contract. It does this by attempting to put him in as good a position as he would have been in had the contract been performed, that is, had there been no breach. The interest protected in this way is called the "expectation interest." It is sometimes said to give the injured party the "benefit of the bargain." This is not, however, the only interest that may be protected.

The promisee may have changed his position in reliance on the contract by, for example, incurring expenses in preparing to perform, in performing, or in foregoing opportunities to make other contracts. In that case, the court may recognize a claim based on his reliance rather than on his expectation. It does this by attempting to put him back in the position in which he would have been had the contract not been made. The interest protected in this way is called "reliance interest." Although it may be equal to the expectation interest, it is ordinarily smaller because it does not include the injured party's lost profit.

In some situations a court will recognize yet a third interest and grant relief to prevent unjust enrichment. This may be done if a party has not only changed his own position in reliance on the contract but has also conferred a benefit on the other party by, for example, making a part payment or furnishing services under the contract. The court may then require the other party to disgorge the benefit that he has received by returning it to the party who conferred it. The interest of the claimant protected in this way is called the "restitution interest." Although it may be equal to the expectation or reliance interest, it is ordinarily smaller because it includes neither the injured party's lost profit nor that part of his expenditures in reliance that resulted in no benefit to the other party.

The interests described in this Section are not inflexible limits on relief and in situations in which a court grants such relief as justice requires, the relief may not correspond precisely to any of these interests. See §§ 15, 87, 89, 90, 139, 158 and 272. **Illustrations:**

1. A contracts to building for B on B's land for $ 100,000. B repudiates the contract before either party has done anything in reliance on it. It would have cost A $ 90,000 to build the building. A has an expectation interest of $ 10,000, the difference between the $ 100,000 price and his savings of $ 90,000 in not having to do the work. Since A has done nothing in reliance, A's reliance interest is zero. Since A has conferred no benefit on B, A's restitution interest is zero.

2. The facts being otherwise as stated in Illustration 1, B does not repudiate until A has spent $ 60,000 of the $ 90,000. A has been paid nothing and can salvage nothing from the $ 60,000 that he has spent. A now has an expectation interest of $ 70,000, the difference between the $ 100,000 price and his saving of $ 30,000 in not having to do the work. A also has a reliance interest of $ 60,000, the amount that he has spent. If the benefit to B of the partly finished building is $ 40,000, A has a restitution interest of $ 40,000.

b. Expectation interest. In principle, at least, a party's expectation interest represents the actual worth of the contract to him rather than to some reasonable third person. Damages based on the expectation interest therefore take account of any special circumstances that are peculiar to the situation of the injured party, including his personal values and even his idiosyncracies, as well as his own needs and opportunities. See

Illustration 3. In practice, however, the injured party is often held to a more objective valuation of his expectation interest because he may be barred from recovering for loss resulting from such special circumstances on the ground that it was not foreseeable or cannot be shown with sufficient certainty. See §§ 351 and 352. Furthermore, since he cannot recover for loss that he could have avoided by arranging a substitute transaction on the market (§ 350), his recovery is often limited by the objective standard of market price. See Illustration 4. The expectation interest is not based on the injured party's hopes when he made the contract but on the actual value that the contract would have had to him had it been performed. See Illustration 5. It is therefore based on the circumstances at the time for performance and not those at the time of the making of the contract. **Illustrations:**

    3. A, who is about to produce a play, makes a contract with B, an actor, under which B is to play the lead in the play at a stated salary for the season. A breaks the contract and has the part played by another actor. B's expectation interest includes the extent to which B's reputation would have been enhanced if he had been allowed to play the lead in A's play, as well as B's loss in salary, both subject to the limitations stated in Topic 2.

    4. A contracts to construct a monument in B's yard for $ 10,000 but abandons the work after the foundation has been laid. It will cost B $ 6,000 to have another contractor complete the work. The monument planned is so ugly that it would decrease the market price of the house. Nevertheless, B's expectation interest is the value of the monument to him, which, under the rule stated in § 348(2)(b), would be measured by the cost of completion, $ 6,000.

    5. A makes a contract with B under which A is to pay B for drilling an oil well on B's land, adjacent to that of A, for development and exploration purposes. Both A and B believe that the well will be productive and will substantially enhance the value of A's land in an amount that they estimate to be $ 1,000,000. Before A

has paid anything, B breaks the contract by refusing to drill the well. Other exploration then proves that there is no oil in the region. A's expectation interest is zero.

    c. Reliance interest. If it is reliance that is the basis for the enforcement of a promise, a court may enforce the promise but limit the promisee to recovery of his reliance interest. See §§ 87, 89, 90, 139. There are also situations in which a court may grant recovery based on the reliance interest even though it is consideration that is the basis for the enforcement of the promise. These situations are dealt with in §§ 349 and 353.

    d. Restitution interest. Since restitution is the subject of a separate Restatement, this Chapter is concerned with problems of restitution only to the extent that they arise in connection with contracts. Such problems arise when a party, instead of seeking to enforce an agreement, claims relief on the ground that the other party has been unjustly enriched as a result of some benefit conferred under the agreement. In some cases a party's choice of the restitution interest is dictated by the fact that the agreement is not enforceable, perhaps because of his own breach (§ 374), as a result of impracticability of performance or frustration of purpose (§ 377(1)), under the Statute of Frauds (§ 375), or in consequence of the other party's avoidance for some reason as misrepresentation, duress, mistake or incapacity (§ 376). Occasionally a party chooses the restitution interest even though the contract is enforceable because it will give a larger recovery than will enforcement based on either the expectation or reliance interest. These rare instances are dealt with in § 373. Sometimes the restitution interest can be protected by requiring restoration of the specific thing, such as goods or land, that has resulted in the benefit. See § 372. Where restitution in kind is not appropriate, however, a sum of money will generally be allowed based on the restitution interest. See § 371.

§ 345. Judicial Remedies Available

    The judicial remedies available for the protection of the interests stated in § 344 include a judgment or order

    (a) awarding a sum of money due under the contract or as damages,

    (b) requiring specific performance of a contract or enjoining its non-performance,

    (c) requiring restoration of a specific thing to prevent unjust enrichment,

    (d) awarding a sum of money to prevent unjust enrichment,

    (e) declaring the rights of the parties, and

(f) enforcing an arbitration award.

Comment:

a. Nature of remedies. This Section enumerates the principal judicial remedies available for the protection of the interests defined in the preceding section. It is not intended to be exhaustive, since other remedies such as replevin of a chattel or reformation or cancellation of a writing supplement those listed here. As to reformation, see §§ 155, 166. Nor are the remedies listed mutually exclusive, since a court may in the same action, for example, both require specific performance of a promise and award a sum of money as damages for delay in its performance. The details of the procedure by which such remedies are obtained and enforced vary from one jurisdiction to another and are beyond the scope of this Restatement. In some circumstances a party to a contract is empowered to protect himself or to obtain satisfaction by methods not involving recourse to a court, such as retaking goods or foreclosing on security. The exercise of such a power, whether under a term of the contract or otherwise, is not a judicial remedy and is not dealt with in this Section. But see Topic 5 as to election and avoidance.

b. Enforcement. In most contract cases, what is sought is enforcement of a contract. Enforcement usually takes the form of an award of a sum of money due under the contract or as damages. Damages may be based on either the expectation or reliance interest of the injured party. See § 344. They are subject to the rules stated in Topic 2. A court may also enforce a promise by ordering that it be specifically performed or, in the alternative, by enjoining its nonperformance. In doing so, it protects the promisee's expectation interest. The rules governing the granting of such relief are stated in Topic 3.

c. Restitution. Sometimes a party, instead of seeking to enforce a contract under the rules stated in Topics 2 and 3, seeks protection of his restitution interest. If this can be accomplished by requiring the other party to restore a specific thing that is in his hands, a court may order restoration or make restoration a condition of granting relief to the other party. If restoration of the specific thing is not appropriate, the restitution interest may be protected by requiring the other party to pay a sum of money equivalent to the benefit that he has derived from that thing. The rules relating to the prevention of unjust enrichment by restitution, in either kind or money, are stated in Topic 4.

d. Declaratory judgments. Declaratory judgments play an important and growing role in the resolution of disputes arising out of contracts. Courts may render declaratory judgments under statutes adopted in nearly all states, and, in some instances, without the aid of statute. Such a judgment declares the legal relations between the parties but does not award damages or order other relief and may be rendered even though no breach of contract has occurred. In most states, including those that have adopted the Uniform Declaratory Judgment Act, courts may also render declaratory judgments in conjunction with other relief. In all states, and in the federal courts under the Federal Declaratory Judgment Act, the decision whether to render a declaratory judgment is discretionary. Because questions relating to declaratory judgments depend largely on statute and are not confined to contract cases, they are not considered in detail in this Restatement.

e. Enforcement of arbitration awards. Arbitration also plays an important and growing role in the resolution of contract disputes. Although arbitration is not in itself a judicial remedy, enforcement by a court of an award of an arbitral tribunal is. Statutes relating to the enforcement of such awards, based on either an agreement to arbitrate a future dispute or a submission of an existing dispute, have been enacted in many states. These statutes provide for the transformation of an award into a judgment by means of a summary procedure, without the necessity of bringing an action on the award as was required at common law. This transformation permits the use of the regular judicial process to enforce the arbitration award. The passage of these statutes reflects the increasing use of arbitration to settle private disputes and a decline in the judicial hostility to arbitration that had limited its effectiveness. Because questions concerning the enforcement of arbitration awards depend largely on statute, they are not considered in detail in this Restatement. But see Comment *a* Illustration 2 to § 366.

Introductory Note This Topic contains rules for enforcement of contracts by means of the award of damages. The initial assumption is that the injured party is entitled to full compensation for his actual loss. This is reflected in the general measure of damages set out in § 347. However, important limitations including those of avoidability, unforeseeability and uncertainty follow in §§ 350-53. The limitation of certainty can sometimes be overcome, at least in part, through the use of alternative bases for measuring damages (§ 348) or through the use of reliance as a measure of damages (§ 349). Other sections deal with nominal damages (§ 346), punitive damages (§ 355) and liquidated damages and penalties (§ 356). Except for the restrictions imposed by the rule that proscribes the fixing of penalties (§ 356), parties are free to vary the rules governing damages, subject to the usual limitations on private agreement such as that on unconscionable contracts or terms (§ 208). Although interest may be awarded as damages under the rule stated in § 354, for the sake of simplicity specific references to interest have generally been omitted from the illustrations in this Chapter.

Under the rule stated in § 346, a breach of contract ordinarily gives rise to a claim for damages. For the sake of convenience, the term "a claim for damages" is used in other chapters of this Restatement to refer to a right arising out of breach whether or not it includes a right to specific performance or an injunction as well as damages. See, for example, the use of that term in §§ 243 and 251. Although a claim to the price promised to be paid for something or to a sum of money promised to be repaid is, strictly speaking, not a claim for damages, such money claims are generally enforceable in the same way as those for damages. As to the right of a seller of land to recover the price, see Comment *e* to § 360.

§ 346. Availability of Damages

(1) The injured party has a right to damages for any breach by a party against whom the contract is enforceable unless the claim for damages has been suspended or discharged.

(2) If the breach caused no loss or if the amount of the loss is not proved under the rules stated in this Chapter, a small sum fixed without regard to the amount of loss will be awarded as nominal damages.

Comment:

a. Right to damages. Every breach of contract gives the injured party a right to damages against the party in breach, unless the contract is not enforceable against that party, as where he is not bound because of the Statute of Frauds. The resulting claim may be one for damages for total breach or one for damages for only partial breach. See § 236. Although a judgment awarding a sum of money as damages is the most common judicial remedy for breach of contract, other remedies, including equitable relief in the form of specific performance or an injunction, may be also available, depending on the circumstances. See Topic 3. In the exceptional situation of a contract for transfer of an interest in land that is unenforceable under the Statute of Frauds, action in reliance makes the contract enforceable by specific performance even though it gives rise to no claim for damages for breach. See Comment *c* to § 129. A duty to pay damages may be suspended or discharged by agreement or otherwise, and if it is discharged the claim for

damages is extinguished. See Introductory Note to Chapter 12. When this happens, the right to enforcement by other means such as specific performance or an injunction is also extinguished. If the duty of performance, as distinguished from the duty to pay damages, has been suspended or discharged, as by impracticability of performance or frustration of purpose, there is then no breach and this Section is not applicable.

The parties can by agreement vary the rules stated in this Section, as long as the agreement is not invalid for unconscionability (§ 208) or on other grounds. The agreement may provide for a remedy such as repair or replacement in substitution for damages. See Uniform Commercial Code § 2-719.

b. Nominal damages. Although a breach of contract by a party against whom it is enforceable always gives rise to a claim for damages, there are instances in which the breach causes no loss. See Illustration 1. There are also instances in which loss is caused but recovery for that loss is precluded because it cannot be proved with reasonable certainty or because of one of the other limitations stated in this Chapter. See §§ 350-53. In all these instances the injured party will nevertheless get judgment for nominal damages, a small sum usually fixed by judicial practice in the jurisdiction in which the action is brought. Such a judgment may, in the discretion of the court, carry with it an award of court costs. Costs are generally awarded if a significant right was involved or the claimant made a good faith effort to prove damages, but not if the maintenance of the action was frivolous or in bad faith. Unless a significant right is involved, a court will not reverse and remand a case for a new trial if only nominal damages could result.

Illustration:

1. A contracts to sell to B 1,000 shares of stock in X Corporation for $ 10 a share to be delivered on June 1, but breaks the contract by refusing on that date to deliver the stock. B sues A for damages, but at trial it is proved that B could have purchased 1,000 shares of stock in X Corporation on the market on June 1 for $ 10 a share and therefore has suffered no loss. In an action by B against A, B will be awarded nominal damages.

c. Beneficiaries of gift promises. If a promisee makes a contract, intending to give a third party the benefit of the promised performance, the third party may be an intended beneficiary who is entitled to enforce the contract. See § 302(1)(b). Such a gift promise creates overlapping duties, one to the beneficiary and the other to the promisee. If the performance is not forthcoming, both the beneficiary and the promisee have claims for damages for breach. If the promisee seeks damages, however, he will usually be limited to nominal damages: although the loss to the beneficiary may be substantial, the promisee cannot recover for that loss and he will ordinarily have suffered no loss himself. In such a case the remedy of specific performance will often be an appropriate one for the promisee. See § 307.

Illustration:

2. As part of a separation agreement B promises his wife A not to change the provision in B's will for C, their son. A dies and B changes his will to C's detriment, adding also a provision that C will forfeit any bequest if he questions the change before any tribunal. In an action by A's personal representative against B, the representative can get a judgment for nominal damages. As to the representative's right to specific performance, see Illustration 2 to § 307.

§ 347. Measure of Damages in General

Subject to the limitations stated in §§ 350-53, the injured party has a right to damages based on his expectation interest as measured by

(a) the loss in the value to him of the other party's performance caused by its failure or deficiency, plus

(b) any other loss, including incidental or consequential loss, caused by the breach, less

(c) any cost or other loss that he has avoided by not having to perform.

Comment:

a. Expectation interest. Contract damages are ordinarily based on the injured party's expectation interest and are intended to give him the benefit of his bargain by awarding him a sum of money that will, to the extent possible, put him in as good a position as he would have been in had the contract been performed. See § 344(1)(a). In some situations the sum awarded will do this adequately as, for example, where the injured party has simply had to pay an additional amount to arrange a substitute transaction and can be adequately compensated by damages based on that amount. In other situations the sum awarded cannot adequately compensate the injured party for his disappointed expectation as, for example,

where a delay in performance has caused him to miss an invaluable opportunity. The measure of damages stated in this Section is subject to the agreement of the parties, as where they provide for liquidated damages (§ 356) or exclude liability for consequential damages.

b. Loss in value. The first element that must be estimated in attempting to fix a sum that will fairly represent the expectation interest is the loss in the value to the injured party of the other party's performance that is caused by the failure of, or deficiency in, that performance. If no performance is rendered, the loss in value caused by the breach is equal to the value that the performance would have had to the injured party.

See Illustrations 1 and 2. If defective or partial performance is rendered, the loss in value caused by the breach is equal to the difference between the value that the performance would have had if there had been no breach and the value of such performance as was actually rendered. In principle, this requires a determination of the values of those performances to the injured party himself and not their values to some hypothetical reasonable person or on some market. See Restatement, Second, Torts § 911. They therefore depend on his own particular circumstances or those of his enterprise, unless consideration of these circumstances is precluded by the limitation of foreseeability (§ 351). Where the injured party's expected advantage consists largely or exclusively of the realization of profit, it may be possible to express this loss in value in terms of money with some assurance. In other situations, however, this is not possible and compensation for lost value may be precluded by the limitation of certainty. See § 352. In order to facilitate the estimation of loss with sufficient certainty to award damages, the injured party is sometimes given a choice between alternative bases of calculating his loss in value. The most important of these are stated in § 348. See also §§ 349 and 373. **Illustrations:**

    1. A contracts to publish a novel that B has written. A repudiates the contract and B is unable to get his novel published elsewhere. Subject to the limitations stated in §§ 350-53, B's damages include the loss of royalties that he would have received had the novel been published together with the value to him of the resulting enhancement of his reputation. But see Illustration 1 to § 352.

    2. A, a manufacturer, contracts to sell B, a dealer in used machinery, a used machine that B plans to resell. A repudiates and B is unable to obtain a similar machine elsewhere. Subject to the limitations stated in §§ 350-53, B's damages include the net profit that he would have made on resale of the machine.

c. Other loss. Subject to the limitations stated in §§ 350-53, the injured party is entitled to recover for all loss actually suffered. Items of loss other than loss in value of the other party's performance are often characterized as incidental or consequential. Incidental losses include costs incurred in a reasonable effort, whether successful or not, to avoid loss, as where a party pays brokerage fees in arranging or attempting

to arrange a substitute transaction. See Illustration 3. Consequential losses include such items as injury to person or property resulting from defective performance. See Illustration 4. The terms used to describe the type of loss are not, however, controlling, and the general principle is that all losses, however described, are recoverable. **Illustrations:**

    3. A contracts to employ B for $ 10,000 to supervise the production of A's crop, but breaks his contract by firing B at the beginning of the season. B reasonably spends $ 200 in fees attempting to find other suitable employment through appropriate agencies. B can recover the $ 200 incidental loss in addition to any other loss suffered, whether or not he succeeds in finding other employment.

    4. A leases a machine to B for a year, warranting its suitability for B's purpose. The machine is not suitable for B's purpose and causes $ 10,000 in damage to B's property and $ 15,000 in personal injuries. B can recover the $ 25,000 consequential loss in addition to any other loss suffered. See Uniform Commercial Code § 2-715(2)(b).

d. Cost or other loss avoided. Sometimes the breach itself results in a saving of some cost that the injured party would have incurred if he had had to perform. See Illustration 5. Furthermore, the injured party is expected to take reasonable steps to avoid further loss. See § 350. Where he does this by discontinuing his own performance, he avoids incurring additional costs of performance. See Illustrations 6 and 8. This cost avoided is subtracted from the loss in value caused by the breach in calculating his damages. If the injured party avoids further loss by making substitute arrangements for the use of his resources that are no longer needed to perform the contract, the net profit from such arrangements is also subtracted. See Illustration 9. The value to him of any salvageable materials that he has acquired for performance is also subtracted. See Illustration 7. Loss avoided is subtracted only if the saving results from the injured party not having to perform rather than from some unrelated event. See Illustration 10. If no cost or other loss has been avoided, however, the injured party's damages include the full amount of the loss in value with no subtraction, subject to the limitations stated in §§ 350-53. See Illustration 11. The intended "donee" beneficiary of a gift promise usually suffers loss to the full

extent of the value of the promised performance, since he is ordinarily not required to do anything, and so avoids no cost on breach. See § 302(1)(b).
Illustrations:

    5. A contracts to build a hotel for B for $ 500,000 and to have it ready for occupancy by May 1. B's occupancy of the hotel is delayed for a month because of a breach by A. The cost avoided by B as a result of not having to operate the hotel during May is subtracted from the May rent lost in determining B's damages.

    6. A contracts to build a house for B for $ 100,000. When it is partly built, B repudiates the contract and A stops work. A would have to spend $ 60,000 more to finish the house. The $ 60,000 cost avoided by A as a result of not having to finish the house is subtracted from the $ 100,000 price lost in determining A's damages. A has a right to $ 40,000 in damages from B, less any progress payments that he has already received. See Illustration 2 to § 344.

    7. The facts being otherwise as stated in Illustration 6, A has bought materials that are left over and that he can use for other purposes, saving him $ 5,000. The $ 5,000 cost avoided is subtracted in determining A's damages, resulting in damages of only $ 35,000 rather than $ 40,000.

    8. A contracts to convey land to B in return for B's working for a year. B repudiates the contract before A has conveyed the land. The value to A of the land is subtracted from the value to A of B's services in determining A's damages.

    9. A contracts to employ B for $ 10,000 to supervise the production of A's crop, but breaks his contract by firing B at the beginning of the season. B instead takes another job as a supervisor at $ 9,500. The $ 9,500 is subtracted from the $ 10,000 loss of earnings in determining B's damages. See Illustration 8 to § 350.

    10. A contracts to build a machine for B and deliver it to be installed in his factory by June 30. A breaks the contract and does not deliver the machine. B's factory is destroyed by fire on December 31 and the machine, if it had been installed there, would also have been destroyed. The fact that the factory was burned is not considered in determining B's damages.

    11. A contracts to send his daughter to B's school for $ 5,000 tuition. After the academic year has begun, A withdraws her and refuses to pay anything. A's breach does not reduce B's instructional or other costs and B is unable to find another student to take the place of A's daughter. B has a right to damages equal to the full $ 5,000.

e. Actual loss caused by breach. The injured party is limited to damages based on his actual loss caused by the breach. If he makes an especially favorable substitute transaction, so that he sustains a smaller loss than might have been expected, his damages are reduced by the loss avoided as a result of that transaction. See Illustration 12. If he arranges a substitute transaction that he would not have been expected to do under the rules on avoidability (§ 350), his damages are similarly limited by the loss so avoided. See Illustration 13. Recovery can be had only for loss that would not have occurred but for the breach. See § 346. If, after the breach, an event occurs that would have discharged the party in breach on grounds of impracticability of performance or frustration of purpose, damages are limited to the loss sustained prior to that event. See Illustration 15. Compare § 254(2). The principle that a party's liability is not reduced by payments or other benefits received by the injured party from collateral sources is less compelling in the case of a breach of contract than in the case of a tort. See Restatement, Second, Torts § 920A. The effect of the receipt of unemployment benefits by a discharged employee will turn on the court's perception of legislative policy rather than on the rule stated in this Section. See Illustration 14. **Illustrations:**

    12. A contracts to build a house for B for $ 100,000, but repudiates the contract after doing part of the work and having been paid $ 40,000. Other builders would charge B $ 80,000 to finish the house, but B finds a builder in need of work who does it for $ 70,000. B's damages are limited to the $ 70,000 that he actually had to pay to finish the work less the $ 60,000 cost avoided or $ 10,000, together with damages for any loss caused by the delay. See Illustration 2 to § 348.

    13. A contracts to employ B for $ 10,000 to supervise the production of A's crop. A breaks the contract by firing B at the beginning of the season, and B, unable to find another job, instead takes a job as a farm laborer for the entire season at $ 6,000. The $ 6,000 that he made as a farm laborer is subtracted from the $ 10,000 loss of earnings in determining B's damages. See Illustration 8 to § 350.

    14. A contracts to employ B for $ 10,000 to supervise the production of A's crop, but breaks his contract by firing B at the beginning of the season. B is unable to find another similar job but receives $ 3,000 in state unemployment

benefits. Whether the $ 3,000 will be subtracted from the $ 10,000 loss of earnings depends on the state legislation under which it was paid and the policy behind it.

15. On April 1, A and B make a personal service contract under which A is to employ B for six months beginning July 1 and B is to work for A during that period. On May 1, B repudiates the contract. On August 1, B falls ill and is unable to perform the contract for the remainder of the period. A can only recover damages based on his loss during the month of July since his loss during subsequent months was not caused by B's breach. Compare Illustration 2 to § 254.

f. Lost volume. Whether a subsequent transaction is a substitute for the broken contract sometimes raises difficult questions of fact. If the injured party could and would have entered into the subsequent contract, even if the contract had not been broken, and could have had the benefit of both, he can be said to have "lost volume" and the subsequent transaction is not a substitute for the broken contract. The injured party's damages are then based on the net profit that he has lost as a result of the broken contract. Since entrepreneurs try to operate at optimum capacity, however, it is possible that an additional transaction would not have been profitable and that the injured party would not have chosen to expand his business by undertaking it had there been no breach. It is sometimes assumed that he would have done so, but the question is one of fact to be resolved according to the circumstances of each case. See Illustration 16. See also Uniform Commercial Code § 2-708(2).

Illustration:

16. A contracts to pave B's parking lot for $ 10,000. B repudiates the contract and A subsequently makes a contract to pave a similar parking lot for $ 10,000. A's business could have been expanded to do both jobs. Unless it is proved that he would not have undertaken both, A's damages are based on the net profit he would have made on the contract with B, without regard to the subsequent transaction.

§ 348. Alternatives to Loss in Value of Performance

(1) If a breach delays the use of property and the loss in value to the injured party is not proved with reasonable certainty, he may recover damages based on the rental value of the property or on interest on the value of the property.

(2) If a breach results in defective or unfinished construction and the loss in value to the injured party is not proved with sufficient certainty, he may recover damages based on

(a) the diminution in the market price of the property caused by the breach, or

(b) the reasonable cost of completing performance or of remedying the defects if that cost is not clearly disproportionate to the probable loss in value to him.

(3) If a breach is of a promise conditioned on a fortuitous event and it is uncertain whether the event would have occurred had there been no breach, the injured party may recover damages based on the value of the conditional right at the time of breach.

Comment:

a. Reason for alternative bases. Although in principle the injured party is entitled to recover based on the loss in value to him caused by the breach, in practice he may be precluded from recovery on this basis because he cannot show the loss in value to him with sufficient certainty. See § 352. In such a case, if there is a reasonable alternative to loss in value, he may claim damages based on that alternative. This Section states the rules that have been developed for three such cases.

b. Breach that delays the use of property. If the breach is one that prevents for a period of time the use of property from which profits would have been made, the loss in value to the injured party is based on the profits that he would have made during that period. If those profits cannot be proved with reasonable certainty (§ 352), two other bases for recovery are possible. One is the fair rental value of the property during the period of delay. Damages based on fair rental value include an element of profit since the fair rental value of property depends on what it would command on the market and this turns on the profit that would be derived from its use. For this reason, uncertainty as to profits may result in uncertainty in fair rental value. Another possible basis for recovery, as a last resort, is the interest on the value of the property that has been made unproductive by the breach, if that value can be shown with reasonable certainty. Although these two other bases will ordinarily give a smaller recovery than loss in value, it is always open to the party in breach to show that this is not so and to hold the injured party to a smaller recovery based on loss in value to him. **Illustration:**

    1. A contracts with B to construct an outdoor drive-in theatre, to be completed by June 1. A does not complete the work until September 1. If B cannot prove his lost profits with reasonable certainty, he can recover damages based on the rental value of the theatre property or based on the interest on the value of the theatre property itself if he can prove either of these values with reasonable certainty. See Illustration 2 to § 352.

    c. Incomplete or defective performance. If the contract is one for construction, including repair or similar performance affecting the condition of property, and the work is not finished, the injured party will usually find it easier to prove what it would cost to have the work completed by another contractor than to prove the difference between the values to him of the finished and the unfinished performance. Since the cost to complete is usually less than the loss in value to him, he is limited by the rule on avoidability to damages based on cost to complete. See § 350(1). If he has actually had the work completed, damages will be based on his expenditures if he comes within the rule stated in § 350(2).

    Sometimes, especially if the performance is defective as distinguished from incomplete, it may not be possible to prove the loss in value to the injured party with reasonable certainty. In that case he can usually recover damages based on the cost to remedy the defects. Even if this gives him a recovery somewhat in excess of the loss in value to him, it is better that he receive a small windfall than that he be undercompensated by being limited to the resulting diminution in the market price of his property.

    Sometimes, however, such a large part of the cost to remedy the defects consists of the cost to undo what has been improperly done that the cost to remedy the defects will be clearly disproportionate to the probable loss in value to the injured party. Damages based on the cost to remedy the defects would then give the injured party a recovery greatly in excess of the loss in value to him and result in a substantial windfall.

Such an award will not be made. It is sometimes said that the award would involve "economic waste," but this is a misleading expression since an injured party will not, even if awarded an excessive amount of damages, usually pay to have the defects remedied if to do so will cost him more than the resulting increase in value to him. If an award based on the cost to remedy the defects would clearly be excessive and the injured party does not prove the actual loss in value to him, damages will be based instead on the difference between the market price that the property would have had without the defects and the market price of the property with the defects. This diminution in market price is the least possible loss in value to the injured party, since he could always sell the property on the market even if it had no special value to him. **Illustrations:**

    2. A contracts to build a house for B for $ 100,000 but repudiates the contract after doing part of the work and having been paid $ 40,000. Other builders will charge B $ 80,000 to finish the house. B's damages include the $ 80,000 cost to complete the work less the $ 60,000 cost avoided or $ 20,000, together with damages for any loss caused by delay. See Illustration 12 to § 347.

    3. A contracts to build a house for B for $ 100,000. When it is completed, the foundations crack, leaving part of the building in a dangerous condition. To make it safe would require tearing down some of the walls and strengthening the foundation at a cost of $ 30,000 and would increase the market value of the house by $ 20,000. B's damages include the $ 30,000 cost to remedy the defects.

    4. A contracts to build a house for B for $ 100,000 according to specifications that include the use of Reading pipe. After completion, B discovers that A has used Cohoes pipe, an equally good brand. To replace the Cohoes pipe with Reading pipe would require tearing down part of the walls at a cost of over $ 20,000 and would not affect the market price of the house. In an action by B against A, A gives no proof of any special value that Reading pipe would have to him. B's damages do not include the $ 20,000 cost to remedy the defects because that cost is clearly disproportionate to the loss in value to B. B can recover only nominal damages.

    d. Fortuitous event as condition. In the case of a promise conditioned on a fortuitous event (see Comment *a* to § 379), a breach that occurs before the happening of the fortuitous event may make it impossible to determine whether the event would have occurred had there been no breach. It would be unfair to the party in breach to award damages on the assumption that the event would have occurred, but equally unfair to the injured party to deny recovery of damages on the ground of uncertainty. The injured party has, in any case, the remedy of restitution (see § 373). Under the rule stated in Subsection (3) he also has the alternative remedy of damages based on the value of his conditional contract right at the time of breach, or what may be described as the value of his "chance of winning." The value of that right must itself be proved with reasonable certainty, as it may be if there is a market for such rights or if there is a suitable basis for determining the probability of the occurrence of the event.

The rule stated in this Subsection is limited to aleatory promises and does not apply if the promise is conditioned on some event, such as return performance by the injured party, that is not fortuitous. If, for example, an owner repudiates a contract to pay for repairs to be done by a contractor and then maintains that the contractor could not or would not have done the work had he not repudiated, the contractor must prove that he could and would have performed. If he fails to do this, he has no remedy in damages. He is not entitled to claim damages under the rule stated in Subsection (3). **Illustration:**

> 5. A offers a $ 100,000 prize to the owner whose horse wins a race at A's track. B accepts by entering his horse and paying the registration fee. When the race is run, A wrongfully prevents B's horse from taking part. Although B cannot prove that his horse would have won the race, he can prove that it was considered to have one chance in four of winning because one fourth of the money bet on the race was bet on his horse. B has a right to damages of $ 25,000 based on the value of the conditional right to the prize.

§ 349. Damages Based on Reliance Interest

As an alternative to the measure of damages stated in § 347, the injured party has a right to damages based on his reliance interest, including expenditures made in preparation for performance or in performance, less any loss that the party in breach can prove with reasonable certainty the injured party would have suffered had the contract been performed.

Comment:

a. Reliance interest where profit uncertain. Loss in value and cost or other loss avoided are key components of contract damages. See § 347. If the injured party was to supply services such as erecting a building, for example, the difference between loss in value of the other party's performance and the cost or other loss avoided by the injured party will be equal to the cost of the injured party's expenditures in reliance, up to the time of breach, plus the profit that would have been made had the contract been fully performed. To the extent that "overhead" costs are fixed costs, they are not included in the cost of expenditures in reliance for this purpose. See Illustration 6 to § 347. Under the rule stated in this Section, the injured party may, if he chooses, ignore the element of profit and recover as damages his expenditures in reliance. He may choose to do this if he cannot prove his profit with reasonable certainty. He may also choose to do this in the case of a losing contract, one under which he would have had a loss rather than a profit. In that case, however, it is open to the party in breach to prove the amount of the loss, to the extent that he can do so with reasonable certainty under the standard stated in § 352, and have it subtracted from the injured party's damages. The resulting damages will then be the same as those under the rule stated in § 347. If the injured party's expenditures exceed the contract price, it is clear that at least to the extent of the excess, there would have been a loss. For this reason, recovery for expenditures under the rule stated in this section may not exceed the full contract price. As to the possibility of restitution in such a case, see § 373. Often the reliance consists of preparation for performance or actual performance of the contract, and this is sometimes called "essential reliance." See, for example, Illustration 3. It may, however, also consist of preparation for collateral transactions that a party plans to carry out when the contract in question is performed, and this is sometimes called "incidental" reliance. See Illustration 4.

Illustrations:

1. A gives B a "dealer franchise" to sell A's products in a stated area for one year. In preparation for performance, B spends money on advertising, hiring sales personnel, and acquiring premises that cannot be used for other purposes. A then repudiates before performance begins. If neither party proves with reasonable certainty what profit or loss B would have made if the contract had been performed, B can recover as damages his expenditures in preparation for performance. See Illustration 8 to § 90.

2. A contracts with B to stage a series of performances in B's theater, each to have 50 per cent of the gross receipts. After A has spent $ 20,000 in getting ready for the performances, B rents the theater to others and repudiates the contract, and A stages the performance at another theater. A's expenditures in preparation for performance of the contract with B are worth $ 8,000 to him in connection with staging the performances at the other theater. If neither party proves with reasonable certainty what profit or loss A would have made if the contract had been performed, A can recover as damages the $ 12,000 balance of his expenditures in preparation for performance.

3. A contracts to build for B a factory of experimental design for $ 1,000,000. After A has spent $ 250,000 and been paid $ 150,000 in progress payments, B repudiates the contract and A stops work. A's expenditures include materials worth $ 10,000 that he can use on other jobs. If neither party proves with reasonable certainty what profit or loss A would have made if the contract had been performed, A can recover as damages the $ 90,000 balance of his expenditures in preparation for performance.

. . .

b. Reliance interest in other cases. There are other instances in which damages may be based on the reliance interest. Under the rules stated in §§ 87, 89, 90 and 139, if a promise is enforceable because it has induced action or forbearance, the remedy granted for breach may be limited as justice requires. Under these rules, relief may be limited to damages measured by the extent of the promisee's reliance rather than by the terms of the promise. See Comment *e* to § 87, Comment *d* to § 89, Comment *d* to § 90 and Comment *d* to § 139. Furthermore, even when the contract is enforceable because of consideration, a court may, under the rule stated in § 353, conclude that the circumstances require that damages be limited to losses incurred in reliance. See Comment *a* to § 353.

§ 350. Avoidability as a Limitation on Damages

(1) Except as stated in Subsection (2), damages are not recoverable for loss that the injured party could have avoided without undue risk, burden or humiliation.

(2) The injured party is not precluded from recovery by the rule stated in Subsection (1) to the extent that he has made reasonable but unsuccessful efforts to avoid loss.

Comment:

a. Rationale. The rules stated in this Section reflect the policy of encouraging the injured party to attempt to avoid loss. The rule stated in Subsection (1) encourages him to make such efforts as he can to avoid loss by barring him from recovery for loss that he could have avoided if he had done so. See Comment *b*. The exception stated in Subsection (2) protects him if he has made actual efforts by allowing him to recover, regardless of the rule stated in Subsection (1), if his efforts prove to be unsuccessful. See Comment *h*. See also Comment *c* to § 347.

b. Effect of failure to make efforts to mitigate damages. As a general rule, a party cannot recover damages for loss that he could have avoided by reasonable efforts. Once a party has reason to know that performance by the other party will not be forthcoming, he is ordinarily expected to stop his own performance to avoid further expenditure. See Illustrations 1, 2, 3 and 4. Furthermore, he is expected to take such affirmative steps as are appropriate in the circumstances to avoid loss by making substitute arrangements or otherwise. It is sometimes said that it is the "duty" of the aggrieved party to mitigate damages, but this is misleading because he incurs no liability for his failure to act. The amount of loss that he could reasonably have avoided by stopping performance, making substitute arrangements or otherwise is simply subtracted from the amount that would otherwise have been recoverable as damages. **Illustrations:**

1. A contracts to build a bridge for B for $ 100,000. B repudiates the contract shortly after A has begun work on the bridge, telling A that he no longer has need for it. A nevertheless spends

an additional $ 10,000 in continuing to perform. A's damages for breach of contract do not include the $ 10,000.

2. A contracts to lease a machine to B and to deliver it at B's factory. B repudiates the contract, but A nevertheless ships the machine to B, who refuses to receive it. A's damages for breach of contract do not include the cost of shipment of the machine.

3. A sells oil to B in barrels. B discovers that some of the barrels are leaky, in breach of warranty, but does not transfer the oil to good barrels that he has available. B's damages for breach of contract do not include the loss of the oil that could have been saved by transferring the oil to the available barrels.

4. A contracts to sell flour to B. The flour is defective, in breach of warranty, as B discovers after delivery. B nevertheless uses it to bake bread to supply his customers. B's damages for breach of contract do not include his loss of business caused by delivering inferior bread made from the flour.

c. Substitute transactions. When a party's breach consists of a failure to deliver goods or furnish services, for example, it is often possible for the injured party to secure similar goods or services on the market. If a seller of goods repudiates, the buyer can often buy similar goods elsewhere. See Illustration 5. If an employee quits his job, the employer can often find a suitable substitute. See Illustration 6. Similarly, when a party's breach consists of a failure to receive goods or services, for example, it is often possible for the aggrieved party to dispose of the goods or services on the market. If a buyer of goods repudiates, the seller can often sell the goods elsewhere. See Illustration 7. If an employer fires his employee, the employee can often find a suitable job elsewhere. See Illustration 8. In such cases as these, the injured party is expected to make appropriate efforts to avoid loss by arranging a substitute transaction. If he does not do so, the amount of loss that he could have avoided by doing so is subtracted in calculating his damages. In the case of the sale of goods, this principle has inspired the standard formulas under which a buyer's or seller's damages are based on the difference between the contract price and the market price on that market where the injured party could have arranged a substitute transaction for the purchase or sale of similar goods. See Uniform Commercial Code §§ 2-708, 2-713. Similar rules are applied to other contracts,

such as contracts for the sale of securities, where there is a well-established market for the type of performance involved, but the principle extends to other situations in which a substitute transaction can be arranged, even if there is no well-established market for the type of performance. However, in those other situations, the burden is generally put on the party in breach to show that a substitute transaction was available, as is done in the case in which an employee has been fired by his employer.

Illustrations:

5. A contracts to sell to B a used machine to be delivered at B's factory by June 1 for $ 10,000. A breaks the contract by repudiating it on May 1. By appropriate efforts B could buy a similar machine from another seller for $ 11,000 in time to be delivered at his factory by June 1, but he does not do so and loses a profit of $ 25,000 that he would have made from use of the machine. B's damages do not include the loss of the $ 25,000 profit, but he can recover $ 1,000 from A. See Uniform Commercial Code §§ 2-713(1), 2-715(2)(a).

6. A contracts to supervise the production of B's crop for $ 10,000, but breaks his contract and leaves at the beginning of the season. By appropriate efforts, B could obtain an equally good supervisor for $ 11,000, but he does not do so and the crop is lost. B's damages for A's breach of contract do not include the loss of his crop, but he can recover $ 1,000 from A.

7. A contracts to buy from B a used machine from B's factory for $ 10,000. A breaks the contract by refusing to receive or pay for the machine. By appropriate efforts, B could sell the machine to another buyer for $ 9,000, but he does not do so. B's damages for A's breach of contract do not include the loss of the $ 10,000 price, but he can recover $ 1,000 from A. See Uniform Commercial Code § 2-708(1).

8. A contracts to employ B for $ 10,000 to supervise the production of A's crop, but breaks his contract by firing B at the beginning of the season. By appropriate efforts, B could obtain an equally good job as a supervisor at $ 100 less than A had contracted to pay him, but he does not do so and remains unemployed. B's damages for A's breach of contract do not include his $ 10,000 loss of earnings, but he can recover $ 100 from A. See Illustration 9 to § 347.

d. "Lost volume." The mere fact that an injured party can make arrangements for the disposition of the goods or services that he was to supply under the contract does not necessarily mean that by doing so he will avoid loss. If he would have entered into both transactions but for the breach, he has "lost volume" as a result of the breach. See Comment *f* to § 347. In that case the second transaction is not a "substitute" for the first one. See Illustrations 9 and 10.

Illustrations:

9. A contracts to buy grain from B for $ 100,000, which would give B a net profit of $ 10,000. A breaks the contract by refusing to receive or pay for the grain. If B would have made the sale to A in addition to other sales, B's efforts to make other sales do not affect his damages. B's damages for A's breach of contract include his $ 10,000 loss of profit.

10. A contracts to pay B $ 20,000 for paving A's parking lot, which would give B a net profit of $ 3,000. A breaks the contract by repudiating it before B begins work. If B would have made the contract with A in addition to other contracts, B's efforts to obtain other contracts do not affect his damages. B's damages for A's breach of contract include his $ 3,000 loss of profit.

e. What is a "substitute." Whether an available alternative transaction is a suitable substitute depends on all the circumstances, including the similarity of the performance and the times and places that they would be rendered. See Illustration 11. If discrepancies between the transactions can be adequately compensated for in damages, the alternative transaction is regarded as a substitute and such damages are awarded. See Illustrations 12 and 13. If the party in breach offers to perform the contract for a different price, this may amount to a suitable alternative. See Illustration 14. But this is not the case if the offer is conditioned on surrender by the injured party of his claim for breach. See Illustration 15. **Illustrations:**

11. The facts being otherwise as stated in Illustration 8, by appropriate efforts B could only obtain a job as a farm laborer at $ 6,000, but he does not do so and remains unemployed. B's damages for breach of contract include his $ 10,000 loss of earnings.

12. The facts being otherwise as stated in Illustration 5, the other seller will not deliver the similar machine to B's factory, and insists that B take possession of it two weeks earlier than he can install it in his factory, but B can arrange to have it stored for two weeks and shipped to his factory for $ 1,500. B's damages do not include the loss of the $ 25,000 profit, but he can recover the $ 1,500 as well as the $ 1,000 from A.

13. A contracts to bale hay on B's farm so that B can use it later to feed his livestock. A does the work so defectively that the hay is worthless. B can buy similar hay in bales in Central City, 100 miles from his farm, for $ 10,000. The cost to ship the bales between Central City and his farm is $ 1,000. B's damages include the $ 10,000 market price and the $ 1,000 cost of shipment. If B had intended to ship his bales of hay to Central City for sale there, rather than to feed it to his livestock, the $ 1,000 cost of shipment would be subtracted from the $ 10,000 market price as cost avoided under § 347(c).

14. A contracts to sell to B a used machine from A's factory for $ 10,000. A breaks the contract by refusing to deliver the machine at that price, but offers to sell it to B for $ 11,000 without prejudice to B's right to damages. B refuses to buy it at that price and, since he cannot find a similar machine elsewhere, loses a profit of $ 25,000 that he would have made from use of the machine. B's damages do not include the loss of the $ 25,000 profit, but he can recover $ 1,000 from A.

15. The facts being otherwise as stated in Illustration 14, A's offer to sell the machine at $ 11,000 is conditioned on B's surrendering any claim that he may have against A for breach of contract. B's damages may include the loss of the $ 25,000 profit.

f. Time for arranging substitute transaction. The injured party is expected to arrange a substitute transaction within a reasonable time after he learns of the breach. He is expected to do this even if the breach takes the form of an anticipatory repudiation, since under the rule stated in Subsection (2) he is then protected against the possibility of a change in the market before the time for performance. See Comment *g.* The injured party may, however, make appropriate efforts to urge the repudiating party to perform in spite of his repudiation or to retract his repudiation, and these efforts will be taken into account in determining what is a reasonable time. Although the injured party is expected to arrange a substitute transaction without unreasonable delay following the anticipatory repudiation, the time for performance under the substitute transaction will ordinarily be the same time as it would have been under the original contract.

Illustrations:

16. On May 1, A contracts to sell to B a stated quantity of grain for $ 100,000, delivery and payment to be made on July 1. On July 1, A breaks the contract by refusing to deliver the

grain, but B does not buy substitute grain on the market on that date although he could do so for $ 110,000. On July 10, B buys substitute grain on the market for $ 120,000. B's damages for A's breach of contract do not include the $ 20,000 above the contract price that he paid on July 10, but he can recover $ 10,000 from A.

17. The facts being otherwise as stated in Illustration 16, A breaks the contract by repudiating it on June 1 and on the same day B tells A that he considers the repudiation final. B does not buy substitute grain on the market on that date although he could do so for $ 105,000 for delivery and payment on July 1. B's damages for A's breach of contract do not include the $ 20,000 above the contract price that he paid on July 10, but he can recover $ 5,000 from A.

g. Efforts expected. In some situations, it is reasonable for the injured party to rely on performance by the other party even after breach. This may be true, for example, if the breach is accompanied by assurances that performance will be forthcoming. In such a situation the injured party is not expected to arrange a substitute transaction although he may be expected to take some steps to avoid loss due to a delay in performance. Nor is it reasonable to expect him to take steps to avoid loss if those steps may cause other serious loss. He need not, for example, make other risky contracts, incur unreasonable expense or inconvenience or disrupt his business. In rare instances the appropriate course may be to complete performance instead of stopping. Finally the aggrieved party is not expected to put himself in a position that will involve humiliation, including embarrassment or loss of honor and respect.

Illustrations:

18. A contracts to build a building for B for $ 100,000. B repudiates the contract shortly before A has finished work. Because A has duties to subcontractors and will have difficulty in calculating his damages, A spends an additional $ 10,000 and completes the building. If stopping work would not have been reasonable in the circumstances, A can recover the full $ 100,000, including the $ 10,000 that he spent after B's repudiation. Compare Illustration 1.

19. A contracts to supervise the production of B's crop for $ 10,000, but commits a material breach of the contract by failing to begin on time. By appropriate efforts, B could obtain an equally good supervisor for $ 1,000 more than he had contracted to pay A, but he does not do so because A assures him that the delay is only

temporary. By the time that B discovers that A will be unavailable for the entire season, it is too late to hire another supervisor and the crop is lost. If B's delay in hiring another supervisor was reasonable in the circumstances, B's damages for A's breach of contract may include the loss of his crop.

20. A, a motion picture company, contracts to have B star in a musical comedy for $ 100,000. A breaks the contract and engages C, a rival of B, to star in the musical comedy, but offers B an equally good role under an identical contract as a star in another musical comedy for $ 100,000. Because B would be humiliated to work for A after A hired a rival in B's place, B refuses to accept the offer. If rejection of the offer was reasonable in the circumstances, B can recover the full $ 100,000. Compare Illustration 8.

h. Actual efforts to mitigate damages. Sometimes the injured party makes efforts to avoid loss but fails to do so. The rule stated in Subsection (2) protects the injured party in that situation if the efforts were reasonable. If, for example, a seller who is to manufacture goods for a buyer decides, on repudiation by the buyer, "in the exercise of reasonable commercial judgment for the purpose of avoiding loss" to complete manufacture of the goods, he is protected under Uniform Commercial Code § 2-704(2) even if it later appears that he could have better avoided loss by stopping manufacture. Similarly, if a buyer of goods who decides, on repudiation by the seller, to "'cover' by making in good faith and without unreasonable delay any reasonable purchase of or contract to purchase goods in substitution for those due from the seller," he is protected under Uniform Commercial Code § 2-712. See also Uniform Commercial Code § 2-706 for the seller's comparable right of resale. The rule stated in Subsection (2) reflects the policy underlying these Code provisions, one encouraging the injured party to make reasonable efforts to avoid loss by protecting him even when his efforts fail. To this extent, his failure to avoid loss does not have the effect stated in Subsection (1). Under the rule stated in § 347, costs incurred in a reasonable but unsuccessful effort to avoid loss are recoverable as incidental losses. See Comment *c* to § 347. **Illustrations:**

21. A contracts to sell to B a used machine to be delivered at A's factory by June 1 for $ 10,000. A breaks the contract by repudiating it

on May 1. B makes a reasonable purchase of a similar machine for $ 12,000 in time to be delivered at his factory by June 1. It later appears that, unknown to B, a similar machine could have been found for only $ 11,000. Nevertheless, B can recover $ 2,000 from A. Compare Illustration 5. See Uniform Commercial Code § 2-712.

22. A contracts to supervise the production of B's crop for $ 10,000, but breaks his contract and leaves at the beginning of the season. B makes a reasonable substitute contract with another supervisor for $ 12,000 in time to save his crop. It later appears that, unknown to B, a suitable supervisor could have been found for only $ 11,000. Nevertheless, B can recover $ 2,000 from A. Compare Illustration 6.

23. A pays a premium to B, an insurance company, for a policy of fire insurance on his house for a period of five years. B later repudiates the policy and A reasonably gets a similar policy from another insurer for the balance of the period. A has a right to damages against B based on the cost of the new policy.

§ 351. Unforeseeability and Related Limitations on Damages

(1) Damages are not recoverable for loss that the party in breach did not have reason to foresee as a probable result of the breach when the contract was made.

(2) Loss may be foreseeable as a probable result of a breach because it follows from the breach

(a) in the ordinary course of events, or

(b) as a result of special circumstances, beyond the ordinary course of events, that the party in breach had reason to know.

(3) A court may limit damages for foreseeable loss by excluding recovery for loss of profits, by allowing recovery only for loss incurred in reliance, or otherwise if it concludes that in the circumstances justice so requires in order to avoid disproportionate compensation.

Comment:

a. Requirement of foreseeability. A contracting party is generally expected to take account of those risks that are foreseeable at the time he makes the contract. He is not, however, liable in the event of breach for loss that he did not at the time of contracting have reason to foresee as a probable result of such a breach. The mere circumstance that some loss was foreseeable, or even that some loss of the same general kind was foreseeable, will not suffice if the loss that actually occurred was not foreseeable. It is enough, however, that the loss was foreseeable as a probable, as distinguished from a necessary, result of his breach. Furthermore, the party in breach need not have made a "tacit agreement" to be liable for the loss. Nor must he have had the loss in mind when making the contract, for the test is an objective one based on what he had reason to foresee. There is no requirement of foreseeability with respect to the injured party. In spite of these qualifications, the requirement of foreseeability is a more severe limitation of liability than is the requirement of substantial or "proximate" cause in the case of an action in tort or for breach of warranty. Compare Restatement, Second, Torts § 431; Uniform Commercial Code § 2-715(2)(b). Although the recovery that is precluded by the limitation of foreseeability is usually based on the expectation interest and takes the form of lost profits (see Illustration 1), the limitation may also preclude recovery based on the reliance interest (see Illustration 2). **Illustrations:**

1. A, a carrier, contracts with B, a miller, to carry B's broken crankshaft to its manufacturer for repair. B tells A when they make the contract that the crankshaft is part of B's milling machine and that it must be sent at once, but not that the mill is stopped because B has no replacement. Because A delays in carrying the crankshaft, B loses profit during an additional period while the mill is stopped because of the delay. A is not liable for B's loss of profit. That loss was not foreseeable by A as a probable result of the breach at the time the contract was made because A did not know that the broken crankshaft was necessary for the operation of the mill.

2. A contracts to sell land to B and to give B possession on a stated date. Because A delays a short time in giving B possession, B incurs unusual expenses in providing for cattle that he had already purchased to stock the land as a ranch. A

had no reason to know when they made the contract that B had planned to purchase cattle for this purpose. A is not liable for B's expenses in providing for the cattle because that loss was not foreseeable by A as a probable result of the breach at the time the contract was made.

b. *"General" and "special" damages.* Loss that results from a breach in the ordinary course of events is foreseeable as the probable result of the breach. See Uniform Commercial Code § 2-714(1). Such loss is sometimes said to be the "natural" result of the breach, in the sense that its occurrence accords with the common experience of ordinary persons. For example, a seller of a commodity to a wholesaler usually has reason to foresee that his failure to deliver the commodity as agreed will probably cause the wholesaler to lose a reasonable profit on it. See Illustrations 3 and 4. Similarly, a seller of a machine to a manufacturer usually has reason to foresee that his delay in delivering the machine as agreed will probably cause the manufacturer to lose a reasonable profit from its use, although courts have been somewhat more cautious in allowing the manufacturer recovery for loss of such profits than in allowing a middleman recovery for loss of profits on an intended resale. See Illustration 5. The damages recoverable for such loss that results in the ordinary course of events are sometimes called "general" damages.

If loss results other than in the ordinary course of events, there can be no recovery for it unless it was foreseeable by the party in breach because of special circumstances that he had reason to know when he made the contract. See Uniform Commercial Code § 2-715(2)(a). For example, a seller who fails to deliver a commodity to a wholesaler is not liable for the wholesaler's loss of profit to the extent that it is extraordinary nor for his loss due to unusual terms in his resale contracts unless the seller had reason to know of these special circumstances. See Illustration 6. Similarly, a seller who delays in delivering a machine to a manufacturer is not liable for the manufacturer's loss of profit to the extent that it results from an intended use that was abnormal unless the seller had reason to know of this special circumstance. See Illustration 7. In the case of a written agreement, foreseeability is sometimes established by the use of recitals in the agreement itself. The parol evidence rule (§ 213) does not, however, preclude the use of negotiations prior to the making of the contract to show for this purpose circumstances that were then known to a party. The damages recoverable for loss that results other than in the ordinary course of events are sometimes called "special" or "consequential" damages. These terms are often misleading, however, and it is not necessary to distinguish between "general" and "special" or "consequential" damages for the purpose of the rule stated in this Section. **Illustrations:**

3. A and B make a written contract under which A is to recondition by a stated date a used machine owned by B so that it will be suitable for sale by B to C. A knows when they make the contract that B has contracted to sell the machine to C but knows nothing of the terms of B's contract with C. Because A delays in returning the machine to B, B is unable to sell it to C and loses the profit that he would have made on that sale. B's loss of reasonable profit was foreseeable by A as a probable result of the breach at the time the contract was made.

4. A, a manufacturer of machines, contracts to make B his exclusive selling agent in a specified area for the period of a year. Because A fails to deliver any machines, B loses the profit on contracts that he would have made for their resale. B's loss of reasonable profit was foreseeable by A as a probable result of the breach at the time the contract was made.

5. A and B make a contract under which A is to recondition by a stated date a used machine owned by B so that it will be suitable for use in B's canning factory. A knows that the machine must be reconditioned by that date if B's factory is to operate at full capacity during the canning season, but nothing is said of this in the written contract. Because A delays in returning the machine to B, B loses its use for the entire canning season and loses the profit that he would have made had his factory operated at full capacity. B's loss of reasonable profit was foreseeable by A as a probable result of the breach at the time the contract was made.

6. The facts being otherwise as stated in Illustration 3, the profit that B would have made under his contract with A was extraordinarily large because C promised to pay an exceptionally high price as a result of a special need for the machine of which A was unaware. A is not liable for B's loss of profit to the extent that it exceeds what would ordinarily result from such a contract. To that extent the loss was not foreseeable by A as a probable result of the breach at the time the contract was made.

. . .

c. Litigation or settlement caused by breach. Sometimes a breach of contract results in claims by third persons against the injured party. The party in breach is liable for the amount of any judgment against the injured party together with his reasonable expenditures in the litigation, if the party in breach had reason to foresee such expenditures as the probable result of his breach at the time he made the contract. See Illustrations 8, 10, 11 and 12. This is so even if the judgment in the litigation is based on a liquidated damage clause in the injured party's contract with the third party. See Illustration 8. A failure to notify the party in breach in advance of the litigation may prevent the result of the litigation from being conclusive as to him. But to the extent that the injured party's loss resulting from litigation is reasonable, the fact that the party in breach was not notified does not prevent the inclusion of that loss in the damages assessed against him. In furtherance of the policy favoring private settlement of disputes, the injured party is also allowed to recover the reasonable amount of any settlement made to avoid litigation, together with the costs of settlement. See Illustration 9.

Illustrations:

8. The facts being otherwise as stated in Illustration 3, B not only loses the profit that he would have made on sale of the machine to C, but is held liable for damages in an action brought by C for breach of contract. The damages paid to C and B's reasonable expenses in defending the action were also foreseeable by A as a probable result of the breach at the time he made the contract with B. The result is the same even though they were based on a liquidated damage clause in the contract between B and C if A knew of the clause or if the use of such a clause in the contract between B and C was foreseeable by A at the time he made the contract with B.

9. The facts being otherwise as stated in Illustration 3, B not only loses the profit that he would have made on sale of the machine to C, but settles with C by paying C a reasonable sum of money to avoid litigation. The amount of the settlement paid to C and B's reasonable expenses in settling were also foreseeable by A at the time he made the contract with B as a probable result of the breach.

10. A contracts to supply B with machinery for unloading cargo. A, in breach of contract, furnishes defective machinery, and C, an employee of B, is injured. C sues B and gets a judgment, which B pays. The amount of the judgment and B's reasonable expenditures in defending the action were foreseeable by A at the time the contract was made as a probable result of the breach.

11. A contracts to procure a right of way for B, for a railroad. Because A, in breach of contract, fails to do this, B has to acquire the right of way by condemnation proceedings. B's reasonable expenditures in those proceedings were foreseeable by A at the time the contract was made as a probable result of the breach.

12. A leases land to B with a covenant for quiet enjoyment. C brings an action of ejectment against B and gets judgment. B's reasonable expenditures in defending the action were foreseeable by A as the probable result of the breach at the time the contract was made.

d. Unavailability of substitute. If several circumstances have contributed to cause a loss, the party in breach is not liable for it unless he had reason to foresee all of them. Sometimes a loss would not have occurred if the injured party had been able to make substitute arrangements after breach, as, for example, by "cover" through purchase of substitute goods in the case of a buyer of goods (see Uniform Commercial Code § 2-712). If the inability of the injured party to make such arrangements was foreseeable by the party in breach at the time he made the contract, the resulting loss was foreseeable. See Illustration 13. On the impact of this principle on contracts to lend money, see Comment *e*. **Illustration:**

13. A contracts with B, a farmer, to lease B a machine to be used harvesting B's crop, delivery to be made on July 30. A knows when he makes the contract that B's crop will be ready on that date and that B cannot obtain another machine elsewhere. Because A delays delivery until August 10, B's crop is damaged and he loses profit. B's loss of profit was foreseeable by A at the time the contract was made as a probable result of the breach.

e. Breach of contract to lend money. The limitation of foreseeability is often applied in actions for damages for breach of contracts to lend money. Because credit is so widely available, a lender often has no reason to foresee at the time the contract is made that the borrower will be unable to make substitute arrangements in the event of breach. See Comment *d*. In most cases, then, the lender's liability will be limited to the relatively small additional amount that it would ordinarily cost to get a similar loan from another lender. However, in the less common situation in which the lender has reason to foresee that the borrower will be unable to borrow elsewhere or will be delayed in borrowing elsewhere, the lender may be liable for much heavier damages based on the borrower's inability to take advantage of a specific opportunity (see Illustration 14), his having to postpone or abandon a profitable project (see Illustration 15), or his forfeiture of security for failure to make prompt payment (see Illustration 16). **Illustrations:**

14. A contracts to lend B $ 100,000 for one year at eight percent interest for the stated purpose of buying a specific lot of goods for resale. B can resell the goods at a $ 20,000 profit. A delays in making the loan, and although B can borrow money on the market at ten percent interest, he is unable to do so in time and loses the opportunity to buy the goods. Unless A had reason to foresee at the time that he made the contract that such a delay in making the loan would probably cause B to lose the opportunity, B can only recover damages based on two percent of the amount of the loan.

15. A contracts to lend $ 1,000,000 to B for the stated purpose of enabling B to build a building and takes property of B as security. After construction is begun, A refuses to make the loan or release the security. Because B lacks further security, he is unable to complete the building, which becomes a total loss. B's loss incurred in partial construction of the building was foreseeable by A at the time of the contract as a probable result of the breach.

16. A, who holds B's land as security for a loan, contracts to lend B a sum of money sufficient to pay off other liens on the land at the current rate of interest. A repudiates and informs B in time to obtain money elsewhere on the market, but B is unable to do so. The liens are foreclosed and the land sold at a loss. Unless A knew when he made the contract that B would probably be unable to borrow the money elsewhere, B's loss on the foreclosure sale was not foreseeable as a probable result of A's breach.

f. Other limitations on damages. It is not always in the interest of justice to require the party in breach to pay damages for all of the foreseeable loss that he has caused. There are unusual instances in which it appears from the circumstances either that the parties assumed that one of them would not bear the risk of a particular loss or that, although there was no such assumption, it would be unjust to put the risk on that party. One such circumstance is an extreme disproportion between the loss and the price charged by the party whose liability for that loss is in question. The fact that the price is relatively small suggests that it was not intended to cover the risk of such liability. Another such circumstance is an informality of dealing, including the absence of a detailed written contract, which indicates that there was no careful attempt to allocate all of the risks. The fact that the parties did not attempt to delineate with precision all of the risks justifies a court in attempting to allocate them fairly. The limitations dealt with in this Section are more likely to be imposed in connection with contracts that do not arise in a commercial setting. Typical examples of limitations imposed on damages under this discretionary power involve the denial of recovery for loss of profits and the restriction of damages to loss incurred in reliance on the contract. Sometimes these limits are covertly imposed, by means of an especially demanding requirement of foreseeability or of certainty. The rule stated in this Section recognizes that what is done in such cases is the imposition of a limitation in the interests of justice. **Illustrations:**

17. A, a private trucker, contracts with B to deliver to B's factory a machine that has just been repaired and without which B's factory, as A knows, cannot reopen. Delivery is delayed because A's truck breaks down. In an action by B against A for breach of contract the court may, after taking into consideration such factors as the absence of an elaborate written contract and the extreme disproportion between B's loss of profits during the delay and the price of the trucker's services, exclude recovery for loss of profits.

18. A, a retail hardware dealer, contracts to sell B an inexpensive lighting attachment, which, as A knows, B needs in order to use his tractor at night on his farm. A is delayed in obtaining the attachment and, since no substitute is available, B is unable to use the tractor at night during the delay. In an action by B against A for breach of contract, the court may, after taking into consideration such factors as the absence of an elaborate written contract and the extreme disproportion between B's loss of profits during the delay and the price of the attachment, exclude recovery for loss of profits.

19. A, a plastic surgeon, makes a contract with B, a professional entertainer, to perform plastic surgery on her face in order to improve her appearance. The result of the surgery is, how-

ever, to disfigure her face and to require a second operation. In an action by B against A for breach of contract, the court may limit damages by allowing recovery only for loss incurred by B in reliance on the contract, including the fees paid by B and expenses for hospitalization, nursing care and medicine for both operations, together with any damages for the worsening of B's appearance if these can be proved with reasonable certainty, but not including any loss resulting from the failure to improve her appearance.

§ 352. Uncertainty as a Limitation on Damages

Damages are not recoverable for loss beyond an amount that the evidence permits to be established with reasonable certainty.

Comment:

a. Requirement of certainty. A party cannot recover damages for breach of a contract for loss beyond the amount that the evidence permits to be established with reasonable certainty. See Illustration 1. Courts have traditionally required greater certainty in the proof of damages for breach of a contract than in the proof of damages for a tort. The requirement does not mean, however, that the injured party is barred from recovery unless he establishes the total amount of his loss. It merely excludes those elements of loss that cannot be proved with reasonable certainty. The main impact of the requirement of certainty comes in connection with recovery for lost profits. Although the requirement of certainty is distinct from that of foreseeability (§ 351), its impact is similar in this respect. Although the requirement applies to damages based on the reliance as well as the expectation interest, there is usually little difficulty in proving the amount that the injured party has actually spent in reliance on the contract, even if it is impossible to prove the amount of profit that he would have made. In such a case, he can recover his loss based on his reliance interest instead of on his expectation interest. See § 349 and Illustrations 1, 2 and 3.

Doubts are generally resolved against the party in breach. A party who has, by his breach, forced the injured party to seek compensation in damages should not be allowed to profit from his breach where it is established that a significant loss has occurred. A court may take into account all the circumstances of the breach, including willfulness, in deciding whether to require a lesser degree of certainty, giving greater discretion to the trier of the facts. Damages need not be calculable with mathematical accuracy and are often at best approximate. See Comment 1 to Uniform Commercial Code § 1-106. This is especially true for items such as loss of good will as to which great precision cannot be expected. See Illustration 4. Furthermore, increasing receptiveness on the part of courts to proof by sophisticated economic and financial data and by expert opinion has made it easier to meet the requirement of certainty. **Illustrations:**

1. A contracts to publish a novel that B has written. A repudiates the contract and B is unable to get his novel published elsewhere. If the evidence does not permit B's loss of royalties and of reputation to be estimated with reasonable certainty, he cannot recover damages for that loss, although he can recover nominal damages. See Illustration 1 to § 347.

2. A contracts to sell B a tract of land on which B plans to build an outdoor drive-in theatre. A breaks the contract by selling the land to C, and B is unable to build the theatre. If, because of the speculative nature of the new enterprise the evidence does not permit B's loss of profits to be estimated with reasonable certainty, his recovery will be limited to expenses incurred in reliance or, if none can be proved with reasonable certainty, to nominal damages.

3. A and B make a contract under which A is to construct a building of radical new design for B for $ 5,000,000. After A has spent $ 3,000,000 in reliance, B repudiates the contract and orders A off the site. If the evidence does not permit A's lost profits to be estimated with reasonable certainty, he can recover the $ 3,000,000 that he has spent in reliance. He must, however, then prove that amount with reasonable certainty.

. . .

b. Proof of profits. The difficulty of proving lost profits varies greatly with the nature of the transaction. If, for example, it is the seller who claims lost profit on the ground that the buyer's breach has caused him to lose a sale, proof of lost profit will ordinarily not be difficult. If, however, it is the buyer who claims lost profit on the ground that the seller's breach has caused him loss in other transactions, the task of proof is harder. Furthermore, if the transaction is more complex and extends into the future, as where the seller agrees to furnish all of the buyer's requirements over a period of years, proof of the loss of profits caused by the seller's breach is more difficult. If the breach prevents the injured party from carrying on a well-established business, the resulting loss of profits can often be proved with sufficient certainty. Evidence of past performance will form the basis for a reasonable prediction as to the future. See Illustration 5. However, if the business is a new one or if it is a speculative one that is subject to great fluctuations in volume, costs or prices, proof will be more difficult. Nevertheless, damages may be established with reasonable certainty with the aid of expert testimony, economic and financial data, market surveys and analyses, business records of similar enterprises, and the like. See Illustration 6. Under a contract of exclusive agency for the sale of goods on commission, the agent can often prove with sufficient certainty the profits that he would have made had he not been discharged. Proof of the sales made by the agent in the agreed territory before the breach, or of the sales made there by the principal after the breach, may permit a reasonably accurate estimate of the agent's loss of commissions. However, if the agency is not an exclusive one, so that the agent's ability to withstand competition is in question, such a showing will be more difficult, although the agent's past record may give a sufficient basis for judging this. See Illustration 7. **Illustrations:**

5. A contracts with B to remodel B's existing outdoor drive-in theatre, work to be completed on June 1. A does not complete the work until September 1. B can use records of the theatre's prior and subsequent operation, along with other evidence, to prove his lost profits with reasonable certainty.

6. A contracts with B to construct a new outdoor drive-in theatre, to be completed on June

1. A does not complete the theatre until September 1. Even though the business is a new rather than an established one, B may be able to prove his lost profits with reasonable certainty. B can use records of the theatre's subsequent operation and of the operation of similar theatres in the same locality, along with other evidence including market surveys and expert testimony, in attempting to do this.

7. A contracts with B to make B his exclusive agent for the sale of machine tools in a specified territory and to supply him with machine tools at stated prices. After B has begun to act as A's agent, A repudiates the agreement and replaces him with C. B can use evidence as to sales and profits made by him before the repudiation and made by C after the repudiation in attempting to prove his lost profits with reasonable certainty. It would be more difficult, although not necessarily impossible, for B to succeed in this attempt if his agency were not exclusive.

c. Alternative remedies. The necessity of proving damages can be avoided if another remedy, such as a decree of specific performance or an injunction, is granted instead of damages. Although the availability of such a remedy does not preclude an award of damages as an alternative, it may justify a court in requiring greater certainty of proof if damages are to be awarded. See Illustration 8. **Illustration:**

8. A, a steel manufacturer, and B, a dealer in scrap steel, contract for the sale by A to B of all of A's output of scrap steel for five years at a price fixed in terms of the market price. B's profit will depend largely on the amount of A's output and the cost of transporting the scrap to B's purchasers. A repudiates the contract at the end of one year. Whether B can recover damages based on lost profits over the remaining four years will depend on whether he can prove A's output and the transportation costs with reasonable certainty. If he can do so for part of the remaining four years, he can recover damages based on lost profits for that period. The availability of the remedy of specific performance is a factor that will influence a court in requiring greater certainty.

§ 353. Loss Due to Emotional Disturbance

Recovery for emotional disturbance will be excluded unless the breach also caused bodily harm or the contract or the breach is of such a kind that serious emotional disturbance was a particularly likely result.

Comment:

a. Emotional disturbance. Damages for emotional disturbance are not ordinarily allowed. Even if they are foreseeable, they are often particularly difficult to establish and to measure.

There are, however, two exceptional situations where such damages are recoverable. In the first, the disturbance accompanies a bodily injury. In such cases the action may nearly always be regarded as one in tort, although most jurisdictions do not require the plaintiff to specify the nature of the wrong on which his action is based and award damages without classifying the wrong. See Restatement, Second, Torts §§ 436, 905. In the second exceptional situation, the contract or the breach is of such a kind that serious emotional disturbance was a particularly likely result. Common examples are contracts of carriers and innkeepers with passengers and guests, contracts for the carriage or proper disposition of dead bodies, and contracts for the delivery of messages concerning death. Breach of such a contract is particularly likely to cause serious emotional disturbance. Breach of other types of contracts, resulting for example in sudden impoverishment or bankruptcy, may by chance cause even more severe emotional disturbance, but, if the contract is not one where this was a particularly likely risk, there is no recovery for such disturbance. **Illustrations:**

1. A contracts to construct a house for B. A knows when the contract is made that B is in delicate health and that proper completion of the work is of great importance to him. Because of delays and departures from specifications, B suffers nervousness and emotional distress. In an action by B against A for breach of contract, the element of emotional disturbance will not be included as loss for which damages may be awarded.

2. A, a hotel keeper, wrongfully ejects B, a guest, in breach of contract. In doing so, A uses foul language and accuses B of immorality, but commits no assault. In an action by B against A for breach of contract, the element of B's emotional disturbance will be included as loss for which damages may be awarded.

3. A makes a contract with B to conduct the funeral for B's husband and to provide a suitable casket and vault for his burial. Shortly thereafter, B discovers that, because A knowingly failed to provide a vault with a suitable lock, water has entered it and reinterment is necessary. B suffers shock, anguish and illness as a result. In an action by B against A for breach of contract, the element of emotional disturbance will be included as loss for which damages may be awarded.

. . .

§ 354. Interest as Damages

(1) If the breach consists of a failure to pay a definite sum in money or to render a performance with fixed or ascertainable monetary value, interest is recoverable from the time for performance on the amount due less all deductions to which the party in breach is entitled.

(2) In any other case, such interest may be allowed as justice requires on the amount that would have been just compensation had it been paid when performance was due.

Comment:

a. Scope. This Section deals with an injured party's right to interest as damages in compensation for the deprivation of a promised performance. Had the performance been rendered when it was due, the injured party would have been able to make use of it. Interest is a standardized form of compensation to the injured party for the loss of that use, in the absence of agreement to the contrary. It is payable without compounding at the rate, commonly called the "legal rate," fixed by statute for this purpose. This Section does not deal with the injured party's right to interest to compensate him for expenditures occasioned by the breach. If, following an anticipatory repudiation, he loses the use of money through making reasonable substitute arrangements, he is entitled to interest as incidental damages under the rule stated in § 347. Nor does this Section deal with the injured party's right to interest under the terms of the contract. If the parties have agreed on the payment of interest, it is payable not as damages but pursuant to a contract duty that is enforceable as is any other such duty, subject to legal restrictions on the rate of interest. Nor does this Section deal with interest on a judgment once rendered.

b. Performance must be due. Interest is not payable as damages for non-performance until performance is due. If there is a period of time before performance is due, such as a definite or indefinite period of credit, interest does not begin to run until the period is over. If the performance is to be rendered on demand, interest does not begin to run until a demand is made, even though an action might be maintained without a demand. See Illustration 3 to § 226. If the action itself is considered to be the required demand, interest begins to run from the time the action is brought. If the performance is subject to the occurrence of an event as a condition, interest does not begin to run until that condition occurs or is excused.

c. Where amount due is sufficiently definite. Under the rule stated in Subsection (1), a party is not chargeable with interest on a sum unless its amount is fixed by the contract or he could have determined its amount with reasonable certainty so that he could have made a proper tender. Unless otherwise agreed, interest is always recoverable for the non-payment of money once payment has become due and there has been a breach. This rule applies to debts due for money lent, goods sold or services performed, including installments due on a construction contract. The fact that the breach has spared some expense that is uncertain in amount does not prevent the recovery of interest. The sum due is sufficiently definite if it is ascertainable from the terms of the contract, as where the contract fixes a price per unit of performance, even though the number of units performed must be proved and is subject to dispute. The same is true, even if the contract does not of itself create a money debt, if it fixes a money equivalent of the performance. It is also true, even if the contract does not fix a money equivalent of the performance, if such an equivalent can be determined from established market prices. The fact that the extent of the performance rendered and the existence of the market price must be proved by evidence extrinsic to the contract does not prevent the application of these rules. **Illustrations:**

1. A lends B $ 10,000 to be repaid in 30 days without interest. B fails to pay the debt. A sues B and recovers $ 10,000. A is also entitled to simple interest on the $ 10,000 at the legal rate from the date of maturity.

2. A contracts to sell B goods for $ 10,000 on 30 days credit, nothing being said as to interest. A delivers the goods but B fails to pay for them at the end of 30 days. A sues B and recovers $ 10,000. A is also entitled to simple interest on the $ 10,000 at the legal rate from the expiration of the credit period.

3. A contracts to sell B all the berries to be grown on A's farm during one year for $ 5 a quart. A delivers 2,000 quarts. No part of the price is paid. B wrongly claims that only 1,000 quarts were delivered and that they were all paid for when received. A sues B and recovers $ 10,000. A is also entitled to simple interest on the $ 10,000 at the legal rate from the date when payment was due.

4. A contracts to sell machinery to B for $ 10,000, the price to be paid by B in wheat at the market price on July 1. A delivers the machinery but B fails to deliver the wheat. A sues B and recovers $ 10,000. A is also entitled to simple interest on the $ 10,000 at the legal rate from July 1. The result would be the same if the price were not expressed in dollars but in terms of 1,000 bushels of wheat to be delivered on July 1 and the market price on that day was $ 10 a bushel.

5. On February 1 A makes a contract to sell a ship to B for $ 10,000,000, payment and delivery to be October 1. On September 1, B repudiates the contract and A promptly makes a reasonable contract to resell the ship for $ 8,000,000, payment and delivery to take place on October 1. A sues B and recovers $ 2,000,000. A is entitled to simple interest on the $ 2,000,000 at the legal rate from October 1.

. . .

d. Discretionary in other cases. Damages for breach of contract include not only the value of the promised performance but also compensation for consequential loss. The amount to be awarded for such loss is often very difficult to estimate in advance of trial and cannot be determined by the party in breach with sufficient certainty to enable him to make a proper tender. In such cases, the award of interest is left to judicial discretion, under the rule stated in Subsection (2), in the light of all the circumstances, including any deficiencies in the performance of the injured party and any unreasonableness in the demands made by him. **Illustrations:**

8. A sells seed to B, warranting that it is Bristol cabbage seed. It is an inferior type of cabbage seed instead, and B suffers a loss of profit. B sues A and recovers $ 10,000, the difference between the value to B of a crop of Bristol cabbage and the crop actually grown. That amount was not, however, sufficiently definite to give B a right to interest on it. The allowance of interest is in the discretion of the court.

9. A contracts to build a bungalow for B for $ 30,000. After completion but before B has paid the final $ 6,000, B occupies the bungalow but refuses to pay the balance because the workmanship and materials are unsatisfactory. A sues B and recovers only $ 4,000 on the ground that B's claim entitles him to compensation in the amount of $ 2,000. The sum of $ 4,000 was not sufficiently definite to give A a right to interest on it. The allowance of interest is within the discretion of the court. The fact that A was himself in breach will be considered.

§ 355. Punitive Damages

Punitive damages are not recoverable for a breach of contract unless the conduct constituting the breach is also a tort for which punitive damages are recoverable.

Comment:

a. Compensation not punishment. The purposes of awarding contract damages is to compensate the injured party. See Introductory Note to this Chapter. For this reason, courts in contract cases do not award damages to punish the party in breach or to serve as an example to others unless the conduct constituting the breach is also a tort for which punitive damages are recoverable. Courts are sometimes urged to award punitive damages when, after a particularly aggravated breach, the injured party has difficulty in proving all of the loss that he has suffered. In such cases the willfulness of the breach may be taken into account in applying the requirement that damages be proved with reasonable certainty (Comment *a* to § 352); but the purpose of awarding damages is still compensation and not punishment, and punitive damages are not appropriate. In exceptional instances, departures have been made from this general policy. A number of states have enacted statutes that vary the rule stated in this Section, notably in situations involving consumer transactions or arising under insurance policies. **Illustrations:**

1. A is employed as a school teacher by B. In breach of contract and without notice B discharges A by excluding him from the school building and by stating in the presence of the pupils that he is discharged. Regardless of B's motive in discharging A, A cannot recover punitive damages from B. A can recover compensatory damages under the rule stated in § 347, including any damages for emotional disturbance that are allowable under the rule stated in § 353.

2. A and B, who are neighbors, make a contract under which A promises to supply water to B from A's well for ten years in return for B's promise to make monthly payments and share the cost of repairs. After several years, the relationship between A and B deteriorates and A, in breach of contract and to spite B, shuts off the water periodically. B cannot recover punitive damages from A. B can recover compensation damages under the rule stated in § 347 if he can prove them with reasonable certainty (§ 352), and the court may take into account the willfulness of A's breach in applying that requirement. See Comment *a* to § 352.

b. Exception for tort. In some instances the breach of contract is also a tort, as may be the case for a breach of duty by a public utility. Under modern rules of procedure, the complaint may not show whether the plaintiff intends his case to be regarded as one in contract or one in tort. The rule stated in this Section does not preclude an award of punitive damages in such a case if such an award would be proper under the law of torts. See Restatement, Second, Torts § 908. The term "tort" in the rule stated in this Section is elastic, and the effect of the general expansion of tort liability to protect additional interests is to make punitive damages somewhat more widely available for breach of contract as well. Some courts have gone rather far in this direction. **Illustrations:**

3. A, a telephone company, contracts with B to render uninterrupted service. A, tortiously as well as in breach of contract, fails to maintain service at night and B is unable to telephone a doctor for his sick child. B's right to recover punitive damages is governed by Restatement, Second, Torts § 908.

. . .

§ 356. Liquidated Damages and Penalties

(1) Damages for breach by either party may be liquidated in the agreement but only at an amount that is reasonable in the light of the anticipated or actual loss caused by the breach and the difficulties of proof of loss. A term fixing unreasonably large liquidated damages is unenforceable on grounds of public policy as a penalty.

(2) A term in a bond providing for an amount of money as a penalty for non-occurrence of the condition of the bond is unenforceable on grounds of public policy to the extent that the amount exceeds the loss caused by such non-occurrence.

Comment:

a. Liquidated damages or penalty. The parties to a contract may effectively provide in advance the damages that are to be payable in the event of breach as long as the provision does not disregard the principle of compensation. The enforcement of such provisions for liquidated damages saves the time of courts, juries, parties and witnesses and reduces the expense of litigation. This is especially important if the amount in controversy is small. However, the parties to a contract are not free to provide a penalty for its breach. The central objective behind the system of contract remedies is compensatory, not punitive. Punishment of a promisor for having broken his promise has no justification on either economic or other grounds and a term providing such a penalty is unenforceable on grounds of public policy. See Chapter 8. The rest of the agreement remains enforceable, however, under the rule stated in § 184(1), and the remedies for breach are determined by the rules stated in this Chapter. See Illustration 1. A term that fixes an unreasonably small amount as damages may be unenforceable as unconscionable. See § 208. As to the liquidation of damages and modification or limitation of remedies in contracts of sale, see Uniform Commercial Code §§ 2-718, 2-719.

b. Test of penalty. Under the test stated in Subsection (1), two factors combine in determining whether an amount of money fixed as damages is so unreasonably large as to be a penalty. The first factor is the anticipated or actual loss caused by the breach. The amount fixed is reasonable to the extent that it approximates the actual loss that has resulted from the particular breach, even though it may not approximate the loss that might have been anticipated under other possible breaches. See Illustration 2. Furthermore, the amount fixed is reasonable to the extent that it approximates the loss anticipated at the time of the making of the contract, even though it may

not approximate the actual loss. See Illustration 3. The second factor is the difficulty of proof of loss. The greater the difficulty either of proving that loss has occurred or of establishing its amount with the requisite certainty (see § 351), the easier it is to show that the amount fixed is reasonable. To the extent that there is uncertainty as to the harm, the estimate of the court or jury may not accord with the principle of compensation any more than does the advance estimate of the parties. A determination whether the amount fixed is a penalty turns on a combination of these two factors. If the difficulty of proof of loss is great, considerable latitude is allowed in the approximation of anticipated or actual harm. If, on the other hand, the difficulty of proof of loss is slight, less latitude is allowed in that approximation. If, to take an extreme case, it is clear that no loss at all has occurred, a provision fixing a substantial sum as damages is unenforceable. See Illustration 4. **Illustrations:**

1. A and B sign a written contract under which A is to act in a play produced by B for a ten week season for $ 4,000. A term provides that "if either party shall fail to perform as agreed in any respect he will pay $ 10,000 as liquidated damages and not as a penalty." A leaves the play before the last week to take another job. The play is sold out for that week and A is replaced by a suitable understudy. The amount fixed is unreasonable in the light of both the anticipated and the actual loss and, in spite of the use of the words "liquidated damages," the term provides for a penalty and is unenforceable on grounds of public policy. The rest of the agreement is enforceable (§ 184(1)), and B's remedies for A's breach are governed by the rules stated in this Chapter.

2. A, B and C form a partnership to practice veterinary medicine in a town for ten years. In the partnership agreement, each promises that if, on the termination of the partnership, the practice is continued by the other two members, he will not practice veterinary medicine in the same town during its continuance up to a maximum of

three years. A term provides that for breach of this duty "he shall forfeit $ 50,000 to be collected by the others as damages." A leaves the partnership, and the practice is continued by B and C. A immediately begins to practice veterinary medicine in the same town. The loss actually caused to B and C is difficult of proof and $ 50,000 is not an unreasonable estimate of it. Even though $ 50,000 may be unreasonable in relation to the loss that might have resulted in other circumstances, it is not unreasonable in relation to the actual loss. Therefore, the term does not provide for a penalty and its enforcement is not precluded on grounds of public policy. See Illustration 14 to § 188.

3. A contracts to build a grandstand for B's race track for $ 1,000,000 by a specified date and to pay $ 1,000 a day for every day's delay in completing it. A delays completion for ten days. If $ 1,000 is not unreasonable in the light of the anticipated loss and the actual loss to B is difficult to prove, A's promise is not a term providing for a penalty and its enforcement is not precluded on grounds of public policy.

. . .

c. Disguised penalties. Under the rule stated in this Section, the validity of a term providing for damages depends on the effect of that term as interpreted according to the rules stated in Chapter 9. Neither the parties' actual intention as to its validity nor their characterization of the term as one for liquidated damages or a penalty is significant in determining whether the term is valid. Sometimes parties attempt to disguise a provision for a penalty by using language that purports to make payment of the amount an alternative performance under the contract, that purports to offer a discount for prompt performance, or that purports to place a valuation on property to be delivered. Although the parties may in good faith contract for alternative performances and fix discounts or valuations, a court will look to the substance of the agreement to determine whether this is the case or whether the parties have attempted to disguise a provision for a penalty that is unenforceable under this Section. In determining whether a contract is one for alternative performances, the relative value of the alternatives may be decisive. **Illustration:**

5. A contracts to build a house for B for $ 50,000 by a specified date or in the alternative to pay B $ 1,000 a week during any period of delay. A delays completion for ten days. If $ 1,000 a week is unreasonable in the light of both the anticipated and actual loss, A's promise to pay $ 1,000 a week is, in spite of its form, a term providing for a penalty and is unenforceable on grounds of public policy.

d. Related types of provisions. This Section does not purport to cover the wide variety of provisions used by parties to control the remedies available to them for breach of contract. A term that fixes as damages an amount that is unreasonably small does not come within the rule stated in this Section, but a court may refuse to enforce it as unconscionable under the rule stated in § 208. A mere recital of the harm that may occur as a result of a breach of contract does not come within the rule stated in this Section, but may increase damages by making that harm foreseeable under the rule stated § 351. As to the effect of a contract provision on the right to equitable relief, see Comment *a* to § 359. As to the effect of a term requiring the occurrence of a condition where forfeiture would result, see § 229. Although attorneys' fees are not generally awarded to the winning party, if the parties provide for the award of such fees the court will award a sum that it considers to be reasonable. If, however, the parties specify the amount of such fees, the provision is subject to the test stated in this Section.

e. Penalties in bonds. Bonds often fix a flat sum as a penalty for non-occurrence of the condition of the bond. A term providing for a penalty is not unenforceable in its entirety but only to the extent that it exceeds the loss caused by the non-occurrence of the condition. **Illustration:**

6. A executes a bond obligating himself to pay B $ 10,000, on condition that the bond shall be void, however, if C, who is B's cashier, shall properly account for all money entrusted to him. C defaults to the extent of $ 500. A's promise is unenforceable on grounds of public policy to the extent that it exceeds the actual loss, $ 500.

Introductory Note Specific performance and injunction are alternatives to the award of damages as means of enforcing contracts. Specific performance is by definition limited to the enforcement of contract duties. The remedy of injunction is used in many fields of law, but is dealt with here in connection with contracts only. The general availability of these remedies in contract cases is affirmed in § 357. The power of the court to shape the remedy is stressed in § 358. These remedies originated in courts of equity, and their use is within the discretion of the court and is subject to a number of limitations that are dealt with in §§ 359-69. The most significant is the rule that specific performance or an injunction will not be granted if damages are an adequate remedy (§ 359). This rule, the product of the historical division of jurisdiction between law and equity, has been preserved under the Uniform Commercial Code. See Uniform Commercial Code § 2-716(1) and Official Comment; Introductory Note to this Chapter. Nevertheless, there has been an increasing disposition to find that damages are not adequate and the commentary to the Code reflects this "more liberal attitude." Comment 1 to Uniform Commercial Code § 2-716. Courts have been increasingly willing to order performance in a wide variety of cases involving output and requirements contracts, contracts for the sale of a business or of an interest in a business represented by shares of stock, and covenants not to compete. Factors that bear on the adequacy of damages are listed in § 360. Other limitations on the availability of such equitable relief go to such matters as the need for certainty of terms (§ 362) and for security as to the completion of the agreed exchange (§ 363), and to the impact of unfairness (§ 364), of public policy (§ 365) and of difficulty of enforcement of the decree (§ 366). This Chapter does not deal with other equitable remedies such as reformation or cancellation. See Introductory Note to this Chapter and, as to reformation, §§ 155, 166.

§ 357. Availability of Specific Performance and Injunction

(1) Subject to the rules stated in §§ 359-69, specific performance of a contract duty will be granted in the discretion of the court against a party who has committed or is threatening to commit a breach of the duty.

(2) Subject to the rules stated in §§ 359-69, an injunction against breach of a contract duty will be granted in the discretion of the court against a party who has committed or is threatening to commit a breach of the duty if

(a) the duty is one of forbearance, or

(b) the duty is one to act and specific performance would be denied only for reasons that are inapplicable to an injunction.

Comment:

a. Specific performance. An order of specific performance is intended to produce as nearly as is practicable the same effect that the performance due under a contract would have produced. It usually, therefore, orders a party to render the performance that he promised. (On the form of the order, see § 358.) Such relief is seldom granted unless there has been a breach of contract, either by non-performance or by repudiation. In unusual circumstances, however, it may be granted where there is merely a threatened breach. See Subsection (1).

b. Injunction. A court may by injunction direct a party to refrain from doing a specified act. This is appropriate in two types of cases.

In the first, the performance due under the contract consists simply of forbearance, and the injunction in effect orders specific performance. See Paragraph (2)(a). Duties of forbearance are often imposed not as a matter of agreement but as a matter of law, as is usually the case for the duty not to interfere with the other party's performance of the contract. Duties of forbearance are ordinarily accompanied by other duties that require affirmative action by both parties. The presence of such other duties does not, of itself, preclude issuance of an injunction ordering forbearance only, but an injunction will not be issued if the performance of those other duties cannot be secured. See § 363.

In the second type of case, the performance due under the contract consists of the doing of an act rather than of forbearance, and the injunction is used as an indirect means of enforcing the duty to act. See Paragraph (2)(b). Instead of ordering that the act be done, the court orders forbearance from inconsistent action. This is appropriate in situations where an injunction will afford a measure of relief and the duty to act would have been specifically enforced were it not for some objection that can be avoided by ordering forbearance from inconsistent action. For example, the difficulties involved in supervising compliance with the order may be less in the case of an injunction that in the case of specific performance. See § 366. An injunction will not be issued, however, if the reason for refusing specific performance is not merely that the practical difficulties of such relief are too great but that compelling performance of the duty is itself undesirable. For example, an injunction is not ordinarily appropriate as an indirect means of enforcing a duty to render personal service. See Comment *c* to § 367. **Illustrations:**

1. A contracts with B to give B the "first refusal" of A's house on stated terms. A later offers to sell the house to others without first offering it to B and B sues A to enjoin him from doing this. An injunction may properly be granted.

2. A, B and C form a partnership to practice veterinary medicine in a town for ten years. In the partnership agreement each makes an enforceable promise that if, on the termination of the partnership, the practice is continued by the other two members, he will not practice veterinary medicine in the same town during its continuance up to a maximum of three years. See Illustration 11 to § 188. A leaves the partnership and the practice is continued by B and C. A immediately threatens to begin the practice of veterinary medicine in the same town, and B and C sue to enjoin A from doing so. An injunction may properly be granted.

3. A, the owner of a large factory, contracts to take all of his requirements of electricity from B, who promises to build a new electric plant at a place where it would not otherwise be profitable. A repudiates the contract and B sues A to enjoin him from using electricity that is not supplied by B. An injunction may properly be granted.

4. A makes a contract with B under which A promises to sell exclusively B's dress patterns in A's stores for a period of five years. The contract provides details as to manner of exhibition and division of profits. On anticipatory repudiation of the contract by A, B sues A for specific performance of his duty to sell B's patterns and to enjoin him from selling competing dress patterns. Even if the court refuses specific performance on the ground that enforcement and supervision would be too difficult (§ 366), it may properly grant an injunction.

. . .

c. Discretionary nature of relief. The granting of equitable relief has traditionally been regarded as within judicial discretion. The exercise of that discretion is subject to the rules stated in §§ 359-69. It is also subject to general principles of equity that are not peculiar to contract disputes, such as those that bar relief to one who has been guilty of laches or who has come into court with unclean hands. Furthermore, it is subject to principles of common sense so that, for example, a court will not order a performance that is impossible. In granting relief, as well as in denying it, a court may take into consideration the public interest.

§ 358. Form of Order and Other Relief

(1) An order of specific performance or an injunction will be so drawn as best to effectuate the purposes for which the contract was made and on such terms as justice requires. It need not be absolute in form and the performance that it requires need not be identical with that due under the contract.

(2) If specific performance or an injunction is denied as to part of the performance that is due, it may nevertheless be granted as to the remainder.

(3) In addition to specific performance or an injunction, damages and other relief may be awarded in the same proceeding and an indemnity against future harm may be required.

Comment:

a. Flexibility of order. The objective of the court in granting equitable relief is to do complete justice to the extent that this is feasible. Under the rule stated in Subsection (1), the court has the power to mold its order to this end. The form and terms of the order are to a considerable extent within the discretion of the court. Its order may be directed at the injured party as well as at the party in breach. It may be conditional on some performance to be rendered by the injured party or a third person, such as the payment of money to compensate for defects or the giving of security. It may even be conditional on the injured party's assent to the modification of the contract that he seeks to enforce.

The exact performance that is promised in a contract may be, in whole or in part, very difficult of enforcement, or it may have become unreasonably burdensome or unlawful. Nevertheless, by exercising its discretion in fashioning the order, the court may be able substantially to assure the expectations of the parties, without undue difficulty of enforcement, unreasonable hardship to the party in breach, or violation of the law. It may command a performance by the party in breach that is not identical with the one that he promised to render. It may indirectly induce the party in breach to do an act by enjoining him from doing inconsistent acts. See § 357(2)(b). If a court cannot, because of the promisor's death or disability, compel performance of a contract to give a child rights as an heir, whether by adoption or otherwise, it may nevertheless be able to give the child those rights. Statutes in most states empower the court to transfer the title to land by virtue of its own decree or the deed of an officer of the court without the execution of a deed by the previous owner. In appropriate cases, a court may issue a preliminary injunction to prevent an undesirable change in the situation. **Illustrations:**

    1. A, a water company, contracts with B, a city, to construct a water supply system and to supply sufficient water for public and private use, including any increase in demand. In return B gives A the exclusive right to supply water at rates fixed according to a schedule. A constructs the system substantially as agreed with the exception of a few defects, which can be corrected. B repudiates and A sues B for specific performance. Specific performance may properly be granted, conditional on correction of the defects. See § 369. If changing circumstances require it, the order may also be conditional on A's consent to modification of the terms of the contract, if this should become necessary to avoid unreasonable hardship to B.

    2. A contracts to sell land to B, who promises to pay the price in eight installments on stated dates. Conveyance is to be made on payment of the third installment, and the balance is to be secured by a mortgage and paid with interest in five annual installments. After B has paid the third installment, A delays and finally refuses to convey, and B sues for specific performance. Specific performance may properly be granted. The order will be conditional on execution of the mortgage for the balance and may provide for equitable adjustment of rents and profits, interest on the unpaid part of the price, and extension of the times fixed for the last five payments to allow for time lost by A's delay.

b. Order as to part. Sometimes the requirements are met for specific performance of part of the performance due from the party in breach, but the remaining part of the performance has become impracticable or is otherwise of such a character as to preclude such relief. A court may properly issue an order as to the first part, together with any compensation that is appropriate for non-performance of the second part. This will not be done, however, if compelling performance of only part would impose unreasonable hardship on the party in breach.

c. Damages and other relief. In addition to any equitable relief granted, a court may also award damages or other relief. Since an order seldom results in performance within the time the contract requires, damages for the delay will usually be appropriate. A seller of land who cannot perform as agreed because of a deficiency in area or a defect in title may be ordered to transfer all that he can, with compensation for the resulting claim for partial breach. The compensation may take the form of damages, restitution of money already paid or an abatement of the price not yet paid. A claimant who sues for specific performance or an injunction and who is denied that relief, may be awarded damages or restitution in the same proceeding. In appropriate cases, an indemnity may be required against future harm, and in some cases such an indemnity may be the only remedy that is necessary. **Illustrations:**

    3. A contracts to sell B a tract of land warranted to contain 200 acres for $ 100,000. The tract contains only 160 acres, substantially uniform in value. A refuses to perform and B sues for specific performance. Specific performance will be granted with an abatement of $ 20,000, conditional on B paying $ 80,000. See Illustration 1 to § 369. If the price had already been paid in full, the decree would order the restitution of $ 20,000.

    . . .

§ 359. Effect of Adequacy of Damages

(1) Specific performance or an injunction will not be ordered if damages would be adequate to protect the expectation interest of the injured party.

(2) The adequacy of the damage remedy for failure to render one part of the performance due does not preclude specific performance or injunction as to the contract as a whole.

(3) Specific performance or an injunction will not be refused merely because there is a remedy for breach other than damages, but such a remedy may be considered in exercising discretion under the rule stated in § 357.

Comment:

a. Bases for requirement. The underlying objective in choosing the form of relief to be granted is to select a remedy that will adequately protect the legally recognized interest of the injured party. If, as is usually the case, that interest is the expectation interest, the remedy may take the form either of damages or of specific performance or an injunction. As to the situation in which the interest to be protected is the restitution interest, see § 373.

During the development of the jurisdiction of courts of equity, it came to be recognized that equitable relief would not be granted if the award of damages at law was adequate to protect the interests of the injured party. There is, however, a tendency to liberalize the granting of equitable relief by enlarging the classes of cases in which damages are not regarded as an adequate remedy. This tendency has been encouraged by the adoption of the Uniform Commercial Code, which "seeks to further a more liberal attitude than some courts have shown in connection with the specific performance of contracts of sale." Comment 1 to Uniform Commercial Code § 2-716. In accordance with this tendency, if the adequacy of the damage remedy is uncertain, the combined effect of such other factors as uncertainty of terms (§ 362), insecurity as to the agreed exchange (§ 363) and difficulty of enforcement (§ 366) should be considered. Adequacy is to some extent relative, and the modern approach is to compare remedies to determine which is more effective in serving the ends of justice. Such a comparison will often lead to the granting of equitable relief. Doubts should be resolved in favor of the granting of specific performance or injunction.

Because the availability of equitable relief was historically viewed as a matter of jurisdiction, the parties cannot vary by agreement the requirement of inadequacy of damages, although a court may take appropriate notice of facts recited in their contract. See also Comment *b* to § 361.

b. Damages adequate as to part. The fact that damages would be an adequate remedy for failure to render one part of the promised performance does not preclude specific performance of the contract as a whole. In such a case, complete relief should be granted in a single action and that relief may properly be a decree ordering performance of the entire contract if the other requisites for such relief are met.

. . .

c. Other legal remedies. Common-law remedies other than damages may be available to the injured party, but they will seldom afford as complete relief as will specific performance. Restitution of the value in money of the performance rendered by the injured party is one of those remedies, but it does not purport to be the equivalent of a promised performance, and its availability is not a sufficient reason for denying specific enforcement. Replevin is another of those remedies, but its effectiveness is reduced by rules allowing the giving of a bond in place of surrendering of the goods sought to be replevied. The availability of such a remedy will not preclude the granting of equitable relief, although it may be considered by a court in the exercise of its discretion in that regard. The availability of other forms of equitable relief, such as a decree for specific restitution, for reformation, and for rescission or cancellation, may also be considered in choosing the remedy best suited to the circumstances of the case.

§ 360. Factors Affecting Adequacy of Damages

In determining whether the remedy in damages would be adequate, the following circumstances are significant:

(a) the difficulty of proving damages with reasonable certainty,

(b) the difficulty of procuring a suitable substitute performance by means of money awarded as damages, and

(c) the likelihood that an award of damages could not be collected.

Comment:

a. Principal factors. Under the rule stated in § 359, specific performance or an injunction will not be ordered if damages would be adequate to protect the injured party's expectation interest. This Section lists the principal factors that enter into a decision as to the adequacy of damages. The enumeration does not purport to be exclusive of other factors. A court may also consider, for example, the probability that full compensation cannot be had without multiple litigation, although this is an unusual circumstance in contract cases.

b. Difficulty in proving damages. The damage remedy may be inadequate to protect the injured party's expectation interest because the loss caused by the breach is too difficult to estimate with reasonable certainty (§ 352). If the injured party has suffered loss but cannot sustain the burden of proving it, only nominal damages will be awarded. If he can prove some but not all of his loss, he will not be compensated in full. In either case damages are an inadequate remedy. Some types of interests are by their very nature incapable of being valued in money. Typical examples include heirlooms, family treasures and works of art that induce a strong sentimental attachment. Examples may also be found in contracts of a more commercial character. The breach of a contract to transfer shares of stock may cause a loss in control over the corporation. The breach of a contract to furnish an indemnity may cause the sacrifice of property and financial ruin. The breach of a covenant not to compete may cause the loss of customers of an unascertainable number or importance. The breach of a requirements contract may cut off a vital supply of raw materials. In such situations, equitable relief is often appropriate.

Illustrations:

1. A contracts to sell to B a painting by Rembrandt for $ 1,000,000. A repudiates the contract and B sues for specific performance. Specific performance will be granted.

2. A contracts to sell to B the racing sloop "Columbia," this sloop being one of a class of similar boats manufactured by a particular builder. Although other boats of this class are easily obtainable, their racing characteristics differ considerably and B has selected the "Columbia" because she is regarded as a witch in light airs and, therefore, superior to most of the others. A repudiates the contract and B sues for specific performance. Specific performance may properly be granted.

3. A contracts to sell to B his interest as holder of a franchise to operate a hamburger stand. Because A has not yet opened his stand for business, it would be difficult to prove his expected profits with reasonable certainty. A repudiates the contract and B sues for specific performance. Specific performance may properly be granted.

4. A, a manufacturer of steel, contracts to sell B all of its output of steel scrap for a period of five years. After one year, A repudiates the contract and B sues A for specific performance. The uncertainty in A's output over the remaining four years would make it very difficult for B to prove damages. Specific performance may properly be granted.

. . .

c. Difficulty of obtaining substitute. If the injured party can readily procure by the use of money a suitable substitute for the promised performance, the damage remedy is ordinarily adequate. Entering into a substitute transaction is generally a more efficient way to prevent injury than is a suit for specific performance or an injunction and there is a sound economic basis for limiting the injured party to damages in such a case. Furthermore, the substitute transaction affords a basis for proving damages with reasonable certainty, eliminating the factor stated in Paragraph (a). The fact that the burden of financing the transaction is cast on the injured party can usually be sufficiently compensated for by allowing interest. There are many situations, however, in which no suitable substitute is obtainable, and others in which its procurement would be unreasonably difficult or inconvenient or would impose serious financial burdens or risks on the injured party. A suitable substitute is never available for a performance that consists of forbearance, such as that under a contract not to compete. If goods are unique in kind, quality or personal association, the purchase of an equivalent elsewhere may be impracticable, and the buyer's "inability to cover is strong evidence of" the propriety of granting specific performance. Comment 2 to Uniform Commercial Code § 2-716. Shares of stock in a corporation may not be obtainable elsewhere. Patents and copyrights are unique. In all these situations, damages may be regarded as inadequate. **Illustrations:**

6. A contracts to sell B 10,000 bales of cotton. A repudiates the contract on the day for delivery. B can buy cotton on the market at a somewhat higher price. B will not be granted specific performance.

7. A contracts to sell to B 1,000 shares of stock in the X Corporation for $ 10,000. A repudiates the contract and B sues for specific performance. Other shares of X Corporation are not readily obtainable and B will suffer an uncertain loss as a result of diminished voting power. Specific performance may properly be granted. If other shares were readily obtainable, even though at a considerably higher price, specific performance would be refused.

8. A contracts to obtain a patent for his invention and to assign a half interest in it to B, who promises to pay A's expenses and $ 100,000. A repudiates the contract and threatens to assign the patent when it is issued to others. B sues A for specific performance. Specific performance may properly be granted. The decree may enjoin A from assigning the patent to others and order him to proceed with the application and, on its issuance to execute an assignment to B, all conditional on appropriate payment by B.

d. Difficulty of collecting damages. Even if damages are adequate in other respects, they will be inadequate if they cannot be collected by judgment and execution. The party in breach may be judgment proof or may conceal his assets. Statutes may exempt some or all of his property from execution. If he is insolvent, specific performance may result in a preferential transfer to the party seeking relief and will then be denied on grounds of public policy. See Comment *b* to § 365 and Illustration 4 to that Section. If, however, the contract is unperformed on both sides and provides for a fair exchange, performance will not result in a preferential transfer and may benefit other creditors and help prevent insolvency. **Illustrations:**

9. A contracts to sell his stock of goods together with good will to B for $ 100,000, a fair price, payable on delivery. Before the time for performance, A becomes insolvent and repudiates the contract. B sues A for specific performance. A's insolvency is a factor tending to show that damages are inadequate. But see Illustration 4 to § 365.

10. A owns an interest in a shop, the title to which is held by B in trust for A and others. B is insolvent. A assigns his interest to C and B contracts with C to effectuate the transfer of that interest to C and to terminate his own power. B then refuses to do so and C sues B for specific performance. B's insolvency is a factor tending to show that damages are inadequate.

e. Contracts for the sale of land. Contracts for the sale of land have traditionally been accorded a special place in the law of specific performance. A specific tract of land has long been regarded as unique and impossible of duplication by the use of any amount of money. Furthermore, the value of land is to some extent speculative. Damages have therefore been regarded as inadequate to enforce a duty to transfer an interest in land, even if it is less than a fee simple. Under this traditional view, the fact that the buyer has made a contract for the resale of the land to a third person does not deprive him of the right to specific performance. If he cannot convey the land to his purchaser, he will be held for damages for breach of the resale contract, and it is argued that these damages cannot be accurately determined without litigation. Granting him specific performance enables him to perform his own duty and to avoid litigation and damages.

Similarly, the seller who has not yet conveyed is generally granted specific performance on breach by the buyer. Here it is argued that, because the value of land is to some extent speculative, it may be difficult for him to prove with reasonable certainty the difference between the contract price and the market price of the land. Even if he can make this proof, the land may not be immediately convertible into money and he may be deprived of funds with which he could have made other investments. Furthermore, before the seller gets a judgment, the existence of the contract, even if broken by the buyer, operates as a clog on saleability, so that it may be difficult to find a purchaser at a fair price. The fact that specific performance is available to the buyer has sometimes been regarded as of some weight under the now discarded doctrine of "mutuality of remedy" (see Comment *c* to § 363), but this is today of importance only because it enables a court to assure the vendee that he will receive the agreed performance if he is required to pay the price. The fact that legislation may have prohibited imprisonment as a means of enforcing a decree for the payment of money does not affect the seller's right to such a decree. After the seller has transferred the interest in the land to the buyer, however, and all that remains is for the buyer to pay the price, a money judgment for the amount of the price is an adequate remedy for the seller. **Illustrations:**

11. On February 1, A contracts to sell his farm to B for $ 500,000, of which $ 100,000 is paid when the contract is signed and $ 400,000 is to be paid on A's delivery of a deed on August 1. On March 1, A repudiates the contract. B sues A for specific performance. Specific performance will be granted immediately, A's performance not to take place until August 1 and to be conditional on the simultaneous payment by B of the $ 400,000 balance when the deed is tendered at that time. A may also be enjoined from making a conveyance to anyone else.

12. The facts being otherwise as stated in Illustration 11, B rather than A repudiates the contract on March 1 and A sues B for specific performance. Specific performance will be granted immediately, B's performance not to take place until August 1 and to be conditional on the simultaneous tender by A of the deed when the $ 400,000 balance is tendered at that time.

. . .

§ 361. Effect of Provision for Liquidated Damages

Specific performance or an injunction may be granted to enforce a duty even though there is a provision for liquidated damages for breach of that duty.

Comment:

a. Rationale. A contract provision for payment of a sum of money as damages may not afford an adequate remedy even though it is valid as one for liquidated damages and not a penalty (§ 356). Merely by providing for liquidated damages, the parties are not taken to have fixed a price to be paid for the privilege not to perform. The same uncertainty as to the loss caused that argues for the enforceability of the provision may also argue for the inadequacy of the remedy that it provides. Such a provision does not, therefore, preclude the granting of specific performance or an injunction if that relief would otherwise be granted. If the provision is unenforceable as one for a penalty, the same result follows, but because of the ineffectiveness of the clause rather than the operation of the rule here stated. If equitable relief is granted, damages for such breach as has already occurred may also be awarded in accordance with the rule stated in § 358. These damages will ordinarily be limited to the actual loss suffered unless the provision for liquidated damages affords a suitable basis for calculating such damages. **Illustration:**

1. A, B and C form a partnership to practice veterinary medicine in a town for ten years. In the partnership agreement each makes an enforceable promise that if, on the termination of the partnership, the practice is continued by the other two members, he will not practice veterinary medicine in the same town during its continuance up to a maximum of three years. See Illustration 11 to § 188 and Illustration 2 to § 357. Each also makes an enforceable promise that for breach of this duty he will pay $ 50,000 as liquidated damages. See Illustration 2 to § 356. A leaves the partnership, and the practice is continued by B and C. A immediately begins to practice veterinary medicine in the same town. B and C sue A for an injunction and damages. In spite of the liquidated damage clause, A will be enjoined from practicing veterinary medicine in violation of his promise not to compete. B and C may not then recover damages under the liquidated damage clause but may recover damages for any actual loss caused by A's breach, but not more than $ 50,000.

b. Provision for alternative performance distinguished. Although parties who merely provide for liquidated damages are not taken to have fixed a price for the privilege not to perform, there is no reason why parties may not fix such a price if they so choose. If a contract contains a provision for the payment of such a price as a true alternative performance, specific performance or an injunction may properly be granted on condition that the alternative performance is not forthcoming. But if the obligor chooses to pay the price, equitable relief will not be granted. **Illustration:**

2. A sells his grocery business to B for $ 200,000, of which $ 100,000 is payable immediately and $ 100,000 at the end of a year. Under the agreement A makes an enforceable promise not to engage in a business of the same kind within a hundred miles for three years unless he reduces the balance from $ 100,000 to $ 50,000. See Illustration 1 to § 188. Before the end of the year, A writes B that the balance is reduced to $ 50,000 and immediately opens a competing business. A will not be enjoined from operating the competing business.

§ 362. Effect of Uncertainty of Terms

Specific performance or an injunction will not be granted unless the terms of the contract are sufficiently certain to provide a basis for an appropriate order.

Comment:

a. Reason for requirement. One of the fundamental requirements for the enforceability of a contract is that its terms be certain enough to provide the basis for giving an appropriate remedy. See § 33. If this minimum standard of certainty is not met, there is no contract at all. It may be, however, that the terms are certain enough to provide the basis for the calculation of damages but not certain enough to permit the court to frame an order of specific performance or an injunction and to determine whether the resulting performance is in accord with what has been ordered. In that case there is a contract but it is not enforceable by specific performance or an injunction.

b. Degree of certainty required. If specific performance or an injunction is to be granted, it is important that the terms of the contract are sufficiently certain to enable the order to be drafted with precision because of the availability of the contempt power for disobedience. Before concluding that the required certainty is lacking, however, a court will avail itself of all of the usual aids in determining the scope of the agreement. See Chapter 9, The Scope of Contractual Obligations. Apparent difficulties of enforcement due to uncertainty may disappear in the light of courageous common sense. Expressions that at first appear incomplete may not appear so after

resort to usage (§ 221) or the addition of a term supplied by law (§ 204). A contract is not too uncertain merely because a promisor is given a choice of performing in several ways, whether expressed as alternative performances or otherwise. He may be ordered to make the choice and to perform accordingly, and, if he fails to make the choice, the court may choose for him and order specific performance. Even though subsidiary terms have been left to determination by future agreement, if performance has begun by mutual consent, equitable relief may be appropriate with the court supplying the missing terms so as to assure the promisor all advantages that he reasonably expected. **Illustrations:**

1. A and B make a contract under which A promises to convey part of a tract of land to B and B promises to pay $ 100,000 and to build "a first class theatre" on it. Building the theatre will enhance the value of A's remaining land. A conveys the land to B, who pays the price but refuses to build the theatre. A sues B for specific performance. Specific performance will be refused because of the uncertainty of the terms of the contract, although A can receive damages from B based on the failure to enhance the value of his land if he can prove them with reasonable certainty (§ 352). See also § 366 on the effect of difficulty in supervision.

. . .

§ 363. Effect of Insecurity as to the Agreed Exchange

Specific performance or an injunction may be refused if a substantial part of the agreed exchange for the performance to be compelled is unperformed and its performance is not secured to the satisfaction of the court.

Comment:

a. Importance of security. The rule stated in this Section is intended to make sure that a party is not compelled to render his own performance without receiving substantially the agreed exchange from the other party. This problem does not arise in an action for damages for total breach because the party in breach is only required to pay money, and the amount is always reduced by the amount the injured party saves by not having to proceed with his own performance. If the party in breach is to be required to perform specifically, however, the injured party is expected to do the same, and some security to assure that performance is desirable. Even if performance by the party in breach would have been due under the contract before that of the injured party, such security is desirable since, after controversy has developed, the risk of non-performance is increased. In some situations, the injured party may already have so far partly performed and so committed his funds and labor that his own self-interest furnishes adequate security. In other situations, however, it will be reasonable, in the exercise of judicial discretion, to require the injured party to furnish further security.

b. Means of securing performance. The desired security can often be afforded by the terms of the order itself. If performance by the injured party is already due or will be due simultaneously with the performance of the party in breach, the order may be made conditional on the injured party's rendition of his performance. This can be done even if a series of simultaneous exchanges is involved. If performance by the injured party is not due under the contract until after performance by the party in breach or is not due until an undetermined time, the injured party may nevertheless consent to have the order conditioned on his simultaneous performance, and even absent his consent it may be just to require him to perform simultaneously if he is to be granted equitable relief rather than damages. In such situations a discount may be allowed to compensate the injured party for the advancement in the time for his performance. If security cannot be afforded by fashioning the order in one of these ways, it may be made conditional on the injured party's execution of a mortgage as security for future performance or on his giving other collateral.

If it is impossible to assure performance by the injured party, an order may be refused, especially if there is reason to fear that the injured party will not perform. For example, a contract to render personal service exclusively for one employer will not be indirectly enforced by an injunction against serving another employer unless the court is convinced that the employer is ready and willing to perform his part of the contract.

The question of security does not arise until the time for issuance of an order. At the pleading stage, a mere allegation by the plaintiff that he is ready and willing to perform is usually sufficient in a suit for specific performance or an injunction. Actual performance or tender is not generally required. **Illustrations:**

1. A contracts to sell land to B, part of the purchase price to be paid in installments after the time fixed for the conveyance of the land. A refuses to convey the land and B sues for specific performance. Specific performance may properly be granted, conditional on B executing a mortgage or giving other satisfactory security that the payments will be made. This is so even though the contract provides for no security.

2. A contracts to transfer land to B immediately in return for B's promise to render personal services to A for ten years. A dispute between them causes unfriendly relations, A refuses to convey the land, and B sues for specific performance. Specific performance will be refused because of the increased risk that B's services will not be rendered and because sufficient security that they will be rendered is lacking.

. . .

c. "Mutuality of remedy." It has sometimes been said that there is a requirement of "mutuality of remedy." However, the law does not require that the parties have similar remedies in case of breach, and the fact that specific performance or an injunction is not available to one party is not a sufficient reason for refusing it to the other party. The rationale of the supposed requirement of "mutuality of remedy" is to make sure that the party in breach will not be compelled to perform without being assured that he will receive any remaining part of the agreed exchange from the injured party. It is therefore enough if adequate security can be furnished. **Illustrations:**

> 6. A contracts to sell a tract of land to B for $ 100,000. The contract when made is unenforceable against B because the only memorandum of the contract is signed by A but not B. A repudiates the contract and B sues for specific performance. Specific performance may properly be granted because the commencement of the action by B makes the contract enforceable against him.

> 7. A contracts to sell a tract of land to B for $ 100,000. A is unable to convey the agreed title because C owns a part interest in the tract. A repudiates the contract and B sues for specific performance. Specific performance as to A's interest may properly be granted even though A could not have obtained such a decree against B because of his own breach. See § 369.

d. Assignments. A special application of the rule stated in this Section occurs where a party to a contract assigns his rights to an assignee. The assignee can get specific performance or an injunction on the same terms that the assignor could. The fact that the other party to the contract cannot get such relief against the assignee is not in itself a sufficient reason for refusing it when it is sought by the assignee. The assignment does not relieve the assignor from his contractual duty and may not make it less likely that the agreed exchange will be rendered. However, specific performance or an injunction may be refused if there is no satisfactory security that it will be rendered. The order may, as in any other case, be fashioned to provide this security. Furthermore, if the assignee assumes the assignor's duty, the other party acquires additional security for the performance due him. Even if the assignor repudiates his duty or becomes unable to perform it, the assignee may be able to get an order by making a tender and keeping it good.

§ 364. Effect of Unfairness

(1) Specific performance or an injunction will be refused if such relief would be unfair because

(a) the contract was induced by mistake or by unfair practices,

(b) the relief would cause unreasonable hardship or loss to the party in breach or to third persons, or

(c) the exchange is grossly inadequate or the terms of the contract are otherwise unfair.

(2) Specific performance or an injunction will be granted in spite of a term of the agreement if denial of such relief would be unfair because it would cause unreasonable hardship or loss to the party seeking relief or to third persons.

Comment:

a. Types of unfairness. Courts have traditionally refused equitable relief on grounds of unfairness or mistake in situations where they would not necessarily refuse to award damages. Some of these situations involve elements of mistake (§§ 152, 153), misrepresentation (§ 164), duress (§ 175) or undue influence (§ 177) that fall short of what is required for avoidance under those doctrines. See Paragraph (a) and Illustrations 1, 2 and 3. Others involve elements of impracticability of performance or frustration of purpose that fall short of what is required for relief under those doctrines. See Paragraph (b) and Illustration 4. Still others involve elements of substantive unfairness in the exchange itself or in its terms that fall short of what is required for unenforceability on grounds of unconscionability (§ 208). See Paragraph (c) and Comment *b*. The gradual expansion of these doctrines to afford relief in an increasing number of cases has resulted in a contraction of the area in which this traditional distinction is made between the availability of equitable and legal relief. Nevertheless, the discretionary nature of equitable relief permits its denial when a variety of factors combine to make enforcement of a promise unfair, even though no single legal doctrine alone would make the promise unenforceable. Such general equitable doctrines as those of laches and "unclean hands" supplement the rule stated in this Section. See Comment *c* to § 357. **Illustrations:**

1. A is an aged, illiterate farmer, inexperienced in business. B is an experienced speculator in real estate who knows that a developer wants to acquire a tract of land owned by A and will probably pay a price considerably above the previous market price. B takes advantage of A's ignorance of this fact and of his general inexperience and persuades A not to seek advice. He induces A to contract to sell the land at the previous market price, which is considerably less than the developer later agrees to pay B. A refuses to perform, and B sues A for specific performance. Specific performance may properly be refused on the ground of unfairness.

2. A and B make a contract under which A is to sell B a tract of land for $ 100,000. B does not tell A that he intends to combine the tract with others as part of a large development in order to prevent A from asking a higher price. $ 100,000 is a fair price for the tract at existing market prices. A refuses to perform and B sues A for specific performance. Specific performance will not be refused on the ground of unfairness. Cf. Illustration 2 to § 171.

3. A writes B offering to sell for $ 100,000 a tract of land that A owns known as "201 Lincoln Street." B, who mistakenly believes that this description contains an additional tract of land worth $ 30,000, accepts A's offer. On discovery of his mistake, B refuses to perform and A sues for specific performance. Even if the court determines that enforcement of the contract would not be unconscionable under the rule stated in § 153, specific performance may properly be refused on the ground of unfairness. Cf. Illustration 5 to § 153.

. . .

b. Unfairness in the exchange. Unfairness in the exchange does not of itself make an agreement unenforceable. See Comment *c* to § 208. If it is extreme, however, it may be a sufficient ground, without more, for denying specific performance or an injunction. See Illustration 5. A contract, other than an option contract on fair terms (§§ 25, 87), that is binding solely because of a nominal payment or by reason of some formality such as a seal or a signed writing will not ordinarily be enforced by specific performance or an injunction. It is, however, unusual to find such unfairness in the exchange itself without some mistake or unfairness in its inducement. In determining the fairness of an exchange, account will be taken of the risks taken by both parties at the time the agreement was made. An exchange that might otherwise seem unfairly favorable to one party may in fact be fair if there is a substantial risk that the other party's performance may never become due. This is so for insurance and other aleatory contracts. See also Illustration 6. Where the agreement is one of modification between parties who are already bound by a contract (§ 89), the overriding duty of good faith and fair dealing (§ 205) imposes a requirement of fairness. **Illustrations:**

5. A, an individual, contracts in June to sell at a fixed price per ton to B, a large soup manufacturer, carrots to be grown on A's farm. The contract, written on B's standard printed form, is obviously drawn to protect B's interests and not A's; it contains numerous provisions to protect B against various contingencies and none giving analogous protection to A. Each of the clauses can be read restrictively so that it is not unconscionable, but several can be read literally to give unrestricted discretion to B. In January, when the market price has risen above the contract price, A repudiates the contract, and B seeks specific performance. In the absence of justification by evidence of commercial setting, purpose or effect, the court may determine that the contract as a whole was unconscionable when made and may properly deny specific performance on the ground of unfairness regardless of whether it would award B damages for breach.

. . .

c. Unfair term. Sometimes a party relies upon an unfair term as a defense in a suit for specific performance or injunction. Even if the term is not unconscionable (§ 208), the court may disregard it and grant the relief sought. See Illustration 7. **Illustration:**

7. A contracts to sell land to B for $ 100,000, payable in five annual $ 20,000 installments with conveyance to be at the time of the last payment. The contract contains a term providing that "time is of the essence with respect to each installment, and B shall lose all his rights under the contract if he fails to pay any installment when due." See Comment *d* to § 242. B pays the first installment and takes possession, making improvements and paying the next two installments on time. When he tenders the fourth payment one month late, A refuses it and brings an action of ejectment. B sues for specific performance. The court may refuse to enforce the quoted term on the ground of unfairness. Specific performance may then properly be granted conditional on payment into court of the fourth installment with interest from maturity and on payment of the last installment on conveyance.

§ 365. Effect of Public Policy

Specific performance or an injunction will not be granted if the act or forbearance that would be compelled or the use of compulsion is contrary to public policy.

Comment:

a. Act or forbearance against public policy. If the performance of a contract is contrary to public policy, the contract will often be unenforceable under the rules stated in Chapter 8, Unenforceability on Grounds of Public Policy. Its performance may, for example, involve a breach of a duty to a third person arising under tort law, out of a fiduciary relation or under a contract. See §§ 192, 193 and 194. There are, however, situations in which the contract is enforceable but it would be an improper use of judicial power to grant specific performance or an injunction because the act or forbearance that would be compelled would adversely affect some aspect of the public interest or would otherwise be contrary to public policy. In such situations, equitable relief will be refused even though a judgment for damages will be granted. See Illustration 1. **Illustration:**

    1. A is induced to make a contract to sell land to B, to be paid for out of funds of C that B holds as trustee, by B's false representation that such use of C's money is within B's authority as trustee. A sues B for specific performance. Specific performance will be refused on grounds of public policy, since the act that would be ordered would involve a breach of trust, even though B will be held liable in damage for breach of contract.

b. Compulsion against public policy. Even though the act or forbearance that would be compelled is not contrary to public policy, the use of compulsion to require that act or forbearance may be contrary to public policy. One example of this general principle is the rule under which a court will refuse to grant specific performance if the character of performance is such that enforcement will impose a disproportionate burden on the court (§ 366). Another is the rule under which a court will refuse to grant specific performance of a promise to render personal services or supervision (§ 367). The general principle is not, however, limited to these situations and another important application occurs where equitable relief is denied on the ground that to grant it would give a preference with respect to the assets of an insolvent party. **Illustrations:**

    2. A contracts to give B, a railroad company, a right of way in return for B's promise to locate a station and stop its express trains at a designated place. It later turns out that that place is an inconvenient one for the public and that the disadvantage to B as well as the public of B's promise is performed will be disproportionate to any advantage to A. B refuses to locate the station as promised, and A sues B for specific performance. Specific performance will be refused on grounds of public policy, even though B will be held liable in damages for breach of contract.

. . .

§ 366. Effect of Difficulty in Enforcement or Supervision

A promise will not be specifically enforced if the character and magnitude of the performance would impose on the court burdens in enforcement or supervision that are disproportionate to the advantages to be gained from enforcement and to the harm to be suffered from its denial.

Comment:

a. Burden on court as a factor. Granting specific performance may impose on the court heavy burdens of enforcement or supervision. Difficult questions may be raised as to the quality of the performance rendered under the decree. Supervision may be required for an extended period of time. Specific relief will not be granted if these burdens are disproportionate to the advantages to be gained from enforcement and the harm to be suffered from its denial. A court will not, however, shrink from assuming these burdens if the claimant's need is great or if a substantial public interest is involved. In such cases, for example, structures may be ordered to be built and facilities may be required to be maintained. Experience has shown that potential difficulties in enforcement or supervision are not always realized and the significance of this factor is peculiarly one for judicial discretion. Because of the limited scope appropriate to judicial review of arbitration awards, a court will be less hesitant in confirming such an award that grants specific performance than it would in granting specific performance itself. **Illustrations:**

1. A contracts to modernize and expand B's steel fabricating plant at a cost of $ 50,000,000. A falls behind the schedule fixed in the agreement, and B seeks specific performance to compel A to requisition 300 more workmen for the night shift and take other steps to speed up the work. A court may properly refuse specific performance on the ground that the difficulty of supervision by the court would be disproportionate to the benefits to be gained from enforcement.

. . .

§ 367. Contracts for Personal Service or Supervision

(1) A promise to render personal service will not be specifically enforced.

(2) A promise to render personal service exclusively for one employer will not be enforced by an injunction against serving another if its probable result will be to compel a performance involving personal relations the enforced continuance of which is undesirable or will be to leave the employee without other reasonable means of making a living.

Comment:

a. Rationale of refusal of specific performance. A court will refuse to grant specific performance of a contract for service or supervision that is personal in nature. The refusal is based in part upon the undesirability of compelling the continuance of personal association after disputes have arisen and confidence and loyalty are gone and, in some instances, of imposing what might seem like involuntary servitude. To this extent the rule stated in Subsection (1) is an application of the more general rule under which specific performance will not be granted if the use of compulsion is contrary to public policy (§ 365). The refusal is also based upon the difficulty of enforcement inherent in passing judgment on the quality of performance. To this extent the rule stated in Subsection (1) is an application of the more general rule on the effect of difficulty of enforcement (§ 366).

b. What is personal service. A performance is not a personal service under the rule stated in Subsection (1) unless it is personal in the sense of being non-delegable (§ 318). However, not every non-delegable performance is properly described as a service. An act such as the writing of an autograph or the signing of a diploma may be personal in the sense of being non-delegable even though it is not a personal service, and if that is so specific performance is not precluded. In determining what is a personal service, the policies reflected in the more general rules on the effect of public policy (§ 365) and of the difficulty of enforcement (§ 366) are relevant. The importance of trust and confidence in the relation between the parties, the difficulty of judging the quality of the performance rendered and the length of time required for performance are significant factors. Among the parties that have been held to render what are personal services within the rule stated in Subsection (1) are actors, singers and athletes, and the rule applies generally to contracts of employment that create the intimate relation traditionally known as master and servant. See Restatement, Second, Agency § 2.

The rule that bars specific enforcement of the employee's promise to render personal service has sometimes been extended to bar specific enforcement of the employer's promise where personal supervision is considered to be involved. The policies against compelling an employer to retain an employee have not, however, prevented courts from ordering reinstatement of employees discharged in contravention of statutes prohibiting discrimination or in violation of collective bargaining agreements. **Illustrations:**

1. A, a noted opera singer, contracts with B to sing exclusively at B's opera house during the coming season. A repudiates the contract before the time for performance in order to sing at C's competing opera house, and B sues A for specific performance. Even though A's singing at C's opera house will cause B great loss that he cannot prove with reasonable certainty, and even though A can find suitable jobs singing at opera

houses not in competition with B's, specific performance will be refused.

. . .

c. Availability of injunction. A contract for personal service is usually exclusive in the sense that it imposes not only a duty to render the service to the other party but also a duty to forbear from rendering it to anyone else. Because specific performance of the duty to render the service is precluded by the rule stated in Subsection (1), the availability of injunctive relief to enforce the duty of forbearance takes on special importance. Subsection (2) indicates the application of the general rule on injunctive relief stated in § 357(2) to this important situation. Under that general rule, an injunction will not be ordered if the remedy in damages would be adequate (§ 359). Damages are likely to be adequate to protect the employer's interest unless the employee's services are unique or extraordinary, either because of special skill that he possesses or because of special knowledge that he has acquired of the employer's business.

Even if damages are not adequate, however, an injunction will not be granted if its probable result will be to leave the employee without other reasonable means of making a living. It is not the purpose in granting the injunction to enforce the duty to render the service and, to justify granting it, it should appear that the employee is not being forced to perform the contract as the only reasonable means of making a living. Furthermore, if the probable result of an injunction will be the employee's performance of the contract, it should appear that the employer is prepared to continue the employment in good faith so that performance will not involve personal relations the enforced continuance of which is undesirable. These issues are for the exercise of judicial discretion based on such factors as the character and duration of the service, the probability of the renewal of good relations, the extent to which other remedies are adequate, and the probable hardship that will result from an injunction. **Illustrations:**

3. A contracts to serve exclusively as sales manager in B's clothing store for a year. A repudiates the contract shortly after beginning performance and goes to work for C, a competitor of B. B sues A for an injunction ordering A not to work for C. Unless A's services are unique or extraordinary, the injunction will be refused. If, however, A has special knowledge of B's customers that will cause a substantial number of them to leave B and patronize C, the injunction may properly be granted.

4. The facts being otherwise as stated in Illustration 1, B sues A for an injunction ordering A not to sing in C's opera house. The injunction may properly be granted. If, however, C is not a competitor of B, the injunction will not be granted because its principal effect would be indirectly to compel A to continue in B's service.

§ 368. Effect of Power of Termination

(1) Specific performance or an injunction will not be granted against a party who can substantially nullify the effect of the order by exercising a power of termination or avoidance. (2) Specific performance or an injunction will not be denied merely because the party seeking relief has a power to terminate or avoid his duty unless the power could be used, in spite of the order, to deprive the other party of reasonable security for the agreed exchange for his performance.

Comment:

a. Power in party against whom relief is sought. Specific performance or an injunction will not be granted against a party who, by exercising a power of termination or avoidance, can substantially nullify the effect of the order. The power of termination or avoidance may be derived from a term of the agreement or from a rule of law. If a term of the agreement allows the party to terminate at will so as to make his promise illusory, no contract is created and no question of enforcement arises. See Comment *e* to § 2. Even if the term requires that notice of termination be given some period of time before it takes effect, so that the promise is not illusory and the contract is enforceable, the period may be so short that specific performance or an injunction would be pointless. If, however, the period is a substantial one, for example thirty days, and the performance that would have to be rendered during that period would be substantial even if notice were given immediately, equitable relief may properly be granted. As to the situation in which the power can be exercised only at the cost of rendering some significant alternative performance, see Comment *b* to § 361. **Illustrations:**

    1. A, a noted opera singer, contracts with B to sing exclusively at B's opera house for two seasons, reserving the power to terminate the contract at any time after the end of the first season by giving 24 hours' written notice. A repudiates the contract when the second season is half over in order to sing at C's competing opera house, and B sues to enjoin A from doing so. The injunction will not be granted. If, however, A repudiates when the first season is half over, the injunction may be granted.

    2. A sells his business to B and makes a valid promise not to carry on a competing business, reserving the power to terminate his duty not to compete by paying B $ 50,000. A repudiates his duty not to compete and threatens to operate a competing business, and B sues A to enjoin him from doing so. The injunction may be granted, conditional on A not having paid the $ 50,000.

b. Power in party seeking relief. The existence of a power of termination or avoidance in the party who seeks specific performance or an injunction does not preclude such relief unless the power will seriously threaten the other party's security that the agreed exchange will be rendered. This is a specific application of the general rule stated in § 363. If the power is reserved by a term of the agreement, the court can protect the other party by providing that either the decree itself or the other party's performance shall extinguish the power. If the party seeking relief has already rendered part performance or otherwise materially changed his position in reliance on the contract, this may give him a stronger economic interest in carrying out the agreement and thus increase the other party's security. If the other party's security cannot be reasonably assured, however, equitable relief will be refused. **Illustrations:**

    3. A, a minor, makes a contract to transfer a farm to B for $ 100,000. B repudiates the contract and A sues B for specific performance. Specific performance, even on condition of payment of the $ 100,000, will be refused if A has not reached the age of majority, unless the jurisdiction is one in which the court's decree is conclusive on A so as to terminate his power of avoidance. After A reaches the age of majority and has ratified the contract, specific performance will be granted.

. . .

§ 369. Effect of Breach by Party Seeking Relief

Specific performance or an injunction may be granted in spite of a breach by the party seeking relief, unless the breach is serious enough to discharge the other party's remaining duties of performance.

Comment:

a. Seriousness of breach. If a party has himself committed such a serious breach of contract, whether by non-performance or repudiation, as to discharge the other party's remaining duties under the contract, the party in breach is not entitled to relief, equitable or otherwise, if the other party refuses further performance. Whether a breach is serious enough to have this effect is determined by the rules stated in Chapter 10, Performance and Non-Performance. However, the fact that a party has committed a minor breach, one not serious enough to discharge the other party's remaining duties, does not preclude specific performance or an injunction. The party seeking relief may be required to cure the breach as a condition of the decree (see Illustration 1 to § 358) or may be held accountable for damages caused by his breach, either through a payment of money to the other party or by an abatement in the price that the other party is compelled to pay. **Illustrations:**

    1. A contracts to sell B his farm, said to contain 150 acres and to have a house on it in good repair. The farm contains 149 acres and the house is in slight disrepair. A tenders a deed but B refuses to accept it or pay although the defects are not such as would discharge his remaining duties of performance (see § 241), and A sues B for specific performance. Specific performance may properly be granted with an abatement of the price in an amount equal to damages for the defects. See Illustration 3 to § 358.

. . .

Topic 4. Restitution

Introductory Note Restitution is a common form of relief in contract cases. It has as its objective not the enforcement of contracts through the protection of a party's expectation or reliance interests but the prevention of unjust enrichment through the protection of his restitution interest. See § 344. A party who has received a benefit at the expense of the other party to the agreement is required to account for it, either by returning it in kind or by paying a sum of money. General rules that govern restitution in this context are set out in §§ 370-77.

This Chapter does not deal with restitution in general, because that subject is covered by the Restatement of Restitution. This Topic treats restitution in five situations that are closely related to contracts. The first is that in which the other party is in breach and the party seeking restitution has chosen it as an alternative to the enforcement of the contract between them (§ 373). In the second the party seeking restitution claims the benefit that he has conferred under the contract because he is precluded by his own breach from enforcing the contract (§ 374). In the third situation the party seeking restitution claims the benefit that he has conferred under the contract because he is precluded from enforcing it against the other party because of the Statute of Frauds (§ 375). The fourth situation is that in which a party claims restitution upon avoidance of a contract on the ground, for example, of mistake, misrepresentation or duress (§ 376). The fifth is that in which he claims restitution on the ground that his duty of performance did not arise or was discharged as a result of impracticability of performance, frustration of purpose, non-occurrence of a condition or disclaimer by a beneficiary (§ 377). A party's right to restitution under an agreement that is unenforceable on grounds of public policy is the subject of Topic 5 of Chapter 8, Unenforceability on Grounds of Public Policy. As to the right to restitution following an agreement of rescission, see Comment *c* to § 283. This Chapter does not deal with restitution for benefits during negotiations that do not result in an agreement or under an agreement that is not enforceable because its terms are not sufficiently certain (§ 33). See generally Restatement of Restitution §§ 15, 40, 47, 53.

§ 370. Requirement That Benefit Be Conferred

A party is entitled to restitution under the rules stated in this Restatement only to the extent that he has conferred a benefit on the other party by way of part performance or reliance.

Comment:

a. Meaning of requirement. A party's restitution interest is his interest in having restored to him any benefit that he has conferred on the other party. See § 344(2). Restitution is, therefore, available to a party only to the extent that he has conferred a benefit on the other party. The benefit may result from the transfer of property or from services, including forbearance. See Restatement of Restitution § 1, Comment *b*. The benefit is ordinarily conferred by performance by the party seeking restitution, and receipt by the other party of performance that he bargained for is regarded as a benefit. However, a benefit may also be conferred if the party seeking restitution relies on the contract in some other way, as where he makes improvements on property that does not ultimately become his. However, a party's expenditures in preparation for performance that do not confer a benefit on the other party do not give rise to a restitution interest. See Illustration 1. If, for example, the performance consists of the manufacture and delivery of goods and the buyer wrongfully prevents its completion, the seller is not entitled to restitution because no benefit has been conferred on the buyer. See Illustration 2. The injured party may, however, have an action for damages, including one for recovery based on his reliance interest (§ 349). The requirement of this Section is generally satisfied if a benefit has been conferred, and it is immaterial that it was later lost, destroyed or squandered. See Illustration 3. The benefit must have been conferred by the party claiming restitution. It is not enough that it was simply derived from the breach. See Illustration 4. The other party is considered to have had a benefit conferred on him if a performance was rendered at his request to a third person. See Illustration 5. If the contract is for the benefit of a third person, the promisee is entitled to restitution unless the duty to the beneficiary cannot be varied under the rule stated in § 311. **Illustrations:**

    1. A, who holds a mortgage on B's house, makes a contract with B under which A promises not to foreclose the mortgage for a year. In reliance on this promise, B invests money that he would have used to pay the mortgage in improving other land that he owns. A repudiates the contract and forecloses. B cannot get restitution based on the improvements since making them conferred no benefit on A. But see Illustration 4 to § 373 and Illustration 11 to § 90.

    2. A contracts to sell B a machine for $ 100,000. After A has spent $ 40,000 on the manufacture of the machine but before its completion, B repudiates the contract. A cannot get restitution of the $ 40,000 because no benefit was conferred on B.

    3. A promises to deposit $ 100,000 to B's credit in the X Bank in return for B's promise to render services. A deposits the $ 100,000, the X Bank fails, and B refuses to perform. A can get restitution of the $ 100,000 because a benefit was to that extent conferred on B even though it was lost by B when the X Bank failed. See § 373.

    4. A contracts to work full time for B as a bookkeeper. In breach of this contract, A uses portions of the time that he should spend working for B in keeping books for C, who pays him an additional salary. B sues A for breach of contract. B cannot recover from A the amount of the salary paid by C because it was not a benefit conferred by B.

    5. A, a social worker, promises B to render personal services to C in return for B's promise to educate A's children. B repudiates the contract after A has rendered part of the services. A can get restitution from B for the services, even though they were not rendered to B, because they conferred a benefit on B. See Illustration 3 to § 371.

§ 371. Measure of Restitution Interest

If a sum of money is awarded to protect a party's restitution interest, it may as justice requires be measured by either
(a) the reasonable value to the other party of what he received in terms of what it would have cost him to obtain it from a person in the claimant's position, or
(b) the extent to which the other party's property has been increased in value or his other interests advanced.

Comment:

    a. Measurement of benefit. Under the rules stated in §§ 344 and 370, a party who is liable in restitution for a sum of money must pay an amount equal to the benefit that has been conferred upon him. If the benefit consists simply of a sum of money received by the party from whom restitution is sought, there is no difficulty in determining this amount. If the benefit consists of something else, however, such as services or property, its measurement in terms of money may pose serious problems.

    Restitution in money is available in a wide variety of contexts, and the resolution of these problems varies greatly depending on the circumstances. If, for example, the party seeking restitution has himself committed a material breach (§ 374), uncertainties as to the amount of the benefit may properly be resolved against him.

    A particularly significant circumstance is whether the benefit has been conferred by way of performance or by way of reliance in some other way. See Comment *a* to § 370. Recovery is ordinarily more generous for a benefit that has been conferred by performance. To the extent that the benefit may reasonably be measured in different ways, the choice is within the discretion of the court. Thus a court may take into account the value of opportunities for benefit even if they have not been fully realized in the particular case.

    An especially important choice is that between the reasonable value to a party of what he received in terms of what it would have cost him to obtain it from a person in the claimant's position and the addition to the wealth of that party as measured by the extent to which his property has been increased in value or his other interests advanced. In practice, the first measure is usually based on the market price of such a substitute. Under the rule stated in this Section, the court has considerable discretion in making the choice between these two measures of benefit. Under either choice, the court may properly consider the purposes of the recipient of the benefit when he made the contract, even if those purposes were later frustrated or abandoned.

b. Choice of measure. The reasonable value to the party against whom restitution is sought (Paragraph (a)) is ordinarily less than the cost to the party seeking restitution, since his expenditures are excluded to the extent that they conferred no benefit. See Comment *a* to § 344. Nor can the party against whom restitution is sought reduce the amount for which he may himself be liable by subtracting such expenditures from the amount of the benefit that he has received. See Illustration 5 to § 377. The reasonable value to the party from whom restitution is sought (Paragraph (a)), is, however, usually greater than the addition to his wealth (Paragraph (b)). If this is so, a party seeking restitution for part performance is commonly allowed the more generous measure of reasonable value, unless that measure is unduly difficult to apply, except when he is in breach (§ 374). See Illustration 1. In the case of services rendered in an emergency or to save life, however, restitution based on addition to wealth will greatly exceed that based on expense saved and recovery is invariably limited to the smaller amount. See Illustration 2. In the case of services rendered to a third party as the intended beneficiary of a gift promise, restitution from the promisee based on his enrichment is generally not susceptible of measurement and recovery based on reasonable value is appropriate. See Illustration 3.

Illustrations:

1. A, a carpenter, contracts to repair B's roof for $ 3,000. A does part of the work at a cost of $ 2,000, increasing the market price of B's house by $ 1,200. The market price to have a similar carpenter do the work done by A is $ 1,800. A's restitution interest is equal to the benefit conferred on B. That benefit may be measured either by the addition to B's wealth from A's services in terms of the $ 1,200 increase in the market price of B's house or the reasonable value to B of A's services in terms of the $ 1,800 that it would have cost B to engage a similar carpenter to do the same work. If the work was not completed because of a breach by A and restitution is based on the rule stated in § 374, $ 1,200 is appropriate. If the work was not completed because of a breach by B and restitution is based on the rule stated in § 373, $ 1,800 is appropriate.

2. A, a surgeon, contracts to perform a series of emergency operations on B for $ 3,000. A does the first operation, saving B's life, which can be valued in view of B's life expectancy at $ 1,000,000. The market price to have an equally competent surgeon do the first operation is $ 1,800. A's restitution interest is equal to the benefit conferred on B. That benefit is measured by the reasonable value to B of A's services in terms of the $ 1,800 that it would have cost B to engage a similar surgeon to do the operation regardless of the rule on which restitution is based.

3. A, a social worker, promises B to render personal services to C in return for B's promise to educate A's children. A renders only part of the services and B then refuses to educate A's children. The market price to have a similar social worker do the services rendered by A is $ 1,800. If A recovers in restitution under the rule stated in § 373, an appropriate measure of the benefit conferred on B is the reasonable value to B of A's services in terms of the $ 1,800 that it would have cost B to engage a similar social worker to do the same work.

§ 372. Specific Restitution

(1) Specific restitution will be granted to a party who is entitled to restitution, except that:

(a) specific restitution based on a breach by the other party under the rule stated in § 373 may be refused in the discretion of the court if it would unduly interfere with the certainty of title to land or otherwise cause injustice, and

(b) specific restitution in favor of the party in breach under the rule stated in § 374 will not be granted.

(2) A decree of specific restitution may be made conditional on return of or compensation for anything that the party claiming restitution has received.

(3) If specific restitution, with or without a sum of money, will be substantially as effective

as restitution in money in putting the party claiming restitution in the position he was in before rendering any performance, the other party can discharge his duty by tendering such restitution before suit is brought and keeping his tender good.

Comment:

a. Specific restitution on avoidance or in similar circumstances. A party who has a right to restitution under the rule stated in § 376 because he has avoided the contract, generally has a choice of either claiming a sum of money in restitution or seeking specific restitution if the benefit is something that can be returned to him. The same is true of a party who has a right to restitution under the rule stated in § 377 on one of the grounds there stated, even though this rule does not, strictly speaking, result in avoidance of the contract. The right to specific restitution may, however, be subject to rights of third parties. Their rights are not dealt with in this Restatement. For special rules governing the right of a seller under a contract for the sale of goods, see Uniform Commercial Code §§ 2-507, 2-702. **Illustration:**

1. A is induced by B's misrepresentation to sell a tract of land to B for $ 100,000. On discovery of the misrepresentation, A tenders back the $ 100,000 and sues B for specific restitution of the land. Specific restitution will be granted.

b. Specific restitution on other grounds. A party whose right to restitution is based on the other party's breach also has a right to specific restitution, subject to the limitation stated in Paragraph (a). In the case of a contract for the sale of goods, the Uniform Commercial Code limits much more severely the seller's right to specific restitution, although the seller can protect himself by taking a security interest in the goods. See Uniform Commercial Code § 2-703. The most important problems of specific restitution that remain usually arise in connection with contracts to transfer land. If the buyer of land fails or refuses to pay the price after the transfer of the land to him, the seller is limited to his claim for the price, which may be secured by a vendor's lien as a matter of law or by a security interest that he has reserved. The question of his right to specific restitution does not arise in that situation (§ 373(2)). Specific restitution may, however, be appropriate where there is a right to restitution because the return promise is to do something other than pay money. See Illustrations 2 and 3. In that case, however, a court may refuse specific restitution if it would unduly interfere with the certainty of title to the land. In resolving that question, a court will take into account all the circumstances, including the inadequacy of other relief. A court may also refuse specific restitution if it would otherwise cause injustice as where, for example, it would result in a preference over other creditors in bankruptcy. Specific restitution under the rule stated in this Section is available to the injured party even though enforcement of the contract is barred by the Statute of Frauds. See § 375. Under the exception stated in Paragraph (b), however, it is never available to a party who is himself in breach. See § 374. **Illustrations:**

2. A contracts to transfer a tract of land to B in return for B's promise to transfer a tract of land to A at the same time. After A has transferred his tract to B and received a deed from B, A learns that B does not have title to the other tract. A sues B for specific restitution. Specific restitution will be granted, together with compensation to A for the value to B of the use of the land, because the right to specific restitution will not unduly interfere with the certainty of title to land. If B's promise is to transfer his tract to A ten years after A's transfer of his tract, specific restitution will be denied because a right to specific restitution would unduly interfere with the certainty of title to land during the ten years.

3. A contracts to transfer a tract of land to B in return for B's promise to support A for life. B repudiates the contract after he has supported A for a time and A has transferred the land to him, and A sues B for specific restitution. Specific restitution will be granted, conditional on compensation by A for any support that he has received less the value to B of the use of the land, because the right to specific restitution will not unduly interfere with the certainty of title to land given the inadequacy of A's right to damages because of the difficulty of proving damages with sufficient certainty (§ 352).

. . .

c. Tender off specific restitution. In some circumstances, a party who is liable for restitution can discharge his duty by tendering specific restitution and keeping his tender good. The tender has this result only if specific restitution will be substantially as effective as restitution in money in putting the party claiming restitution in the position he was in before rendering any performance. If tender of a sum of money in addition to specific restitution will do this, such a tender discharges the other party's duty. See Illustration 6. The tender must, however, be made before suit has been brought. **Illustration:**

6. A makes an oral contract with B under which A transfers 1,000 shares of stock to B in return for B's promise to convey a tract of land to A. B repudiates the contract before he has conveyed the land and tenders back the stock and the dividends received from it and keeps his tender good. A rejects the tender and sues B for restitution of the value to B of the stock. A cannot recover the value of the stock.

§ 373. Restitution When Other Party Is in Breach

(1) Subject to the rule stated in Subsection (2), on a breach by non-performance that gives rise to a claim for damages for total breach or on a repudiation, the injured party is entitled to restitution for any benefit that he has conferred on the other party by way of part performance or reliance.

(2) The injured party has no right to restitution if he has performed all of his duties under the contract and no performance by the other party remains due other than payment of a definite sum of money for that performance.

Comment:

a. Restitution as alternative remedy for breach. An injured party usually seeks, through protection of either his expectation or his reliance interest, to enforce the other party's broken promise. See § 344(1). However, he may, as an alternative, seek, through protection of his restitution interest, to prevent the unjust enrichment of the other party. See § 344(2). This alternative is available to the injured party as a remedy for breach under the rule stated in this Section. It is available regardless of whether the breach is by non-performance or by repudiation. If, however, the breach is by non-performance, restitution is available only if the breach gives rise to a claim for damages for total breach and not merely to a claim for damages for partial breach. Compare Illustration 1 with Illustration 2. A party who has lost the right to claim damages for total breach by, for example, acceptance or retention of performance with knowledge of defects (§ 246), has also lost the right to restitution. Restitution is available on repudiation by the other party, even in those exceptional situations in which no claim for damages for total breach arises as a result of repudiation alone. See Comment *d* to § 253. See Illustration 3. The rule stated in this Section applies to all enforceable promises, including those that are enforceable because of reliance. See Illustration 4. An injured party's right to restitution may be barred by election under the rules stated in §§ 378 and 379. **Illustrations:**

1. A contracts to sell a tract of land to B for $ 100,000. After B has made a part payment of $ 20,000, A wrongfully refuses to transfer title. B can recover the $ 20,000 in restitution. The result is the same even if the market price of the land is only $ 70,000, so that performance would have been disadvantageous to B.

2. A contracts to build a house for B for $ 100,000, progress payments to be made monthly. After having been paid $ 40,000 for two months, A commits a breach that is not material by inadvertently using the wrong brand of sewer pipe. B has a claim for damages for partial breach but cannot recover the $ 40,000 that he has paid A.

3. On February 1, A and B make a contract under which, as consideration for B's immediate payment of $ 50,000, A promises to convey to B a parcel of land on May 1. On March 1, A repudiates by selling the parcel to C. On April 1, B commences an action against C. Although under the rule stated in § 253(1), B has no claim against A for damages for breach of contract until performance is due on May 1, B can recover $ 50,000 from A in restitution. See Illustration 4 to § 253.

. . .

b. When contract price is a limit. The rule stated in Subsection (1) is subject to an important exception. If, after one party has fully performed his part of the contract, the other party then refuses to pay a definite sum of money that has been fixed as the price for that performance, the injured party is barred from recovery of a greater sum as restitution under the rule stated in Subsection (2). Since he is entitled to recover the price in full together with interest, he has a remedy that protects his expectation interest by giving him the very thing that he was promised. Even if he asserts that the benefit he conferred on the other party exceeds the price fixed by the contract, justice does not require that he have the right to recover this larger sum in restitution. To give him that right would impose on the court the burden of measuring the benefit in terms of money in spite of the fact that this has already been done by the parties themselves when they made their contract. See Illustration 5. If, however, the performance to be rendered by the party in breach is something other than the payment of a definite sum in money, this burden is less of an imposition on the court since, even if damages were sought by the injured party, the court would have to measure the value to him of the performance due from the party in breach. The clearest case occurs where the injured party has paid the full price in money for the performance that the party in breach has subsequently failed to render. To allow restitution of the sum paid in that case imposes no burden of measurement on the court and relieves it of the burden that it would have if damages were awarded of measuring the value to the injured party of the performance due from the party in breach. See Illustration 6. For this reason, the rule stated in Subsection (2) is limited to the situation where the only remaining performance due from the party in breach is the payment of a definite sum of money. See Illustrations 6 and 7. If the performance promised by the party in breach consists in part of money and in part of something else, full performance by the injured party does not bar him from restitution unless the party in breach has rendered all of his performance except a money payment. **Illustrations:**

    5. A contracts to work for B for one month for $ 10,000. After A has fully performed, B repudiates the contract and refuses to pay the $ 10,000. A can get damages against B for $ 10,000, together with interest, but cannot recover more than that sum even if he can show that the benefit to B from the services was greater than $ 10,000.

    6. A contracts to sell a tract of land to B for $ 100,000. After B has paid the full $ 100,000, A repudiates and refuses to transfer title. B has a right to $ 100,000 in restitution.

    . . .

    c. Effect of "divisibility." Sometimes a contract is "divisible" in the sense that parts of the performances to be exchanged on each side are properly regarded as a pair of agreed equivalents. See § 240. The rule stated in Subsection (2) applies by analogy to such contracts. If one party has fully performed his side of such a pair and all that remains on the other side is for the other party to pay a definite sum of money, recovery for the performance rendered is limited to that sum. Restitution is not available as an alternative even if there has been a breach as to other parts of the contract. See Illustration 8. If both parties have fully performed, so that nothing with respect to the pair of agreed equivalents remains to be done on either side, no recovery can be had as to that pair. **Illustrations:**

    8. A contracts to work as a consultant for B for a fee of $ 50,000, payable at the end of the year, together with a payment of $ 200 a month for A's use of his own car and reimbursement of A's expenses. B wrongfully discharges A at the end of six months. A cannot recover in restitution for the use of his car or for his expenses, but can recover for these items as provided in the contract. As to his recovery for his services, see Illustration 12.

    9. A contracts to build a house for B for $ 50,000, progress payments to be made monthly in an amount equal to 85% of the price of the work performed during the preceding month, the balance to be paid on the architect's certificate of satisfactory completion of the house. B makes the first three payments and then repudiates the contract and has another builder finish the house. A can recover in restitution for the reasonable value of his work, labor and materials, less the amount of the three payments. The performance during each month and the corresponding progress payments are not agreed equivalents under the rule stated in § 240. See Illustration 7 to § 240.

    d. Losing contracts. An injured party who has performed in part will usually prefer to seek damages based on his expectation interest (§ 347) instead of a sum of money based on his restitution interest because such damages include his net profit and will give him a larger recovery. Even if he cannot prove what his net profit would have been, he will ordinarily seek damages based on his reliance interest (§ 348), since this will compensate him for all of his expenditures, regardless of whether they resulted in a benefit to the party in breach. See Comment *a* to § 344. In the case of a contract on which he would have sustained a loss instead of having made a profit, however, his restitution interest may give him a larger recovery than would damages on either basis. The right of the injured party under a losing contract to a greater amount in restitution than he could have recovered in damages has engendered much controversy. The rules stated in this Section give him that right. He is entitled to such recovery even if the contract price is stated in terms of a rate per unit of work and the recovery exceeds that rate. There are, however, two important limitations. The first limitation is one that is applicable to any claim for restitution: the party in breach is liable only to the extent that he has benefited from the injured party's performance. If he has, for example, taken advantage of the injured party's part performance by having the rest of the work completed after his breach, the extent of his benefit is easy to measure in terms of the reasonable value of the injured party's performance. See Illustration 10. If, however, he has abandoned the project and not completed the work, that measurement will be more difficult. See Illustration 11. In that situation, the court may exercise its sound discretion in choosing between the two measures stated in § 371. In doing so it will take account of all the circumstances including the observance by the parties of standards of good faith and fair dealing during any negotiations leading up to the rupture of contractual relations (§ 208). See Introductory Note to Chapter 10. Since a contract that is a losing one for the injured party is often an advantageous one for the party in breach, the possibility should not be overlooked that the breach was provoked by the injured party in order to avoid having to perform. The second limitation is that stated in Subsection (2). If the injured party has completed performance and nothing remains for the party in breach to do but to pay him the price, his recovery is limited to the price. See Comment *b*. **Illustrations:**

10. A, a plumbing subcontractor, contracts with B, a general contractor, to install the plumbing in a factory being built by B for C. B promises to pay A $ 100,000. After A has spent $ 40,000, B repudiates the contract and has the plumbing finished by another subcontractor at a cost of $ 80,000. The market price to have a similar plumbing subcontractor do the work done by A is $ 40,000. A can recover the $ 40,000 from B in restitution.

11. A contracts to build a house for B for $ 100,000. After A has spent $ 40,000, B discovers that he does not have good title to the land on which the house is to be built. B repudiates the contract and abandons the project. A's work results in no actual benefit to B. A cannot recover in restitution from B, but under the rule stated in § 349 he can recover as damages the $ 40,000 that he has spent unless B proves with reasonable certainty that A would have sustained a net loss if the contract had been performed. See Illustration 4 to § 349.

12. A contracts to work as a consultant for B for a fee of $ 50,000, payable at the end of the year. B wrongfully discharges A at the end of eleven months. A can recover in restitution based on the reasonable value of his services. The terms of the contract are evidence of this value but are not conclusive.

e. Avoidability as a limit on restitution. The rule that precludes restitution for a benefit that has been conferred officiously (Restatement of Restitution § 2), applies to preclude recovery for performances that a party has rendered following a repudiation by the other party. Compare the rule stated in § 350. **Illustration:**

13. A contracts to build a bridge for B for $ 100,000. B repudiates the contract shortly after A has begun work on the bridge, telling A that he no longer has need for it. A nevertheless spends an additional $ 10,000 in continuing to perform. A's restitution interest under the rule stated in § 370 does not include the benefit conferred on B by the $ 10,000. See Illustration 1 to § 350.

§ 374. Restitution in Favor of Party in Breach

(1) Subject to the rule stated in Subsection (2), if a party justifiably refuses to perform on the ground that his remaining duties of performance have been discharged by the other party's breach, the party in breach is entitled to restitution for any benefit that he has conferred by way of part performance or reliance in excess of the loss that he has caused by his own breach.

(2) To the extent that, under the manifested assent of the parties, a party's performance is to be retained in the case of breach, that party is not entitled to restitution if the value of the performance as liquidated damages is reasonable in the light of the anticipated or actual loss caused by the breach and the difficulties of proof of loss.

Comment:

a. Restitution in spite of breach. The rule stated in this Section applies where a party, after having rendered part performance, commits a breach by either non-performance or repudiation that justifies the other party in refusing further performance. It is often unjust to allow the injured party to retain the entire benefit of the part performance rendered by the party in breach without paying anything in return. The party in breach is, in any case, liable for the loss caused by his breach. If the benefit received by the injured party does not exceed that loss, he owes nothing to the party in breach. If the benefit received exceeds that loss, the rule stated in this Section generally gives the party in breach the right to recover the excess in restitution. If the injured party has a right to specific performance and remains willing and able to perform, he may keep what he has received and sue for specific performance of the balance.

The rule stated in this Section is of particular importance in connection with breach by the buyer under a land sale contract (see Illustration 1) and breach by the builder under a construction contract (see Illustrations 2, 3 and 4). It is less important in the case of the defaulting employee, who has the protection afforded by statutes that require salary payments at relatively short intervals. The case of defaulting buyer of goods is governed by Uniform Commercial Code § 2-718(2), which generally allows restitution of all but an amount fixed by that section. Furthermore, to the extent that the contract is "divisible" so that pairs of part performances on each side are agreed equivalents (§ 240), the party in breach can recover under the terms of the contract and does not need restitution to obtain relief.

b. Measurement of benefit. If the party in breach seeks restitution of money that he has paid, no problem arises in measuring the benefit to the other party. See Illustration 1. If, however, he seeks to recover a sum of money that represents the benefit of services rendered to the other party, measurement of the benefit is more difficult. Since the party seeking restitution is responsible for posing the problem of measurement of benefit, doubts will be resolved against him and his recovery will not exceed the less generous of the two measures stated in § 370, that of the other party's increase in wealth. See Illustration 3. If no value can be put on this, he cannot recover. See Illustration 5. Although the contract price is evidence of the benefit, it is not conclusive. However, in no case will the party in breach be allowed to recover more than a ratable portion of the total contract price where such a portion can be determined.

A party who intentionally furnishes services or builds a building that is materially different from what he promised is properly regarded as having acted officiously and not in part performance of his promise and will be denied recovery on that ground even if his performance was of some benefit to the other party. This is not the case, however, if the other party has accepted or agreed to accept the substitute performance. See §§ 278, 279. **Illustrations:**

1. A contracts to sell land to B for $ 100,000, which B promises to pay in $ 10,000 installments before transfer of title. After B has paid $ 30,000 he fails to pay the remaining installments and A sells the land to another buyer for $ 95,000. B can recover $ 30,000 from A in restitution less $ 5,000 damages for B's breach of contract, or $ 25,000. If A does not sell the land to another buyer and obtains a decree of specific performance against B, B has no right to restitution.

2. A contracts to make repairs to B's building in return for B's promise to pay $ 10,000 on completion of the work. After spending $ 8,000 on the job, A fails to complete it because of insolvency. B has the work completed by another builder for $ 4,000, increasing the value of the building to him by a total of $ 9,000, but he loses $ 500 in rent because of the delay. A can recover $ 5,000 from B in restitution less $ 500 in damages for the loss caused by the breach, or $ 4,500.

3. A contracts to make repairs to B's building in return for B's promise to pay $ 10,000 on completion of the work. A makes repairs costing him $ 8,000 but inadvertently fails to follow the specifications in such material respects that there is no substantial performance. See Comment *d* to § 237. The defects cannot be corrected with-

out the destruction of large parts of the building, but the work confers a benefit on B by increasing the value of the building to him by $ 4,000. A can recover $ 4,000 from B in restitution.

...

c. Exception for money paid. Instead of promising to pay a fixed sum as liquidated damages in case of breach, a promisor may actually pay a sum of money that the parties understand is to be retained by the promisee if the promise is not performed. If the sum is a reasonable one that would be sustained as liquidated damages under the rule stated in § 356, the promisee is entitled to retain it. If it is not, the promisor is entitled to restitution under the rule stated in Subsection (1). The test of reasonableness is the same as that applicable to a provision for liquidated damages. See Comment *b* to § 356. The understanding of the parties may be shown by the terms of their agreement, by description of the sum as "earnest money" or by usage. The sum may or may not be part of the price to be paid by the promisor. The same principle applies if what is to be retained by the promisee is property other than money. **Illustrations:**

6. The facts being otherwise as stated in Illustration 1, the contract provides that on default by B, A has the right to retain the first $ 10,000 installment paid by B. If $ 10,000 is a reasonable amount, B can recover only $ 20,000 from A in restitution.

7. The facts being otherwise as stated in Illustration 1, the contract provides that on default by B, A has the right to retain any installments paid by B. The provision is not valid, and B can still recover $ 30,000 from A in restitution less $ 5,000 damages for B's breach of contract, or $ 25,000.

§ 375. Restitution When Contract Is Within Statute of Frauds

A party who would otherwise have a claim in restitution under a contract is not barred from restitution for the reason that the contract is unenforceable by him because of the Statute of Frauds unless the Statute provides otherwise or its purpose would be frustrated by allowing restitution.

Comment:

a. Restitution generally available. Parties to a contract that is unenforceable under the Statute of Frauds frequently act in reliance on it before discovering that it is unenforceable. A party may, for example, render services under the contract or may make improvements on land that is the subject of the contract. The rule stated in this Section allows restitution in such cases. See Illustrations 1 and 2. If the party claiming restitution is in breach, the right to restitution is subject to the rule stated in § 374. If the other party is in breach it is subject to the rule stated in § 373. Since allowing restitution does not amount to enforcement of the contract, it ordinarily does not contravene the policy behind the Statute. Restitution will not be allowed, however, if the Statute so provides or if restitution would frustrate the purpose of the Statute. See Illustration 3. However, the mere fact that the particular wording of the Statute makes the contract "void" is not controlling in this respect.

For the purposes of this Section, the measure of the benefit conferred is generally the same as that applicable to similar situations under enforceable contracts. See Comment *b* to § 373 and Comment *b* to § 374. The agreement, although unenforceable, may be evidence of this benefit. As to the possibility of recovery based on the reliance interest, see § 139. **Illustrations:**

1. A makes an oral contract to furnish services to B that are not to be performed within a year (§ 130). After A has worked for two months B discharges him without paying him anything. A can recover from B as restitution the reasonable value of the services rendered during the two months.

2. A makes an oral contract to sell a tract of land to B for $ 100,000 (§ 125). B pays $ 50,000, takes possession and makes improvements. A then refuses to convey the land to B, and B sues A for restitution of $ 50,000 plus $ 20,000, the reasonable value of the improvements, less $ 5,000, the value to B of the use of the land. B can recover $ 65,000 from A.

3. A, a home owner, makes an oral contract with B, a real estate broker, to pay B the usual 5% commission if B succeeds in selling A's house. The state Statute of Frauds contains a provision providing that a real estate broker shall have no right to such a commission unless there is a written memorandum of the contract. B sells A's house for $ 100,000 and sues A in restitution for

$ 5,000, the reasonable value of B's services. B cannot recover in restitution because the purpose of the Statute would be frustrated if B were allowed to recover as restitution the same amount that had been promised under the contract.

b. Limits on restitution. The rule stated in this Section gives a right to restitution only to one who would have such a right if the contract were enforceable. It is therefore subject to the rules stated in §§ 370-72. A party's right to restitution may, for example, be terminated by the other party's tender of specific restitution. See § 373(4). Furthermore, the rule stated in this Section governs the right to restitution only if the Statute makes the contract unenforceable. If the party seeking restitution under a land sale contract has a right to enforce the contract by a suit for specific performance on the ground of reliance (§ 129), his right to restitution is governed by the rules stated in §§ 373 and 374. Similarly, if a party seeking restitution under a contract not to be performed within a year has a right to enforce it because he has completely performed, his right to restitution is governed by the rule stated in § 373. Finally, under the rule stated in § 138(1), the right to restitution is subject to the same defenses that would be available if the Statute were satisfied. A party has no right to restitution, therefore, if the other party is not in breach and is prepared to perform, except to the extent that such a right would exist if the Statute were satisfied. A party has, however, a right to restitution under the rule stated in § 141 if the other party will neither perform nor sign a sufficient memorandum. See Illustration 4.

The rule stated in this Section is not intended as an exclusive statement of the right to restitution under provisions of the Statute of Frauds other than those contained in Chapter 5 of this Restatement. For example, in the case of a contract that is unenforceable because of a statutory requirement that contracts not performable within a life-time be evidenced by a writing, full performance by one party may not make such a contract enforceable by him. He may therefore be unable to enforce the contract and yet not be entitled to restitution under the rule stated in § 373 because of the limitation in Subsection (2) of that section. His right to restitution is not dealt with in this Restatement.

Illustration:

> 4. A makes an oral contract to buy a tract of land from B for $ 100,000 (§ 125). Payment is to be made in $ 10,000 installments, conveyance to be made on the payment of the third installment. A pays $ 10,000 and then refuses to pay any more and sues B to recover in restitution the $ 10,000 that he has paid. If B signs a sufficient memorandum, A's refusal to pay is a defense to his action under the rule stated in § 141(1) and A cannot get restitution. See Illustration 6 to § 374. If B refuses to sign a sufficient memorandum, A's refusal to pay is not a defense under the rule stated in § 141(2) and A can get restitution. See Illustration 1 to § 373.

§ 376. Restitution When Contract Is Voidable

A party who has avoided a contract on the ground of lack of capacity, mistake, misrepresentation, duress, undue influence or abuse of a fiduciary relation is entitled to restitution for any benefit that he has conferred on the other party by way of part performance or reliance.

Comment:

a. Recovery of benefit on avoidance. A party who exercises his power of avoidance is entitled to recover in restitution for any benefit that he has conferred on the other party through part performance of or reliance on the contract. The benefit from his part performance includes that resulting from the use by the other party of whatever he has received up to the time that it is returned on avoidance. Furthermore, under the rule stated in § 384, a party seeking restitution must generally return any benefit that he has himself received. If he has received and must return land, for example, he may have made improvements on the land in reliance on the contract and he is entitled, on avoidance and return of the land, to recover the reasonable value of those improvements (§ 371(b)). The rule stated in this Section applies to avoidance on any ground, including lack of capacity (§§ 14-16), mistake (§§ 152, 153), misrepresentation (§ 164), duress (§ 175), undue influence (§ 177) or abuse of a fiduciary relation (§ 173). Uncertainties in measuring the benefit, however, are more likely to be resolved in favor of the party seeking restitution if the other party engaged in misconduct, as in cases of fraudulent misrepresentation, duress or undue influence. In cases of mental incompetency the rule stated in this Section is supplemented by that stated in § 15(2) and in cases of mistake it is supplemented by that stated in § 158. **Illustrations:**

1. A contracts to sell an automobile to B, an infant, for $ 2,000. After A has delivered the automobile and B has paid the $ 2,000, B disaffirms the contract on the ground of infancy (§ 14), tenders the automobile back to A, and sues A for $ 2,000. B can recover the $ 2,000 from A in restitution.

2. A contracts to sell and B to buy for $ 100,000 a tract of land, the value of which has depended mainly on the timber on it. Both A and B believe that the timber is still there, but in fact it has been destroyed by fire. After A has conveyed the land to B and B has paid the $ 100,000, B discovers the mistake. B disaffirms the contract for mistake (§ 152), tenders a deed to the land to A, and sues A for $ 100,000. B can recover $ 100,000 from A in restitution. See Illustration 1 to § 152.

3. A submits a $ 150,000 offer in response to B's invitation for bids on the construction of a building. A believes that this is the total of a column of figures, but he has made an error by inadvertently omitting $ 50,000, and in fact the total is $ 200,000. Because B had estimated the expected cost as $ 180,000 and the 10 other bids were all in the range between $ 180,000 and $ 200,000, B had reason to know of A's mistake. A discovers the mistake after he has done part of the work, disaffirms the contract on the ground of mistake (§ 153), and sues B in restitution for the benefit conferred on B as measured by the reasonable value of A's performance. A can recover the reasonable value of his performance in restitution and if the cost of the work done can be determined under the next lowest bid, that cost is evidence of its reasonable value. See Illustration 9 to § 153.

. . .

§ 377. Restitution in Cases of Impracticability, Frustration, Non-Occurrence Of Condition or Disclaimer by Beneficiary

A party whose duty of performance does not arise or is discharged as a result of impracticability of performance, frustration of purpose, non-occurrence of a condition or disclaimer by a beneficiary is entitled to restitution for any benefit that he has conferred on the other party by way of part performance or reliance.

Comment:

a. Scope. A party whose duty of performance is discharged on grounds of supervening impracticability of performance (§ 261) or frustration of purpose (§ 265) may already have performed in part or otherwise relied on the contract before the occurrence of the supervening event. A party whose duty never arises on those grounds (§ 266) may have taken similar action before discovery of the relevant circumstances. Under the rule stated in this Section such a party is entitled to restitution. Furthermore, in cases of impracticability or frustration the other party is also ordinarily relieved of any obligation of rendering the return performance that he has promised on the ground of failure of performance (§ 267). Under the rule stated in this Section that party is also entitled to restitution. The same is true where the parties are relieved of their obligations on the ground of the non-occurrence of a condition (§ 225) or because of a disclaimer by a beneficiary (§ 306). If both parties have rendered some performance, each is entitled to restitution against the other. The rule stated in this Section is subject to contrary agreement to the extent that the agreement does not violate the rules relating to unfairness (§ 364), unconscionability (§ 208) and forfeiture (§ 229).

Illustrations:

1. A contracts to employ B as a confidential secretary for a month for $ 2,000, to be paid at the end of that time. B falls ill after working for two weeks and the duties of performance of both A and B are discharged as a result of impracticability of performance (§ 262). B is entitled to restitution from A for the services that he has performed. See Illustration 1 to § 262. The result is the same if B's duty is discharged as a result of A's illness rather than B's. See Illustration 2 to § 262.

2. A contracts to employ B as a confidential secretary for a month for $ 2,000, to be paid in advance. B falls ill after A has paid the $ 2,000 but before B has begun work and the duties of performance of both A and B are discharged as a result of impracticability of performance (§ 262). A is entitled to restitution of $ 2,000 from B. If

B had fallen ill after working for two weeks, B would also be entitled to restitution from A for the services that he has performed.

. . .

b. Measure of benefit. Cases of impracticability and frustration may pose particularly difficult problems of adjustment after the occurrence of a disruptingevent that was ordinarily unforeseeable when the contract was made. The rule stated in § 272(2) gives a court discretion in an extreme case to do justice by supplying a term that is reasonable in the circumstance. In most cases, however, restitution is all that is required, given the choice open to the court in measuring benefit (§ 371). Usually the measure of reasonable value is appropriate. A benefit may be found if it was conferred before the occurrence of the event even though the event later resulted in its destruction, and in that case recovery may be limited to the measure of increase in wealth prior to the event, if this is less than reasonable value. Compare Illustrations 4 and 6. A party cannot, however, recover his reliance interest under the rule stated in this Section, and his expenditures in reliance are not subtracted from what he has received in calculating the benefit for which he is liable. See

Illustration 5; see also Comment *b* to § 371. Furthermore, to the extent that the contract price can be roughly apportioned to the work done, recovery will not be allowed in excess of the appropriate amount of the price. **Illustrations:**

4. A contracts with B to shingle the roof of B's house for $ 5,000, payable as the work progresses. After A has spent $ 2,000 doing part of the work and has been paid $ 1,800, much of the house including the roof is destroyed by fire without his fault, and the duties of performance of both A and B are discharged as a result of impracticability of performance (§ 263). The work done before the fire increased the market price and the insurable value of the house by $ 1,500. A is entitled to restitution of $ 1,500 from B and B is entitled to restitution of $ 1,800 from A. See Illustration 3 to § 263.

5. The facts being otherwise as stated in Illustration 4, the fire also destroyed shingles that had cost A $ 500 and that were piled near the house for the rest of the work. A is not entitled to restitution of this loss from B. Nor can A subtract the $ 500 from the $ 1,800 he has been paid in determining the benefit that he has received. The court may, however, take this loss into consideration in deciding whether to allow A restitution of $ 1,500 or $ 2,000. See also § 272.

. . .

Topic 5. Preclusion by Election and Affirmance

Introductory Note Sometimes a party who has a choice of alternative remedies is precluded by his action or inaction from pursuing one of those remedies on the ground that he has "elected" the other. The rules governing this are dealt with in §§ 378 and 379. They reflect the trend against preclusion by election that has resulted from the merger of law and equity and the reform of rules of procedure.

A party who has a power of avoidance on the ground, for example, of mistake, misrepresentation or duress, may be precluded by his action or inaction from exercising it on the ground that he has ratified the contract by affirming it. The rules governing this are dealt with in §§ 380-85. This Topic does not contain the substantive rules that determine whether a party has a power of avoidance. Those rules appear in other chapters of this Restatement that deal with the various grounds for avoidance. See §§ 14-16, 152-53, 164, 173, 175 and 177.

§ 378. Election Among Remedies

If a party has more than one remedy under the rules stated in this Chapter, his manifestation ˙ of a choice of one of them by bringing suit or otherwise is not a bar to another remedy unless the remedies are inconsistent and the other party materially changes his position in reliance on the manifestation.

Comment:

a. Election among remedies. The rules stated in this Chapter give a party three basic types of remedies: damages (Topic 2), specific performance or an injunction (Topic 3), and restitution (Topic

4). The rule stated in this Section precludes a party who has manifested his choice of one of those remedies from shifting to another remedy if such a shift would be unjust because of the other party's reliance on the earlier manifestation. The mere manifestation of an intention to pursue one remedy rather than another does not, however, preclude a party from making such a shift. Nor must the shift be made within any particular time. Only if the other party has materially changed his position in reliance on the original choice is a shift to another remedy precluded by the election of the first. A change of position is "material" within the meaning of this Section if it is such that in all the circumstances a shift in remedies would be unjust. This rejection of any doctrine of election in the absence of reliance is consistent with a similar policy in the Uniform Commercial Code. See Uniform Commercial Code § 2-703 and Comment 1; § 2-711 and § 2-721. Even if the bringing of an action for one remedy is a manifestation of choice of that remedy, it does not preclude the plaintiff from shifting to another remedy as long as the defendant has not materially changed his position. Alternative counts seeking inconsistent remedies are generally permitted in the same complaint and a change in remedy may often be made by amendment of the complaint, even at an advanced stage of the action.

Illustrations:

    1. A contracts to sell a tract of land to B. A repudiates and B brings an action for damages. While this action is pending, A makes valuable improvements on the land reasonably believing that B does not intend to pursue his remedy of specific performance. B then amends his complaint to ask specific performance. If A's change of position is material, B's claim for specific performance is precluded.

    2. A contracts to transfer his farm to B in return for B's promise to support A for life. After A has transferred the farm, B repudiates the contract and A sues for specific restitution. Before any change in B's position, A learns that a part of the farm has been sold by B and amends his complaint to ask for damages for the breach. A's claim for damages is not precluded.

    3. A contracts to transfer his farm to B in return for B's promise to support A for life. After A has transferred the farm, B repudiates the contract and A sues for damages. Before any change in B's position, A discovers that it will be difficult to prove his damages with reason-

able certainty and that a judicial sale of B's property including the farm would be unlikely to realize enough to satisfy a judgment and amends his complaint to ask specific restitution. Specific restitution is not precluded.

    b. Additional circumstances. In two situations a party is not precluded from seeking a different remedy, even after reliance on his first choice by the other party, because his shift is justified by additional circumstances. The first situation is that in which the party made his original choice while ignorant of facts that give him a remedy based on, for example, misrepresentation or mistake and later discovers those facts. In that situation he is not bound by his original choice because he made it when mistaken. The second situation is that in which after a party makes his original choice, a later breach by the other party occurs. In that situation he can pursue any remedy based on the later breach without regard to his original choice.

    c. Remedy not available. The rule stated in this Section applies only where a party pursues a remedy that he actually has. A party is not precluded from pursuing other remedies by the fact that he has made a mistaken attempt to obtain a remedy that is not available to him, even if his original choice has been relied on by the other party. **Illustrations:**

    4. A makes an oral contract to transfer his farm to B in return for B's promise to support A for life. After A has transferred the farm, B repudiates the contract and A sues for damages. B pleads the Statute of Frauds and A's action is about to be dismissed. A then amends his complaint to ask specific restitution. Regardless of whether B has changed his position, specific restitution is not precluded.

    5. A makes a written contract to sell a tract of land to B. A repudiates the contract and B, claiming that both parties were mistaken as to the contents of the writing, sues A for reformation of the writing and for specific performance of the contract as reformed. The court refuses to reform the writing on the ground that mistake was not proved and B amends his complaint to ask damages for breach of the contract as written. B's claim for damages is not precluded.

    d. Other remedy not inconsistent. The rule stated in this Section applies only where a party seeks to shift to a remedy that is inconsistent with the one he has chosen. A party who seeks specific performance or an injunction may, for example, be entitled to damages to compensate him for delay in performance. See Comment c to § 358. Similarly, a party who seeks restitution may, for example, be entitled to damages to compensate him for costs of transportation of goods that he has incurred. A later request for such damages in a suit for specific performance or an injunction or in one for restitution is not precluded because it is not inconsistent with that suit. However, the remedy of specific performance or an injunction and that of damages for total breach of contract are inconsistent. The remedy of specific performance or an injunction and that of restitution are also inconsistent. And the remedy of restitution and that of damages for total breach are inconsistent. **Illustration:**

> 6. A contracts to sell a tract of land to B. A fails to convey the tract and B sues A for specific performance. B later amends his complaint to add a claim for damages resulting from the delay caused by A's failure. Regardless of whether A has changed his position, such a further claim is not precluded.

e. Other situations distinguished. The rule stated in this Section applies only as among the remedies provided for in this Chapter. It does not, for example preclude a party from pursuing a claim in tort for misrepresentation or a claim for breach of warranty in the sale of goods. See Uniform Commercial Code § 2-721. It does not determine whether a party is barred by election from treating his remaining duties of performance as discharged (§ 379). Nor does it apply in the many instances in which a party makes a choice that affects his substantive rights, such as the choice of an offeree between acceptance (§ 50) and rejection (§ 38), the choice of an intended beneficiary between disclaiming the contract and not doing so (§ 306), or the choice of an infant between affirmance and disaffirmance (§§ 14, 380). Furthermore, this rule does not apply to situations in which a party is precluded by his delay from enforcing a substantive right, as is the case where one having the power of avoidance loses it by delay (§ 381). Finally this Section is inapplicable to matters of procedure, such as the requirement that a party choose between inconsistent remedies at some stage of a judicial proceeding, and to matters governed by the law of judgments, such as merger and bar. See Restatement, Second, Judgments §§ 17, 18, 19.

§ 379. Election to Treat Duties of Performance Under Aleatory Contract as Discharged

If a right or duty of the injured party is conditional on an event that is fortuitous or is supposed by the parties to be fortuitous, he cannot treat his remaining duties to render performance as discharged on the ground of the other party's breach by non-performance if he does not manifest to the other party his intention to do so before any adverse change in the situation of the injured party resulting from the occurrence of that event or a material change in the probability of its occurrence.

Comment:

a. Election under an aleatory contract. An aleatory contract is one in which at least one party is under a duty that is conditional on the occurrence of an event that, so far as the parties to the contract are aware, is dependent on chance. Its occurrence may be within the control of third persons or beyond the control of any person. The event may have already occurred, as long as that fact is unknown to the parties. It may be the failure of something to happen as well as its happening. Common examples are contracts of insurance and suretyship, as well as gambling contracts. If the injured party's duty is conditional on such an event, it would be unfair if, after the breach, he were allowed to take advantage of a material change in the likelihood of its occurrence when deciding whether to treat his remaining duties as discharged. If it was more likely that it would occur it would be to his advantage to treat those duties as discharged. For this reason, he is precluded from treating them as discharged if there has been an adverse change in his situation because the event has occurred or because there has been a material increase in the probability of its occurrence. The same principle applies to the case where a right rather than a duty of the injured party is conditional on the occurrence of such an event.

. . .

§ 380. Loss of Power of Avoidance by Affirmance

(1) The power of a party to avoid a contract for incapacity, duress, undue influence or abuse of a fiduciary relation is lost if, after the circumstances that made the contract voidable have ceased to exist, he manifests to the other party his intention to affirm it or acts with respect to anything that he has received in a manner inconsistent with disaffirmance.

(2) The power of a party to avoid a contract for mistake or misrepresentation is lost if after he knows or has reason to know of the mistake or of the misrepresentation if it is non-fraudulent or knows of the misrepresentation if it is fraudulent, he manifests to the other party his intention to affirm it or acts with respect to anything that he has received in a manner inconsistent with disaffirmance.

(3) If the other party rejects an offer by the party seeking avoidance to return what he has received, the party seeking avoidance if entitled to restitution can, after the lapse of a reasonable time, enforce a lien on what he has received by selling it and crediting the proceeds toward his claim in restitution.

Comment:

a. Ratification by affirmance. A party who has the power of avoidance may lose it by action that manifests a willingness to go on with the contract. Such action is known as "affirmance" and has the effect of ratifying the contract. See Restatement of Restitution § 68. The rule stated in this Section is a special application of that stated in § 85, under which a promise to perform a voidable duty is binding. On ratification, the affirming party is bound as from the outset and the other party continues to be bound.

b. Manner and time of affirmance. A party may manifest his intention to affirm by words or other conduct, including the exercise of dominion over what he has received in a manner inconsistent with avoidance of the contract. Compare Uniform Commercial Code § 2-606. If he offers to return the performance that he has received and if such an offer is rejected, he must hold that performance for the other party. Because the party seeking restitution has a lien on any performance that he has himself received, however, he is entitled to enforce that lien under the rule stated in Subsection (3) after he has waited a reasonable time. A party's power of avoidance for incapacity, duress, undue influence or abuse of a fiduciary relation is not lost by conduct while the circumstances that made the contract voidable continue to exist. Nor is his power of avoidance for misrepresentation or mistake lost until he knows of the misrepresentation if it is fraudulent, or knows or ought to know of a non-fraudulent misrepresentation or mistake. **Illustrations:**

1. A is induced by B's misrepresentation to make a contract to repair B's house, payment to be made when the services have been rendered. When A discovers the facts, he accuses B of fraud and threatens to avoid the transaction unless B pays in advance or furnishes security. Before A receives any response from B, A notifies B that he avoids the contract. A's conduct did not amount to affirmance and the contract is avoided. The result would be different, however, if A demanded that B perform the contract or accepted security from B.

2. A is induced by B's misrepresentation to make a contract to employ B for a year. When A discovers the facts, he continues to employ B for two weeks and then discharges him in violation of the contract, notifying B that he avoids the contract. A's conduct amounted to affirmance and he is liable to B for breach of contract. The result would not be affected if A did not learn until the end of the two weeks that the law gave him the power to avoid the contract. The result would be different, however, if B had persuaded A to continue the employment for another two weeks as a trial period and A discharged B at the end of that time because A was still dissatisfied.

3. A is induced by B's fraudulent and material misrepresentation to buy land from B. When A discovers the fraud he brings an action in deceit against B. A later discontinues the action and notifies B that he avoids the contract. Since A's bringing of the action was a manifestation of his intention to affirm the contract only if damages are paid, it did not without more amount to affirmance. A's subsequent attempt to avoid the contract was effective.

. . .

§ 381. Loss of Power of Avoidance by Delay

(1) The power of a party to avoid a contract for incapacity, duress, undue influence or abuse of a fiduciary relation is lost if, after the circumstances that made it voidable have ceased to exist, he does not within a reasonable time manifest to the other party his intention to avoid it.

(2) The power of a party to avoid a contract for misrepresentation or mistake is lost if after he knows of a fraudulent misrepresentation or knows or has reason to know of a non-fraudulent misrepresentation or mistake he does not within a reasonable time manifest to the other party his intention to avoid it. The power of a party to avoid a contract for non-fraudulent misrepresentation or mistake is also lost if the contract has been so far performed or the circumstances have otherwise so changed that avoidance would be inequitable and if damages will be adequate compensation.

(3) In determining what is a reasonable time, the following circumstances are significant:

(a) the extent to which the delay enabled or might have enabled the party with the power of avoidance to speculate at the other party's risk;

(b) the extent to which the delay resulted or might have resulted in justifiable reliance by the other party or by third persons;

(c) the extent to which the ground for avoidance was the result of any fault by either party; and

(d) the extent to which the other party's conduct contributed to the delay.

(4) If a right or duty of the party who has the power of avoidance for non-fraudulent misrepresentation or mistake is conditional on an event that is fortuitous or is supposed by the parties to be fortuitous, a manifestation of intention under Subsection (1) or (2) is not effective unless it is made before any adverse change in his situation resulting from the occurrence of that event or a material change in the probability of its occurrence.

Comment:

a. Effect of delay. A party who has the power to avoid a contract may lose that power by delay alone, even without such conduct as amounts to affirmance (§ 380). Under the rule stated in this Section the power is lost if it is not exercised within a reasonable time. The rule is similar in its purpose to that stated in § 380 on the loss of the power to treat one's remaining duties as discharged on breach. Here, as under § 379, what time is reasonable depends on all the circumstances, including the extent to which the delay was or was likely to be prejudicial to the other party or to third persons. Such prejudice may result if the delay enables the party with the power of avoidance to speculate at the other party's risk, affirming if the course of the market makes the contract advantageous to him and disaffirming if it makes it disadvantageous. Such prejudice may also result from reliance or the likelihood of reliance by the other party or by third persons. The reliance must be justifiable and the fact that the one who relied knew of the ground for avoidance is a consideration in this connection. If the ground for avoidance was to any extent the fault of either party, this is also a

factor. For example, the fault of the party with the power of avoidance in not discovering a mistake or a misrepresentation will shorten the period for avoidance. Compare §§ 157, 172. The misconduct of the other party in cases of fraudulent misrepresentation or duress will lengthen it. A consumer is not generally expected to avoid as promptly as is a merchant in similar circumstances. Furthermore, if the other party contributes to the delay, as by promising to remedy defects or by urging a further period of testing before avoidance, this will lengthen the period. Ordinarily, if the party with the power of avoidance retains during the delay something that he has received from the other party, avoidance will be precluded by the rule stated in § 380. The importance of the present Section is, therefore, chiefly in cases in which the party with that power has received nothing.

b. When reasonable time begins. A party who has the power of avoidance for incapacity, duress, undue influence or abuse of a fiduciary relation is not expected to act until the circumstances that have made the contract voidable have ceased to exist, and the reasonable time does not begin to run until then. In the case of a party who has the power of avoidance for misrepresentation or mistake, it does not begin to run until he knows of the misrepresentation if it is fraudulent, or knows or has reason to know of a non-fraudulent misrepresentation or mistake. However, in determining whether a party acted within a reasonable time once he was expected to do so, the fact that a considerable period of time had elapsed after the original transaction is significant. Nevertheless, if the power of avoidance is then exercised within a reasonable time, avoidance is not ordinarily precluded even though the other party has relied. Compare Illustration 2 with Illustration 3. But see Comment c. The rights of third parties who may have relied are not dealt with in this Restatement. See Introductory Note to this Chapter. Where a party seeks to avoid a contract on the ground of a mistake that he alone has made, he must show that enforcement of the contract would be unconscionable, unless the other party had reason to know of the mistake or his fault caused it. See § 153. The lapse of time before the mistaken party discovers his mistake may invite reliance by the other party that will make it more difficult to show unconscionability even though it would not preclude avoidance under the present Section. A party need not specify in detail the bases of his disaffirmance unless this is necessary in order for the other party to know the ground of avoidance or to take appropriate action in response. Compare Illustration 5 with Illustration 6. As to the requirement that he return what he has received, see § 384. **Illustrations:**

    1. A is induced by B's misrepresentation to contract in January to sell B 1,000 shares of stock in the X Corporation for $ 100,000, delivery and payment to be on May 1. A discovers the fraud in February but does not manifest his intention to avoid the transaction until April. In view of the extent to which A's delay of two months enabled him to speculate at B's expense, A has lost his power of avoidance, and his manifestation is not effective to avoid the transaction. Compare Illustration 2 to § 379. The result does not depend on whether the market price of the stock has risen or fallen.

    . . .

c. When avoidance would be inequitable. In some situations where a party has a power of avoidance for non-fraudulent misrepresentation or mistake, the circumstances may have so changed after the contract was made that it would be inequitable to allow avoidance if damages would adequately compensate him. This may be so where performance in whole or in part makes avoidance excessively burdensome for the other party. It may also be so where, because of a drastic shift in market prices, avoidance will throw onto the other party a heavy loss unrelated to the misrepresentation or mistake. In such situations the party having the power of avoidance loses it and is limited to a claim for damages under the rule stated in Subsection (2). A similar rule as to avoidance for mental incompetency is stated in § 15(2). **Illustration:**

    7. A, seeking to induce B to make a contract to buy his house for $ 50,000, tells B that the roof is in "good condition." A is mistaken and unknown to him the roof has a hidden defect that can be fully remedied for $ 1,000. B is induced by the statement to make the proposed contract, and, two years after taking possession, he discovers the defect. Even if the court considers the statement a material misrepresentation, it may conclude that the contract is no longer voidable and limit B's relief to the recovery of $ 1,000 in damages from A.

d. Aleatory contracts. Under an aleatory contract, at least one party is under a duty that is conditional on the occurrence of an event that, so far as the parties are aware, is dependent on chance. See Comment a to § 379. If the duty of the party having a power of avoidance for non-fraudulent misrepresentation or mistake is conditional on such an event, it would be unfair if he could take advantage of a material change in the likelihood of its occurrence when deciding whether to exercise that power. If it were more likely that it would occur it would be to his advantage to exercise it. If it were less likely that it would occur, it would be to his advantage not to exercise it. For this reason, he is precluded from exercising it if there has been an adverse change in his situation because the event has occurred or because there has been a material increase in the probability of its occurrence. The same principle applies to the case when a right of the party with the power of avoidance is conditional on the occurrence of such an event.

    . . .

§ 382. Loss of Power to Affirm by Prior Avoidance

(1) If a party has effectively exercised his power of avoidance, a subsequent manifestation of intent to affirm is inoperative unless the other party manifests his assent to affirmance by refusal to accept a return of his performance or otherwise.

(2) A party has not exercised his power of avoidance under the rule stated in Subsection (1) until

(a) he has regained all or a substantial part of what he would be entitled to by way of restitution on avoidance,

(b) he has obtained a final judgment of or based on avoidance, or

(c) the other party has materially relied on or manifested his assent to a statement of disaffirmance.

Comment:

a. Conclusive effect of avoidance. Effective exercise of the power of avoidance is conclusive and precludes subsequent affirmance. An exercise of the power is not effective if it is itself avoided on such grounds as mistake, misrepresentation, duress or mental incompetency. Exercise of the power by an infant is not, however, voidable on the ground of his infancy. Even after a party's effective exercise of the power of avoidance, the other party may wish to have the transaction sustained and, if both parties manifest this intention their new agreement is effective.

b. What amounts to exercise of power. A mere statement of disaffirmance, even if coupled with ineffective attempts to regain what one has given, is not such an exercise of the power of avoidance as will preclude affirmance. There is no exercise of the power by a party until he has regained all or part of what he gave, has obtained a judgment that will put him back into his original position, has caused the other party to change his position in reliance on the disaffirmance, or has contracted with the other party on the basis of the disaffirmance.

. . .

§ 383. Avoidance in Part

A contract cannot be avoided in part except that where one or more corresponding pairs of part performances have been fully performed by one or both parties the rest of the contract can be avoided.

Comment:

a. No avoidance in part. A party who has the power of avoidance must ordinarily avoid the entire contract, including any part that has already been performed. He cannot disaffirm part of the contract that is particularly disadvantageous to himself while affirming a more advantageous part, and an attempt to do so is ineffective as a disaffirmance. The rule stated in this Section does not preclude avoidance of only one of two or more entirely separate contracts. Nor does it prevent reformation of a part of a contract for either mistake or misrepresentation. See §§ 155 and 166. **Illustration:**

1. A makes a contract to work for B for a year and is induced by B's fraud to assent to a covenant under which he agrees to refrain from entering into a similar business in the same town for three years after the termination of the employment. A discovers the fraud after he has worked for a month. A cannot avoid the covenant not to compete without avoiding the rest of the contract.

b. Exception for "divisible" contracts. There is an exception to the general rule stated in this Section if the contract is "divisible" in the sense that the performances to be exchanged can be apportioned into corresponding pairs of part performances under the rule stated in § 240. In that situation, if one or more pairs of part performances have been fully performed by one or both parties, the party who has the power of avoidance can avoid the rest of the contract only or can avoid the whole contract.

. . .

§ 384. Requirement That Party Seeking Restitution Return Benefit

(1) Except as stated in Subsection (2), a party will not be granted restitution unless

(a) he returns or offers to return, conditional on restitution, any interest in property that he has received in exchange in substantially as good condition as when it was received by him, or

(b) the court can assure such return in connection with the relief granted.

(2) The requirement stated in Subsection (1) does not apply to property

(a) that was worthless when received or that has been destroyed or lost by the other party or as a result of its own defects,

(b) that either could not from the time of receipt have been returned or has been used or disposed of without knowledge of the grounds for restitution if justice requires that compensation be accepted in its place and the payment of such compensation can be assured, or

(c) as to which the contract apportions the price if that part of the price is not included in the claim for restitution.

Comment:

a. Duty to return benefit. A party who seeks restitution of a benefit that he has conferred on the other party is expected to return what he has received from the other party. The objective is to return the parties, as nearly as is practicable, to the situation in which they found themselves before they made the contract. If a party has received land, goods or other property, he is expected to return it. The fact that he has benefited from possession of them does not preclude restitution since he can compensate the other party in money for this benefit. The property itself, however, must generally be returned. If it has been used, destroyed or substantially altered in character while in his possession, restitution is generally not available. Mere depreciation in market value, however, is not such a change as will preclude restitution. Cf. Uniform Commercial Code § 2-608.

b. Necessity of offer to return. If a party seeking restitution offers to return what he has received, he may make his offer conditional on restitution being made to him. To this end, the law gives him a lien on what he has received. See § 380(3). In equity, his failure to make such an offer before commencing a suit for rescission did not preclude relief. The decree could be made conditional on an offer. At law, however, an offer was traditionally regarded as a condition of the right to commence an action based on rescission. The merger of law and equity and modern procedural reforms have made this distinction undesirable, and the rule stated in this Section reflects the increasing criticism of the rule at law. If the court has the power to assure the required return in connection with the relief that it grants,

it is not necessary that there have been a prior return or offer to return. If all that is to be returned is money, a credit against a larger sum allowed in restitution will suffice. In other cases a conditional judgment will be proper. A court may, in awarding costs, take account of any failure by the party seeking restitution to afford the other party an adequate opportunity to make restitution without the commencement of legal process. This is particularly appropriate in cases, such as mutual mistake, impracticability of performance or frustration of purpose, in which the other party is in no way at fault. Even though an offer to return property is not necessary under the rule stated in this Section, the retention of property together with the exercise of dominion over it may preclude avoidance under the rule stated in § 380. **Illustrations:**

1. A contracts to sell to B a factory and a patent and B makes a part payment of $ 100,000. A assigns the patent but fails to transfer the factory to B. B sues A asking restitution of $ 100,000 without offering to reassign the patent. B is entitled to a judgment for that amount conditional on his tender of a reassignment of the patent.

2. A is induced by B's fraudulent misrepresentations to contract to sell to B for $ 10,000 an antique worth $ 100,000. A delivers the antique and B pays the $ 10,000. On discovery of the fraud, A demands the return of the antique without offering to repay the $ 10,000. On B's refusal, A sues B in conversion for the value of the antique. A is entitled to a judgment for $ 90,000, the value of the antique less $ 10,000.

3. The facts being otherwise as stated in Illustration 2, A sues B in replevin and posts a bond. If the procedure in replevin does not per-

mit an adequate opportunity for the determination of A's claim of fraud before return of the antique to him, replevin will be denied on the ground that he has not offered to return the $ 10,000.

c. *Where no offer of return required.* In some instances there is no requirement of an offer to return. This is so if the property was worthless when received or if its destruction or loss was caused by the other party or by its own defects. See Illustration 4. It may also be so if it was never possible to return the property or if it has become impossible because the recipient used or disposed of it before he had knowledge of the grounds for restitution. See Illustrations 5 and 6. In those cases no offer need to be made if justice requires that compensation be accepted in place of the property and if the payment of such compensation can be assured. In determining what justice requires, consideration will be given to all the circumstances, including any misconduct such as fraud or duress by the other party. A party who receives only property that he already owned receives no interest and is not subject to the rule stated in Subsection (1) at all. Furthermore, if the contract apportions the price among various pieces of property, restitution of the price as to part of the property may be had on a return of only that part if the price as to the unreturned property is not included in the claim for restitution. See Illustration 7. **Illustrations:**

4. A contracts to work on B's ranch in return for a number of cattle warranted by B to be sound. After A has done the work and B has delivered the cattle, they are discovered to have hoof and mouth disease and are destroyed by government order. A is entitled to restitution of the reasonable value of his services.

5. A puts his son in B's private school, paying a year's tuition in advance. During the first month of school, the son is wrongfully expelled by B. A is entitled to restitution of the amount of tuition paid less the benefit to A of B's services during the first month.

. . .

§ 385. Effect of Power of Avoidance on Duty of Performance or on Duty Arising Out of Breach

(1) Unless an offer to restore performance received is a condition of avoidance, a party has no duty of performance while his power of avoidance exists.

(2) If an offer to restore performance received is a condition of avoidance, a duty to pay damages is terminated by such an offer made before the power of avoidance is lost.

Comment:

a. *No duty of performance.* If a party has the power to avoid the contract simply by disaffirmance, without offering to restore performance received, his refusal or failure to perform is not a breach under the rule stated in Subsection (1). This is so even if he is ignorant of his power of avoidance and believes that his refusal or failure is a breach. As a general rule, the legal consequences of a party's refusal or failure to perform are not affected by the fact that he is ignorant of some justification or excuse for his refusal or failure. See Comment e to § 225 and Comment c to § 237. **Illustrations:**

1. A is induced by B's fraud to make a contract to buy goods from B. While A is still ignorant of the fraud and before he has received the goods from B, A writes a letter telling him that he refuses to perform. B sues A for damages for total breach by repudiation. A is not liable to B because, since A has no duty of performance, his letter was not a repudiation.

. . .

b. *Duty arising out of breach terminated.* If an offer to restore performance received is a condition of avoidance (§ 384), a party with a power of avoidance is under a duty of performance until such an offer is made. His refusal or failure to perform is therefore a breach. A subsequent offer to restore performance, however, terminates the duty to pay damages that arises from that breach if the offer is made before the power of avoidance is lost. **Illustration:**

3. A is induced by B's fraud to make a contract to buy goods from B. While A is still ignorant of the fraud but after he has received the goods from B, A commits a material breach by failure to pay B. A then discovers the fraud and tenders the goods back to B. B sues A for damages for total breach of contract. Even if an offer to return the goods was a condition of avoidance by A, A is not liable to B because A's breach was nullified by the tender of what he had received.

UNIDROIT PRINCIPLES
OF INTERNATIONAL
COMMERCIAL CONTRACTS

UNIDROIT Principles of
International Commercial Contracts
[1994]

FOREWORD

It is with the utmost pleasure that the International Institute for the Unification of Private Law

(UNIDROIT) announces the completion of the drawing up of the UNIDROIT Principles of International Commercial Contracts. This achievement represents the outcome of many years of intensive research and deliberations involving the participation of a large number of eminent lawyers from all five continents of the world.

Tribute must first be paid to the members of the Working Group primarily entrusted with the preparation of the UNIDROIT Principles and, among them, especially to the Rapporteurs for the different chapters. Without their personal commitment and unstinting efforts, so ably coordinated throughout by Michael Joachim Bonell, this ambitious project could not have been brought to its successful conclusion.

We must also express gratitude for the most valuable input given by the numerous practising lawyers, judges, civil servants and academics from widely differing legal cultures and professional backgrounds, who became involved in the project at various stages of the drafting process and whose constructive criticism was of the greatest assistance.

In this moment of great satisfaction for the Institute we cannot but evoke the memory of Mario Matteucci, who for so many years served UNIDROIT as Secretary-General and then as President and whose belief in the Principles as a vital contribution to the process of international unification of law was a source of constant inspiration to us all.

Malcolm Evans Secretary-General

Riccardo Monaco President

INTRODUCTION

Efforts towards the international unification of law have hitherto essentially taken the form of binding instruments, such as supranational legislation or international conventions, or of model laws. Since these instruments often risk remaining little more than a dead letter and tend to be rather fragmentary in character, calls are increasingly being made for recourse to non-legislative means of unification or harmonisation of law.

Some of those calls are for the further development of what is termed "international commercial custom", for example through model clauses and contracts formulated by the interested business circles on the basis of current trade practices and relating to specific types of transactions or particular aspects thereof.

Others go even further and advocate the elaboration of an international restatement of general principles of contract law.
UNIDROIT's initiative for the elaboration of "Principles of International Commercial Contracts" goes in that direction.
It was as long ago as 1971 that the Governing Council decided to include this subject in the Work Programme of the Institute. A small Steering Committee, composed of Professors René David, Clive M. Schmitthoff and Tudor Popescu, representing the civil law, the common law and the socialist systems, was set up with the task of conducting preliminary inquiries into the feasibility of such a project.

It was not until 1980, however, that a special Working Group was constituted for the purpose of preparing the various draft chapters of the Principles. The Group, which included representatives of all the major legal systems of the world, was composed of leading experts in the field of contract law and international trade law. Most of them were academics, some high ranking judges or civil servants, who all sat in a personal capacity.

The Group appointed from among its members Rapporteurs for the different chapters of the Principles, who were entrusted with the task of submitting successive drafts together with Comments. These were then discussed by the Group and circulated to a wide range of experts, including UNIDROIT's extensive network of correspondents. In addition, the Governing Council offered its advice on the policy to be followed, especially in those cases where the Group had found it difficult to reach a consensus. The necessary editorial work was entrusted to an Editorial Committee, assisted by the Secretariat.

For the most part the UNIDROIT Principles reflect concepts to be found in many, if not all, legal systems. Since however the Principles are intended to provide a system of rules especially tailored to the needs of international commercial transactions, they also embody what are perceived to be the best solutions, even if still not yet generally adopted.

The objective of the UNIDROIT Principles is to establish a balanced set of rules designed for use throughout the world irrespective of the legal traditions and the economic and political conditions of the countries in which they are to be applied. This goal is reflected both in their formal presentation and in the general policy underlying them.

As to their formal presentation, the UNIDROIT Principles deliberately seek to avoid the use of terminology peculiar to any given legal system. The international character of the Principles is also stressed by the fact that the comments accompanying each single provision systematically refrain from referring to national laws in order to explain the origin and rationale of the solution retained. Only where the rule has been taken over more or less literally from the world wide accepted United Nations Convention on Contracts for the International Sale of Goods (CISG) is explicit reference made to its source.

With regard to substance, the UNIDROIT Principles are sufficiently flexible to take account of the constantly changing circumstances brought about by the technological and economic developments affecting cross-border trade practice. At the same time they attempt to ensure fairness in international commercial relations by expressly stating the general duty of the parties to act in accordance with good faith and fair dealing and, in a number of specific instances, imposing standards of reasonable behaviour.

Naturally, to the extent that the UNIDROIT Principles address issues also covered by CISG, they follow the solutions found in that Convention, with such adaptations as were considered appropriate to reflect the particular nature and scope of the Principles(*).

In offering the UNIDROIT Principles to the international legal and business communities, the Governing Council is fully conscious of the fact that the Principles, which do not involve the endorsement of Governments, are not a binding instrument and that in consequence their acceptance will depend upon their persuasive authority. There are a number of significant ways in which the UNIDROIT Principles may find practical application, the most important of which are amply explained in the Preamble.

The Governing Council is confident that those to whom the UNIDROIT Principles are addressed will appreciate their intrinsic merits and derive full advantage from their use.

THE GOVERNING COUNCIL OF UNIDROIT

Rome, May 1994

PREAMBLE – Purpose of the Principles

These Principles set forth general rules for international commercial contracts.

They shall be applied when the parties have agreed that their contract be governed by them.

They may be applied when the parties have agreed that their contract be governed by "general principles of law", the "*lex mercatoria*" or the like.

They may provide a solution to an issue raised when it proves impossible to establish the relevant rule of the applicable law.

They may be used to interpret or supplement international uniform law instruments.

They may serve as a model for national and international legislators.

COMMENT

The Principles set forth general rules which are basically conceived for "international commercial contracts".

1. "International" contracts

The international character of a contract may be defined in a great variety of ways. The solutions adopted in both national and international legislation range from a reference to the place of business or habitual residence of the parties in different countries to the adoption of more general criteria such as the contract having "significant connections with more than one State", "involving a choice between the laws of different States", or "affecting the interests of international trade".

The Principles do not expressly lay down any of these criteria. The assumption, however, is that the concept of "international" contracts should be given the broadest possible interpretation, so as ultimately to exclude only those situations where no international element at all is involved, i.e. where all the relevant elements of the contract in question are connected with one country only.

2. "Commercial" contracts

The restriction to "commercial" contracts is in no way intended to take over the distinction traditionally made in some legal systems between "civil" and "commercial" parties and/or transactions, i.e. to make the application of the Principles dependent on whether the parties have the formal status of "merchants" (*commerçants*, *Kaufleute*) and/or the transaction is commercial in nature. The idea is rather that of excluding from the scope of the Principles so-called "consumer transactions" which are within the various legal systems being increasingly subjected to special rules, mostly of a mandatory character, aimed at protecting the consumer, i.e. a party who enters into the contract otherwise than in the course of its trade or profession.

The criteria adopted at both national and international level also vary with respect to the distinction between consumer and non-consumer contracts. The Principles do not provide any express definition, but the assumption is that the concept of "commercial" contracts should be understood in the broadest possible sense, so as to include not only trade transactions for the supply or exchange of goods or services, but also other types of economic transactions, such as investment and/or concession agreements, contracts for professional services, etc.

3. The Principles and domestic contracts between private persons

Notwithstanding the fact that the Principles are conceived for international commercial contracts, there is nothing to prevent private persons from agreeing to apply the Principles to a purely domestic contract. Any such agreement would however be subject to the mandatory rules of the domestic law governing the contract.

4. The Principles as rules of law governing the contract

a. *Express choice by the parties*

As the Principles represent a system of rules of contract law which are common to existing national legal systems or best adapted to the special requirements of international commercial transactions, there might be good reasons for the parties to choose them expressly as the rules applicable to their contract, in the place of one or another particular domestic law. Parties who wish to adopt the Principles as the rules applicable to their contract would however be well advised to combine the reference to the Principles with an arbitration agreement. The reason for this is that the freedom of choice of the parties in designating the law governing their contract is traditionally limited to national laws. Therefore, a reference by the parties to the Principles will normally be considered to be a mere agreement to incorporate them in the contract, while the law governing the contract will still have to be determined on the basis of the private international law rules of the forum. As a result, the Principles will bind the parties only to the extent that they do not affect the rules of the applicable law from which the parties may not derogate.

The situation may be different if the parties agree to submit disputes arising from their contract to arbitration. Arbitrators are not necessarily bound by a particular domestic law. This is self-evident if they are authorised by the parties to act as *amiable compositeurs* or *ex aequo et bono*. But even in the absence of such an authorisation there is a growing tendency to permit the parties to choose "rules of law" other than national laws on which the arbitrators are to base their decisions. See in particular Art. 28(1) of the *1985 UNCITRAL Model Law on International Commercial Arbitration*; see also Art. 42(1) of the *1965 Convention on the Settlement of Investment Disputes between States and Nationals of other States (ICSID Convention)*. In line with this approach, the parties would be free to choose the Principles as the "rules of law" according to which the arbitrators would decide the dispute, with the result that the Principles would apply to the exclusion of any particular national law, subject only to the application of those rules of domestic law which are mandatory irrespective of which law governs the contract (see Art. 1.4). In disputes falling under the ICSID Convention, the Principles might even be applicable to the exclusion of any domestic rule of law.

b. *The Principles applied as lex mercatoria*

Parties to international commercial contracts who cannot agree on the choice of a particular domestic law as the law applicable to their contract sometimes provide that it shall be governed by the "general principles of law", by the "usages and customs of international trade", by the *lex mercatoria*, etc.

Hitherto, such reference by the parties to not better identified principles and rules of a supranational or transnational character has been criticised, among other grounds, because of the extreme vagueness of such concepts. In order to avoid, or at least considerably to reduce, the uncertainty accompanying the use of such vague concepts for the determination of their content, it might be advisable to have recourse to a systematic and well-defined set of rules such as the Principles.

5. The Principles as a substitute for the domestic law otherwise applicable

The Principles may however become relevant even where the contract is governed by a particular domestic law. This is the case whenever it proves extremely difficult if not impossible to establish the relevant rule of that particular domestic law with respect to a specific issue and a solution can be found in the Principles. The reasons for such a difficulty generally lie in the special character of the legal sources and/or the cost of access to them.

Recourse to the Principles as a substitute for the domestic law otherwise applicable is of course to be seen as a last resort; on the other hand it may be justified not only in the event of the absolute impossibility of establishing the relevant rule of the applicable law, but also whenever the research involved would entail disproportionate efforts and/or costs. The current practice of courts in such situations is that of applying the *lex fori*. Recourse to the Principles would have the advantage of avoiding the application of a law which will in most cases be more familiar to one of the parties.

6. The Principles as a means of interpreting and supplementing existing international instruments

Any legislation, whether of international or national origin, raises questions concerning the precise meaning of its individual provisions. Moreover, such legislation is by its very nature unable to anticipate all the problems to which it will be applied. When applying domestic statutes it is possible to rely on long established principles and criteria of interpretation to be found within each legal system. The situation is far more uncertain with respect to instruments which, although formally incorporated into the various national legal systems, have been prepared and agreed upon at international level. According to the traditional view recourse should, even in such cases, be had to the principles and criteria provided in domestic law, be it the law of the forum or that which would, according to the relevant rules of private international law, be applicable in the absence of the uniform law.

At present, both courts and arbitral tribunals tend more and more to abandon such a "conflictual" method and seek instead to interpret and supplement international instruments by reference to autonomous and internationally uniform principles. This approach, which has indeed been expressly sanctioned in the most recent conventions (see, e.g., Art. 7 of the *1980 UN Convention on Contracts for the International Sale of Goods (CISG)*), is based on the assumption that uniform law, even after its incorporation into the various national legal systems, only formally becomes an integrated part of the latter, whereas from a substantive point of view it does not lose its original character of a special body of law autonomously developed at international level and intended to be applied in a uniform manner throughout the world. Until now, such autonomous principles and criteria for the interpretation and supplementing of international instruments have had to be found in each single case by the judges and arbitrators themselves on the basis of a comparative survey of the solutions adopted in the different national legal systems. The Principles could considerably facilitate their task in this respect.

7. The Principles as a model for national and international legislators

In view of their intrinsic merits the Principles may in addition serve as a model to national and international law-makers for the drafting of legislation in the field of general contract law or with respect to special types of transactions. At a national level, the Principles may be particularly useful to those countries which lack a developed body of legal rules relating to contracts and which intend to update their law, at least with respect to foreign economic relationships, to current international standards. Not too different is the situation of those countries with a well-defined legal system, but which after the recent dramatic changes in their socio-political structure have an urgent need to rewrite their laws, in particular those relating to economic and business activities. At an international level the Principles could become an important term of reference for the drafting of conventions and model laws. So far the terminology used to express the same concept differs considerably from one instrument to another, with the obvious risk of misunderstandings and misinterpretations. Such inconsistencies could be avoided if the terminology of the Principles were to be adopted as an international uniform glossary.

UNIDROIT Principles of International Commercial Contracts [1994]

CONTENTS

CHAPTER 1 – GENERAL PROVISIONS

ARTICLE 1.1 – Freedom of contract

The parties are free to enter into a contract and to determine its content.

COMMENT

1. Freedom of contract as a basic principle in the context of international trade

The principle of freedom of contract is of paramount importance in the context of international trade. The right of business people to decide freely to whom they will offer their goods or services and by whom they wish to be supplied, as well as the possibility for them freely to agree on the terms of individual transactions, are the cornerstones of an open, market-oriented and competitive international economic order.

2. Economic sectors where there is no competition

There are of course a number of possible exceptions to the principle laid down in the present article.

As concerns the freedom to conclude contracts with any other person, there are economic sectors which States may decide in the public interest to exclude from open competition. In such cases the goods or services in question can only be requested from the one available supplier, which will usually be a public body, and which may or may not be under a duty to conclude a contract with whoever makes a request, within the limits of the availability of the goods or services.

3. Limitation of party autonomy by mandatory rules

With respect to the freedom to determine the content of the contract, in the first instance the Principles themselves contain provisions from which the parties may not derogate. See Art. 1.5.

Moreover, there are both public and private law rules of mandatory character enacted by States (e.g. anti-trust, exchange control or price laws; laws imposing special liability regimes or prohibiting grossly unfair contract terms, etc.), which may prevail over the rules contained in the Principles. See Art. 1.4.

ARTICLE 1.2 – No form required

Nothing in these Principles requires a contract to be concluded in or evidenced by writing. It may be proved by any means, including witnesses.

COMMENT

1. Contracts as a rule not subject to formal requirements

This article states the principle that as a rule the conclusion of a contract is not subject to any requirement as to form. Although the article mentions only the requirement of writing, it may be extended to other requirements as to form. The rule also covers the subsequent modification or termination of a contract by agreement of the parties. The principle, which is to be found in many, although not in all, legal systems, seems particularly appropriate in the context of international trade relationships where, thanks to modern means of communication, many transactions are concluded at great speed and are not paper-based. The first sentence of the article takes into account the fact that some legal systems regard formal requirements as matters relating to substance, while others impose them for evidentiary purposes only. The second sentence is intended to make it clear that to the extent that the principle of freedom of form applies, it implies the admissibility of oral evidence in judicial proceedings.

2. Possible exceptions under the applicable law

The principle of freedom of form may of course be overridden by the applicable law. See Art. 1.4. National laws as well as international instruments may impose special requirements as to form with respect either to the contract as a whole or to individual terms (e.g. arbitration agreements; jurisdiction clauses).

3. Form requirements agreed by the parties

Moreover, the parties may themselves agree on a specific form for the conclusion, modification or termination of their contract. In this context see Arts. 2.13, 2.17 and 2.18.

ARTICLE 1.3 – Binding character of contract

A contract validly entered into is binding upon the parties. It can only be modified or terminated in accordance with its terms or by agreement or as otherwise provided in these Principles.

COMMENT

1. The principle *pacta sunt servanda*

This article lays down another basic principle of contract law, that of *pacta sunt servanda*.

The binding character of a contractual agreement obviously presupposes that an agreement has actually been concluded by the parties and that the agreement reached is not affected by any ground of invalidity. The rules governing the conclusion of contractual agreements are laid down in Chapter 2 of the Principles, while the grounds of invalidity are dealt with in Chapter 3. Additional requirements for the valid conclusion of contracts may be found in the applicable national or international mandatory rules.

2. Exceptions

A corollary of the principle of *pacta sunt servanda* is that a contract may be modified or terminated whenever the parties so agree. Modification or termination without agreement are on the contrary the exception and can therefore be admitted only when in conformity with the terms of the contract or when expressly provided for in the Principles. See Arts. 3.10(2), 3.10(3), 3.13, 5.8, 6.1.16, 6.2.3, 7.1.7, 7.3.1 and 7.3.3.

3. Effects on third persons not dealt with

While as a rule a contract produces effects only between the parties, there may be cases where it also affects third persons. Thus, a seller may under some domestic laws be under a contractual duty to protect the physical integrity and property not only of the buyer but also of accompanying persons during their presence on the seller's premises; equally, the consignee of a cargo may be entitled to sue the carrier for non-performance of a contractual duty undertaken by the latter in its contract of carriage with the sender. By stating the principle of the binding force of the contract between the parties, this article does not intend to prejudice any effect which that contract may have vis-à-vis third persons under the applicable law.

Similarly the Principles do not deal with the effects of avoidance and termination of a contract on the rights of third persons.

ARTICLE 1.4 – Mandatory rules

Nothing in these Principles shall restrict the application of mandatory rules, whether of national, international or supranational origin, which are applicable in accordance with the relevant rules of private international law.

COMMENT

1. Mandatory rules prevail

Given the particular nature of the Principles, they cannot be expected to prevail over applicable mandatory rules, whether of national, international or supranational origin. In other words, mandatory provisions, whether enacted by States autonomously or to implement international conventions, or adopted by supranational organisations, cannot be overruled by the Principles.

2. Mandatory rules applicable in the event of mere incorporation of the Principles in the contract

In cases where the parties' reference to the Principles is considered to be only an agreement to incorporate them in the contract, the Principles will first of all encounter the limit of the mandatory rules of the law governing the contract, i.e. they will bind the parties only to the extent that they do not affect the rules of the applicable law from which parties may not contractually derogate. In addition, the mandatory rules of the forum, and possibly also those of third States, will likewise prevail, provided that they claim application whatever the law governing the contract and, in the case of the rules of third States, there is a close connection between those States and the contract in question.

3. Mandatory rules applicable if the Principles are the law governing the contract

Yet, even where, as may be the case if the dispute is brought before an arbitral tribunal, the Principles are applied as the law governing the contract, they cannot prejudice the application of those mandatory rules which claim application irrespective of which law is applicable to the contract (*lois d'application nécessaire*). Examples of such mandatory rules, the application of which cannot be excluded simply by choosing another law, are to be found in the field of foreign exchange regulations (see Art. VIII(2)(b) of the *Agreement of the International Monetary Fund, (Bretton Woods Agreement)*), import-export licences (see Arts. 6.1.14 - 6.1.17 of these Principles on public permission requirements), regulations pertaining to restrictive trade practices, etc.

4. Recourse to the rules of private international law relevant in each individual case

Both courts and arbitral tribunals differ considerably in the way in which they determine the mandatory rules applicable to international commercial contracts. For this reason the present article deliberately refrains from entering into the merit of the various questions involved, in particular whether in addition to the mandatory rules of the forum and of the *lex contractus* those of third States are also to be taken into account and if so, to what extent and on the basis of which criteria. These questions are to be settled in accordance with the rules of private international law which are relevant in each particular case (see, for instance, Art. 7 of the *1980 Rome Convention on the Law applicable to Contractual Obligations*).

ARTICLE 1.5 – Exclusion or modification by the parties

The parties may exclude the application of these Principles or derogate from or vary the effect of any of their provisions, except as otherwise provided in the Principles.

COMMENT

1. The non-mandatory character of the Principles

The rules laid down in the Principles are in general of a non-mandatory character, i.e. the parties may in each individual case either simply exclude their application in whole or in part or modify their content so as to adapt them to the specific needs of the kind of transaction involved.

2. Exclusion or modification may be express or implied

The exclusion or modification of the Principles by the parties may be either express or implied. There is an implied exclusion or modification when the parties expressly agree on contract terms which are inconsistent with provisions of the Principles and it is in this context irrelevant whether the terms in question have been negotiated individually or form part of standard terms incorporated by the parties in their contract.

If the parties expressly agree to the application of some only of the chapters of the Principles (e.g. "As far as the performance and non-performance of this contract is concerned, the UNIDROIT Principles shall apply"), it is presumed that the chapters concerned will be applied together with the general provisions of Chapter 1.

3. Mandatory provisions to be found in the Principles

A few provisions of the Principles are of a mandatory character, i.e. their importance in the system of the Principles is such that parties should not be permitted to exclude or to derogate from them as they wish. It is true that given the particular nature of the Principles the non-observance of this precept may have no consequences. On the other hand, it should be noted that the provisions in question reflect standards of behaviour and rules which are of a mandatory character under most domestic laws also.

Those provisions of the Principles which are mandatory are normally expressly indicated as such. This is the case with Art. 1.7 on good faith and fair dealing, with the provisions of Chapter 3 on substantive validity, except in so far as they relate or apply to mistake and to initial impossibility (see Art. 3.19), with Art. 5.7(2) on price determination and with Art. 7.4.13(2) on agreed payment for non-performance. Exceptionally, the mandatory character of a provision is only implicit and follows from the content and purpose of the provision itself (see Art. 7.1.6).

ARTICLE 1.6 – Interpretation and supplementation of the Principles

(1) In the interpretation of these Principles, regard is to be had to their international character and to their purposes including the need to promote uniformity in their application.

(2) Issues within the scope of these Principles but not expressly settled by them are as far as possible to be settled in accordance with their underlying general principles.

COMMENT

1. Interpretation of the Principles as opposed to interpretation of the contract

The Principles, like any other legal text, be it of a legislative or of a contractual nature, may give rise to doubts as to the precise meaning of their content. The interpretation of the Principles is however different from that of the individual contracts to which they apply. Even if the Principles are considered to bind the parties only at contractual level, i.e. their application is made dependent on their incorporation in individual contracts, they remain an autonomous set of rules worked out with a view to their application in a uniform manner to an indefinite number of contracts of different types entered into in various parts of the world. As a consequence they must be interpreted in a different manner from the terms of each individual contract. The rules for the interpretation of the latter are laid down in Chapter 4 of the Principles. The present article deals rather with the manner in which the Principles are to be interpreted.

2. Regard to the international character of the Principles

The first criterion laid down by this article for the interpretation of the Principles is that regard is to be had to their "international character". This means that their terms and concepts are to be interpreted autonomously, i.e. in the context of the Principles themselves and not by reference to the meaning which might traditionally be attached to them by a particular domestic law.

Such an approach becomes necessary if it is recalled that the Principles are the result of thorough comparative studies carried out by lawyers coming from totally different cultural and legal backgrounds. When drafting the individual provisions, these experts had to find sufficiently neutral legal language on which they could reach a common understanding. Even in the exceptional cases where terms or concepts peculiar to one or more national laws are employed, the intention was never to use them in their traditional meaning.

3. Purposes of the Principles

By stating that in the interpretation of the Principles regard is to be had to their purposes, this article makes it clear that they are not to be construed in a strict and literal sense but in the light of the purposes and the rationale underlying the individual provisions as well as the Principles as a whole. The purpose of the individual provisions can be ascertained both from the text itself and from the comments thereon. As to the purposes of the Principles as a whole, this article, in view of the fact that the Principles' main objective is to provide a uniform framework for international commercial contracts, expressly refers to the need to promote uniformity in their application, i.e. to ensure that in practice they are to the greatest possible extent interpreted and applied in the same way in different countries. As to other purposes, see the remarks contained in the Introduction. See further Art. 1.7 which, although addressed to the parties, may also be seen as an expression of the underlying purpose of the Principles as such to promote the observance of good faith and fair dealing in contractual relations.

4. Supplementation of the Principles

A number of issues which would fall within the scope of the Principles are not settled expressly by them. In order to determine whether an issue is one that falls within the scope of the Principles even though it is not expressly settled by them, or whether it actually falls outside their scope, regard is to be had first to what is expressly stated either in the text or in the comments (see e.g. Art. 3.1, comment 3 on Art. 1.3 and comment 4 on Art. 1.4). A useful additional guide in this respect is the subject-matter index of the Principles.

The need to promote uniformity in the application of the Principles implies that when such gaps arise a solution should be found, whenever possible, within the system of the Principles itself before resorting to domestic laws. The first step is to attempt to settle the unsolved question through an application by analogy of specific provisions. Thus, Art. 6.1.6 on place of performance should also govern restitution. Similarly, the rules laid down in Art. 6.1.9 with respect to the case where a monetary obligation is expressed in a currency other than that of the place for payment may also be applied when the monetary obligation is expressed by reference to units of account such as the Special Drawing Right (SDR) or the European Currency Unit (ECU). If the issue cannot be solved by a mere extension of specific provisions dealing with analogous cases, recourse must be made to their underlying general principles, i.e. to the principles and rules which may be applied on a much wider scale because of their general character. Some of these fundamental principles are expressly stated in the Principles (see, e.g., Arts. 1.1, 1.3, 1.5 and

1.7). Others have to be extracted from specific provisions, i.e. the particular rules contained therein must be analysed in order to see whether they can be considered an expression of a more general principle, and as such capable of being applied also to cases different from those specifically regulated.

Parties are of course always free to agree on a particular national law to which reference should be made for the supplementing of the Principles. A provision of this kind could read "This contract is governed by the UNIDROIT Principles supplemented by the law of country X", or "This contract shall be interpreted and executed in accordance with the UNIDROIT Principles. Questions not expressly settled therein shall be settled in accordance with the law of country X".

ARTICLE 1.7 – Good faith and fair dealing

(1) Each party must act in accordance with good faith and fair dealing in international trade.

(2) The parties may not exclude or limit this duty.

COMMENT

1. "Good faith and fair dealing" as a fundamental idea underlying the Principles

There are a number of provisions throughout the different chapters of the Principles which constitute a direct or indirect application of the principle of good faith and fair dealing. See, for instance, Articles 2.4(2)(b), 2.15, 2.16, 2.18, 2.20, 3.5, 3.8, 3.10, 4.1(2), 4.2(2), 4.6, 4.8, 5.2, 5.3, 6.1.3, 6.1.5, 6.1.16(2), 6.1.17(1), 6.2.3(3)(4), 7.1.2, 7.1.6, 7.1.7, 7.2.2(b)(c), 7.4.8 and 7.4.13. This means that good faith and fair dealing may be considered to be one of the fundamental ideas underlying the Principles. By stating in general terms that each party must act in accordance with good faith and fair dealing para. (1) of this article makes it clear that even in the absence of special provisions in the Principles the parties' behaviour throughout the life of the contract, including the negotiation process, must conform to good faith and fair dealing. **Illustrations**

1. A grants B forty-eight hours as the time within which B may accept its offer. When B, shortly before the expiry of the deadline, decides to accept, it is unable to do so: it is the weekend, the fax at A's office is disconnected and there is no telephone answering machine which can take the message. When on the following Monday A refuses B's acceptance A acts contrary to good faith since when it fixed the time-limit for acceptance it was for A to ensure that messages

could be received at its office throughout the forty-eight hour period.

2. A contract for the supply and installation of a special production line contains a provision according to which A, the seller, is obliged to communicate to B, the purchaser, any improvements made by A to the technology of that line. After a year B learns of an important improvement of which it had not been informed. A is not excused by the fact that the production of that particular type of production line is no longer its responsibility but that of C, a wholly-owned affiliated company of A. It would be against good faith for A to invoke the separate entity of C, which was specifically set up to take over this production in order to avoid A's contractual obligations vis-à-vis B.

3. A, an agent, undertakes on behalf of B, the principal, to promote the sale of B's goods in a given area. Under the contract A's right to compensation arises only after B's approval of the contracts procured by A. While B is free to decide whether or not to approve the contracts procured by A, a systematic and unjustified refusal to approve any contract procured by A would be against good faith.

4. Under a line of credit agreement between A, a bank, and B, a customer, A suddenly and inexplicably refuses to make further advances to B whose business suffers heavy losses as a consequence. Notwithstanding the fact that the agreement contains a term permitting A to

accelerate payment "at will", A's demand for payment in full without prior warning and with no justification would be against good faith.

2. "Good faith and fair dealing in international trade"

The reference to "good faith and fair dealing in international trade" first makes it clear that in the context of the Principles the two concepts are not to be applied according to the standards ordinarily adopted within the different national legal systems. In other words, such domestic standards may be taken into account only to the extent that they are shown to be generally accepted among the various legal systems. A further implication of the formula used is that good faith and fair dealing must be construed in the light of the special conditions of international trade. Standards of business practice may indeed vary considerably from one trade sector to another, and even within a given trade sector they may be more or less stringent depending on the socio-economic environment in which the enterprises operate, their size and technical skill, etc.

It should be noted that the provisions of the Principles and/or the comments thereto at times refer only to "good faith" or to "good faith and fair dealing". Such references should always be understood as a reference to "good faith and fair dealing in international trade" as specified in this article. **Illustrations**

5. Under a contract for the sale of high-technology equipment the purchaser loses the right to rely on any defect in the goods if it does not give notice to the seller specifying the nature of the defect without undue delay after it has discovered or ought to have discovered the defect. A, a buyer operating in a country where such equipment is commonly used, discovers a defect in the equipment after having put it into operation, but in its notice to B, the seller of the equipment, A gives misleading indications as to the nature of the defect. A loses its right to rely on the defect since a more careful examination of the defect would have permitted it to give B the necessary specifications.

6. The facts are the same as in Illustration 5, the difference being that A operates in a country where this type of equipment is so far almost unknown. A does not lose its right to rely on the defect because B, being aware of A's lack of technical knowledge, could not reasonably have expected A properly to identify the nature of the defect.

3. The mandatory nature of the principle of good faith and fair dealing

The parties' duty to act in accordance with good faith and fair dealing is of such a fundamental nature that the parties may not contractually exclude or limit it (para. (2)). As to specific applications of the general prohibition to exclude or limit the principle of good faith and fair dealing between the parties, see Arts. 3.19, 7.1.6 and 7.4.13. On the other hand, nothing prevents parties from providing in their contract for a duty to observe more stringent standards of behaviour.

ARTICLE 1.8 – Usages and practices

(1) The parties are bound by any usage to which they have agreed and by any practices which they have established between themselves.

(2) The parties are bound by a usage that is widely known to and regularly observed in international trade by parties in the particular trade concerned except where the application of such a usage would be unreasonable.

COMMENT

1. Practices and usages in the context of the Principles

This article lays down the principle according to which the parties are in general bound by practices and usages which meet the requirements set forth in the article. Furthermore, these same requirements must be met by practices and usages for them to be applicable in the cases and for the purposes expressly indicated in the Principles. See, for instance, Arts. 2.6(3), 4.3, and 5.2.

2. Practices established between the parties

A practice established between the parties to a particular contract is automatically binding, except where the parties have expressly excluded its application. Whether a particular practice can be deemed to be "established" between the parties will naturally depend on the circumstances of the case, but behaviour on the occasion of only one previous transaction between the parties will not normally suffice.

Illustration

1. A, a supplier, has repeatedly accepted claims from B, a customer, for quantitative or qualitative defects in the goods as much as two weeks after their delivery. When B gives another notice of defects only after a fortnight, A cannot object that it is too late since the two-weeks' notice amounts to a practice established between A and B which will as such be binding on A.

3. Agreed usages

By stating that the parties are bound by usages to which they have agreed, para. (1) of this article merely applies the general principle of freedom of contract laid down in Art. 1.1. Indeed, the parties may either negotiate all the terms of their contract, or for certain questions simply refer to other sources including usages. The parties may stipulate the application of any usage, including a usage developed within a trade sector to which neither party belongs, or a usage relating to a different type of contract. It is even conceivable that the parties will agree on the application of what are sometimes misleadingly called usages, i.e. a set of rules issued by a particular trade association under the title of "Usages", but which only in part reflects established general lines of conduct.

4. Other applicable usages

Para. (2) lays down the criteria for the identification of usages applicable in the absence of a specific agreement by the parties. The fact that the usage must be "widely known to and regularly observed [...] by parties in the particular trade concerned" is a condition for the application of any usage, be it at international or merely at national or local level. The additional qualification "in international trade" is intended to avoid usages developed for, and confined to, domestic transactions also being invoked in transactions with foreigners. **Illustration**

2. A, a real estate agent, invokes a particular usage of the profession in its country vis-à-vis B, a foreign customer. B is not bound by such a usage if that usage is of a local nature and relates to a trade which is predominantly domestic in character.

Only exceptionally may usages of a purely local or national origin be applied without any reference thereto by the parties. Thus, usages existing on certain commodity exchanges or at trade exhibitions or ports should be applicable provided that they are regularly followed with respect to foreigners as well. Another exception concerns the case of a businessperson who has already entered into a number of similar contracts in a foreign country and who should therefore be bound by the usages established within that country for such contracts. **Illustration**

3. A, a terminal operator, invokes a particular usage of the port where it is located vis-à-vis B, a foreign carrier. B is bound by this local usage if the port is normally used by foreigners and the usage in question has been regularly observed with respect to all customers, irrespective of their place of business and of their nationality.

4. A, a sales agent from country X, receives a request from B, one of its customers in country Y, for the customary 10% discount upon payment of the price in cash. A may not object to the application of such a usage on account of its being restricted to country Y if A has been doing business in that country for a certain period of time.

5. Application of usage unreasonable

A usage may be regularly observed by the generality of business people in a particular trade sector but its application in a given case may nevertheless be unreasonable. Reasons for this may be found in the particular conditions in which one or both parties operate and/or the atypical nature of the transaction. In such cases the usage will not be applied. **Illustration**

5. A usage exists in a commodity trade sector according to which the purchaser may not rely on defects in the goods if they are not duly certified by an internationally recognised inspection agency. When A, a buyer, takes over the goods at the port of destination, the only internationally recognised inspection agency operating in that port is on strike and to call another from the nearest port would be excessively costly. The application of the usage in this case would be unreasonable and A may rely on the defects it has discovered even though they have not been certified by an internationally recognised inspection agency.

6. Usages prevail over the Principles

Both courses of dealing and usages, once they are applicable in a given case, prevail over conflicting provisions contained in the Principles. The reason for this is that they bind the parties as implied terms of the contract as a whole or of single statements or other conduct on the part of one of the parties. As such, they are superseded by any express term stipulated by the parties but, in the same way as the latter, they prevail over the Principles, the only exception being those provisions which are specifically declared to be of a mandatory character. See comment 3 on Art. 1.5.

ARTICLE 1.9 – Notice

(1) Where notice is required it may be given by any means appropriate to the circumstances.
(2) A notice is effective when it reaches the person to whom it is given.
(3) For the purpose of paragraph (2) a notice "reaches" a person when given to that person orally or delivered at that person's place of business or mailing address.
(4) For the purpose of this article "notice" includes a declaration, demand, request or any other communication of intention.

COMMENT

1. Form of notice

This article first lays down the principle that notice or any other kind of communication of intention (declarations, demands, requests, etc.) required by individual provisions of the Principles are not subject to any particular requirement as to form, but may be given by any means appropriate in the circumstances. Which means are appropriate will depend on the actual circumstances of the case, in particular on the availability and the reliability of the various modes of communication, and the importance and/or urgency of the message to be delivered. Thus, if the postal service is unreliable, it might be more appropriate to use fax, telex or other forms of electronic communication for a communication which has to be made in writing, or the telephone if an oral communication is sufficient. In choosing the means of communication the sender must as a rule take into account the situation which exists both in its own and in the addressee's country.

2. Receipt principle

With respect to all kinds of notices the Principles adopt the so-called "receipt" principle, i.e. they are not effective unless and until they reach the person to whom they are given. For some communications this is expressly stated in the provisions dealing with them: see Arts. 2.3(1), 2.3(2), 2.5, 2.6(2), 2.8(1) and 2.10. The purpose of para. (2) of the present article is to indicate that the same will also be true in the absence of an express statement to this effect: see Arts. 2.9, 2.11, 3.13, 3.14, 6.1.16, 6.2.3, 7.1.5, 7.1.7, 7.2.1, 7.2.2, 7.3.2 and 7.3.4.

3. Dispatch principle to be expressly stipulated

The parties are of course always free expressly to stipulate the application of the dispatch principle. This may be appropriate in particular with respect to the notice a party has to give in order to preserve its rights in cases of the other party's actual or anticipated non-performance when it would not be fair to place the risk of loss, mistake or delay in the transmission of the message on the former. This is all the more true if the difficulties which may arise at international level in proving effective receipt of a notice are borne in mind.

4. "Reaches"

It is important in relation to the receipt principle to determine precisely when the communications in question "reach" the addressee. In an attempt to define the concept, para. (3) of this article draws a distinction between oral and other communications. The former "reach" the addressee if they are made personally to it or to another person authorised by it to receive them. The latter "reach" the addressee as soon as they are delivered either to the addressee personally or to its place of business or mailing address. The particular communication in question need not come into the hands of the addressee. It is sufficient that it be handed over to an employee of the addressee authorised to accept it, or that it be placed in the addressee's mailbox, or received by the addressee's fax, telex or computer.

ARTICLE 1.10 – Definitions

In these Principles — "court" includes an arbitral tribunal; — where a party has more than one place of business the relevant "place of business" is that which has the closest relationship to the contract and its performance, having regard to the circumstances known to or contemplated by the parties at any time before or at the conclusion of the contract; — "obligor" refers to the party who is to perform an obligation and "obligee" refers to the party who is entitled to performance of that obligation. — "writing" means any mode of communication that preserves a record of the information contained therein and is capable of being reproduced in tangible form.

COMMENT

1. Courts and arbitral tribunals

The importance of the Principles for the purpose of the settlement of disputes by means of arbitration has already been stressed (see above the comments on the Preamble). In order however to avoid undue heaviness of language, only the term "court" is used in the text of the Principles, on the understanding that it covers arbitral tribunals as well as courts.

2. Party with more than one place of business

For the purpose of the application of the Principles a party's place of business is of relevance in a number of contexts such as the place for the delivery of notices (Art. 1.9(3)); a possible extension of the time of acceptance because of a holiday falling on the last day (Art. 2.8(2)); the place of performance (Art. 6.1.6) and the determination of the party who should apply for a public permission (Art. 6.1.14(a)).

With reference to a party with multiple places of business (normally a central office and various branch offices) the present article lays down the rule that the relevant place of business should be considered to be that which has the closest relationship to the contract and to its performance. Nothing is said with respect to the case where the place of the conclusion of the contract and that of performance differ, but in such a case the latter would seem to be the more relevant one. In the determination of the place of business which has the closest relationship to a given contract and to its performance, regard is to be had to the circumstances known to or contemplated by both parties at any time before or at the conclusion of the contract. Facts known only to one of the parties or of which the parties became aware only after the conclusion of the contract cannot be taken into consideration.

3. "Obligor" - "obligee"

Where necessary, to better identify the party performing and the party receiving performance of obligations the terms "obligor" and "obligee" are used, irrespective of whether the obligation is non-monetary or monetary.

4. "Writing"

In some cases the Principles refer to a "writing" or a "contract in writing". See Arts. 1.2, 2.9(2), 2.12, 2.17 and 2.18. The Principles define this formal requirement in functional terms. Thus, a writing includes not only a telegram and a telex, but also any other mode of communication that preserves a record and can be reproduced in tangible form. This formal requirement should be compared with the more flexible form of a "notice". See Art. 1.9(1).

CHAPTER 2 – FORMATION

ARTICLE 2.1 – Manner of formation

A contract may be concluded either by the acceptance of an offer or by conduct of the parties that is sufficient to show agreement.

COMMENT

1. Offer and acceptance

Basic to the Principles is the idea that the agreement of the parties is, in itself, sufficient to conclude a contract (see Art. 3.2). The concepts of offer and acceptance have traditionally been used to determine whether, and if so when, the parties have reached agreement. As this article and this chapter make clear, the Principles retain these concepts as essential tools of analysis.

2. Conduct sufficient to show agreement

In commercial practice contracts, particularly when related to complex transactions, are often concluded after prolonged negotiations without an identifiable sequence of offer and acceptance. In such cases it may be difficult to determine if and when a contractual agreement has been reached. According to this article a contract may be held to be concluded even though the moment of its formation cannot be determined, provided that the conduct of the parties is sufficient to show agreement. In order to determine whether there is sufficient evidence of the parties' intention to be bound by a contract, their conduct has to be interpreted in accordance with the criteria set forth in Art. 4.1 *et seq.* **Illustration**

A and B enter into negotiations with a view to setting up a joint venture for the development of a new product. After prolonged negotiations without any formal offer or acceptance and with some minor points still to be settled, both parties begin to perform. When subsequently the parties fail to reach an agreement on these minor points, a court or arbitral tribunal may decide that a contract was nevertheless concluded since the parties had begun to perform, thereby showing their intention to be bound by a contract.

ARTICLE 2.2 – Definition of offer

A proposal for concluding a contract constitutes an offer if it is sufficiently definite and indicates the intention of the offeror to be bound in case of acceptance.

COMMENT

In defining an offer as distinguished from other communications which a party may make in the course of negotiations initiated with a view to concluding a contract, this article lays down two requirements: the proposal must (i) be sufficiently definite to permit the conclusion of the contract by mere acceptance and (ii) indicate the intention of the offeror to be bound in case of acceptance.

1. Definiteness of an offer

Since a contract is concluded by the mere acceptance of an offer, the terms of the future agreement must already be indicated with sufficient definiteness in the offer itself. Whether a given offer meets this requirement cannot be established in general terms. Even essential terms, such as the precise description of the goods or the services to be delivered or rendered, the price to be paid for them, the time or place of performance, etc., may be left undetermined in the offer without necessarily rendering it insufficiently definite: all depends on whether or not the offeror by making the offer, and the offeree by accepting it, intends to enter into a binding agreement, and whether or not the missing terms can be determined by interpreting the language of the agreement in accordance with Arts. 4.1 *et seq.*, or supplied in accordance with Arts. 4.8 or 5.2. Indefiniteness may moreover be overcome by reference to practices established between the parties or to usages (see Art. 1.8), as well as by reference to specific provisions to be found elsewhere in the Principles (e.g. Arts. 5.6 (Determination of quality of performance), 5.7 (Price determination), 6.1.1 (Time of performance), 6.1.6 (Place of performance), and 6.1.10 (Currency not expressed)). **Illustration**

1. A has for a number of years annually renewed a contract with B for technical assistance for A's computers. A opens a second office with the same type of computers and asks B to provide assistance also for the new

computers. B accepts and, despite the fact that A's offer does not specify all the terms of the agreement, a contract has been concluded since the missing terms can be taken from the previous contracts as constituting a practice established between the parties.

2. Intention to be bound

The second criterion for determining whether a party makes an offer for the conclusion of a contract, or merely opens negotiations, is that party's intention to be bound in the event of acceptance. Since such an intention will rarely be declared expressly, it often has to be inferred from the circumstances of each individual case. The way in which the proponent presents the proposal (e.g. by expressly defining it as an "offer" or as a mere "declaration of intent") provides a first, although not a decisive, indication of possible intention. Of even greater importance are the content and the addressees of the proposal. Generally speaking, the more detailed and definite the proposal, the more likely it is to be construed as an offer. A proposal addressed to one or more specific persons is more likely to be intended as an offer than is one made to the public at large. **Illustrations**

2. After lengthy negotiations the Executive Directors of two companies, A and B, lay down the conditions on which B will acquire 51% of the shares in company C which is totally owned by A. The "Memorandum of Agreement" signed by the negotiators contains a final clause stating that the agreement is not binding until approved by A's Board of Directors. There is no contract before such approval is given by them.

3. A, a government agency, advertises for bids for the setting up of a new telephone network. Such an advertisement is merely an invitation to submit offers, which may or may not be accepted by A. If, however, the advertisement indicates in detail the technical specifications of the project and states that the contract will be awarded to the lowest bid conforming to the specifications, it may amount to an offer with the consequence that the contract will be concluded once the lowest bid has been identified.

A proposal may contain all the essential terms of the contract but nevertheless not bind the proponent in case of acceptance if it makes the conclusion of the contract dependent on the reaching of agreement on some minor points left open in the proposal. See Art. 2.13.

ARTICLE 2.3 – Withdrawal of offer

(1) An offer becomes effective when it reaches the offeree.

(2) An offer, even if it is irrevocable, may be withdrawn if the withdrawal reaches the offeree before or at the same time as the offer.

COMMENT

1. When an offer becomes effective

Para. (1) of this article, which is taken literally from Art. 15 CISG, provides that an offer becomes effective when it reaches the offeree (see Art. 1.9(2)). For the definition of "reaches" see Art. 1.9(3). The time at which the offer becomes effective is of importance as it indicates the precise moment as from which the offeree can accept it, thus definitely binding the offeror to the proposed contract.

2. Withdrawal of an offer

There is, however, a further reason why it may in practice be important to determine the moment at which the offer becomes effective. Indeed, up to that time the offeror is free to

change its mind and to decide not to enter into the agreement at all, or to replace the original offer by a new one, irrespective of whether or not the original offer was intended to be irrevocable. The only condition is that the offeree is informed of the offeror's altered intentions before or at the same time as the offeree is informed of the original offer. By expressly stating this, para. (2) of the present article makes it clear that a distinction is to be drawn between "withdrawal" and "revocation" of an offer: before an offer becomes effective it can always be withdrawn whereas the question of whether or not it may be revoked (see Art. 2.4) arises only after that moment.

ARTICLE 2.4 – Revocation of offer

(1) Until a contract is concluded an offer may be revoked if the revocation reaches the offeree before it has dispatched an acceptance.

(2) However, an offer cannot be revoked (a) if it indicates, whether by stating a fixed time for acceptance or otherwise, that it is irrevocable; or (b) if it was reasonable for the offeree to rely on the offer as being irrevocable and the offeree has acted in reliance on the offer.

COMMENT

The problem of whether an offer is or is not revocable is traditionally one of the most controversial issues in the context of the formation of contracts. Since there is no prospect of reconciling the two basic approaches followed in this respect by the different legal systems, i.e. the common law approach according to which an offer is as a rule revocable, and the opposite approach followed by the majority of civil law systems, the only remaining possibility is that of selecting one approach as the main rule, and the other as the exception.

1. Offers as a rule revocable

Para. (1) of this article, which is taken literally from Art. 16 CISG, states that until the contract is concluded offers are as a rule revocable. The same paragraph, however, subjects the revocation of an offer to the condition that it reach the offeree before the offeree has dispatched an acceptance. It is thus only when the offeree orally accepts the offer, or when the offeree may indicate assent by performing an act without giving notice to the offeror (see Art. 2.6(3)), that the offeror's right to revoke the offer continues to exist until such time as the contract is concluded. Where, however, the offer is accepted by a written indication of assent, so that the contract is concluded when the acceptance reaches the offeror (see Art. 2.6(2)), the offeror's right to revoke the offer terminates earlier, i.e. when the offeree dispatches the acceptance. Such a solution may cause some inconvenience to the offeror who will not always know whether or not it is still possible to revoke the offer. It is, however, justified in view of the legitimate interest of the offeree in the time available for revocation being shortened.

2. Irrevocable offers

Para. (2) provides for two important exceptions to the general rule as to the revocability of offers: (i) where the offer contains an indication that it is irrevocable and (ii) where the offeree, having other good reasons to treat the offer as being irrevocable, has acted in reliance on that offer.

a. Indication of irrevocability contained in the offer

The indication that the offer is irrevocable may be made in different ways, the most direct and clear of which is an express statement to that effect by the offeror (e.g. "This is a firm offer"; "We shall stand by our offer until we receive your answer"). It may, however, simply be inferred from other statements by, or conduct of, the offeror. The indication of a fixed time for acceptance may, but need not necessarily, amount by itself to an implicit indication of an irrevocable offer. The answer must be found in each case through a proper interpretation of the terms of the offer in accordance with the various criteria laid down in the general rules on interpretation in Chapter 4. In general, if the offeror operates within a legal system where the fixing of a time for acceptance is considered to indicate irrevocability, it may be assumed that by specifying such a fixed time the offeror intends to make an irrevocable offer. If, on the other hand, the offeror operates in a legal system where the fixing of a time for acceptance is not sufficient to indicate irrevocability, the offeror will not normally have had such an intention.

Illustrations

1. A, a travel agency, informs a client of a cruise in its brochure for the coming New Year holidays. It urges the client to book within the next three days, adding that after that date there will probably be no more places left. This statement by itself will not be considered to indicate that the offer is irrevocable during the first three days.

2. A invites B to submit a written offer of the terms on which B is prepared to construct a building. B presents a detailed offer containing the statement "Price and other conditions are not good after 1 September". If A and B operate within a legal system where such a statement is considered to be an indication that the offer is irrevocable until the specified date, B can expect the offer to be understood as being irrevocable. The same may not necessarily be the case if the offeree operates in a legal system where such a

statement is not considered as being sufficient to indicate that the offer is irrevocable.

b. *Reliance by offeree on irrevocability of offer*

The second exception to the general rule regarding the revocability of offers, i.e. where "it was reasonable for the offeree to rely on the offer as being irrevocable", and "the offeree has acted in reliance on the offer", is an application of the general principle of good faith and fair dealing laid down in Art. 1.7. The reliance of the offeree may have been induced either by the conduct of the offeror, or by the nature of the offer itself (e.g. an offer whose acceptance requires extensive and costly investigation on the part of the offeree or an offer made with a view to permitting the offeree in turn to make an offer to a third party). The acts which the offeree must have performed in reliance on the offer may consist in making preparations for production, buying or hiring of materials or equipment, incurring expenses etc., provided that such acts could have been regarded as normal in the trade concerned, or should otherwise have been foreseen by, or known to, the offeror.

Illustrations

3. A, an antique dealer, asks B to restore ten paintings on condition that the work is completed within three months and that the price does not exceed a specific amount. B informs A that, so as to know whether or not to accept the offer, B finds it necessary to begin work on one painting and will then give a definite answer within five days. A agrees, and B, relying on A's offer, begins work immediately. A may not revoke the offer during those five days.

4. A seeks an offer from B for incorporation in a bid on a project to be assigned within a stated time. B submits an offer on which A relies when calculating the price of the bid. Before the expiry of the date, but after A has made the bid, B informs A that it is no longer willing to stand by its offer. B's offer is irrevocable until the stated date since in making its bid A relied on B's offer.

ARTICLE 2.5 – Rejection of offer

An offer is terminated when a rejection reaches the offeror.

COMMENT

1. Rejection may be express or implied

An offer may be rejected either expressly or impliedly. A frequent case of implied rejection is a reply to an offer which purports to be an acceptance but which contains additions, limitations or other modifications (see Art. 2.11(1)). In the absence of an express rejection the statements by, or the conduct of, the offeree must in any event be such as to justify the belief of the offeror that the offeree has no intention of accepting the offer. A reply on the part of the offeree which merely asks whether there would be a possible alternative (e.g. "Is there any chance of the price being reduced?", or "Could you deliver a couple of days earlier?") would not normally be sufficient to justify such a conclusion. It should be recalled that a rejection will bring about the termination of any offer, irrespective of whether it was revocable or irrevocable according to Art. 2.4. **Illustration**

A receives an offer from B stating that the offer will be firm for two weeks. A replies by return of post asking for partially different conditions which B does not accept. A may no longer accept the original offer even though there are still several days left before the expiry of the two week period since by making a counter-offer A implicitly rejected the original offer.

2. Rejection only one cause of termination of an offer

Rejection by the offeree is only one of the causes of termination of an offer. Other causes are dealt with in Arts. 2.4(1) and 2.7.

ARTICLE 2.6 – Mode of acceptance

(1) A statement made by or other conduct of the offeree indicating assent to an offer is an acceptance. Silence or inactivity does not in itself amount to acceptance.

(2) An acceptance of an offer becomes effective when the indication of assent reaches the offeror.

(3) However, if, by virtue of the offer or as a result of practices which the parties have established between themselves or of usage, the offeree may indicate assent by performing an act without notice to the offeror, the acceptance is effective when the act is performed.

COMMENT

1. Indication of assent to an offer

For there to be an acceptance the offeree must in one way or another indicate "assent" to the offer. The mere acknowledgement of receipt of the offer, or an expression of interest in it, is not sufficient. Furthermore, the assent must be unconditional, i.e. it cannot be made dependent on some further step to be taken by either the offeror (e.g. "Our acceptance is subject to your final approval") or the offeree (e.g. "We hereby accept the terms of the contract as set forth in your Memorandum and undertake to submit the contract to our Board for approval within the next two weeks"). Finally, the purported acceptance must contain no variation of the terms of the offer or at least none which materially alters them (see Art. 2.11).

2. Acceptance by conduct

Provided that the offer does not impose any particular mode of acceptance, the indication of assent may either be made by an express statement or be inferred from the conduct of the offeree. Para. (1) of this article does not specify the form such conduct should assume: most often it will consist in acts of performance, such as the payment of an advance on the price, the shipment of goods or the beginning of work at the site, etc.

3. Silence or inactivity

By stating that "[s]ilence or inactivity does not in itself amount to acceptance", para. (1) makes it clear that as a rule mere silence or inactivity on the part of the offeree does not allow the inference that the offeree assents to the offer. The situation is different if the parties themselves agree that silence shall amount to acceptance, or if there exists a course of dealing or usage to that effect. In no event, however, is it sufficient for the offeror to state unilaterally in its offer that the offer will be deemed to have been accepted in the absence of any reply from the offeree. Since it is the offeror who takes the initiative by proposing the conclusion of the contract, the offeree is free not only to accept or not to accept the offer, but also simply to ignore it.

Illustrations

1. A requests B to set out the conditions for the renewal of a contract for the supply of wine, due to expire on 31 December. In its offer B includes a provision stating that "if we have not heard from you at the latest by the end of November, we will assume that you have agreed to renew the contract on the conditions as indicated above". A finds the proposed conditions totally unacceptable and does not even reply. The former contract expires on the fixed date without a new contract having been agreed between the parties.

2. Under a long-term agreement for the supply of wine B regularly met A's orders without expressly confirming its acceptance. On 15 November A orders a large stock for New Year. B does not reply, nor does it deliver at the requested time. B is in breach since, in accordance with the practice established between the parties, B's silence in regard to A's order amounts to an acceptance.

4. When acceptance becomes effective

According to para. (2) an acceptance becomes effective at the moment the indication of assent reaches the offeror (see Art. 1.9(2)). For the definition of "reaches" see Art. 1.9(3). The reason for the adoption of the "receipt" principle in preference to the "dispatch" principle is that the risk of transmission is better placed on the offeree than on the offeror, since it is the former who chooses the means of communication, who knows whether the chosen means of communication is subject to special risks or delay, and who is consequently best able to take measures to ensure that the acceptance reaches its destination.

As a rule, an acceptance by means of mere conduct likewise becomes effective only when notice thereof reaches the offeror. It should be noted, however, that special notice to this effect by the offeree will be necessary only in cases where the conduct will not of itself give notice of acceptance to the offeror within a reasonable period of time. In all other cases, e.g. where the conduct consists in the payment of the price, or the shipment of the goods by air or by some other rapid mode of transportation, the same effect may well be achieved simply by the bank or the carrier informing the offeror of the funds transfer or of the consignment of the goods.

An exception to the general rule of para. (2) is to be found in the cases envisaged in para. (3), i.e. where "by virtue of the offer or as a result of practices which the parties have established between themselves or of usage, the offeree may indicate assent by performing an act without notice to the offeror". In such cases the acceptance is effective at the moment the act is performed, irrespective of whether or not the offeror is promptly informed thereof. **Illustrations**

    3. A asks B to write a special program for the setting up of a data bank. Without giving A notice of acceptance, B begins to write the program and, after its completion, insists on payment in accordance with the terms set out in A's offer. B is not entitled to payment since B's purported acceptance of A's offer never became effective as B never notified A of it.

    4. The facts are the same as in Illustration 3, the difference being that in the offer B is informed of A's absence for the following two weeks, and that if B intends to accept the offer B should begin writing the program immediately so as to save time. The contract is concluded once B begins to perform, even if B fails to inform A thereof either immediately or at a later stage.

This article corresponds to paras. (1), (2) first part and (3) of Art. 18 CISG.

ARTICLE 2.7 – Time of acceptance

An offer must be accepted within the time the offeror has fixed or, if no time is fixed, within a reasonable time having regard to the circumstances, including the rapidity of the means of communication employed by the offeror. An oral offer must be accepted immediately unless the circumstances indicate otherwise.

COMMENT

With respect to the time within which an offer must be accepted, this article, which corresponds to the second part of para. (2) of Art. 18 CISG, distinguishes between oral and written offers. Oral offers must be accepted immediately unless the circumstances indicate otherwise. As to written offers, all depends upon whether or not the offer indicated a fixed time for acceptance: if it did, the offer must be accepted within that time, while in all other cases the indication of assent must reach the offeror "within a reasonable time having regard to the circumstances, including the rapidity of the means of communication employed by the offeror".

It is important to note that the rules laid down in this article also apply to situations where, in accordance with Art. 2.6(3), the offeree may indicate assent by performing an act without notice to the offeror: in these cases it is the act of performance which has to be accomplished within the respective periods of time. For the determination of the precise starting point of the period of time fixed by the offeror, and the calculation of holidays occurring during that period of time, see Art. 2.8; as to cases of late acceptance and of delay in transmission, see Art. 2.9.

ARTICLE 2.8 – Acceptance within a fixed period of time

(1) A period of time for acceptance fixed by the offeror in a telegram or a letter begins to run from the moment the telegram is handed in for dispatch or from the date shown on the letter or, if no such date is shown, from the date shown on the envelope. A period of time for acceptance fixed by the offeror by means of instantaneous communication begins to run from the moment that the offer reaches the offeree.

(2) Official holidays or non-business days occurring during the period for acceptance are included in calculating the period. However, if a notice of acceptance cannot be delivered at the address of the offeror on the last day of the period because that day falls on an official holiday or a non-business day at the place of business of the offeror, the period is extended until the first business day which follows.

COMMENT

The offeror may fix a deadline within which the offeree must accept the offer. As long as this is done by indicating a precise date (e.g. "In case you intend to accept my offer, please do so no later than 1 March"), no special problems arise.

If, on the other hand, the offeror merely indicates a period of time (e.g. "You have ten days to accept this offer"), the problem may arise as to when the period starts to run as well as as to the effect of holidays occurring during, or at the expiry of, that period. The present article, which corresponds to Art. 20 CISG, is intended to provide an answer to these two questions when nothing is said in the offer itself.

ARTICLE 2.9 – Late acceptance. Delay in transmission

(1) A late acceptance is nevertheless effective as an acceptance if without undue delay the offeror so informs the offeree or gives notice to that effect.

(2) If a letter or other writing containing a late acceptance shows that it has been sent in such circumstances that if its transmission had been normal it would have reached the offeror in due time, the late acceptance is effective as an acceptance unless, without undue delay, the offeror informs the offeree that it considers the offer as having lapsed.

COMMENT

1. Late acceptance normally ineffective

According to the principle laid down in Art. 2.7 for an acceptance to be effective it must reach the offeror within the time fixed by the latter or, if no time is fixed, within a reasonable time. This means that as a rule an acceptance which reaches the offeror thereafter is without effect and may be disregarded by the offeror.

2. Offeror may nevertheless "accept" late acceptance

Para. (1) of this article, which corresponds to Art. 21 CISG, states that the offeror may nevertheless consider a late acceptance as having arrived in time and thus render it effective, provided that the offeror "without undue delay [...] so informs the offeree or gives notice to that effect". If the offeror takes advantage of this possibility, the contract is to be considered as having been concluded as soon as the late acceptance reaches the offeror and not when the offeror informs the offeree of its intention to consider the late acceptance effective. **Illustration**

1. A indicates 31 March as the deadline for acceptance of its offer. B's acceptance reaches A on 3 April. A, who is still interested in the contract, intends to "accept" B's late acceptance, and immediately informs B of its intention. Notwithstanding the fact that this notice only reaches B on 5 April the contract is concluded on 3 April.

3. Acceptance late because of delay in transmission

As long as the acceptance is late because the offeree did not send it in time, it is natural to consider it as having no effect unless the offeror expressly indicates otherwise. The situation is different when the offeree has replied in time, but the acceptance reaches the offeror late because of an unexpected delay in transmission. In such a case the reliance of the offeree on the acceptance having arrived in time deserves protection, with the consequence that the late acceptance is considered to be effective unless the offeror objects without undue delay. The only condition required by para. (2) is that the letter or other writing containing the late acceptance shows that it has been sent in such circumstances that, had its transmission been normal, it would have reached the offeror in due time. **Illustration**

2. The facts are the same as in Illustration 1, the difference being that B, knowing that the normal time for transmission of letters by mail to A is three days, sends its letter of acceptance on 25 March. Owing to a strike of the postal service in A's country the letter, which shows the date of its mailing on the envelope, only arrives on 3 April. B's acceptance, though late, is nevertheless effective unless A objects without undue delay.

ARTICLE 2.10 – Withdrawal of acceptance

An acceptance may be withdrawn if the withdrawal reaches the offeror before or at the same time as the acceptance would have be-come effective.

COMMENT

With respect to the withdrawal of an acceptance the present article lays down the same principle as that contained in Art. 2.3 concerning the withdrawal of an offer, i.e. that the offeree may change its mind and withdraw the acceptance provided that the withdrawal reaches the offeror before or at the same time as the acceptance. It should be noted that while the offeror is bound by the offer and may no longer change its mind once the offeree has dispatched the acceptance (see Art. 2.4(1)), the offeree looses its freedom of choice only at a later stage, i.e. when the notice of acceptance reaches the offeror. This article corresponds to Art. 22 CISG.

ARTICLE 2.11 – Modified acceptance

(1) A reply to an offer which purports to be an acceptance but contains additions, limitations or other modifications is a rejection of the offer and constitutes a counter-offer.

(2) However, a reply to an offer which purports to be an acceptance but contains additional or different terms which do not materially alter the terms of the offer constitutes an acceptance, unless the offeror, without undue delay, objects to the discrepancy. If the offeror does not object, the terms of the contract are the terms of the offer with the modifications contained in the acceptance.

COMMENT

1. Acceptance with modifications normally to be considered a counter-offer

In commercial dealings it often happens that the offeree, while signifying to the offeror its intention to accept the offer ("acknowledgement of order"), nevertheless includes in its declaration terms additional to or different from those of the offer. Para. (1) of this article provides that such a purported acceptance is as a rule to be considered a rejection of the offer and that it amounts to a counter-offer by the offeree, which the offeror may or may not accept either expressly or impliedly, e.g. by an act of performance.

2. Modifications which do not alter the nature of the acceptance

The principle according to which the acceptance must be the mirror image of the offer implies that even unimportant differences between the offer and the acceptance permit either party at a later stage to question the existence of the contract. In order to avoid such a result, which a party may well seek merely because market conditions have changed unfavourably, para. (2) provides for an exception to the general rule laid down in para. (1) by stating that if the additional or modified terms contained in the acceptance do not "materially" alter the terms of the offer, the contract is concluded with those modifications unless the offeror objects without undue delay.

What amounts to a "material" modification cannot be determined in the abstract but will depend on the circumstances of each case.

Additional or different terms relating to the price or mode of payment, place and time of performance of a non-monetary obligation, the extent of one party's liability to the other or the settlement of disputes, will normally, but need not necessarily, constitute a material modification of the offer. An important factor to be taken into account in this respect is whether the additional or different terms are commonly used in the trade sector concerned and therefore do not come as a surprise to the offeror. **Illustrations**

1. A orders a machine from B to be tested on A's premises. In its acknowledgement of order B declares that it accepts the terms of the offer, but adds that it wishes to be present at the testing of the machine. The additional term is not a "material" modification of the offer and will therefore become part of the contract unless A objects without undue delay.

2. The facts are the same as in Illustration 1, the difference being that in its acknowledgement of order B adds an arbitration clause. Unless the circumstances indicate otherwise, such a clause amounts to a "material" modification of the terms of the offer, with the result that B's purported acceptance would constitute a counter-offer.

3. A orders a stated quantity of wheat from B. In its acknowledgement of order B adds an arbitration clause which is standard practice in the commodity sector concerned. Since A cannot be surprised by such a clause, it is not a "material" modification of the terms of the offer and, unless A objects without undue delay, the arbitration clause becomes part of the contract.

ARTICLE 2.12 – Writings in confirmation

If a writing which is sent within a reasonable time after the conclusion of the contract and which purports to be a confirmation of the contract contains additional or different terms, such terms become part of the contract, unless they materially alter the contract or the recipient, without undue delay, objects to the discrepancy.

COMMENT

1. "Writings in confirmation"

This article deals with the situation where a contract has already been concluded either orally or by the exchange of written communications limited to the essential terms of the agreement, and one party subsequently sends the other a document intended simply to confirm what has already been agreed upon, but which in fact contains terms which are additional to or different from those previously agreed by the parties. In theory, this situation clearly differs from that envisaged in Art. 2.11, where a contract has not yet been concluded and the modifying terms are contained in the offeree's purported acceptance. Yet, since in practice it may be very difficult if not impossible to distinguish between the two situations, the present article adopts with respect to modifying terms contained in a writing in confirmation the same solution as that envisaged in Art. 2.11. In other words, just as for the modifications contained in an acknowledgement of order, it is provided that terms additional to or different from those previously agreed by the parties contained in a writing in confirmation become part of the contract, provided that they do not "materially" alter the agreement and that the recipient of the document does not object to them without undue delay.

It goes without saying that also in the context of writings in confirmation the question of which of the new terms "materially" alter the terms of the previous agreement can be answered definitely only in the light of the circumstances of each individual case. On the other hand, the present article clearly does not apply to cases where the party sending the writing in confirmation expressly invites the other party to return it duly counter-signed for acceptance. In such circumstances it is irrelevant whether the writing contains modifications, and if so whether or not these modifications are "material" since the writing must in any case be expressly accepted by the addressee if there is to be a contract. **Illustrations**

1. A orders by telephone a machine from B, who accepts the order. The following day A receives a letter from B confirming the terms of their oral agreement but adding that B wishes to be present at the testing of the machine on A's premises. The additional term is not a "material" modification of the terms previously agreed between the parties and will therefore become part of the contract unless A objects without undue delay.

2. The facts are the same as in Illustration 1, the difference being that the modification contained in B's writing in confirmation consists in the addition of an arbitration clause. Unless the circumstances indicate otherwise such a clause amounts to a "material" modification of the terms previously agreed between the parties with the result that it will not become part of the contract.

3. A orders by telex a stated quantity of wheat and B accepts immediately by telex. Later on the same day B sends a letter to A confirming the terms of their agreement but adding an arbitration clause which is standard practice in the commodity sector concerned. Since A cannot be surprised by such a clause, it is not a "material" modification of the terms previously agreed and, unless A objects without undue delay, the arbitration clause becomes part of the contract.

2. Writing in confirmation to be sent within a reasonable time after conclusion of the contract

The rule according to which silence on the part of the recipient amounts to acceptance of the content of the writing in confirmation, including any non-material modifications of the terms previously agreed, presupposes that the writing is sent "within a reasonable time after the conclusion of the contract". Any writing of this kind sent after a period of time which, in the circumstances, appears to be unreasonably long, loses any significance, and silence on the part of the recipient may therefore no longer be interpreted as acceptance of its content.

3. Invoices

For the purposes of this article, the term "writing in confirmation" is to be understood in a broad sense, i.e. as covering also those cases where a party uses the invoice or another similar document relating to performance to specify the conditions of the contract concluded either orally or by informal correspondence, provided that such use is customary in the trade sector and/or country concerned.

ARTICLE 2.13 – Conclusion of contract dependent on agreement on specific matters or in a specific form

Where in the course of negotiations one of the parties insists that the contract is not concluded until there is agreement on specific matters or in a specific form, no contract is concluded before agreement is reached on those matters or in that form.

COMMENT

1. Conclusion of contract dependent on agreement on specific matters

As a rule, a contract is concluded if the parties reach agreement on the terms which are essential to the type of transaction involved, while minor terms which the parties have not settled may subsequently be implied either in fact or by law. See comment 1 on Art. 2.2 and also Arts. 4.8 and 5.2. **Illustration**

1. A agrees with B on all the terms which are essential to their intended contract for the distribution of A's goods. When the question subsequently arises of who should bear the costs of the publicity campaign, neither party may claim that no contract has come into existence by reason of the silence of the contract on this point, as the missing term is not essential to the type of transaction in question and will be implied in fact or by law.

Parties may, however, in a given case consider specific matters to be of such importance that they do not intend to enter into a binding agreement unless these matters are settled in a satisfactory manner. If the parties, or one only of them, make such an intention explicit, the contract as such does not come into existence without agreement on those matters. By using the word "insists", the present article makes it clear that it is not sufficient for the parties to manifest their intention to this effect simply in passing, but that it must be done unequivocally. **Illustration**

2. The facts are the same as in Illustration 1, the difference being that during the negotiations B repeatedly declares that the question of who should bear the cost of the publicity campaign must be settled expressly. Notwithstanding their agreement on all the essential terms of the contract, no contract has come into existence between A and B since B had insisted that the conclusion of the contract was dependent on agreement regarding that specific term.

2. Conclusion of contract dependent on agreement in a specific form

In commercial practice, particularly when transactions of considerable complexity are involved, it is quite frequent that after prolonged negotiations the parties sign an informal document called "Preliminary Agreement", "Memorandum of Understanding", "Letter of Intent" or the like, containing the terms of the agreement so far reached, but at the same time state their intention to provide for the execution of a formal document at a later stage ("Subject to Contract", "Formal Agreement to follow"). In some cases the parties consider their contract as already being concluded and the execution of the formal document only as confirmation of the already complete agreement. If, however, both parties, or only one of them, make it clear that they do not intend to be bound unless the formal document has been drawn up, there will be no contract until that time even if the parties have agreed on all the relevant aspects of their transaction. **Illustrations**

3. After prolonged negotiations A and B sign a "Memorandum of Understanding" containing the terms of an agreement for a joint venture for the exploration and exploitation of the continental shelf of country X. The parties agree that they will at a later stage draw up the agreement in formal documents to be signed and exchanged at a public ceremony. If the "Memorandum" already contains all the relevant terms of the agreement and the subsequent documents are intended merely to permit the agreement to be properly presented to the public, it may be taken that the contract was already concluded when the first written document was signed.

4. The facts are the same as in Illustration 3, the difference being that the "Memorandum of Understanding" contains a clause such as "Not binding until final agreement is executed" or the like. Until the signing and the exchange of the formal documents there is no binding contract.

ARTICLE 2.14 – Contract with terms deliberately left open

(1) If the parties intend to conclude a contract, the fact that they intentionally leave a term to be agreed upon in further negotiations or to be determined by a third person does not prevent a contract from coming into existence.

(2) The existence of the contract is not affected by the fact that subsequently (a) the parties reach no agreement on the term; or (b) the third person does not determine the term, provided that there is an alternative means of rendering the term definite that is reasonable in the circumstances, having regard to the intention of the parties.

COMMENT

1. Contract with terms deliberately left open

A contract may be silent on one or more issues because the parties simply did not think of them during the negotiations. Provided that the parties have agreed on the terms essential to the type of transaction concerned, a contract will nonetheless have been concluded and the missing terms will be supplied on the basis of Arts. 4.8 or 5.2. See comment 1 on Art. 2.2. Quite different is the case dealt with in the present article: here the parties intentionally leave open one or more terms because they are unable or unwilling to determine them at the time of the conclusion of the contract, and refer for their determination to an agreement to be made by them at a later stage, or to a third person. This latter situation, which is especially frequent in, although not confined to, long-term transactions, gives rise in essence to two problems: first, whether the fact that the parties have intentionally left terms open prevents a contract from coming into existence and second, if this is not the case, what will happen to the contract if the parties subsequently fail to reach agreement or the third person fails to make the determination.

2. Open terms not in themselves an impediment to valid conclusion of contract

Para. (1) states that if the parties intended to conclude a contract, the fact that they have intentionally left a term to be agreed upon in further negotiations or to be determined by a third person does not prevent a contract from coming into existence. In cases where it is not expressly stated, the parties' intention to conclude a contract notwithstanding the terms left open may be inferred from other circumstances, such as the non-essential character of the terms in question, the degree of definiteness of the agreement as a whole, the fact that the open terms relate to items which by their very nature can be determined only at a later stage, the fact that the agreement has already been partially executed, etc. **Illustration**

1. A, a shipping line, enters into a detailed agreement with B, a terminal operator, for the use of B's container terminal. The agreement fixes the minimum volume of containers to be discharged or loaded annually and the fees payable, while the fees for additional containers are left to be determined if and when the minimum volume is reached. Two months later A learns that B's competitor would offer better conditions and refuses to perform, claiming that the agreement with B never resulted in a binding contract because the question of the fees had not been settled. A is liable for non-performance because the detailed character of the agreement as well as the fact that both A and B began performance immediately indicate clearly that their intention was to enter into a binding agreement.

3. Failure of mechanism provided for by parties for determination of open terms

If the parties are unable to reach agreement on the open terms or the third person does not determine them, the question arises as to whether or not the contract comes to an end. According to para. (2) of this article the existence of the contract is not affected "provided that there is an alternative means of rendering the term definite that is reasonable in the circumstances, having regard to the intention of the parties". A first alternative exists whenever the missing term may be supplied on the basis of Art. 5.2; if the parties have deferred the determination of the missing term to a third person to be nominated by an instance such as the President of the Tribunal, or of the Chamber of Commerce, etc., it may also consist in the appointment of a new third person. The cases in which a given contract may be upheld by resorting to such alternative means will, however, be quite rare in practice. Few problems should arise as long as the term to be implemented is of minor importance. If, on the other hand, the term in question is essential to the type of transaction concerned, there must be clear evidence of the intention of the parties to uphold the contract: among the factors to be taken into account in this connection are whether the term in question relates to items which by their very nature can be determined only at a later stage, whether the agreement has already been partially executed, etc. **Illustration**

> 2. The facts are the same as in Illustration 1, the difference being that when the minimum volume of containers to be loaded or unloaded is

reached the parties fail to agree on the fees payable in respect of the additional containers. A stops performing, claiming that the contract has come to an end. A is liable for non-performance, since the fact that the parties have started performing without making future agreement on the missing term a condition for the continuation of their business relationship is sufficient evidence of their intention to uphold the contract even in the absence of such agreement. The fees for the additional containers will be determined according to the criteria laid down in Art. 5.7.

ARTICLE 2.15 – Negotiations in bad faith

(1) A party is free to negotiate and is not liable for failure to reach an agreement.

(2) However, a party who negotiates or breaks off negotiations in bad faith is liable for the losses caused to the other party.

(3) It is bad faith, in particular, for a party to enter into or continue negotiations when intending not to reach an agreement with the other party.

COMMENT

1. Freedom of negotiation

As a rule, parties are not only free to decide when and with whom to enter into negotiations with a view to concluding a contract, but also if, how and for how long to proceed with their efforts to reach an agreement. This follows from the basic principle of freedom of contract enunciated in Art. 1.1, and is essential in order to guarantee healthy competition among business people engaged in international trade.

2. Liability for negotiating in bad faith

A party's right freely to enter into negotiations and to decide on the terms to be negotiated is, however, not unlimited, and must not conflict with the principle of good faith and fair dealing laid down in Art. 1.7. One particular instance of negotiating in bad faith which is expressly indicated in para. (3) of this article is that where a party enters into negotiations or continues to negotiate without any intention of concluding an agreement with the other party. Other instances are where one party has deliberately or by negligence misled the other party as to the nature or terms of the proposed contract, either by actually misrepresenting facts, or by not disclosing facts which, given the nature of the parties and/or the contract, should have been disclosed. As to the duty of confidentiality, see Art. 2.16.

A party's liability for negotiating in bad faith is limited to the losses caused to the other party

(para. (2)). In other words, the aggrieved party may recover the expenses incurred in the negotiations and may also be compensated for the lost opportunity to conclude another contract with a third person (so-called reliance or negative interest), but may generally not recover the profit which would have resulted had the original contract been concluded (so-called expectation or positive interest). **Illustrations**

> 1. A learns of B's intention to sell its restaurant. A, who has no intention whatsoever of buying the restaurant, nevertheless enters into lengthy negotiations with B for the sole purpose of preventing B from selling the restaurant to C, a competitor of A's. A, who breaks off negotiations when C has bought another restaurant, is liable to B, who ultimately succeeds in selling the restaurant at a lower price than that offered by C, for the difference in price.

> 2. A, who is negotiating with B for the promotion of the purchase of military equipment by the armed forces of B's country, learns that B will not receive the necessary export licence from its own governmental authorities, a pre-requisite for permission to pay B's fees. A does not reveal this fact to B and finally concludes the contract, which, however, cannot be enforced by reason of the missing licences. A is liable to B for the costs incurred after A had learned of the impossibility of obtaining the required licences.

> 3. A enters into lengthy negotiations for a bank loan from B's branch office. At the last minute the branch office discloses that it had no authority to sign and that its head office had

decided not to approve the draft agreement. A, who could in the meantime have obtained the loan from another bank, is entitled to recover the expenses entailed by the negotiations and the profits it would have made during the delay before obtaining the loan from the other bank.

3. Liability for breaking off negotiations in bad faith

The right to break off negotiations also is subject to the principle of good faith and fair dealing. Once an offer has been made, it may be revoked only within the limits provided for in Art. 2.4. Yet even before this stage is reached, or in a negotiation process with no ascertainable sequence of offer and acceptance, a party may no longer be free to break off negotiations abruptly and without justification. When such a point of no return is reached depends of course on the circumstances of the case, in particular the extent to which the other party, as a result of the conduct of the first party, had reason to rely on the positive outcome of the negotiations, and on the number of issues relating to the future contract on which the parties have already reached agreement. **Illustration**

4. A assures B of the grant of a franchise if B takes steps to gain experience and is prepared to invest US$ 150,000. During the next two years B makes extensive preparations with a view to concluding the contract, always with A's assurance that B will be granted the franchise. When all is ready for the signing of the agreement, A informs B that the latter must invest a substantially higher sum. B, who refuses, is entitled to recover from A the expenses incurred with a view to the conclusion of the contract.

ARTICLE 2.16 – Duty of confidentiality

Where information is given as confidential by one party in the course of negotiations, the other party is under a duty not to disclose that information or to use it improperly for its own purposes, whether or not a contract is subsequently concluded. Where appropriate, the remedy for breach of that duty may include compensation based on the benefit received by the other party.

COMMENT

1. Parties in general not under a duty of confidentiality

Just as there exists no general duty of disclosure, so parties, when entering into negotiations for the conclusion of a contract, are normally under no obligation to treat the information they have exchanged as confidential. In other words, since a party is normally free to decide which facts relevant to the transaction under negotiation to disclose, such information is as a rule to be considered non-confidential, i.e. information which the other party may either disclose to third persons or use for purposes of its own should no contract be concluded.

Illustration

1. A invites B and C, producers of air-conditioning systems, to submit offers for the installation of such a system. In their offers B and C also provide some technical details regarding the functioning of their respective systems, with a view to enhancing the merits of their products. A decides to reject B's offer and to continue negotiations only with C. A is free to use the information contained in B's offer in order to induce C to propose more favourable conditions.

2. Confidential information

A party may have an interest in certain information given to the other party not being divulged or used for purposes other than those for which it was given. As long as that party expressly declares that such information is to be considered confidential, the situation is clear, for by receiving the information the other party implicitly agrees to treat it as confidential. The only problem which may arise is that if the period during which the other party is not to disclose the information is too long, this might contravene the applicable laws prohibiting restrictive trade practices. Yet even in the absence of such an express declaration the receiving party may be under a duty of confidentiality. This is the case where, in view of the particular nature of the information or the professional qualifications of the parties, it would be contrary to the general principle of good faith and fair dealing for the receiving party to disclose it, or to use it for its own purposes after the breaking off of negotiations. **Illustrations**

2. The facts are the same as in Illustration 1, the difference being that in its offer B expressly

requests A not to divulge certain technical specifications contained therein. A may not use this information in its negotiations with C.

...

3. Damages recoverable

The breach of confidentiality implies first liability in damages. The amount of damages recoverable may vary, depending on whether or not the parties entered into a special agreement for the non-disclosure of the information. Even if the injured party has not suffered any loss, it may be entitled to recover from the non-performing party the benefit the latter received by disclosing the information to third persons or by using it for its own purposes. If necessary, for example when the information has not yet been disclosed or has been disclosed only partially, the injured party may also seek an injunction in accordance with the applicable law.

ARTICLE 2.17 – Merger clauses

A contract in writing which contains a clause indicating that the writing completely embodies the terms on which the parties have agreed cannot be contradicted or supplemented by evidence of prior statements or agreements. However, such statements or agreements may be used to interpret the writing.

COMMENT

If the conclusion of a contract is preceded by more or less extended negotiations, the parties may wish to put their agreement in writing and declare that document to constitute their final agreement. This can be achieved by an appropriately drafted "merger" or "integration" clause (e.g. "This contract contains the entire agreement between the parties"). However, the effect of such a clause is not to deprive prior statements or agreements of any relevance: they may still be used as a means of interpreting the written document. See also Art. 4.3(a).

A merger clause of course covers only prior statements or agreements between the parties and does not preclude subsequent informal agreements between them. The parties are, however, free to extend an agreed form even to future amendments. See Art. 2.18.

This article indirectly confirms the principle set out in Art. 1.2 in the sense that, in the absence of a merger clause, extrinsic evidence supplementing or contradicting a written contract is admissible.

ARTICLE 2.18 – Written modification clauses

A contract in writing which contains a clause requiring any modification or termination by agreement to be in writing may not be otherwise modified or terminated. However, a party may be precluded by its conduct from asserting such a clause to the extent that the other party has acted in reliance on that conduct.

COMMENT

Parties concluding a written contract may wish to ensure that any modification or termination by agreement will also be in writing and to this end include a special clause in the contract. This article states that as a rule such a clause renders any oral modification or termination ineffective, thus rejecting the idea that such oral modification or termination of the contract may be seen as an implied abrogation of the written modification clause. The article however provides for an exception to the general rule by specifying that a party may be precluded by its conduct from invoking the written modification clause to the extent that the other party has acted in reliance on that conduct.

Illustration

A, a contractor, contracts with B, a school board, for the construction of a new school building. The contract provides that the second floor of the building is to have sufficient bearing capacity to support the school library. Notwithstanding a written modification clause in the same contract, the parties orally agree that the second floor of the building should be of non-bearing construction. A completes construction according to the modification, and B, who has observed the progress of the construction without making any objections, only at this point objects to how the second floor has been constructed. A court may decide that B is not entitled to invoke the written modification clause as A reasonably relied on the oral modification, and is therefore not liable for non-performance.

ARTICLE 2.19 – Contracting under standard terms

(1) Where one party or both parties use standard terms in concluding a contract, the general rules on formation apply, subject to Articles 2.20 - 2.22.

(2) Standard terms are provisions which are prepared in advance for general and repeated use by one party and which are actually used without negotiation with the other party.

COMMENT

1. Contracting under standard terms

This article is the first of four articles (Arts. 2.19 - 2.22) which deal with the special situation where one or both parties use standard terms in concluding a contract.

2. Notion of "standard terms"

"Standard terms" are to be understood as those contract provisions which are prepared in advance for general and repeated use by one party and which are actually used without negotiation with the other party (para. (2)). What is decisive is not their formal presentation (e.g. whether they are contained in a separate document or in the contract document itself; whether they have been issued on pre-printed forms or whether they are only on computer, etc.), nor who prepared them (the party itself, a trade or professional association, etc.), nor their volume (whether they consist of a comprehensive set of provisions covering almost all the relevant aspects of the contract, or of only one or two provisions regarding, for instance, exclusion of liability and arbitration). What is decisive is the fact that they are drafted in advance for general and repeated use and that they are actually used in a given case by one of the parties without negotiation with the other party. This latter requirement obviously relates only to the standard terms as such, which the other party must accept as a whole, while the other terms of the same contract may well be the subject of negotiation between the parties.

3. General rules on formation apply

Usually, the general rules on formation apply irrespective of whether or not one or both parties use standard terms (para. (1)). It follows that standard terms proposed by one party bind the other party only on acceptance, and that it depends upon the circumstances of the case whether the two parties must refer to the standard terms expressly or whether the incorporation of such terms may be implied. Thus, standard terms contained in the contract document itself will normally be binding upon the mere signature of the contract document as a whole, at least as long as they are reproduced above that signature and not, for instance, on the reverse side of the document. On the other hand, standard terms contained in a separate document will normally have to be referred to expressly by the party intending to use them. Implied incorporation may be admitted only if there exists a practice established between the parties or usage to that effect. See Art. 1.8. **Illustrations**

1. A intends to conclude an insurance contract with B covering the risk of liability for accidents of A's employees at work. The parties sign a model contract form presented by B after filling in the blank spaces relating, among other matters, to the premium and to the maximum amount insured. By virtue of its signature, A is bound not only by the terms which it has individually negotiated with B, but also by the General Conditions of the National Insurers' Association, which are printed on the form.

2. A normally concludes contracts with its customers on the basis of its own standard terms which are printed as a separate document. When making an offer to B, a new customer, A fails to make an express reference to the standard terms. B accepts the offer. The standard terms are not incorporated in the contract unless A can prove that B knew or ought to have known of A's intention to conclude the contract only on the basis of its own standard terms, e.g. because the same standard terms had regularly been adopted in previous transactions.

3. A intends to buy grain on the commodity exchange in London. In the contract concluded between A and B, a broker on that exchange, no express reference is made to the standard terms which normally govern brokerage contracts concluded at the exchange in question. The standard terms are nevertheless incorporated in the contract because their application to the kind of contract in question amounts to a usage.

ARTICLE 2.20 – Surprising terms

(1) No term contained in standard terms which is of such a character that the other party could not reasonably have expected it, is effective unless it has been expressly accepted by that party.

(2) In determining whether a term is of such a character regard shall be had to its content, language and presentation.

COMMENT

1. Surprising terms in standard terms not effective

A party which accepts the other party's standard terms is in principle bound by them irrespective of whether or not it actually knows their content in detail or fully understands their implications. An important exception to this rule is, however, laid down in this article which states that, notwithstanding its acceptance of the standard terms as a whole, the adhering party is not bound by those terms which by virtue of their content, language or presentation are of such a character that it could not reasonably have expected them. The reason for this exception is the desire to avoid a party which uses standard terms taking undue advantage of its position by surreptitiously attempting to impose terms on the other party which that party would scarcely have accepted had it been aware of them. For other articles intended to protect the economically weaker or less experienced party, see Arts. 3.10 and 4.6.

2. Terms "surprising" by virtue of their content

A particular term contained in standard terms may come as a surprise to the adhering party first by reason of its content. This is the case whenever the content of the term in question is such that a reasonable person of the same kind as the adhering party would not have expected it in the type of standard terms involved. In determining whether or not a term is unusual, regard must be had on the one hand to the terms which are commonly to be found in standard terms generally used in the trade sector concerned, and on the other to the individual negotiations between the parties. Thus, for example, a term excluding or limiting the contractual liability of the proponent may or may not be considered to be "surprising", and in consequence ineffective in a particular case, its effectiveness depending on whether or not terms of that kind are common in the trade sector concerned, and are consistent with the way in which the parties conducted their negotiations.

Illustration

1. A, a travel agency, offers package tours for business trips. The terms of the advertisement give the impression that A is acting as a tour operator who undertakes full responsibility for the various services comprising the package. B books a tour on the basis of A's standard terms. Notwithstanding B's acceptance of the terms as a whole, A may not rely on a term stating that, with respect to the hotel accommodation, it is acting merely as an agent for the hotelkeeper, and therefore declines any liability.

3. Terms "surprising" by virtue of their language or presentation

Other reasons for a particular term contained in standard terms being surprising to the adhering party may be the language in which it is couched, which may be obscure, or the way in which it is presented typographically, for instance in minute print. In order to determine whether or not this is the case, regard is to be had not so much to the formulation and presentation commonly used in the type of standard terms involved, but more to the professional skill and experience of persons of the same kind as the adhering party. Thus, a particular wording may be both obscure and clear at the same time, depending on whether or not the adhering party belongs to the same professional category as the party using the standard terms. The language factor may also play an important role in the context of international transactions. If the standard terms are drafted in a foreign language it cannot be excluded that some of its terms, although fairly clear in themselves, will turn out to be surprising for the adhering party who could not reasonably have been expected fully to appreciate all their implications. **Illustrations**

2. A, an insurance company operating in country X, is an affiliate of B, a company incorporated in country Y. A's standard terms comprise some 50 terms printed in small type. One of the terms designates the law of country Y as the applicable law. Unless this term is presented in bold letters or in any other way apt to attract the attention of the adhering party, it will be without effect since customers in country

X would not reasonably expect to find a choice-of-law clause designating a foreign law as the law governing their contracts in the standard terms of a company operating in their own country.

3. A, a commodity dealer operating in Hamburg, uses in its contracts with its customers standard terms containing, among others, a provision stating "Hamburg - Freundschaftliche Arbitrage". In local business circles this clause is normally understood as meaning that possible disputes are to be submitted to a special arbitration governed by particular rules of procedure of local origin. In contracts with foreign customers this clause may be held to be ineffective, notwithstanding the acceptance of the standard terms as a whole, since a foreign

customer cannot reasonably be expected to understand its exact implications, and this irrespective of whether or not the clause has been translated into its own language.

4. Express acceptance of "surprising" terms

The risk of the adhering party being taken by surprise by the kind of terms so far discussed clearly no longer exists if in a given case the other party draws the adhering party's attention to them and the adhering party accepts them. The present article therefore provides that a party may no longer rely on the "surprising" nature of a term in order to challenge its effectiveness, once it has expressly accepted the term.

ARTICLE 2.21 – Conflict between standard terms and non-standard terms

In case of conflict between a standard term and a term which is not a standard term the latter prevails.

COMMENT

Standard terms are by definition prepared in advance by one party or a third person and incorporated in an individual contract without their content being discussed by the parties (see Art. 2.19(2)). It is therefore logical that whenever the parties specifically negotiate and agree on particular provisions of their contract, such provisions will prevail over conflicting provisions contained in the standard terms since they are more likely to reflect the intention of the parties in the given case.

The individually agreed provisions may appear in the same document as the standard terms, but may also be contained in a separate document. In the first case they may easily be recognised on account of their being written in characters different from those of the standard

terms. In the second case it may be more difficult to distinguish between the provisions which are standard terms and those which are not, and to determine their exact position in the hierarchy of the different documents. To this effect the parties often include a contract provision expressly indicating the documents which form part of their contract and their respective weight.

Special problems may however arise when the modifications to the standard terms have only been agreed upon orally, without the conflicting provisions contained in the standard terms being struck out, and those standard terms contain a provision stating the exclusive character of the writing signed by the parties, or that any addition to or modification of their content must be in writing. For these cases see Arts. 2.17 and 2.18.

ARTICLE 2.22 – Battle of forms

Where both parties use standard terms and reach agreement except on those terms, a contract is concluded on the basis of the agreed terms and of any standard terms which are common in substance unless one party clearly indicates in advance, or later and without undue delay informs the other party, that it does not intend to be bound by such a contract.

COMMENT

1. Parties using different standard terms

It is quite frequent in commercial transactions for both the offeror when making the offer, and the offeree when accepting it, each to refer to its own standard terms. In the absence of express acceptance by the offeror of the

offeree's standard terms, the problem arises as to whether a contract is concluded at all and if so, which, if either, of the two conflicting sets of standard terms should prevail.

2. "Battle of forms" and general rules on offer and acceptance

If the general rules on offer and acceptance were to be applied, there would either be no contract at all since the purported acceptance by the offeree would, subject to the exception provided for in Art. 2.11(2), amount to a counter-offer, or if the two parties have started to perform without objecting to each other's standard terms, a contract would be considered to have been concluded on the basis of those terms which were the last to be sent or to be referred to (the "last shot").

3. The "knock-out" doctrine

The "last shot" doctrine may be appropriate if the parties clearly indicate that the adoption of their standard terms is an essential condition for the conclusion of the contract. Where, on the other hand, the parties, as is very often the case in practice, refer to their standard terms more or less automatically, for example by exchanging printed order and acknowledgement of order forms with the respective terms on the reverse side, they will normally not even be aware of the conflict between their respective standard terms. There is in such cases no reason to allow the parties subsequently to question the very existence of the contract or, if performance has commenced, to insist on the application of the terms last sent or referred to.

It is for this reason that the present article provides, notwithstanding the general rules on offer and acceptance, that if the parties reach an agreement except on their standard terms, a contract is concluded on the basis of the agreed terms and of any standard terms which are common in substance ("knock-out" doctrine).

Illustration

1. A orders a machine from B indicating the type of machine, the price and terms of payment, and the date and place of delivery. A uses an order form with its "General Conditions for Purchase" printed on the reverse side. B accepts by sending an acknowledgement of order form on the reverse side of which appear its own "General Conditions for Sale". When A subsequently seeks to withdraw from the deal it claims that no contract was ever concluded as there was no agreement as to which set of standard terms should apply. Since, however, the parties have agreed on the essential terms of the contract, a contract has been concluded on those terms and on any standard terms which are common in substance.

A party may, however, always exclude the operation of the "knock-out" doctrine by clearly indicating in advance, or by later and without undue delay informing the other, that it does not intend to be bound by a contract which is not based on its own standard terms. What will in practice amount to such a "clear" indication cannot be stated in absolute terms but the inclusion of a clause of this kind in the standard terms themselves will not normally be sufficient since what is necessary is a specific declaration by the party concerned in its offer or acceptance.

Illustrations

2. The facts are the same as in Illustration 1, the difference being that A claims that the contract was concluded on the basis of its standard terms since they contain a clause which states that "Deviating standard terms of the party accepting the order are not valid if they have not been confirmed in writing by us". The result will be the same as in Illustration 1, since merely by including such a clause in its standard terms A does not indicate with sufficient clarity its determination to conclude the contract only on its own terms.

3. The facts are the same as in Illustration 1, the difference being that the non-standard terms of A's offer contain a statement to the effect that A intends to contract only on its own standard terms. The mere fact that B attaches its own standard terms to its acceptance does not prevent the contract from being concluded on the basis of A's standard terms.

CHAPTER 3 – VALIDITY

ARTICLE 3.1 – Matters not covered

These Principles do not deal with invalidity arising from (a) lack of capacity; (b) lack of authority; (c) immorality or illegality.

COMMENT

This article makes it clear that not all the grounds of invalidity of a contract to be found in the various national legal systems fall within the scope of the Principles. This is in particular the case of lack of capacity, lack of authority and immorality or illegality. The reason for their exclusion lies both in the inherent complexity of questions of status, agency and public policy and the extremely diverse manner in which they are treated in domestic law. In consequence, matters such as *ultra vires*, the authority of an agent to bind its principal as well as the authority of directors to bind their company, and the illegal or immoral content of contracts will continue to be governed by the applicable law.

ARTICLE 3.2 – Validity of mere agreement

A contract is concluded, modified or terminated by the mere agreement of the parties, without any further requirement.

COMMENT

The purpose of this article is to make it clear that the mere agreement of the parties is sufficient for the valid conclusion, modification or termination by agreement of a contract, without any of the further requirements which are to be found in some domestic laws.

1. No need for consideration

In common law systems, consideration is traditionally seen as a prerequisite for the validity or enforceability of a contract as well as for its modification or termination by the parties.

However, in commercial dealings this requirement is of minimal practical importance since in that context obligations are almost always undertaken by both parties. It is for this reason that Art. 29(1) CISG dispenses with the requirement of consideration in relation to the modification and termination by the parties of contracts for the international sale of goods. The fact that the present article extends this approach to the conclusion, modification and termination by the parties of international commercial contracts in general can only bring about greater certainty and reduce litigation.

2. No need for *cause*

This article also excludes the requirement of cause which exists in some civil law systems and is in certain respects functionally similar to the common law "consideration". **Illustration**

1. At the request of its French customer A, bank B in Paris issues a guarantee on first demand in favour of C, a business partner of A in England. Neither B nor A can invoke the possible absence of consideration or cause for the guarantee.

It should be noted however that this article is not concerned with the effects which may derive from other aspects of cause, such as its illegality. See comment 2 on Art. 3.3.

3. All contracts consensual

Some civil law systems have retained certain types of "real" contract, i.e. contracts concluded only upon the actual handing over of the goods concerned. Such rules are not easily compatible with modern business perceptions and practice and are therefore also excluded by the present article. **Illustration**

2. Two French businessmen, A and B, agree with C, a real estate developer, to lend C 300,000 French francs on 2 July. On 25 June, A and B inform C that, unexpectedly, they need the money for their own business. C is entitled to receive the loan, although the loan is generally considered a "real" contract in France.

ARTICLE 3.3 – Initial impossibility

(1) The mere fact that at the time of the conclusion of the contract the performance of the obligation assumed was impossible does not affect the validity of the contract.

(2) The mere fact that at the time of the conclusion of the contract a party was not entitled to dispose of the assets to which the contract relates does not affect the validity of the contract.

COMMENT

1. Performance impossible from the outset

Contrary to a number of legal systems which consider a contract of sale void if the specific goods sold have already perished at the time of conclusion of the contract, para. (1) of this article, in conformity with the most modern trends, states in general terms that the mere fact that at the time of the conclusion of the contract the performance of the obligation assumed was impossible does not affect the validity of the contract. A contract is valid even if the assets to which it relates have already perished at the time of contracting, with the consequence that initial impossibility of performance is equated with impossibility occurring after the conclusion of the contract. The rights and duties of the parties arising from one party's (or possibly even both parties') inability to perform are to be determined according to the rules on non-performance. Under these rules appropriate weight may be attached, for example, to the fact that the obligor (or the obligee) already knew of the impossibility of performance at the time of contracting.

The rule laid down in para. (1) also removes possible doubts as to the validity of contracts for the delivery of future goods. If an initial impossibility of performance is due to a legal prohibition (e.g. an export or import embargo), the validity of the contract depends upon whether under the law enacting the prohibition the latter is intended to invalidate the contract or merely to prohibit its performance. Para. (1) moreover departs from the rule to be found in some civil law systems according to which the object (*objet*) of a contract must be possible. The paragraph also deviates from the rule of the same systems which requires the existence of a *cause*, since, in a case of initial impossibility, the *cause* for a counter-performance is lacking. See Art. 3.2.

2. Lack of legal title or power

Para. (2) of this article deals with cases where the party promising to transfer or deliver assets was not entitled to dispose of the assets because it lacked legal title or the right of disposition at the time of the conclusion of the contract. Some legal systems declare a contract of sale concluded in such circumstances to be void. Yet, as in the case with initial impossibility, and for even more cogent reasons, para. (2) of this article considers such a contract to be valid. Indeed, a contracting party may, and often does, acquire legal title to, or the power of disposition over, the assets in question after the conclusion of the contract. Should this not occur, the rules on non-performance will apply. Cases where the power of disposition is lacking must be distinguished from those of lack of capacity. The latter relate to certain disabilities of a person which may affect all or at least some types of contract concluded by it, and falls outside the scope of the Principles. See Art. 3.1(a).

ARTICLE 3.4 – Definition of mistake

Mistake is an erroneous assumption relating to facts or to law existing when the contract was concluded.

COMMENT

1. Mistake of fact and mistake of law

This article equates a mistake relating to facts with a mistake relating to law. Identical legal treatment of the two types of mistake seems justified in view of the increasing complexity of modern legal systems. For cross-border trade the difficulties caused by this complexity are exacerbated by the fact that an individual transaction may be affected by foreign and therefore unfamiliar legal systems.

2. Decisive time

The article indicates that the mistake involves an erroneous assumption relating to the factual or legal circumstances that exist at the time of the conclusion of the contract.

The purpose of fixing this time element is to

distinguish cases where the rules on mistake with their particular remedies apply from those relating to non-performance. Indeed, a typical case of mistake may, depending on the point of view taken, often just as well be seen as one involving an obstacle which prevents or impedes the performance of the contract. If a party has entered into a contract under a misconception as to the factual or legal context and therefore misjudged its prospects under that contract, the rules on mistake will apply. If, on the other hand, a party has a correct understanding of the surrounding circumstances but makes an error of judgment as to its prospects under the contract, and later refuses to perform, then the case is one of non-performance rather than mistake.

ARTICLE 3.5 – Relevant mistake

(1) A party may only avoid the contract for mistake if, when the contract was concluded, the mistake was of such importance that a reasonable person in the same situation as the party in error would only have concluded the contract on materially different terms or would not have concluded it at all if the true state of affairs had been known, and

(a) the other party made the same mistake, or caused the mistake, or knew or ought to have known of the mistake and it was contrary to reasonable commercial standards of fair dealing to leave the mistaken party in error; or

(b) the other party had not at the time of avoidance acted in reliance on the contract.

(2) However, a party may not avoid the contract if

(a) it was grossly negligent in committing the mistake; or

(b) the mistake relates to a matter in regard to which the risk of mistake was assumed or, having regard to the circumstances, should be borne by the mistaken party.

COMMENT

This article states the conditions necessary for a mistake to be relevant with a view to avoidance of the contract. The introductory part of para. (1) determines the conditions under which a mistake is sufficiently serious to be taken into account; sub-paras. (a) and (b) of para. (1) add the conditions regarding the party other than the mistaken party; para. (2) deals with the conditions regarding the mistaken party.

1. Serious mistake

To be relevant, a mistake must be serious. Its weight and importance are to be assessed by reference to a combined objective/subjective standard, namely what "a reasonable person in the same situation as the party in error" would have done if it had known the true circumstances at the time of the conclusion of the contract. If it would not have contracted at all, or would have done so only on materially different terms, then, and only then, is the mistake considered to be serious. In this context the introductory part of para. (1) relies on an open-ended formula, rather than indicating specific essential elements of the contract to which the mistake must relate. This flexible approach allows full account to be taken of the intentions of the parties and the circumstances of the case. In ascertaining the parties' intentions, the rules of interpretation laid down in Chapter 4 must be applied. General commercial standards and relevant usages will be particularly important. Normally in commercial transactions certain mistakes, such as those concerning the value of goods or services or mere expectations or motivations of the mistaken party, are not considered to be relevant. The same is true of mistakes as to the identity of the other party or its personal qualities, although special circumstances may sometimes render such mistakes relevant (e.g. when services to be rendered require certain personal qualifications or when a loan is based upon the credit-worthiness of the borrower). The fact that a reasonable person would consider the circumstances erroneously assumed to be essential is however not sufficient, since additional requirements concerning both the mistaken and the other party must be met if a mistake is to become relevant.

2. Conditions concerning the party other than the mistaken party

A mistaken party may avoid the contract only if the other party satisfies one of four conditions laid down in para. (1). The first three conditions indicated in sub-para. (a) have in common the fact that the other party does not deserve protection because of its involvement in one way or another with the mistaken party's error. The first condition is that both parties laboured under the same mistake. **Illustration**

> 1. A and B, when concluding a contract for the sale of a sports car, were not and could not have been aware of the fact that the car had in the meantime been stolen. Avoidance of the contract is admissible.

However, if the parties erroneously believe the object of the contract to be in existence at the time of the conclusion of the contract, while in reality it had already been destroyed, Art. 3.3 has to be taken into account. The second condition is that the error of the mistaken party is caused by the other party. This is the case whenever the error can be traced to specific representations made by the latter party, be they express or implied, negligent or innocent, or to conduct which in the circumstances amounts to a representation. Even silence may cause an error. A mere "puff" in advertising or in negotiations will normally be tolerated. If the error was caused intentionally, Art. 3.8 applies.

The third condition is that the other party knew or ought to have known of the error of the mistaken party and that it was contrary to reasonable commercial standards of fair dealing to leave the mistaken party in error. What the other party ought to have known is what should have been known to a reasonable person in the same situation as that party. In order to avoid the contract the mistaken party must also show that the other party was under a duty to inform it of its error. The fourth condition is laid down in sub-para. (b) and is that the party other than the mistaken party had not, up to the time of avoidance, acted in reliance on the contract. For the time of avoidance, see Arts. 3.15 and 1.9.

3. Conditions concerning the mistaken party

Para. (2) of the present article mentions two cases in which the mistaken party may not avoid the contract.

The first of these, dealt with in sub-para. (a), is that the error is due to the gross negligence of the mistaken party. In such a situation it would be unfair to the other party to allow the mistaken party to avoid the contract. Sub-para. (b) contemplates the situation where the mistaken party either has assumed the risk of mistake or where this risk should in the circumstances be borne by it. An assumption of the risk of mistake is a frequent feature of speculative contracts. A party may conclude a contract in the hope that its assumption of the existence of certain facts will prove to be correct, but may nevertheless undertake to assume the risk of this not being so. In such circumstances it will not be entitled to avoid the contract for its mistake. **Illustration**

> 2. A sells to B a picture "attributed" to the relatively unknown painter C at a fair price for such paintings. It is subsequently discovered that the work was painted by the famous artist D. A cannot avoid its contract with B on the ground of its mistake, since the fact that the picture was only "attributed" to C implied the risk that it might have been painted by a more famous artist.

Sometimes both parties assume a risk. However, speculative contracts involving conflicting expectations of future developments, e.g. those concerning prices and exchange rates, may not be avoided on the ground of mistake, since the mistake would not be one as to facts existing at the time of the conclusion of the contract.

ARTICLE 3.6 – Error in expression or transmission

An error occurring in the expression or transmission of a declaration is considered to be a mistake of the person from whom the declaration emanated.

COMMENT

This article equates an error in the expression or transmission of a declaration with an ordinary mistake of the person making the declaration or sending it and thus the rules of Art. 3.5 and of Arts. 3.12 to 3.19 apply also to these kinds of error.

1. Relevant mistake

If an error in expression or transmission is of sufficient magnitude (especially if it has resulted in the misstatement of figures), the receiver will be, or ought to be, aware of the error. Since nothing in the Principles prevents the receiver/ offeree from accepting the erroneously expressed or transmitted offer, it is for the sender/offeror to invoke the error and to avoid the contract provided that the conditions of Art. 3.5 are met, in particular that it was contrary to reasonable commercial standards of fair dealing for the receiver/offeree not to inform the sender/offeror of the error.

In some cases the risk of the error may have been assumed by, or may have to be imposed upon, the sender if it uses a method of transmission which it knows or ought to know to be unsafe either in general or in the special circumstances of the case. **Illustration**

> A, a potential Italian client, asks B, an English law firm, for legal advice and by way of reply receives a telegram indicating that B's hourly rate is "££ 150", whereas the form handed by B to the English post office had read "££ 250". Since it is well known that numbers in telegrams are often wrongly transmitted, B is considered to have assumed that risk and is not entitled to invoke the error in the transmission, even if the other conditions of Art. 3.5 are met.

2. Mistakes on the part of the receiver

Transmission ends as soon as the message reaches the receiver. See Art. 1.9. If the message is correctly transmitted, but the receiver misunderstands its content, the case falls outside the scope of the present article. If the message is correctly transmitted to the receiver's machine which, however, due to a technical fault, prints out a mutilated text, the case is again outside the scope of this article. The same is true if, at the receiver's request, a message is given orally to the receiver's messenger who misunderstands it or transmits it wrongly. In the two above-mentioned situations the receiver may however be entitled to invoke its own mistake in accordance with Art. 3.5, if it replies to the sender and bases its reply upon its own misunderstanding of the sender's message and if all the conditions of Art. 3.5 are met.

ARTICLE 3.7 – Remedies for non-performance

A party is not entitled to avoid the contract on the ground of mistake if the circumstances on which that party relies afford, or could have afforded, a remedy for non-performance.

COMMENT

1. Remedies for non-performance preferred

This article is intended to resolve the conflict which may arise between the remedy of avoidance for mistake and the remedies for non-performance. In the event of such a conflict, preference is given to the remedies for non-performance since they seem to be better suited and are more flexible than the radical solution of avoidance.

2. Actual and potential conflicts

An actual conflict between the remedies for mistake and those for non-performance arises whenever the two sets of remedies are invoked in relation to what are essentially the same facts.

Illustration

> A, a farmer, who finds a rusty cup on the land sells it to B, an art dealer, for 100,000 Austrian schillings. The high price is based upon

the assumption of both parties that the cup is made of silver (other silver objects had previously been found on the land). It subsequently turns out that the object in question is an ordinary iron cup worth only 1,000 schillings. B refuses to accept the cup and to pay for it on the ground that it lacks the assumed quality. B also avoids the contract on the ground of mistake as to the quality of the cup. B is entitled only to the remedies for non-performance. It may be that the conflict between the two sets of remedies is only potential, since the mistaken party could have relied upon a remedy for non-performance, but is actually precluded from doing so by special circumstances, for example because a statutory limitation period has lapsed. Even in such a case the present article applies with the consequence that the remedy of avoidance for mistake is excluded.

ARTICLE 3.8 – Fraud

A party may avoid the contract when it has been led to conclude the contract by the other party's fraudulent representation, including language or practices, or fraudulent non-disclosure of circumstances which, according to reasonable commercial standards of fair dealing, the latter party should have disclosed.

COMMENT

1. Fraud and mistake

Avoidance of a contract by a party on the ground of fraud bears some resemblance to avoidance for a certain type of mistake. Fraud may be regarded as a special case of mistake caused by the other party. Fraud, like mistake, may involve either representations, whether express or implied, of false facts or non-disclosure of true facts.

2. Notion of fraud

The decisive distinction between fraud and mistake lies in the nature and purpose of the defrauding party's representations or non-disclosure. What entitles the defrauded party to avoid the contract is the "fraudulent" representation or non-disclosure of relevant facts. Such conduct is fraudulent if it is intended to lead the other party into error and thereby to gain an advantage to the detriment of the other party. The reprehensible nature of fraud is such that it is a sufficient ground for avoidance without the need for the presence of the additional conditions laid down in Art. 3.5 for the mistake to become relevant. A mere "puff" in advertising or negotiations does not suffice.

ARTICLE 3.9 – Threat

A party may avoid the contract when it has been led to conclude the contract by the other party's unjustified threat which, having regard to the circumstances, is so imminent and serious as to leave the first party no reasonable alternative. In particular, a threat is unjustified if the act or omission with which a party has been threatened is wrongful in itself, or it is wrongful to use it as a means to obtain the conclusion of the contract.

COMMENT

This article permits the avoidance of a contract on the ground of threat.

1. Threat must be imminent and serious

Threat of itself is not sufficient. It must be of so imminent and serious a character that the threatened person has no reasonable alternative but to conclude the contract on the terms proposed by the other party. The imminence and seriousness of the threat must be evaluated by an objective standard, taking into account the circumstances of the individual case.

2. Unjustified threat

The threat must in addition be unjustified. The second sentence of the present article sets out, by way of illustration, two examples of an unjustified threat. The first envisages a case where the act or omission with which the contracting party has been threatened is wrongful in itself (e.g. a physical attack). The second refers to a situation where the threatened act or omission is in itself lawful, but the purpose to be achieved is wrongful (e.g. the bringing of a court action for the sole purpose of inducing the other party to conclude the contract on the terms proposed).

Illustration

1. A, who is in default with the repayment of a loan, is threatened by B, the lender, with proceedings for the recovery of the money. The only purpose of this threat is to obtain on particularly advantageous terms a lease of A's warehouse. A signs the lease, but is entitled to avoid the contract.

3. Threat affecting reputation or economic interests

For the purpose of the application of the present article, threat need not necessarily be made against a person or property, but may also affect reputation or purely economic interests.

Illustration

2. Faced with a threat by the players of a basketball team to go on strike unless they receive a much higher bonus than had already been agreed for winning the four remaining matches of the season, the owner of the team agrees to pay the requested bonus. The owner is entitled to avoid the new contract with the players, since the strike would have led automatically to the team being relegated to a minor league and therefore represented a serious and imminent threat to both the reputation and the financial position of the club.

ARTICLE 3.10 – Gross disparity

(1) A party may avoid the contract or an individual term of it if, at the time of the conclusion of the contract, the contract or term unjustifiably gave the other party an excessive advantage. Regard is to be had, among other factors, to

(a) the fact that the other party has taken unfair advantage of the first party's dependence, economic distress or urgent needs, or of its improvidence, ignorance, inexperience or lack of bargaining skill, and

(b) the nature and purpose of the contract.

(2) Upon the request of the party entitled to avoidance, a court may adapt the contract or term in order to make it accord with reasonable commercial standards of fair dealing.

(3) A court may also adapt the contract or term upon the request of the party receiving notice of avoidance, provided that that party informs the other party of its request promptly after receiving such notice and before the other party has acted in reliance on it. The provisions of Article 3.13(2) apply accordingly.

COMMENT

1. Excessive advantage

This provision permits a party to avoid a contract in cases where there is a gross disparity between the obligations of the parties, which gives one party an unjustifiably excessive advantage. The excessive advantage must exist at the time of the conclusion of the contract. A contract which, although not grossly unfair when entered into, becomes so later may be adapted or terminated under the rules on hardship contained in Chapter 6, Section 2. As the term "excessive" advantage denotes, even a considerable disparity in the value and the price or some other element which upsets the equilibrium of performance and counter-performance is not sufficient to permit the avoidance or the adaptation of the contract under this article. What is required is that the disequilibrium is in the circumstances so great as to shock the conscience of a reasonable person.

2. Unjustifiable advantage

Not only must the advantage be excessive, it must also be unjustifiable. Whether this requirement is met will depend upon an evaluation of all the relevant circumstances of the case. Para. (1) of the present article refers in particular to two factors which deserve special attention in this connection.

a. *Unequal bargaining position*

The first factor is that one party has taken unfair advantage of the other party's dependence, economic distress or urgent needs, or its improvidence, ignorance, inexperience, or lack of bargaining skill (sub-para. (a)). As to the dependence of one party vis-à-vis the other, superior bargaining power due to market conditions alone is not sufficient. **Illustration**

A, the owner of an automobile factory, sells an outdated assembly line to B, a governmental agency from a country eager to set up its own automobile industry. Although A makes no

representations as to the efficiency of the assembly line, it succeeds in fixing a price which is manifestly excessive. B, after discovering that it has paid an amount which corresponds to that of a much more modern assembly line, may be entitled to avoid the contract.

b. *Nature and purpose of the contract*

The second factor to which special regard must be had is the nature and purpose of the contract (sub-para. (b)). There are situations where an excessive advantage is unjustifiable even if the party who will benefit from it has not abused the other party's weak bargaining position.

Whether this is the case will often depend upon the nature and purpose of the contract. Thus, a contract term providing for an extremely short period for giving notice of defects in goods or services to be supplied may or may not be excessively advantageous to the seller or supplier, depending on the character of the goods or services in question. Equally, an agent's fee expressed in terms of a fixed percentage of the price of the goods or services to be sold or rendered, although justified in the event of the agent's contribution to the conclusion of the transaction being substantial and/or the value of the goods or services concerned not being very high, may well turn out to confer an excessive advantage on the agent if the latter's contribution is almost negligible and/or the value of the goods or services are extraordinarily high.

c. *Other factors*

Other factors may need to be taken into consideration, for example the ethics prevailing in the business or trade.

3. Avoidance or adaptation

The avoidance of the contract or of any of its individual terms under this article is subject to the general rules laid down in Arts. 3.14 - 3.18. However, according to para. (2) of the present article, at the request of the party who is entitled to avoidance, the court may adapt the contract in order to bring it into accord with reasonable commercial standards of fair dealing. Similarly, according to para. (3) the party receiving notice of avoidance may also request such adaptation provided it informs the avoiding party of its request promptly after receiving the notice of avoidance, and before the avoiding party has acted in reliance on that notice. If the parties are in disagreement as to the procedure to be adopted, it will be for the court to decide whether the contract is to be avoided or adapted and, if adapted, on which terms. If, in its notice or subsequently, a party entitled to avoidance requests adaptation only, its right to avoidance will be lost. See Art. 3.13(2).

ARTICLE 3.11 – Third persons

(1) Where fraud, threat, gross disparity or a party's mistake is imputable to, or is known or ought to be known by, a third person for whose acts the other party is responsible, the contract may be avoided under the same conditions as if the behaviour or knowledge had been that of the party itself.

(2) Where fraud, threat or gross disparity is imputable to a third person for whose acts the other party is not responsible, the contract may be avoided if that party knew or ought to have known of the fraud, threat or disparity, or has not at the time of avoidance acted in reliance on the contract.

COMMENT

This article deals with situations, frequent in practice, in which a third person has been involved or has interfered in the negotiation process, and the ground for avoidance is in one way or another imputable to that person.

1. Third person for whom a party is responsible

Para. (1) is concerned with cases in which fraud, threat, gross disparity or a party's mistake is caused by a third person for whose acts the other party is responsible, or cases in which, without causing the mistake, the third person knew or ought to have known of it. A party is responsible for the acts of a third person in a variety of situations ranging from those in which that person is an agent of the party in question to those where the third person acts for the benefit of that party on its own initiative. In all such cases it seems justified to impute to that party the third person's acts or its knowledge, whether actual or constructive, of certain circumstances, and this irrespective of whether the party in question knew of the third person's acts.

2. Third person for whom a party is not responsible

Para. (2) deals with cases where a party is defrauded, threatened or otherwise unduly influenced by a third person for whom the other party is not responsible. Such acts may be imputed to the latter party only if it knew or ought to have known of them. There is however one exception to this rule: the defrauded, threatened or otherwise unduly influenced party is entitled to avoid the contract, even if the other party did not know of the third person's acts, whenever the latter party has not acted in reliance on the contract before the time of avoidance. This exception is justified because in this situation the other party is not in need of protection.

ARTICLE 3.12 – Confirmation

If the party entitled to avoid the contract expressly or impliedly confirms the contract after the period of time for giving notice of avoidance has begun to run, avoidance of the contract is excluded.

COMMENT

This article lays down the rule according to which the party entitled to avoid the contract may either expressly or impliedly confirm the contract. For there to be an implied confirmation it is not sufficient, for example, for the party entitled to avoid the contract to bring a claim against the other party based on the latter's non-performance. A confirmation can only be assumed if the other party acknowledges the claim or if a court action has been successful. There is also confirmation if the party entitled to avoidance continues to perform the contract without reserving its right to avoid the contract.

ARTICLE 3.13 – Loss of right to avoid

(1) If a party is entitled to avoid the contract for mistake but the other party declares itself willing to perform or performs the contract as it was understood by the party entitled to avoidance, the contract is considered to have been concluded as the latter party understood it. The other party must make such a declaration or render such performance promptly after having been informed of the manner in which the party entitled to avoidance had understood the contract and before that party has acted in reliance on a notice of avoidance.

(2) After such a declaration or performance the right to avoidance is lost and any earlier notice of avoidance is ineffective.

COMMENT

1. Performance of the contract as understood by the mistaken party

According to this article a mistaken party may be prevented from avoiding the contract if the other party declares itself willing to perform or actually performs the contract as it was understood by the mistaken party. The interest of the other party in so doing may lie in the benefit to be derived from the contract, even in its adapted form.

Such regard for the interests of the other party is only justified in the case of mistake and not in other cases of defective consent (threat and fraud) where it would be extremely difficult to expect the parties to keep the contract alive.

2. Decision to be made promptly

The other party has to declare its decision to perform or actually to perform the contract in its adapted form promptly after having been informed of the manner in which the mistaken party had understood the contract. How the other party is to receive the information about the erroneous understanding of the terms of the contract will depend on the circumstances of the case.

3. Loss of right to avoid

Para. (2) expressly states that after the other party's declaration or performance the right of the mistaken party to avoid the contract is lost and that any earlier notice of avoidance becomes ineffective. Conversely, the other party is no longer entitled to adapt the contract if the mistaken party has not only given notice of avoidance but has also acted in reliance on that notice.

4. Damages

The adaptation of the contract by the other party does not preclude the mistaken party from claiming damages in accordance with Art. 3.18 if it has suffered loss which is not compensated by the adaptation of the contract.

ARTICLE 3.14 – Notice of avoidance

The right of a party to avoid the contract is exercised by notice to the other party.

COMMENT

1. The requirement of notice

This article states the principle that the right of a party to avoid the contract is exercised by notice to the other party without the need for any intervention by a court.

2. Form and content of notice

No provision is made in this article for any specific requirement as to the form or content of the notice of avoidance. It follows that in accordance with the general rule laid down in Art. 1.9(1), the notice may be given by any means appropriate to the circumstances. As to the content of the notice, it is not necessary that the term "avoidance" actually be used, or that the reasons for avoiding the contract be stated expressly. However, for the sake of clarity a party would be well advised to give some reasons for the avoidance in its notice, although in cases of fraud or gross disparity the avoiding party may assume that those reasons are already known to the other party. **Illustration**

A, B's employer, threatens B with dismissal if B does not sell A a Louis XVI chest of drawers. B ultimately agrees to the sale. Two days later A receives a letter from B announcing B's resignation and stating that B has sold the chest of drawers to C. B's letter is sufficient notice of avoidance of the contract of sale with A.

3. Notice must be received

The notice of avoidance becomes effective when it reaches the other party. See Art. 1.9(2).

ARTICLE 3.15 – Time limits

(1) Notice of avoidance shall be given within a reasonable time, having regard to the circumstances, after the avoiding party knew or could not have been unaware of the relevant facts or became capable of acting freely.

(2) Where an individual term of the contract may be avoided by a party under Article 3.10, the period of time for giving notice of avoidance begins to run when that term is asserted by the other party.

COMMENT

According to para. (1) of this article notice of avoidance must be given within a reasonable time after the avoiding party became aware or could not have been unaware of the relevant facts or became capable of acting freely. More precisely, the mistaken or defrauded party must give notice of avoidance within a reasonable time after it became aware or could no longer be unaware of the mistake or fraud. The same applies in cases of gross disparity which result from an abuse of the innocent party's ignorance, improvidence or inexperience. In cases of threat or abuse of the innocent party's dependence, economic distress or urgent needs the period runs from the time the threatened or abused party becomes capable of acting freely. In case of avoidance of an individual term of the contract in accordance with Art. 3.10, para. (2) of this article states that the period of time for giving notice begins to run when that term is asserted by the party.

ARTICLE 3.16 – Partial avoidance

Where a ground of avoidance affects only individual terms of the contract, the effect of avoidance is limited to those terms unless, having regard to the circumstances, it is unreasonable to uphold the remaining contract.

COMMENT

This article deals with situations where the grounds of avoidance affect only individual terms of the contract. In such cases the effects of avoidance will be limited to the terms affected unless it would in the circumstances be unreasonable to uphold the remaining contract. This will generally depend upon whether or not a party would have entered into the contract had it envisaged that the terms in question would have been affected by grounds of avoidance.

Illustrations

1. A, a contractor, agrees to build two houses on plots of land X and Y for B, one of which B intends to live in and the other to rent. B was mistaken in assuming that it had a licence to build on both plots, since in fact the licence covered only plot X. Unless the circumstances indicate otherwise, notwithstanding the avoidance of the contract concerning the building of the house on plot Y, it would be reasonable to uphold the remaining contract concerning the building of the house on plot X.

. . .

ARTICLE 3.17 – Retroactive effect of avoidance

(1) Avoidance takes effect retroactively.

(2) On avoidance either party may claim restitution of whatever it has supplied under the contract or the part of it avoided, provided that it concurrently makes restitution of whatever it has received under the contract or the part of it avoided or, if it cannot make restitution in kind, it makes an allowance for what it has received.

COMMENT

1. Avoidance generally of retroactive effect

Para. (1) of this article states the rule that avoidance takes effect retroactively. In other words, the contract is considered never to have existed. In the case of a partial avoidance under Art. 3.16 the rule applies only to the avoided part of the contract. There are however individual terms of the contract which may survive even in cases of total avoidance. Arbitration, jurisdiction and choice-of-law clauses are considered to be different from the other terms of the contract which may be upheld notwithstanding the avoidance of the contract in whole or in part. Whether in fact such clauses remain operative is to be determined by the applicable domestic law.

2. Restitution

According to para. (2) of the present article either party may claim restitution of what it has supplied under the contract or the part of it avoided. The only condition for such restitution is that each party makes restitution of whatever it has received under the contract or the part of it avoided. If restitution in kind is not possible, as is typically the case with services, a party must make an allowance for what it has received, except where the performance received is of no value to it. **Illustration**

A commissions B to decorate a restaurant. B begins the work. When A later discovers that B is not the famous decorator who had made similar decorations in a number of another restaurants, A avoids the contract. Since the decorations so far made cannot be returned and they have no value for A, B is not entitled to any allowance from A for the work done.

ARTICLE 3.18 – Damages

Irrespective of whether or not the contract has been avoided, the party who knew or ought to have known of the ground for avoidance is liable for damages so as to put the other party in the same position in which it would have been if it had not concluded the contract.

COMMENT

1. Damages if ground for avoidance known to the other party

This article provides that a party which knew or ought to have known of a ground for avoidance is liable for damages to the other party. The right to damages arises irrespective of whether or not the contract has been avoided.

2. The measure of damages

Unlike the damages in case of non-performance under Chapter 7, Section 4, the damages contemplated by the present article are intended simply to put the other party in the same position in which it would have been if it had not concluded the contract. **Illustration**

A sells software to B, and could not have been unaware of B's mistake as to its appropriateness for the use intended by B. Irrespective of whether or not B avoids the contract, A is liable to B for all the expenses incurred by B in training its personnel in the use of the software, but not for the loss suffered by B as a consequence of the impossibility to use the software for the intended purpose.

ARTICLE 3.19 – Mandatory character of the provisions

The provisions of this Chapter are mandatory, except insofar as they relate to the binding force of mere agreement, initial impossibility or mistake.

COMMENT

This article declares the provisions of this Chapter relating to fraud, threat and gross disparity to be of a mandatory character. It would be contrary to good faith for the parties to exclude or modify these provisions when concluding their contract. However, nothing prevents the party entitled to avoidance to waive that right once it learns of the true facts or is able to act freely. On the other hand, the provisions of this Chapter relating to the binding force of mere agreement, to initial impossibility or to mistake are not mandatory. Thus the parties may well reintroduce special requirements of domestic law, such as consideration or cause; they may likewise agree that their contract shall be invalid in case of initial impossibility, or that mistake by one of them is not a ground for avoidance.

ARTICLE 3.20 – Unilateral declarations

The provisions of this Chapter apply with appropriate adaptations to any communication of intention addressed by one party to the other.

COMMENT

This article takes account of the fact that apart from the contract itself the parties, either before or after the conclusion of the contract, often exchange a number of communications of intention which may likewise be affected by invalidity. a commercial setting, the most important example of unilateral communications of intention which are external, but preparatory, to a contract are bids for investment, works, delivery of goods or provision of services. Communications of intention made after the conclusion of a contract take a variety of forms, such as notices, declarations, demands and requests. In particular, waivers and declarations by which a party assumes an obligation may be affected by a defect of consent.

CHAPTER 4 – INTERPRETATION

ARTICLE 4.1 – Intention of the parties

(1) A contract shall be interpreted according to the common intention of the parties.

(2) If such an intention cannot be established, the contract shall be interpreted according to the meaning that reasonable persons of the same kind as the parties would give to it in the same circumstances.

COMMENT

1. Common intention of the parties to prevail

Para. (1) of this article lays down the principle that in determining the meaning to be attached to the terms of a contract, preference is to be given to the intention common to the parties. In consequence, a contract term may be given a meaning which differs both from the literal sense of the language used and from the meaning which a reasonable person would attach to it, provided that such a different understanding was common to the parties at the time of the conclusion of the contract. The practical importance of the principle should not be over-estimated, first because parties to commercial transactions are unlikely to use language in a sense entirely different from that usually attached to it, and secondly because even if this were to be the case it would be extremely difficult, once a dispute arises, to prove that a particular meaning which one of the parties claims to have been their common intention was in fact shared by the other party at the time of the conclusion of the contract.

2. Recourse to the understanding of reasonable persons

For those cases where the common intention of the parties cannot be established, para. (2) provides that the contract shall be interpreted in accordance with the meaning which reasonable persons of the same kind as the parties would give to it in the same circumstances. The test is not a general and abstract criterion of reasonableness, but rather the understanding which could reasonably be expected of persons with, for example, the same linguistic knowledge, technical skill, or business experience as the parties.

3. How to establish the common intention of the parties or to determine the understanding of reasonable persons

In order to establish whether the parties had a common intention and, if so, what that common intention was, regard is to be had to all the relevant circumstances of the case, the most important of which are listed in Art. 4.3. The same applies to the determination of the understanding of reasonable persons when no common intention of the parties can be established.

4. Interpretation of standard terms

Both the "subjective" test laid down in para. (1) and the "reasonableness" test in para. (2) may not always be appropriate in the context of standard terms. Indeed, given their special nature and purpose, standard terms should be interpreted primarily in accordance with the reasonable expectations of their average users irrespective of the actual understanding which either of the parties to the contract concerned, or reasonable persons of the same kind as the parties, might have had. For the definition of "standard terms", see Art. 2.19(2).

ARTICLE 4.2 – Interpretation of statements and other conduct

(1) The statements and other conduct of a party shall be interpreted according to that party's intention if the other party knew or could not have been unaware of that intention.

(2) If the preceding paragraph is not applicable, such statements and other conduct shall be interpreted according to the meaning that a reasonable person of the same kind as the other party would give to it in the same circumstances.

COMMENT

1. Interpretation of unilateral acts

By analogy to the criteria laid down in Art. 4.1 with respect to the contract as a whole, this article states that in the interpretation of unilateral statements or conduct preference is to be given to the intention of the party concerned, provided that the other party knew (or could not have been unaware) of that intention, and that in all other cases such statements or conduct are to be interpreted according to the understanding that a reasonable person of the same kind as the other party would have had in the same circumstances. In practice the principal field of application of this article, which corresponds almost literally to Art. 8(1) and (2) CISG, will be in the process of the formation of contracts where parties make statements and engage in conduct whose precise legal significance may have to be established in order to determine whether or not a contract is ultimately concluded. There are however also unilateral acts performed after the conclusion of the contract which may give rise to problems of interpretation: for example, a notification of defects in goods, notice of avoidance or of termination of the contract, etc.

2. How to establish the intention of the party performing the act or to determine the understanding of a reasonable person

In applying both the "subjective" test laid down in para. (1) and the "reasonableness" test in para. (2), regard is to be had to all the relevant circumstances, the most important of which are listed in Art. 4.3.

ARTICLE 4.3 – Relevant circumstances

In applying Articles 4.1 and 4.2, regard shall be had to all the circumstances, including (a) preliminary negotiations between the parties; (b) practices which the parties have established between themselves; (c) the conduct of the parties subsequent to the conclusion of the contract; (d) the nature and purpose of the contract; (e) the meaning commonly given to terms and expressions in the trade concerned; (f) usages.

COMMENT

1. Circumstances relevant in the interpretation process

This article indicates circumstances which have to be taken into consideration when applying both the "subjective" test and the "reasonableness" test in Arts. 4.1 and 4.2. The list mentions only those circumstances which are the most important and is in no way intended to be exhaustive.

2. "Particular" and "general" circumstances compared

Of the circumstances listed in the present article some relate to the particular relationship which exists between the parties concerned, while others are of a more general character. Although in principle all the circumstances listed may be relevant in a given case, the first three are likely to have greater weight in the application of the "subjective" test. **Illustrations**

    1. A contract for the writing of a book between A and B, a publisher, indicates that the book should consist of "about 300 pages". During their negotiations B had assured A that an approximate indication of the number of pages was necessary for administrative reasons and that A was not bound to stick precisely to that number of pages, but could exceed it, substantially if need be. A submits a manuscript of 500 pages. In interpreting the meaning of "about 300 pages" due consideration should be given to these preliminary negotiations. See Art. 4.3(a).

    2. A, a Canadian manufacturer, and B, a United States retailer, conclude a number of contracts for the delivery of optical lenses in which the price is always expressed in Canadian dollars. A makes B a new offer indicating the price in "dollars" without further specification, but intending to refer again to Canadian dollars. In the absence of any indication to the contrary, A's intention will prevail. See Art. 4.3(b).

The remaining circumstances listed in this article, i.e. the nature and purpose of the contract, the meaning commonly given to terms and expressions in a trade concerned and usages, are important primarily, although not exclusively, in the application of the "reasonableness" test. The criteria in sub-paras. (e) and (f) may at first sight appear to overlap. There is however a difference between them: while the "usages" apply only if they meet the requirements laid down in Art. 1.8, the "meaning commonly given [...] in the trade concerned" can be relevant even if it is peculiar to a trade sector to which only one, or even neither, party belongs, provided that the expression or term concerned is one which is typical in that trade sector. **Illustrations**

    3. A and B conclude a contract for the sale of a cargo of oil at US$ 20.5 per barrel. The parties subsequently disagree on the size of the barrel to which they had referred, A having intended a barrel of 42 standard gallons and B one of 36 Imperial gallons. In the absence of any

indications to the contrary, A's understanding prevails, since in the international oil trade it is a usage to measure barrels in standard gallons. See Art. 4.3(f).

4. A, a shipowner, concludes a charterparty agreement with B for the carriage of grain containing the standard term "whether in berth or not" with respect to the commencement of the lay-time of the ship after its reaching the port of destination. When it subsequently emerges that the parties attached different meanings to the term, preference should, in the absence of any indication to the contrary, be given to the meaning commonly attached to it in the shipping trade since the term is typical in the shipping trade. See Art. 4.3(e).

3. "Merger" clauses

Parties to international commercial transactions frequently include a provision indicating that the contract document completely embodies the terms on which they have agreed. For the effect of these so-called "merger" or "integration" clauses, in particular whether and to what extent they exclude the relevance of preliminary negotiations between the parties, albeit only for the purpose of the interpretation of the contract, see Art. 2.17.

ARTICLE 4.4 – Reference to contract or statement as a whole

Terms and expressions shall be interpreted in the light of the whole contract or statement in which they appear.

COMMENT

1. Interpretation in the light of the whole contract or statement

Terms and expressions used by one or both parties are clearly not intended to operate in isolation but have to be seen as an integral part of their general context. In consequence they should be interpreted in the light of the whole contract or statement in which they appear.

Illustration

A, a licensee, hears that, despite a provision in their contract granting A an exclusive licence, B, the licensor, has concluded a similar contract with C, one of A's competitors. A sends B a letter complaining of B's breach and ending with the words "your behaviour has clearly demonstrated that it was a mistake on our part to rely on your professional correctness. We hereby avoid the contract we have with you". Despite the use of the term "avoid", A's words interpreted in the light of the letter as a whole, must be understood as a notice of termination.

2. In principle no hierarchy among contract terms

In principle there is no hierarchy among contract terms, in the sense that their respective importance for the interpretation of the remaining part of the contract is the same regardless of the order in which they appear. There are, however, exceptions to this rule. First, declarations of intent made in the preamble may or may not be of relevance for the interpretation of the operative provisions of the contract. Secondly, it goes without saying that, in cases of conflict, provisions of a specific character prevail over provisions laying down more general rules. Finally, the parties may themselves expressly establish a hierarchy among the different provisions or parts of their contract. This is frequently the case with complex agreements consisting of different documents relating to the legal, economic and technical aspects of the transaction.

ARTICLE 4.5 – All terms to be given effect

Contract terms shall be interpreted so as to give effect to all the terms rather than to deprive some of them of effect.

COMMENT

It is to be expected that when drafting their contract parties do not use words to no purpose. It is for this reason that this article lays down the rule that unclear contract terms should be interpreted so as to give effect to all the terms rather than to deprive some of them of effect.

The rule however comes into play only if the terms in question remain unclear notwithstanding the application of the basic rules of interpretation laid down in Arts. 4.1 - 4.3. **Illustration**

A, a commercial television network, enters into an agreement with B, a film distributor, for the periodic supply of a certain number of films to be transmitted on A's network in the afternoon, when only those films that are admissible for all viewers may be transmitted. According to the contract the films submitted must "have passed the admission test" of the competent censorship commission. A dispute arises between A and B as to the meaning of this term. B maintains that

it implies only that the films must have been released for circulation, even if they are X-rated, while A insists that they must have been classified as admissible for everybody. If it is not possible otherwise to establish the meaning to be attached to the term in question, A's understanding prevails since B's interpretation would deprive the provision of any effect.

ARTICLE 4.6 – Contra proferentem rule

If contract terms supplied by one party are unclear, an interpretation against that party is preferred.

COMMENT

A party may be responsible for the formulation of a particular contract term, either because that party has drafted it or otherwise supplied it, for example, by using standard terms prepared by others. Such a party should bear the risk of possible lack of clarity of the formulation chosen. It is for this reason that the present article states that if contract terms supplied by one party are unclear, there is a preference for their interpretation against that party. The extent to which this rule applies will depend on the circumstances of the case; the less the contract term in question was the subject of further negotiations between the parties, the greater the justification for interpreting it against the party who included it in the contract. **Illustration**

A contract between A, a contractor, and B for the construction of an industrial plant contains a provision drafted by A and not discussed further stating that "[t]he Contractor shall be liable for and shall indemnify the Purchaser for all losses, expenses and claims in respect of any loss of or damage to physical property (other than the works), death or personal injury caused by negligence of the Contractor, its employees and agents". One of A's employees plays around with some of B's equipment after working hours and damages it. A denies liability, contending that the provision in question covers only cases where A's employees act within the scope of their employment. In the absence of any indication to the contrary, the provision will be interpreted in the manner which is less favourable to A, i.e. as also covering cases where his employees are not acting within the scope of their employment.

ARTICLE 4.7 – Linguistic discrepancies

Where a contract is drawn up in two or more language versions which are equally authoritative there is, in case of discrepancy between the versions, a preference for the interpretation according to a version in which the contract was originally drawn up.

COMMENT

International commercial contracts are often drawn up in two or more language versions which may diverge on specific points. Sometimes the parties expressly indicate which version shall prevail. If all versions are equally authoritative the question arises of how possible discrepancies should be dealt with. The present article does not lay down a hard and fast rule, but merely indicates that preference should be given to the version in which the contract was originally drawn up or, should it have been drawn up in more than one original language version, to one of those versions. **Illustration**

1. A and B, neither of them native English speakers, negotiate and draw up a contract in English before translating it into their respective languages. The parties agree that all three versions are equally authoritative. In case of divergencies between the texts, the English version will prevail unless circumstances indicate the contrary.

A situation where a different solution may be preferable could arise where the parties have contracted on the basis of internationally and widely known instruments such as INCOTERMS or the *Uniform Customs and Practices on Documentary Credits*. In case of divergencies between the different versions used by the parties it may be preferable to refer to yet another version if that version is much clearer than the ones used.

Illustration

    2. A contract between a Mexican and a Swedish company drawn up in three equally authoritative versions, Spanish, Swedish and English, contains a reference to INCOTERMS 1990. If the French version of INCOTERMS is much clearer than the other three on a point in dispute, that version might be referred to.

ARTICLE 4.8 – Supplying an omitted term

(1) Where the parties to a contract have not agreed with respect to a term which is important for a determination of their rights and duties, a term which is appropriate in the circumstances shall be supplied.

(2) In determining what is an appropriate term regard shall be had, among other factors, to (a) the intention of the parties; (b) the nature and purpose of the contract; (c) good faith and fair dealing; (d) reasonableness.

COMMENT

1. Supplying of omitted terms and interpretation

    Articles 4.1 - 4.7 deal with the interpretation of contracts in the strict sense, i.e. with the determination of the meaning which should be given to contract terms which are unclear. This article addresses a different though related issue, namely that of the supplying of omitted terms. Omitted terms or gaps occur when, after the conclusion of the contract, a question arises which the parties have not regulated in their contract at all, either because they preferred not to deal with it or simply because they did not foresee it.

2. When omitted terms are to be supplied

    In many cases of omitted terms or gaps in the contract the Principles will themselves provide a solution to the issue. See, for example, Arts. 5.6, (Determination of quality of performance), 5.7 (Price determination), 6.1.1 (Time of performance), 6.1.4 (Order of performance), 6.1.6 (Place of performance) and 6.1.10 (Currency not expressed). See also, in general, Art. 5.2 on implied obligations. However, even when there are such suppletive, or "stop-gap", rules of a general character they may not be applicable in a given case because they would not provide a solution appropriate in the circumstances in view of the expectations of the parties or the special nature of the contract. This article then applies.

3. Criteria for the supplying of omitted terms

    The terms supplied under the present article must be appropriate to the circumstances of the case. In order to determine what is appropriate, regard is first of all to be had to the intention of the parties as inferred from, among other factors, the terms expressly stated in the contract, prior negotiations or any conduct subsequent to the conclusion of the contract. **Illustration**

    1. The parties to a construction contract agree on a special interest rate to be paid by the purchaser in the event of delay in payment of the price. Before the beginning of the work, the parties decide to terminate the contract. When the constructor delays restitution of the advance payment the question arises of the applicable interest rate. In the absence of an express term in the contract dealing with this question, the circumstances may make it appropriate to apply the special interest rate agreed for delay in payment of the price by the purchaser also to delay in restitution by the constructor.

    If the intention of the parties cannot be ascertained, the term to be supplied may be determined in accordance with the nature and purpose of the contract, and the principles of good faith and fair dealing and reasonableness. **Illustration**

    2. A distribution franchise agreement provides that the franchisee may not engage in any similar business for a year after the termination of the agreement. Although the agreement is silent on the territorial scope of this prohibition, it is, in view of the particular nature and purpose of a franchise agreement, appropriate that the prohibition be restricted to the territory where the franchisee had exploited the franchise.

CHAPTER 5 – CONTENT

ARTICLE 5.1 – Express and implied obligations
The contractual obligations of the parties may be express or implied.
COMMENT

This provision restates the widely accepted principle according to which the obligations of the parties are not necessarily limited to that which has been expressly stipulated in the contract. Other obligations may be implicit (see Art. 5.2, comments and illustrations).

Close links exist between this rule and some of the other provisions of the Principles. Thus Art. 5.1 is a direct corollary of the rule according to which "[e]ach party must act in accordance with good faith and fair dealing in international trade" (Art. 1.7). Insofar as the rules on interpretation (Chapter 4) provide criteria for filling lacunae (besides criteria for solving ambiguities), those rules may assist in determining the precise content of the contract and therefore in establishing the terms which must be considered as implied.

ARTICLE 5.2 – Implied obligations
Implied obligations stem from (a) the nature and purpose of the contract; (b) practices established between the parties and usages; (c) good faith and fair dealing; (d) reasonableness.
COMMENT

Art. 5.2 describes the sources of implied obligations. Different reasons may account for the fact that they have not been expressly stated. The implied obligations may for example have been so obvious, given the nature or the purpose of the obligation, that the parties felt that the obligations "went without saying". Alternatively, they may already have been included in the practices established between the parties or prescribed by trade usages according to Art. 1.8. Yet again, they may be a consequence of the principles of good faith and fair dealing and reasonableness in contractual relations.
Illustrations

1. A rents a full computer network to B and installs it. The contract says nothing as to A's possible obligation to give B at least some basic information concerning the operation of the system. This may however be considered to be an implied obligation since it is obvious, and necessary for the accomplishment of the purpose of such a contract, that the provider of sophisticated goods should supply the other party with a minimum of information. See Art. 5.2(a).

2. A broker who has negotiated a charterparty claims the commission due. Although the brokerage contract is silent as to the time when the commission is due, the usages of the sector can provide an implied term according to which the commission is due, for example only when the hire is earned, or alternatively when the charterparty was signed, regardless of whether or not the hire will effectively be paid. See Art. 5.2(b).

3. A and B, who have entered into the negotiation of a co-operation agreement, conclude an agreement concerning a complex feasibility study, which will be most time-consuming for A. Long before the study is completed, B decides that it will not pursue the negotiation of the co-operation agreement. Even though nothing has been stipulated regarding such a situation, good faith requires B to notify A of its decision without delay. See Art. 5.2(c).

ARTICLE 5.3 – Co-operation between the parties
Each party shall cooperate with the other party when such co-operation may reasonably be expected for the performance of that party's obligations.
COMMENT

A contract is not merely a meeting point for conflicting interests but must also, to a certain extent, be viewed as a common project in which each party must cooperate. This view is clearly related to the principle of good faith and fair dealing (Art. 1.7) which permeates the law of contract, as well as to the obligation to mitigate harm in the event of non-performance (Art. 7.4.8).

The duty of co-operation must of course be confined within certain limits (the provision refers to reasonable expectations), so as not to upset the allocation of duties in the performance of the contract. Although the principal concern of the provision is the duty not to hinder the other party's performance, there may also be circumstances which call for more active co-operation. **Illustrations**

1. A, after contracting with B for the immediate delivery of a certain quantity of oil, buys all the available oil on the spot market from another source. Such conduct, which will hinder B in performing its obligation, is contrary to the duty of co-operation.

. . .

ARTICLE 5.4 – Duty to achieve a specific result; Duty of best efforts

(1) To the extent that an obligation of a party involves a duty to achieve a specific result, that party is bound to achieve that result.

(2) To the extent that an obligation of a party involves a duty of best efforts in the performance of an activity, that party is bound to make such efforts as would be made by a reasonable person of the same kind in the same circumstances.

COMMENT

1. Distinction between the duty to achieve a specific result and the duty of best efforts

The degree of diligence required of a party in the performance of an obligation varies considerably depending upon the nature of the obligation incurred. Sometimes a party is bound only by a duty of best efforts. That party must then exert the efforts that a reasonable person of the same kind would exert in the same circumstances, but does not guarantee the achievement of a specific result. In other cases, however, the obligation is more onerous and such a specific result is promised.

The distinction between a "duty to achieve a specific result" and a "duty of best efforts" corresponds to two frequent and typical degrees of severity in the assumption of a contractual obligation, although it does not encompass all possible situations.

Obligations of both types may coexist in the same contract. For instance, a firm that repairs a defective machine may be considered to be under a duty of best efforts concerning the quality of the repair work in general, and under a duty to achieve a specific result as regards the replacement of certain spare parts.

2. Distinction provides criteria for determining whether a party has performed its obligations

Taken together, the two paragraphs of this article provide judges and arbitrators with criteria by which correct performance can be evaluated. In the case of an obligation to achieve a specific result, a party is bound simply to achieve the promised result, failure to achieve which amounts in itself to non-performance, subject to the application of the force majeure provision (Art. 7.1.7). On the other hand, the assessment of non-performance of an obligation of best efforts calls for a less severe judgment, based on a comparison with the efforts a reasonable person of the same kind would have made in similar circumstances. This distinction signifies that more will be expected from a highly specialised firm selected for its expertise than from a less sophisticated partner. **Illustrations**

1. A, a distributor, promises that it will reach a quota of 15,000 sales within a year in the contract zone. If at the end of the period A has sold only 13,000 items, it has clearly failed to perform its obligation. See Art. 5.4(1).

. . .

ARTICLE 5.5 – Determination of kind of duty involved

In determining the extent to which an obligation of a party involves a duty of best efforts in the performance of an activity or a duty to achieve a specific result, regard shall be had, among other factors, to

(a) the way in which the obligation is expressed in the contract;

(b) the contractual price and other terms of the contract;

(c) the degree of risk normally involved in achieving the expected result;

(d) the ability of the other party to influence the performance of the obligation.

COMMENT

1. Criteria for determining the nature of the obligation

It is important to determine whether an obligation involves a duty to achieve a specific result or simply a duty of best efforts, as the obligation is more onerous in the former case. Such a determination may sometimes be difficult. This article therefore establishes criteria which may offer guidance to parties, judges and arbitrators, although the list is not exhaustive. The problems involved are frequently matters of interpretation.

2. Nature of the obligation as expressed by the contract

The way in which an obligation is expressed in the contract may often be of assistance in determining whether the parties intended to create a duty to achieve a specific result or a duty of best efforts. **Illustration**

> 1. A, a contractor, agrees to build storage facilities for B, who is most keen that the work be finished in an unusually short time. If A undertakes that "the work will be completed before 31 December", it assumes an obligation to achieve the specific result of meeting that deadline. If it merely undertakes "to try to complete the work before 31 December", its obligation involves a duty of best efforts to

attempt to meet the deadline, but no guarantee that it will definitely be met. See Art. 5.5(a).

. . .

4. Degree of risk in performance of an obligation

When a party's performance of an obligation normally involves a high degree of risk it is generally to be expected that that party does not intend to guarantee a result, and that the other party does not expect such a guarantee. The opposite conclusion will be drawn when the desired result can as a rule be achieved without any special difficulty. See Art. 5.5(c).

Illustrations

> 2. A space agency undertakes to put a telecommunication satellite into orbit, the rate of failure of past launchings having been 22%. The space agency cannot be expected to guarantee that the orbiting will be successful. The obligation is merely to observe the degree of diligence required for such launchings in view of the present state of technology.
>
> 3. A promises to deliver 20 tons of steel to B on 30 June. Such a relatively simple operation is subject to no special risk. A is committed to the specific result of delivering the required quantity of steel on the date specified and not merely to attempting to do so.

. . .

Article 5.6 – Determination of quality of performance

Where the quality of performance is neither fixed by, nor determinable from, the contract a party is bound to render a performance of a quality that is reasonable and not less than average in the circumstances.

COMMENT

Standards have been set in Art. 5.4 concerning the exercise of "best efforts", but quality of performance is a wider problem addressed by Art. 5.6. If goods are to be supplied, or services rendered, it is not sufficient to supply those goods or to render those services; they must also be of a certain quality.

The contract will often be explicit as regards the quality due ("grade 1 oil"), or it will provide elements making that quality determinable. In other cases, the rule established by Art. 5.6 is that the quality must be "reasonable and not less than average in the circumstances". Two criteria are thus combined. **Illustration**

1. A undertakes to build a hotel next to a busy railway station. The contract provides for "adequate sound isolation", the quality of which is not more precisely determined. It is, however, determinable from the contract that the sound isolation must meet the high standards needed in view of the hotel's proximity to a railway station.

1. Performance must be of average quality

The minimum requirement is that of providing goods of average quality. The supplier is not bound to provide goods or services of superior quality if that is not required by the contract, but neither may it deliver goods or services of inferior quality. This average quality is determined according to the circumstances, which normally means that which is available on the relevant market at the time of performance (there may for example have been a recent technological advance). Other factors may also be of relevance, such as the specific qualifications for which the performing party was chosen.

Illustration

2. A buys 500 kgs. of oranges from B. If the contract says nothing more precise, and no other circumstances call for a different solution, those oranges may not be of less than average quality. Average quality will however suffice unless it is unreasonably defective.

2. Performance must be reasonable

The additional reference to reasonableness is intended to prevent a party from claiming that it has performed adequately if it has rendered an "average" performance in a market where the average quality is most unsatisfactory and is intended to give the judge or arbitrator an opportunity to raise those insufficient standards.

Illustration

3. A company based in country X organises a banquet to celebrate its 50th anniversary. Since the cuisine in country X is mediocre, the company orders the meal from a renowned restaurant in Paris. In these circumstances the quality of the food provided must not be less than the average standards of the Parisian restaurant; it would clearly not be sufficient simply to meet the average standards of country X.

ARTICLE 5.7 – Price determination

(1) Where a contract does not fix or make provision for determining the price, the parties are considered, in the absence of any indication to the contrary, to have made reference to the price generally charged at the time of the conclusion of the contract for such performance in comparable circumstances in the trade concerned or, if no such price is available, to a reasonable price.

(2) Where the price is to be determined by one party and that determination is manifestly unreasonable, a reasonable price shall be substituted notwithstanding any contract term to the contrary.

(3) Where the price is to be fixed by a third person, and that person cannot or will not do so, the price shall be a reasonable price.

(4) Where the price is to be fixed by reference to factors which do not exist or have ceased to exist or to be accessible, the nearest equivalent factor shall be treated as a substitute.

COMMENT

1. General rule governing price determination

A contract usually fixes the price to be paid, or makes provision for its determination. If however this is not the case, para. (1) of this article presumes that the parties have made reference to the price generally charged at the time of the conclusion of the contract for such performance in comparable circumstances in the trade concerned. All these qualifications are of course significant. The provision also permits the rebuttal of the presumption if there is any indication to the contrary. This article is inspired by Art. 55 CISG. The rule has the necessary flexibility to meet the needs of international trade. It is true that in some cases the price usually charged on the market may not satisfy the reasonableness test which prevails elsewhere in this article. Recourse would then have to be made to the general provision on good faith and fair dealing (Art. 1.7), or possibly to some of the provisions on mistake, fraud and gross disparity (Chapter 3).

Some international contracts relate to operations which are unique or at least very specific, in respect of which it is not possible to refer to the price charged for similar performance in comparable circumstances. According to para. (1) the parties are then deemed to have made reference to a reasonable price and the party in question will fix the price at a reasonable level, subject to the possible review by courts or arbitral tribunals. **Illustrations**

> 1. A, a firm specialised in express mailing throughout the world, receives from B a parcel to be delivered as soon as possible from France to the United States. Nothing is said as to the price. A should bill B with the price usually charged in the sector for such a service.

> 2. The next order which A receives from B is one to deliver another parcel as soon as possible to Antarctica where a team of explorers is in need of urgent supplies. Again, nothing is said as to price, but since no possible market comparison can be made A must act reasonably when fixing the price.

2. Determination of price by one party

In some cases the contract expressly provides that the price will be determined by one of the parties. This happens frequently in several sectors, for example the supply of services. The price cannot easily be determined in advance, and the performing party is in the best position to place a value on what it has done.

In those cases where the parties have made such a provision for determining the price, it will be enforced. To avoid possible abuses however, para. (2) enables judges or arbitrators to replace a manifestly unreasonable price by a reasonable one. This provision is mandatory.

3. Determination of price by third person

A provision that the price will be determined by a third person can give rise to serious difficulty if that third person is unable to accomplish the mission (not being the expert he or she was thought to be) or refuses to do so. Para. (3) provides that the price, possibly determined by judges or arbitrators, shall be reasonable. If the third person determines the price in circumstances that may involve fraud, gross disparity or threat, Art. 3.11(2) may apply.

4. Determination of price by reference to external factors

In some situations the price is to be fixed by reference to external factors, typically a published index, or quotations on a commodity exchange. In cases where the reference factor ceases to exist or to be accessible, para. (4) provides that the nearest equivalent factor shall be treated as a substitute. **Illustration**

> 3. The price of a construction contract is linked to several indexes, including the "official index of charges in the construction sector", regularly published by the local Government. Several instalments of the price still have to be calculated when that index ceases to be published. The Construction Federation, a private trade association, decides however to start publishing a similar index to replace the former one and in these circumstances the new index will serve as a substitute.

gives rise, at least in the first instance, to renegotiations. The rule in Art. 5.8 requires no special condition to be met, except that the

ARTICLE 5.8 – Contract for an Indefinite Period

A contract for an indefinite period may be ended by either party by giving notice a reasonable time in advance.

COMMENT

The duration of a contract is often specified by an express provision, or it may be determined from the nature and purpose of the contract (e.g. technical expertise provided in order to assist in performing specialised work). However, there are cases when the duration is neither determined nor determinable. Parties can also stipulate that their contract is concluded for an indefinite period. This article provides that in such cases either party may end the contractual relationship by giving notice a reasonable time in advance. What a reasonable time in advance will be will depend on circumstances such as the period of time the parties have been cooperating, the

importance of their relative investments in the relationship, the time needed to find new partners, etc. The rule can be understood as a gap-filling provision in cases where parties have failed to specify the duration of their contract. More generally, it also relates to the widely recognised principle that contracts may not bind the parties eternally and that they may always opt out of such contracts provided they give notice a reasonable time in advance.

This situation is to be distinguished from the case of hardship which is covered by Arts. 6.2.1 - 6.2.3. Hardship requires a fundamental change of the equilibrium of the contract, and duration of the contract be indefinite and that it permit unilateral cancellation. **Illustration**

A agrees to distribute B's products in country X. The contract is concluded for an indefinite period. Either party may cancel this arrangement unilaterally, provided that it gives the other party notice a reasonable time in advance.

CHAPTER 6
PERFORMANCE

SECTION 1: PERFORMANCE IN GENERAL

ARTICLE 6.1.1 – Time of performance

A party must perform its obligations:
(a) if a time is fixed by or determinable from the contract, at that time;
(b) if a period of time is fixed by or determinable from the contract, at any time within that period unless circumstances indicate that the other party is to choose a time;
(c) in any other case, within a reasonable time after the conclusion of the contract.

COMMENT

With a view to determining when a contractual obligation is to be performed, this article, which is inspired by Art. 33 CISG, distinguishes three situations. The first is where the contract stipulates the precise time for performance or makes it determinable. If the contract does not specify a precise moment but a period of time for performing, any time during that period chosen by the performing party will be acceptable unless circumstances indicate that the other party is to choose the time. Finally, in all other cases, performance is due within a reasonable time. **Illustrations**

1. A offers to advise B in the latter's plans to buy computer equipment and software, and it is agreed that A's experts will visit B "in May" It is in principle for A to announce when precisely in May that visit will take place. The circumstances may however leave the option to B, as would be the case if the contract expressly left to B the choice of the precise dates, or where, for example, it was understood that some of B's staff who are often absent on business trips must be present when A's experts arrive. See Art. 6.1.1(b).

2. A, a building contractor, encounters unusual difficulties when excavating a site, and needs special equipment to continue the work which it does not have. A immediately telephones B, another contractor, who has the necessary equipment and agrees to lend it to A. Nothing however is said as to when the equipment should be delivered to A. Performance is then to take place "within a reasonable time" in the circumstances. Since the work has been interrupted because of the above-mentioned difficulties, A urgently needs to receive the equipment and in such a case "within a reasonable time" probably means that performance is due almost immediately. See Art. 6.1.1(c).

ARTICLE 6.1.2 – Performance at one time or in instalments

In cases under Article 6.1.1(b) or (c), a party must perform its obligations at one time if that performance can be rendered at one time and the circumstances do not indicate otherwise.

COMMENT

A party's performance is of necessity sometimes rendered at one time (e.g. delivery of a single object), or, alternatively, must take place over a period of time (e.g. construction). There are however also cases where it can be rendered either at one time or in instalments (e.g. delivery of quantities of goods). Art. 6.1.2 addresses the latter situation, in circumstances where there is no contractual provision as to how such performance should be rendered, or where it is not determinable from the contract. The principle stated is that performance is due at one time, unless the circumstances indicate otherwise. **Illustrations**

1. A promises to deliver 100 tons of coal to B "in March". It would be materially possible and perhaps convenient for A to deliver the 100 tons in instalments, for instance 25 tons each week of the month. In principle however, according to Art. 6.1.2, A must deliver the 100 tons at one time.

2. The facts are the same as in Illustration 1, the difference being that B needs the coal

gradually, to meet the needs of its operations. B also has limited storage facilities and could not cope adequately with a consignment of 100 tons at any one time. A knows of B's specific needs. Here the circumstances suggest that A should instead deliver in instalments during the month of March.

ARTICLE 6.1.3 – Partial performance

(1) The obligee may reject an offer to perform in part at the time performance is due, whether or not such offer is coupled with an assurance as to the balance of the performance, unless the obligee has no legitimate interest in so doing.

(2) Additional expenses caused to the obligee by partial performance are to be borne by the obligor without prejudice to any other remedy.

COMMENT

1. Partial performance distinguished from performance at one time or in instalments

The situation covered by Art. 6.1.3 should be distinguished from that of Art. 6.1.2. The provision on "[p]erformance at one time or in instalments" attempts to solve a preliminary question which concerns only certain special cases. If a party's performance can be rendered at one time or in instalments and if the contract does not make it clear or determinable how that party is to perform, it must in principle perform at one time.

Art. 6.1.3 (Partial performance) has a more general scope. It provides that at the time performance is due the obligee may in principle reject an offer of partial performance. This applies at maturity, irrespective of whether what is due then is a global performance or an instalment of a wider obligation (which, in some cases, has been previously determined on the basis of Art. 6.1.2). **Illustration**

> 1. A owes US$ 1,000,000 to a bank and it has been agreed that A will pay back US$ 100,000 on the first day of each month, starting in January. On 1 April A offers to reimburse only US$ 50,000, and the balance two weeks later. In principle, the bank is entitled to refuse A's proposal.

2. Obligee entitled in principle to reject partial performance

When performance is due at maturity (be it the whole performance or an instalment), that which is due must be performed completely. In principle, the obligee may reject an offer of partial performance, whether or not it is coupled with an assurance as to the balance of the performance, since it is entitled to receive the whole of what was stipulated. Subject to what will be said below, partial performance normally constitutes a breach of contract. A party who does not obtain full performance at maturity may resort to the available remedies. As a rule, the obligee has a legitimate interest in requiring full performance of what was promised at the time that performance is due. The obligee may of course also refrain from rejecting the offer to perform in part, while reserving its rights as to the breach, or may accept it without any reservation, in which case partial performance can no longer be treated as a non-performance. **Illustration**

> 2. A wishes to open a branch office in Brussels and rents the necessary office space in a building under construction, due to be finished in time for the move on 1 September. On that date, only four of the ten offices are made available for A, with an assurance that the remaining six will be ready in one month. In principle, A may refuse to move into those four offices.

3. Obligee's right to reject partial performance conditional on its legitimate interest in so doing

There may be situations where the obligee's legitimate interest in receiving full performance is not apparent and where temporary acceptance of partial performance will not cause any significant harm to the obligee. If the party tendering partial performance proves this to be the case, the obligee cannot then refuse such partial performance (subject to para. (2)), and there is no non-performance in such cases. This may be seen as a consequence of the general principle of good faith and fair dealing enunciated in Art. 1.7. **Illustration**

> 3. An airline promises to transport 10 automobiles from Italy to Brazil in one single consignment due to be delivered on a definite date. When performance is due, some circumstances make it difficult, although not impossible, for the airline to find sufficient space in a single aircraft. The airline suggests making two successive deliveries within a week. It is

established that this will cause no inconvenience to the purchaser of the cars, which will not actually be used before the following month. In such a case the obligee has no legitimate interest in refusing partial performance.

4. Additional expenses entailed by partial performance to be borne by obligor

If partial performance is accepted, it may entail additional expenses for the obligee. In all cases, such expenses are to be borne by the other party. If partial performance amounts to a non-performance (as it usually does), these expenses will be part of the damages, without prejudice to any other available remedy. If partial performance does not amount to a non-performance (the obligee has been shown not to have any legitimate interest in rejecting the offer of partial performance, or has found the offer to be acceptable without reservation), it will only be entitled to those expenses. **Illustration**

> 4. The facts are the same as in Illustration 3. If the purchaser has to meet additional expenses on account of having to make double arrangements for picking up the cars at the airport, those extra costs will be borne by the airline.

ARTICLE 6.1.4 – Order of performance

(1) To the extent that the performances of the parties can be rendered simultaneously, the parties are bound to render them simultaneously unless the circumstances indicate otherwise.

(2) To the extent that the performance of only one party requires a period of time, that party is bound to render its performance first, unless the circumstances indicate otherwise.

COMMENT

In bilateral contracts, where both parties have obligations towards the other, the basic but complex question arises of which party is to perform first. If the parties have not made any specific arrangements, then in practice much will depend on usages and it must also be recalled that there are often several obligations on each side which may have to be performed at different times.

Art. 6.1.4 states two broad principles, while recognising that in both cases the circumstances may indicate otherwise. In effect, the main purpose of this article is to draw the parties' attention to the problem of order of performance, and to encourage them, where necessary, to draft appropriate contractual provisions.

A distinction is drawn between cases where the parties' performances can be rendered simultaneously and those where the performance of only one party requires a period of time.

1. Simultaneous performance to be made when possible

In the first situation, the rule is that the parties are bound to perform simultaneously (para. (1)). A seller is entitled to payment on delivery but circumstances may indicate otherwise, for example any exception originating from the terms of the contract or from usages which may allow a party to perform some time after the other. **Illustration**

> 1. A and B agree to barter a certain quantity of oil against a certain quantity of cotton. Unless circumstances indicate otherwise, the commodities should be exchanged simultaneously.

2. Exception where performance requires a period of time

If the performance of only one party's obligation by its very nature requires a period of time, for example in construction and most service contracts, the rule established in para. (2) is that that party is bound to render its performance first. Circumstances may frequently however indicate the contrary. Thus, insurance premiums are normally paid in advance, as also are rent and freight charges. In construction contracts, payments are usually made in agreed instalments throughout the duration of the work. **Illustration**

> 2. A promises to write a legal opinion to assist B in an arbitration. If no arrangement is made as to when A should be paid for the services, A must prepare the opinion before asking to be paid.

3. Relation of order of performance to withholding of performance

This article sets out the rules which will condition the application of Art. 7.1.3 concerning the withholding of performance.

ARTICLE 6.1.5 – Earlier performance

(1) The obligee may reject an earlier performance unless it has no legitimate interest in so doing.

(2) Acceptance by a party of an earlier performance does not affect the time for the performance of its own obligations if that time has been fixed irrespective of the performance of the other party's obligations.

(3) Additional expenses caused to the obligee by earlier performance are to be borne by the obligor, without prejudice to any other remedy.

COMMENT

1. Obligee in principle entitled to reject earlier performance

When performance is due at a certain moment (to be determined in accordance with Art. 6.1.1), it must take place at that time and in principle the obligee may reject an earlier performance. Usually, the time set for performance is geared to the obligee's activities, and earlier performance may cause it inconvenience. The obligee has therefore a legitimate interest in refusing it. Earlier performance, in principle, constitutes non-performance of the contract. The obligee may of course also abstain from rejecting an earlier performance while reserving its rights as to the non-performance. It may also accept such performance without reservation, in which case earlier performance can no longer be treated as non-performance. **Illustration**

> 1. A agrees to carry out the annual maintenance of all lifts in B's office building on 15 October. A's employees arrive on 14 October, a day on which important meetings, with many visitors, are taking place in the building. B is entitled to refuse such earlier performance which would cause it obvious inconvenience.

2. Obligee's right to reject earlier performance conditional on its legitimate interest in so doing

Situations may arise in which the obligee's legitimate interest in timely performance is not apparent and when its accepting earlier performance will not cause it any significant harm. If the party offering earlier performance proves this to be the case, the other party cannot reject earlier performance.

. . .

3. Effect of acceptance by obligee on its own performance of earlier performance of the other party's obligations

If one party accepts earlier performance by the other, the question arises of whether this affects the time for performance of its own obligations. Para. (2) deals with cases where obligations are due at a certain time which is not linked to the performance of the other party's obligations; that time for performance remains unchanged.

This provision does not however deal with the converse case where the performances are linked in time. Several situations may then arise. This circumstance may in itself establish the obligee's legitimate interest in rejecting earlier performance. If earlier performance is thus rejected, the obligee's time of performance is unaffected. If earlier performance is accepted with all due reservations as to the non-performance involved, the obligee may also reserve its rights as to its time for performance. If earlier performance is acceptable to the obligee it may at the same time decide whether or not to accept the consequences as regards its own obligations.

Illustrations

> 3. B undertakes to deliver goods to A on 15 May and A to pay the price on 30 June. B wishes to deliver the goods on 10 May and A has no legitimate interest in refusing such earlier performance. This will however have no effect on the time agreed for payment of the price, which was determined irrespective of the date of delivery.

> 4. B undertakes to deliver goods to A on 15 May and A to pay the price "on delivery". If B tenders the goods on 10 May, A, depending on the circumstances, may reject such earlier performance, claiming that it is not in a position to pay at that date, take delivery of the goods subject to observing the original deadline for payment of the price, or decide to accept the goods and pay for them immediately.

4. Additional expenses entailed by earlier performance to be borne by the performing party

If earlier performance is accepted, it may entail additional expenses for the obligee. In all cases, such expenses are to be borne by the other party. If earlier performance amounts to non-performance (the normal case), those expenses will be part of the damages, without prejudice to any other remedy available. If earlier performance does not amount to non-performance (the obligee has been shown not to have any legitimate interest in rejecting the offer of earlier performance, or has found that offer to be acceptable without reservation), the obligee will only be entitled to those expenses.

. . .

ARTICLE 6.1.6 – Place of performance

(1) If the place of performance is neither fixed by, nor determinable from, the contract, a party is to perform:

(a) a monetary obligation, at the obligee's place of business;

(b) any other obligation, at its own place of business.

(2) A party must bear any increase in the expenses incidental to performance which is caused by a change in its place of business subsequent to the conclusion of the contract.

COMMENT

1. Place of performance fixed by, or determined from, the contract when possible

The place where an obligation is to be performed is often determined by an express term of the contract or is determinable from it. It is obvious, for instance, that an obligation to build must be performed on the construction site, and that an obligation to transport goods must be performed in accordance with the agreed route.

2. Need for suppletive rules

Rules are however needed to cover cases where the contract is silent on the matter and circumstances do not indicate where performance should take place. Art. 6.1.6(1) provides two solutions.

The general rule is that a party is to perform its obligations at its own place of business. The second rule is specific to monetary obligations where the converse solution applies, namely that the obligor is to perform its obligations at the obligee's place of business (subject to the application of Art. 6.1.8 concerning payments by funds transfers). These solutions may not be the most satisfactory in all cases, but they do reflect the need for rules where the parties have not made any other arrangement or where the circumstances do not indicate otherwise.

Illustrations

1. A wishes some of its engineers to learn the language of country X, where they will be employed for some time. It agrees with B, a language school, for a series of intensive lessons. If nothing else is stipulated, the lessons are to take place at B's place of business. See Art. 6.1.6(1)(b).

2. The facts are the same as in Illustration 1. The language school sends its bill to A. The cost of the lessons must, in principle, be paid at B's place of business. See Art. 6.1.6(1)(a).

. . .

ARTICLE 6.1.7 – Payment by cheque or other instrument

(1) Payment may be made in any form used in the ordinary course of business at the place for payment.

(2) However, an obligee who accepts, either by virtue of paragraph (1) or voluntarily, a cheque, any other order to pay or a promise to pay, is presumed to do so only on condition that it will be honoured.

COMMENT

Discharge of monetary obligations is frequently made by cheques or similar instruments, or by transfers between financial institutions. The problems involved have however very seldom been the subject of codification, one notable exception being the *UNCITRAL Model Law on International Credit Transfers*. Without attempting to provide a detailed regulation, which would not be compatible with the very rapid evolution of techniques in this field, Arts. 6.1.7 and 6.1.8 establish some basic principles which should be of assistance in regard to international payments.

1. General rule regarding form of payment

Para. (1) allows for payment to be made in any form that is usual at the place for payment. Subject to the reservation contained in para. (2), the obligor may for instance pay in cash, by cheque, banker's draft, a bill of exchange, credit card, or in any other form such as the newly developing electronic means of payment, provided it chooses a mode that is usual at the place for payment, i.e. normally at the obligee's place of business. In principle, the obligee should be satisfied to receive payment in a form that is customary at its place of business. **Illustration**

1. A, an importer in Luxembourg, receives a bill for goods bought from B, a firm in Central America, and sends a eurocheque in payment. B may reject this mode of payment if the banks in its country are not familiar with eurocheques.

. . .

ARTICLE 6.1.8 – Payment by funds transfer

(1) Unless the obligee has indicated a particular account, payment may be made by a transfer to any of the financial institutions in which the obligee has made it known that it has an account.

(2) In case of payment by a transfer the obligation of the obligor is discharged when the transfer to the obligee's financial institution becomes effective.

COMMENT

1. Admissibility of funds transfers

Although the principle enunciated in Art. 6.1.6 that payment of a monetary obligation should be made at the obligee's place of business still stands, para. (1) of this article provides that it can also be made to one of the financial institutions in which the obligee has made it known that it keeps an account. If however the obligee has indicated a particular account, payment should then be made to that account.

Naturally, the obligee can also make it known that it does not wish payment to be made by transfer. **Illustration**

1. A, a shipyard established in Helsinki, repairs a ship belonging to B, a Swedish company, and the bill is sent on a letter-head that mentions a bank account in Finland and another in Sweden. Unless A states that payment has to be made to the Finnish account, or by a means other than a bank transfer, B is entitled to make payment to the Swedish account.

. . .

ARTICLE 6.1.9 – Currency of payment

(1) If a monetary obligation is expressed in a currency other than that of the place for payment, it may be paid by the obligor in the currency of the place for payment unless

(a) that currency is not freely convertible; or

(b) the parties have agreed that payment should be made only in the currency in which the monetary obligation is expressed.

(2) If it is impossible for the obligor to make payment in the currency in which the monetary obligation is expressed, the obligee may require payment in the currency of the place for payment, even in the case referred to in paragraph (1)(b).

(3) Payment in the currency of the place for payment is to be made according to the applicable rate of exchange prevailing there when payment is due.

(4) However, if the obligor has not paid at the time when payment is due, the obligee may require payment according to the applicable rate of exchange prevailing either when payment is due or at the time of actual payment.

COMMENT

Monetary obligations are usually expressed in a certain currency (currency of account), and payment must normally be made in the same currency. However, when the currency of the place for payment is different from the currency of account, paras. (1) and (2) of this article provide for those cases where the obligor may or must make payment in the former currency.

1. Monetary obligation expressed in currency different from that of place for payment

As a general rule, the obligor is given the alternative of paying in the currency of the place for payment, which may have definite practical advantages and, if that currency is freely convertible, this should cause no difficulty to the obligee.

If, however, the currency of the place for payment is not freely convertible, the rule does not apply. Parties may also exclude the application of the rule by agreeing that payment is to be made only in the currency in which the monetary obligation is expressed (*effectivo* clause). If it has an interest in the payment actually being made in the currency of account, the obligee should specify this in the contract. **Illustrations**

1. A French firm receives an order for machinery from a Brazilian buyer, the price being expressed in United States dollars. According to Art. 6.1.6, payment of that monetary obligation must in principle be made at the obligee's place of business, i.e. France. If the Brazilian firm finds it more convenient, it may pay the price in French francs. See Art. 6.1.9(1).

2. The same French firm frequently needs to buy from United States sources certain parts to be included in the machines, and has stipulated that the Brazilian buyer should pay only in dollars. In this case, payment may only be made in dollars. See Art. 6.1.9(1)(b).

. . .

3. Determination of applicable rate of exchange

Paras. (3) and (4) deal with the problem of the determination of the rate of exchange to be chosen when payment is made in the currency of the place for payment rather than in a different currency stipulated in the contract. This may occur when the obligor avails itself of para. (1), or the obligee the provisions of para. (2).

Two widely accepted solutions are offered. In normal cases, the rate of exchange is that prevailing when payment is due. If, however, the obligor is in default, the obligee is given an option between the rate of exchange prevailing when payment was due or the rate at the time of actual payment.

The double reference to the "applicable" rate is justified by the fact that there may be different rates of exchange depending on the nature of the operation. **Illustration**

5. The facts are the same as in Illustration 4. A chooses to be reimbursed in Swiss francs and payment, which was due on 10 April, actually takes place on 15 September. The rate of exchange on 10 April was Sfrs. 2 to US\$ 1. By 15 September it has become Sfrs. 2,15 to US\$ 1. A is entitled to apply the latter rate. If the dollar had depreciated rather than increased in value, A would have chosen the rate applicable on 10 April.

ARTICLE 6.1.10 – Currency not expressed

Where a monetary obligation is not expressed in a particular currency, payment must be made in the currency of the place where payment is to be made.

. . .

ARTICLE 6.1.11 – Costs of performance

Each party shall bear the costs of performance of its obligations.

COMMENT

The performance of obligations often entails costs, which may be of different kinds: transportation costs in delivering goods, bank commission in making a monetary transfer, fees to be paid when applying for a permission, etc. In principle, such costs are to be borne by the performing party. Other arrangements may of course be made by the parties and there is nothing to prevent the performing party from including those costs in advance in the price it quotes. The rule set out in Art. 6.1.11 applies in the absence of such arrangements.

The provision states who shall bear the costs, not who shall pay them. Usually, it will be the same party, but there may be different situations, for example where tax regulations place the burden of payment on a specific party; in such cases, if the person who has to pay is different from the person who must bear the costs under Art. 6.1.11, the latter must reimburse the former. **Illustration**

A, a consultant, agrees to send five experts to perform an audit of B's firm. Nothing is said concerning the experts' travel expenses, and A does not take those costs into account when determining its fees. A may not add the travel expenses to the bill.

ARTICLE 6.1.12 – Imputation of payments

(1) An obligor owing several monetary obligations to the same obligee may specify at the time of payment the debt to which it intends the payment to be applied. However, the payment discharges first any expenses, then interest due and finally the principal.

(2) If the obligor makes no such specification, the obligee may, within a reasonable time after payment, declare to the obligor the obligation to which it imputes the payment, provided that the obligation is due and undisputed.

(3) In the absence of imputation under paragraphs (1) or (2), payment is imputed to that obligation which satisfies one of the following criteria in the order indicated:

(a) an obligation which is due or which is the first to fall due;

(b) the obligation for which the obligee has least security;

(c) the obligation which is the most burdensome for the obligor;

(d) the obligation which has arisen first.

If none of the preceding criteria applies, payment is imputed to all the obligations proportionally.

COMMENT

Arts. 6.1.12 and 6.1.13 deal with the classic problem of imputation of payments. If an obligor owes several monetary obligations at the same time to the same obligee and makes a payment the amount of which is not sufficient to discharge all those debts, the question arises of the debts to which that payment applies.

Art. 6.1.12, which is inspired by widely recognised principles, offers the obligor the possibility of imputing its payment to a particular debt, provided that any expenses and interest due are discharged before the principal. In the absence of any imputation by the obligor, this provision enables the obligee to impute the payment received, although not to a disputed debt. Para. (3) lays down criteria which will govern in the absence of any imputation by either party.

Illustration

A receives under separate contracts three loans, each of US$ 100,000, from bank B payment of which is due on 31 December. B receives US$ 100,000 from A on 2 January with the imprecise message: "Reimbursement of the loan". B pays little attention to the matter and at first does not react, but three months later sues A for payment of the remaining US$ 200,000 and the parties disagree as to which of the loans had been reimbursed by the January payment. B had similar security in each case, but the interest rates were not the same: 8% on the first loan, 8,50% on the second and 9% on the third. The January payment will be imputed to the third loan.

ARTICLE 6.1.13 – Imputation of non-monetary obligations

Article 6.1.12 applies with appropriate adaptations to the imputation of performance of non-monetary obligations.

. . .

ARTICLE 6.1.14 – Application for public permission

Where the law of a State requires a public permission affecting the validity of the contract or its performance and neither that law nor the circumstances indicate otherwise

(a) if only one party has its place of business in that State, that party shall take the measures necessary to obtain the permission;

(b) in any other case the party whose performance requires permission shall take the necessary measures.

COMMENT

If the validity or the performance of a contract is subject to compliance with public permission requirements, several issues arise as to who has the burden of filing the application (Art. 6.1.14), the time for filing (Art. 6.1.15), the legal consequences of failure to obtain an administrative decision in due time (Art. 6.1.16) and the rejection of the application (Art. 6.1.17)

1. Scope of the permission requirement

The Principles do not deal with the relevance of public permission requirements. What kind of public permission is required, if any, is to be determined under the applicable law, including the rules of private international law.

National courts tend to give effect only to the public permission requirements of the *lex fori*, and sometimes to those prescribed by the *lex contractus*. Arbitral tribunals may enjoy wider discretion than national courts in deciding which public permissions are relevant to the contract. Under Art. 7(2) of the 1980 Rome Convention and other conflict of laws rules, public permission requirements of the law of other jurisdictions connected with the contract may also come into play. Long-arm statutes in some jurisdictions may also impose public permission requirements on licensees or subsidiaries of companies located abroad. This article assumes that the requirements prescribed by the applicable law are to be observed.

a. *Broad notion of "public permission"*

The term "public permission" is to be given a broad interpretation. It includes all permission requirements established pursuant to a concern of a public nature, such as health, safety, or particular trade policies. It is irrelevant whether a required licence or permit is to be granted by a governmental or by a non-governmental institution to which Governments have delegated public authority for a specific purpose. Thus, the authorisation of payments by a private bank pursuant to foreign exchange regulations is in the nature of a "public permission" for the purposes of this article.

b. *Timing of public permission*

The provisions on public permissions refer primarily to those required by the applicable law or by a regulation in force at the time of the conclusion of the contract. However, these provisions may also apply to public permissions that may be introduced after the conclusion of the contract.

c. *Public permission may affect the contract in whole or in part*

The provisions on public permissions apply both to those requirements affecting the contract as a whole and to those merely affecting individual terms of the contract. However, where the legal consequences of failing to obtain a public permission differ according to whether such permission affects the contract in whole or in part, different rules are established. See Arts. 6.1.16 (2) and 6.1.17.

...

3. Which party is bound to take measures to obtain a public permission

a. *Party with place of business in State requiring public permission*

The rule set out in sub-para. (a) of this article which places the burden to apply on the party who has its place of business in the State which requires the relevant public permission reflects current international trade practices. It is that party who is in the best position to apply promptly for a public permission, since it is probably more familiar with the application requirements and procedures.

If a party needs further information from the other to file an application (e.g. information relating to the final destination of the goods, or information as to the purpose or subject matter of the contract), the other party must furnish such information pursuant to the duty of co-operation (Art. 5.3). Should that party not furnish such information it may not rely on the obligation of the first party. This duty to cooperate with the other party applies even if the contract stipulates that one of the parties bears the burden of applying for a public permission. Thus, if the parties have incorporated in their contract the term "ex works", which imposes far-reaching obligations on the buyer, the seller is nevertheless bound to provide the buyer, "at the latter's request, risk and expense, every assistance in obtaining any export licence or other official authorisation necessary for the exportation of the goods" (INCOTERMS 1990, A 2, see also B 2).

b. *Party whose performance requires public permission*

Sub-para. (b) of this article contemplates those cases where none of the parties has a place of business in the State requiring the permission. It also envisions a contract which is truly international notwithstanding the fact that both parties have their places of business in that State. In either case, the party whose performance requires the public permission is bound to take the necessary measures to obtain such a permission.

. . .

c. *Suppletory nature of provisions on public permissions*

The purpose of this article is to determine the party who must apply for a public permission in those cases where it is not clear who is to bear that burden. It is a suppletory rule to be applied when neither the contract, nor the law requiring the permission or the circumstances specify which party is under an obligation to apply for the required public permission.

. . .

4. Nature of obligation to take the "necessary measures"

The party who has to apply for the permission must take the "necessary measures" to obtain such permission, but is not responsible for the outcome of the application. That party is bound to exhaust available local remedies to obtain the permission, provided that they have a good chance of success and that resorting to local remedies appears reasonable in view of the circumstances of the case (e.g. the value of the transaction, time constraints).

Which measures have to be taken depends on the relevant regulations and the procedural mechanisms available in the State where the permission is to be granted. The obligation is in the nature of an obligation of best efforts (see Art. 5.4(2)).

. . .

ARTICLE 6.1.15 – (Procedure in applying for permission)

(1) The party required to take the measures necessary to obtain the permission shall do so without undue delay and shall bear any expenses incurred.

(2) That party shall whenever appropriate give the other party notice of the grant or refusal of such permission without undue delay.

COMMENT

1. Time for filing an application

The party under an obligation to obtain a public permission must take action immediately after the conclusion of the contract and pursue this action as necessary under the circumstances.

2. Expenses

According to Art. 6.1.11, each party shall bear the costs of performance of its obligations. This rule has been restated in para. (1) of the present article for the sake of clarity.

3. Duty to give prompt notice of the grant or refusal of the permission

The parties to the contract need to know as soon as possible whether the permission can be obtained. Accordingly, para. (2) of this article provides that the party required to take the necessary measures must inform the other of the outcome of the application. This duty of

information extends to other relevant facts, such as for example the timing and outcome of the application, whether a refusal is subject to appeal and whether an appeal is to be lodged.

. . .

5. Consequences of the failure to inform

Failure to provide information regarding the grant or refusal of the permission amounts to non-performance. Accordingly, the general consequences of non-performance, as set forth in Chapter 7, apply. The duty to give notice of the grant of the public permission is a contractual obligation arising at the time the contract comes into existence. The duty to give notice of the refusal of the permission is part of the duty to take the "necessary measures" to obtain the permission under Art. 6.1.14 (see comment 4).

. . .

ARTICLE 6.1.16 – Permission neither granted nor refused

(1) If, notwithstanding the fact that the party responsible has taken all measures required, permission is neither granted nor refused within an agreed period or, where no period has been agreed, within a reasonable time from the conclusion of the contract, either party is entitled to terminate the contract.

(2) Where the permission affects some terms only, paragraph (1) does not apply if, having regard to the circumstances, it is reasonable to uphold the remaining contract even if the permission is refused.

COMMENT

Whereas Arts. 6.1.14 and 6.1.15 are concerned with the duties of the contracting parties, Arts. 6.1.16 and 6.1.17 deal with the legal consequences in cases respectively where there has been no decision on the application within a given period or where the public permission has been refused.

1. No decision taken as regards the permission

Para. (1) of the present article deals with the "nothing happens" situation, that is to say a situation where permission has neither been granted nor refused within the agreed period or, where no period has been agreed, within a reasonable time from the conclusion of the contract. The reasons for the absence of a pronouncement may vary, for example the slow pace of processing the application, a pending appeal, etc. In any event there is no longer any reason to keep the parties waiting and either party is entitled to terminate the contract.

2. Termination of the contract

Remedies other than termination may be appropriate depending on the legal role played by the permission in the creation of the contractual obligations. This is in particular the case where the granting of the public permission is a condition for the validity of the contract, since in the absence of the permission either party may simply disregard the contract. The reason why this article provides also in these cases for the termination of the contract is that the parties are, with a view to obtaining the permission, under a number of obligations which cannot be allowed to exist indefinitely. The entitlement of the party responsible for obtaining the permission to terminate the contract under this article is conditional on that party's having taken "the necessary measures" to that effect.

Illustration

1. A, situated in country X, sells rifles to B for resale by B in the hunting season starting in four months. The validity of the sale is subject to a public permission to be granted by the authorities of country X. No period is agreed for obtaining that permission. Notwithstanding the fact that A takes all the necessary measures to obtain the permission, after three months no decision has yet been taken on A's application. Either party may terminate the contract.

The termination envisaged under this article has no consequences for the expenses so far incurred by the parties for the purpose of obtaining the permission. The expenses will be borne by the party who has assumed the risk of not obtaining the permission.

3. Permission affecting individual terms only

Where the permission affects some terms only of the contract, para. (2) of this article excludes the right of termination in cases where, even if the permission had been refused, it would according to Art. 6.1.17(1) nevertheless be reasonable to uphold the contract. **Illustration**

2. A, situated in country X, enters into a contract with B, containing a penalty clause for delay, the validity of which is subject to a public permission to be granted by the authorities of country X. Notwithstanding the fact that A takes all the necessary measures to obtain the permission, time continues to pass without any decision being taken. It would be reasonable in the circumstances to uphold the contract. Even if the permission were to have been refused, neither party may terminate the contract.

ARTICLE 6.1.17 – Permission refused

(1) The refusal of a permission affecting the validity of the contract renders the contract void. If the refusal affects the validity of some terms only, only such terms are void if, having regard to the circumstances, it is reasonable to uphold the remaining contract.

(2) Where the refusal of a permission renders the performance of the contract impossible in whole or in part, the rules on non-performance apply.

COMMENT

1. Application for permission rejected

This article contemplates the situation where the application for a permission is expressly refused. The nature of the obligation imposed on the responsible party with respect to the application for the permission is such that a refusal under this article is one which is not subject to an appeal which has a reasonable prospect of success. See comment 4 on Art. 6.1.14. Moreover, means of recourse against the refusal need not be exhausted whenever a final decision on the permission would be taken only after the time at which the contract could meaningfully be performed.

2. Legal consequences of a refusal of permission

The consequences of a refusal to grant the permission vary depending on whether the permission affects the validity of the contract or its performance.

a. *Refusal of permission affecting validity of the contract*

Where the permission affects the validity of the whole contract, a refusal renders the whole contract void, i.e. the contract is considered as never having come into being. **Illustration**

1. A, situated in country X, enters into a contract with B, the validity of which is subject to a public permission to be granted by the authorities of country X. Notwithstanding the fact that A takes all the necessary measures to obtain the permission, A's application is refused. The contract is considered never to have come into existence.

Where, on the other hand, a refusal affects the validity of some terms only of the contract, only such terms are void, while the remaining part of the contract may be upheld provided that such a result is reasonable in the circumstances. **Illustration**

2. A, situated in country X, enters into a contract with B, containing a penalty clause for delay, the validity of which is subject to a public permission to be granted by the authorities of country X. Notwithstanding the fact that A takes all the necessary measures to obtain the permission, A's application is refused. If it is reasonable in the circumstances, the contract will be upheld without the penalty clause.

b. *Refusal rendering performance of the contract impossible*

If the refusal of the permission renders the performance impossible in whole or in part, para. (2) of this article refers to the rules on non-performance embodied in Chapter 7. **Illustration**

3. Under a contract entered into with B, A owes B US$ 100,000. The transfer of the sum from country X, where A is situated, to B's bank account in country Y is subject to a permission by the Central Bank of country X. Notwithstanding the fact that A takes all the necessary measures to obtain the permission, A's application is refused. The refusal of the permission renders it impossible for A to pay B. The consequences of A's non-performance are determined in accordance with the provisions of Chapter 7.

The refusal of the permission may render impossible the performance of a party only in the State imposing the permission requirement, while it may be possible for that party to perform the same obligation elsewhere. In such cases the general principle of good faith (see Art. 1.7) will prevent that party from relying on the refusal of the permission as an excuse for non-performance. **Illustration**

4. The facts are the same as in Illustration 3, the difference being that A has in country Z, where no such permission requirement exists, sufficient funds to pay B. A may not rely on the refusal of the permission by the authorities of country X as an excuse for not paying B.

SECTION 2: HARDSHIP

ARTICLE 6.2.1 – Contract to be Observed

Where the performance of a contract becomes more onerous for one of the parties, that party is nevertheless bound to perform its obligations subject to the following provisions on hardship.

COMMENT

1. Binding character of the contract the general rule

The purpose of this article is to make it clear that as a consequence of the general principle of the binding character of the contract (see Art. 1.3) performance must be rendered as long as it is possible and regardless of the burden it may impose on the performing party. In other words, even if a party experiences heavy losses instead of the expected profits or the performance has become meaningless for that party the terms of the contract must nevertheless be respected.

Illustration

In January 1990 A, a forwarding agent, enters into a two-year shipping contract with B, a carrier. Under the contract B is bound to ship certain goods from Hamburg to New York at a fixed price, on a monthly basis throughout the two-year period. Alleging a substantial increase in the price of fuel in the aftermath of the 1990 Gulf crisis, B requests a five per cent increase in the rate for August 1990. B is not entitled to such an increase because B bears the risk of its performance becoming more onerous.

2. Change in circumstances relevant only in exceptional cases

The principle of the binding character of the contract is not however an absolute one. When supervening circumstances are such that they lead to a fundamental alteration of the equilibrium of the contract, they create an exceptional situation referred to in these Principles as "hardship" and dealt with in the following articles of this section. The phenomenon of hardship has been acknowledged by various legal systems under the guise of other concepts such as frustration of purpose, *Wegfall der Geschäftsgrundlage*, *imprévision*, *eccessiva onerosità sopravvenuta*, etc. The term "hardship" was chosen because it is widely known in international trade practice as confirmed by the inclusion in many international contracts of so-called "hardship clauses".

ARTICLE 6.2.2 – Definition of hardship

There is hardship where the occurrence of events fundamentally alters the equilibrium of the contract either because the cost of a party's performance has increased or because the value of the performance a party receives has diminished, and

(a) the events occur or become known to the disadvantaged party after the conclusion of the contract;

(b) the events could not reasonably have been taken into account by the disadvantaged party at the time of the conclusion of the contract;

(c) the events are beyond the control of the disadvantaged party; and (d) the risk of the events was not assumed by the disadvantaged party.

COMMENT

1. Hardship defined

This article defines hardship as a situation where the occurrence of events fundamentally alters the equilibrium of the contract, provided that those events meet the requirements which are laid down in sub-paras. (a) to (d).

2. Fundamental alteration of equilibrium of the contract

Since the general principle is that a change in circumstances does not affect the obligation to perform (see Art. 6.2.1), it follows that hardship may not be invoked unless the alteration of the equilibrium of the contract is fundamental. Whether an alteration is "fundamental" in a given case will of course depend upon the circumstances. If, however, the performances are capable of precise measurement in monetary terms, an alteration amounting to 50% or more of the cost or the value of the performance is likely to amount to a "fundamental" alteration.

Illustration

1. In September 1989 A, a dealer in electronic goods situated in the former German Democratic Republic, purchases stocks from B, situated in country X, also a former socialist country. The goods are to be delivered by B in December 1990. In November 1990, A informs B that the goods are no longer of any use to it, claiming that after the unification of the German Democratic Republic and the Federal Republic of Germany there is no longer any market for such goods imported from country X. Unless the circumstances indicate otherwise, A is entitled to invoke hardship.

a. *Increase in cost of performance*

In practice a fundamental alteration in the equilibrium of the contract may manifest itself in two different but related ways. The first is characterised by a substantial increase in the cost for one party of performing its obligation. This party will normally be the one who is to perform the non-monetary obligation. The substantial increase in the cost may, for instance, be due to a dramatic rise in the price of the raw materials necessary for the production of the goods or the rendering of the services, or to the introduction of new safety regulations requiring far more expensive production procedures.

b. *Decrease in value of the performance received by one party*

The second manifestation of hardship is characterised by a substantial decrease in the value of the performance received by one party, including cases where the performance no longer has any value at all for the receiving party. The performance may be that either of a monetary or of a non-monetary obligation. The substantial decrease in the value or the total loss of any value of the performance may be due either to drastic changes in market conditions (e.g. the effect of a dramatic increase in inflation on a contractually agreed price) or the frustration of the purpose for which the performance was required (e.g. the effect of a prohibition to build on a plot of land acquired for building purposes or the effect of an export embargo on goods acquired with a view to their subsequent export). Naturally the decrease in value of the performance must be capable of objective measurement: a mere change in the personal opinion of the receiving party as to the value of the performance is of no relevance. As to the frustration of the purpose of the performance,

this can only be taken into account when the purpose in question was known or at least ought to have been known to both parties.

3. Additional requirements for hardship to arise

a. *Events occur or become known after conclusion of the contract*

According to sub-para. (a) of this article, the events causing hardship must take place or become known to the disadvantaged party after the conclusion of the contract. If that party had known of those events when entering into the contract, it would have been able to take them into account at that time and may not subsequently rely on hardship.

b. *Events could not reasonably have been taken into account by disadvantaged party*

Even if the change in circumstances occurs after the conclusion of the contract, sub-para. (b) of this article makes it clear that such circumstances cannot cause hardship if they could reasonably have been taken into account by the disadvantaged party at the time the contract was concluded. **Illustration**

2. A agrees to supply B with crude oil from country X at a fixed price for the next five years, notwithstanding the acute political tensions in the region. Two years after the conclusion of the contract, a war erupts between contending factions in neighbouring countries. The war results in a world energy crisis and oil prices increase drastically. A is not entitled to invoke hardship because such a rise in the price of crude oil was not unforeseeable.

Sometimes the change in circumstances is gradual, but the final result of those gradual changes may constitute a case of hardship. If the change began before the contract was concluded, hardship will not arise unless the pace of change increases dramatically during the life of the contract. **Illustration**

3. In a sales contract between A and B the price is expressed in the currency of country X, a currency whose value was already depreciating slowly against other major currencies before the conclusion of the contract. One month afterwards a political crisis in country X leads to a massive devaluation of the order of 80% of its currency. Unless the circumstances indicate otherwise, this constitutes a case of hardship, since such a dramatic acceleration of the loss of value of the currency of country X was not foreseeable.

c. *Events beyond the control of disadvantaged party*

Under sub-para. (c) of this article a case of hardship can only arise if the events causing the hardship are beyond the control of the disadvantaged party.

d. *Risks must not have been assumed by disadvantaged party*

Under sub-para. (d) there can be no hardship if the disadvantaged party had assumed the risk of the change in circumstances. The word "assumption" makes it clear that the risks need not have been taken over expressly, but that this may follow from the very nature of the contract. A party who enters into a speculative transaction is deemed to accept a certain degree of risk, even though it may not have been fully aware of that risk at the time it entered into the contract.

Illustration

4. A, an insurance company specialised in the insurance of shipping risks, requests an additional premium from those of its customers who have contracts which include the risks of war and civil insurrection, so as to meet the substantially greater risk to which it is exposed following upon the simultaneous outbreak of war and civil insurrection in three countries in the same region. A is not entitled to such an adaptation of the contract, since by the war and civil insurrection clause insurance companies assume these risks even if three countries are affected at the same time.

4. Hardship relevant only to performance not yet rendered

By its very nature hardship can only become of relevance with respect to performances still to be rendered: once a party has performed, it is no longer entitled to invoke a substantial increase in the costs of its performance or a substantial decrease in the value of the performance it receives as a consequence of a change in circumstances which occurs after such performance.

If the fundamental alteration in the equilibrium of the contract occurs at a time when performance has been only partially rendered, hardship can be of relevance only to the parts of the performance still to be rendered. **Illustration**

5. A enters into a contract with B, a waste disposal company in country X, for the purpose of arranging the storage of its waste. The contract provides for a four-year term and a fixed price per ton of waste. Two years after the conclusion of the contract, the environmental movement in country X gains ground and the Government of country X prescribes prices for storing waste which are ten times higher than before. B may successfully invoke hardship only with respect to the two remaining years of the life of the contract.

5. Hardship normally relevant to long-term contracts

Although this article does not expressly exclude the possibility of hardship being invoked in respect of other kinds of contracts, hardship will normally be of relevance to long-term contracts, i.e. those where the performance of at least one party extends over a certain period of time.

6. Hardship and force majeure

In view of the respective definitions of hardship and force majeure (see Art. 7.1.7) under these Principles there may be factual situations which can at the same time be considered as cases of hardship and of force majeure. If this is the case, it is for the party affected by these events to decide which remedy to pursue. If it invokes force majeure, it is with a view to its non-performance being excused. If, on the other hand, a party invokes hardship, this is in the first instance for the purpose of renegotiating the terms of the contract so as to allow the contract to be kept alive although on revised terms.

7. Hardship and contract practice

The definition of hardship in this article is necessarily of a rather general character. International commercial contracts often contain much more precise and elaborate provisions in this regard. The parties may therefore find it appropriate to adapt the content of this article so as to take account of the particular features of the specific transaction.

ARTICLE 6.2.3 – Effects of hardship

(1) In case of hardship the disadvantaged party is entitled to request renegotiations. The request shall be made without undue delay and shall indicate the grounds on which it is based.

(2) The request for renegotiation does not in itself entitle the disadvantaged party to withhold performance.

(3) Upon failure to reach agreement within a reasonable time either party may resort to the court.

(4) If the court finds hardship it may, if reasonable,

(a) terminate the contract at a date and on terms to be fixed, or

(b) adapt the contract with a view to restoring its equilibrium.

COMMENT

1. Disadvantaged party entitled to request renegotiations

Since hardship consists in a fundamental alteration of the equilibrium of the contract, para. (1) of this article in the first instance entitles the disadvantaged party to request the other party to enter into renegotiation of the original terms of the contract with a view to adapting them to the changed circumstances. **Illustration**

> 1. A, a construction company situated in country X, enters into a lump sum contract with B, a governmental agency, for the erection of a plant in country Y. Most of the sophisticated machinery has to be imported from abroad. Due to an unexpected devaluation of the currency of country Y, which is the currency of payment, the cost of the machinery increases by more than 50%. A is entitled to request B to renegotiate the original contract price so as to adapt it to the changed circumstances.

A request for renegotiations is not admissible where the contract itself already incorporates a clause providing for the automatic adaptation of the contract (e.g. a clause providing for automatic indexation of the price if certain events occur). **Illustration**

> 2. The facts are the same as in Illustration 1, the difference being that the contract contains a price indexation clause relating to variations in the cost of materials and labour. A is not entitled to request a renegotiation of the price.

However, even in such a case renegotiation on account of hardship would not be precluded if the adaptation clause incorporated in the contract did not contemplate the events giving rise to hardship. **Illustration**

> 3. The facts are the same as in Illustration 2, the difference being that the substantial increase in A's costs is due to the adoption of new safety regulations in country Y. A is entitled to request B to renegotiate the original contract price so as to adapt it to the changed circumstances.

2. Request for renegotiations without undue delay

The request for renegotiations must be made as quickly as possible after the time at which hardship is alleged to have occurred (para. (1)). The precise time for requesting renegotiations will depend upon the circumstances of the case: it may, for instance, be longer when the change in circumstances takes place gradually (see comment 3(b) on Art. 6.2.2).

The disadvantaged party does not lose its right to request renegotiations simply because it fails to act without undue delay. The delay in making the request may however affect the finding as to whether hardship actually existed and, if so, its consequences for the contract.

3. Grounds for request for renegotiations

Para. (1) of this article also imposes on the disadvantaged party a duty to indicate the grounds on which the request for renegotiations is based so as to permit the other party better to assess whether or not the request for renegotiations is justified. An incomplete request is to be considered as not being raised in time, unless the grounds of the alleged hardship are so obvious that they need not be spelt out in the request. Failure to set forth the grounds on which the request for renegotiations is based may have similar effects to those resulting from undue delay in making the request (see comment 2 on this article).

4. Request for renegotiations and withholding of performance

Para. (2) of this article provides that the request for renegotiations does not of itself entitle the disadvantaged party to withhold performance. The reason for this lies in the exceptional character of hardship and in the risk of possible abuses of the remedy. Withholding performance may be justified only in extraordinary circumstances. **Illustration**

4. A enters into a contract with B for the construction of a plant. The plant is to be built in country X, which adopts new safety regulations after the conclusion of the contract. The new regulations require additional apparatus and thereby fundamentally alter the equilibrium of the contract making A's performance substantially more onerous. A is entitled to request renegotiations and may withhold performance in view of the time it needs to implement the new safety regulations, but it may also withhold the delivery of the additional apparatus, for as long as the corresponding price adaptation is not agreed.

5. Renegotiations in good faith

Although nothing is said in this article to that effect, both the request for renegotiations by the disadvantaged party and the conduct of both parties during the renegotiation process are subject to the general principle of good faith (Art. 1.7) and to the duty of co-operation (Art. 5.3). Thus the disadvantaged party must honestly believe that a case of hardship actually exists and not request renegotiations as a purely tactical manoeuvre. Similarly, once the request has been made, both parties must conduct the renegotiations in a constructive manner, in particular by refraining from any form of obstruction and by providing all the necessary information.

6. Resort to the court upon failure to reach an agreement

If the parties fail to reach agreement on the adaptation of the contract to the changed circumstances within a reasonable time, para. (3) of the present article authorises either party to resort to the court. Such a situation may arise either because the non-disadvantaged party completely ignored the request for renegotiations or because the renegotiations, although conducted by both parties in good faith, did not achieve a positive outcome.

How long a party must wait before resorting to the court will depend on the complexity of the issues to be settled and the particular circumstances of the case.

7. Court measures in case of hardship

According to para. (4) of this article a court which finds that a hardship situation exists may react in a number of different ways. A first possibility is for it to terminate the contract.

However, since termination in this case does not depend on a non-performance by one of the parties, its effects on the performances already rendered might be different from those provided for by the rules governing termination in general (Arts. 7.3.1. *et seq.*). Accordingly, para. (4)(a) provides that termination shall take place "at a date and on terms to be fixed" by the court.

Another possibility would be for a court to adapt the contract with a view to restoring its equilibrium (para. (4)(b)). In so doing the court will seek to make a fair distribution of the losses between the parties. This may or may not, depending on the nature of the hardship, involve a price adaptation. However, if it does, the adaptation will not necessarily reflect in full the loss entailed by the change in circumstances, since the court will, for instance, have to consider the extent to which one of the parties has taken a risk and the extent to which the party entitled to receive a performance may still benefit from that performance.

Para. (4) of this article expressly states that the court may terminate or adapt the contract only when this is reasonable. The circumstances may even be such that neither termination nor adaptation is appropriate and in consequence the only reasonable solution will be for the court either to direct the parties to resume negotiations with a view to reaching agreement on the adaptation of the contract, or to confirm the terms of the contract as they stand. **Illustration**

    5. A, an exporter, undertakes to supply B, an importer in country X, with beer for three years. Two years after the conclusion of the contract new legislation is introduced in country X prohibiting the sale and consumption of alcoholic drinks. B immediately invokes hardship and requests A to renegotiate the contract. A recognises that hardship has occurred, but refuses to accept the modifications of the contract proposed by B. After one month of fruitless discussions B resorts to the court. If B has the possibility to sell the beer in a neighbouring country, although at a substantially lower price, the court may decide to uphold the contract but to reduce the agreed price.

If on the contrary B has no such possibility, it may be reasonable for the court to terminate the contract, at the same time however requiring B to pay A for the last consignment still en route.

CHAPTER 7
NON-PERFORMANCE
SECTION 1: NON-PERFORMANCE IN GENERAL

ARTICLE 7.1.1 – Non-performance defined

Non-performance is failure by a party to perform any of its obligations under the contract, including defective performance or late performance.

COMMENT

This article defines "non-performance" for the purpose of the Principles. Particular attention should be drawn to two features of the definition.

The first is that "non-performance" is defined so as to include all forms of defective performance as well as complete failure to perform. So it is non-performance for a builder to erect a building which is partly in accordance with the contract and partly defective or to complete the building late. The second feature is that for the purposes of the Principles the concept of "non-performance" includes both non-excused and excused non-performance.

Non-performance may be excused by reason of the conduct of the other party to the contract (see Arts. 7.1.2 (Interference by the other party) and 7.1.3 (Withholding performance) and comments) or because of unexpected external events (Art. 7.1.7 (Force majeure) and comment).

A party is not entitled to claim damages or specific performance for an excused non-performance of the other party but a party who has not received performance will as a rule be entitled to terminate the contract whether or not the non-performance is excused. See Art. 7.3.1 *et seq.* and comment.

There is no general provision dealing with cumulation of remedies. The assumption underlying the Principles is that all remedies which are not logically inconsistent may be cumulated. So, in general, a party who successfully insists on performance will not be entitled to damages but there is no reason why a party may not terminate a contract for non-excused non-performance and simultaneously claim damages. See Arts. 7.2.5 (Change of remedy), 7.3.5 (Effects of termination in general) and 7.4.1 (Right to damages).

ARTICLE 7.1.2 – Interference by the other party

A party may not rely on the non-performance of the other party to the extent that such non-performance was caused by the first party's act or omission or by another event as to which the first party bears the risk.

COMMENT

1. Non-performance caused by act or omission of the party alleging non-performance

This article can be regarded as providing two excuses for non-performance. However conceptually, it goes further than this. When the article applies, the relevant conduct does not become excused non-performance but loses the quality of non-performance altogether. It follows, for instance, that the other party will not be able to terminate for non-performance.

Two distinct situations are contemplated. In the first, one party is unable to perform either wholly or in part because the other party has done something which makes performance in whole or in part impossible. **Illustration**

1. A agrees to perform building work on B's

land beginning on 1 February. If B locks the gate to the land and does not allow A entry, B cannot complain that A has failed to begin work. B's conduct will often amount to non-excused non-performance either because of an express provision entitling A to access to the land or because B's conduct infringes the obligations of good faith and co-operation. This result does not however depend on B's non-performance being non-excused. The result will be the same where B's non-performance is excused, for instance because access to the land is barred by strikers.

The Principles contemplate the possibility of one party's interference acting only as a partial impediment to performance by the other party and in such cases it will be necessary to decide the extent to which non-performance was caused by the first party's interference and that to which it was caused by other factors.

2. Non-performance caused by event for which party alleging non-performance bears the risk

Another possibility is that non-performance may result from an event the risk of which is expressly or impliedly allocated by the contract to the party alleging non-performance.

Illustration

> 2. A, a builder, concludes a construction contract to be performed on the premises of B who already has many buildings on those

premises which are the subject of an insurance policy covering any damage to the buildings. If the parties agree that the risk of accidental damage is to fall on B as the person insured, there would normally be no reason to reject the parties' allocation of risk since risks of this kind are normally covered by insurance. Even therefore if a fire were to be caused by A's negligence, the risk may be allocated to B although it would clearly need more explicit language to carry this result than would be the case if the fire which destroyed the building were the fault of neither party.

ARTICLE 7.1.3 – Withholding performance

(1) Where the parties are to perform simultaneously, either party may withhold performance until the other party tenders its performance.

(2) Where the parties are to perform consecutively, the party that is to perform later may withhold its performance until the first party has performed.

COMMENT

This article must be read together with Art. 6.1.4 (Order of performance). The present article is concerned with remedies and corresponds in effect to the civil law concept of exceptio non adimpleti contractus. **Illustration**

> A agrees to sell to B a thousand tons of white wheat, cif Rotterdam, payment to be made by confirmed letter of credit opened in German marks on a German bank. A is not obliged to

ship the goods unless and until B opens the letter of credit in conformity with its contractual obligations.

The text does not explicitly address the question which arises where one party performs in part but does not perform completely. In such a case the party entitled to receive performance may be entitled to withhold performance but only where in normal circumstances this is consonant with good faith (Art. 1.7).

ARTICLE 7.1.4 – Cure by non-performing party

(1) The non-performing party may, at its own expense, cure any non-performance, provided that

(a) without undue delay, it gives notice indicating the proposed manner and timing of the cure;

(b) cure is appropriate in the circumstances;

(c) the aggrieved party has no legitimate interest in refusing cure; and (d) cure is effected promptly.

(2) The right to cure is not precluded by notice of termination.

(3) Upon effective notice of cure, rights of the aggrieved party that are inconsistent with the non-performing party's performance are suspended until the time for cure has expired.

(4) The aggrieved party may withhold performance pending cure.

(5) Notwithstanding cure, the aggrieved party retains the right to claim damages for delay as well as for any harm caused or not prevented by the cure.

COMMENT

1. General principle

Para. (1) of this article provides that, if certain conditions are met, the non-performing party may cure by correcting the non-performance. In effect, by meeting these conditions, the non-performing party is able to extend the time for performance

for a brief period beyond that stipulated in the contract, unless timely performance is required by the agreement or the circumstances. This article thus favours the preservation of the contract. It also reflects the policy of minimising economic waste, as incorporated in Art. 7.4.8

(Mitigation of harm), and the basic principle of good faith stated in Art. 1.7. This article is related to the cure provisions contained in Arts. 37 and 48 CISG and in some domestic laws governing contracts and sales. Even many of those legal systems that do not have a rule permitting cure would normally take a reasonable offer of cure into account in assessing damages.

2. Notice of cure

Cure may be effected only after the non-performing party gives notice of cure. The notice must be reasonable with regard to its timing and content as well as to the manner in which it is communicated. Notice of cure must be given without undue delay after the non-performing party learns of the non-performance. To the extent information is then available, the notice must indicate how cure is to be effected and when. Notice must also be communicated to the aggrieved party in a manner that is reasonable in the circumstances.

Notice of cure is considered to be "effective" when the requirements of para. (1)(a) - (c) have been met.

3. Appropriateness of cure

Whether cure is appropriate in the circumstances depends on whether it is reasonable, given the nature of the contract, to permit the non-performing party to make another attempt at performance. As indicated in para. (2), cure is not precluded merely because the failure to perform amounts to a fundamental non-performance. The factors to be considered in determining the appropriateness of cure include whether the proposed cure promises to be successful in resolving the problem and whether the necessary or probable delay in effecting cure would be unreasonable or would itself constitute a fundamental non-performance. However, the right to cure is not defeated by the fact that the aggrieved party subsequently changes its position. If the non-performing party gives effective notice of cure, the aggrieved party's right to change position is suspended. Nonetheless, the situation may be different if the aggrieved party has changed position before receiving notice of cure.

4. The aggrieved party's interest

The non-performing party may not cure if the aggrieved party can demonstrate a legitimate interest in refusing cure. However, if notice of cure is properly given and if cure is appropriate in the circumstances, it is presumed that the non-performing party should be permitted to cure. A legitimate interest may arise, for example, if it is likely that, when attempting cure, the non-performing party will cause damage to person or property. On the other hand, a legitimate interest is not present if, on the basis of the non-performance, the aggrieved party has simply decided that it does not wish to continue contractual relations. **Illustration**

1. A agrees to construct a road on B's property. When the road is complete, B discovers that the road grade is steeper than the contract permits. B also discovers that, during construction, A's trucks caused damage to B's timber. A gives notice of cure to regrade the road. Even if cure would otherwise be appropriate in the circumstances, B's desire to prevent further damage to the timber may provide a legitimate interest for refusing cure.

5. Timing of cure

Cure must be effected promptly after notice of cure is given. Time is of the essence in the exercise of the right to cure. The non-performing party is not permitted to lock the aggrieved party into an extended waiting period. The lack of inconvenience on the part of the aggrieved party does not justify the non-performing party in delaying cure.

6. Proper forms of cure

Cure may include repair and replacement as well as any other activities that remedy the non-performance and give to the aggrieved party all that it is entitled to expect under the contract. Repairs constitute cure only when they leave no evidence of the prior non-performance and do not threaten the value or the quality of the product as a whole. It is left to the courts to determine the number of times the non-performing party may attempt a cure. **Illustration**

2. A agrees to install an assembly line for high temperature enamel painting in B's factory. The motors are installed with insufficient lubricant and as a result "lock up" after a few hours of operation. A replaces the motors in a timely fashion, but refuses to examine and test the rest of the equipment to ensure that other parts of the line have not been damaged. A has not effectively cured.

7. Suspension of other remedies

When the non-performing party has given effective notice of cure, the aggrieved party may, in accordance with para. (4), withhold its own performance but, pursuant to para. (3), may not exercise any remedies inconsistent with the non-performing party's right to cure until it becomes clear that a timely and proper cure has not been or will not be effected. Inconsistent remedies include giving notice of termination, entering into replacement transactions and seeking damages or restitution.

8. Effect of a notice of termination

If the aggrieved party has rightfully terminated the contract pursuant to Arts. 7.3.1(1) and 7.3.2(1), the effects of termination (Art. 7.3.5) are also suspended by an effective notice of cure. If the non-performance is cured, the notice of termination is inoperative. On the other hand, termination takes effect if the time for cure has expired and any fundamental non-performance has not been cured.

9. Right of aggrieved party to damages

Under para. (5) of this article, even a non-performing party who successfully cures is liable for any harm that, before cure, was occasioned by the non-performance, as well as for any additional harm caused by the cure itself or by the delay or for any harm which the cure does not prevent. The principle of full compensation for damage suffered, as provided in Art. 7.4.2, is fundamental to these Principles.

10. The aggrieved party's obligations

The decision to invoke this article rests on the non-performing party. Once the aggrieved party receives effective notice of cure, it must permit cure and, as provided in Art. 5.3, cooperate with the non-performing party. For example, the aggrieved party must permit any inspection that is reasonably necessary for the non-performing party to effect cure. If the aggrieved party refuses to permit cure when required to do so, any notice of termination is ineffective. Moreover, the aggrieved party may not seek remedies for any non-performance that could have been cured.

Illustration

3. A agrees to construct a shed on B's property in order to protect B's machinery from the weather. The roof is constructed in a defective manner. During a storm, water leaks into the shed and B's machinery is damaged. B gives notice of termination. A gives timely notice of cure. B does not wish to deal further with A and refuses the cure. If cure is appropriate in the circumstances and the other conditions for cure are met, B cannot invoke remedies for the faulty construction but can recover for damage caused to the machinery before the cure was to be effected. If cure is inappropriate in the circumstances, or if the proposed cure could not have solved the problem, the contract is terminated by B's notice.

ARTICLE 7.1.5 – Additional period for performance

(1) In a case of non-performance the aggrieved party may by notice to the other party allow an additional period of time for performance.

(2) During the additional period the aggrieved party may withhold performance of its own reciprocal obligations and may claim damages but may not resort to any other remedy. If it receives notice from the other party that the latter will not perform within that period, or if upon expiry of that period due performance has not been made, the aggrieved party may resort to any of the remedies that may be available under this Chapter.

(3) Where in a case of delay in performance which is not fundamental the aggrieved party has given notice allowing an additional period of time of reasonable length, it may terminate the contract at the end of that period. If the additional period allowed is not of reasonable length it shall be extended to a reasonable length. The aggrieved party may in its notice provide that if the other party fails to perform within the period allowed by the notice the contract shall automatically terminate.

(4) Paragraph (3) does not apply where the obligation which has not been performed is only a minor part of the contractual obligation of the non-performing party.

COMMENT

This article deals with the situation where one party performs late and the other party is willing to give extra time for performance. It is inspired by the German concept of Nachfrist although similar results are obtained by different conceptual means in other legal systems.

1. Special characteristics of late performance

The article recognises that late performance

is significantly different from other forms of defective performance. Late performance can never be remedied since once the date for performance has passed it will not occur again, but nevertheless in many cases the party who is entitled to performance will much prefer even a late performance to no performance at all. Secondly, at the moment when a party fails to perform on time it is often unclear how late performance will in fact be. The commercial interest of the party receiving performance may often therefore be that a reasonably speedy completion, although late, will be perfectly acceptable but that a long delayed completion will not. The procedure enables that party to give the performing party a second chance without prejudicing its other remedies.

2. Effects of granting extension of time for performance

The party who grants the extension of time cannot terminate or seek specific performance during the extension time. The right to recover damages arising from late performance is not affected. The position at the end of the period of extension depends on whether the late performance was already fundamental at the time when the extension was granted. In this situation, if the contract is not completely performed during the extension, the right to terminate for fundamental non-performance simply springs into life again as soon as the extension period expires. On the other hand, if the late performance was not yet fundamental, termination would only be possible at the end of the period of extension if the extension was reasonable in length.

Illustrations

1. A agrees to construct a special bullet-proof body for B's Rolls Royce. The contract provides that the body is to be finished by 1 February so that the car can be shipped to B's country of residence. On 31 January the car is needed but not yet quite finished. A assures B that it will be able to complete the work if given another week and B agrees to a week's extension of time. If the car is finished within the week B must accept it but may recover any damages, for example extra shipping charges. If the work is not finished within the week, B may refuse to accept delivery and terminate the contract.

2. A, a company in country X, concludes a contract with B, a company in country Y, to build 100 km. of motorway in the latter country. The contract provides that the motorway will be finished within two years from the start of the work. After two years, A has in fact built 85 km. and it is clear that it will take at least three more months to finish the motorway. B gives A notice to complete within a further month. B is not entitled to terminate at the end of the month because the additional period of time is not reasonable; it shall be extended to the reasonable period of three months.

ARTICLE 7.1.6 – Exemption clauses

A clause which limits or excludes one party's liability for non-performance or which permits one party to render performance substantially different from what the other party reasonably expected may not be invoked if it would be grossly unfair to do so, having regard to the purpose of the contract.

COMMENT

1. The need for a special rule on exemption clauses

The Principles contain no general rule permitting a court to strike down abusive or unconscionable contract terms. Apart from the principle of good faith and fair dealing (Art. 1.7) which may exceptionally be invoked in this respect, there is only one provision permitting the avoidance at any time of the contract as a whole as well as of any of its individual terms when they unjustifiably give one party an excessive advantage (Art. 3.10).

The reason for the inclusion of a specific provision on exemption clauses is that they are particularly common in international contract practice and tend to give rise to much controversy between the parties.

Ultimately, the present article has opted in favour of a rule which gives the court a broad discretionary power based on the principle of fairness. Terms regulating the consequences of non-performance are in principle valid but the court may ignore clauses which are grossly unfair.

2. "Exemption clauses" defined

For the purpose of this article exemption clauses are in the first instance those terms which directly limit or exclude the non-performing party's liability in the event of non-performance.

Such clauses may be expressed in different ways (e.g. fixed sum, ceiling, percentage of the performance in question, deposit retained).

Exemption clauses are further considered to be those which permit a party to render a performance substantially different from what the other party reasonably expected. In practice clauses of this kind are in particular those whose purpose or effect is to allow the performing party unilaterally to alter the character of the performance promised in such a way as to transform the contract. Such clauses are to be distinguished from those which are limited to defining the performance undertaken by the party in question. **Illustration**

> 1. A tour operator offers at a high price a tour providing for accommodation in specifically designated luxury hotels. A term of the contract provides that the operator may alter the accommodation if the circumstances so require. If the operator puts up its clients in second class hotels, it will be liable to them notwithstanding the contractual term since the clients expected to be accommodated in hotels of a category similar to that which had been promised.
>
> 2. A hotelkeeper exhibits a notice to the effect that the hotel is responsible for cars left in the garage but not for objects contained in the cars. This term is not an exemption clause for the purpose of this article since its purpose is merely that of defining the scope of the hotelkeeper's obligation.

3. Exemption clauses to be distinguished from forfeiture clauses

Exemption clauses are to be distinguished from forfeiture clauses which permit a party to withdraw from a contract on payment of an indemnity. In practice, however, there may be forfeiture clauses which are in reality intended by the parties to operate as disguised exemption clauses.

4. Exemption clauses and agreed payment for non-performance

A contract term providing that a party who does not perform is to pay a specified sum to the aggrieved party for such non-performance (see Art. 7.4.13) may also have the effect of limiting the compensation due to the aggrieved party. In such cases the non-performing party may not be entitled to rely on the term in question if the conditions laid down in the present article are satisfied. **Illustration**

> 3. A enters into a contract with B for the building of a factory. The contract contains a penalty clause providing for payment of 10,000 Australian dollars for each week of delay. The work is not completed within the agreed period because A deliberately suspends the work for another project which was more lucrative for it and in respect of which the penalty for delay was higher. The actual harm suffered by B as a result of the delay amounts to 20,000 Australian dollars per week. A is not entitled to rely on the penalty clause and B may recover full compensation of the actual harm sustained, as the enforcement of that clause would in the circumstances be grossly unfair in view of A's deliberate non-performance.

5. Cases where exemption clauses may not be relied upon

Following the approach adopted in most national legal systems this article starts out from the assumption that in application of the doctrine of freedom of contract (Art. 1.1) exemption clauses are in principle valid. A party may not however invoke such a clause if it would be grossly unfair to do so.

This will above all be the case where the term is inherently unfair and its application would lead to an evident imbalance between the performances of the parties. Moreover, there may be circumstances in which even a term that is not in itself manifestly unfair may not be relied upon: for instance, where the non-performance is the result of grossly negligent conduct or where the aggrieved party could not have obviated the consequences of the limitation or exclusion of liability by taking out appropriate insurance. I n all cases regard must be had to the purpose of the contract and in particular to what a party could legitimately have expected from the performance of the contract. **Illustrations**

> 4. A, an accountant, undertakes to prepare B's accounts. The contract contains a term excluding any liability of A for the consequences arising from any inaccuracy whatsoever in A's performance of the contract. As a result of a serious mistake by A, B pays 100% more taxes than were due. A may not rely on the exemption clause which is inherently unfair.
>
> 5. A, a warehouse operator, enters into a contract with B for the surveillance of its premises. The contract contains a term limiting B's liability. Thefts occur in the terminal resulting in loss exceeding the amount of the limitation.

Although the term, agreed upon by two professional parties, is not inherently unfair, it may not be relied upon by B if the thefts are committed by B's servants in the course of their employment.

6. Consequence of inability to rely on exemption clauses

If a party is not entitled to rely on an exemption clause, its liability is unaffected and the aggrieved party may obtain full compensation for the non-performance. Contrary to the rule laid down with respect to agreed payment for non-performance in Art. 7.4.13, the court has no power to modify the exemption clause.

ARTICLE 7.1.7 – Force majeure

(1) Non-performance by a party is excused if that party proves that the non-performance was due to an impediment beyond its control and that it could not reasonably be expected to have taken the impediment into account at the time of the conclusion of the contract or to have avoided or overcome it or its consequences.

(2) When the impediment is only temporary, the excuse shall have effect for such period as is reasonable having regard to the effect of the impediment on the performance of the contract.

(3) The party who fails to perform must give notice to the other party of the impediment and its effect on its ability to perform. If the notice is not received by the other party within a reasonable time after the party who fails to perform knew or ought to have known of the impediment, it is liable for damages resulting from such non-receipt.

(4) Nothing in this article prevents a party from exercising a right to terminate the contract or to withhold performance or request interest on money due.

COMMENT

1. The notion of force majeure

This article covers the ground covered in common law systems by the doctrines of frustration and impossibility of performance and in civil law systems by doctrines such as force majeure, *Unmöglichkeit*, etc. but it is identical with none of these doctrines. The term "force majeure" was chosen because it is widely known in international trade practice, as confirmed by the inclusion in many international contracts of so-called "force majeure" clauses. **Illustration**

1. A, a manufacturer in country X, sells a nuclear power station to B, a utility company in country Y. Under the terms of the contract A undertakes to supply all the power station's requirements of uranium for ten years at a price fixed for that period, expressed in United States dollars and payable in New York. The following separate events occur: (1) After five years the currency of country Y collapses to 1% of its value against the dollar at the time of the contract. B is not discharged from liability as the parties have allocated this risk by the payment provisions. (2) After five years the government of country Y imposes foreign exchange controls which prevent B paying in any currency other than that of country Y. B is excused from paying in United States dollars. A is entitled to terminate the contract to supply uranium. (3) After five years the world uranium market is cornered by a group of Texan speculators. The price of uranium on the world market rises to ten times the contract figure. A is not excused from delivering uranium as this is a risk which was foreseeable at the time of making the contract.

2. Effects of force majeure on the rights and duties of the parties

The article does not restrict the rights of the party who has not received performance to terminate if the non performance is fundamental. What it does do, where it applies, is to excuse the non-performing party from liability in damages.

In some cases the impediment will prevent any performance at all but in many others it will simply delay performance and the effect of the article will be to give extra time for performance. It should be noted that in this event the extra time may be greater (or less) than the length of the interruption because the crucial question will be what is the effect of the interruption on the progress of the contract. **Illustration**

2. A contracts to lay a natural gas pipeline across country X. Climatic conditions are such that it is normally impossible to work between 1 November and 31 March. The contract is timed to finish on 31 October but the start of work is delayed for a month by a civil war in a neighbouring country which makes it impossible

to bring in all the piping on time. If the consequence is reasonably to prevent the completion of the work until its resumption in the following spring, A may be entitled to an extension of five months even though the delay was itself of one month only.

3. Force majeure and hardship

The article must be read together with Chapter 6, section 2 of the Principles dealing with hardship. See comment 6 on Art. 6.2.2.

4. Force majeure and contract practice

The definition of force majeure in para. (1) of this article is necessarily of a rather general character. International commercial contracts often contain much more precise and elaborate provisions in this regard. The parties may therefore find it appropriate to adapt the content of this article so as to take account of the particular features of the specific transaction.

SECTION 2: RIGHT TO PERFORMANCE

ARTICLE 7.2.1 – Performance of monetary obligation

Where a party who is obliged to pay money does not do so, the other party may require payment.

COMMENT

This article reflects the generally accepted principle that payment of money which is due under a contractual obligation can always be demanded and, if the demand is not met, enforced by legal action before a court. The term "require" is used in this article to cover both the demand addressed to the other party and the enforcement, whenever necessary, of such a demand by a court.

The article applies irrespective of the currency in which payment is due or may be made. In other words, the right of the obligee to require

payment extends also to cases of payment in a foreign currency. For the determination of the currency in which a monetary obligation is due or payment may be made, see Arts. 6.1.9, 6.1.10 and 7.4.12.

Exceptionally, the right to require payment of the price of the goods or services to be delivered or rendered may be excluded. This is in particular the case where a usage requires a seller to resell goods which are neither accepted nor paid for by the buyer. For the applicability of usages, see Art. 1.8.

ARTICLE 7.2.2 – Performance of non-monetary obligation

Where a party who owes an obligation other than one to pay money does not perform, the other party may require performance, unless

(a) performance is impossible in law or in fact;

(b) performance or, where relevant, enforcement is unreasonably burdensome or expensive;

(c) the party entitled to performance may reasonably obtain performance from another source;

(d) performance is of an exclusively personal character; or (e) the party entitled to performance does not require performance within a reasonable time after it has, or ought to have, become aware of the non-performance.

COMMENT

1. Right to require performance of non-monetary obligations

In accordance with the general principle of the binding character of the contract (see Art. 1.3), each party should as a rule be entitled to require performance by the other party not only of monetary, but also of non-monetary obligations, assumed by that party. While this is not controversial in civil law countries, common

law systems allow enforcement of non-monetary obligations only in special circumstances.

Following the basic approach of CISG (Art. 46) this article adopts the principle of specific performance, subject to certain qualifications. The principle is particularly important with respect to contracts other than sales contracts. Unlike the obligation to deliver something, contractual obligations to do something or to abstain from doing something can often be performed only by the other contracting party itself. In such cases the only way of obtaining performance from a party who is unwilling to perform is by enforcement.

2. Remedy not discretionary

While CISG provides that "a court is not bound to enter a judgement for specific performance unless the court would do so under its own law in respect of similar contracts of sale not governed by [the] Convention" (Art. 28), under the Principles specific performance is not a discretionary remedy, i.e. a court must order performance, unless one of the exceptions laid down in the present article applies.

3. Exceptions to the right to require performance

a. *Impossibility*

A performance which is impossible in law or in fact, cannot be required (sub-para. (a)). However, impossibility does not nullify a contract: other remedies may be available to the aggrieved party. See Arts. 3.3 and 7.1.7(4). The refusal of a public permission which is required under the applicable domestic law and which affects the validity of the contract renders the contract void (see Art. 6.1.17(1)), with the consequence that the problem of enforceability of the performance cannot arise. When however the refusal merely renders the performance impossible without affecting the validity of the contract (see Art. 6.1.17(2)), sub-para. (a) of this article applies and performance cannot be required.

b. *Unreasonable burden*

In exceptional cases, particularly when there has been a drastic change of circumstances after the conclusion of a contract, performance, although still possible, may have become so onerous that it would run counter to the general principle of good faith and fair dealing (Art. 1.7) to require it. **Illustration**

> 1. An oil tanker has sunk in coastal waters in a heavy storm. Although it would be possible to lift the ship from the bottom of the sea, the shipper may not require performance of the contract of carriage if this would involve the shipowner in expense vastly exceeding the value of the oil. See Art. 7.2.2(b).

The words "where relevant, enforcement" take account of the fact that in common law systems it is the courts and not the obligees who supervise the execution of orders for specific

performance. As a consequence, in certain cases, especially those involving performances extended in time, courts in those countries refuse specific performance if supervision would impose undue burdens upon courts.

As to other possible consequences arising from drastic changes of circumstances amounting to a case of hardship, see Arts. 6.2.1 *et seq.*

c. *Replacement transaction*

Many goods and services are of a standard kind, i.e. the same goods or services are offered by many suppliers. If a contract for such staple goods or standard services is not performed, most customers will not wish to waste time and effort extracting the contractual performance from the other party. Instead, they will go into the market, obtain substitute goods or services and claim damages for non-performance.

In view of this economic reality sub-para. (c) excludes specific per-formance whenever the party entitled to performance may reasonably obtain performance from another source. That party may terminate the contract and conclude a replacement transaction. See Art. 7.4.5.

The word "reasonably" indicates that the mere fact that the same performance can be obtained from another source is not in itself sufficient, since the aggrieved party could not in certain circumstances reasonably be expected to have recourse to an alternative supplier. **Illustration**

> 2. A, situated in a developing country where foreign exchange is scarce, buys a machine of a standard type from B in Tokyo. In compliance with the contract, A pays the price of US$ 100,000 before delivery. B does not deliver. Although A could obtain the machine from another source in Japan, it would be unreasonable, in view of the scarcity and high price of foreign exchange in its home country, to require A to take this course. A is therefore entitled to require delivery of the machine from B.

d. *Performance of an exclusively personal character*

Where a performance has an exclusively personal character, enforcement would interfere with the personal freedom of the obligor. Moreover, enforcement of a performance often impairs its quality. The supervision of a very personal performance may also give rise to insuperable practical difficulties, as is shown by the experience of countries which have saddled their courts with this kind of responsibility. For all these reasons, sub-para. (d) excludes enforcement of performance of an exclusively personal character.

The precise scope of this exception depends essentially upon the meaning of the phrase "exclusively personal character". The modern tendency is to confine this concept to performances of a unique character. The exception does not apply to obligations undertaken by a company. Nor are ordinary activities of a lawyer, a surgeon or an engineer covered by the phrase for they can be performed by other persons with the same training and experience. A performance is of an exclusively personal character if it is not delegable and requires individual skills of an artistic or scientific nature or if it involves a confidential and personal relationship.

Illustrations

3. An undertaking by a firm of architects to design a row of 10 private homes can be specifically enforced as the firm can delegate the task to one of the partners or employ an outside architect to perform it.

4. By contrast, an undertaking by a world-famous architect to design a new city hall embodying the idea of a city of the 21st century cannot be enforced because it is highly unique and calls for the exercise of very special skills. The performance of obligations to abstain from doing something does not fall under sub-para. (d).

e. *Request within reasonable time*

Performance of a contract often requires special preparation and efforts by the obligor. If the time for performance has passed but the obligee has failed to demand performance within a reasonable time, the obligor may be entitled to assume that the obligee will not insist upon performance. If the obligee were to be allowed to leave the obligor in a state of uncertainty as to whether performance will be required, the risk might arise of the obligee's speculating unfairly, to the detriment of the obligor, upon a favourable development of the market.

For these reasons sub-para. (e) excludes the right to performance if it is not required within a reasonable time after the obligee has become, or ought to have become, aware of the non-performance.

For a similar rule concerning the loss of the right to terminate the contract, see Art. 7.3.2(2).

ARTICLE 7.2.3 – Repair and replacement of defective performance

The right to performance includes in appropriate cases the right to require repair, replacement, or other cure of defective performance. The provisions of Articles 7.2.1 and 7.2.2 apply accordingly.

COMMENT

1. Right to performance in case of defective performance

This article applies the general principles of Arts. 7.2.1 and 7.2.2 to a special, yet very frequent, case of non-performance, i.e. defective performance. For the sake of clarity the article specifies that the right to require performance includes the right of the party who has received a defective performance to require cure of the defect.

2. Cure of defective performance

Under the Principles cure denotes the right both of the non-performing party to correct its performance (Art. 7.1.4) and of the aggrieved party to require such correction by the non-performing party. The present article deals with the latter right.

The article expressly mentions two specific examples of cure, namely repair and replacement.

Repairing defective goods (or making good an insufficient service) is the most common case and replacement of a defective performance is also frequent. The right to require repair or replacement may also exist with respect to the payment of money, for instance in case of an insufficient payment or of a payment in the wrong currency or to an account different from that agreed upon by the parties.

Apart from repair and replacement there are other forms of cure, such as the removal of the rights of third persons over goods or the obtaining of a necessary public permission.

3. Restrictions

The right to require cure of a defective performance is subject to the same limitations as the right to performance in general. Most of the exceptions to the right to require performance that are set out in Art. 7.2.2 are easily applicable to the various forms of cure of a defective performance. Only the application of sub-para. (b) calls for specific comment. In many cases involving small, insignificant defects, both replacement and repair may involve "unreasonable effort or expense" and are therefore excluded. **Illustration**

A new car is sold which has a small painting defect which decreases the value of the car by 0,01 % of the purchase price. Repainting would cost 0,5% of the purchase price. A claim for repair is excluded but the buyer is entitled to require a reduction in the purchase price.

ARTICLE 7.2.4 – Judicial penalty

(1) Where the court orders a party to perform, it may also direct that this party pay a penalty if it does not comply with the order.

(2) The penalty shall be paid to the aggrieved party unless mandatory provisions of the law of the forum provide otherwise. Payment of the penalty to the aggrieved party does not exclude any claim for damages.

. . .

ARTICLE 7.2.5 – Change of remedy

(1) An aggrieved party who has required performance of a non-monetary obligation and who has not received performance within a period fixed or otherwise within a reasonable period of time may invoke any other remedy.

(2) Where the decision of a court for performance of a non-monetary obligation cannot be enforced, the aggrieved party may invoke any other remedy.

COMMENT

1. Aggrieved party entitled to change of remedy

This article addresses a problem which is peculiar to the right to require performance. The aggrieved party may abandon the remedy of requiring performance of a non-monetary obligation and opt instead for another remedy or remedies.

This choice is permitted on account of the difficulties usually involved in the enforcement of non-monetary obligations. Even if the aggrieved party first decides to invoke its right to require performance, it would not be fair to confine that party to this single option. The non-performing party may subsequently become unable to perform, or its inability may only become evident during the proceedings.

2. Voluntary change of remedy

Two situations must be addressed.

In the first case, the aggrieved party has required performance but changes its mind before execution of a judgment in its favour, perhaps because it has discovered the non-performing party's inability to perform. The aggrieved party now wishes to invoke one or more other remedies. Such a voluntary change of remedy can only be admitted if the interests of the non-performing party are duly protected. It may have prepared

for performance, invested effort and incurred expense. For this reason para. (1) of this article makes it clear that the aggrieved party is entitled to invoke another remedy only if it has not received performance within a fixed period or otherwise within a reasonable period of time.

How much additional time must be made available to the non-performing party for performance depends upon the difficulty which the performance involves. The non-performing party has the right to perform provided it does so before the expiry of the additional period.

For similar conditions which restrict the right of termination in case of delay in performance, see Art. 7.3.2(2).

3. Unenforceable decision

Para. (2) addresses the second and less difficult case in which the aggrieved party has attempted without success to enforce a judicial decision or arbitral award directing the non-performing party to perform. In this situation it is obvious that the aggrieved party may immediately pursue other remedies.

4. Time limits

In the event of a subsequent change of remedy the time limit provided for a notice of termination under Art. 7.3.2(2) must, of course, be extended accordingly. The reasonable time for giving notice begins to run, in the case of a voluntary change of remedy, after the aggrieved party has or ought to have become aware of the non-performance at the expiry of the additional period of time available to the non-performing party to perform; and in the case of para. (2) of this article, it will begin to run after the aggrieved party has or ought to have become aware of the unenforceability of the decision or award requiring performance.

SECTION 3: TERMINATION

ARTICLE 7.3.1 – Right to terminate the contract

(1) A party may terminate the contract where the failure of the other party to perform an obligation under the contract amounts to a fundamental non-performance.

(2) In determining whether a failure to perform an obligation amounts to a fundamental non-performance regard shall be had, in particular, to whether

(a) the non-performance substantially deprives the aggrieved party of what it was entitled to expect under the contract unless the other party did not foresee and could not reasonably have foreseen such result;

(b) strict compliance with the obligation which has not been performed is of essence under the contract;

(c) the non-performance is intentional or reckless;

(d) the non-performance gives the aggrieved party reason to believe that it cannot rely on the other party's future performance;

(e) the non-performing party will suffer disproportionate loss as a result of the preparation or performance if the contract is terminated.

(3) In the case of delay the aggrieved party may also terminate the contract if the other party fails to perform before the time allowed it under Article 7.1.5 has expired.

COMMENT

1. Termination even if non-performance is excused

The rules set out in this Chapter are intended to apply both to cases where the non-performing party is liable for the non-performance and to those where the non-performance is excused so that the aggrieved party can claim neither specific performance nor damages for non-performance.

Illustration

1. A, a company located in country X, buys wine from B in country Y. The Government of country X subsequently imposes an embargo upon the import of agricultural products from country Y. Although the impediment cannot be attributed to A, B may terminate the contract.

2. Right to terminate the contract dependent on fundamental non-performance

Whether in a case of non-performance by one party the other party should have the right to terminate the contract depends upon the weighing of a number of considerations. On the one hand, performance may be so late or so defective that the aggrieved party cannot use it for its intended purpose, or the behaviour of the non-performing party may in other respects be such that the aggrieved party should be permitted to terminate the contract. On the other hand, termination will often cause serious detriment to the non-performing party whose expenses in preparing and tendering performance may not be recovered.

For these reasons para. (1) of this article provides that an aggrieved party may terminate the contract only if the non-performance of the other party is "fundamental", i.e. material and not merely of minor importance. See also Arts. 7.3.3. and 7.3.4.

3. Circumstances of significance in determining whether non-performance is fundamental

Para. (2) of this article lists a number of circumstances which are relevant to the determination of whether, in a given case, failure to perform an obligation amounts to fundamental non-performance.

a. *Non-performance substantially depriving the other party of its expectations*

The first factor referred to in para. 2(a) is that the non-performance is so fundamental that the aggrieved party is substantially deprived of what it was entitled to expect at the time of the conclusion of the contract. **Illustration**

> 2. On 1 May A contracts to deliver standard software before 15 May to B who has requested speedy delivery. If A tenders delivery on 15 June, B may refuse delivery and terminate the contract.

The aggrieved party cannot terminate the contract if the non-performing party can show that it did not foresee, and could not reasonably have foreseen, that the non-performance was fundamental for the other party. **Illustration**

> 3. A undertakes to remove waste from B's site during 1992. B fails to inform A that B has hired excavators at high cost to begin work on the site on 2 January 1993. B cannot terminate its contract with A on the ground that A had not cleared the site on 2 January.

b. *Strict performance of contract of essence*

Para. (2)(b) looks not at the actual gravity of the non-performance but at the nature of the contractual obligation for which strict performance might be of essence. Such obligations of strict performance are not uncommon in commercial contracts. For example, in contracts for the sale of commodities the time of delivery is normally considered to be of the essence, and in a documentary credit transaction the documents tendered must conform strictly to the terms of the credit.

c. *Intentional non-performance*

Para. (2)(c) deals with the situation where the non-performance is intentional or reckless. It may, however, be contrary to good faith (Art. 1.7) to terminate a contract if the non-performance, even though committed intentionally, is insignificant.

d. *No reliance on future performance*

Under para. (2)(d) the fact that non-performance gives the aggrieved party reason to believe that it cannot rely on the other party's future performance is of significance. If a party is to make its performance in instalments, and it is clear that a defect found in one of the earlier performances will be repeated in all performances, the aggrieved party may terminate the contract even if the defects in the early instalment would not of themselves justify termination.

Sometimes an intentional breach may show that a party cannot be trusted. **Illustration**

> 4. A, the agent of B, who is entitled to reimbursement for expenses, submits false vouchers to B. Although the amounts claimed are insignificant, B may treat A's behaviour as a fundamental non-performance and terminate the agency contract.

e. *Disproportionate loss*

Para. (2)(e) deals with situations where a party who fails to perform has relied on the contract and has prepared or tendered performance. In these cases regard is to be had to the extent to which that party suffers disproportionate loss if the non-performance is treated as fundamental. Non-performance is less likely to be treated as fundamental if it occurs late, after the preparation of performance, than if it occurs early before such preparation. Whether a performance tendered or rendered can be of any benefit to the non-performing party if it is refused or has to be returned to that party is also of relevance. **Illustration**

> 5. On 1 May A undertakes to deliver software which is to be produced specifically for B. It is agreed that delivery shall be made before 31 December. A tenders delivery on 31 January, at which time B still needs the software, which A cannot sell to other users. B may claim damages from A, but cannot terminate the contract.

4. Termination after *Nachfrist*

Para. (3) makes reference to Art. 7.1.5, para. (3) of which provides that the aggrieved party may use the *Nachfrist* procedure to terminate a contract which may not otherwise be terminated in case of delay. See comment 2 on Art. 7.1.5.

ARTICLE 7.3.3 – Anticipatory non-performance

Where prior to the date for performance by one of the parties it is clear that there will be a fundamental non-performance by that party, the other party may terminate the contract.

COMMENT

This article establishes the principle that a non-performance which is to be expected is to be equated with a non-performance which occurred at the time when performance fell due. It is a requirement that it be clear that there will be non-performance; a suspicion, even a well-founded one, is not sufficient. Furthermore, it is necessary that the non-performance be fundamental and that the party who is to receive performance give notice of termination.

An example of anticipatory non-performance is the case where one party declares that it will not perform the contract; however, the circumstances also may indicate that there will be a fundamental non-performance. **Illustration**

A promises to deliver oil to B by M/S Paul in Montreal on 3 February. On 25 January M/S Paul is still 2000 kilometres from Montreal. At the speed it is making it will not arrive in Montreal on 3 February, but at the earliest on 8 February. As time is of the essence, a substantial delay is to be expected, and B may terminate the contract before 3 February.

ARTICLE 7.3.2 – Notice of termination

(1) The right of a party to terminate the contract is exercised by notice to the other party.
(2) If performance has been offered late or otherwise does not conform to the contract the aggrieved party will lose its right to terminate the contract unless it gives notice to the other party within a reasonable time after it has or ought to have become aware of the offer or of the non-conforming performance.

COMMENT

1. The requirement of notice

Para. (1) of this article reaffirms the principle that the right of a party to terminate the contract is exercised by notice to the other party. The notice requirement will permit the non-performing party to avoid any loss due to uncertainty as to whether the aggrieved party will accept the performance. At the same time it prevents the aggrieved party from speculating on a rise or fall in the value of the performance to the detriment of the non-performing party.

2. Performance overdue

When performance is due but has not been made, the aggrieved party's course of action will depend upon its wishes and knowledge.

It may be the case that the aggrieved party does not know whether the other party intends to perform, and either it no longer wants the performance or is undecided. In this case the aggrieved party may wait and see whether performance is ultimately tendered and make up its mind if and when this happens (see para. (2)). Alternatively, it may still want the other party to perform, in which case it must seek performance within a reasonable time after it has or ought to have become aware of the non-performance. See Art. 7.2.2(e).

This article does not deal with the situation where the non-performing party asks the aggrieved party whether it will accept late performance. Nor does it deal with the situation where the aggrieved party learns from another source that the non-performing party intends nevertheless to perform the contract. In such cases good faith (Art. 1.7) may require that the aggrieved party inform the other party if it does not wish to accept the late performance. If it does not do so, it may be held liable in damages.

3. "Reasonable time"

An aggrieved party who intends to terminate the contract must give notice to the other party within a reasonable time after it becomes or ought to have become aware of the non-performance (para. (2)).

What is "reasonable" depends upon the circumstances. In situations where the aggrieved party may easily obtain a substitute performance and may thus speculate on a rise or fall in the price, notice must be given without delay. When it must make enquiries as to whether it can obtain substitute performance from other sources the reasonable period of time will be longer.

4. Notice must be received

The notice to be given by the aggrieved party becomes effective when the non-performing party receives it. See Art. 1.9.

ARTICLE 7.3.4 – Adequate assurance of due performance

A party who reasonably believes that there will be a fundamental non-performance by the other party may demand adequate assurance of due performance and may meanwhile withhold its own performance. Where this assurance is not provided within a reasonable time the party demanding it may terminate the contract.

COMMENT

1. Reasonable expectation of fundamental non-performance

This article protects the interest of a party who has reason to believe that the other will be unable or unwilling to perform the contract at the due date but who cannot invoke Art. 7.3.3 since there is still a possibility that the other party will or can perform. In the absence of the rule laid down in the present article the former party would often be in a dilemma. If it were to wait until the due date of performance, and this did not take place, it might incur loss. If, on the other hand, it were to terminate the contract, and it then became apparent that the contract would have been performed by the other party, its action will amount to non-performance of the contract, and it will be liable in damages.

2. Right to withhold performance pending adequate assurance of performance

Consequently this article enables a party who reasonably believes that there will be a fundamental non-performance by the other party to demand an assurance of performance from the other party and in the meantime to withhold its own performance. What constitutes an adequate assurance will depend upon the circumstances. In some cases the other party's declaration that it will perform will suffice, while in others a request for security or for a guarantee from a third person may be justified. **Illustration**

> A, a boatbuilder with only one berth, promises to build a yacht for B to be delivered on 1 May, and no later. Soon afterwards, B learns from C that A has promised to build a yacht for C during the same period. B is entitled to ask A for an adequate assurance that the yacht will be delivered on time and A will then have to give B a satisfactory explanation of how it intends to perform its contract with B.

3. Termination of the contract

If adequate assurance of due performance is not given the other party may terminate the contract.

ARTICLE 7.3.5 – Effects of termination in general

(1) Termination of the contract releases both parties from their obligation to effect and to receive future performance.

(2) Termination does not preclude a claim for damages for non-performance.

(3) Termination does not affect any provision in the contract for the settlement of disputes or any other term of the contract which is to operate even after termination.

COMMENT

1. Termination extinguishes future obligations

Para. (1) of this article states the general rule that termination has effects for the future in that it releases both parties from their duty to effect and to receive future performance.

2. Claim for damages not affected

The fact that, by virtue of termination, the contract is brought to an end, does not deprive the aggrieved party of its right to claim damages for non-performance in accordance with the rules laid down in section 4 of this Chapter (Arts. 7.4.1. et seq.). **Illustration**

> 1. A sells B specified production machinery. After B has begun to operate the machinery serious defects in it lead to a shutdown of B's assembly plant. B declares the contract terminated but may still claim damages (Art. 7.3.5(2)).

3. Contract provisions not affected by termination

Notwithstanding the general rule laid down in para. (1), there may be provisions in the contract which survive its termination. This is the case in particular with provisions relating to dispute settlement but there may be others which by their very nature are intended to operate even after termination. **Illustration**

> 2. The facts are the same as in Illustration 1, the difference being that A discloses to B confidential information which is necessary for the production and which B agrees not to divulge for as long as it does not become public

knowledge. The contract further contains a clause referring disputes to the courts of A's country. Even after termination of the contract by B, B remains under a duty not to divulge the confidential information, and any dispute relating to the contract and its effects are to be settled by the courts of A's country (Art. 7.3.5(3)).

ARTICLE 7.3.6 – Restitution

(1) On termination of the contract either party may claim restitution of whatever it has supplied, provided that such party concurrently makes restitution of whatever it has received. If restitution in kind is not possible or appropriate allowance should be made in money whenever reasonable.

(2) However, if performance of the contract has extended over a period of time and the contract is divisible, such restitution can only be claimed for the period after termination has taken effect.

COMMENT

1. Entitlement of parties to restitution on termination

Para. (1) of this article provides for a right for each party to claim the return of whatever it has supplied under the contract provided that it concurrently makes restitution of whatever it has received. **Illustration**

> 1. A sells a Renoir painting to B for US$ 2,000,000. B does not pay for the picture when it is delivered. A can claim back the picture.

If the non-performing party cannot make restitution it must make allowance in money for the value it has received. Thus, in the case described in Illustration 1, B has to make allowance for the value of the picture if B has sold and delivered it to a purchaser from whom it cannot be reclaimed.

The rule also applies when the aggrieved party has made a bad bargain. If in the case mentioned in Illustration 1 the true value of the picture is US$ 3,000,000, A may still require the return of the picture and, if it cannot be returned, claim the true value of US$ 3,000,000.

The present article also applies to the situation where the aggrieved party has supplied money in exchange for property, services etc. which it has not received or which are defective. **Illustration**

> 2. The "Renoir" painting for which B has paid US$ 2,000,000 was not a Renoir but a copy. B can claim back the money and must return the copy to A.

Money returned for services or work which have not been performed or for property which has been rejected should be repaid to the party who paid for it and the same principle applies to custody of goods and to rent and leases of property.

2. Restitution not possible or appropriate

There are instances where instead of restitution in kind, allowance in money should be made. This is the case first of all where restitution in kind is not possible. **Illustration**

> 3. A, who has contracted to excavate B's site, leaves it after only half the work has been performed. B, who then terminates the contract, will have to pay A a reasonable sum for the work done, measured by the value that work has for B.

Allowance in money is further envisaged by para. (1) of this article whenever restitution in kind would not be "appropriate". This is so in particular when the aggrieved party has received part of the performance and wants to retain that part.

The purpose of specifying that allowance should be made in money "whenever reasonable" is to make it clear that allowance should only be made if, and to the extent that, the performance received has conferred a benefit on the party claiming restitution. **Illustration**

> 4. A, who has undertaken to decorate a bedroom suite for B, a furniture maker, abandons the work after having completed about half of the decorations. B can claim back the advance payments, but as the decorations made have no value for B, B does not have to pay for the work which has been done.

3. Contracts to be performed over a period of time

If the performance has extended over a period of time, restitution can, in accordance with para. (2) of this article, only be claimed in respect of the period after termination. **Illustration**

> 5. A contracts to service B's computer hardware and software for a period of five years. After three years of regular service A is obliged

by illness to discontinue the services and the contract is terminated. B, who has paid A for the fourth year, can claim return of the advance payment for that year but not the money paid for the three years of regular service.

This rule only applies if the contract is divisible. **Illustration**

> 6. A undertakes to paint ten pictures depicting a historical event for B's festival hall. After delivering and having been paid for five paintings, A abandons the work. B can claim return of the advances paid to A and must return the five paintings to A.

4. Other rules applicable to restitution

Both the rule in Art. 7.1.3 on the right to withhold performance and Art. 7.2.2 on specific performance of non-monetary obligations apply with appropriate adaptations to a claim for the restitution of property. Thus the aggrieved party cannot claim the return of goods when this has become impossible or would put the non-performing party to unreasonable effort or expense (see Art. 7.2.2 (a) and (b)). In such cases the non-performing party must make allowance for the value of the property. See Art. 7.3.6(1).

5. Rights of third persons not affected

In common with other articles of the Principles, Art. 7.3.6 deals with the relationship between the parties and not with any rights which third persons may have acquired on the goods concerned. Whether, for instance, an obligee of the buyer, the buyer's receivers in bankruptcy, or a purchaser in good faith may oppose the restitution of goods sold is to be determined by the applicable national law.

SECTION 4: DAMAGES

ARTICLE 7.4.1 – Right to damages

Any non-performance gives the aggrieved party a right to damages either exclusively or in conjunction with any other remedies except where the non-performance is excused under these Principles.

COMMENT

1. Right to damages in general

This article establishes the principle of a general right to damages in the event of non-performance, except where the non-performance is excused under the Principles, as in the case of force majeure (Art. 7.1.7) or of an exemption clause (Art. 7.1.6). Hardship (Art. 6.2.1 et seq.) does not in principle give rise to a right to damages.

The article recalls that the right to damages, like other remedies, arises from the sole fact of non-performance. It is enough for the aggrieved party simply to prove the non-performance, i.e. that it has not received what it was promised. It is in particular not necessary to prove in addition that the non-performance was due to the fault of the non-performing party. The degree of difficulty in proving the non-performance will depend upon the content of the obligation and in particular on whether the obligation is one of best efforts or one to achieve a specific result. See Art. 5.4.

The right to damages exists in the event of failure to perform any of the obligations which arise from the contract. Thus it is not necessary to draw a distinction between principal and accessory obligations.

2. Damages may be combined with other remedies

This article also states that the aggrieved party may request damages either as an exclusive remedy (for example damages for delay in the case of late performance or for defective performance accepted by the aggrieved party; damages in the event of impossibility of performance for which the non-performing party is liable), or in conjunction with other remedies. Thus, in the case of termination of the contract, damages may be requested to compensate the loss arising from such termination, or again, in the case of specific performance, to compensate for the delay with which the aggrieved party receives performance and for any expenses which might have been incurred. Damages may also be accompanied by other remedies (cure, publication in newspapers of, for example, an admission of error, etc.).

3. Damages and pre-contractual liability

The right to damages may arise not only in the context of non-performance of the contract, but also during the pre-contractual period. See, for instance, Art. 2.15 in case of negotiations in bad faith, Art. 2.16 in the event of breach of the duty of confidentiality, or Art. 3.18 in the case of mistake, fraud, threat or gross disparity. The rules governing damages for non-performance as laid down in this Section may be applied by analogy to those situations.

ARTICLE 7.4.2 – Full compensation

(1) The aggrieved party is entitled to full compensation for harm sustained as a result of the non-performance. Such harm includes both any loss which it suffered and any gain of which it was deprived, taking into account any gain to the aggrieved party resulting from its avoidance of cost or harm.

(2) Such harm may be non-pecuniary and includes, for instance, physical suffering or emotional distress.

COMMENT

1. Aggrieved party entitled to full compensation

Para. (1) of this article establishes the principle of the aggrieved party's entitlement to full compensation for the harm it has sustained as a result of the non-performance of the contract. It further affirms the need for a causal link between the non-performance and the harm. See also comment 3 on Art. 7.4.3. Non-performance must be a source neither of gain nor of loss for the aggrieved party. The solution to be found in some legal systems which allows the court to reduce the amount of damages having regard to the circumstances has not been followed, since in international situations it could risk creating a considerable degree of uncertainty and its application might moreover vary from one court to another.

2. Damages cover loss suffered, including loss of profit

In specifying the harm for which damages are recoverable, para. (1) of this article, following the rule laid down in Art. 74 CISG, states that the aggrieved party is entitled to compensation in respect not only of loss which it has suffered, but also of any gain of which it has been deprived as a consequence of the non-performance.

The notion of loss suffered must be understood in a wide sense. It may cover a reduction in the aggrieved party's assets or an increase in its liabilities which occurs when an obligee, not having been paid by its obligor, must borrow money to meet its commitments. The loss of profit or, as it is sometimes called, consequential loss, is the benefit which would normally have accrued to the aggrieved party if the contract had been properly performed. The benefit will often be uncertain so that it will frequently take the form of the loss of a chance. See Art. 7.4.3(2). **Illustrations**

1. The *Bibliothèque de France* sends a rare manuscript by special courier to New York for an exhibition. The manuscript is irreparably damaged during transport. Its loss in value is estimated at 50,000 French francs and it is this sum which is due by the courier.

2. A, who has not been paid by B under the terms of their contract, must borrow money from its bank at a high rate of interest. B must compensate A for the interest due by the latter to its bank.

3. A, a construction company, hires a crane from company B. The boom of the crane, which has been poorly maintained, breaks and in falling crushes the architect's car and results in an interruption of work on the site for eight days, for which A must pay a penalty for delay of 70,000 French francs to the owner. B must reimburse A for the expenses incurred as a consequence of the interruption of the work, the amount of the penalty and the cost of repairing the architect's car which A has had to pay.

4. A, a singer, cancels an engagement with B, an impresario. A must pay damages to B in respect not only of the expenses incurred by B in preparing the concert, but also of the loss of profit resulting from the cancellation of the concert.

3. Damages must not enrich the aggrieved party

However, the aggrieved party must not be enriched by damages for non-performance. It is for this reason that para. (1) also provides that account must be taken of any gain resulting to the aggrieved party from the non-performance, whether that be in the form of expenses which it has not incurred (e.g. it does not have to pay the cost of a hotel room for an artist who fails to appear), or of a loss which it has avoided (e.g. in the event of non-performance of what would have been a losing bargain for it). **Illustration**

> 5. A hires out excavating machinery to B for two years at a monthly rental of 50,000 French francs. The contract is terminated after six months for non-payment of the rentals. Six months later, A succeeds in renting out the same machinery at a monthly charge of 55,000 French francs. The gain of 60,000 French francs realised by A as a result of the reletting of the machinery for the remainder of the initial contract, that is to say one year, should be deducted from the damages due by B to A.

4. Damages in case of changes in the harm

In application of the principle of full compensation regard is to be had to any changes in the harm, including its expression in monetary terms, which may occur between the time of the non-performance and that of the judgment. The rule however is not without exceptions: for example, if the aggrieved party has itself already made good the harm at its own expense, the damages awarded will correspond to the amount of the sums disbursed.

5. Compensation of non-material harm

Para. (2) of this article expressly provides for compensation also of non-pecuniary harm. This may be pain and suffering, loss of certain amenities of life, aesthetic prejudice, etc. as well as harm resulting from attacks on honour or reputation.

The rule might find application, in international commerce, in regard to contracts concluded by artists, outstanding sportsmen or women and consultants engaged by a company or by an organisation. In these cases also, the requirement of the certainty of harm must be satisfied (see Art. 7.4.3), together with the other conditions for entitlement to damages. **Illustration**

> 6. A, a young architect who is beginning to build up a certain reputation, signs a contract for the modernisation of a municipal fine arts museum. The appointment receives wide press coverage. The municipal authorities subsequently decide to engage the services of a more experienced architect and terminate the contract with A. A may obtain compensation not only for the material loss suffered but also for the harm to A's reputation and the loss of the chance of becoming better known which the commission would have provided.

The compensation of non-material harm may assume different forms and it is for the court to decide which of them, whether taken alone or together, best assures full compensation. The court may not only award damages but also order other forms of redress such as the publication of a notice in newspapers designated by it (e.g. in case of breach of a clause prohibiting competition or the reopening of a business, defamation etc.).

ARTICLE 7.4.3 – Certainty of harm

(1) Compensation is due only for harm, including future harm, that is established with a reasonable degree of certainty.

(2) Compensation may be due for the loss of a chance in proportion to the probability of its occurrence.

(3) Where the amount of damages cannot be established with a sufficient degree of certainty, the assessment is at the discretion of the court.

COMMENT

1. Occurrence of harm must be reasonably certain

This article reaffirms the well-known requirement of certainty of harm, since it is not possible to require the non-performing party to compensate harm which may not have occurred or which may never occur. Para. (1) permits the compensation also of future harm, i.e. harm which has not yet occurred, provided that it is sufficiently certain. Para. (2) in addition covers loss of a chance, obviously only in proportion to the probability of its occurrence: thus, the owner of a horse which arrives too late to run in a race as a result of delay in transport cannot recover the whole of the prize money, even though the horse was the favourite.

2. Determination of extent of harm

Certainty relates not only to the existence of the harm but also to its extent. There may be harm whose existence cannot be disputed but which it is difficult to quantify. This will often be the case in respect of loss of a chance (there are not always "odds" as there are for a horse, for example a student preparing for a public examination) or of compensation for non-material harm (detriment to someone's reputation, pain and suffering, etc.). **Illustration**

> A entrusts a file to B, an express delivery company, in response to an invitation to submit tenders for the construction of an airport. B undertakes to deliver the file before the closing date for tenders but delivers it after that date and A's application is refused. The amount of compensation will depend upon the degree of probability of A's tender having been accepted and calls for a comparison of it with the applications which were admitted for consideration. The compensation will therefore be calculated as a proportion of the profit which A might have made.

According to para. (3), where the amount of damages cannot be established with a sufficient degree of certainty then, rather than refuse any compensation or award nominal damages, the court is empowered to make an equitable quantification of the harm sustained.

3. Harm must be a direct consequence of non-performance as well as certain

There is a clear connection between the certainty and the direct nature of the harm. Although the latter requirement is not expressly dealt with by the Principles, it is implicit in Art. 7.4.2(1) which refers to the harm sustained "as a result of the non-performance" and which therefore presupposes a sufficient causal link between the non-performance and the harm. Harm which is too indirect will usually also be uncertain as well as unforeseeable.

ARTICLE 7.4.4 – Foreseeability of harm

The non-performing party is liable only for harm which it foresaw or could reasonably have foreseen at the time of the conclusion of the contract as being likely to result from its non-performance.

COMMENT

The principle of limitation of recoverable harm to that which is foreseeable corresponds to the solution adopted in Art. 74 CISG. This limitation is related to the very nature of the contract: not all the benefits of which the aggrieved party is deprived fall within the scope of the contract and the non-performing party must not be saddled with compensation for harm which it could never have foreseen at the time of the conclusion of the contract and against the risk of which it could not have taken out insurance.

The requirement of foreseeability must be seen in conjunction with that of certainty of harm set out in Art. 7.4.3.

The concept of foreseeability must be clarified since the solution contained in the Principles does not correspond to certain national systems which allow compensation even for harm which is unforeseeable when the non-performance is due to wilful misconduct or gross negligence. Since the present rule does not provide for such an exception, a narrow interpretation of the concept of foreseeability is called for. Foreseeability relates to the nature or type of the harm but not to its extent unless the

extent is such as to transform the harm into one of a different kind. In any event, foreseeability is a flexible concept which leaves a wide measure of discretion to the judge. What was foreseeable is to be determined by reference to the time of the conclusion of the contract and to the non-performing party itself (including its servants or agents), and the test is what a normally diligent person could reasonably have foreseen as the consequences of non-performance in the ordinary course of things and the particular circumstances of the contract, such as the information supplied by the parties or their previous transactions. **Illustrations**

> 1. A cleaning company orders a machine which is delivered five months late. The manufacturer is obliged to compensate the company for lost profit caused by the delay in delivery as it could have foreseen that the machine was intended for immediate use. On the other hand the harm does not include the loss of a valuable government contract that could have been concluded if the machine had been delivered on time since that kind of harm was not foreseeable.
>
> 2. A, a bank, usually employs the services of a security firm for the conveyance of bags

containing coins to its branches. Without informing the security firm, A sends a consignment of bags containing new coins for collectors worth fifty times the value of previous consignments. The bags are stolen in a hold-up. A can only recover compensation corresponding to the value of the normal consignments as this was the only kind of harm that could have been foreseen and the value of the items lost was such as to transform the harm into one of another kind.

Unlike certain international conventions, particularly in the field of transport, the Principles follow CISG in not making provision for full compensation of harm, albeit unforeseeable, in the event of intentional non-performance.

ARTICLE 7.4.5 – Proof of harm in case of replacement transaction

Where the aggrieved party has terminated the contract and has made a replacement transaction within a reasonable time and in a reasonable manner it may recover the difference between the contract price and the price of the replacement transaction as well as damages for any further harm.

COMMENT

1. Amount of harm presumed in case of replacement transaction

It seems advisable to establish, alongside the general rules applicable to the proof of the existence and of the amount of the harm, presumptions which may facilitate the task of the aggrieved party.

The first of these presumptions is provided by this article which corresponds in substance to Art. 75 CISG. It concerns the situation where the aggrieved party has made a replacement transaction, for instance because so required by the duty to mitigate harm or in conformity with usages. In such cases, the harm is considered to be the difference between the contract price and the price of the replacement transaction.

The presumption comes into play only if there is a replacement transaction and not where the aggrieved party has itself performed the obligation which lay upon the non-performing party (for example when a shipowner itself carries out the repairs to its vessel following the failure to do so of the shipyard which had been entrusted with the work).

Nor is there replacement, and the general rules will apply, when a company, after the termination of a contract, uses its equipment for the performance of another contract which it could have performed at the same time as the first ("lost volume").

The replacement transaction must be performed within a reasonable time and in a reasonable manner so as to avoid the non-performing party being prejudiced by hasty or malicious conduct.

2. Further damages recoverable for additional harm

The rule that the aggrieved party may recover the difference between the two contract prices establishes a minimum right of recovery. The aggrieved party may also obtain damages for additional harm which it may have sustained.

Illustration

A, a shipyard, undertakes to accommodate a ship belonging to B, a shipowner, in dry dock for repairs costing US$ 500,000 as from 1 July. B learns on 1 June that the dry dock will only be available as from 1 August. B terminates the contract and after lengthy and costly negotiations concludes with C, another shipyard, an identical contract at a price of US$ 700,000. B is entitled to recover from A not only the difference in the price of US$ 200,000 but also the expenses it has incurred and compensation for the longer period of unavailability of the ship.

ARTICLE 7.4.6 – Proof of harm by current price

(1) Where the aggrieved party has terminated the contract and has not made a replacement transaction but there is a current price for the performance contracted for, it may recover the difference between the contract price and the price current at the time the contract is terminated as well as damages for any further harm.

(2) Current price is the price generally charged for goods delivered or services rendered in comparable circumstances at the place where the contract should have been performed or, if there is no current price at that place, the current price at such other place that appears reasonable to take as a reference.

COMMENT

1. Amount of harm presumed when no replacement transaction

The purpose of this article, which corresponds in substance to Art. 76 CISG, is to facilitate proof of harm where no replacement transaction has been made, but there exists a current price for the performance contracted for. In such cases the harm is presumed to be equal to the difference between the contract price and the price current at the time the contract was terminated.

2. Determination of "current price"

According to para. (2) "current price" is the price generally charged for the goods or services in question. The price will be determined in comparison with that which is charged for the same or similar goods or services. This will often, but not necessarily, be the price on an organised market. Evidence of the current price may be obtained from professional organisations, chambers of commerce etc.

For the purpose of this article the place relevant for determining the current price is that where the contract should have been performed or, if there is no current price at that place, the place that appears reasonable to take as a reference.

3. Further damages recoverable for additional harm

The rule that the aggrieved party may recover the difference between the contract price and the current price at the time of termination establishes only a minimum right of recovery. The aggrieved party may also obtain damages for additional harm which it may have sustained as a consequence of termination.

ARTICLE 7.4.7 – Harm due in part to aggrieved party

Where the harm is due in part to an act or omission of the aggrieved party or to another event as to which that party bears the risk, the amount of damages shall be reduced to the extent that these factors have contributed to the harm, having regard to the conduct of each of the parties.

COMMENT

1. Contribution of the aggrieved party to the harm

In application of the general principle established by Art. 7.1.2 which restricts the exercise of remedies where non-performance is in part due to the conduct of the aggrieved party, the present article limits the right to damages to the extent that the aggrieved party has in part contributed to the harm. It would indeed be unjust for such a party to obtain full compensation for harm for which it has itself been partly responsible.

2. Ways of contributing to the harm

The contribution of the aggrieved party to the harm may consist either in its own conduct or in an event as to which it bears the risk. The conduct may take the form of an act (e.g. it gave a carrier a mistaken address) or an omission (e.g. it failed to give all the necessary instructions to the constructor of the defective machinery). Most frequently such acts or omissions will result in the aggrieved party failing to perform one or another of its own contractual obligations; they may however equally consist in tortious conduct or non-performance of another contract. The external events for which the aggrieved party bears the risk may, among others, be acts or omissions of persons for whom it is responsible such as its servants or agents. **Illustrations**

1. A, a franchisee bound by an "exclusivity" clause contained in the contract with B, acquires stock from C because B has required immediate payment despite the fact that the franchise agreement provides for payment at 90 days. B claims payment of the penalty stipulated for breach of the exclusivity clause. B will obtain only part of the sum due thereunder as it was B who provoked A's non-performance.

2. A, a passenger on a liner effecting a luxury cruise, is injured when a lift fails to stop at the floor requested. B, the shipowner, is held liable for the consequences of A's injury and seeks recourse against C, the company which had checked the lifts before the liner's departure. It is proved that the accident would have been

avoided if the floor had been better lit. Since this was B's responsibility, B will not obtain full recovery from C.

3. Apportionment of contribution to the harm

The conduct of the aggrieved party or the external events as to which it bears the risk may have made it absolutely impossible for the non-performing party to perform. If the requirements of Art. 7.1.7 (Force majeure) are satisfied, the non-performing party is totally exonerated from liability. Otherwise, the exoneration will be partial, depending on the extent to which the aggrieved party contributed to the harm. The determination of each party's contribution to the harm may well prove to be difficult and will to a large degree depend upon the exercise of judicial discretion. In order to give some guidance to the court this article provides that the court shall have regard to the respective behaviour of the parties. The more serious a party's failing, the greater will be its contribution to the harm.

Illustrations

3. The facts are the same as in Illustration 1. Since it was B who was the first not to observe the terms of the contract, B is deemed to have caused A's failure to respect the exclusivity clause. B may only recover 25% of the amount stipulated in the penalty clause.

4. The facts are the same as in Illustration 2. Since the failings of B and C seem to be equivalent, B can only recover from C 50% of the compensation it had to pay A.

4. Contribution to harm and mitigation of harm

This article must be read in conjunction with the following article on mitigation of harm (Art. 7.4.8). While the present article is concerned with the conduct of the aggrieved party in regard to the cause of the initial harm, Art. 7.4.8 relates to that party's conduct subsequent thereto.

ARTICLE 7.4.8 – Mitigation of harm

(1) The non-performing party is not liable for harm suffered by the aggrieved party to the extent that the harm could have been reduced by the latter party's taking reasonable steps.

(2) The aggrieved party is entitled to recover any expenses reasonably incurred in attempting to reduce the harm.

COMMENT

1. Duty of aggrieved party to mitigate harm

The purpose of this article is to avoid the aggrieved party passively sitting back and waiting to be compensated for harm which it could have avoided or reduced. Any harm which the aggrieved party could have avoided by taking reasonable steps will not be compensated. Evidently, a party who has already suffered the consequences of non-performance of the contract cannot be required in addition to take time-consuming and costly measures. On the other hand, it would be unreasonable from the economic standpoint to permit an increase in harm which could have been reduced by the taking of reasonable steps.

The steps to be taken by the aggrieved party may be directed either to limiting the extent of the harm, above all when there is a risk of it lasting for a long time if such steps are not taken (often they will consist in a replacement transaction: see Art. 7.4.5), or to avoiding any increase in the initial harm. **Illustrations**

1. On 2 May, A requests B, a travel agency, to reserve a hotel room in Paris for 1 June, at a cost of 500 French francs. On 15 May, A learns that B has not made the reservation. A waits however until 25 May before making a new reservation and can only find a room costing 700 francs, whereas accommodation could have been secured for 600 francs if A had already taken action on 15 May. A can recover only 100 francs from B.

2. A, a company which has been entrusted by B with the building of a factory, suddenly stops work when the project is nearing completion. B looks for another company to finish the building of the factory but takes no steps to protect the buildings on the site whose condition deteriorates as a result of bad weather. B cannot recover compensation for such deterioration as it is attributable to its failure to take interim protective measures.

2. Reimbursement of expenses

The reduction in damages to the extent that the aggrieved party has failed to take the necessary steps to mitigate the harm must not however cause loss to that party. The aggrieved party may therefore recover from the non-performing party the expenses incurred by it in mitigating the harm, provided that those expenses were reasonable in the circumstances (para. (2)).

Illustrations

3. The facts are the same as in Illustration 2, the difference being that B has the necessary work carried out to ensure the interim protection of the buildings. The cost of such work will be added to the damages due by A for non-performance of the contract on condition that those costs were reasonable. If they were not, they will be reduced.

4. The facts are the same as in Illustration 1, the difference being that A takes a room costing 2,000 French francs in a luxury hotel. A may only recover the hundred franc difference in respect of the room which A could have obtained for 600 francs.

ARTICLE 7.4.9 – Interest for failure to pay money

(1) If a party does not pay a sum of money when it falls due the aggrieved party is entitled to interest upon that sum from the time when payment is due to the time of payment whether or not the non-payment is excused.

(2) The rate of interest shall be the average bank short-term lending rate to prime borrowers prevailing for the currency of payment at the place for payment, or where no such rate exists at that place, then the same rate in the State of the currency of payment. In the absence of such a rate at either place the rate of interest shall be the appropriate rate fixed by the law of the State of the currency of payment.

(3) The aggrieved party is entitled to additional damages if the non-payment caused it a greater harm.

COMMENT

1. Lump sum compensation for failure to pay a sum of money

This article reaffirms the widely accepted rule according to which the harm resulting from delay in the payment of a sum of money is subject to a special regime and is calculated by a lump sum corresponding to the interest accruing between the time when payment of the money was due and the time of actual payment.

Interest is payable whenever the delay in payment is attributable to the non-performing party, and this as from the time when payment was due, without any need for the aggrieved party to give notice of the default.

If the delay is the consequence of force majeure (e.g. the non-performing party is prevented from obtaining the sum due by reason of the introduction of new exchange control regulations), interest will still be due not as damages but as compensation for the enrichment of the debtor as a result of the non-payment as the debtor continues to receive interest on the sum which it is prevented from paying.

The harm is calculated as a lump sum. In other words, subject to para. (3) of this article, the aggrieved party may not prove that it could have invested the sum due at a higher rate of interest or the non-performing party that the aggrieved party would have obtained interest at a rate lower than the average lending rate referred to in para. (2).

The parties may of course agree in advance on a different rate of interest (which would in effect subject it to Art. 7.4.13).

2. Rate of interest

Para. (2) of this article fixes in the first instance as the rate of interest the average bank short-term lending rate to prime borrowers. This solution seems to be that best suited to the needs of international trade and most appropriate to ensure an adequate compensation of the harm sustained. The rate in question is the rate at which the aggrieved party will normally borrow the money which it has not received from the non-performing party. That normal rate is the average bank short-term lending rate to prime borrowers prevailing at the place for payment for the currency of payment.

No such rate may however exist for the currency of payment at the place for payment. In such cases, reference is made in the first instance to the average prime rate in the State of the currency of payment. For instance, if a loan is made in pounds sterling payable at Tunis and there is no rate for loans in pounds on the Tunis financial market, reference will be made to the rate in the United Kingdom.

In the absence of such a rate at either place, the rate of interest will be the "appropriate" rate fixed by the law of the State of the currency of payment. In most cases this will be the legal rate of interest and, as there may be more than one, that most appropriate for international transactions. If there is no legal rate of interest, the rate will be the most appropriate bank rate.

3. Additional damages recoverable

Interest is intended to compensate the harm normally sustained as a consequence of delay in payment of a sum of money. Such delay may however cause additional harm to the aggrieved party for which it may recover damages, always provided that it can prove the existence of such harm and that it meets the requirements of certainty and foreseeability (para. (3)).

Illustration

A concludes a contract with B, a specialised finance company, for a loan which will permit the renovation of its factory in Singapore. The loan specifically mentions the use of the funds. The money lent is transferred three months later than agreed. During that period the cost of the renovation has increased by ten percent. A is entitled to recover this additional sum from B.

ARTICLE 7.4.10 – Interest on damages

Unless otherwise agreed, interest on damages for non-performance of non-monetary obligations accrues as from the time of non-performance.

COMMENT

This article determines the time from which interest on damages accrues in cases of non-performance of obligations other than monetary obligations. In such cases, at the time of non-performance the amount of damages will usually not yet have been assessed in monetary terms. The assessment will only be made after the occurrence of the harm, either by agreement between the parties or by the court.

The present article fixes as the starting point for the accrual of interest the date of the occurrence of the harm. This solution is that best suited to international trade where it is not the practice for businesspersons to leave their money idle. In effect, the aggrieved party's assets are diminished as from the occurrence of the harm whereas the non-performing party, for as long as the damages are not paid, continues to enjoy the benefit of the interest on the sum which it will have to pay. It is only natural that this gain passes to the aggrieved party.

However, when making the final assessment of the harm, regard is to be had to the fact that damages are awarded as from the date of the harm, so as to avoid double compensation, for instance when a currency depreciates in value.

The present article takes no stand on the question of compound interest, which in some national laws is subject to rules of public policy limiting compound interest with a view to protecting the non-performing party.

ARTICLE 7.4.11 – Manner of monetary redress

(1) Damages are to be paid in a lump sum. However, they may be payable in instalments where the nature of the harm makes this appropriate.

(2) Damages to be paid in instalments may be indexed.

COMMENT

1. Lump sum or instalments

Although this article does not impose a fixed rule as to the manner in which damages are to be paid, the payment of damages as a lump sum is in general considered to be the mode of payment best suited to international trade. There are however situations in which payment by instalments will be more appropriate, having regard to the nature of the harm, for instance when the harm is on-going. **Illustrations**

1. A, a consultant, is retained by B for the purpose of checking the safety of its factories. A is killed when travelling by helicopter to one of B's factories, for which accident B is held responsible. A leaves two children aged twelve and eight. So as to compensate for the loss of the maintenance of the family, a monthly allowance will be payable to the children until they reach the age of majority.

2. A, a consultant in safety matters, is recruited by B for a three year period. The remuneration is fixed at 0.5% of the production. A is wrongfully dismissed after six months. It may be appropriate that B be ordered to pay A monthly a sum corresponding to the agreed salary until A has found new employment or, at the most, for thirty months.

2. Indexation

Para. (2) of this article contemplates the possibility of indexation of damages to be paid in instalments so as to avoid the complex mechanism of a review of the original judgment in order to take account of inflation. Indexation may however be prohibited by the law of the forum. **Illustration**

> 3. The facts are the same as in Illustration 1. The monthly allowance may be adjusted in accordance with the cost of living index applicable where the children live.

ARTICLE 7.4.12 – Currency in which to assess damages

Damages are to be assessed either in the currency in which the monetary obligation was expressed or in the currency in which the harm was suffered, whichever is more appropriate.

COMMENT

The harm resulting from the non-performance of an international contract may occur in different places and the question therefore arises of the currency in which it is to be assessed. This question is dealt with by the present article and should be kept distinct from that of the currency of payment of the damages addressed in Art. 6.1.9.

The article offers a choice between the currency in which the monetary obligation was expressed and that in which the harm was suffered, whichever is more appropriate in the circumstances.

While the first alternative calls for no particular comment, the second takes account of the fact that the aggrieved party may have incurred expenses in a particular currency to repair damage which it has sustained. In such a case it should be entitled to claim damages in that currency even if it is not the currency of the contract. Another currency which may be considered the most appropriate is that in which the profit would have been made.

The choice is left to the aggrieved party, provided that the principle of full compensation is respected. Finally, it may be noted that in the absence of any indication to the contrary, a party is entitled to interest and to liquidated damages and penalties in the same currency as that in which the main obligation is expressed.

ARTICLE 7.4.13 – Agreed payment for non-performance

(1) Where the contract provides that a party who does not perform is to pay a specified sum to the aggrieved party for such non-performance, the aggrieved party is entitled to that sum irrespective of its actual harm.

(2) However, notwithstanding any agreement to the contrary the specified sum may be reduced to a reasonable amount where it is grossly excessive in relation to the harm resulting from the non-performance and to the other circumstances.

COMMENT

1. Agreed payment for non-performance defined

This article gives an intentionally broad definition of agreements to pay a specified sum in case of non-performance, whether such agreements be intended to facilitate the recovery of damages (liquidated damages according to the common law) or to operate as a deterrent against non-performance (penalty clauses proper), or both.

2. Agreed payment for non-performance in principle valid

National laws vary considerably with respect to the validity of the type of clauses in question, ranging from their acceptance in the civil law countries, with or without the possibility of judicial review of particularly onerous clauses, to the outright rejection in common law systems of clauses intended specifically to operate as a deterrent against non-performance, i.e. penalty clauses. In view of their frequency in international contract practice, para. (1) of this article in principle acknowledges the validity of any clauses providing that a party who does not perform is to pay a specified sum to the aggrieved party for such non-performance, with the consequence that the latter is entitled to the agreed sum irrespective of the harm actually suffered by it. The non-performing party may not allege that the aggrieved party sustained less harm or none at all. **Illustration**

1. A, a former Brazilian international player, is recruited for three years to train the players of B, an Australian football team, at a monthly salary of 10,000 Australian dollars. Provision is made for a severance allowance of 200,000 Australian dollars in the event of unjustified dismissal. A is dismissed without any justification after six months. A is entitled to the agreed sum, even though A was immediately recruited by another team at double the salary received from B.

Normally, the non-performance must be one for which the non-performing party is liable, since it is difficult to conceive a clause providing for the payment of an agreed sum in case of non-performance operating in a force majeure situation. Exceptionally, however, such a clause may be intended by the parties also to cover non-performance for which the non-performing party is not liable.

In the case of partial non-performance, the amount may, unless otherwise agreed by the parties, be reduced in proportion.

3. Agreed sum may be reduced

In order to prevent the possibility of abuse to which such clauses may give rise, para. (2) of this article permits the reduction of the agreed sum if it is grossly excessive "in relation to the harm resulting from the non-performance and to the other circumstances". The same paragraph makes it clear that the parties may under no circumstances exclude such a possibility of reduction.

The agreed sum may only be reduced, but not entirely disregarded as would be the case were the judge, notwithstanding the agreement of the parties, to award damages corresponding to the exact amount of the harm. It may not be increased, at least under this article, where the agreed sum is lower than the harm actually sustained (see however comment 4 on Art. 7.1.6). It is moreover necessary that the amount agreed

be "grossly excessive", i.e. that it would clearly appear to be so to any reasonable person. Regard should in particular be had to the relationship between the sum agreed and the harm actually sustained. **Illustration**

2. A enters into a contract with B for the purchase of machinery which provides for 48 monthly payments of 30,000 French francs. The contract contains a clause allowing immediate termination in the event of non-payment by A of one instalment, and authorises B to keep the sums already paid and to recover future instalments as damages. A fails to pay the eleventh instalment. B keeps the 300,000 francs already paid and claims, in addition to the return of the machinery, the 1,140,000 francs representing the 38 outstanding instalments. The court will reduce the amount since A's non-performance would result in a grossly excessive benefit for B.

4. Agreed payment for non-performance to be distinguished from forfeiture and other similar clauses

The type of clauses dealt with in the present article must be distinguished from forfeiture and other similar clauses which permit a party to withdraw from a contract either by paying a certain sum or by losing a deposit already made. On the other hand a clause according to which the aggrieved party may retain sums already paid as part of the price falls within the scope of this article. **Illustrations**

3. A undertakes to sell real estate to B for 900,000,000 Italian lire. B must exercise the option to purchase within three months and must pay a deposit of 50,000,000 lire, which A is entitled to retain if B does not exercise the option. Since this is not an agreed payment for non-performance it does not fall under the present article and the sum cannot be reduced thereunder even if grossly excessive in the circumstances.

4. A enters into a contract with B for the lease of a machine. The contract provides that in the event of A's failure to pay one single rental the contract will be terminated and that the sums already paid will be retained by B as damages. The clause falls under the present article and the agreed amount may be subject to reduction.

APPENDIX

INDEX:

RESTATEMENT 2d OF THE LAW: CONTRACTS

INDEX

Third person's duty to promisee, § 114.

-E-

ELECTION OF REMEDIES
See Remedies.

EMOTIONAL DISTURBANCE
Damages, § 353.

EMPLOYMENT CONTRACTS
See also Personal Service Contract.
Post-employment restraints, § 188c, g.
Promises not to compete, § 188(2)g.

EQUITABLE RELIEF
See Cancellation; Equity; Injunction; Reformation; Specific Performance.

EQUITY
Judicial discretion, § 357c.
Married woman's capacity to contract, § 12d.
Mental illness or defect, § 15e.
Party requirements, § 10a.
Self-dealing, § 11b.

ERROR
Manifestation of assent, § 20d.

ESCROW
Delivery of written promise, § 103.

ESTOPPEL
See Reliance.

EVENT
See Aleatory Contracts; Condition.

EVIDENCE
Contradiction of integrated terms, § 215.
Integrated agreements, § 214.

EXCHANGE
See also Bargain; Bargained for Exchange.
Bargain's essential element, § 17b, d.

EXCUSABLE IGNORANCE
See Ignorance; Legislation.

EXCUSE
See Condition; Forfeiture.

EXECUTOR OR

ADMINISTRATOR
Statute of Frauds, §§ 110(1), 111.

EXECUTORY ACCORD
See Accord.

EXECUTORY CONTRACTS
Agreement of rescission, § 283a.
Assignment, § 338f.
Incompetency's effect, § 15d.
Intoxicated persons, § 16b.
Modification as consideration, § 89.
Oral agreement to rescind, § 148a.

EXPECTATION INTEREST
See also Reliance; Restitution.
Damages preferred to specific performance or injunction, § 359(l).
Defined, § 344(a).
Foreseeability based on, § 351a.
Measure of damages, § 347a.

EXPRESS CONTRACT
Implied contract distinguished, § 4a.

EXTRINSIC EVIDENCE
Interpretation of integrated agreements, § 212b, e.

-F-

FACT
See also Assertion of Intention; Assertion of Opinion; Misrepresentation.
Concealment, § 160.
Law as, § 170a.
Law not distinguished from, § 151b.
Meaning of "fact," § 159c.
Non-disclosure of, § 161.
Promises made in ignorance of, § 93.
State of mind as, § 159d.
Unconscionable contract or term, § 208f.

FACTOR
Contract of not within Statute of Frauds, § 121.

FAILURE TO PERFORM
See Performance.

FAIR DEALING
See Good Faith and Fair Dealing.

FAULT
Impracticability's effect, § 261d.
Misrepresentation's effect, § 163b.
Party seeking relief, effect of, § 157.
Unjustified reliance, § 172.

FIDUCIARY RELATIONS
Creditor's capacity, application of payments, §§ 259d, 260b.
Loss of power of avoidance by, Affirmance, § 380(1).
Delay, § 381(1).
Non-disclosure of fact, § 161f.
Promises inducing violation of duty, § 193.
Reliance on assertion of opinion, § 169.
Restitution when contract voidable by abuse of, § 376.
Self-dealing, § 9b.

FIXTURES
Security interests in, § 127d.

FORBEARANCE
Claim settlement as consideration, §§ 74d, 75c.
Injunction to effect, § 357h.
Promise inducing as binding, § 90.

FOREIGN LAW
Assertions or statements of, § 170C.

FORESEEABILITY
See also Damages; Frustration; Impracticability.
Impracticability, § 261c.
Supervening frustration, § 265a.

FORFEITURE
Disproportionate, §§ 229b, 271a.
Excuse of condition to avoid, §§ 229, 271.
Impracticability, condition's non-occurrence excused, § 271.
Material failure to perform, § 241d.

Marriage, §§ 189-90.

Non-ancillary restraints, § 187.

Partial enforcement, §§ 183-184.

Performance's effect where intended use is improper, § 182.

Restitution generally unavailable, § 197.

Exceptions, §§ 197-99.

Sources of court derived rules, § 179.

Specific performance or injunction, § 365.

Unenforceable bargain, illustration, § 8b3.

When terms are unenforceable, 178.

PUBLICATION

General offer revoked, § 46.

PUNITIVE DAMAGES

See Damages.

-Q-

QUASI-CONTRACTS

Defined, § 4b.

Infant's obligations, § 14b.

Liability for necessaries, § 12f.

Ward's obligations, § 13b.

QUOTATION OF PRICE

Invitation to an offer, § 26c.

-R-

RATIFICATION

Affirmance, § 380.

Effect, in voidable contract, § 7e.

Intoxicated persons, § 16c.

Unenforceable contract, § 8.

REAL PARTY IN INTEREST

Beneficiary as, § 307a-b.

State practice, Stat. note prec. § 316.

REALTY

Sale of minerals severed from, § 127c.

REASON TO KNOW

Effect of misunderstanding, § 20.

Elements of, § 26a.

Knowledge and "should

know" distinguished, § 19b.

Mistake, § 153(b)e.

Non-occurrence of condition, §§ 246-248.

Suretyship under Statute of Frauds, § 112d.

Third persons, application of payments, § 258(2).

Usage, §§ 201(2)b, 220-22.

See also Usage.

REASONABLE TIME

See also Time.

Assurance of due performance, § 251e.

Creditor's application of payment by debtor, § 259b.

Delay, loss of power of avoidance by, § 381.

Uncertain time of performance, §§ 33d, 204d.

RECEIPT

See Acceptance; Rejection; Revocation.

RECITAL

Facts in integrated agreement, § 218.

RECOGNIZANCES

Definition and uses, § 6c.

REFORMATION

See also Mistake; Remedies.

Availability, § 359c.

Court's equitable discretion, § 155d.

Misrepresentation as to writing justifies, § 166.

Mistake of both parties as to writing, § 155.

Relief by, in mistake, § 152(2)d.

Statute of Frauds doesn't preclude, § 156.

Who is entitled. § 155e.

REGULATION

See Legislation; Licensing.

REJECTION

See also Counter-offer; Offer.

Counter-offer as, § 39a.

Insufficient reason excuses non-occurrence of condition, § 248.

Offeree's termination of power of acceptance, §§ 36(1)(a),

38(1).

Receipt, what constitutes, § 68.

Subsequent acceptance's effect, § 40b.

RELEASE

Common law rules, states retaining, Stat. note prec. § 288.

Defined, § 284(1).

Grounds for attacking, § 152f.

Joint debtor, § 284c.

RELIANCE

See also Breach of Contract; Offer; Performance; Promise; Remedies.

Action in as overcoming uncertainty, § 34(3).

Assertion of intention, § 171.

Consideration by virtue of, § 17e.

Damages, § 349.

Effect on unconscionability in mistake, § 153d.

Election of remedies, § 378

Enforcement notwithstanding Statute of Frauds, § 139.

Estoppel,

Creation of, § 84b.

Enforcement of waiver, § 84b.

Facts in integrated agreements, § 218c.

Promises inducing action or forbearance as binding, §§ 90, 139a, 336g.

Fault making reliance unjustified, § 172.

Guaranty, § 88d.

Justifiable in misrepresentation, § 164d.

Land provision of Statute of Frauds, § 129.

Law, assertions as to matters of, § 170.

Modification of executory contract as consideration, § 89d.

Oral modification of contract, § 150.

Rejection's effect on offeror, § 38a.

Reliance interest,

INDEX:

UNIDROIT PRINCIPLES OF INTERNATIONAL COMMERCIAL CONTRACTS

INDEX

Entries are keyed to the comments which follow each article, the number in square brackets indicating the number of the comment, where applicable.